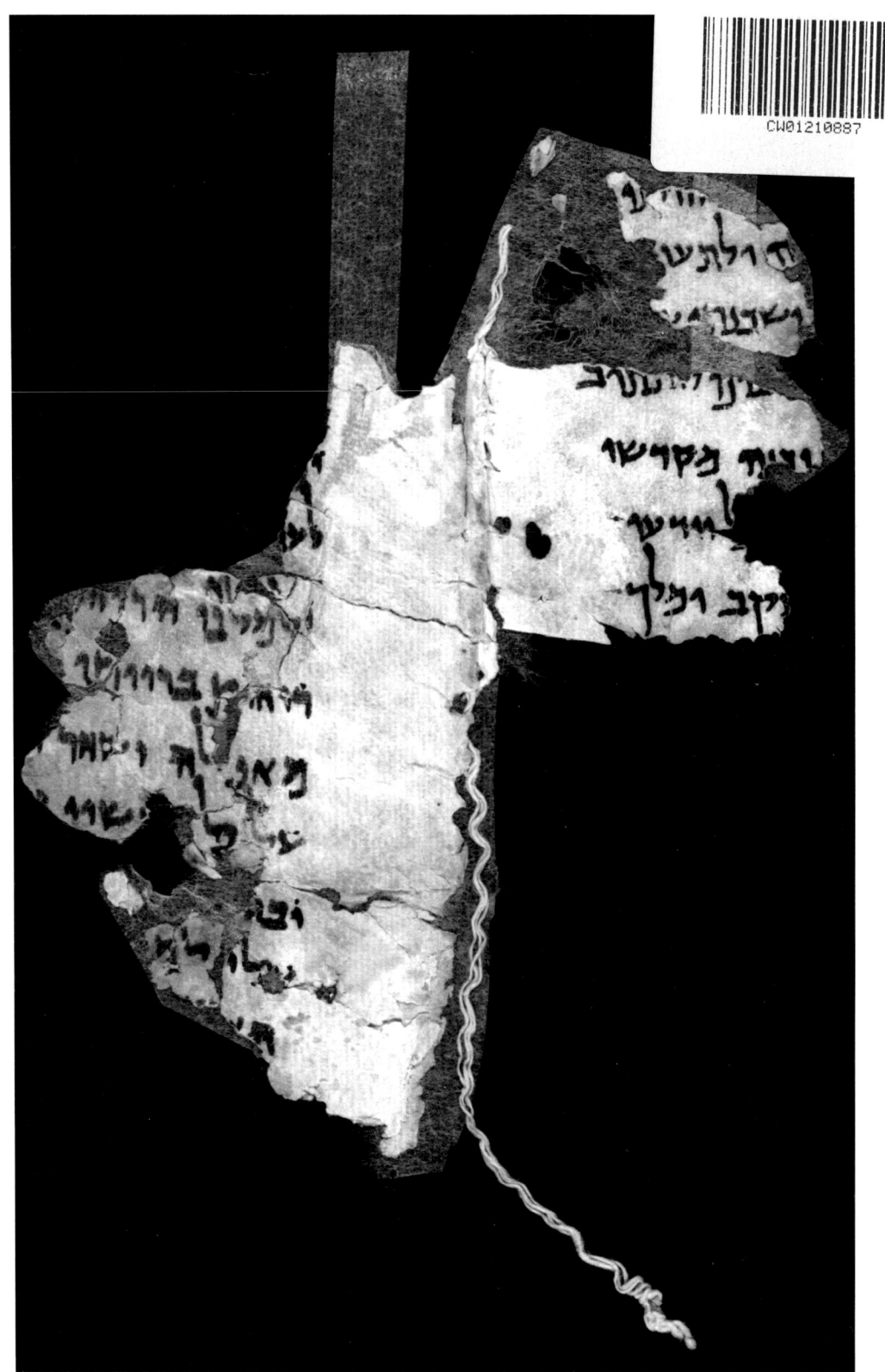

Jubilees 2

hermeneia

**Hermeneia
—A Critical
and Historical
Commentary
on the Bible**

Old Testament Editorial Board

Peter Machinist, Harvard University, chair
Sidnie White Crawford, University of Nebraska
Paul D. Hanson, Harvard University, emeritus
Thomas Krüger, University of Zurich
S. Dean McBride Jr., Union Theological Seminary
  in Virginia, emeritus
Andreas Schuele, University of Leipzig
David Vanderhooft, Boston College
Molly Zahn, University of Kansas

New Testament Editorial Board

Harold W. Attridge, Yale University, chair
Adela Yarbro Collins, Yale University
Eldon Jay Epp, Case Western Reserve University
Hans-Josef Klauck, University of Chicago
AnneMarie Luijendijk, Princeton University
Laura S. Nasrallah, Harvard University

Jubilees 2

A Commentary
on the Book of Jubilees
Chapters 22–50

by James C. VanderKam

Edited by
Sidnie White Crawford

**Fortress
Press** Minneapolis

Jubilees
A Commentary

Copyright © 2018 Fortress Press, an imprint of 1517 Media

All rights reserved. Except for brief quotations in critical articles or reviews, no part of this book may be reproduced in any manner without prior written permission from the publisher. Write: Permissions, Fortress Press, Box 1209, Minneapolis, MN 55440-1209.

Scripture quotations from the New Revised Standard Version of the Bible are copyright © 1989 by the Division of Christian Education of the National Council of the Churches of Christ in the U.S.A. and are used by permission.

Cover and interior design by Kenneth Hiebert
Typesetting and page composition by
The HK Scriptorium

Print ISBN: 978-0-8006-6035-2

eISBN: 978-1-5064-3848-1

The paper used in this publication meets the minimum requirements of American National Standard for Information Sciences—Permanence of paper for Printed Library Materials, ANSI Z329.48–1984.

Manufactured in the U.S.A.

■ *To Mary, for an abundance of love and support over many years, and to a generation of Notre Dame students who have enjoyed Mary's hospitality and taught me a bunch*

The Author

James C. VanderKam is John A. O'Brien Professor of Hebrew Scriptures emeritus at the University of Notre Dame. He has edited thirteen volumes in the series Discoveries in the Judaean Desert and is an editor-in-chief of the *Encyclopedia of the Dead Sea Scrolls* (2000). He is the author of the prize-winning *The Dead Sea Scrolls Today* (1994, 2010), *From Joshua to Caiaphas: High Priests after the Exile* (Fortress Press, 2004), *The Meaning of the Dead Sea Scrolls* (2002), *An Introduction to Early Judaism* (2001), and *From Revelation to Canon: Studies in the Hebrew Bible and Second Temple Literature* (2000), and the coauthor of *1 Enoch 2: A Commentary on the Book of 1 Enoch Chapters 37–82* (Fortress Press, 2012).

Endpapers

Front endpapers show a black-and-white photograph of fragments from 4Q216, the oldest copy of Jubilees from Qumran Cave 4. Back endpapers show a black-and-white photograph of another fragment from 4Q216. Courtesy of The Leon Levy Dead Sea Scrolls Digital Library; IAA photo: Shai Halevi.

Contents
Jubilees 2

Reference Codes	xiii
1. Abbreviations	xiii
2. Symbols and Procedures	xvi
3. Editions of Ancient Texts	xvii
4. Short Titles	xviii

■ Commentary

22 Abraham's Last Festival and His Testament to Jacob — 647
- 1-6 The Family Celebrates the Festival of Weeks — 652
- 7-9 Abraham's Prayer — 655
- 10-15 Abraham Prays for Jacob — 657
- 16-24 Abraham Gives Commands to Jacob — 661
- 25-26 Abraham and Jacob Lie Down Together — 667
- 27-30 Abraham Blesses the Sleeping Jacob — 668

23 Abraham's Death and the Pattern of Human Life Spans — 670
- 1-7 The Death of Abraham — 676
- 8-31 The Pattern of Human Life Spans — 679
  - 8-10 Abraham's Short Life in a Period of Decreasing Longevity — 680
  - 11-15 Continual Decline in Life Spans — 681
  - 16-25 Low Point in the Time of the Evil Generation — 686
  - 26-31 The Children and the Reversal in Longevity — 694
- 32 Command That Moses Write the Message — 702
- Excursus: Werman's Theory about Chapter 23 — 703
- Excursus: The Chronology of Abraham's Life — 705

24 Isaac and the Philistines — 708
- 1-2 Narrative Setting (Gen 26:11; 26:1a) — 713
- 3-7 Jacob Gains the Right of Firstborn (Gen 25:29-34) — 714
- 8-11 Famine, Journey to Gerar, Blessing (Gen 26:1-5) — 716
- 12-17 Isaac in Gerar (Gen 26:6, 11-16) — 718
- 18-20 Isaac and His Wells in the Valleys of Gerar (Gen 26:17-22) — 719
- 21-23 Blessing and Sacrifice in Beersheba (Gen 26:23-25) — 720
- 24-33 Isaac's Oath with the Philistines and Curse upon Them (see Gen 26:26-33) — 721

25 Rebekah and Jacob — 728
- 1-10 Dialogue between Rebekah and Jacob — 731
  - 1-3 Rebekah Instructs Jacob about a Fitting Marriage Partner — 731
  - 4-10 Jacob Explains His Behavior and View of Marriage — 733
- 11-23 Rebekah Blesses God and Prays for Jacob — 735
- Excursus: Patterns in Jubilees 25:11-23 — 741

26 Jacob, Not Esau, Receives Isaac's Blessing — 742
- 1-2 Isaac's Instructions to Esau — 746
- 3-9 Rebekah and Jacob — 746
  - 3-6 Rebekah's Plan — 746

		7-9	Jacob's Reply and Rebekah's Insistence	747
	10-25ab	Isaac's Unwitting Blessing of Jacob		749
	25c-34	Isaac and Esau		753
	35	Esau's Plot to Kill Jacob		756

27	Jacob Leaves Home and Encounters the Lord in Bethel	757
	1-7 Rebekah and Jacob Discuss Plans	760
	8-11 Isaac Carries Out Rebekah's Instructions and Blesses Jacob (Gen 27:6—28:4)	762
	12-18 Jacob Leaves and His Parents Cope (Gen 28:5)	764
	19-27 The Theophany at Luz/Bethel (Gen 28:10-22)	766

28	Jacob Gains a Family and Acquires Wealth	773
	1-10 The Marriages and the Law of the Firstborn Daughter (see Gen 29:1, 21-22, 24, 23, 25, 18, 17, 26-27, 28-30)	777
	11-24 The Births of Twelve Children	783
	25-30 Jacob's Work for Laban	788
	Excursus: The Chronology in Jubilees 28:10-24	790

29	Jacob Leaves Haran and Deals with Laban, Esau, and His Parents (Genesis 31–33)	796
	1-4 Jacob and His Family Leave Laban's Home and Go to Gilead	799
	5-8 The Encounter between Jacob and Laban in Gilead	801
	Excursus: Laban in Jubilees	803
	9-11 A Digression on the Previous Name and Inhabitants of Gilead	804
	Excursus: Jubilees 29:9-11 and Hasmonean History	806
	12-20 Jacob Meets Esau and Cares for Isaac and Rebekah	807

30	Dinah, Shechem, Exogamy, and Levi the Priest (Genesis 34)	813
	1-4 The Story about the Rape of Dinah and the Response by Jacob and His Sons	819
	Excursus: Dinah's Age	821
	5-10 There Is to Be No Such Defilement in Israel	824
	11-16 No Marriage with Non-Israelites	830
	17-23 The Example of Simeon and Levi	834
	Excursus: Source Texts	835
	24-26 The End of the Episode	840
	Excursus: An Interpolator?	841

31	Bethel (1): Jacob Sees His Parents and Isaac Blesses Levi and Judah (Genesis 35)	843
	1-3a Preparations and Travel to Bethel	847
	3b-30a Jacob, His Parents, and His Two Sons Levi and Judah	849
	3b-7 Invitations, Arrival with Levi and Judah, and Meeting with Rebekah	849
	8-23 Meeting with Isaac and Blessing of Levi and Judah	851
	14b-15 Blessing on Levi's Descendants	855
	16-17 Blessing on Levi	857
	18-20 Isaac's Blessing of Judah	858

		24-30a Further Conversation with Isaac	862
		30b-32 Return to Bethel and Joyful Reflection on His Father's Blessings	864
32	Bethel (2): Tithing, Temple-Building, and Departure (Genesis 35)		866
	1-29	Bethel	871
		1 Levi's Dream	871
	Excursus: Levi, Levites, and the Levi Tradition		874
		2-9 Jacob's Tithes	875
	Excursus: Levi as the Tenth		877
		10-15 Tithes	883
		16-26 Night Appearances to Jacob	885
	Excursus: No Temple in Bethel		890
	Excursus: The Angel Vision from Another Writer?		891
		27-29 An Extra Day	893
	Excursus: An Interpolator in vv. 27-29?		894
		30-34 Departure from Bethel	895
33	Reuben's Sin with Bilhah and Jacob's Move to the House of Abraham		898
	1-9a	Jacob and Leah's Absence and Reuben's Sin with Bilhah (Gen 35:21-22a; cf. v. 27)	902
	9b-20	The Angel's Address to Moses	906
		9b-12 The Law regarding the Sin	906
		13-17 Commands for Israel and the Special Case of Reuben	908
		18-20 Israel as a Holy Nation	912
	Excursus: An Interpolator in 33:10-20?		913
	21-23	Jacob and His Family Move to the House of Abraham (Gen 35:22b-25, 27)	914
34	War with the Amorite Kings, Joseph and His Brothers, the Day of Atonement, and the Wives of Jacob's Sons		916
	1-9	War with Seven Amorite Kings	918
	Excursus: War with the Amorite Kings		925
	Excursus: Jubilees 34:1-9 and Hasmonean Sites		926
	10-19	Joseph and His Brothers (Gen 37:13-14, 17-18, 28, 36, 31, 32, 35)	928
		10 Joseph's Mission to His Brothers	929
		11 Their Harsh Treatment of Joseph	929
		12-19 Jacob's Grief and the Day of Atonement	929
	20-21	The Wives of Jacob's Sons	934
35	The Last Instructions and Death of Rebekah		936
	1-8	Conversation between Rebekah and Jacob	941
	9-17	Conversation between Rebekah and Isaac	944
	18-24	Conversation between Rebekah and Esau	949
	25-26	Esau and Jacob with Rebekah	951
	27	Esau and Jacob's Final Meal with Rebekah and Her Death	951
36	Isaac's Last Day and the Death of Leah		953
	1-11	Isaac's Instructions regarding His Burial and His Testament to Esau and Jacob	957
	12-18	Isaac Divides His Estate, Dies, and Is Buried	963

		19-20	Esau and Jacob Go to Their Homes	966
		21-24	Jacob's Beloved Wife Leah Dies	968

37	Hostilities Break Out between Esau and Jacob		971
	1-8	Esau's Sons Want to Fight Jacob for the Birthright but Esau Opposes Their Plan	975
	9-10	Esau's Sons Assemble an Army of Foreign Mercenaries	979
	11-13	Esau Changes His Mind and Agrees to Attack Jacob	980
	14-23	Jacob Is Surprised by the Attack and Has an Unpleasant Exchange with Esau	982
	24-25	Jacob Orders a Strike against Esau and His Army	988

38	War between Esau and Jacob and an Edomite King List		989
	1-14	The War between the Forces of Jacob and Esau	992
	Excursus: The War with Esau and His Sons and Maccabean History		999
	15-24	The Kings Who Ruled in Edom (Gen 36:31-39)	1001

39	The Humble Beginnings of Joseph's Career in Egypt		1003
	1-2ab	Jacob in Canaan (Gen 37:1-2a)	1006
	2c-4	Joseph Succeeds in Potiphar's House (Gen 39:1-6a)	1007
	5-11	Joseph and Potiphar's Wife (Gen 39:6b-20)	1008
	12-13	Joseph Succeeds in Prison (Gen 39:21-23)	1015
	14-18	Joseph Successfully Interprets Two Dreams (Genesis 40)	1016

40	Joseph Interprets Pharaoh's Dreams and Becomes Ruler of Egypt		1019
	1-7	Pharaoh's Dreams and Joseph's Appointment as Second Ruler in Egypt	1021
	8-13	Joseph's Just Rule over Egypt	1026

41	Judah and Tamar (Genesis 38)			1033
	1-7	Judah's Sons and Tamar (Gen 38:6-12a)		1037
	8-21	Judah and Tamar (Gen 38:12b-26)		1041
		8-12	Tamar Misleads Judah (Gen 38:12b-18)	1041
		13-15	Tamar Disappears (Gen 38:19-23)	1043
		16-21	The Truth Emerges and Twins Are Born (Gen 38:24-30)	1045
	22	The Seven Years of Abundance End (Gen 41:53)		1049
	23-28	Legal Issues		1049
		23-25	Judah's Remorse and Pardon	1050
		26-28	The Law for Israel	1053

42	Joseph's Brothers Travel to Egypt		1056
	1-3	The Famine Begins (Gen 41:54, 56)	1059
	4-12	The Brothers Make Their First Trip to Egypt, Encounter a Harsh Joseph, and Return Home (Gen 42:1, 3-5, 8, 7, 9, 17, 25, 29, 30, 36, 38)	1061
	13-14	The Famine Grows More Severe and the Egyptians Cope by Imitating Joseph (Gen 43:1)	1065
	15-20	Jacob Agrees to Send Benjamin with His Brothers on Their Second Trip to Egypt (Gen 43:1-2; 42:37-38; 43:8-9, 11)	1066

	21-25	The Brothers Meet Joseph, Who Devises a Plan to Test Them (Gen 43:15, 29, 23, 26, 34; 44:1-2)	1068
43		Joseph Tests His Brothers and Reveals His Identity	1072
	1-13	The Cup as an Instrument for Testing Relations between the Brothers (Genesis 44)	1074
		1-8a Placing and Finding the Cup in Benjamin's Sack (Gen 44:1-13)	1074
		8b-10 Confrontation with Joseph (Gen 44:14-17)	1077
		11-13 Judah's Speech (Gen 44:18-34)	1079
	14-20	Joseph Reveals His Identity (Gen 45:1-20)	1081
	21-24	The Return Trip and Announcement of the Good News to Jacob (Gen 45:21-28)	1084
44		The Descent to Egypt by Jacob and His Family	1087
	1-6	From Hebron to the Well of the Oath (Gen 46:1-4)	1089
	7-10	From the Well of the Oath toward Goshen (Gen 46:5, 6, 28)	1093
	11-34	The Seventy Who Descended to Egypt (Gen 46:8-27)	1095
45		Reunion of the Family and Death of Jacob	1103
	1-5	The Reunion of Jacob and Joseph (Gen 46:28-30)	1105
	6-7	Joseph's Provisions for His Father and Brothers (Gen 46:31—47:12)	1108
	8-12	Joseph's Supervision of the Famine Relief (Gen 47:13-26)	1110
	13-16	Jacob's Last Days (Gen 47:28—50:14)	1112
46		From Harmony to Oppression	1117
	1-2	Harmonious Relations in Egypt	1120
	3-11	Deaths of the Twelve Brothers with Burials Delayed by Warfare	1122
	12-16	The Egyptian King Initiates Oppressive Measures against the Israelites	1130
		Excursus: The War between Egypt and Canaan	1131
47		From Moses's Birth to His Escape from Egypt	1136
	1-8	Moses's Birth and Rescue by Pharaoh's Daughter (Exod 1:22: 2:1-9)	1138
	9-10a	Life at Home and in the Royal Court (Exod 2:10)	1143
	10b-12	Danger and Flight from Egypt (Exod 2:11-15a)	1145
48		Moses's Return to Egypt, the Plagues, and the Exodus	1147
	1-3	Moses to Midian and Back (Exod 2:15b—4:31)	1150
	4-8	Revenge through Ten Plagues (Exod 5:1—11:10; 12:29-32)	1153
	9-19	Defeat of Mastema and the Egyptians (Exod 12:33-36; 14)	1157
49		The First Passover and the Laws of Passover	1166
	1	The Timing of Passover	1170
	2-6	The First Passover	1171
		Excursus: The Agent of the Tenth Plague	1173

	7-15	The Proper Time for Celebrating Passover	1176
	16-21	The Proper Place for Celebrating Passover	1183
	Excursus: The Heavenly Tablets Reference in 49:8		1185
	22-23	The Festival of Unleavened Bread	1188
50		Sabbaths, Weeks, and Jubilees	1192
	1	Sabbath Laws in the Wilderness of Sin	1194
	2-5	Sabbaths of Years, Jubilees, and the Chronological System	1194
	Excursus: The Chronology in the Book of Jubilees		1199
	6-13	Sabbath Laws	1201
	Excursus: The Number of Prohibited Kinds of Labor		1210
	Excursus: Is the Unit 50:6-13 Part of the Original Text?		1212

■ Back Matter

Bibliography	1215
Index	1251
1. Passages	1251
2. Names	1307

Reference Codes

1. Abbreviations

AB	Anchor Bible
ABD	David Noel Freedman, ed., *The Anchor Bible Dictionary* (6 vols.; New York: Doubleday, 1992).
ABRL	Anchor Bible Reference Library
acc.	accusative
ACCS	Ancient Christian Commentary on Scripture
ACEBT	*Amsterdamse Cahiers voor Exegese en bijbelse Theologie*
adj.	adjective
AGJU	Arbeiten zur Geschichte des antiken Judentums und des Urchristentums
AJEC	Ancient Judaism and Early Christianity
AJSL	*American Journal of Semitic Languages and Literatures*
ALD	Aramaic Levi Document
ALGHJ	Arbeiten zur Literatur und Geschichte des hellenistischen Judentums
AnBib	Analecta Biblica
ANF	Alexander Roberts and James Donaldson, eds., *Ante-Nicene Fathers: The Writings of the Fathers down to A.D. 325* (10 vols.; Buffalo: Christian Literature Publishing, 1887–96; repr., Peabody, MA: Hendrickson, 1994).
AOT	Hedley F. D. Sparks, ed., *The Apocryphal Old Testament* (Oxford: Clarendon, 1984).
APOT	R. H. Charles, ed., *The Apocrypha and Pseudepigrapha of the Old Testament* (2 vols.; Oxford: Clarendon, 1913).
Aram.	Aramaic
ArBib	Aramaic Bible
As. Mos.	Assumption of Moses
ASTI	*Annual of the Swedish Theological Institute*
AUSS	*Andrews University Seminary Studies*
AYB	Anchor Yale Bible
AYBRL	Anchor Yale Bible Reference Library
BAG	Walter Bauer, *A Greek-English Lexicon of the New Testament and Other Early Christian Literature* (trans. and ed. William F. Arndt and F. Wilbur Gingrich; Chicago: University of Chicago Press, 1957).
BASOR	*Bulletin of the American Schools of Oriental Research*
BBB	Bonner biblische Beiträge
BDB	Francis Brown, S. R. Driver, and Charles A. Briggs, *A Hebrew and English Lexicon of the Old Testament* (Oxford: Clarendon, 1907).
BETL	Bibliotheca ephemeridum theologicarum lovaniensium
BGBE	Beiträge zur Geschichte der biblischen Exegese
Bib	*Biblica*
BibOr	Biblica et Orientalia
Bijdr	*Bijdragen: Tijdschrift voor filosofie en theologie*
BJS	Brown Judaic Studies
BN	*Biblische Notizen*
BO	Bibliotheca Orientalis
BSO(A)S	*Bulletin of the School of Oriental and African Studies*
BZ	*Biblische Zeitschrift*
BZAW	Beihefte zur Zeitschrift für die alttestamentliche Wissenschaft
CBQ	*Catholic Biblical Quarterly*
CBQMS	Catholic Biblical Quarterly Monograph Series
CC	Continental Commentaries
ConBNT	Coniectanea Biblica: New Testament Series
CSCO	Corpus Scriptorum Christianorum Orientalium
CurBR	*Currents in Biblical Research*
DCH	David J. A. Clines, ed., *Dictionary of Classical Hebrew* (9 vols.; Sheffield: Sheffield Phoenix, 1993–2014).
DDD²	Karel van der Toorn, Bob Becking, and Pieter W. van der Horst, *Dictionary of Deities and Demons in the Bible* (2nd rev. ed.; Grand Rapids: Eerdmans, 1999).
DJD	Discoveries in the Judaean Desert
1	D. Barthélemy and J. T. Milik, *Qumran Cave 1* (DJD 1; Oxford: Clarendon, 1955).
3	M. Baillet, J. T. Milik, and R. de Vaux, *Les 'petites grottes' de Qumrân* (DJD 3; Oxford: Clarendon, 1962).
4	J. A. Sanders, *The Psalms Scroll of Qumrân Cave 11 (11QPsᵃ)* (DJD 4; Oxford: Clarendon, 1965).
5	J. M. Allegro with A. A. Anderson, *Qumrân Cave 4.I (4Q158–4Q186)* (DJD 5; Oxford: Clarendon, 1968).

7	M. Baillet, *Qumrân grotte 4.III (4Q482–4Q520)* (DJD 7; Oxford: Clarendon, 1982).		*1QHodayot*[a], with Incorporation of *4QHodayot*[a-f] and *1QHodayot*[b] (DJD 40; Oxford: Clarendon, 2009).
9	P. W. Skehan, E. Ulrich, and J. E. Sanderson, *Qumran Cave 4.IV: Palaeo-Hebrew and Greek Biblical Manuscripts* (DJD 9; Oxford: Clarendon, 1992).	DSD DSSR	*Dead Sea Discoveries* Donald W. Parry and Emanuel Tov, eds., *The Dead Sea Scrolls Reader* (6 vols.; Leiden: Brill, 2004–5).
13	H. Attridge et al., in consultation with J. VanderKam, *Qumran Cave 4.VIII: Parabiblical Texts, Part 1* (DJD 13; Oxford: Clarendon, 1994).	EBib EJL EMML Eng.	Etudes bibliques Early Judaism and Its Literature Ethiopic Manuscript Microfilm Library English
14	E. Ulrich, F. M. Cross, et al., *Qumran Cave 4.IX: Deuteronomy, Joshua, Judges, Kings* (DJD 14; Oxford: Clarendon, 1995).	Epiphanius Pan. Eth. *EThL*	*Panarion* Ethiopic *Ephemerides theologicae lovanienses*
18	J. Baumgarten, *Qumran Cave 4.XIII: The Damascus Document (4Q266–273)* (DJD 18; Oxford: Clarendon, 1996).	*Exod. Rab.* FAT FC	*Exodus Rabbah* Forschungen zum Alten Testament Fathers of the Church
19	M. Broshi et al., in consultation with J. VanderKam, *Qumran Cave 4.XIV: Parabiblical Texts, Part 2* (DJD 19; Oxford: Clarendon, 1995).	fem. frg. FRLANT	feminine fragment Forschungen zur Religion und Literatur des Alten und Neuen Testaments
21	S. Talmon, J. Ben-Dov, and U. Glessmer, *Qumran Cave 4.XVI: Calendrical Texts* (DJD 21; Oxford: Clarendon, 2001).	GCS *Gen. Rab.*	Die griechischen christlichen Schriftsteller der ersten drei Jahrhunderte *Genesis Rabbah*
22	G. J. Brooke et al., in consultation with J. VanderKam, *Qumran Cave 4.XVII: Parabiblical Texts, Part 3* (DJD 22; Oxford: Clarendon, 1996).	Gk. HALOT	Greek Ludwig Koehler, Walter Baumgartner, and Johann J. Stamm, *The Hebrew and Aramaic Lexicon of the Old Testament* (trans. and ed.
23	F. García Martínez, E. J. C. Tigchelaar, and A. S. van der Woude, *Qumran Cave 11.II (11Q2–18, 11Q20–31)* (DJD 23; Oxford: Clarendon, 1998).	HAR HB HBS	Mervyn E. J. Richardson; 4 vols.; Leiden: Brill, 1994–99). *Hebrew Annual Review* Hebrew Bible Herders biblische Studien
30	D. Dimant, *Qumran Cave 4.XXI: Parabiblical Texts, Part 4: Pseudo-Prophetic Texts* (DJD 30; Oxford: Clarendon, 2001).	Heb. *Hen Hermen* hma. hmt.	Hebrew *Henoch Hermenêutica* homoioarcton homoioteleuton
31	É. Puech, *Qumrân Grotte 4.XXII: Textes araméens, première partie: 4Q529–4Q549* (DJD 31; Oxford: Clarendon, 2001).	HRCS	Edwin Hatch and Henry A. Redpath, *Concordance to the Septuagint and Other Greek Versions of the Old Testament* (2 vols.; Oxford: Clarendon, 1897; 2nd ed.; Grand Rapids: Baker, 1998).
35	J. Baumgarten et al., *Qumran Cave 4.XXV: Halakhic Texts* (DJD 35; Oxford: Clarendon, 1999).		
36	S. J. Pfann, *Qumran Cave 4.XXVI: Cryptic Texts;* P. S. Alexander et al., in consultation with J. VanderKam and M. Brady, *Miscellanea, Part 1* (DJD 36; Oxford: Clarendon, 2000).	HSM HSS HTR HTS *HUCA* HUCM	Harvard Semitic Monographs Harvard Semitic Studies *Harvard Theological Review* Harvard Theological Studies *Hebrew Union College Annual* Monographs of the Hebrew Union College
40	C. Newsom, H. Stegemann, and E. Schuller, *Qumran Cave 1.III:*	impf.	imperfect

impv.	imperative	MT	Masoretic Text
indic.	indicative	NETS	*A New English Translation of the Septuagint, and the Other Greek Translations Traditionally Included under That Title* (ed. Albert Pietersma and Benjamin G. Wright; New York: Oxford University Press, 2007).
JAJSup	Journal of Ancient Judaism Supplements		
Jastrow	Marcus Jastrow, *A Dictionary of the Targumim, the Talmud Babli and Yerushalmi, and the Midrashic Literature* (2 vols.; New York: Pardes, 1950).		
		NHMS	Nag Hammadi and Manichaean Studies
JBL	*Journal of Biblical Literature*		
JBW	*Jahrbücher der biblischen Wissenschaft*	NHS	Nag Hammadi Studies
		NICOT	New International Commentary on the Old Testament
JJS	*Journal of Jewish Studies*		
Josephus		NRSV	New Revised Standard Version
Ant.	*Antiquities*	NTAbh	Neutestamentliche Abhandlungen
Ap.	*Against Apion*		
Bell.	*Bellum Judaicum*	*NTT*	*Norsk Teologisk Tidsskrift*
JQR	*Jewish Quarterly Review*	OBO	Orbis biblicus et orientalis
JSHRZ	Jüdische Schriften aus hellenistisch-römischer Zeit	OG	Old Greek
		OL	Old Latin
JSJ	*Journal for the Study of Judaism in the Persian, Hellenistic, and Roman Period*	*OLP*	*Orientalia Lovaniensia Periodica*
		OLZ	*Orientalistische Literaturzeitung*
		om.	omit(s)
JSJSup	Supplements to the Journal for the Study of Judaism	OTL	Old Testament Library
		OTP	James H. Charlesworth, ed., *The Old Testament Pseudepigrapha* (2 vols.; New York: Doubleday, 1983–85).
JSNTSup	Journal for the Study of the New Testament: Supplement Series		
JSOTSup	Journal for the Study of the Old Testament: Supplement Series		
JSP	*Journal for the Study of the Pseudepigrapha*	*PAAJR*	*Proceedings of the American Academy of Jewish Research*
		pass.	passive
JSPSup	Supplements to the Journal for the Study of the Pseudepigrapha	perf.	perfect
		Philo	
JSQ	*Jewish Studies Quarterly*	Abr.	*On the Life of Abraham*
JSS	*Journal of Semitic Studies*	Alleg. Interp.	*Allegorical Interpretation*
JTS	*Journal of Theological Studies*	Migr.	*Migration of Abraham*
Jud	Judaica	Somn.	*On Dreams*
K&D	Carl Friedrich Keil and Franz Delitzsch, *Biblical Commentary on the Old Testament* (trans. James Martin et al.; 25 vols.; Edinburgh, 1857–78; repr., 10 vols.; Peabody, MA: Hendrickson, 1996).	Spec.	*On the Special Laws*
		pl.	plural
		P.Oxy.	Oxyrhynchus papyri
		pr.	preceded by
		ptc.	participle
		PTSDSSP	Princeton Theological Seminary Dead Sea Scrolls Project
L.A.B.	Liber antiquitatum biblicarum (Pseudo-Philo)		
		PVTG	Pseudepigrapha Veteris Testamenti Graece
LCL	Loeb Classical Library		
LHBOTS	Library of Hebrew Bible/Old Testament Studies	QL	Qumran literature
		Rabbinic writings	
lit.	literally	b.	Babylonian Talmud
LSJ	Henry George Liddell, Robert Scott, and Henry Stuart Jones, *A Greek-English Lexicon* (9th ed., with revised supplement; Oxford: Clarendon, 1996).	m.	*Mishnah*
		Mek.	*Mekilta*
		Pesaḥ.	*Pesaḥim*
		Šabb.	*Šabbat*
		RB	*Revue biblique*
LSTS	Library of Second Temple Studies	*REJ*	*Revue des études juives*
LXX	Septuagint	*RevQ*	*Revue de Qumran*
masc.	masculine	*RHPhR*	*Revue d'histoire et de philosophie religieuses*
MGWJ	*Monatschrift für Geschichte und Wissenschaft des Judenthums*		

RHR	*Revue de l'histoire des religions*
SAOC	Studies in Ancient Oriental Civilization
SBL(A)SP	Society of Biblical Literature (Abstracts and) Seminar Papers
SBLDS	Society of Biblical Literature Dissertation Series
SBLEJL	Society of Biblical Literature Early Judaism and Its Literature
SBLTT	Society of Biblical Literature Texts and Translations
SBLSCS	Society of Biblical Literature Septuagint and Cognate Studies
SDSSRL	Studies in the Dead Sea Scrolls and Related Literature
SEÅ	*Svensk exegetisk årsbok*
sg.	singular
Sib. Or.	Sibylline Oracles
SIDIC	*SIDIC (Journal of the Service internationale de documentation judeo-chrétienne)*
SJLA	Studies in Judaism in Late Antiquity
SJOT	*Scandinavian Journal of the Old Testament*
SNTSMS	Society for New Testament Studies Monograph Series
SP	Samaritan Pentateuch
SPAW	*Sitzungsberichte der preussischen Akademie der Wissenschaften*
STDJ	Studies on the Texts of the Desert of Judah
StPB	Studia Post-biblica
SVTP	Studia in Veteris Testamenti Pseudepigraphica
Syr.	Syriac
Syr. Chr.	Syriac Chronicle
Targums	
Tg. Neof.	*Targum Neofiti*
Tg. Onq.	*Targum Onqelos*
Tg. Ps.-J.	*Targum Pseudo-Jonathan*
TBN	Themes in Biblical Narrative
TDOT	G. Johannes Botterweck and Helmer Ringgren, eds., *Theological Dictionary of the Old Testament* (trans. John T. Willis et al.; 15 vols.; Grand Rapids: Eerdmans, 1974–2006).
ThR	*Theologische Rundschau*
ThStK	*Theologische Studien und Kritiken*
tr.	transpose(s)
TSAJ	Texte and Studien zum antiken Judentum
VT	*Vetus Testamentum*
VTSup	Supplements to Vetus Testamentum
WBC	Word Biblical Commentary
WMANT	Wissenschaftliche Monographien zum Alten und Neuen Testament
WUNT	Wissenschaftliche Untersuchungen zum Neuen Testament
ZABR	*Zeitschrift für altorientalische und biblische Rechtsgeschichte*
ZAW	*Zeitschrift für die alttestamentliche Wissenschaft*
ZDMG	*Zeitschrift der deutschen morgenländischen Gesellschaft*
ZDPV	*Zeitschrift des deutschen Palästina-Vereins*
ZRGG	*Zeitschrift für Religions- und Geistesgeschichte*
ZWTh	*Zeitschrift für wissenschaftliche Theologie*

2. Symbols and Procedures

Translation

( ) Parentheses   Words or letters within parentheses are supplied for the sake of the English translation

___   Underlining   Underlined words and letters are translations of words and letters on the Hebrew fragments of Jubilees from Qumran

Italics   Words in italics represent emendations of the text, as explained in the textual notes.

[ ] Brackets   Brackets surround places where something appears to be missing from the text, as explained in the textual notes. Where there is no evidence for what might have stood in the text, the bracketed space is left blank. Where there is evidence, as explained in the textual notes, a word or words are supplied within the brackets. Brackets also surround dates that are the equivalents in years from creation for the ones expressed in the system of jubilees, weeks, and/or years in the text. In some passages where the text refers to a period of time, say, four weeks of years, the equivalent in numbers is indicated between brackets.

{{ }} Double braces   Double braces surround text represented by a witness but about which there is strong doubt whether it actually belongs in the text. The unusual situation is explained in the textual notes. This happens only at 2:19.

Superscript letters   The raised letters in the translation, marking the location of a lemma, are placed after the word or words in question. The letters indicate that there is a textual note on the word or words. The exception to this procedure is when a lemma involves several words or another lemma consists of one or two words within that longer lemma. In those instnaces, the letter marking the location of the longer lemma is placed after the first word in it, while the shorter lemma is then marked with the next letter after the relevant word or words. The exact words involved in each lemma will be clear from the textual note where the superscript letter is repeated, followed by the lemma.

Textual Notes

( ) Parentheses   Quotation of a lemma at the beginning of a textual note may include a word or words enclosed in parentheses, although in the translation itself the word or words are not in parentheses. In the lemmas, the parentheses indicate that the word or words are not part of the textual variant that is explained in the textual notes. The same is true when a word or words are within parentheses in the translation. If they are part of a lemma, it will still be the case that the variant does not involve the word/words in parentheses since they are not actually in the text.

A lemma may include in parentheses a word before or after the variant in question. These terms from the context are provided to make it easier for the reader to locate the lemma in the translation of a verse where the term may occur several times, where the word affected is a short one (e.g., "and," "her"), or where there is an implied object of a verb not realized in the translation (say, in a sequence of verbs where the subject is not repeated). As with all words in parentheses in the lemma as cited at the beginning of a textual note, they are not part of the textual unit for which there is a variant reading. Ethiopic manuscript numbers are explained in the introduction.

Superscript Letters after a Manuscript Number
  t = text
  c = corrector
  mg. = a different reading in the margin not marked as a correction

Superscript Number after a Word in the Lemma: In a few cases a superscript 2 will be appended to a word in the lemma if that word is the second occurrence of it in the verse or if two uses of it occur in very close proximity to each other. The superscript number is meant to indicate more clearly which occurrence is the one in the lemma.

— The dash between words in the lemma indicates that the lemma includes all the words that intervene as well.

... The presence of periods separating words in a lemma indicates that the lemma involves only those terms, not the word or words intervening between them.

/ A slash or solidus marks the separation of two items in the lemma whose order is reversed in a variant or variants.

→ The arrow indicates that the word before the arrow was corrupted/developed into the one after it.

om. Is omitted by
pr. Is preceded by
+ Add(s)

Ethiopic Transcription

In transcriptions of Ethiopic words, the labialized consonants are represented as *qw, ḫw, kw, gw*, rather than with a superscript –w.

3. Editions of Ancient Texts

MT   Masoretic Text
Karl Elliger and Wilhelm Rudolph, eds., *Biblia Hebraica Stuttgartensia* (5th ed.; Stuttgart: Deutsche Bibelgesellschaft, 1997).

SP   Samaritan Pentateuch
H. von Gall, ed., *Der hebräische Pentateuch der Samaritaner* (5 vols.; Giessen: Alfred Töpelmann, 1914–18).

Syr   Syriac (Peshitta)
T. Jansma and M. D. Koster, eds., *The Old Testament in Syriac, according to the Peshiṭta Version,* part 1, fascicle 1, *Genesis–Exodus* (Leiden: Brill, 1977).

LXX   Septuagint
John William Wevers, ed., *Genesis* (Septuaginta: Vetus Testamentum Graecum Auctoritate Academiae Scientiarum Gottingensis editum 1; Göttingen: Vandenhoeck & Ruprecht, 1974).
John William Wevers, ed., *Exodus* (Septuaginta: Vetus Testamentum Graecum Auctoritate Academiae Scientiarum Gottingensis editum II.1; Göttingen: Vandenhoeck & Ruprecht, 1991).
Alfred Rahlfs, ed., *Septuaginta* (2 vols.; Stuttgart: Württembergische Bibelanstalt, 1935).

OL   Old Latin
Bonifacius Fischer, ed., *Genesis* (Vetus Latina: Die Reste der altlateinischen Bibel 2; Freiburg: Herder, 1951).

Eth.   Ethiopic
J. Oscar Boyd, ed., *The Octateuch in Ethiopic according to the Text of the Paris Codex, with the Variants of Five Other Manuscripts* (2 vols.; Bibliotheca Abessinica 3-4; Leiden: Brill; Princeton: University Library, 1909–11).

Tg.   Targum
Targum Pseudo-Jonathan, Targum Neofiti
Alexandro Díez Macho, ed., *Genesis* (Biblia Polyglotta Matritensia, IV: Targum Palaestinense in Pentateuchum 1; Madrid: Consejo Superior de Investigaciones Científicas, 1988).
Alexandro Díez Macho, ed., *Exodus* (Biblia Polyglotta Matritensia, IV: Targum Palaestinense in Pentateuchum 2; Madrid: Consejo Superior de Investigaciones Científicas, 1980).

Targum Onqelos
Alexander Sperber, ed., *The Pentateuch according to Targum Onkelos* (Bible in Aramaic 1; Leiden: Brill, 1959).

Fragment Targum
Michael L. Klein, *The Fragment-Targums of the Pentateuch according to Their Extant Sources* (2 vols.; AnBib 76; Rome: Biblical Institute Press, 1980).

M. Ginsburger, ed., *Das Fragmententhargum* (Berlin: S. Calvary, 1899).

4. Short Titles

Aalen, *Heilsverlangen*
Sverre Aalen, *Heilsverlangen und Heilsverwirklichung: Studien zur Erwartung des Heils in der apokalyptischen Literatur des antiken Judentums und im ältesten Christentum* (ALGHJ 21; Leiden: Brill, 1990).

Adler, "Burning"
William Adler, "Abraham and the Burning of the Temple of Idols: Jubilees Traditions in Christian Chronography," *JQR* 77 (1986-87) 95-117.

Adler, "Jacob of Edessa"
William Adler, "Jacob of Edessa and the Jewish Pseudepigrapha in Syriac Chronography," in John C. Reeves, ed., *Tracing the Threads: Studies in the Vitality of Jewish Pseudepigrapha* (SBLEJL 6; Atlanta: Scholars Press, 1994) 143-71.

Adler/Tuffin, *Chronography*
William Adler and Paul Tuffin
The Chronography of George Synkellos: A Byzantine Chronicle of Universal History from the Creation (Oxford: Oxford University Press, 2002).

Albani et al., *Studies in the Book of Jubilees*
Matthias Albani, Jörg Frey, and Armin Lange, eds., *Studies in the Book of Jubilees* (TSAJ 65; Tübingen: Mohr Siebeck, 1997).

Albeck, *Jubiläen*
Chanoch Albeck, *Das Buch der Jubiläen und die Halacha* (Sieben und vierziger Bericht der Hochschule für die Wissenschaft des Judentums in Berlin; Berlin-Schöneberg: Siegfried Scholem, 1930).

Alexander, "Imago Mundi"
Philip Alexander, "Notes on the 'Imago Mundi' of the Book of Jubilees," *JJS* 33 (1982) 197-213.

Alexander and Dan, "Complete"
Tamar Alexander and Yosef Dan, "The Complete Midrash Va-yissa'u," *Folklore Research Center Studies* 3 (1972) 67-76.

Anderson, "Celibacy"
Gary A. Anderson, "Celibacy or Consummation in the Garden? Reflections on Early Jewish and Christian Interpretations of the Garden of Eden," *HTR* 82 (1989) 121-48.

Anderson, "Torah before Sinai"
Gary A. Anderson, "The Status of the Torah before Sinai: The Retelling of the Bible in the Damascus Covenant and the Book of Jubilees," *DSD* 1 (1994) 1-29.

Baillet, "Remarques"
Maurice Baillet, "Remarques sur le manuscrit du Livre des Jubilés de la grotte 3 de Qumrân," *RevQ* 5/19 (1964-66) 423-33.

Baumgarten, "265. 4QMiscellaneous Rules"
Joseph Baumgarten, "265. 4QMiscellaneous Rules," in *Qumran Cave 4 XXV: Halakhic Texts* (DJD 35; Oxford: Clarendon, 1999) 57-78.

Baumgarten, "Beginning of the Day"
Joseph Baumgarten, "The Beginning of the Day in the Calendar of Jubilees," *JBL* 77 (1958) 355-60.

Baumgarten, "First and Second Tithes"
Joseph Baumgarten, "The First and Second Tithes in the *Temple Scroll*," in Ann Kort and Scott Morschauer, eds., *Biblical and Related Studies Presented to Samuel Iwry* (Winona Lake, IN: Eisenbrauns, 1985) 5-15.

Baumgarten, "Laws of 'Orlah"
Joseph Baumgarten, "The Laws of 'Orlah and First Fruits in the Light of Jubilees, the Qumran Writings, and Targum Ps. Jonathan," *JJS* 38 (1987) 195-202.

Baumgarten, "Purification"
Joseph Baumgarten, "Purification after Childbirth and the Sacred Garden in 4Q265 and Jubilees," in George Brooke and Florentino García Martínez, eds., *New Qumran Texts and Studies* (STDJ 15; Leiden: Brill, 1994) 3-10.

Baumgarten, "Some Problems"
Joseph Baumgarten, "Some Problems of the Jubilees Calendar in Current Research," *VT* 32 (1982) 485-89.

Baumgarten, *Studies in Qumran Law*
Joseph Baumgarten, *Studies in Qumran Law* (SJLA 24; Leiden: Brill, 1977).

Bautch, "Afterlife"
Richard Bautch, "Afterlife in Jubilees: Through a Covenantal Prism," in Tobias Nicklas, Friedrich Reiterer, and Jozef Verheyden, eds., *The Human Body in Death and Resurrection* (Deuterocanonical and Cognate Literature Yearbook 2009; Berlin: de Gruyter, 2009) 205-19.

Beckwith, *Old Testament Canon*
Roger Beckwith, *The Old Testament Canon of the New Testament Church and Its Background in Early Judaism* (Grand Rapids: Eerdmans, 1985).

Beer, *Jubiläen*
Bernhard Beer, *Das Buch der Jubiläen und sein Verhältniss zu den Midraschim* (Leipzig: Wolfgang Gerhard, 1856).

Ben-Dov, "Tradition and Innovation"
Jonathan Ben-Dov, "Tradition and Innovation in the Calendar of Jubilees," in Gabriele Boccaccini and Giovanni Ibba, eds., *Enoch and the Mosaic Torah: The Evidence of Jubilees* (Grand Rapids: Eerdmans, 2009) 276-93.

Berger, *Jubiläen*
Klaus Berger, *Das Buch der Jubiläen* (JSHRZ 2.3; Gütersloh: Gütersloher Verlagshaus Gerd Mohn, 1981).

Bergsma, *Jubilee*
John Bergsma, *The Jubilee from Leviticus to Qumran: A History of Interpretation* (VTSup 115; Leiden: Brill, 2007).

Bergsma, "Jubilees and the Early Enochic Books"
: John Bergsma, "The Relationship between Jubilees and the Early Enochic Books (Astronomical Book and Book of the Watchers)," in Gabriele Boccaccini and Giovanni Ibba, eds., *Enoch and the Mosaic Torah: The Evidence of Jubilees* (Grand Rapids: Eerdmans, 2009) 36–51.

Berner, *Jahre*
: Christoph Berner, *Jahre, Jahrwochen und Jubiläen: Heptadische Geschichtskonzeptionen im Antiken Judentum* (BZAW 363; Berlin: de Gruyter, 2006).

Blenkinsopp, *Isaiah 1–39*
: Joseph Blenkinsopp, *Isaiah 1–39: A New Translation with Introduction and Commentary* (AB 19; New York: Doubleday, 2000).

Blenkinsopp, *Isaiah 55–66*
: Joseph Blenkinsopp, *Isaiah 55–66: A New Translation with Introduction and Commentary* (AB 19B; New York: Doubleday, 2003).

Boccaccini, *Enoch and Qumran Origins*
: Gabriele Boccaccini et al., eds., *Enoch and Qumran Origins: New Light on a Forgotten Connection* (Grand Rapids: Eerdmans, 2005).

Boccaccini and Ibba, *Mosaic Torah*
: Gabriele Boccaccini and Giovanni Ibba, eds., *Enoch and the Mosaic Torah: The Evidence of Jubilees* (Grand Rapids: Eerdmans, 2009).

Bohn, "Bedeutung"
: Friedrich Bohn, "Die Bedeutung des Buches der Jubiläen: Zum 50 jährigen Jubiläen der ersten, deutschen Übersetzung," *ThStK* 73 (1900) 167–84.

Bousset, "Die Testamente der zwölf Patriarchen"
: Wilhelm Bousset, "Die Testamente der zwölf Patriarchen," *ZNW* 1 (1900) 141–75, 187–209.

Boxel, "God of Rebekah"
: Piet van Boxel, "The God of Rebekah," *SIDIC* 9 (1976) 14–18.

Brin, "Sources"
: Gershon Brin, "The Sources of the Saying of Esau in Jubilees 37 according to 4Q PapJubilees[h], unit 2, col. IV," in Rimmon Kasher and Moshe Sippor, eds., *Memorial Volume for Yehudah Qomlosh* (Studies in Bible and Exegesis 6; Ramat-Gan: University of Bar-Ilan, 2003) 17–24.

Brock, "Abraham and the Ravens"
: Sebastian Brock, "Abraham and the Ravens: A Syriac Counterpart to Jubilees 11–12 and Its Implications," *JSJ* 9 (1978) 135–52.

Brooke, "Exegetical Strategies"
: George J. Brooke, "Exegetical Strategies in Jubilees 1–2: New Light from 4QJubilees[a]," in Matthias Albani, Jörg Frey, and Armin Lange, eds., *Studies in the Book of Jubilees* (TSAJ 65; Tübingen: Mohr Siebeck, 1997) 39–57.

Büchler, "Studies"
: Adolph Büchler, "Studies in the Book of Jubilees," *REJ* 82 (1926) 253–74.

Büchler, "Traces"
: Adolph Büchler, "Traces des idées et des coutumes hellénistiques dans le Livre des Jubilés," *REJ* 89 (1930) 321–48.

Byron, *Cain and Abel*
: John Byron, *Cain and Abel in Text and Tradition: Jewish and Christian Interpretations of the First Sibling Rivalry* (TBN 14; Leiden: Brill, 2011).

Caquot, "Deux notes"
: André Caquot, "Deux notes sur la géographie des Jubilés," in Gérard Nahon and Charles Touati, eds., *Hommages à Georges Vajda: Études d'histoire et de pensée juives* (Louvain: Peeters, 1980) 37–42.

Caquot, "Jubilés"
: André Caquot, "Jubilés," in André Dupont-Sommer and Marc Philonenko, eds., *La Bible: Écrits Intertestamentaires* (Paris: Gallimard, 1987) 627–810.

Caquot, "'Loi' et 'Temoignage'"
: André Caquot, "'Loi' et 'Témoignage' dans le Livre des Jubilés," in Christian Robin, ed., *Mélanges linguistiques offerts à Maxime Rodinson par ses élèves, ses collègues et ses amis* (Comptes rendus du Groupe linguistique d'études chamito-sémitiques, supplément 12; Paris: Geuthner, 1985) 137–45.

Caquot, "Les protecteurs"
: André Caquot, "Les protecteurs des tribus d'Israël: Notes d'angelologie à propos de Testament de Juda 25, 2," in *La vie de la parole: De l'Ancien au Nouveau Testament: Études d'exégèse et d'herméneutique bibliques offert à Pierre Grelot professeur à l'Institut Catholique de Paris* (Paris: Desclée, 1987) 49–59.

Cavallin, *Life after Death*
: Hans Clemens Cavallin, *Life after Death: Paul's Argument for the Resurrection of the Dead in 1 Cor. 15* (ConBNT 7.1; Lund: Gleerup, 1974).

Ceriani, *Monumenta Sacra et Profana*
: Antonio Maria Ceriani, *Monumenta Sacra et Profana* (2 vols.; Milan: Bibliotheca Ambrosiana, 1861–63).

Charles, *Eschatology*
: Robert Henry Charles, *Eschatology: The Doctrine of a Future Life in Israel, Judaism, and Christianity: A Critical History* (New York: Schocken Books, 1963; original, 1899; 2nd ed., 1913).

Charles, *Ethiopic Version*
: Robert Henry Charles, *Maṣḥafa Kufālē or the Ethiopic Version of the Hebrew Book of Jubilees* (Anecdota Oxoniensia; Oxford: Clarendon, 1895).

Charles, *Jubilees*
: Robert Henry Charles, *The Book of Jubilees or the Little Genesis* (London: Adam & Charles Black, 1902).

Christiansen, *Covenant*
: Ellen Juhl Christiansen, *The Covenant in Judaism and Paul: A Study of Ritual Boundaries as Identity Markers* (AGJU 27; Leiden: Brill, 1995).

Cohen, "Intermarriage"
: Shaye J. D. Cohen, "From the Bible to the Talmud: The Prohibition of Intermarriage," *HAR* 7 (1983) 23–39.

Collins, "Genre"
John J. Collins, "The Genre of the Book of *Jubilees*," in Eric F. Mason, Kelley Coblentz Bautch, Angela Kim Harkins, and Daniel A. Machiela, eds., *A Teacher for All Generations: Essays in Honor of James C. VanderKam* (2 vols.; JSJSup 153/I-II; Leiden: Brill, 2012) 737-55.

Crawford, "Exegetical Function"
Cory D. Crawford, "On the Exegetical Function of the Abraham/Ravens Tradition in Jubilees 11," *HTR* 97 (2004) 91-97.

Crislip, "*Book of Jubilees* in Coptic"
Andrew Crislip, "The *Book of Jubilees* in Coptic: An Early Christian *Florilegium* on the Family of Noah," *Bulletin of the American Society of Papyrologists* 40 (2003) 27-44.

Cross, "Jewish Scripts"
Frank Moore Cross, "The Development of the Jewish Scripts," in George Ernest Wright, ed., *The Bible and the Ancient Near East: Essays in Honor of William Foxwell Albright* (Garden City, NY: Doubleday, 1961) 133-202.

Davenport, *Eschatology*
Gene L. Davenport, *The Eschatology of the Book of Jubilees* (StPB 20; Leiden: Brill, 1971).

Dean, *Epiphanius' Treatise*
James Elmer Dean, *Epiphanius' Treatise on Weights and Measures: The Syriac Version* (The Oriental Institute of the University of Chicago, SAOC 11; Chicago: University of Chicago Press, 1935).

Deichgräber, "Fragmente"
Reinhard Deichgräber, "Fragmente einer Jubiläen-Handschrift aus Höhle 3 von Qumran," *RevQ* 5/19 (1964-66) 415-22.

Delcor, "La fête des huttes"
Mathias Delcor, "La fête des huttes dans le Rouleau du Temple et dans le livre des Jubilés," *RevQ* 15/57-58 (1991) 181-98.

Denis, *Fragmenta*
Albert-Marie Denis, *Fragmenta pseudepigraphorum quae supersunt graeca* (PVTG 3; Leiden: Brill, 1970).

Dillmann, *Grammar*
August Dillmann, *Ethiopic Grammar* (2nd ed.; trans. Carl Bezold; London: Williams & Norgate, 1907).

Dillmann, "Jubiläen"
August Dillmann, "Das Buch der Jubiläen oder die kleine Genesis," *Jahrbücher der Biblischen Wissenschaft* 2 (1850) 230-56; 3 (1851) 1-96.

Dillmann, *Lexicon*
August Dillmann, *Lexicon Linguae Aethiopicae* (1865; repr., New York: Frederick Ungar, 1955).

Dillmann, *Liber Jubilaeorum*
August Dillmann, *Maṣḥafa Kufālē sive Liber Jubilaeorum* (Kiel: C. G. L. van Maack; London: Williams & Norgate, 1859).

Dimant, "Binding of Isaac"
Devorah Dimant, "The Biblical Basis of Non-Biblical Additions: The Binding of Isaac in Jubilees in Light of the Story of Job," in Devorah Dimant, *Connected Vessels: The Dead Sea Scrolls and the Literature of the Second Temple Period* (Asuppot 3; Jerusalem: Bialik Institute, 2010) 348-68.

Dimant, "Biography of Enoch"
Devorah Dimant, "The Biography of Enoch and the Books of Enoch," *VT* 33 (1983) 19-24.

Dimant, "Fallen Angels"
Devorah Dimant, "The 'Fallen Angels' in the Dead Sea Scrolls and in the Apocryphal and Pseudepigraphic Books Related to Them" (PhD diss., Hebrew University of Jerusalem, 1974).

Dimant, "Judah and Tamar"
"Judah and Tamar in Jubilees 41," in Eric F. Mason, Kelley Coblentz Bautch, Angela Kim Harkins, and Daniel A. Machiela, eds., *A Teacher for All Generations: Essays in Honor of James C. VanderKam* (JSJSup 153/I-II; Leiden: Brill, 2012) 783-97.

Dimant, "Sons of Heaven"
Devorah Dimant, "The Sons of Heaven—The Teaching about the Angels in the Book of Jubilees in Light of the Writings of the Qumran Community," in Moshe Idel, Devorah Dimant, and Shalom Rosenberg, eds., *A Tribute to Sarah: Studies in Jewish Philosophy and Kabbalah* (Jerusalem: Magnes Press, 1994) 97-118.

Dimant, "Two 'Scientific Fictions'"
Devorah Dimant, "Two 'Scientific Fictions': The So-Called Book of Noah and the Alleged Quotation of Jubilees in CD 16:3-4," in Peter Flint, James VanderKam, and Emanuel Tov, eds., *Studies in the Hebrew Bible, Qumran, and the Septuagint Presented to Eugene Ulrich* (VTSup 101; Leiden: Brill, 2006) 230-49.

Dobos, "Consolation of History"
Károly Daniel Dobos, "The Consolation of History: A Reexamination of the Chronology of the Abraham Pericope in the Book of Jubilees," *Hen* 31 (2009) 84-91.

Docherty, "Joseph the Patriarch"
Susan Docherty, "Joseph the Patriarch: Representations of Joseph in Early Post-Biblical Literature," in Martin O'Kane, ed., *Borders, Boundaries and the Bible* (JSOTSup 313; Sheffield: Sheffield Academic Press, 2002) 194-216.

Doering, "Concept of the Sabbath"
Lutz Doering, "The Concept of the Sabbath in the Book of Jubilees," in Matthias Albani, Jörg Frey, and Armin Lange, eds., *Studies in the Book of Jubilees* (TSAJ 65; Tübingen: Mohr Siebeck, 1997) 179-205.

Doering, "*Jub.* 50:6-13"
Lutz Doering, "*Jub.* 50:6-13 als Schlussabschnitt des Jubiläenbuchs: Nachtrag aus Qumran oder ursprünglicher Bestandteil des Werks," *RevQ* 20/79 (2002) 359-87.

Doering, *Schabbat*
Lutz, Doering, *Schabbat: Sabbathalacha und –praxis im antiken Judentum und Urchristentum* (TSAJ 78; Tübingen: Mohr Siebeck, 1999).

Doran, "Non-Dating"
   Robert Doran, "The Non-Dating of Jubilees: Jub 34–38; 23:14-32 in Narrative Context," *JSJ* 20 (1989) 1–11.
Dorman, "Commit Injustice"
   Anke Dorman, "'Commit Injustice and Shed Innocent Blood': Motives behind the Institution of the Day of Atonement in the Book of Jubilees," in Thomas Hieke and Tobias Nicklas, eds., *The Day of Atonement: Its Interpretations in Early Jewish and Christian Traditions* (TBN 15; Leiden: Brill, 2012) 51–62.
Drawnel, *Aramaic Wisdom Text*
   Henryk Drawnel, *An Aramaic Wisdom Text from Qumran: A New Interpretation of the Levi Document* (JSJSup 86; Leiden: Brill, 2004).
Driver, *Deuteronomy*
   Samuel Rolles Driver, *A Critical and Exegetical Commentary on Deuteronomy* (ICC; Edinburgh: Clark, 1902).
Ego, "Heilige Zeit"
   Beate Ego, "Heilige Zeit—heiliger Raum—heiliger Mensch: Beobachtungen zur Struktur der Gesetzesbegründung in der Schöpfungs- und Paradiesgeschichte des Jubiläenbuchs," in Matthias Albani, Jörg Frey, and Armin Lange, eds., *Studies in the Book of Jubilees* (TSAJ 65; Tübingen: Mohr Siebeck, 1997) 207–19.
Eiss, "Das Wochenfest"
   Werner Eiss, "Das Wochenfest im Jubiläenbuch und im antiken Judentum," in Matthias Albani, Jörg Frey, and Armin Lange, eds., *Studies in the Book of Jubilees* (TSAJ 65; Tübingen: Mohr Siebeck, 1997) 165–78.
Endres, *Biblical Interpretation*
   John C. Endres, *Biblical Interpretation in the Book of Jubilees* (CBQMS 18; Washington, DC: Catholic Biblical Association of America, 1987).
Endres, "Prayers in Jubilees"
   John C. Endres, "Prayers in Jubilees," in Lynn LiDonnici and Andrea Lieber, eds., *Heavenly Tablets: Interpretation, Identity and Tradition in Ancient Judaism* (JSJSup 119; Leiden: Brill, 2007) 31–47.
Epstein, "Jubilés"
   A. Epstein, "Le Livre des Jubilés, Philon, et le Midrasch Tadsché," *REJ* 20 (1890) 80–97; 22 (1891) 1–25.
Eshel, "Demonology"
   Esther Eshel, "Demonology in Palestine During the Second Temple Period" (Diss., Hebrew University of Jerusalem, 2000).
Eshel, "*Imago Mundi* of the *Genesis Apocryphon*"
   Esther Eshel, "The *Imago Mundi* of the *Genesis Apocryphon*," in Lynn LiDonnici and Andrea Lieber, eds., *Heavenly Tablets: Interpretation, Identity and Tradition in Ancient Judaism* (JSJSup 119; Leiden: Brill, 2007) 111–31.
Eshel, "*Jubilees* 32"
   Esther Eshel, "*Jubilees* 32 and the Bethel Cult Traditions in Second Temple Literature," in Esther Chazon, David Satran, and Ruth Clements, eds., *Things Revealed: Studies in Early Jewish and Christian Literature in Honor of Michael E. Stone* (JSJSup 89; Leiden: Brill, 2004) 21–36.
Eshel, "Three New Fragments"
   Hanan Eshel, "Three New Fragments from Qumran Cave 11," *DSD* 8 (2001) 1–8 (English version of "Three New Fragments from Cave 11 at Qumran," *Tarbiz* 68 [1998] 273–78).
Finkelstein, "Pre-Maccabean Documents"
   Louis Finkelstein, "Pre-Maccabean Documents in the Passover Haggadah," *HTR* 36 (1943) 1–38 (Appendix: "The Date of the Book of Jubilees," 19–24).
Finkelstein, "Rabbinic Halaka"
   Louis Finkelstein, "The Book of Jubilees and the Rabbinic Halaka," *HTR* 16 (1923) 39–61.
Flint and VanderKam, *Dead Sea Scrolls after Fifty Years*
   Peter W. Flint and James C. VanderKam, eds., *The Dead Sea Scrolls after Fifty Years: A Comprehensive Assessment* (2 vols.; Leiden: Brill, 1998, 1999).
Flusser, *Judaism*
   David Flusser, *Judaism and the Origins of Christianity* (Jerusalem: Magnes Press, 1988).
Francis, "Excluded Middle"
   Michael Francis, "Defining the Excluded Middle: The Case of Ishmael in *Jubilees*," *JSP* 21 (2012) 259–83.
Frankel, "Das Buch der Jubiläen"
   Zecharias Frankel, "Das Buch der Jubiläen," *MGWJ* 5 (1856) 311–16, 380–400.
Freedman, *Midrash Rabbah*
   Harry Freedman and Maurice Simon, eds., *Midrash Rabbah* (10 vols.; 3rd ed.; London/New York: Soncino, 1983).
Frevel, "Intermarriage"
   Christian Frevel, "'Separate Yourself from the Gentiles' (*Jubilees* 22:16): Intermarriage in the Book of *Jubilees*," in Christian Frevel, ed., *Mixed Marriages: Intermarriage and Group Identity in the Second Temple Period* (LHBOTS 547; London: T&T Clark, 2011) 220–50.
Frey, "Weltbild"
   Jörg Frey, "Zum Weltbild im Jubiläenbuch," in Matthias Albani, Jörg Frey, and Armin Lange, eds., *Studies in the Book of Jubilees* (TSAJ 65; Tübingen: Mohr Siebeck, 1997) 261–92.
Friedlander, *Pirḳê de Rabbi Eliezer*
   Gerald Friedlander, *Pirḳê de Rabbi Eliezer* (1916; repr., New York: Hermon, 1970).
García Martínez, "Heavenly Tablets"
   Florentino García Martínez, "The Heavenly Tablets in the Book of Jubilees," in Matthias Albani, Jörg Frey, and Armin Lange, eds., *Studies in the Book of Jubilees* (TSAJ 65; Tübingen: Mohr Siebeck, 1997) 243–60.

García Martínez, *Qumran and Apocalyptic*
  Florentino García Martínez, *Qumran and Apocalyptic: Studies on the Aramaic Texts from Qumran* (STDJ 9; Leiden: Brill, 1992) 1-44.

Geist and VanderKam, "Four Places"
  Andrew Geist and James VanderKam, "Four Places That Belong to the Lord (*Jubilees* 4.26)," *JSP* 22 (2012) 146-62.

Gelzer, "Die apokryphischen Reste"
  Heinrich Gelzer, "Die apokryphischen Reste der Byzantiner und ihre Abstammung aus Pandorus und Africanus," in idem, *Sextus Julius Africanus und die byzantinische Chronographie*, vol. 2: *Die Nachfolger des Julius Africanus* (Leipzig: Teubner, 1885) 249-97.

Gilders, "Blood and Covenant"
  William K. Gilders, "Blood and Covenant: Interpretive Elaboration on Genesis 9.4-6 in the Book of *Jubilees*," *JSP* 15 (2006) 83-118.

Gilders, *Blood Ritual*
  William K. Gilders, *Blood Ritual in the Hebrew Bible: Meaning and Power* (Baltimore: Johns Hopkins University Press, 2004).

Gilders, "Concept of Covenant"
  William K. Gilders, "The Concept of Covenant in Jubilees," in Gabriele Boccaccini and Giovanni Ibba, eds., *Enoch and the Mosaic Torah: The Evidence of Jubilees* (Grand Rapids: Eerdmans, 2009) 178-92.

Ginzberg, *Legends*
  Louis Ginzberg, *The Legends of the Jews* (7 vols.; Philadelphia: Jewish Publication Society of America, 1909-38; repr., Baltimore: Johns Hopkins University Press, 1998).

Ginzberg, *Unknown Jewish Sect*
  Louis Ginzberg, *An Unknown Jewish Sect* (Moreshet Series 1; New York: Jewish Theological Seminary of America, 1970 [German original, 1922]).

Glessmer, "Explizite Aussagen"
  Uwe Glessmer, "Explizite Aussagen über kalendarische Konflikte im Jubiläenbuch: Jub 6, 22-32.33-38," in Matthias Albani, Jörg Frey, and Armin Lange, eds., *Studies in the Book of Jubilees* (TSAJ 65; Tübingen: Mohr Siebeck, 1997) 127-64.

Goldmann, "Jubilees"
  Moshe Goldmann, "The Book of Jubilees," in Avraham Kahana, ed., *The Apocryphal Books* (2 vols.; 1956; repr., Jerusalem: Maqor, 1970) 1:216-313.

Goldstein, "Date"
  Jonathan Goldstein, "The Date of the Book of Jubilees," *PAAJR* 50 (1983) 63-86. Reprinted in Jonathan Goldstein, *Semites, Iranians, Greeks and Romans* (BJS 217; Atlanta: Scholars Press, 1990) 161-80.

van Goudoever, *Biblical Calendars*
  J. van Goudoever, *Biblical Calendars* (2nd ed.; Leiden: Brill, 1961).

Grabbe, *Etymology*
  Lester Grabbe, *Etymology in Early Jewish Interpretation: The Hebrew Names in Philo* (BJS 115; Atlanta: Scholars Press, 1988).

Greenberg, *Biblical Prose Prayers*
  Moshe Greenberg, *Biblical Prose Prayers as a Window to the Popular Religion of Ancient Israel* (The Taubman Lectures in Jewish Studies, 6th Series; Berkeley: University of California Press, 1983).

Greenfield, Stone, and Eshel, *Aramaic Levi Document*
  Jonas Greenfield, Michael Stone, and Esther Eshel, *The Aramaic Levi Document: Edition, Translation, Commentary* (SVTP 19; Leiden: Brill, 2004).

Gregory, "Death and Legacy of Leah"
  Bradley Gregory, "The Death and Legacy of Leah in Jubilees," *JSP* 17 (2008) 99-120.

Grelot, "Hénoch et ses écritures"
  Pierre Grelot, "Hénoch et ses écritures," *RB* 92 (1975) 481-500.

Grossfeld, *Targum Onqelos to Exodus*
  Bernard Grossfeld, *The Targum Onqelos to Exodus* (ArBib 7; Wilmingtom, DE: Michael Glazier, 1988).

Grossfeld, *Targum Onqelos to Genesis*
  Bernard Grossfeld, *The Targum Onqelos to Genesis* (ArBib 6; Wilmington, DE: Michael Glazier, 1988).

Gunkel, *Genesis*
  Hermann Gunkel, *Genesis* (trans. Mark E. Biddle; Mercer Library of Biblical Studies; Macon, GA: Mercer University Press, 1997; translated from the 9th German printing, 1977 = 3rd ed., 1910).

Haile, "Homily of Aṣe Zärʾa Yaʿəqob"
  Getatchew Haile, "The Homily of Aṣe Zärʾa Yaʿəqob of Ethiopia in Honour of Saturday," *OLP* 13 (1982) 185-231.

Halpern-Amaru, "Bilhah and Naphtali"
  Betsy Halpern-Amaru, "Bilhah and Naphtali in Jubilees: A Note on 4QTNaphtali," *DSD* 6 (1999) 1-10.

Halpern-Amaru, "Burying the Fathers"
  Betsy Halpern-Amaru, "Burying the Fathers: Exegetical Strategies and Source Traditions in *Jubilees* 46," in Esther Chazon, Devorah Dimant, and Ruth Clements, eds., *Reworking the Bible: Apocryphal and Related Texts at Qumran* (STDJ 58; Leiden: Brill, 2005) 135-52.

Halpern-Amaru, *Empowerment*
  Betsy Halpern-Amaru, *The Empowerment of Women in the Book of Jubilees* (JSJSup 60; Leiden: Brill, 1999).

Halpern-Amaru, "Festivals"
  Betsy Halpern-Amaru, "The Festivals of Pesaḥ and Massot in the Book of Jubilees," in Gabriele Boccaccini and Giovanni Ibba, eds., *Enoch and the Mosaic Torah: The Evidence of Jubilees* (Grand Rapids: Eerdmans, 2009) 309-22.

Halpern-Amaru, "First Woman, Wives"
  Betsy Halpern-Amaru, "The First Woman, Wives, and Mothers in *Jubilees*," *JBL* 113 (1994) 609-26.

Halpern-Amaru, "Joy as Piety"
  Betsy Halpern-Amaru, "Joy as Piety in the 'Book of Jubilees,'" *JJS* 56 (2005) 185-205.

Halpern-Amaru, "Naming of Levi"
Betsy Halpern-Amaru, "The Naming of Levi in the Book of Jubilees," in Esther G. Chazon and Michael E. Stone, eds., *Pseudepigraphic Perspectives: The Apocrypha and Pseudepigrapha in Light of the Dead Sea Scrolls. Proceedings of the International Symposium of the Orion Center, 12–14 January 1997* (STDJ 31; Leiden: Brill, 1999) 59–69.

Halpern-Amaru, "Portrait of Sarah"
Betsy Halpern-Amaru, "The Portrait of Sarah in Jubilees," in Ulf Haxen, Hanne Trautner-Kromann, and Karen Lisa Goldschmidt Salamon, eds., *Jewish Studies in a New Europe: Proceedings of the Fifth Congress of Jewish Studies in Copenhagen 1994 under the auspices of the European Association for Jewish Studies* (Copenhagen: C. A. Rietzel, 1998) 336–48.

Halpern-Amaru, "Protection from Birds"
Betsy Halpern-Amaru, "Protection from Birds in the *Book of Jubilees*," in Aren Maeir, Jodi Magness, and Lawrence Schiffman, eds., *'Go Out and Study the Land' (Judges 18:2): Archaeological, Historical and Textual Studies in Honor of Hanan Eshel* (JSJSup 148; Leiden: Brill, 2012) 59–67.

Halpern-Amaru, *Rewriting the Bible*
Betsy Halpern-Amaru, *Rewriting the Bible: Land and Covenant in Post-Biblical Jewish Literature* (Valley Forge, PA: Trinity Press International, 1994).

Halpern-Amaru, "Use of Bible"
Betsy Halpern-Amaru, "The Use of Bible in *Jubilees* 49: The Time and Date of the Pesaḥ Celebration," *Meghillot* 5–6 (2007) 81–100.

Hamilton, *Genesis 1–17*
Victor P. Hamilton, *The Book of Genesis: Chapters 1–17* (NICOT; Grand Rapids: Eerdmans, 1990).

Hamilton, *Genesis 18–50*
Victor P. Hamilton, *The Book of Genesis: Chapters 18–50* (NICOT; Grand Rapids: Eerdmans, 1995).

Hanneken, "Angels and Demons"
Todd Hanneken, "Angels and Demons in the Book of Jubilees and Contemporary Apocalypses," *Hen* 28 (2006) 11–25.

Hanneken, "Status"
Todd Hanneken, "The Status and Interpretation of *Jubilees* in 4Q390," in Eric F. Mason, Kelley Coblentz Bautch, Angela Kim Harkins, and Daniel A. Machiela, eds., *A Teacher for All Generations: Essays in Honor of James C. VanderKam* (2 vols.; JSJSup 153/I-II; Leiden: Brill, 2012) 407–28.

Hanneken, *Subversion*
Todd Hanneken, *The Subversion of the Apocalypses in the Book of Jubilees* (SBLEJL 34; Atlanta: Society of Biblical Literature, 2012).

Hanneken, "Watchers"
Todd Hanneken, "The Watchers in Rewritten Scripture: The Use of the *Book of the Watchers* in *Jubilees*," in Angela Harkins, Kelley Coblentz Bautch, and John Endres, eds., *The Fallen Angels Traditions: Second Temple Developments and Reception History* (CBQMS 53; Washington, DC: Catholic Biblical Association of America, 2014) 25–68.

Hartom, "Jubilees"
Eliyahu S. Hartom, "The Book of Jubilees," in idem, *The Apocryphal Literature* (7 vols.; 3rd ed.; Tel Aviv: Yavneh, 1969) 5b.7–147.

Hayes, "Intermarriage and Impurity"
Christine E. Hayes, "Intermarriage and Impurity in Ancient Jewish Sources," *HTR* 92 (1999) 3–36.

Hayward, "Genesis and Its Reception in *Jubilees*"
C. T. R. Hayward, "Genesis and Its Reception in *Jubilees*," in Craig A. Evans, Joel N. Lohr, and David L. Petersen, eds., *The Book of Genesis: Composition, Reception, and Interpretation* (VTSup 152; Leiden: Brill, 2012) 375–404.

Hayward, *Jerome's Hebrew Questions*
C. T. R. Hayward, *Jerome's Hebrew Questions on Genesis* (Oxford Early Christian Studies; Oxford: Clarendon, 1995).

Hempel, "*Book of Jubilees* at Qumran"
Charlotte Hempel, "The Place of the *Book of Jubilees* at Qumran and Beyond," in Timothy Lim, ed., *The Dead Sea Scrolls in Their Historical Context* (Edinburgh: T&T Clark, 2000) 187–96.

Herrmann, *Erdkarte*
Albert Herrmann, *Die Erdkarte der Urbibel mit einem Anhang über Tartessos und die Etruskerfrage* (Braunschweig: Georg Westermann, 1931).

Himmelfarb, "Echoes"
Martha Himmelfarb, "Some Echoes of Jubilees in Medieval Hebrew Literature," in John Reeves, ed., *Tracing the Threads: Studies in the Vitality of the Jewish Pseudepigrapha* (SBLEJL 6; Atlanta: Scholars Press, 1994) 127–35.

Himmelfarb, *Kingdom of Priests*
Martha Himmelfarb, *A Kingdom of Priests: Ancestry and Merit in Ancient Judaism* (Jewish Culture and Contexts; Philadelphia: University of Pennsylvania Press, 2006).

Himmelfarb, "Levi, Phinehas"
Martha Himmelfarb, "Levi, Phinehas, and the Problem of Intermarriage at the Time of the Maccabean Revolt," *JSQ* 6 (1999) 1–24.

Himmelfarb, "Sexual Relations"
Martha Himmelfarb, "Sexual Relations and Purity in the Temple Scroll and the Book of Jubilees," *DSD* 6 (1999) 11–36.

Hoffmann, *Die Toten*
Paul Hoffmann, *Die Toten in Christus: Eine religionsgeschichtliche und exegetische Untersuchung zur paulinischen Eschatologie* (NTAbh n.F. 2; Münster: Aschendorff, 1966).

Holladay, *Jeremiah*
William L. Holladay, *Jeremiah: A Commentary on the Book of the Prophet Jeremiah* (2 vols.; Hermeneia; Minneapolis: Fortress Press, 1986, 1989).

Hollander and de Jonge, *Testaments*
Harm W. Hollander and Marinus de Jonge, *The Testaments of the Twelve Patriarchs: A Commentary* (SVTP 8; Leiden: Brill, 1985).

Hölscher, *Drei Erdkarten*
  Gustav Hölscher, *Drei Erdkarten: Ein Beitrag zur Erkenntnis des hebräischen Altertums* (Sitzungsberichte der Heidelberger Akademie der Wissenschaften, Philosophisch-historische Klasse, 1944–48; Heidelberg: Carl Winter, Universitäts-Verlag, 1949).

Houtman, *Exodus*
  Cornelis Houtman, *Exodus* (3 vols.; Historical Commentary on the Old Testament; Kampen: Kok, 1993, 1996 [vols. 1–2]; Louvain: Peeters, 2006 [vol. 3]).

Huizenga, "Battle for Isaac"
  Loren A. Huizenga, "The Battle for Isaac: Exploring the Composition and Function of the *Aqedah* in the Book of *Jubilees*," *JSP* 13 (2002) 33–59.

Hultgård, *L'eschatologie*
  Anders Hultgård, *L'eschatologie des Testaments des Douze Patriarches*, vol. 1: *Interprétation des textes* (Acta Universitatis Upsaliensis Historia Religionum 6; Uppsala: Almqvist & Wiksell, 1977).

Jaubert, *Date of the Last Supper*
  Annie Jaubert, *La date de la cène: Calendrier biblique et liturgie chrétienne* (Paris: Librairie LeCoffre, 1957); Eng. trans., *The Date of the Last Supper: The Biblical Calendar and Christian Liturgy* (trans. I. Rafferty; New York: Society of St. Paul, 1965).

Jaubert, *La notion d'alliance*
  Annie Jaubert, *La notion d'alliance dans le Judaisme* (Patristica Sorbonensia 6; Paris: Seuil, 1963).

Jellinek, *Bet ha-Midrasch*
  Adolph Jellinek, *Bet ha-Midrasch: Sammlung kleiner Midraschim und vermischter Abhandlungen aus der ältern jüdischen Literatur* (2 vols., 6 parts; Leipzig: C. W. Vollrath, 1855; repr., Jerusalem: Wahrmann, 1967).

Jones, *Ancient Jewish Christian Source*
  F. Stanley Jones, *An Ancient Jewish Christian Source on the History of Christianity: Pseudo-Clementine Recognitions 1.27-71* (SBLTT 37, Christian Apocrypha Series 2; Atlanta: Scholars Press, 1995).

Kister, "Body and Purification"
  Menahem Kister, "Body and Purification from Evil: Prayer Formulas and Concepts in Second Temple Literature and Their Relationship to Later Rabbinic Literature," *Meghillot* 8–9 (2010) 243–84.

Kister, "Essene Sect"
  Menahem Kister, "Towards the History of the Essene Sect: Studies in the Animal Apocalypse, the Book of Jubilees, and the Damascus Document," *Tarbiz* 56 (1986–87) 1–18.

Kister, "Newly-Identified Fragments"
  Menahem Kister, "Newly-Identified Fragments of the Book of Jubilees: Jub. 23:21-23, 30-31," *RevQ* 12 (1987) 529–36.

Kister, "Qumran Halakhah"
  Menaham Kister, "Some Aspects of Qumran Halakhah," in Julio Trebolle Barrera and Luis Vegas Montaner, eds., *The Madrid Qumran Congress: Proceedings of the International Congress on the Dead Sea Scrolls, Madrid, 18–21 March, 1991* (2 vols.; STDJ 11; Leiden: Brill, 1992) 2:571–88.

Kister, "Syncellus"
  Menaham Kister, "Syncellus and the Sources of *Jubilees* 3: A Note on M. Segal's Article," *Meghillot* 1 (2003) 127–33.

Kister, "*Tohu wa-Bohu*"
  Menahem Kister, "*Tohu wa-Bohu*, Primordial Elements and *Creatio ex Nihilo*," *JSQ* 14 (2007) 229–56.

Kister, "Two Formulae"
  Menahem Kister, "Two Formulae in the Book of Jubilees," *Tarbiz* 70 (2001) 289–300.

Klein, "Palästinisches im Jubiläenbuch"
  S. Klein, "Palästinisches im Jubiläenbuch," *ZDPV* 57 (1934) 7–27.

Knibb, "Jubilees and the Origins"
  Michael Knibb, "Jubilees and the Origins of the Qumran Community," An Inaugural Lecture Delivered in the Department of Biblical Studies, King's College (London, January 17, 1989).

Knibb, "Which Parts?"
  Michael Knibb, "Which Parts of *1 Enoch* Were Known to *Jubilees*? A Note on the Interpretation of *Jubilees* 4.16-25," in J. Cheryl Exum and Hugh G. M. Williamson, eds., *Reading from Right to Left: Essays on the Hebrew Bible in Honour of David J. A. Clines* (JSOTSup 373; Sheffield: Sheffield Academic Press, 2003) 254–62.

Knowles, "Abram and the Birds"
  Michael P. Knowles, "Abram and the Birds in *Jubilees* 11: A Subtext for the Parable of the Sower," *NTS* 41 (1995) 145–51.

Krüger, "Chronologie"
  M. J. Krüger, "Die Chronologie im Buche der Jubiläen, auf ihre biblische Grundlage zurückgeführt und berichtigt," *ZDMG* 12 (1858) 279–99.

Kugel, "4Q369"
  James L. Kugel, "4Q369 'Prayer of Enosh' and Ancient Biblical Interpretation," *DSD* 5 (1998) 119–48.

Kugel, "Biblical Apocrypha"
  James L. Kugel, "Biblical Apocrypha and Pseudepigrapha and the Hebrew of the Second Temple Period," in Takamitsu Muraoka and John F. Elwolde, eds., *Diggers at the Well: Proceedings of the Third International Symposium on the Hebrew of the Dead Sea Scrolls and Ben Sira* (STDJ 36; Leiden: Brill, 2000) 166–77.

Kugel, *In Potiphar's House*
  James L. Kugel, *In Potiphar's House: The Interpretive Life of Biblical Texts* (San Francisco: HarperSanFrancisco, 1990; 2nd ed.; Cambridge, MA: Harvard University Press, 1994).

Kugel, "Intended Replacement"
  James L. Kugel, "Is the Book of Jubilees a Commentary on Genesis or an Intended Replacement?," in Christl M. Maier, ed., *Congress Volume: Munich 2013* (VTSup 163; Leiden: Brill, 2014) 67–91.

Kugel, "Interpolations"
James L. Kugel, "On the Interpolations in the *Book of Jubilees*," *RevQ* 94 (2009) 215–72.

Kugel, "Jubilees"
James L. Kugel, "Jubilees," in *Outside the Bible: Ancient Jewish Writings Related to Scripture*, ed. Louis H. Feldman, James L. Kugel, and Lawrence H. Schiffman (3 vols.; Philadelphia: Jewish Publication Society, 2013) 1:272–465.

Kugel, "Jubilees Apocalypse"
James L. Kugel, "The Jubilees Apocalypse," *DSD* 1 (1994) 322–37.

Kugel, "Levi's Elevation"
James L. Kugel, "Levi's Elevation to the Priesthood in Second Temple Writings," *HTR* 86 (1993) 1–64.

Kugel, "Reuben's Sin"
James L. Kugel, "Reuben's Sin with Bilhah in the Testament of Reuben," in David Wright, David N. Freedman, and Avi Hurvitz, eds., *Pomegranates and Golden Bells: Studies in Biblical, Jewish, and Near Eastern Ritual, Law, and Literature in Honor of Jacob Milgrom* (Winona Lake, IN: Eisenbrauns, 1995) 525–54.

Kugel, "Story of Dinah"
James L. Kugel, "The Story of Dinah in the *Testament of Levi*," *HTR* 85 (1992) 1–34.

Kugel, *Traditions*
James L. Kugel, *Traditions of the Bible: A Guide to the Bible as It Was at the Start of the Common Era* (Cambridge, MA: Harvard University Press, 1998).

Kugel, *Walk through* Jubilees
James L. Kugel, *A Walk through* Jubilees: *Studies in the* Book of Jubilees *and the World of Its Creation* (JSJSup 156; Leiden: Brill, 2012).

Kugel, "Which Is Older?"
James L. Kugel, "Which Is Older, *Jubilees* or the *Genesis Apocryphon*?," in *A Walk through* Jubilees: *Studies in the* Book of Jubilees *and the World of Its Creation* (JSJSup 156; Leiden: Brill, 2012) 305–42.

Kugler, *From Patriarch to Priest*
Robert Kugler, *From Patriarch to Priest: The Levi-Priestly Tradition from* Aramaic Levi *to* Testament of Levi (SBLEJL 9; Atlanta: Scholars Press, 1996).

Kvanvig, "Jubilees—Read as a Narrative"
Helge Kvanvig, "Jubilees—Read as a Narrative," in Gabriele Boccaccini, ed., *Enoch and Qumran Origins: New Light on a Forgotten Connection* (Grand Rapids: Eerdmans, 2005) 75–83.

Lambert, "Did Israel Believe?"
David Lambert, "Did Israel Believe That Redemption Awaited Its Repentance? The Case of Jubilees 1," *CBQ* 68 (2006) 631–50.

Lambert, "Last Testaments"
David Lambert, "Last Testaments in the Book of Jubilees," *DSD* 11 (2004) 82–107.

Lange, "Divinatorische Träume"
Armin Lange, "Divinatorische Träume und Apokalyptik im Jubiläenbuch," in Matthias Albani, Jörg Frey, and Armin Lange, eds., *Studies in the Book of Jubilees* (TSAJ 65; Tübingen: Mohr Siebeck, 1997) 25–38.

Lange, "Magic and Divination"
Armin Lange, "The Essene Position on Magic and Divination," in Moshe Bernstein, Florentino García Martínez, and John Kampen, eds., *Legal Texts and Legal Issues: Proceedings of the Second Meeting of the International Organization for Qumran Studies, Published in Honour of Joseph M. Baumgarten* (STDJ 23; Leiden: Brill, 1997) 377–435.

Lavee, "Noahide Laws"
Moshe Lavee, "The Noahide Laws: The Building Blocks of a Rabbinic Conceptual Framework in Qumran and the Book of Acts," *Meghillot* 10 (2013) 73–114.

Le Déaut, *La nuit pascale*
Roger Le Déaut, *La nuit pascale* (AnBib 22; Rome: Pontifical Biblical Institute, 1963).

Leslau, *Comparative Dictionary*
Wolf Leslau, *Comparative Dictionary of Ge'ez (Classical Ethiopic)* (Wiesbaden: Harrassowitz, 1991).

Leslau, *Concise Dictionary*
Wolf Leslau, *Concise Dictionary of Ge'ez (Classical Ethiopic)* (Wiesbaden: Harrassowitz, 1989).

Levenson, "Rewritten Aqedah"
Jon D. Levenson, "The Rewritten Aqedah of Jewish Tradition," in idem, *The Death and Resurrection of the Beloved Son: The Transformation of Child Sacrifice in Judaism and Christianity* (New Haven: Yale University Press, 1993) 173–99.

Levine, *Numbers 1–20*
Baruch Levine, *Numbers 1–20: A New Translation with Introduction and Commentary* (AB 4A; New York: Doubleday, 1993).

Levine, *Numbers 21–36*
Baruch Levine, *Numbers 21–36: A New Translation with Introduction and Commentary* (AB 4B; New Haven: Yale University Press, 2000).

Levinson, *Twice Told Tale*
Joshua Levinson, *The Twice Told Tale: A Poetics of the Exegetical Narrative in Rabbinic Midrash* (Jerusalem: Magnes Press, 2005).

Levison, *Portraits of Adam*
Jack R. Levison, *Portraits of Adam in Early Judaism: From Sirach to 2 Baruch* (JSPSup 1; Sheffield: JSOT Press, 1988).

Lewis and Short, *Latin Dictionary*
Charlton T. Lewis and Charles Short, *A Latin Dictionary* (Oxford: Clarendon, 1969).

Licht, *Testing*
Jacob S. Licht, *Testing in the Hebrew Scriptures and in Judaism of the Second Temple Period* (Jerusalem: Magnes Press, 1973).

Licht, *Thanksgiving Scroll*
Jacob S. Licht, *The Thanksgiving Scroll: A Scroll from the Wilderness of Judaea: Text, Introduction, Commentary and Glossary* (Jerusalem: Bialik, 1957).

Lichtenberger, "Bedeutung von יצר"
  Hermann Lichtenberger, "Zu Vorkommen und Bedeutung von יצר im Jubiläenbuch," *JSJ* 14 (1983) 1–10.
LiDonnici and Lieber, *Heavenly Tablets*
  Lynn LiDonnici and Andrea Lieber, eds., *Heavenly Tablets: Interpretation, Identity and Tradition in Ancient Judaism* (JSJSup 119; Leiden: Brill, 2007).
Lipscomb, "Tradition"
  W. Lowndes Lipscomb, "A Tradition from the Book of Jubilees in Armenian," *JJS* 29 (1978) 149–63.
Littmann, "Jubiläen"
  Enno Littmann, "Das Buch der Jubiläen," in Emil Kautsch, ed., *Die Apokryphen und Pseudepigraphen des Alten Testaments*, vol. 2: *Die Pseudepigraphen des Alten Testaments* (Tübingen: Greiburg i. B. and Leipzig: J. C. B. Mohr [Paul Siebeck], 1900) 31–119.
Livneh, "*Jubilees* 34:1-9"
  Atar Livneh, "*Jubilees* 34:1-9: Joseph, the 'House of Joseph,' and the Josephites' Portion," *JSJ* 43 (2012) 22–41.
Livneh, "'Love Your Fellow'"
  Atar Livneh, "'Love Your Fellow as Yourself': The Interpretation of Leviticus 19:17-18 in the Book of *Jubilees*," *DSD* 18 (2011) 173–99.
Livneh, "Not at First Sight"
  Atar Livneh, "Not at First Sight: Gender Love in *Jubilees*," *JSP* 23 (2013) 3–20.
Livneh, "With My Sword"
  Atar Livneh, "With My Sword and Bow: Jacob as Warrior in *Jubilees*," in Devorah Dimant and Reinhard Kratz, eds., *Rewriting and Interpretation: The Biblical Patriarchs in Light of the Dead Sea Scrolls* (BZAW 439; Berlin: de Gruyter, 2013) 189–213.
Loader, *Sexuality*
  William R. G. Loader, *Enoch, Levi, and Jubilees on Sexuality: Attitudes towards Sexuality in the Early Enoch Literature, the Aramaic Levi Document, and the Book of Jubilees* (Grand Rapids: Eerdmans, 2007).
Machiela, *Genesis Apocryphon*
  Daniel A. Machiela, *The Dead Sea Genesis Apocryphon: A New Text and Translation with Introduction and Special Treatment of Columns 13–17* (STDJ 79; Leiden: Brill, 2009).
Maher, *Targum Pseudo-Jonathan: Genesis*
  Michael Maher, *Targum Pseudo-Jonathan: Genesis* (ArBib 1B; Collegeville, MN: Liturgical Press, 1992).
Maier, "Überlieferungen"
  J. Maier, "Zu ethnographisch-geographischen Überlieferungen über Japhetiten (Gen 10,2-4) im frühen Judentum," *Hen* 13 (1991) 157–94.
Maori, *Peshitta Version*
  Yeshayahu Maori, *The Peshitta Version of the Pentateuch and Early Jewish Exegesis* (Jerusalem: Magnes Press, 1995).
Marmorstein, "Die Namen der Schwestern"
  A. Marmorstein, "Die Namen der Schwestern Kains und Abels in der midraschischen und in der apokryphen Literatur," *ZAW* 25 (1905) 141–44.
Martin, "Jubilés"
  François Martin, "Le Livre des Jubilés: But et procédés de l'auteur. Ses Doctrines," *RB* 8 (1911) 321–44, 502–33.
Mason et al., *Teacher for All Generations*
  Eric F. Mason, Kelley Coblentz Bautch, Angela Kim Harkins, and Daniel A. Machiela, eds., *A Teacher for All Generations: Essays in Honor of James C. VanderKam* (2 vols.; JSJSup 153/I-II; Leiden: Brill, 2012).
McNamara and Hayward, *Neofiti 1: Exodus*
  Martin McNamara and Robert Hayward, *Targum Neofiti 1: Exodus* (ArBib 2; Collegeville, MN: Liturgical Press, 1994).
McNamara and Hayward, *Neofiti 1: Genesis*
  Martin McNamara and Robert Hayward, *Targum Neofiti 1: Genesis* (ArBib 1; Collegeville, MN: Liturgical Press, 1992).
Mermelstein, *Creation, Covenant*
  Ari Mermelstein, *Creation, Covenant, and the Beginnings of Judaism: Reconceiving Historical Time in the Second Temple Period* (JSJSup 168; Leiden: Brill, 2014).
Meyer, "Emanzipationsbestrebungen"
  R. Meyer, "Levitische Emanzipationsbestrebungen in nachexilischer Zeit," *OLZ* 41 (1938) 721–28.
Milgrom, "Impurity"
  Jacob Milgrom, "The Concept of Impurity in *Jubilees* and the *Temple Scroll*," *RevQ* 16/62 (1993) 277–84.
Milgrom, *Leviticus*
  Jacob Milgrom, *Leviticus: A New Translation with Introduction and Commentary* (3 vols.; AB 3, 3A, 3B; New York: Doubleday, 1991, 2000, 2010).
Milik, "Version grecque"
  J. T. Milik, "Recherches sur la version grecque du Livre des Jubilés," *RB* 78 (1971) 545–57.
Milikowsky, *Seder Olam*
  Chaim Milikowsky, *Seder Olam: Critical Edition, Commentary, and Introduction* (2 vols.; Jerusalem: Yishaq Ben Zvi, 2013).
Mimouni, *La circoncision*
  Simon Claude Mimouni, *La circoncision dans le monde judéen aux époques grecque et romaine: Histoire d'un conflit interne au judaïsme* (Collection de la Revue des études juives 42; Paris-Louvain: Peeters, 2007).
Müller, "Die hebräische Sprache"
  Karlheinz Müller, "Die hebräische Sprache der Halacha als Textur der Schöpfung: Beobachtungen zum Verhältnis von Tora und Halacha im Buch der Jubiläen," in Helmut Merklein, Karlheinz Müller, and Günter Stemberger, eds., *Bibel in jüdischer und christlicher Tradition* (BBB 88; Frankfurt: Anton Hain, 1993) 157–76.
Najman, *Seconding Sinai*
  Hindy Najman, *Seconding Sinai: The Development of Mosaic Discourse in Second Temple Judaism* (JSJSup 77; Leiden: Brill, 2003).

Nickelsburg, *1 Enoch 1*
  George W. E. Nickelsburg, *1 Enoch 1: A Commentary on the Book of 1 Enoch Chapters 1–36, 81–108* (Hermeneia; Minneapolis: Fortress Press, 2001).
Nickelsburg, *Resurrection*
  George W. E. Nickelsburg, *Resurrection, Immortality, and Eternal Life in Intertestamental Judaism* (HTS 26; Cambridge, MA: Harvard University Press, 1972).
Nickelsburg and VanderKam, *1 Enoch 2*
  George W. E. Nickelsburg and James C. VanderKam, *1 Enoch 2: A Commentary on the Book of 1 Enoch Chapters 37–82* (Hermeneia; Minneapolis: Fortress, 2012).
Niehoff, *Figure of Joseph*
  Maren Niehoff, *The Figure of Joseph in Post-Biblical Jewish Literature* (AGJU 16; Leiden: Brill, 1992).
Nitzan, "Liturgy at Qumran"
  Bilhah Nitzan, "The Liturgy at Qumran: Statutory Prayers," in Menahem Kister, ed., *The Qumran Scrolls and Their World* (2 vols.; Between Bible and Mishnah; Jerusalem: Yisḥaq Ben Zvi, 2009) 1:225–60.
Paz, "Before the Giving of the Torah"
  Yaqir Paz, "Before the Giving of the Torah: The Fathers and the Statutes of Moses in Rabbinic Literature against the Backround of Second Temple Literature and the Fathers of the Church" (MA thesis, Hebrew University of Jerusalem, 2009).
Peters, *Noah Traditions*
  Dorothy M. Peters, *Noah Traditions in the Dead Sea Scrolls: Conversations and Controversies of Antiquity* (SBLEJL 26; Atlanta: Society of Biblical Literature, 2008).
Petit, *La chaîne sur la Genèse*
  Françoise Petit, *La chaîne sur la Genèse: Édition integrale I–IV* (Traditio Exegetica Graeca 1–4 (Louvain: Peeters, 1992–96).
Rabin, "Jubilees"
  Chaim Rabin, "Jubilees," in H. F. D. Sparks, ed., *The Apocryphal Old Testament* (Oxford: Clarendon, 1984) 1–139.
Rapp, *Jakob in Bet-El*
  Hans Rapp, *Jakob in Bet-El: Gen 35, 1-15 und die jüdische Literatur des 3. und 2. Jahrhunderts* (HBS 29; Freiburg: Herder, 2001).
Ravid, "Issues"
  Liora Ravid, "Issues in the Book of Jubilees" (PhD diss., Bar-Ilan University, 2001).
Ravid, "Jubilees and Its Calendar"
  Liora Ravid, "The Book of Jubilees and Its Calendar—A Reexamination," *DSD* 10 (2003) 371–94.
Ravid, "Purity"
  Liora Ravid, "Purity and Impurity in the Book of *Jubilees*," *JSP* 13 (2002) 61–86.
Ravid, "Sabbath Laws"
  Liora Ravid, "The Sabbath Laws in Jubilees 50:6-13," *Tarbiz* 69 (2000) 161–66.
Reeves, *Tracing the Threads*
  John C. Reeves, ed., *Tracing the Threads: Studies in the Vitality of Jewish Pseudepigrapha* (SBLEJL 6; Atlanta: Scholars Press, 1994).

Rönsch, *Jubiläen*
  Hermann Rönsch, *Das Buch der Jubiläen oder die Kleine Genesis* (Leipzig: Fue, 1874; repr., Amsterdam: Editions RODOPI, 1970).
Rook, "Names of the Wives"
  John T. Rook, "The Names of the Wives from Adam to Abraham in the Book of *Jubilees*," *JSP* 7 (1990) 105–17.
Rook, "Twenty-Eight-Day Month"
  John T. Rook, "A Twenty-Eight-Day Month Tradition in the Book of Jubilees," *VT* 31 (1981) 83–87.
Rothstein, "'And Jacob Came (in)to'"
  David Rothstein, "And Jacob came (in)to [אל + בוא] . . .': Spousal Relationships and the Use of a Recurring Syntagm in Genesis and Jubilees," *Hen* 29 (2007) 91–103.
Rothstein, "Jubilees' Formulation of Gen 2:23"
  David Rothstein, "Jubilees' Formulation of Gen 2:23: A Literary Motif Viewed against the Legal Matricies of the Hebrew Bible and the Ancient Near East," *Zeitschrift für Altorientalische und Biblische Rechtsgeschichte* 11 (2005) 4–11.
Rothstein, "Sexual Union"
  David Rothstein, "Sexual Union and Sexual Offences in *Jubilees*," *JSJ* 35 (2004) 363–84.
Rothstein, "Text and Context"
  David Rothstein, "Text and Context: Domestic Harmony and the Depiction of Hagar in Jubilees," *JSP* 17 (2008) 243–64.
Rubenstein, *History of Sukkot*
  Jeffrey Rubenstein, *The History of Sukkot in the Second Temple and Rabbinic Periods* (BJS 302; Atlanta: Scholars Press, 1995).
van Ruiten, *Abraham*
  Jacques T. A. G. M. van Ruiten, *Abraham in the Book of Jubilees: The Rewriting of Genesis 11:26–25:10 in the Book of Jubilees 11:14–23:8* (JSJSup 161; Leiden: Brill, 2012).
van Ruiten, "Abraham, Job"
  Jacques T. A. G. M. van Ruiten, "Abraham, Job and the Book of *Jubilees*: The Intertextual Relationship of Genesis 22:1-19, Job 1:1–2:13 and *Jubilees* 17:15—18:19," in Ed Noort and Eibert Tigchelaar, eds., *The Sacrifice of Isaac: The Aqedah (Genesis 22) and Its Interpretations* (TBN 4; Leiden: Brill, 2002) 58–85.
van Ruiten, "Abraham's Last Day"
  Jacques T. A. G. M. van Ruiten, "Abraham's Last Day according to the Book of *Jubilees* (*Jub.* 22:1-23:8)," in Erkki Koskenniemi and Pekka Lindqvist, eds., *Rewritten Biblical Figures* (Studies in Rewritten Bible 3; Turku, Finland: Åbo Akademi University, 2010) 57–88.
van Ruiten, "Abram's Prayer"
  Jacques T. A. G. M. van Ruiten, "Abram's Prayer: The Coherence of the Pericopes in Jubilees 12:16-27," in Gabriele Boccaccini and Giovanni Ibba, eds., *Enoch and the Mosaic Torah: The Evidence of Jubilees* (Grand Rapids: Eerdmans, 2009) 211–28.

van Ruiten, "Angels and Demons"
Jacques T. A. G. M. van Ruiten, "Angels and Demons in the Book of Jubilees," in Friedrich V. Reiterer, Tobias Nicklas, and Karin Schöpflin, eds., *Angels: The Concept of Celestial Beings. Origins, Development and Reception* (Deuterocanonical and Cognate Literature Yearbook 2007; Berlin: de Gruyter, 2007) 585–609.

van Ruiten, "Between Jacob's Death and Moses' Birth"
Jacques T. A. G. M. van Ruiten, "Between Jacob's Death and Moses' Birth: The Intertextual Relationship between Genesis 50:15—Exodus 1:14 and Jubilees 46:1-16," in Anthony Hilhorst, Émile Puech, and Eibert Tigchelaar, eds., *Flores Florentino: Dead Sea Scrolls and Other Early Jewish Studies in Honour of Florentino García Martínez* (JSJSup 122; Leiden: Brill, 2007) 467–89.

van Ruiten, "Covenant of Noah"
Jacques T. A. G. M. van Ruiten, "The Covenant of Noah in *Jubilees* 6.1-38," in Stanley Porter and Jacqueline de Roo, eds., *The Concept of the Covenant in the Second Temple Period* (JSJSup 71; Leiden: Brill, 2003) 167–90.

van Ruiten, "Eden and Jubilees 3:1-31"
Jacques T. A. G. M. van Ruiten, "The Garden of Eden and Jubilees 3:1-31," *Bijdr* 57 (1996) 305–17.

van Ruiten, "Eden and the Temple"
Jacques T. A. G. M. van Ruiten, "Eden and the Temple: The Rewriting of Genesis 2:4—3:24 in the *Book of Jubilees*," in Gerard Luttikhuizen, ed., *Paradise Interpreted: Representations of Biblical Paradise in Judaism and Christianity* (TBN 2; Leiden: Brill, 1999) 63–94.

van Ruiten, "Exod 31, 12-17"
Jacques T. A. G. M. van Ruiten, "The Relationship between Exod 31, 12-17 and Jubilees 2, 1.17-33," in Marc Vervenne, ed., *Studies in the Book of Exodus: Redaction – Reception – Interpretation* (BETL 126; Leuven: University Press/Peeters, 1996) 567–75.

van Ruiten, "Genesis 6:1-12"
Jacques T. A. G. M. van Ruiten, "The Interpretation of Genesis 6:1-12 in Jubilees 5:1-19," in Matthias Albani, Jörg Frey, Armin Lange, eds., *Studies in the Book of Jubilees* (TSAJ 65; Tübingen: Mohr Siebeck, 1997) 57–73.

van Ruiten, "Literary Dependency"
Jacques T. A. G. M. van Ruiten, "A Literary Dependency of Jubilees on 1 Enoch?," in Gabriele Boccaccini, ed., *Enoch and Qumran Origins: New Light on a Forgotten Connection* (Grand Rapids: Eerdmans, 2005) 90–93.

van Ruiten, "Moses and His Parents"
Jacques T. A. G. M. van Ruiten, "Moses and His Parents: The Intertextual Relationship between Exodus 1:22–2:10 and Jubilees 47:1-9," in Antti Laato and Jacques van Ruiten, eds., *Rewritten Bible Reconsidered: Proceedings of the Conference in Karkku, Finland, August 24–26, 2006* (Studies in Rewritten Bible 1; Turku: Åbo Akademi University; Winona Lake, IN: Eisenbrauns, 2008) 43–78.

van Ruiten, *Primaeval History*
Jacques T. A. G. M. van Ruiten, *Primaeval History Interpreted: The Rewriting of Genesis 1–11 in the Book of Jubilees* (JSJSup 66; Leiden: Brill, 2000).

van Ruiten, "Rewriting of Exodus 24:12-18"
Jacques T. A. G. M. van Ruiten, "The Rewriting of Exodus 24:12-18 in Jubilees 1:1-4," *BN* 79 (1995) 25–29.

van Ruiten, "Van tekst"
Jacques T. A. G. M. van Ruiten, "Van tekst tot tekst: Psalm 90 en Jubileeën 23:12-15," *NTT* 47 (1993) 177–85.

Schäfer, "Götzendienst"
Peter Schäfer, "Der Götzendienst des Enosch: Zur Bildung und Entwicklung aggadischer Traditionen im nachbiblischen Judentum," in idem, *Studien zur Geschichte und Theologie des rabbinischen Judentums* (AGJU 15; Leiden: Brill, 1978) 134–52.

Schafer, "'One Language'"
Rachel Schafer, "'One Language and One Tongue': Animal Speech in *Jubilees* 3:27-31" (Unpublished seminar paper, University of Notre Dame, 2010).

Schechter, *Fragments*
Solomon Schechter, *Fragments of a Zadokite Work* (Documents of Jewish Sectaries 1; Cambridge: University Press, 1910; repr. New York: Ktav, 1970).

Schiffman, *Courtyards*
Lawrence H. Schiffman, *The Courtyards of the House of the Lord: Studies on the Temple Scroll* (ed. F. García Martínez; STDJ 75; Leiden: Brill, 2008).

Schiffman, *Halakhah*
Lawrence H. Schiffman, *The Halakhah at Qumran* (SJLA 16; Leiden: Brill, 1975).

Schiffman, "Jubilees and the Temple Scroll"
Lawrence H. Schiffman, "The Book of Jubilees and the Temple Scroll," in Gabriele Boccaccini and Giovanni Ibba, eds., *Enoch and the Mosaic Torah: The Evidence of Jubilees* (Grand Rapids: Eerdmans, 2009) 99–115.

Schiffman, "Sacrificial System"
Lawrence H. Schiffman, "The Sacrificial System of the *Temple Scroll* and the Book of Jubilees," *SBLSP* (1985) 217–33.

Schmidt, "Jewish Representations"
Francis Schmidt, "Jewish Representations of the Inhabited Earth during the Hellenistic and Roman Periods," in Aryeh Kasher, Uriel Rappaport, and Gideon Fuks, eds., *Greece and Rome in Eretz Israel: Collected Essays* (Jerusalem: Yishaq Ben Zvi/IES, 1990) 119–34.

Schmidt, "Imago Mundi"
Francis Schmidt, "Première Partie, Imago Mundi et Pèlerinage: Naissance d'une Géographie Juive," in Alain Desreumaux and Francis Schmidt, eds., *Moïse Géographe: Recherches sur les représentations juives et chrétiennes de l'espace* (Paris: J. Vrin, 1988) 13–30.

Schreiber, "Halakhic Redactor"
Sarah Schreiber, "Is a Halakhic Redactor Necessary? A Closer Look at Jubilees 41" (Unpublished seminar paper, University of Notre Dame, 2010).

Schubert, "'El 'Æljôn"
Friedemann Schubert, "'El 'Æljôn' als Gottesname im Jubiläenbuch," *Mitteilungen und Beiträge* 8 (1994) 3–18.

Schubert, *Tradition*
Friedemann Schubert, *Tradition und Erneuerung: Studien zum Jubiläenbuch und seinem Trägerkreis* (Europäische Hochschulschriften, Reihe III: Geschichte und ihre Hilfswissenschaften 771; Frankfurt: Lang, 1998).

Schulz, "Two Views"
Joseph P. Schulz, "Two Views of the Patriarchs: Noahides and Pre-Sinai Israelites," in Michael A. Fishbane and Paul R. Florh, eds., *Texts and Responses: Studies Presented to Nahum N. Glatzer on the Occasion of His Seventieth Birthday by His Students* (Leiden: Brill, 1975) 43–59.

Schwartz, "Jubilees, Bethel"
J. Schwartz, "Jubilees, Bethel and the Temple of Jacob," *HUCA* 56 (1985) 63–85.

Schwarz, *Identität*
Eberhard Schwarz, *Identität durch Abgrenzung: Abgrenzungsprozesse in Israel im 2. vorchristlichen Jahrhundert und ihre traditionsgeschichtlichen Voraussetzungen. Zugleich ein Beitrag zur Erforschung des Jubiläenbuches* (Europäische Hochschulschriften 162; Frankfurt am Main: Peter Lang, 1982).

Scott, *Geography*
James Scott, *Geography in Early Judaism and Christianity: The Book of Jubilees* (SNTSMS 113; Cambridge: Cambridge University Press, 2002).

Scott, *On Earth as in Heaven*
James Scott, *On Earth as in Heaven: The Restoration of Sacred Time and Sacred Space in the Book of Jubilees* (JSJSup 91; Leiden: Brill, 2005).

Segal, *Jubilees*
Michael Segal, *The Book of Jubilees: Rewritten Bible, Redaction, Ideology and Theology* (JSJSup 117; Leiden: Brill, 2007).

Segal, "Law and Narrative"
Michael Segal, "Law and Narrative in Jubilees: The Story of the Entrance into the Garden of Eden Revisited," *Meghillot* 1 (2003) 111–25.

Segal, "Literary Relationship"
Michael Segal, "The Literary Relationship between the Genesis Apocryphon and Jubilees: The Chronology of Abram and Sarai's Descent to Egypt," *Aramaic Studies* 8 (2010) 71–88.

Segal, "Rewriting"
Michael Segal, "Rewriting the Story of Dinah and Shechem: The Literary Development of Jubilees 30," in Nora David, Armin Lange, Kristin De Troyer, and Shani Tzoref, eds., *The Hebrew Bible in Light of the Dead Sea Scrolls* (FRLANT 239; Göttingen: Vandenhoeck & Ruprecht, 2012) 337–56.

Segal, "Shechem and Dinah"
Michael Segal, "The Story of Shechem and Dinah in *Jubilees* 30," *Meghillot* 8 (2010) 227–41.

Segal, *Ben Sira*
Moshe Segal, *The Complete Book of Ben Sira* (2nd ed.; Jerusalem: Bialik, 1972).

Shemesh, "4Q265"
Aharon Shemesh, "4Q265 and the Authortiative Status of Jubilees at Qumran," in Gabriele Boccaccini and Giovanni Ibba, eds., *Enoch and the Mosaic Torah: The Evidence of Jubilees* (Grand Rapids: Eerdmans, 2009) 247–60.

Shemesh "4Q265 and the Status"
Aharon Shemesh, "4Q265 and the Status of the Book of Jubilees in the Qumran Community," *Zion* 73 (2008) 5–20.

Singer, *Jubiläen*
Wilhelm Singer, *Das Buch der Jubiläen oder die Leptogenesis* (Stuhlweissenburg, Hungary: Singer, 1898).

Skehan, "Qumran Psalter"
Patrick Skehan, "*Jubilees* and the Qumran Psalter," *CBQ* 37 (1975) 343–47.

Skinner, *Genesis*
John Skinner, *A Critical and Exegetical Commentary on Genesis* (ICC; 2nd ed.; Edinburgh: T&T Clark, 1930).

Sokoloff, *Dictionary of Jewish Babylonian Aramaic*
Michael Sokoloff, *A Dictionary of Jewish Babylonian Aramaic of the Talmudic and Geonic Periods* (Ramat-Gan: Bar Ilan University Press; Baltimore: Johns Hopkins University Press, 2002).

Sollamo, "Creation of Angels"
Raija Sollamo, "The Creation of Angels and Natural Phenomena Intertwined in the *Book of Jubilees* (4QJub[a])," in Charlotte Hempel and Judith Lieu, eds., *Biblical Traditions in Transition: Essays in Honour of Michael A. Knibb* (JSJSup 111; Leiden: Brill, 2006) 273–90.

Söllner, "Ismael und Isaak"
Peter Söllner, "Ismael und Isaak—muss der eine den anderen denn immer nur verfolgen? Zum Verhältnis der beiden Abrahamsöhne im Jubiläenbuch," in Axel von Dobbeler, Kurt Erlemann, and Roman Heiligenthal, eds., *Religionsgeschichte des Neuen Testaments: Festschrift für Klaus Berger zum 60. Geburtstag* (Tübingen: Francke, 2000) 357–78.

Steck, "Aufnahme"
Odil Hannes Steck, "Die Aufnahme von Genesis 1 in Jubiläen 2 und 4. Esra 6," *JSJ* 8 (1977) 154–82.

Steck, "Die getöteten 'Zeugen' (I)
Odil Hannes Steck, "Die getöteten 'Zeugen' und die verfolgten 'Tora-Sucher' in Jub 1,12: Ein Beitrag zur Zeugnis-Terminologie des Jubiläenbuches (I)," *ZAW* 107 (1995) 445–65.

Steck, "Die getöteten 'Zeugen' (II)
Odil Hannes, Steck, "Die getöteten 'Zeugen' und die verfolgten 'Tora-Sucher' in Jub 1,12: Ein Beitrag zur Zeugnis-Terminologie des Jubiläenbuches (II)," *ZAW* 108 (1996) 70–86.

Stökl Ben Ezra, *Yom Kippur*
  Daniel Stökl Ben-Ezra, *The Impact of Yom Kippur on Early Christianity: The Day of Atonement from Second Temple Judaism to the Fifth Century* (WUNT 163; Tübingen: Mohr Siebeck, 2003).

Stuckenbruck, "Origin of Evil"
  Loren Stuckenbruck, "The Book of Jubilees and the Origin of Evil," in Gabriele Boccaccini and Giovanni Ibba, eds., *Enoch and the Mosaic Torah: The Evidence of Jubilees* (Grand Rapids: Eerdmans, 2009) 294–308.

Tabory, *Festivals*
  Joseph Tabory, *Jewish Festivals in the Time of the Mishnah and Talmud* (3rd ed.; Jerusalem: Magnes Press, 2000).

Tafel, *Theodosii Meliteni*
  Gottlieb Tafel, *Theodosii Meliteni qui fertur Chronographia ex codice graeco Regiae Bibliothecae monacensis* (Munich: G. Franz, 1859).

Ta-Shema, "Interpretation"
  Y. Ta-Shema, "On the Interpretation of a Section of the Book of Jubilees," *Bet Miqra* 11 (1966) 99–102.

Tchernowitz, *History of Hebrew Law*
  Chaim Tchernowitz, *History of Hebrew Law: The Transmission and Development of the Oral Law from Its Inception to the Compilation of the Talmud*, vol. 4: *From the Period of the Scribes and the Zugot to the End of the Second Commonwealth* (New York: Committee for the Publication of Rav Tzair's Collected Works, 1950) 348–88.

Teeter, "Exegetical Function"
  D. Andrew Teeter, "On 'Exegetical Function' in Rewritten Scripture: Inner-Biblical Exegesis and the Abram/Ravens Narrative in *Jubilees*," *HTR* 106 (2013) 373–402.

Teeter, "Wisdom, Torah"
  D. Andrew Teeter, "Wisdom, Torah, and Rewritten Scripture: *Jubilees* and 11QPs[a] in Comparative Perspective," in Bernd U. Schipper and D. Andrew Teeter, eds., *Wisdom and Torah: The Reception of 'Torah' in the Wisdom Literature of the Second Temple Period* (JSJSup 163; Leiden: Brill, 2013) 233–72.

Testuz, *Idées*
  Michel Testuz, *Les idées religieuses du Livre des Jubilés* (Geneva: E. Droz; Paris: Librairie Minard, 1960).

Tigchelaar, "Cave 4 Fragment"
  Eibert J. C. Tigchelaar, "A Cave 4 Fragment of Divre Mosheh (4QDM) and the Text of 1Q22 1:7-10 and *Jubilees* 1:9, 14," *DSD* 12 (2005) 303–12.

Tisserant, "Fragments"
  Eugène Tisserant, "Fragments syriaques du Livre des Jubilés," *RB* 30 (1921) 55–86, 206–32.

van der Toorn and van der Horst, "Nimrod"
  Karel van der Toorn and Pieter van der Horst, "Nimrod before and after the Bible," *HTR* 83 (1990) 1–29.

Treuenfels, "Die kleine Genesis"
  A. Treuenfels, "Die kleine Genesis בראשית זוטא," *Fürst's Literaturblatt des vorderen Orients* number 1 (1846) 7–12; number 2 (1846) 28–32; number 4 (1846) 59–64; number 5 (1846) 65–71; number 6 (1846) 81–86.

Ulfgard, *Story of Sukkot*
  Håkan Ulfgard, *The Story of Sukkot: The Setting, Shaping, and Sequel of the Biblical Feast of Tabernacles* (BGBE 34; Tübingen: Mohr Siebeck, 1998).

VanderKam, "Adam's Incense Offering"
  James C. VanderKam, "Adam's Incense Offering (Jubilees 3:27)," *Meghillot* 5-6 (2007) 141–56.

VanderKam, "Angel of the Presence"
  James C. VanderKam, "The Angel of the Presence in the Book of Jubilees," *DSD* 7 (2000) 378–93.

VanderKam, "Angel Story"
  James C. VanderKam, "The Angel Story in the Book of Jubilees," in Esther Chazon and Michael E. Stone, eds., *Pseudepigraphic Perspectives: The Apocrypha and Pseudepigrapha in Light of the Dead Sea Scrolls: Proceedings of the International Symposium of the Orion Center, 12–14 January 1997* (STDJ 31; Leiden: Brill, 1999) 151–70.

VanderKam, "Another Citation"
  James C. VanderKam, "Another Citation of Greek *Jubilees*," in Andrés Piquer Otero and Pablo A. Torijano Morales, eds., *Textual Criticism and Dead Sea Scrolls Studies in Honour of Julio Trebolle Barrera: Florilegium Complutense* (JSJSup 157; Leiden: Brill, 2012) 377–92.

VanderKam, "Anthropological Gleanings"
  James C. VanderKam, "Anthropological Gleanings from The Book of Jubilees," in Ulrike Mittmann-Richert, Friedrich Avemarie, and Gerbern S. Oegema, eds., *Der Mensch vor Gott: Forschungen zum Menschenbild in Bibel, antikem Judentum und Koran: Festschrift für Hermann Lichtenberger zum 60. Geburtstag* (Neukirchen-Vluyn: Neukirchener Verlag, 2003) 117–31.

VanderKam, *Aqedah*
  James C. VanderKam, "The *Aqedah*, *Jubilees*, and PseudoJubilees," in Craig A. Evans and Shemaryahu Talmon, eds., *The Quest for Context and Meaning: Studies in Biblical Intertextuality in Honor of James A. Sanders* (Biblical Interpretation Series; Leiden: Brill, 1997) 241–61.

VanderKam, *Book of Jubilees*
  James C. VanderKam, *The Book of Jubilees* (Guides to Apocrypha and Pseudepigrapha; Sheffield: Sheffield Academic Press, 2001).

VanderKam, "Chronology"
  James C. VanderKam, "Das chronologische Konzept des Jubiläenbuches," *ZAW* 107 (1995) 80–100. An English version is "Studies in the Chronology of the Book of Jubilees" in VanderKam, *From Revelation to Canon: Studies in the Hebrew Bible and Second Temple Literature* (JSJSup 62; Leiden: Brill, 2000) 522–44.

VanderKam, "Covenant and Biblical Interpretation"
  James C. VanderKam, "Covenant and Biblical Interpretation in Jubilees 6," in Lawrence Schiffman, Emanuel Tov, and James C. VanderKam, eds.,

The Dead Sea Scrolls Fifty Years after Their Discovery: Proceedings of the Jerusalem Congress, July 20–25, 1997 (Jerusalem: Israel Exploration Society and the Shrine of the Book, Israel Museum, 2000) 92–104.

VanderKam, "Demons"
James C. VanderKam, "The Demons in the Book of Jubilees," in Armin Lange, Hermann Lichtenberger, and K. F. Diethard Römheld, eds., *Die Dämonen: Die Dämonologie der israelitisch-jüdischen und frühchristlichen Literatur im Kontext ihrer Umwelt / Demons: The Demonology of the Israelite-Jewish and Early Christian Literature in the Context of Their Environment* (Tübingen: Mohr Siebeck, 2003) 339–64.

VanderKam, "End of the Matter?"
James C. VanderKam, "The End of the Matter? Jubilees 50:6-13 and the Unity of the Book," in Lynn LiDonnici and Andrea Lieber, eds., *Heavenly Tablets: Interpretation, Identity and Tradition in Ancient Judaism* (JSJSup 119; Leiden: Brill, 2007) 267–84.

VanderKam, *Enoch*
James C. VanderKam, *Enoch: A Man for All Generations* (Studies on Personalities of the Old Testament; Columbia: University of South Carolina Press, 1995).

VanderKam, *Enoch and the Growth*
James C. VanderKam, *Enoch and the Growth of an Apocalyptic Tradition* (CBQMS 16; Washington: Catholic Biblical Association of America, 1984).

VanderKam, "Enoch Traditions"
James C. VanderKam, "Enoch Traditions in Jubilees and Other Second-Century Sources," *SBLASP* (1978) 1:229–51.

VanderKam, "Exegetical Creation"
James C. VanderKam, "Jubilees' Exegetical Creation of Levi the Priest," *RevQ* 17/65-68 (1996) 359–73.

VanderKam, *From Revelation to Canon*
James C. VanderKam, *From Revelation to Canon: Studies in the Hebrew Bible and Second Temple Literature* (JSJSup 62; Leiden: Brill, 2000).

VanderKam, "Genesis 1 in Jubilees 2"
James C. VanderKam, "Genesis 1 in Jubilees 2," *DSD* 1 (1994) 300–321.

VanderKam, "Isaac's Blessing"
James C. VanderKam, "Isaac's Blessing of Levi and His Descendants in *Jubilees* 31," in Donald W. Parry and Eugene Ulrich, eds., *The Provo International Conference on the Dead Sea Scrolls: Technological Innovations, New Texts, and Reformulated Issues* (STDJ 30; Leiden: Brill, 1999) 497–519.

VanderKam, *Jubilees*
James C. VanderKam, *The Book of Jubilees* (2 vols.; CSCO 510-11; Scriptores Aethiopici 87-88; Louvain: E. Peeters, 1989).

VanderKam, "*Jubilees* 46:6–47:1"
James C. VanderKam, "*Jubilees* 46:6–47:1 and 4QVisions of Amram," *DSD* 17 (2010) 141–58.

VanderKam, "Jubilees and Hebrew Texts"
James C. VanderKam, "Jubilees and Hebrew Texts of Genesis–Exodus," *Textus* 14 (1988) 71–85.

VanderKam, "Jubilees as Prophetic History"
James C. VanderKam, "Jubilees as Prophetic History" in Donald W. Parry, Stephen D. Ricks, and Andrew C. Skinner, eds., *The Prophetic Voice at Qumran: The Leonardo Museum Conference on the Dead Sea Scrolls, 11–12 April 2014* (STDJ 120; Leiden: Brill, 2017) 167–88.

VanderKam, "Made to Order"
James C. VanderKam, "Made to Order: Creation in Jubilees," in Lance Jenott and Sarit Kattan Gribetz, eds., *In the Beginning: Jewish and Christian Cosmogony in Late Antiquity* (TSAJ 155; Tübingen: Mohr Siebeck, 2013) 23–38.

VanderKam, "Manuscript Tradition"
James C. VanderKam, "The Manuscript Tradition of Jubilees," in Gabriele Boccaccini and Giovanni Ibba, eds., *Enoch and the Mosaic Torah: The Evidence of Jubilees* (Grand Rapids: Eerdmans, 2009) 3–21.

VanderKam, "Mastema"
James C. VanderKam, "Mastema in the Qumran Literature and the Book of Jubilees," in Joel Baden, Hindy Najman, and Eibert Tigchelaar, eds., *Sibyls, Scriptures, and Scrolls: John Collins at Seventy* (JSJSup 175; Leiden: Brill, 2017) 1346–60.

VanderKam, "Moses"
James C. VanderKam, "Moses Trumping Moses: Making the Book of Jubilees," in Sarianna Metso, Hindy Najman, and Eileen Schuller, eds., *The Dead Sea Scrolls: Transmission of Tradition and Publication of Texts* (STDJ 92; Leiden: Brill, 2010) 25–44.

VanderKam, "One Author?"
James C. VanderKam, "Jubilees as the Composition of One Author?," *RevQ* 26/104 (2014) 501–16.

VanderKam, "Origins"
James C. VanderKam, "The Origins and Purposes of the Book of Jubilees," in Matthias Albani, Jörg Frey, and Armin Lange, eds., *Studies in the Book of Jubilees* (TSAJ 65; Tübingen: Mohr Siebeck, 1997) 3–24.

VanderKam, "Pentateuchal Legislation"
James C. VanderKam, "Exegesis of Pentateuchal Legislation in Jubilees and Related Texts Found at Qumran," in Akio Moriya and Gohei Hata, eds., *Pentateuchal Traditions in the Late Second Temple Period: Proceedings of the International Workshop in Tokyo, August 28–31, 2007* (JSJSup 158; Leiden: Brill, 2012) 177–200.

VanderKam, "Priestly Messiah"
James C. VanderKam, "*Jubilees* and the Priestly Messiah of Qumran," *RevQ* 13 (1988) 353–65.

VanderKam, "Putative Author"
James C. VanderKam, "The Putative Author of the Book of Jubilees," *JSS* 26 (1981) 209–17.

VanderKam, "Putting Them in Their Place"
James C. VanderKam, "Putting Them in Their Place: Geography as an Evaluative Tool," in John C. Reeves and John Kampen, eds., *Pursuing the Text: Studies in Honor of Ben Zion Wacholder on the Occasion of his Seventieth Birthday* (JSOTSup 184; Sheffield: Sheffield Academic Press, 1994) 47–69.

VanderKam, "Rebekah's Patriarchal Prayers"
James C. VanderKam, "Rebekah's Patriarchal Prayers," in Jeremy Penner, Ken M. Penner, and Cecilia Wassen, eds., *Prayer and Poetry in the Dead Sea Scrolls and Related Literature: Essays in Honor of Eileen Schuller on the Occasion of her 65th Birthday* (STDJ 98; Leiden: Brill, 2012) 421-36.

VanderKam, "Righteousness of Noah"
James C. VanderKam, "The Righteousness of Noah," in George W. E. Nickelsburg and John J. Collins, eds., *Ideal Figures in Ancient Judaism* (SBLSCS 12; Chico, CA: Scholars Press, 1980) 13-32.

VanderKam, "Studies"
James C. VanderKam, "Studies on the Prologue and Jubilees 1," in Randal A. Argall, Beverly A. Bow, and Rodney A. Werline, eds., *For a Later Generation: The Transformation of Tradition in Israel, Early Judaism, and Early Christianity* (Harrisburg, PA: Trinity Press International, 2000) 266-79.

VanderKam, "Temple Scroll"
James C. VanderKam, "The Temple Scroll and the Book of Jubilees," in George J. Brooke, ed., *Temple Scroll Studies* (JSPSup 7; Sheffield: JSOT Press, 1989) 211-36.

VanderKam, *Textual*
James C. VanderKam, *Textual and Historical Studies in the Book of Jubilees* (HSM 14; Missoula, MT: Scholars Press, 1977).

Vermes, "Leviticus 18:21"
Geza Vermes, "Leviticus 18:21 in Ancient Jewish Bible Exegesis," in Jacob J. Petuchowski and Ezra Fleischer, eds., *Studies in Aggadah, Targum and Jewish Liturgy in Memory of Joseph Heinemann* (Jerusalem: Magnes/Hebrew Union College Press, 1981) 108-24.

Vermes, *Scripture and Tradition*
Geza Vermes, *Scripture and Tradition in Judaism: Haggadic Studies* (2nd ed.; StPB 4; Leiden: Brill, 1973).

Volz, *Jüdische Eschatologie*
Paul Volz, *Jüdische Eschatologie von Daniel bis Akiba* (Tübingen: Mohr Siebeck, 1903).

Wacholder, "Date of the Eschaton"
Ben-Zion Wacholder, "The Date of the Eschaton in the Book of Jubilees: A Commentary on Jub. 49:22—50:5, CD 1:1-10, and 16:2-3," *HUCA* 59 (1988) 87-101.

Wacholder, "*Jubilees* as the Super Canon"
Ben-Zion Wacholder, "*Jubilees* as the Super Canon: Torah-Admonition versus Torah-Commandment," in Moshe J. Bernstein, Florentino García Martínez, and John Kampen, eds., *Legal Texts and Legal Issues: Proceedings of the Second Meeting of the International Organization for Qumran Studies, Cambridge 1995. Published in Honour of Joseph M. Baumgarten* (STDJ 23; Leiden: Brill, 1997) 195-211.

Weinfeld, *Deuteronomy 1-11*
Moshe Weinfeld, *Deuteronomy 1-11: A New Translation with Introduction and Commentary* (AB 5; New York: Doubleday, 1991).

Werman, "Aramaic Sources"
Cana Werman, "The Book of Jubilees and Its Aramaic Sources," *Meghillot* 8 (2010) 135-74.

Werman, "Attitude"
Cana Werman, "The Attitude towards Gentiles in The Book of Jubilees and Qumran Literature Compared with the Early Tannaic Halakha and Contemporary Pseudepigrapha" (PhD diss., Hebrew University of Jerusalem, 1995).

Werman, *Jubilees*
Cana Werman, *The Book of Jubilees: Introduction, Translation, and Interpretation* (Between Bible and Mishnah; Jerusalem: Yishaq Ben Zvi, 2015).

Werman, "*Jubilees* 30"
Cana Werman, "*Jubilees* 30: Building a Paradigm for the Ban on Intermarriage," *HTR* 90 (1997) 1-22.

Werman, "Jubilees in the Hellenistic Context"
Cana Werman, "Jubilees in the Hellenistic Context," in Lynn LiDonnici and Andrea Lieber, eds., *Heavenly Tablets: Interpretation, Identity and Tradition in Ancient Judaism* (JSJSup 119; Leiden: Brill, 2007) 133-58.

Werman, "Meaning"
Cana Werman, "Te'udah: On the Meaning of the Term," in Gershon Brin and Bilhah Nitzan, eds., *Fifty Years of Dead Sea Scrolls Research: Studies in Memory of Jacob Licht* (Jerusalem: Yishaq Ben Zvi, 2001) 231-43.

Werman, "Qumran and the Book of Noah"
Cana Werman, "Qumran and the Book of Noah," in Esther Chazon and Michael E. Stone, eds., *Pseudepigraphic Perspectives: The Apocrypha and Pseudepigrapha in Light of the Dead Sea Scrolls* (STDJ 31; Leiden: Brill, 1999) 171-81.

Werman, "Rules"
Cana Werman, "The Rules of Consuming and Covering the Blood in Priestly and Rabbinic Law," *RevQ* 16 (1995) 621-36.

Werman, "Shaping"
"The Shaping of the Events of the Generation of the Flood," *Tarbiz* 64 (1995) 183-202.

Werman, "תורה"
Cana Werman, "The תורה and the תעודה Engraved on the Tablets," *DSD* 9 (2002) 75-103.

Werman and Shemesh, *Revealing*
Cana Werman and Aharon Shemesh, *Revealing the Hidden: Exegesis and Halakha in the Qumran Scrolls* (Jerusalem: Bialik, 2011).

Westermann, *Genesis 1-11*
Claus Westermann, *Genesis 1-11: A Commentary* (Minneapolis: Augsburg, 1984).

Westermann, *Genesis 12-36*
Claus Westermann, *Genesis 12-36: A Commentary* (Minneapolis: Augsburg, 1985).

Westermann, *Genesis 37-50*
Claus Westermann, *Genesis 37-50: A Commentary* (Minneapolis: Augsburg, 1986).

Wiesenberg, "Jubilee of Jubilees"
:   Ernest Wiesenberg, "The Jubilee of Jubilees," *RevQ* 3 (1961-62) 3-40.

Williams, Panarion *of Epiphanius*
:   Frank Williams, *The* Panarion *of Epiphanius of Salamis Book I [Sects 1-46]* (2nd ed.; NHMS 63; Leiden: Brill, 2009); *The* Panarion *of Epiphanius of Salamis, Books II and III [Sects 47-80, De Fide]* (NHMS 36; Leiden: Brill, 1994).

Wintermute, "Jubilees"
:   O. S. Wintermute, "Jubilees," in James Charlesworth, ed., *The Old Testament Pseudepigrapha* (2 vols.; Garden City, NY: Doubleday, 1983, 1985) 2:35-142.

Wise, Abegg, and Cook, *Dead Sea Scrolls*
:   Michael O. Wise, Martin G. Abegg Jr., and Edward M. Cook, *The Dead Sea Scrolls: A New Translation* (rev. and updated ed.; New York: Harper, 2005).

Yadin, *Temple Scroll*
:   Yigael Yadin, *The Temple Scroll* (3 vols.; Jerusalem: Israel Exploration Society, 1983).

Zahn, *Rewritten*
:   Molly Zahn, *Rethinking Rewritten Scripture: Composition and Exegesis in the 4QReworked Pentateuch Manuscripts* (STDJ 95; Leiden: Brill, 2011).

Zeitlin, "'Jubilees' and the Pentateuch"
:   Solomon Zeitlin, "The Book of 'Jubilees' and the Pentateuch," *JQR* 48 (1957) 218-35.

Zeitlin, "Jubilees, Its Character"
:   Solomon Zeitlin, "The Book of Jubilees, Its Character and Its Significance," *JQR* 30 (1939-40) 1-31.

Zuurmond, "De misdaad"
:   Rochus Zuurmond, "De misdaad van Ruben volgens Jubileeën 33:1-9," *Amsterdamse Cahiers* 8 (1987) 108-16.

Zuurmond, "Het Oordeel"
:   Rochus Zuurmond, "Het Oordeel over Kain in de Oud-Joodse Traditie," *Amsterdamse Cahiers* 3 (1982) 107-16.

Commentary

22

Abraham's Last Festival and His Testament to Jacob

1/ In <u>the first week</u>[a] in the forty-<u>third</u>[b] jubilee, during the second year[c] [2109]— it was <u>the year</u>[d] in which Abraham died—Isaac and Ishmael <u>came</u> from the well of the oath to their father Abraham to celebrate <u>the Festival</u> of Weeks[e]—<u>this is the Festi</u>val of the Firstfruits of the harvest. Abraham[f] was happy that[g] his two sons had come. 2/ For Isaac's possessions in Beersheba were numerous. Isaac used to go[a] and inspect his possessions[b] and then return to his father. 3/ At that time Ishmael came to see his father, and both of them[a] came[b] together. Isaac slaughtered a sacrifice for the offering; he offered (it) on[c] his father's altar that he had made in Hebron. 4/ He sacrificed[a] a peace offering and prepared[b] a joyful feast[c] in front of his brother Ishmael. Rebekah made fresh[d] bread out of new[e] wheat. She gave it[f] to her son Jacob to bring[g] to his father Abraham some of the firstfruits of the land so that he would eat (it) and bless the Creator[h] of everything[i] before he died. 5/ Isaac, too, sent through Jacob his excellent peace offering and wine to his father[a] Abraham for him to eat and drink.[b] 6/ He[a] ate and drank. Then he blessed the Most High God who created the heavens and the earth, who made[b] all the fat things[c] of the earth, and gave them to humanity to eat, drink, and bless[d] their Creator.

7/ "Now I pay homage[a] to you,[b] my God, because you have shown me[c] this day. I am now[d] 175 years of age, old and satisfied with (my) days. All of my days have proved to be peace for me. 8/ The enemy's sword[a] has not subdued me in anything at all[b] that you have given me[c] and my sons[d] during all my lifetime until today. 9/ May[a] your kindness and peace[b] rest on your servant[c] and on the descendants of his sons[d] so that they,[e] out of all the nations[f] of the earth, may be your acceptable[g] people and heritage from now until all the time of the earth's history[h] throughout all ages."

10/ He[a] <u>summoned Jacob</u>[b] and said to him,[c] "My son Jacob, may the God of all bless and strengthen you to do before him what is right and what he wills. May he choose you and[d] your descendants to be his people for his heritage in accord with[e] his will throughout all time. Now you, my son Jacob, come close[f] and kiss me." 11/ So he[a] came close[b] and kissed him.[c] Then he said, "May <u>my son Jacob and all his sons be blessed to</u> the Most High God throughout all ages.[d] May the Lord give you righteous descendants, and[e] may he sanctify[f] some of your sons in the entire earth. May the nations serve you, and may all the nations bow before your descendants.[g] 12/ Be strong before people and[a] exercise power among all of Seth's descendants.[b] Then your ways and the ways of your sons will be justified[c] so that they may be a holy people. 13/ May the Most High God give you all the blessings with which he blessed me and with which he blessed Noah and Adam. May they[a] come to rest on the sacred[b] head[c] of your descendants throughout each and every generation[d] and[e] forever.[f] 14/ May he purify[a] you from all filthy pollution[b] so that you may be pardoned[c] for every sin you have committed in ignorance.[d] May he strengthen and bless you; may you possess the entire earth. 15/ May he renew his covenant with you[a] so that you may be for him[b] the people[c] of his[d] heritage throughout all ages. May he truly and rightly be God[e] for you[f] and your descendants throughout all the time of the earth.

16/ "Now you, my son Jacob,
  remember what I say[a]
  and keep the commandments of[b] your father Abraham.
  Separate from the nations,
  and do not eat with them.
  Do not act as they do,[c]
  and do not become their companion,
  for their actions are something that is impure,[d]
  and all their ways are defiled[e] and something abominable and detestable.
17/ They[a] offer their sacrifices[b] to the dead,[c]
  and[d] they worship demons.
  They eat in tombs,
  and everything they do is empty and worthless.[e]

647

18/ They have no mind to think,
and their eyes do not see what they do
and how they err in saying to (a piece of) wood,
'You are my god';[a]
or to a stone,
'You are my lord;[b]
you are my[c] deliverer.'
They have[d] no mind.
19/ "As for you, my son Jacob,
may the Most High God help you[a]
and the God of heaven[b] bless you.

"May he remove you[c] from their impurity[d] and from all their error. 20/ Be careful, my son[a] Jacob, not to marry a woman from all the descendants of[b] Canaan's daughters,[c] because all of his[d] descendants are (meant) for being uprooted[e] from the earth. 21/ For through[a] Ham's sin Canaan erred. All of his descendants and all of his (people) who remain will be destroyed from the earth; on the day of judgment there will be no one (descended) from him[b] who will be saved. 22/ There is no hope in the land of the living for all who worship idols[a] and for those who are odious.[b] For they will descend to Sheol and[c] will go to the place of judgment. There will be no memory of any of them[d] on the earth. As the people of Sodom were taken from the earth, so all[e] who worship idols will be destroyed.[f]

23/ "Do not be afraid, my son Jacob,
and do not be upset, son of Abraham.
May the Most High God keep you[a] from corruption;
and from every erroneous way[b] may he rescue you.[c]

24/ This house I have built[a] for myself[b] to put my name on it upon the earth.[c] It has been given to you and to your descendants forever.[d] It will be called Abraham's house. It has been given to you and your descendants forever because you will build my house and will establish[e] my name[f] before God[g] until eternity. Your descendants and[h] your name will remain throughout all[i] the history of the earth."

25/ Then he finished[a] commanding and blessing him. 26/ The two of them[a] lay down together[b] on one bed. Jacob slept in the bosom of his grandfather Abraham. He kissed him[c] seven times,[d] and his feelings[e] and mind were happy about him. 27/ He blessed him[a] wholeheartedly and said:[b] "The Most High God[c] is the God of all and Creator of everything[d] who brought me[e] from Ur[f] of the Chaldeans to give me[g] this land[h] in order that I should possess it[i] forever and raise up[j] holy descendants so that they may be blessed[k] forever." 28/ Then he blessed[a] Jacob:[b] "My son,[c] with whom[d] I[e] am *exceedingly* happy[f] with all my mind[g] and feelings[h]—may your grace and mercy continue[i] on him and his descendants for all time. 29/ Do not leave or neglect him from now until the time of[a] eternity. May your eyes[b] be open on him and his descendants[c] so that they may watch over them[d] and so that you may bless and sanctify them as the people of your heritage.[e] 30/ Bless him[a] with all[b] your[c] blessings from now until all the time of eternity. With[d] your entire will renew your covenant[e] and your grace with him and[f] with his descendants throughout all the generations of the earth."

Textual Notes

1a week] om. 20.
b (forty-)third] 4Q219 ii:35 שלושה. Eth. "fourth"; "its fourth" 12 42.
c year] "its year" 12 17 21 39 44 48 58 63; + "and" 39 44.
d the year] om. 12; "its year" 58; 4Q219 ii:36 השנה.
e Weeks] 4Q219 ii:37 ת[ו]עבש[ה]; "7" 9 47 48; "week" 20 25 35[c] (om. 35[f]) 38 58.

f Abraham] + "their father" 20.
g that] om. 47.
2a used to go] "they used to go" 9.
b his possessions] Lat. "what he still possessed."
3a both of them] = Lat. (*utrique*). Eth. = "all." Charles (*Ethiopic Version*, 77 n. 24; *Jubilees*, 138) emended Eth. to read *kel'ēhomu* = the two of them/both of them, instead of *kwellomu* = all of them (see VanderKam, *Jubilees* 2:127).

648

b came] + "to him" 35 58.
c on] Eth. *diba* = "on" agrees with Lat. *super*; some Eth. mss. read *westa* = lit., "in."
4a sacrificed] + "a sacrifice" 35 38 58; Latin expresses with *fecit sacrificium* what the Eth. verb *šo'a* accomplishes; it does not require a cognate accusative.
b prepared] + "it" (?) 9.
c a joyful feast (lit., "a feast of joy")] "a feast and joy" 12; "and made/prepared joy" 44; Lat. *convivium laetitiae*, "a feast of joy."
d fresh (lit., "new")] om. 12; Lat. *novam*.
e new] om. 20; Lat. *novo*.
f it] om. 44 63; Lat. *eam*.
g bring] "give" 9 39; Lat. *inferret*.
h the Creator] "the fruit" 63.
i everything] om. 38; Lat. *omnium*.
5a his excellent peace offering and wine to his father] The words "his" and "and wine to his father" come from the Latin text, which at the end of the verse reads:
Ethiopic: *'abrehām yeblā' wa-yestay*,
Latin: *et vinum patri suo Abraham ut manducet et bibat*.
The extra words "and wine to his father" in Lat. make the verb "drink" meaningful (see v. 6 for the two verbs). It may be that, if the Greek text behind the Eth. read as the Lat. does, there was omission of several words due to the repetition of αυτου (VanderKam, *Jubilees* 2:127).
b eat/drink] Mss. 9 20 25 35 38 39 42 47 48 63 transpose the verbs, while the other copies have the order "eat/drink" of Lat.
6a He] Lat. "Abraham."
b who made] "and" 39 42 47 48 58; Lat. *qui fecit*.
c fat things] Eth. *sebḥa* = Lat. *pinguedinis*; mss. 17 35 39 42 47 48 58 63 have *sefḥa*, "width, spaciousness" (Leslau, *Comparative Dictionary*, 487).
d and bless] "and they blessed" 17 21 25 42 47 63; Lat. agrees with the majority text: *et benedicant*.
7a I pay homage] "I will pay homage" 21; "let me pay homage" 38; Lat. *confiteor ego* ("I acknowledge") seems similar in meaning to the majority Eth. reading.
b to you] Lat. lacks the phrase.
c me] om. 38 (Lat. *mihi*).
d now] pr. "and" 20 38 = Lat. *et*.
8a The enemy's sword] pr. "and" 17 44 (= Lat. *et*).
b in (this 44; om. 63; Lat. *in*) anything at all] A conjunction precedes the phrase, perhaps meaning "even" (rendered "at all"); it is lacking in 12 38 and Lat. Lat. has *in omnibus diebus*. Rönsch (*Jubiläen*, 122) thought it entered the text under the influence of its use later in the verse (VanderKam, *Jubilees* 2:128).
c you have given me] "he has given me" 44; Lat. "you have given me."
d my sons] The Eth. mss. read "to my sons," except 58 = "in/among"; Lat. *in*.

9a May] + "O My God" 35 39 42 47 48 58. Lat. has a short gap followed by *nunc*, "now."
b and peace (= "and your peace")] om. 9 12 17 21 38 39 42 44 47 48 58 63; Lat. *et pax tua*.
c servant] "seed/descendants" 21; Lat. *puerum istum*, "this young man/servant" (see VanderKam, *Jubilees* 2:128). Lat. adds *domini*, "Lord/O Lord" (see note 9a on *May* above).
d the descendants of his sons] Lat. "his descendants."
e they . . . may be] The verb is singular in form, but with seed (= descendants) as the subject it has a plural meaning. Mss. 21 35 read a plural, as does Lat.
f nations] Lat. "sons."
g acceptable] "blessed" 17; = Lat. "acceptable." Eth. *ḥeruya* means "chosen," but it also has the meaning "acceptable," which seems more appropriate in the context.
h history] + "and" 20 38 44 (Lat. lacks a conjunction here).
10a He] Lat. *abraham*.
b Jacob] Lat. "his son and/even Jacob." See VanderKam, *Jubilees* 2:129.
c to him] om. 20 25 35 58; Lat. also lacks it.
d and (your descendants)] om. 12 25; Lat. *et*.
e his heritage in accord with] Lat. lacks.
f close] Lat. adds "to me" (*ad me*).
11a he] Lat. *iacob*.
b close] + "to him" 12 17 21 (and 63 with a different spelling); Lat. also lacks "to him."
c him] om. 58; Lat. *eum*.
d ages] Lat. lacks an equivalent. Ms. 12 "(every) age."
e and (may)] om. 20 25 38 39 42 47 48; Lat. *et*.
f may he sanctify] + "him" 39 42; several mss. read different passive forms, but Lat. *santificabis* (to be corrected to *sanctificabit*) agrees with the majority Eth. reading.
g descendants] Lat. "name"—a confusion of *nominis* and *seminis*.
12a and (exercise)] Eth. "when you exercise."
b Seth's (Lat. *et* is a mistake for *set*) descendants] "the descendants of the land/earth and to the seed of Seth" 38.
c will be justified (or: true/faithful)] There is considerable variation in the mss., with some reading passive/reflexive forms. Lat. has *iustificabuntur*, a future passive form.
13a May they] Lat. places *et* before the verb (VanderKam, *Jubilees* 2:130). The Eth. mss. have no trace of a conjunction here; Charles (*Ethiopic Version*, 79 n. 4) changed *et* to *ut*, but there is no support for the alteration.
b sacred head (lit., "head of sacredness/holiness")] 21 39c 48 "head and sacredness"; 58 "head for sacredness"; ms. 17 reads a verb: "and he will be holy/and so that he may be holy"; ms. 44 omits "sacredness."
c head] "your head" 17 and 21 35 39 48 58 with a differ-

ent spelling. Ms. 49 has "on your head and on the head of."

d each and every generation (lit., "all generations of generations")] Lat. reads only *in omni generatione*; MSS. 42 47 lack "generations of."

e and] Lat. lacks *et*, and MS. 21 om. *wa-*.

f forever] 39 48 58 have "age(s) of age(s)"; see also 42. Lat. *in saeculum* agrees with Eth. *la-'ālam*.

14a May he purify] "He will purify" 9 47 (and 58 with a different spelling); Lat. also reads a future indicative as it often does where Eth. has a subjunctive form.

b filthy pollution] The best Eth. reading is two nouns in a construct relation. Several copies read a conjunction between them (44: "filth and from all pollution"; 35: "filth and pollution"), while 12 17 38 47 63 have a noun + adjective: "polluted filth"; 21 reads only the first noun. Lat. also places a conjunction between the two nouns. With any of the readings, the meaning is not much affected. See VanderKam, *Jubilees* 2:130.

c you may be pardoned] Lat. *ut propitius sit*, "he may forgive." Charles (*Ethiopic Version*, 78 n. 16) changed the Eth. to a third-person form, but that would fit poorly with the preposition *'em-* that follows, so he had to remove it. See VanderKam, *Jubilees* 2:130.

d sin you have committed in ignorance] Lat. seems to have a roughly equivalent expression to the one in Eth., but it places a conjunction between the units: "your unjust acts and your sins of negligence."

15a May he renew his covenant with you] Lat. "You will renew his covenant with him"—that is, it reverses the subject and the object of the preposition, leaving an awkward expression. Cf. 22:30 and VanderKam, *Jubilees* 2:131.

b for him] om. 17 44; Lat. *illi*.

c the people] "his people" 38; Lat. *plebem*.

d his] Lat. lacks a possessive.

e God] om. 12; Lat. *deum*.

f for you] om. 39 58; Lat. *tibi*.

16a what I say (lit., "my word")] om. 38; Lat. *sermonum meorum*.

b the commandments of] There is variation of an odd sort in the Eth. copies, with several reading "my command of" (12; see 44 58); Lat. *praecepta* (followed by a noun in the genitive).

c act as they do (lit., "according to their actions")] "their action" 20 21 38 44 58 63; Lat. *operas eorum*.

d something that is impure] While most MSS. read a noun, 9 12 38 39 47 63 read an adjective. Lat. has a noun, *pollutio*.

e defiled] Several copies read a noun, *gemmānē*, as does Lat. (*inmunditia*).

17a They] pr. "and" 9 17 38 39 42ᶜ 44 58.

b offer their sacrifices] Eth. uses a noun + verb construction, while Lat. expresses the idea with a verb alone placed at the beginning of the sentence.

c the dead] Some Eth. copies read an unusual form *'abdām* (9 21 38) rather than *'abdent*. Presumably it too is a pl. for "the dead."

d and] om. 9 38; Lat. *et*. Ms. 38 places the conjunction before the verb rather than at the beginning of the clause.

e and worthless] om. 9 38.

18a my god] "our lord, saying" 44; "our god" 38ᶜ; Lat. *deus meus*.

b my lord] "our lord" 38ᶜ 44; "my god" 63; Lat. *dominus meus*.

c my (deliverer)] Lat. lacks an equivalent of "my" (*meus*). Ms. 38ᶜ has "our (deliverer)."

d They have] Eth. lacks "They have," though Lat. correctly supplies it (*illis*).

19a may the Most High God help you] "may he guard you and help you" 12 (it om. "bless you" in the next line); "may the Most High God bless you and help you" 21; "may the Most High God guard you" 44.

b the God of heaven] Lat. the God of *adae*. The reading is puzzling, but it may be a remnant of *saddae* = שדי (see VanderKam, *Jubilees* 2:132).

c remove you] "return you" 12; Lat. *separabit te*.

d impurity] Lat. "all their abominable acts" (*omnibus abominationibus ipsorum*); pr. "their wickedness and from" 58.

20a my son] pr. "you, O" 12; pr. "O" 21.

b all the descendants of] om. 21 44.

c daughters] om. 25 35; pr. "from" 38.

d his] "their" 35 58; "Canaan's" 63.

e being uprooted] "being obliterated" 44.

21a through] om. 38 63.

b (from) him] "them" 9 38 39 42 48 58.

22a idols] om. 25.

b odious (*ṣelu'ān*)] "strong" (*ṣenu'ān*) 42 47.

c and (will go)] om. 39 63.

d of any of them] = 4Q221 2 i:2; Eth. "of them."

e all] om. 21; 4Q221 2 i:3 reads "all."

f destroyed] So 4Q221 2 i:3; Eth. "taken."

23a May . . . keep you] "will keep you" 9 38.

b erroneous way (lit., "way of error")] "error of the way" 38.

c may he rescue you] "he will rescue you" 9 38 44; "you have rescued" 21.

24a I have built] "you have built" 39 42ᶜ(?) 47 48 63; + "for you and" 17ᶜ.

b for myself] om. 12.

c the earth] + "which" 38.

d It has been given (the subj. is fem.; masc. subject 17 38, and the same is the case in the second instance of the verb in the verse) to you and to your descendants (+ "after you" 20; + "until" 44) forever] Charles (*Jubilees*, 142) bracketed these words, considering them a dittography of the same clause later in the verse. Werman

e	will establish] "will stand/rise/be established (my name will arise)" 38.	d	with whom] om. 38.
		e	I] "he" 9 12 17 20 21 25 39 42 44 47 48 58 63; cf. 35.
f	my name] om. 35; + "forever" 17.	f	*exceedingly* happy] There are serious problems with the text. The translation is based on accepting the poorly attested first-person sg. verb "I am happy" (most MSS. read "he is happy) and in explaining *ba-'ella* ("in them") as a reflection of באשר where אשר is actually the noun "happiness," not the familiar relative pronoun as in the Eth. expression (hence *exceedingly* in the translation for "I am happy with *happiness*"). See VanderKam, *Jubilees* 2:134–35, for a fuller discussion. Werman (*Jubilees*, 344 n. 22) also suggests several corruptions in the text. She takes v. 27 as an address to God, not as a sentence (as in the present translation); then v. 28 begins with an imperative, calling on God to bless Jacob: "bless my son Jacob with whom I am happy with all my heart and my soul." In this way she removes the somewhat awkward situation in which in v. 28 Abraham first addresses Jacob and then calls on God to bless Jacob. But it is possible that the patriarch mentioned Jacob first to emphasize him and continued the sentence by calling on God to bless him.
g	God] "the Lord" 58.		
h	Your descendants and] om. 44.		
i	all] om. 63 + "forever in all" 35; + "the earth and in all" 44.		
25a	finished] + "speaking with him and" 38.		
26a	The two of them] om. 21.		
b	together] om. 12 20.		
c	He kissed him] Ms. 47 makes "his mind" the subject of the verb.		
d	seven times] "a kiss" 12; "70 times" (?) 44.		
e	his feelings] pr. "in" 35 44.		
27a	him] om. 12.		
b	said] + "to him" 63.		
c	The Most High God] "May the Most High God bless you" 63.		
d	of everything] om. 21.		
e	who brought me] "you brought us" 9; "you brought me" 17ᶜ 20 25 35 42 47 58. Despite the strong support for "you," it makes poor sense in the context where Abraham is speaking to Jacob.		
		g	my mind] om. 12.
		h	feelings] pr. "all and in" 12; pr. "all" 35 58.
		i	continue] + "O Lord" 63.
		29a	the time of] om. 21 38 44; pr. "all" 35. Mss. 38 and 44 add the expression after "eternity."
f	Ur] "Sur" 9 12 17 20 21 25 39 42 47 48 (graphic confusion?).	b	your eyes] "my eyes" 25.
		c	and his descendants] om. 63.
g	to give me] "you should give me" 20 35 58.	d	they may watch over them] "you may watch over them" 12 38 63.
h	land] + "of Ham" = *kām* 39 42 47 48; *kama* (it introduces a purpose clause) 44 58. *Kām* must be a development from the unneeded *kama*.	e	as the people (your people 39 58) of your heritage] om. 9 12 17 21 38 44 63.
i	that I should posses it] om. 21; "that I should take it up" (?) 12 17.	30a	Bless him] "You will/are to bless him" 12; + "O Lord" 63; om. 44.
j	raise up] + "my name" 12.	b	with all] om. 21.
k	that they may be blessed] "that the Most High may be blessed" 9 38.	c	your] om. 12 38.
		d	With your entire will—with his descendants] om. 25.
28a	he blessed] "I will bless" 17 21 48 63; "bless" (pl. imperative) 35; "bless" (sg. imperative) 58.	e	covenant] + "with him" 12.
		f	with him and] om. 12.
b	Jacob] + "and said" 38.		
c	My son] om. 21.		

Commentary

Abraham directs the final testament in the series of three in chaps. 20–22 not to any of his actual sons but to Jacob, his true heir. Verses 1-9 describe the last Festival of Weeks that occurred in Abraham's life, the extraordinary joy he felt on the occasion when his two sons Isaac and Ishmael joined him for the celebration, and the prayer he then offered. The festivities serve as the setting for Abraham's testamentary words to Jacob, who was also present for the holiday (vv. 10-24). In this section the aged patriarch speaks again about the holiness of Jacob and his descendants and delivers his most explicit, developed teachings about separation from the nations and about not intermarrying with Canaanites (vv. 16-22). Once he concludes his final address, he and Jacob settle down for the night, and while the young man sleeps Abraham prays for an eternal blessing on him (vv. 25-30). The beginning of Jubilees 23 (vv. 1-7) is, in a sense, part of the same literary unit because it forms the direct continuation of the action in chap. 22,[1] but, since it also functions as an introduction to the apocalyptic section that dominates the chapter, it will be treated with 23:8-32.

The chapter may be outlined as follows:
1-6   The family celebrates the Festival of Weeks
7-9   Abraham's prayer
10-15 Abraham prays for Jacob
16-24 Abraham gives commands to Jacob
25-26 Abraham and Jacob lie down together
27-30 Abraham blesses the sleeping Jacob

None of these sections has a parallel in Genesis.

There are several textual witnesses for Jubilees 22. Besides the Ethiopic manuscripts that contain the full text, the Latin translation is available for vv. 2-19, and two highly fragmentary Hebrew copies preserve small parts of the chapter:

4Q219 ii:35-37 contain some of v. 1, 4Q221 2 i:1-3 have parts of v. 22, and 2 ii:1 may have two letters from v. 30.[2]

1-6 The Family Celebrates the Festival of Weeks

■ **1-2** The beginning of a new unit at v. 1 is apparent from the date formula that locates the events to follow sometime after those of chap. 21. The date itself, however, has long been recognized as a problem because it is wildly out of harmony with the others for Abraham's life. Jubilees 21:1 places Abraham's address to Isaac in the year 172 of his life (see the commentary on the passage for the textual issue), while the formula in the Ethiopic version of 22:1 claims the events of the chapter occurred when Abraham was 233 years of age (jubilee 44, week 1, year 2). The verse also reports that this was the year of his death when, according to v. 7 and 23:8, he was 175 years. Dillmann changed the jubilee number to 43, which would place the action of chap. 22 in the year 2060, when Abraham would have been 184.[3] Charles took a more drastic approach: he changed all three numbers in v. 1 so that they become jubilee 42, week 6, year 7 = 2051, when Abraham would have been 175.[4] 4Q219 ii:35 happens to preserve the first words of the date formula and assigns the events to the first week of jubilee 43—just as Dillmann had proposed.[5] Even this date leaves one with an age nine years too high (Abraham would be 184), but it is consistent with the preceding dates and not as utterly improbable as the Ethiopic reading.[6] The number in the Ethiopic manuscript tradition, expressed as four-and-forty, may have arisen when the word *forty* induced a scribe to write *four* instead of *three* before it. As a result, one can at least say that Abraham and his sons celebrated the festival and the patriarch instructed Jacob several years after his speech to his actual son and heir Isaac. The unusual multiplicity of testaments (three of them) culminates in the one for Abraham's true successor and "son," Jacob.[7] The final

---

1   Berger (*Jubiläen*, 434 n. a to chap. 22) includes 23:1-8 with chap. 22, as does van Ruiten ("Abraham's Last Day according to the Book of *Jubilees* [*Jub*. 22:1–23:8]," in Erkki Koskenniemi and Pekka Lindqvist, eds., *Rewritten Biblical Figures* [Studies in Rewritten Bible 3; Turku, Finland: Abo Akademi University, 2010] 57-88, here 58-59; *Abraham*, 295-98) because it has "a unity of time and space as well as continuity of the actors." The theme, however, differs.

2   In DJD 13:70, it is suggested that the only two surviving letters (בר) may be from ברית (covenant) in v. 30. Because of the great uncertainty in identifying the correct location for just two letters, there is no underlining to mark them in the translation.

3   Dillmann, "Jubiläen," 71 n. 14. The last several year numbers in the stories about Abraham's life have been nine higher than their counterparts in Genesis.

4   Charles, *Jubilees*, 137; Hartom ("Jubilees," 75) follows Charles.

5   In Jubilees one does not reach the first year of jubilee 44 until 24:21.

6   See DJD 13:53; VanderKam, "Chronology," 539; cf. van Ruiten, "Abraham's Last Day," 58; *Abraham*, 296.

7   As van Ruiten indicates, "Jacob is mentioned by name fourteen times, and is mostly referred to as 'my son Jacob' (22.10c, e, 11d, 16a, 19a, 20a), but also as 'son of Abraham' (22.23b), or simply 'my son' (22.28b). Abraham is referred to as 'your father Abraham' (22:16c). When Jacob awakened and realised Abraham was dead he said 'father, father' (23.3d). Only twice is Abraham referred to

testament came most appropriately in the very last year of Abraham's life, in fact, in its very last full day.

The scene in v. 1 is heartwarming. Abraham's two oldest sons—the only ones who are not merely names in a list in Genesis and Jubilees—traveled from their places to be with their elderly father for the holiday. They appear in the order Isaac-Ishmael, but Ishmael plays a positive role in the scene. Their arrival delighted Abraham, showing that both meant much to him, just as they did in the story of Isaac's weaning (Jub 17:3). The last place that Jubilees had mentioned as a residence for Abraham was "Hebron—that is, Kiriath Arba" (19:1),[8] and it is to Hebron that the two brothers journey for the occasion (see v. 3). The reader learns that Isaac had large holdings in Beersheba (v. 2); Gen 26:23 says he pitched his tent in this place where there was a well. But, as a dutiful son, his practice was to tend to his business there—his wealth is highlighted (see Gen 26:12-14 // Jub 24:14-15)—and then go to be with Abraham in the Hebron area. This is a passage where both "well of the oath" and the name *Beersheba* appear in the text. The wording of v. 1 indicates that the half-brothers came from Beersheba to visit their father; the implication is that Ishmael went to Beersheba first and the two made the trip to Hebron together. The exact place where Ishmael resided is never stated in Jubilees, but the area of Paran is mentioned twice in connection with him (Jub 17:12 [// Gen 21:12, where he lived in "the wilderness of Paran"]; 20:12 [cf. Gen 25:18]).

The occasion for the reunion is the Festival of Weeks[9]—called by this name and by its other designation, "the Festival of the Firstfruits of the harvest" (see Exod 23:16a; 34:22 [both names]; cf. Lev 23:16; Num 28:26 [both names]).[10] Jubilees 6:21 had also referred to it in the two ways ("it is the Festival of Weeks and it is the Festival of Firstfruits"),[11] and the writer had employed the second name in 15:1 as well ("in the third month, in the middle of the month—Abram celebrated the Festival of the Firstfruits of the wheat harvest").[12]

■ **3** Although he had already mentioned the arrival of Ishmael in the company of Isaac in v. 1, the author saw fit to say it again at the beginning of v. 3. The fact that he had talked about Isaac's regular travels in v. 2 may have induced him to treat Ishmael in v. 3a, but the notice does signify that Ishmael is no afterthought in the context—he is part of the family, and he is a good son. Indeed, his presence for the festival "reintroduces him to the heartbeat of covenant life."[13] The Ethiopic text follows the notice about Ishmael with "and all of them came together," perhaps meaning that the three were in one place, but the Latin translation reads *utrique* ("both"), so that the text says "both of them came together,"[14] that is, Isaac and Ishmael arrived together.

The two sons, though they traveled together, play

---

as 'his grandfather' (22.26b; 23.2b)" ("Abraham's Last Day," 59; *Abraham*, 297).

8   In Gen 22:19 (// Jub 18:17) Abraham returned to his home in Beersheba, but Sarah died in Kiriath Arba = Hebron (Gen 23:2 // Jub 19:2) and Abraham buried her in the cave located in the field of Machpelah that is opposite Hebron (Gen 23:19 // Jub 19:5). For their move back to Hebron, see Jub 19:1.

9   The festival also happened to be Isaac's birthday (16:13).

10 Enough ink survives on 4Q219 ii:37 to indicate that the Hebrew text utilized both names for the festival.

11 In the context the angel tells Moses that Abraham, Isaac, and Jacob kept the festival, just as they do here in chap. 22.

12 The passage is one of the places in Jubilees that contradicts Kugel's thesis about two separate festivals. He, however, considers the identification of the two in the present passage as a "small but telling error" made by his interpolator ("Interpolations, 247-48; *Walk through* Jubilees, 255-56 (cf. 125); "Jubilees," 370).

13 Francis, "Excluded Middle," 269. Kugel thinks the writer makes "a subtle dig at Ishmael" (*Walk through* Jubilees, 125-26 [quotation from p. 125]; "Jubilees," 370). This seems a misreading of the text, where nothing negative is said about him. It is true that Isaac is the one who visits his father regularly, but Ishmael lives farther away—in fact in a place to which Abraham sent him (20:11-12)—and still takes the trouble to see him in Hebron. The only meaningful distinction between the brothers is that Isaac is a priest and Ishmael is not.

14 Ms. 44 adds "his children," but that term would also include Keturah's sons, who play no role in the present scene. Charles considered *kwellomu* ("all of them") to be a mistake for *kel'ēhomu* ("the two of them") (*Ethiopic Version*, 77 n. 24; in *Jubilees*, 138,

653

different roles in Hebron. The writer makes it clear that Isaac is the one who assumes the priestly function for which Abraham had prepared him in chap. 21. At first he simply reports Isaac's slaughtering of a victim—or so it seems. In the Ethiopic text Isaac executes a victim for an offering (*senḥaḥ*), a term used in chap. 21 in connection with the peace/well-being offering. The Latin uses *fructuum*, another word employed in chap. 21 regarding the peace offering (see v. 7). Neither term is the actual name of the sacrifice, but the writer may be hinting in v. 3 about the nature of the sacrifice that in v. 4 he will call a peace/well-being offering. The altar used was the one that Abraham had constructed at Hebron (see Jub 14:10-11);[15] this is the only indication in the chapter about where the events take place.

■ **4** The writer leaves no doubt about roles when he says Isaac was the one who made the peace offering and prepared the festival meal in the presence of Ishmael, though Ishmael is part of the celebration. Leviticus 23:19 prescribes that the Israelites were to bring a peace offering on the Festival of Weeks. The author of Jubilees also echoes Deut 16:11, which commands that on the holiday the Israelites are to rejoice before the Lord,[16] a command that he apparently understands in the sense of eating a celebratory meal together. Since the peace offering was shared among God, the priest, and the one presenting it, a meal was a natural event in the circumstances. Leviticus 7:11-36 (see Jub 21:10) provides the rules for consuming the items sacrificed.

Rebekah and Isaac each sent a peace offering through Jacob to Abraham. Rebekah's offering, mentioned first, more nearly reflects the legislation for the holiday. She "made fresh bread out of new wheat."[17] The festival was the time for bringing the first of the wheat harvest, and she used the wheat to bake bread. Leviticus 23:17 and 20 refer to the two loaves of bread made from the new wheat; they function as an elevation offering. The purpose for presenting Rebekah's bread to Abraham was so that before he died he could bless the Creator who made the crops grow from the earth (see v. 6). Years later, under different circumstances, she would prepare bread and food for Isaac and send them through Jacob so that his father could pronounce a blessing on his son before he died (Gen 27:17)—one of a series of parallels between Jubilees 22 and Genesis 27.[18]

■ **5** Isaac too sent his peace offering to his father through Jacob, and his sacrifice included wine according to the Latin translation; the phrase "for him to eat and drink" presupposes that he received an appropriate liquid.[19] Exactly why the parents send their offerings

---

he simply includes the change in his translation without explaining what he had done), and in this Littmann, Goldmann, Hartom, and Wintermute have followed him. The two words would be easy to confuse. Werman, who prefers "all of them," notes that here the brothers are following Abraham's command in 20:2 regarding unity among his sons and grandsons (*Jubilees*, 343 n. 2, 345).

15 Jubilees does not say that Abra(ha)m built an altar at Hebron, only that he constructed one at the oak of Mamre that is near Hebron (14:10-11). Genesis 13:18 relates that Abram built an altar at Hebron, but Jub 13:21 does not reproduce the statement, although the present verse presupposes it.

16 See Halpern-Amaru, "Joy as Piety," 196–97; she draws attention to 2 Chr 15:10-15, dated to the third month in the fifteenth year of King Asa and thus reminding one of Jubilees' date for the Festival of Weeks, when the people enter into covenant with an oath and rejoice. For the joyful occasion, see also Söllner, "Ismael und Isaak," 370–71.

17 Syncellus records a similar account: "After making little bread cakes, as Josephus says, Rebecca gave them to Jacob. And he brought them, along with other gifts sent through Isaac, to Abraham" (120.4-5; Adler/Tuffin, *Chronography*, 148). He then refers to the blessings Abraham gave to Jacob. This is one of the instances in which Syncellus attributes to Josephus material coming from Jubilees.

18 These have been noticed before, but van Ruiten provides a convenient summary of them and places the parallel passages side by side ("Abraham's Last Day," 63–65; *Abraham*, 302–4). He adds that there are important differences between Jubilees 22 and Genesis 27, but Jubilees 22 more significantly illustrates a practice of the author who raids similar situations in Genesis for words and phrases to use in the episode he is creating. Werman too supplies a chart showing the agreements between the two passages (*Jubilees*, 342).

19 The reference to wine is an additional similarity with Genesis 27 where Jacob brought wine, among other items, to his father (v. 25).

through their son Jacob the text does not say; it is simply another indication of how important he is in the story (Esau does not figure in chap. 22). Jacob is identified as Rebekah's son in v. 4; in v. 5 he is not called Isaac's son. Rebekah, who had a better understanding of Jacob than Isaac did, also has a deeper grasp of Abraham's character: the reason she sends him the bread is "so that he would eat (it) and bless the Creator of everything before he died." She may have known that Abraham had done this before—when he saw his two sons Ishmael and Isaac at the time of Isaac's weaning. At that time too he blessed the Creator of all (with a loud voice according to 17:3; see also 11:17; 12:19; 16:26; and v. 27 below).[20] The only purposes listed for Isaac's gift are so that his father could eat and drink.

■ 6 Abraham did consume the food and drink the wine[21] and, as Rebekah intended, he did bless the Creator who had given the abundance of the earth to humanity so that they in turn could, like Abraham, eat, drink, and bless him. The language reminds one of what Israel was to do on the Sabbath: "In this way he made a sign on it by which they, too, would keep Sabbath with us on the seventh day to eat, drink, and bless the Creator of all as he had blessed them and sanctified them for himself as a treasured people out of all the nations; and to be keeping Sabbath together with us" (2:21; see also 2:31-32).[22] "Most High" is a frequent title for God in Jubilees: in the Abraham chapters it occurs elsewhere in 12:19; 13:16, 29; 16:18, 27; 20:9; 21:20, 22, 23, 25; 22:11, 13, 19, 23, 27. Among these it is coupled with the title "Creator" or a paraphrase of it in 12:19 and 22:27 (see too 25:11)—reminiscent of its use in Gen 14:18-24, where, also in a context in which bread and wine play a role (v. 18), Melchizedek says, "Blessed be Abram by God Most High, / maker of heaven and earth; / and blessed be God Most High, / who has delivered your enemies into your hand" (vv. 19-20). In Gen 14:20 Abram too invokes "God Most High, maker of heaven and earth." By speaking of God as the one who made "all the fat things of the earth," Abraham uses a term that will figure in Isaac's mistaken blessing of Jacob in Genesis 27. In 27:28 he says of the disguised Jacob, "May God give you of the dew of heaven, / and of the fatness of the earth, / and plenty of grain and wine" (in v. 39 Esau will lack that "fatness of the earth").

7-9 Abraham's Prayer

■ 7 Once he had eaten and drunk the nourishment given to him by Jacob, Abraham offered a prayer of thanks to "my God" for bringing him to this time and situation, a time when he was 175 years of age (both the Ethiopic and Latin versions document the number). The verb he uses (Ethiopic *'etgānay*;[23] Latin *confiteor*) suggests he is acknowledging this God; it does not seem likely in the context that he is "submitting himself," as he had done throughout his lifetime. Here he is recognizing or acknowledging that God was the one who had

---

20 Cf. Charles, *Jubilees*, 138.
21 The same is said about Isaac in Gen 27:25.
22 The passage occurs just after the deity said he had chosen the descendants of Jacob who would be the ones keeping the Sabbath (2:20). Endres cites Sir 24:8; 2 Macc 1:24-25; 7:22-23, where the title "the creator of all" or the like also occurs (*Biblical Interpretation*, 41-42). He finds deep theological meaning in it in the present context: "Belief in divine election was rooted in an experience of salvation, both of which proceed from a theology of creation. This notion had already occurred in Sirach, a work noted for its acute Torah-consciousness and concern for cultic observance. It also arose in literature of self-preservation, especially in 2 Maccabees. Moreover it related creation, liberation, and covenant to the promises made by God to Noah (Genesis 9): God promised never again to destroy that which he had created. The feast of Shabuot celebrates that saving act, and it grounded the responsibilities of the elect people in this theologoumenon: the God who saved/liberated Israel is the God who creates/re-creates Israel. This conception of the divine corresponds to the program of the priestly writers and one with which the author of Jubilees was highly enamored" (p. 42). Perhaps it is enough to say that creation language is at home in the context of the festival but that the title has to do with God's power in making the earth fertile.
23 For the form Leslau lists "humble oneself, worship, humbly entreat, beseech, give praise, pay homage, laud, submit oneself, supplicate, confess sins, ask forgiveness" (*Concise Dictionary*, 208). It shares with *confiteor* the nuance of confession but also the idea of acknowledging (Lewis and Short, *Latin Dictionary*, 415).

made events take place as they had. And it was a truly happy day: his two sons had joined him, and together with Rebekah and Jacob they were celebrating the Festival of Weeks, the holiday of the covenant.[24] Abraham uses for himself the expression the Genesis narrator employs for him in 25:8—literally, that he is "old and full" (MT); almost all the other versions of Gen 25:8 (including SP LXX) place "of days" after "full," as in the present verse (see Gen 35:29, where it is used regarding Isaac). Abraham adds a summary statement about the nature of his many years: "All of my days have proved to be peace for me." The assertion is surprising in light of several events in his life, including nearly losing Sarai in Egypt (Jub 13:11-15), the battle with the kings to release Lot (13:22-29), the distress he experienced over the treatment of Hagar and Ishmael (17:4-14), and the nightmare of almost killing Isaac (17:15–18:19). Of course, Ishmael and Isaac, both of whom had received some rough treatment from their father, were listening to his words. What he means by the assertion Abraham explains in v. 8.

■ 8 That all his days became or proved to be peace for him meant that enemies had never conquered him or gained control over the bounties God had given him or his children. Taken in this sense, his claim in v. 7 is accurate. So, for example, Pharaoh had returned Sarai to a very rich Abram; he managed to rescue Lot from the kings; Ishmael received a blessing; and Isaac was saved at the last moment.

■ 9 At this very late stage in his life, the patriarch asks God to continue showering divine grace on both himself and his descendants. Determining exactly which descendants he included in his prayer is difficult. The Ethiopic reads literally "on your servant and on the seed of his sons" where the Latin has "on this young man, Lord, and on his seed." According to the Ethiopic version, Abraham is referring to himself as "your servant," and "the seed of his sons" makes no differentiation between any of his offspring or at least includes both Isaac and Ishmael with their children. The Latin translation entails that Abraham is speaking about Jacob as "this young man," and Jacob's descendants are the ones for whom he requests grace and peace.[25] Narrowing the blessing to Jacob and his descendants is consistent with the stance of the author, yet in the narrative sequence of the chapter the blessing of Jacob does not begin until v. 10, when Abraham has to summon him; moreover, both Latin and Ethiopic had just mentioned Abraham's sons as ones who had received gifts from God, benefits they had not lost. Consequently, the Ethiopic reading, it seems, should be retained and the Latin rejected as a misplaced anticipation of the blessing on Jacob and his descendants. In v. 9, then, Abraham would be praying for divine grace on both of his sons and their children. The chief difficulty with the Ethiopic version is the sequel where Abraham asks that the descendants of his sons become "your acceptable people[26] and heritage" in preference to all other nations. That sounds like the language used only for Israel in the book.

The difference between the versions may first have arisen over the interpretation of a form of παις in their base texts: it can mean "child, boy, youth" or "slave,

---

24 The above seems a more likely reading of Abraham's thanks to God for letting him see this day than Werman's interpretation that he is talking about achieving the age of 175 years (*Jubilees*, 345). She thinks that he is accepting the context sketched in chap. 23 according to which at the time of Abraham the final ages of humans were becoming lower than those of their ancestors. She does have to admit that, by characterizing his days as peaceful, Abraham would be an exception to the description in 23:9-10. Rather, he is grateful, it seems, because his sons and grandson are present to celebrate the covenantal festival with him.

25 Though the choice of reading makes a significant difference in the interpretation of the text, the translators and commentators regularly ignore the issue. A partial exception is Rabin in his revision of Charles's translation, where he renders the passage "upon thy servant, and upon his descendants," with a footnote after the last phrase indicating this is the Latin reading and also giving a translation of the Ethiopic text. So, oddly enough, he has adopted the Ethiopic version's "thy servant" and the Latin's "upon his descendants," but he says nothing about the problem with "thy servant."

26 See the textual discussion below. The term used in the Ethiopic version (ḥeruya) also means "chosen." Similar language occurs in 2:20 בחר is used in 4Q216 vii:11); 15:30; 19:18 (Ethiopic yaḥarri; Latin *elegit*); 33:11.

servant." In the LXX, forms of παις most frequently render עבד,[27] an association that favors seeing עבד as the preferred reading. Once the Latin translator selected the wrong sense for παις, he may have added the demonstrative and reworked the sequel (making it "and his descendants") so that it would fit Jacob. However, while a strong textual case can be made for the Ethiopic readings, the words "your chosen people and heritage" are enough to refute that case and render the Latin readings earlier in v. 9 the more likely ones. But here too there is a problem. The two versions read:

Ethiopic: ḥezba ḥeruya wa-resta 'em-kwellu 'aḥzāba medr
Latin: in populum acceptabilem et hereditas ex omnibus filiis terrae

A potential difference involves Ethiopic ḥeruya and Latin *acceptabilem*. The Ethiopic term is used in the sense of "chosen, elect," but it can also have the meanings "excellent, pleasing, acceptable, preferable."[28] If Abraham were requesting that the descendants of Ishmael and Isaac become a people acceptable to the Lord to a greater extent than the other nations, it would be consistent with what is said not only about Israel but also about Ishmael and his descendants. The book never uses the language of "chosen people" regarding Ishmael or his offspring, and it separates him and his line from Israel (e.g., 15:30-32). In fact, 15:30 says explicitly that God did not choose them but chose Israel. Nevertheless, the writer has positive things to say about Ishmael. In 17:7 the deity promises to make him into a great nation since he was Abraham's son, and 17:13 declares that the Lord was with him. Ishmael and his sons were among the recipients of Abraham's testamentary address in chap. 20, where instructions about mutual love, circumcision, purity, and monotheism are prominent. The patriarch there predicts that if they live by his commands to them, they "will be a blessing on the earth, and all the nations of the earth will be delighted with you. They will bless your sons in my name so that they may be blessed as I am" (20:10). That is, all of Abraham's descendants are distinguished from the nations. The Latin in v. 9 and perhaps also the Ethiopic, then, would be calling Abraham's descendants "pleasing/acceptable," not chosen.[29]

10-15 Abraham Prays for Jacob[30]

The major part of the chapter contains Abraham's final words to Jacob, a character who has been mentioned in vv. 4-5 as the bearer of gifts to Abraham but one the reader already knows as the true successor to Abraham, the descendant through whom the promises and blessings will continue (see 19:17-29). In the grand design of the book, it is only fitting that he would be the one to receive Abraham's final words of blessing and instruction.[31] In Genesis there is no contact between Abraham and Jacob, though the chronology entails that Abraham lived until Jacob was fifteen years of age. The author of Jubilees here crafts another scene to enhance the stature of Jacob and uses elements from Genesis 27 to structure it (for parallels with Genesis 27 in the previous verses, see above).

---

27 HRCS, 1049-51.
28 Leslau, *Concise Dictionary*, 113.
29 Forms of the adjective *acceptabilis* usually figure in contexts that deal with acceptable sacrifices (21:9; 32:4; 49:9) or festivals (16:27, 29). In 49:15 it modifies "testimony." Most of the passages that speak of Israel's election are in the places where the Latin translation is not available, but, as noted above, in 19:18 it uses a form of *elegit* ("to choose") where Ethiopic has *yaḥarri*, not a form of *accipio*. According to Werman, v. 9 yields the possibility that Ishmael and Keturah's sons are included (*Jubilees*, 345-46), but v. 10 shows that this is not the case. Hers is an appealing way of reading the evidence, but it does not explain why Abraham refers to the seed of his "sons" (pl.) in v. 9.
30 There is disagreement regarding how much of the unit in which Abraham speaks of and to Jacob is poetic. Here none of the blessing in vv. 10-15 is set as verse—only vv. 16-18 below, part of v. 19, and v. 23—but others have seen poetry from v. 10 to v. 24. For a study of the issue, see van Ruiten, "Abraham's Last Day," 79-80; *Abraham*, 308-9. It is often not easy to decide whether sections are poetic when only granddaughter translations (Ethiopic and Latin) of the original Hebrew text are available.
31 See van Ruiten ("Abraham's Last Day," 67-68; *Abraham*, 306) for the alternation between blessing and commandment in these speeches of Abraham. He also outlines the similarities between the beginnings of the two blessings in vv. 10-24 ("Abraham's Last Day," 68; *Abraham*, 307-8).

■ **10-11a** Abraham calls to Jacob, but he may not have been very far away because he had just delivered bread and wine to his grandfather (vv. 4-5). He begins his interaction with Jacob by calling him "my son." He was, of course, not Abraham's actual son, but he nearly functions as one in Jubilees (see 19:21, where the patriarch loves Jacob much more than all his sons). For this select descendant he asks a blessing from the "God of all." The title is not very common in Jubilees (here and in v. 27; 30:19; 31:32; for "the Lord of all" see 31:13),[32] but it conveys clearly the capability of this deity to do what he intends to do, since he controls everything. Abraham asks for both blessing and strength for Jacob so that he can act in the correct way and do what God wants—he needs divine help to conduct himself according to God's will (see v. 15 below). In that way God will choose him and his progeny "to be his people for his heritage" lasting forever. The words "people" and "heritage," both of which appeared in v. 9, are often paired in the HB. In Deut 4:20 Moses says the Lord led Israel out of Egyptian bondage "to become a people of his very own possession [לעם נחלה], as you are now" (see also 9:26, 29; related are 7:6; 14:2).

With Abraham's powerful, authoritative words ringing in Jacob's ears, the elderly man told him to come nearer and kiss him. This is another reminder that Genesis 27, where the "dying" Isaac intends to bless Esau but is deceived so that he blesses Jacob, serves as a literary basis for the scene in Jubilees 22—this time with Jacob being a much more admirable character. In fact the end of 22:10 and the beginning of 22:11 practically cite Gen 27:26-27, with Abraham playing the role Isaac takes in Genesis 27 but improving considerably on his performance there (see also Gen 48:10):

Jubilees 22:10-11: Now you, my son Jacob,[33] come close
    and kiss me. So he came close and kissed him.
Genesis 27:26-27: Come near and kiss me, my son. So he
    came near and kissed him.

With this prelude, Abraham begins his words of prayerful blessing on Jacob

■ **11b** He again (as in v. 10) refers to Jacob as "my son" and asks for blessings on him and his descendants forever. In addressing the deity with the title "Most High" attached to a divine name, Abraham is using a term to which he has resorted frequently. The descriptor appears twenty-four times in Jubilees, sixteen of them in the Abraham chapters and six in chap. 22 (see also vv. 6, 13, 19, 23, 27). He prays that Jacob may be the ancestor of righteous descendants (Ethiopic *zar'a ṣedq*; Latin *semen veritatis*),[34] some of whom would be sanctified. That Jacob and his descendants would be blessed and holy is a theme met already in chap. 2, where Israel, unlike the nations, is blessed and holy as is the Sabbath that they alone among humanity keep with God and his great angels (2:19, 20, 21, 24, 28, 31). God sanctified Israel out of all humanity (15:31). Abraham had earlier learned that one of Isaac's sons would become a holy progeny and people (16:17-18). When Jacob was a child, his grandfather recognized that he would prove a blessing among humanity forever (19:17, 20), and at that time he asked that all the blessings the Lord had bestowed on him and his offspring would belong eternally to Jacob and his line (19:23). In requesting that the Lord sanctify "some of your sons in the entire earth," Abraham could be implying that not all of Jacob's descendants would prove to be holy, but perhaps it is more likely that he is praying for a continuation of the priestly line among Jacob's progeny. The line had begun with Adam, and Isaac had just assumed the role of priest as his father had before him. The verb "sanctify" (piel קדש) is used for setting apart priests (e.g., Exod 28:3, 41; 29:1, 33) and is now employed by Abraham in this sense. The final lines of v. 11 nearly quote Gen 27:29a, part of Isaac's blessing on "Esau":[35]

Jubilees 22:11: May the nations serve you, and may all
    the nations[36] bow before your descendants.

---

32   "Lord of all" occurs in 4Q409 1 i:8 and possibly in line 6; in 11QPs^a xxviii:8 "God of all" is a likely reading, and "Lord of all" is probable in line 7. See also As. Mos. 4:2.

33   In Genesis 27, Isaac properly calls Jacob "my son," whereas in Jubilees 22 "son" could take on the meaning of "descendant" but seems even more suggestive.

34   The expression occurs in Jer 2:21: "Yet I planted you as a choice vine, / from the purest stock [זרע אמת]." "Seed of holiness" occurs in Isa 6:13 and Ezra 9:2.

35   Charles, *Jubilees*, 139; Endres, *Biblical Interpretation*, 43.

36   This is one of many examples illustrating Ethiopic Jubilees' independence from Ethiopic Genesis.

Genesis 27:29a: Let the peoples serve you, and the nations bow down to you.

"You" in both instances in Gen 27:29a is singular, referring to Jacob; Jubilees uses a singular form in the first clause but refers the second one to Jacob's progeny. The wish envisages a time when Israel will be a nation. Here Abraham does not call for separation from the peoples as he will in v. 16 but merely wants the nations to be useful to the offspring of Jacob. It is worth noting that at this point Abraham does not include the words immediately following Gen 27:29a: "Be lord over your brothers, / and may your mother's sons bow down to you."

■ **12** Abraham continues to deal with the relations between Jacob and the nations in v. 12. In this context he adopts language reminiscent of Balaam's oracle in Num 24:17-18.[37] There Balaam sees a star/scepter arising from Jacob/Israel and overpowering opponents, including the "sons of Seth [בני שת]." Abraham calls on Jacob to be strong (*kun ḥayyāla*/ *efficere fortis*);[38] Balaam speaks of Israel "doing valiantly [עשה חיל]." Jubilees interprets the much-discussed "sons of Seth" in the sense of all humanity, in line with the midrashic interpretation of this Seth as the third child of Adam and Eve and the ancestor of humanity (*Tg. Onq.* Num 24:17: "and rule over all of humanity"; Jubilees shares its understanding of קרקר as "rule"). The book does not, however, deal with the star/scepter image as pointing to a messiah; it simply does not broach the issue here. Abraham declares that, if Jacob and his progeny act in this fashion, their ways "will be justified" or proper (cf. Josh 1:8; Isa 48:15, though these passages speak of prospering in one's way).[39] They will be conducting themselves in the appropriate manner leading to their becoming a holy people. Israel as a holy people is an idea expressed a number of times in Deuteronomy. For example, Deut 7:6 reads: "For you are a people holy to the LORD your God; the LORD your God has chosen you out of all the peoples on the earth to be his people, his treasured possession"[40] (see also Deut 14:2, 21; 26:19; Isa 63:18; Dan 12:7).

■ **13** In v. 13 Abraham prays for the second time that the blessings he and his ancestors received should be transferred to Jacob. In his first prayer for Jacob, the patriarch had asked that a blessing accrue to him and his ancestors through Jacob's descendants (19:24). There he listed Shem, Noah, Enoch, Malaleel, Enosh, Seth, and Adam. In the same context he requested that the blessings he, Adam, Enoch, Noah, and Shem enjoyed should belong to Jacob (19:27). But now, though the petition is the same, he names only Noah and Adam (in reverse order again, as in 19:24). So, the number of forefathers he mentions continues to dwindle, yet he still asks that the ancestral blessings be imparted to Jacob, his successor. He resorts to an unusual expression for where the blessings are to fall: "on the sacred head[41] of your descendants." As Charles noted, the phrasing seems to be influenced by Gen 49:26, part of Jacob's blessing for Joseph. "The blessings of your father / are stronger than the blessings of the eternal mountains, / the bounties of the everlasting hills; / may they be on the head of Joseph, / on the brow of him who was set apart from his brothers" (see also Deut 33:16, part of another blessing of Joseph). The rendition of the verse in *Targum Neofiti* (*Targum Pseudo-Jonathan* is similar but somewhat more

---

In the clause, following the LXX's αρχοντες, Eth Gen 27:29a reads *malā'ekt* (here probably meaning "princes/rulers"; cf. Leslau, *Comparative Dictionary*, 303) rather than another word for "nations."

37 Genesis 27:27-29 and Numbers 24 share a number of elements (Westermann, *Genesis 12–36*, 441).

38 Latin *potestatem exerce*, which appears in the next clause, even more closely reflects עשה חיל in Num 24:18.

39 Werman draws attention to the conditional element in the statement (*Jubilees*, 346).

40 Regarding the passage in context (a context that will be reflected later in Jubilees 22), Weinfeld comments: "This is the reason for the previous commandments about abstaining from contact with the Canaanites and their worship: Israel is of separate status to God, is set apart from other nations, and therefore should not behave like them" (*Deuteronomy 1–11*, 367). As he indicates, a similar point is made in Exod 19:5-6.

41 The Ethiopic term is *demāḥ*, not the normal one for "head" (*re's*); Latin reads *vertex* (the form here is *verticem*). Both words suggest the top of the head or crown (Dillmann, *Lexicon*, 1085; Leslau, *Concise Dictionary*, 192) and probably reflect an original קדקד, the second term for "head" ("brow" in NRSV) in Gen 49:26 (it is the word Hartom uses in his translation).

elaborate) gives an idea of how it could be seen as appropriate to Jubilees 22:

> May the blessings of your father *be added for you*, to the blessings *with which my fathers Abraham and Isaac blessed me, which the lords of the world Ishmael and Esau longed for from the beginning. Let all these blessings come; let them become a crown of dignity* on the head of Joseph, and on the brow of the *pious* man.

In Jubilees Abraham makes the point repeatedly that Jacob and his line, that is, Israel, are the rightful recipient of all his and the ancestral blessings. The concluding words in the verse emphasize that this is no one- or two-generation arrangement; it is emphatically eternal.

■ **14** Abraham next turns to the ongoing need for Jacob to be pure as he comes to occupy the extraordinary position envisaged for him. In the Ethiopic version he prays that God will purify or keep him pure from "all filthy pollution [lit., all the impurity of filth]," while the Latin translation uses two nouns: "filth and injustice." His words may imply that such unfortunate actions will occur and will have to be addressed through the means available for the purpose. Both pollution/filth/impurity and sins/iniquities serve as phenomena that are purified in the HB: for impurity, see, e.g., Ezek 24:13; 36:25; for sins, see, e.g., Lev 16:30; Jer 33:8; Ps 51:4 (Eng. v. 2). Abraham moves from the thought of purification to that of atonement. Here too the versions differ in their formulations. In Ethiopic, Jacob is the subject of a verbal form meaning "make atonement, obtain remission of sins," but in Latin God is the subject of *propitius sit*: so that he may be favorable/kind/gracious.[42] Both express the idea that the impairment is to be removed in some way, once Jacob has been cleansed from impurity and other wrongs. The expression for the kinds of faults from which he would experience pardon reads differently in the two versions:

Ethiopic: sin[43] you have committed in ignorance
Latin: your unjust acts and your sins of negligence.

They agree that inadvertent sins are involved, but they disagree about how the first noun relates to the second: are they joined in a single expression as in Ethiopic, or are they two separate entities joined by a conjunction as in Latin? There is reason to believe that the Ethiopic version has retained the better reading. In Leviticus 4 and Numbers 15, chapters where inadvertent sins are treated, a recurring expression (see Lev 4:2, 27; Num 15:27) includes the verb "sin" (חטא) and "in negligence" (בשגגה). Numbers 15:28 is a parallel, and in it the verb "atone" also figures: "And the priest shall make atonement before the LORD for the one who commits an error, when it is unintentional, to make atonement for the person, who then shall be forgiven."[44]

Abraham concludes v. 14 with a repetition of his requests in v. 10 that the Lord would bless and strengthen Jacob, though he reverses the order of the verbs. These two petitions stand before a third one that he had not yet mentioned to Jacob, either in chap. 22 or 19—inheriting the land/earth. This was, of course, a prominent blessing or promise in the Abraham stories (e.g., Jub 13:3), and in harmony with his prayer that all the blessings given to him fall upon Jacob and his progeny he now includes it (the other major promises of numerous descendants and proving a blessing he had adduced in 19:17, 19, 21-22, 24). As in 19:21, where his descendants are to fill the entire earth/land, so here

---

42 Leslau, *Concise Dictionary*, 68; Lewis and Short, *Latin Dictionary*, 1471. Charles changed the Ethiopic verb to a third-person form to agree with the Latin (*Ethiopic Version*, 78 n. 16; cf. *Jubilees*, 140, where he reverts to the second person), but, as Littmann ("Jubiläen," 77 n. f) objected, the meaning Charles attributed to his revised form ("forgive") would be unusual.

43 The Ethiopic word here is *'abbasā*: "transgression, serious fault, iniquity, offense, sin, crime, guilt" (Leslau, *Concise Dictionary*, 139).

44 Frevel thinks the reference to sins committed in ignorance may point forward to Jacob's passive role in the Shechem episode (Genesis 34 // Jubilees 30) ("'Separate Yourself,'" 228–29), but there seems to be no hint to this effect in v. 14. Werman finds in the verse a leap to eschatological times because of the shared language with 1:21-23 (note too possession of the entire earth) (*Jubilees*, 346), a likely reading because Abraham's blessing clearly includes Jacob's descendants despite his continued use of the singular pronoun "you."

the term *medr/terra* is not further defined as pertaining specifically to the later territory of Israel.

■ **15** In v. 15, the last one in this section, Abraham expresses in other terms the meaning of what he has been saying throughout: he asks that the covenantal relationship with God and all it entails continue with Jacob and eventually with the nation that will descend from him. He uses the verb "renew," the appropriate one in the theology of the covenant in Jubilees. There is one agreement between God and the humans he selects. It is first noted in connection with Noah directly after the flood (6:4, 10-11), and it was renewed every year on the Festival of Weeks (6:17). A specific renewal on the holiday appears in Jub 14:18-20 (// Gen 15:18-21) where, in the middle of the third month, "we concluded a covenant with Abram like the covenant that we concluded during this month with Noah. Abram renewed the festival and the ordinance for himself forever" (14:20). On the same date Moses and Israel will renew the covenant at Mount Sinai (6:19).[45] It is fitting that Abraham should speak of renewing the covenant (see also 22:30 and 19:29), as he is speaking to Jacob while they celebrate the Festival of Weeks. Another expression that parallels his words in v. 10 is "so that you may be for him the people of his heritage throughout all ages" (see the commentary on v. 10). The final sentence in v. 15 recalls the words of God to Abraham in Gen 17:7 just after mentioning the eternal covenant he was establishing with Abraham and his descendants: "to be God to you and to your offspring after you."[46] The HB passage that most nearly resembles Abraham's words is Zech 8:8: "They shall be my people and I will be their God, in faithfulness and in righteousness [באמת ובצדקה]." The Lord made a similar promise to Moses in Jub 1:17 when speaking about Israel after punishment and exile: "I will be their God and they will be my true and righteous people." In several ways, then, vv. 10 and 15 form brackets around the initial section in Abraham's words to Jacob.

16-24 Abraham Gives Commands to Jacob

Abraham's second direct address to Jacob as his son (see v. 10 for the first one) marks the beginning of the second section in the speech (vv. 16-18), one in which he gives crucial instructions to Jacob. Having established the unique calling and role of Jacob and his descendants in vv. 10-15, he underscores an important concomitant of it. In vv. 16-18 he orders a radical separation from the nations and their idolatrous behavior.[47] His words have a poetic balance to them as he imparts a crucial teaching in the book. Though Abraham now commands separation from the other peoples, the reader should recall that already in 2:19, a verse that shares some of the language found in 22:15, God himself had said to the angels at the end of the first week: "I will now separate a people for myself among my nations. They, too, will keep Sabbath. I will sanctify a people for myself and will bless them {{as I sanctified the Sabbath day. I will sanctify them for myself; in this way I will bless them.}} They will be my people and I will be their God." Separation of Israel from the nations was God's intention from the beginning.[48]

---

45 See Jaubert, *La notion d'alliance*, 102–4.
46 The expression recurs frequently; see Skinner, *Genesis*, 293, for a list.
47 Schwarz (*Identität*, 20–22) sees it as the most important covenantal stipulation in the book. He emphasizes, and the evidence will be adduced below, that two kinds of passages influenced the author in his teachings about separation: those in Ezra and Nehemiah in which the two leaders try to establish and consolidate the post-exilic community, and the ones forbidding any covenant with the nations in Canaan such as Deut 7:1-6 (see, e.g., p. 35 and the second chapter of his book, pp. 37–84, where he treats these two kinds of texts). Consequently, Jubilees uses existing materials as it formulates the teaching about separation but applies them to the circumstances of the author's time. A. Shemesh ("4Q265 and the Authoritative Status of Jubilees at Qumran," 255–59) contends that 1QS v:13-20, especially the shorter form of the passage in some of the cave 4 copies, is a reworking of Jub 22:16-22. The sectarian text commands separation from the men of deceit; Jubilees orders separation from the nations. There are parallels in language and in concepts as well (e.g., not eating together). While the passages deal with a similar topic and draw upon some of the same passages, it is not easy to see the Serek unit as a *rewriting* of Jub 22:16-22.
48 Schwarz (*Identität*, 21–23) highlights the passage from chap. 2 as offering the theoretical background for the practical consequences set forth in chap. 22 and as demonstrating through its language the covenantal nature of the command to separate. See also van Ruiten, "Abraham's Last

■ **16** Abraham first instructs him to remember his words and keep his (his "father's") commandments. As he did with all his sons in chap. 20 and Isaac in chap. 21, he now provides Jacob with guidance for his life and that of his progeny. Abraham's words take poetic form, and the two parallel terms "what I say" and "the commandments of your father Abraham" point to him as the source for the instructions to follow. It is doubtful that the Jubilean Abraham means to distinguish his orders from those of God; rather, he communicates the revealed tradition to his grandson. The first command is to separate from the nations. The words resemble those Ezra addressed to his contemporaries: ". . . separate yourselves from the peoples of the land" (Ezra 10:11; see also v. 16 and 6:21; 9:1; Neh 9:2). Ezra's imperative form matches the one in Jub 22:16, but the teaching of separation is more widespread in the HB. In a series of passages, the Lord directed Israel to make no covenant with the residents of the land of Canaan (Exod 23:31-33; 34:12, 15; Deut 7:2-5). He declares in Lev 20:24: "I have separated you from the peoples" (cf. Num 23:9; Deut 32:9, 17; 1 Kgs 8:53), and in v. 26 he repeats the idea in connection with another topic central to Jubilees 22: "You shall be holy to me; for I the LORD am holy, and I have separated you from the other peoples to be mine." In the sequel, the writer focuses on the objectionable practices of the other peoples as reasons for separation from them and leaves out the injunctions about violent treatment of them and their cultic apparatuses.[49]

It seems as if the context of Leviticus 20 continues to influence the passage in the next prohibition—"do not eat with them."[50] After the Lord talks about the abominable practices of the nations in Lev 20:1-21, he exhorts Israel to keep his commands and statutes so that they may remain in the land and tells them not to imitate the practices just enumerated. Since he has separated Israel from the nations, "[y]ou shall therefore make a distinction between the clean animal and the unclean, and between the unclean bird and the clean; you shall not bring abomination on yourselves by animal or by bird or by anything with which the ground teems, which I have set apart for you to hold unclean" (Lev 20:25). The nations apparently ate the forbidden foods, and Israel was to be separate from them and their disgusting dietary practices.[51] At least some expositors understood the separation to involve not eating with people from

---

Day," 71; *Abraham*, 310-11; he additionally refers to Abram's separation from his family over the issue of idolatry, just as Jacob and his seed are to distance themselves from idolaters.

49 That is, in this context Jubilees does not borrow the instructions about smashing altars and idols found in several passages such as Exod 34:13; Deut 7:2, 5; Judg 2:2.

50 See Schwarz, *Identität*, 23-25. He notes that the food laws of Leviticus 11 and Deuteronomy 14 serve a separatist function, as does the law about not consuming blood; and he wonders whether the meals to which v. 16 refers might be cultic (comparing Exod 34:15). Cf. van Ruiten, "Abraham's Last Day," 73-74; *Abraham*, 313-14. As Shemesh notes (Werman and Shemesh, *Revealing*, 247-49), one of the Cave 4 copies of the Rule of the Community (4Q256 4 ix:8-10) offers similar instructions to the ones Abraham here gives to Jacob: "and to be separated from [al]l the men of injustice, Further[more, they shall not touch the purity of the men of] holiness, and he shall not eat with him [in com]munity. Furthermore, n[o man of the men of the Community shall give answer in accordance with their opinion] relating to any Torah or judgement. [Further]more, he shall not be united [with him in possessions or in work]" (trans. Abegg, *DSSR* 1:143).

51 Milgrom, *Leviticus 17-22*, 1762. He maintains that the passage "does not categorically mean that Israelites may not dine at the same table with others . . . , but that they must be wary of the meat being served." He then refers to later texts that did draw this inference, including Jub 22:16 and the passage from the Letter of Aristeas cited below. Tobit claims that he, unlike his fellow captives from Israel, refrained from eating the Gentiles' food (1:10-11), and Daniel and his friends also resolved not to defile themselves with the royal food; but in neither of these cases is the issue of eating with non-Jews addressed directly. The two chapters (Leviticus 11 and Deuteronomy 14) that contain the food laws include sections relating them to Israel's holiness (Lev 11:41-45; Deut 14:21). The latter passage says that Israelites were not to consume the meat of anything that was not slaughtered properly but that they could give it as food to foreigners living among them or sell it to them; Israel could not eat such meat because they are a holy people. See Schwarz, *Identität*, 23-24.

the nations. One of them is the author of the Letter of Aristeas. As the high priest Eleazar explains the meaning of the dietary laws, he includes these comments about them:

> The symbolism conveyed by these things [e.g., the separation taught by the cloven hoof] compels us to make a distinction in the performance of all our acts, with righteousness as our aim. This moreover explains why we are distinct from all other men. The majority of other men defile themselves in their relationships, thereby committing a serious offense. . . . We are quite separated from these practices. (151-52; trans. Shutt, *OTP* 2:23).

Jubilees, which stresses the importance of separation, here mentions a practical situation in which such separation would be violated and categorically prohibits it.[52]

The next prohibition covers actions more generally. Jacob (with his descendants) is not to behave as the nations do.[53] Here again Leviticus 20 seems to be in the background: "You shall not follow the practices of the nation[54] that I am driving out before you. Because they did all these things, I abhorred them" (v. 23; see also 18:2-3, 24, 27). The prohibition in Leviticus becomes a general ban on imitating the actions of the nations. The injunction precedes what appears to be an inference about the teachings regarding relations with the nations: Jacob and his progeny were to have nothing to do with them; hence they were not to associate or be friendly with them.[55] The prohibition reminds one of Peter's words to Cornelius and his household in Acts 10:28:

"You yourselves know that it is unlawful for a Jew to associate with or to visit a Gentile." The reason is not chauvinistic or nationalistic. As the sequel in Jubilees relates, there is to be no companionship or close association with the nations because of how impure and abominable their actions are. This is the message of Leviticus 18 and 20 (cf. 2 Kgs 16:3; Ezra 9:11), which list various vile practices, especially in sexual relations, and say that the previous inhabitants of Canaan defiled the land through such abominations. Israel, the holy people, was not to follow their example. In his prayer regarding mixed marriages, Ezra appeals to commands delivered by the prophets to the effect that Israel was never to "seek their peace and prosperity" (Ezra 9:12).[56]

■ **17** The ways of the nations that are to be avoided include the religious exercises that are the focus of vv. 17-18. The writer had seized the opportunity to disdain idols and idolaters before (e.g., 12:1-8; 20:7-8), but here he prefaces his criticisms with references to deviant rites of which the nations are guilty. Abraham charges them with sacrificing to the dead, a subject mentioned elsewhere in ancient Jewish literature.[57] Psalm 106:28 says of the Israelites in the wilderness that "they attached themselves to the Baal of Peor, / and ate sacrifices offered to the dead." Apparently they were imitating their Moabite and Midianite hosts in doing so (see Num 25:1-5, esp. v. 2: "These invited the people to the sacrifices of their gods, and the people ate and bowed down to their gods"). Ben Sira refers to offering food on a grave and follows it with words that make it seem as if it was sacrificed to gods: "Of what use to an idol is

---

52 The story in Acts 10–11, where Peter eats with Gentiles, admits how it was contrary to his practice, and is criticized for it, serves as another early source for the view that Jews and non-Jews were not to eat together.

53 Schwarz, *Identität*, 25–29. He draws attention to the fact that the prohibition of being like the nations is associated in the sequel with their idolatry. A series of positive commands contrast the worship of the one God with the service of idols and thus entail separation from the nations (see Jub 20:7-9; 21:3, 5; 36:5; cf. also 7:20; 20:2; 36:7).

54 The SP, LXX, and the other versions read a plural form (cf. MT Lev 18:24).

55 Shemesh thinks the prohibition refers to economic relations as in 4Q256 4 ix:10 (cf. 1QS v:14-15) (Werman and Shemesh, *Revealing*, 248). Schwarz considers various options for interpreting this general instantiation of the command to separate from the nations, among which is that political associations are meant (*Identität*, 29–30). However, though remaining uncertain, he accepts Goldmann's translation תתרע as illustrated by Prov 22:24: "Make no friends [תתרע] with those given to anger, / and do not associate with hotheads." Van Ruiten seems to think the text prohibits making a political covenant ("Abraham's Last Day," 74–75; *Abraham*, 314–15). The expression is too general to allow a specific conclusion.

56 Ezra's demand resembles the one in Deut 23:6 regarding the treatment of the Ammonites and Moabites (Blenkinsopp, *Ezra-Nehemiah*, 185).

57 For references, see Charles, *Jubilees*, 140–41; Frevel, "'Separate Yourself,'" 227.

a sacrifice? For it can neither eat nor smell" (30:18-19; here v. 19). Jubilees also charges the nations with worshiping demons. In the book the demons or evil spirits who came from the pre-flood giants were responsible for causing all sorts of ills in society. They dominate people's thoughts and misguide them (12:20). According to 15:31, God made such spirits rule the nations "to lead them astray from following him," and he guards Israel from their influence (v. 32). Just after mentioning images that people worship, the author wrote that depraved spirits led people to commit sins and impurities (11:4). God predicts to Moses that Israelites will sacrifice their children to demons (1:11). The HB accuses Israel of making offerings to demons: "They made him jealous with strange gods, / with abhorrent things they provoked him. / They sacrificed to demons, not God, / to deities they had never known, / to new ones recently arrived, / whom your ancestors had not feared" (Deut 32:16-17; see also Lev 17:7). Psalm 106 again offers language that appears in this context in Jubilees—this time including offering children to demons:

> They did not destroy the peoples,
>   as the Lord commanded them,
> but they mingled with the nations
>   and learned to do as they did.
> They served their idols,
>   which became a snare to them.
> They sacrificed their sons
>   and their daughters to the demons;
> they poured out innocent blood,
>   the blood of their sons and daughters,
> whom they sacrificed to the idols of Canaan;
>   and the land was polluted with blood.
> Thus they became unclean by their acts,
>   and prostituted themselves in their doings.
>   (Ps 106:34-39)[58]

The notion of eating in tombs is related to sacrificing to the dead: the deceased and the living apparently were thought to share the food placed upon graves. Psalm 106:28 mentions eating food sacrificed to the dead, and in Deut 26:14 the Israelite farmer presenting his produce declares that he has "not offered any of it to the dead." Abraham's verdict on all of these practices that he attributes to the nations is that they are "empty and worthless." The phrase may reflect some biblical passages that condemn the Israelites' idolatry. 2 Kings 17:15 says of northern Israel: "They went after false idols [הבל] and became false [ויהבלו]; they followed the nations that were around them, concerning whom the Lord had commanded them that they should not do as they did." Jeremiah used the words הבל ואין בם מועיל ("worthless things in which there is no profit"; see also Jer 10:15 = 51:18) for idols.[59]

■ **18** The words "empty and worthless" lead smoothly to v. 18, which contains an emphatic critique of those who worship idols. The verse begins and ends with a line about a total lack of understanding on the part of those engaged in such practices—a thought at home in the parodies of idolatry in the HB and elsewhere (Isa 44:9, 18; 45:20; Jer 10:8, 14; Ep Jer 41). The next charge—"their eyes do not see what they do"—refers to those who make and serve idols, not to the idols themselves as in the biblical passages (cf. Ps 135:16; Ep Jer 19, but see Isa 44:9). Abraham also charges the nations with calling a piece of wood or a stone a god; in doing so he reflects the language of Jer 2:27, where it says of Israelites that they "say to a tree, 'You are my father,' / and to stone, 'You gave me birth'" (see Jer 10:1-10, which depicts the idolatrous ways of the nations). But more exactly he echoes the sentiments of Hab 2:19. In a context where the prophet is speaking of idolatry (see v. 18), he proclaims: "Alas for you who say to the wood, 'Wake up!' / to silent stone, 'Rouse yourself!' / Can it teach? / See, it is gold and silver plated, / and there is no breath in it at all."[60] For calling on an idol to deliver or save, see Isa

---

58   See Charles, *Jubilees*, 141, who also lists 1 Enoch 19:1; VanderKam, "Demons," 353-54.

59   Kugel thinks this is an allusion to הבל וריק in Isa 30:7 ("worthless and empty," NRSV) (*Walk through Jubilees*, 127); this would be more plausible if it were not for the fact that there the words apply to Egypt, not idols (as Kugel recognizes).

60   For these passages, see Berger, *Jubiläen*, 437 n. c to v. 18. He also mentions Wis 14:21, where the sage, discussing the origins of idolatry, refers to people

44:19. So Abraham's emphasis lies on those who worship inert idols and their utter senselessness in doing so.[61]

■ **19** With his third direct appeal to Jacob (v. 19), again as his son, Abraham resumes the theme of separation and relates it to impurity and the worship of idols—the issues he has just treated. Once again he pleads that God will help and bless Jacob and returns to the title "the Most High God" (as in vv. 6 and 11). The two epithets for the deity—the Most High God and the God of heaven—form a poetic pair. Abraham is appealing to the one who is over all, in charge of the world, to assist his successor Jacob. He asks that the great God keep Jacob away ("remove you") from the impurity and error of the nations that he has described in vv. 16-18. Jacob, who is destined to be the ancestor of a holy people, was to distance himself from the destructive ways of the nations.

■ **20-21** In this setting Abraham warns Jacob about marrying a Canaanite woman.[62] The theme of avoiding such marriages arises several times in Genesis.[63] Abraham made his servant swear "that you will not get a wife for my son from the daughters of the Canaanites among whom I live" (Gen 24:3) before dispatching him to the old family center to fetch a more suitable wife for Isaac. Esau's marriage to Hittite women was a problem for Isaac and Rebekah (26:34-35),[64] and Rebekah was insistent that Jacob not follow suit in marrying "one of the women of the land" (27:46). Isaac himself ordered Jacob not to marry "one of the Canaanite women" (28:1, 6); even Esau tried to do better by marrying a daughter of Ishmael (28:6-9). That marriage with Canaanites continued to pose a problem in the next generation is evident from Judah's taking Shua, the daughter of a Canaanite, as a wife (38:2; cf. Jub 41:2). So Abraham now lends his considerable authority to a command that Rebekah will be anxious to enforce.

The reason Abraham adduces for not marrying such a woman is that the Canaanites have a sentence of doom hanging over them.[65] The behavior of their eponymous ancestor had brought this upon them. Noah had cursed Canaan (Gen 9:25-27 // Jub 7:10-12), and Canaan himself had only made the situation worse for himself and his progeny by refusing to migrate to the territory assigned to them (the north coast of Africa bordering the Atlantic Ocean) and settling instead in the land that would bear his name. When his father and brothers warned him that he and his children "will fall in the land and be cursed with dissension, because you have settled in dissension and in dissension your children will fall and be uprooted forever" (10:30), he paid no attention to the dire prediction and thus brought a second curse on himself and his descendants (10:32). Abraham alluded to the first curse on Canaan to document the need for Jacob not to intermarry with the doomed race and hinted at the second by citing from 10:30 the punishment of being uprooted. Jubilees is as vague in v. 21 and 7:10-12 as Genesis regarding why Canaan received severe punishment when his father Ham sinned.[66] Abraham knew that Canaan's progeny continued to pose a threat and pointed to the future, to the judgment, by which time all Canaanites will have suffered destruction. They will not be among those "who will be saved" or delivered on that occasion, that is, the ones who continue to live on the earth after it.

---

who "bestowed on objects of stone or wood the name that ought not to be shared."

61 The first and last lines of v. 18 are very similar, enclosing the ones between them (see Werman, *Jubilees*, 348).

62 Schwarz, *Identität*, 32-34. Abraham had so instructed all of his sons in 20:4.

63 It surfaces elsewhere in the HB as well. See, e.g., Deut 7:3-4.

64 In Jub 25:1, Rebekah says that Esau's wives were Canaanites and mentions their impurity. In 25:7, Jacob references Abraham's teachings to him about "lewdness and sexual impurity." See also 27:8-10.

65 As Schwarz notes, the same reason is given in 20:4 in very similar language (*Identität*, 32-33). He thinks it possible that the author is dealing with the hellenizing situation in the time of Antiochus IV—the period to which he dates the book—though he realizes one cannot demonstrate the point. See also Endres, *Biblical Interpretation*, 43-45; van Ruiten, "Abraham's Last Day," 75-78.

66 Kugel writes: "Perhaps *Jubilees*, like other ancient interpreters, means that Canaan was complicit in Ham's sin. . . . Alternately, *Jubilees*' author may mean that Ham's sin was simply the beginning of a chain of misdeeds" (*Walk through* Jubilees, 127; cf. "Jubilees," 373, where he considers the latter more likely). Van Ruiten sees the reference to Ham as possibly relating to the general command in 7:20—about keeping oneself from fornication, uncleanness, and injustice ("Abraham's Last Day," 76; *Abraham*, 316).

■ **22** The subject of a day for judgment leads Abraham to deal with all those with no hopeful prospects on that momentous occasion. He names two groups that may be coterminous: those who worship idols and those who are odious (ṣeluʾān).[67] He declares that these people have no hope of remaining in the "land of the living," that is, on earth, but will descend to Sheol, identified as a place of judgment. The Hebrew word Sheol appears four times in the Ethiopic text of Jubilees (5:14; 7:29; and 24:31 are the others). Jubilees 5:14 refers to it between "the darkness" and "the deep" in a context describing judgment; in 7:29 Noah predicts that those who shed or consume blood will be left with no survivors on the earth "because they will go into Sheol and will descend into the place of judgment. All of them will depart into deep darkness through an evil death."[68] According to 24:31 the Caphtorites, among whom are the Philistines, will be uprooted and will go down to Sheol for punishment. Those in Sheol leave no remembrance, no trace on the earth. Abraham compares the fate of idolaters to the one suffered by the inhabitants of Sodom—removal, erasure from the earth (see 16:5-9, where the judgment of these people for their sins, including their sexual impurity, comes under consideration). When Sodom met its end, the angel reported (16:6): "The Lord will execute judgment in the same way in the places where people commit the same sort of impure actions as Sodom—just like the judgment on Sodom"[69]—a fate decreed for Lot and his descendants after his sin with his daughters (16:8-9). Sheol is a nether place to which the wicked go, and Jacob and his descendants will avoid it by separating from the ways of the nations.[70]

■ **23** Abraham marks the concluding section of his speech to and for Jacob (vv. 23-24) just as he did the other three—by naming Jacob and calling him "my son" (his words in v. 23 have a poetic rhythm to a greater extent than the lines in the verses that precede and follow). At this point he seems concerned that young Jacob will fear the dangers posed by the world of the nations; consequently he tells him not to worry.[71] He calls on God to provide the protection he will need. The two kinds of situations from which he will need divine rescue are ones characterized by corruption and error. "Corruption" (musennā) figures in 20:5, where Abraham warns his sons about the punishment visited on the giants and Sodom because of sexual immorality (in v. 4

---

67 Charles emended to ṣeʾulān ("profane") (*Jubilees*, 142); why one should do this is not clear, and his references to Lev 21:7, 14 are not helpful, as they concern women whom priests were not to marry. Kugel says that 4Q221 frg. 2, col. i lacks "for all who worship idols and for those who are odious" (*Walk through* Jubilees, 127 n. 228; he does not repeat the claim in "Jubilees," 373). As a matter of fact, these words are the first ones in the Ethiopic text and would have appeared before the letters and words preserved in line 1. So they may have been present, but the spot where they would have appeared has not survived.

68 For Sheol as a place of darkness, see, e.g., Job 17:13; as a place to which one goes down, see Gen 37:35; Num 16:30; Isa 57:9; etc.

69 Hanneken comments regarding the use of Sodom in Jubilees: "Whereas Jubilees mentions the flood only once after Noah, as a chronological reference point (Jub. 23:9), Jubilees mentions Sodom in five different passages, three of which refer to Sodom as an example of judgment beyond the Genesis narrative (Jub. 13; 16; 20:5-6; 22:22; 36:10). Jubilees includes the flood as an example of judgment but prefers the example of Sodom. The emphasis on the judgment of an individual city contrasts sharply with the deferred cosmic judgment in Daniel and especially the flood typology of the Enochic apocalypses. Of course, the idea of using Sodom as evidence of the real threat of God's punishment is not novel to Jubilees, but it is unprecedented in apocalypses. Sodom is a clear case of judgment that has already happened in a noneschatological framework that could happen again at any time" (*Subversion*, 161–62). On the passage, see also Davenport, *Eschatology*, 53–54.

70 Schwarz thinks the author, in 22:16-22, is engaging two fronts: the nations and Israelites who serve idols (*Identität*, 35–36). The words of v. 22 he may be directing against the latter group. The point is less obvious here but clearer in other passages (e.g., 21:4, as Schwarz indicates).

71 Kugel draws attention to the close similarity between Abraham's words to Jacob here and Jer 30:10: "But as for you, have no fear, my servant Jacob, says the Lord, / and do not be dismayed, O Israel" (*Walk through* Jubilees, 127–28; "Jubilees," 373). As he indicates, Jubilees could not use "Israel" here as a name for Jacob because it had not yet been given to him.

he had forbidden marriage with Canaanite women and mentioned that they will be uprooted from the earth; see also 23:17, 21). In v. 19 he had asked that God remove Jacob from the impurity and error of the nations, just as he does here. The perils are present, but with the Lord's help Jacob will be delivered from them.

■ 24 The image Abraham adopts in v. 24 is most expressive of the subject he has been treating. He speaks about the house he has built for himself and on which he has placed his name. That house he gives to Jacob and his progeny, who will continue to construct it.[72] Through the ongoing process, they will establish Abraham's name forever, and, unlike the nations, who will vanish from the surface of the earth, the name of Jacob and his descendants will remain eternally. The description of the house and of the way in which the generations descended from Abraham will continue to build it indicates that this is not a literal house but rather a covenantal household or family line. In the HB there are usages of "house" attached to a person's name that to some extent resemble the concept here: for example, there is "the house/household of Jacob" (e.g., Gen 46:27; Exod 19:3) or "the house/household of Israel" (e.g., Exod 16:31; 40:38). It is possible, however, that Jub 22:24 alludes to Gen 18:19, where the Lord says of Abraham: "I have chosen [lit., known] him, that he may charge his children and his household after him to keep the way of the LORD by doing righteousness and justice; so that the LORD may bring about for Abraham what he has promised him." The Lord had, of course, promised him many descendants and a great name (as in Gen 12:2) as well as making an eternal covenant with him and those born in his line (Gen 17:5-8). As he now gives a member of his household—Jacob—the kind of charge envisaged in Gen 18:19, Abraham incorporates the eternal covenant God made with him and his family into the image of a house that lasts forever.[73]

25-26 Abraham and Jacob Lie Down Together

Despite all that he taught Jacob and everything he requested for him in vv. 10-24, Abraham could not stop expressing his love and prayers for him and his offspring. The short v. 25 announces the end of the previous scene by reworking Gen 27:30 ("As soon as Isaac had finished blessing Jacob") to fit the present context. Since Abraham had given Jacob orders as well as blessing him, the writer adds that he had also finished delivering commands. One then learns that the 175-year-old patriarch and his fifteen-year-old grandson Jacob lie down together on a single bed—a literal instance of the familiar phrase "slept with his fathers." Jacob fell asleep "in the bosom" of Abraham. Though New Testament scholars seem not to have paid much attention to it, this is an early attestation of the phrase later found in the parable of the Rich Man and Lazarus where Lazarus is pictured in the afterlife as being in Abraham's bosom (Luke 16:22-23).[74] In Jubilees, "the bosom of Abraham" is clearly a special place, the place where his dearest grandchild and successor lies. Abraham expresses his warm

---

72   See Kugel for the possibility that Abraham, in saying, "This house I have built for myself to put my name on it upon the earth," may be referring to the land of Israel and that Abraham's name is therefore connected with only one of his descendants, Jacob, and his line (*Walk through* Jubilees, 128; cf. "Jubilees," 373-74). While possible, this seems unlikely. The land promise is not a theme in chap. 22, whereas the one regarding descendants is to the fore. Note that in v. 14 Abraham possibly speaks about his descendants possessing the entire earth.

73   It is possible that the sections about "sure houses" influenced the writer, as Berger suggests (*Jubiläen*, 438 nn. b-c to v. 24). He mentions the one promised to David in 2 Samuel 7 (he could have added the great name for David as another parallel [e.g., v. 9]). There is also the sure house of the priesthood in 1 Sam 2:35. For Werman, the statement shows that Jacob is the true firstborn in the household (*Jubilees*, 349). She adduces earlier parallels for the practice that the firstborn inherited the father's house. Yet, in this context, "house" is not being used in its literal sense.

74   Joseph A. Fitzmyer writes: "This designation is unknown elsewhere in pre-Christian Jewish literature, finding its way (from here?) into late midrashim (*Echa Rabb.* 1.85; *Pesiqta rabb.* 43 §108b) and the Babylonian Talmud (*b. Qidd.* 72a-b)" (*The Gospel according to Luke X–XXIV: A New Translation with Introduction and Commentary* [AB 28A; New York: Doubleday, 1985], 1132). In the same place he mentions the idea that "the bosom of Abraham" may be "a development of the OT idea of sleeping with one's fathers or ancestors."

and complete affection for the sleeping Jacob by kissing him seven times—an affection involving both his feelings and his thoughts.

27-30 Abraham Blesses the Sleeping Jacob

■ **27** It is no wonder that the narrator says in v. 27 that the elderly man blessed him with his entire heart. With overflowing feelings, Abraham returns to some of the topics about which he had spoken before. He begins with an appeal to God to whom he gives three titles found elsewhere in the book and in the present chapter: the Most High God (vv. 6, 11, 13, 19, 23), the God of all (v. 10), and the Creator of everything (see v. 6). This God, so utterly distinct from the worthless idols worshiped by the nations, is the one to whom he turns in this extraordinary moment just before he dies.[75] He initially recalls the deliverance he had received from God, who took him from Ur to this land, and the promises of the land and descendants he had given to him. The promises are familiar from Genesis and Jubilees, but the phrasing of the one regarding numerous offspring is different: "raise up holy descendants so that they may be blessed forever."[76] Jubilees has already referred to one of Isaac's progeny who would be a holy people (16:17-18), and in the present chapter Abraham spoke about the ways in which Jacob and his sons should act to become a holy people (v. 12). Yet the wording makes one suspect that Gen 18:19 continues to exercise influence: God knew Abraham so "that he may charge his children and his household after him to keep the way of the Lord by doing righteousness and justice; so that the Lord may bring about for Abraham what he has promised him." In chaps. 20–22 the patriarch carried out this pedagogical function and thus did what he could to help his descendants to be holy. Abraham now blessed the almighty God who had brought about all these astonishing developments. For blessing his progeny forever, see, among other passages, 22:11, 13, 15; 21:25 (one of the parallels between the blessings Abraham pronounced on Isaac in 21:25 and here on Jacob).

■ **28-30** Abraham begins as if he is speaking to Jacob. Perhaps his first words, "My son," should be understood not as a vocative (Jacob is sleeping) but in the sense of "As for my son." In the blessing itself, which again takes the form of a prayer and repeats themes mentioned earlier in the chapter, Abraham highlights Jacob and his seed and asks for divine providence upon them forever.[77] He not only requests that God's grace (in vv. 28 and 30) and mercy (cf. 1:20; 10:3 [twice]; 12:29—all in prayers; see also 31:25; 45:3) rest on them, but he also prays that God will be with them and protect them. The negated verbs "leave" and "neglect" are paired a number of times in the HB. In Deut 31:6, 8 Moses tells Israel that the Lord will neither fail nor forsake them, in Josh 1:15 the Lord himself promises such care to Joshua, and in 1 Kgs 8:57 Solomon prays that the Lord will neither leave nor abandon his people (see Isa 42:16; 49:14-15). Abraham adopts another expression from the HB when he requests that God's eyes be open over them. Solomon had prayed that God's eyes would be open to the temple and to the pleas offered by him and the people (1 Kgs 8:29, 52 = 2 Chr 6:20, 40; see also 2 Chr 7:15; Neh 1:6). The image is one of protective watching and solicitude, similar to the language Abraham had used earlier when he urged that Rebekah's eyes rest lovingly on him (19:20). Abraham asks that all God's blessings fall to Jacob and his progeny, as he had earlier prayed that the ones given to him and his ancestors would belong to them (e.g., 19:27; 22:13). He had already spoken several times about Israel

---

75 Charles suspected that v. 27 was an interpolation because it "professes to give Abraham's blessing of Jacob, and yet does not mention him at all. Jacob's blessing begins in ver. 28" (*Jubilees*, 143). The verse does not claim to give his blessing of Jacob, and, as Charles admitted, there must have been a mention of God's name before v. 28, but there would not be if one jettisoned v. 27.

76 Charles followed MS. 38 in which *le'ul* is the subject of the verb: "blessed be the Most High for ever" (*Jubilees*, 143). He recognized that a better translation would be "that the Most High may be blessed for ever" but thought it left the sentence with no main verb. The reading of MS. 38 (and of MS. 9) is clearly wrong, as blessing for Abraham's seed ("descendants") is under consideration.

77 Werman charts the parallels between earlier verses in chap. 22 in which he blessed Jacob in a volitive form (she includes vv. 11, 13-15, 23) and vv. 28-30 in which he addresses God directly (*Jubilees*, 350).

as holy and as the people of his heritage (see vv. 9, 10, 12, 15) and reiterates the themes here. It is most appropriate that his last wish, and one uttered on the festival associated with the covenant, is for God to renew his covenant with Jacob and his descendants forever (see v. 15; in vv. 28-30 he uses phrases such as "for all time," "eternity" or "throughout all the history of the world" four times). The eternal race, enriched by divine blessing and care, contrasts sharply with the nations, who will vanish from the face of the earth. No day of judgment will mark the end of the covenantal relationship between God and Jacob along with his offspring.

23

Abraham's Death and the Pattern of Human Life Spans

1/ He put two of Jacob's fingers on his eyes[a] and blessed the God of gods. He covered his face,[b] stretched out his feet, fell asleep forever, and was gathered[c] to his ancestors.[d] 2/ During all of this Jacob[a] was lying in his bosom and was unaware that his grandfather Abraham had died.[b] 3/ When Jacob awakened from his sleep, there was Abraham cold as ice. He said, "Father, father!"[a] But he said nothing to him.[b] Then he knew that he[c] was dead. 4/ He got up from his bosom and ran and told his mother Rebekah. Rebekah went to Isaac at night and told him. They went[a] together—and Jacob[b] with them (carrying) a lamp in his hands.[c] When they came they found Abraham's corpse lying (there). 5/ Isaac fell on his father's face,[a] cried,[b] and kissed him. 6/ After the report[a] was heard in the household of Abraham, his son Ishmael set out and came[b] to his father[c] Abraham. He mourned[d] for[e] his father[f] Abraham—he and all the men of Abraham's household.[g] They mourned[h] very much. 7/ They—both of[a] his sons[b] Isaac and Ishmael—buried him in the cave of Machpelah near his wife Sarah. All the people of his household as well as Isaac, Ishmael, and all[c] their sons and Keturah's sons[d] in their places mourned for him for 40 days. Then the tearful mourning for Abraham was completed.

8/ He had lived for three[a] jubilees and four[b] weeks of years—175 years—when[c] he completed[d] his lifetime. He had grown old and was satisfied with (his) days.[e] 9/ For the times of the ancients were 19[a] jubilees for their lifetimes.[b] After[c] the flood they started[d] to decrease from 19 jubilees,[e] to be fewer with respect to jubilees,[f] to age quickly,[g] and to have their times be completed[h] because of the numerous difficulties[i] and through the wickedness of their ways—with the exception of Abraham. 10/ For Abraham was perfect with the Lord in everything that he did[a]—being properly[b] pleasing[c] throughout all his lifetime. And yet (even) he had not completed four[d] jubilees during his lifetime by the time[e] he became old—because of wickedness[f]—and reached the end of his time. 11/ All[a] the generations that[b] will come into being[c] from now until[d] the great day[e] of judgment will grow old quickly—before they complete two[f] jubilees. It will be their knowledge[g] that[h] will leave them because of their old age;[h] all of their knowledge will depart[i]. 12/ In those days, if a man lives a jubilee and one-half of years,[a] it will be said about him: "He has lived for a long time." But the greater part of his time[b] will be (characterized by) difficulties, toil, and distress without[c] peace 13/ because (there will be) blow upon blow,[a] trouble upon trouble,[b] distress upon distress,[c] bad news upon bad news, disease upon disease, and every (kind of) bad punishment like this,[d] one with the other:[e] disease[f] and stomach pains;[g] snow, hail, and frost; fever,[h] cold,[i] and numbness;[j] famine, death, sword, captivity, and every (sort of) blow and difficulty.[k] 14/ All of this[a] will happen to the evil[b] generation that makes the earth commit sin[c] through sexual impurity,[d] contamination, and their detestable actions.[e] 15/ Then[a] it will be said: "The days of the ancients[b] were numerous—as many as 1000 years—and good.[c] But now[d] the days of our lives, if a man has lived for a long time, are 70 years, and, if he is strong, 80 years."[e] All[f] are evil and there is no peace during the days of that evil generation.

16/ During that generation the children will find fault[a] with their fathers and elders because of sin and injustice, because of what they say and the great evils that they commit, and because of their abandoning the covenant that the Lord had made between them and himself[b] so that they should observe and perform all his commands, ordinances, and all his laws without deviating[c] to the left or right.[d] 17/ For[a] all have acted wickedly; every mouth speaks what is sinful.[b] Everything that they do is impure[c] and something detestable;[d] all their ways are (characterized by) contamination, impurity, and destruction. 18/ The[a] earth will indeed be destroyed because of all that they do. There will be no produce, wine,[b] or oil[c] because what they do (constitutes) complete apostasy.[d] All will be destroyed[e] together[f]—animals, cattle, birds, and all fish of the sea—because of[g] humanity. 19/ One group will struggle with another—the young[a] with the old, the old with the young; the poor with the rich,[b] the lowly with the great; and^c the needy with the ruler—regarding the law and^d the covenant. For they have forgotten commandment, covenant, festival, month, Sabbath, jubilee, and every verdict.^e 20/ They will stand up with swords^a and warfare in order to bring them back to the way;^b but they will not be brought back until much blood is shed on the earth^c by each group.

21/ Those who escape will not turn^a from their wickedness to the right way because all of them will elevate themselves for (the purpose of) cheating and^b through wealth so that one takes everything that belongs to another. They will mention^c the great name but neither tru<u>ly nor rightly</u>. They^d will defile the holy things of the holy one^e with the impur<u>e c</u>orruption^f of their contamination.^g 22/ <u>There will be great anger</u>^a from the Lord <u>for the actions of</u> that <u>generation</u>. He will deliver th<u>em</u>^b <u>to the sword, judgment</u>, captivity, <u>plundering, and devouring</u>.^c 23/ <u>He will arouse</u>^a <u>against them</u> the sinful nations^b who will have no mercy or kind<u>ness for them</u>^c <u>and</u> who will sh<u>ow</u> partiality <u>to no one</u>,^d whether old or young, or anyone at all, because they are evil and strong so that they are more evil^e than all humanity. They will cause^f chaos^g in Israel and sin against Jacob. Much blood will be shed on the earth, and there will be no one who gathers up (corpses) or who buries (them).

24/ At that time they will cry out and call and pray to be rescued from the power of the sinful nations, but there will be no one who rescues (them). 25/ The children's^a heads will turn white with gray hair. A child who is three^b weeks of age will look old like one whose years are 100, and their condition will be destroyed through distress and pain.

26/ In those days the children will begin to study^a the laws,^b to seek out the commands, and to return to the right way. 27/ The days will begin to become numerous and increase, and humanity^a as well—generation^b by generation and day by day^c until their lifetimes approach 1000 years^d and to more years than the number of days (had been).^e 28/ There will be no old man, nor anyone who has lived out (his) lifetime,^a because all of them will be infants and children. 29/ They will complete^a and live their entire lifetimes peacefully and joyfully. There will be neither a satan nor any evil one^b who will destroy.^c For their entire lifetimes will be times of blessing and healing.

30/ Then the Lord will heal his servants. They will rise^a and see^b great peace. He will expel^c his^d enemies. The righteous will see (this), offer praise, and be very happy forever and ever. <u>They will see</u> all their punishments and <u>curse</u>s <u>on</u> their enemies.^e 31/ Their bones will rest in the earth and <u>their spirits will</u> be very happy. They will know^a that <u>there is a God who executes</u> judgment but shows^b kindness <u>to</u> hundred<u>s and tens of thousands</u>^c and to all who love him.

32/ Now you,^a Moses, write^b down these words^c because this is how it is written^d and^e entered^f in the testimony of the heavenly tablets for the history of eternity.

Textual Notes

1a on his eyes] om. 20 25.
b his face] + "forever and ever" 39.
c was gathered] "they were gathered" 17 38 44.
d his ancestors (lit., "fathers")] "his father" 9 63; "his children" 38^c.
2a Jacob] + "and" 25 48; + "in all" 47.
b had died] "was asleep" 21.
3a father] om. 47.
b to him] om. 9 12 17 20 42 48 63.

c he (was dead)] "Abraham" 39 42 47 48 58.
4a They went] "The two of them went" 44.
b and Jacob] om. 44.
c in his hands] "with him" 20; "in their hands" 44.
5a face] "bosom" 63; MS. 35 inserts "Abraham" in the expression here so that it reads "on the face of his father Abraham." Ms. 38 does the same but with a different word order.
b cried] "blessed him" 12 17 21 44 63; + "and blessed him" 42 47.
6a the report] "a/the cry of the voice" (?) 63.

b came] 3Q5 3 2 (יבוא) agrees with most Eth. copies, but 63 has a pl. form.
c his father] "their father" 38 (this MS. had read "Ishmael and his son" as the subject of "set out").
d He mourned] "They mourned" 38ᶜ 42 47.
e for his father Abraham] om. 17 44.
f his father] om. 21 38ᶜ 44 48ᵗ.
g the men of Abraham's household] 3Q5 3 3 has אנ[שי בית א]ברהם.
h They mourned] "He mourned" 21.
7a both of] om. 12 17 39 42 44 47 48 58 63.
b his sons] "his son" 21 42 47 48.
c all] pr. "and" 25 35 38; 2Q19 2 כול.
d Keturah's sons] "all of Keturah's sons" 12.
8a three] The number is the first word in the verse in both Eth. and 2Q19 4. All Eth. copies prefix "and" to it except MS. 25; 2Q19 4 agrees with MS. 25.
b lived/and four] This is the order of the Eth. copies and 2Q19 4, but MS. 17 transposes them.
c when (lit., "and")] Mss. 21 63 om. "and," as does Lat., but the beginning of the verse is illegible on the Lat. MS. so that the full construction here is not known.
d he completed] = Lat. complevit. Mss. 17ᶜ 38 39 58 read a passive form.
e days] = Lat. Ms. 25 has "his days," as do 39 48 58 but with a different spelling. 2Q19 5 ימים.
9a 19] pr. "and" 48; Lat. et. If "and" has the sense of "even," it could be similar in meaning to the copies of the text lacking a conjunction here but more emphatic; see VanderKam, Jubilees 2:138.
b their lifetimes] So Ethiopic; Lat. "his life/lifetime." "His" makes little sense in the context.
c After] + "this" 47; + "the waters of" 58. Lat. post.
d they started] "he started" 35; Lat. coeperunt.
e to decrease from 19 jubilees] Lat. lacks, perhaps by haplography (VanderKam, Jubilees 2:139); but it is also possible that Eth. has a dittography (so Charles, Ethiopic Version, 82 n. 1; Jubilees, 145; cf. Werman, Jubilees, 352 n. 9).
f jubilees] Lat. "these jubilees." See VanderKam, Jubilees 2:139.
g quickly] Lat. "more quickly," which may in effect be the meaning of Eth.
h their times be completed] Lat. "the times of their life to decrease."
i numerous difficulties] Lat. "difficulties of many" (literally).
10a that he did (lit., "his deeds")] om. 12; "his deed" 21; Lat. operibus suis.
b properly (lit., "in righteousness")] "in his righteousness" 38; + "in his every deed" 12; Lat. in veritate.
c pleasing] + "to him" 12 21 35 58 (cf. 12).
d four] "nine" 17; Lat. quattuor.
e by the time] 4Q221 3 1 has אשר with עד written above it = "until/by the time," which is probably the sense of quousque.
f wickedness] Lat. "evil ones." For an argument against Baillet's suggestion that 3Q5 frg. 4 contains words from 23:10 ("Remarques sur le manuscrit du Livre des Jubilés de la grotte 3 de Qumran," RevQ 5/19 [1964–66] 423–33, here 429), see VanderKam, Textual, 100–101; Jubilees 2:139. Berger (Jubiläen, 441 n. d to v. 10) also rejects Baillet's placement of the fragment.
11a All] Lat. has no equivalent.
b that] "and" 21; Lat. quae.
c will come into being] The Lat. surrexerunt (past tense) has to be changed to a future form (surrexerint; Rönsch, Jubiläen, 36).
d until (lit., "and until")] om. "and" 25 35 58; 4Q221 3 2 also lacks a conjunction, though Lat. reads et.
e great day] The fem. 'abāy should modify 'elat ("day") = "the great day." Mss. 17 38 read a masc. 'abiy = "the day of the great judgment"; this is the reading of Lat. in diem iudicii magni. The place in 4Q221 3 3 where the equivalent would have been has not survived. In this line it may be that Heb. had a longer text. The same is the case in line 4, though Milik suggested that there may have been a defect in the leather where the scribe could not write (see DJD 13:72).
f two] "one" 35; Lat. duobus; 4Q221 3 3 שנ[ים.
g their knowledge] Lat. reads spiritus intellectus ipsorum, which is very likely a rendering of the same base text. See Charles, Jubilees, 145; VanderKam, Jubilees 2:140.
h because of their old age (reš'omu = reš'omu)] Lat. lacks the expression, as do MSS. 9 38. It is meaningful in that the writer has just said they will age quickly. The omission in Lat. is part of a longer one (also in Eth. MS. 21), possibly caused by haplography; see below.
i all of their knowledge will depart] Lat. lacks, having omitted (?) from "their knowledge"[1] to "their knowledge"[2].
12a years] Lat. annorum. Ms. 44 "year"; 35 42 47 48 "jubilee," and 39 58 have "jubilee" but with different spellings.
b his time (lit., "days")] Lat. dierum ipsius; 4Q221 3 5 ימו; MS. 12 reads "their days."
c without] The word 'albo ("there is not") is preceded by a conjunction, and both Lat. and 3Q5 1 2 also read one; MSS. 25 44 lack a conjunction.
13a upon blow] om. 20 25; 3Q5 1 2 על מכה; Lat. super vulnus.
b trouble upon trouble] Eth. ṣel'ān (or ṣel') diba ṣel'ān = "wound upon wound" (Leslau, Comparative Dictionary, 554): ṣal'a = "be wounded"; ṣal' = "wound, sore"; ṣal'at = "wound"). 3Q5 1 2 ומהו]מה = "tumult, confusion, trouble, distress" (the first word in the expression). Lat. et dolor super dolor = "trouble upon trouble." All may be attempts at עמל in Ps 90:10 = "trouble, labor, toil" (BDB, 765). In the LXX the term is rendered with κόπος, "striking, beating, trouble, suffering, pain."

c   distress upon distress] The Eth. and Heb. have the same words as in v. 12; there Lat. read *augustiae* but here *tribulationem*.
d   bad punishment like this] Lat. seems to have had a slightly different word order: after *iudicia* there is *eius* . . . ; Rönsch properly filled the space with *-modi* so that the reading is *iudicia eiusmodi maligna* (*Jubiläen*, 36, 126). Ms. 44 moves *za-kamāhu* ("like this") earlier in the text (after "all/every" just before the lemma). Rather than *za-kamāhu*, MS. 12 has: evil with evil.
e   one with the other] Eth. reads "this with this" where Lat. has *secundum hoc ipsud cum*: "according to this itself with." Rönsch takes *secundum hoc ipsud* to mean *simul, una, iunctim* (*Jubiläen*, 127).
f   disease] "punishment/judgment" 44; om. 63. Lat. *corruptione* may be, according to Rönsch (*Jubiläen*, 126) a mistake for *correptione* = epilepsy? (general sickness?).
g   stomach pains] The Eth. term *gabaṭbāṭ* Leslau defines as "stomach disease" (*Comparative Dictionary*, 180). Lat. *clades* means "calamity," and "destroyer, scourge, pest." Littmann suggested reading *zebṭatāt*, "beating, whipping, punishment, plague, blow, stroke, scourge" (Leslau, *Comparative Dictionary*, 631).
h   fever] Eth. *nabarṣāw* (Leslau, *Comparative Dictionary*, 384: "heat, fever, kind of disease").
i   cold] Eth. *sakaḥkāḥ* is a problem, apparently a word not attested elsewhere. Lat. *frigora* is the term Dillmann used for it in *Lexicon*, 378.
j   numbness] Eth. *saʿozāz* seems related to the verb Leslau gives as *ʾasʿozaza*, "become cramped, grow stiff, be benumbed" (*Comparative Dictionary*, 81). Here Lat. reads *provocatio*, which makes little sense. Rönsch thought it was an error for *praefocatio*, "choking" (*Jubiläen*, 36, 126). The Greek for it would have been αγχνη, which the Eth. translator misread as αργια (see VanderKam, *Jubilees* 2:142).
k   difficulty] Eth. *ḥemām* (Leslau, *Comparative Dictionary*, 233: "illness, disease, pain, suffering, grief, distress, affliction, tribulation, passion"). Lat. *planctus*, "beating."
14a All of this] The words "all" and "this" ("is" is implied) are transposed in 20 21 44; Lat. *omnia haec*.
b   evil] om. 38; Lat. *qui est iniqua*.
c   makes the earth commit sin] Lat. *iniquitatem facit in terra*. Several Eth. copies read a non-causative form of the verb, and they, with others, read *medr* instead of *medra* (accus.) so that in them "the earth commits sin." Charles, without support in any of the copies, revises the Eth. text to agree with Lat., so that the evil generation commits sin on the earth (*Ethiopic Version*, 82 nn. 22-23).
d   through sexual impurity] Lat. *et inmunditia et fornicationis*. The Lat. offers the same order of nouns as Eth., but it introduces the first with *et*, not *in*, and places a conjunction between them, whereas in Eth. they are in construct with each other. The nominative forms of these and the remaining nouns in the verse show the translator did not understand them as objects of the verb. The Eth. version introduces each of the nouns with the preposition *ba-* ("in/with").

e   detestable actions (lit., "and in disgust their action[s]")] It seems likely that *saqorār* ("horror, abomination, disgust"; Leslau, *Comparative Dictionary*, 444) should have the construct ending *-a* suffixed to it, and thus it would be read with "their actions," that is, "the disgust of their actions." This is the way in which Dillmann, Berger, VanderKam (*Jubilees* 2:147) have construed the relationship between the nouns.
15a Then] pr. "and" 9 12 35 38 39 42 47 48 58; Lat. *tunc*.
b   of the ancients] Lat. *antiqui* seems wrong; Charles suggested *antiquorum* (*Ethiopic Version*, 83 n. 12 to Latin), although why this form would have been altered to *antiqui* is not evident. VanderKam proposed *antiquibus* (= Eth.), hypothesizing that the ending's similiarity to that of *dies* caused a disturbance (*Jubilees* 2:143). As the Lat. now stands, "the ancients" would be the subject of the verb of speaking = "the ancients say/will say."
c   and good] Lat. "and good days."
d   But now] om. 21 38; Lat. *Nam ecce* seems to have the same sense as Eth. *wa-nāhu* (against Charles, *Ethiopic Version*, 83 n. 13 to Latin, who wished to change Lat. *nam* to *sed* or *et*).
e   80 years] Lat. lacks "years."
f   All] Lat. *isti*, "they." Psalm 90:10 has, as Jub reflects it, רבם, and perhaps *kwellu* echoes it. Charles changed Eth. *kwellu* to *ʾellu* to agree with Lat. (*Ethiopic Version*, 83 n. 35). See VanderKam, *Jubilees* 2:143.
16a will find fault] The form *tezzālafu* has the strongest backing and agrees with Lat. *arguent*. Several Eth. copies read other forms of the same verb (*tazzallafu*, 17 20 21 48; *yezallefu* 12 35 38 39 44 [it would have about the same meaning as *yezzālafu*]).
b   them and himself] Lat. "himself and them."
c   without deviating] Lit., "and there is not to depart/deviate/turn aside." Lat. uses almost the same words and order: "and there is not one who departs." Rönsch revised to *ut non sit qui* (*Jubiläen*, 36, 128; cf. Charles, *Ethiopic Version*, 85 n. 1 to Latin), but *qui* is the word that differs from the Eth. reading.
d   left or right] Lat. (with MSS. 12 21 38 63) has the more common "right or left" and is therefore unlikely to be the superior reading.
17a For] Rather than *ʾesma* ("for/because"), MSS. 9 12 20 25 35 42 44 47 63 read *ʾeska*, "until"; Lat. *propter quod* agrees with *ʾesma*.
b   what is sinful = Lat. *maligne*] MS. 44 reads *ʿammaḍa*, "what is unjust, lawless."
c   impure] Lat. reads a noun *inmunditia*, as do MSS. 9 20 39 47 48 58 (it has the noun with an accusative ending). But the adjectival form *rekus* seems to function as a noun.
d   something detestable (*saqorār*)] Lat. *odium*. The two may render the same Heb. or Greek word (VanderKam, *Jubilees* 2:144).
18a The] Ms. 21 prefixes a conjunction = Lat. *et*.
b   produce, wine] Eth. "produce of/from the vine" (a construct phrase); MSS. 17 44 place a conjunction between the two nouns = Lat. *semen et vinum*.
c   or oil (lit., "and not oil")] om. 12. Lat. does not repeat the negative, but this does not change the meaning.
d   apostasy] Lat. *m . . . tata*. Rönsch (*Jubiläen*, 38, 128) and Charles (*Ethiopic Version*, 85) read and restored *m[align]ata*,

though this involves a change of one letter from what Ceriani read (VanderKam, *Jubilees* 2:144).

e   will be destroyed] Lat. . . . *reunt* should be restored as *pereunt* (Rönsch, *Jubiläen*, 38; Charles, *Ethiopic Version*, 85), which agrees with Eth.

f   together] Lat. lacks.

g   because of (lit., "from before")] "from all" 21; Lat. "from the evil." Possibly the two versions represent Heb. מפני (Eth.) and מפשע (Lat.; VanderKam, *Jubilees* 2:145).

19a   the young] Lat. places *nam* before *iubenes* (= *iuvenes*); MS. 9 reads a conjunction here, but the other copies have nothing like *nam*. Cf. VanderKam, *Jubilees* 2:145.

b   the rich] Many MSS. add "and" after "rich" (9 12 17 21 39 42 44 47 48 58 63), but Lat. lacks an equivalent for the unnecessary word.

c   and (the needy)] om. 20 25 35 38 42 47 48 58, but Lat. reads *et*.

d   and (the covenant)] Lat. lacks.

e   verdict] "his verdict" 38; Lat. *iudicia*.

20a   with swords] Lat. "with bow and with swords." The Eth. equivalent of Lat. would be *ba-qast wa-ba-'asyeft*. This is what Charles placed in his text, with *ba-qast wa-* marked as a change (*Ethiopic Version*, 84 n. 13). It is difficult to decide which text is preferable. Littmann added a translation of Lat.'s extra words in brackets (see "Jubiläen," 80 n. a), but Hartom, without a note, makes them part of his text. See VanderKam, *Jubilees* 2:145.

b   the way] "the way of the wicked one" 9; "the wicked way" 17c (?) 21 38 (39 48 ?); "their way" 12 35 58; 35 58 = "their honorable way and those who keep the statute"; Lat. *viam*.

c   the earth] om. 20 25; Lat. *terra*.

21a   will not turn] "have not turned" 38; Lat. "will not depart"; Lat. places the verb "will not turn" after "from their wickedness."

b   and (through wealth)] om. 39 42 47 48 58; Lat. *et*.

c   mention (lit., "name" = Lat.)] pr. "place and" 38 (it could be a miscopying of a form of *samaya*, "to name"). Ms. 9 reads "place" instead of "name." Lat. has only *nominabunt*. It is likely that *yessammayu* (the best Eth. reading; it is a passive form) is a misspelling of *yesammeyu*, "they will name" (so Charles, *Ethiopic Version*, 84 n. 18; *Jubilees*, 148; Littmann, "Jubiläen," 80 n. b; Hartom; Berger, *Jubiläen*, 444 n. d to v. 21; VanderKam, *Jubilees* 2:145–46). Ms. 44 reads a jussive *yesmayu*.

d   They will defile . . . with the impure] The Eth. and Lat. agree. 4Q176 19 + 20 1 offers a few letters in this vicinity, but the interpretation of them is not clear. Kister ("Newly-Identified Fragments," 530–32) read the letters in question as א בח and suggested that the words around them should be טמ[א בח]ילולי; this yields a text at variance with both Eth. and Lat., which presuppose a pl. verb followed by "in/with" and a noun for "impurity/abomination" (Lat. has *abominationibus*; VanderKam, *Jubilees* 2:146). G. W. Nebe's suggestion ("Ergänzende Bemerkung zu *4Q176*, Jubiläen 23,21," *RevQ* 14/53 [1989] 129–30) that one reconstruct בח[ו]בל (= חבל = "destruction") is even more unlikely. Perhaps the letter Kister read as *ḥet* is a *taw*: בת may be for בת[ו]עבות (cf. 4Q221 5, where this Hebrew noun appears where Eth. has *rekwsomu*). Werman (*Jubilees*, 353) reads, without comment: בטמא בהבל (by dots above the *aleph* and *bet-he* she indicates that they are the legible ones on the fragment); her suggestion agrees with neither Eth. nor Lat. and takes the last visible letter as *he*, which seems unlikely.

e   holy things of the holy one] Most copies read a pl. construct form (*qeddesāta*) of the adj. "holy" (12 39 42 44 have a sg. *qeddesta*), followed by *qeddus* (a pl. form in 12 39 42 44 47 48 58); Lat. *sanctificationem sanctam*. Leslau (*Comparative Dictionary*, 423): *qeddusa qeddusān* = "holy of holies." So neither version uses standard expressions for "the holy of holies."

f   impure corruption] In Eth. there is a construct formation between two nouns = "impurity of corruption." Lat. also has two nouns, with the second in the genitive case. Mss. 25 38 48 63 (and 47, but with a different spelling) lack the construct ending on the first noun so that the two nouns are simply juxtaposed. Lat. *veritatis* ("of truth") is unexpected in this pejorative context; Rönsch (*Jubiläen*, 38) and Charles (*Ethiopic Version*, 85 n. 9 to Latin) altered it to *pravitatis*, "perverseness, depravity."

g   of their contamination] Lat. has no possessive, and it reads a conjunction before *inmunditiis*. Ms. 38: and the contamination of their fornication and their contamination.

22a   anger] Lat. *ire* and Heb. קצף indicate that the meaning is "anger." Eth. *maqšaft* regularly means "punishment, beating," but it can also have the sense of "wrath, anger, fury" (Leslau, *Comparative Dictionary*, 448). As Kister indicated, in 1 Enoch 13:8 *maqšaft* and ὀργή are paired ("Newly-Identified Fragments," 532).

b   them] Lat. *illis* seems a mistake for *illos* (Charles, *Ethiopic Version*, 85 n. 10 to Latin). The quite understandable mistake after the verb "give" yields the meaning for Lat.: He will deliver to them the sword. Consequently, Charles (ibid.) also inserted *in* before *gladium*. Note that Lat. does have *in* before *captivitatem* a couple of words later.

c   devouring] The Eth. and Lat. agree on the form, but the reading in the Heb. frg. 4Q176 19-20 3 is difficult. Allegro (DJD 5:65) read ולאיבו with the next word beginning with לה. Kister ("Newly-Identified Fragments," 53) saw ולאוכולה. The form may actually be ולאיכולה (VanderKam, *Jubilees* 2:147). At any rate, it is probably a form related to אכל, as the Eth. and Lat. presuppose.

23a will arouse] It is likely that Eth. and Heb. agree. The probable reading in 4Q176 19–20 3 is ויער (see Kister, "Newly-Identified Fragments," 530; VanderKam, *Jubilees* 2:147). Lat. *obdormire faciet*, "he will make fall asleep," must be wrong. Rönsch (*Jubiläen*, 38, 129) changed the infinitive to *oboriri*, "he will make spring up," a simple change and one yielding a sense in line with the Heb. and Eth. Rönsch (*Jubiläen*, 129) wondered whether νψωσει and υπνωσει were confused, while Charles thought the mistaken Lat. form arose when the prefix εξ- was omitted from εξυπνωσει (*Ethiopic Version*, 85 n. 11 to Latin).
b sinful nations] Lat. repeats *peccatores*; Lat. and Eth. read a pl. *nations*, but MS. 38 has a sg. form.
c mercy or kindness for them] 4Q176 19–20 4 may place "for/on them" (om. 9 38) after the nouns rather than before them as in Eth. The Lat. segment ends just before the phrase.
d will show partiality to no one] The verb is pl. in 17 38. The reading of 4Q176 19–20 4 is difficult. Allegro saw ובל after an unidentifiable letter at the end of the previous word (DJD 5:65), but Kister ("Newly-Identified Fragments," 534) suggested פני כן[ו]ל but thought it would be better to read ולכול. The first legible letter is very close to the next one, but it is possible they come from two words. Kister's first suggestion would produce a text in agreement with Eth. If וכול is read, then פני did not precede it. Otherwise, the remaining letters on the line can be read as agreeing with Eth. if the dot of ink after]שא is indeed only a dot and not a remnant of a *vav* for the pl. See VanderKam, *Jubilees* 2:147.
e they are more evil] "they cause more evil" 12 63.
f will cause (or: do)] "are to cause/do" 39 42 48 58.
g chaos] *ḥakak*, "tumult, sedition, riot, revolt, trouble, turmoil, terror, alarm, uproar, quarrel, discord, dissension, consternation, commotion, chaos, disorder" (Leslau, *Comparative Dictionary*, 216). The translators have, however, preferred *Gewalt* (Dillmann, Littmann, Berger), violence (Charles), חמס (Goldmann, Hartom).

3Q5 frg. 2, according to A. Rofé ("Fragments," 334–35), holds words and letters from 23:23, and Baillet agreed with his identification ("Remarques," 431 n. 39). Deichgräber ("Fragmente," 421) was not able to find a location for it. The disagreements with the Eth., the only witness to the text here, are too many to make Rofé's identification plausible. See VanderKam, *Textual*, 99–100; *Jubilees* 2:148; Berger, *Jubiläen*, 444 n. c. to v. 23.
25a The children's] "Their children's" 21 38.
b three] "7" 21.
26a study] For *taḥašša/taḥasasa* Leslau (*Comparative Dictionary*, 266) gives the meanings (besides the passive and reflexive of the simple stem = "seek out for themselves, investigate/scrutinize for themselves"): "dispute, debate, demand." For *taḥasasa* he lists "inquire collectively, discuss with one another"; this is the form in MSS. 9 12 35 39 42 48 58 63.
b laws] sg. 20 44.
27a and humanity (lit. "the children of people")] "in those children of people" 12; om. "and" 44. In this difficult expression Werman (*Jubilees*, 353 n. 23) alters "and the children of [ובני]" to "the days of [ימי]," so that it would read "the days of people." The new expression would, however, be repetitive with the words that precede it besides eliminating a conjunction.
b generation] Several MSS. (9 12 20 38) read verbal forms (the four copies read three different forms) of *walada*, which can hardly be correct in the context.
c by day] One might expect *'em-'elat* to match the previous *'elat* (day), but only 39 42 47 48 58 read it rather than *mawā'el* ("days, time").
d years] om. 12.
e to more years than the number of days (had been)] For the awkwardness of the phrasing, see Dillmann, "Jubiläen," 71 n. 21. It reads literally, "to many more years than many days." See VanderKam, *Jubilees* 2:148; cf. Werman, *Jubilees*, 354 n. 24.
28a who has lived out (his) lifetime] Lit., "who is full of days/filled with days" ("their days" 12). Oddly, Charles (*Ethiopic Version*, 85 n. 42; *Jubilees*, 150) inserted a negative before the verb: "nor one who is not satisfied with his days." Littmann ("Jubiläen," 80 n. e) and Berger (*Jubiläen*, 445 n. c to v. 28) have rejected his unsupported emendation.
29a will complete] "are to complete" 42 47.
b evil one] "evil" 21 35 38 39 42 47 48 58.
c who will destroy] Werman (*Jubilees*, 354 n. 25) curiously leaves out the relative clause, not because there is manuscript support for omitting it but because she thinks the passage reflects 1 Kgs 5:18 (Eng. v. 4), which lacks it. The Kings verse also does not refer to an "evil one" but to פגע רע ("misfortune" [NRSV]).
30a They will rise] "They will take/receive" 21 63.
b see] + "eternally" 21 42ᵗ 47 48; + "in eternity" 35ᶜ 58; + "forever" 39 42ᶜ.
c He will expel] "They will expel" 9 38 58; "he is to expel" 47.
d his] "their" 38 42 44 47 48 58 63.
e They (He 17 63) will see all their punishments and curses on their enemies] Kister ("Newly-Identified Fragments," 534–36), who identified the text of 4Q176 frg. 21 as containing the end of Jub 23:30 and v. 31, proposed to read the first line as וראו ש]ונאיהם את כל [משפטם (with circlets over all letters but the first). The verb is a reasonable reading, but ש is doubtful and hardly supplies a secure basis for changing the subject of the verb: in Eth. the righteous see the punishments of their enemies, while according to Kister's reconstruction the enemies see their punishments. Werman (*Jubilees*, 354) more plausibly reads the letter as

bet, which agrees with Eth. where "on their enemies" immediately follows "They will see."

31a know] "make known" 20 21 35 38 39; "are to know" 25; "is to make known" 63.
b shows] "again shows/again will show" 12.
c hundreds and tens of thousands] 4Q176 frg. 21 5 may have read מאו]ת (Kister ["Newly-Identified Fragments," 534] prefers אלפי]ם; so also Werman, *Jubilees*, 354); the next word begins with ולר, so that his reading ולר]בבות is very likely. If Kister's proposals are correct, the translation would be "thousands and tens of thousands."

32a you] "I" 9.
b write] "I have written" 9.
c these words] "this word" 39 42 47 48.
d it is written] om. 25 39ʹ 42 47.
e and] om. 39 42 47 48.
f entered] "they enter" 12 21 42 47 48; "he enters it" 9; "they enter it" 38. The Eth. form is actually "they go up/they will go up," but the pl. probably represents a passive meaning (VanderKam, *Jubilees* 2:149).

Commentary

The first section of chap. 23 continues the story from chap. 22 by relating the death of Abraham and the rites of mourning that it set in motion (vv. 1-7). A notice about his age at the time of his death introduces a unit (vv. 8-31) that reflects on the changes in human longevity—how the long lives of the antediluvians gave way to progressively shorter ones as human sin continued and intensified after the flood. Following an event that triggers a change—when "the children" begin studying the laws and commandments (v. 26), the lives of the righteous will begin to lengthen until they exceed the number of years enjoyed by the first people. The chapter concludes with the angel commanding Moses to record these words that are written on the heavenly tablets (v. 32).

Jubilees 23 falls into these parts:

1-7 The death of Abraham
8-31 The pattern of human life spans
    8-10 Abraham's short life in a period of decreasing longevity
    11-15 Continual decline in life spans
    16-25 Low point in the time of the evil generation
    26-31 The children and the reversal in longevity
32 Command that Moses write the message

For the chapter, the textual witnesses, besides the Ethiopic copies, are these:
Latin: vv. 8-23
Hebrew:

3Q5 frg. 3:	23:6-7
2Q19:	23:7-8
4Q221 frg. 3:	23:10-13
3Q5 frg. 1:	23:12-13
4Q176 frgs. 19-20:	23:21-23
4Q176 frg. 21:	23:30-31

The number of preserved letters and words on each of the Hebrew fragments is small, but they provide a valuable witness to the original Hebrew level of the text. That fragments from four manuscripts preserve material from Jubilees 23 may be due to the fact that the chapter would have appeared near the middle of a scroll, a place where the parchment would have been more protected from damage than the leaves on the outer parts.

1-7 The Death of Abraham[1]

The writer draws a few words from Gen 25:8 (for the end of v. 1) and 25:9 (for v. 7a) but mostly crafts a scene far more detailed than the one in Genesis.

■ **1-2** As Jacob apparently remains asleep, Abraham places one of the young man's fingers on each of his own eyes. The action resembles the one mentioned in Gen

---

[1] For this section, see Endres, *Biblical Interpretation*, 45-48 (he finds it ironic that the author, who regularly drains the drama from the stories of Genesis, heightens it relative to Genesis 25—to emphasize Jacob and also the familial harmony evident in the events); van Ruiten, "Abraham's Last Day," 78-86; *Abraham*, 318-28.

46:4 where God reassures Jacob that he will accompany him to Egypt and "Joseph's own hand shall close your eyes."[2] It is meant to be, as commentators on Genesis write, a tender, moving gesture,[3] and in Jubilees it appears to be that—another sign of the close relationship between Abraham and Jacob. With Jacob's fingers covering his eyes, the grandfather reaches the end of his life while blessing God one more time. This time he blesses "the God of gods." The only other time the title appears in the book is in 8:20, where Noah blesses the God of gods for placing his word in his mouth. With his face covered, Abraham realizes that the end has come. He manages to stretch out before an eternal sleep descends upon him; that is, he dies. The scene adopts language from Gen 49:33, where Jacob, after making final arrangements, "drew up his feet into the bed, breathed his last, and was gathered to his people."[4] The first expression "drew up his feet into the bed" is phrased in Syr and Eth Gen 49:33 as it is here in Jubilees: he "stretched out his feet."[5] Since he and Jacob were already lying in a bed, there was no need for him to lift his feet into it (as Jacob apparently did when he died). That Abraham slept forever[6] is a telling comment consistent with the book's teachings about the future: the writer does not anticipate a bodily resurrection even for someone so virtuous as Abraham (see v. 31 below). Genesis 25:8 says that he "was gathered to his people," whereas Jubilees has "was gathered to his ancestors," a reading also found in some Greek witnesses to Gen 25:8 and attested in Judg 2:10. It resembles the prediction to him in Gen 15:15 (// Jub 14:15): "As for yourself, you shall go to your ancestors in peace; you shall be buried in a good old age." According to v. 2, Jacob was unaware of what was happening because he was asleep in his grandfather's bosom (for the expression, see 22:26).

■ 3 Jacob awakened at some point and noticed that Abraham's body had turned cold in death.[7] He called out to him but received no reply—a confirmation that Abraham had died. In this last time he called to the elderly man, Jacob twice addressed him as "father."[8] So, Jacob rather than Isaac or Ishmael was the one with Abraham at his death and therefore the first to learn of it; their extraordinary relationship extended to the very last moment, a moment that is depicted as Jacob's death will be later in Genesis.[9]

---

2   See Charles, *Jubilees*, 144. As he notes, Singer (*Jubiläen*, 107 n. 1) pointed to *b. Šabb.* 151b, in a passage commenting on *m. Šabb.* 23:5: "They may not close a corpse's eyes on the Sabbath; nor may they do so on a weekday at the moment when the soul is departing; and he that closes the eyes [of the dying man] at the moment when the soul is departing, such a one is a shedder of blood." In the talmudic commentary, the practice is compared to putting out a flickering flame by placing a finger on it. Cf. also Endres, *Biblical Interpretation*, 46 (the author "deliberately altered the tradition to enhance Jacob's status"); van Ruiten, "Abraham's Last Day," 81, 85; *Abraham*, 326.

3   E.g., Westermann, *Genesis 37–50*, 156; Hamilton, *Genesis 18–50*, 592.

4   See van Ruiten, "Abraham's Last Day," 83–86; *Abraham*, 322–26, for a series of parallels with Gen 49:33—50:4: "Most likely, the author of *Jubilees* used the extensive deathbed scene of Jacob in Genesis as a basic structure for his description of Abraham's deathbed scene" ("Abraham's Last Day," 83; *Abraham*, 323).

5   Charles, *Jubilees*, 144. For the expression here and in the Testaments of the Twelve Patriarchs, see van Ruiten, "Abraham's Last Day," 84–85; *Abraham*, 325–26. He reacts critically to the suggestion by Patricia Robinson ("To Stretch Out the Feet: A Formula for Death in the Testaments of the Twelve Patriarchs," *JBL* 97 [1978] 369–74) that the reading "extend" rather than "raise" the feet arises from confusion between forms of אסף ("gather") and יסף ("add"). In addition, as van Ruiten points out, her claim (p. 371) that some Greek manuscripts of Jubilees read "stretched out" and others "drew up" is curious, since there are no Greek copies of this part of Jubilees.

6   Charles (*Jubilees*, 144) drew attention to the same expression in Jer 51:39, 57, where the prophet predicts this fate for the Babylonians when they are drunk.

7   Endres, *Biblical Interpretation*, 47: "The graphic simile ('cold as ice') and the tenderness of the scene strike one as uncharacteristic of this author; precisely for that reason these details focus attention on Jacob."

8   Van Ruiten lists the instances of father–son language in 22:1–23:8 ("Abraham's Last Day," 59; *Abraham*, 297).

9   Van Ruiten comments: "Perhaps one could con-

■ **4-5** The sequence in which Jacob informs family members is striking and characteristic of the author: he first goes to his mother Rebekah, and she then relays the message to Isaac.[10] The son of Abraham's old age, the one he loved so much but who did not recognize Jacob's superiority over his brother Esau, was merely the third to discover that Abraham had died. Genesis has none of this: 25:9 says only that Isaac and Ishmael buried him (see below, on Jub 23:7). In Jubilees, Isaac, Rebekah, and Jacob (not Esau) all go to where his body lay, with Jacob helpfully carrying a light because the death occurred at night. When they arrive, Isaac expresses his strong feelings for his father: the writer, quoting words from Gen 50:1, where Joseph threw himself on Jacob's dead body, relates that he "fell on his father's face, cried, and kissed him."

The powerful reactions to Abraham's death reveal the admiration and love that these three family members had for him, but they also introduce a legal problem: both Jacob and Isaac touched the dead body of Abraham and thus rendered themselves impure through corpse contamination. Purity is an important topic in Jubilees, but the author, who has created the scene, seems oblivious to the problem in 23:1-5. In a passage without parallel in Genesis 25, he makes both of the patriarch's special descendants defile themselves. The issue has been emphasized by Ravid, who sees this as an instance in which the writer shows no concerns for matters of *ritual* purity. She draws attention to the gravity of corpse impurity in Numbers 19, where a person who has touched a dead body (rendering him impure for seven days) and yet has not purified himself at the right times with cleansing water is to be cut off from his people because he has defiled the tabernacle (e.g., 19:11-13). The Temple Scroll (see 11Q19 xlix:5-21; l:10-15) also indicates the severity of such impurity. In light of the teachings in the Torah and in the scrolls (and she adds that in Jubilees the priests Abram and Levi ran the danger of coming into contact with dead bodies in battle),[11] it is peculiar that the writer allows such actions and provides no remedy for purification after them.[12] Ravid thinks the author opposed the priesthood of his time and its system of ritual purity and impurity.

While her case may seem convincing, it neglects an important feature of Jubilees. It is a book that retells stories in Genesis–Exodus and in which the writer reflects the texts and what he takes to be the situation in them. In his statements he is not necessarily reacting to a problem in his own time. That is, the book deals with an age when there was no sanctuary, and a sanctuary is a prerequisite for the ritual purity system (see the mention of the tabernacle in Num 19:13). In the patriarchal period as described in Genesis and Jubilees that presupposition was lacking, so there was nothing that could be defiled by such instances of ritual impurity. Just as one should not see in the example in Gen 50:1 where Joseph touches his father's dead body an attack on the purity system practiced at the time of J, so one should not interpret this case in Jubilees as an anti-sacerdotal gesture on the part of the author. It is simply a believable scene from family life in the patriarchal age before there was a tabernacle or temple.[13]

■ **6-7** Verses 1-5 describe the reactions to Abraham's death in the closest circle of his family, while vv. 6-7 deal with the ensuing events within the larger clan. The writer uses a passive expression—"the report was

---

clude that *Jubilees* wanted to stress that Abraham and Jacob were united both in their lives and in their deaths. Jacob was not only with Abraham at the end of Abraham's life, but Abraham's end resembled that of Jacob in Genesis" ("Abraham's Last Day," 87–88; *Abraham*, 329).

10   The text says, "Rebekah went to Isaac at night and told him." So they are not in the very same place, but there is no indication of how far apart they were (cf. Werman, *Jubilees*, 354).

11   Abram did so when he rescued Lot (13:22-25), and Levi, after his appointment as priest (32:1-3), would have encountered the same problem by participating in the battle against the Amorite kings (34:1-9) and in the war against Esau and his allies (38:6).

12   Ravid, "Purity," 65–67; "Issues," 66–68.

13   These arguments derive from VanderKam, "Viewed from Another Angle: Purity and Impurity in the Book of *Jubilees*," *JSP* 13 (2002) 209–15; cf. also van Ruiten, "Abraham's Last Day," 86; *Abraham*, 327–28.

heard"[14]—to indicate that news of his death reached all members of his household (for the phrase "the house[hold] of Abraham," see 22:24). Here again the author takes the opportunity to place Ishmael, Abraham's oldest son, in a favorable light.[15] Isaac was nearby when Abraham died so he did not have to travel, but v. 6 could suggest that Ishmael received the news in his homeland and set out from there for Abraham's residence. But it seems unlikely that he had returned home after the events of chap. 22, since Abraham died on the night directly after the Festival of Weeks, and Ishmael was present for the celebration of the holiday (22:1-3).[16] Wherever he was, he came from that place to mourn for his father—perhaps the only other member of the larger family to be there (see v. 7). In v. 7 the author rewrites the text of Genesis regarding the burial, moving the sons' names to the end of the clause and expanding the notice about the burial place:

Genesis 25:9 (literally) and they buried him, Isaac and Ishmael his sons, at the cave of Machpelah

Jubilees 23:7 (literally) and they buried him in the double cave [= Machpelah] near Sarah his wife, even his sons Isaac and Ishmael.[17]

Genesis places both sons at the burial and adds later (in v. 10) that Abraham was interred with Sarah; Jubilees combines the notices and in the context says more about the roles of the sons in the event. Ishmael's filial devotion is apparent from the text. Indeed, he and all the men of Abraham's household mourned a great deal, so strong was their affection for him. The elderly man may have sent them away and designated Isaac his special heir in preference to them, but he still meant much to them. There was unity on this in the entire clan. Exactly which household members carried out the mourning rites "in their places" (cf. 20:12) is less evident. Minimally, the sons of Keturah are the ones who did not journey to Hebron for the occasion, but the number may include Ishmael's sons and Esau (obviously Jacob is an exception). The period of mourning lasts for forty days (the number survives on 2Q19 line 2). However frequent the number *forty* is in the HB, it is not an attested time span for such rites;[18] Genesis gives no information about the matter. The Ethiopic text uses two nouns for mourning (translated "tearful mourning"), and Charles thought they reflected Hebrew נהי בכי as in Jer 31:15, where the first word, he suggested, was a corruption of ימי ("days of").[19] This is the translation Hartom gives, but there is no manuscript support for it. The statement regarding the end of the mourning period is reminiscent of Gen 50:4, where the conclusion of the time of weeping for Jacob is noted.

8-31 The Pattern of Human Life Spans[20]

Verse 8 should be considered part of the section that follows (see the introductory section in the commentary on chap. 22). It gives Abraham's age at death, and in that sense it concludes the long unit covering his life (11:16–23:7); but the number of years in his life serves as a springboard for the next verses because the great hero's age at death required some explanation. Why did a person who was a friend of God and had proved extraordinarily faithful to him throughout his days live for only 175 years when his ancestors, some of them with

---

14 The verb נשמע is legible on 3Q5 3 1. The same expression occurs in Gen 45:16 where a report (the term is הקל in Genesis, while Eth Jubilees uses the cognate *qāl*) was heard in Pharaoh's house regarding the arrival of Joseph's brothers (Werman, *Jubilees*, 354).

15 Endres (*Biblical Interpretation*, 47) draws attention to *Tg. Ps.-J.* Gen 25:8: "Abraham expired and died in a good old age, old and satisfied *with every good; even Ishmael had repented in his days*; and *then* he was gathered to his people."

16 See van Ruiten, "Abraham's Last Day," 59; *Abraham*, 297.

17 Van Ruiten, "Abraham's Last Day," 80–82; *Abraham*, 320–22.

18 Even Aaron and Moses received only thirty-day periods of mourning (Num 20:29; Deut 34:8). The process of embalming Jacob took forty days, but the Egyptian mourning period lasted seventy days (Gen 50:3). Cf. Endres, *Biblical Interpretation*, 48; van Ruiten, "Abraham's Last Day," 85–86; *Abraham*, 326–27.

19 Charles, *Jubilees*, 144; cf. van Ruiten, "Abraham's Last Day," 85; *Abraham*, 326.

20 Davenport thinks Jub 23:14-31 and 1:4b-26 were added to an original Angelic Discourse by the same redactor (R_1) (*Eschatology*, 32–46). There is ample evidence for a relation between the two passages, but to claim they are from an editor rather than the author is unconvincing. See the Introduction.

dubious religious credentials, lived longer than he did? In order to clarify the matter, the author contextualizes his modest years in the sweep of world history, locating them relative to the ages of those before him and the ones who would come after him.[21]

8-10 Abraham's Short Life in a Period of Decreasing Longevity

■ 8 The section opens with a double indication of how long Abraham lived—in jubilees (three = 147) and weeks (four = 28), and in numbers (175).[22] So he has the distinction of having lived to an age that is exactly divisible by seven. His grandson Jacob will trump him by living exactly three jubilees of years. His final age derives from Gen 25:7 and had been mentioned in Jub 22:1-7. For the problem the total poses in Jubilees' chronology, see the excursus "The Chronology of Abraham's Life" (pp. 705-7). Once he has provided these data, the writer borrows language from the end of Gen 25:8 that reads literally, "he was old and full of days" ("of days" is missing from the MT but present in the other ancient versions of Genesis). The Ethiopic reading "of days" in Jubilees is confirmed by 2Q19 line 5 and the Latin translation.

■ 9 The author then takes up the remarkable longevity attained by "the ancients," that is, the prediluvian patriarchs. As he phrases it, they lived for nineteen jubilees (= 931 years, one more than the number of years Adam lived [Gen 5:5]).[23] He points out that after the flood the lengths of people's lives began a long period of decline—a point abundantly clear from Gen 11:10-32, where, after Shem (600 years), the longest-lived patriarch is Eber with 464 (LXX 504) years and the shortest-lived is Nahor with 148 (LXX 208).[24] Whatever the exact numbers were in each of the ancient chronologies for the period from Shem to Abram, the dropoff in ages at death is dramatic. The author attributes the decline to "the numerous difficulties and . . . the wickedness of their ways." Jubilees 5:13-16 had spoken of judgment for evil after the flood, and the narratives about events since the flood document the presence of widespread idola-

---

21 Scholars have proposed different ways of outlining the section. Davenport maintains that vv. 9-13 are from his Angelic Discourse (as identified by the use of jubilee language), while vv. 14-31 are from his R₁, who added them to "relate the judgment passage, as well as the commands in xxii, 16-22, to the day of the one who added them" (*Eschatology*, 32 n. 1). He continues by analyzing vv. 14-31 into two sections: an eschatological poem in vv. 24-31 and a prose interpretation of it in vv. 14-23 (less v. 21, which is supposed to be later yet). The prose and poetry present three related items in reverse order: vv. 14-15, judgment on the present generation // vv. 24-25, Gentile oppression; vv. 16-20, uprising of sons against fathers for violating Torah // vv. 26-29, children return to the Torah; and vv. 22-23, coming of the Gentiles // vv. 30-31, victory of Israel (ibid., 33-46). He is correct in seeing that the material covers the same period, and there are correspondences in the units he isolates, but there is no sufficient reason for thinking vv. 24-31 are poetic or that vv. 14-23 comment on them. As he does for the survey in Jubilees 1, Nickelsburg finds in Jub 23:16-31 a fourfold pattern, influenced by the last chapters of Deuteronomy (31-34): sin (vv. 16-21), punishment (vv. 22-25), turning point (v. 26), and salvation (vv. 27-31) (*Resurrection, Immortality, and Eternal Life in Intertestamental Judaism* [HTS 26; Cambridge, MA: Harvard University Press, 1972] 46). Why he thinks "sin" begins in v. 16 is not clear, as it dominates the previous verses as well. Endres (*Biblical Interpretation*, 53-61) elaborates on the pattern Nickelsburg finds and comments on vv. 14-31 under those four headings. Although he adduces Nickelsburg's scheme, van Ruiten ("Van tekst tot tekst: Psalm 90 en Jubileën," *NTT* 47 [1993] 177-85, here 180) properly notes that 23:9-15 should be included, as the statements there about diminishing life spans find their counterpart in the lengthening ones in vv. 27-31.

22 2Q19 line 4 preserves and confirms the reading "three jubilees" and has the first two letters of the number "four" for the weeks.

23 For the first ten generations, Jubilees provides the final ages of only Adam (4:29 [930 years]) and Noah (10:16 [950 years]) and allows one to calculate quite closely that of Cain (compare 4:1 and 4:31) and possibly that of Enoch (see 4:16, 20, 21), although in neither of the last two cases does the writer give enough evidence to determine the exact age at death.

24 The numbers in Jubilees' chronology (see chaps. 10 and 11) probably differed somewhat, as is evident from the ages of the fathers when their first sons were born. See the helpful chart in Skinner, *Genesis*, 233 (it includes data from Jubilees) with his analysis, pp. 233-34; and Scott, *On Earth as in Heaven*, 108-9.

try, violence, and immorality. The decline in life spans results from and reflects that fact. The phrase at the end of v. 9—"with the exception of Abraham"—does not refer to his final age but to the fact that the modest length of his life had a different cause—the general wickedness that characterized the rest of humanity after the flood.

■ **10** The point is explicit in v. 10, where the author explains that even his close relationship with God and his success in pleasing him throughout his days (cf. 15:3; 17:17-18; 18:14-16; 21:2) did not exempt Abraham from a lifetime shorter than those of the ancients. He words it in his own way—his age at death did not reach four jubilees (= 196 years). This was no criticism of Abraham, only of the depraved era in which he lived. For the expression "because of wickedness," see Isa 57:1 (where the righteous one is gathered up מפני הרעה, "from calamity" NRSV). The concern is somewhat different in Wis 4:10-14, but the poet there explains why the righteous Enoch (not named), one who pleased God, lived so short a life compared to those of other antediluvian patriarchs. The Lord took him quickly to remove him from the wickedness all around him. The author of Jubilees does not say God removed Abraham sooner than expected to distance him from evil; he says rather that he attained a relatively low number of years at death because of the wicked era in which he lived.

11-15 Continual Decline in Life Spans

Having broached the subject of lower ages, the writer next explains how the process is ongoing and the depths it will reach.

■ **11** The angel who is revealing the book to Moses turns to the future—to the time from the era of Moses onward: "from now until the great day of judgment." All the generations that populate the earth in the post-Mosaic age will die "before they complete two jubilees [= 98 years]." Moses achieved an age of 120 years (Deut 34:7), Aaron reached 123 (Num 33:38-39), and after them Joshua died at 110 years. In the periods following those great founding leaders, no one except the high priest Jehoiada (2 Chr 24:15), who lived to 130 years, reached 100.[25] The angel reports that the trait of swift aging will characterize human life "until the great day of judgment." The context here is an important clue to the meaning of the term: that special "day" of judgment marks the point where diminishing life spans give way to increasing ones—a change that occurs at 23:26 and that seems already to have occurred at the time of the author. It is not an eschatological event in the sense that it will transpire at one future, definitive time of cosmic change and new creation. It is a period after which improvement commences.[26]

The angel stresses—he mentions it twice[27]—that people's knowledge will abandon them in their old age, and they will quickly reach a late stage in their lives. This passage may underlie CD x:7-10:[28] "No man over the age of sixty shall hold office as Judge of the Congregation, for 'because man sinned his days have been shortened, and in the heat of His anger against the inhabitants of the earth God ordained that their understanding should depart even before their days are completed' (Jubilees,

---

25   Scott, *On Earth as in Heaven*, 114. Job died at 140 years (Job 42:16), but he was often thought to have lived in the patriarchal era.

26   Hanneken, *Subversion*, 148-49, 153-57. Note his explanation in connection with Jub 23:11: "Jubilees uses the language of 'great day of judgment' in an eschatological framework but inverts the meaning to refer to covenantal chastisement rather than final destruction of evil. In Jub. 23 the great day of judgment is not the reversal of the 'final' woes that Israel suffers but the woes themselves. Judgment does not follow but precedes the turning point of history and thus is eschatological only in a very atypical sense" (pp. 155-56). As he sees it, Jubilees has a "rolling" notion of judgment that has already happened to some nations (e.g., Sodom and Gomorrah) and will happen to others in the course of history. For the entire book he finds two themes: "judgment is a rolling process, and judgment is realized" (p. 156). See also the commentary on v. 30 below. Misunderstanding what chap. 23 says about the "great day of judgment" has led to dubious theories about eschatology in the book, a messianic kingdom, and the like (e.g., Charles, *Jubilees*, lxxxvii, 9-10, 150; Testuz, *Idées*, 170-72).

27   Charles thought the second instance was a dittography (the Latin translation lacks it) (*Jubilees*, 145), but the Latin reading may be the result of haplography (VanderKam, *Jubilees* 2:140).

28   See Charles, "Fragments of a Zadokite Work," *APOT* 2:826; de Vaux, "La grotte des manuscrits hébreux," *RB* 56 (1949) 586-609, here 604 n. 4 (in these works the passage is called col. xi:3-4). Cf. also C. Rabin, *The Zadokite Documents* (2nd ed.;

xxiii, 11)" (trans. Vermes).[29] The thought in the Damascus Document is surely related—senility sets in early—but the wording is not close enough to justify the quotation marks Vermes places around the last part of the passage.[30]

■ **12** The sequel in v. 12 makes it especially clear that Psalm 90 is a key source text for the writer; its wording and teachings will be reflected in several places in chap. 23.[31] It should be noted that Psalm 90 is the only one in the Psalter attributed to Moses (the title reads: "A Prayer of Moses, the man of God"), and the revelation by the angel to Moses in Jub 23:8-31 may be presented as the circumstance that led to Moses's writing Psalm 90.[32] The angel predicts that in the days to come "if a man lives a jubilee and one-half of years, it will be said about him: 'He has lived for a long time.' But the greater part of his time will be (characterized by) difficulties, toil, and distress without peace."[33] A jubilee and one-half would be 73.5 years, reminding one of the familiar line in Ps 90:10: "The days of our life are seventy years, / or perhaps eighty, if we are strong; / even then their span is only toil and trouble; / they are soon gone, and we fly away" (see below, v. 15, where more of Ps 90:10 is cited). In the future, people will regard a life lasting some seventy years as an impressive accomplishment, but even those few years will be spent in unrelieved suffering. The terms the writer uses to characterize the few years allotted to humans build on but are more extensive than the ones found at the end of Ps 90:10.[34] The MT mentions two kinds of difficulties: עמל and און; in Eth Ps 89:11 ḥemām (the first term of the three in Jub 23:12)[35] stands where Hebrew און does. Serāḥ (the second noun) appears to be a reasonable equivalent of עמל. The two Hebrew nouns are paired in Hab 1:3, where the same Ethiopic terms render them (cf. also Jer 20:18). The second and third of the three nouns in the Ethiopic version of 23:12 (serāḥ and mendābē [Latin: angustiae;[36] 3Q5 1 2: perhaps צרה])[37] are coupled in eschatological contexts in 1 Enoch 45:2; 63:8; 103:9 ("the day of affliction and tribulation" in 45:2).[38] As a result, the short lives to which the angel points have a decidedly negative cast to them. The final clause "without peace [lit., and there is no peace]" echoes words found frequently in the prophets (Isa 48:22 ["'There is no peace,' says the Lord, 'for the wicked'"]; 57:21; Jer 6:14; 8:11; 12:12; 30:5; Ezek 7:25 [in a context dealing with the day of the Lord's wrath, v. 19], etc.). The sequel highlights such traits even more emphatically.

■ **13** The angel predicts a series of calamities that will befall the people at the time of which he is speaking.

      Oxford: Oxford University Press, 1958) 51 n. 3 to line 8. Rabin claimed that it was quoted from Jub 23:11 "in a different recension" (see also p. 51 n. 2 to line 9).

29   The lines are also attested in 4Q266 8 iii:6–9 and 270 6 iv:18–19.

30   Kugel ("The Jubilees Apocalypse," 335–36) may have the best explanation: loss of knowledge relates to an interpretation of נבהלנו in Ps 90:7 (NRSV "overwhelmed") as meaning "confused." If so, both Jub 23:11 and CD x:7-10 may be witnesses to this understanding of the verb.

31   Psalm 90:4 underlies Jub 4:30 as well (see the commentary to the passage), and see above on v. 11. For studies of the role played by Psalm 90 in Jubilees 23, see van Ruiten, "Van tekst tot tekst," 177–85; Kugel, "The Jubilees Apocalypse," DSD 1 (1994) 322–37; VanderKam, "Psalm 90 and Isaiah 65 in Jubilees 23," in John Ashton, ed., Revealed Wisdom: Studies in Apocalyptic in Honour of Christopher Rowland (AJEC 88; Leiden: Brill, 2014) 73–81.

32   See van Ruiten, "Van tekst," 181–85; Kugel, "Jubilees Apocalypse," 323–24. As Kugel observes, in Jubilees 23 one finds a reversal of the normal way of interpreting a scriptural text. The writer "purports to give the real message of which the biblical verse is merely a poetic restatement" (p. 324). He thinks the angel's command that Moses write down these words in 23:31 refers to writing Psalm 90; that is, the revelation narrated in Jubilees 23 led to his composing Psalm 90.

33   As Kugel comments, the writer took Psalm 90 not as a description of the human condition—the way it has always been—but as a prophecy ("Jubilees Apocalypse," 331–32). The superscription on the psalm identifies Moses as "the man of God," a prophetic title. The psalm, according to Jubilees, served as the requisite fair warning about the consequences of sin in the post-Mosaic era.

34   Van Ruiten treats especially the evidence from LXX Ps 89:10 in connection with the rendering of the verse in Jubilees ("Van tekst," 182).

35   A verbal form related to the same root represents עניתנו in 90:15 (Eth 89:17); for the noun, see also Deut 28:59.

36   The Vulgate for Ezek 7:25 uses angustiae where the MT has קפדה; the context in Ezekiel 7 offers more parallels with Jubilees 23.

37   צרה and mendābē again are equivalents in v. 13.

38   The references come from Dillmann, Lexicon, 342.

The author had as sources several units in the HB enumerating hardships that would afflict those who persistently violate the covenantal law,[39] in particular Deuteronomy 28.[40] The woes he names are the following:

Blow upon blow. The Hebrew (מכה), Latin (*vulnus*), and Ethiopic (*maqšaft*) terms suggest that Deuteronomy 28 was a resource for expanding on Ps 90:10. In Deut 28:22, 27, 35 the verb "(the Lord) will strike you [יככה]" introduces punishments God will bring upon violators of the covenant, and the noun מכה occurs in v. 61. In the Ethiopic version of Deuteronomy 28, the verb *yeqaššefaka* stands in vv. 22, 27, 35 and the related noun *maqšaft* in v. 61.[41]

Trouble upon trouble. It is likely that 3Q5 1 2 reads מהומה (the first three letters are legible at the left edge of the fragment); the noun means "tumult, confusion, panic, disturbance, commotion, trouble," and the like. Latin *dolor* seems a reasonable translation of it ("pain, distress, affliction, trouble," etc.). The Ethiopic *ṣelʿān*, however, is problematic. The nearest form to it listed in the dictionaries is *ṣalʿ* or *ṣelʿ*, meaning "abscess, wound, ulcer, sore."[42] It may be that מהומה in Hebrew Jubilees was meant as a near equivalent for עמל in Ps 90:10; the Greek translator of Jubilees could have rendered it with κοπος, "trouble, difficulty; striking, beating, pain."[43] The person who translated Greek Jubilees into Latin opted for the first meaning, while the one who rendered it into Ethiopic chose the second and less fitting one.[44] מהומה occurs in Deut 28:20 as the second of the woes to come: "The Lord will bring upon you disaster, *panic*, and frustration in everything you attempt to do, until you are destroyed and perish quickly,[45] on account of the evil of your deeds, because you have forsaken me" (cf. Isa 22:5).

Distress upon distress. Again the terms in all three versions survive. Hebrew צרה and Ethiopic *mendābē* are equivalents in v. 12 (rendered "distress" there as well), while Latin resorts to a noun (*tribulatio*) different from but synonymous with *angustia* in v. 12. For the word in a list of punishments, see Deut 31:17, 21 (plural in both places).

Bad news upon bad news. The three versions are extant and in harmony for the reading. The expression may have been influenced by Ezek 7:26: "Disaster comes upon disaster, / rumor [ושמעה] follows rumor."

Disease upon disease. 3Q5 frg. 1 breaks off before the phrase, but the Latin and Ethiopic texts attest the reading. A source for it may be Deut 28:59-61:

> ... then the Lord will overwhelm both you and your offspring with severe and lasting afflictions and grievous and lasting maladies. He will bring back upon you all the diseases of Egypt, of which you were in dread, and they shall cling to you. Every other malady and affliction, even though not recorded in the book of this law, the Lord will inflict on you until you are destroyed.

And every (kind of) bad punishment [or: judgment] like this, one with the other. The phrase could be taken as an introduction to the list of afflictions that follows, but it may also be understood as a summary statement regarding the preceding pairs of terms (lit., "this with this"[46]).

The list that concludes v. 13 encompasses fourteen items, though the final two could sum up all the others. The remaining twelve woes fall into four categories.

---

39 Hanneken underscores the thesis that the woes in vv. 13-14 and elsewhere in the chapter are seen as just punishments for violating the covenant, as the heavy reliance on Deuteronomy 28 shows (*Subversion*, 41, 138–44).

40 Van Ruiten ("Van tekst," 183) quite understandably says he cannot avoid the impression that the woes enumerated in vv. 13-14 are an expanded paraphrase of Ps 90:10, especially in the form of the text attested in LXX Ps 89:10: "The days of our years—in them are seventy years, / but if in acts of dominance eighty years, / and the greater part of them is toil and trouble, / because meekness came upon us, and we shall become disciplined." Verse 13 picks up on the notion of being punished, and v. 14 ("the evil generation") on the words "meekness came upon us." The latter is questionable, but for v. 13 he seems right, though the writer clearly drew on other texts as well.

41 In Psalm 89 (90) the Ethiopic version twice uses *maqšaft* where the MT has nouns for "anger" (vv. 9, 13 [MT 11]).

42 Leslau, *Concise Dictionary*, 224.

43 It translates עמל in Ps 89 (90):10.

44 VanderKam, *Jubilees* 2:141–42.

45 The thought of perishing quickly would also be appropriate to the context in Jubilees 23.

46 Werman interprets "this with this" as meaning: as soon as one finishes the next begins (she compares Jub 6:29) (*Jubilees*, 356).

Disease and stomach pains. The first Ethiopic word—*dawē*—was used earlier in v. 13; the Latin *corruptio* may be, according to Rönsch, an error for *correptio*, which he says means "bei den Aertzen nicht blos im Allgemeinen jeder Krankheitsanfall . . . , sondern es könnte auch hier speciell, als wörtliche Uebersetzung von ἐπιληψία."[47] Lewis and Short suggest general meanings for *corruptio* ("corrupt condition") and also for *correptio* ("a laying hold of, seizing [of a disease]").[48] The nouns in the second position in the two versions also do not seem well matched. Latin *clades* means "calamity," but the Ethiopic word is unparalleled elsewhere—*gabaṭbāṭ*. Leslau lists a noun spelled either *gabṭ* or *gabaṭ* and meaning "colic, stomach ache."[49] The form in Jubilees should be related to it. The term that stood in the Hebrew original is unknown: Goldmann uses אבדן and Hartom repeats מכה from earlier in the verse, both of which seem influenced by the Latin reading while ignoring the Ethiopic one (see the textual note).

Snow, hail, and frost. For the next grouping, the two versions correspond more closely. The words "snow, hail, and frost" reproduce ones found in Jub 2:2: among the angels God created on the first day were "the angels of the spirits of the clouds for darkness, ice, hoar-frost, dew, snow, hail, and frost." All of them occur in Ps 147:16-17 but in a context praising the Lord's power, not exactly as punishments.

Fever,[50] cold,[51] and numbness (Latin: choking?). These maladies recall the first category (disease and stomach pains) but are of a distinguishable kind. The first term likely represents Hebrew קדחת (so Goldmann, Hartom); it figures in Deut 28:22, a passage that seems to underlie parts of Jub 23:13: "The LORD will afflict you with consumption, fever, inflammation, with fiery heat and drought, and with blight and mildew; they shall pursue you until you perish" (cf. Lev 26:16).

Famine, death, sword, captivity. Famine ("drought") or hunger occurs in Deut 28:22 (quoted above), 48, while sword, pestilence, famine are mentioned in Ezek 7:15. For the sword, see Lev 26:33; Deut 32:25, 41-42; for captivity, see Deut 28:36, 41. Jeremiah and Ezekiel several times combine the three nouns "sword, famine, pestilence" (e.g., Jer 42:16-17; Ezek 5:12). Needless to say, death is likely to accompany famine, sword, or captivity.

And every (sort of) blow [*maqšaft*] *and difficulty* [*ḥemām*].[52] The expression seems to gather terms from Ps 90:10 and Deut 28:61. *Maqšaft* has appeared several times in this context ("blow upon blow" at the beginning of v. 13) and represents מכה in Deut 28:61; in the psalm *ḥemām* stands where the MT reads און. In the Greek version of the psalm (89:10), the two nouns at the end of the verse are κόπος ("striking, beating; toil, trouble, suffering") and πόνος ("striking, beating; toil, trouble, suffering pain")—possibly the words that appeared here in Greek Jubilees.

■ **14** The initial words of v. 14 echo expressions from the beginning of several verses in Deuteronomy 28. Examples are 28:15: if Israel does not obey, "all these curses shall come upon you" (see also v. 45); and v. 61, which uses a causative: "Every other malady and affliction, even though not recorded in the book of this law, the LORD will inflict on you until you are destroyed."[53] As in Deuteronomy 28 where the evils Moses predicts will befall the disobedient Israelites, in Jubilees 23 they will punish "the evil generation." The HB knows of an evil generation—the Israelites of the wilderness wanderings (cf. Jub 1:7). Psalm 78:8 exhorts Israel to tell the next generation not "to be like their ancestors, / a stubborn and rebellious generation, / a generation whose heart was not steadfast, / whose spirit was not faithful to God" (see v. 33, where "their days vanish like a breath, / and their years in terror"; 95:10; also Deut 32:5, 20; Jer

---

47 Rönsch, *Jubiläen*, 126 (= "among the physicians not merely each attack of disease in general . . . , but it could also here be [used] specifically as a literal translation of ἐπίληψια [seizure]").

48 Lewis and Short, *Latin Dictionary*, 473-74.

49 Leslau, *Concise Dictionary*, 207.

50 Ethiopic *nabaršāw* means "heat, fever, kind of disease" (Leslau, *Concise Dictionary*, 123).

51 Latin *frigora* provides the only guidance regarding the meaning of the otherwise unattested Ethiopic noun *sakaḥkāḥ*. The same is the case for *provocatio* (it should be emended to *praefocatio* [Rönsch, *Jubiläen*, 36, 126]), which stands where the Ethiopic version has the unknown *saʿozāz*.

52 Latin reads *plaga* where Ethiopic has *maqšaft*, lacks a conjunction, and has *planctus* ("beating, wailing") where Ethiopic gives *ḥemām*.

53 For the expression, see Jub 1:6.

2:31; 7:29).[54] That epithet, referring to people of the past, the writer transposes to the post-Mosaic future.[55] The Latin and Ethiopic versions differ regarding what the evil generation will do. The former speaks about the evil deeds they will perform on the earth, while the latter claims they will make the earth sin. The Ethiopic reading sounds like Deut 24:4: after forbidding a woman's first husband to take her back after her second husband, too, has divorced her ("after she has been defiled"), the legislator writes: "for that would be abhorrent to the Lord, and you shall not bring guilt [תחטיא] on the land that the Lord your God is giving you as a possession" (see also Jer 3:1).[56] Jubilees 7:33 (cf. also v. 18 below) contains Noah's instructions about purifying the earth from the blood shed on it, just as Lev 18:25 says the earth/land was defiled by immoral practices.[57] In keeping with the precedents for this language, Jubilees points to sins of a sexual nature as rendering the land or earth guilty or sinful. The vocabulary for the offenses of which they will be guilty ("sexual impurity, contamination, and their detestable actions"[58]) is reminiscent of Leviticus 18, where the Lord instructs Israel not to act as did the population that preceded them in the land. Verbs and nouns related to the word for "impurity" (*rekws*) occur in Ethiopic Lev 18:19, 21-24, 26-30;[59] and the verb related to the noun "contamination" figures in 18:25, 27. The fundamental command in Lev 18:24-25 is: "Do not defile yourselves in any of these ways, for by these practices the nations I am casting out before you have defiled themselves. Thus the land became defiled; and I punished it for its iniquity, and the land vomited out its inhabitants." The "evil generation" of Jubilees 23 is guilty of the disgusting practices against which Leviticus 18 warns.

■ 15 The depths to which the people of that time ("the evil generation") will sink serve as the background for another borrowing from Ps 90:10. The verse from the psalm stands in a context that seems appropriate for the purposes of Jubilees.

For we are consumed by your anger;
    by your wrath we are overwhelmed.
You have set our iniquities before you,
    our secret sins in the light of your countenance.
For all our days pass away under your wrath;
    our years come to an end like a sigh. (Ps 90:7-9)

Jubilees introduces its version of words from Ps 90:10 by quoting again from the people of that generation: "Then it will be said:[60] 'The days of the ancients were numerous—as many as 1000 years—and good." In v. 9 the author had mentioned "the ancients" as people who lived nineteen jubilees of years. Here he adduces an even greater number of years as an echo of Ps 90:4: "For a thousand years in your sight / are like yesterday when it is past, / or like a watch in the night."[61] The psalmist and his community then lament the words of Ps 90:10. The

---

54 The NT attributes the expression "evil generation" or one similar to it to Jesus in reference to his contemporaries (Matt 12:39, 45; 16:4; cf. 17:17; Mark 8:38; 9:19; Luke 9:41; 11:29). See also Acts 2:40; Phil 2:15; Wis 3:19.

55 For Werman (*Jubilees*, 356), v. 14 depicts the sins of Moses's generation, but there is no indication that the verse applies to any such limited period. The sins characterize all the time after Moses (see the excursus at the end of the commentary on this chapter).

56 Ethiopic Deuteronomy 24:4 uses verbs related to *rekws* (the noun for "impurity" near the end of 23:14) to render "after she has been defiled" and "you shall not bring guilt upon the land."

57 Driver, *Deuteronomy*, 272.

58 For the translation, see VanderKam, *Jubilees* 2:143. As it stands the text reads "and in abomination are their deeds." For Ethiopic *saqorār*, see Dillmann,

Lexicon, 353 (among passages where it appears is Hos 9:10); Leslau, *Concise Dictionary*, 83: "horror, abomination, disgust."

59 The Latin of Jubilees uses *pollutiones abominationes* (with no grammatical indication of how the two nouns relate to each other); forms of these words appear in the Vulgate of Leviticus 18 in vv. 13-14, 21-22, 24-27, 29-30.

60 Literally the text reads "they will say," just as in v. 12.

61 Van Ruiten, "Van tekst," 183–84. He has shown that Jub 23:12-15 reworks Ps 90:10 in its entirety: v. 12c cites the second part of the verse and it is paraphrased in vv. 13-14, while 23:15 cites the first part of the verse. As a result, vv. 12-15 present a chiastic reworking of Ps 90:10. He also finds reflections of other parts of the psalm in Jubilees 23. For example, the notion of diminishing lifetimes could echo Ps 90:9 (he thinks the reading in the Vulgate

similarity in wording between the psalm and Jubilees is especially clear when the Hebrew and Ethiopic texts are aligned:

Psalm 90:10   yĕmê šĕnôtênû bāhem
    šibʿîm šānâ
Jubilees 23:15   mawāʿela ḥeywatena ʾemma ʾabzeḫa
    sabʾ ḥayewa sabʿā ʿāmata
Psalm 90:10   ʾim bigbûrōt šĕmônîm šānâ wĕrohbām
    ʿāmāl wā-ʾāwen
Jubilees 23:15   wa-ʾemma ḫayyala samāneya ʿāmat
    wa-kwellu[62] ʾekuy

The writer of Jubilees places in the mouths of the speakers the claim that attaining seventy years was deemed to be living a long time,[63] while reaching eighty required even more fortitude. Its formulation ("All are evil") more nearly reflects the reading רובם, known from the LXX ("the greater part of them"), rather than the MT's curious רהבם.[64] As was said in v. 12, there will be no peace during their short lifetimes—"during the days of that evil generation." Psalm 90:10 speaks about the human condition—pitiful in comparison with God's eternity—and vv. 7-9 locate the statement in a context of sin and punishment. The writer of Jubilees 23 took these elements and transformed them to picture the ultimate level of decline in human longevity, a low point reached because of sin.

Kugel and Scott think the period from Moses on marks another distinctive stage in the decline of life spans,[65] but that view fails to appreciate fully a basic feature of the text: there is simply one long decline from the antediluvians through the post-Mosaic period, with no indication that it takes a sharper turn for the worse after Moses. Verses 9 (regarding the post-flood generations) and 11 (the time from Moses to the great judgment) both refer to people aging quickly. "The shape of the curve is the opposite of the exponential decline typical of apocalypses. The present generation stands not in the freefall of a catastrophic plummet but at a relatively flat point along a decline spread across history. In this way Jubilees diffuses the urgency that is so essential to the apocalyptic view of history."[66]

16-25: Low Point in the Time of the Evil Generation

The phrase "that evil generation" at the end of v. 15 launches the writer into a section about the sinful people of the future (relative to the time when the angel is speaking with Moses).

■ 16 One striking theme in the section is a conflict between young and old—between "the children" and "their fathers and elders." The older people, rather than advising and correcting the youth, are subject to criticism from them.[67] Perhaps this is one aspect of what the author means when he says "there is no peace during the days of that evil generation" (v. 15). The verb used for "finding fault" may come from Lev 19:17: "you shall reprove[68] your neighbor, or you will incur guilt yourself." According to the Leviticus passage, it is one's duty to offer such reproof rather than hating another person in one's heart; by rebuking, one avoids taking vengeance or bearing a grudge. From the language he uses, it sounds as if the author thinks the children are doing the right thing—following a scriptural injunction. However, questions have arisen regarding his attitude toward the children. Collins thinks he is "ambivalent" about them or that he may disapprove of them.[69] Hanneken agrees:

---

    suggests a lessening of human years), and Ps 90:13-17 offer some of the themes that characterize Jubilees 23 (e.g., the days "you have afflicted us" in v. 15). The psalmist places the emphasis on God's wrath and calls upon him to change; the author of Jubilees accents human sin and expects people to reform.

62 The Latin translation reads *et isti* here.
63 He also adds an expression denoting special circumstances into the first line ("if a man has lived for a long time") where the psalm lacks one.
64 4Q221 3 5 reads רוב at v. 12.
65 Kugel, "Jubilees Apocalypse," 326-27; Scott, *On Earth as in Heaven*, 106-19. It is also not easy to agree with Kugel that for Jubilees declining human ages "solved the problem of the missing requital for grave infractions" (p. 327). The entire period covered was marked by "requitals," probably right to the time of the writer.
66 Hanneken, *Subversion*, 126.
67 Testuz compares the effort of the youth to that of the young Abram to turn his father away from idolatry (12:1-8) (*Idées*, 166).
68 The Latin translation of Jub 23:16 uses *arguant*, while the Vulgate of Lev 19:17 uses *argue*; the Ethiopic of Jubilees has *yezzālafu*, and a form of the same verb figures in Lev 19:17 (*tezzālafo*).
69 John J. Collins, "Pseudepigraphy and Group Formation in Second Temple Judaism," in Esther Chazon and Michael E. Stone, eds., *Pseudepigraphic Perspec-

"There are no good reasons to assume that Jubilees has anything nice to say about these militants [see v. 20], although there are bad reasons, and good reasons to think the opposite."[70] If the passage echoes Lev 19:17, Collins and Hanneken would have to modify their positions. In addition, one can read the punishment as falling on the opponents who are left (v. 21), not on the children. See below on "the children" in v. 26 and the problem of whether they are the same as "the children" of v. 16.

Experts have often compared "the children" and the situation in which they find themselves with the group mentioned in 1 Enoch 90:6-7, part of the Animal Apocalypse: "And look, lambs were born of those white sheep, and they began to open their eyes and to see and to cry out to the sheep. But they did not listen to them nor attend to their words, but they were extremely deaf, and their eyes were extremely and excessively blinded." A younger group attempts to call back their Judean elders on the basis of the insight they had (their opened eyes), but their efforts, like those of the children in Jub 23:16, failed. Charles, among others, understood the lambs of 1 Enoch as the Hasidim, while the sheep are traditional Israelites who cling to an older way.[71] It is noteworthy that both texts appeal to a younger, reforming group and their lack of success in dealing with their fellow Israelites. But that the group was the Hasidim of 1 Maccabees seems less certain. Kister has maintained that in 1 Enoch 90 and Jubilees 23, with the first column of the Damascus Document, the origins of the Essenes are being pictured.[72] It is, of course, very difficult to identify the group behind the label, but at least it is clear that the text is describing an internal struggle regarding the covenantal law.

If the young are following the law of reproof, they obey the prescription and present their charges—ones that the text expresses in fairly general terms.

Sin. The group received its name from their penchant for sin—the evil generation.

Injustice. The Hebrew term may have been חמס (so Goldmann). If the word was used, Gen 6:11 could lie behind it: "the earth was filled with violence [חמס]" (cf. v. 13).

What they say (lit., the words of their mouths). See Deut 32:1; Job 8:2 (Bildad); Pss 19:15 (Eng. 14); 54:4 (Eng. 2); 36:4 (Eng. 3): "The words of their mouths are mischief and deceit"; cf. Eccl 10:12.

Great evils that they commit. See Deut 28:20: "the evil of your deeds"; 31:18: "all the evil they have done." See also Gen 39:9; Jer 16:10.

Their trespasses are all-encompassing—embracing their actions and their words—and they constitute "abandoning the covenant[73] that the Lord had made between them and himself." "Abandoning the covenant" reminds one of Deut 29:24 (Eng. 29:25), where the nations who witness the severe punishments the Lord will impose upon Israel say: "It is because they abandoned the covenant of the Lord, the God of their ancestors, which he made with them when he brought them out of the land of Egypt." It is especially interesting that another group joins the nations in making this assessment: "The next [האחרון] generation, your children who rise up after you" (Deut 29:21 [Eng. 22]; cf. also Deut 31:21). The situation resembles the one in Jubilees 23, where the children criticize the previous generation for what it has done. The purpose for which God established the covenant—"so that they should observe and perform all his commands, ordinances, and all his laws"—echoes Deut 30:16 (cf. vv. 8, 10): "If you obey the commandments of the Lord your God [MT lacks this first part of the verse] that I am commanding you today, by loving the Lord your God, walking in his ways, and observing his commandments, decrees, and ordinances. . . ."[74] God had predicted to Moses that Israel would "forget all my laws, all

---

tives: *The Apocrypha and Pseudepigrapha in Light of the Dead Sea Scrolls* (STDJ 31; Leiden: Brill, 1999) 43–58, here 53.

70 Hanneken, *Subversion*, 101. He adds that in vv. 16-21 neither side is in the right as nothing favorable is said about either of them (102).

71 Charles, *Jubilees*, 146. See also Berger, *Jubiläen*, 442 n. a to v. 16.

72 See Kister, "Essene Sect," 1–18. Davenport accepts the idea that the Hasidim and the Maccabean revolt are being pictured here (*Eschatology*, 41–42). The "fathers" would be the people who held positions of authority, and the young people would be the ones who objected to their ways.

73 The two versions of the verse use *testamentum* and *šerʿāta* respectively for "covenant."

74 In Jub 21:5 Abraham commanded Isaac to "keep his commandments, ordinances, and verdicts." As

my commandments, and all my verdicts" (Jub 1:14) and in the evil generation the forecast finds its fulfillment (cf. 1:9). The expression for not deviating to the left or right reverses the directions found in places such as Deut 28:13-14 (cf. Deut 5:32), where Moses predicts blessings "if you obey the commandments of the LORD your God, which I am commanding you today, by diligently observing them, and if you do not turn aside from any of the words that I am commanding you today, either to the right or to the left, following other gods to serve them" (cf. 1QS i:15). It is noteworthy that, while in the general context in Deuteronomy idolatry is a major evil, the angel does not mention it in Jubilees 23.[75] That fact and the charge that "the evil generation" abandoned the covenant are consistent with the thesis that Jubilees here is speaking about an inner-Jewish conflict, not about one between Jews and sinners from other nations.

■ 17 The text continues its general condemnation of Israelites in the evil generation. It is not that a few have spoiled the era for the many; all are guilty. The comprehensive verdict makes it sound as if the conditions before the flood are reappearing, and the impression grows stronger in the sequel. At that time "God saw that the earth was corrupt; for all flesh had corrupted its ways upon the earth" (Gen 6:12 [cf. v. 5]; see Jub 5:2-3; Rom 3:23). The blanket indictment allows the writer to repeat some of his characteristic terms for the wrongs people will commit: all their actions are impurity (*rekus/inmunditia*), an abomination (*saqorār/odium*; see v. 14 above); and all their ways are "contamination [*gemmānē/pollution..*], impurity [*rekws/abominatio*],[76] and destruction [*musennā/exterminium*]." One meets these words in other contexts in which the writer condemns a group or characters are warned not to act in this fashion. Three examples are (ordered by the number of parallel terms that occur in them):

22:16 (regarding separating from the nations): "for their actions are something that is impure [*rekws/pollutio*], / and all their ways are defiled [*gemmun/inmunditia*] and something abominable [*mennānē/abominatio*] and detestable [*saqorār/spurcitia*]"

33:19 (after Reuben's sin with Bilhah): "For all who commit it on the earth before the Lord are impure [*rekus/inmunditia*], something detestable [*saqorār/abominatio*], a blemish, and something contaminated [*gemmānē/pollutio*]"

20:6 (to Abraham's sons, after warnings about the descendants of Canaan, the giants, and the punishment of Sodom in vv. 4-5, where *rekws* and *musennā* occur): "Now you keep yourselves from all sexual impurity and uncleanness [*rekws*] and from all the contamination [*gemmānē*] of sin"

So these terms are distinguished entries in the author's vocabulary of disgust; they focus on the corrupting influence of impurity, especially sexual misconduct. The behavior of the evil generation mimics that of impure sinners in the historical account.

The charge "For all have acted wickedly; every mouth speaks what is sinful" picks up words from Isa 9:17 (Eng. 16). There, when severe punishment does not induce the people to seek the Lord, the prophet writes: "That is why the Lord did not have pity on their young people, / or compassion on their orphans and widows; / for everyone was godless and an evildoer, / and every mouth spoke folly. / For all this his anger has not turned away; / his hand is stretched out still."[77]

■ 18 Verse 18 continues the use of language reminding one of material in the flood account. The angel predicts that the earth will be destroyed because of what the evil generation does. Before the flood God said he would destroy the earth (Gen 6:13), and after it he promised never to do so again with a flood (Gen 9:11; cf. 8:21; see Jub 6:4). As a result, when destruction of the earth is forecast in v. 18, nothing is said about a flood. The destruction will take another form: the sequel speaks of no seed, wine, or oil—a trio of staples mentioned in Hos 2:10 (Eng. v. 8; cf. Lev 26:20; Deut 7:13; 11:14; 28:51): "She did not know that it was I who gave her the

---

he put it in 21:4, God "exercises judgment against all who transgress his commands and despise his covenant."

75 See Kister, "Essene Sect," 6–7.
76 This term was mistakenly omitted from the translation in VanderKam, *Jubilees* 2. The periods after *pollution* represent illegible traces of letters.
77 Davenport, *Eschatology*, 42 n. 3; Kister, "Essene Sect," 6 n. 22.

grain, the wine, and the oil." According to Hos 2:24 (Eng. v. 22) they will be restored in the future.[78] The Ethiopic text characterizes the evildoers' actions as total rebellion or apostasy (the Latin term is only partially legible).[79] Once again, as in the flood, destruction will overwhelm all living things because of human actions: the text mentions animals, cattle, birds, and fish. The fish are an interesting category, as they are not likely to be destroyed by water and are not mentioned in Genesis 6–8, but in the future, when destruction comes through a different means, they too will meet their end. Jubilees 5:20 (// Gen 6:7; cf. Gen 6:17; 7:4, 22-23; 8:21) says that God decreed that he would destroy, besides people, "cattle, animals, birds, and whatever moves about on the ground" (see 5:2, where they too are guilty of corrupting their ways). Verse 18 generally seems also to reflect the influence of Hos 4:1-3, especially v. 3: "Therefore the land mourns, / and all who live in it languish; / together with the wild animals / and the birds of the air, / even the fish of the sea are perishing."[80] The word "together" (v. 18; it is not in the Latin version) suggests that the destructive punishment will happen at one time.

■ **19**[81] Verses 19-20 deal with the conflicts between different groups in society, and here too the struggles are within the Jewish population because the issues are the law and covenant that all of them were supposed to obey (cf. 4Q390 2 i:6). The struggle is pictured as more complex than between one generation and the next, as the writer mentions several pairs to indicate that the entire society became involved in the violence: not only people separated by age but also ones at the two extremes of the economic and social spectrums.[82] The fights raged over the law and the covenant (Latin: in the law regarding the covenant). Those who violated the covenantal law neglected the essential elements that God had predicted they would cease practicing: "They will forget all my laws, all my commandments, and all my verdicts. They will forget beginning(s) of the month, Sabbath, festival, jubilee, and covenant" (1:14; see also 1:10; 6:34-35, 38).[83] Calendar is a central part of the covenantal law, and the people who forget the law go astray in these extraordinarily important matters.

■ **20** While v. 19 could be read as an account of social tensions resulting from differing approaches to the covenant and what was involved in living by it, v. 20 describes a civil war. One group, whose aim was to turn the other back to "the way," resorts to the sword (cf. Lev 26:25, 33);[84] their military efforts encounter resistance that leads to bloodshed, and they fail to accomplish their goal (see v. 21). The "way" in v. 19 must refer to the

---

78   Berger adduces 1 Enoch 10:19 as also mentioning the three in a context describing eschatological blessing (*Jubiläen*, 443 n. b to v. 18).
79   Leslau lists as the senses of *kāḥd*: "lack of faith, apostasy, impiety, heresy, perfidy, denial, rebellion, contention, controversy, contradiction" (*Concise Dictionary*, 150).
80   Kister, "Essene Sect," 6 n. 23.
81   There is a series of verbal or content parallels between 4Q390 and Jubilees 23, particularly from 23:19-26. For a full list of these, see Hanneken, "Status," 410-13. As his list shows, many of these are also paralleled in the related survey in Jubilees 1.
82   Berger thinks the clear direction of the conflict is from below upward: "Trägerkreis des Jub sind nach eigenem Selbstverständnis Arme, Niedrige und Gesetzestreue (vgl. auch die Erwähnung des Reichtums in V. 21 ["The circle responsible for Jubilees was, according to its own self-understanding, poor, lowly, and faithful to the law; cf. also the mention of wealth in v. 21"])" (*Jubiläen*, 443 n. b to v. 19). The wording of the text favors the idea that the conflict affected all parts and levels of society, not that the righteous, the people who transmitted Jubilees, thought of themselves as lowly or poor. The reference to greed in v. 21 is a general charge, not a social statement. Kister suggests that Isa 3:5 lies behind the text: "The people will be oppressed, / everyone by another / and everyone by a neighbor; / the youth will be insolent to the elder, / and the base to the honorable" ("Essene Sect," 6 n. 24).
83   The correspondence between what God predicts regarding Israel in chap. 1 and what will happen according to chap. 23 is another indication that chap. 23 largely envisages conflicts and failures in Israel, not ones between Israel and people from other nations. For the parallel in 4Q390 1 8-9, see Knibb, "A Note on 4Q372 and 4Q390," in F. García Martínez, A. Hilhorst, and C.J. Labuschagne, eds., *The Scriptures and the Scrolls: Studies in Honour of A.S. van der Woude on the Occasion of his 65th Birthday* (VTSup 49; Leiden: Brill, 1992) 164-77, here 175-76; Hanneken, "Status," 414-17.
84   And the bow, in Latin.

behavior—the manner of covenantal life—the writer considers correct (see "the right way" in v. 21).[85] Isaiah 30, a passage that also speaks of a disobedient people who would be punished before the divine grace reappeared, may have conditioned its use here—Isaiah 30 sounds much like Jubilees at times (recall the importance of the related passage, Isa 8:16-20, for Jubilees 1). In 30:8-9 the prophet receives orders:

> Go now, write it before them on a tablet,
>   and inscribe it in a book,
> so that it may be for the time to come
>   as a witness forever.
> For they are a rebellious people,
>   faithless children,
> children who will not hear
>   the instruction of the LORD.

These people in Isaiah, who wish to silence the seers and visionaries, say, "leave the way; turn aside from the path, let us hear no more about the Holy One of Israel" (v. 11).[86] Much like the ones who rise up in Jub 23:19, the Lord tells those deviating from the path: "In returning and rest you shall be saved" (Isa 30:15), though Isaiah does not refer to violent means. As he describes the future return of God's mercy, the prophet says: "And when you turn to the right or when you turn to the left, your ears shall hear a word behind you, saying, 'This is the way; walk in it'" (v. 21). Before God raised up the Teacher of Righteousness, those who would later follow him were groping for the way (CD i:9).

The inner-Jewish warfare of v. 20 has given rise to the theory that Jubilees alludes in a prophecy after the fact to circumstances in the time of Judas the Maccabee. As Charles phrased it, "This verse describes the warlike efforts of Judas the Maccabee to force the apostates to return to Judaism."[87] He added that after 162 BCE, when the Jews had achieved religious independence so that they could follow their own laws (1 Macc 6:55-62), the conflict was no longer with external foes but with internal ones. The question became "whether the Hellenising faction or the national party should control the nation."[88] His hypothesis honors the fact that the struggle is presented as being between Jewish groups, and, according to 1 Macc 7:21-25 (cf. 2:42-48), Judas and his forces turned violently against Alcimus and his supporters. For more on the subject, see below.

■ 21 The writer continues the prediction by dealing with those who survive the warfare of v. 20. They will fail to learn a lesson from their harrowing experience and will not return to the way to which their opponents tried to coerce them. Instead they will conduct themselves in thorough violation of the covenant by acting fraudulently with goods and inappropriately in religious matters.

Financial misdeeds. The eighth commandment forbids stealing, but the people who deviated from the way acted immorally in economic matters by greedily pursuing wealth and by robbing the goods of others (cf. 4Q390 2 i:8-9).

Religious infractions. The angel charges them with misusing God's name in violation of the third commandment—a commandment that was often interpreted as referring to unnecessary or false oaths.[89] Verse 21 predicts only that they will not say or use it as they should. Nothing is said about a prohibition of actually pronouncing the divine name; the accusation is that they will use it improperly—without truth or righteousness. The

---

85 Hanneken thinks the writer "condones none of the factions fighting in the civil war. Closely related is the fact that Jubilees views the 'shedding of much blood' not as a glorious thing but as an inherently wicked thing that arouses punishment from God" (*Subversion*, 116). However, if the one group is trying to bring the other back to the "way," and if this way is a positive image as shown in the commentary, their military efforts are not being criticized.

86 Charles drew attention to Isa 30:21 and also to the NT designation "the Way" for the earliest followers of Jesus (e.g., Acts 9:2) (*Jubilees*, 148).

87 *Jubilees*, 147–48. See also Testuz, *Idées*, 167 (the description is so lively that the author may have been a participant), and Davenport (*Eschatology*, 43) who believes v. 20 depicts the Maccabean revolt but that the writer makes no distinction between it and the resistance in v. 16; for him it was a single struggle.

88 Charles, *Jubilees*, 148.

89 See the sources assembled in Kugel, *Traditions*, 649–51.

language here and in the context is closely related to Isa 48:1-2: "Hear this, O house of Jacob, / who are called by the name of Israel, / and who came forth from the loins [MT: waters] of Judah; / who swear by the name of the Lord, / and invoke the God of Israel, / but not in truth or right."[90] It also somewhat resembles Jer 4:1-2: "If you return, O Israel, says the Lord, / if you return to me, / if you remove your abominations from my presence, / and do not waver, / and if you swear, 'As the Lord lives!' / in truth, in justice, and in uprightness...."[91]

Identifying the second religious infraction is rendered difficult by a textual and translation problem. The Latin phrase is *sanctificationem sanctam*, "the holy holiness"; the Ethiopic is *qeddesāta qeddus*,[92] "the holy things of the holy one." To what do the expressions refer? The practice has been to see a reference to the holy of holies here, but Rönsch objected that in the Vulgate *sanctum sanctorum* was the expression for that inner room; he thought the words in v. 21 referred to the holiness or sanctity of the temple.[93] Caquot employs "les choses très saintes" in his translation and considers these the parts of sacrifices eaten by the priests.[94] The coupling of terms found in both the Latin and Ethiopic suggests that two words from the root קדש figured here in the original text, but the forms in the two translations are not literal reflections of קדש קדשים. The Ethiopic of Jub 8:19, where there definitely is a reference to the holy of holies, reads *qeddesta qeddusān*. It may be that by the present expression the temple in general is meant and that the evildoers defile it by their actions.[95] In this case, the referent would not be the holy of holies, a place accessible only to the high priest. The terms in the expression "the impure corruption of their contamination"[96] have been used several times before—e.g., in 22:16 and 23:14, 17.

In this connection it is helpful to adduce another passage from the Damascus Document that appears related to Jubilees. That text cites Isa 24:17—"Terror, and the pit, and the snare / are upon you, O inhabitant of the earth"[97]—and explains it (CD iv:14-18): "Interpreted, these are the three nets of Belial with which Levi son of Jacob said that he catches Israel by setting them up as three kinds of righteousness. The first is fornication, the second is riches, and the third is profanation of the temple [טמא המקדש]" (trans. Vermes). The second and the third nets of Belial are two faults that Jub 23:21 finds in the survivors of the war, while the first net of Belial is incorporated in the charge about defiling the sanctuary.[98]

Jubilees 23:21 too (see above on v. 20) has played a role in the attempt to find historical events behind the predictions in the chapter. Charles, for example, thought that Alcimus and his hellenizing party were the ones charged with improperly naming the great name and defiling the sanctuary.[99] In 1 Macc 7:9 Alcimus, who is called "ungodly," became high priest. When a band of

---

90 Kister, "Essene Sect," 7 n. 27; "Newly-Identified Fragments," 531 n. 9.
91 Note the references near the end of the preceding chapter to the people perverting their way and forgetting the Lord who calls them to return (3:21-22).
92 For the first term, mss. 12 39 42 44 read a singular form, and for the second these copies and 47 48 58 read a plural form.
93 Rönsch, *Jubiläen*, 129.
94 Caquot, "Jubilés," 728. An example is Lev 2:3.
95 Davenport understands the reference to be to the temple hierarchy (comparing 1QpHab xii:8-10) (*Eschatology*, 44-45 n. 2).
96 Werman, who renders the last word in the verse as תועבותם, adduces 4QMMT C 5-7, in which Deut 7:25 is referenced in connection with bringing any abominable thing into one's house (*Jubilees*, 360). She follows a suggestion of Kister ("Studies on MMT," 347-48) that this resembles the charge against the Wicked Priest (1QpHab viii:10-13, where תועבות also occurs) that he took the wealth of nations, possibly violating thereby the prohibition against idolatry, since the gold and silver taken as spoils of war could have been associated with it.
97 The context in CD iv is similar to the one in Jubilees 23: "when the age is completed" (line 10), and "During all those years Belial shall be unleashed against Israel" (lines 12-13).
98 See Catherine M. Murphy, *Wealth in the Dead Sea Scrolls and in the Qumran Community* (STDJ 40; Leiden: Brill, 2002) 38.
99 Charles, *Jubilees*, 148; Davenport (*Eschatology*, 43-45), while recognizing the force of Charles's case, maintains that v. 21 is an interpolation referring to the Hasmoneans Simon and John Hyrcanus and that it was placed in the text by someone at Qumran. The verse, however, fits comfortably in its setting and seems to belong; there is no reason for thinking that v. 21 was added to transform vv. 16-20 from a depiction of the dawn of a new day in his-

Hasidim met with him (vv. 12-18), he swore an oath to them and then promptly broke it, leading to the charge against him and his group that there was "no truth or justice in them, for they have violated the agreement and the oath that they swore" (v. 18).[100] Judas then led his troops "into all the surrounding parts of Judea, taking vengeance on those who had deserted and preventing those in the city from going out into the country" (v. 24). Later (1 Macc 9:54-57) Alcimus wanted to tear down a wall in the inner court of the temple but became paralyzed and died. Clearly, a number of terms in Jub 23:21 could find a meaningful reference in these characters and events, but the description is quite general so that it is difficult to be very confident that the author had the misdeeds of Alcimus and Judas's reaction in mind.

■ **22** The next two verses picture the Lord's response to the unremitting evil perpetrated by those who survived the war of v. 20. The actions of that generation will arouse his anger[101] so that he hands them over for five kinds of punishment. Of the five terms, four are present on 4Q176 19-20 3 (the third—captivity—is lost in a gap), and all of them are present in both the Ethiopic and Latin translations. The terms used are sword, judgment, captivity, plundering, and devouring. The list is related to the one in Ezra 9:7: "From the days of our ancestors to this day we have been deep in guilt, and for our iniquities we, our kings, and our priests have been handed over to the sword, to captivity, to plundering, and to utter shame, as is now the case"[102] (for handing over to the sword, see 4Q390 1 9-10; 2 i:4). The enumeration in Jub 1:13 includes captivity, devastation, and devouring.[103]

■ **23** Verse 23 provides the first mention of the nations and their role with respect to the offending Israelites. God will arouse against the evil generation "the sinful nations," who will make a devastating and merciless (see Jer 6:23) assault on them. Several passages in the HB picture the Lord arousing or stirring up the nations for such a purpose.[104] For example, Isa 13:17-18 (cf. also Isa 9:11; Jer 50:9; 51:1, 11; Ezek 23:22) expresses frightening predictions similar to those in Jub 23:23:

> See, I am stirring up the Medes against them [Babylon],
>   who have no regard for silver
>   and do not delight in gold.
> Their bows will slaughter the young men;
>   they will have no mercy on the fruit of the womb;
>   their eyes will not pity children.

Psalm 79:1-3, part of which 1 Macc 7:17 cites in connection with Alcimus and his actions, also furnishes some of the details:

> O God, the nations have come into your inheritance;
>   they have defiled your holy temple;
>   they have laid Jerusalem in ruins.
> They have given the bodies of your servants
>   to the birds of the air for food,
>   the flesh of your faithful to the wild animals of the earth.
> They have poured out their blood like water
>   all around Jerusalem,
>   and there was no one to bury them.[105]

---

tory to a unit to be followed by more corruption. It is also difficult to believe "those who escape" would be a designation for leaders of a successful revolt. Cf. also Schubert who relates the verse to the events depicted in 1 Maccabees 7 (*Tradition*, 148-49), after a detailed study of who the Hasidim in the chapter were (pp. 144-47).

100 The writer cites Ps 79:2-3, including the phrase ""there was no one to bury them" (7:17); Jub 23:23 uses similar language (see below).

101 In VanderKam, *Jubilees* 2, the word is translated "punishment," a meaning of Ethiopic *maqśaft* though Latin reads *ira*. קצף in 4Q176 19-20 2 confirms the Latin reading but also suggests that this is a case in which the Ethiopic term means "wrath, fury" (Leslau, *Concise Dictionary*, 82), as

Kister noted ("Newly-Identified Fragments," 532). For another instance in which the Lord displays his "great anger," see 15:34, where the failure of Israelites to circumcise their sons is the cause: "Then there will be great anger from the Lord against the Israelites because they abandoned his covenant."

102 See Kister, "Newly-Identified Fragments," 532. He also refers to 11QT[a] lix:7-8.

103 The passage is partly preserved on 4Q216 ii:14-15. See DJD 13:8, 11.

104 Werman points to Deut 28:49-50 as a parallel; the passage speaks of a single foreign nation that will show no partiality to the old or young (*Jubilees*, 360).

105 See Schubert, *Tradition*, 149-50.

The description in v. 23 is also reminiscent of the ways in which Habakkuk presents the action of the Lord and the ways of his punishing instruments (1:6-9):

> For I am rousing the Chaldeans,
>   that fierce and impetuous nation,
> who march through the breadth of the earth
>   to seize dwellings not their own.
> Dread and fearsome are they;
>   their justice and dignity proceed from themselves.
> Their horses are swifter than leopards,
>   more menacing than wolves at dusk;
>   their horses charge.
> Their horsemen come from far away;
>   they fly like an eagle swift to devour.
> They all come for violence,
>   with faces pressing forward;
>   they gather captives like sand [note v. 17, where he destroys "nations without mercy"].[106]

Appropriate to their place in the flow of history, the nations who will effect the punishments are "more evil than all humanity." The result will be the tumult or chaos[107] of war and evil deeds against Israel/Jacob (a poetic pair). Naturally, blood will flow (Ps 79:3; cf. Hab 2:8, 17), and there will be no one to perform the normal dignities for those slain in battle—collecting their bodies and burying them (see above, Ps 79:3 [= 1 Macc 7:17], 10; Jer 8:2: [regarding the bones of leaders] "and they shall not be gathered or buried").[108] The destruction caused by the sinful nations will be simply horrible (although the writer does not say the results will be unique in the annals of warfare).

■ **24** Verse 24 relates directly to the conditions in v. 23, as the introductory "At that time [*ba-we'etu mawā'el*]" indicates.[109] The frightening, destructive attack of the sinful nations will elicit a cry for help, a prayer for rescue from the devastating conditions, but the cry will bring no relief. A number of passages in the HB may have influenced the phrasing in v. 24, but a close parallel, as noted by Berger, can be found in 11QT^a lix:5-8,[110] a part of its paraphrase of Deuteronomy 28 (e.g., 28:29):

> And in the land of their enemies they (will) groan and cry out because of a heavy yoke, and they will call, and I will not hear; and they will cry out, and I will not answer them because of their evil doings. And I will hide my face from them, and they will become food and prey and spoil, and there shall be no one to help because of their wickedness by breaking my covenant and spurning my law, until they will be guilty of all sins.

(See also Jub 1:13-14.) The situation will differ from the one in the days of the judges, when Israel would cry out and the Lord would raise up a deliverer for them (e.g., Judg 2:11-22). The divine refusal to answer is the antithesis of the promise for the new creation in Isa 65:24: "Before they call I will answer, / while they are yet speaking I will hear."[111]

■ **25** The final lines in the description of the future woes destined to befall the evil generation speak of a situation

---

[106] Kister places Jub 23:23 and lines from various places in Pesher Habakkuk side by side ("Essene Sect," 13-14). The most helpful parallel in the pesher is in the comment on Hab 1:17 (which reads in the pesher: "Therefore he keeps his sword [MT: net] always drawn to kill nations without pity") in 1QpHab vi:8-9: "This refers to the Kittim who destroy many people with the sword, including boys, the weak, old men, women, and children. Even on the child in the womb they have no mercy" (vi:10-12; trans. Abegg, *DSSR* 2:85).

[107] For *hakak*, Leslau lists: "tumult, alarm, uproar, turmoil, commotion, dissension, consternation, chaos, disorder" (*Concise Dictionary*, 2). It is used several times in reference to the frightening chaos caused by invading armies (Isa 22:5; Jer 14:19; 49:2; Ezek 23:46 [Dillmann, *Lexicon*, 9-10]). *Hakak* is used three times in Jub 10:30 in connection with the destruction of Ham's children because their ancestor took land that did not belong to him.

[108] Charles noticed the use of language from Jer 8:2 (*Jubilees*, 149).

[109] The connecting phrase is a reason why Davenport's division between vv. 14-23 (prose) and 24-31 (poetry) does not fit the evidence. He writes that it marks a new unit (*Eschatology*, 36); rather, it ties v. 24 to the preceding context.

[110] Berger, *Jubiläen*, 445 n. b to v. 24. See Yadin, *Temple Scroll*, 2:267 for the following translation and for references to scriptural sources and parallels.

[111] Isaiah 65:20 influenced other passages in chap. 23: vv. 28-29 and also, perhaps, v. 25 (see below).

diametrically opposed to the pre-flood period when the ancients lived nineteen jubilees of years. In the evil generation children will have the gray hair that marks the elderly; in fact, a child of three weeks will appear to be one hundred years of age. Especially the word translated "child" (ḥeḍān)[112] suggests that when referring to "three weeks of age" the writer means exactly that, not three units of seven years.[113] The translators and commentators have drawn attention to intriguing parallels in Greek literature, especially in Hesiod and the Sibylline Oracles.[114] Hesiod describes the unfortunate conditions of the fifth generation, a race of iron: "And Zeus will destroy this race of mortal men also when they come to have grey hair on the temples at their birth" (*Works and Days* 180-81). He continues by speaking about conflicts between children and fathers and within other groups, of people growing old quickly, and of false words and oaths. When the deities Aidos and Nemesis depart from the earth, humans will have great sorrows, "and there will be no one to help against evil" (201; trans. H. G. Evelyn-White, LCL). Similarly, Sib. Or. 2:154-59, speaking of the last times, says:

> But whenever this sign appears throughout the world,
> children born with gray temples from birth,
> afflictions of men, famines, pestilence, and wars,
> change of times, lamentations, many tears;
> alas, how many people's children in the countries will feed
> on their parents, with piteous lamentations.
> (trans. J. Collins, *OTP* 1:349)

So the idea of children looking old in later periods of distress is more widespread, but the author of Jubilees may here be painting a picture that is the opposite of the conditions in the new creation in Isaiah 65, just as he may have done in v. 24.[115]

> No more shall there be in it
>   an infant that lives but a few days,
>   or an old person who does not live out a lifetime;
> for one who dies at a hundred years will be considered a youth,
>   and one who falls short of a hundred will be considered accursed. (Isa 65:20)

In claiming "[a] child who is three weeks of age will look like one whose years are 100" in a negative context, the writer may be reflecting the interpretation of Third Isaiah's "one who falls short of [חוטא] a hundred" in the sense of "a sinner who is one hundred years," as in the LXX[116] and the targum (the imprint of Isa 65:20 will reappear in 23:27-28 below). The low ages are associated with the distress (see v. 13) and pain of that time.

26-31 The Children and the Reversal in Longevity

Only when conditions have reached the lowest point and human life spans are correspondingly the shortest ever (see v. 25) does a reversal come about.

■ **26** Typical of this apocalypse, that change is not instantaneous, dramatic, or cosmic: it is introduced by the same expression as in v. 24 ("In those days," *ba-weʾetu mawāʿel*) relating it to the preceding context, and it is marked by the fact that "the children will begin to study [*yetḥaśśaśu*] the laws, to seek out [*la-ḥāśiśa*] the commands, and to return to the right way" (v. 26).[117] The two verbal forms enclosed in brackets are related to

---

112 Leslau, *Comparative Dictionary*, 226: "infant, young child."
113 Werman understands the reference to mean twenty-one years (*Jubilees*, 357).
114 Examples are Charles, *Jubilees*, 149; Caquot, "Les enfants aux cheveux blancs (Remarques sur *Jubilés* XXIII, 25)," *RHR* 177 (1970) 131-32; Berger, *Jubiläen*, 445 n. a to v. 25. Caquot's comments about these infants as albinos and the horrors such people would produce for the Essenes, who were so concerned about purity, miss the point, as does his section about Noah in 1 Enoch 106:2. Hanneken calls them gnomes, since the text pictures them as old men and infants at the same time (*Subversion*, 46). See also pp. 145-48, where he discusses whiteness and children in other apocalypses and thinks Jubilees is here subverting the normally favorable images and criticizing groups who may identify with such images. Davenport thinks v. 25 evokes a picture of starvation (*Eschatology*, 37-38).
115 For the influence of Isaiah 65 on Jubilees 23, see VanderKam, "Psalm 90 and Isaiah 65 in Jubilees 23," 81-86.
116 ". . . for the young person will be a hundred years old, but the one who dies a sinner will be a hundred years old and accursed."
117 On the passage, see Testuz, *Idées*, 168-69; Davenport, *Eschatology*, 38.

the same root and have similar meanings.[118] Goldmann renders both with forms of דרש, but Hartom preferred למד for the first and דרש for the second.[119] If a distinction in Hebrew words ultimately underlies the two Ethiopic verbs, perhaps forms of בקש and דרש appeared in the text (Werman uses לדרוש for the first and לבקש for the second). Both figure in Qumran literature with objects such as law, statutes, and commands. Examples are 1QS v:11 ("They have neither inquired [בקשו] nor sought after Him [דרשהו] concerning His laws" [trans. Vermes]); 4Q306 (Men of the People Who Err) 2 3 ("they sought the Torah and the co[mmandment" [trans. Lim, *DSSR* 6:288–89]); and 4Q398 11–13 7 (= C 24) ("these were the seekers of the Torah" [trans. Qimron and Strugnell, *DSSR* 1:334–35]). A number of texts refer to a special דורש התורה (e.g., CD vi:7). In Jub 1:12 God predicts that the Israelites "will persecute those who study the law" (4Q216 ii:13: מבקשי התורה). The children here will reverse the trend predicted in 1:16, 19-20, where many will forget the laws and commandments and fail to return to the proper path, though forceful attempts are made. Here too (see also 23:20-21) the writer calls it "the right way [*fenota ṣedq*]."

The children (*daqiq*—the same word as in v. 16) are the ones who bring about the transformation through seeking the divine will and a concomitant return to the proper way of life. Are these the same characters as the children of v. 16? The text does not address the question explicitly, but the same common word is used for them and they exist at the time of the same evil generation.[120] One reason for not equating them is that the children in v. 16 rebuke their elders and in v. 19 "the young" (if they are the children) engage in warfare against the older people, while in v. 26 they study the Torah and return to the right way. Actually, there is no contradiction in claiming the same people performed all of these actions, so it is possible that "the children" in vv. 16, 19, 26 are one group.

Friedemann Schubert has written a detailed study of who the ones studying the laws and seeking the commandments might have been if Jubilees, in this part of chap. 23, is dealing with circumstances in early Hasmonean times.[121] To do so, he also draws on references in chap. 1, especially 1:12, which mentions "witnesses" and those who seek the Torah. He develops his view in contrast to Odil Hannes Steck, for whom the witnesses and generally the ones seeking the Torah were Hasidim (see 1 Macc 2:42), scholars of the Torah who preached repentance; Steck identified the seekers in 23:26 with this group.[122] Schubert investigates the evidence from 1 Maccabees 2 and concludes that two groups are under consideration: the Hasidim in 2:42, and another set of people in 2:29-41. The latter are described as "many who were seeking righteousness and justice" (v. 29); they with their families and livestock fled to the wilderness to escape the decree of King Antiochus that the peoples of his kingdom become one and give up their "particular customs" (1:41). So as not to profane the Sabbath they did not defend themselves when attacked on the seventh day by the forces sent to implement the royal wishes and perished as a result. Their fate induced Mattathias and his followers to permit military defense on the Sabbath.

---

118 Leslau, *Concise Dictionary*, 112.
119 Kugel ("Jubilees Apocalypse," 333 n. 13) thinks the second verb would have been דרש ("interpret"), and in this he follows the view of J. Baumgarten ("The Unwritten Law in the Pre-Rabbinic Period," in his *Studies in Qumran Law*, 13–35, esp. 32–33). Baumgarten writes about usage of the verb in Qumran texts: "Such searching was a regular aspect of the cultic life of the community and derives from the expectation that 'from time to time' a new revelation might be disclosed to an earnest seeker. While scriptural readings and exposition of the Law were part of the devotional pattern, the esoteric illuminations of the Qumran teachers were looked upon as an indispensable source of *halakha*" (p. 33).
120 The temporal indicators in the apocalyptic section do not suggest any significant change of time: v. 12 "In those days"; v. 15 "Then"; v. 16 "During that generation"; v. 24 "At that time"; and v. 26 "In those days." See Davenport, *Eschatology*, 41; and Paul Hoffmann, *Die Toten in Christus: Eine religionsgeschichtliche und exegetische Untersuchung zur paulinischen Eschatologie* (NTAbh n.F. 2; Münster: Aschendorff, 1966) 95–97 (where he highlights the author's focus on the final generation).
121 Schubert, *Tradition*, 124–51.
122 Steck, *Israel und das gewaltsame Geschick der Propheten* (WMANT 23; Neukirchen-Vluyn: Neukirchener Verlag, 1967) 160–61.

This group in 1 Macc 2:29-41 is of transparent interest for Jubilean studies because Jub 50:12-13 includes in a list of Sabbath violations deserving capital punishment anyone who "makes war on the Sabbath day." Though this seems to reflect an older halakhic view, the group in 1 Macc 2:29-41 and the writer of Jubilees (with his community) were adherents of it at the time.[123] The shared stance on Sabbath fighting and the related terminology for the two led Schubert to infer that there was an overlap between the community of Jubilees and the sort of people described in 1 Macc 2:29-41. From his study of the verb בקש and other data, he concluded that they were people who were concerned with understanding the law as interpreted in Jubilees and putting it into practice. The people in Jub 23:26, like those in 1:12 and the ones in 1 Macc 2:29-41, had the same goal. In this he disagrees with Steck who, as noted above, thought they were Torah scholars, scribal experts on the text. Schubert, like Davenport, thinks the terms "children" and "fathers/elders" are not meant in a literal sense: the fathers/elders are people in positions of authority in society, and the young are the ones who protest against their ways. Thus, the fathers/elders are the apostates, and the children or the young are the pious in this apocalyptic scenario. Interestingly, he with a number of others (e.g., Berger) thinks that "rich" and "poor" in 23:19 reflect social realities.

The designations "children" and those who "study the laws" and "seek out the commands" are rather general. They do not adequately circumscribe the social entity or entities involved, but the evidence does indicate that the roles and views of the people presented as producing the great turning point in history in Jubilees 23 could fit well with the type of people who believed and acted like the refugees in 1 Maccabees 2.

■ **27** The turning point introduced in v. 26 is not a spectacular, cataclysmic event—not one preceded by or connected with a universal day of ultimate judgment[124]—and the era that follows consists of gradual, ongoing change.[125] The ages attained by people will increase incrementally ("generation by generation and day by day") once the children begin their study and return to the right way. It may be that the writer also thinks the human population will grow if that is what "and humanity as well" conveys.[126] The upward trend in longevity will continue until humans achieve ages matching the numbers enjoyed by the antediluvians and even exceed them. An age of one thousand years was reached by no patriarch before the flood (although Jub 4:30 could imply that one thousand years was the original ideal for humanity), and certainly by no one after it.[127] Possibly the reference to one thousand years is another echo of Psalm 90, this time of v. 4: "For a thousand years in your sight are like yesterday when it is past, or like a watch in the night."[128] However that may be, the number serves to communicate the idea that the long process of decline in ages will be matched by a lengthy movement of increase in them so that eventually one arrives back at the starting point. The future ideal is to return to the original situation, not to replace it.[129] The parallel movements of similar length appear to be related to Ps 90:15: "Make us glad as many days as you have afflicted us, / and as many years as we have seen evil."[130] The author states his point in extreme form: the number of years people live will be greater than the number of days in their lives at the lowest point (v. 25).[131]

---

123 See Doering, *Schabbat*, 540-47, regarding the sources for the prohibition.
124 Hanneken, *Subversion*, 155-56.
125 See, e.g., Charles, *Jubilees*, 149-50; Hanneken, *Subversion*, 172-73: "Not only is the restoration gradual; it has already begun" (p. 172).
126 See the note in VanderKam, *Jubilees* 2:148. On the grounds that the text as it stands does not make sense, Werman changes בני in the phrase בני אדם to ימי so that it reads "the days of humanity" rather than, literally, "the sons of humanity" (*Jubilees*, 352 n. 23). But the text mentions days at the beginning of the verse and would hardly need to repeat the term in this location just a few words later.
127 In 23:15, however, people are quoted as saying that the "days of the ancients were numerous—as many as 1000 years—and good."
128 Cf. van Ruiten, "Van tekst," 183.
129 Hanneken, *Subversion*, 171-73.
130 Kugel notes the connection with Ps 90:15 (and v. 16) ("Jubilees Apocalypse," 333-34).
131 Kugel suggests that the line develops the words "the days you have afflicted us" in Ps 90:15 ("Jubilees Apocalypse," 334). For the writer it means "make us joyful by giving us 'more years than the number of days,' that is, the days that you took away from us." A human age of one thousand years finds no parallel in the HB, though the number is

■ **28** Verse 28[132] returns to the language of Isa 65:20, though in a paraphrastic and interpretive way. The first part ("There will be no old man, nor anyone who has lived out [his] lifetime") relates to the opening of 65:20: "No more shall there be in it / an infant that lives but a few days [MT: עול ימים], / or an old person who does not live out a lifetime." Jubilees may take both statements—about the child and about the elderly—as referring to an older person. The LXX read the beginning of the verse as "And there shall not be there one who dies untimely [αωρος]"[133]—a reading more compatible with the way Jubilees apparently understood the words. At any rate, the writer moves the word for "old person" to the beginning of the sentence and applies both parts of the Isaian saying to that subject. The second part of Jub 23:28 takes up the latter part of Isa 65:20, again with some interpretation.[134]

Jub 23:28: because all of them will be infants and children.

Isa 65:20: for one who dies at a hundred years will be considered a youth,
and one who falls short of a hundred will be considered accursed.

The picture is one of ideal conditions, with people living for a very long time but suffering none of the ills that normally accompany extreme old age. Where Third Isaiah speaks about people living to an advanced age, Jubilees talks of a population that does not age as its years increase. Rather than Third Isaiah's "one who dies at a hundred years will be considered a youth," Jubilees says everyone will remain young as the years pass by ("infants and children"). Blenkinsopp, who calls attention to the parallels between Jub 23:27-28 and Isa 65:20, also refers to 1 Enoch 25:6, which speaks of the time when God visits the earth and gives the tree of life as food to the righteous: "Its fragrances <will be> in their bones, / and they will live a long life on the earth, / such as your fathers lived also in their days, / and torments and plagues and suffering will not touch them."[135]

In describing the long lives of blessing people will enjoy, the author may again have drawn on Isa 65:22: "They shall not build and another inhabit; / they shall not plant and another eat; / for like the days of a tree shall the days of my people be, / and my chosen shall long enjoy the work of their hands." The "tree" in the verse arouses curiosity, and both the LXX and the targum to Isaiah identify it as the tree of life (see 1 Enoch 25:6 above), an understandable inference in a context envisaging lengthy life spans.

■ **29** The fact that people will attain such remarkable ages does not mean they will live forever. Their lives will have limits ("They will complete and live their entire

---

used in connection with long life. In the Decalogue, one reads (Exod 20:5-6 // Deut 5:9-10): "You shall not bow down to them or worship them; for I the Lord your God am a jealous God, punishing children for the iniquity of parents, to the third and fourth generation of those who reject me, but showing steadfast love to the thousandth generation of those who love me and keep my commandments" (also Deut 7:9; the Decalogue is referenced in Jub 23:31). In 1 Enoch 10, the eschatological picture includes several references to one thousand but not in connection with ages: "And now all the righteous will escape, / and they will live until they beget thousands, / and all the days of their youth and their old age will be completed in peace" (10:17; v. 19 says every vine will yield 1000 jugs of wine and every seed 1000 measures). There is also the millennium in Rev 20:1-6, and Ps.-Clem. *Recognitions* 4.9, referring to the original state of humanity, says that "a life of a thousand years did not fall into the frailty of old age" (ANF 8; cf. Berger, *Jubiläen* 445 n. a to v. 27).

132 For the use of Isaiah 65 and 66 in vv. 28-31, see Endres, *Biblical Interpretation*, 59–61.

133 The adjective figures in Job 22:19, where the MT reads לא עת. In Isa 65:20, 1QIsa[a] has עויל where the MT reads עול; the former means "young boy" or possibly "unjust one" (BDB, 732).

134 E.g., Charles, *Jubilees*, 150; Cf. Bautch, "Afterlife in Jubilees: Through a Covenantal Prism," in Tobias Niklas, Friedrich Reiterer, and Jozef Verheyden, eds., *The Human Body in Death and Resurrection* (Deuterocanonical and Cognate Literature Yearbook 2009; Berlin: de Gruyter, 2009) 205–19, here 212. Davenport suggests that Isa 65:20 and its context were influential on v. 27 as well (*Eschatology*, 38 n. 2).

135 Blenkinsopp, *Isaiah 56–66: A New Translation with Introduction and Commentary* (AB 19B; New York: Doubleday, 2003) 288. For 1 Enoch 25:6, see Nickelsburg, *1 Enoch 1*, 314–16.

lifetimes"),[136] but they will live the many days allotted to them in blissful conditions—"peacefully and joyfully," in "times of blessing and healing." The writer here continues to work with material toward the end of Isaiah 65 (vv. 21-25), which depicts ideal circumstances of harmony and fulfillment and where "[t]hey shall not hurt or destroy on all my holy mountain" (v. 25).[137] But it is also likely that Psalm 90 reasserts itself in v. 29. The psalmist prays in vv. 14-15: "Satisfy us in the morning with your steadfast love, / so that we may rejoice and be glad all our days. / Make us glad as many days as you have afflicted us, / and as many years as we have seen evil." Several times the author of Jubilees marks an ideal period by saying there will be no satan or evil one (twice in Egypt during Joseph's reign [40:9; 46:2]; in the future when Israel is purified in the land, 50:5).[138] For the lack of one who destroys, see above on Isa 65:25.[139] The prediction about the renewal of the luminaries in Jub 1:29 says they will be for "healing, health, and blessing for all the elect ones of Israel" (and see v. 30 below). Healing is among the eschatological blessings in Isa 57:18-19; 58:8; Jer 3:22; 30:17; 33:6; 1QS iv:6-7 (where long life is also mentioned) and stands in marked contrast to the maladies mentioned in v. 13.

■ **30-31**[140] The final two verses in the section furnish more detail about the situation in the future age. At this point the language of Isaiah 65-66, and of Isa 66:14 in particular, contributes significantly to the wording.[141]

Jubilees 23:30-31	Isaiah 66:14
Then the Lord will heal his servants. They will rise and see great peace. He will expel his enemies. The righteous will see (this), offer praise, and be very happy forever and ever. They will see all their punishments and curses on their enemies. Their bones will rest in the earth and their spirits will be very happy. They will know that there is a God who executes judgment.	You shall see, and your heart shall rejoice; your bodies [lit., bones] shall flourish like the grass;[142] and it shall be known that the hand of the Lord is with his servants, and his indignation is against his enemies.

Terms or expressions shared by the two include:

1. The Lord will heal his servants (see also Isa 57:18-19; Jer 33:6; Mal 3:20 [Eng. 4:2]) // the hand of the Lord is with his servants
2. See great peace, (will see [this]), punishments and curses on their enemies // You shall see
3. He will expel his enemies, punishments and curses on their enemies // his indignation is against his enemies
4. Be very happy forever and ever, their spirits will be very happy // your heart shall rejoice

---

136 Hoffmann, *Die Toten in Christus*, 100; Davenport, *Eschatology*, 38. Hanneken ("Watchers," 28-29) draws attention to parallels between 1 Enoch 5:8-9 and parts of Jub 23:29 and 30 in particular: "Then wisdom will be given to all the chosen; / and they will all live, / and they will sin no more through godlessness or pride. / In the enlightened man there will be light, / and in the wise man, understanding. / And they will transgress no more, / nor will they sin all the days of their life, / nor will they die in the heat of <God's> wrath. / But the number of the days of their life they will complete, / and their life will grow in peace, / and the years of their joy will increase in rejoicing and eternal peace / all the days of their life."

137 Note the concentration of words for joy in Isa 65:18-19 in connection with the new heavens and earth.

138 Charles has an odd comment on the expression "no satan": "This statement need not mean very much" (he then refers to the other three passages in which it occurs) (*Jubilees*, 150). As Davenport indicates, this is not a use of *satan* as a title or name (*Eschatology*, 39 n. 1).

139 Nickelsburg, *Resurrection*, 21; Bautch, "Afterlife," 212, commenting that the blessings pictured here counter the covenantal curses of v. 22.

140 Werman (*Jubilees*, 358) maintains that v. 30 and the end of v. 31 do not belong to the document the author has incorporated into chap. 23 (see the excursus at the end of the commentary on this chapter) because v. 30 repeats the healing mentioned at the end of v. 29 and both v. 30 and the end of v. 31 introduce a distinction between the righteous and others—a distinction not relevant to the devolution of humanity pictured in the chapter. On all of this, see the excursus below.

141 E.g., Nickelsburg, *Resurrection*, 22.

142 Though they do not share vocabulary for this expression, Ps 90:5 and Isa 66:14 speak of grass flourishing but to make different points.

5. Their bones will rest in the earth // your bones shall flourish like the grass
6. They will know that the Lord is one who executes judgment // it shall be known that the hand of the LORD is with his servants

The passage, following after v. 29, which notes the joyful way in which blessed people will complete their lives, speaks about the Lord healing his servants. The notion of divine healing at a future, better time comes to expression in several passages in the HB. One that is intriguing in the present context is Isa 57:18-19:

> I have seen their ways, but I will heal them;
>   I will lead them and repay them with comfort,
>   creating for their mourners the fruit of the lips.
> Peace, peace, to the far and near, says the LORD;
>   and I will heal them.[143]

Isaiah 57 begins by speaking about the righteous (singular, though the NRSV renders as a plural)[144] and his removal because of wickedness: "For the righteous are taken away from calamity, / and they enter into peace; / those who walk uprightly / will rest on their couches [משכבותם]" (vv. 1e-2). The term "couches" is a euphemism for graves;[145] hence, these righteous people are pictured as resting in death.

"Servants" is a term that is familiar from Third Isaiah, especially chap. 65, where it occurs seven times, with several instances of it clustered in vv. 13-14.[146] In these verses, which contrast the fate of the servants with that of the ones who forsake the Lord, the poet says the servants will rejoice and sing for joy. Isaiah 66:14 (cited above) also declares that the Lord is with his servants. Thus, as he speaks about the wonderful conditions coming into existence, the writer of Jubilees echoes Third Isaiah's language in the chapters that deal with the new creation. Jubilees does not use terms so striking as "new creation" in this context (though see 1:29), but it words its depiction of the transformed circumstances in the future in such a way as to remind one of the original state of humans whose health allowed them to live to extraordinary ages.

"They will rise" is an expression that has stimulated debate about whether the writer envisages a physical resurrection of the dead (see also the comments on v. 31 below). It is reasonable to think that the verb "rise" is related to Isa 26:19:[147] "Your dead shall live, their corpses [MT: my corpse] shall rise [יקומון]. / O dwellers in the dust, awake and sing for joy! / For your dew is a radiant dew, / and the earth will give birth to those long dead." There is a long tradition of interpreting Isa 26:19 as predicting a physical resurrection,[148] but the fact that the poet had just written "The dead do not live" (v. 14) coupled with the wider context in Isaiah and the HB raises the possibility that the passage should be read differently—as "a metaphorical reference to the reestablishment of Israel."[149] The manner in which the author of Jubilees understood the passage, if it underlies the present one, is the point under discussion, but the verb itself

---

143 The Hebrew of Isa 26:19, which has influenced the context in Jubilees, makes no reference to healing, but the Greek translation of the line where the MT has "For your dew is a radiant dew" is "for the dew for you is healing for them." Davenport understands the healing in v. 30 as a healing not of individuals' physical bodies but of the nation as a unit (*Eschatology*, 40).
144 The parallel term "the devout" (57:1) is, however, plural.
145 Blenkinsopp, *Isaiah 56–66*, 152.
146 Bautch ("Afterlife," 215), who stresses the covenantal character of Jub 23:29-31 (see pp. 206–7), thinks the servants embody "covenantal kinship" and that their healing is a restoration to the covenant.
147 MT Dan 12:2 reads יקיצו, but the Old Greek has αναστησονται (Theodotion: εξεγερθησονται). The Ethiopic version reflects the Old Greek, using the same verb as the one Jubilees has here. For the connection of "rise up" with Isa 26:19, see Bautch, "Afterlife," 215–16. He thinks the two authors have quite similar traditions about an afterlife that does not include a bodily resurrection. "Rising up" in the two works is "a type of revivification emphasizing peace and the absence of pain, with concomitant joy and rejoicing" (p. 216).
148 So the Isaiah targum and *b. Sanh.* 90b.
149 H. Wildberger, *Isaiah 13–27* (CC; Minneapolis: Fortress, 1997) 568 (see 567–70); cf. Blenkinsopp, *Isaiah 1–39*, 370–71. A. Hakham provides citations from several traditional Jewish commentators regarding a figurative interpretation (*The Book of Isaiah* [2 vols.; Da'at Miqra'; Jerusalem: Mossad Harav Kook, 1984] 1:272–73, esp. n. 40).

in Isa 26:19 is open to more than one interpretation. Similarly, "they will rise" in Jub 23:30 is not sufficiently specific to allow one to infer that the author anticipated a resurrection of bodies. The servants, who are the ones who rise or stand up, could be the faithfully obedient people who happen to be living at the time depicted in v. 30. They now stand up to commence a new activity.

The servants will not only rise but will also "see great peace."[150] The verb of seeing may come from Isa 66:14 ("You shall see"), and "great peace" as the object observed may reflect a line from the same context—"For thus says the LORD: I will extend prosperity [שלום] to her like a river" (v. 12). In addition, the righteous/devout people in Isa 57:1-2 "enter into peace" (v. 2)—a sort of wholeness characterizing the future time but unavailable to the wicked (Isa 57:21). The great peace that the servants will experience contrasts with the harsh divine treatment of their enemies whom the Lord will expel, or, as Isa 66:14 puts it, "his indignation is against his enemies" (LXX: "he shall threaten those who disobey him"). Isaiah 66:15 further elaborates the violent fashion in which God will turn against his foes.[151] The divine treatment of the enemies who have punished Israel—expulsion from the land—suggests that their fate is to return to their homes and continue to experience the vicissitudes of human life, including, presumably, short life spans.[152]

As v. 30 continues, one reads "the righteous [plural] will see (this), offer praise, and be very happy forever and ever." Both seeing and rejoicing are present in Isa 66:14: "You shall see and your heart shall rejoice," although the wording comes close to matching a line from a speech of Eliphaz in Job 22:19-20 (the context describes how the wicked misperceive God and his judgment): "The righteous see it and are glad; / the innocent laugh them to scorn, / saying, 'Surely our adversaries are cut off, / and what they left, the fire has consumed.'" The joy of the righteous also comes to expression in several psalms (e.g., 32:11; 33:1; 68:4 [Eng. v. 3]; 97:12). That the righteous in the transformed circumstances of Jubilees 23 should be happy is expected, but the writer does not clarify whether "the righteous" are the same people as "the servants" who rise and "see great peace" at the beginning of the verse. The point may seem picayune, but it affects one's interpretation of vv. 30-31. Early commentators did not deal with whether "the servants" and "the righteous" were identical; they seem to have assumed that they were two designations for the same people. The view is understandable, but the writer offers somewhat differing predictions for them:

Servants: God heals them, they rise, see great peace, and God expels his enemies.

Righteous: They see, praise, rejoice, and see their punishments/curses on their enemies.

In his analysis of the passage, Paul Volz argued that the two labels designated two groups. That is, he thought the servants at the beginning of v. 30 and the righteous mentioned later in the verse were not the same people. For him, Jub 23:30-31 does not stand in chronological continuity with vv. 26-29, whose coverage of the future extends to the time when people live to one thousand years of age; rather, they speak of the situation at the beginning of the time of deliverance as one can tell from the references to defeating or removing enemies and healing of the servants.[153] The righteous (whose bones rest in the earth while their spirits rejoice according to v. 31) may have been martyrs who had died just before the time of deliverance pictured in v. 30. They had suffered violent deaths, and for that reason the writer notes that their bones are at rest (in v. 31). Their spirits are,

---

150 For Werman, Ps 37:11, 10 underlie the reference here to "peace" for the righteous and later to their not seeing the wicked (*Jubilees*, 361); throughout this section of her commentary on chap. 23 she does not refer to Isaiah 65 or 66.

151 Although Charles and others translate "they [the servants] will drive out their enemies," the preferred readings are singular forms so that God is the one who drives out his enemies (see the textual notes). This means that one should not understand the rising of the servants as their setting out for warfare against their foes.

152 Hanneken, *Subversion*, 155-56, 164.

153 Davenport too thinks vv. 24-31 are not sequential (*Eschatology*, 39, 41); "Then" at the beginning of v. 30 (or "At that time," as he translates it) points to the same periods to which vv. 24 and 26 refer—"the end of Israel's predicament and of the return to Torah" (p. 39).

however, in a blessed place (not specified, perhaps with God) from which they see the good happening to the Lord's servants and delight in what they observe.[154]

Most experts have read the first sentence in v. 31—"Their bones will rest in the earth, and their spirits will be very happy"—as referring to physical death and ongoing spiritual life (cf. 1 Enoch 100:5). The term "bones" probably comes from Isa 66:14 ("your *bones* [NRSV: bodies] shall flourish like the grass"). The bodies of the righteous dead remain entombed but their spirits live on. As Charles wrote, "when the righteous die, their spirits will enter into a blessed immortality."[155] Volz came to a similar conclusion,[156] but Davenport maintains on rather general grounds that there is no division of the person here into body and soul. Rather, the righteous dead remain in their graves yet are somehow restless until they have been avenged.[157]

Berger has advanced a different proposal: he wonders whether the bodies in the earth are those of the enemies whom God expels in v. 30, as they are the last group named before the references to "Their bones" and "their spirits" in v. 31.[158] Read in this way, there would be no conflict between what happens to the bones and the spirits: the bones would be those of the enemies, and the spirits would designate the righteous people who continue to live. Berger thinks that the servants and the righteous are the same groups, and the joy they experience (vv. 30 and 31) is that mentioned in v. 29. Consequently, the passage deals not with the topic of resurrection but with the people living at the time; they are the ones who see punishments executed on the wicked. Though Berger's creative proposal has advantages, its decisive flaw is that it assumes an abrupt but unmarked change of subject from the first verb in v. 31 to the second. On Berger's reading the sentence would say: "Their [the enemies'] bones will rest in the earth and [but] their [the righteous'] spirits will be very happy." Just as it is implausible that "the enemies" would be the subject of "will be very happy," so it is unlikely that they are the referent of "Their bones will rest in the earth." It makes better sense of the passage to understand "the righteous," the subject of the preceding verb ("They will see," v. 30), as the subject of both "will rest" and "will be very happy."[159] The passage, therefore, does not speak about the resurrection of the righteous but only about the ongoing existence of their spirits. As noted above, the writer says regarding Abraham that he "fell asleep forever, and was gathered to his ancestors" (23:1); he will say the same about Isaac (36:18) and Jacob (45:13), and for none of them does he mention a resurrection. The eschatology of the author in this respect is consistent with the implications of his base text, Isaiah,[160] which

---

154 Volz, *Jüdische Eschatologie von Daniel bis Akiba* (Tübingen: Mohr Siebeck, 1903) 24-25. Hoffmann (*Die Toten*, 100-101), Hans Clemens Cavallin (*Life after Death: Paul's Argument for the Resurrection of the Dead in 1 Cor 15* [ConBNT 7.1; Lund: Gleerup, 1974] 38), and Sverre Aalen (*Heilsverlangen und Heilsverwirklichung: Studien zur Erwartung des Heils in der apokalyptischen Literatur des antiken Judentums und im ältesten Christentum* [ALGHJ 21; Leiden: Brill, 1990] 18-19) accept Volz's explanation. Aalen thinks it unlikely, however, that the martyrs are with God; rather, they are in Sheol (understanding it as a place for the righteous and the wicked). If they are in Sheol, the picture of it would differ from the joyless place depicted in the HB, since the righteous are happy here (see Hoffmann, *Die Toten*, 102). Nickelsburg refers to Volz's interpretation and considers it plausible (*Resurrection*, 32-33).

155 Charles, *Eschatology*, 240; *Jubilees*, 150-51. Others who have adopted the position are Hoffmann, *Die Toten*, 101-4; Nickelsburg, *Resurrection*, 31-33; Caquot, "Jubilés," 729 n. to v. 30; Endres, *Biblical Interpretation*, 59-60 (though he seems hesitant); Émile Puech, *La croyance des Esséniens en la vie future: Immortalité, resurrection, vie éternelle? Histoire d'une croyance dans le Judaïsme ancien* (2 vols.; EBib 21-22; Paris: Gabalda, 1993) 1:103-5; Bautch, "Afterlife," 217.

156 Volz, *Jüdische Eschatologie*, 25. He refers to *b. Šabb.* 152b, where various passages are under discussion, including Eccl 12:7: "and the dust returns to the earth as it was, and the breath [spirit] returns to God who gave it." This too could be interpreted as envisaging a corpse in the ground and a spirit remaining alive. See also Aalen, *Heilsverlangen*, 18.

157 Davenport, *Eschatology*, 40, esp. n. 2. He thinks the bones and spirits are somehow parallel to each other and that "[m]an is a unity, even in death." For a negative reaction to Davenport's reading, see Cavallin, *Life after Death*, 37-38.

158 Berger, *Jubiläen*, 446 n. e to v. 30.

159 For another negative verdict on Berger's view, see Puech, *La croyance*, 1:104 n. 14.

160 So Aalen, *Heilsverlangen*, 20-21.

also speaks of people someday living long times but eventually dying though their descendants and name endure far into the future (e.g., Isa 66:14, 22; see also 26:19).[161]

The final line in v. 31 is in part a reworking of Exod 20:5-6 // Deut 5:9-10. As in the Decalogue, so here the line pairs divine punishment on some with his favor toward others: "punishing children for the iniquity of parents, to the third and fourth generation of those who reject me, but showing steadfast love to the thousandth generation [lit., to thousands] of those who love me and keep my commandments." The children of Jubilees 23 had inaugurated the great change by beginning "to study the laws, to seek out the commands, and to return to the right way" (v. 26). The Lord rewards such actions by showing his kindness to thousands, just as people now live to one thousand years.[162] In Isaiah 66 too the Lord promises judgment on his enemies and his reassuring presence with his servants (v. 14 and vv. 15-16), but again Jubilees does not adopt the fiery, military vocabulary of judgment in Isa 66:15-16.

32 Command That Moses Write the Message

The unusual chapter ends with the angel once more turning directly to Moses with a command that he record "these words." The phrasing of the verse makes it clear that Moses is to write something regarding what he has just heard from the angel, material etched on the heavenly tablets. Since the message is on the tablets (which contain information not only about the past but about the future as well), it is certain and unchangeable forever. In most of Jubilees 2-50 Moses is pictured as writing down the contents of Genesis 1–Exodus 24, either in the form they take in Genesis–Exodus or in Jubilees; that would not apply in the present case since most of chap. 23 falls outside the contents of what one finds in Genesis–Exodus. As a result, Kugel's suggestion that the angel in v. 32 is telling Moses to write down Psalm 90 is very appealing. That Psalm, attributed to Moses, the man of God, exercised a heavy influence on Jub 23:8-31 and may reasonably be seen as Moses's subsequent record of what the angel had revealed to him in chap. 23.[163] Since Moses is writing down the contents of Jubilees as well, he has also penned Jubilees 23 at the angel's dictation.

Kugel's suggestion that v. 32 is to be attributed to his interpolator is less appealing. True, the verse mentions the heavenly tablets, but there seems to be no compelling reason for assigning it to anyone but the author. He offers two reasons: (1) "In keeping with the Interpolator's ideology, the predictions of this chapter must all appear on the Heavenly Tablets; he therefore inserted this one sentence attribution."[164] (2) "In keeping with the traditional role of the 'tablets of heaven' before *Jubilees*, the angel of the presence could not simply have told Moses of the future of humanity on his own authority; he must have learned all this from the Heavenly Tablets. The Interpolator therefore inserted this one-sentence attribution at the end of the original author's predictions."[165] A question is why anyone would feel a need to assert this sentence, much less add it, in a text that has presupposed this setting for all revelations since the end of chap. 1. If someone interpolated 23:32, he was not supplying new or helpful information. The author of the book had written similar words in 1:29 where he was first describing the revelatory situation and where he also used "testimony" in connection with the contents of the tablets.

---

161 How and whether the teaching here harmonizes with Jub 5:13-16 and 36:9-10 regarding a "great day of judgment" is a problem discussed in the Introduction. Cavallin thinks there is no relation between the present passage and the statements about a future judgment elsewhere in the book (*Life after Death*, 38).

162 Bautch draws attention to the covenantal nature of the blessing articulated in Exod 20:6 ("Afterlife," 217).

163 Kugel, "Jubilees Apocalypse," 331-33, 336-37.

164 Kugel, "Interpolations," 264.

165 Kugel, *Walk through* Jubilees, 287. On p. 133 he says, "This last sentence was intended to assert that Moses' knowledge of future events (as evidenced in Psalm 90, authored by him) derived from the Heavenly Tablets." For the same as this last suggestion, see Kugel, "Jubilees," 379.

Excursus: Werman's Theory about Chapter 23[166]

Werman, who advocates for a greater Hellenistic impact on Jubilees than other scholars have, finds not Hellenistic but Classical Greek influence in Jub 23:9-31. She has reconstructed behind this section a Jewish work that she names a "Composition on the Division of the Times" that was written to defend the veracity of the Bible regarding the great ages of the prediluvians. The author of Jubilees, she thinks, adopted the source and added to it a layer having to do with the events of his age and the struggles taking place in it. The Jewish-Hellenistic work "Composition on the Division of the Times" itself contains a reworking of Hesiod's four ages of human history in *Works and Days* (Gold, Silver, Bronze, Iron; Hesiod himself reworked yet earlier Persian models).

Her theory involves several distinguishable theses that should be evaluated.

1. The author of Jubilees drew on a source in chap. 23. The thesis is quite plausible in that the section has some unusual features compared with the remainder of Jubilees.[167] One is that it does not, in its survey of history, employ the chronological units of jubilees and weeks of years so frequent elsewhere in the book. There are several references to jubilees in chap. 23, but they do not function as units of world chronology but measure the lengths of individuals' lives. The only instance in which this is not true is v. 19, where "jubilee" figures in a list of calendrical items sinners will forget. Also, the text does not refer to angels or to Prince Mastema and his demons when it speaks about the behavior of people.[168] Omission of the latter group and its leader is surprising because so much of the section treats human wickedness—something that Mastema and the demons cause and encourage.

2. The source "Composition on the Division of the Times" was written by a Hellenistic Jew who reworked Hesiod's scheme of the four ages in human history. Werman detects influence from Hesiod because (a) 23:9-31 divides history into four ages and (b) there are strong similarities between the descriptions of them and the ways in which Hesiod writes about his four. In the "Composition on the Division of the Times" she finds these four ages:

From creation to the flood (referenced in v. 9)
From the flood to Moses (vv. 9-10)
From Moses to the time of the author (vv. 11-14; on p. 26 she includes v. 15)
From the time of the author to the eschaton (vv. 17-19, 25; on p. 26 she includes vv. 25, 18-19a, 17, 16a).[169]

The sections on the last two ages are arranged chiastically.

A fundamental flaw in Werman's case regarding a composition influenced by the four ages in Hesiod is that Jub 23:9-31 does not seem to separate history into four units. It does indeed refer to the times before and after the flood and it speaks about the time after Moses and a great reversal in the future, but it does not give any hint of a division of eras around the time of the author. There is more likely one long period of ever-worsening decline that commences after the flood, passes through the time of Abraham and that of Moses, and continues until the reversal of ages in the eschaton. There is no indication that anything changed significantly in the time of Moses or in that of the author,[170] such that ages took a sharper drop downward when they were living (see the commentary on v. 15 above).

Regarding the similarities with Hesiod's scheme—they extend even to the level of language—she offers

---

166 She presents her views in *Jubilees*, 25-27 (part of her introduction in which she surveys sources the author used), 64-65 (on the debt of Jubilees to what she calls "Pseudo-Moses"), and 351-52, 355-61 (parts of her commentary on chap. 23).

167 Werman infers that the author of Jubilees did not compose the work because he inserted into it another layer of material and did so in an inelegant fashion (*Jubilees*, 25). The unusual features noted in the paragraph above are not ones to which she draws attention.

168 Hanneken, *Subversion*, e.g., 84-88.

169 She groups vv. 27-29, 31 (at least in part) as belonging to the earlier text (*Jubilees*, 355, 361), but v. 30 and part of v. 31 are sectarian additions in which a distinction between the righteous and others is introduced. Her ascription of v. 29 to the source is strange in that the verse contains language characteristic of the author (no satan or evil one).

170 In the case of Moses one could appeal to v. 11, where the angel predicts "All the generations that will come into being from now [when Moses is on Mount Sinai] until the great day of judgment" as suggesting the time of Moses as marking a change of eras (although no such claim is made), but the same verse shows there is no such change at the time of the author since the pattern it predicts is to prevail from the time of Moses to the day of judgment.

a table (p. 27) in which she suggests parallels between vv. 12-13 (regarding the present) and Hesiod's Age of Iron (*Works and Days* 176-78); vv. 19a, 25 (the future) and his Age of Iron (183-89; cf. line 180); v. 28 (the eschaton) and his Ages of Gold (113-14) and Silver (130-31); and v. 31 and his Age of Gold (121-22). In other words, there are on her reckoning parallels only for the first two and the last of Hesiod's four ages and they do not appear separately (note parallels with both the Golden and Silver ages for v. 28) or in the same order—the largest difference is that the Golden Age traits appear not at the beginning, as in Hesiod, but at the end in Jubilees 23. Moreover, while there are indeed some parallels (e.g., people of the Age of Gold after living wonderful lives become spirits, or in the Age of Iron they grow old quickly and there is strife between groups [though it is especially between parents and children]), the differences far outweigh them. For example, Hesiod's pure spirits (the form in which the people of the Golden Age survive) rove over the earth and act as guardians of humanity; Zeus destroys the people of the Silver Age; the Age of Iron is actually a fifth for Hesiod; and there is no blessed future in *Works and Days*. If there were a "Composition on the Division of the Times," it divided history into two ages (pre- and post-flood), not into four and thus was very likely not influenced by Hesiod's pattern.

3. The author of Jubilees inserted into the "Composition on the Division of the Times" another, sectarian layer in which he describes the difficulties of his own day and makes halakhic charges that would apply only to Israel, not to all of humanity as in the older composition. In these places he was influenced by the text Werman calls "Pseudo-Moses" from Qumran.[171] The author of Jubilees took from this earlier work material dealing with two particular generations. In "Pseudo-Moses" the first of these generations lived in the period before the decrees of Antiochus IV and the second in the time after them. The author of Jubilees speaks of this first generation in vv. 16b and 19b, and the second comes under consideration in vv. 21-24. In vv. 23-24, however, he fails to follow the paradigm in Pseudo-Moses. In Jubilees the first evil generation gives rise to a civil war and leads to the emergence of an additional sinful generation—the one that receives punishment. No punishing enemy separates the two as in "Pseudo-Moses" (Jubilees does not mention Antiochus's decrees in chap. 23).

There is no doubting that Jubilees and 4Q390 share vocabulary in chap. 23 as they do in chap. 1 (see the commentary on these chapters).[172] The questions are whether one borrowed from the other and, if so, which did the borrowing. However those questions are answered,[173] there appears to be an insufficient basis for claiming that Jubilees is borrowing from the historical sketch in 4Q390. The two differ considerably. 4Q390, for instance, speaks of various jubilee periods in its sketch of the future, whereas Jubilees, as noted above, does not. In addition, where 4Q390 refers to the angels of Mastemot several times, the section in Jubilees refers neither to Mastema nor to angels. In addition, Jubilees 23 may not differentiate between two generations in the passages Werman assigns to the added set of verses. They refer to an evil generation in vv. 14, 15, 16 (called just "that generation"), and 22 and never distinguish between them by indicating that one preceded the other.

Finally, Werman's understanding of the material that she assigns to the author rather than to the "Composition on the Division of the Times" seems inaccurate. It is probably not the case that the author of Jubilees added to the source text charges that apply only to Israel or an inappropriate distinction between the righteous and the wicked. Right from the beginning of the unit vv. 9-31 the writer indicated that not all people fell under the heavy condemnations: Abraham was an exception, as he notes,

---

171 Dimant, at an early stage in her work on 4Q390, labeled it "Pseudo-Moses"; in the official edition she determined that it belonged to the Apocryphon of Jeremiah C that she identified in a number of other copies (see DJD 30). Werman has argued that Dimant's original identification was correct and therefore calls 4Q390 "Pseudo-Moses" ("Epochs and End-Time: The 490-Year Scheme in Second Temple Literature," *DSD* 13 [2006] 229-55; this is an English translation of the essay "Times and End-Time in Second Temple Literature," *Tarbiz* 72 [2004] 37-57). Whether 4Q390 is a separate Mosaic work or part of the Apocryphon of Jeremiah is not germane to the question under discussion here.

172 A clear instance is 4Q390 1 8 ("they will forget statute and festival and Sabbath and covenant" [trans. Dimant, *DSSR* 6:113]) compared with Jub 23:19: "For they have forgotten commandment, covenant, festival, month, Sabbath, jubilee, and every verdict."

173 Hanneken details points of contact between the two and considers Jubilees the older work ("Status," 407-28).

and one may assume that Moses was as well. Both of these characters figure in the verses that Werman assigns to the "Composition on the Division of the Times" (vv. 9-11). It is reasonable to regard the children mentioned in vv. 16 and 26 as further examples of righteous exceptions, so that the references to the righteous in v. 30 and to those who love God in v. 31 are not inappropriate. There were probably all along, as the HB indicates and Jubilees 23 suggests, righteous people who, like Abraham, kept the covenant when all others fell away.

In summary, the author of Jubilees may well have incorporated a source into 23:9-31, but that source appears not to have divided history into four ages or units. As a result it is unlikely the writer of the source was working with Hesiod's Ages of Gold, Silver, Bronze, and Iron in surveying history. Moreover, while there are parallels in language between parts of 23:9-31 and 4Q390, there is no clear evidence that the writer of Jubilees took those words and phrases from 4Q390 and none at all that he borrowed or reshaped what 4Q390 has to say about two generations that lived before and after the time of Antiochus IV's decrees against Judaism. In fact, the verses and parts of verses that Werman identifies as additions of the author of Jubilees fit within the scheme of vv. 9-31.

Excursus: The Chronology of Abraham's Life[174]

Several dates in Abraham's life proved important to chronographers who were grappling with issues such as when the 400 years to the exodus mentioned in Gen 15:13 or the 430 years named in Exod 12:41 had begun. That complicated problem seems not to have been a major concern for the author of Jubilees, as neither of these numbers, if subtracted from 2410, the year of the exodus, leads one back to a significant event in Abraham's life. The only connection between an important date in his life and the later history of the nation seems to be that he received the call to go to Canaan in 1951, five hundred years before Israel would enter it.

While the 400/430 years calculations were not his focus, the writer clearly was interested in the chronology of Abraham's life. He took over several numbers from Genesis and added a series of dates to them to document when key events occurred. From Genesis he took these numbers:

1. Abram was 75 when the order to leave Haran came (cf. Gen 12:4; Jub 12:16-24—his age can be deduced from the chronological formula in v. 16)
2. Abram was 86 when Ishmael was born/named (Gen 16:16; Jub 14:24)
3. Abraham was 100 and Sarah 90 when Isaac was born (Gen 17:24 and 21:5; see Jub 15:17)
4. Abraham died at age 175 (Gen 25:7; Jub 22:7; 23:8).

Other dates in his life could be inferred. For instance, Sarah died at age 127 (Gen 23:1; Jub 19:7) so that Abraham, her senior by ten years, would have been 137 at the time. Isaac was 40 when he married Rebekah (Gen 25:20) so that Abraham would have been 140; and Isaac was 60 when the twins were born (Gen 25:26), so that Abraham would have been 160.

The fact that the writer of Jubilees took a series of numerical figures from Genesis, including Abraham's age at death, suggests that he was intentionally following the chronology present in the older text.

Nevertheless, if one examines the dates that the author expressed through his system of jubilee periods, weeks of years, and years, discrepancies with the explicit ages he claimed for Abraham arise.

1. Abraham received the summons to go to Canaan when he was 75 (Jub 12:16), but he did not leave Haran until two years later when he would have been 77 (12:28). So there is a two-year difference with Genesis.
2. Although both texts say explicitly that Abram was 86 when Ishmael was born/named, the date that the author specifies in his jubilean system (14:24) makes him 89. The gap between it and the explicit age is now three years.
3. Where Genesis and Jubilees say that Abraham was 100 years of age when Isaac was born, in the jubilean system he was 111 (16:15 [year of the world 1987]). That is, the three-year gap has widened by eight more.
4. A series of subsequent dates are largely consistent with the one in 16:15 (eleven higher than in Genesis). So, for example, Abraham was 148 years when Sarah died, when he should have been 137, and he was 151 (19:10) when Isaac married (at age 40) when he should have been 140. At the time when Esau and Jacob were born (Isaac was 60, Gen 25:26) his age is given as 170 (Jub 19:13) while according to Genesis he should have been 160. So, the date in the jubilee system is one year closer now to the explicit or implied age of Abraham.
5. Both texts put Abraham's final age at 175, but the date expressed in the jubilee system yields an age of 184. The number in the system is now one year closer to the expected year, just nine years above

---

174 See VanderKam, "Chronology," 532–40.

it, than it was for the date when Esau and Jacob arrived.

Experts have advanced different theories to account for the divergences between the explicit ages and the ones entailed by the overall chronology. Wiesenberg, as noted before, thinks a series of revisions to the chronology occurred,[175] while Segal maintains that the compiler of Jubilees imposed his comprehensive chronology upon rewritten stories whose internal dates at times conflicted with the larger chronology.[176] Neither of these theories provides a likely solution to the problems presented above. They either assume arbitrary date changes or carelessness by the author in not noticing that his system disagreed with his sources.

K. Dobos thinks that the writer of Jubilees composed a kind of imaginary history supplied with dates that often made little chronological sense but served to separate events in Abraham's life by seven years or multiples of seven.[177] So, it is a mistake to think the author was trying to follow the numbers of Genesis; his dates had other aims. There is no doubt that in the Abraham stories (and elsewhere) sevens were important to the writer—something that has been noted[178]—but some of the date pairings that Dobos cites leave one wondering why the author would associate them. For example, Abram invented a plow in the year of the world 1891 when he was 15 (note, not 14); this event precedes by 63 (9 × 7) years Abram's first stay at Bethel (1954).[179] True enough, but is there any connection between the events? It seems unlikely there is.

It may not be possible to explain how all the numbers now in the text of Jubilees arose, but some suggestions can be made. It is difficult to believe that the writer was careless about numbers and failed to notice contradictions when his jubilees system was so important to his message. Further, it does not seem as if the discrepancies are haphazard when, once a year was established (say, Abraham's age at Isaac's birth), the calculations for the dates over the next several chapters build on it.

The readings from Hebrew fragments offer support for dates in the Ethiopic text of Jubilees at some points (12:16, 28; 21:1) but also reveal that, to no one's surprise, mistakes occurred in the process of transmission. 4QJub^d (4Q219) ii:35 (Jub 22:1) shows that, as Dillmann had hypothesized,[180] the jubilee number in the Ethiopic copies (44) was one too high. Is there a similar way to account for the other discrepancies in the dates for Abraham's life? Or could orthographic or similar minor confusions have led to mistakes, if they are mistakes?

The dates listed above should now be examined with these considerations in mind.

1. For Abram's age at his departure from Haran (77 rather than the 75 of Gen 12:4), Jub 12:16 does place his call to leave in the year when he was 75. That call came on 7/1 at the beginning of the six-month rainy season during which the angel taught Hebrew to Abram and assisted him in studying the books of his ancestors. Hence, the teaching period (months 7–12) prevented him from leaving until the next year. By delaying his departure still another year, the writer was able to place a key event in Abram's life in the seventh year of a week of years (12:28; the reading "seven" is supported by a Hebrew fragment). So, this two-year deviation may actually be a deliberate move by the author who still retained the age of 75 for when the Angel of the Presence summoned Abram to leave for Canaan. In this case, one might wonder whether there was another benefit for the author in delaying his departure. If he accepted the chronology according to which his father Terah lived 145 years as in the SP, then he would have died in the year Abram received his call. The dutiful Abram thus would have tended to his father's remains and departed a reasonable time after his death. However, this theory does not fit the facts, since his father was still alive the year Abram left (Abram, aged 77, requested his permission to leave in 12:28).

2. In the case of the next divergence, when Ishmael was born—an additional one year besides the two years from #1—the surplus year could have been added when the author inferred that Ishmael's birth must have occurred in the year after the covenant between the pieces described earlier in the same chapter. The agreement took place on 3/15

---

175 Wiesenberg, "Jubilee of Jubilees," 3–40.
176 Segal, *Jubilees*, 45–82.
177 Dobos, "Consolation of History," 84–91.
178 VanderKam, "Chronology," 539. The writer is fond of dating events to the first or the seventh year of a week of years (see the chart for the dates in the Abraham chapters of Jubilees on pp. 533–34). There are twenty-seven dates in these chapters, and in seven of them the event occurs in year 1 of a week and in five it takes place in year 7. So, almost half (twelve) of the dates fall in these years.
179 Dobos, "Consolation of History," 88.
180 Dillmann, "Jubiläen," 71 n. 14.

in the fourth year of a week of years, and Abram took Hagar as a wife after this. Hence Ishmael would very likely have been born early the following year. In this case there is another possibility: a mistake occurred with the previous date (for the covenant) that perhaps should have been in the third rather than the fourth year of the week (the Greek ordinals "third" [τριτος] and "fourth" [τεταρτος] could have been confused).

3. For the eleven-year gap at the time of Isaac's birth, that is, eight years beyond the three-year margin at the birth of Ishmael, a simple suggestion is that both the year number and the week number were mistakenly increased by one (year 6, week 4 should be year 5 week 3).

4. For each of the remaining two instances—Abraham's age at the birth of the twins and at his death—the eleven-year gap shrinks by one, so that one could posit a simple mistake by a copyist or translator.

The numbers could have resulted in these ways, but there is at present no way to check the suggestions. Whatever the reasons for them may be, the gaps, some of which may indeed have resulted from errors in transmission, did not affect the comprehensive chronology in the book, according to which Israel leaves Egypt in 2410 and arrives at the border of Canaan in 2450. One reason that the discrepancies did not ruin the entire system is that there is insufficient information in Genesis and Exodus for the chronology of Jacob's sons and their offspring until Moses's time. Hence, the chronology for the period after Jacob could be adjusted to fit the writer's aims.

24

1/ After Abraham's death, the Lord blessed his son Isaac. He set out from Hebron and went and lived during the first year of the third week[a] of this jubilee [2073] at the well of the vision[b] for seven years. 2/ During the first year of the fourth week [2080] a famine — different than the first famine[a] that had occurred in Abraham's lifetime — began in the land.

3/ When Jacob was cooking lentil porridge, Esau came hungry[a] from the field. He said to his brother Jacob, "Give me[b] some of this *red*[c] porridge." But Jacob said to him, "Hand over to me your birthright that belongs to the firstborn, and then I will give you food and some of this porridge as well." 4/ Esau said to himself, "I will die.[a] What good[b] will this right of the firstborn do?" So he[c] said to Jacob, "I (hereby) give (it) to you." 5/ Jacob said to him,[a] "Swear to me today." So he swore to him. 6/ Then Jacob gave the food and porridge to his brother Esau,[a] and he ate until he was full. Esau repudiated the right of the firstborn. This is why he was named Esau and Edom:[b] because of the *red* porridge that[c] Jacob[d] gave him in exchange for his right of the firstborn. 7/ So Jacob became the older one, but Esau was lowered from his prominent position.

8/ As there was a famine over the land, Isaac[a] set out[b] to go down to Egypt during the second year of this[c] week [2081]. He went to Gerar to the Philistine king Abimelech. 9/ The Lord appeared to him and told him, "Do not go down to Egypt.[a] Stay in the land that I will tell you.[b] Live as a foreigner in this[c] land. I will be with you and bless you, 10/ because I will give this entire land to you and your[a] descendants. I will carry out the terms of my oath that I swore to your father Abraham. I will make your descendants as numerous as the stars of the sky. I will give this entire land to your descendants. 11/ All the peoples of the earth will be blessed through your descendants because of the fact that your father obeyed me and kept my obligations,[a] commands,[b] laws,[c] statutes, and covenant. Now obey me[d] and live in this[e] land."

12/ He lived in Gerar for three[a] weeks of years. 13/ Abimelech gave orders[a] as follows regarding him and everything that belonged to him: "Anyone[b] who touches him[c] or[d] anything that belongs to him is to die." 14/ Isaac prospered among the Philistines and possessed much property:[a] cattle, sheep, camels, donkeys, and much property.[b] 15/ He planted[a] seeds in the land of the Philistines,[b] and he harvested one hundredfold.[c] When Isaac had become very great, the Philistines grew jealous of him. 16/ (As for) all the wells[a] that Abraham's servants had dug during Abraham's lifetime — the Philistines covered[b] them up after Abraham's death and filled them with dirt. 17/ Then Abimelech told Isaac, "Leave us because you have become much too great for us." So Isaac left that place[a] during the first year of the seventh[b] week [2102]. He lived as a foreigner[c] in the valleys of Gerar.

18/ They again dug the water wells[a] which the servants of his father Abraham had dug and[b] the Philistines had covered up after his father Abraham's[c] death. He called them by the names that his father Abraham[d] had given them. 19/ Isaac's servants dug wells[a] in the wadi[b] and found flowing water.[c] Then the shepherds of Gerar quarreled with Isaac's shepherds and said, "This[d] water is ours." So Isaac named that well Difficult[e] "because they have been difficult for us."[f] 20/ They[a] dug a second well,[b] and they fought about it[c] too. He named it Hostility.[d] When he had set out,[e] they dug[f] another well[g] but did not quarrel about it. He named it Wide.[h] Isaac said, "Now the Lord has enlarged (a place) for us, and we have increased[i] in numbers on the land."

21/ He went up from there to the well of the oath during the first year of the first week in the forty-fourth jubilee [2108]. 22/ The Lord appeared to him that night — on the first of the first month — and said to him, "I am the God of your father Abraham. Do not[a] be afraid because I am with you and will bless you. I will certainly make your descendants as numerous[b] as the sand of the earth[c] for the sake of my servant[d] Abraham." 23/ There[a] he built the altar that[b] his father Abraham[c] had first built. He called on the Lord's name and offered a sacrifice to the God of his father Abraham.

24/ They[a] dug a well[b] and found[c] flowing water. 25/ But when Isaac's servants[a] dug another well,[b] they did not find water. They went and told Isaac that they had not found water. Isaac said, "On this very day[c] I have sworn an oath to the Philistines; now this has happened[d] to us." 26/ He named that place the well[a] of the oath because there he had sworn an oath to[b] Abimelech, his companion Ahuzzath, and his guard[c] Phicol. 27/ On that day[a] Isaac realized that he had sworn an oath to them[b] under pressure[c] to make peace with them.[d] 28/ On that day Isaac cursed the Philistines and said, "May the Philistines be cursed from among all peoples at the day[a] of anger and wrath.[b] May the Lord make them into (an object of) disgrace and a curse, into (an object of) anger and wrath in the hands of the sinful nations[c] and[d] in the hands of the Kittim.[e] 29/ Whoever[a] escapes[b] from the enemy's sword and from the Kittim may the just nation[c] in judgment eradicate from beneath the sky, for they will become enemies and opponents to my sons during their times[d] on the earth. 30/ They[a] will have no one left[b] or anyone who is rescued[c] on the day of judgmental anger,[d] for[e] all the descendants of the Philistines (are meant) for destruction, eradication, and removal[f] from the earth.[g] All of Caphtor[h] will no longer[i] have either name or descendants[j] left[k] upon the earth.

31/ For[a] even if he should go up to the sky,
from there he would come down;[b]
even if he should become powerful on the earth,[c]
from there he will be torn out.
Even if he should hide himself among the nations,[d]
from there[e] he will be uprooted;
even if he should go down to Sheol,
there[f] his punishment will increase.[g]
There he will have no peace.

32/ Even if he should go[a] into captivity through the power of those[b] who seek his life,[c]
they will kill him[d] along the way.[e]
There will remain for him neither name nor descendants[f] on the entire earth,
because he is going to an eternal curse."

33/ This[a] is the way it has been written and inscribed[b] regarding him[c] on the heavenly tablets—to do[d] (this) to him on the day of judgment so that he may be eradicated[e] from the earth.[f]

Textual Notes

1a the third week] "its third week" 9.
b   the vision] "his vision and" 21. pr. "the oath of" 38.
2a famine] om. 38.
3a hungry] A number of MSS. attest a suffix on the adj. form: *reḥubu* (12 17 39 44 48 63), *reḥibo* (an infinitive 38), or *reḥbu* (42 47). They seem to express the idea "he, being hungry," but it does not affect the meaning.
b   his brother . . . Give me] "give me, my brother, so I can eat" 44.
c   red] As Dillmann ("Jubiläen," 71 n. 23) observed, the mistaken reading "wheat" in Eth. resulted from confusing πυρον ("of wheat") and πυρρον ("red") in Gen 25:30. The same mistake occurs in v. 6. See VanderKam, *Jubilees* 2:150.
4a die] + "in hunger" 35 44 58.
b   What good] + "to me" 35.
c   he] "Esau" 63.
5a to him] om. 12 17 20 39[c] 47 48 63.
6a to his brother Esau (om. Esau 12)] om. 17 (it adds these words later in the sentence.
b   Edom] There are variations on the name in the copies. Ms. 12 reads: "his birthright/right of firstborn was not pleasing."
c   that] "and" 12.
d   Jacob] pr. "to" 12 44.
8a Isaac] om. 38.
b   set out] "wanted" 63.
c   this] om. 21.
9a Egypt] pr. "the region of" 44.
b   I will tell you] "I will give you" 38; "I will show you" 44.
c   this] om. 44.
10a your] pr. "all" 63.

11a my obligations] "my voice/word" 21 42 47 48; om. 39 58.
b commands] "command" 21 38 44 58ᵗ 63.
c laws] "law" 21 38 39 44 58 63.
d me (lit., "my voice/word")] + "and my commandment" 21.
e this] om. 9 21 38.
12a three] "one" 17.
13a gave orders] + "to him" 9 20 21 39; + "to them" 42 47; Lat. reads neither plus.
b (any)one (lit., "[every] man"))] om. 12; Lat. *homo*. Ms. 12 reads "from a man/people" after "touches him."
c touches him] om. "him" 21; "quarrels with him" 48 (this verb involves a switch of consonants from "touches": *zlf* instead of *lkf* (*z* and *k* have also been confused). Lat. *molestaverit eum*, "troubles him." Eth. agrees with Gen 26:11 (VanderKam, *Jubilees* 2:152).
d or] om. 21; Lat. *aut*.
14a much property] Eth. lacks a conjunction after "much property," suggesting that the following nouns are a list of what was meant by the general "much property." Lat. reads *et* after "property," implying that the following nouns are in addition to "much property" (VanderKam, *Jubilees* 2:152). Possibly *et* means "even, namely" here. Both Eth. and Lat. phrase the matter differently than Gen 26:14.
b and much property] om. 44. Lat.: "and many servants" (*et ministerium magnum*). Both may represent understandings of עבדה in Gen 26:14. Lat. *ministerium*, like Hebrew עבדה, can mean "occupation, work" and "retinue." Eth. *ṭerit* means "property, possessions" and may render מקנה, which also appears in Gen 26:14. See VanderKam, *Jubilees* 2:152.
15a He planted] 21 38 48 58 63 and Lat. (*seminavit*) read a sg., as does Gen 26:12. Although the pl. has strong backing in the Eth. copies, the sg. is to be preferred in this context (against VanderKam, *Jubilees* 2:152).
b the Philistines] "the people of the Philistines" 20.
c one hundredfold] So Lat.; Eth. "one hundred ears." The two renderings are reflections of the same original read differently. שערים was interpreted by the Old Latin and possibly Syriac Gen 26:12 as "barley, grains." This reading is the one in Eth. Jubilees. The other versions read it as "measures" as in Lat. Jubilees (VanderKam, *Jubilees* 2:153).
16a the wells] "the well" 9 12 17 38 42 44 63; om. 21.
b covered] "would cover" 39 47.
17a that place (lit., "from there")] om. 44; Lat. *inde*.
b seventh] 9 25 38 read "seven."
c He lived as a foreigner] "They lived as foreigners" 21; "he lived" 12. Lat. reads instead of the clause "He lived as a foreigner in the valley of Gerar" only the words "with his own (people)." It is likely that a form of the verb גר and the place-name גרר led to omission of the unit; *cum suis* may have been added to fill in for the missing text (VanderKam, *Jubilees* 2:153).
18a wells] "well" 9 12 17 21 38 42ᶜ(?) 44 (+ 63 with a slightly different spelling).
b and] "which" 35 58.
c his father Abraham's] The Eth. copies have the order "of Abraham his father"; MS. 44 and Lat. reverse the two ("his father Abraham").
d Abraham] Lat. lacks the name.
19a wells] "well" 9 21 38 42ᶜ(?) 44 63.
b wadi] The form in the best Eth. copies is *ferānegā*, while 9 12 17 21 42 47 48 58 63 have *fānegā*. Both are attempts at φαραγγι in Gen 26:19, with the latter transcription being defective. Leslau (*Comparative Dictionary*, 162) has a curious entry *fangā* (the spelling in 38 39 44 = "decayed, spoiled, fetid"), adding that Charles translated it "valley" here in Jubilees. Leslau did not notice it is a transcription of a Greek word. See Lat. *torrente*.
c found flowing water] Lat. "found in flowing water"; Rönsch (*Jubiläen*, 40) and Charles (*Ethiopic Version*, 89 n. 5 to Latin) emended *in* to *ibi* ("there").
d This] Lat. lacks the word. Charles (*Jubilees*, 153) explained the Eth. demonstrative as a reflection of a Greek definite article (see το υδωρ in Gen 26:20). The same explanation may apply to the word "that" before "well" (ibid.).
e Difficult ('*eṣub*)] Lat. "Difficulty" = 12 21 ('*eḍab*).
f for us (lit., "with us")] "for them" 21; "for him" 44 (= Gen 26:20); Lat. *nobiscum*.
20a They] "He" 9 38; Lat. has "They."
b well] "wells" 20 25 39 42 47 48ᶜ 58; Lat. has sg.
c it] "them" 9 39 (the former has a fem. pl. form, the latter a masc. pl.); Lat. has "it."
d Hostility] The Eth. *ṣabāb* ("narrow") disagrees with Lat. "Hostility" and the versions of Gen 26:21 ("Contention" = NRSV note). The translator may have selected *ṣabāb* to form an antonym with the name of the next well ("Wide"; so Charles, *Jubilees*, 154). Charles emended *ṣabāb* to *ṣel'*, "Enmity" (*Ethiopic Version*, 88 n. 22; *Jubilees*, 154).
e he had set out] Lat. om; perhaps through parablepsis (see VanderKam, *Jubilees* 2:154). The form '*anśe'a* is not the usual one for this meaning (though an acceptable one; see Dillmann, *Lexicon*, 637); as a result, several MSS. substitute the normal form *tanśe'a* 20 21 35 39 42 47 48 58, while 44 63 have a pl. form of it. Many Eth. copies also add "from there" 12 17 21 35 38 39 42 44 47 48 58 63 as in all the versions of Gen 26:22. Both Dillmann (necessarily) and Charles included it in their texts.
f they dug (= SP Syr Gen 26:22)] "he dug" 9 38 58; Lat. "they dug."
g another well] Lat. improves the nonspecific "another"

of Eth. and the versions of Gen 26:22 to "third." Some Eth. copies again read "wells" 20 25 39 42ᵗ(?) 47 48.
h   Wide] Lat. *capacitas* is in harmony with the versions of Gen 26:22 in reading a noun here; the form in Eth. is an adjective, just as adjectives were employed for the names of the previous two wells (vv. 19, 20).
i   we have increased (= MT SP Syr Gen 26:22)] "who has increased me" 63. Lat., in agreement with LXX OL Eth Gen 26:26, has *multiplicavit nos*.
22a Do not] pr. "and" 25 35 38; Lat. lacks "and."
b   will certainly make . . . numerous] The Eth. text reads an intensifying infinitive (like the Hebrew infinitive absolute), while Lat. and the versions of Gen 26:24 lack one. Its presence may reflect the influence of parallel promises, e.g., Gen 22:17.
c   the sand of the earth] Lat. agrees. It too may come from Gen 22:17, though MT reads "sea" there instead of "earth." Mss. 38 44 58 read "sea" here; oddly, Goldmann and Hartom place הים in their translations.
d   servant] "friend" 21; Lat. *puerum*.
23a There . . . the altar . . . first] Lat. has a lacuna of c. twenty-five letters here. See VanderKam, *Jubilees* 2:155 for proposals for filling in the gap.
b   that . . . first] om. 38 44 (both add "first" later in the sentence).
c   his father Abraham] om. 58; Lat. "his father."
24a They] "He" 9 12 17 21 38ᶜ 39 42 44 48 63; Lat. reads "They."
b   a well] "wells" 20 25; Lat. "a well."
c   (they) found] "(he) found" 9 12 17 21 38 39 42 44 47 48 58 63; Lat. "(they) found." Ms. 21 = "He did not find" (see v. 25).
25a Isaac's servants] Eth. begins the verse with "and" followed by these words; Lat. puts them at the end of the clause. Lat. also reads "once more" (*iterum*), but Eth. lacks such a word.
b   well] "wells" 20 25; Lat. "well."
c   day] "night" 21; Lat. "day."
d   I have sworn . . . now this has happened] Lat. places "Because" before "I have sworn" and lacks a conjunction before "now this has happened." Hence, the meaning in Lat. is "Because I have sworn . . . this has happened." It may be that the original Hebrew read כי before "I have sworn" to mark the following words as a quotation, a fact not recognized in the text behind the Lat. This may have led to omission of a conjunction before "now this has happened." See VanderKam, *Jubilees* 2:156.
26a the well] "the wells" 25; Lat. also reads a sg.
b   to (Abimelech)] om. 21 38ᶜ 47 (this would make Abimelech the subject of "swore," as in Lat., but these copies do not omit "to" before the next two names, thus disagreeing with Lat. The case endings in Lat., where they can be determined, indicate that all three names are in the nominative rather than dative case. The Lat. readings make little sense here, as v. 27 shows.
c   his guard] The Eth. copies have several spellings. *'aqābihu* ("his guard"); but several older copies have forms with -yo- inserted: *'aqabiyohu* 9 25 44; *'aqābāyohu* 12 17; *'eqabayyo* 21—forms not appearing in the lexica. The Latin text has "the leader of his army," which in Eth. would be *'aqābē serwēhu*, an emendation Charles made (*Ethiopic Version*, 90 n. 7). See VanderKam, *Jubilees* 2:156.
27a On that day] om. 21 (added later in the verse); Lat. "on that day."
b   to them] om. 21; "to him" 38. Lat. *ille*, "he" (the subject of *iuravit*). Rönsch (*Jubiläen*, 42) preferred the Latin reading, but Charles (*Ethiopic Text*, 91 n. 1 to Latin) changed *ille* to *illis*.
c   under pressure] Text-critically, the preferred reading is *gefu'*, "oppressed, harmed, wronged" (see Leslau, *Comparative Dictionary*, 183), but a better sense emerges from the noun *gef'*, "oppression, violence, wrongdoing, wrong, etc." (ibid.) read by 9 21 35 39 42 44 47 48 58 63. Lat. is illegible here (see VanderKam, *Jubilees* 2:156).
d   with them] Lat. *cum ipso* ("with him"), which Charles (*Ethiopic Version*, 91 n. 2 to Latin) changed to *cum ipsis* ("with them").
28a at the day] + "of their toil/hardship/trouble at the day of" 21. Lat. agrees with the shorter reading of the other Eth. copies.
b   anger and wrath] "wrath" 9 38; "day of wrath" 44. Lat. *indignatione ire* is odd; *ire*, with no conjunction between the two nouns, should be *irae* (genitive).
c   the sinful nations] "sinful nation" (?) 20 25. Lat. reads two sg. forms: *peccatoris populi*, "the sinful nation."
d   and (in the hands)] om. 17 21 44; Lat. *et*.
e   Kittim] + "to uproot them" (lit., "so that he may uproot them" [in several spellings]) 35ᶜ 39 42 47; 58 has a pl. subj. ("so that they . . ."). It is difficult to understand why Littmann, Goldmann, and Hartom render as "Hittites."
29a Whoever . . . Kittim] Lat. lacks these words, probably through parablepsis with "Kittim" at the end of v. 28. The uncertain *et* read by Ceriani in this space could be a conjunction added after the omission occurred (VanderKam, *Jubilees* 2:157).
b   escapes] The form is past tense, so it could be rendered "Whoever has escaped," but the meaning would not be affected. Mss. 20 25 35 38 read *'amṣeṭo*, "having escaped"?
c   just nation] Both Eth. and Lat. have sg. forms.
d   times (lit., "days")] Lat. "generations." Charles (*Ethiopic Version*, 90 n. 18; *Jubilees*, 155) changed *mawā'elihomu* to *tewleddomu* to match Lat., and Hartom seems to have accepted the change. With either word, the meaning is really the same.

30a They] "He" 9 25; Lat. "To them (they will not leave)."
b left] "who will leave to him" 12 25 (a misspelling of the infinitive).
c who is rescued] Lat. *salus sevadens* is strange—two words, both misspelled and saying largely the same thing. See Rönsch, *Jubiläen*, 42; Charles, *Ethiopic Version*, 91 n. 5 to Latin.
d judgmental anger (om. "anger" 9 38; Lat. *irae*)] "anger and judgment" 12 21 35 63; "angry judgment" 39 42 47 48. Lat. agrees with the majority Eth. reading.
e for] Lat. *sed*, "but." Both Eth. and Lat. appear to reflect כי.
f and removal] Lat. makes this a purpose clause and thus not the third in a balanced list as in Eth.
g from the earth] Lat. "from the face/surface of the earth."
h All of Caphtor] Lat. has just *illis* ("to them" = "they will not have").
i no longer] Lat. lacks.
j or descendants] Lat. lacks. See VanderKam, *Jubilees* 2:157-58.
k left (lit., "which is left")] "and is left" 9 12 17 21 35 38 44 58 63; Lat. *relictum*.
31a For] om. 21; Lat. "And."
b he would come down] "they would bring him down" 38; Lat. "he would be brought down." See Amos 9:2, where, regarding Caphtor, אורידם is used.
c even if he should become powerful on the earth] Lat. "where(ver) he would flee." The significant difference for this line resulted from an unknown cause or causes.
d the nations] "the mountains" 21.
e from there] om. Lat.
f there] om. 21; Lat. *ibi*.
g will increase] "would increase" 9 12 17 63; Lat. *abundabit*.
32a go] Lat. *vadens abierit* = "going, will (?) go away."
b those] Lat. "all those" (*omnium*).
c his life] Lat. has *eum* (some Eth. MSS. agree 20 25 42 47 48) as object of the verb "seek," and it is followed by *anima eius*. *Eum* makes little sense here; see VanderKam, *Jubilees* 2:158.
d will kill him] "would kill" 9 12 35 44 63; om. 20 25; Lat. "he will die."
e along the way] "in Sheol" = Lat. (*inferni*). Possibly *inferni* is an error for *itinere*, "way" (as in Eth.). So Charles, *Ethiopic Version*, 91 n. 7 to Latin.
f name/descendants] Lat. "descendants/name."
33a This] Lat. "For," where Eth. has "and" (not realized in the translation).
b and inscribed] om. 12 58. Lat. *et consignatum*, "recorded."
c regarding him] om. 12. Lat. *adversus eum*, "against him."
d to do] Lat. *fiat*, "that it may happen"; perhaps *fiat* is a mistake for *faciat*.
e he may be eradicated] "they may be eradicated" 17 21; "they will be eradicated" 58; Lat. "he may be eradicated."
f from the earth] "from the surface of the earth" = Lat.

Commentary

Following the lengthy expansion of the Genesis story about the end of Abraham's life and the unit regarding the pattern of human life spans (chaps. 20–23), the writer of Jubilees returns to the patriarchal narratives with a section centering on Isaac. Chapter 24 rewrites material in Gen 25:11–26:32, but a number of distinctions separate the two accounts as the writer adapts the earlier stories to his purposes. The contents of chap. 24 align with Genesis 25–26 in this way:

1-2 Narrative setting (Gen 25:11; 26:1a)
3-7 Jacob gains the right of firstborn (Gen 25:29-34)
8-11 Famine, journey to Gerar, blessing (Gen 26:1-5)
12-17 Isaac in Gerar (Gen 26:6, 11-16)
18-20 Isaac and his wells in the valleys of Gerar (Gen 26:17-22)
21-23 Blessing and sacrifice in Beersheba (Gen 26:23-25)
24-33 Isaac's oath with the Philistines and curse upon them (Gen 26:26-33)

Chapter 24 actually omits a major part of Genesis 25 (vv. 12-28), and in representing chap. 26 it turns the varying relations between Isaac and the Philistines in Genesis into an opportunity for Isaac to curse them roundly. The language of the imprecation draws on oracles elsewhere in the HB, most notably in Amos 9 (where Philistines are not explicitly the subject).

For the chapter, the Ethiopic manuscript tradition alone preserves the entire text, but from the last word of v. 12 to the end of the chapter the Latin translation has survived.

1-2 Narrative Setting (Gen 25:11; 26:1a)

The first two verses of the chapter contain citations from Gen 25:11 and 26:1. The writer here omits almost all of the intervening verses and does so for understandable reasons. Genesis 25:11 introduces the time after Abraham's death when God blessed his son Isaac but moves quickly from that notice to a section about Ishmael and his descendants (25:12-18). Jubilees does not reproduce the unit (although see 20:12) because Ishmael no longer serves a function in the story; the focus is now on Isaac and soon will return to Jacob. Genesis 25:19-28 deals with the circumstances around the births of Esau and Jacob; the author of Jubilees had introduced a version of this material in 19:10, 13-14 and so bypasses it here. Genesis 25 concludes with the story about Jacob gaining the birthright from Esau (vv. 29-34); Jubilees presents it in 24:3-7 but prefaces to it the famine notice in Gen 26:1 that follows the birthright story in Genesis.

■ 1 As he sets forth the information in Gen 25:11, the author supplements the base text in typical ways:

Genesis 25:11	Jubilees 24:1
After the death of Abraham, God blessed his son Isaac.	After Abraham's death, The Lord blessed his son Isaac. He set out from Hebron and went and lived during the first year of the third week of this jubilee [2073] at the well of the vision for seven years.
And Isaac settled at Beer-lahai-roi.	

Verse 1 clarifies for the reader that when he last appeared in the story Isaac, to whom the divine blessing now passes, was at Hebron (22:3) helping Abraham celebrate the Festival of Weeks and soon afterwards mourning the death of his father. In this way it contextualizes the notice about where Isaac lived after Abraham died. The place-name "the well of the vision" is an abbreviated translation of באר לחי ראי as it appears in the textual tradition represented in LXX (το φρεαρ της ορασεως) OL Eth Gen 25:11. Neither Genesis nor Jubilees elaborates on the name, although it seems significant because of the other references to it in Genesis.

According to [Gen] 16:14 Beer-lahai-roi is where Yahweh's messenger appeared to the distraught and pregnant Hagar, and where subsequently Ishmael was born. That Isaac settles in the place where Ishmael was born indicates that, geographically, Isaac is indeed the one chosen by Yahweh to be blessed, and that Ishmael is to be either displaced, or more likely, replaced.[1]

Since the story about the birth of Ishmael is severely abbreviated in Jubilees, the place-name did not occur in it (see Jub 14:22-24); thus 24:1 is its first appearance in Jubilees.[2] As one would expect, the writer dates the onset of the new narrative in his familiar categories. Abraham died in 2060 (22:1); now some thirteen years later the story resumes with a new patriarch in another place. If Sarah bore Isaac in 1987 (16:15), he would be eighty-six years of age, the very age of Abram when Ishmael was born (Gen 16:16 // Jub 14:24). Genesis does not specify how long Isaac resided in Beer-lahai-roi, but Jub 24:1 says he lived there for seven years (see v. 2).

■ 2 At the end of the seven-year period, a natural disaster struck the land.[3] Here the text draws on Gen 26:1, where a famine is mentioned and where it is distinguished from the earlier one in the time of Abra(ha)m (in Gen 12:10-20 // Jub 13:10-15). In Genesis the new famine introduces the story about Isaac's leaving his current residence and moving to Gerar. The author of Jubilees will later use it for the same purpose (see v. 8 below) but also cites it here to provide a suitable setting for the story concerning Esau's hunger and the birth-

---

1 Hamilton, *Genesis 18–50*, 169. In Gen 25:11, where it immediately precedes the Ishmael section in vv. 12-18, the connection is more apparent than in Jubilees, where vv. 12-18 are lacking. Genesis also refers to the place-name in 24:62, where it is a location from which Isaac had departed before Rebekah arrived.

2 According to Werman, the writer fixes Hebron as the family home and thus has to explain what Isaac was doing away from the city—he was spending time in the south because of God's blessing mentioned just before the geographical notice (*Jubilees*, 369). It is not so clear, however, that the blessing has anything to do with his living at the well of the vision.

3 One could translate Jubilees as saying either that the famine began or that it prevailed (see Dillmann, *Lexicon*, 767; VanderKam, *Jubilees* 2:150). For *'aḥaza*, Leslau includes the senses of "hold, take hold of, seize" (*Concise Dictionary*, 140).

right in vv. 3-7. The notice about the famine follows the story regarding the birthright in Genesis and apparently has no connection with it.

3-7 Jacob Gains the Right of Firstborn (Gen 25:29-34)[4]

The fact that a famine prevailed in the land explains why Esau was so hungry in the story in Gen 25:29-34, although it leaves one wondering why Jacob had food enough for himself and his brother.[5]

■ 3 Verse 3 reproduces Gen 25:29 but provides a closer identification of the food Jacob was cooking than Genesis does—a lentil porridge (as in LXX[b] and *Targums Neofiti* and *Pseudo-Jonathan*). "Lentil" is borrowed from Gen 25:34; in the parallel to Gen 25:34—Jub 24:6—"lentil" is lacking. In Jubilees, Esau is hungry as in most ancient versions, while the LXX seems to say more: he was "languishing." There is no hint in the text that the author accepts the midrashic interpretation that Esau was weary[6] because of all the serious sinning he had accomplished that day (*Tg. Ps.-J.* Gen 25:29; *Gen. Rab.* 63:12).[7] That he was hungry was enough for the story to proceed; in this instance it was apparently not thought necessary to present Esau in a worse light than Genesis does.

In the latter part of the verse, the wording in Jubilees may even make Esau look a little more refined than he does in Genesis.

Genesis 25:30	Jubilees 24:3b
Esau said to Jacob, "Let me eat some of that red stuff, for I am famished!" (Therefore he was called Edom.)	He said to his brother Jacob: "Give me some of this *red* porridge."

Genesis 25:30 places the verb הלעיטני ("let me swallow, make me gulp down") on Esau's lips. Skinner says of the verb: "a coarse expression suggesting bestial voracity."[8] Jubilees has the more neutral imperative "give me" (as does the Vulgate). Where all the versions of Genesis have him demanding "some of that red stuff," the Ethiopic text of v. 3b has "some of this wheat porridge." Dillmann and after him Charles and others have observed that Ethiopic *šernāy* ("wheat") translates Greek πυρον, and LXX Gen 25:30 reads πυρρον ("red"). This is an instance in which the Ethiopic version clearly rests on a mistake made in Greek Jubilees or in reading it,[9] since a term meaning "red" is vital to the etymology of "Edom" in the story. Jubilees lacks the extra reference to "red" found in Gen 25:30 (lit., "some of the red, this red [stuff]"), and it postpones the explanation of "Edom" until the end of the unit.

Jacob's response to Esau's demand may also be slightly gentler in Jubilees than in Gen 25:31.

Genesis 25:31	Jubilees 24:3c
Jacob said, "First sell me your birthright."	But Jacob said to him: "Hand over to me your birthright that belongs to the firstborn,[10] and then I will give you food and some of this porridge as well."

The Jacob of Genesis insists that Esau sell (a financial term) him the birthright "today/now [כיום]." Rather than requiring that his slightly older brother sell it immediately, the Jacob of Jubilees tells him simply to hand it over. The Ethiopic verb *'agbe'a* (also employed in Eth Gen 25:31) reflects Greek αποδου. The Ethiopic copies have an elaborate way of indicating the right of the firstborn: *leḥqānika za-qedma ledat*, "your seniority of the precedence of birth" (Eth. Gen 25:31 uses one word:

---

4 On the section, see Endres, *Biblical Interpretation*, 63-65.
5 Cf. ibid., 63-64.
6 The adjective used to describe Esau's condition in Gen 25:29 is עיף, "faint, weary" (from exercise or hunger) (cf. BDB, 746).
7 In *Genesis Rabbah* word associations lead to the identification of wrongs Esau is supposed to have committed. For example, he came in "from the field," and the word "field" is used in a law in Deut 22:25 as the place where an engaged young woman is raped. Hence Esau was guilty of this sin.
8 Skinner, *Genesis*, 361 n. to v. 29. Cf. *Gen. Rab.* 63:12, where the word is used for feeding a camel.
9 Dillmann, "Jubiläen," 71 n. 23; Charles, *Ethiopic Version*, 86 n. 20; cf. *Jubilees*, 152. Many LXX witnesses also omit one *rho* and thus have the same confusion.
10 Cf. Werman, who thinks Jacob is not asking for the birthright but only the rights of the firstborn (*Jubilees*, 369); but the sequel hardly bears out such a distinction.

bekwrennāka).[11] Here, unlike Gen 25:31, Jubilees extends Jacob's response to Esau by having him say what Genesis, three verses later (25:34), phrases in the third person: "Then Jacob gave Esau bread and lentil stew" (see Jub 24:6a). In this way the writer prepares for what Jacob will give Esau—more kinds of food than he had demanded.

■ **4-5** The next two verses rework Gen 25:32-33 in interesting ways:

Genesis 25:32-33	Jubilees 24:4-5
Esau said, "I am about to die; of what use is a birthright to me?"	Esau said to himself: "I will die. What good will this right of the firstborn do?" So he said to Jacob: "I (hereby) give (it) to you."
Jacob said, "Swear to me first."	Jacob said to him: "Swear to me today."
So he swore to him.	So he swore to him.

The answer Esau gives to Jacob in Gen 25:32 is a continuation of the conversation: "Esau said, 'I am about to die; of what use is a birthright to me?'" The rewriting of it in Jub 24:4 conceives of it differently: it is something Esau says to himself (lit., "in his heart"),[12] not aloud to Jacob. Jubilees also gives a line to Esau that makes his act of ceding his right of firstborn more explicit and formal: "So he said to Jacob, 'I (hereby) give (it) to you.'" In Genesis he never actually says he is turning it over to Jacob; the act is merely implied by his question. The extra words in Jub 24:4 furnish a better context for Jacob's demand that Esau swear to him about the transfer. In Jubilees, Esau first gives his word to Jacob that he is transferring the birthright to him, and Jacob, who knows his brother and wants to be sure about the transaction, then orders him to confirm his declaration with an oath. This is the point where the author introduces "today" that he had left out of v. 3 (it is in Gen 25:31 and here in v. 33 [NRSV: "first"]; see above). The formal oath sworn by Esau is the action to which the "today/now" is attached, and the oath verifies the words Esau has actually uttered.

■ **6** Jacob keeps his side of the bargain by providing Esau with the kinds of food he had promised in v. 3 ("bread/food" does not appear until Jacob feeds Esau in Gen 25:34). Earlier the text had mentioned "lentil porridge" (v. 3); here it has only "porridge" (Gen 25:34 has "lentil stew"). Where Gen 25:34 says that Esau "ate and drank, and rose and went his way," v. 6 reports "he ate until he was full." Jacob fed him well.

Genesis 25:34 concludes the story with a negative comment: "Thus Esau despised his birthright" ("his" is not in the Hebrew text). Jubilees reproduces the verdict in v. 6: "Esau repudiated [or: despised][13] the right of the firstborn." The subject of the birthright arises two more times in the immediate sequel, neither of which has a parallel in Genesis. In the first instance, the writer appends it to the name explanation, an etymology that had occurred already in Gen 25:30 but without reference to the birthright. The sentence in v. 6 is odd: "This is why he was named Esau and Edom:[14] because of the *red* porridge that Jacob gave him in exchange for his right of the firstborn."[15] The statement clearly presupposes that the original text had "red porridge" to explain the name "Edom," not "wheat porridge" as in the Ethiopic copies (see above on the same mistaken reading in v. 3). But, more importantly, the writer says again that the birthright passed from one brother to the other.

■ **7** The second additional reference to it is indirect: the text explains that, because of the transfer, Jacob became senior to his brother, who now assumed a more junior status. He does not say that before the transaction Jacob had a lower standing; he says only that Jacob is now the older brother[16] and Esau has suffered a demotion. In

---

11 In Jub 24:4, 6 the expression is *qadima tawāledo*, and at the end of v. 6 it is *qedmata ledatu*.
12 Syriac Gen 25:32 reads similarly (*b-npšh*).
13 Leslau gives both meanings for *mannana* (*Concise Dictionary*, 38).
14 It is reasonable to think the text once said "This is the reason why Esau was named Edom," but the rendering given here is true to the preferred reading in the Ethiopic witnesses. See VanderKam, *Jubilees* 2:150-51.
15 Kugel wonders whether the etymological explanation was delayed to suggest that it was not the stew but his ceding the birthright that gave rise to the name Edom (*Walk through* Jubilees, 133; "Jubilees," 379-80).
16 *Genesis Rabbah* 63:14, where Gen 25:34 is the subject, cites a number of passages, among which is Exod 4:22 where the Lord says "Israel is my firstborn son," thus divinely confirming Jacob's acquisition of the birthright.

Genesis the transfer recalls and partially instantiates the pre-birth prediction from the Lord to Rebekah: "Two nations are in your womb, / and two peoples born of you shall be divided; / the one shall be stronger than the other, / the elder shall serve the younger" (Gen 25:23). Jubilees does not reproduce the passage but devotes large amounts of space in the preceding chapters (19:13–23:8) to establishing Jacob as the true heir of Abraham and to documenting his superiority to Esau. Both Abraham and Rebekah assessed him accurately at an early time (Jub 19:16-31; 22:10-29); the present episode simply offers an acknowledgment of Jacob's right to the first position—something the author had already given him when he mentioned their births in the order Jacob–Esau (19:13-15).[17] The fact that Jacob has now obtained the status of the older brother means that he is the one whom Isaac really should bless in Genesis 27 // Jubilees 26, as Abraham had prayed in 19:23, 27; 22:10-15, 19, 23-24 (see 16:17-18). Oddly enough, however, when it comes time to bless his older son, Isaac will be oblivious to their change in status, as if he did not know about it. Esau's reaction to ceding the right of firstborn to Jacob is not treated in this context, but he will remember the event both negatively (Gen 27:36 // Jub 26:30) and perhaps more positively (Jub 36:14; although see 37:1-4) in years to come.

8-11 Famine, Journey to Gerar, Blessing (Gen 26:1-5)

At this point the text of Jubilees continues to follow the sequence in Genesis.

■ **8** The writer furnishes an abbreviated version of the famine notice in Gen 26:1, the second occurrence of it in chap. 24 (see v. 2).

Genesis 26:1	Jubilees 24:8
Now there was a famine in the land, besides the former famine that had occurred in the days of Abraham.	As there was a famine over the land.
And Isaac went to Gerar, to King Abimelech of the Philistines.	Isaac set out to go down to Egypt during the second year of this week [2081]. He went to Gerar to the Philistine king Abimelech.

This time he uses the famine notice as Genesis does—to explain why Isaac left his residence in Beer-lahai-roi to go to Gerar: he was leaving a famine-plagued area (he had referred to the earlier famine in Abraham's time in v. 2). Presumably the territory of Gerar where the Philistines lived would afford relief, as wells feature prominently in the story (etymologically, there could hardly be a better place for a temporary resident [a גר] to live than Gerar [גרר]). Jubilees offers a typical change in v. 8: "Isaac set out to go down to Egypt. . . . He went to Gerar," where Gen 26:1 reads simply "Isaac went to Gerar." The reason for introducing Egypt is the divine order in Gen 26:2 that he not descend to Egypt. Readers of Gen 26:1 would have no reason for suspecting Egypt as his destination (unless they remembered his father Abram's response to the earlier famine). In this way Jubilees provides the context for the Lord's prohibition (as does *Tg. Ps.-J.* Gen 26:2). Verse 8 also dates the journey to the year following completion of his seven years in Beer-lahai-roi (the well of the vision).

■ **9-10** The next verses (including v. 11 and the first clause in v. 12) are a sustained, verbatim citation of Gen 26:2-6—one of the longest of these in Jubilees. The passage conveys the Lord's confirmation of the patriarchal blessings to Isaac and explains what they entailed at the present time. As in Genesis, this is, however, the first time the promise "I will be with you" is given to a patriarch (see also v. 22 // Gen 26:24).[18] Isaac and his line would someday possess the entire land as God's gift; he was, therefore, not to leave it by traveling to Egypt. Rather, he was to reside in the land designated by God. Gerar, itself part of the land promised to Abraham, was a place in which he would merely live temporarily as an alien.[19] In the blessing itself, every time "the land" is

---

17　See Werman, "Attitude," 187–89.
18　Hamilton *Genesis 18–50*, 193. In Jubilees, Terah had asked that God be with Abram (12:29), but the promise has not occurred in a context of blessing or covenant.
19　The Ethiopic text of Jubilees maintains the distinction in Gen 26:2-3 between the land in which he would live (שכן/*nebar*) and the one in which he would be a temporary resident (גור/*feles*). The expression "settle in the land that I shall show you"

716

mentioned, the word "all" accompanies it (v. 10 // Gen 26:3-4). Genesis twice (vv. 3 and 4) speaks of "all these lands," but in those instances Jubilees (24:10), with the LXX tradition, uses a singular form that may express the same meaning as the Hebrew plural.[20] The wording of the promises closely resembles the ones made to Abraham in Gen 22:17-18 // Jub 18:15-16, and the formulation of the passage also links them with Abraham: "I will carry out the terms of my[21] oath that I swore to your father Abraham" (v. 10 // Gen 26:3). As in Genesis, bestowal of the promises to Isaac depends on his father Abraham.[22]

■ 11 The strongest connection with Abraham comes in v. 11 // Gen 26:5: the blessings, including the derivative one the nations will experience through the chosen line, now belong to Isaac because Abraham was unfailingly obedient:

Genesis 26:4b-5	Jubilees 24:11
and all the nations of the earth shall gain blessing for themselves through your your offspring because Abraham obeyed my voice and kept my charge, my commandments, my statutes, and my laws.	All the peoples of the earth will be blessed through your descendants because of the fact that your father obeyed me and kept my obligations, commands, laws, statutes, and covenant.

The texts agree word for word (not always obvious in the translations) apart from two differences: where the MT uses the name Abraham alone and the SP, LXX, and OL have "Abraham your father," Jubilees reads "your father"; and at the end of the verse its words "and covenant" are unique to it (they may come from Gen 17:9-10 // Jub 15:11).[23] Nouns such as "commands, statutes, and laws" are surprising in connection with Genesis, where Abraham received very few orders that were legal in nature. There is no question that he was obedient, as he demonstrated when he nearly sacrificed Isaac (see esp. 18:15-16 // Gen 22:16-18), and he was unswervingly loyal to the covenant (e.g., through circumcision); but "obligations, statutes, and laws" (terms that sound Deuteronomic; see Deut 11:1, for example) point to legal matters. The only legal requirement placed on Abraham in Genesis was circumcision (17:9-14), but in Jubilees he receives and/or keeps other legal obligations.

From the ancestral books he knew of the legislation for:
    the Festival of Weeks/Firstfruits of the Wheat Harvest (chap. 14; 22:1-6)
    the sacrificial practices he taught Isaac (chap. 21).
New legislation revealed in his time included:
    the law of the tithe (13:25-27)
    circumcision (15:11-14, with vv. 25-34)
    the Festival of Tabernacles (16:20-31)
    the Festival of Unleavened Bread (18:17-19 [not named]).

In every case Abraham proved obedient to the demands placed upon him or that arose from the tradition or his experiences. As a result, the Abraham of Jubilees seems a better fit for the terms in Gen 26:5 than the Abraham of Genesis. The writer does not go so far as to say Abraham obeyed the entire law, as, for example, in the statement cited in *m. Qidd.* 4:14: "And we find that Abraham our father had performed the whole law before it was given, for it is written . . ." (Gen 26:5 is then cited).[24] In Jubilees he obeys the laws revealed before and in his time, and his virtue entails that the promised blessings now fall on his son Isaac and his descendants. Addition of "and covenant" in Jubilees reminds the reader that the laws belong in the context of the ongoing agreement between God and his chosen ones. A passage such as Gen 26:5[25] probably influenced the thesis represented in Jubilees that a number of pentateuchal laws could be traced back to the time of the ancestors.

    (Gen 26:2 // Jub 24:9) seems to fit better with the situation of Abram, to whom the Lord would show the land to which he was traveling. It is strange in connection with Isaac.
20 The plural forms in Gen 26:3-4 seem to designate the various parts of the land promised (see Skinner, *Genesis*, 364 n. to v. 3).
21 The possessive "my" agrees with the reading in the LXX tradition at Gen 26:3.
22 See Halpern-Amaru, *Rewriting the Bible*, 36.
23 Jubilees may also have the words "statutes/laws" in reverse order, though the terms used have ranges of meanings in the legal sphere.
24 VanderKam, "Exegesis of Pentateuchal Legislation," 178–80. Cf. Philo, *Abr.* 275-76.
25 The same could be said about Gen 18:19, but Jubilees does not cite the passage.

Jubilees places an additional command at the end of the deity's address to Isaac: "Now obey me and live [*ḥeder*—a more permanent kind of residence] in this land" (v. 11). The Lord's demand relates to the example of obedient Abraham: Isaac should now imitate his father's conduct in order that the blessings could later be transmitted to his children as they had now come to him.[26]

12-17 Isaac in Gerar (Gen 26:6, 11-16)

The rewriting of this section is remarkable and an instructive example of the author's approach.

■ **12-13** Verse 12 begins by citing the first clause from Gen 26:6: "So Isaac settled in Gerar." To it the writer adds a typical chronological phrase—"for three weeks of years"—to indicate that his stay in the area where the Philistines lived was not a short one (twenty-one years). Genesis supplies only a vague note about the length of his sojourn there: "When Isaac had been there a long time" (26:8). Verse 13 follows with the next borrowing, this time from Gen 26:11, so that Gen 26:7-10 is omitted almost entirely. The reason is obvious. Those verses tell the story about Isaac's lie regarding his wife and how he lost her, apparently to King Abimelech of the Philistines, who discovered only later that she was his wife. The writer here omits an episode that places one of the patriarchs in a bad light—a time when Isaac chose the wrong example from his father for imitation.[27] He betrays the fact that he knows the full account by reworking the last verse in it.

Genesis 26:11	Jubilees 24:13
So Abimelech warned all the people, saying,	Abimelech gave orders as follows regarding him and everything that belonged to him:[28]
"Whoever touches this man or his wife shall be put to death."	"Anyone who touches him or anything that belongs to him is to die."

The references to his wife have been replaced by "everything that belonged to him" and "anything that belongs to him."[29] A reader who saw just v. 13 in Jubilees would have no idea that there had been any problem involving Rebekah. The treatment of the story is more radical than the way in which the author handled Gen 12:10-20. There in his rewriting he told much of the story but not Abram's request that Sarai misrepresent their relationship, and he focused on the fact that Pharaoh took her forcibly (13:11-15). Here he deletes any suggestion of contact between a foreign ruler and a patriarchal wife and modifies the royal command that ends the incident. He also avoids having a Philistine lecture a patriarch about his lack of truthfulness (as the king does in Gen 26:9-10). Abimelech's edict now functions as background for Isaac's prosperity in Gerar, not as a response to the nearly disastrous situation brought on by a less-than-admirable Isaac. A disadvantage of leaving out the story of taking Rebekah is that Abimelech's orders regarding Isaac and his property have no motivation.

As the story proceeds in vv. 14-17, the writer generally follows the narrative about Isaac's wealth in Gen 26:12-17, but he rearranges it slightly.

■ **14-15** Verse 14 makes a general statement about his riches (twice, at the beginning and at the end [on the term here see the textual note]) and supplies some details beyond what Gen 26:14 includes (note the camels and donkeys); the list of items resembles the one for Abram's possessions in Jub 13:14 (cf. Gen 12:16). After enumerating the livestock he owned, the text backtracks and takes up material in Gen 26:12-13 concerning his agricultural prowess and only then, after the full survey of his diverse wealth, does the writer report that the Philistines grew jealous of him (from Gen 26:14, where it follows the summary statement reflected in Jub 24:14). Isaac had moved to Gerar to escape the famine, and there he had become an extraordinarily successful farmer. To

---

26 Endres, *Biblical Interpretation*, 66.
27 In fact he omits the lie in all three accounts of patriarchs losing their wives to foreign rulers—Gen 12:10-20; Genesis 20; and the present passage. See Jub 13:11-15, where he tells the Abram-Sarai story but alters it considerably; 16:10 (he omits the entire story from Genesis 20); and here in 24:12-13.
28 The Latin translation lacks "and everything that belonged to him." It does, however, contain the corresponding expression in Abimelech's command ("or anything that belongs to him"). For the shorter Latin reading as a result of parablepsis, either in Hebrew or Greek, see VanderKam, *Jubilees* 2:152.
29 Endres, *Biblical Interpretation*, 66-67.

this point in Jubilees he had caused no trouble, and he profited richly from Abimelech's protection of him and his property.

■ **16-17** Wells become an issue in v. 16, which rewrites Gen 26:15. The text is not explicit about it, but it would have been natural for Isaac to settle where his father had lived before and had dug wells to support his livestock (see Gen 20:1; 21:25, 30-34). The Philistine residents of Gerar took to attacking the indispensable basis of Isaac's wealth—the wells that supplied his many animals and supported the crops that were highlighted in the two preceding verses (14-15). Jubilees 24:16 states explicitly, unlike Gen 26:15 (the words do appear in v. 18), that the campaign of stopping up the wells transpired after Abraham's death. Apparently as a continuation of the natives' actions, Abimelech in v. 17 expelled Isaac on the grounds that he had become too great[30] for the people of Gerar. In Genesis, Isaac's earlier deception had not caused Abimelech to order him out of the country; his annoying prosperity now apparently does exactly that.[31] There must have been serious issues between Isaac and the Philistines. Isaac complied with the royal decree, but he did not move very far away, as the next area where he resides temporarily (*falasa*; but "camped [ויחן]" and "settled [וישב]" in Gen 26:17) is said to be the valleys[32] of Gerar. The chronological notice in v. 17 is consistent with the one in v. 12, where his stay in Gerar is said to have lasted twenty-one years (2081–2102).

18-20 Isaac and His Wells in the Valleys of Gerar (Gen 26:17-22)

It is strange that, though he left Gerar, where the local population had plugged Abraham's wells, Isaac and his men in their new place of residence clear out wells of Abraham that the Philistines had stopped up. However the problem arose in the text of Genesis 26,[33] the writer of Jubilees had to deal with the finished text, but he does not say anything about the issue. Perhaps he assumed these water sources were different from the ones in v. 16.

■ **18-19** Isaac's servants[34] made the set of Abrahamic wells in question usable again, and Isaac himself rechristened them with the names the older patriarch had assigned to them. In this way Isaac staked a claim to his father's heritage and supported his entourage and livestock. The wells, however, may not have proved adequate because Isaac's servants dug new ones that tapped into fresh water. In this way Isaac was no longer dependent only on what his father left him; through his initiative he supported his own household. In this case, too, Isaac's successes led to problems with the indigenous population, this time with "the shepherds of Gerar" (v. 19; Gen 26:19), who claimed ownership of the water.

The dispute over the precious water forms the background for naming the wells (vv. 19-20 // Gen 26:20-21).[35] The name of the first is עשק = "contention" (pointed with a *sin* in MT Gen 26:20 [the only place where the word

---

30 The verb *'abya* means "to be great, famous, important, powerful" (Leslau, *Concise Dictionary*, 175); Latin Jubilees has *magnus factus es*. Genesis 26:16 uses עצמת, which means "you have become powerful," although it could be translated "you have become numerous" (*DCH* 6:533–34). Nothing in the immediate context, however, suggests that the problem was the number of people associated with Isaac. The first reference to an increase in Isaac's group is in Jub 24:20 (Gen 26:22).

31 Cf. Hamilton, *Genesis 18–50*, 200–201.

32 The Ethiopic copies support reading a plural form; the Latin translation seems to have suffered from a loss of text at this point so that it has no indication of where Isaac went (see VanderKam, *Jubilees* 2:153). The term in Gen 26:17, נחל, can be used for a river valley (*DCH* 5:657). Jubilees reproduces the next instance of this word in v. 19 (Gen 26:19).

33 Cf. Westermann, *Genesis 12–36*, 426; he comments that Gen 26:15 and 18 belong together and that at an earlier stage vv. 19-25 had no connection with vv. 12-17.

34 Where MT Gen 26:18 says that the Philistines had stopped up the wells "in the days of his father Abraham," Jubilees (Ethiopic and Latin) reads "the servants of his father Abraham," as do SP LXX and the other ancient versions (even *Targum Pseudo-Jonathan*). Syriac Gen 26:18 reads both: the servants of his father in the days of his father Abraham. In Gen 26:18 Isaac is the one who is said to have dug the wells, but, in harmony with the context and situation (see Gen 26:19 // Jub 24:19), the writer of Jubilees attributes the work to Isaac's servants.

35 For a list comparing the names of the wells in Jubilees, LXX, and MT, see Endres, *Biblical Interpretation*, 67 n. 35.

occurs in the HB]), but in both versions of Jub 24:19 the term is taken to mean "difficult/difficulty ['eṣub/difficultatem]."[36] The Syriac cognate to the Hebrew verb in fact means "difficult."[37] Where the versions of Gen 26:20 explain that Isaac chose the name because of their actions "with him," in Jubilees he says that they had been difficult "for us."

■ **20** To the second new and successful well that led to fighting Isaac gave the name "Narrow," or so the Ethiopic has it. The word ṣabāb does mean "narrow," but the Latin translation has *inimicitias* ("hostility/enmity"), which is an equivalent of שנאה in Gen 26:21. Charles emended the Ethiopic form to ṣel', "enmity." He wrote: "The corruption is native to the text. It [i.e., "Narrow"] most probably arose from a scribe's wishing to make an antithesis between the name of this well and that of the next 'Room.'"[38]

Subsequent to the incidents concerning the two wells named after the conflicts they caused, Isaac went to a place at least somewhat removed from the problem area ("When he had set out"; see Gen 26:22). In the new location a third well[39]—for whatever reason—produced no altercation. As a result, Isaac gave it a positive name. The form in Ethiopic is again an adjective (*sefuḥ*), but the Latin has a noun (*capacitas*, "capacity"). Both words clearly reflect רחבת in Gen 26:22, and the significance of the name, as the texts explain, is that it expresses Isaac's belief that God was the one who has now provided a place, sufficient space, for him and his household in this temporary residence. He also adds that the Lord has increased the size of his household. The growth was not an indication that the patriarchal blessing of a numerous progeny was coming true (see v. 22 // Gen 26:24) but rather another sign that he was prospering. His relief, however, was to be short-lived.

21-23 Blessing and Sacrifice in Beersheba (Gen 26:23-25)

Isaac changed locations again, this time to a place with family associations and a little more removed from the Philistines, though not by much.

■ **21** Isaac next migrated to the former patriarchal residence of Beersheba (the well of the oath), obviously a good place to go in this context much concerned with wells. Jubilees 22:1-2 reported that Isaac had large holdings in Beersheba, and it was from there that he and Ishmael had come to celebrate the Festival of Weeks with Abraham just before he died. Abraham himself had lived there at an earlier time (Jub 16:11, 15; 18:17). To the travel notice the writer adds a chronological note: the move occurred six years after Isaac left Gerar (see v. 17).[40]

■ **22** Back in the familiar place, the patriarch received the privilege of having the Lord appear to him. During the theophany, the deity reiterated the promise, mentioned first in v. 9 (see Gen 26:3; cf. also 28:15 // Jub 27:24), to be with him and also to multiply his progeny. The wording, however, differs from the versions of Gen 26:24 due to the influence of parallel blessing formulas. Both Gen 26:24 and Jub 24:22 indicate that the appearance occurred "that night," the night when he arrived at Beersheba. Typically, Jubilees then explains exactly which night it was: the first of the first month. The information, combined with the date in v. 21, shows that the Lord appeared to Isaac on the very first day of jubilee 44—surely an auspicious occasion in the chronology. The date (1/1) was also one of the memorial days instituted in connection with the flood and the date on which the Lord would later appear at night to Jacob (27:19). In v. 22 the deity identifies himself as "the God of your father

---

36   The versions of Genesis handle the name differently: the LXX's "injustice" (αδικια) is translated literally in Eth. Gen 26:20 ('ammaḍā). The rendering in the LXX may presuppose עשק, with the sibilant understood as śin (= "oppression, extortion" [BDB, 799]). Werman wonders whether the writer of Jubilees reworked the understanding of the term in LXX because the idea of Isaac as the one oppressed/extorted did not fit the picture he wished to convey (*Jubilees*, 371).

37   J. Payne Smith, *A Compendious Syriac Dictionary* (Oxford: Clarendon, 1903) 421.

38   Charles, *Jubilees*, 154; cf. *Ethiopic Version*, 88 n. 22; VanderKam, *Jubilees* 2:154.

39   Jubilees again attributes the digging to Isaac's servants ("they"), as do SP Syr Gen 26:22; MT and the others read "he."

40   For most of v. 21 the Latin manuscript is illegible, but it does contain the words "during the first year of the first week."

Abraham," and, after reassuring Isaac that there was no need to fear because he was with him, he promises to bless him and make the number of his descendants large. The Ethiopic version of the promise of progeny reflects a Hebrew infinitive absolute construction (*'abzeḥ o 'abazzeḥ*), as in an earlier parallel, Gen 22:17; the Latin version has only a future-tense verb as in Gen 26:24. Both texts of Jubilees supply the phrase "as the sand of the earth," drawn, presumably, from passages such as Gen 13:16; 28:14 (also pronounced during a nocturnal appearance). At this time there has not been much progress in fulfilling the promise of many descendants, so therefore it was important to renew it for Isaac. The assurance to Isaac is encased in references to Abraham: the deity calls himself the God of Abraham and says he will bless and multiply Isaac because of his servant[41] Abraham. Perhaps the fundamental message here as with the wells is one of continuity: "God is not initiating anything with Isaac. He is perpetuating what he started with Abraham."[42]

■ **23** Isaac responded to the theophany by building an altar as his father had in Gen 12:7 (Jub 13:4); 13:18, after receiving similar promises. In this instance the writer reinforces the connection with Abraham beyond what is done in Gen 26:25: the altar that Isaac constructed was the one his father had first built. The reference is to Jub 16:10-31, where Abraham built an altar in Beersheba after Sarah became pregnant with Isaac and on the occasion of the first Festival of Tabernacles. Once he has tied the altar to Abraham, the author returns briefly to the text of Gen 26:25 with the report that Isaac called on the Lord's name. He then once again departs from the base text by adding that he offered a sacrifice to the God of his father Abraham. His procedure here is the same as, for example, in 13:4: where Genesis (12:7) says only that a patriarch built an altar, Jubilees adds that he made an offering on it. The writer locates these words where Genesis says that Isaac pitched his tent at that place. Isaac was qualified to make an offering because he, like Abraham, was a priest, and he had received from his father careful, detailed instructions about procedures in sacrificing (see chap. 21 above).

24-33 Isaac's Oath with the Philistines and Curse upon Them (Gen 26:26-33)

Genesis 26:26-33, the second instance of an agreement between a patriarch and Philistine officials that led to the naming of Beersheba (see Gen 21:22-34 for the first), becomes in Jubilees a text with a very different message.

■ **24-25** Verse 24 begins as if it is continuing the text of Genesis 26, where at the end of v. 25 Isaac's servants dig yet another well that in vv. 32-33 becomes the reason for (the initial part of) the place name "Beersheba." Genesis at this point introduces a meeting between Isaac and three Philistine dignitaries, Abimelech, Ahuzzath, and Phicol, and a solemn agreement between them (vv. 26-31). The scene ends amicably: "In the morning they rose early and exchanged oaths; and Isaac sent them on their way, and they departed from him in peace" (v. 31; the Philistines call their agreement a "covenant" in v. 28). The sequel in Jubilees, though, reads much differently than in the Hebrew texts (MT SP) of Genesis 26. The author of Jubilees finds two wells in this episode: the well mentioned in Gen 26:25 ("And there Isaac's servants dug a well" [nothing is said about finding water in it]) is the one in which, according to Jub 24:24, they found flowing water. The second is the well about which the servants speak seven verses later (and after the meeting with the Philistines) in Gen 26:32. There the Hebrew texts of Genesis read: "That same day Isaac's servants came and told him about the well that they had dug, and said to him, 'We have found water!'" As it is phrased in Jub 24:25 the verse reads: "But when Isaac's servants dug another well, they did not find water. They went and told Isaac that they had not found water." The reason for the contradiction between the Hebrew versions of Genesis and Jubilees is in part textual:[43]

---

41 Both versions of Jubilees read with MT SP Gen 26:24, not with the LXX tradition that has "your father" instead of "my servant."

42 Hamilton, *Genesis 18–50*, 204.

43 Rönsch, *Jubiläen*, 131; Charles, *Ethiopic Version*, 90 n. 1; *Jubilees*, 154; VanderKam, *Jubilees* 2:155. In *Gen. Rab.* 64:10 the expositors show their awareness of the two possible readings. Commenting on Gen 26:32, they say: "Now from this we do not know whether they have found it [water] or not. But from the verse, '*And found there a well of living water*' (ib. 19), it follows that they had found water."

721

Genesis 26:32: (they) said to him [לוֹ], "We have found water!"

Jubilees 24:25 (= LXX tradition): (they) told Isaac that they had not [לֹא] found water.

The reading can be explained as resulting from the difference between two Hebrew words that sound alike and can be spelled in the same way, but the negative sentence is also more appropriate for what follows in Jubilees 24, where something clearly incited Isaac to become furious at the Philistines—as if they were responsible for the failure of Isaac's servants to locate water in the well they had just dug (24:25): "Isaac said, 'On this very day I have sworn an oath to the Philistines; now this has happened to us.'"

Genesis 26:26-31[44] must have pained the writer of Jubilees because it pictured Isaac, with whom the promises to Abraham had just been renewed, swearing a covenantal oath with representatives of the Philistines and sealing the agreement by eating a meal with them. His conduct directly contradicted Abraham's commands to Jacob: "Separate from the nations, / and do not eat with them" (22:16). It also conflicted with Exod 23:32 ("You shall make no covenant with them [the peoples of Canaan]"); 34:12, 15 (no covenant with them); and Deut 7:2 (no covenant with the seven Canaanite peoples).[45] The writer of Jubilees had omitted the earlier story where Abraham made a covenant with the same people (Gen 21:32 uses "covenant" for their sworn agreement), but he included the one involving Isaac and thus had to find a fitting explanation for what the second patriarch had done.

■ **26-27** As a result, he attributes Isaac's regrettable action to bad behavior on the part of the Philistine leaders. That is, he acknowledged that Isaac swore to the agreement and named the Philistines with whom he had done so. In addition, he accounted for the (latter part of the) name "Beersheba" as arising from the oath, as in Gen 26:33 (this is clearer in Gen 21:31).[46] But, unlike Genesis 26, he maintained that Isaac did not enter the covenant with full awareness of the situation or by his free choice. A close look at the words attributed to the Philistines in Genesis shows that they not only flattered Isaac (they recognized that the Lord was with him, as he promised in 26:24, and they called him "the blessed of the LORD" in v. 29) but also made a false claim: the agreement was to assure that Isaac would not harm them "just as we have not touched you and have done to you nothing but [רַק] good and have sent you away in peace" (v. 29). As *Gen. Rab.* 64:10 notes, "RAḲ is a limitation, for they did not do him a complete favour." The Philistines had, of course, expelled him from their territory when he became too great for them, and they had grown jealous of him (Gen 26:14-16); moreover, there were the quarrels about wells (vv. 17-21). Perhaps based on their misleading words, therefore, and his abhorrence of agreements with foreigners, the author of Jubilees concluded that Isaac made a covenant (though he does not use the word) with a party that wronged him—he, an individual however mighty, was compelled to ally with an entire nation to ensure peace ("under pressure to make peace with them" [v. 27]). The exact charge about the Philistines' conduct is not clear: at the key point in the text the preferred Ethiopic reading is *ba-gefuʿ* (a strongly supported variant is *ba-gefʿ*—with a noun instead of the passive participle). *Gefuʿ* should mean "oppressed, harmed, afflicted" or "one who suffers wrong"; if the noun is preferred the meaning would be: (with) "oppression, violence, wrongdoing, wrong, persecution, vexation, injustice."[47] So, he entered the agreement under wrongful conditions, possibly with a hint of violence,[48]

---

44 See Endres, *Biblical Interpretation*, 68–70.

45 The Philistines are not listed among the seven nations, but, as Exod 34:12 dictates, the Israelites were to make no covenants with "the inhabitants of the land."

46 Since the writer of Jubilees had omitted Gen 21:22-34, the text to this point has not provided an explanation for the city name Beersheba, "the well of the oath."

47 Leslau, *Concise Dictionary*, 214; Dillmann, *Lexicon*, 1213. Goldmann renders with בלחץ ("under pressure/compulsion"), Hartom with נאנס ("was forced"), and Werman with באונס ("with compulsion").

48 Genesis 26:26 identifies Phicol as the commander of Abimelech's army; Eth. Jub 24:26 calls him "his guard," and the Latin text "the leader of this army" (for the reading here, see VanderKam, *Jubilees* 2:156). Why Berger thinks that the term "guard" ("Wächter") has any theological significance (he

but, as the Latin is illegible here, little more can be said about the matter. The essential point is that Isaac did swear the oath and thus made a covenant, but the agreement was not valid because Isaac did not enter it under proper circumstances. The failure to find water in the well was a sign that the Philistines were not reliable covenant partners; instead they remained opponents of Isaac.

■ **28** The next five verses of the chapter cite the words Isaac spoke after he perceived he had been duped. Once he was aware of what had happened—on that very day— Isaac "cursed the Philistines."[49] There is no parallel to such an action in the ancient versions of Genesis 26, so the passage is an addition by the author or the tradition on which he was drawing.[50] For this reason, some scholars, for example, Charles, have seen in it a reflection of events in the author's time about which he harbored very strong feelings.[51] Methodologically, however, it is preferable to look first to other passages in the HB regarding the Philistines to test whether they are the sources for the vituperative language in Isaac's speech.[52] If that approach fails to account for his words, then one could look for other explanations, including the one formulated by Charles.

The writer leaves no doubt in the reader's mind that he understood the interaction between Isaac and the three Philistine leaders in a highly negative sense—they forced or misled him into an agreement to live at peace with them. Isaac became aware of their misbehavior only later when his servants told him about the well in which they found no water. The Philistines, of course, fare poorly in the HB, where they are pictured as a long-standing enemy of Israel—from the days of the judges and through much of monarchic period. Consequently, one is not surprised to find expressions of hostility toward them in a text such as Jubilees. Philistia figures in the prophetic oracles against the nations, though it is hardly the most frequent entry in the lists. Nevertheless, several expressions in Isaac's words about the Philistines derive from or echo prophetic denunciations of them.

Isaac cursed the Philistines. In Jeremiah 25 the Philistine "kings" (v. 20) are included among those from several nations on whom Jeremiah pours the cup of the Lord's wrath "to make them a desolation and a waste, an object of hissing and of cursing, as they are today" (v. 18). Perhaps this is what is meant in Jub 24:28 by "May the Philistines be cursed from among all peoples" unless

---

	refers to the use of "Watcher" as an angel title) is puzzling (*Jubiläen*, 449–50 n. b to v. 26).
49	Davenport says that "Jub. xxiv, 8-27, 33 is a prose narrative which provides the context for a curse on the Philistines" (*Eschatology*, 54). Testuz designates 24:28b (from "May the Philistines be cursed . . .")-30 (end) as one of the three passages that are additions to the original text of Jubilees (inserted into the text at some point between 65 and 38 BCE) (*Idées*, 39–42). Among the reasons is the heaping up of nearly synonymous terms and the sheer hatred of a gentile nation found in it—features hardly distinctive to this and the other two passages he excises.
50	Kugel suggests the following: "An oath, even an oath with the Philistines, cannot be undone. *Jubilees* thus has Isaac do the next best thing, uttering a curse (in the biblical world, a kind of negative oath, and an equally effective one) against the Philistines" (*Walk through* Jubilees, 135; cf. "Jubilees," 381).
51	Charles, *Jubilees*, 154–55. He thought that the "hatred expressed in these verses is hardly intelligible save in a contemporary of the wars waged by the Maccabeans against the Philistine cities" (p. 154). He then listed the passages attesting to Hasmonean conflicts with the remaining Philistine cities. It will be recalled that Charles believed the author of Jubilees was a supporter of the Maccabean high priesthood (ibid., lxxiii). See Endres's comments on Charles's view (*Biblical Interpretation*, 72–73 n. 47); for a very negative attitude toward the Philistines, Endres also refers to Sir 50:25-26, where they are among the three peoples the poet detests. The Philistines appear in the Qumran literature just a few times. Examples of places where the context is preserved are the following: in 1QM i:1-2 they are among the peoples first attacked by the sons of light (with the Edomites, Moabites, Ammonites, and the Kittim of Asshur); and 1QM xi:3 recalls that David defeated the Philistines many times by God's holy name. Philistines will also be among those who come to the aid of Esau and his sons in Jub 37:10 (with troops of the Kittim); in 38:7 they are among the slain.
52	Cf. Endres, *Biblical Interpretation*, 70–73.

the sense is that they are to be cursed "more than" all the nations.

On[53] *the day of anger and wrath.* Jeremiah's cup of wrath is identified as "the cup of the wine of wrath" in Jer 25:15, but the language here in Jubilees is closer to Jer 47:4 (part of the chapter about the Philistines in Jeremiah's oracles against the nations):

> because of the day that is coming
>   to destroy all the Philistines,
> to cut off from Tyre and Sidon
>   every helper that remains.
> For the LORD is destroying the Philistines,
>   the remnant of the coastland of Caphtor.

See also Zeph 1:14, which refers to "the great day of the LORD," a day characterized in v. 15 as "a day of wrath," and in v. 18 as "the day of the LORD's wrath." In Zephaniah 2, in dealing with the day of divine anger, the prophet refers to the Philistines first (after a reference to the "shameless nation" in v. 1): "before there comes upon you the fierce anger of the LORD, / before there comes upon you the day of the LORD's wrath." See too Jub 36:10.

May the Lord make them into (an object of) disgrace and a curse, into (an object of) anger and wrath. See Jer 25:18 (quoted above), especially "an object of hissing and cursing" when God pours out his anger on them.

In the hands of the sinful nations and in the hands of the Kittim.[54] In Jeremiah 47 the destruction and devastation that are coming on the Philistines are presented as the results of Pharaoh's attack on Gaza (v. 1)—a destruction that is ultimately from the hand of God. The phrase "the sinful nations" should remind one of Jub 23:23-24, where the sinful nations are the ones who invade and punish Israel (v. 24 employs the very expression used here in 24:28).[55] The text offers no more information about who, in the estimation of the author, the Kittim might be (see also v. 29 below). They are well known as enemies in the Qumran literature; see also Dan 11:30. However, in the only other occurrence of the term in Jubilees, they are not enemies of the Philistines as here but allies with them in the war of Esau and his sons against Jacob and his family (37:10, where the name is spelled *kētēwon*; they do not figure in the account of the actual battle in chap. 38). Since "Kittim" is used in tandem with "the sinful nations" and "the enemy" (v. 29), it may have a more general meaning for enemies from the west, perhaps the Greeks.[56]

■ 29 *Whoever escapes from the enemy's sword* (Latin lacks the expression) *and from the Kittim.*[57] In Jeremiah 25 the sword that the Lord is sending among the nations to punish them is mentioned in the verse directly before and after (vv. 16, 27, also v. 38) the section where Jeremiah pours out the cup of the Lord's wrath (vv. 17-26). The idea resembles some of the wording in Amos 9:1, a verse directly preceding the part of the chapter that influenced Jub 24:31-32: "and those who are left I will kill with the sword; / not one of them shall flee away, / not one of them shall escape." It is true that the divine words in Amos 9:1 are addressed to "the capitals" ("Strike the capitals") near the altar so that the temple in question shakes and shatters, but it is possible that the author of Jubilees

---

53 Davenport translates *la-ʿelata/in die* as "until the day" and explains that it reflects Hebrew עדה [*sic*], which means "up to and including" (p. 55 n. 3). This is a most unlikely suggestion regarding the Hebrew preposition, and understandably neither of the translations of Jubilees into Hebrew agrees with it: Goldmann ליום and Hartom ביום. Oddly, Berger translates the preposition as "bis zum."

54 Kittim is the most likely understanding of *kēteʾēm/cettin* (see Rönsch, *Jubiläen*, 132; Charles, *Jubilees*, 155), but Littmann, Goldmann, Hartom, and Berger think they are the Hittites. Hittites, to whom the writer refers in 19:4 as *weluda kēt/filiis geth*, are implausible in this context.

55 Puech thinks, therefore, that a universal war is intended, when the just will defeat these enemies (see v. 29 and 23:30) (*La croyance*, 1:102). It is more likely, however, that Jub 23:30 pictures God as expelling the enemies (see the commentary there).

56 Kugel suggests that it refers to the Macedonian troops of Alexander (*Walk through* Jubilees, 135; cf. "Jubilees," 382).

57 Davenport thinks that vv. 28-32 are poetic, apart from v. 29 (*Eschatology*, 55, 99). It is difficult to classify the uneven lines of vv. 28 and 30 as metrical, while vv. 31-32 are poetic and are based on a poetic passage—Amos 9:2-4 (see below). It is not clear why Davenport believes the passage moves from a curse in v. 28 to a judgment saying, and it is more challenging to see why he writes that v. 29 "is not concerned with the curse *until* the day of judgment, but with the plight of the Philistines on that day" (p. 55 n. 1). For the interpretation of the day of judgment, see the comments on v. 33 below.

saw some connection to his topic here since the word for "capitals" is הכפתור, a term that echoes "Caphtor" in 9:7, the place from which the Philistines are said to have come.[58] Isaiah 14:29 is also worth noting: "Do not rejoice, all you Philistines, / that the rod that struck you is broken, / for from the root of the snake will come forth an adder, / and its fruit will be a flying fiery serpent."

May the just nation in judgment eradicate from beneath the sky (cf. 31:20; 36:9). The vocabulary recalls words from passages such as Exod 17:14 (cf. Jub 24:33), although it concerns a different people: "Then the LORD said to Moses, 'Write this as a reminder in a book and recite it in the hearing of Joshua: I will utterly blot out the remembrance of Amalek from under heaven.'" Or Deut 7:24 could have provided some inspiration (regarding the nations in the land): "He will hand their kings over to you and you shall blot out their name from under heaven; no one will be able to stand against you, until you have destroyed them." The "just nation" should mean Israel, but the expression is not attested in the HB. They too will have a part in annihilating the Philistines.

For they will become enemies and opponents to my sons during their times (Latin: generations) *on the earth* [or: in the land]. The statement is a prediction by Isaac that the Philistines will prove to be foes to Israel as they were in the time the descendants of Isaac lived in the land (or on the earth).[59] The Israelites were, of course, the offspring of Isaac.

■ 30 Isaac promises complete destruction for the Philistines, leaving none to survive. The lines draw on the vocabulary and themes of several sections in the HB. Jeremiah 47:4 again lies behind the expression: "to destroy all the Philistines, / to cut off from Tyre and Sidon / every helper that remains. / For the LORD is destroying the Philistines, / the remnant of the coastland of Caphtor." Amos 1:8 is similar: "I will cut off the inhabitants from Ashdod, / and the one who holds the scepter from Ashkelon; / I will turn my hand against Ekron, / and the remnant of the Philistines shall perish, / says the LORD God." See also Isa 14:30; Ezek 25:16. The expression "name or descendants," another way of saying no person or memory of them will survive, sounds like the punishment predicted for Babylon in Isa 14:22: "I will rise up against them, says the LORD of hosts, and will cut off from Babylon name and remnant, offspring and posterity,[60] says the LORD."

Thus much, even if not all, of the language in Isaac's curse upon the Philistines can be traced in various ways to scriptural models, and it is motivated by a problem the writer spotted in the text of Genesis 26. For these reasons the passage need not be read as a reflection of Hasmonean hatred of the Philistines. More important is the message the writer communicates through the passage: "The main concern . . . behind the harshness in Jub. 24 has less to do with the Philistines per se and more to do with making covenants with surrounding nations."[61]

■ 31-32 In vv. 31-32, however, the base for Isaac's words in the HB is clearer: here the writer draws directly on Amos 9:2-4. In the comment above on v. 29, it was noted that the writer may have been attracted to the last chapter in the prophecy by the fact that Caphtor, the place from which the Philistines originated, makes two appearances in it: in v. 1, where the term for "the capitals" is הכפתור, and in v. 7, where it is the place-name: "Did I not bring Israel up from the land of Egypt, / and the Philistines from Caphtor and the Arameans from Kir?" The twofold occurrence of the noun may have encouraged the writer of Jubilees to adapt other parts of the chapter to his formulation of the curse upon the Philistines, even though Amos 9 seems not to be directed toward them.[62]

---

58 Kister, "Biblical Phrases and Hidden Biblical Interpretations and *Pesharim*," in Devorah Dimant and Uriel Rappaport, eds., *The Dead Sea Scrolls: Forty Years of Research* (STDJ 10; Leiden: Brill, 1992), 27–39, here 28–29.

59 The Deuteronomistic History is full of stories about wars between Philistines and Israelites; cf. also Ezek 25:15.

60 Where the two words נין and נכד figure in the MT, the LXX uses σπερμα. "Name and seed" appear together in other passages such as 1 Sam 24:21, where Saul asks David to swear he will not cut off "my descendants" and "my name."

61 Hanneken makes this comment, after recognizing that the passage could refer to second-century circumstances (*Subversion*, 163).

62 As Wintermute indicates ("Jubilees," 104 n. h), the reference to "the way of Beer-sheba" in Amos 8:14

The writer cites a number of expressions from Amos 9:2-4, but the elements do not always appear in the same order. Here are the two passages in parallel columns.

Amos 9:2-4	Jubilees 24:31-32
Though they dig into Sheol,	For even if he should go up to the sky,
from there shall my hand take them;	from there he would come down;
though they climb up to heaven,	even if he should become powerful on the earth,[63]
from there I will bring them down.	from there he will be torn out.
Though they hide themselves on the top of Carmel,	Even if he should hide himself among the nations,
from there I will search out and take them;	from there he will be uprooted;
and though they hide from my sight at the bottom of the sea,	even if he should go down to Sheol,
there I will command the sea-serpent,	there his punishment will increase.
And it shall bite them.	There he will have no peace.
And though they go into captivity in front of their enemies,	Even if he should go into captivity through the power of those who seek his life,
there I will command the sword, and it shall kill them;	they will kill him along the way.[64]
and I will fix my eyes on them for harm and not for good.	There will remain for him neither name nor descendants on the entire earth, because he is going to an eternal curse.

While the structure of the two texts differs,[65] from the comparison one can see that their message is similar. The people in question will have no place to escape; wherever they go, the punishment meant for them will find them and bring about their death (as Amos 9:1 indicates).[66] In Jubilees there are a few extra elements that make the point about the unavoidable fate of the Philistines even more emphatically:

His punishment will increase (Amos: from there shall my hand take them).

There he will have no peace (see Jub 23:12, 15, where this is a characteristic of evil times, the times of "the evil generation").

There will remain for him neither name nor descendants (see v. 30) *on the entire earth because he is going to an eternal curse* (this line, with "There he will have no peace," may be an elaboration or interpretation of the words "and I will fix my eyes on them for harm and not for good" in Amos 9:4). The source of the expression "an eternal curse" is not clear.

■ **33** At the conclusion of Isaac's curse, the angel explains that the words uttered by the patriarch conform to what is etched on the tablets of heaven. That is, the dire fate he has prescribed for them will come to pass because those words are part of the eternal, unchanging record in the celestial composition.[67] The future of the Philistines is fixed and unalterable. In v. 33 the angel comments that the terrible events Isaac has predicted will befall them "on the day of judgment so that he may be eradicated from the earth." This is the third reference in the unit to a day of this kind. In v. 28 it was the "day of anger and wrath," and in v. 30 the "day of judgmental anger." All of these designations sound as if they refer to a specific time in the future when the Philistines will receive their just reward, the time when all others will as well. It is not likely, however, that the

---

may also have caught the attention of the writer, as Isaac was there when he cursed the Philistines (Wintermute confuses Isaac and Jacob in his note). One may add that Amos also makes two of the three prophetic references to Isaac (7:9, 16).

63   The Latin version reads *et ubi fugiens erit* ("where[ver] he would flee").

64   For this line Latin has "he will die in Sheol."

65   In Amos 9:2-4 there are two elements with opposite terms (Sheol/heaven; top of Carmel/bottom of the sea) followed by the reference to captivity; in Jubilees there is a progression from sky to earth to Sheol before the reference to captivity.

66   In Ps 139:7-12 some similar language is used to a different end as the psalmist confesses—in a context of praise—that there is no place he can flee from the Lord's presence.

67   Since the heavenly tablets are mentioned, Kugel attributes v. 33 to his interpolator ("Interpolations," 264; *Walk through* Jubilees, 135, 287; "Jubilees," 382). His explanation is the same as for the reference in 23:32—the angel could not make the prediction, which came true in history, on his own authority. However, as noted in the commentary on 23:32, the author is merely proceeding with the same framework he has adopted since the end of chap. 1. There is no need to hypothesize intervention by another hand where the text expresses what the author characteristically writes.

writer means this by his various terms for that "day." Hanneken has made a solid case for the thesis that in Jubilees there is a "rolling" process of judgment for the nations: each one of them experiences the judgment appropriate to it, but the punishment of each nation is not tied to one specific temporal point at the end of the present world. The "day" to which the writer refers here is a time, however extended, when the Philistines gain their deserved rewards; the process was carried out in the course of history.[68] Each nation has its own "day." For other instances of "the day of judgment" in Jubilees, see the excursus on the subject in the commentary on chap. 4.

---

68 This is part of his larger thesis about how Jubilees subverts the genre apocalypse, but on this specific passage see *Subversion*, 161–65. Davenport seems to take the "day" to be an eschatological one (*Eschatology*, 55), but later he states that the purpose of the passage is "not to teach eschatological doctrine, but to show why the Philistines have fared as they have among the nations" (p. 56).

Rebekah and Jacob

25

1/ In the second year of this[a] week, in this[b] jubilee [2109], Rebekah summoned her son[c] Jacob and spoke to him: "My son, do not marry any of the Canaanite women like your brother Esau who has married two wives from the descendants[d] of Canaan. They have embittered my life with all the impure things that they do because everything that they do (consists of) sexual impurity[e] and lewdness. They have no decency because[f] (what they do) is evil. 2/ I, my son, love you very much; my heart[a] and my affection bless you[b] at all times of the day and[c] watches of the nights.[d] 3/ Now, my son, listen to me. Do[a] as your mother wishes.[b] Do not marry any of the women of this land but (someone) from my father's[c] house and from[d] my father's[e] clan. Marry[f] someone from my father's house.[g] The Most High God will bless you;[h] your family[i] will be a righteous family and your[j] descendants (will be) holy."

4/ Then Jacob spoke with his mother[a] Rebekah and said to her, "Mother, I am now nine[b] weeks of years [= 63 years] and have known[c] no woman. I have neither touched (one) nor have I even considered marrying any woman of[d] all the descendants of[e] Canaan's daughters.[f] 5/ For I recall, mother, what[a] our father[b] Abraham ordered me—that I should not marry anyone from all the descendants of[c] Canaan's house.[d] For I will marry[e] (someone) from the descendants of my father's house[f] and from my family.[g] 6/ Earlier I heard, mother,[a] that daughters had been born to your brother Laban. I have set my mind on them for the purpose of marrying one of them. 7/ For this reason I have kept myself from sinning and from becoming corrupted[a] in any ways[b] during my entire lifetime[c] because father[d] Abraham gave me many orders about lewdness and sexual impurity. 8/ Despite everything he ordered me, my brother has been quarreling with me[a] for the last 22 years and has often said to me, 'My brother, marry one of the sisters of my two wives.' But I have not been willing to do as he did.[b] 9/ I swear in your presence, mother, that during <u>my</u> entire <u>lifetime</u>[a] I will <u>not</u>[b] marry any[c] of the descendants of[d] Canaan's daughters nor will I do what is wrong as <u>my brother Esau</u>[e] has done. 10/ <u>Do not be afraid, mother, and be assured</u>[a] that I will do[b] as you wish. I will behave rightly and will <u>never conduct myself corruptly</u>."

11/ <u>Then she lifted her face</u>[a] to heaven, extended her fingers,[b] <u>and opened her mouth. She blessed the Most High God</u>[c] <u>who had created</u> the heavens and the earth and gave him tha<u>nks and praise</u>. 12/ <u>She said, "May the Lord God</u>[a] <u>be blessed</u>, and may his name[b] be blessed forever and e<u>ver—he who gave me Ja</u>cob, a pure son and a holy offspring, for he belongs to you. May his descendants[c] <u>be yours</u> throughout all time, throughout[d] the history of[e] eternity. 13/ Bless him,[a] Lord, and place a righteous blessing in my mouth[b] so that I may bless him."[c] 14/ At that time[a] the spirit of righteousness[b] descended[c] into her mouth. She put her two hands on Jacob's head and said:

15/ "Blessed are you, righteous Lord,[a] God[b] of the ages;[c]
and may he bless you more than all the human race.[d]
My son, may he provide the right path for you
and reveal[e] what is right to your descendants.
16/ May he multiply your sons during your lifetime;
may they rise[a] in number to the months of the year.[b]
May their children be more numerous[c] and great[d] than the stars of the sky;
may their number be larger[e] than the sands of the sea.
17/ May he give them[a] this pleasant land
as he said[b] he would give it[c] for all time
to Abraham and his descendants[d] after him;
may they own it as an eternal possession.
18/ Son, may I see your blessed children[a] during my lifetime;
may all[b] your descendants be blessed and[c] holy descendants.
19/ As you have given rest[a] to your mother's spirit during her lifetime,
so may the womb of the one who gave birth to you bless you.[b]
My affection and my breasts bless you;[c]
my mouth and my tongue praise you greatly.

20/ Increase and spread out[a] in[b] the land;
may your descendants be[c] perfect throughout all eternity
in the joy of[d] heaven and earth.
May your descendants[e] be delighted,[f]
and, on the great day of peace, may they have peace.
21/ May your name and your descendants[a] continue until[b] all ages.
May the Most High God be their God;[c]
may the righteous God[d] live with them;
and may[e] his[f] sanctuary be built among them into all[g] ages.
22/ May the one who blesses you be blessed
and anyone[a] who curses you falsely be cursed.[b]"

23/ She then kissed him and said to him, "May[a] the eternal Lord[b] love you[c] as your mother's heart and her affection are delighted with you and bless you." She then[d] stopped blessing (him).

Textual Notes

1a this] om. 20 25; Lat. *huius*.
b this (jubilee)] om. 44; Lat. lacks it.
c her son] om. 20 25; Lat. *filium suum*.
d descendants (lit., "seed")] "daughters" 9 12 38.
e because . . . impurity] om. 12 21.
f because²] om. 21.
2a my heart (*wa-lebbeya*)] "my son" (*waldeya*) 42 47 48.
b bless you] "have blessed you" 9 38ᵗ.
c day and] om. 9 38.
d the nights] om. 9 38.
3a listen . . . Do] "keep . . . do" 63; "listen . . . keep and do" 44.
b your mother wishes] "as I wish" 21 48 (phrased slightly differently).
c my father's] "your father's" 9 12 17 21 38 39 42 44 47 48 58 63.
d from²] om. 44 48 58 63; "of" 9 12 38 39 42 47.
e my father's²] "your father's" 9 12 17 38 39 42 44 47 48 58 63.
f Marry (lit., "take")] "you will marry" 12 20 25 35.
g from my (your 21 44 58) father's house²] om. 25.
h will bless you] "may bless" (i.e., "may the Most High God bless you") 9 21 38 42 44 48; "will bless" 20 25 39 47 58.
i your family] "your sons/children" 38 39 58.
j your (descendants)] om. 9 12 21 38 63.
4a his mother] om. 25.
b nine] "seven" 9 12; "two" 38; "four" 58. For "nine weeks" MS. 20 reads "seventy."
c known] The best reading of *ya'ammer*, though *ya'ammer* as in 9 12 17 44 would be the more likely spelling of the causative form.
d of] "among" 9 38.
e all the descendants of] om. 12 63.
f daughters (lit., "daughters of")] "his family" 9; "family of" 38; + "of the descendants of" 63.
5a what] "because" 12 38; "which" 63.
b our father] "my father" 44.
c the descendants of] "the daughters of" 12.
d house] om. 12 20 25 35.
e I will marry] "I am to marry/let me marry" 12 17.
f house] om. 9 38 63.
g my family] Mss. 20 25 35 use a different word for "family"; "the family of my father's house" 12.
6a mother] The form *'emmu* is one kind of vocative (see Dillmann, *Grammar*, 319-20 §142). Some MSS. express the same meaning through various forms (e.g., *'emmo* 12; *'emmeya* 44, while the others use the simple nominative form (but 9 has *'emma*). Ms. 38 om.
7a becoming corrupted] "corrupting" 9 21 35 44.
b ways] "my ways" 20 34 42 44 47 48 58.
c father] om. 9 12 20 38; "my father" 21 39 42 47 48; "our father" 63.
8a with me] om. 42 47 48.
b he did] om. 21; "my brother" 38; "I will not do" 35; + "my brother" (= "my brother did") 39 42 44 47 48 58 (see v. 9).
9a lifetime] + "mother" (vocative) 21.
b not] In DJD 13 the traces of letters at the left edge of frg. 1 are read as לא, but Werman (*Jubilees*, 375) reads only the *aleph* of what she thinks is אם (= "if"; the meaning of the oath would not be affected by the reading). One can be quite sure that the traces of letters are not from an *aleph*.
c any] om. 12 44.
d descendants of] "generations of the descendants (of Canaan)" 20 25 35.
e my brother Esau] So 4Q222 1 2. The Eth. copies lack "Esau."
10a and be assured] Eth. *ta'amani* seems a good equivalent of *hḥlmy* (4Q222 1 2). The Heb. verb has a conjunction before it, unlike Eth.
b I will do] "let me do/I am to do" 12 20.
11a lifted her face] "extended (?) her hands" 12.
b fingers] + "to heaven" 38 63.
c God] + "of heaven" 25 35.
12a God] "My God" 39 42 47 48 58.
b his name] "his holy name" 12.

c	his descendants] "descendants" 42 47.	c	blessed and] om. 47.
d	throughout] pr. "and" 20 25 35 44.	19a	you have given rest] "has given rest to you" 21 (with "your mother's spirit" as subject).
e	of] "until" 25 35.		
13a	him] om. 20 25 35 44.	b	may . . . bless you] "bless him" 9 17; "bless" 21 25 44 47 58; "will bless you" 35 63.
b	my mouth] "his mouth" 9; "her mouth" 38.		
c	him] om. "him" 25 35; "(bless) her" 58.	c	(my breasts bless) you] "thus bless you and" 12.
14a	time] + "when" 20 25.	20a	spread out] Though most copies read a sg. form, as with "increase," 9 and 17 read pl. forms (spelled differently).
b	spirit of righteousness] "holy spirit" 39 42ᵗ 47 48 58.		
c	descended] + "upon her" 12.		
15a	righteous Lord] "Lord of righteousness" 12 21 42 47 48 58 63.	b	in] "on" 21.
		c	be] "will be" 38.
b	God] pr. "and" 9 17 21 39 42 44 47 48 58 63.	d	in the joy of] om. 12.
c	ages] + "she lifted and said" 12.	e	your descendants] "in your descendants" 12.
d	race] om. 21. After "human(s)" it then adds "and than all the sons of people."	f	be delighted] pl. in 21 44; "will rejoice" 12.
		21a	your name and your descendants] om. 44.
e	reveal] Mss. 9 12 17 read an indicative: "he will reveal."	b	and your descendants continue (om. 12; pr. "and" 44; + "to them" 35) until] om. 9 17 63; "continue in" 12; "in" 21 38 44.
16a	may they rise] "may he rise" 20 21 25 35 38.		
b	year] "years" 20 44 58.	c	be their God] om. 35; ms. 21 om. from "God"—"God."
c	May . . . be . . . numerous] "will be numerous" 9.		
d	(may . . . be . . .) great] "will be great" 9; "will cause to be great" 38; om. 20 (it adds the verb in "and be greater than the sands").	d	God] "may he give you" 9 38.
		e	may . . . be built] "may build" 17.
		f	his] om. 9 38; "the Lord's" 21.
e	may . . . be larger] "will be larger" 9 21 25.	g	all] om. 21.
17a	them] "her/it" 42 47; "him/it" 48.	22a	anyone (lit., "all flesh")] Ms. 12 om. "flesh"; "all your flesh" 38.
b	he said] om. 25.		
c	would give it] The suffix is fem., referring to the land; 9 17 35 39 44 48 read a masc. sg. suffix; "would give them" 21; "would give" 42 47 63; om. 38.	b	be cursed] + "in everything" 12.
		23a	May . . . love] "will love" 9; "may love you" 12.
		b	the eternal Lord] "the Lord for ever" 39 44 58.
d	his descendants] + "to eternity and" 38; + "who" 63.	c	you] om. 12.
18a	children] "son" 39 42 47 48 58.	d	then] om. 20 25 35.
b	all] om. 21 58.		

Commentary

After a chapter devoted to Isaac and concluding with his curse on the Philistines, the text of Jubilees turns to Rebekah, the issue of marriage for Jacob, and the extraordinary blessing his mother requested for him. The subject of a wife for Jacob, a key topic in the chapter and one related to a fundamental concern in Jubilees (see 20:4; 22:20), first arises in Genesis once Rebekah hears that Esau wants to kill Jacob for stealing his father's blessing (in 27:1-40). She instructs Jacob to flee to her brother Laban in Haran (vv. 41-45); in the Genesis context she says nothing about taking a wife from among Laban's daughters. Escape to safety is the only concern. When in the next verse she speaks to Isaac, marriage takes center stage: "Then Rebekah said to Isaac, 'I am weary of my life because of the Hittite women. If Jacob marries one of the Hittite women such as these, one of the women of the land, what good will my life be to me?'" (v. 46). Isaac dutifully complied with her wish by dispatching Jacob to find a suitable wife in the ancestral home (Gen 28:1-5). In Genesis it seems as if marriage is Rebekah's excuse for sending Jacob away, not the real reason.[1]

The author of Jubilees relocates a form of the story before Isaac mishandles the blessing of the older son

---

[1] The standard way to explain the difference separating 27:41-45 and v. 46 is to appeal to sources (the former from J, the latter from P). For a discussion, see Hamilton, *Genesis 18–50*, 233–34; cf. Endres, *Biblical Interpretation*, 93.

(found in Genesis 27 // Jubilees 26) and the ensuing events. As a result, the account (Jub 25:1-10) is unaffected by Esau's desire for revenge and the danger in which it placed Jacob. Rather, Rebekah's instructions to Jacob, spoken directly to him, build on the negative example of Esau's marriages.[2] Genesis mentions those unions at the end of chap. 26, after Isaac's dealings with the Philistines: "When Esau was forty years old, he married Judith daughter of Beeri, the Hittite, and Basemath daughter of Elon, the Hittite; and they made life bitter for Isaac and Rebekah" (26:34-35). Following the blessing story in Gen 27:1-40, she expressed concern about her daughters-in-law and gave voice to her fear that Jacob would repeat Esau's nuptial mistakes (see above for 27:46). Jubilees to this point has made no reference to Esau's marriages; the reader first learns about them from Rebekah's words to Jacob (vv. 1-3), where she pre-empts Isaac's role in Gen 28:1-5.[3] In Jubilees, Jacob's planned trip to Haran initially has nothing to do with fear. Its goal is to find a proper wife for him. Once Rebekah and Jacob have expressed their agreement about marriage within the clan, she follows the example of Abraham by blessing God, Jacob, and his future descendants.

Chapter 25 falls into these parts:
1-10 Dialogue between Rebekah and Jacob
    1-3 Rebekah instructs Jacob about a fitting marriage partner
    4-10 Jacob explains his conduct and view of marriage
11-23 Rebekah blesses God and prays for Jacob and his descendants

Apart from the full Ge'ez text of the chapter, there is only a little evidence from the versions: part of v. 1 is legible on the Latin manuscript, and 4Q222 frg. 1 has words and letters from vv. 9-12.

1-10 Dialogue between Rebekah and Jacob

The only verbal interactions Genesis records between the mother and favored son are their exchange when she wants him to deceive Isaac (Gen 27:5-13) and as she speaks to him when she wishes to send him away from Esau (27:41-45; Jacob makes no reply). The author of Jubilees, in contrast, incorporates a sustained and moving encounter between them; it has a far more appealing tenor than the words between them in Genesis.

1-3 Rebekah Instructs Jacob about a Fitting Marriage Partner

In Genesis, Rebekah never speaks to Jacob about whom he should marry; only Isaac gives him such instructions. In Gen 28:1 Isaac sends for him, although he does so after prodding by Rebekah in 27:46. The author of Jubilees had noted several times that Rebekah, like Abraham, favored Jacob far more than Esau (19:16-31; 22:4; 23:4). Moreover, Abraham had charged her to take special care of him (19:17-21), and now she senses a need and opportunity to do precisely that.

■ 1 The year after Isaac's unfortunate encounter with the Philistine leaders (compare the dates in 24:21 and 25:1) Rebekah took charge of matters by summoning Jacob. In bidding him to come to her, this redoubtable mother did something that no other woman does in Genesis (she summons Jacob in 27:42), where patriarchs are the ones who require the presence of others. Her command that Jacob come to her is modeled on Isaac's action in Gen 28:1, and her words to him are also based on Isaac's instructions to his younger son in Gen 28:2-4. Those words, however, the writer transforms into a more characteristically Jubilean speech.

Genesis 28:1	Jubilees 25:1
Then Isaac called Jacob and blessed him, and charged him, "You shall not marry one of the Canaanite women."	. . . Rebekah summoned her son Jacob and spoke to him: "My son, do not marry any of the Canaanite women."

The writer of Jubilees does not reproduce "and blessed him" here because the expression will become appropriate only later in the chapter (vv. 11-23). Otherwise, the version in Jubilees for the most part simply replaces *Isaac* with *Rebekah* and reduces the number of verbs of speaking from three to two (from four to three in the Hebrew and Ethiopic texts).[4] It is noteworthy that in

---

2   See Halpern-Amaru, *Empowerment*, 84–85; Endres, *Biblical Interpretation*, 74–76.
3   Jubilees presents the contents of Gen 27:40–28:5 for a second time in 26:35–27:11; there Rebekah and Isaac play the roles they have in Genesis. The result is that in Jubilees 27 Isaac merely reaffirms what Rebekah said in chap. 25.
4   Both employ verbs of speaking that simply intro-

Genesis and Jubilees the forbidden women are identified as Canaanites.

After these introductory words, Rebekah continues her speech to Jacob in a way that is typical in Jubilees. She draws on the contents of the two notices about Esau's wives (Gen 26:34-35; 27:46; neither passage has appeared yet in Jubilees) and invokes him as a negative example. Isaac in Gen 28:1 tells Jacob not to marry Canaanite women. Rebekah in Jubilees says the same words and adds that Esau's wives fall into that category. Her claim is consistent with the implication of Gen 23:3-7, 10, 16, 18, 20 (see Jub 19:4-5) that Hittites lived in and owned part of the land.[5] Genesis 23:12 and 13 call them "the people of the land," and Rebekah had said to Isaac that she did not want Jacob to marry "one of the Hittite women such as these, one of the women of the land" (Gen 27:46; see Jub 27:8). This she now declares to Jacob in Jub 25:1. Using direct speech, she takes up the notice from Gen 26:35 that the Hittite wives of Esau made the lives of Isaac and Rebekah bitter, but, unlike in Gen 26:35, she zeroes in on how they embittered *her* life: "with all the impure things that they do because everything that they do (consists of) sexual impurity and lewdness. They have no decency because (what they do) is evil."[6] These women, according to Rebekah, behave as Abraham had told Jacob the nations habitually conducted themselves (22:16-17; cf. 23:17).[7] Their behavior matches their unfortunate ethnic origin. Quite understandably, she does not want her son Jacob, the one who had received extraordinary blessings and promises from Abraham and was to be his successor on earth (19:17-18), to corrupt the chosen line through fateful mismatches.

■ **2** She followed up her basic thesis by expressing the deep, sincere love she felt for her younger son (cf. v. 23). Abraham had observed that Rebekah "loved Jacob much more than Esau" (19:16; see v. 19), and the writer said that "Rebekah loved Jacob with her entire heart and her entire being very much more than Esau" (19:31). As she puts it, she has his welfare in mind throughout every day and night (for watches of the night, see Ps 90:4; Lam 2:19). Regarding her actions during the day she nearly quotes Ps 34:2a (Eng. v. 1): "I will bless the Lord at all times"; but Jacob is the one she blesses unceasingly.

■ **3** Out of her warm affection for him, she gives him proper instructions about marriage; those directions are related to but not lifted verbatim from Gen 28:1-3.

Genesis 28:1-3	Jubilees 25:3
Then Isaac called Jacob and blessed him, and charged him, "You shall not marry one of the Canaanite women. Go at once to Paddan-aram to the house of Bethuel, your mother's father; and take as wife from there one of the daughters of Laban, your mother's brother. May God Almighty bless you and make you fruitful and numerous, that you may become a company of peoples."	"Now, my son, listen to me. Do as your mother wishes.[8] Do not marry any of the women of this land but (someone) from my father's house and from my father's clan. Marry someone from my father's house. The Most High God will bless you; your family will be a righteous family and your and your descendants (will be) holy."

Jacob is not to take "any of the women of this land" but is to wed someone from within the family. The book of Jubilees is adamant about endogamy, and Rebekah is the one who commends it forcefully to her all-important son. If he obeys her orders, she asserts, it will unleash the patriarchal blessing of descendants who will also

---

duce quotations and thus are not rendered in the translations.

5 Genesis 10:15 lists Heth as a son of Canaan, and Josh 1:4 calls the entire promised land "the land of the Hittites." The Hittites are the first of the seven nations in the land with whom Deut 7:1-6 forbids intermarriage. There the concern is idolatry, while here Rebekah speaks of sexual improprieties.

6 Loader observes how Rebekah speaks only of herself as having her life embittered without mentioning Isaac (unlike Gen 26:35) and correctly suggests her words may be influenced by Gen 27:46 (*Enoch, Levi*, 162).

7 VanderKam, "Rebekah's Patriarchal Prayers," 426. See also 35:14. Endres thinks the failure of Rebekah to name Esau's wives is intentional: "The author showed his disdain for these foreign wives by avoiding even the mention of their names; this constitutes the height of insult" (*Biblical Interpretation*, 75). Yet it could be simply a result of abbreviating.

8 Note that Rebekah, though she summoned Jacob and addresses him with imperatives, is not said to command him, as Isaac does, but to urge him to do her wishes.

be righteous and holy. Her instructions mirror those Abraham had given when arranging for a wife for Isaac: he had ordered the senior servant on his staff to swear that "you will not get a wife for my son from the daughters of the Canaanites among whom I live, but will go to my country and to my kindred and get a wife for my son Isaac" (Gen 24:3-4). Isaac, at Rebekah's behest, did the same in Gen 28:1-2 when he spoke to Jacob. Here again Isaac's words that Jubilees will reproduce in 27:10 are placed in Rebekah's mouth first. She does not, however, mention the family of her brother Laban but in part echoes the words of Isaac in Gen 28:2 ("the house of Bethuel, your mother's father") and of Abraham in Gen 24:4 ("to my kindred"). Where in Gen 28:3 Isaac calls on God Almighty to bless Jacob, Rebekah addresses the Most High God for this purpose (the divine title appears in other blessings in Jub 20:9; 21:25; 22:11, 13, 19, 23, 27; in chap. 25, see vv. 11, 21). Between the expected benediction on the individual himself and the gift of descendants she interposes the prediction that his family (*tewledd*)[9] will be righteous (see Pss 14:5; 112:2). For holy descendants, see Deut 7:6 (part of a passage forbidding exogamy [vv. 3-6]); Isa 6:13; Ezra 9:2 (also against exogamy).[10] While Rebekah utters words familiar from blessings in Genesis, the noteworthy fact is that a woman speaks them. This passage and the prayers in vv. 11-23 below are the most outstanding instances in Jubilees of the enhanced stature she attains in the book.[11] She perceived Jacob's character and place before Isaac did, and she again precedes her husband, this time in seeking the welfare of Jacob and of the chosen family.

4-10 Jacob Explains His Behavior and View of Marriage

In Genesis 28 Jacob does not reply to his father's orders about going to Paddan-aram; he simply goes. Here in Jubilees he makes a lengthy, self-promoting response to his mother, indicating his complete agreement with her and declaring his unceasing vigilance in the matter.

■ 4 He declares that he has reached the age of sixty-three[12] yet remains unsullied by contact with women and by any wish at all to marry Canaanite ladies. He was pure in action and in thought. Rebekah had told him not to marry "any of the Canaanite women" (v. 1); Jacob answers that he had had no sexual contact with

---

9   Leslau lists "race, tribe, family, species, offspring, generation" as its meanings (*Concise Dictionary*, 159).

10 Jacob Milgrom notes that Rebekah refers three times in this chapter (vv. 3, 12, 18) to the holiness of Jacob's seed—an indication in the book that in the pre-Sinaitic period Israel is holy ("The Concept of Impurity in *Jubilees* and the *Temple Scroll*," *RevQ* 16/62 [1993] 277-84, here 282). "And if Jacob and his descendants are to remain holy they must always eschew intermarriage" (p. 282).

11 For a summary of the evidence, see VanderKam, *Book of Jubilees*, 116.

12 His age is correct. Jubilees 19:13 places the birth of the twins in 2046, and 25:1 dates the present episode to 2109. In *Gen. Rab.* 68:5, R. Hezekiah says, "Our father Jacob was sixty-three years old when he received the blessings." In *b. Meg.* 17a and *Seder Olam* 2 one finds the reasoning behind the number, and it proceeds in this way. Ishmael's life span (137 years [Gen 25:17, where the notice is anticipatory]) is recorded in Genesis to relate it to Jacob. Ishmael was fourteen years older than Isaac (he was born when Abram was eighty-six, while Abram was one hundred when Isaac arrived); Isaac was sixty when the twins were born; at that time Ishmael would have been seventy-four, leaving sixty-three more years in his life. It was assumed that the next episode in Genesis after Isaac sent Jacob to Haran—"Esau went to Ishmael and took Mahalath daughter of Abraham's son Ishmael, and sister of Nebaioth, to be his wife in addition to the wives he had" (28:9)—happened at the same time as Jacob's departure and that the text implied that Ishmael died at this time, since that is why Nebaioth his son is mentioned: when his father passed away, he was the one who gave Mahalath to Esau. Hence Jacob was sixty-three at the time. The author of Jubilees must have arrived at the number sixty-three, not for his father's blessing and the departure for Haran but for the present incident, in a different way; also, when it reproduces Gen 28:9 (in 29:18), it omits any reference to Nebaioth. There Mahalath is identified only as Ishmael's daughter. Syncellus reported: "Josephos says that when Jacob was 63, he had never had relations with a woman, as he himself declared to his mother Rebecca" (120.16–17; Adler/Tuffin, *Chronography*, 149). This is one of the instances where the historian confuses what came from Jubilees and what came from Josephus; Josephus says nothing about this in *Ant.* 1.276-77. See Rönsch, *Jubiläen*, 298; Charles, *Jubilees*, 157.

any woman[13] and had not even thought of marriage with "any woman of all the descendant's of Canaan's daughters" (v. 4). Genesis 28 several times refers to בנות כנען (vv. 1, 6, 8, 9) but does not resort to the full phrase Jacob uses. Rather, Jacob echoes the words of his grandfather Abraham, who had exhorted him not to "marry a woman from all the descendants of Canaan's daughters" (Jub 22:20). Jacob states explicitly in the sequel (vv. 5, 7) that he based his marital views on the teachings of Abraham; in v. 4 he simply recalls his words without mentioning the source.

■ 5 He uses almost the same phrase in v. 5, where he does attribute the teaching to Abraham. The occasion to which Jacob appeals was when Abraham gave his final orders to his grandson, especially the ones about separating from the nations (22:16-22). In Jub 22:20 he had said to Jacob, "Be careful, my son Jacob, not to marry a woman from all the descendants of Canaan's daughters, because all of his descendants are (meant) for being uprooted from the earth" (cf. 20:4; for the curse and uprooting of Canaan's descendants, see 10:30). Jacob, Abraham's true "son," of course obeyed what his grandfather commanded him. As a result, he announces that he will marry someone from "the descendants of my father's house and from my family." By "my father's house" he should mean Abraham's clan because his own father's house contained no marriageable women. Abraham had not demanded that he marry within the family (Jubilees does not reproduce Abraham's instructions to his servant on the matter in Gen 24:2-4; cf. vv. 37-38, 48), but it was an easy inference from avoiding marriage with Canaan's daughters. On this score he echoes Rebekah's words in v. 3.

■ 6 In further response to Rebekah, Jacob refers to the news he had received "that daughters had been born to your brother Laban." Genesis 28:2 has Isaac say only that he was to take one of Laban's daughters as his spouse without saying how Isaac knew Laban had daughters. The author of Jubilees anticipates the problem through Jacob's words in v. 6, but the model for the idea may come from Gen 22:20-24. There one reads: "Now after these things it was told Abraham, 'Milcah has also borne children, to your brother Nahor'" (v. 20). News passed between the two branches of the family, so it was only natural that Jacob learned his uncle was the father of daughters. Apparently he had resolved to find a spouse among them even before his mother broached the subject. His plans at this stage call for only one wife.

■ 7 The Abrahamic curriculum included warnings about avoiding impurity and sexual offenses. Jacob in v. 7 may be alluding to the instructions Abraham gave to all his sons in 20:3-7, but several references in chap. 22 are more likely to lie behind the verse. Abraham prayed that God would "purify you from all filthy pollution" (22:14); Jacob was to separate from the peoples "for their actions are something that is impure, / and all their ways are defiled and something abominable and detestable" (22:16); and he asked that God would remove Jacob from "their impurity and from all their error" (22:19). In 25:1 Rebekah asserted that Esau's wives had "embittered my life with all the impure things that they do because everything that they do (consists of) sexual impurity and lewdness." Jacob, unlike Esau, had learned and applied his grandfather's lessons.

■ 8 Jacob further incriminates his brother by charging that Esau had been badgering him for the last twenty-two years to marry a sister of his Hittite wives. According to Gen 26:34-35 Esau married the two when he—and thus his twin Jacob as well—was forty years of age. If Jacob is now sixty-three years, he would be saying that almost immediately after he became a husband Esau started pressuring Jacob to emulate his example.[14] True to his character, Esau disobeyed Abraham's instructions on so vital a matter as marriage (he was present for the scene in chap. 20). He was already overwhelmingly unfit to be the recipient of the patriarchal promises and blessings. Genesis says nothing about Esau's urging his brother to marry into his wives' families. Jacob, as one would expect, proved immune to his brother's misguided attempts, despite his persistence over so many years. The influence of Abraham outweighed that of Esau.

---

13 Loader thinks the passage implies that sex before marriage is included in what the author means by sexual misbehavior (*Enoch, Levi*, 163).

14 The charge that Esau had been pestering Jacob about marrying into his wives' families for years may seem to be news to Rebekah, but, as Kugel writes, it may be meant to supply a reason why

■ **9-10** In view of Esau's efforts, Jacob swears an oath before his mother that he will maintain his noble resolve. Again using Abraham's expression, he asserts he will never marry "any of the descendants of Canaan's daughters." He makes the same pledge by saying to her that he will never do as his brother had done. So he in effect tells her that she need not fret as she did in Gen 27:46 (but see Jub 27:8): "If Jacob marries one of the Hittite women such as these, one of the women of the land, what good will my life be to me?" Jacob promises he will always be obedient to her. He will do what is right (lit., "I will walk in the right [*wa-ba-retu' 'aḥawwer*]") and avoid what is corrupt (lit., "I will not corrupt my ways forever [*wa-'i-yāmāsen fenāwiya la-'ālam*]").[15] Abraham had so commanded all his sons (20:2-3, 9) and Isaac (21:25) and Jacob (22:10) individually; moreover, he had characterized his own conduct in much the same terms (21:2). There is a way ordained by God in which the line of Abraham is to walk, and Jacob has trod that path and vows he always will. Jacob's powerful reassurances to his mother express in crystal-clear terms what the book teaches about such marriages.

11-23 Rebekah Blesses God and Prays for Jacob

As a response to the reassuring words from Jacob, Rebekah assumes an additional patriarchal role: she pronounces blessings and asks that God bless her son with the gifts promised to Abraham. The section divides into several parts: v. 11, a prose description; vv. 12-13, her blessing of God and prayer for Jacob; v. 14, a prose description; vv. 15-22, another blessing of God and prayer for Jacob and his descendants; and v. 23, a prose description in which a one-line prayer for Jacob is included.

■ **11** Verse 11 is a narrative introduction to her words that are quoted in vv. 12-13. To mark how important her blessing/prayer is, the writer takes the time to describe her bodily motions as she spoke. She looked upward and extended the fingers of her hands.[16] A near parallel occurs in ALD 3:1–2, where Levi says, "Then I lifted up my eyes and my countenance [lit., face] to heaven, and I opened my mouth and spoke. I stretched out the fingers of my hands for truth over against [or: towards] the holy ones. And I prayed."[17] Like Levi, she "opened her mouth" and first blessed the one who was responsible for the happy situation in which she found herself as mother of a quintessentially virtuous son. In her prayer, she addresses "the Most High God [4Q222 1 4: אל עליון]," just as Melchizedek had done when blessing Abram. And, like the priest-king of Salem, she appeals to the one "who had created the heavens and the earth."[18] In addition to blessing him, "(she) gave him thanks and praise" for his wonderful gift (for thanks/praise paired, see, e.g., Ps 69:31 [Eng. 30]; and esp. 100:4).[19]

■ **12-13** In the posture depicted in v. 11, she directed her thanks and praise to this almighty God who had not only bestowed rich blessings on her and her son but could also do the same in the future.

The words of her first prayer[20] in this context begin

Rebekah was worried Jacob would marry as Esau had (*Walk through* Jubilees, 136; cf. "Jubilees," 383).

15 Almost all of the latter expression survives on 4Q222 1 3: ול[א אשחית דרכי לעולם]. Loader draws attention to the fact that corrupting ways is the expression used for the sin of the Watchers, humans, and animals before the flood (Jub 5:2-3) (*Enoch, Levi*, 163).

16 4Q222 1 3-4 preserves the verb "she raised [נשאה]" and the reference to her hands (די[הא]').

17 Greenfield, Stone, and Eshel, *Aramaic Levi Document*, 61; see Drawnel, *Aramaic Wisdom Text*, 211; VanderKam, "Rebekah's Patriarchal Prayers," 428–29.

18 Only a trace of the first letter survives on 4Q222 1 4, and it may be the *qoph* in קונה ("Creator"); see DJD 13:90 for a discussion of the difficulty in reading the letter. Werman reads בורא without comment (*Jubilees*, 375, 378), although when citing the passage on p. 375 n. 5 she uses קנה. Endres notes that God as Creator is a theme in other such texts in the book ("Prayers," 34, 46–47). For his prayer when dedicating the temple, Solomon "spread out his hands to heaven" (1 Kgs 8:22) and blessed God with whom no other deities in heaven or on earth could compare (v. 23).

19 See also 1QHª xix:4–5 (Werman, *Jubilees*, 378).

20 For categorizing her words in vv. 12-13 as a prayer, though the text does not use the term for it, see VanderKam, "Rebekah's Patriarchal Prayers," 430. Rebekah's prayers in this chapter, though not found in the HB, fit Moshe Greenberg's description of biblical prose prayer, despite their being rather poetic. Greenberg writes about the prose prayers:

in v. 12 and conclude in v. 13. The terms by which she invokes the deity survive on 4Q222 1 5: ברוך יהוה אלוה[ים. In the HB, addresses or references to God often begin with "Blessed" (e.g., Gen 9:26; 14:20; 24:27, etc.), and, as here, forms of ברך are also used with his "name" (Job 1:21; Pss 96:2; 100:4; 113:2; 145:1, 21 [where "forever" follows]). Rebekah attaches to the divine names a relative pronoun that explains the action for which she is blessing him. While her words mimic the pattern in Melchizedek's blessing ("and *blessed be God Most High, / who has delivered your enemies into your hand*," Gen 14:20) and in others in the HB,[21] the matter she records is the gift of Jacob. Her description of Jacob is truly fitting in the context and in the book: he is "a pure son" (cf. 22:14, 19), "a holy offspring/child" (see 22:27, 29; 25:3)—quite unlike his brother Esau. She asserts that Jacob belongs to God (here she switches from the third to the second person, speaking directly to the deity) and asks that his descendants too may be the Lord's eternal possession (cf. 2:19-21). In so doing she echoes sentiments that Abraham had expressed regarding her son and his offspring; see 19:18, 29; 22:10, 11, 15, 24, 28-30. The other petitions that she makes in her prayer are that God would bless Jacob (see 19:27; 22:10, 11, 14, 19, 30, where Abraham makes the same request) and that she would receive the ability to bless him in the proper way (to utter a "righteous" blessing, that is, an "appropriate" or "true" one). Apparently, she realized she needed assistance to do something so momentous on her own. Her request received an immediate, positive answer. Though her words will take the form of a prayer, through her prayer and with God's help she will be blessing Jacob.

■ **14** Verse 14 serves as the narrative bridge to the longest of her prayers regarding Jacob. She had requested that God place "a righteous blessing" in her mouth, and now the deity does precisely that. The inspiration accorded her is termed "the/a spirit of righteousness." No Hebrew survives at this point so that one cannot determine whether the expression was רוח אמת (see 1QS iii:18, 21; iv:23; 4Q177 12–13 i:5; Werman uses this translation) or רוח צדקה/צדק (see 4Q444 1–4 i + 5 3). Whichever phrase appeared in the original Hebrew text, Rebekah receives the divine inspiration for which she had asked (cf. Abram in 12:22). The picture of her in the context anticipates the rabbinic notion that Rebekah, like the other matriarchs, was a prophetess.[22] Once again the placement of her hands is noted: she put both of them on Jacob's head (see Gen 48:14, 17).[23]

■ **15** She begins a second time by speaking directly to God—that is, she prays—but she does this for just one line. Once more she places "Blessed" first in the prayer and then refers to the deity as righteous (Deut 32:4; Pss 119:137; 129:4; etc.; Jub 21:4; for "God of righteousness," see Ps 4:2; 1QH[a] xxvii:8; 4Q427 7 ii:14; 4Q511 1 5). The adjective is well chosen in a context where Rebekah wants to say the right blessing; that is, she will bless Jacob, who is not her older son. Consequently, she appeals to the God who is righteous; he will assure that the blessing be communicated to the right person with the appropriate benefits. Moreover, she refers to him as the "God of the ages." Her request will be that he should bless Jacob forever (see vv. 17, 20-21), and the Lord who rules for all ages is fully capable of doing that.

After her one-line blessing of God, she starts speaking directly to Jacob and continues the second-person form through the end of her words (v. 22).[24] Her requests for him are wide-ranging and comprehensive. Indeed, as

---

"What distinguishes all these prayers is that they appear to be freely composed in accordance with particular life-settings; their putative authors and their function are supplied by their context" (*Biblical Prose Prayers as a Window to the Popular Religion of Ancient Israel* [The Taubman Lectures in Jewish Studies, 6th series; Berkeley: University of California Press, 1983] 7).

21 Cf. Greenberg, *Biblical Prose Prayer*, 30–32. The pattern occurs in expressions of gratitude for benefits conferred by God.

22 As recounted in *Gen. Rab.* 67:9, the idea was attached to Gen 27:42, where Rebekah learns of Esau's threatening words that he had said *to himself* (in Jub 27:1 she learns this in a dream). See Halpern-Amaru, *Empowerment*, 86 n. 24; Endres, *Biblical Interpretation*, 78–79.

23 VanderKam, "Rebekah's Patriarchal Prayers," 432–33. Endres tentatively suggests that Rebekah is ordaining Jacob as a rabbi (*Biblical Interpretation*, 80), but how the words of her blessing would fit with such a setting is not readily apparent.

24 For examples of this switch in persons in such prayer/blessings, see Greenberg, *Biblical Prose*

Halpern-Amaru notes, she is passing on the patriarchal promises.

> The scene marks the third occasion in Jubilees when the blessings of the covenant are transmitted to Jacob. Rebekah, however, does not convey them in the summary form of "the blessing of Abraham" or even as she herself heard them from the mouth of that patriarch [19:23, 27]. . . . Directly inspired by God, she sets them forth in a full formulation that frequently reflects the language of the promises as they had been made on multiple occasions to Abraham and as they would eventually be made to Jacob at Bethel.[25]

The individual requests Rebekah makes are these:

May he bless you more than all the human race (the force of the preposition *'em-* in *'em-kwellu tewledda sab'* appears to be comparative).[26] There is no direct parallel in Genesis, but the words express well the sentiments of a mother determined that her son, whose virtues she had recognized long before, should receive the full abundance of the promises made to his ancestors. The implication of those blessings was that the chosen line would fare better than any other people.[27] The line may also echo the teachings in Deuteronomy 32 (vv. 6b-14) and 33 (esp. vv. 28-29: "So Israel lives in safety, / untroubled is Jacob's abode / in a land of grain and wine, / where the heavens drop down dew. / Happy are you, O Israel! Who is like you, / a people saved by the Lord, / the shield of your help, / and the sword of your triumph! / Your enemies shall come fawning to you, / and you shall tread on their backs").

Provide the right path [fenota ṣedq] *for you / and reveal what is right* [ṣedqa] *to your descendants*. See Jub 20:2; Ps 23:3; 1QS iv:2. Revealing what is right calls to mind the Lord's words about Abraham in Gen 18:19: "I have chosen him, that he may charge his children and his household after him to keep the way of the Lord by doing righteousness and justice" (cf. Isa 45:19).

■ 16 Having introduced the subject of Jacob's descendants, Rebekah develops it in her next lines.

May he multiply your sons during your lifetime; / may they rise in number to the months of the year. The phrasing of the first line in v. 16 is unusual in that Rebekah asks the Lord to multiply Jacob's sons while he is alive, but the intent of it is to contrast his immediate sons with those of future generations, who come in for consideration in the next sentence. The entire verse constitutes a more detailed statement of the traditional blessing/request for descendants. Perhaps it is not surprising that Rebekah already designates a specific number of sons—"may they rise in number to the months of the year"—as she is speaking under the influence of "the spirit of righteousness."[28]

May their children be more numerous and great than the stars of the sky; / may their number be larger than the sands of the sea. As for his children, she prays that their descendants will attain the numbers mentioned in the patriarchal promises: more numerous (she adds: "and great")[29] than the stars (Gen 15:5; 22:17; 26:4), of greater numbers than the sands on the beach (Gen 22:17). She asks for more than the number of stars and sands, not for "as many as" in the promises in Genesis.

■ 17 From innumerable offspring she turns to the place where they will reside.

May he give them this pleasant land . . . as an eternal possession: Naturally, Rebekah mentions the land promise that is prominent in Genesis and in Jubilees (e.g., Jub 13:3, 19-21 ["forever"]; 14:18; 15:10 ["forever"]; 19:9; 22:14, 27; 24:10). For Canaan as a pleasant land, see Jub 13:2, where Abram saw that "the land . . . was very pleasant" (cf. 12:30; 13:6). Abraham had anticipated her

---

Prayers, 33–34. Werman raises the possibility that a sentence has dropped out (*Jubilees*, 378), though she realizes one cannot reconstruct what it might have been.
25 Halpern-Amaru, *Empowerment*, 86.
26 Charles: "beyond all the generations of men"; Wintermute: "more than all the generations of man."
27 Cf. VanderKam, "Rebekah's Patriarchal Prayers," 433–34.
28 God predicted the same for Ishmael in Gen 17:20 // Jub 15:20.
29 The word "great" is used in Gen 15:1 in a context where Abram's progeny is the subject ("your reward shall be very great").

blessing by requesting that the promises of progeny and land be given to Jacob; she now reinforces what he said, as will Isaac in Gen 28:4 // Jub 27:11. The latter part of the verse, appealing to the promises made to Abraham, sounds very much like Luke 1:55 (the translations are literal):

Jubilees: as he said he would give it to Abraham and his descendants after him for all time
Luke: as he said to our fathers, to Abraham and to his descendants for all time.[30]

■ **18** Rebekah, due to the nature of the situation, is speaking about future gifts, but she herself wants to be able to experience some of them. So she makes a request for herself.

May I see your blessed children during my lifetime; / may all your descendants be blessed and holy descendants.
Rebekah's maternal side comes to the fore in this request. Just as she wanted Jacob to have many sons "during your lifetime" (v. 16), so now she asks for the privilege of seeing his children—a blessing that Sarah and the Rebekah of Genesis never enjoyed. She will indeed see his sons Levi and Judah in Jub 31:5-7, perhaps the other nine in 31:30—32:31, and all of them including Benjamin in 33:21-23. Regarding all his descendants, she reiterates the prediction she made in 25:3 in connection with a proper marriage for him: "your family will be a righteous family and your descendants (will be) holy."[31]

Abraham too had requested righteous, holy descendants for Jacob (22:11-12, 29).

■ **19** Rebekah next reverts to the relationship between herself and her special son. She begins by mentioning a benefit he has given her—he has "given rest[32] to your mother's spirit." She may be referring to his reassuring words about marriage in vv. 4-10. She continues by employing a series of terms several of which name feminine anatomical features, to express the depth of her love for him.

womb (*ḥemś*)
my affection (*meḥrateya*)
my breasts (*'aṭbāteya*)

After these, she mentions her mouth and tongue. The middle term in the list above, "my affection," has troubled commentators. Charles bracketed it "for it comes in awkwardly between 'womb,' 'breasts,' 'mouth,' and 'tongue.' We should expect an 'and' to precede it. It may be a dittography and have originated as a false alternative rendering of רחם, 'womb.'"[33] It is not possible to trace the term farther back in the transmission history of Jubilees, since the Ethiopic version is the only one available here, but *meḥrateya* means "my affection," not "my womb."[34] It may be that the term underlying the Ethiopic noun was a form of σπλαγχνα, "inward parts, entrails," a noun serving as a figure for "the seat of emotions."[35] A helpful parallel occurs in the description of the mother

---

30 Charles, *Jubilees*, 159 n.: "The words in Luke recall both Mic. vii.20 and our text. Observe that this statement in Luke is added parenthetically or explanatorily as in our text."

31 Halpern-Amaru draws attention to the prediction made by angels to Abraham that "one of Isaac's sons would become a holy progeny" and his descendants would be "a holy people" (16:17-18) (*Empowerment*, 86).

32 Both Goldmann and Hartom render as השיבות נפש אמך, "you have refreshed your mother" (for the expression, see BDB, 999, s.v. שוב). They may be correct (Charles, *Jubilees*: "as thou hast refreshed thy mother's spirit"), although that does not seem to be the sense of the Ethiopic phrase (see Dillmann, *Lexicon*, 970-71). If "refresh" is what Rebekah means, she would be contrasting Jacob's behavior with Esau's marriages that had led her to despair (see v. 1).

33 Charles, *Jubilees*, 159. Endres agrees and places "My *womb*" in his translation (*Biblical Interpretation*, 82). In a subsequent essay, Endres suggests the translation "compassion" as more appropriate than "affection" ("Revisiting the Rebekah of the Book of *Jubilees*," in Mason et al., *Teacher for All Generations*, 765-82, here 777). Both Goldmann and Hartom use רחמי, but Werman (*Jubilees*, 375) opts for נפשי and offers no explanation for the unusual choice. She also points (p. 379) to Gen 49:25, where some of these terms recur in Jacob's blessing of his son Joseph: "by the Almighty who will bless you / with the blessings of heaven above, / the blessing of the deep that lies beneath, / blessings of the breasts and of the womb."

34 Leslau, *Concise Dictionary*, 31: "compassion, pardon, mercy, pity, clemency."

35 BAG, 770; cf. Dillmann, *Lexicon*, 158.

whose seven sons Antiochus tortured to death (4 Macc 14:13 ["an emotion felt in her inmost parts"; 15:23). Possibly, the original text of Jubilees read קרבי (BDB, 899). If so, Rebekah would have used a word for a bodily part here as well. The verse is an effusive statement that she blesses and praises Jacob with her entire motherly being (see 22:26, where *meḥratu* is used in connection with Abraham, and in v. 23 below, where Rebekah voices it = "her affection").

■ **20** In v. 20 she once again speaks about his descendants and their character. The first sentence relates to the promise of many offsping in that she speaks about his (the verb is singular) increasing and spreading abroad in the land (cf. 19:21). God himself will make a similar promise in Jub 27:23 // Gen 28:14.[36] But she soon turns to the kind of people she wants his progeny to be. She mentions two virtues—they should be perfect (*feṣṣuma*) and be delighted or happy (*yetḥaššay*).[37] The first word said about Jacob after his birth was that he was perfect (*feṣṣum*, 19:13; see 35:12), so she wants his offspring to be like him (and like Abraham, Jub 23:10). In 22:11 Abraham had asked God to give Jacob righteous descendants. There are many statements about joy in Jubilees, although the common verb for such happiness is *tafaššeḥa* or the related noun used in the preceding phrase "in the joy [*feššeḥā*] of heaven and earth" (e.g., 16:20; 23:29). What does "the joy of heaven and earth" mean? The fact that she has just spoken of their being perfect "throughout all eternity" places the phrase in a certain context. It reminds one to some extent of the words in Ps 96:11: "Let the heavens be glad, and let the earth rejoice; / let the sea roar, and all that fills it; / let the field exult, and everything in it." The psalm makes these exhortations in a context speaking of the Lord being recognized as king among the nations, coming and executing judgment. It may be that Rebekah is hoping that Jacob's progeny will join the happiness of this natural chorus (cf. Jub 19:25).[38] Or passages that mention שמחת עולם ("everlasting joy") in connection with restoration from exile may have influenced her words: "And the ransomed of the Lord shall return, / and come to Zion with singing; / everlasting joy shall be upon their heads; / they shall obtain joy and gladness, / and sorrow and sighing shall flee away" (Isa 35:10). It may be significant that in Jubilees joy, mentioned frequently in the context of celebrating festivals, is also a trait of the righteous in the new age (e.g., 7:3 [festival]; 23:30-31 [new age]). The latter point is especially important in view of her request that they enjoy peace on "the great day of peace." In chap. 23, when describing the future "in those days" (v. 26), the promise is that the people then "will complete and live their entire lifetimes peacefully and joyfully" (v. 29), the same terms as the ones Rebekah wishes for Jacob's offspring (see also vv. 30-31). What exactly the "great day of peace" is she does not explain, but the conditions for which she calls are those described in chap. 23 for the new age.[39]

■ **21** The eschatological ring of her words, begun in v. 20, carries over into v. 21. The patriarchal promises at times include reference to the *name* of the person in question: "and make your name great" (Gen 12:2 // Jub 12:23; see also 21:12). Abraham, speaking of Jacob, had asked that his and his ancestors' names be blessed through Jacob, but his words to Jacob about his own house (22:24) come closest to Rebekah's prayer here:

> This house I have built for myself to put my name on it upon the earth. It has been given to you and to your descendants forever. It will be called Abraham's house. It has been given to you and your descendants forever because you will build my house and will establish my name before God until eternity. Your

---

36 See Halpern-Amaru, *Empowerment*, 86. In n. 25 she observes that *medr* ("land") could also be translated "earth" and thinks the author could mean both, citing in support the promise in Jub 32:19, where the meaning is probably "earth." Endres finds a hint of the Priestly blessing to multiply and fill the earth (Gen 1:28) in her words (*Biblical Interpretation*, 82).

37 Rebekah uses the same verb for her delight in Jacob in v. 23.

38 Werman attaches importance to 19:25 in explaining this line (*Jubilees*, 379). It reads: "May they serve (the purpose of) laying heaven's foundations, making the earth firm, and renewing all the luminaries which are above the firmament." It indicates, in her estimation, that heaven and earth are dependent on the offspring of Jacob.

39 See Halpern-Amaru, "Joy as Piety," 204–5.

descendants and your name will remain throughout all the history of the earth.

To this hope for a long history she adds the first part of the covenantal formulary by praying that "the Most High God" be their God. She alters the second part (and you will be his people), however, by praying that he would live with them, that is, that his sanctuary would remain among them for all time. Here she echoes words from chap. 1 where the Lord tells Moses that once the people have returned to him and he has transformed them into a righteous plant, "I will build my temple among them and will live with them; I will be their God and they will be my true and righteous people. I will neither abandon them nor become alienated from them, for I am the Lord their God" (1:17-18; cf. also vv. 26-29). For "righteous God" see 25:15 ("righteous Lord"). She thus asks for a blessed future for Jacob's descendants but does not, of course, deal with Israel's time of wickedness that precedes it in the overview of chap. 1.

■ 22 The final words of the blessing/prayer that she pronounces over Jacob repeat with a slight change the ones recorded in Gen 12:3 // Jub 12:23 (right after the blessing of making Abram's name great): "I will bless those who bless you, and the one who curses you I will curse" (see also Gen 27:29, where the clauses are reversed; Num 24:9). The curse line she modifies to "curses you falsely," possibly because Jub 1:16 implies that Israel became subject to God's curse after they abandoned him and committed all sorts of evil. That was an appropriate curse, unlike the one she mentions here. Her request expresses the desire that God side with Jacob (and his descendants) in preference to all others and that he respond to those others in line with the way they treat Jacob.

■ 23 The scene comes to an end with a short statement about her next action before she offers a last, brief blessing. The mother who harbored such strong emotions about her son kissed him, just as Abraham had done on three occasions (19:26; 22:10-11, 26). And like Abraham in chap. 22 (see vv. 25-30), she seems hardly able to stop asking for blessings on her perfect son. Her concluding request is that God love him as she, his mother, does (see v. 2).[40] For the first time in the chapter she mentions her heart and then repeats the term "affection" that she had used in v. 19 (see also v. 2). She also speaks of her delight in Jacob, employing the verb applied to his descendants in v. 20. Then at last she managed to stop her inspired prayer on his behalf.

Halpern-Amaru sums up the situation in these words:

> Thus Rebekah gives voice to the full triad of promises that comprise the patriarchal covenant—multiple numbers, land, and election. But her blessing prayer also extends beyond the traditional covenant. She speaks of the twelve sons that Jacob will have (25:16), of joy and peace for his descendants (25:20), and of the sanctuary that will be built (25:21). Moreover, the divine "spirit of righteousness" that inspires her employs the maternal images of a female speaker. The matriarch talks of the womb that bore her son, of the breasts that bless him (25:19), and of the maternal nature of God's love (25:23). The striking imagery clearly indicates that Rebekah here acts neither as a substitute for Abraham nor as an extension of her husband. She has her own voice and in that voice she conveys what properly can be termed a "matriarchal blessing."[41]

Rebekah had with overwhelming clarity perceived Jacob's place in the divine plan and has now taken steps to ensure that nothing will go wrong in effecting that plan. Isaac has shown no such insight to this point and will attempt to thwart providence in the next chapter. Once again Rebekah will have to intervene on behalf of Jacob. Only later will Isaac, at last acting as head of the clan, recognize the true situation (see 35:13; cf. 27:14-18). Rebekah is the one who saves the day and the future; Rebekah functions as the true successor of Abraham. She joins him in blessing Jacob with the great promises and in interceding for his descendants, that is, Israel.[42] She has adopted the role of the patriarch at this point

---

40 Halpern-Amaru compares Isa 49:14-15 (*Empowerment*, 87 n. 27); cf. Endres, *Biblical Interpretation*, 83.
41 Halpern-Amaru, *Empowerment*, 87.
42 See van Boxel, "God of Rebekah," 17-18.

in the story while speaking very much as a mother and under the influence of "the spirit of righteousness."

Excursus: Patterns in Jubilees 25:11-23

Werman[43] finds several patterns in the section that offers Rebekah's blessings of God, Jacob, and his descendants. She divides the section into two parts.
First Part (two corresponding units)
>11-12 Rebekah enlists anatomical features to express thanks and praise to God for giving her a son like Jacob
>18-19 She expresses the hope to see his sons, and her bodily parts give thanks and praise to Jacob

The comparison between God and Jacob and his offspring prepares the reader for the second part of the blessing where it becomes eschatological.
Second Part (vv. 15-22), where there is a chiastic arrangement
>15 and 21 The verses contain earthly promises, with the terms "righteousness" and "the ages/ generations" shared
>16-17 and 20 The verses offer eschatological blessings, with terms such as "increase," "heaven," "earth," and "eternity" figuring prominently.

While there are similarities between the units that she details (Rebekah covers the same topics several times), it seems the section divides differently. The most prominent structural element—something that does not figure in Werman's arrangement—is that Rebekah utters three blessings/prayers, though the third is very brief.

Verse 11 Prose introduction (her posture is noted) and summary of her words
>1. Prayer 1 (12-13) She blesses God, thanks him for Jacob, and prays for his descendants; she asks for a spirit of righteousness so she can bless him appropriately.

Verse 14 Prose notice that her request is granted (her posture is noted)
>2. Prayer 2 (15-22) She blesses God and prays that he will bless Jacob with the patriarchal promises of a numerous progeny (who will be holy) and the land; she prays for the eternal validity of their covenantal association.

Verse 23a A short prose notice that she ceased her blessing by kissing Jacob
>3. Prayer 3 (23b) She adds a brief prayer for the Lord's love and blessing on Jacob.

Two short prayers (vv. 12-13 and 23b), the first of which centers on blessing the Lord (who gave Jacob to her) and the second on blessing Jacob, enclose her lengthier blessing/prayer focused on granting the patriarchal promises to Jacob and his offspring forever. That longer prayer moves through the promises/blessings more than once and expands upon them. A result is that it is somewhat repetitious, although there does not seem to be a strict pattern of organization for the repetitions.

---

43 Werman, *Jubilees*, 377–78.

Jacob, Not Esau, Receives Isaac's Blessing

26

1/ During the seventh year of this[a] week[b] [2114] Isaac summoned his older[c] son Esau and said to him, "My son, I have grown old and now have difficulty seeing,[d] but I do not know when I will die. 2/ Now then,[a] take[b] your hunting gear[c]—your quiver and your bow—and go to the field. Hunt on my behalf and catch (something) for me,[d] my son. Then prepare (some) food for me[e] just as I like (it) and bring (it) to me[f] so that[g] I may eat (it) and bless you before I die."[h] 3/ Rebekah was listening[a] as Isaac was talking to Esau. 4/ When Esau went out early to the open country to[a] trap (something), catch (it), and bring (it) to his father, 5/ Rebekah summoned her son Jacob and said to him, "I have just[a] heard your father Isaac[b] saying to your brother Esau, 'Trap (something) for me, prepare me (some) food, bring (it) to me,[c] and let me eat (it). Then I will bless you in the Lord's presence before I die.'[d] 6/ Now, therefore,[a] listen, my son, to what I am ordering you. Go[b] to your flock and take for me[c] two excellent kids. Let me prepare them[d] as food for your father just as he likes (it). You are to take[e] (it) to your father, and[f] he is to eat it so that[g] he may bless you in the Lord's presence before he dies and you may be[h] blessed." 7/ But Jacob said to his mother Rebekah, "Mother,[a] I will not be sparing about anything[b] that my father eats and that pleases[c] him, but I am afraid, mother,[d] that he will recognize my voice and wish to touch me. 8/ You know that I am smooth while my brother[a] Esau is hairy. I will look to him like a mocker. I would be doing something that he did not order me[b] (to do), and he would get angry[c] at me. Then I would bring a curse on myself, not a blessing." 9/ But his mother[a] Rebekah said to him, "Let your curse be on me, my son; just obey me."

10/ So Jacob obeyed his mother Rebekah.[a] He went and took two[b] excellent, fat[c] kids and brought them to his mother.[d] His mother[e] prepared them[f] as he liked (them). 11/ Rebekah then took her older son Esau's[a] favorite clothes that were present with her in the house.[b] She dressed her younger son Jacob (in them) and placed the goatskins[c] on his forearms[d] and on the exposed parts of his neck. 12/ She then put[a] the food and bread that she had prepared[b] in her son Jacob's hand. 13/ He[a] went in to his father and said,[b] "I am your son. I have done as you told me. Get up, have a seat, and eat some of what I have caught, father, so that you may bless me." 14/ Isaac said to his son, "How have you[a] managed to find (it) so quickly, my son?" 15/ Jacob said,[a] "It was your God[b] who made me find[c] (it) in front of me." 16/ Then Isaac said to him,[a] "Come close[b] and let me touch you, my son,[c] (so that I can tell) whether you are my son[d] Esau or not."[e] 17/ Jacob came close[a] to his father Isaac. When he touched him he said,[b] 18/ "The voice[a] is Jacob's voice, but the forearms[b] are Esau's forearms." He did not recognize him because[c] there was a turn of affairs from heaven to distract his mind. Isaac[d] did not recognize (him) because his forearms were hairy like Esau's[e] forearms so that he should bless him.[f] 19/ He said,[a] "Are you my son Esau?" He said,[b] "I am your son." Then he said,[c] "Bring (it) to me and let me eat some of what you have caught, my son, so that I may bless you."[d] 20/ He then brought him (food)[a] and he ate; he brought him wine and he drank.

21/ His father Isaac said to him, "Come close[a] and kiss me, my son."[b] He came close[c] and kissed him. 22/ When he[a] smelled the fragrant aroma[b] of his clothes, he blessed him and said, "Indeed the aroma of my son is like the aroma of a full field[c] that the Lord has blessed.

23/ May the Lord grant to you and multiply for you[a]
(your share) of the dew of heaven and the dew of[b] the earth;
may he multiply grain and oil[c] for you.
May the nations serve you,
and the peoples bow[d] to you.
24/ Become lord of your brothers;[a]
may the sons of your mother bow[b] to you.
May all[c] the blessings with which the Lord has blessed me and blessed
  my father Abraham
belong to you and your descendants forever.

May the one who curses you be cursed,
and the one who blesses you be blessed."

25/ After Isaac had finished blessing his son Jacob and Jacob had left[a] his father Isaac, he hid and his brother[b] Esau arrived from his hunting. 26/ He, too, prepared food and brought (it) to his father. He said to his father,[a] "Let my father rise[b] and eat some of what I have caught and[c] so that you may bless me." 27/ His father Isaac[a] said to him, "Who are you?" He said to him, "I am your firstborn, your son Esau. I have done as[b] you ordered me." 28/ Then Isaac was absolutely dumbfounded and said, "Who was the one who hunted, caught (something) for me, and brought (it)?[a] I ate some of everything before you came and blessed him. He and all his descendants are to be blessed forever." 29/ When Esau heard what his father Isaac said, he cried out very[a] loudly and bitterly and said to his father,[b] "Bless me too, father!" 30/ He said to him, "Your brother came deceptively and took your blessings." He said,[a] "Now I know the reason why he was named Jacob. This is now the second time that he has cheated me. The first time he took my birthright and now he has taken my blessing."[b] 31/ He said, "Have you not saved a blessing for me, father?" Isaac said in reply to Esau, "I have just now designated him as your lord. I have given him all his brothers to be his servants. I have strengthened him[a] with an abundance of grain, wine, and oil.[b] So, what shall I now[c] do for you, my son?" 32/ Esau said to his father Isaac, "Do you have just[a] one blessing, father? Bless me[b] too, father!" Then Esau cried loudly. 33/ Isaac said in reply to him,[a] "The place where you live[b] is indeed[c] to be (away) from the dew of the earth and from the dew of heaven above. 34/ You will live[a] by your sword and will serve[b] your brother. May it be[c] that, if you become great[d] and remove his yoke from your neck, then you will commit an offense fully worthy of death and your descendants[e] will be eradicated from beneath the sky."

35/ Esau kept threatening Jacob[a] because of the blessing with which his father had blessed him. He said to himself, "The time of mourning for my father is now approaching.[b] Then I will kill[c] my brother Jacob."

Textual Notes

1a this] om. 9 38.
 b week] "seventh week" 12.
 c older] om. 12.
 d seeing] The more strongly attested reading is an infinitive (*re'ey*) as in LXX Gen 27:1; mss. 9 38 read a related noun (*rā'y*) meaning "sight."
2a Now then] "Get up and" 44.
 b take] om. 58 63.
 c gear] + "and" 35 38 44 58 63.
 d catch (something) for me] + "and *trap* for me" (see vv. 4, 5) 35 58; 44 63 om. "for me."
 e (food) for me] om. 21 38 63; + "my son" 58.
 f and bring (it) to me] om. 48.
 g so that] "and" 12.
 h I die] "it" (i.e., "my soul," which Isaac uses twice in place of "I" whereas the versions of Gen 27:4 have it once) "dies" 20 25 39 42 47 48 63. See VanderKam, *Jubilees* 2:163.
3a listening] + "to his speech" 39 42 47 48 58.
4a to] + "bring and" 12.

5a just (*nāhu*)] "hunt" 58; om. 38.
 b your father Isaac] om. 44 (it reads "Isaac" after "saying").
 c to me] om. 21 25.
 d I die] "he dies" 39.
6a therefore (-*kē*)] om. 9 12 17 21 38 44 48ᵗ 63.
 b Go] pr. "and" 21 38 (cf. 44).
 c for me] om. 9 39; "for you" 12 21.
 d Let me prepare them] "Make them" 12 20 21 38 63 (cf. 9).
 e You are to take] "You will take" 12 44.
 f and (he is to eat)] "so that (he may eat)" 44.
 g so that] "and" 12; pr. "and" 58.
 h you may be] "you will be" 35 58 63.
7a Mother] om. 9 21 38 58 63.
 b anything] "any food" 20.
 c pleases] "would please" 12 17 20 25 35.
 d mother] om. 12.
8a my brother] om. 21.
 b he did not (om. 12) order me] Lat. begins to be legible here but reads *consilii eius*, "of his advice." For suggestions about confusions that may have caused the dif-

ference, see VanderKam, *Jubilees* 2:164. The lack of the preceding words makes the Lat. difficult to interpret.
c and he would get angry] Lat. repeats the expression.
9a his mother] om. 12; Lat. *mater sua*.
10a his mother Rebekah] The Eth. order is "Rebekah his mother," while Lat. and MS. 44 reverse to "his mother Rebekah."
b two] om. 38; Lat. *duos*.
c excellent, fat] Lat. "tender, excellent"; *teneros* ("tender") is present in Gen 27:9 (LXX OL^E). Werman (*Jubilees*, 380 n. 2) prefers the Lat. reading because the word "tender" is attested in Gen 18:6 (actually in 18:7) for a calf, while the term in Eth. ("fat") is not used. That in itself could be an argument in favor of the Eth. reading, and Ezek 34:16 shows the word can be used for members of a flock.
d to his mother] om. 25; Lat. *matri suae*.
e His mother] om. 12 21 35 44.
f them] + "as good" = Lat. = Gen 27:14. Charles inserted *mable'a* into the Eth. text to harmonize it with the Lat. (*Ethiopic Version*, 95 n. 36; so Littmann, Hartom as well). See VanderKam, *Jubilees* 2:164.
11a her (older) son Esau's] Lat. and MS. 63 reverse the order of her son/Esau.
b the house] lit., "her house"; Lat. and MSS. 9 12 17 21 63 lack a possessive. The suffix in Eth. may render a Greek definite article (LXX: εν τω οικω). See VanderKam, *Jubilees* 2:164.
c goatskins] Lat. has only *hedorum* rather than *hedos caprarum* as in 26:10 (there is an error in VanderKam, *Jubilees* 2:164 where *caprarum* should be *hedorum*).
d forearms] + "and shoulders" Lat. (against Eth. and the versions of Genesis).
12a She then put] Eth. *wa-wahabato*, lit., "she gave to him"; Lat. *obtendidit*, "she extended." Rönsch (*Jubiläen*, 44, 134) emended to *et dedit*. Gen 27:17 has ותתן. What exactly the suffix on *wahabat* accomplishes is not clear. See VanderKam, *Jubilees* 2:165.
b the food (her food 25; Lat. *cibos*) and bread that she had prepared] Mss. 20 25 35 lack "and" and read a construct phrase; Lat. "food that she had prepared and bread."
13a He] "Jacob" 12 = Lat. *iacob*. It seems unlikely to be original as it is an obvious kind of addition to a text that really does not need it.
b said] "Jacob said to his father" 44; + "here I am" 38. Lat. has neither of these pluses.
14a you] + "my son" 25 35; Lat. lacks "my son" here. These two MSS. lack "my son" at the end of the verse where the other Eth. copies and Lat. have it.
15a said] + "to him" 20 25 35 38 44 58. Lat. lacks "to him."
b your God] "the Lord your God" = Lat.; "God" 21 35 44. The versions of Gen 27:20 also read a double divine name.
c made me find] "helped me" 12 21 44 63 (= 17 but with a different form); "showed me" 38. Lat. *direxit*, "guided (it)." See VanderKam, *Jubilees* 2:165–66 for the various readings in the versions of Genesis.
16a to him] om. 12 38; Lat. *ad illum*.
b Come close] + "to me" 12 38; = Lat. *mihi* = LXX OL Eth Gen 27:21.
c my son] + "Esau" 58; "son" 63; om. 25 35; Lat. *nate*.
d my son²] om. 21 58; Lat. *filius meus*.
e or not (lit., "or if it is not he")] "or if you are he" 9 38; "or if you are not he" 35 39^c 44 58 63; Lat. lacks the expression.
17a came close] + "to him" 12 17; Lat. *adproximavit*.
b he said] + "to him" 17 21 44; Lat. *dixit*.
18a The voice] "Your voice" 21 35 58; om. 9; Lat. *vox*.
b the forearms] om. 9; Lat. *manus*; "your forearms" 44.
c because] om. 9; Lat. *quoniam*.
d Isaac] Lat. lacks.
e Esau's²] + "his brother" Lat. = Gen 27:23 (except Eth. Gen).
f so that he should bless him] Lat. "and he blessed him" = Gen 27:23.
19a He said] "Isaac said to him" 63; Lat. *dixit*.
b He said²] + "to him: 'indeed'" 35 58; + "to him" 63; Lat. "Jacob said." Gen 27:24: "He said."
c he said] + "to him" 21 25 35 44 63; Lat. "Isaac said." Gen 27:25: "he said."
d bless you] "bless him" 20 25; "bless" 42 47; Lat. = "bless you."
20a (food)] Mss. 38 39^c 48 supply the understood term "food"; Lat., with the other Eth. copies, lacks it.
21a Come close] + "my son" 20; Lat. + "to me" = LXX OL Gen 27:26.
b my son] om. 20 58; Lat. *nate*.
c came close] + "to him" 12; Lat. "came close."
22a he] "his father" 63; Lat. "he."
b the fragrant aroma] Eth. uses two nouns, while Lat. has just one = Gen 27:27 ("aroma"). Werman suggests that the Eth. reading resulted from a double translation of a Greek term (*Jubilees*, 381 n. 11).
c full field] Lat. *agri pleni* = SP LXX OL Gen 27:27; Eth. lacks "full." Charles (*Ethiopic Version*, 97 n. 9) added *melu'* to the Eth. text to make it agree with the Lat. See VanderKam, *Jubilees* 2:166–67.
23a multiply for you] "multiply" 17.
b dew of²] "blessings of" 12. Gen 27:28: "fat things of," except Eth Gen = "dew of."
c oil] pr. "wine and" 44.
d (may) . . . bow] "will bow" 9 63.
24a brothers] "brother" 17 21 35 38 39 42 44 47 48 58 = LXX OL Eth Gen 27:29. See VanderKam, *Jubilees* 2:167.
b (may) . . . bow] "will bow" 9 12 58 63.
c all] In some MSS. *kwellon* ("all [of them]") has morphed into a form of the verb "be/become" (*kwen* [i.e., *kun*] = "be" 9; *yekun laka* = "may be for you" 12; *yekun* = "may be" 17 21 44 63; *yekawwen* = "will be" 63).

25a had left] om. 12 20 21 35 38 44.
 b his brother] om. 12 38 44 (44 places the words after the verb "arrived," while the other copies place them before the verb and with "Esau").
26a (said) to his father] om. 44.
 b Let . . . rise] "Rise" 35 38 44 58 63. The same MSS. use an imperative for the verb "eat" as well.
 c and (so that)] om. 12 21 35 38 39ᶜ 44 58 63.
27a Isaac] om. 12 20.
 b as] + "you said to me and as" 44.
28a brought (it)] + "to me" 17.
29a very] om. 21.
 b to his father] om. 20 25 35 (= "to him"). LXX OL Eth Gen 27:34 have a verb of speaking with no indirect object.
30a He said²] om. 38 42 47 48.
 b he has taken my blessing] om. 21.
31a I have strengthened him] + "more than every nation of the earth" 44.
 b and oil] om. 63 (also not in Gen 27:37).
 c now] om. 17.
32a just] Most MSS. read *kemma*, but several turn it into the more familiar *kama* (9 38 47 48); om. 12; "of" = "one of your blessing(s)" 63.
 b me] om. 9 38 39ᵗ.
33a to him] om. 12.
 b The place where you live] "your blessing" 39 47ᵗ 58 63.
 c indeed] "let there be to him" 9 38 (they omit "be" later in the verse).
34a You will live] "Live" 35 38 (= Eth Gen 27:40); om. 21.
 b will serve] "serve" (imperative) 12 21 35.
 c May it be] "Be" 39 48 58; + "a servant" (i.e., "May he be a servant") 39ᶜ 48ᶜ 58; om. 35. Cf. εσται in Syncellus.
 d become great (*'abayka*)] "disobey/rebel" (*'abayka*) 12 20 21 44 47.
 e your descendants] pr. "all" 9 38 42 47 (with a different form also 44 48 58 63); + "all" 17.
35a Jacob] + "his brother" 35; om. 25.
 b is . . . approaching] "let . . . approach for him" 12; "let . . . approach" 17 21 38 58 63.
 c I will kill] "let me kill" 25 38 42 44 47.

Commentary

Jubilees 26 rewrites the story in Gen 27:1-41 in which Isaac thinks he is blessing Esau but actually blesses Jacob, who was carrying out the deception designed by his mother. In Genesis the story follows a note about the marriages of Esau to the two Hittite women who "made life bitter for Isaac and Rebekah" (Gen 26:35). To this stage in Genesis, the writer had said little about their two sons other than to record Isaac's preference for Esau and Rebekah's for Jacob and Jacob's gaining the right of firstborn from Esau. Neither the birthright story nor the marriage notice put Esau in a very good light, but Isaac's intent to bless the older son still appears to be a reasonable option and only crafty, underhanded behavior thwarts the effort. The situation is far different in Jubilees. After the introduction of Jacob as "perfect and upright" (19:13), Abraham's potent and repeated endorsement of him as his successor and heir of the promises to him (19:15-29; 22:10-30), Jacob's becoming the elder in place of Esau (24:7), and Rebekah's enthusiastic prayers/blessings for him in the previous chapter (25:11-23), Isaac's plan to bestow the blessing on Esau seems almost inconceivable. How could he have ignored all that had happened—he may have been a witness to Abraham's blessing of Jacob in 22:10-30—and still show preference for Esau, who had yet to do anything right? No wonder Rebekah had to seize control of the situation and orchestrate events so that the will of God, Abraham, and herself would be done.

The major units in chap. 26 are:

1-2	Isaac's instructions to Esau
3-9	Rebekah and Jacob
	3-6 Rebekah's plan
	7-9 Jacob's reply and Rebekah's insistence
10-25ab	Isaac's unwitting blessing of Jacob
25c-34	Isaac and Esau
35	Esau's plan to kill Jacob

For Jubilees 26 the Ethiopic tradition alone preserves the full text. The Latin translation for vv. 8-23 (first three words) survives, and Syncellus may allude to Jub 26:34. Though no Hebrew text for any of the verses is available, the wording in Jubilees 26 is often very close to that of Genesis 27; one has, therefore, a strong indication in those places of how the original Hebrew text of Jubilees read.

1-2 Isaac's Instructions to Esau

Genesis 27 begins with a statement explaining the reason Isaac summoned Esau and, indirectly, for the difficulties he would have in carrying out his plan: "Isaac was old and his eyes were dim so that he could not see." The writer of Jubilees, who dates the event five years after Rebekah's blessing (compare 25:1 and 26:1),[1] incorporates the words about eye problems into Isaac's first-person address to Esau[2] whom the text labels "his older son" though in Jubilees he had lost that status (see 24:3-7). The author also dispenses with Genesis's formulaic "'My son'; and he answered, 'Here I am'" in v. 1. Otherwise, vv. 1-2 are a fairly close citation of Gen 27:1-4.[3] Earlier, Jubilees had passed over the statement in Gen 25:28 that Isaac loved Esau "because he was fond of game" (Jub 19:14 says Esau was "a rustic man and a hunter," reflecting Gen 25:27: "Esau was a skillful hunter, a man of the field"). Now Isaac orders him to use his native talent to procure the meat for a pre-blessing dinner. There is no indication in Jubilees that Isaac is aware of any earlier event that might have induced him to bless Jacob rather than Esau. The chronological gap by which Jubilees separates chap. 25 from chap. 26 produces the awkward result that, despite his mother's wishes and his own strong resolve, Jacob has after five years still not set out to find a wife from Laban's family. The problem does not arise in Genesis, where the marriage issue surfaces later, in chap. 28, after the blessing story in chap. 27.

3-9 Rebekah and Jacob

The much more perceptive Rebekah was not only attuned to the situation with respect to her sons but also up-to-date on household news. Naturally, she had to prevent her clueless husband from ruining all that had been put in place for Jacob as it is set forth so fully in the previous chapters of Jubilees.

3-6 Rebekah's Plan

Jubilees again follows the text of Genesis closely in the section regarding Rebekah's intervention (Gen 27:5-10). There was little need to rework it, especially because of the wider context in which the writer had placed the story.

■ **3-4** For v. 3 (// Gen 27:5) the two texts coincide word for word apart from Jubilees' lack of "his son" in the expression "his son Esau" and the unexpected placement of the name "Isaac" where "his son" occurs in the MT and SP, that is, at the end of the sentence (lit., "as [he] was talking to Esau Isaac").[4] Jubilees does not adopt the explanation attested in *Tg. Ps.-J.* Gen 27:5 (see also

---

1. Genesis indicates that many years passed between the scene in chap. 27 and the death of Isaac in 35:27-29 by placing between the two passages the story about Jacob's twenty years in Haran and his return. In the chronology of Jubilees, the present story occurs in 2114 and Isaac dies in 2162 (36:1-18), forty-eight years later. So in both he wildly miscalculates how close his death is when arranging to bless his older son.
2. For Werman, the writer of Jubilees, by making the statement part of Isaac's words rather than leaving them to the narrator, changes its meaning (*Jubilees*, 382). Rather than a physical ailment, his is now a mental blindness. His confession that he was not able to assess the situation accurately makes Rebekah and Jacob innocent of wrongdoing. They do not mislead a blind man but direct a person who admits his ability to judge has been taken from him. How exactly moving the same words from narrative to direct speech accomplishes all this is exceedingly difficult to perceive.
3. There are a few differences worth noting: Gen 27:3 has "hunt game for me," where Jub 26:2 has "Hunt on my behalf and catch (something) for me, my son." The extra words appear where the MT and SP read a cognate direct object, ציד. Charles concluded there was no reason to think Hebrew Jubilees differed from the MT here (*Ethiopic Version*, 94 n. 4), but it is difficult to see how "and catch (something) for me, my son" would have resulted from ציד even if it was read as a verb. Similar readings occur in 26:4 // Gen 27:5; cf. 26:28 // 27:33. Where the Hebrew versions of Gen 27:4 read "such as I like," Jub 26:2 has, literally, "such as my soul likes." Using "my soul" here seems modeled on the expression later in the verse (literally) "that my soul may bless you." In these cases "my soul" is clearly another way of saying "I" and is regularly translated that way (hence the rendering here, "just as I like [it]").
4. Only the late ms. 63 reverses "to Esau" and "Isaac."

on v. 42) and elsewhere that "Rebekah heard *through the Holy Spirit* while Isaac spoke with Esau his son." In Jubilees she simply overheard a household conversation that must have astonished her. Unlike any ancient version of Gen 27:5 where Esau simply goes (וילך), Jub 26:4 says that Esau "went out early [*wa-gēsa*]."[5] The verb may suggest that Esau was being prompt in obeying his father's orders; then too, he was likely to gain from acting swiftly, lest anything go wrong. In this verse the combination צוד ציד stands where Jubilees has two verbs—"trap/catch." The reading "and bring (it) to his father" may be a doublet: "bring" agrees with the MT and SP להביא, and "to his father [לאביו]" coincides with the reading of the LXX and dependent versions. The two terms could easily have been confused, or, if both are to be read, it would not have been difficult for a scribe of Hebrew Genesis to omit one of the nearly look-alike terms.[6]

■ **5** Rebekah summons Jacob—apparently a stronger word than "call" in Genesis; possibly it represents a stylistic variation to avoid the repetition of "say" (forms of אמר occur three times in Gen 27:6). In Jubilees this is the second time she summons Jacob (see 25:1); it is the first time in Genesis. The LXX tradition identifies Jacob as "her younger son" in Gen 27:6, but Jub 26:5 lacks "younger," as do the MT and SP.[7] The adjective would not be helpful in this context, although strangely enough the writer does call Jacob Rebekah's younger son in 26:11 // Gen 27:15 and in the next chapter (27:1 // Gen 27:42).

The close association in wording between Jubilees and Genesis continues in 26:5b // Gen 27:7, although the writer again makes a stylistic change: Genesis lists as the verbs in Isaac's instructions (quoted by Rebekah): "bring . . . prepare . . . eat," but the order seems wrong, so Jubilees rephrases more logically as "trap . . . prepare . . . bring . . . eat." This is also the order of the verbs in Gen 27:4 where Isaac himself utters them.

■ **6** Rebekah in both Genesis and Jubilees issues commands to Jacob; she does not merely urge him to act. When she tells him what to do in v. 6b (// Gen 27:9), there is a small difference from the versions of Genesis: in Genesis she commands him to "Go to the flock," but in Jubilees she says "Go to your flock."[8] This is the first indication that he owns animals. The purpose of the reading is probably to explain how he was able to procure the goats so quickly, but it also absolves him of guilt for having taken animals from his father's flock in order to deceive him with his own property. The continuation of Rebekah's plan contains additional language that departs from the Hebrew versions of Gen 27:10:

Genesis: so that he may bless you before he dies
Jubilees: so that he may bless you in the Lord's presence before he dies and you may be blessed.

The additional words "before the Lord" come from the parallel in Gen 27:7 // Jub 26:5 and are also present in Syr. Gen 27:10 (and *Targum Neofiti*). The last expression "and you may be blessed" is unique to Jubilees in this place. With it Rebekah points to the actual result that will obtain from her plan and in so doing echoes what Isaac will say when Esau arrives: ". . . and I have blessed him . . . and blessed he shall be" (27:33 // Jub 26:28). Both she and Isaac therefore affirm that, despite the dubious circumstances, the blessing, pronounced "before the Lord," will indeed be valid.

■ **7-9**[9] **Jacob's Reply and Rebekah's Insistence**
Rebekah formulated her words to Jacob as a command, but the virtuous son found it appropriate to argue with

---

5 This is the verb's primary sense (Leslau, *Concise Dictionary*, 211), but Dillmann (*Lexicon*, 1196) also lists "to set out [*proficisci*]" as a meaning for it. At this point Eth Gen 27:5 uses the simple *wa-ḥora* ("and he went").
6 Cf. Skinner, *Genesis*, 369.
7 Actually Jubilees and the Hebrew versions of Gen 27:6 have a verb of speaking at this point; it introduces the words quoted from Rebekah in the remainder of the verse. Possibly the Greek reading (ελασσω) is a corruption or variation of ελεξεν or λεγουσα.
8 This is an instance in which Jubilees and part of the manuscript tradition of Ethiopic Genesis agree against the other ancient versions. Where some copies of Eth. Gen 27:9 read "your flock," others have "our flock." Jubilees and the Ethiopic Genesis also uniquely lack "from there" (not translated in NRSV) after "get me."
9 On these verses, see Endres, *Biblical Interpretation*, 87–88.

her about her demands that put him in a complicated situation.

■ **7-8** At the beginning of Jacob's answer to his mother, Jubilees contains a supplement to the text of Genesis. Rather than simply fearing that his father will discover who he is (as in Genesis), the Jacob of Jubilees affirms his respect for his father: "Mother, I will not be sparing about anything that my father eats and that pleases him." Since Rebekah had told him to take goats from his own flock, Jacob makes clear that it was not a matter of the expense he would incur from using his own animals; he would not withhold from his father any food he would like, whatever the cost. The note is typical of the author and his project of burnishing Jacob's image. Jacob's entire answer to his mother serves this purpose.

Genesis 27:11-12	Jubilees 26:7-8
But Jacob said to his mother Rebekah,[10]	But Jacob said to his mother Rebekah: "Mother, I will not be sparing about anything that my father eats and that pleases him, but I am afraid, mother, that he will recognize my voice and wish to touch me. You know that I am smooth while my brother Esau is hairy.
"Look, my brother Esau is a hairy man, and I am a man of smooth skin.	
Perhaps my father will feel me, and I shall seem to be mocking him,	I will look to him like a mocker. I would be doing something that he did not order me (to do), and he would get angry at me.
and bring a curse on myself and not a blessing."	Then I would bring a curse on myself, not a blessing."

Besides his good will toward his father, Jacob draws attention to his voice. The point anticipates Isaac's comment in Gen 27:22 // Jub 26:18 that the voice of the son visiting him was Jacob's but the arms or hands were those of Esau.[11] In other words, each of the twins could be recognized by his distinctive voice. Jacob mentions his smoothness before referring to Esau's hairiness, reversing the order of Genesis. In Genesis he fears that, if detected, he will appear to be disrespecting his father rather than honoring him. Ethiopic Jubilees uses the verb 'asta'akaya, "hold as evil, declare bad, treat badly, do evil." Though the spelling is consistent in the copies, the virtually identical form 'asta'ākaya means despise, scorn, mock, dishonor,[12] like the verb in Gen 27:12, and it supplies the sense needed here. That this is the nuance he conveys is consistent with his next comment (also not present in Genesis)—he would be doing something his father had not commanded him to do (see Jub 27:6 for a similar case). Jacob is obedient and respectful to his father, however misguided and befuddled Isaac may seem to be.[13] Such behavior, he realizes, will make Isaac angry (also not in Genesis) with the result that he will place a curse on him rather than a blessing. The author of Jubilees will present the scene as if Jacob actually does not lie to Isaac about being Esau (see below). In the book he tells the truth and, moreover, obeys his mother. So in the rewritten story why should he fear being cursed by Isaac, who would have no reason to punish him in this way? The answer is: he would not be acting in harmony with his father's wishes. The writer has in mind what Jacob will say in Jub 26:13 // Gen 27:19: "I have done as *you* told me."[14] That would not be true, and so he has Jacob anticipate the problem. That is all he does at this point, because Jacob still says those words about doing Isaac's bidding in v. 13. At least in Jubilees Jacob is aware of the problem; in Genesis he is not.

■ **9** Rebekah's[15] remarkable response reads as it does in Genesis. She agrees to take on herself the nega-

---

10 *Targum Pseudo-Jonathan* Gen 27:11 begins: "*Because Jacob feared sin, he was afraid that his father might curse him*; and he said." See also *Pirqe R. El.* 32.
11 Hartom, "Jubilees," 85 n.
12 Leslau, *Concise Dictionary*, 144. It is translated "does what is wrong" in VanderKam, *Jubilees* 2. Ethiopic Genesis 27:12 uses a form of 'astaḥaqara, "disdain, look down on, esteem lightly, profane, humiliate, treat with contempt, etc." (*Concise Dictionary*, 20).
13 Endres, *Biblical Interpretation*, 88. He thinks the passage also fills "an apparent lacuna in Jubilees, the lack of an explicit command to respect one's parents." He refers to Testuz (*Idées*, 117), who notes the lack but thinks the idea is known, as indicated in Jub 35:9-13. Both seem to have overlooked Jub 7:20.
14 Hartom, "Jubilees," 85 n.
15 Jubilees uses "Rebekah" as the subject, not just "his mother," as in Gen 27:13, because Jacob's longer speech separated the line too far from the last reference to her name.

tive consequences that may result from her plan and absolves Jacob, who would, of course, simply be obeying his mother. *Targum Pseudo-Jonathan* Gen 27:13 tries to clarify what she is saying: "But his mother said to him, '*If he blesses you with blessings, let them come upon you and upon your children. But if he curses you with curses, let them come* upon me *and upon my soul*; only *obey me*, and go and bring (them) to me.'"[16] Read in this way, she too would probably be safe from the curse, since Isaac was most unlikely to utter one. The author of Jubilees allows her frightening statement to stand as it is in Genesis. Now, throughout the episode about to unfold, Jacob will be blameless for misleading his father and depriving his brother.[17] The writer does not reproduce Rebekah's final two imperatives "and go, get them for me," perhaps because they are superfluous after her general order that he was to obey her.

10-25ab Isaac's Unwitting Blessing of Jacob

The largest part of the chapter relates the story about the preparations for and the actual encounter between Isaac and the disguised Jacob, including the patriarch's transmission of the blessing for the firstborn.

■ **10** The section begins with a statement not present in Gen 27:14: "So Jacob obeyed his mother Rebekah."[18] The sequel shows he heeded her (the verbs she used in her orders are repeated in Gen 27:14), but Jubilees makes it explicit. This could be another hint in the story that Jacob was innocent; the deception was his mother's idea, and he was merely doing as she told him.[19] To show that he did indeed obey her, the text specifies that he went and took two excellent, fat (Latin: tender) kids—words drawn from Gen 27:9 // Jub 26:6 ("fat" is added here; cf. LXX Gen 27:9: "two kids from there, tender and good").[20] The Ethiopic for v. 10 substitutes "them"[21] for the term for "food" (the Hebrew word underlying the translation "savory food" is plural) in the versions of Gen 27:14.

■ **11-12** Rebekah's idea is the same seemingly implausible one in Jubilees as it is in Genesis: she puts some of Esau's finest[22] clothing on him and lays the hides of the kids/goats on his hands or arms[23] and on the exposed parts of his neck. A remarkable feature in Jub 26:11 // Gen 27:15 is that Esau is called "her older son" and Jacob "her younger son." There is no real problem with those designations in Genesis, but they are strange in Jubilees, where Jacob has already obtained seniority (24:7) and where the writer would have reason to omit the adjectives. Once her son had the clothing and skins on him, she placed the food she had prepared in his hands for delivery to his father.

---

16   Though "obey me" is italicized in Maher's translation, it should not be since it is in Gen 27:13.

17   Syncellus records a way of mitigating Jacob's guilt that probably derives from Jubilees, despite his claim about the source: "... Jacob stole the blessings of Esau in accordance with his mother's advice. But he had received them previously from the patriarch Abraham, as Josephos has confirmed, and his statement is trustworthy" (120.13-15; Adler/Tuffin, *Chronography*, 149).

18   Josephus, *Ant.* 1.269: "And Jacob obeyed his mother, taking all his instructions from her" (Thackeray, LCL).

19   Endres writes: "One suspects that the author desired to point once again to Rebekah's stature as the real leader of the family; Jacob's acquiescence to her command also corresponds well with her authority as prophetess" (*Biblical Interpretation*, 88). Possibly the author implies that Rebekah's command is more authoritative than the word of Isaac and that Jacob should not worry about doing something not ordered by him.

20   There is no discussion in Genesis or Jubilees about why two kids/goats were needed rather than one. Later sources identify one as for Passover (e.g., *Tg. Ps.-J.* Gen 27:9; *Pirqe R. El.* 32), a festival also mentioned in the midrashic elaboration of v. 1 (Isaac's poor vision was due to seeing the throne of glory at the Aqedah, which occurred on the date of Passover).

21   The Latin translation has *cibas* ("food"); see VanderKam, *Jubilees* 2:164.

22   Nothing in either text has led one to expect that Esau had any high-quality clothing; in fact in Gen 27:27 // Jub 26:22 the aroma from his clothes convinces Isaac that Esau was standing in front of him. The term in Ethiopic Jubilees, *za-yetfattaw*, means "desirable," and the Latin reads *optimas*.

23   The Hebrew texts of Gen 27:16 use ידי, the reading reflected in Ethiopic Jubilees (*'edawihu*), but the LXX tradition has "his arms [βραχιονας]." Latin Jubilees has "forearms and shoulders [*brachia et humeros*]."

■ **13** The scene in which Jacob and Isaac are together is in 26:13-25ab. The first words between them read as follows in Genesis and Jubilees:

Genesis 27:18-19	Jubilees 26:13
So he went in to his father, and said, "My father"; and he said, "Here I am; who are you, my son?" Jacob said to his father, "I am Esau your firstborn. I have done as you told me."	He went in to his father and said, "I am your son. I have done as you told me."

As he did for the conversation between Isaac and Esau in Gen 27:1, so here the author of Jubilees leaves out the "My . . . Here I am" exchange, but by deleting "My father" he makes Jacob's first statement more meaningful. It would be strange, if Jacob had just addressed Isaac as father, that he would promptly inform him he was his son. The change also required that he omit "who are you, my son," as "I am your son" would not have been a helpful answer to that question. The most obvious rewriting in Jubilees is, of course, the use of only the words "your son" where Genesis has "I am Esau your firstborn," thus sparing Jacob an outright lie. This solution to the problem presented by Genesis resembles one attested in some rabbinic sources that Gen 27:19 be punctuated as: "I am; Esau is your firstborn."[24] "I am" is Jacob's reply to the same question in Gen 27:24 (in the parallel, Jub 26:19, he again says "I am your son"). His declaration that he had done as Isaac commanded perhaps could be construed as a general statement about how Jacob had throughout his life been obedient to Isaac. Read in this way, both answers would be true but in a contextually strained fashion. With Gen 27:19, Jubilees has Jacob use three verbs in the invitation to his father: rise, sit, eat. "Rise [קום]" in the context supplies the sense of urging him to begin an action, in this case sitting up and eating. Jacob had not addressed him as "my father" upon entering the room (contrary to all versions of Genesis), but in v. 13 he does say "father" in the course of his invitation—again contrary to the versions.

■ **14-15** Jacob was still not safe from detection because his father had the sense to ask a further question: how did it happen that he executed his assignment so quickly? He had expected his son to go on a hunting expedition, not to visit his flock, in order to procure an animal for butchering. Isaac still does not call him Esau in v. 14 (// Gen 27:20), only "my son." Jacob's explanation for his swift success is worded differently in the ancient versions of Genesis. The MT and SP read הקרה, meaning "cause to occur" (BDB, 899), that is, God made things happen as they did.[25] The LXX (παρέδωκεν) and dependent translations express the notion of "giving, handing over" (LXX: "the Lord your God delivered up before me"), and the targums use the verb "arrange." In Jubilees there is a difference between the two versions: Ethiopic 'arkabani, "made me find," and Latin direxit, "guided." Charles emended 'arkabani to 'arte'ani = direxit,[26] although he still translated as if he had retained 'arkabani. In all of these readings—whatever their nuances—the quick conclusion of the project is attributed to the Lord himself; in fact, Jacob even refers to him as "your God" (Latin, with the versions of Gen 27:20, has "the Lord, your God"). Also, Jacob, in the Ethiopic readings, attaches the divine causation to himself: he caused *me* to find, where the versions of Genesis have a more impersonal or indirect expression.[27]

■ **16-18** Despite Jacob's appeal to divine assistance, Isaac continues to harbor doubts because he next wants to do what Jacob suspected he would (26:7-8)—he wishes to touch him (v. 16 // Gen 27:21)—since that would be

---

24 For references, see Kugel, *Traditions*, 360. Rashi interprets that statement as: the word "I" means that Jacob was identifying himself as the one who was bringing the food to Isaac; with the other two words he was declaring that Esau was Isaac's firstborn. In *Gen. Rab.* 65:18, R. Levi reads the statement as: "I am to receive the Ten Commandments, but Esau [is] your firstborn." As Freedman explains (*Midrash Rabbah: Genesis*, 594 n. 1), the correlation of "I" with the Ten Commandments probably arose from the fact that the latter begins with the same pronoun. Josephus, by omitting the opening exchange between father and son, also saves Jacob's moral reputation (*Ant.* 1.270-73).

25 *DCH* 7.318: "grant success, lit. 'cause (something favourable) to occur.'"

26 Charles, *Ethiopic Version*, 95 n. 46.

27 In the versions of Genesis, he mentions himself only in the phrase (literally): "before me" at the end of the verse. Jubilees includes it as well.

the simplest way in which to distinguish the hirsute son from the smooth one. Amazingly, his disguise proved successful. The visually impaired Isaac became sufficiently convinced of his identity, although he realized that not everything seemed in order: the person with whom he was conversing sounded like Jacob but felt like Esau (vv. 16-18a are quotations of Gen 27:21-22). So, despite the conflicting evidence, he could not fathom exactly what was happening and went forward with the all-important blessing nevertheless. Isaac is not a very impressive character to this stage in the account.

The writer of Jubilees, like any reader of Genesis, was surprised that Isaac failed to notice he was touching animal skins on Jacob's forearms/hands. Then, too, could he not have done a little more investigating before botching something so momentous as the blessing? Genesis provides no explanation for this latest failure on Isaac's part, but Jub 26:18b does: "He did not recognize him because [these first words are from Gen 27:23][28] there was a turn of affairs from heaven [*miṭat 'em-samāy/aversio erat de caelo*] to distract his mind."[29] The word for divine interference with his mind (his spirit, *manfasu*) seems to derive from 1 Kgs 12:15 // 2 Chr 10:15,[30] where King Rehoboam, ignoring sound counsel and acting on foolish advice, spoke harshly to Jeroboam and the people of the north. The historian explains his baffling behavior: "So the king did not listen to the people, because it was a turn of affairs brought about by the LORD [סבה מעם יהוה; 2 Chr 10:15: נסבה מעם האלהים] that he might fulfill his word, which the LORD had spoken by Ahijah the Shilonite to Jeroboam son of Nebat."[31] Just as the event that drove a final wedge between the northern and southern sections of the nation Israel may seem to have occurred through human actions and folly though God directed it,[32] so the plan of Rebekah, however deceptive and clumsy, was actually the will of the Lord, who intervened to make sure it succeeded in order that Jacob, not Esau, would receive the blessing.[33] Isaac would have made a disastrous mistake had God not forced events such that he acted contrary to his original intent; as a result, even the implausible disguise concocted by Rebekah was successful.

■ **19-20** Nevertheless, Isaac tried one more time to clear the last uncertainty from his troubled mind. In Gen 27:24 he asks directly, "Are you really my son Esau?" to which Jacob replies with his second bald lie, "I am." The Isaac of Jubilees puts the same question to him, but for the second time Jacob resorts to the evasive "I am your son." The result is the same in Jubilees and Genesis, and in identical words in both Isaac orders Jacob to present the food (Jacob adds wine for him to drink) so that he could eat and then bless him (26:19-20 = Gen 27:25). In this way Isaac proceeds as Abraham did just before he blessed the Lord and Jacob (Jub 22:4-6)—an occasion when Jacob also brought food and wine to a patriarch who sensed he was about to die.

■ **21-22** The verses agree word for word with Gen 27:26-27, which introduces the blessing scene itself.[34] As

---

28 Jubilees repeats them in the next sentence.
29 For *miṭat*, Leslau gives: "turning away, returning, return, answer, change, transformation, conversion, revolution (going around)" (*Concise Dictionary*, 44).
30 Charles, *Jubilees*, 162.
31 Apart from the Hebrew phrase cited, the version in Chronicles is identical except for small variations in the divine name and its placement. Hartom uses נסבה in his translation of Jubilees, and Werman chooses סבה, but Goldmann has שומה, as in 2 Sam 13:32 ("determined" [so NRSV]), where the word is of uncertain meaning and textual status (it was likely not in 4QSam[a] and is not reflected in the LXX). סבה or נסבה is much more likely to have appeared in Jub 26:18, as the Ethiopic and Latin terms express the same sense of turning found in the Hebrew words.
32 See Sara Japhet, *I & II Chronicles: A Commentary* (OTL; Louisville: Westminster John Knox, 1993) 656.
33 Cf. Kugel, *Traditions*, 361 (where he adduces other texts that attempt to explain why the deception worked); *Walk through Jubilees*, 137.
34 In v. 22 the Ethiopic text says, "When he smelled the fragrant aroma [*sēnā ma'azā*] of his clothes," while the Latin translation has simply *et odoratus est odorem vestimentorum eius*, that is, it lacks an equivalent of "fragrant," just as the versions of Genesis fail to have one. It is as if the Hebrew underlying the Ethiopic reading is ריח נחוח ("a fragrant aroma"), an unlikely description of Esau's clothing. When Isaac refers to the smell of the clothing in the next line, he uses just one word, and in this case Ethiopic Jubilees does as well. Genesis and Ethiopic Jubilees refer to the "aroma of a field,"

Abraham did to Jacob in Jub 22:10 (where he calls him "my son"), Isaac orders him to approach and kiss him. As he did in 22:11 with Abraham, Jacob complies with his father's command. The two scenes involving blessing of a son by a patriarch proceed in a formally parallel fashion. Now the aroma exuded by the clothing of Esau worn by Jacob inspires Isaac to bless him and no longer to suspect that he may be speaking with the wrong person. The smell of the clothing reminds Isaac of a field blessed by the Lord and leads him to pray for agricultural plenty for his son.[35]

■ **23-24** Isaac's blessing in the two works reads as follows.

Genesis 27:28-29	Jubilees 26:23-24
May God give you of the dew of heaven,	May the Lord grant to you and multiply for you (your share) of the dew of heaven
and of the fatness of the earth,	and the dew of the earth;
and plenty of grain and wine.	may he multiply grain and oil for you.
Let peoples serve you,	May the nations serve you,
and nations bow down to you.	and the peoples bow to you.
Be lord over your brothers,	Become lord of your brothers;[36]
and may your mother's sons bow down to you.	may the sons of your mother bow to you.
	May all the blessings with which the Lord has blessed me and blessed my father Abraham belong to you and your descendants forever.
Cursed be everyone who curses you,	May the one who curses you be cursed,
and blessed be everyone who blesses you!	and the one who blesses you be blessed.[37]

At the beginning, Jubilees uniquely reads "grant to you and multiply for you,"[38] where the versions of Genesis have only a verb of giving or granting. "Multiplying" is mentioned frequently in patriarchal blessings (for example, Isaac uses the verb in Gen 28:3 // Jub 27:11); perhaps such diction has influenced the writer here. Instead of using an equivalent of "the fatness," the writer repeats "the dew" before "of the earth." Genesis 27:28 speaks of "plenty of grain and wine"; Jubilees has a word for plenty but it is a cognate accusative with a second instance of "multiply": literally, "may he multiply a multiplying/multitude of grain and oil." This appears to be an intensifying expression like the one in the first sentence of the blessing ("grant and multiply"). All of the versions of Gen 27:28 have "wine," but Jubilees reads "oil." *Targum Neofiti* Gen 27:28 has "wine and oil." Grain, wine, and oil are, of course, a triad repeated a number of times in the HB to refer to the principal crops.

The major difference from Genesis is the extra line in which Isaac gives to Jacob all the blessings that Abraham and he had received before him. The author seems to have sensed that something was missing from Isaac's words, which focused on agricultural plenty and dominance over others. Rebekah had bestowed the patriarchal blessings on Jacob (25:15-22), but in Gen 27:28-29 Isaac says nothing about the familiar and crucial gifts of land and offspring (he will in Gen 28:3-4 // Jub 27:11). Since this is the first and most solemn occasion on which Isaac blesses Jacob, it made sense to think that at this time he passed along the promises made to him[39] and

---

but Latin Jubilees, with SP LXX OL, reads the "aroma of a full field."

35 The connection between Isaac's words here and in the blessing itself is commonly noted in commentaries; see, e.g., Skinner, *Genesis*, 371.

36 The plural, which is strange in view of Jacob's having just one brother, is retained by Jubilees; the LXX reads singular forms for "brother" but curiously has a plural for the parallel term "sons" and uses "your father" in place of "your mother." See Hamilton, *Genesis 18–50*, 222; he thinks "your brothers" may be "poetic craft" rather than a reference to actual male siblings.

37 In Jubilees singular forms appear; the MT (unlike the NRSV translation) reads plurals in "those who curse/those who bless" but singular forms of the adjectives "cursed/blessed." Jubilees agrees in the numbers with the LXX tradition.

38 The legible part of the Latin translation ends with *et det tibi*; thus, whether it had the second verb is not known.

39 Werman notes that, by adding the blessings given to him as well, Isaac here exceeds what he will say in Gen 28:4 (// Jub 27:11), where he mentions only "the blessing of Abraham" (*Jubilees*, 382).

to Abraham.[40] Consequently, on this occasion Isaac officially, if unintentionally, blesses Jacob with the gifts meant for Esau and with the patriarchal promises as well. Isaac, after Abraham and Rebekah, becomes the third one to pray that the great benefits of land and progeny would accrue to Jacob. He does not yet know what he has done, but his insight will eventually sharpen so that he becomes the supporter of Jacob he should have been all along. His education in being a true patriarch has only begun.

■ **25ab** Genesis closes the scene of blessing by reporting simply that Isaac concluded his words and Jacob left the room (27:30a). Jubilees 26:25a says the same but adds the detail that Jacob hid. It would seem a cowardly thing for him to do, considering that in 27:4 he will show no fear of his older brother. Perhaps one is to imagine that he knew, if the two met at the door, it would be awkward to explain to Esau why he had borrowed his best clothes and was wearing animal hides as accessories. Such an encounter was a real possibility, since the phrasing in Gen 27:30 implies that Esau arrived just after Jacob left.[41]

25c-34 Isaac and Esau

Esau is the one who in fact obeyed his father's instructions but lost the blessing in spite of his virtuous efforts.

■ **25c-26** He had gone hunting and returned with game, and now he set about preparing it for his father to eat, totally unaware that he was too late. He apparently did his own cooking without the benefit of Rebekah's special touch (see Gen 27:9 // Jub 26:6). As in Genesis, he invites his father to eat what he has caught so that he will be able to bless him. Jubilees 26:26 is a citation of Gen 27:31, but where Esau uses an indirect, polite expression "Let my father . . . and eat of his son's game," Jubilees substitutes a first-person phrase: "Let my father . . . eat some of what I have caught."

■ **27** There is surely some irony in the fact that when Isaac asks "Who are you?"[42] Esau, with no need to be evasive, replies with the unvarnished truth. Jubilees even expands on his answer in Genesis:

Genesis 27:32	Jubilees 26:27
His father Isaac said to him, "Who are you?" He answered, "I am your firstborn son, Esau."	His father Isaac said to him, "Who are you?" He said to him, "I am your firstborn, your son Esau. I have done as you ordered me."

In the last clause, which is unique to Jubilees in this place (it comes from Gen 27:19 // Jub 26:13), Esau could honestly say he had followed his father's instructions—something Jacob could do only in a loose sense in v. 13.

■ **28** Jubilees 26:28 reproduces Gen 27:33 verbatim[43] in describing Isaac's stunned reaction and confession of what he had just done. Naturally, he wondered whom he had blessed—an action that involved more than just words. "Upon discovering that he has been tricked, Isaac makes no attempt to rescind his earlier blessing on Jacob. Abrogation is not an option for Isaac, for the essence of an oracle is that it is irrevocable. Isaac says here, 'What I have said, I have said.'"[44] The author of Jubilees highlights the point with additional words.

Genesis 27:33	Jubilees 26:28
. . . and I have blessed him—yes, and blessed he shall be!	. . . and [I have] blessed him. He and all his descendants are to be blessed forever.

---

40 Endres thinks the addition of the Abrahamic blessings was meant to be encouraging for all of Israel, right down to the time of the author (*Biblical Interpretation*, 90, 92). That may be true, but the blessing to Jacob and his descendants appeared in Gen 28:3-4, so Jubilees would in essence be adding nothing to the scriptural message here, just moving it to a place a little earlier in the narrative.

41 See BDB, 36, s.v. אַךְ: "*only just* (or *scarcely*) had Jacob gone out, . . . and (= when) Esau came in"; Hamilton, *Genesis 18–50*, 226; and Josephus, *Ant.* 1.274: "but scarce had he ended them [his prayers for Jacob] when Esau came in from his hunting" (Thackeray, LCL). In *Gen. Rab.* 66:5 there are similar explanations: "R. Aibu said: The tent of our father Isaac was open at both ends (one [Esau] entered by one and the other [Jacob] left by the other). The Rabbis said: The doors were hinged and could be folded backwards: Jacob stood behind the door until Esau came in and then he departed." The latter option sounds much like what happens in Jubilees.

42 Unlike his earlier question in Gen 27:19, here Isaac does not ask "who are you, my son?"

43 Here again, where the Hebrew versions of Gen 27:33 have the cognate accusative construction צוּד צַיִד Jubilees renders with two verbs ("hunted, caught").

44 Hamilton, *Genesis 18–50*, 226.

In Jubilees it is not only Jacob but also his offspring who for all time have gained a blessing that could not be recalled. The expanded form of the sentence involves inserting in Isaac's blessing the lines regarding the promises made to Isaac and Abraham (26:24). Isaac had spoken the solemn words under false pretenses, but the unchangeable result was that Jacob and thus Israel were the beneficiaries of the eternal promises. Just as surely, Esau and his progeny were not.

■ **29** Esau's response to the shattering news parallels that of his father: as Isaac had (literally) trembled a very great trembling, so Esau cried out a very great and bitter cry[45] (Gen 27:34 // Jub 26:29). The pitiful cry of the older, obedient hunter is a desperate plea for whatever may be left.

■ **30** By this time Isaac realized that Jacob was the one whom he had blessed before Esau arrived. It is understandable that in Gen 27:35 Isaac says that Jacob "came deceitfully [במרמה]";[46] less understandably, the writer of Jubilees (v. 30) did not alter his assessment of Jacob's act. He may not have thought it needed to be softened, as it was by other interpreters,[47] because it was merely Isaac's evaluation, not that of the Lord or even of Rebekah. Isaac also refers to the words he had pronounced over Jacob as "your [Esau's] blessing," and Jubilees follows suit. Isaac still has not caught on to the fact that anything but an innocent mistake has been made; he fails to see the hand of God guiding events to protect him from a serious error and to produce a better result.

Esau was justifiably angry with his brother, and, as in the story about the right of the firstborn son (see Jub 24:6), here too a name finds its explanation. The meaning of the expression in the MT and SP (הכי קרא שמו יעקב, translated "Is he not rightly named Jacob?" in NRSV) is unclear, and the other ancient versions seem to reflect a somewhat different base text. The LXX, for example, reads: δικαιως εκληθη το ονομα αυτου Ιακωβ, literally, "rightly is his name called Jacob." Jubilees also resorts to a passive verb but introduces it differently: *ye'ezē 'a'marku ba-za tasamya semu yā'qob*, "Now I know the reason why he was named Jacob." Charles thought *ye'ezē 'a'marku* ("Now I know") resulted from a mistake in Greek Jubilees: η δικαιως was misread as οιδα ως.[48] His suggestion fails to account for "Now" and is probably unnecessary; the writer simply paraphrased a difficult text.[49] On the occasion of transferring the birthright,[50] the etymologies of (Esau and) Edom were given; in the present verse Esau supplies a less flattering twist to his brother's name: he is Jacob (יעקוב) because he supplanted (יעקב).[51] The verb employed in the Ethiopic text of Jubilees is *'a'qaṣa*, "ensnare, defraud"[52] (Eth. Gen 27:36 uses the same form). The author could allow this second unfavorable reflection on Jacob to stand because it was merely Esau's opinion, hardly one to cause concern.

■ **31** For the second time the distraught Esau begs for any blessing his father might have retained, and poor Isaac could offer him nothing more than to tell him what he had given Jacob. Those blessings had exhausted his arsenal; there was no provision for a second set. Jacob now had everything and Esau was left with the consequences. Jubilees 26:31a exactly reproduces Gen 27:36b-37a. There Isaac concentrates rather uncharitably on the part of the blessing most pertinent to Esau: he had made Jacob lord or master of Esau and all his broth-

---

45 Jubilees, with the LXX tradition, uses "voice" rather than a cognate accusative as in the Hebrew versions of Genesis.

46 As commentators often note, Jacob becomes the victim of deception a few chapters later when Laban gives him Leah instead of Rachel (the related verb is used, Gen 29:25).

47 The expression is *ba-ḥebl*, "with cunning/guile/deceit" (Leslau, *Concise Dictionary*, 20). Some texts reveal attempts to reinterpret what Isaac said. *Targum Neofiti* Gen 27:35 has "great wisdom" (rendered "great cunning" by McNamara, who considers it "a euphemistic rendering" of the Hebrew text); *Pseudo-Jonathan* and *Onqelos* both have "with wisdom," which Bernard Grossfeld thinks means "cleverly" (*The Targum of Onqelos to Genesis* [Aramaic Bible 6; Wilmington, DE: Michael Glazier, 1988] 101 n. 12). *Genesis Rabbah* 67:6 suggests that something else was meant: "R. Johanan said: He came with the wisdom of his Torah."

48 Charles, *Ethiopic Version*, 97 n. 36; *Jubilees*, 163.

49 See VanderKam, *Jubilees* 2:168-69.

50 Though he had not objected at the time, now (Jub 26:30 // Gen 27:36) Esau claims that Jacob took the birthright from him (Hamilton, *Genesis 18-50*, 227).

51 Genesis provides explanations for both *Esau* and *Jacob* in 25:25-26, but Jubilees did not reproduce the passage.

52 Leslau, *Concise Dictionary*, 175.

ers. Again the plural points to kinsfolk (see Gen 31:46), but in this case Isaac emphasizes the fact that Jacob will be lord by placing the term first in the sentence and by saying, not merely that he had made Jacob ruler over his brothers, but had appointed him "your lord" and had assigned all his brothers to him as his servants. The Isaac of Jubilees says nothing to Esau about imparting the traditional patriarchal blessings to Jacob; he recalls only the ones found in Gen 27:28-29 but in reverse order: Jacob as ruler over his kin and as recipient of agricultural bounty. In Gen 27:28 he had referred to grain and wine, where Jubilees had him speak of grain and oil (v. 23). Here Isaac repeats those two items, but Jubilees mentions the traditional three: an abundance of grain, wine, and oil. Genesis again employs the verb שמתיו, used with making Jacob lord, in connection with the grain and wine, but Ethiopic Jubilees has 'aṣnā'kewwo, reflecting the interpretation "strengthen" found in LXX εστηριϲα. There was nothing left for Esau but to submit and accept the reality that had been ordained through the blessing.

■ **32-34** Oddly enough, though he had been rebuffed twice, Esau asks a third time whether something might remain for him (v. 32 // Gen 27:38). Jubilees with the Hebrew versions of Gen 27:38 says nothing about Isaac's reaction, but the LXX says that he "was cut to the quick." With no reply forthcoming from his father, Esau cried. The whole scene makes him look pathetic and Jacob the victor.

When Isaac does reply, he utters a sort of negative blessing over his weeping son, words that incorporate the reverse of the benefits granted to Jacob.

Genesis 27:39-40	Jubilees 26:33-34
See, away from the fatness of the earth shall your home be, and away from the dew of heaven on high.	The place where you live is indeed to be (away) from the dew[53] of the earth and from the dew of heaven above.
By your sword you shall live, and you shall serve your brother;	You will live by your sword and will serve your brother.[54]
but when you break loose, you shall break his yoke from your neck.	May it be[55] that, if you become great and remove his yoke from your neck, then you will commit an offense fully worthy of death[56] and your descendants will be eradicated from beneath the sky.

The two read similarly until the words of Genesis translated "when you break loose" that stand alongside "if you become great" in Jubilees. The form in the MT is a crux: תריד has been related to a root רוד, "wander restlessly, roam" (in the hiphil, "show restlessness" [?]).[57] The reading in Ethiopic Jubilees—'abayka, "you have become great"—more likely reflects the reading in the SP, תאדר, "become wide/great."[58] The line provides for a time

---

53 Here, as in 26:23 // Gen 27:28, Jubilees repeats "dew" (so Eth. Gen 27:39); Gen 27:39 distinguishes "fatness" and "dew," as in v. 28, but switches the order of earth and heaven.

54 These words confirm what the Lord told Rebekah when she was pregnant: "Two nations are in your womb, / and two peoples born of you shall be divided; / the one shall be stronger than the other, / the elder shall serve the younger" (Gen 25:23). It is puzzling that Jubilees omitted the passage, but it does give the confirmation of it here. See Kugel, *Traditions*, 361, where he cites Ephraem, *Commentary on Genesis* 25:2: "Isaac could not change his blessings . . . because he knew that the word of God had been fulfilled, just as it had been told to Rebekah."

55 Kugel has rightly objected that "may it be" followed by a negative consequence seems strange in what Isaac says about his son (*Walk through* Jubilees, 137 n. 29), but the text does read *yekun*, not *yekawwen*, which would be a literal rendering of ויהיה.

56 Syncellus (123.23-25; Adler/ Tuffin, *Chronography*, 154) wrote: "Isaac said to Esau in his blessings, 'There will be a time when you shall break and loosen his yoke from your neck, and you shall commit a sin to death [πλημμελησης εις θανατον].'" He claims this is from Genesis, yet the last clause is not in Gen 27:40 but is in Jub 26:34 (see the note in Adler/ Tuffin, 154-55). As they point out, Michael Glycas noticed the mistake in Syncellus but claimed the material was from Josephus—another misattribution.

57 So BDB, 923; cf. *DCH* 7:426, where for the hiphil the meanings in BDB are given, followed by "perh. break loose." The LXX tradition renders a form of ירד (καθελης). Cf. Charles, *Jubilees*, 164; Endres, *Biblical Interpretation*, 90-91.

58 BDB, 12.

when the descendants of Esau would become powerful enough to free themselves from subjection to Jacob's progeny; that is the end of the prediction in Genesis. But in Jubilees extricating themselves will be the prelude to disaster. By revolting against their rightful lot of subservience, they will be violating the divine order as established in the blessing—Jacob should rule over his kin. Their refusal to accept what God had ordained for them would be a mortal sin, and it would lead to the extermination of Esau's line. A partial fulfillment of the prediction will come in Jubilees 37–38. This is no blessing for Esau; it is a forecast[59] of doom for him and his offspring (see 24:32 for eradication of the Philistines).

35 Esau's Plot to Kill Jacob

Jubilees 26 ends with a reproduction of Gen 27:41. Esau now realized nothing could be done about the blessing; it was a *fait accompli*. A better way of handling the situation was, in his opinion, to eliminate Jacob, who had become and would always be his master. Perhaps he calculated that if he killed Jacob, who had no children, there would be no one to rule him and his descendants and they would be free of the burden Isaac had placed upon them. The text indicates that he laid his plans secretly—literally, "he said in his heart." Yet even in his scheming Esau was a dutiful son. After all the harm his father had brought upon him, he decided not to carry out the plan during his lifetime. It was to remain a secret until Isaac's death. Jubilees 27:1 will show how a greater force was at work to foil that plan too (see below). The better reading in v. 35 is the imperfect form *yebaṣṣeḥ* ("is approaching"), not the subjunctive *yebṣāḥ*; as a result, Charles was incorrect in claiming the writer gave "a malicious turn" to Esau's words (he translated: "May the days of mourning for my father now come").[60] The son who had lost so much could wait until then to kill his brother and did not ask that the time come soon, though it could since Isaac at the time believed he was at death's door (Gen 27:1-2 // Jub 26:1).

---

59 Hamilton comments that, though Isaac's eyesight is poor, his "prophetic insight is as sharp as ever" since this will happen in the course of history (see 2 Kgs 8:20-22) (*Genesis 18–50*, 228).

60 *Jubilees*, 165. There were interpreters who read Esau's words in Gen 27:41 (where the verb could be jussive or imperfect [LXX read it in the jussive sense, εγγισατωσαν]) in such a negative fashion. *Targum Pseudo-Jonathan* (the same is in *Targum Neofiti*) reads: "And Esau *harbored* hatred *in his heart* against *his brother* Jacob because of *the order of* blessings with which his father had blessed him. And Esau said to himself, '*I will not do as Cain did, who killed Abel while his father was alive; but his father then begot Seth. Rather, I will restrain myself until the time when* the days of mourning *for the death* of my father *come*, and then I will kill my brother Jacob, *and I will be murderer and heir*'." Cf. also *Gen. Rab.* 67:8.

27

Jacob Leaves Home and Encounters the Lord in Bethel

1/ Rebekah was told[a] in a dream[b] what her older son Esau had said. So Rebekah sent[c] and summoned her younger son Jacob and said to him, 2/ "Your brother Esau will[a] now try to get revenge against you by killing you. 3/ So then, my son,[a] listen to me. Set out and run away to my brother Laban—to Haran. Stay with him for a few days until your brother's anger turns away and he stops[b] being angry at you and forgets[c] everything that you have done to him.[d] Then I will send and take you back from there." 4/ Jacob[a] said,[b] "I am not afraid. If he wishes to kill me, I will kill him."[c] 5/ She said to him,[a] "May I not[b] lose my two sons[c] in one day." 6/ Jacob said to his mother Rebekah, "You are of course aware that my father has grown old, and I notice[a] that he has difficulty seeing. If I left him, he would consider it a bad thing be<u>cause I would be leaving</u> him[b] and going away from you. My father would be angry and curse me. <u>I will</u> n<u>ot go. If he</u> sends me, only then[c] will I go." 7/ Rebekah said to Jacob, "I will go in and te<u>ll him</u>.[a] Then he will send[b] you."

8/ Rebekah went in[a] and said to Isaac,[b] "I despise my life[c] because of the two Hittite women whom Esau has married. If Jacob marries one of the women of the land[d] who are like them,[e] why should I remain alive any longer, because the Canaanite women are evil." 9/ So Isaac summoned his son Jacob, blessed[a] and instructed him,[b] and said to him, 10/ "Do not marry any[a] of the Canaanite women. Set out, go[b] to Mesopotamia, to the house of Bethuel, your mother's father. From there[c] take a wife from the daughters of Laban, your mother's brother. 11/ May the God of Shaddai[a] bless you;[b] may he make you increase, become numerous, and be a throng of nations. May he give the blessings of my father Abraham to you and to your descendants after you[c] so that you may possess the land where you wander as a foreigner—and[d] all the land that the Lord gave to Abraham. Have a safe trip, my son."

12/ So Isaac sent Jacob away. He went to Mesopotamia, to Laban, the son of Bethuel the Aramean—the brother of Rebekah, Jacob's mother. 13/ After Jacob had set out to go[a] to Mesopotamia, Rebekah grieved for her son[b] and kept crying.[c] 14/ Isaac said to Rebekah, "My sister,[a] do not cry for my son Jacob because he will go[b] safely and return safely. 15/ The Most High God will guard[a] him from every evil and will be with him because[b] he will not abandon[c] him throughout his entire lifetime.[d] 16/ For I well know[a] that his ways[b] will be directed favorably[c] wherever he goes until[d] he returns safely to us[e] and we see[f] that he is safe. 17/ Do not[a] be afraid for him, my sister, because he is just in his way.[b] He is perfect;[c] he is a true man.[d] He will not be abandoned.[e] Do not cry." 18/ So Isaac was consoling Rebekah regarding her son[a] Jacob, and he blessed him.[b]

19/ Jacob[a] left the well of the oath to <u>go to Haran during the first</u> year of the second week of the forty-fourth[b] jubilee [2115]. He arrived at Luz th<u>at is on the mountain—that is, Bethel</u>—on the first of the first month of[c] this week. He arrived at the pla<u>ce</u>[d] in the eve<u>ning, turned off the road</u>[e] <u>to the we</u>st[f] of the highway during this night, and slept[g] there because the sun had set. 20/ He too<u>k one of the stones of</u> that <u>place</u> and se<u>t it</u>[a] at the place (for) his head[b] beneath that[c] tree. <u>He was traveling</u> <u>alone</u> and fell asleep.[d] 21/ That night he dreamed[a] that[b] a ladder was set up on the earth and its top was reaching heaven; that angels of the Lord[c] were going up and down on it; and that the Lord[d] was standing[e] on it. 22/ He spoke with Jacob and said, "I am the God[a] of Abraham your father and the God of Isaac. The land[b] on which you are sleeping[c] I will give to you and your descendants after you. 23/ Your descendants will be like the sands of the earth.[a] You will become numerous[b] toward the west,[c] the east, the north, and the south. All the families[d] of the nations[e] will be blessed through you and[f] your descendants. 24/ As for me, I will be[a] with you. I will guard you wherever you go. I will bring you back safely to this[b] land because[c] I will not abandon you until I have done everything[d] that I have said to you." 25/ Jacob said in (his) sleep:[a] "This place is indeed the house of the Lord but I did not know (it)." He was afraid and said, "This place, which is nothing but the house of the Lord, is awe-inspiring; and this is the gate of heaven."

26/ Jacob, upon arising early in the morning, took the stone that he had placed[a] at his head[b] and set it[c] up as a pillar for a marker.[d] He poured oil on top of it and named that place Bethel. But[e] at first the name of this[f] area was Luz. 27/ Jacob vowed to the Lord, "If[a] the Lord is with me and guards me on this road on which I am traveling and gives[b] me food to eat and clothes to wear so that I return[c] safely to my father's house,[d] then the Lord will be[e] my God. Also, this stone that I have set up as a pillar for a marker in this place is to become[f] the house of the Lord. All[g] that you have given me[h] I will indeed[i] tithe to you, my God."

Textual Notes

1a   was told (lit., "it was told to")] "We told" 20; "he said to" 38.
b   in a dream] om. 21.
c   So Rebekah sent] om. 21.
2a   will] "is to" (?) 9 42 47.
3a   my son] om. 12 47 (MS. 12 places it at the end of the sentence).
b   stops] "is to stop" 12 17 63.
c   forgets] pr. "until" 44.
d   to him] om. 17 21.
4a   Jacob] om. 12.
b   said] + "to her" 35.
c   I will kill him] "let me kill him" 9 47; pr. "or" 44.
5a   She said to him] "Rebekah said to Jacob" 12; "His mother said to him" 35; + "Go 58.
b   May I not] "I will not" 20; + "my son" 44.
c   my two sons] "two sons" 38; om. "my sons" 44.
6a   I notice] The form is *'erē'*, "I see"; MSS. 20 25 35 58 read *'i-yerē'i*, "he does not see." As this may be the smoother reading, it is suspect (VanderKam, *Jubilees* 2:171).
b   because I would be leaving him] om. 12. 4Q222 frg. 2 1: עׄל אשר עזבתןׄ. The Eth. imperfect and Heb. perfect have the same meaning in this hypothetical statement (see DJD 13:92–93).
c   then] om. 21 25 35 (but 25 reads it earlier in the clause).
7a   him] om. 58.
b   he will send] "I will send" 38; pr. "I will tell you and" 21.
8a   went in] + "to Isaac" 17 35 58 63.
b   to Isaac] om. 17 35 63.
c   life] + "my lord/husband" 63.
d   the land] "this land" 21 63 (with different demonstrative forms); "Canaan" 38.
e   who are like them] om. 38.
9a   blessed] om. 20.
b   instructed him] "instructed" 35 47.
10a any] om. 44.
b   go] Many MSS. prefix a conjunction (which mistakenly appears in the translation in VanderKam, *Jubilees* 2:172) 12 17 21 35 38 39 42 44 47 48 58 63.

c   From there] om. 12 20 25 (but 12 adds it later).
11a of Shadday (*sadday*)] "of heaven" (*samāy*) 20 21 25 35 39 42 47 48 58.
b   (bless) you] om. 9 58; + "and" 20 21 35 38 39 42 47 48 58 63.
c   (after) you] "me" 17; Lat. *te*.
d   and (all the land)] om. 20 25; Lat. *et*.
13a After Jacob had set out to go] Lat. "When he was going."
b   her son] pr. "Jacob" Lat.; pr. "went" 35c 38 (Lat. does not support "went").
c   kept crying] Lat. "cried."
14a My sister] Lat. "sister."
b   he will go] "he will make him go" 12; Lat. "he will go" (*ibit*).
15a will guard] "is to guard/let (him) guard" 9 21 39 42 47 48; "let (him) bless and guard" 44; Lat. "will guard."
b   because] Lat. "and."
c   will not abandon] "is not to abandon" 9 17; Lat. "will not abandon."
d   his entire lifetime] Lat. lacks "his"; "the days of his life" 38. Werman (*Jubilees*, 384 n. 5) regards the possessive as a substitute for the definite article.
16a I well know (Lat. *scio* seems weaker = "I know")] "let me affirm" 21; "I know" 20 25 35 39 42 47 48; "know" (imperative) 58.
b   his ways] Lat. "all his ways"; "his way" 21; om. 20 25.
c   be directed favorably (*yeššērāḥ*)] The MSS. attest a variety of verbal forms, many of them active in meaning, but a passive sense is needed in the context, as in Lat. *dirigentur*. Cf. VanderKam, *Jubilees* 2:173.
d   until] om. 12; Lat. *quousque*.
e   safely to us] Lat. and MS. 20 switch the order: "to us safely."
f   we see] "I see" 21; "we are to see" 63; Lat. *videbimus*.
17a Do not] Lat. adds *ergo*.
b   just in his way] "in peace and in justice are his ways" 12; Lat. "he is on/in the right way." Cf. VanderKam, *Jubilees* 2:173.
c   He is perfect] om. 44.
d   he is a true man] pr. "and" 20 25 35 58 (no conjunction in Lat.).

e He will not be abandoned] "You are not to abandon/lose and" 38; Lat. agrees with the other Eth. mss.
18a her son] "his son" 58 (Lat. is ambiguous).
b him] Jacob 63; Lat. *eum*.
19a Jacob] Lat. places the date formula as the first element in the sentence, giving the same date as Eth., though the units within it are in a different order. 1Q17 1 confirms the placement of the date formula in Eth. after "Haran": חרן באחד. How exactly the Hebrew expressed the remainder of "in the first year" is not clear. If it read שנה after אחד, they would not match in gender (see VanderKam, *Jubilees* 2:174).
b (forty-)fourth] "ninth" 12 58.
c of the first (month) of] om. 9 38; Lat. *primi*.
d the place] For Hebrew למק[ום = 1Q17 4, see VanderKam, *Textual*, 77–78.
e the road] "his road" 25; Lat. *via*; 1Q17 4 הדרך. Most Eth. copies read a construct form (= "the road of the west"), but the form without the construct ending attested in ms. 17 agrees with the two older versions (see VanderKam, *Jubilees* 2:174).
f to the west] For the reading למע[רב in 1Q17 4, see VanderKam, *Textual*, 77–78.
g and slept] Lat. lacks a conjunction so that the line says "During this night he slept there," while Eth. directly connects his sleeping there with the fact that he sun had set.
20a and set it] om. 12 63; Lat. lacks a conjunction because it relates this finite verb with the participle it used for the first verb in the sentence. It (with all versions of Gen 28:11) also lacks a pronominal object for "set," though 1Q17 5 likely has it (see VanderKam, *Textual*, 79; *Jubilees* 2:175).
b at the place (for) his head] Lat. *ad caput sibi* reflects מראשתיו in Gen 28:11. There is space for the word in 1Q17 5 (VanderKam, *Textual*, 79–80). See also Jub 27:26, where *diba re'su* appears in the text; and Charles, *Jubilees*, 167; VanderKam, *Jubilees* 2:175. The lack of the expression in the Eth. mss. tradition here may seem the preferred reading, and perhaps it is. But there is no obvious scribal trigger for omission of *diba re'su*.
c that (tree)] om. 21 and Lat. There is space for a demonstrative in 1Q17 6 (see VanderKam, *Textual*, 80), although the Eth. demonstrative may represent a Greek definite article (VanderKam, *Jubilees* 2:175). Werman (*Jubilees*, 385 n. 9) thinks one should add וישכב שם after the reference to the tree to fill up the available space in 1Q17 6 (as in *DSSR* 3:38), but it is doubtful the extra words are needed.
d and fell asleep] Lat. continues the use of participles from the previous expression: *iter faciens* [these words are confirmed by 1Q17 6] *et dormiens sibi*. Rönsch (*Jubiläen*, 46) read it with the next verse so that it would say "as he was sleeping he dreamed." See VanderKam, *Jubilees* 2:175.

21a he dreamed] Lat. reads *sibi* before *somniavit*. Its function is unclear, while Eth. reads a conjunction with the versions of Gen 28:12.
b that (*nāhu/ecce* = [traditionally] "behold")] + "a ladder and" 12.
c of the Lord] om. 12 (Lat. *dei*).
d the Lord] Lat. lacks *ecce* here = LXX OL Eth. Gen 28:13.
e standing] "sitting" 21 = Lat. *incumbebat*. Possibly LXX Gen 28:13 επεστηρικτο ("leaned upon") is the source of Lat.'s reading. See VanderKam, *Jubilees* 2:175.
22a the God] pr. "the Lord" 38; pr. "your" 12. Lat. *dominus deus* = Gen 28:13. Many LXX witnesses, however, lack "the Lord" here. See VanderKam, *Jubilees* 2:176.
b The land] pr. "from/of" 42 47 48 (Lat. *terram*).
c sleeping] Lat. *ordomis* is a mistake for *obdormis* (Rönsch, *Jubiläen*, 46).
23a earth] "sea" 17 35 38 44 58; Lat. *terrae*.
b You will become numerous] Lat. "It [= his seed/descendants] will become numerous"; this is the reading of the LXX tradition.
c the west (= the sea)] "the earth" 9 17 38; Lat. *mare*.
d the families] om. 12 44; Lat. *tribus*.
e of the nations] Lat. *terrae* = Gen 28:14; + "each in their families" 12; + "the land" 44. The Eth. reading is the more difficult one in respect of content (cf. Werman, *Jubilees*, 385 n. 12).
f and (your)] om. 9 12 17 20 21 38 44; Lat. *et*.
24a I will be] "I have been" 21.
b this] om. 21 58.
c because] "and" 20; om. 21.
d everything] "my voice/word" 9 21 38; om. 35.
25a Jacob said in (his) sleep] Lit., the text says, "Jacob slept a sleep and said." For the textual issue, see the commentary.
26a that he had placed at] om. 38.
b his head] The best reading is *re'su*, "his head," but several copies have *ter'asu*, "at the place of his head" 17c 21 44 63 (cf. 38); others add *wa-ter'asu*, "and at the place of his head" 39 42 47 48, while ms. 58 adds simply *ter'asu*.
c it] om. 12 20 38.
d marker] + "in this place" 47.
e But] "Its name" (= "as for its name at first") 12 25 39 42 47 58 (cf. 48).
f this] om. 12.
27a If ('*emma*)] "Because" ('*esma*) 20.
b gives] "the Lord gives" 38.
c return] "returned" 9 38.
d my father's house] "to my father" 44.
e the Lord will be] "may the Lord be" 12 21 38.
f is to become] "will be" 58; om. 21.
g All] om. 9 21.
h you have given me] "he has given me" 25 35t 38.
i I will indeed] "I will" 35 42 44 47 48 58.

Commentary

The end of chap. 26 left Jacob in a precarious position. He had obtained the patriarchal blessings under questionable circumstances, and his brother wanted to kill him as a result. The current chapter shows how Jacob escaped the dangerous situation at home and set out on a journey that would introduce the next major phase in his life. As the reader would expect by now, the ever-vigilant and resourceful Rebekah was the one who made the arrangements to protect her favored son. Once he reached Bethel in his flight from Esau, Jacob experienced a theophany in which he received from the Lord himself the full set of patriarchal promises. Jubilees 27 rewrites most of the material in Gen 27:42-46; 28:1-22, with the major parts being:

- 1-7 Rebekah and Jacob discuss plans (Gen 27:42-45)
- 8-11 Isaac carries out Rebekah's instructions and blesses Jacob (Gen 27:6—28:4)
- 12-18 Jacob leaves and his parents cope (Gen 28:5)
- 19-27 The theophany at Luz/Bethel (Gen 28:10-22).

The only part of Gen 27:42—28:22 that fails to appear in Jubilees 27 is 28:6-9. The short section deals with Esau's marriage to Mahalath daughter of Ishmael, a union meant to appease his parents, who disapproved of his Canaanite spouses. The writer of Jubilees defers mention of the marriage until a later context (29:18), where any positive implications for Esau that are present in Gen 28:6-9 fade from view.

As for the textual witnesses, the full Ethiopic version is joined by the Latin translation for vv. 11-24 (first two words) and by 1Q17 and 4Q222 frg. 2. 4Q222 frg. 2 preserves parts of vv. 6-7, while 1Q17 has letters and words from vv. 19-20. Little of the Hebrew text survives on these pieces, but the chapter once again closely follows the wording of Genesis so that one can often infer the Hebrew original from the MT and SP.

1-7 Rebekah and Jacob Discuss Plans

Rebekah, not Isaac, takes the initiative to thwart another disaster in the family, one that threatened the life of Jacob and thus of his descendants.

■ 1 The previous chapter ended with Esau plotting to kill Jacob but keeping his plan private—he said it to himself (Jub 26:35 // Gen 27:41). Yet according to the very next verse in Genesis (27:42), "the words of her elder son Esau were told to Rebekah," with no explanation for how she acquired the private information. One could speculate that Esau, among his other problems, could not keep a secret, but there is no hint of this in the text. The writer of Jubilees and other ancient expositors took different approaches to explaining how Rebekah learned of Esau's intentions: in Jubilees she was told in a dream what Esau was threatening; in *Tg. Ps.-J.* Gen 27:42 she learned it through the Holy Spirit (see also *Gen. Rab.* 67:9, where she and the other matriarchs appear to be prophetesses).[1] As a result, Rebekah once more summoned Jacob. Both Genesis and Jubilees refer to Esau as her elder and Jacob as her younger son in this context, as though the birthright and now the blessing had not really affected Jacob's status.

■ 2-3 Rebekah realized from her dream that prompt action was in order, as no one knew when Isaac would die and, consequently, when Esau would attempt to carry out his murderous plan. She emphasized to Jacob that Esau at this very time (הנה = *nāhu*) was plotting his revenge. Interpretations of the participle she uses to express what her older son was doing, מתנחם, vary. BDB (637) suggests "*ease oneself,* by taking vengeance."[2] "Take vengeance, threaten, or hold a grudge" are meanings of the verb in the Ethiopic text (*yetqēyamaka*, an imperfect tense form),[3] and the LXX and OL take it in the sense of threatening. Whatever Esau was doing, Jacob's life was in danger.

As she had in 26:6 after getting disturbing news, here again Rebekah orders Jacob to listen to her. She tells him

---

1 Cf. Endres, *Biblical Interpretation*, 93-94.
2 Skinner, *Genesis*, 374: "to take satisfaction"; Westermann, *Genesis 12–36*, 433: "will take vengeance."
3 Leslau, *Concise Dictionary*, 89. Werman translates as מתנקם (*Jubilees*, 386); cf. VanderKam, *Jubilees* 2:170.

to flee to her brother Laban in Haran.[4] She says nothing about marriage at this stage (contrast 25:1-3); she speaks only of flight for safety. Rebekah has access to otherwise inaccessible information (Esau's plan), but on this occasion she shows no gift for prediction—she claims Jacob is to remain in Haran only a few days (NRSV "a while"). As Genesis presents it, his stay in Haran lasted twenty years.[5] Her assessment of Esau and his resolve is telling: if Jacob stays at a distance for a short time, Esau will get over his anger[6] and forget all Jacob had done to him. The prediction nearly cites the words of Gen 27:44-45 verbatim, but it is noteworthy that Rebekah seems to place the responsibility for Jacob's deceptive behavior in the previous chapter on Jacob himself—when Esau "forgets everything[7] *you have done to him*." She could simply be reflecting what Esau might be thinking, as he may not have known about Rebekah's role in procuring the blessing for Jacob. The immediate danger is grave, but, Rebekah believed, the whole problem should disappear very soon, and then she would notify Jacob that it was safe to come home. As it turns out, she never sent word to him there, leading one to wonder whether she had misjudged the level and staying power of Esau's fury at Jacob.[8]

■ **4-5** Genesis 27:45 ends with Rebekah's question to Jacob: "Why should I lose both of you in one day?" Her concern had been that Esau would kill Jacob, but why is she worried about losing Esau as well? Is he too in danger? Genesis supplies no explanation for including both brothers in her question, but the writer of Jubilees does.[9] Jubilees 27:4, a verse lacking a parallel in Genesis, contains Jacob's reply to his mother (she is the only speaker in the context in Genesis): "I am not afraid. If he wishes to kill me, I will kill him."[10] Jacob seems suddenly to have become braver than when he hid after receiving the blessing (26:25), but the purpose of the insertion in Jubilees is to clarify why Rebekah worried she would lose both sons at the same time: each would try to kill the other, and maybe both would succeed. Now there was all the more reason to send Jacob away from home. The formulation of her words in Jub 27:5 is slightly different than in the Hebrew versions of Gen 27:45:

Genesis | Jubilees
Why should I lose both of you in one day? | May I not lose my two sons in[11] one day.

The words "may I not [*kama-'i-*]" (or: lest) agree with the phrasing in the LXX tradition ($\mu\eta\pi o\tau\epsilon$) rather than the למה of the MT and SP, and in Jubilees she uses "my two sons" where Genesis has, lit., "the two of you."

■ **6-7** Rebekah's maternal desire not to lose her only two sons in a single tragedy still does not persuade the Jacob of Jubilees. The reader could have concluded from chap. 26 that Jacob had not treated his father with appropriate respect when he took advantage of his failing eyesight to steal the blessing. True, he had objected when Rebekah broached the scheme (26:7-8), but he obeyed her nevertheless and deceived Isaac. Now, however, one learns that he really does honor his father and needs his approval before he obeys his mother in this important matter. In Jub 27:6 he objects to abandoning both the infirm Isaac and the anxious Rebekah, two aging parents:[12] "You are of course aware that my father

---

4 After the verb "flee," the LXX tradition reads "into Mesopotamia."

5 *Genesis Rabbah* 67:10, explaining the few days she mentions, adduces Gen 29:20: "So Jacob served seven years for Rachel, and they seemed to him but a few days because of the love he had for her." The same expression is used in both places; hence "a few days" means "seven years."

6 Genesis twice uses forms of שוב for the turning of Esau's anger; in Jubilees the first instance is rendered as expected, but the second (Gen 27:45 // Jub 27:3b) reads: (literally) "he will stop/leave off [*yaḥaddeg*] his anger." At this point the Vulgate has *cesset*.

7 There is no equivalent of "everything" in Gen 27:45.

8 *Genesis Rabbah* 67:10 notes that Esau's anger must not have disappeared and cites Amos 1:11: "Thus says the Lord: / For three transgressions of Edom, / and for four, I will not revoke the punishment; / because he pursued his brother with the sword / and cast off all pity; / he maintained his anger perpetually, / and kept his wrath forever." The passage from Amos will also play a role in Jubilees 37–38.

9 Endres, *Biblical Interpretation*, 94.

10 This is exactly what Jacob will eventually do (38:2) when Esau tries to kill him (e.g., 37:24).

11 There is no preposition in MT SP, but the other ancient versions (not the targums) of Gen 27:45 read "in."

12 Werman finds an analogy here with Jub 12:28-31, where Abram leaves his aged father Terah with the latter's permission (*Jubilees*, 386). Jacob will later

has grown old, and I notice that he has difficulty seeing. If I left him, he would consider it a bad thing because I would be leaving[13] him and going away from you." In this line he recalls the information about Isaac's condition from Gen 27:1-2 // Jub 26:1. By this time Jacob certainly would have been most aware of his father's ocular issues. In fact, however, he is concerned not only about abandoning Isaac and Rebekah in shameful fashion but also with nullifying all his and his mother's scheming to gain the blessing: "My father would be angry and curse me.[14] I will not go. If he sends me, only then will I go" (see Gen 27:12 // Jub 26:8).[15] Leaving home under the present circumstances would require approval of both parents, not just Rebekah. Jacob does not want to pit one parent against the other; he will obey both (cf. Gen 28:7). This statement from Jacob, not present in Genesis, also functions to explain the sudden transition from Gen 27:45 to 27:46: in v. 45 Rebekah is speaking with Jacob ("Why should I lose both of you in one day?"), but suddenly in v. 46 she is telling Isaac how difficult Esau's Hittite wives make her life. In Jubilees there is an explanatory transition: after Jacob said he would leave home only if his father told him to go, "Rebekah said to Jacob: 'I will go in and tell him.[16] Then he will send you'" (v. 7). She is confident of her ability to persuade Isaac. In this scene Rebekah is the catalyst but Isaac is the final authority.

Singer suggested that the emphasis on Jacob's filial piety in the present passage arose from the fact that in the interpretive tradition his abandoning aging parents for what proved to be a very long time raised questions about his loyalty to them and cast him in an unfavorable light compared with Esau who remained with Isaac and Rebekah during all those years. Singer also pointed to the several passages later in Jubilees where Jacob proves to be a much better son than Esau does (e.g., 29:13-19).[17] As he and Charles observed, the passage is yet another attempt to polish the image of Jacob as he appears in Genesis. He did in fact leave Isaac and Rebekah for many years, but he went only because both of them sent him away, and they dispatched him only because of Esau's murderous intent. He would have come home after a short absence had Esau been able to get himself under control (see Jub 29:17-19; 35:9-16 for how badly Esau treated his parents).

8-11 Isaac Carries Out Rebekah's Instructions and Blesses Jacob (Gen 27:6–28:4)

Verses 8-11 form an unusual section in Jubilees because much of the material in it occurs for the second time in the book. Rebekah's address to Jacob in 25:1-3 was based on Gen 28:1, 3, and some of her words of blessing in that

---

care for the infirm Isaac (29:15-20 [both parents]; 34:3).

13 4Q222 frg. 2 1 agrees with the Ethiopic text: ע[ל אשר עזבתנ]י (see DJD 13:92–93 for how the Hebrew perfect tense verb and the Ethiopic imperfect have the same value in this context).

14 The writer of Jubilees says nothing about the implication of Gen 27:29 // Jub 26:24 or Jub 25:22—that the one who curses Jacob is to be cursed. In other words, if Isaac cursed Jacob, he would bring a curse on himself (see also Jub 25:22).

15 4Q222 frg. 2 2 (ל[וא אלך כי אם י]שלחני) and the Ethiopic text agree (see DJD 13:93).

16 4Q222 frg. 2 3 preserves the equivalent of "and tell him": וא[ג]יד לו (DJD 13:93).

17 Singer supplies several references to pertinent midrashic texts (*Jubiläen*, 170); see also Charles, *Jubilees*, 165 (who cites Singer). Chronological calculations, given in, for example, *Seder Olam* 2 and *b. Meg.* 17a and based on the scriptural year numbers in the lives of Jacob and Joseph, reveal a fourteen-year gap in Jacob's life for which there is no account. Jacob was 63 when he received the blessing (see Jub 25:4 and the commentary there), and Joseph was born fourteen years later, when Jacob was 77 (at the end of the two units of seven years in Haran). Genesis 41:46 says Joseph was 30 when he stood before Pharaoh; at that time Jacob would have been 107. If one adds the seven years of plenty and two years of famine, Jacob would be 116. Then in Gen 47:8-9 Jacob tells the Pharaoh he is 130, when he should be 116. The sources claim he spent the extra fourteen years studying Torah in the house of Eber; they did not count in his time away from his parents. The result was that Jacob, who did not go back home for thirty-six years, was in effect gone for only twenty-two years, exactly the amount of time Joseph would be away from his father Jacob. Neither was apparently guilty of dishonoring his father. Jubilees does not take this approach but shows that Jacob was a virtuous son when he finally returned to the land.

chapter resemble Isaac's blessings in Gen 28:3-4 (cf. Jub 25:16-17). The main difference is that now Isaac, ever the slower of the married couple, gives the instructions and blessing, not Rebekah.

■ **8** Even here, though Isaac gives Jacob the patriarchal blessings and this time is fully aware he is speaking to Jacob, he still does so only at Rebekah's urging. She went to Isaac and made her case by reminding him of the Hittite wives whom Esau had married (Gen 27:46 mentions only the wives, not Esau) and how they made her despair of her life (Jub 27:8 // Gen 27:46). She underscored the point by adding a description of the women to the end of the sentence in Gen 27:46: "because the Canaanite women are evil." She by no means wanted Jacob to repeat Esau's error, although in Jubilees, it seems, she had no need to fear he would because of his earnest assurances to her in 25:4-10, including his strong intention ("I have set my mind," v. 6) of marrying one of Laban's daughters. Either she feared that with the passage of time (five years) he forgot his pledge or she was again manipulating Isaac into doing what she wanted him to do.

■ **9-11** Whatever her motives, she succeeded and Isaac finally got things right. The three versions of the scene—one in Genesis and two in Jubilees—read as follows.

Genesis 28:1-4	Jubilees 27:9-11	Jubilees 25:1, 3 (cf. 16-17)
Then Isaac called Jacob and blessed him, and charged him, "You shall not marry one of Canaanite women. Go at once to Paddan-aram to the house of Bethuel, your mother's father; and take as wife from there one of the daughters of Laban, your mother's brother. May God almighty bless you and make you fruitful and numerous, that you may become a company of peoples. May he give to you the blessing of Abraham, to you and to your offspring with you, so that you may take possession of the land where you now live as an alien—land that God gave to Abraham."	So Isaac summoned his son Jacob, blessed and instructed him, and said to him, "Do not marry any of the Canaanite women. Set out, go to Mesopotamia, to the house of Bethuel, your mother's father. From there take a wife from the daughters of Laban, your mother's brother. May the God of Shaddai bless you; may he make you increase, become numerous, and be a throng of nations. May he give the blessings of my father Abraham to you and to your descendants after you so that you may possess the land where you wander as a foreigner—and all the land that the Lord gave to Abraham. Have a safe trip, my son."[18]	. . . Rebekah summoned her son Jacob and spoke to him, "My son, do not marry any of the Canaanite women. . . . Do not marry any of the women of this land but (someone) from my father's house and from my father's clan. Marry someone from my father's house. The Most High God will bless you; your family will be a righteous family and your descendants (will be) holy." (See 25:16-17 for blessings of many descendants and the land.)

Isaac commands Jacob to follow the practice set forth by Abraham when he ordered his servant to fetch a wife for Isaac from his extended family, the family of Nahor and Bethuel, who had remained in Haran (Genesis 24). After the instructions and blessings that Isaac gave to Jacob on this occasion, there could be no question whether Jacob was the rightful patriarchal heir: Isaac asked that his descendants become many—a throng/company of nations—and that Jacob and they possess the land. Here he joins Abraham (19:21-25; 22:10-15, 24, 27-30) and Rebekah (25:15-22), both of whom had

---

18 Few actual variant readings, that is, ones not due to the different English translations cited for Genesis and Jubilees, separate Gen 28:1-4 from Jub 27:9-11. Verse 9 (Gen 28:1): *his son* Jacob (addition of "his son" agrees with Rebekah's way of referring to Jacob in 25:1 where she also addresses him directly as "my son"). Verse 10 (Gen 28:1): *any* of the Canaanite women (this too agrees with Rebekah's phrasing in 25:1). *Mesopotamia* (not Paddan-aram; see also v. 12 // Gen 28:5); here Jubilees agrees with the LXX tradition. Verse 11 (Gen 28:4): *blessings* (plural), a reading found in Syr. Gen 28:4; *my father* Abraham (not just Abraham); LXX agrees, while the SP and Eth. Genesis have "your father"; *after you* (= Latin Jubilees as well; not *with you*), as in the LXX tradition; *and all the land* (despite the NRSV rendering quoted above, *land* appears just once in the text), a reading unique here to Jubilees (in both Ethiopic and Latin).

already pronounced the blessings on Jacob, as he himself had in 26:23-24, though he did not realize it at the time. The wording in 27:11—"so that you may possess the land where you wander as a foreigner—and all the land that the Lord gave to Abraham"—makes it seem as if Isaac is talking about two geographical entities where Genesis gives two descriptions of the same territory. If so, in Jubilees the land where Jacob sojourned was only a part of what he and his descendants would own.[19] His added wish—"Have a safe trip, my son [lit., Go in peace, my son]"—reminds one of the words Terah said to Abram as the latter prepared to go in the opposite direction Jacob will now travel (Jub 12:29; cf. 18:16).

12-18 Jacob Leaves and His Parents Cope (Gen 28:5)

■ **12** Jubilees 27:12 quotes Gen 28:5 verbatim, except for one deletion at the end (see below). Isaac sent Jacob away to Mesopotamia—this is all Rebekah had asked him to do—but he had done much more by blessing him. The names *Mesopotamia* and the gentilic used for Laban (*soryāwi*; Latin *syri*)[20] are indicators that a Greek translation of Jubilees underlies both the Ethiopic and Latin versions of the book. After identifying Laban as Bethuel's son, the text adds that he is the brother of Rebekah who is the mother of Jacob, where Gen 28:5 says she is the mother of Jacob and Esau (in that order). It may be that the author of Jubilees dropped the mention of Esau because of his dislike for him, but it may also be the case that he omitted his name when he left the following unit, Gen 28:6-9, out of his text. These verses portray Esau in a relatively favorable light. When he saw that his first two marriages displeased his parents who had just indicated they wanted Jacob to marry within the clan, he went to another branch of the family to find a third wife. He married Mahalath, the daughter of Ishmael. There was no doubt Ishmael was part of Abraham's family, and his daughter was not a Canaanite woman (her mother was an Egyptian according to Gen 21:21). However, Gen 28:9 adds that he took her "in addition to the wives he had." As a result, while he made a better choice for a wife than he had before, he remained married to the other two who so strongly offended Isaac and Rebekah. The author, who was deeply concerned about proper marriages, could hardly countenance his behavior and omitted the episode here.[21] He will mention the marriage in 29:18 but in a very negative context: Esau, the son who in Genesis actually stays with his elderly parents, is said to have "left his father Isaac alone at the well of the oath" after stealing all his flocks. Isaac finally settled at a distance from him to put a safe space between them (29:17). In the same context, Jacob, the son who left his aging parents for decades, is credited with taking exceptionally good care of them upon finally returning to the land (29:15-16, 20). Esau cannot win in Jubilees.

■ **13-18** Once he has reproduced Gen 28:5, the writer of Jubilees fashions a scene without parallel in Genesis. He probably sensed a gap in Genesis where, after Rebekah and Jacob have had a special bond for sixty-nine years (see the date in 27:19), there is no hint they ever saw each other again or even communicated. There is no indication she ever sent for him during the twenty years he was with her brother, and she is not mentioned when he returns to the land. The only remaining occurrences of her name after chap. 28 are in Gen 29:1 (Laban is named as her brother),[22] 12 (Jacob tells Rachel he is Rebekah's son), 35:8 (Deborah is identified as "Rebekah's nurse"), and 49:31 (her burial place is noted). Whenever the idea of Jacob's going home surfaces in the Jacob stories, the purpose is to see his father (Gen 31:18, 30, 53; 32:9). Genesis does not record the death of Rebekah, only that of Isaac, whom Jacob apparently visited just before he died (Gen 35:27-29). All of this must have been difficult for an ancient expositor to accept. Surely Rebekah did not simply forget her beloved

---

19 See Werman, *Jubilees*, 386. It is also possible that "and" here means "even," in which case the sense would be that of Gen 28:4.
20 Where MT SP read פדנה ארם the LXX tradition has "Mesopotamia," and where MT SP have הארמי the same tradition has "the Syrian."
21 Cf. Endres, *Biblical Interpretation*, 94.
22 The Hebrew version of Gen 29:1 used by Jubilees contained this information; it is not in the MT and SP but is in the LXX tradition.

son and never see him again. And did she never see her grandchildren? Had she not prayed "Son, may I see your blessed children during my lifetime" (Jub 25:18)? The author of Jubilees, who has emphasized the strong feelings of Rebekah for Jacob, assigns her a prominent role in later chapters, once Jacob returns to the land (31:5-7, 30; 33:21-23; 35).

In the present context in Jubilees, Rebekah is crushed by the departure of "her son." Her strong feelings for him overflow in unending tears. Isaac, showing a side of his character not evident before, now becomes the stronger of the two and demonstrates that he has truly come to understand the extraordinary character of Jacob. When Rebekah cannot stop crying, Isaac addresses her as "My sister" and tells her not to cry for "my son Jacob" (v. 14)—he claims him as his own. His consoling words focus on Jacob's safety, success, and return; he is sure of a favorable outcome because the Lord will accompany him. In v. 14 he assures her that Jacob will travel safely in both directions. He knows that God will be with him (he expressed a wish for this in v. 11) not only on the present journey but also throughout his life. Isaac does not say that all the promises about descendants would prove hollow if harm came to Jacob before he had children, nor does he say that Abraham had asked God not to leave or neglect Jacob (22:29). Instead, he declares his own confident faith: the Most High God will guard him and never abandon him. Moreover, God will direct his ways "until he returns safely to us and we see that he is safe" (v. 16). Both of them will be alive when that happens—the Isaac of Jubilees believes he and Rebekah will see Jacob again. The scene allows the author to introduce another glowing description of Jacob because Isaac concludes his loving words of comfort by saying, "Do not be afraid for him, my sister, because he is just [rāteʿ] in his way. He is perfect [feṣṣum]; he is a true [meʾman] man. He will not be abandoned. Do not cry" (v. 17). The attributes Isaac assigns to Jacob recall the description of him at birth: "Jacob was perfect [feṣṣum] and upright [rāteʿ]" (19:13; cf. Jub 25:12 [in 25:20 Rebekah asks for perfect descendants for Jacob]; Gen 25:27). In describing Jacob as a true/faithful (meʾman/verax) man, Isaac adopts an adjective that puts Jacob on a par with Abraham, who proved faithful in every test the Lord imposed on him (17:15-18; 18:16 [meʾman appears in vv. 15, 17, 18 (twice) and in 18:16; the related form mahaymen figures in vv. 15, 16, 17). Isaac's words also prepare for the ones the deity says to Jacob just a few verses later: "I will be with you. I will guard you wherever you go. I will bring you back safely to this land because I will not abandon you until I have done everything that I have said to you" (27:24; Jacob repeats some of this in v. 27). The narrator realizes that Isaac both comforts Rebekah (regarding "her son Jacob") and blesses Jacob with the words he pronounces (v. 18).[23]

Another text in which it appears that Isaac comforts Rebekah in the same context is 4Q364 (4QRewritten Pentateuch) 3 ii:1-6 (the sequel in lines 7-9 appears to begin the unit about Esau's marriage after Jacob's departure [Gen 28:6-9]). Only the beginnings of the lines are preserved:

1 him you shall see [
2 you shall see (him) in good health [
3 your death, and unto [your] eyes [
4 both of you and [Isaac] called [
5 her all [these] thin[gs
6 after Jacob her son [[24]

---

23 Werman finds influence from the priestly blessing in Isaac's words in vv. 14-15 (*Jubilees*, 387). There is some shared language between the passages (bless, keep/watch, peace), but the stronger influences come from the other descriptions of Jacob in Jubilees (see above), and closer parallels are available elsewhere (see below).

24 Translation of Abegg in *DSSR* 3:247 with some adjustment of brackets and without his restorations after the preserved words on lines 3, 4, and 6. For analyses of the section, see Daniel Falk, *The Parabiblical Texts: Strategies for Extending the Scriptures among the Dead Sea Scrolls* (LSTS 63, Companion to the Qumran Scrolls 8; London: T&T Clark, 2007) 115-16 (perhaps an angel is speaking to Isaac in the first lines); Hanna Tervanotko, "'You Shall See': Rebekah's Farewell Address in 4Q364 3 ii 1-6," in Nóra Dávid, Armin Lange, Kristin De Troyer, and Shani Tzoref, eds., *The Hebrew Bible in Light of the Dead Sea Scrolls* (FRLANT 239; Göttingen: Vandenhoeck & Ruprect, 2012) 413-26, here 423-26 (Rebekah is speaking in the first four lines—an unlikely interpretation in view of line 5, where someone is telling her "all [these] thin[gs"); and Molly Zahn, *Rethinking Rewritten Scripture: Composition and Exegesis in the 4QReworked Pentateuch*

The context is probably that of Jub 27:13-18, although "both of you" in line 4 makes it likely someone else is speaking to Isaac (the pronouns "you/your" in lines 1-3 are masculine) and that he then reports what he had learned to Rebekah. If so, the situation would not be exactly that of Jubilees, though the setting is the same.

Isaac's calling Rebekah "my sister" (vv. 14, 17) could remind one of the story in Gen 26:6-11 (almost all of it is omitted from Jubilees), where Isaac, after the men of Gerar notice Rebekah, tells them "She is my sister." Yet in Jub 27:14, 17 he is not trying to mislead anyone about the identity of his wife but aims only to comfort her and uses an endearing term for her. As a number of experts have noted, the scene has a near parallel in the book of Tobit, although commentators have not always spelled out the extent of the similarities.[25] There, Tobit, also an aging father who cannot see, and his wife Anna send their son Tobias on a long journey to another branch of the family, not specifically to find a wife though he gains one in the process. When Tobias is set to leave home, "he kissed his father and mother. Tobit then said to him, 'Have a safe journey.' But his mother began to weep, and said to Tobit, 'Why is it that you have sent my child away? Is he not the staff of our hand as he goes in and out before us?'" (5:17-18) After she makes a few more statements to this effect, "Tobit said to her, 'Do not worry; our child will leave in good health and return to us in good health. Your eyes will see him on the day when he returns to you in good health. Say no more! Do not fear for them, my sister. For a good angel will accompany him; his journey will be successful, and he will come back in good health.' So she stopped weeping" (5:21–6:1).[26] Tobit, like Isaac, calls his wife "my sister" as he comforts her when their son leaves, assures her he will be safe and successful, predicts she will see him when he returns, claims he will have supernatural protection, and of course wishes his son a safe trip.[27]

The scene in Jubilees, though not unique to the book, is a moving description of two parents who care deeply for their son and for each other. Endres describes the function of the unit well:

> [I]n Jubilees this section plays an important role, since it binds together the various scenes between Jacob and his parents, and concludes the whole with a type of familial compassion and tenderness which offsets the parents' previous differences over their children. Finally, this segment also portends the eventual concurrence of minds and joining of sympathies in Jubilees 35.[28]

19-27 The Theophany at Luz/Bethel (Gen 28:10-22)

The section offers a close reproduction of Gen 28:10-22 with some additional notes characteristic of Jubilees.

■ **19** The writer dates Jacob's departure to the year 2115, the year after the previous major event in the text (26:1, the date for the story about blessing the "wrong" son). He may have left shortly after his and Rebekah's deception in Genesis 27 // Jubilees 26—an event that may have occurred late in the previous year, because, according to the end of v. 19, Jacob arrives at Luz/Bethel on the first day of the first month of the year 2115. This should,

---

Manuscripts (STDJ 95; Leiden: Brill, 2011) 77–81 (she surveys the various views, their weaknesses and strengths).

25 Rönsch, *Jubiläen*, 135; Singer, *Jubiläen*, 168 n. 6; Charles, *Jubilees*, 166; Hartom, "Jubilees," 84; Endres, *Biblical Interpretation*, 95–97. Of these scholars, only Rönsch and Endres point to the wider parallels in the two works, with the latter printing the texts side by side. Carey A. Moore indicates the parallels by italics in his translation of Tobit and discusses them (*Tobit: A New Translation with Introduction and Commentary* [AB 40A; New York: Doubleday, 1996] 193–95). His arguments for Jubilees as later and as therefore borrowing from Tobit are too general to be conclusive. Jubilees is probably the later text, but there is no need to infer that the writer fashioned the scene, which fits so well with his major teachings, under the influence of Tobit (with thanks to Dr. Joseph Khalil for his e-mail comments on the issue).

26 4Q197 (4QTob[b]) 4 i:1-4 preserves some words from Tob 5:19–6:1, including "my sister [אחתי]" in line 3.

27 As Endres points out, Isaac differs from Tobit by "moralizing his optimistic prediction" for Jacob through the description of him in v. 17 (*Biblical Interpretation*, 96).

28 Ibid., 97.

therefore, be the very day on which he had left Beer-sheba—also dated to 2115. The danger posed by Esau's need for revenge must have remained serious enough to force Jacob from his home—and to cover a lot of territory in one day of walking.[29] This time the place for which he departs[30] is called Haran (it was Mesopotamia in v. 12). According to Jubilees, "He arrived at Luz that is on the mountain—that is, Bethel." Genesis says "He came to a certain place" (v. 11; actually "*the* place" in the MT) and supplies no information about its two names until eight verses later (Gen 28:19 // Jub 27:26). So, the author at the beginning removes any uncertainty about the site in question, though the date on which Jacob arrived—the first day of the first month—implies that something significant was likely to happen there.[31] The geographical fact that Bethel is on a mountain is mentioned in Josh 16:1; 1 Sam 13:2 (cf. Gen 12:8; see also Josh 18:12-13; Judg 1:22-26).

Jubilees further supplements the terse narrative in Genesis as it describes the situation:

Genesis 28:11
He came to a certain place

and stayed there for the night, because the sun had set.

Jubilees 27:19
He arrived at the place in the evening, turned off the road to the west of the highway during this night, and slept there because the sun had set.

Reference to the west in connection with Bethel reminds one of Abram's initial visit to the site: "From there he moved on to the hill country on the east of Bethel, and pitched his tent, with Bethel on the west and Ai on the east; and there he built an altar to the LORD and invoked the name of the LORD" (Gen 12:8; see Jub 13:5). Abram approached Bethel from the north and Jacob from the south, but both encountered the Lord there and built altars afterwards (Gen 12:8; Gen 35:7 // Jub 31:3).

■ 20 The rewritten text continues to cite the wording of Gen 28:11 until the last words of 27:20.

Genesis 28:11
Taking one of the stones of the place,
he put it under his head

and lay down in that place.

Jubilees 27:20
He took one of the stones of that place
and set it at the place (for) his head[32] beneath that tree.
He was traveling alone and fell asleep.

The reference to "that tree" is intriguing. There is no tree in Gen 28:11, and prior to the notice Jubilees had also not mentioned one. It is likely that the tree where he stopped is the one recorded in Gen 35:8 // Jub 32:30. When Deborah, Rebekah's nurse, died in Bethel, "she was buried under an oak below Bethel. So it was called Allon-bacuth" (Gen 35:8). In Jubilees the verse reads: "They buried her below the city, beneath the oak (near) the stream. He named that place the Stream of Deborah

---

29 The distance is too great to walk in one day. The author clearly did not adopt the interpretation, found in *Gen. Rab.* 68:10, that God made the sun set two hours early that day.

30 Both the Ethiopic and Latin of Jubilees use a purpose clause (*kama yeḥor/ut iret*), as SP Gen 28:10 (ללכת) does; MT has וילך. 1Q17 2 preserves enough letters to indicate that Hebrew Jubilees also read an infinitive (לל[כת).

31 Werman calls this Rosh Ha-Shanah and speaks of it as the time of change from summer to fall (*Jubilees*, 388). In the calendar of Jubilees, of course, the first of the first month occurs in the spring. After misdating the occasion, she next writes about how, at the change of seasons, one angel (responsible for the season just ending) gives way to the one in charge of the next season. The angels ascending and descending on the ladder are these very angels in the process of trading positions with each other. To support this remarkable claim she refers to 6:29; 12:20, neither of which says anything about an angelic change of shifts. She thinks the days of calendrical transfer between seasons (and thus of angels as well) were called ימי פיגועים (she does not say where in Jubilees they are so named; they are called memorial days in Jubilees 6) and that the verb ויפגע ("He came to a certain place," Gen 28:11) motivated the author to make the association. It hardly needs to be said that the text bears no trace of such an interpretation.

32 The English translations of Genesis and Jubilees read differently but render the same text. The word for the place where his head was in Gen 28:11—מראשתיו—likely appeared in the Hebrew of Jubilees as there is space for it in the reconstructed line 5 of 1Q17 (VanderKam, *Textual*, 80 [where it is line 4]). The Latin translation includes *ad caput sibi*, but the Ethiopic copies lack an equivalent. The term reappears in Gen 28:18, and there Eth. Jubilees (27:26) has it as well (*ḫaba re'su*).

and the oak the Oak of Mourning for Deborah" (Jub 32:30).[33] The two visits of Jacob to Bethel are tied together in a number of ways, and this may be another, if small, example of the connections between them in Jubilees. That Jacob was traveling alone could easily be inferred from the context in Genesis (cf. also Gen 32:10), though the text does not make it explicit. When he returns to Bethel his large family and many possessions will accompany him.

■ 21-24 The solitary and no doubt weary traveler with a stone next to his head experienced a vivid dream. There are only minor differences between the dream passages in Gen 28:12-15 and Jub 27:21-24. Jubilees 27:21 supplies a direct quotation of Gen 28:12, with just the superfluous "That night" representing an addition to it. The Hebrew texts of Gen 28:12 are ambiguous about where the angels ascend and descend—on the ladder or on Jacob—since the suffix of בו could refer to either;[34] both the Ethiopic and Latin texts of Jubilees use feminine suffixes identifying the ladder as the place of angelic travel. The same sharing of text prevails in Jub 27:21b-22, which quotes Gen 28:13 but with two extra expressions: at the beginning Jubilees reads: "He spoke with Jacob," a clause hardly needed but filling out the short narrative of Genesis; and at the end "your descendants after you" expands in a familiar way on the term "your offspring/descendants" in Genesis. It is worth adding that while in Genesis the Lord could be understood as standing at the top of the ladder/staircase or above Jacob (עליו), Jubilees (both Ethiopic and Latin) clearly opts for the former interpretation, as the suffix/object of the preposition is feminine (*westētā/ea*). In v. 23 // Gen 28:14 the close textual relationship continues, though the verb ופרצת ("and you shall spread abroad") stands where Jubilees reads *tebazzeḥ/abundabit*, "you will become numerous/it [= your seed] will become numerous."[35] Farther along, where Genesis has משפחת האדמה, "the families of the earth," Ethiopic Jubilees has *baḥāwerta 'aḥzāb*, "the families of the nations" (Latin *tribus terrae* agrees with Genesis).[36] Finally in v. 24 there is full agreement with Gen 28:15 apart from the extra "safely (lit., in peace)" echoing Isaac's words to Jacob in Jub 27:16.[37]

Consequently, the pericope about the dream Jacob saw at Bethel is a passage that the writer of Jubilees felt no need to alter or enhance in any significant way.[38] It is the first time the Lord speaks directly to Jacob in Genesis and in Jubilees, and the promises he makes to him constitute a full statement of the patriarchal blessings with no conditions attached. They stand in a relation to the ones accorded to Abram in Genesis 12 and 13 (at Bethel). Genesis 12:3 (Jub 12:23) and 28:14 are the only passages using "families of the earth" ("nations of the earth," Jub 12:23); Gen 13:14 (Jub 13:19) and 28:14 refer to the four cardinal directions in connection with promises; and 13:16 (Jub 13:20) and 28:14 compare the patriarchs' offspring to the dust of the earth. Both the place and the promises, then, pair Abram and Jacob, but in Jubilees alone the blessings confirm words spoken earlier by Abraham regarding Jacob (19:17-23; 22:11-15, 24, 28-30). Abraham prayed to the Lord more than once that the blessings given him would accrue to Jacob (19:23, 27; 22:13; cf. 22:24); now the deity has guaranteed they would. In some

---

33 Though Gen 35:8 uses אלון for the tree, the word לוז can refer to an almond tree (BDB, 531; *Gen. Rab.* 69:8). It is not obvious why Charles and Endres think the tree was an *asherah* (Charles, *Jubilees*, 167; Endres, *Biblical Interpretation*, 98). Why would Jubilees add to the text of Genesis a reference to a suspect kind of tree?

34 See the debate about these options in *Gen. Rab.* 68:12, 13.

35 Syriac Gen 28:14 agrees with the reading (*tsg'*), and Eth. Gen 28:14 uses the same verb as Jubilees but is otherwise different: *yebazzeḥ zar'eka wa-yemalle'*, "your seed/descendants will be numerous and fill up/multiply."

36 Endres suggests that the change produces a more pointed reference to the gentiles (*Biblical Interpretation*, 99).

37 The word "everything" in "everything that I have said to you" agrees with the text represented in the LXX tradition; the Hebrew versions of Gen 28:15 have "what I have promised/said to you."

38 For elaborations of the story in other works, see Kugel, *The Ladder of Jacob: Ancient Interpretations of the Biblical Story of Jacob and His Children* (Princeton: Princeton University Press, 2006) 9-35.

ways, Jacob's blessings are even more remarkable than Abraham's: Jacob has not yet left the land but is assured he will come back to it, and he is not yet married but is promised his descendants will be huge in number.[39] The close similarities between the promises in 27:22-24 and the ones given to Isaac in 24:9-11, 22 were noted in the commentary on chap. 24. The present passage shares with the ones in chap. 24, besides the promises of land and progeny, the assurance that God would be with the recipient (24:9, 22), the peoples of the earth would be blessed through his descendants (24:11), and his descendants would be as numerous as the sands of the earth (24:22). By this time in Jubilees, then, Jacob has received words of blessing from Abraham, Rebekah, and Isaac, and God himself has set his imprimatur on them. Jacob is definitely the chosen descendant and successor of Abraham and Isaac.

Promises are a familiar element in the patriarchal stories, but the assurance that God will accompany the hero on a difficult journey and return him in safety relates to the special circumstances of Jacob once he left home.[40] Perhaps the promise that God will be with him is meant as a clarification of Jubilees' earlier report that Jacob was traveling alone (v. 20).[41] It turns out he was by no means alone on the road but was accompanied by God and perhaps also the angels who moved between heaven and earth.[42]

■ 25 Jacob's response to the stunning dream revelation (vv. 25-27 // Gen 28:16-22), like the story of the dream itself, closely parallels the one in Genesis, but with some noteworthy differences. The first distinction is at the beginning of v. 25 (Gen 28:16), where Genesis (in all the ancient versions) offers: "Then Jacob woke from his sleep and said." In Jubilees the reading literally is "Jacob slept a sleep and said." Since the Ethiopic is the only version available here, it cannot be confirmed or contrasted with other textual evidence for the book. Jacob in Jubilees is pictured as talking in his sleep. A natural reaction is to think something has happened to alter the text, and this is the conclusion some scholars have drawn.[43] In his edition, Charles changed the Ethiopic text so that it matched Genesis,[44] but in his commentary he offered a hypothesis about how Jubilees's reading originated: ἐξυπνωσε ἐξ ὑπνου was misread as ὑπνωσε ὑπνου.[45] The proposal has obvious appeal (though it would involve leaving out ἐξ twice), but it may not be needed. Gold-

---

39 Hamilton, *Genesis 18–50*, 242-43.
40 In direct speech the Lord tells Isaac he will be/is with him in Gen 26:3, 24, but there Isaac is pictured as a resident alien, not as a traveler.
41 *Genesis Rabbah* 68:10 contains the interpretation that the words "the sun had set" in 28:11 suggested God made the sun set early that day so that he could speak with Jacob in private.
42 If the writer meant to say the angels were accompanying him, he only implied it. It is explicit in the Palestinian targums. They build on the fact that Gen 28:12 says angels were "ascending and descending," that is, "ascending" comes first and entails that some angels were on the earth before the ladder appeared. "And he dreamed, and behold, a ladder was fixed on the earth and its head reached *to the height of* the heavens; and behold, the angels *that had accompanied him from the house of his father* ascended *to bear good tidings to the angels on high, saying: 'Come and see the pious man whose image is engraved in the throne of Glory, whom you desired to see.'* And behold, the angels *from before the Lord* ascended and descended *and observed him*" (*Tg. Neof.* Gen 28:12). Cf. *Gen. Rab.* 68:12.
43 However, both Dillmann ("u. Jakob schlief [aus]") and Schodde ("and Jacob finished his sleep") worked with the text as it stands.
44 Charles, *Ethiopic Version*, 100 nn. 16-17; Littmann ("Jubiläen," 87 n. b) agreed but thought it difficult to discern how the reading arose. Wintermute, Caquot (both without a note), and Rabin also change the text as Charles indicated. Kugel believes the text is clearly a mistake for what Gen 28:16 says (*Walk through* Jubilees, 139), but he does not indicate why one should think it was a mistake. He does not repeat this statement about the text in his "Jubilees," and allows the translation of Wintermute ("And Jacob awoke from his sleep and he said") to stand in his text without a note. Werman (*Jubilees*, 385 n. 13) considers it impossible to retain the Ethiopic text, since he speaks and looks about and there is no indication in the sequel that he awoke (but see the view of Goldmann below). She reads ויקץ יעקב משנתו ("And Jacob awoke from his sleep").
45 Charles, *Jubilees*, 168.

mann, who rendered the Ethiopic text as it stands (וישן יעקב את שנתו), rejected Charles's hypothesis. He noted that Jacob was speaking these words in a dream, from which he does not awaken until the next verse.[46] His observation may reveal the author's thought process: Gen 28:18 ("So Jacob rose early in the morning" // Jub 27:26) could be taken to imply that Jacob awakened only at that point, not already here in Gen 28:16.

His next words contain a minor deviation from Genesis. In Genesis (v. 16) Jacob first exclaims, "Surely the LORD is in this place," but in Jubilees he says, "This place is indeed the house of the Lord." One could search for significance in the different wordings,[47] but the author has simply taken an expression from Gen 28:17 and inserted it in Jacob's first words after seeing the dream. In 28:17 he declares, "This is none other than the house of God" (see the next sentence in Jubilees). In Jubilees the writer forefronts the play on the name Bethel, a name that he, unlike Genesis, has already given to the place in this context. The remainder of Jub 27:25 offers a word-for-word reproduction of the last clause in Gen 28:16 and of Gen 28:17. For the second time in one verse, therefore, Jacob refers to the location as the house of the Lord[48] and also calls it the gate of heaven.

■ 26 Jacob apparently awakens only in Jub 27:26 (Gen 28:18). When he does, he takes the stone that he had lodged near his head and puts it to a certain use. In Genesis (see also 35:14) he "set it up for a pillar [מצבה]," but in Jubilees he "set it up as a pillar for a marker [*la-te'mert*]." The writer will do the same in v. 27b, where Gen 28:22 again refers simply to a pillar. It may be that the author, in distinction from Genesis, felt some unease at the idea of a patriarch erecting a מצבה, a term suffused with idolatrous associations (e.g., 1 Kgs 14:23; 2 Kgs 17:10) and designating objects that were supposed to be smashed (Deut 7:5; 12:2-4). The addition of "for a marker" or "for a sign" would then indicate that there was nothing cultic about the pillar, even though Jacob set it up at a place named Bethel, a city that would have its own sanctuary in later times.[49] It merely marks a place.[50] This is the point where Genesis finally discloses its former and present name. Jubilees had dispelled any mystery about the location by introducing them at the beginning of the story (v. 19), but the writer copies the text of Genesis and thus repeats them at this juncture. In v. 19 he had mentioned Luz first and identified it with Bethel; here he follows Gen 28:19 in saying that it first had the name Luz but Jacob renamed it Bethel after the revelation to him. The expression in the Hebrew versions of Genesis אולם לוז (SP: אולם לוזה), in which אולם means "but," was read by the LXX translator as though it were a two-word place-name: ουλαμλουζ. In Jubilees the words were properly understood so that only *luzā* (= the SP spelling) is given as the original name of the area.[51]

---

46 Goldmann, "Jubilees," 276; cf. VanderKam, *Jubilees* 2:176.

47 Hartom thinks the writer may have made the change to avoid giving the impression that the Lord occupied this place ("Jubilees," 89), but that seems unlikely because in both Genesis and Jubilees Jacob calls the place "the house of God." Endres (*Biblical Interpretation*, 99) agrees with Hartom. Kugel claims the writer "omits Jacob's 'Surely the Lord is present in this place, and I did not know it'" (*Walk through* Jubilees, 139; "Jubilees," 389), but he does not actually leave it out. The only difference from Gen 28:16 is the one noted above, one that does not picture Jacob as hesitant about implying the place was holy.

48 In both references to the house, the Ethiopic text uses the same term for the deity (*'egzi'abḥēr*, rendered "the Lord"), whereas Genesis has the Tetragrammaton in v. 16 and אלהים in v. 17.

49 Hartom, "Jubilees," 89; Endres, *Biblical Interpretation*, 99; Kugel, *Walk through* Jubilees, 139; "Jubilees," 389 (he references Deut 16:22, which prohibits setting up a מצבה). This is the third time in the story that a related form is used: מצב (for the ladder/staircase being "set up"; note that it has a top—ראשו, v. 12), and נצב (for the Lord standing, v. 13). Like the ladder, Jacob's pillar has a top, and on it he pours oil. See Hamilton, *Genesis 18-50*, 246.

50 Kugel ("Levi's Elevation," 19-21) maintains that the addition of "for a marker/sign" frees Jacob from the charge that he failed to carry out his vow (see v. 27). Since he was not a priest, he had to wait until one could come to offer sacrifice at Bethel, and that one was his son Levi. The issue of whether Jacob was a priest will be treated in the commentary on chap. 31. At this point there was no need for anyone to perform a priestly function.

51 For calling it an area (*beḥēru*), see Syr. Gen 28:18 ('tr'), though the Syriac term could simply repeat

■ **27** The verse (// Gen 28:20-22) takes up Jacob's more specific response to the Lord's promises to him. Genesis terms his words a vow, and Jubilees seems to do the same, although *ṣallaya* can also mean "pray."[52] The conditional formulation favors the sense of vow. And a bold vow it is. He sets conditions for the Lord to meet, conditions that, once satisfied, will lead him to respond in a certain way. As commentators on Genesis note, Jacob leaves out of his vow anything about the traditional patriarchal promises that God gave to him in Gen 28:13-14 // Jub 27:22-23 and focuses instead on the more personal assurances the deity provided in Gen 28:15 // Jub 27:24. To those assurances he even adds a few (the provision of food and clothing). Since Genesis and Jubilees agree nearly verbatim in these places, the two passages from the latter will illustrate the details:

Jubilees 27:24	Jubilees 27:27
As for me, I will be with you. I will guard you wherever you go.	If the Lord is with me and guards me on this road on which I am traveling and gives me food to eat and clothes to wear
I will bring you back safely to this land because I will not abandon you until I have done everything that I have said to you.	so that I return[53] safely to my father's house

Scholars debate the structure of the oath Jacob takes: does the protasis end with the clause regarding safe return to his father's house[54] so that the apodosis begins with "then the Lord will be my God"? Or does the protasis include the next clause—"(and if) the Lord will be my God"? Most translations of Genesis follow the first option (NRSV: "then the Lord shall be my God") and translators of Jubilees do the same. There is no grammatical or syntactical problem with the translation,[55] but a theological issue does arise: is Jacob saying that only if the Lord lives up to his words will he be Jacob's God? Despite the daring implications, there is adequate warrant for thinking that "then the Lord will be my God" is the beginning of the apodosis.[56] The previous statements in the protasis are taken from the Lord's words earlier in the passage, while "the Lord will be my God" is new. The verb והיה that introduces the clause was taken in this sense in *Gen. Rab.* 70:6, where R. Levi cites other promises introduced by the same form.

Jacob, then, vows that the Lord will be his God and makes two other promises besides this one. First, he declares that the stone he had set up (adding again that it was "for a marker in this place," cf. v. 26) "is to become the house of the Lord" (Gen 28:22: "shall be God's house"). The clause sounds like a vow to build a temple on that very spot, yet it is a declaration, however provocative, that is left hanging in Genesis. The issue never arises when Jacob returns to Bethel many years later (35:1-15), but the author of Jubilees remembers it. When Jacob returns to Bethel, he says he wants to build a sacred place there (Jub 32:16; in v. 22 it is called a temple), but an angel tells him not to construct one "because

---

the word for *place* found several times in the unit. Ethiopic Genesis 28:18 has *beḥēr*.

52   Leslau, *Concise Dictionary*, 224.
53   The translation attempts to cope with the fact that in the Ethiopic text the previous verbs are in the perfect tense (*'emma hallo . . . wa-'aqabani . . . wa-wahabani*) but this one is in the imperfect tense (*wa-'etmayyaṭ* [MSS. 9 38 read perfect tense forms]). Perhaps the change could signal that the apodosis begins here, but that seems wrong, since the element in question, like the ones preceding it, is mentioned in the divine speech. The non-causative form in Jubilees agrees with the one in the Hebrew texts of Gen 28:21 (ושבתי), not with the causative verb in the LXX tradition.
54   The place of return is more exactly defined in Jubilees. Jacob will reenter the land long before he reaches Isaac's house, but home is understandably where he wants to go.
55   Hamilton maintains that the switch from converted perfect verbs to an imperfect form in "this stone, which I have set up for a pillar, shall be God's house" indicates that the protasis starts here (*Genesis 18–50*, 248). However, as he is aware, the imperfect form is required by the fact that the subject of the clause is pre-posed for emphasis so that the tense of the verb is not determinative for locating the beginning of the protasis.
56   Werman (*Jubilees*, 389) considers it part of the protasis, since in Jubilees the Lord is already Jacob's God before this (see v. 25) (*Jubilees*, 389). She also thinks that in Genesis the statement is part of the apodosis, but in it Jacob also recognizes the Lord before this (see 28:16) just as in Jubilees.

this is not the place" (v. 22). At least in Jubilees Jacob recalls his vow and tries to fulfill it. The second vow is to tithe all that the Lord had given to him.[57] This is the second time the subject of a tithe has arisen in Genesis and Jubilees. In the Melchizedek story, someone, often thought to be Abram, gives a tithe to another, presumably Melchizedek who was a priest (Gen 14:20). Jubilees makes much more of the tithe in the passage. Though the first part of it seems to have fallen from the text through scribal error, Jub 13:25-27 speak of it as a tithe of firstfruits incumbent on Abram and his descendants forever. They were to give the priest a tenth of everything, and the list includes "seed, the vine, oil, cattle, and sheep" (v. 26). At Bethel, Jacob does not appeal to the earlier legislation about the tithe, which was there called "an eternal ordinance" (13:25), but vows to offer a tenth of everything, as Jub 13:26 prescribes. This is another vow that plays no part in the passage regarding Jacob's return to Bethel in Gen 35:1-15. It will, however, play a significant role in Jubilees. When he returns to Bethel Jacob will tithe everyone and everything with him in fulfillment of the promise (32:2, 5-8; cf. also vv. 10-15), and the notion of the tenth will prove significant in the choice of Levi for the priesthood (32:3).

---

57 Jubilees uses a past tense verb—*wahabkani*—where Genesis has a future tense form—תתן. At the end of the sentence it adds a reference to the deity that is found in no ancient version of Gen 28:22: "I will indeed tithe to you, *my God*."

Jacob Gains a Family and Acquires Wealth

28

1/ He set out on foot and went^a to the eastern land, to Laban, Rebekah's^b brother. He remained with him and served him in exchange for his daughter Rachel for one week. 2/ During the first year of the third week [2122] he said to him,^a "Give me my wife for whom I have served you seven years." Laban said to Jacob, "I will give you your wife." 3/ Laban^a prepared a banquet, took^b his older daughter Leah, and gave (her) to Jacob as a wife. He gave her^c Zilpah, his servant girl,^d as a maid. But Jacob was not aware (of this) because^e Jacob thought^f she was Rachel. 4/ He went in to her, and, to his surprise, she was Leah. Jacob was angry at Laban and said to him,^a "Why have you acted^b this way? Was it not for Rachel that I served you and not for Leah? Why have you wronged me?^c Take your daughter and I will go^d because you have done a bad thing to me." 5/ For Jacob loved Rachel more than Leah because Leah's^a eyes were weak, though her figure was very lovely;^b but Rachel's eyes were beautiful, her figure was lovely,^c and^d she was very^e pretty. 6/ Laban^a said to Jacob, "It is not customary in our country to give the younger daughter before the older one." It is not right to do this because this is the way it is ordained and written on the heavenly tablets: that no one should give^b his^c younger daughter before his older one, but^d he should first give the older and after her the younger. Regarding the man who acts in this way they enter a sin in heaven.^e There is no one who is just and does this because this action is evil in the Lord's presence. 7/ Now you order the Israelites not to do this.^a They are neither to take nor give^b the younger before giving precedence^c to the older because it is very wicked. 8/ Laban said to Jacob, "Let the seven days of the banquet for this one go by;^a then I will give you Rachel so that you serve me^b a second^c (term of) seven years by tending my flocks as you did during the first week." 9/ At the time when the seven^a days of^b Leah's banquet had passed by, Laban gave Rachel to Jacob so that he would serve him a second^c (term of) seven years. He gave her^d Bilhah, Zilpah's^e sister, as a maid. 10/ He^a served^b seven years a second time for Rachel because Leah had been given to him^c for nothing.

11/ When the Lord opened Leah's^a womb, she became pregnant and gave birth to a son for Jacob. He named him Reuben on^b the fourteenth day of the ninth month during the first year of the third week [2122]. 12/ Now Rachel's womb was closed because the Lord saw that Leah was hated^a but Rachel was loved. 13/ Jacob again went in to Leah. She became pregnant^a and gave birth to a second son for Jacob. He named him Simeon on the twenty-first of the tenth month, during^b the third year of this week [2124]. 14/ Jacob again went in to Leah. She became pregnant and gave birth to a third son for him. He named him Levi on^a the first of the first month during the sixth year of this week [2127]. 15/ He^a went in yet another time to her^b and she gave birth^c to a fourth son.^d He named him Judah on the fifteenth of the third month during the first year of the fourth week^e [2129].

16/ Throughout all this Rachel was jealous of Leah, since she was not bearing children.^a She said to Jacob, "Give me children." Jacob said to her,^b "Have I withheld the product of your womb from you?^c Have^d I abandoned you?" 17/ When^a Rachel^b saw that Leah^c had given birth to four sons for Jacob—Reuben, Simeon, Levi, and Judah—she said to him,^d "Go in to my servant girl Bilhah. Then she will become pregnant^e and give birth^f to a son for me."^g 18/ So he went in,^a she became pregnant, and gave birth to a son^b for him.^c He^d named him Dan on the ninth^e of the sixth month during the sixth year of the third week^f [2127]. 19/ Jacob once again^a went in to Bilhah. She became pregnant and gave birth to a second son^b for Jacob. Rachel named^c him Naphtali on the fifth of the seventh month during the second year of the fourth week^d [2130]. 20/ When Leah saw that she had become barren^a and was not bearing children, she grew jealous of Rachel^b and also gave her maid Zilpah to Jacob as a wife. She became pregnant and gave birth to a son. Leah named him Gad on the twelfth of the eighth month during the third year of the fourth week^c [2131]. 21/ He again^a went in to her, and she became pregnant and^b gave birth to a second^c son for him. Leah^d named him Asher on the second of the eleventh month^e during the fifth year of the fourth[f] week [2133]. 22/ Then[a] Jacob[b] went in to Leah.[c] She became pregnant and gave birth to a son for Jacob.[d] He[e] named him Issachar on[f] the fourth[g] (day) of the fifth month during the fourth[h] year of the fourth week [2132]. She gave him to a nurse. 23/ Again Jacob went in to her.[a] She became pregnant and gave birth to twins: a son and a daughter.[b] She named the son Zebulun and the daughter Dinah on the seventh[c] (of the) seventh month, during the sixth year, the fourth week [2134]. 24/ Then the Lord was kind to Rachel.[a] He opened her womb, and she became pregnant and gave birth to a son. She named him Joseph on the first of the fourth month, during the sixth year[b] in this[c] fourth week [2134].

25/ At the time when Joseph was born,[a] Jacob said to Laban, "Give me my wives and my children so that I may go[b] to my father Isaac and make[c] a house for myself, because I have completed the years[d] during which I served you in exchange for your two daughters. Then I will go to my father's house."[e] 26/ Laban said to Jacob, "Stay with me[a] in exchange for your wages. Tend my flocks for me[b] again and take[c] your wages." 27/ They agreed among themselves[a] that he would give him his wages: all[b] the lambs[c] and kids that were born a dark gray color and dark mixed with[d] white were to be his wages.[e] 28/ All the dark-colored sheep kept giving birth to all with variously colored spots of every kind and various shades of dark gray.[a] The sheep would again give birth to (lambs) that looked like them. All with spots belonged to Jacob and those without spots to Laban. 29/ Jacob's[a] possessions grew very large; he acquired cattle, sheep, donkeys, camels, and male and female servants. 30/ When Laban and his sons became jealous of Jacob, Laban took back his sheep from him and kept his eye on him[a] for evil purposes.

Textual Notes

1a went] + "to Mesopotamia" 39 42 47 48 58.
b Rebekah's] + "his mother" 35 (38 different word order) 63.
2a he said to him] "he said" 17; "he said to Laban" 63.
3a Laban] "He" 38.
b took] "Laban took" 48.
c He gave her] "He gave him" 9 12 17 21 38 48 63.
d his servant girl] om. 20; "her servant girl" 44.
e because] om. 17 20.
f thought ('amsalā)] The verbal form that means "regard as, hold as equivalent, consider someone so and so, think, compare, believe," has spawned variant readings in which the form was taken as a noun 'amsāl, "aspect, form, figure, likeness, etc." (see Leslau, *Comparative Dictionary*, 365). Only the verb makes sense here. Werman (*Jubilees*, 390 n. 1) objects to the formulation in Eth., which she thinks reflects a piel form of דמה, since the root in that conjugation is not present in the Qumran literature. She reads a niphal: she looked to Jacob like Rachel. Qumran usage would not be decisive for a text-critical decision in Jubilees; in addition, she has to change more than the verb when she makes "Jacob" the object of a preposition, since "Jacob" is the subject of the sentence.

4a to him] "to them" 21.
b have you acted] + "to me" 20 25.
c wronged me] + "in this way" 12.
d I will go] "Let me go" 21.
5a Leah's] "her" 21.
b very lovely] + "pretty" 21 63.
c (was) lovely] om. 44.
d and (she was)] om. 35 44 63.
e very] om. 25.
6a Laban] "He" 21.
b should give] The more strongly supported reading is *yehub*, "will give"; mss. 12 20 25 35 read the expected jussive form (*yahab*).
c his] "the" 17 44 63.
d but (he should first give) the older] om. 9 12 17 21 38 39 42 44 48 58. Littmann ("Jubiläen," 88 n. a) correctly noted that these copies om. by homoioteleuton (against Charles, *Ethiopic Version*, 102 n. 1). In *Jubilees* (169) Charles accepted Littmann's explanation. See VanderKam, *Jubilees* 2:178.
e heaven] pr. "the tablets of" 20 25 35 39 42 48 58.
7a this (= this sound/statement/thing = *qāla*)] om. *qāla* 12; "this deed" 35 63; "this thing" (*nagara*) 58.
b nor give] om. 38.
c giving precedence] Many mss. read a simple imperfect

(9 12) or jussive (17 20 21 25 35 39 44 48 58 63), but the causative makes sense here.
8a Let . . . go by] "Will . . . go by" 12 63.
b me] "her" 44.
c second] "two" 9.
9a seven] "seventh" 12 42ᶜ 58.
b of] "and" 42 47.
c second] "two" 9 (cf. 58).
d (gave) her] "him" 9 38; "to Rachel" 39 42 47 48 58.
e Zilpah's] "Rachel's" 20 25; + "to Rachel" 44.
10a He] "Jacob" 63.
b served] "made serve" 9.
c to him] om. 39 42 58.
11a Leah's] "her" 25.
b on] pr. "and" 21.
12a was hated] "was hostile" 9 12.
13a pregnant] + "(with a) son" 20 25.
b during] Most Eth. MSS. prefix a conjunction, but 20 25 35 44 lack one.
14a on] pr. "and" 21 38; "and" 44.
15a He] Mss. 39 42 47 48 58 misread *kāʿeba*, "yet," as *yāʿqob*. Thus they read "Jacob again went in. . . ." Dillmann, Charles, Littmann, Goldmann, and Hartom have the erroneous reading (VanderKam, *Jubilees* 2:179).
b to her] "to Leah" 21 39 42 47 48 58; "and became pregnant" 38.
c gave birth] pr. "became pregnant and" 39 42 47 48 58.
d a fourth son] pr. "to him" 39 42 47 48 58 63.
e the fourth (seventh 63) week] "this fourth week" 12.
16a children] "a child/son" 9 12 17 38 63.
b said to her (om. to her 12)] om. 42 47.
c from you] om. 21.
d Have²] Eth. repeats an interrogative particle after "I" in both Jacob's questions in the verse; here Lat. reads *aut*, "or." Perhaps the two versions express the same sense. See VanderKam, *Jubilees* 2:180.
17a When] Lat. "Since/Because." The Eth. reading reflects בראות, the Lat. כי ראתה (VanderKam, *Jubilees* 2:180).
b Rachel] "Leah" 9 12 17 21 38; om. 63; Lat. *rachel*.
c Leah] "she" 9 12 17 21 38; Lat. *lia*.
d she said to him] "Rachel said to him" 42ᶜ 47; "Leah said to Jacob" 63; Lat. "Rachel said to Jacob."
e she will become pregnant] "let her become pregnant" 21 39 42 47 48; Lat. "she will become pregnant."
f give birth] "let her give birth" 21 25 39 42 47 48; Lat. "give birth."
g to a son for me] om. 9 38; Lat. "to a son for me."
18a So he went in] + "to her" 20 38; Lat. "She gave her servant girl Bilhah as a wife." Both the clause in Eth. and the one in Lat. are found in Gen 30:4. The textual situation could be explained in different ways, but the Eth. reading is perhaps preferable in that it makes Jacob do as Rachel ordered him in v. 17; see VanderKam, *Jubilees* 2:180. Werman (*Jubilees*, 391 nn. 4-5) prefers the Lat. reading because it parallels the one for Zilpah in v. 20.

She adds that the verb "went in" is used for sexual relations leading to pregnancies other than with the first child of a wife; hence the lack of "went in" from Lat. is also preferred, since this is Bilhah's first child. See the commentary on vv. 11-24.
b son] om. 39 42ᵗ 48 58; Lat. *filium*.
c for him] lacking in Lat.
d He] "She" 42 47 48; Lat. is ambiguous (*vocavit*). Genesis 30:6 has "She."
e ninth] "fourth" 58; Lat. *nono*.
f of the sixth month during the sixth year of the third week] Lat. has lost several of the words in the date formula: "of this sixth year of the week." See VanderKam, *Jubilees* 2:180.
19a once again] Both versions indicate repetition, but the Eth. MSS. have an additional word for it (rendered "once" here).
b son] om. 39 58; Lat. *filium*.
c Rachel named] The reading is also preserved in Lat. Mss. 39 63 have "He named," and 20 38 48 63 lack "Rachel" (48 places it after "Naphtali").
d on the fifth of the seventh month during the second year of the fourth week] Lat. seems to have the same date, but several of the words have the wrong case endings. See Rönsch, *Jubiläen*, 48; Charles, *Ethiopic Version*, 103 nn. 4-5 to Latin.
20a had become barren] Lat. "was held back." Genesis 30:9 (מלדת) עמדה. For the ways in which commentators have explained the discrepancy, see VanderKam, *Jubilees* 2:181. Possibly the Eth. reading resulted from confusion between εστη (= LXX) and στειρα ("barren"), or the visual similarity between עמדה and עקרה could have led to the present reading. Werman (*Jubilees*, 391 n. 7) points to Isa 54:1 for the expression that may lie behind the Eth. reading. Lat. may reflect a form of εφιστημι (some LXX MSS. read επεστη in Gen 30:9).
b she grew jealous of Rachel] The words are not reflected in Lat. They do, however, parallel the statement about Rachel in Jub 28:16 (= Gen 30:1).
c on the twelfth . . . week] The two versions give the same date if one alters several case endings in the Lat. text, with the exception of the week number—fourth in the Eth., fifth in the Lat. But Lat. prefixes *et* to the date formula, indicating that it relates not to the birth of Gad but to the event recorded at the beginning of 28:21.
21a again] Lat. lacks an equivalent of Eth. *dagama* ("to do something again"), which is also absent from Gen 30:12. The Eth. verb is preceded by a conjunction; Lat. reads a conjunction before the date at the end of v. 20 and does not repeat it here.
b she became pregnant and] Lat. lacks. It is present in LXX OL Eth. Gen 30:12.
c second] Lat. lacks.
d Leah] Lat. "She/He" (= Gen 30:13).

e eleventh month] Lat. *mense decimi diei* seems wrong. The equivalent of Eth. would be *mensis undecimi* (Rönsch, *Jubiläen*, 48; Charles, *Ethiopic Version*, 105 nn. 1-2 to Latin).
f fourth] seventh 9 38.
22a Then (lit., "and")] Lat. lacks, since in it the date at the end of v. 21 relates to the events of v. 22.
b Jacob] "He" Lat.
c to Leah] Lat. *ad illam* may be a mistake for *ad liam* = Eth. (Rönsch, *Jubiläen*, 48; Charles, *Ethiopic Version*, 105 n. 4 to Latin).
d for Jacob] om. 12 20 38; Lat. lacks. It is present in Gen 30:17 (but not in Eth. Gen 30:17).
e He] Lat. is ambiguous, but 12 38 42 47 48 read "She." Genesis 30:18 also uses a fem. verbal form.
f on (the fourth)] Lat. prefaces *et* to the date and thus relates it to the events of v. 23 (though Lat. also introduces v. 23 with *et*).
g fourth] + "year" = Lat. Rönsch (*Jubiläen*, 48) and Charles (*Ethiopic Version*, 105 n. 6 to Latin) suggest omitting *anno* here where it does not belong (see *anni* three words later).
h fourth (year)] Lat. *die* should have appeared where *anno* now stands; at this spot one expects *quarti*.
23a to her] Lat. *ad liam*. There again could be a confusion in Lat. between the look-alike *ad illam* and *ad liam*.
b a son and a daughter] Lat. "a male and a female."
c on the seventh] Lat. and Eth. appear to have the same date, but Lat. again places a conjunction before "on the seventh" so that the whole date may relate to v. 24.
24a Rachel] "her" 21; Lat. *rachel*.
b year] Lat. lacks.
c this] om. 21 58; Lat. *huius*.
25a when Joseph was born] The Eth. wording, in most copies, lacks a relative pronoun after "the days" (= when), while Lat. has *quo*; MSS. 20 25 63 supply a relative pronoun *za-*.
b I may go] "I will go" 9 21 38 48; Lat. *abibo*, "I will go." Cf. אלכה in Gen 30:26.

c and make] "and will make" 9 21 38 39 58 ("he will make" 42 47 48); Lat. *faciam*, "I will make."
d the years] "the seven years" 12 (Lat. *annos*).
e my father's house] om. 20; Lat. *domum patris mei*.
26a Stay with me ("here" 35)] Lat. "Wait for me." The expression in Gen 30:28 probably underlies the divergent readings: נקבה שכרך עלי. As Charles (*Jubilees*, 174) commented, Lat. *expecta* may reflect קוה, and Eth. *nebar* may render קום ("stand" in the sense of "maintain oneself, endure"; BDB, 878). Though this may seem doubtful, it is possible, and the two forms could be explained as miscopyings of נקבה (see VanderKam, *Jubilees* 2:183).
b for me] Lat. lacks.
c take] "I will give you" = Lat. Lat. echoes אתנה in Gen 30:28. See VanderKam, *Jubilees* 2:183.
27a They agreed among themselves] Lat. "they agreed about the wages." The Eth. copies place "his wages" after the verb "give," not here. The Lat. becomes illegible before that point. Some Eth. copies read *tabahhalu* ("they spoke together" [?]) rather than *takāhalu* (some MSS. have *-ka-*), "they agreed" 38 42 47 48 63.
b all] om. 25.
c the lambs] om. 25 35.
d with] om. 12; "and" 35 38 58 63.
e his wages] + "all the lambs and kids that were born a dark gray and dark mixed with white were to be his wages" 21.
28a All—gray] There are variants around the unfamiliar terms, but none seems to produce a different text. Charles (*Ethiopic Version*, 104 nn. 21, 26-27; *Jubilees*, 104) made numerous changes that do not appear helpful, although Littmann, Goldmann, and Hartom have accepted them. See VanderKam, *Jubilees* 2:184.
29a Jacob's] "His" 20 38.
30a on him] om. 9 17 21 38 (12 63 with another spelling and a third person subject). Mss. 42 47 48 read a past tense form.

Commentary

Jubilees 28 rewrites significant parts of Genesis 29–30 and the beginning of 31 (vv. 1-2). The chapters in Genesis describe Jacob's meeting Laban's daughter Rachel at a well, his arrival at the home of Laban, his marriages to Laban's two daughters, the births of their children, and Jacob's further work for Laban. In chap. 28 the writer of Jubilees offers a condensed version of the Genesis stories in which he omits these parts:

the entire encounter with Rachel at the well (Gen 29:2-14)[1]
the explanations of the eleven sons' names
the mandrake story (Gen 30:14-16)

---

1   Cf. Endres, *Biblical Interpretation*, 100, where he comments that the writer also omitted the story about the encounter at the well when Abraham's servant went to find a wife for Isaac in the same locale. Note too that he left out a third such story—Moses's meeting with his future wife (Exod 2:15-22).

He also severely curtails the lengthy discussion between Jacob and Laban about the terms of his employment and the results of it (the nineteen verses of Gen 30:25-43 become just five—Jub 28:25-29). Yet, with all the excisions from the text, the author expands significantly on the law about giving the older daughter in marriage first (Gen 29:26 // Jub 28:6-7) and adds dates for when a parent named each of the children born to Jacob and his wives.

The major components in the chapter are:
1-10   The marriages and the law of the firstborn daughter
11-24 The births of twelve children
25-30 Jacob's work for Laban

The textual witnesses are the full Ethiopic version and the Latin translation for vv. 16-27.

1-10 The Marriages and the Law of the Firstborn Daughter (Gen 29:1, 21-22, 24, 23, 25, 18, 17, 26-27, 28-30)[2]

Jubilees 28:1 should convince readers that the author is not interested in telling good stories for their own sake. He skips over the meeting with Rachel at the well so thoroughly that one would never guess from Jubilees that the event took place. He could, of course, assume that his audience would know the full story in Genesis 29; his purpose was to draw the essential points from it for understanding the message of Genesis as he read it. Hence he gives only the basic details and sacrifices the literary appeal of the story in the process.

■ 1 The author uses the expression that Gen 29:1 employs for Jacob's travel: literally, he lifted his feet and went. Where the Hebrew versions of Gen 29:1 say he reached the land of "the sons of the east," Jubilees, with the LXX tradition, uses simply the land of "the east" (translated here as "the eastern land"). It also extends the verse beyond the text of the MT and SP, again in agreement with the LXX tradition, by adding "to Laban, Rebekah's brother." Unlike that textual tradition, Jubilees includes nothing about Bethuel or about Rebekah's being the mother of Jacob and Esau (cf. 27:12 where, of all the names in the Genesis parallel [28:5], only Esau's is omitted).[3]

The next item reported is that Jacob remained with Laban and worked in exchange for Rachel for seven years. The reader might recall that Laban had daughters from Jacob's report to his mother in 25:6: "Earlier I heard, mother, that daughters had been born to your brother Laban. I have set my mind on them for the purpose of marrying one of them." It appears from v. 1 that he is carrying out what he intended to do and what his parents ordered, though this is the first time Rachel's name surfaces in Jubilees. There is no hint of why she is the one, if Laban had more than one daughter ("daughters had been born," but he had "set his mind" on marrying one of them), for whom Jacob labored seven years, and one does not know why the price was seven years of work. Genesis explains all of that by telling the tender story of their first encounter at the well and of Jacob's special feelings for the lovely Rachel. It informs the reader:

> Leah's eyes were lovely, and Rachel was graceful and beautiful. Jacob loved Rachel; so he said, "I will serve you [Laban] seven years for your younger daughter Rachel." Laban said, "It is better that I give her to you than that I should give her to any other man; stay with me." So Jacob served seven years for Rachel, and they seemed to him but a few days because of the love he had for her. (Gen 29:17-20)

This would have been helpful information to include in Jubilees, but the writer bypassed it.[4]

■ 2 Jacob left his home in the year 2115 (27:19), worked for Rachel for seven years, and at the end of the period, in 2122 (28:2), demanded from Laban that she be given to him in marriage. Here the author slightly reworks the passage in Genesis:

---

2 See the alignment of Jubilees and Genesis passages in Endres, *Biblical Interpretation*, 100.

3 The LXX has: "to the land of the east, to Laban the son of Bathouel the Syrian and brother of Rebekka, mother of Iakob and Esau."

4 See Halpern-Amaru, *Empowerment*, 42–43.

Genesis 29:21	Jubilees 28:2
Then Jacob said to Laban, "Give me[5] my wife that I may go in to her, for my time is completed."	. . . he said to him, "Give me my wife for whom I have served you seven years." Laban said to Jacob, "I will give you your wife."

He deletes the sexual motivation for Jacob's wish to have Rachel[6] and is more explicit about the length of time Jacob had served. Laban gives no response to Jacob's blunt words in Genesis, but in Jubilees he answers in a vague manner reminiscent of the misleading reply Jacob had given to Isaac: "I am your son" (Jub 26:13, 19). He promises to give him his wife but does not name her, just as Jacob did not ("Give me my wife").[7] It is a first hint that the deception Jacob played on his father is coming to haunt him, as he deals with another father of two children and becomes part of a second conflict between younger and older.[8]

■ 3 The parallels with the deception of Isaac continue in v. 3 (Gen 29:22b, 23-24) where Laban prepares a meal to celebrate the marriage. A meal in connection with a deception is strongly reminiscent of Jubilees 26 // Genesis 27, where Jacob brought food and drink to his father to eat before he blessed him. Laban, of course, substituted his older daughter Leah for Rachel, the reverse of the scene where Jacob had replaced his older brother Esau. Like Gen 29:24, Jubilees mentions in this setting Laban's gift of his maid Zilpah to Leah as her servant girl. Genesis says nothing about how the substitution of Leah for Rachel took place, much less how it succeeded.[9] Jubilees adds to the end of its citation of Gen 29:24: "But Jacob was not aware (of this) because Jacob thought she was Rachel." *Targum Pseudo-Jonathan* appends a similar explanation to the next verse, Gen 29:25: "At morning *time he looked at her*, and behold it was Leah! *During the whole night he had thought that it was Rachel*."[10]

■ 4 Verse 4, which reflects the end of Gen 29:23 and the beginning of 29:25, relates that Jacob "went in to her" (a common expression for having sex)[11] and records the surprise he felt upon discovering the identity of the woman he had just married. It does not say he learned of this only in the morning but rather when "he went in to her." Genesis does not say Jacob was angry; rather it reproduces his irate words to Laban for tricking him. Jubilees does both.

Genesis 29:25	Jubilees 28:4
And Jacob said to Laban, "What is this you have done to me? Did I not serve with you for Rachel? Why then have you deceived me?"	Jacob was angry at Laban and said to him, "Why have you acted this way? Was it not for Rachel that I served you and not for Leah? Why have you wronged me? Take your daughter and I will go because you have done a bad thing to me."

---

5   The forcefulness, not to say rudeness, of Jacob's words, however one translates הבה, has caught the attention of exegetes ancient and modern. See as examples *Gen. Rab.* 70:18; Hamilton, *Genesis 18–50*, 260.

6   See Rothstein, "'And Jacob Came (in)to [בוא + אל] . . .': Spousal Relationships and the Use of a Recurring Syntagm in Genesis and Jubilees," *Henoch* 29 (2007) 91–103, here 100–101, where he also refers to later reinterpretations of Jacob's rather crude language (e.g., *Gen. Rab.* 70:18). As Rothstein argues, avoidance of the "go/come into her" expression is characteristic of the way in which the author of Jubilees treats the relationship between Jacob and Rachel (see below).

7   See Endres, *Biblical Interpretation*, 101.

8   In *Tg. Ps.-J.* Gen 29:12, where Jacob identifies himself to Rachel at the well, the text reads: "Jacob told Rachel that *he had come to dwell with* her father *and to take one of his daughters*. Rachel answered and said, 'It is not possible for you to dwell with him, for he is a deceitful man.' Jacob said to her, 'I am more deceitful *and more clever than he, and he has no power to harm me, because the Memra of the Lord is at my assistance*.' *And when she knew that* he was Rebekah's son, she ran and told her father." In this way the targumist places the issue of deception at the beginning of the account.

9   Werman thinks the text of Jubilees leaves the impression that Leah was given to Jacob during the banquet, not after it (*Jubilees*, 393). So, for example, it does not mention the cover of darkness ("in the evening") as Gen 29:23 does. In fact, Jub 28:3 is so terse that it gives no clear indication of when, relative to the banquet, Laban gave Leah to Jacob.

10   The targum continues by explaining about the identifying markers Jacob had given to Rachel to prevent just such a switch of daughters—a switch that Rachel suspected her father would attempt. Nevertheless, Rachel, out of sympathy for her sister, gave the markers to Leah. The same story appears in *b. B. Bat.* 123a; *b. Meg.* 13b (in both Jacob calls himself Laban's "brother in deceit").

11   Werman interprets the expression in a literal way—

Genesis has Jacob use precisely the verb (רמיתני)[12] that would remind the reader about his deception of his father whom he misled into thinking he was the older brother; now he wonders why he was treated in the same way by Laban. If Laban has done something wrong, as Jacob tells him, then it would seem to follow that Jacob had misbehaved in deceiving his father. But he draws no such inference. Jacob was so terribly upset, however, that he wanted to return Leah to her father and leave the household.[13] There is no parallel in Genesis for this frightening prospect that would undo the agreement about marriage reached by Jacob and Rebekah and contradict the command of Isaac to marry a daughter of Laban.[14]

■ 5 The writer next reverts to earlier verses in Genesis 29, where the narrator spoke about Jacob's feelings for Rachel and described the sisters. He reports that Jacob loved Rachel (see Gen 29:18a), adding from Gen 29:30 that he loved her more than Leah.[15] The traits of Rachel and Leah (see Gen 29:17) then serve as reasons for Jacob's greater affection for Rachel.

Genesis 29:17	Jubilees 28:5
Leah's eyes were lovely,	... because Leah's eyes were weak, though her figure was very lovely;
and Rachel was graceful and beautiful.	but Rachel's eyes were beautiful, her figure was lovely, and she was very pretty.

The issue of what exactly Genesis says about Leah's eyes (רכות) has elicited varied proposals. The adjective can mean "tender, delicate, soft, weak" (BDB, 940; *DCH* 7:486), so it could be a positive (as in the NRSV rendering cited above) or a negative trait; and, from the context, one could defend either interpretation.[16] In Jubilees it is a negative trait,[17] although the writer does

---

Jacob went from one place to another where Leah was; here it does not refer to sexual intercourse (*Jubilees*, 393, 396). Her reasoning is that elsewhere in this context "went in to" is used for the times other than when his wives became pregnant for the first time. In part she follows the analysis of Rothstein ("'And Jacob Came [in]to,'" 91–103), who maintains that the expression, which is not used in connection with Rachel but is employed for the other three, indicates that Jacob had to go to the places where Leah, Bilhah, and Zilpah were but maintained regular sexual relations with Rachel and thus did not have to go to the place where she was. It seems unlikely, however, that in v. 4 "He went in to her" refers only to geographical movement from one place to another. See below.

12 The verb in Eth. Jubilees is *gafā'kani*, "you have harmed me" (Leslau also lists "oppress, press, afflict, treat violently, do violence, wrong, vex, push" [*Concise Dictionary*, 214]), while Eth. Gen 29:25 has *'astāḥqarkani*, "you have disdained/profaned/treated me with contempt" (ibid., 20). In Gen 27:35 Isaac characterized Jacob's action as מרמה (Jub 26:30 uses *ḥebl*). The narrator will use a synonymous expression in Gen 31:19 (lit., "he stole the heart of Laban") to indicate he deceived him in return when he left Paddan-aram with his family without telling Laban (see also 31:26-27).

13 Since sexual relations constitute marriage in Qumran law, Werman thinks that Jacob's willingness to return Leah to her father and to leave shows that the marriage had not been consummated in v. 4 and that therefore "He went in to her" does not mean they had intercourse (*Jubilees*, 393). The point hardly follows; one could as well say that Jacob is offering to divorce Leah after their admittedly short marriage.

14 Kugel (*Walk through* Jubilees, 139; "Jubilees," 390) suggests: "But the author no doubt found the whole tale distasteful, in part because of the implication that Leah, future mother of six of Israel's tribes, had cooperated in the deception. He thus had Jacob take a principled stand against Laban and say what he does not in Genesis, 'Take your daughter and I will go . . . .'" For Endres, "perhaps the author downplayed the courtesies of familial relationships here in order to depict the righteous indignation of his hero of the ancestral period" (*Jubilees*, 393).

15 As Werman comments, the note occurs in Genesis after Jacob has had sexual relations with both of the sisters (*Jubilees*, 393).

16 Skinner, *Genesis*, 383: "weak"; Westermann, *Genesis 12–36*, 462–63: "without lustre"; Hamilton, *Genesis 18–50*, 258–59: "tender" in a positive sense.

17 Leslau, *Concise Dictionary*, 198: "weak, feeble, tired, exhausted, wretched." The same understanding is present in LXX: ἀσθενεῖς. The writer of Jubilees does not, however, express the more elaborate thesis found in *Genesis Rabbah* (see 70:16; 71:2) and some targums—that Leah's eyes had become weak because of her crying over the possibility (the custom of the time) that she, the older daughter, would be given in marriage to Esau, the older son, just as the two younger siblings Rachel and Jacob were to wed (see *Tg. Ps.-J.* and *Frg. Tg.* Gen 29:17; cf. *Tg. Neof.* Gen 29:17; *T. Onq.* Genesis 29:17, however,

describe Leah as an attractive woman otherwise. Leah will go on to become a major character in Jubilees; as a result, the author may have felt he should say something positive about her beyond what the ambiguous text of Genesis implied.[18] Leah was a very marriageable woman, but Rachel was beautiful in every way, including her eyes (not included in Genesis).

■ 6-7 Chapter 28 continues to reflect the text of Genesis in v. 6 but takes a surprising turn in v. 7. Verse 6 is a verbatim quotation of Gen 29:26: Laban explains to Jacob that he was following the local custom in not giving his younger daughter in marriage before the older one. The narrator in Genesis may imply that he was fabricating an excuse for his shameful behavior, or, if Laban accurately represented the practice in Haran, the narrator may be suggesting he was blameworthy for not informing Jacob about it before the wedding festivities.[19] There is no trace of any of this in Jubilees. To the contrary, the writer not only considers Laban's claim a straightforward statement about the law in Haran but also asserts that it is so written on the heavenly tablets.[20] It is a divine law, not one manufactured by Laban to cover his perfidy, and it applies beyond the city limits of Haran. By giving Leah first, Laban prevented the violation of an eternal law. The passage is another instance in which the full language of heavenly tablets is employed and where the Angel of the Presence turns more directly to Moses (he does not use his name) with an order for him to communicate the law to the people of Israel,[21] although there is no hint of such a rule in the HB. Neither the laws about marital partners in Leviticus (18:6-21 and 20:10-14, 17, 19-21) nor the marriage sections in Deuteronomy (22:13-30; 24:1-5; 25:5-10) include legislation to this effect.[22] Yet violating it is considered a serious offense ("it is very wicked"). This is the only time in Jubilees in which someone outside the chosen line enunciates a law on the heavenly tablets.

Once he has cited Laban's words about the local custom, the Angel of the Presence comments on the legal situation. He does not say the law in question originated from the events that have just unfolded; he says only "this is the way it is ordained and written on the heavenly tablets." The law was there beforehand, but Jacob must not have known about it while Laban somehow did. The angel then spells out exactly what is recorded on the heavenly tablets:

---

claims that her eyes were beautiful). Josephus, who says Jacob was drunk on the wedding night, refers to Leah as "devoid of beauty" (*Ant.* 1.301). Cf. Endres, *Biblical Interpretation*, 102–3.

18 Cf. Halpern-Amaru, *Empowerment*, 44. Werman suggests Leah's attractiveness softens the negative impact of Laban's act of substituting Leah for Rachel (*Jubilees*, 393).

19 See Skinner, *Genesis*, 383–84; Hamilton, *Genesis 18–50*, 263. The *Fragment Targum*, *Pseudo-Jonathan*, and *Neofiti* Gen 29:22 present the plan to replace Rachel with Leah as one formulated by Laban and the men of the place, and they label it a deceit. The purpose was to make sure Jacob served a second set of seven years because of the prosperity he had brought to the area during the first seven years of his residence there.

20 Beer already indicated that there was no trace of such a law elsewhere in Jewish literature (*Jubiläen*, 49). Deuteronomy 21:15-17 ("If a man has two wives, one of them loved and the other disliked" [v. 15]) looks as if it might apply to Jacob's situation, but it deals with the right of the son born first and also does not specify that the women are sisters. Kugel attributes this section to his interpolator (it mentions the heavenly tablets) ("Interpolations," 264; *Walk through* Jubilees, 140, 287; "Jubilees," 390), but he does not identify a very plausible reason why someone would have interpolated the text. He thinks his interpolator saw here a chance to "suggest that a story in Genesis reflected one of the eternal teachings that are inscribed on high" ("Jubilees," 390 = *Walk through* Jubilees, 140). But does the text of Jubilees lead one to think someone was so eager to find such opportunities that he seized on this curious text? When Genesis provided a much better opportunity in Gen 32:32 ("the Israelites do not eat the thigh muscle that is on the hip socket") the text fails to refer to the law. It seems unlikely someone would latch onto Laban's law for such a purpose.

21 The last time he addressed Moses by name was in 23:32.

22 There is no such law in the Qumran texts either; see Werman, who mentions that King Saul wanted to marry his older daughter Merab to David before the younger Michal (1 Sam 18:17-27) though the latter loved David (*Jubilees*, 393–94). The case is not an exact parallel with the one in Jubilees because there is no indication in it that there was any legal problem with marrying a younger daughter before an older one.

[N]o one should/is to give his younger daughter before his older one,
but he should first give the older and after her the younger.

Laban obeyed this law. In this form, however, it did not apply to Jacob because it is directed to fathers of daughters—it deals with giving daughters in marriage and says nothing about guilt for taking a younger daughter first. The angel adds that if one violates the ruling another piece of information is incised in the tablets: the guilty party is charged with a sin. No just individual acts in this way because the Lord considers such behavior wicked. Furthermore, the law engraved on the celestial record is, the angel explains, one that Moses must transmit to Israel when he descends from Mount Sinai. The wording of the law that he articulates for Israel, in distinction from the way Laban stated it and the angel first formulated it in v. 6, makes it directly relevant to Jacob's case: "They are neither to take nor give the younger before giving precedence to the older" (v. 7). Since Jacob was going to take the younger woman first, he would have violated this eternal law and committed an act that was "very wicked." Oddly enough, Laban saved the otherwise extraordinarily virtuous Jacob from making a big mistake. Halpern-Amaru correctly discerns here a parallel to the divine intervention that prevented Isaac from recognizing Jacob (Jub 26:18). The heavenly law provides sanction for the marriage with Leah and thus elevates her status as a proper wife, not the unwanted spouse she is in Genesis.[23]

■ 8 Verse 8 reproduces the content of Gen 29:27, in which Laban urges Jacob to complete the week-long wedding celebration[24] for Leah; after that he[25] would give Rachel—the name is used pointedly in Jubilees, not a pronoun as in Gen 29:27 (גם את זאת, "also this one")—to him in exchange for another seven years of labor. Under the proposed arrangement, at the end of the seven-day party Jacob would, in addition to Leah, receive Rachel as a wife, and he would begin a second set of seven years in Laban's employ. That he did not have to wait another seven years for Rachel is evident from v. 8 and from the section about the births of the children later in the chapter. For the writer of Jubilees, who frequently antedates Mosaic law to the time of the patriarchs, it is strange that he says nothing about the fact that marriage to sisters is forbidden in Lev 18:18: "And you shall not take a woman as a rival to her sister, uncovering her nakedness while her sister is still alive."[26] The law poses no problem in Genesis, since the Sinaitic legislation lay in the future; one might have expected the author of Jubilees to make some mention of it, even if only to say it had not yet been revealed.

■ 9 The verse reflects material from Gen 29:28, 30. The writer once again makes clear that the "seven" or the "week" that passed were the seven days of the festival for Leah; after the celebration Laban gave Rachel to Jacob (this time Genesis also mentions her name and adds that she was Laban's daughter). But where Genesis says he gave her to him as a wife, Jubilees states as the purpose that he was to serve Laban a second unit of seven years (cf. Gen 29:30). The verse concludes with words from

---

23 Halpern-Amaru, *Empowerment*, 45–46.
24 With *Targums Neofiti* and *Pseudo-Jonathan*, Jub 28:8 speaks of "the seven days of the banquet for this one." The MT and SP have only "the week of this one." The Peshitta also mentions the banquet but not the days, while the OL and Eth. Genesis have "seven years of this one" (see also Josephus, *Ant.* 1.302)—an interpretation that can hardly be correct as Jacob had already completed those years. Cf. Endres, *Biblical Interpretation*, 104.
25 The MT reads the niphal form נתנה (differently interpreted by NRSV, "we will give"), but the other ancient versions, including the SP, have first-person singular forms, as Jubilees does ("I will give").
26 Charles, *Jubilees*, 169–70. See Milgrom, *Leviticus*, 2:1548–49, for a survey of the various interpretations of Lev 18:18, Jacob's violation of it, and the discussions of the issue. One way of exonerating Jacob was to assert that the law applied only in Canaan (so Ibn Ezra; see Lev 18:2-5). Endres suggests that the author of Jubilees and his community may have found this offense less important than marrying the younger daughter first or marrying a non-Jew (*Biblical Interpretation*, 104). He adds: "Perhaps social customs in the author's day so successfully prevented the marriage of one man to two sisters that the author felt no need to polemicize against a practice that he considered obsolete." The suggestion is interesting but the issue is treated in the Temple Scroll (11Q19) lvii:17–18 and CD iv:21 and thus may have been a contemporary concern.

Gen 29:29—Laban gave Rachel his servant girl Bilhah as her maid—and adds that she was Zilpah's sister.[27] That Zilpah and Bilhah were sisters is asserted more widely in the interpretive tradition. Jubilees provides perhaps the first attestation of it, and another early witness is 4Q215 (4QNaph):

1. with 'Ahiyot, Bilhah's father '[   ]. *h*, Deborah who nursed Reb[ecca
2. And he went into captivity. And Laban sent and redeemed him, and he gave him Hannah, one of [his] maidservants[
3. first Zilpah. And he made her name Zilpah, after the name of the city to which he was taken captive[
4. And she conceived, and she bore Bilhah, my mother. And Hannah called her name Bilhah, for when she was born[
5. hastening to nurse, and she said, "How my daughter hastens!" And she called (her) Bilhah again[
6. *vacat*
7. And when Jacob my father came to Laban, fleeing from before Esau his brother and when [
8. father of Bilhah, my mother. And Laban brought Hannah, my mother's mother and her two daughters[
9. [   ] and one to Rachel. And when Rachel was barren[28] [
10. [Jaco]b my father and gave him Bilhah my mother, and she bore Dan [my] brother[

(trans. M. Stone, *DSSR* 3:563).

From the broken lines one can infer that 'Ahiyot and Hannah were the parents of the older Zilpah and the younger Bilhah. In the Testaments of the Twelve Patriarchs, Naphtali says that Rotheus, a member of Abraham's family and a servant of Laban, married Aina, another of his servants, and the two became parents of first Zilpah, then Bilhah (T. Naph. 1:10-12), the latter being Naphtali's mother.[29] In this text, the assertion that the father of Zilpah and Bilhah was a member of Abraham's family points to the intent of the tradition: to give a legitimate genealogy to the mothers of four Israelite tribes. More evidence for this concern comes from *Tg. Ps.-J.* Gen 29:24, 29, where Zilpah and Bilhah are Laban's daughters with an unnamed concubine. The idea that they were Laban's daughters is connected with his words regarding Jacob's *entire* family in Gen 31:43: "Then Laban answered and said to Jacob, 'The daughters are my daughters, the children are my children, the flocks are my flocks, and all that you see is mine. But what can I do today about these daughters of mine, or about their children whom they have borne?'"[30] It is surprising indeed in a book like Jubilees, where the maternal side of the genealogy is so vital, that the writer makes no mention of Zilpah and Bilhah's family, though he agrees they were sisters. True, the lineage of their mother in 4Q215 and the Testament of Naphtali would still not be clear, but at least the sisters would have been members of the correct household, just as Hagar was a member of Abra(ha)m's house.

■ **10** The author informs the reader that Jacob did in fact serve Laban another seven years for Rachel, just as the end of Gen 29:30 says. However, he adds a twist to the words of Gen 29:30: by saying that he worked another seven years "for Rachel," he draws a reasonable inference from Genesis—that this was the second unit of seven years Jacob had worked for Rachel. In other words, he had worked the first seven for her, as Jacob himself said in Gen 29:18, 25 and as the narrator disclosed in 29:20, and the second set of seven years were also in exchange for her (Gen 29:27-28). So, Jacob

---

27 Manuscripts 9 and 20 say she was the sister of Rachel, but that reading is a confusion of names as the other copies show. A number of the manuscripts make the recipient of the gift of Bilhah explicit by reading "to Rachel" (as in Gen 29:29), and the scribes of 9 and 20 have mistakenly written "Rachel" where "Zilpah" should stand.
28 The text says she was not bearing children.
29 See Charles, *Jubilees*, 170.
30 For use of Gen 31:43, see *Gen. Rab.* 74:13, where the first reference to "daughters"—"The daughters are my daughters"—is understood as referring to Leah and Rachel and the second ("these daughters of mine") as designating Zilpah and Bilhah. The same interpretation is applied to his double use of "daughters" in Gen 31:50. See also *Pirqe R. El.* 36, where, one learns, the females born to a man's wife are called daughters and ones born to a concubine are termed handmaidens. Gerald Friedlander explains, "The Midrashic reading of Gen. xxix.29 seems to be: 'And Laban gave to Rachel his daughter Bilhah (by) his handmaid (to be) her handmaid'" (*Pirķê de Rabbi Eliezer* [1916; repr., New York: Hermon, 1970] 272 n. 3).

labored fourteen years as payment for receiving Rachel as his wife. The claim entailed that Leah had come to him free of charge; he never served Laban to obtain her as a spouse. While the result need not be taken as a criticism of Leah—it is simply a conclusion drawn from givens in the text—it presumably did not contribute to family harmony.[31]

11-24 The Births of Twelve Children

The section follows the sequence of the births in Gen 29:31–30:24 but omits much of the material that surrounds them. Endres describes the pattern in Jubilees for the birth sections thus: "(1) Jacob 'went in to,' i.e., had *sexual intercourse* with his respective mate; (2) the woman '*conceived and bore*' a child; (3) the *naming* of the child; (4) the *date of birth*."[32] There are exceptions to the pattern: in the cases of the first child for both Leah and Rachel, the Lord opens the woman's womb and she becomes pregnant (vv. 11, 24); it does not say Jacob went in to them (on Leah, see below). And for Zilpah's first pregnancy (with Gad) she simply becomes pregnant (v. 20).[33] The presence or absence of the formula "went in to" is significant because it may follow a pattern. In Genesis it is used in connection with the wedding nights of Leah (29:23 // Jub 28:4) and Rachel (29:30), but otherwise it is absent from the birth list except in the cases of Dan (30:3-4 [Rachel tells Jacob to do so and he does]) and Issachar (30:16 [Leah tells him to do so]). In Jubilees the formula is used in the list in all cases except Leah's pregnancy with Reuben (but see 28:4) and Zilpah's first pregnancy (with Gad; for Bilhah's first pregnancy, see the textual discussion at 28:18). The two exceptions may not actually fall outside the pattern since in both instances for the next pregnancy with Leah and Zilpah the text says that Jacob "again went in" to the respective wife (28:13, 21). The only certain exception to use of the formula is in the case of Rachel (28:24). Rothstein highlights the contrast with Genesis and the author's leveling of the birth notices such that he employs the formula for the pregnancies of Leah, Bilhah, and Zilpah but not for Rachel. Rothstein concludes:

> [T]he author of *Jubilees* has, I submit, employed the phrase "ויבא אל X" to convey the point that the particular act of conjugal congress/intercourse was not part of a regular, daily relationship between the two participants. That is, use of the formula implies that the man must come to the woman—or her house—precisely because he is normally not found with/alongside her; in cases involving spouses who live together and, presumably, are physically intimate on a regular basis, there is no need to specify that the husband "came (in)to" his wife. Given this understanding, the data preserved in *Jubilees* are readily explained. The author systematically employed this formula in connection with three of Jacob's wives, while pointedly avoiding this usage in connection with Rachel, so as to highlight the fact that Jacob's primary, ongoing relationship—emotional and physical—was with Rachel alone; his sexual contact with the other wives constituted exceptions to his regular routine of living and sleeping with Rachel.[34]

The nature of the pattern makes his conclusion possible, although in the list Rachel has just one pregnancy (her pregnancy with Benjamin is described differently in 32:3—she became pregnant with him) and the notice for

---

31 "Leah had been given to him for nothing" seems the proper translation, though the word translated "for nothing"—*baka*—can have the sense of "in vain, uselessly, fortuitously, without cause, for no purpose, in idleness, by mere chance" (Leslau, *Concise Dictionary*, 101). Hartom translated it as חנם and explained that the meaning is she was given to him "not according to his wish/contrary to his wish" ("Jubilees," 90 n. to v. 10). Jacob, of course, wanted Rachel, not Leah, but in context the point of the passage is to say that both periods of seven years were ones Jacob worked for the right to marry Rachel; Leah came to him without any such price attached. Endres thinks this makes no sense (he translates: "against his wishes") (*Biblical Interpretation*, 105) but misinterprets the context and the use of *baka* in another passage in Jubilees—21:19.

32 Endres, *Biblical Interpretation*, 106. As he notes, numbers 1 (apart from the case of Dan in Gen 30:4) and 4 are not found in the parallel sections in Genesis.

33 Cf. Halpern-Amaru, *Empowerment*, 65–67.

34 Rothstein, "And Jacob Came (in)to," 96 (see 93–96).

it is formulated in a way parallel with the one for Leah's first pregnancy in v. 11.

■ **11-15** As in Genesis, the unit begins with Leah's first four sons, after a notice that the Lord opened her womb. Jubilees does not reproduce at this point the beginning of Gen 29:31: "When the Lord saw that Leah was unloved." Jubilees delays the indication that she was the subject of such a strong feeling (שנואה, "hated") until it mentions in v. 12 that Rachel's womb was closed. The span during which the children were born begins in the year of the weddings—2122. For the birth of Reuben,[35] the text repeats expressions from Gen 29:31-32, but, rather than having Leah name him as in Gen 29:32, Jubilees uses a masculine singular verb and thus indicates Jacob took on that responsibility.[36] The choice of name in Genesis was dictated by Leah's feelings ("Because the Lord has looked on my affliction; surely now my husband will love me") so that she was the natural one to name him. Jubilees, however, omits all the explanations for the children's names and thus could be more flexible about which parent named the child. The date—9/14 in the year 2122 (the weddings must therefore have occurred very early in the year)—is attached specifically to the time of the naming (as in all the other cases in the chapter) yet probably refers to the date of birth as well. The author then (v. 12) mentions that, unlike Leah, who was hated but, by God's favor, gave birth to a son, Rachel's womb was closed (Gen 29:31: "Rachel was barren").

The birth of Simeon, the second[37] son, followed two years later; Jacob named him as well, while in Gen 29:33 Leah again gives a son a name related to her experience ("Because the Lord has heard that I am hated, he has given me this son also"). The birth of the third son, Levi, generally follows the separate patterns established in Jubilees and Genesis, but, since the third son is Levi, who will become the priest in Jubilees (see 30:18-20; 31:13-17; 32:1-9), he is treated a little differently: Jacob gave him his name on a highly significant date—the first day of the first month, in the third year after the birth of Simeon. The date is one on which other significant events in the priestly realm would occur: the birth of Qahat (ALD 11:5-7) along with the erection of the tabernacle and installation of the priesthood (Exodus 40).[38] MT Genesis 29:34 uses a masculine singular verb (קרא), indicating that Jacob named Levi, but the SP employs a feminine form (קראה) while the LXX and OL are ambiguous. It is strange that the MT should have Jacob name Levi, as the meaning of *Levi* is also related to Leah's experience ("Now this time my husband will be joined to me, because I have borne him three sons"). The question of who named Levi in Jubilees is more complicated than in the other cases because it is mentioned a second time in the book. When Isaac blesses Levi in Jub 31:13-17, he includes these words: "Your mother named you Levi, / and she has given you the right name. / You will become one who is joined to the Lord / and a companion of all Jacob's sons" (v. 16). So, who named Levi—Jacob (28:14) or Leah (31:16)? Halpern-Amaru concludes that both did, just as the parents share the naming of their other children, with the father naming some and the mother others (as in the present list). It may indeed be true that this is one of the several ways in which the writer of Jubilees, as Halpern-Amaru maintains, emphasizes the roles of the mothers and paints a portrait of patriarchal marriages as "ideal unions of co-partners."[39] The rapid sequence of the first four births concludes in Jub 28:15 with the arrival of Judah. On this occasion Leah

---

35 The Ethiopic copies spell the name *robēl*; the final *-l* is likewise attested in the Peshitta, Eth. Genesis, and Josephus, *Ant.* 1.304.

36 The ancient versions of Gen 29:32 are unanimous that Leah named Reuben. It may be that the masculine singular form in Jubilees arose from the ambiguity of εκαλεσεν in the Greek base of the Ethiopic version.

37 With the LXX tradition, Jubilees reads "a second son for Jacob" where the Hebrew versions of Gen 29:33 read simply "a son."

38 Rapp, *Jakob in Bet-El*, 203.

39 Halpern-Amaru, "The Naming of Levi in the Book of Jubilees," in Esther G. Chazon and Michael E. Stone, eds., *Pseudepigraphic Perspectives: The Apocrypha and Pseudepigrapha in Light of the Dead Sea Scrolls* (STDJ 31; Leiden: Brill, 1999) 59-69 (quotation from p. 62). She writes that the case of Benjamin is a parallel in that both Rachel and Jacob name him, but in that case, unlike the instance of Levi, they give him different names (Gen 35:18 // Jub 32:33). For the significance of Leah's naming Levi in 31:16 and providing explanations for his name, see the commentary there.

names her son (Gen 29:35, explaining: "This time I will praise the Lord"), but in Jubilees Jacob again does the honors. The date for Judah's birth is also noteworthy: the fifteenth day of the third month, that is, the date for the Festival of Weeks, a little more than two years after Levi's birth. The attentive reader could glean from the dates when they were named that Levi and Judah were destined to be special characters in the story.

■ **16-19** Genesis 30:1-14 covers the circumstances in which the two maids of Jacob's wives became mothers of four more sons. The writer of Jubilees condenses the material into the six verses of 28:16-21. The dispute between Rachel, who envied her sister's fertility, and Jacob and the provision of Bilhah to bear children for Jacob are largely repeated in Jubilees (Gen 30:1-8 // Jub 28:16-19) but without the explanations of the two sons' names and with other editorial modifications. The changes in v. 16 are interesting.

Genesis 30:1-2	Jubilees 28:16
When Rachel saw that she bore Jacob no children, she envied her sister; and she said to Jacob, "Give me children, or I shall die!" Jacob became very angry with Rachel and said, "Am I in the place of God, who has withheld from you the fruit of the womb?"	Throughout all this[40] Rachel was jealous of Leah, since she was not bearing children. She said to Jacob, "Give me children." Jacob said to her, "Have I withheld the product of your womb from you? Have I abandoned you?"

The transparent changes are that Rachel in Jubilees does not attach "or I shall die" to her demand, that Jacob does not get angry, and that Jacob omits "Am I in the place of God?" but adds "Have I abandoned you?"[41] These strong statements in Genesis caused some discomfort in the interpretive tradition. In *Tg. Ps.-J.* Gen 30:1 Rachel's demand appears as: "*Pray before the Lord that he may give me children; and if not, I shall be reckoned as dead.*" Her words should have met with the kind of response Isaac made when Rebekah was unable to bear children—he prayed (Gen 25:21; see *Gen. Rab.* 71:7,[42] where Rachel is said to mention what Isaac did). Jubilees 28:16 does not transform her words into a request for prayer or soften the last part; it simply leaves out the claim she will die. As for Jacob's anger, *Gen. Rab.* 71:7 presents a negative evaluation of it. Some of the words of Eliphaz in Job 15:2 are applied to Jacob: "Should the wise answer with windy knowledge, / and fill themselves with the east wind?" The Rabbis related the first line to Abram in his dealings with Sarai (see Gen 16:2) and the second to Jacob in Gen 30:2. God himself takes offense at his wrath: "Said the Holy One, blessed be He, to him: 'Is that a way to answer a woman in distress? By your life, your children will one day stand [in supplication] before her son [Joseph], (who will answer them, *Am I in the place of God?*' [Gen. L, 19])."[43] Quite understandably, then, the notice about Jacob's anger is lacking in Jubilees. Jacob's question "Am I in the place of God, who has withheld from you the fruit of the womb" also called for rephrasing. *Targum Pseudo-Jonathan* (see also *Tgs. Onq.* and *Neof.* Gen 30:2) renders Jacob's question: "*For how long will you beseech me? Beseech from before the Lord, for it is from before him that children (come), and it is he* who has withheld from you the fruit of the womb." The Jacob of Jubilees asks rhetorically whether he is responsible for her failure to have children and also sounds more compassionate toward her when he asks, again rhetorically, whether he has abandoned her? He is not the enraged spouse of Genesis and seems less concerned to correct the theology of his distraught

---

40 The expression in Jubilees could suggest that Rachel's jealousy continued for a longer time than the wording in Gen 30:1 (so Werman, *Jubilees*, 394), but Genesis may imply the same ongoing feeling because it does not attach the jealousy to any specific time, only to the fact that her sister was having babies when she was not.

41 On the passage, see Halpern-Amaru, *Empowerment*, 64–65. As she comments, Jacob's last question in Jubilees suggests that the two continued to have conjugal relations.

42 In the same place Rachel also appeals to how Sarai responded to childlessness—she brought her rival Hagar into the home and had a child through her. Rachel then does something similar by giving Bilhah to Jacob so she could be "built up" through her.

43 See Freedman, *Midrash Rabbah: Genesis*, 2:658 n. 2 for the textual situation (his translation as cited above is slightly modernized). Joseph's use of the same expression—"am I in the place of God?"—will also not appear in Jubilees.

wife. He also refrains from charging God directly with preventing Rachel from having children (but see v. 12).[44]

Verse 17 may appear unimportant, little more than a restatement of Gen 30:3, but it does more: it establishes a chronological order for the births of Leah's and Bilhah's sons. Genesis presents all the children in a sequence, of course, but it does not rule out the possibility that more than one of the mothers would be pregnant at the same time. The narrator in Jubilees states that it was after Leah had given birth to four sons, all of whom are named in order, that Rachel told Jacob to have relations with Bilhah. So Bilhah's children arrived after the births of Reuben, Simeon, Levi, and Judah (Judah was born in 2129 according to 28:15).

The Bilhah paragraph in Gen 30:3-8 receives a summary in Jub 28:17b-19. The writer does not use Rachel's colorful expression—that Bilhah will bear a child "upon my knees" (Gen 30:3)—but paraphrases with "give birth to a son for me" (v. 17b). Bilhah, like Hagar, will bear a son on behalf of her mistress who was unable to become a mother. Jubilees 28:18 combines words from Gen 30:4-6[45] in describing the relations between Jacob and Bilhah that led to the birth of Dan. In Genesis, Rachel explains the meaning of the name that she gives to the child; in Jubilees, Jacob names Dan and says nothing about the reason for the name. The date on which Jacob names Dan is listed as the sixth month, the ninth day, in 2127, a year number that poses a problem because Dan was supposed to be born after Reuben, Simeon, Levi, and Judah—and Judah's naming/birth year is given as 2129. The chronology, then, contradicts the order in which the story says the sons were born.[46] See the excursus below for a discussion of this and other problematic dates in the list.

The pattern with Dan almost repeats itself in the lines devoted to Bilhah and Jacob's second son (Gen 30:7-8 // Jub 28:19). In Genesis, Rachel names him Naphtali in honor of her successful "wrestlings" with her sister; in Jubilees, Rachel also gives him the name but provides no explanation for it. The date for his naming—2130—seems like the one that should have designated the date for Dan, as it follows Judah's birth by a little more than one year.

■ **20-21** Jubilees 28:20-21 parallels Gen 30:9-13 in which

---

44 Rothstein, "'And Jacob Came (in)to,'" 97-99. He understands the passage to express "an atmosphere of caring and warmth on the part of Jacob towards Rachel" (p. 98) but also "the importance of spousal devotion" (p. 99). He thinks that the verse contains one of the indications regarding the special relationship between Jacob and Rachel as Jacob's "central wife" (p. 98; see below).

45 It includes a clause from Gen 30:4 if one reads the first part of the verse with Latin, *Et dedit ballam ancillam suam in uxorem*, words lacking in the Ethiopic copies, and/or reads *wa-boʾa ḥabēhā* with the Ethiopic copies—words lacking in the Latin translation. See the textual note and VanderKam, *Jubilees* 2:180. In view of the uncertain textual situation at this point, one should be hesitant about drawing inferences from the way in which Bilhah is presented in the Ethiopic text, where it is not said that she is given to Jacob as a wife. Halpern-Amaru thinks the omission of the Genesis expression "So she gave him her maid Bilhah as a wife" (30:4) was deliberate because Bilhah, who will be defiled by Reuben, is a problematic character for the author of Jubilees, who is deeply concerned about sexual purity ("Bilhah and Naphtali in Jubilees: A Note on 4QTNaphtali," *DSD* 6 [1999] 1-10, here 8-9). If the Latin reading should be the correct one, the writer of Jubilees would here be presenting her as a wife for Jacob. In Jub 33:10-12 the law applied to the situation when Reuben defiled Bilhah has to do with a father's wife. Application of that law presupposes that she was Jacob's wife.

46 Werman accepts the dates of birth for Judah (the year 2129) and for Dan (2127) and infers from them that the statement in v. 17—"When Rachel saw that Leah had given birth to four sons for Jacob—Reuben, Simeon, Levi, and Judah—she said to him: 'Go in to my servant girl Bilhah'"—actually relates to the birth of Bilhah's second son, Naphtali, because he was born in 2130, after the birth years for Leah's first four sons (*Jubilees*, 395). For Werman, Rachel's instructions that Jacob have conjugal relations with Bilhah had taken place in the past, before the birth of Judah (she does some rewriting of the verse to make it conform to the sequence she defends; see p. 391 nn. 5-6 and her commentary on v. 18 on p. 395). So she gives more weight to the year numbers than to the explicit sequence in the text that puts the birth of Bilhah's first child after that of Judah. For more on the chronological issue, see the excursus at the end of the commentary on this chapter.

Leah, in response to her failure to have any more children, gives Zilpah to Jacob. Genesis says nothing about her imitating her sister or being jealous of her; Leah acted because she had stopped achieving pregnancies. Jubilees 28:20 at first agrees closely with Gen 30:9, but the Ethiopic version, not the Latin, reports: "she grew jealous of Rachel." In this way the text makes Leah's reaction parallel her sister's envy when she saw Leah giving birth to son after son (Gen 30:1 // Jub 28:16).[47] Since the extra clause figures in no ancient version of Gen 30:9, it is likely to be original in Jubilees; the Latin version is suspect because it agrees with the versions of Gen 30:9.[48] On this occasion, Leah is the one who assigns the name Gad to the child because she said, "Good fortune!" (30:11). Leah also names him in Jubilees although she provides no etymology for *Gad*. His naming date of 8/12 in the year 2131 fits nicely in the chronology. The second son of Jacob and Zilpah is Asher, whom Leah in Genesis names in harmony with her declaration "Happy am I! For the women will call me happy" (30:13). The author of Jubilees simply notes her pregnancy, the child's birth, and the name Asher that Leah gave him on 11/2 in the year 2133.

■ **22-24** At this point Genesis tells the mandrake story (30:14-16a). Jubilees lacks the account, whose purpose is to explain why Jacob and Leah again had relations—she gained the right by giving to Rachel her son Reuben's mandrakes. The son born to Jacob and Leah received the name Issachar from his mother, who related it to her hiring of her husband from Rachel (30:17-18). The writer of Jubilees records only that Jacob "went in to Leah" and she gave birth to Issachar, whom Jacob named on 5/2 in the year 2132 (28:22)—a number that is strange because it would mean that Issachar's birth preceded that of Asher, although the sequence suggests it followed it.

There is an additional note in Jubilees—that Leah gave Issachar to a nurse. Among the twelve children born in this section only for Issachar is a nurse mentioned. It may be that the note is an echo of the way in which Leah explains his name as derived from שכר ("hire") since she had hired her husband for the night with her son Reuben's mandrakes (Gen 30:14-18). In Exod 2:9 Pharaoh's daughter hires Moses's mother to nurse him (שכר is the word for her wages). Just possibly, then, the reference to a nurse reflects the etymology of Issachar's name in Genesis. After Issachar, Gen 30:19-21 relates the birth of Zebulun, whom Leah named (she explains the choice), and apparently later the birth of Dinah, whom Leah also named (with no explanation). In Jubilees, when next Leah became pregnant she bore twins—Zebulun and Dinah—both of whom she named on 7/7 in 2134. Perhaps the inference that they were twins arose from the fact that Genesis says nothing about an additional pregnancy for Leah before Dinah's birth—she simply bore her after bearing Zebulun.[49]

At last Rachel's turn arrived. In Gen 30:22-24 she becomes pregnant when the Lord remembers her, listens to her, and opens her womb. Jubilees 28:24 notes that the Lord was kind to her[50] and opened her womb. In both texts Rachel gives the child the name *Joseph*; Gen 30:21 contains her explanation of the name, while Jub 28:24 dates the naming to 4/1 in the year 2134. This is the first time a child is born on a significant date since Judah's arrival; the first of the fourth month is one of the festivals that commemorates an event during the flood and marks one of the four seasons (6:23-31).[51]

Since, according to the text, Reuben was named on 9/14 in 2122 and Joseph arrived on 4/1 in 2134, the time span during which the eleven sons and one daughter were born was just short of twelve years. In Genesis the

---

47 See Halpern-Amaru, "Naming of Levi," 64.
48 Charles emended to "and she took" (*Ethiopic Version*, 103 n. 46). But the emendation makes the text agree with Genesis. This would be the easier reading and, for that reason, the less likely one.
49 The only other instances in which Genesis fails to mention the woman's becoming pregnant are for the two children of Zilpah (Gen 30:10, 12).
50 The writer of Jubilees does not repeat the Genesis-Exodus passages in which God/the Lord is said to remember (Gen 8:1; 9:15, 16; Exod 2:24; 6:25) with the exception of his remembering Abraham in the Lot/Sodom story (Gen 19:29 // Jub 16:7).
51 *Genesis Rabbah* 73:1 cites R. Eleazar as saying that Sarah, Rachel, and Hannah were remembered on the New Year. The rabbinic *Roš Haššanah* falls on 7/1 so that, if one adds nine months of pregnancy to it, the date would be 4/1 of the next year—the date for Joseph's naming in Jub 28:24.

mother names each child (a passive verb is used for naming Levi), but in Jubilees Jacob names Reuben, Simeon, Levi, Judah, Dan, and Issachar, while Rachel names Naphtali and Joseph, and Leah names Gad, Asher, Zebulun, and Dinah. Why there is a difference from the text of Genesis is not apparent.[52] Werman advances an intriguing if ultimately unsuccessful argument to explain the evidence of the text.[53] She thinks that the discussion between Jacob and Laban in vv. 25-30 (see below) is not what it may seem to be. She correctly notes that the second seven-year period for which Jacob served to gain Rachel ended during the time when the children were being born. The births in Jubilees took place over a twelve-year stretch that began at the time Jacob received Rachel (the year 2122) and ended with the arrival of Joseph in 2134. The seven-year period reached its conclusion in 2129. Hence, there must have been negotiations at that time about wages for Jacob so that he would remain with Laban past the second seven-year span (vv. 25-28 summarize those wages). All that happens at the time Joseph was born five years later was that Laban convinced Jacob to stay longer while continuing to receive his wages. This is also why, in v. 25 (see below), Jacob does not have to request his children and wives from Laban. The situation Werman describes relates to the issue of who names the children: since Jacob was away working the last five years when the children were born, he was not present to name them; hence the wives took over that duty. Against her arguments one should note that there is no indication in the birth section of chap. 28 regarding negotiations about wages five years before Joseph's birth; they are explicitly connected with the time of his birth. In addition there is no suggestion that when the younger children were born Jacob was not present to name them. He had to have been present for their conception, so why not at the times they were named? It is true that nearly all of the younger children were christened by a mother, but Issachar, whose name could have suggested wages, is an exception in that he was born in the time after the second seven-year period ended and Jacob named him (28:22). Perhaps the author did imagine Jacob working for wages the last five years when the children were born along with the following year to reach the six years of paid labor Jacob mentions in Gen 31:41, but he never says as much. The impression left by the text is that Jacob worked for wages for only one year (see 29:5, where he leaves Laban's employ in 2135).[54]

25-30 Jacob's Work for Laban

The chapter concludes with an abbreviated version of Gen 30:25-43 in Jub 28:25-29 and a final verse that summarizes the reaction of Laban and his sons to Jacob's ever-growing wealth (see Gen 31:1-2). In a sense, one might expect Jubilees to reproduce more of the account because it details how Jacob outwitted Laban, after Laban had tricked Jacob in the marriage with his daughter Leah in Genesis 29 (though it was not a deceptive act according to Jubilees).[55] However, the Genesis passage also pays an abundance of attention to animal colors, may refer to divination (30:27),[56] and includes improbable, not to say dubious[57] techniques for making animals produce offspring whose coats had the desired traits. Whatever the motivation for condensing the section may

---

52 See Endres, *Biblical Interpretation*, 106-7; he notes the facts given above and comments: "Although the pattern is clear, I detect no particular tendency in it" (p. 107). See, however, the note on 28:11 // Gen 29:32 above regarding the ambiguity in gender of εκαλεσεν.

53 Werman, *Jubilees*, 395-97.

54 The extant text is resistant to her readings in other places in the unit. She notes that in v. 17 Rachel tells Jacob to have relations with Bilhah, who will give birth to a son "for me." Werman claims that "for me" refers not to Bilhah's first son Dan (who is mentioned next) but to Naphtali, her second son, since this is the one Rachel names (Jacob names Dan). In Naphtali's case, however, Rachel does not refer to Bilhah's having a son *for her*, so the text opposes Werman's theory. Also, in both vv. 18 (for Dan) and 19 (for Naphtali) Bilhah is said to have borne a son for Jacob.

55 Westermann, *Genesis 12-36*, 480.

56 Though Laban is usually quoted as saying "I have learned by divination [נחשתי]," the verb could mean "I have become rich" (*DCH* 5:667).

57 Westermann, *Genesis 12-36*, 484: "We witness an experiment in breeding that relies as much on ancient magical notions as on observations of the habits of animals."

have been, the writer of Jubilees spares the reader many of the details in the Genesis account.

■ **25** Verse 25 parallels Gen 30:25-26 but alters the order and changes the focus of Jacob's reason for wanting to leave Laban's household.

Genesis 30:25-26	Jubilees 28:25
When Rachel had borne Joseph, Jacob said to Laban, "Send me away, that I may go to my own home [מקומי] and country.	At the time when Joseph was born, Jacob said to Laban,
Give me my wives and my children for whom I have served you, and let me go; for you know very well the service I have given you."	"Give me my wives and my children so that I may go to my father Isaac and make a house for myself, because I have completed the years during which I served you[58] in exchange for your two daughters.[59] Then I will go to my father's house."

Jacob in Jubilees does not request or need his father-in-law's permission to leave. The strong emphasis in it on returning to Isaac draws on Gen 31:18, where Jacob in fact loads up his family and drives all his animals from Paddan-aram "to go to his father Isaac in the land of Canaan" (cf. Jub 29:4). In Gen 30:25 he wishes only to return home, with no mention of Isaac or his father's house. The Jacob of Jubilees seems to be a more loyal son of his aging father than he appears to be in Genesis.[60] He wishes to establish his own house away from that of his father-in-law and with his own father (cf. Gen 30:30).

■ **26-27** Laban's response in Genesis triggers extended, detailed negotiations between himself and Jacob (Gen 30:27-35). As Laban politely relates, he had learned, perhaps by divination, that his prosperity was caused by Jacob's presence. So he invites Jacob to name his wages and remain with him. Jacob replies by rehearsing how Laban "had little before I came, and it has increased abundantly" (30:30); now, however, he wants to provide for his own household. When Laban repeats his invitation that Jacob name his price, he asks only for the right to be able to remove animals with coats of certain colors from Laban's flocks. Laban agrees but, true to his character in Genesis, promptly identifies those animals and hands them over to his sons. He then "set a distance of three days' journey between himself and Jacob, while Jacob was pasturing the rest of Laban's flock" (30:36). There are no negotiations in Jubilees. Laban promises to pay Jacob if he stays and tends his flocks (v. 26), and the two agree about what the wages would be: "all the lambs and kids that were born a dark gray color and dark mixed with white were to be his wages" (v. 27).[61] In Jubilees, Laban does not take those sheep and goats from his flock to give them to his sons, nor does he keep a three-day distance between himself and Jacob.[62]

■ **28** Verse 28 parallels Gen 30:39b. That is, the author skips over the section in Genesis regarding Jacob's resort to intriguing tactics to induce births of animals with the requisite colors—taking the wood of certain trees, exposing the white of them, and placing them where the animals would see them as they came to the drinking troughs and mated (Gen 30:37-39a). Without telling the cause for it, Jubilees gives only the outcome: reproduction led to animals with the right traits. The writer also omits Jacob's further gimmick of having his animals face the ones in Laban's flock that had the colors he desired, a plan that also succeeded. Jubilees 28:28 stands where

---

58 It seems as if both Genesis and Jubilees have Jacob refer to his service to Laban, but Werman (*Jubilees*, 397) thinks the reference to service in Genesis suggests that he was liable to be considered a servant who did not have a right to wives and children whereas this suggestion is eliminated in Jubilees. The contrast is not there.

59 See Gen 31:41, where Jacob tells Laban, "I served you fourteen years for your two daughters." In echoing the Genesis passage, Jub 28:25 presents a different picture from 28:10 that claims he served fourteen years for Rachel but "Leah had been given to him for nothing."

60 In Gen 31:30 Laban recognizes that Jacob left him "because you longed greatly for your father's house."

61 For Werman, the wages are mentioned as something known and agreed between the two men because, on her view, they had settled on them five years earlier (*Jubilees*, 397). Verses 27-28 make that reading improbable.

62 Laban is generally a more positive character in Jubilees than in Genesis (see the excursus in the commentary on chap. 29). Endres attributes the omissions in this section to the writer's penchant for whitewashing the ancestors (*Biblical Interpretation*, 108).

Gen 30:37-42 gives a much more elaborate text. Most of that detail was not needed or perhaps better not mentioned, so the writer of Jubilees offers only the essentials: the dark-colored sheep produced ones with the various spots and shades that made them part of Jacob's wages, and they in turn bore ones that looked like them.[63] It all sounds like a natural process in Jubilees, not the outcome of bizarre, even magical ploys by Jacob as in Genesis.

■ **29** With v. 29, the two texts come together again.

Genesis 30:43	Jubilees 28:29
Thus the man grew exceedingly rich, and had large flocks, and male and female slaves, and camels and donkeys.	Jacob's possessions grew very large; he acquired cattle, sheep, donkeys, camels, and male and female servants.[64]

Jubilees says he had cattle and sheep, where Genesis mentions simply "flocks" (צאן), and it provides a more orderly sequence by listing the servants/slaves at the end rather than within the list of animals (see Gen 12:16 // Jub 13:14 for a similar case).[65] The man who arrived alone in Paddan-aram now has gained a large family and vast possessions. Genesis uses the verb the Lord adopted when making a promise to Jacob at Bethel: "and you shall spread abroad" to the four directions (28:14; see also 30:30); now he has "spread abroad," that is, has expanded or increased (BDB, 829, s.v. פרץ) spectacularly.[66]

■ **30** The last verse of the chapter summarizes and rephrases some of the words in Gen 31:1-2 and 30:35. The idea that Laban and his sons became jealous when they saw how Jacob's herds multiplied (apparently more than theirs did) is an inference from Gen 31:1-2: "Now Jacob heard that the sons of Laban were saying, 'Jacob has taken all that was our father's; he has gained all this wealth from what belonged to our father.' And Jacob saw that Laban did not regard him as favorably as he did before." The sons viewed Jacob's wealth as unmerited, while Laban himself was more negatively inclined toward Jacob than he had been, now that his son-in-law was independently wealthy. It is at this point, according to Jubilees, that Laban took back his own sheep from Jacob because of his astonishing success (see Gen 30:35, where he does this at the beginning of the period covered by their agreement [note: "that day" in v. 35]).[67] The statement may relate as well to what Jacob says to his wives after charging Laban with continually changing his wages: "Thus God has taken away the livestock of your father, and given them to me" (Gen 31:9). Verse 30 also charges that Laban "kept his eye on him for evil purposes"—possibly a conclusion drawn from the phrase וירא יעקב את פני לבן in Gen 31:2 (lit., "Jacob saw the face of Laban").[68] In Jubilees, Laban had not conducted himself poorly toward Jacob before this, though in Genesis he had. It is worth adding that the unit Jub 28:25-30 contains no explicit date; there is only the opening clause "[a]t the time when Joseph was born" (v. 25). Since, according to Jub 29:5, Jacob returned to Gilead in 2135, the year after Rachel bore Joseph (2134), he did not work an additional six years for Laban after the births of the children as he seems to do in Genesis (see Gen 31:41). Moreover, the bad feelings of Laban and his sons are confined to a shorter period than in Genesis.[69]

Excursus: The Chronology in Jubilees 28:10-24

From Gen 31:38, 41 the reader learns that Jacob spent a total of twenty years with Laban: the fourteen years he worked in exchange for his two wives, and the six years of paid shepherding. The impression given by Gen 29:15–30:24 is that the twelve children (including one set of twins) were born in the seven-year period when Jacob was working in return for Rachel the second time. This is the interpretation adopted in *Seder Olam* 2: "He spent 20 years in Laban's house: seven before he married the mothers,

---

63 The end of Jub 28:28 sounds like a reversed and revised version of Gen 30:42b:
Genesis 30:42b | Jubilees 28:28c
so the feebler were | All with spots belonged to
Laban's, and the | Jacob and those without
stronger Jacob's. | spots to Laban.

64 As Berger comments, similar statements are made in describing the wealth of Abraham (Jub 13:14) and Isaac (Jub 24:14) (*Jubiläen*, 466 n. a to v. 29).

65 Werman points out that some of the terms Jubilees uses for his wealth come from Gen 31:18; 33:13, which are here anticipated (*Jubilees*, 397).

66 See Hamilton, *Genesis 18–50*, 284.

67 See Endres, *Biblical Interpretation*, 108–9.

68 So Kugel, *Walk through* Jubilees, 140; "Jubilees," 392; Werman, *Jubilees*, 398.

69 Werman, *Jubilees*, 397–98.

seven after he married the mothers, and six after eleven tribes and Dinah were born. So all the tribes were born in seven years, each one at seven months" (trans. VanderKam).[70]

Jubilees is typically more generous with dates than Genesis and furnishes an example of how the Genesis sequence was read in the second century by at least one perceptive expositor. The book relates that Jacob went from his home to Haran in 2115 (27:19; 2115 = year 1, week 2, jubilee 44). He worked for Laban for one "week" before requesting his wife in 2122 (28:1-2 = year 1, week 3). The second unit of seven years is mentioned in 28:8-10, and the births of the children follow. The dates given are not specifically for when they are born but rather when they received their names (perhaps both occurred on the same day).

Name (passage)	day	month	year	week	A.M.[71]
Reuben (28:11)	14	9	1	3	2122
Simeon (28:13)	21	10	3	[3]	2124
Levi (28:14)	1	1	6	[3]	2127
Judah (28:15)	15	3	1	4	2129

These dates provide a possible span of time for one woman to bear four children, though she would have been busy. Unlike Genesis, Jubilees next makes explicit that Rachel became jealous and gave Bilhah to Jacob *after* the births of Leah's first four sons: "When Rachel saw that Leah had given birth to four sons for Jacob—Reuben, Simeon, Levi, and Judah— she said to him: 'Go in to my servant girl Bilhah. Then she will become pregnant and give birth to a son for me'" (28:17). The data for Bilhah's sons are:

Dan (28:18)	9	6	6	3	2127
Naphtali (28:19)	5	7	2	4	2130

Leah's jealousy regarding Rachel, the writer implies without saying, was motivated by the fact that Bilhah bore sons to Jacob on behalf of Rachel. At any rate, she responded in kind by giving Zilpah to him (28:20). The information for her children is:

Gad (28:20)	12	8	3	4	2131
Asher (28:21)	2	11	5	4	2133

Leah's fertility returned (28:22) and she had a son followed by twins:

Issachar (28:22)	4	5	4	4	2132
Twins (28:23)[72]	7	7	6	4	2134

At last Rachel herself became a mother:

Joseph (28:24)	1	4	6	4	2134

Jubilees 28 contains no more dates, but Jacob and Laban did agree that the former would continue to work (28:25-30), this time for nonhuman wages. The next date is the one for the arrival of Jacob and his family in Gilead in the year 2135 (29:5); as 29:1 says, this was after Joseph's birth. So Jubilees does not assign a six-year period of work to Jacob after the children's births. Rather, Jubilees largely incorporates Genesis's six years of additional employment into the childbearing period and thus does not have to posit the unusually rapid sequence of births implied in Genesis. All told, Jacob spent twenty years in Haran (2115-2135), with the births of the twelve children continuing over a span of nearly twelve years. These are the basic chronological givens for the twenty years in question:

Departure from home (2115)
Seven years before his first marriage (2115-2121)
Births of children (2122-2134)
Departure (?) and arrival in Gilead (2135)

Three of the birth/naming dates are problematic because they are out of sequence:

Dan. Though the text says that Bilhah bore her children after Leah had given birth to *four* sons, the date for Dan's birth (2127) is earlier than that of Judah, Leah's fourth son (2129). The two claims constitute an outright conflict.[73]

Issachar. The fact that the date of 2132 for Issachar is earlier than the one for Zilpah's second son, Asher (2133), puts it out of sequence although it does not contradict an explicit statement in the text (again there are no variant numbers in the Ethiopic copies).

Joseph. He would have been born in the same year as the twins but three months before them.

The numbers for the date regarding Dan read this way in the Latin version: *et vocavit nomen eius dan nono mense huius sexti anni septimanarum,*

---

70 *Pirqe de Rabbi Eliezer* 36 expresses the same view: "Leah bare her sons after seven months, and in seven years there were born unto Jacob eleven sons and one daughter. And all of them were born, each with his partner [apparently meaning his future wife], except Joseph, whose partner was not born with him, for Asenath, the daughter of Dinah, was destined to be his wife, and (also) except Dinah, whose partner was not born with her" (trans. G. Friedlander).

71 A.M. = anno mundi (year of the world); numbers in brackets are presupposed by the context but not stated; bold font indicates an entry that is problematic and treated below.

72 Genesis 30:19-21 may separate the births of the two.

73 The Ethiopic copies offer no variant numbers.

"S/he named him Dan in the ninth month of this sixth year of the week." Something seems amiss in the text (there is no week number), but it does attest the number *six* for the year in question. For Issachar, the Latin text reads: *et vocavit nomen eius isacahar et in quarto anno mense quinti anni <die> septimanarum quarto*, "S/he named him Issachar and in the fourth year, in the month of the fifth year <in the day> of the fourth week." Again, something is wrong here, and the conjunction suggests that the confusing date formula actually belongs with the following clause that, in the Latin, lacks an initial conjunction. If the reference to the fifth year were correct, it would move him one year later and mean he would not be out of sequence in year number, though he still would have been named earlier in that year than Asher, who precedes him in the list. In the case of Joseph, the Latin text and the Ethiopic are in agreement, although again the date in the Latin text may be connected with the following verse.

The dates for the births/naming in Jubilees have given rise to different proposals for handling the problems they pose. It should be noted that the book gives the names in the order in which Genesis presents them in the parallel section. Rönsch, in a section of his book treating ancient works that attest to Jubilees and its content without naming it as a source, adduced the Testaments of the Twelve Patriarchs and the chronological information the composition supplies regarding the sons of Jacob.

Testaments of the Twelve Patriarchs

Name	Year in Jacob's Life When the Son Was Born
Reuben	76
Simeon	79
Levi	81
Judah	84
Dan	85
Issachar	86
Naphtali	86
Gad	86
Zebulun	87
Asher	87
Dinah	88
Joseph	89
Benjamin	101

He compared various data, including the information the Testaments offered about the birth dates of the protagonists, with those in Jubilees and realized that they did not agree completely. He also pointed out the situation described above—that the year numbers for three characters in the Jubilees list did not agree with the stories to which they were attached: Dan, Issachar, and Joseph. It turns out that he added Joseph to his list for a nontextual reason:

Joseph. Jubilees 28:24 places his birth in 2134, but Rönsch thought the author would have located it in a heptadically significant year—not the sixth but the seventh year of a week (of years). He therefore moved his birth date one year later to 2135 (the Hebrew numbers 6 [ו] and 7 [ז] could easily be confused).

Judah and Dan. The author would have placed Judah's birth one week of years before Joseph, that is, in the seventh year of a week. He thought a copyist had switched the birth dates of Judah and Dan. So, rather than being born in the first year of the fourth week, Judah received his name in the seventh year of the third week (2128). Dan followed in year 1 of week 4 (2129).

Asher and Issachar. A simple switch of the numbers 4 and 5 led to the problem. Asher was born in year 4, not 5 (2132), while Issachar came along in year 5, not 4 (2133).[74]

With these changes, all twelve are in sequence, with Jacob leaving Paddan-aram in the year in which Joseph was born (2135), not in the following year.

Rönsch's solution commended itself to Charles, who accepted it in a long footnote, although he did not alter his translation to reflect the changes. Rather, in his rendering he marked the offending numbers with daggers. He also added to the discussion the data from *Midrash Tadshe* 8, lines 2-4 and from Syncellus.[75]

Midrash Tadshe (it supplies only the sons' dates of birth [not the year] and ages at death)

Reuben: born day 14, month 9 (dies at age 125)
Simeon: born day 21, month 10 (dies at 120)
Levi: born day 16, month 1 (dies at 137)
Dan: born day 9, month 6 (dies at 125)
Judah: born day 15, month 3 (dies at 119)
Naphtali: born day 5, month 3 (dies at 133)
Gad: born day 10, month 7 (dies at 128)
Issachar: born day 10, month 5 (dies at 122)
Asher: born day 20, month 11 (dies at 123)
Joseph: born day 21, month 7 (dies at 110)

---

[74] Rönsch, *Jubiläen*, 331 (325-31). Caquot agrees with the suggestions for Judah-Dan, for Asher-Issachar, and for Joseph; he even introduces the changes into his translation, with angle brackets < > around them ("Jubilés," 745-46). Note that in the list of dates from the Testaments (where the period of childbearing is thirteen years long, and twenty-five if Benjamin is included), Issachar was born before Asher.

[75] Charles, *Jubilees*, 170-73.

The information for the remaining two sons comes from an external citation of *Midrash Tadshe*; they are not in the manuscript of the work itself:
Zebulun: born day 7, month 7 (dies at 114)
Benjamin: born day 11, month 8 (dies at 109)
The day and month numbers agree in the midrash and Jubilees for Reuben, Simeon, Dan, Judah, Zebulun, and Benjamin (for him, see Jub 32:33). In the cases of Levi (month), Naphtali (day), Issachar (month), Asher (month), the two agree on one of the numbers, and the other number (the one on which they disagree) can probably be explained through simple confusion of similar-looking numerals except in the instance of Levi. Gad and Joseph are the ones for which the midrash and Jubilees disagree about both numbers. The list may depend on the one in Jubilees (so Charles, Epstein),[76] but the interesting feature is that Dan and Judah appear in reversed order, and Issachar and Asher are switched—just as their birth dates in Jubilees imply. So, if Jubilees was its source, the midrash seems to have known a text of Jubilees, presumably a Hebrew one, that already had the problematic dates attested in the Ethiopic and Latin versions.

Syncellus supplies only the year in Jacob's life when each child was born.

Reuben	80
Simeon	81
Levi	82
Judah	83
Dan	85
Naphtali	86
Gad	87
Asher	88
Issachar	89
Twins	90
Joseph	91
Departure from Laban	93[77]

So he assigns eleven years for childbearing and two extra years before Jacob leaves his uncle's service. Syncellus has the births in the Genesis-Jubilees order. He places Dan's birth two years after that of Judah and that of Issachar one year after Asher's birth, while Joseph appeared the year after Leah bore the twins.

Rönsch and others have opted for textual solutions—assuming that copyists' errors caused the problematic dates—to explain Jubilees' numbers that are inconsistent in their context. Segal has challenged this textual approach, finding it inadequate to deal with the data.[78] The numbers in this section of Jubilees, as he understands them, are important evidence for his theory about the relation between the chronology of Jubilees and the rewritten scriptural stories it encases.

On the basis of the first five names in the list, Segal concludes that Jubilees contains a contradiction caused by the fact that it combines two approaches to the Genesis section: one that takes the births in Genesis as a single chronological sequence, and another that assumes more than one wife was pregnant/bearing children at the same time. Since Dan was born before Judah according to the dates in Jubilees, it looks as if the compiler has taken the second (overlapping pregnancies) approach in his chronology, not the first since his birth is out of sequence. Nevertheless, the text retains the order of sons from Genesis as if they were in sequence (this would be the rewritten story part). Segal also notes how the chronology contradicts the statement in 28:17 (part of the rewritten story) that Dan's birth followed those of Leah's first four sons. "The rewritten story therefore clearly contradicts the dates in the chronological framework, as the addition to the biblical narrative in v. 17 explicitly establishes that Jacob's first four sons were born before Bilhah was given to Jacob."[79] He draws a similar conclusion from the chronological problem with Issachar relative to the overall sequence taken from Genesis.

Segal devotes some attention to Rönsch's textual solution and accuses him of the "preconceived notion that the chronological data and rewritten stories are

---

76 Caquot, "Jubilés," 87.
77 See Adler/Tuffin, *Chronography*, 150.
78 Segal, *Jubilees*, 83–94, esp. 85–91.
79 Ibid., 88. Werman, who devotes a short appendix to the dates in the list (*Jubilees*, 398–99) and, as noted above, regards the birth dates that other scholars consider problematic as expressing points the author wishes to convey, makes no reference to Segal's theory apart from a short footnote to her commentary on 28:19 (p. 395 n. 19). There, after citing the fact that Rachel named Naphtali, Werman explains that she did so because he was the son who was born for her (actually, Dan was that son according to the text, not Naphtali). She then maintains that there is enough in this detail to prove that the author of Jubilees was responsible for what is reported and that there is no pileup of textual layers as in Segal's theory. Rewriting a passage in Jubilees is an unusual basis for opposing his theory.

indeed completely consistent."[80] He thinks, moreover, that Rönsch failed to take into consideration the pattern for expressing dates in Jubilees: they are given in triple numbers—jubilee, week, year in the week. "In this system, a successive date does not repeat any information that is already contained in its predecessor." So a jubilee, week, or year is listed "only when it differs from that of the preceding date."[81] He is clearly wrong about this last point, as in 28:19-24 the "fourth week" is mentioned in six consecutive cases. It is a fact that the writer uses more than one pattern in expressing series of dates.

Segal may be right that Rönsch's particular solution does not work, but his own conclusion from the Dan/Issachar problems is both surprising and radical:

> In my opinion, the necessary conclusion from the contradiction between the chronological details and the rewritten story is not that the text is corrupt (as suggested by Rönsch), but that ch. 28 developed through a complex literary process. The chronological editor of *Jubilees* copied a rewritten story, which reflected a specific approach to understanding the order of the births (v. 17), and superimposed a chronological framework upon this base that reflected a different approach to the interpretation of the biblical story (vv. 15, 18). Any attempt to resolve the tension between the two will necessarily fail, because the two approaches reflect two exegetical traditions arising from two different sources.[82]

One might ask why anyone would do something so odd as to impose a chronological framework on stories it does not fit. Would a person as keen on chronology as the writer of Jubilees not notice the rather obvious point that modern students of the text have repeatedly highlighted? And why should one opt for such a radical solution as separating chronology and rewritten story in the entire book of Jubilees when in this case—which seems to be Segal's major one—only three dates are out of order in a lengthy sequence? It is hardly, to use his language, a "necessary" inference. Would it not be better to search for a simpler solution, especially given how badly numbers can be corrupted in manuscript transmission? All one has to do is look at the Latin translation for this section (Segal does not refer to it) to see how confusions and mistakes can arise.

If one takes the more economical approach of assuming that errors involving numbers have slipped into the text—the Hebrew fragments from Qumran documents confirm that this happened elsewhere in Jubilees—the following proposal may be advanced, one that closely resembles Charles's hypothesis.[83]

If there were eleven births in somewhat less than a twelve-year period and on no occasion was more than one mother pregnant, there would not be many years left without a birth.

Name (passage)	day	month	year	week	A.M.
Reuben (28:11)	14	9	1	3	2122
Simeon (28:13)	21	10	3	[3]	2124
Levi (28:14)	1	1	6	[3]	2127
Judah (28:15)	*15*	*3*	*7*	*[3]*	*2128*
Dan (28:18)	*9*	*6*	*1*	*4*	*2129*
Naphtali (28:19)	5	7	2	4	2130
Gad (28:20)	12	8	3	4	2131
Asher (28:21)	*2*	*11*	*4*	*4*	*2132*
Issachar (28:22)	*4*	*5*	*5*	*4*	*2133*
Twins (28:23)	7	7	6	4	2134
Joseph (28:24)	*1*	*4*	*7*	*4*	*2135*

It may be that the numbers for Judah and Dan simply got switched in transmission: if numerals were used, it would be easy to understand how year 7 [in week 3] became year 6 [in week 3] through the interchange of ז and ו.[84] A similar, accidental switch of dates for Asher and Issachar would account for the problem with them,[85] and in the case of Joseph another ו/ז confusion would explain how his year was one too

---

80 Segal, *Jubilees*, 89.
81 Ibid., 90 (for the last two quotations).
82 Ibid., 91.
83 Charles, *Jubilees*, 171. The chart presented here differs from Charles's in the date for Naphtali, which he mistakenly gives as 2131 when it should be 2130, as he correctly notes in the margin of his translation on p. 173; his total for Gad is also off by one year (2132; again the correct 2131 appears in the margin of the translation); for Asher he lists 2133, which should be 2132 (here the note in the margin of the translation is also wrong); for Issachar he has miscalculated the year by one.
84 The list from the Testaments of the Twelve Patriarchs has the order Judah–Dan, with the two born one year apart; Syncellus has the same order, with two years separating them.
85 In Syncellus's list, they appear in the order Asher–Issachar and are one year apart

low.[86] If Joseph was born in 2135, it would make good sense of the subsequent chronology in which the departure from Laban's home takes place "[a]fter Rachel had given birth to Joseph" (29:1), with the arrival in Gilead occurring in the same year (2135; Jub 29:5).

Plausible mistakes like these allow one to account for the data about the births/namings of the children without having to resort to a major and highly unlikely theory positing contradictions between the chronology in Jubilees and the stories it is meant to organize.[87]

---

[86] In the list from the Testaments, Joseph is born one year after Dinah (Zebulun came one year before her); in Syncellus he is born one year after the twins.

[87] For the argument presented in this excursus, see VanderKam, "One Author?," 510–15.

29

Jacob Leaves Haran and Deals with Laban, Esau, and His Parents

1/ After[a] Rachel had given birth to Joseph,[b] Laban went off to shear his sheep[c] because they were a three-day journey removed from him. 2/ Jacob saw that Laban was going off to shear his sheep and summoned Leah and Rachel. He spoke tenderly with them so that they would come with him to the land of Canaan.[a] 3/ For he told them how he had seen everything in a dream and everything about his statement to him[a] that he should return to his father's house.[b] They said,[c] "We will go with you wherever you go."[d] 4/ Jacob blessed the God of his father Isaac and the God of his grandfather Abraham. He set about loading up his wives and his children and took all his[a] possessions. After he had crossed the river, he reached the land of Gilead. But Jacob had concealed his plan from Laban[b] and had not told him.

5/ During the seventh year of the fourth week [2135] Jacob returned to Gilead on the twenty-first[a] day of the first month. Laban pursued him[b] and found Jacob[c] on the mountain[d] of Gilead on the thirteenth[e] (day) in the third[f] month. 6/ But the Lord did not allow him to harm Jacob because[a] he had appeared to him at night in a dream,[b] and Laban told Jacob. 7/ On the fifteenth of those days[a] Jacob prepared a banquet for Laban and all who had come with him.[b] That day Jacob swore to Laban and Laban to Jacob that neither would commit an offense against the other on the mountain[c] of Gilead with bad intentions. 8/ There he made a mound as a testimony: for this reason[a] that place is named the mound of testimony after this mound.[b] 9/ But[a] at first the land of Gilead was named the land of *Rafaem*[b] because it was the land of the Rafaim. The Rafaim were born there,[c] giants[d] whose heights were ten cubits, nine cubits, eight cubits,[e] and (down) to[f] seven cubits. 10/ The places where they lived[a] (extended) from the land of[b] the Ammonites as far as Mount Hermon. Their royal centers were Karnaim, Ashtaroth,[c] Edrei, Misur, and Beon.[d] 11/ The Lord destroyed them because of the evil things[a] they did,[b] for they were very wicked. The Amorites—evil and sinful—lived[c] in their place. Today[d] there is no nation that[e] has matched all their sins. They no longer have length of life on the earth.

12/ Jacob sent Laban away, and he went[a] to Mesopotamia,[b] to the eastern country.[c] But Jacob returned to the land of Gilead. 13/ He crossed[a] the Jabbok on the eleventh of the ninth month,[b] and on the same day his brother Esau came to him. They were reconciled with each other.[c] Then he went[d] from him[e] to the land of Seir, while Jacob lived in tents. 14/ In the first year of the fifth week during this jubilee [2136] he crossed the Jordan. He settled on the other side of the Jordan[a] and was tending[b] his sheep from the sea[c] of Fahahat[d] as far as Bethshan, Dothan, and[e] the forest[f] of Akrabbim. 15/ He sent[a] his father Isaac some of all his possessions: clothing, food, meat, things to drink, milk,[b] butter, cheese, and some dates from the valley.[c] 16/ To his mother Rebekah, too, (he sent goods) four times per year—between the seasons of the months, between plowing[a] and[b] harvest, between autumn and the rain(y season),[c] and between winter and spring[d]—to Abraham's tower. 17/ For Isaac had returned from the well of the oath, had gone up to the tower of his father Abraham, and had settled there away from his son Esau,[a] 18/ because, at the time when[a] Jacob went to Mesopotamia, Esau had married Mahalath, Ishmael's daughter. He had gathered[b] all[c] his father's flocks and his wives and had gone up and lived[d] in Mount Seir. He had left his father Isaac alone[e] at the well of the oath. 19/ So Isaac had gone up from the well of the oath and settled[a] at the tower of his father Abraham in the mountain of Hebron. 20/ There[a] Jacob would send everything that he was sending[b] to his father and[c] mother from time to time—everything they needed.[d] Then they would bless Jacob with all their mind and with all their being.

Textual Notes

1a After (*'em-za*)] "When" (*'enza*) 9 17 38 39 42 47 48 (63 has *'ama soba*, "when").
b Rachel . . . Joseph] "Leah . . . Issachar" 9 12 17 21 38 63; pr. "Leah . . . Issachar and" 44.
c his sheep] + "a three-day journey" 25 35. These MSS. lack "a three-day journey" later in the verse.
2a the land of Canaan] "his land because his father was living (in) the land of Canaan" 38 (this MS. omits the first part of v. 3, through "his father's house").
3a to him] + "in a dream" 25.
b house] The phrase is literally "(to) the house of his father." Mss. 25 35 replace *bēta* ("house of") with *westa* ("in, to"), while 44 places *westa* before *bēta*.
c They said] + "to him" 38 63.
d you go] "you have gone" 38 (it also reads "we will go" in place of "with you"); "we will go" 42 47 48.
4a his (possessions)] "their" 9 21.
b concealed his plan from Laban] The text reads: "concealed the heart of Laban." However, as with Gen 31:20 it is expressing the idea that Jacob hid what was in his own heart (his plan) from Laban. Apparently, by failing to reveal his plan to Laban, Jacob was "hiding the heart of Laban," that is, keeping information from him. The translation assumes this interpretation. See VanderKam, *Jubilees* 2:185; Werman, *Jubilees*, 400 n. 2.
5a (twenty-) first] "second" 21.
b him] "Jacob" 21 (12 has "Jacob him"); using a different formulation, 20 63 also have "Jacob."
c Jacob] om. 20 21 63.
d mountain (*dabra*)] "land" (*medra*) 17 20.
e thirteenth] "twenty-third" 39.
f third] "second" 38.
6a because] "and" 25 35.
b at night in a dream] "in a dream of the night" 35 47 (cf. 21); "in a dream in the night" 12.
7a those days] "that month of days" 21.
b with him] + "who went out" 38.
c on the mountain] "and the mountain" 9 12 17 63.
8a for this reason] Lat. "because" (*quod*).
b after this mound] om. 35 58; Lat. "after that hill"; om. "after this" 20 25; om. "mound" 48.
9a But (*wa-*)] Lat. "For" (*enim*); om. 25 35.
b the land of *Rafaem*] Most MSS. read a form that more nearly resembles the name Raphael; MSS. 35 58 have a more accurate *rāfā'ēm*. Lat. *terrafaim* blends *terra* and *rafaim* (Rönsch, *Jubiläen*, 50, 138; Charles, *Ethiopic Version*, 107 n. 1 to Latin).
c there] Lat. reads *illic*, "there"; there is no equivalent among the Eth. copies, though it seems to be needed here.
d giants] The noun is juxtaposed with *Rafaim* in the Eth. copies; Lat. inserts *id est* before it.
e eight cubits] om. 20 25 35; Lat. "eight cubits."
f (down) to] om. 20 25 35 58; Lat. *etiam*, "also, even."
10a lived] + "in the land" 35.
b the land of] om. 20 25 35; "the mountain of" 63; Lat. *a terra*.
c Ashtaroth] Lat. *mastaroth*.
d and Beon] om. 21; Lat. *et seo*. See VanderKam, *Jubilees* 2:186–87.
11a because of the evil things] om. 38; Lat. *de malitia*.
b they did (lit., their deeds)] Lat. *studiorum*. The word seems to have a meaning similar to the Eth. *megbāromu* but is not followed by a possessive.
c lived] "they left him/it" 39 42 48ᵗ (cf. 47). Lat. has a causative wording "made (the Amorites) live." The sg. form of the Eth. verb (*ḫadara*) could imply that "the Lord" should be the subject, suggesting that the Lat. may have preserved an earlier reading (see VanderKam, *Jubilees* 2:187).
d Today] The Eth. copies introduce the clause with "and," but Lat. has *sicut* ("so"). Lat. *odio* appears where Eth. reads *yom*, "today." Rönsch (*Jubiläen*, 50) recognized a distortion of *odie/hodie* ("today") in the word; see Charles, *Ethiopic Version*, 107 n. 6 to Latin.
e that] Eth. *za-* seems correct, while Lat. *quia* is likely to be a mistake for *qui* (so Charles, *Ethiopic Version*, 107 n. 7 to Latin).
12a he went] "he sent him" 39; "he sent" 42 47 48; Lat. *abiit*, "he went."
b Mesopotamia] pr. "the land of" 9 12 17 21 38 39 42 47 48 58 63; Lat. also lacks "the land of."
c to the (eastern) country] "toward" 39 58; Lat. *terram*. As the accusative ending on *terram* indicates, the preposition *a* should be *ad* = Eth. reading.
13a He crossed the Jabbok] Lat. "Jacob crossed," confusing *iacob* and *iaboc*.
b on the eleventh of the ninth month] For the difference between this reading in the Eth. version and the one in the Lat. translation, see the commentary.
c They were reconciled with each other] Lat. "He (Esau?) was reconciled" (perhaps *est* fell out of the text before the following *et*). Rönsch (*Jubiläen*, 50) altered the following *et* to *ei*, "to him," while Charles (*Ethiopic Version*, 107) added *ei* before *et*. As it stands, the Lat. can hardly be correct since it would use a participle in a sequence of finite verbs (see VanderKam, *Jubilees* 2:188). The meaning is little affected.
d he went (Lat. *abiit*)] "they went" 9 21 38 39 42 47 48.
e from him (Lat. *ab ipso*)] "from them" 9 21 38.
14a He settled on the other side of the Jordan] om. 12 20 35 38 (the omission is from the first to the second instance of "Jordan"). Lat. has the full text.
b and was tending] Both Eth. and Lat. suggest continuing action. Mss. 9 21 38 44 have "in order to tend."
c sea (*bāḥra*)] "district 9" (= *beḥēr*) 21 38 63 (= *beḥēra*); Lat. *mare*.
d Fahahat] Several MSS. read *fešḥet(a)* 9 12 21 38 58 (cf. 44)

or *fešḥat* 35 39 48, all of which should mean "mound." Lat. *salso*. For a defense of "the Sea of Galilee" as the original reading here, see VanderKam, *Jubilees* 2:188.

e   as far—and] Lat. omits from 'eska¹ to 'eska³ (each of the place-names is preceded by 'eska).

f   forest] The MSS. spell the word with an initial *alf* (') rather than the expected '*om* = forest (Leslau, *Comparative Dictionary*, 62 = "tree, grove, forest, woodland"). The older copies contain an additional confusion of '*oma* with '*ama* ("when"). The Lat. *aggruum* is unexplained (for options, see VanderKam, *Jubilees* 2:188).

15a sent] Eth. *yefēnu*, "sent," but Lat. *tradidit* has the sense of "deliver, transmit." The two are very close in meaning.

b   milk] Eth. places a conjunction before the word and before all the remaining items in the list, while Lat. places one before only the last two.

c   dates from the valley] lit., "some dates of the valley"; Lat. "dates from the valley," that is, Eth. places "from" = "some" before "dates of the valley," and Lat. puts the preposition after "dates." Mss. 39 42 47 48 58 read "from *all* the dates of the valley."

16a plowing] Lat. *area* ("threshing floor") is strange, since the context calls for a time of the year. It should be related to the verb *arare*, "to plow, till." The expected noun would be *arationis* (Rönsch, *Jubiläen*, 140; Charles, *Ethiopic Version*, 109 n. 3 to Latin).

b   and (harvest)] Lat. *usque ad* seems wrong, as specific times, not spans of time, are under consideration. The Eth. reflects a Heb. בין ... ל-; the Lat. may represent a misunderstanding of it.

c   autumn and the rain(y season)] Eth. literally: "harvest season/season of the small rains (= April–July [Leslau, *Comparative Dictionary*, 548]) and rains"; Lat. *autumni pluvias*, "autumn rains."

d   winter and spring] Lat. "its rains" (after mentioning the rains just before this). Rönsch (*Jubiläen*, 52, 140) and Charles (*Ethiopic Version*, 109 n. 5 to Latin) suggested that *eius* was an error for *veris*, "of spring." The Latin probably omitted a few words because of the repeated use of *pluvia* in the verse.

17a away from his son Esau] The Eth. reading differs from Lat. *in terra sua et filii sui*. *Filii sui* could be the equivalent of *waldu*, "his son." The Greek behind the two would be: Eth./Greek: εκ ησαυ υιου αυτου, Lat/Greek: εν γη αυτου και υιον αυτου. If και is an addition, the two would be very close (see VanderKam, *Jubilees* 2:189). Eth. expresses an idea more widespread in Jubilees—portraying Esau negatively (and Jacob positively); so Berger, *Jubiläen*, 469 n. a to v. 17.

18a because, at the time when (= Lat.)] + "he lived and" 17; "and when" 20 25 35 58; "when in the time" 39 42 47 48.

b   He had gathered] Lat. has *uxor eius*, "his wife" (nominative). As it lacks the verb "he gathered," it reads as if Esau took Mahalath as a wife and all his father's flocks, but the nominative *uxor eius* has no function in the sentence (Eth. refers to "his wives" after "his flocks"). Rönsch (*Jubiläen*, 52) suggested *et uxores suas* [*et*] = "his wives (accusative) [and]"; Charles (*Ethiopic Version*, 109) read *et* (*ad se recepit*) *uxores suas et*. The Eth. makes better sense than the Lat., which, at any rate, requires some emendation. See VanderKam, *Jubilees* 2:190. Ms. 12 repeats the verb "gathered" before "his wives."

c   all] = Lat.; om. 9 38.

d   and lived] om. 9 38.

e   alone] Lat. lacks the word. Perhaps the idea of "alone" is implied by the verb *dereliquid*?

19a and settled] Lat. lacks, so that it has Isaac going up into/to the tower of Abraham. Perhaps the presence of the words וישב שבע in sequence led to omission of the verb (so VanderKam, *Jubilees* 2:190).

20a There] = Lat. Eth. "from there" does not fit the context, which requires that Jacob send goods to where his father was.

b   everything that he was sending] Lat. "whatever things were." A verb seems to have gone missing from Lat.

c   and (mother)] Lat. "or."

d   they needed] Lat. + *in omni usu suo*, "in their every want"? The words seem superfluous after *necessaria*, although Werman (*Jubilees*, 401 n. 20), who translates *usu suo* as חפצם, prefers the expression because it shows Jacob's generosity.

Commentary

Jubilees 29 spans the time of transition from when Jacob leaves Paddan-aram until he returns to the land; once he reaches it he encounters Laban and Esau and he cares for Isaac and Rebekah, though he does so from a distance. The stretch of Genesis on which the writer primarily bases the account is chaps. 31–33, but he introduces major changes mostly through omissions but also through additions. So, for example, the long story about the meeting between Jacob and Laban in Gen 31:22-55 he treats in 29:5-8, 12a, and the extended, dramatic encounter between Jacob and Esau in Gen 32:3 (Heb. 32:4)–33:17 he summarizes in 29:13.[1] These episodes, which occurred in the course of the journey home, contributed little to the author's message and may in places have detracted from it, so he largely ignored them. Yet to the account in Genesis he adds a section about the former name and residents of Gilead (29:9-11) and one about the gifts that Jacob regularly sent to his parents (29:15-20). In this latter unit he references Esau's marriage to Mahalath (Gen 28:6-9)—something he had earlier omitted when recounting the story of Jacob's departure from home (Jubilees 27).

The major divisions in the chapter are these:

1-4 Jacob and his family leave Laban's home and go to Gilead
5-8 The encounter between Jacob and Laban in Gilead
9-11 A digression on the previous name and inhabitants of Gilead
12-20 Jacob meets Esau and cares for Isaac and Rebekah.

The full Ethiopic text for the chapter is joined by the Latin translation for vv. 8-20.

1-4 Jacob and His Family Leave Laban's Home and Go to Gilead

The all-important stage of Jacob's life in Haran comes to a close in a way closely analogous to the one in Genesis but with some special Jubilean touches.

■ 1 For the second time the writer begins a section by referring to the time after Rachel gave birth to Joseph. Genesis uses the notice just once (30:25 // Jub 28:25) to introduce the negotiations between Laban and Jacob regarding his continued work for his father-in-law. Very little time passes between Joseph's birth and the present occasion in the chronology of Jubilees. If the dates in 28:24 and 29:5 (see below) are retained, they would occur in the successive years 2134 (fourth month) and 2135 (first month); if the revised chronology is accepted, the years would be 2135 and 2136. In either case, there is no six-year separation as there is in Genesis. The author of Jubilees inserts into this context the notice that Laban was separated by a three-day distance from Jacob, information he had passed over in chap. 28. According to Gen 30:36, Laban removed from his flocks the animals that should have belonged to Jacob, "and he set a distance of three days' journey between himself and Jacob, while Jacob was pasturing the rest of Laban's flock." He combines this notice with the one in Gen 31:19: "Now Laban had gone to shear his sheep." As his animals were a journey of three days away, he did not learn of Jacob's departure until the third day afterwards (31:22). For Jubilees, these time indicators precede and supply the occasion for Jacob's departure with his wives and children; in Genesis, they follow it.

■ 2 Jacob exploited Laban's absence to formulate a plan with Leah and Rachel (note the order of the names; in Gen 31:4 it is Rachel–Leah)[2] whom he summons for a conference. It is noteworthy that the writer fails to include a Genesis section about a direct encounter between the Lord and Jacob. "Then the LORD said to Jacob, 'Return to the land of your ancestors and to your kindred, and I will be with you'" (Gen 31:3). The divine message is the immediate cause for calling Rachel and Leah together in Genesis (see 31:4), while in Jubilees Laban's absence to shear his sheep serves that purpose. The writer adds a comment characterizing the tone of the meeting between Rachel, Leah, and Jacob: "He spoke tenderly with them [lit., into/upon their heart—*westa lebbon*[3]] so that they would come with him to the land of Canaan" (v. 2). The expression *westa lebbon* reflects a Hebrew idiom that occurs in Isa 40:2: "Speak tenderly [על לב] to Jerusalem [Eth. Isa 40:2 reads *westa lebbā*]." The same phrase will be used for the manner in which Joseph speaks to his brothers in Gen 50:21 and the way in which Ruth characterizes Boaz's words to her (Ruth 2:13). There is no rivalry or quarreling among the three spouses, and Jacob does not play favorites. He is not about to abandon his family and naturally wants the consent of the wives to leave their birthplace and father's house and to move to his homeland.

---

1 On the condensed versions of the stories in Jubilees, see Endres, *Biblical Interpretation*, 109.
2 Halpern-Amaru, *Empowerment*, 69.
3 The Hebrew for "their heart"—לבן—allows a wordplay on their father's name.

■ **3** As he speaks with his two wives in Genesis, Jacob recites a litany of offenses their father had committed against him and also draws attention to a revelation he received from "the angel of the LORD" in a dream (31:11 [cf. v. 10]).[4] The content of that dream revelation occupies Gen 31:12-13, where, surprisingly, God himself, not the angel, speaks: "Look up and see that all the goats that leap on the flock are striped, speckled, and mottled; for I have seen all that Laban is doing to you. I am the God of Bethel, where you anointed a pillar and made a vow to me. Now leave this land at once and return to the land of your birth.'" This revelation would seem to be the one Jacob mentions to his wives in v. 3: "For he told them how he had seen everything in a dream and everything about his statement to him that he should return to his father's house." Charles understood the reference to the dream to be to the one mentioned in Gen 31:10, and Endres agrees with him.[5] Halpern-Amaru, however, objects:

> The content of the dream that Jacob describes to his wives in Gen 31:10-13 reflects the earlier narrative of Jacob's efforts to combat Laban's schemes (Gen 30:37-43) and refers to the divine command to return home in Gen 31:3. None of that background to the conversation is preserved in *Jubilees*. The reader knows of a dream in which the patriarch is told he would return to his father's house; but it comes out of a totally different context. It is the dream vision years earlier at Bethel when Jacob, in flight from Esau's anger, was on his way to the home of his uncle. In that vision God conveyed the promises of the patriarchal covenant and assured Jacob that he would bring him back to Canaan (27:22-24).[6]

It is true that Laban's machinations with wages are absent from Jubilees and that the first part of the revealing dream (Gen 31:12) refers to them; but in Gen 31:13 the deity identifies himself as "the God of Bethel" (MT)[7] or "the God who appeared to you in Bethel" (LXX), and in Jub 29:3 Jacob includes in his summary the directive ("his" in "his statement" refers to God) that he should return to his father's house. Neither the Bethel scene in Gen 28:13-15 // Jub 27:22-24 nor the revelation in Gen 31:3 contains a divine promise to return him to his father's house. Jacob includes such a provision in his conditional vow (Gen 28:21 // Jub 27:27), but God does not promise to carry it out. The nearest he comes to doing so is in Gen 31:3, but there he says he is to return to the land of his fathers (plural). Jacob is probably recalling the Bethel scene and the reminder of it in Gen 31:12-13, but he gives his own interpretation of the two revelations.

As Jacob did not detail the deceptions Laban had practiced on him, so the wives refrain from recalling how he had abandoned them and used up the money paid for them (Gen 31:14-16). In Jubilees they agree to go wherever Jacob goes.[8] In Genesis they are less explicit about this because they end their reply with "now, then, do whatever God has said to you" (31:16).

■ **4** Their assent to Jacob's wishes leads Jacob to bless "the God of his father Isaac" in v. 4. Genesis has no equivalent at this juncture, but the clause in Jubilees may reflect Gen 31:6, where Jacob has just mentioned to his wives a change for the worse in Laban's attitude toward him: "But the God of my father has been with me." His charges against Laban follow (Gen 31:7-9). The Genesis stories make two other references in the near context to the God of Isaac: he forbade Laban to harm Jacob (Gen 31:29; cf. v. 24 // Jub 29:6), and Jacob, referring to that message, says to Laban, "If the God of my father, the God of Abraham and the Fear of Isaac, had not been on my side, surely now you would have sent me away empty-handed. God saw my affliction and the labor of my hands, and rebuked you last night" (31:42; cf. also v. 53). Once he has blessed the ancestral God, Jacob loads up his wives and children (MT Gen 31:17 reverses wives and children, but Jubilees reads with the SP and the LXX tradition) along with his possessions; the caravan leaves, crosses the river (the Euphrates), and eventually reaches

---

4   This is an instance where the Angel of the Presence in Jubilees does not identify himself as "the angel of the LORD" in Genesis.

5   Charles, *Jubilees*, 175 n.; Endres, *Biblical Interpretation*, 110.

6   Halpern-Amaru, *Empowerment*, 69–70.

7   Both the MT and SP read the curious האל בית אל.

8   Endres notes the resemblance to Ruth's response to Naomi: "Where you go, I will go" (Ruth 1:16) (*Biblical Interpretation*, 110-11).

Gilead.[9] Jacob disclosed none of this to Laban of course.[10] In this verse the writer has combined words from Gen 31:17, 18 ("all his property/possessions"), 21, and 20. He did not reproduce v. 19, the first part of which he had used in 29:1 ("Now Laban had gone to shear his sheep"); the second part of it he understandably omitted: "and Rachel stole her father's household gods." Jubilees makes no mention of the theft here nor will it in the story about the meeting with Laban in Gilead. The only reference to it will come in 31:1-2, where at Bethel Jacob tells his family members to hand over their foreign gods and Rachel surrenders the ones she stole from Laban.[11] Failure to reproduce the various instances of the verb "steal" in Genesis 31 removes one of the literary touches that reveals its artistry.[12]

5-8 The Encounter between Jacob and Laban in Gilead

The short section contains a greatly condensed version of the story in Gen 31:22-55, where Laban overtakes Jacob, the two have an angry exchange regarding what has happened, they come to an agreement, and they separate. Jubilees 29:5-8 (with v. 12) includes all of these elements except the angry exchange between Jacob and his father-in-law, but in much shorter form.

■ 5 The verse contains notices about the time when Jacob and his fellow travelers arrived in Gilead and when Laban overtook them (see Gen 31:23). The writer, who regularly marks important events by dating them, has Jacob and his party reach Gilead on the twenty-first of the first month[13] in the year 2135 and has Laban catch up with them on 3/13 of the same year. Since Joseph, according to 28:24, was born or named on the first of the fourth month in the year 2134, the dates are compatible. However, if one accepts the revised chronology presented above in which Rachel names Joseph on 4/1 the next year, that is, 2135, then the dates would conflict because Joseph's birth would follow rather than precede the arrival in Gilead as 29:1-5 requires. It may seem a telling blow against the revised chronology, but there are good reasons for suspecting something is amiss with at least one of the dates in 29:5. First, why did it take Laban, who caught up with Jacob on 3/13, so long to cover roughly the same distance that Jacob, the women and their children (some of them very small), and the herds traveled? The contexts in Genesis and Jubilees suggest that as soon as he heard about Jacob's departure, he set out in pursuit,[14] and he had no young families or herds of animals to slow him down (he chases after them for seven days according to Gen 31:23). Even in the unlikely circumstance that he and his men ("his kinsfolk," v. 23; cf. vv. 32, 37) journeyed at the same pace Jacob did, they would have arrived only a few days later, not some two months later. Consequently, it is reasonable to suggest that Jacob and his caravan reached Gilead several days before Laban did; that is, they would have been in Gilead on perhaps 3/10 and no earlier.[15]

---

9   Genesis 31:21 says that after crossing the river he "set his face toward the hill country [הר] of Gilead." Jubilees offers an interpretation: "he reached the land of Gilead." It shares with LXX and OL the idea of proceeding toward or going to Gilead, but it is unique in mentioning "the land of Gilead." It will refer to the mountain of Gilead in 29:5 (// Gen 31:25).

10 According to v. 4, Jacob, literally, "hid the heart of Laban" in agreement with the LXX tradition (εκρυψεν), where Gen 31:20 says literally, "he stole the heart of Laban." The difference likely occurred through a confusion of εκρυψεν and εκλεψεν ("he stole").

11 Cf. Endres, *Biblical Interpretation*, 110.

12 On the use of the verb in Genesis 31, see Hamilton, *Genesis 18–50*, 295-96.

13 Van Goudoever thinks that, by crossing the river on 1/21, Jacob's act is "a 'type' analogous to the later crossing of the Red Sea," on the same date in some texts (*Biblical Calendars*, 125). However, the date at this point in Jubilees is probably incorrect (see below) so that the analogy likely does not exist.

14 The point is not explicit in Jubilees, but in Gen 31:36 Jacob asks Laban, "What is my sin, that you have hotly pursued me?"

15 See VanderKam, *Book of Jubilees*, 65. There it is also noted that 1/21 would be an unlikely date on which to arrive as it is the last of the seven days of the Festival of Unleavened Bread (see 18:18-19), when travel would have been forbidden. The date for Laban's arrival (3/13) is likely to be correct because it allows the two men to make their agreement on 3/15, the Festival of Weeks. Endres thinks Jubilees is correcting Gen 31:23 (Laban pursues for seven days) on the grounds that the writer could not

Yet, if one moves the date to 3/10, it would still be before Joseph's birth on 4/1 in the revised chronology, so the year number in 29:5 would have to be changed to 2136, the year after Joseph's birth (see below for the dates in 29:13-14).

■ **6** Once the two men are together, they do not engage in the lengthy exchange of charge and countercharge found in Gen 31:26-42 and certainly not in the intense argument regarding Rachel's theft of Laban's gods (Gen 31:30-37), as that episode plays no part in the context in Jubilees. The author merely reports that the Lord had prevented Laban from doing any harm to Jacob. In Gen 31:29 Laban gives his own account of the experience: "It is in my [Laban's] power to do you harm; but the God of your father spoke to me last night, saying, 'Take heed that you speak to Jacob neither good nor bad'" (cf. v. 24, where it is called "a dream by night"[16]). This is the verse to which 29:6 refers with the phrase "Laban told Jacob."

■ **7-8** Rather than quarrel,[17] the two men and Laban's companions eat together and swear to a nonaggression pact between them. The two verses drastically abbreviate and somewhat recast the contents of Gen 31:44-54. In Genesis the two men first make what Laban terms a covenant (v. 44) and set up a heap and pillar as markers that Jacob will not mistreat Laban's daughters and that neither of them will cross this geographical line to harm the other. Jacob then sacrifices and celebrates an overnight meal with "his kinsfolk [lit., brothers: אחיו]" (v. 54; they first appeared in vv. 32, 37, 46; a meal for them also figures in v. 46). In the scene Laban is the one who states the stipulations regarding his daughters and the boundary markers, and Jacob is the only one who actually swears an oath to abide by the agreement (31:53).

In Jubilees the situation is different. The agreement with Laban, which is not termed a covenant, is dated to 3/15, the Festival of Weeks. The expression in the text is a bit unusual: "On the fifteenth of those days" (*wa-'ama 'ašuru wa-ḥamusu la-we'etu mawā'el*); but in a context where 3/13 has just been mentioned, it is difficult to see what else could be meant. It will be recalled that this holiday is the time for making and renewing the covenant (its date is usually phrased as "the middle of the third month" in Jubilees, but 44:1-5 demonstrates that the date was the fifteenth). Naturally, this is not the covenant made first with Noah and renewed and expanded with Abraham, Isaac, and Jacob; it is a different agreement altogether, but the author still follows his practice of dating agreements to 3/15. Having supplied the date for the event, he records the meal Jacob prepared for Laban and his retinue. Genesis never explicitly has the two of them sharing a meal. Genesis 31:46 could be taken as saying that Jacob and his kin ate together; in 31:54 the same appears to be the case.[18] What is indefinite in Genesis becomes explicit in Jubilees: both parties

---

believe Jacob and his retinue had covered so much territory in just a few days (*Biblical Interpretation*, 111), but he does not comment on the fact that the dates in Jubilees imply that Laban and his men moved far more slowly than Jacob and his large caravan. Werman recognizes that the date 1/21 is problematic and wonders whether 1/26 (after completion of the Festival of Unleavened Bread; it is the date for waving the barley omer in the Qumran calendar texts) was the original reading (*Jubilees*, 402), but her revised date would still encounter the problem of the long time between Jacob's and Laban's arrivals at Gilead. She adds that Jubilees lacks information about when Laban heard about the flight of Jacob and his company. The seven weeks (or more) between when Jacob reached Gilead and Laban's arrival there suggest that Jacob settled at Mount Gilead and that Laban set out in pursuit only much later. Her view is possible, but the immediate juxtaposition of Jacob's trip and Laban's pursuit in v. 5 may imply that there was no such time gap.

16 Where Gen 31:24 says God "came" to Laban in a dream, Jubilees reads "he had appeared to him," as *Targum Neofiti* does.

17 Endres writes about the omission of Laban's words: subtracting his speech "divested it entirely of its plaint against Jacob. The author eschewed these criticisms against Jacob, especially since they possessed enough truth to rouse the audience's sympathy. Once again the author preferred a stage direction instead of a narration which expressed the depth and drama of the situation" (*Biblical Interpretation*, 111).

18 Skinner takes the meal in v. 54 to be one eaten by Jacob and his kinsmen only, although he seems to understand the one in v. 46 as involving Laban and Jacob (*Genesis*, 401–2). For Westermann, the meal in v. 54 is for Jacob and his people and for Laban and his (*Genesis 12–36*, 500). About the one in v. 46

to the agreement share the one meal Jacob supplies; nothing is said about Jacob's kinsfolk, who are mystery characters in Genesis 31.[19] Next the author records that Jacob and Laban swore to each other "that neither would commit an offense against the other on the mountain of Gilead with bad intentions" (for Jacob's swearing an oath, see Gen 31:53). Nothing appears here regarding Laban's demand that Jacob not harm his daughters or take additional wives. The focus is on the agreement stated in Gen 31:51-52: "See this heap and see this pillar, which I have set between you and me. This heap is a witness, and the pillar is a witness, that I will not pass beyond this heap to you, and you will not pass beyond this heap and this pillar to me, for harm." With this subject of the agreement, it is only fitting that the writer next mentions (v. 8) that Jacob made a "mound as a testimony: for this reason that place is named the mound of testimony after this mound."[20] Here again something unclear in Genesis becomes clear in Jubilees. In Gen 31:46 Jacob is the one who has his kinsfolk gather stones and make a heap or mound, but in v. 51 Laban refers to the heap and pillar he set up. In Jubilees only Jacob erects a heap. The name the place acquires from this act is the Hebrew one that Jacob gives it (Galeed/Gilead) in Gen 31:47 (Jubilees does not reproduce the Aramaic equivalent Laban supplies—*Jegar-sahadutha* [as NRSV transliterates it]).[21]

Excursus: Laban in Jubilees

Laban is an unusual character in Genesis. Although he was not as closely related as Ishmael, he belonged to the family of Abraham—he was a grandson of Abraham's brother Nahor (Gen 22:20-24; 24:29)— and he proved instrumental in delivering his sister Rebekah as a wife for Isaac (Gen 24:28-61). He was the one to whom Isaac dispatched Jacob to find a wife (Gen 28:1-2); he was the head of a household in the extended family of Abraham; and he was the father of Jacob's wives, Leah and Rachel, who bore eight of the twelve sons from whom Israel would spring. Yet, in spite of all these family ties and roles, he proves to be a negative character in his relations with his nephew Jacob. He takes advantage of the younger man by inducing him to work for him for fourteen years in exchange for Leah and Rachel—a process aided by his deceptive substituting of Leah for Rachel—and he supplements those fourteen years with six more in which he regularly manipulates Jacob's wages (ten times [Gen 31:7]). As they plan to leave his household, Jacob and his two wives make strong charges against Laban for theft, deception, and abandonment (31:4-16). Once they leave, he vigorously pursues them to take back the wives, their children, and the animals—all, he claims, belong to him (31:43). Only divine intervention keeps him from harming Jacob and presumably taking back his offspring and the flocks and herds accompanying them. He was, moreover, terribly concerned to recover the gods stolen from him (31:30-35); that is, he carried on the family tradition of serving other gods beyond the river (Josh 24:2-3).

The writer of Jubilees removes most of Laban's negative traits. Exactly what this entails is not obvious, since he could assume that the readers of the book would be familiar with the Genesis stories about Laban as a dangerous schemer. Nevertheless, he chose not to reproduce those negative traits and even asserted that he acted in accordance with legislation etched on the heavenly tablets when he gave Leah before Rachel. He was not deceiving Jacob; he was obeying an eternal law. As Werman has shown in her analysis of the Laban of Genesis in comparison

he writes: "The common meal (a doublet of v. 54) has its place at the end of the rite; it has no meaning before the oath" (p. 498). Cf. Endres, *Biblical Interpretation*, 112.

19 In a comment on Gen 31:46 ("And Jacob said to his kinsfolk"), *Gen. Rab.* 74:13 (Rashi gives the same interpretation) raises and answers the obvious question about who the relatives might be: "How many brothers had he then—but one, and would that he had buried him! It refers, however, to his sons, whom he calls brethren in the Holy Tongue."

20 Since the etymology is taken over from Genesis, the passage does not seem significant for determining what "testimony" means in Jubilees in phrases such as "the law and the testimony."

21 Werman thinks that in Jubilees Laban speaks Hebrew and for that reason the Aramaic terms do not appear in the text (*Jubilees*, 403; cf. 76). Christopher T. Begg compares Jub 28:25—29:12 with the relevant passages in Genesis, noting many differences in Jubilees (e.g., instances of abbreviation) ("Jacob's Escape from Laban in Josephus and Jubilees," *Hermen* 9 [2009] 26-36). He concludes that in Jubilees "Jacob and Laban's roles get approximately 'equal treatment'" (p. 37)—a questionable inference in view of Jacob's status in the story in comparison with Genesis.

with the Laban of Jubilees, he is not a deceiver in Jubilees. Instead, he has appropriate relations with Jacob until Jacob grows exceptionally rich. At that point he becomes jealous of him and attempts to limit his wealth and openly favors his sons over his son-in-law.[22] This understandable reaction was, no doubt, the reason why Jacob concealed from Laban his plans to leave. The Lord appeared to Laban and ordered him not to harm Jacob. The two simply make an agreement to stay in their own territories and not cross over a fixed point, Gilead, to injure the other. Laban makes no claim on his daughters and their families or on the animals Jacob has in his possession, and the subject of the household gods is absent from the section of the text that deals with Laban. It seems likely, as Werman maintains, that the writer of Jubilees polished Laban's image because of his role as father of Jacob's wives and grandfather of his children, the ancestors of Israel. More harmony reigned in the wider family than Genesis entails.

9-11 A Digression on the Previous Name and Inhabitants of Gilead

Having just explained the meaning of *Gilead* (the mound/heap of testimony), the writer departs from his base text in Genesis for a short section about Gilead and its past. He formulates the aside on the pattern of the one in Deut 2:19-21. There, after the Lord warns the people of Israel not to bother the Ammonites when they pass their border with Moab (Deut 2:19), he gives way to an editor who inserts some information about the country of Ammon: "It is also usually reckoned as a land of Rephaim. Rephaim formerly inhabited it, though the Ammonites call them Zamzummim, a strong and numerous people, as tall as the Anakim. But the Lord destroyed them from before the Ammonites so that they could dispossess them and settle in their place" (2:20-21). The territory of Ammon could be thought to extend into the region of Gilead. For example, in Judg 10:8 the Ammonites "crushed and oppressed the Israelites that year. For eighteen years they oppressed all the Israelites that were beyond the Jordan in the land of the Amorites, which is in Gilead." The career of the judge Jephthah the Gileadite follows.

■ **9** In Jubilees, the narrating angel first notes that, as in Deut 2:20, the territory once bore the name of its early inhabitants, the Rephaim,[23] and they were giants.[24] Deuteronomy does not supply their specific height (saying only that they were "as tall as the Anakim"), but Jubilees does. It may be that the writer took one indication of their statures—nine cubits—from the notice about the length of the bed belonging to King Og of Bashan (who is "of the remnant of the Rephaim" [Deut 2:11]). If the Rephaim ranged in height from ten down to seven cubits, even the shortest among them were taller than Goliath, who, according to the MT, was six cubits and a span (1 Sam 17:4).

■ **10** The angel also provides a short statement about the geographical extent of their land (from the territory of the Ammonites as far north as Mount Hermon). While Mount Hermon seems a point rather far north for the region of Gilead, he may be following the givens in Josh 12:1-6, where the territory east of the Jordan that the Israelites conquered and in which Reuben, Gad, and the half-tribe of Manasseh settled is under consideration (see also Num 32:1, 26, 29; 21:13). There the extent of the land is "from the Wadi Arnon to Mount Hermon" (v. 1). In vv. 4-5 there is mention of "King Og of Bashan, one of the last of the Rephaim, who lived at Ashtaroth and at Edrei and ruled over Mount Hermon and Salecah and all Bashan to the boundary of the Geshurites and the Maacathites and over half of Gilead to the boundary of King Sihon of Heshbon." See also Deut 3:8, where the land Israel took from the two Amorite kings, Sihon and Og, stretches from "the Wadi Arnon to Mount Hermon."

The author also saw fit to have the Angel of the Presence mention their five royal cities in v. 10.

---

22   Werman, "Attitude," 159–76.
23   For another case in which the previous name of a city is given, see Jub 27:26, where the ancient name of Bethel is said to be Luz (// Gen 28:19).
24   Werman connects these giants with the offspring of the Watchers (*Jubilees*, 403), but the writer of Jubilees leaves no hint suggesting a connection with the time of the flood and merely reproduces pentateuchal references to the Anakim/giants in the affected areas.

Karnaim. The name is regularly combined with the next one (Ashteroth-karnaim); Gen 14:5 says that Chedorlaomer and the allied kings defeated "the Rephaim in Ashteroth-karnaim (for the name alone, see Amos 6:13).

Ashtaroth. Besides being coupled with Karnaim, Ashtaroth appears alone as the place where King Og ruled (Deut 1:4; Josh 13:12; cf. also Josh 9:10; 12:4).

Edrei. This too was a city of King Og (Deut 1:4; Josh 13:12 [another passage where he is called a remnant of the Rephaim]; see also Num 21:33; Deut 3:1, 10 [in v. 11 Og is a remnant of the Rephaim]; Josh 12:4).

Misur (Eth. *misur*; Latin *msum*). This is the only one of the five that is not attested in the HB as a city name. Dillmann and Charles made the sensible suggestion that Misur reflects מישור, the name for the "elevated plateau or *table-land* between the Arnon and Heshbon" (BDB, 449; see the references there).[25] It is located in the correct area. Deuteronomy 3:10, where Moses is speaking about the victories over Sihon and Og, the two kings of the Amorites, lists the areas conquered: "all the towns of the tableland [המישר], the whole of Gilead, and all of Bashan, as far as Salecah and Edrei, towns of Og's kingdom in Bashan."

Beon. The city is the one mentioned in Num 32:3. In that context, the tribes of Reuben and Gad who settled in the Transjordan saw that Gilead was a good place for their cattle and requested several cities there, among which is Beon.[26] Nothing more is said about it.

■ 11 The learned aside concludes by describing the next stage in the history of the area. The evil of the Rephaim led the Lord himself to destroy them (Deut 2:21),[27] and he replaced them with the Amorites.[28] Both Kings Sihon and Og, though the latter is said to be a survivor of the Rephaim, are called Amorite kings (Deut 3:8), and Og's land of Bashan incorporated an area—the Argob—that once had the name "a land of Rephaim" (Deut 3:13). It seems from the continuation of v. 11 that the Amorites, who were "evil and sinful," are being described: no contemporary nation has matched their level of wickedness and, as a result, they "no longer have length of life on the earth." The name "Amorite" is used in more than one sense in the HB,[29] but their wickedness is noted in Gen 15:16: "And they [the descendants of Abram] shall come back here in the fourth generation; for the iniquity of the Amorites is not yet complete" (see Jub 14:16, which uses a passive form of the verb employed in 29:11). Their massive level of evildoing triggered the punishment expressed in the next sentence (see below). In their conquests of Sihon and Og, the Amorite kings, Moses and the Israelites, by the Lord's power, annihilated them and took over their territories (Num 21:21-35; Deut 2:26–3:7; Josh 12:1-6; Judg 11:14-23). Though Israel won the battle, the accounts stress it was God who gave

---

25 Dillmann, "Jubiläen," 72 n. 39; Charles, *Jubilees*, 176.

26 Levine writes that Beon should probably be Meon, part of the city name Beth-baal-meon (e.g., Josh 13:17) or just Baal-meon (Num 32:38) (*Numbers 21–36*, 485). According to Ceriani, the Latin manuscript has the letters . . . . *et seo* at this point; possibly the last three letters he read should be *beo* (for *beon*; see VanderKam, *Jubilees* 2:186–87). Ethiopic Numbers 32:3 spells the name *bēyān*.

27 The adjective in the expression "they were very wicked" is *ḍawwāgān*, a form of the word used to describe the spirits or demons during and after the time of Noah (10:5, 11; 11:4) and for the residents of Sodom and neighboring cities whom the Lord destroyed (16:5). Werman, who notes that Deuteronomy supplies no reason why the Lord destroyed the Rephaim, thinks that the author of Jubilees, who identifies them with the ancient giants who were guilty of eating and shedding blood, thus clarifies the covenant and oath between Laban and Jacob: the festival they mark is the sign of keeping the prohibitions regarding blood (*Jubilees*, 404). Her interpretation reads too much into the word "giants" in a context where the writer fails to mention blood.

28 Deuteronomy 2:21 declares about the Rephaim: "But the LORD destroyed them from before the Ammonites so that they could dispossess them and settle in their place." One could suspect confusion between *Ammonite* and *Amorite* here, but the Amorites too lived in the region the Rephaim had once inhabited. The Ethiopic and Latin versions of Jub 29:11 differ: in the Ethiopic copies, the Amorites live in the place of the Rephaim, but in the Latin translation the Lord makes the Amorites live in their place.

29 There were Amorites east and west of the Jordan; at times the gentilic refers to ancient residents of Canaan in general (see BDB, 57).

her the victory; see also Amos 2:9: "Yet I destroyed the Amorite before them, / whose height was like the height of cedars, / and who was as strong as oaks; I destroyed his fruit above, / and his roots beneath." The Amorites came to represent a terrible level of evil. The writer of 1 Kgs 21:26 says about King Ahab of Israel: "He acted most abominably in going after idols, as the Amorites had done, whom the Lord drove out before the Israelites." King Manasseh of Judah, who acted more wickedly than the Amorites, became the cause for the destruction of Jerusalem and Judah (2 Kgs 21:11-15). Eventually the Transjordanian tribes Reuben, Gad, and the half-tribe of Manasseh took over the land of Sihon and Og, and the Manassites specifically went to Gilead, where they dispossessed the Amorites, according to Num 32:33-42.

The final sentence of the unit in 29:9-11 is: "Today there is no nation that has matched [lit., completed] all their sins. They no longer have length of life on the earth." The meaning is probably that the exceedingly wicked Amorites no longer existed because they had been decimated in the past.[30] The author used a similar expression in 4:4 when speaking about the length of life on the earth that God had allowed to Cain after he killed his brother.[31] The Amorites, pre-Israelite inhabitants of Canaan and the Transjordan, practically disappear from the HB in the later history of Israel/Judah (Ezra 9:1 is an exception, but the list of Canaanite nations there is a traditional one). Jubilees is therefore able to speak about their disappearance, their lack of continuation on the earth. Yet the writer limits their former territory to the area of Gilead, the place under discussion in the previous section.

Excursus: Jubilees 29:9-11 and Hasmonean History

Charles, who believed that several passages in Jubilees not found in Genesis were based on or in some sense reflected battles during early Hasmonean times, wrote about the five royal cities in 29:10: "It is difficult to understand why our author mentions these seats of the Rephaim unless it is that certain victories of the Maccabees over the Amorites who succeeded the Rephaim are connected with them."[32] In support of his hypothesis, he was able to adduce the following references:

Karnaim (he seems to include Ashtaroth with it). Judas the Maccabee conquered it (1 Macc 5:43-44; 2 Macc 12:21, 26). About this evidence Charles commented: "The Rephaim were succeeded by the Amorites (v. 11), and of these our text grimly declares that 'they have no longer length of life on the earth.' Judas must have nearly annihilated them." He neglected to say that 1 and 2 Maccabees say nothing about Amorites here and certainly not about Rephaim.

Edrei. There is no reference to a Hasmonean conquest of the city, but Charles drew his own conclusion from the silence of the historical record: "Although this town is not mentioned as attacked by Judas in his eastern campaign (1 Macc. v) the fact that it is mentioned here [i.e., in Jubilees] as having been destroyed makes it probable that it did suffer at the hands of Judas."

Beon. He identified the city with βαιαν: "Beon and its inhabitants were utterly destroyed by Judas (1 Macc. v. 4, 5; Joseph. *Ant*. xii.8, 1)."

There are several objections that should be made to Charles's attempt to read the list of cities against a Maccabean background. First, the cities are the royal centers of the Rephaim, according to Jubilees, not of the Amorites; second, the text says nothing about the destruction of these cities; third, the sources for Judas's campaign east of the Jordan do not refer to either Rephaim or Amorites. More importantly, Charles appears to have misunderstood the purpose served by Jub 29:9-11: the author is providing a justification for Israel's conquest of the extraordinarily wicked Amorites as they advanced to take back the land misnamed Canaan.[33] To make the point, he assembled givens from the HB and added to them words to the effect that Amorites in his time no longer occupied the territory of Gilead that had received its name when Jacob and Laban made an agreement there.

---

30 Cf. Hanneken, *Subversion*, 113.
31 For a similar expression—length of days—see, e.g., Deut 30:20; Ps 21:5 (Eng. 4).
32 Charles, *Jubilees*, 176. All citations in this excursus are from this page (cf. also p. lxiii).
33 VanderKam, *Textual*, 239–40; *Book of Jubilees*, 66. See also Endres, *Biblical Interpretation*, 113. In Jub 34:1-9 Jacob and his sons defeat and kill seven Amorite kings and subject the surviving population to tribute.

12-20 Jacob Meets Esau and Cares for Isaac and Rebekah

At the close of the story about their encounter in Gilead, Genesis says, "Early in the morning Laban rose up, and kissed his grandchildren and his daughters and blessed them; then he departed and returned home" (31:55 [Heb. 32:1]). The passage shows that Laban left promptly after the agreement (the next morning) but only after first showing his feelings for his family by kissing and blessing them. Laban is, therefore, the first person to bless the sons of Jacob.

■ **12** In Jubilees all of this takes a different form: "Jacob sent Laban away." From this it sounds as if Jacob is the one in charge, the one giving orders, and the reader learns nothing about any farewell tenderness on Laban's part. Genesis rests content with saying Laban went home; Jubilees specifies that he went to Mesopotamia, the land of the easterners (see Gen 28:2; 29:1; Jub 27:10, 12; 28:1). Genesis 32:1 (Heb. 32:2) has Jacob simply resuming his journey, but the writer of Jubilees says he returned to Gilead—a difficult thing to do since he was already in Gilead. Possibly the meaning is that he traveled to another part of the large area of Gilead.[34] From now on a great distance will separate Laban and Jacob, and Laban will never again see his daughters and grandchildren.

■ **13** The writer marks the end of the Laban-Gilead unit (and the aside in vv. 9-11) with the movements of the two men in v. 12, and in v. 13 he resumes the story of Jacob's journey that the episode had interrupted. He crossed the Jabbok, a stream that flows in the area discussed in vv. 9-11 and whose name appears in some of the passages about it. For instance, Num 21:24 reports that the Israelites defeated Sihon "and took possession of his land from the Arnon to the Jabbok," and Josh 12:2 defines his territory as extending "from Aroer, which is on the edge of the Wadi Arnon, and from the middle of the valley as far as the river Jabbok, the boundary of the Ammonites, that is, half of Gilead."

Verse 13 contains one of the writer's most remarkable abbreviations of a section in Genesis—the one verse stands where Gen 32:3 (Heb. 4)–33:17 relates the long story about the preparations for and the meeting with Esau.[35] In fact, he simply alludes to it (he cites a clause from Gen 32:23 and one from 33:16) and otherwise skips it. It is not difficult to imagine why he would not reproduce the elaborate account.[36] The Jacob of this section is frightened, timid, fearful of Esau, and Esau, though powerful, proves magnanimous and brotherly. Jacob repeatedly calls Esau "my lord" (32:4, 5, 18; 33:8, 13, 14 [twice], 15) and refers to himself as Esau's servant (32:4, 18, 20; 33:5, 14); moreover, he is terribly afraid of his brother and seemingly powerless to oppose him. When he hears about Esau's approach with four hundred men, "Then Jacob was greatly afraid and distressed" (Gen 32:7). He prays, "Deliver me, please, from the hand of my brother, from the hand of Esau, for I am afraid of him; he may come and kill us all, the mothers and the children" (32:11). He tried to appease his brother with presents, and he shielded himself from Esau by sending group after group of his traveling band in front of him.[37] If this were not bad enough, when he met Esau he bowed seven times as he approached (33:3), and he even declared after Esau refused his lavish gifts: "for truly to see your face is like seeing the face of God[38]—since you have received me with such favor" (33:10). Esau, for his

---

34   The reading "returned" is present in both the Ethiopic and Latin versions so that it goes back at least to the Greek translation of Jubilees that underlies them. It is possible that forms of שוב and ישב were confused. If so, the original text would have said that Jacob remained in Gilead (he apparently leaves the area several months later because he does not cross the Jabbok until 9/11 according to v. 13). Werman proposes that Jacob here accompanies Laban part of the way on his journey, just as Abraham had done in sending off the men who visited him (Gen 18:16) (*Jubilees*, 404). Perhaps that is the meaning, but in Gen 18:16 the text is explicit that Abraham accompanied them, whereas v. 12 here does not say that.

35   The writer also omits the short passage in Gen 32:1-2 (Heb. 2-3) about the angels of God meeting Jacob and the name Mahanaim that he gave to the place.

36   See Werman, "Attitude," 191–92.

37   See Hamilton, *Genesis 18–50*, 325–26, where he emphasizes Jacob's lack of bravery and the implications of the frequent uses of the word "face" in the context.

38   Jacob had just seen the face of God at Peniel (32:30).

part, embraces and kisses his brother when they meet (33:4) and seems to find the elaborate approach of Jacob and his party puzzling (see 33:8). At first he refuses any presents but he finally accepts them at Jacob's insistence (33:9-11) and offers to accompany his brother's caravan to provide protection (33:12, 15). None of this harmonizes at all well with the impression left the last time the two were together in Jubilees. On that occasion a pathetic Esau was plotting his brother's death, and a resourceful Jacob said, "I am not afraid. If he wishes to kill me, I will kill him" (27:4).

The large unit in Genesis also includes the story about Jacob wrestling with a man all night long (32:22-32). The wrestling match was one thing, but the consequences were another. The man said to Jacob, "You shall no longer be called Jacob, but Israel, for you have striven with God and with humans, and have prevailed" (32:28).[39] Jacob himself named the place Peniel, "For I have seen God face to face, and yet my life is preserved" (33:30). These lines offer some challenging theology, and Jacob at the end is left with a damaged hip. Verse 32, one of the rare places in Genesis where an Israelite law, or at least a practice, is instituted, the author of Jubilees omits along with the story. He must have been very eager to bypass the whole narrative if he was willing to sacrifice an opportunity to emphasize a law in Genesis.[40]

All that the author of Jubilees writes in v. 13 is that Jacob crossed the Jabbok, his brother Esau met him on that very day, they were reconciled, and they went their own ways. The date for the river crossing involves a curious text-critical issue, as the Ethiopic and Latin readings are quite different:

Ethiopic: wa-taʿadawa ʾiyābok-hā ba-tāseʿ warḫ ʾama ʿašuru wa-ʾamiru, "and he crossed the Jabbok in the ninth month on the eleventh"

Latin: et in mense nono transivit iacob undecim filii ipsius, "and in the ninth month Jacob crossed, his eleven sons

The Latin places the reference to the ninth month before, and the Ethiopic, after the verb. In the Ethiopic *he* crosses the Jabbok, while in Latin *Jacob* crosses (what he crosses the text does not say). There is probably confusion between *iaboc* and *iacob*, with the Latin copy having the wrong reading (*iacob*). Where the Ethiopic then gives a specific date—the eleventh—in the ninth month, the Latin reads "his eleven sons," which makes no sense in the context and lacks a conjunction before it.[41] In all likelihood, the Latin version contains a misunderstanding in which the number eleven in the date was taken to refer to Jacob's eleven sons. The passage in Genesis that underlies the text is in 32:23, where Jacob rises at night, takes his two wives, his two maids, and his eleven children (he actually has twelve, including his daughter Dinah), and crosses the ford of the Jabbok. So the base text in Genesis does mention eleven children, but it is unlikely Jubilees did as the verb for crossing is singular in both versions. In Jubilees' calendar, 9/11 has no particular significance (apart from placing the event some six months after the agreement with Laban)—a fact that favors it as the better reading.[42]

The meeting with Esau took place "on the same day" as the fording of the stream.[43] The writer inferred the timing from the indicators in Genesis 32–33. After Jacob and his family crossed the Jabbok at night, Jacob had the wrestling match with the man, one that lasted all that night (32:24, 26). When the sun rose he passed Penuel (32:31; cf. vv. 24, 26), and around that time Jacob saw Esau approaching (33:1). Hence, the arrival of Esau was on the very day of the river crossing, since in Jubilees the day begins in the evening.[44]

---

39 As Kugel comments, "disturbing enough was the idea that a man could wrestle with a divine being at all—not to speak of defeating him!" (*Walk through* Jubilees, 142; "Jubilees," 394).

40 Endres thinks that, while the Peniel story serves in part to legitimate Jacob, "such affirmation was apparently deemed unnecessary by this author" (*Biblical Interpretation*, 114).

41 Rönsch, however, preferred the Latin text (*Biblical Interpretation*, 114). See also VanderKam, *Jubilees* 2:187.

42 Kugel makes the plausible suggestion that the date was selected to show that the reconciliation that occurred on it was similarly unimportant (*Walk through* Jubilees, 141; "Jubilees," 393).

43 Latin lacks an equivalent of "same" (actually, a demonstrative "this" is used in Ethiopic) but seems not to differ in meaning. See Gen 33:16.

44 The example should, therefore, be added to Baumgarten's list of passages demonstrating the point ("Beginning of the Day," 355–60).

Esau arrives, and the two brothers are reconciled. The Ethiopic verb is *takwānanu* ("they were reconciled"),[45] and the Latin has *propitiatus* ("he was reconciled/appeased"—the participle modifies Esau), possibly followed by *ei* (see the textual note).[46] The Ethiopic reading expresses a mutual effort, but the Latin seems to say that Esau was the one who had to be reconciled to Jacob or to be appeased—perhaps because of what Jacob had done to him in snatching the blessing from him. Whichever reading is preferred (the Ethiopic one fits better in Jubilees), the result is that the two brothers were now at peace with each other.

Verse 13 takes up words from Gen 33:16 regarding Esau's departure for his home territory of Seir. This is where Genesis uses the expression "[on] that day" to mark when Esau and his men departed from Jacob and his company. Genesis then records a trip for Jacob and also a clear indication of his plan to settle on the east side of the Jordan: "But Jacob journeyed to Succoth, and built himself a house, and made booths for his cattle; therefore the place is called Succoth" (33:17).[47] In contrast, the writer of Jubilees attributes no travel to him and certainly no intent to settle down where he was: "Jacob lived in tents." He is clearly working with the term סכות, which, in different spellings, occurs three times in Gen 33:17. Neither the Ethiopic nor the Latin version transliterates the term, implying that it was not understood as a place-name in this instance. It conveniently also suggests that Jacob has not yet reached his destination; his present place is only a temporary dwelling (note Jub 19:13 // Gen 25:27, where Jacob lives in tents, unlike his brother).

■ **14** Verse 14 shows why Jacob lived in tents. At some point in the next year (the text puts it in 2136, but the revised chronology would have it in 2137) Jacob crossed another river, this time the Jordan, so that he finally arrived back in the part of the promised land to which his ancestors had migrated. It was appropriate that the writer date an event of such importance, although Genesis does not even mention Jacob's crossing the Jordan. After noting his residence in Succoth in 33:17, it next reports "Jacob came safely to the city of Shechem which is in the land of Canaan on his way from Paddan-aram" (33:18; cf. Jub 30:1). To go from Succoth to Shechem, he had to ford the Jordan, but the narrator said nothing about it. It was on the west side of the Jordan that he settled and pastured his flocks. The writer of Jubilees circumscribes the exact area in which Jacob decided to live and shepherd his animals by four geographical designations (Latin omits two of them by parablepsis). The two cities Bethshan (Judg 1:27; 1 Sam 31:10; 1 Kgs 4:12) and Dothan (Gen 37:17) are familiar enough: both lie in the territory west of the Jordan, a little to the north of the latitude where Succoth is in the Transjordan. Bethshan is north of Dothan. The other two names pose problems.

Ethiopic: Sea of Faḥaḥat *(or* Fešḥat*)/Latin: Sea of Salt*. The Sea of Salt should be the Dead Sea, but the Ethiopic name is peculiar (there is no known word or name Fahahat). Most of the manuscripts read *fešḥat* (or *fešḥet*), a word for heap, mound, pillar—a form of the word for *mound* that appears in v. 8. The word *sea* is supported by both versions, so it should be secure, although there are not many seas in the general area demarcated by the place-names later in the verse. The Latin name designates one of them, and the only other is the Sea of Galilee. The Dead Sea is too far south for this list, or so it seems, and a decent case can be made for seeing the Sea of Galilee behind the Ethiopic readings. It will be recalled that in the Jacob–Laban story the place received its name Gilead from the mound (גל) of witness/testimony erected there. If the Hebrew text of Jubilees read ים גליל, it is possible that the Jacob–Laban story led the writer of Jubilees to see in the name Sea of Galilee another place named after the heap or mound in Gilead—an area that borders on the Sea of Galilee.[48]

---

45 See Dillmann, *Lexicon*, 855: *sibi invicem reconciliari*. As he indicates, the same verb appears in Eth. Matt 5:24 ("first be reconciled to your brother") and Luke 23:12 ("Herod and Pilate became friends with each other").

46 Charles preferred the (slightly emended) Latin reading and translated: "he was reconciled to him" (*Jubilees*, 177).

47 Skinner, *Genesis*, 415: "showing that he contemplated a lengthy sojourn."

48 VanderKam, *Jubilees* 2:188. A difficulty, though not an insuperable one, for finding the Sea of Galilee behind the Sea of Fahahat or *fešḥat* is that *Sea of Galilee* as a name for the lake is not attested until the Gospel of Mark (1:16; 7:31; see the parallels in Matt 4:18; 15:29; John 6:1). The place-name Galilee

Forest[49] *of Akrabbim.* The practice of the translators has been to take the name as referring to the area that in the HB is termed the ascent of Akrabbim that lies in the extreme south of Judah, southwest of the Dead Sea (Num 34:4; Josh 15:3; Judg 1:36). Neither the Ethiopic nor the Latin version uses a word for "ascent" before Akrabbim. A problem with the location, if the ascent of Akrabbim is meant, is that Jub 29:14 would be claiming that Jacob pastured his flocks over a vast area—almost all of the territory west of the Jordan. Another difficulty is that he would have been tending them in places near where his father and mother lived, though he does not visit them. The narratives around the passage leave one thinking that Jacob and his sons traversed a small area in the center of the land, not one encompassing the far south.[50] This raises the possibility that the Akrabbim in question is not the ascent of Akrabbim in the HB but the territory called Akrabattene in Greek sources. Josephus knows of a district with this name and lying to the north of Jerusalem; it is a name derived from the city Akrabatta that lies within it (*Bell.* 2.234-35, 568, 652; 3.48; 4.504, 511, 551).[51] If it is the place in question, and the identification of the sea as the Sea of Galilee is correct, then a more reasonable and well-ordered list of place-names would result. Reading from north to south, there would be the Sea of Galilee, Bethshan, Dothan, and Akrabattene.

The final six verses of the chapter center on Jacob's renewed relations with his parents whom he still does not visit in person though he had been away for more than twenty years and now resided west of the Jordan. The writer follows the narrative in Genesis, where Jacob likewise does not return to the family home until some time—how long is not said—after his arrival in the Cisjordan. In Genesis, he is back in the land in 33:18; he soon purchases the area near Shechem where he pitched his tent (33:19-20); and the Shechem-Dinah episode ensues (chap. 34). Subsequent to this Jacob goes back to Bethel (35:1-15), Benjamin is born and Rachel dies (35:16-21), and Reuben sleeps with Bilhah (35:22). Finally, in 35:27-29 Jacob visits his father Isaac in Hebron and is there for his death and burial. Genesis furnishes no information about any contact between Jacob and his parents in the period between his leaving Haran and the death of Isaac, just as it supplies none for the years he was with Laban. Jacob does not seem to be a dutiful son in the Genesis narrative.

■ **15-16** Jubilees inserts a section that puts Jacob in a better light. True, he did not visit his parents during the time in question, but he took very good care of Isaac and Rebekah from a distance, unlike Esau, who exploited them. To his father and mother Jacob sent the products a herder of animals would be likely to have. The first terms in the list are general ones: clothing along with what was needed for nourishment. The only item that would not come from the animals in a flock is "dates from the valley." These would have grown naturally; nothing in the list suggests that Jacob had settled down to till the land. All of these goods came from Jacob's vast possessions, and he made them available to Isaac and also to Rebekah, whose name comes after that of Isaac.

The text provides some extra detail about when Jacob sent the supplies. It does not say that he made a one-time donation to his parents; on the contrary, Jacob transmitted the clothing and food to them four times per year.[52] In this section the author sets forth the most extensive

---

is, of course, attested in the HB (e.g., Josh 20:7; Isa 8:23).

49 The Latin text has *aggruum* (the two instances of "g" are uncertain). Rönsch (*Jubiläen*, 50, 139) proposed to read *acervum* ("a heap"), and Charles (*Ethiopic Version*, 107 n. 11 to Latin and n. 48 to Ethiopic) *arborem* ("tree"). Neither seems helpful. On the issue, see VanderKam, *Jubilees* 2:188.

50 This makes better sense of the text than does Endres's proposal that the writer is trying to impress the readers with Jacob's wealth and consequent ability to help his parents (*Biblical Interpretation*, 115).

51 The Ethiopic manuscripts spell the word '*aqrābēt* or '*aqrābit* (Lat. *acrabin*). Dillmann proposed the talmudic name עקרבת (see Jastrow, 1109: "a place at a day's distance north of Jerusalem") and referred to ἀκραβατηνη in Josephus ("Jubiläen," 72 n. 46; cf. Rönsch, *Jubiläen*, 139); Mendels has suggested the same (*Land of Israel*, 72 n. 37). Ethiopic Jubilees calls it the "forest of Akrabbim," and Josephus writes about how well wooded the area was (*Bell.* 3.49).

52 It seems clear enough that the intent of the writer is to say that Jacob sent clothing, food, and drink to both parents and did so four times per year. It

statement about the annual seasons since his words in chap. 6. Rönsch maintained that he would have wished to present Jacob as following the calendar of seasons instituted by Noah in 6:23-31, where the first days of the first, fourth, seventh, and tenth months are "written down and ordained at the four divisions of the year as an eternal testimony" (6:23). The writer of Jubilees marks out four points at which Jacob sends provisions by repeating the preposition "between" in each case:
1. between the seasons of the months (*gizēyātihomu la-'awrāḥ/temporum mensuum*)
2. between plowing and harvest (*ḥaris* and *'aḍid/area*[53] *usque ad messem autumnun*)
3. between autumn and rain(y season) (*ṣadāy* and *zenām/ autumni pluvias*)
4. between winter and spring (*keramt* and *ḥagāy/ pluviarum eius*[54])

Rönsch saw in these descriptions references to 4/1, 7/1, 10/1, and 1/1.[55] His identifications are probably correct, with only the first of them being worded in a peculiar fashion. He hypothesized that the writer designated it as "between the seasons of the months" because this day lies at the midway point between the two months that begin the sacred and agricultural years (1/1 and 1/7). The other dates fit reasonably well with the descriptions supplied here.

In each season of the year Jacob sent large gifts to his parents at the tower (*māḥfad/barin*) of Abraham (note, both Isaac and Rebekah are there in v. 20). Genesis depicts Abraham as living in Hebron or its environs (13:18; 14:13; 18:1; 23:2, 19; 25:9), just as Jubilees does (e.g., 13:10; 16:10; 19:1; 22:3), but it never refers to his place of residence as a tower.[56] The term *tower* makes one think that his residence was an impressively strong and high structure from which one could keep an eye on the surrounding territory for any approaching danger.[57]

■ 17 In the case of Isaac, as the sequel explains, such a place served a protective function. The last time the narrators of Genesis and Jubilees had mentioned Isaac and Rebekah, they lived in Beersheba = the well of the oath (Gen 28:10 // Jub 27:19). But Gen 35:27-29 indicates that at his death Isaac was "at Mamre, or Kiriath-arba (that is, Hebron), where Abraham and Isaac had resided as aliens." Consequently, an explanation was needed for the move to Hebron. It turns out that they had left Beersheba and relocated to Hebron to put some distance between themselves and Esau. It should be remembered that Esau in Genesis is the son who remained with his elderly parents when Jacob left them for more than two decades. He appears to be the more loyal of the two, and Jacob adds to his guilt by not coming to his parents and visiting them after he returns from Haran. Jubilees counters that impression vigorously. Esau remained with his parents, but, says the writer, he was anything but a solicitous son. He had disrespected, even abused his parents in two ways.

■ 18 Verse 18 recounts first the marriage of Esau with Ishmael's daughter Mahalath, an event recorded in Gen

---

does not say that he sent these items to his father but sent other goods to his mother and did the latter four times in a year. Endres seems to think two kinds of gifts, ones for Isaac and ones for Rebekah, are under consideration and writes about the products in v. 15: "For a nomad, this seems a tenable list; in contrast, the gifts for Rebekah at the 'four times' of the year (29:16) suggest the agricultural festivals of a more sedentary people. Such a mixing of types appears natural for this author; in his era such distinctions were neither noticeable nor significant" (*Biblical Interpretation*, 115; Kugel also finds two kinds of gifts here [*Walk through Jubilees*, 142; "Jubilees," 394]). Since the text leaves the impression that the same gifts were sent to both parents at the four times, it is not at all evident how the conclusion follows.

53 The word *area* should be *arationis*; see the textual note.

54 The word should be *veris*, and something has dropped from the text before it. See the textual note.

55 Rönsch, *Jubiläen*, 140.

56 Jubilees 31:5 says that Isaac and Rebekah were living "in the house of his father Abraham." The next verse refers to the tower and tower gates of the place. According to 36:20, Jacob will also live there. Kugel is likely not correct in saying that the place is probably the "Tower of Eder" mentioned in Gen 35:21, as it was not located at Hebron (*Walk through Jubilees*, 142; "Jubilees," 394).

57 The Latin word *barin* suggests that the Greek version of Jubilees read βαρις; in the LXX it normally renders either ארמון (e.g., 2 Chr 36:19) or בירה (e.g., Ezra 6:2). See Rönsch, *Jubiläen*, 140-41. Cf. also Jub 38:1-8 for Jacob's tower in a military context.

28:6-9, immediately after the scene in which Jacob left for Haran. Genesis presents the third marriage of Esau as an attempt by him to please his parents. He heard the instructions of Isaac that Jacob was not to marry a Canaanite woman but rather someone from the family. He too tried to obey: he married Mahalath who, as a daughter of Ishmael, was part of Abraham's family and thus seemingly a suitable marriage partner. But he took her "to be his wife in addition to the wives he had" (Gen 28:9) so that he did not divorce the offending women. The reader does not hear more concerning the marriage or the feelings of Isaac and Rebekah about it, but the author of Jubilees puts it in a negative context.[58] He does not assess the propriety of the union but leaves no doubt that Esau continued to live with his Canaanite wives. With no basis in Genesis, he charges that Esau "gathered all his father's flocks and his wives" and moved to Mount Seir. The writer knew that when Jacob was returning from Paddan-aram and met Esau, Esau was "in the land of Seir, the country of Edom" (Gen 32:3; see also 33:14, 16). Genesis explains several chapters later (and following the notice about Isaac's death in 35:27-29) why Esau moved to Mount Seir. After listing the children born to his three wives in Canaan (the wives have different names here than in Gen 26:34; 28:9), the narrator says:

> Then Esau took his wives, his sons, his daughters, and all the members of his household, his cattle, all his livestock, and all the property he had acquired in the land of Canaan; and he moved to a land some distance from his brother Jacob. For their possessions were too great for them to live together; the land where they were staying could not support them because of their livestock. So Esau settled in the hill country of Seir; Esau is Edom (Gen 36:6-8).

Like Abram and Lot in Genesis 13, Jacob and Esau were too wealthy for one place to sustain their own (not their father's) flocks. Jubilees, however, transfers the move to an earlier time—a time when Esau should have been caring for Isaac and Rebekah. It seems to have happened soon after Jacob left home because immediately after noting the marriage with Mahalath the writer mentions the move to Seir. Most importantly, Esau "had left his father Isaac alone at the well of the oath." So, contrary to impressions, Esau had not been a dutiful son. He had stolen his father's wealth and abandoned him in order to live elsewhere in his own territory with all his wives and his father's herds.[59] He was a thief and showed his parents no honor.[60]

■ 19-20 Consequently, if a reader of Genesis wanted to know why Isaac had moved from Beersheba to Hebron, Jubilees had an answer: it was to protect himself from his son Esau who had stolen his property and abandoned him. He had moved to a fortified location so that he would be safe from him. It was to this changed residence that Jacob sent clothing and food at the four times of the year.[61] In complete contrast to Esau, who deprived them of all they had, Jacob supplied them with everything they needed. He was the son who honored his parents by supporting them in their old age. It is small wonder that they blessed him wholeheartedly for all he was doing on their behalf. That is, they blessed him with the same enthusiasm manifested earlier by Abraham (22:27-28) and Rebekah (19:31; 25:2; cf. 25:19, 23). Isaac now joins that illustrious duo in blessing Jacob.[62]

---

58 Cf. Werman, "Attitude," 191; Endres, *Biblical Interpretation*, 116.
59 Possibly the author was puzzled about Esau's possessions. How would he have acquired the animals and other property if Jacob was his father's heir? He thus inferred that he had such large herds because he stole his father's many animals (Gen 26:14 says Isaac had so many flocks and herds along with a great household that the Philistines envied him; see Jub 24:14). Apart from Gen 36:6-9, there is no reference to Esau's owning herds and flocks of animals.
60 As Caquot remarks, Esau is "un parangon d'impiété" ("Jubilés," 749 n. 18).
61 The phrase rendered "from time to time" could, in the context, mean "from season to season." Latin, however, reads a more general expression: *per singula tempora*, "at each time." The point appears to be that he sent their necessities at the right time, not missing any occasion.
62 Cf. Werman, *Jubilees*, 405.

Dinah, Shechem, Exogamy, and Levi the Priest

30

1/ During the first year of the sixth week[a] [2143] he went up safely to Salem,[b] which is on the east side of Shechem, in the fourth month. 2/ There Jacob's daughter Dinah was taken by force to the house[a] of Shechem, the son of Hamor the Hivite, the ruler[b] of the land. He lay with her and defiled her.[c] Now she was a small girl,[d] twelve years of age. 3/ He begged[a] her father[b] and her brothers[c] that she become his wife. Jacob and his sons were angry with the Shechemites because they had defiled their sister Dinah. They spoke deceptively with them, acted in a crafty way toward them, and deceived them.[d] 4/ Simeon and Levi entered Shechem unexpectedly[a] and effected a punishment on all[b] the Shechemites. They killed every man[c] whom they found in it. They left absolutely no one in it. They killed everyone in a painful way[d] because they had violated their sister Dinah.

5/ Nothing like this[a] is to be done[b] anymore from now on[c]—to defile[d] an Israelite woman. For the punishment had been decreed[e] against them in heaven that they were to annihilate[f] all the Shechemites[g] with the sword,[h] since they had done something shameful in Israel. 6/ The Lord handed them over to Jacob's sons for them to uproot[a] them with the sword and to effect punishment[b] against them and so that there should not again be something like this within[c] Israel—defiling an Israelite virgin.[d] 7/ If there is a man in[a] Israel who wishes to give his daughter or his sister[b] to any foreigner, he is to die. He is to be stoned because he has done something[c] shameful within Israel. The woman is to be burned because she has defiled the reputation of[d] her father's house; she is to be uprooted from Israel. 8/ No prostitute[a] or impurity[b] is to be found within Israel throughout all the time of the earth's history, for Israel is holy to the Lord. Any man who has defiled it[c] is to die; he is to be[d] stoned.[e] 9/ For this is the way it has been ordained and written[a] on the heavenly tablets regarding any descendant of Israel who[b] defiles (it):[c] "He is to die; he is to be stoned." 10/ This law has no temporal end. There is no remission[a] or any[b] forgiveness; but rather the man who has defiled his daughter within all of[c] Israel is to be eradicated[d] because he has given one of his descendants[e] to Molech[f] and has sinned[g] by defiling[h] it.

11/ Now you, Moses, order the Israelites and testify to them that they are not to give any of their daughters to foreigners and that they are not to marry[a] any foreign[b] women because it is despicable before the Lord. 12/ For this reason I have written[a] for you in the words[b] of the law everything that the Shechemites did[c] to Dinah and how Jacob's sons said: "We will not give[d] our daughter to a man who has a foreskin because for us[e] that would be a disgraceful thing." 13/ It is a disgraceful thing[a] for the Israelites who give or take (in marriage) one of the foreign women because it is too impure and despicable for[b] Israel. 14/ Israel will not become clean from this impurity while it has one of the foreign women[a] or if anyone has given one of his daughters to any foreign man.[b] 15/ For it is blow upon blow and curse upon curse. Every punishment, blow,[a] and curse[b] will come.[c] If[d] one does this or shuts his eyes[e] to those who do impure things and who defile[f] the Lord's sanctuary and to those who profane his holy name, then the entire nation will be condemned together because of all this impurity and this contamination.[g] 16/ There will be no favoritism nor partiality;[a] there will be no receiving from him of fruit,[b] sacrifices, offerings, fat,[c] or the aroma of a pleasing fragrance so that he should accept it. (So) is any man or woman[d] in Israel to be who defiles his sanctuary.[e] 17/ For this reason I have ordered you: "Proclaim this testimony to Israel: 'See[a] how it turned out for the Shechemites[b] and their children—how they were handed over to Jacob's two[c] sons. They killed them in a painful way.[d] It was a just act for them and was recorded as a just act for them.' 18/ Levi's descendants were chosen[a] for the priesthood and as Levites to serve before the Lord[b] as we (do) for all time. Levi and his sons will be blessed forever because he was eager[c] to carry out justice, punishment,[d] and revenge on all who rise[e] against Israel. 19/ So blessing and justice before the God of all are entered[a] for him as a testimony[b] on the heavenly tablets. 20/ We ourselves remember[a] the justice that the man performed[b] during his lifetime[c] at[d] all times of the year.[e] As far as 1000 generations[f] will they enter (it).[g] It will come to him and his family[h] after him. He has been recorded on the heavenly tablets as a friend and[i] a just man."[j]

21/ I have written this entire message for you and have ordered you[a] to tell the Israelites not to sin or transgress the statutes or violate the covenant that was established for them so that they should perform it[b] and be recorded as friends.[c] 22/ But if they transgress[a] and behave in any impure ways,[b] they will be recorded on the heavenly tablets as enemies.[c] They will be erased from the book of the living[d] and will be recorded in the book of those who will be destroyed[e] and[f] with those who will be uprooted from the earth. 23/ On the day that Jacob's sons killed (the people of) Shechem, a written notice was entered in heaven for them (to the effect) that they had carried out[a] what was right, justice, and revenge against the sinners.[b] It was recorded[c] as a blessing.

24/ They led[a] their sister Dinah from Shechem's house and captured everything[b] that was in Shechem—their sheep, cattle,[c] and donkeys; all their property and all their flocks[d]—and brought everything to their father Jacob. 25/ He spoke with them about the fact that[a] they had killed[b] (the people of) a city because he was afraid[c] of the people who were living in the land[d]—of the Canaanites and the Perizzites. 26/ A fear of the Lord was in all the cities which were around Shechem. They did not set out to pursue[a] Jacob's sons[b] because terror had fallen on them.

Text Notes

1a week] pr. "this" 12 (Lat. also lacks "this").

b Salem] *Salām* 25; Lat. *salem*.

2a house] Lat. *dom* should be *domum* (Rönsch, *Jubiläen*, 52; Charles, *Ethiopic Version*, 109).

b ruler] + "of the city and" 12 (Lat. also lacks this plus).

c He lay with her and defiled her] Lat. "He defiled her since he slept with her." The two versions have the same verbs but in reverse order, and where Latin joins them with *quia* Eth. reads a conjunction. The Eth. version is closer to Gen 34:2 (see Charles, *Ethiopic Version*, 109 n. 12 to Lat.). The words "with her" in both versions of Jubilees agree with the reading of the LXX tradition, where MT has the unusual אֹתָהּ.

d girl] The word *nestit* means small; several mss. add *walatt* ("daughter"), so that the word is used twice ("small daughter, a daughter of 12 years," 25 35 39 42 44 47 48). Lat. uses only *adulescens* here.

3a begged] Lat. + *illam* ("begged her/for her"); mss. 12 35 38 39 42 47 48 58 63 have *-ā* at the end of the word; it could be the fem. third person sg. suffix, as in Lat., or it could be a lengthened vowel with a guttural consonant (see VanderKam, *Jubilees* 2:191). It seems unnecessary with the wording of the sequel in Eth. but makes sense in Lat.

b her father] "his father" 9 12 39 47; + "that she be given to him as a wife" 9 12 17 20 25 35 39 42 44 47 48 58 63.

Lat. lacks these oddly positioned words (between "her father" and "her brothers"); they are likely an addition. Ms. 38 also lacks the expression though it adds "to give" after "her brothers."

c her brothers] "his brothers" 12 28 58; "her fathers" 20; + "to give" 38; "all her brothers" Lat.

d acted in a crafty way toward them, and deceived them] "Simeon and Levi mocked them in a crafty way" Lat. For "deceived them," 38 reads *'at fe'ewwomu*, "they extinguished/destroyed them." Cf. the next phrase in Lat.

4a Simeon and Levi entered Shechem unexpectedly (see Gen 34:25)] "Simeon and Levi resolved to destroy them" Lat.

b all] om. Lat.

c They killed every man] om. Lat.; om. "every" 17.

d in a painful way] "in judgment" Lat. (cf. Gen 34:25).

5a like this] There is a gap in the Lat. ms.; it could be filled with the equivalent of Eth. (*et ita*; Rönsch, *Jubiläen*, 52; Charles, *Ethiopic Version*, 111).

b be done] "will be" (reading difficult) Lat.; "you are to do" 21 39 42 47 (cf. 58); "you will do" 48.

c from now on] + "and to eternity" 38.

d to defile] "that Israelite women should be defiled" Lat.

e had been decreed] "is to be punishment" Lat. (*iudicum* should be *iudicatum*; Rönsch, *Jubiläen*, 52). So Lat. has no equivalent for "decreed."

f to annihilate] *pungent* ("to fight") Lat. Perhaps

one should read *expungent* ("to blot out/erase"; VanderKam, *Jubilees* 2:192), although Werman (*Jubilees*, 408 n. 13) seems to attribute the readings in Eth. and Lat. to different interpretations of an original ישמדו.

g all the Shechemites] "against Shechem" Lat. Rönsch (*Jubiläen*, 54) and Charles (*Ethiopic Version*, 111) proposed reading *univers]um* after "Shechem." In that case, the only difference would be "the men of" before "Shechem." Ms. 21 om. "the men of."

h with the sword] om. 20 21 25 35 38 63 (21 38 add it later, and 20 25 35 add it later still); *in gladio* Lat.

6a to uproot (lit., "in order that they might uproot")] Eth. and Lat. agree on the plural "they," but MSS. 21 25 39ᵗ 42 47 have "he" as the subject.

b to effect punishment] "to be a punishment" Lat.

c like this within] Lat. is difficult to read (*erit in . . .*) so that one cannot tell whether it had an equivalent for these words. Cf. VanderKam, *Jubilees* 1:193.

d defiling an Israelite virgin] Lat. has a passive verb with *virgo* as subject: "that an Israelite virgin should be defiled" (see v. 5).

7a in] "of" (lit., "from") Lat. Note *'em-* ("from") in MS. 21.

b or his sister] om. 38ᵗ; *sororem suam* Lat. Several MSS. add after "or": "in it who gave to him his daughter or" 9 17 39 42 47 48 63. The longer reading is manifestly secondary (see the commentary), but the shorter reading (lacking "or his sister") is the result of haplography ("his daughter . . . his sister"). The odds of MS. 38ᵗ preserving a more original reading against all other Eth. copies and Lat. are astronomical despite Segal's claim to the contrary (*Jubilees*, 236-38).

c done something] + "sinful and" 25 35 39 42 44 (it lacks "and") 47 48 58. The words *ḫaṭi'ata wa-* ("sinful and") should not have been included in the translation in VanderKam, *Jubilees* 2:193.

d the reputation of] om. Lat. (perhaps *nomen* was omitted with *domum*).

8a prostitute] *fornicaria* Lat. The two could be synonyms. For *zammā* Leslau gives "harlot, prostitute, adulteress" (*Comparative Dictionary*, 640).

b impurity] *abominatio* Lat. Again the words may be synonyms, since *rekus* ("unclean, polluted, impure, defiled, profane, abominable" [Leslau, *Comparative Dictionary*, 470]) can be another spelling of the noun *rekws*, "filth, impurity, defilement, uncleanness, pollution, abomination" (ibid.).

c it] Lat. reads *eum*, whereas Eth. lacks a pronoun.

d he is to be] In Eth. a conjunction precedes the clause; it is lacking in Lat. and in 9 12 21 38. See the next note.

e is to be stoned] Lat. lacks the verb (it couples "with stones" with "is to die"). Rönsch (*Jubiläen*, 143) thought the Lat. preferable, since it reflected מות באבנים, but Charles (*Ethiopic Version*, 111 n. 4 to Lat.) preferred the Eth., comparing v. 9.

9a ordained and written] "written and ordained" Lat.

b who] Lat. reads *quoniam*, possibly reflecting ultimately כי, which can introduce direct quotations. It seems too early in the sentence, as the citation probably begins with "He is to die"; see VanderKam, *Jubilees* 2:194.

c (it)] MSS. 17 20 (cf. 12) read a masc. suffix, and MS. 58 a fem. suffix; Lat. and the other Eth. MSS. lack one.

10a remission] Lat. adds *illi* ("to it").

b any] "no" 12 20 25 35 39 44 48 58; the other Eth. MSS. and Lat. have "any" (*kwello/omnis*).

c all of (Israel)] om. 63; Lat. *hominis* is probably an error for *omnis* (Rönsch, *Jubiläen*, 54; Charles, *Ethiopic Version*, 111 n. 5).

d is to be eradicated] "will be eradicated" 12 38 39 42 47 48 58; "they are to be eradicated" 17; "they will eradicate" 63.

e one of his descendants (lit., "of/from his seed")] "one of all his descendants" Lat.

f to Molech] *aliengena* ("to a foreigner") Lat.; the form should be *aliengenae* (Rönsch, *Jubiläen*, 54; Charles, *Ethiopic Version*, 111 n. 6 to Lat.). Lat. offers an interpretation of Lev 18:21; 20:2, according to which giving to Molech was understood to mean giving to a non-Israelite/non-Jew (so Rönsch, *Jubiläen*, 143). Charles (*Ethiopic Version*, 110 n. 22) wanted to change Eth. to agree with Lat., but later corrected his proposal (*Jubilees*, 181, where he refers to T. Levi 18:21; *m. Sanh.* 9:6; *b. Sanh.* 82a; *b. Meg.* 25a; see VanderKam, *Jubilees* 2:194.

g has sinned] Lat. has a pl. verb *egerunt*, possibly resulting from misreading εποιησεν as εποιησαν.

h defiling] For Lat. *intaminare*, see Rönsch, *Jubiläen*, 143.

11a marry] + "for his sons" Lat. MS. 12 alone adds a word here: *lālihomu*. Charles "corrected" the form to *laweludomu* = the Lat. reading (*Ethiopic Version*, 110 n. 23). Littmann wondered whether the Lat. translator read υιοις instead of αυτοις ("Jubiläen," 91 n. b). The word *lālihomu* is a form of *lala* and occurs only with suffixes = *ipsi* = "they themselves were not to marry" (see Charles, *Jubilees*, 181). But it is highly unlikely that MS. 12 alone has preserved the text properly, and *filiis suis* may have been added to yield a smooth text.

b foreign (lit., "of the nations")] Lat. reads *eorum* rather than "of the nations" and adds "for/to their sons."

12a I have written] "write" (impv.) 12 17.

b the words] "all the words" 39 42 47 48.

c everything that the Shechemites did] "the full account of what the Shechemites did" Lat. The only additional word, *sermones*, may have entered the text through the attraction of *sermonibus* just two words earlier.

d We will not give] "We are not about to give" 9 38 (cf. MS. 21).

e for us] om. 20 25 35; *nobis* Lat.

13a disgraceful thing] *obprobrium* Lat. Mss. 12 20 21 25 35 om. the word, but this omission is due to parablepsis from *we'etu* (v. 12) . . . *we'etu* that includes "for us" at the end of v. 12.

b too . . . for] Eth. has either one noun and one adjective or two adjectives (impurity/impure and despicable), while Lat. has two nouns. The versions differ about the preposition before "Israel." Ethiopic MSS. have *'em-* ("from"), *la-* ("for"; 21 38 39 42 47 48 58), or nothing (9ᵗ 12 17 33 63); Lat. has *in*. The word *'em-* has stronger backing and favors a comparative understanding: too impure . . . for Israel. Lat. also reads "all" before Israel.

14a foreign women (lit., "the daughters of the nations")] "the sons of the nations" 21; "the nations" Lat.

b or if anyone (om. Lat.; "anyone who" 9 12 17 21 39 42 44 47 48) has given one of his daughters to (any foreign) man] The Lat. has "and we will not become clean (from?) one of our daughters." The sizable differences have elicited varied proposals. If one aligns the two they look this way:

wa-'emma-bo   'em-'awālēdihu za-wahabo la-be'si 'em kwellu 'aḥzāb

et non mundabimus de filiabus nostris   omnibus gentibus

Charles (*Ethiopic Version*, 111 n. 11) and Rönsch (*Jubiläen*, 54, 143–44) proposed changes that would retain the first-person statement of Lat.

Rönsch: *et non mun*dabitur *si* dabimus: the similar letters led to the omission of *-dabitur si*.

Charles: *non mundabimus* should be *si dabimus*. See VanderKam, *Jubilees* 2:195–96.

But the first-person forms are unexpected here and possibly influenced by the ones in v. 12. Also, *mundabimus* may have been affected by *mundabitur* earlier in the verse. The Lat. and Eth. would look much alike if *mundabimus* were changed from *-dabimus* to *-dabitur*. *Filiabus nostris* may represent an adjustment to the mistaken verb. Perhaps the lack of an equivalent of *la-besi 'em-* can be explained by positing a haplography *homini de omnibus*.

15a punishment, blow] The Eth. copies, except for 17, read a conjunction between the two nouns; Lat. lacks a conjunction and places the second noun in the gen. case ("punishments of blows").

b curse] "curse of curses" Lat.

c will come] "will bring" 38; + "upon him" 63 (cf. *super illum* Lat., and see the next note).

d If] om. 21 63; *super illum* Lat., but the Lat. seems defective here—something seems to be missing before the next verb "he does this," which is otherwise left with nothing introducing it. Rönsch (*Jubiläen*, 54) inserted *qui* before *faciet*, and Charles (*Ethiopic Version*, 113) added *si* (= [*si*] *faciet*) = Eth. Perhaps *lā'lēhu wa-la-'emma* led to haplography.

e shuts his eyes] "disregards and looks away" Lat. The text reflects Lev 20:4 ואם העלם יעלימו עם הארץ את עיניהם. The Eth. retains the wording more nearly, while the Lat. seems to paraphrase (see VanderKam, *Jubilees* 2:196).

f those who do . . . defile] Eth. reads pl. forms, Lat. sg. ones. Cf. Lev 20:3. Both Rönsch (*Jubiläen*, 56) and Charles (*Ethiopic Version*, 113 nn. 2-3 to Lat.) changed Lat. to pl. forms (*facientes* and [*qui*] *polluerit*).

g and this contamination] Lat. lacks the expression. The word "this" it places in the gen. case (= "of this one") with the preceding noun.

16a nor partiality] Lat. lacks the phrase (lit., "to favor the face"), probably skipping from *personam et non* to the following *personam et non*. This explanation is simpler than the suggestion of Charles (*Ethiopic Version*, 112 n. 13), Littmann ("Jubiläen," 91 n. d), and Berger (*Jubiläen*, 473 n. a to v. 16) that the phrase is dittographic.

b from him of fruit] om. "of fruit" 25 44. Lat. lacks the phrase.

c fat] Lat. lacks (in a series of nouns preceded by a conjunction).

d or woman] om. 17.

e his sanctuary] om. "his" 17. Lat. has a pl. *sanctificationes*.

17a See] om. 12; pr. "and" 21 Lat.

b for the Shechemites] "for Shechem" Eth.; "for the Shechemites" Lat. The difference is carried through in the sequel (where Eth. has lit., "and her children," but Lat. reads "and their children") and in the next verb.

c two] Lat. *hominum* is a mistake for *duorum* (Rönsch, *Jubiläen*, 56; Charles, *Ethiopic Version*, 113 n. 5 to Lat.).

d in a painful way] Lat. "in judgment." See 30:4 for the same terms in the two versions.

18a chosen] "appointed" Lat.

b the Lord] + "at his house" 12.

c he was eager] 42 47 read pl. forms ("they were"), probably of *qan'a*, though they use *'ayn* as the third radical.

d to carry out justice, punishment] Lat. reads slightly differently: "truth to carry out justice/judgment."

e rise] "were placed" Lat. Eth. may presuppose קם (so Goldmann and Hartom), while Lat. may reflect a passive form of שם.

19a are entered] Lit. "they cause to go up" in the sense of a passive (Lat. *refertur*). Mss. 20 38 58 read the simple stem: "they go up," and MS. 63 has "they are to cause to go up."

b for him as a testimony] om. 21, though it later (after "heavenly tablets") adds "as a testimony."

20a We (pr. "to/for all" 21) ourselves remember] "it (justice) will be remembered" Lat. Charles (*Ethiopic Version*, 113 nn. 8-9 to Lat.) changed *memorabitur* to *memoramur*, but the easier emendation to *memorabimur* would make it agree with the Ethiopic form (VanderKam, *Jubilees* 2:198).

b performed] "will perform" Lat. (*faciet* should be *fecit*; Charles, *Ethiopic Version*, 113 n. 9 to Lat.).

c   his lifetime] Lat. agrees, but 9 12 17 39 63 add a conjunction after "his lifetime."
d   at] Lat. agrees, but 42 47 48 read a conjunction.
e   of the year] Lat. agrees, but 17 reads "forever," which Berger accepts; however, *la-ʿālam* is probably a mistake for *la-ʿāmat*.
f   generations] "years" Lat. (its *annos* could have been influenced by *anni* just a few words before; VanderKam, *Jubilees* 2:198).
g   will they enter (it)] Eth. *yāʾarregu* is the normal verb for placing something on the heavenly tablets. Lat. *offeretur* is unexpected (see *refertur* in v. 19); Charles (*Ethiopic Version*, 113 n. 11 to Lat.) understandably emended to *referetur*.
h   his family] "his seed/descendants" Lat. Eth. *tewleddu* is perhaps not the expected term here, but it can mean, besides "generation, family," "offspring," so it may be correct. In that case the Lat. reading may mistakenly give the expected but nonoriginal word with "after him." Segal (*Jubilees*, 294) thinks the passage draws on Deut 7:9, where one reads ". . . the faithful God who maintains covenant loyalty with those who love him and keep his commandments, to a thousand generations [דור]." If so, "his generations" may be the correct rendering here (so Werman, *Jubilees*, 409 n. 21 [referencing Segal]: ולדורותיו).
i   friend and] Lat. lacks the conjunction. Mss. 25 35 39 47 have "his friend and."
j   a just man] *iustus* Lat. Most Eth. copies have "justice," but a few read an adjectival form with Lat.
21a   (ordered) you] Lat. lacks "you."
b   (perform) it] The fem. sg. suffix seems correct (referring to *kidāna/testamentum*), but Lat. has *ea* (pl.), which may refer back to *praecepta*.
c   friends] om. 25; "friends of God" Lat. (see 19:9 and v. 22 below).
22a   transgress] + *testamentum* Lat.—as a clarification of what is not to be transgressed. In the context it is unnecessary.
b   impure ways] If Lat. *abominationem* were changed to the gen. pl. (*abominationum*), it would agree with Eth.
c   they will be recorded on the heavenly tablets as enemies] Lat. appears to understand either "ways" or "abominations" as being recorded on the heavenly tablets—an unlikely reading in the context. See VanderKam, *Jubilees* 2:199.
d   the living] Lat. "life" = ms. 12. The same Hebrew consonants (חיים) underlie both readings.
e   those who will be destroyed] *perditionum* ("destructions") Lat.—possibly a mistake for a pl. ptc. as in Eth.
f   and (with those)] Lat. and ms. 20 lack the conjunction.
23a   they had carried out] "they should carry out/that they might carry out" 9 17 21 38 63. Lat. *facientes* ("doers"; that is, they were ones who do/carry out). 17 58 add "to them."
b   against the sinners] "on them" (*in ipsis*) Lat.
c   It was recorded] A strong case exists for reading "they were recorded" = Lat. and mss. 17 20 39 42 44 47 48 58. See VanderKam, *Jubilees* 2:199–200. Werman (*Jubilees*, 409 n. 25) prefers the pl. form.
24a   They led] "He led" 46 48; "He led him" 42; *eiecerunt* Lat.
b   everything] Lat. uses a pl. (*universa quae erant*), but the meaning is the same.
c   cattle (= their cattle)] Lat. uses a possessive only after the second, fourth, and fifth of the items plundered; Eth. places a suffix on all five forms.
d   flocks] "land" Lat. Rönsch (*Jubiläen*, 58, 145) and Charles (*Ethiopic Version*, 115 n. 3 to Lat.) emended *terram* to *armentam* to make it agree with the Eth. reading.
25a   about the fact that] "why" Lat. The two may be alternative renderings of an original על אשר, understood in the tradition behind Eth. as δια το + inf., and in the one behind Lat. as δια τι. See VanderKam, *Jubilees* 2:200.
b   killed] "destroyed" Lat. In VanderKam, *Jubilees* 2:200 it is suggested that the two verbs Jacob uses in Gen 34:30 regarding what he feared the inhabitants of the land would do to him—הכה and שמד—may lie behind the two readings. Werman (*Jubilees*, 409 n. 26) accepts the Latin reading because it forms a closure with vv. 5-6 (in both of which she uses forms of שמד) and alludes to Gen 34:30.
c   he was afraid (= Lat.)] "they were afraid" 21 39 42 47 48; + "Jacob" 35.
d   the land] "its (fem.) land" 20 25.
26a   set out to pursue] "pursue . . . to harm" Lat. The versions of Gen 35:5 read as Lat. does ("pursue" without "set out/rise up"), but "to harm him" is found in no version of the verse.
b   Jacob's sons] "Jacob" Lat. The Eth. reading agrees with MT SP LXX OL Gen 35:5; Syr. Gen 35:5, like Lat., lacks "sons" here but uses "and his sons" after Jacob's name. Using the name "Jacob" aligns Jubilees with MT SP Syr.; the LXX tradition reads "Israel."

Commentary

Jubilees 30 is related to Genesis 34, the story about the rape of Jacob and Leah's daughter Dinah by Shechem, the son of Hamor the Hivite prince of the region. After the act of violence, Shechem wished to marry Dinah, and he and his father attempted to make nuptial arrangements with Jacob and his sons. As they talked, Hamor proposed that there should be a wider association: "Make marriages with us; give your daughters to us, and take our daughters for yourselves. You shall live with us; and the land shall be open to you; live and trade in it, and get property in it" (Gen 34:9-10). The sons of Jacob (not Jacob himself) decided on a deceptive plan to punish the inhabitants of Shechem: they insisted that before any marriages could take place the men of Shechem had to undergo circumcision. If they complied, "[t]hen we will give our daughters to you, and we will take your daughters for ourselves, and we will live among you and become one people" (34:16). The men of the area agreed, went through with the operation, and, while suffering from the effects, met their deaths when Jacob's sons Simeon and Levi, full brothers of Dinah, attacked the town, killed all its male inhabitants, and liberated their sister (vv. 18-26). Their other brothers plundered the city and took the women and children as captives (vv. 27-29). The savage retaliation produced tension between Jacob and the two ringleaders, Simeon and Levi. "Then Jacob said to Simeon and Levi, 'You have brought trouble on me by making me odious to the inhabitants of the land, the Canaanites and the Perizzites; my numbers are few, and if they gather themselves against me and attack me, I shall be destroyed, both I and my household.' But they said, 'Should our sister be treated like a whore?'" (Gen 34:30-31).

Werman captures the situation by speaking of three viewpoints present in Genesis 34, no one of which is unambiguously adopted or rejected by the narrator.

1. That of Shechem and Hamor: there was no crime, and the social difference between the nomadic family and city dwellers could be overcome through intermarriage
2. That of Jacob: Dinah did suffer defilement, but the cultic problem could be handled through circumcision
3. That of the brothers: intermarriage with natives of the land is abhorrent.[1]

The story takes on a decidedly different cast in Jubilees. The writer swiftly tells what for him were the essentials of the episode (primarily in vv. 1-4,[2] 24-26) but dwells particularly on the horrors of defiling an Israelite woman and marriage with non-Israelites. The rape of Dinah becomes a springboard for a vigorous attack on exogamy,[3] and the revenge exacted by Simeon and Levi becomes a reason for Levi's appointment to the priesthood. Parts of Genesis 34 must have alarmed the author of Jubilees—Jacob and his sons discussing intermarriage with residents of Canaan and contemplating becoming one people with them. The incident illustrated how immediate the danger of marrying with the peoples of Canaan was and how narrowly it had been averted. As a result, he devoted most of chap. 30 to the meaning of the event for Israel and enunciated an absolute ban on such contact and marriages. The impurity involved in the practice would defile the sanctuary and render sacrificial worship unacceptable (30:14-16); the guilty parties would be deleted from the book of the living and uprooted from the earth—punishments normally reserved for the nations (v. 22). Much of the chapter understandably takes the form of the angel directly addressing Moses and in this way underscoring the centrality of the issue for the author. With his turn to Moses, the angel could speak about Israel in a nonanachronistic way, though he was dealing with the patriarchal period.[4]

---

1   Werman, "*Jubilees* 30: Building a Paradigm for the Ban on Intermarriage," *HTR* 90 (1997) 1-22, here 3-6 (cf. *Jubilees*, 406-7). She adds that Jubilees adopts the position of the brothers (pp. 6-9), but it is not so evident that it accepts the position of any but Simeon and Levi. Cf. Frevel, "Intermarriage," 231-33, 240-42; he repeats Werman's three viewpoints but for the third focuses on Simeon and Levi.

2   As Endres points out, the first four verses of chap. 30 abbreviate thirty-two verses in Genesis (*Biblical Interpretation*, 121).

3   Werman writes that the author's purpose was "to provide a paradigmatic example for the law prohibiting intermarriage with Gentiles" ("*Jubilees* 30," 9; cf. *Jubilees*, 407).

4   Whether the author emphasized the ban on

The major divisions in the chapter are these:
1-4   The story about the rape of Dinah and the response by Jacob and his sons
5-10 There is to be no such defilement in Israel
11-16 No marriage with non-Israelites
17-23 The example of Simeon and Levi
24-26 The end of the episode.

The full text of Jubilees 30 is extant in the Ethiopic copies and, for the first time, a chapter in its entirety survives on the Latin manuscript. No other evidence from the versions is available.

1-4 The Story about the Rape of Dinah and the Response by Jacob and His Sons

The section swiftly summarizes the story, leaving out many of the details present in Genesis 34.

■ **1** The writer dates the event, obviously a significant one, to the fourth month of the year 2143, seven years after Jacob had forded the Jordan River (or six years later, in the revised chronology). The span of time between the two events is remarkable because Jacob, after more than twenty-five years away from home, still does not visit his parents.[5] Genesis gives no chronological indicators for the time between his return and when he saw Isaac,[6] but by indicating how long the period was the writer of Jubilees seems to exacerbate the problem, despite the fact that in the previous chapter he has Jacob sending provisions to his parents on a regular basis (29:15-20).

Jubilees introduces the story by citing a line from Gen 33:18: "Jacob came safely to the city of Shechem." The translation in the NRSV offers an interpretation of a potentially confusing text. The MT and SP read:

MT: ויבא יעקב שלם עיר שכם
SP: ויבא יעקב שלום עיר שכם

The problem faced by readers was how to interpret שלם: is it the word for "peace," as SP spells it, or is it the name of a city—Salem?[7] The author of Jubilees with the LXX tradition took it as a place-name, but he also parsed it as meaning "safely/peacefully," so that Jacob went up to Salem in safety/peace. That left the problem of how the reference to "the city of Shechem" could be worked into the sentence. The writer uniquely adds that Salem was east of Shechem, thus indicating they were two different places. In doing so he was probably interpreting the last clause in Gen 33:18: "and he camped before [את פני] the city."[8] As the story begins, there is no conflict with the

---

exogamy because it was a major problem at his time has been debated by scholars. Schwarz (*Identität*, 108–11; it is specifically directed against marriage with Samaritans) and Endres (*Biblical Interpretation*, 133–39) think it was, but others (e.g., Himmelfarb, "Levi, Phinehas, and the Problem of Intermarriage at the Time of the Maccabean Revolt," *JSQ* 6 [1999] 1–24) deny the claim (intermarriage is not mentioned frequently in literature from the relevant period) and prefer to explain the emphasis on a thematic basis. The safest conclusion is that we have too little evidence to determine the frequency of such mixed marriages at the time of the author. Reinhard Pummer ("The *Book of Jubilees* and the Samaritans," *Eglise et théologie* 10 [1979] 147–78, here 167–77) has shown that Jubilees 30 does not concern the Samaritans.

5   Werman suggests that Jubilees, by its dating, removes the impression in Genesis (33:18) that the family of Jacob were newcomers in the area ("*Jubilees* 30," 8–9; *Jubilees*, 410).

6   The story in Genesis 34 does, however, presuppose that Jacob's children, who were frail and unable to travel very fast in 33:13-14 (though he was making an excuse to get rid of Esau when he described them in this way), are now much older (see Westermann, *Genesis 12–36*, 537). According to the chronology in Jubilees, Simeon (born 2124 [28:13]) would be nineteen and Levi (born 2127 [28:14]) sixteen years when they slaughtered the men of the city.

7   For the two interpretations, see Westermann, *Genesis 12–36*, 528 (a place-name); Hamilton, *Genesis 18–50*, 350 (in peace, thus coming near to fulfilling his request in Gen 28:21: "so that I come again to my father's house in peace"). Cf. Charles, *Jubilees*, 178–79; Endres, *Biblical Interpretation*, 122. If it is the name of a city, it is different from the Salem of Melchizedek (Gen 14:18), which was understood to be Jerusalem (see Ps 76:3 [Eng. 2]; 1QapGen xxii:13; the targums to Gen 14:18). Jubilees does not adopt the view expressed in *Gen. Rab.* 79:5 that שלם means "whole, complete, healthy, intact"—that is, whole in body, in his children, in wealth, and in learning.

8   Skinner, *Genesis*, 416: "in the vale to the E[ast] of it."

inhabitants of Shechem, since Jacob and his family live in a neighboring but separate place.

■ **2** Verse 2 takes up some of the words in Gen 34:2; that is, the writer leaves out Gen 34:1: "Now Dinah the daughter of Leah, whom she had borne to Jacob, went out to visit the women of the region." Whatever that sentence suggests about Dinah's activity, it was understood in a negative sense in the discussion about it in, for example, *Gen. Rab.* 80:1-5, where the proverb in Ezek 16:44 ("Like mother, like daughter") is applied to her. As Leah went out (the same verb as the one used for Dinah) to meet Jacob after purchasing the right to sleep with him (the mandrake incident in Gen 30:16), so Dinah went out looking like a prostitute.[9] The verse suggests a surprising freedom on her part, one that had terrible consequences; for that reason, the writer of Jubilees left it out of his retelling. But omission of v. 1 is also consistent with his view that no one in Jacob's family established relations with the local inhabitants.[10] Her actions and motivation in Gen 34:1 had nothing to do with the message he wanted to extract from the story. He reports simply that she was taken forcibly—without saying under what circumstances or why—and was raped in Shechem's house. Genesis does not disclose where the crime occurred, but later Dinah's brothers lead her out of the house of Shechem (34:26), so one could assume it happened there.

It is noteworthy that the writer of Jubilees reproduces the gentilic for Hamor: he is a Hivite,[11] and the Hivites are among the seven nations with whom Deut 7:2-6 forbids Israel to have any positive relations. Among the commands of that passage are these:

> when the LORD your God gives them over to you and you defeat them, then you must utterly destroy them. Make no covenant with them and show them no mercy. Do not intermarry with them, giving your daughters to their sons or taking their daughters for your sons, for that would turn away your children from following me, to serve other gods. Then the anger of the LORD would be kindled against you, and he would destroy you quickly. (Deut 7:2-4)

The passage lies behind a number of points made in Jubilees 30 and forbids precisely what Hamor and Shechem propose and Jacob and his eleven sons apparently consider in Genesis 34. It also contains authorization for the response of Simeon and Levi ("you must utterly destroy them").[12]

The author alters two words in Gen 34:2 and appends an important note. First, where Gen 34:2 says "he took [ויקח] her," Jub 30:2 reads literally "they seized Dinah violently [*masaṭewwā la-dinā/rapuerunt dinam*]." It not only supplies the notion of force with this verb but also makes the subject plural—the first of several indications in the chapter that the people of Shechem, not just Shechem himself, were complicit in the crime. The plural subject was not a free invention of the author of

---

9   For early interpretations of her actions, see Kugel, *Traditions*, 415.

10 See Halpern-Amaru, *Empowerment*, 127-28. Frevel ("Intermarriage," 239-40) regards the role of Dinah as one of the "significant modifications" in Jubilees relative to Genesis 34. Apart from omitting v. 1, however, the writer does not modify her part; she is as passive in Jubilees as in Genesis 34.

11 The text reads with the Hebrew versions of Gen 34:2 against the LXX tradition, which has *Horite*. Presumably, the fact that Hamor and thus his son Shechem were Hivites, not Israelites, explained why the law of Deut 22:28-29, despite its similarities with the situation in Genesis 34 (e.g., the young woman in both is a נערה, the deed in both is termed ענה), did not apply in the case of Shechem and Dinah. Those verses say, "If a man meets a virgin who is not engaged, and seizes her and lies with her, and they are caught in the act, the man who lay with her shall give fifty shekels of silver to the young woman's father, and she shall become his wife. Because he violated her he shall not be permitted to divorce her as long as he lives." See Kugel, "The Story of Dinah in the *Testament of Levi*," *HTR* 85 (1992) 1-34, here 15-17. Frevel thinks the passage was not applicable to this case in Jubilees ("Intermarriage," 241).

12 In this sense and because it mentions Hivites, it is reasonable to think that Deut 7:2-4 influenced the writer in Jubilees 30, contrary to Shaye J. D. Cohen, who rightly observes his more explicit use of Lev 18:21 (see below) but says he did not attach his rhetoric to Deut 7:3-4 ("From the Bible to the Talmud: The Prohibition of Intermarriage," *HAR* 7 [1983] 23-39, here 24-26).

Jubilees because Gen 34:27 also places the guilt on the entire population: "And the other sons of Jacob came upon the slain, and plundered the city, because their sister had been defiled [lit., they had defiled their sister]."[13] Second, where Genesis says literally "and he humbled her [ויענה],"[14] the writer charges that Shechem "defiled her ['arkwasā/polluit eam]." The verb is significant for the case the author will make. It reflects the one used in Gen 34:5, 13, 27 (טמא), but he pre-poses it to announce up front the nature of what Shechem did. The rape involved not merely humbling her but defiling her. Finally, he augments the enormity of the offense by writing that Dinah was just twelve years of age at the time. The age given is, naturally, meant to emphasize what an outrageous act Shechem committed,[15] and a similarly young age for Dinah is documented in other texts. Charles noted that T. Levi 12:5 gives Levi's age as eighteen when he killed Shechem;[16] that number is present also in ALD 12:6. In Jubilees, Levi is seven years older than Dinah, so on this reckoning (i.e., if one combines numbers from the two texts) she would have been eleven years old at the time. According to Jub 28:23, however, she and her brother Zebulun were born in 2134. If the year of the Shechem story is 2143, as v. 1 states, she would have been only nine years.[17] Whatever her age, Shechem did not violate a woman; he defiled a child. It may also be relevant that, in the rabbinic understanding, the age of majority for a girl is twelve.[18]

Excursus: Dinah's Age

Michael Segal, after the publication of his book, added the discrepancy about Dinah's age (was she twelve [Jub 30:2] or was she nine [Jub 28:23 with 30:1]?) to the examples in support of his thesis about the chronological framework of Jubilees—an editor imposed it on previously existing rewritten stories, some of which already contained within them independent chronological data.[19] In this instance, the rewritten version of Genesis 34 contains the age of twelve (v. 2), while the chronological framework entails the age of nine. That Dinah was twelve in the rewritten story serves a halakhic purpose: Segal believes that the definition of a נערה as a girl twelve years and a day, though it is literarily attested only at a much later time, prevailed when Jubilees was written. As a result, he thinks that Dinah's age relates the story to the law of rape in Deut 22:28-29, where the woman is termed a נערה as Dinah is in Gen 34:3, 12 (see the references to Deut 22:28-29 in the commentary on v. 2 above).

---

13 The inference from 34:27, especially from the reading טמאו, is often noted by commentators and is attested in some of the ancient versions (SP Syr and the LXX tradition read a plural form of the verb in v. 13 against the singular in MT). See Kugel, "Story of Dinah," 20; Yeshayahu Maori, *The Peshitta Version of the Pentateuch and Early Jewish Exegesis* (Jerusalem: Magnes, 1995) 67–68; Kugel, *Traditions*, 409–10, 422–23. Endres deals with the corporate guilt of the Shechemites for the rape of Dinah in *Biblical Interpretation*, 124–25.

14 The NRSV translates the word with the preceding verb as "lay with her by force." Jubilees incorporates the idea of force into the first verb—he took her forcibly (with the LXX tradition and other ancient versions, the text assumes that אתה after וישכב is the preposition "with" plus suffix; the MT points it as the direct object marker with suffix). In the commentary below on vv. 17-23, the influence of Exodus 32 on the passage is explained; in that chapter the Israelites are said to be "revelers" (as the NRSV renders the word); the Hebrew verb is ענה (v. 18).

15 Endres, *Biblical Interpretation*, 127.

16 Charles, *Jubilees*, 179. Demetrius the Chronographer gives Dinah's age as sixteen years and four months, Simeon's as twenty-one years and four months, and Levi's as twenty years and six months (frg. 2, 9). They had reached these ages after living near Hamor for ten years.

17 See Endres, *Biblical Interpretation*, 125–27. In *Gen. Rab.* 80:10 the brothers are thirteen years each.

18 Finkelstein ("Rabbinic Halaka," 55 n. 69) points to *m. Nid.* 5:6 (he writes 5:9) and comments that this is implied by Dinah's age in Jub 30:2. "This seems to be based on the use of the word נערה, which is always interpreted by the Rabbis to refer to a girl for the first six months after reaching her twelfth birthday." Cf. Kugel, *Walk through Jubilees*, 142–43; Michael Segal, "The Story of Shechem and Dinah in *Jubilees* 30," *Meghillot* 8 (2010) 227–41, here 230–31; "Rewriting the Story of Dinah and Shechem: The Literary Development of Jubilees 30," in Nora David, Armin Lange, Kristin De Troyer, and Shani Tzoref, eds., *The Hebrew Bible in Light of the Dead Sea Scrolls* (FRLANT 239; Göttingen: Vandenhoeck & Ruprecht, 2012) 337–56, here 342–43; Loader, *Sexuality*, 166.

19 Segal, "Shechem and Dinah," 230–31; "Rewriting," 343–44.

Several comments are in order. First, as Segal and others have noted, there is indeed a contradiction regarding the age of Dinah: the age of twelve is explicit in v. 2 (the Latin and Ethiopic texts agree about her age), and the age of nine is easily inferred by comparing the date in 30:1 with her birthdate in 28:23. Second, however, the conflict joins a series of other ones in the book (see, for example, the discussion of the chronological problems in the account of Abra[ha]m's life). No explanation seems to account for many of the chronological discrepancies other than errors in copying or even authorial mistakes in calculation within a complicated chronological system. Would it not be simpler to explain the twelve/nine discrepancy for Dinah in the same way? Third, it is not very helpful to bring the law in Deut 22:28-29 into the discussion because it probably deals with a case involving an Israelite man and an Israelite woman, not like the situation in the Dinah–Shechem incident, where a Hivite man was the violator. Fourth, the solution adopted by Segal does not account for the textual situation adequately. The date in Jub 30:1 (the event occurred in the year 2143 of the world) is, of course, unmotivated by any given in the text of Genesis, and it is not required by any other factor in Jubilees. Hence, by recording this number in v. 1 and the age for Dinah in v. 2, someone rendered the text inconsistent, but who? Why would a chronological editor be more liable to tolerate the divergence in ages or be less likely to notice it than the author of the entire book? Must one presuppose that editors are more careless about such details than authors? Why? The different ages for Dinah are consistent with Segal's thesis but open to other avenues of explanation.

■ 3 Jubilees 30:3 summarizes several verses in Genesis 34 but omits more of them. Genesis 34:3 presents a more positive picture of Shechem than his treatment of Dinah would indicate: "And his soul was drawn to Dinah daughter of Jacob; he loved the girl, and spoke tenderly to her."[20] These feelings motivated a request to his father to "[g]et this girl to be my wife" (v. 4). Hamor's negotiations with Jacob and his sons occupy Gen 34:6-10. The writer of Jubilees bypasses all of these verses with their suggestion of greater unity between the Shechemites and the family of Jacob. He has nothing good to say about the young man and jumps immediately to his discussion with Jacob and his sons (Gen 34:11-12) where he offers to pay any price they name, "only give me the girl to be my wife" (v. 12). This encounter he summarizes by saying Shechem begged them to give Dinah to him in marriage. The summary makes it unlikely that Deut 22:28-29, which stipulates a payment of fifty shekels of silver, somehow lurks behind the rewritten version, since the writer removes any hint of payment from the Genesis version.

The second sentence in v. 3 introduces a change relative to Genesis 34. In Gen 34:13 the ones who answer Shechem are Jacob's sons, not Jacob. Jacob speaks with both Hamor and Shechem in Genesis, but his reactions are decidedly subdued compared with his sons. When he first heard about the rape, "his sons were with his cattle in the field, so Jacob held his peace until they came" (34:5). The brothers, when they heard about the outrage, "were indignant and very angry" (v. 7). They are the ones who replied to Shechem's offer to pay anything they asked for Dinah: "The sons of Jacob answered Shechem and his father Hamor deceitfully, because he had defiled their sister Dinah" (v. 13). Jubilees 30:3 includes the sons' two responses (from vv. 7 and 13) but makes both Jacob and the eleven the subject: "Jacob and his sons were angry with the Shechemites because they had defiled their sister Dinah." The surprisingly neutral Jacob of Genesis 34 becomes the deeply offended father of Jubilees 30, and all the Shechemites are now guilty of defiling Dinah, not just Shechem. Strangely, the writer did not modify the sentence to read just "Dinah" rather than "their sister Dinah," as the expression fits a speech by the brothers, not by Jacob and his sons. Both Jacob and the eleven are the ones who then speak deceitfully with the young man and the residents of the area—the guilty parties.[21]

The author of Jubilees transparently knew about the painful trick the sons of Jacob played on the men of the area—requiring that they be circumcised before the marriage could take place. Genesis characterizes their words as deceitful (במרמה, v. 13), but their ostensibly careless

---

20 This is the phrase used for the way in which Jacob spoke to Leah and Rachel in Jub 29:2.
21 Cf. Werman, "*Jubilees* 30," 7; *Jubilees*, 410.

approach to circumcision would have made the author of Jubilees uneasy:

> We cannot do this thing, to give our sister to one who is uncircumcised, for that would be a disgrace [חרפה] to us. Only on this condition will we consent to you: that you will become as we are and every male among you be circumcised. Then we will give our daughters to you, and we will take your daughters for ourselves, and we will live among you and become one people. But if you will not listen to us and be circumcised, then we will take our daughter[22] and be gone. (Gen 34:14-17)

Circumcision marked Israel off from the nations (see Jub 15:28-34), but it sounds as if the brothers, though the reader knows they are being deceptive, are willing to ignore that barrier and incorporate one of the forbidden peoples of Deuteronomy 7 into their fellowship. Nothing of the brothers' offer or of the Shechemites' agreement to circumcision (Gen 34:14-24) appears in Jubilees;[23] the writer glosses over it with the general words: "They [Jacob and his sons] spoke deceptively with them, acted in a crafty way[24] toward them, and deceived them." Jacob, no stranger to deceit in dealing with Isaac, Esau, and, to some extent, Laban, now deceives again as do his eleven sons.[25]

■ 4 The intervention of Simeon and Levi is the subject of v. 4 (despite Levi's greater reward in Jub 30:18-20, the writer retains Genesis's order with Simeon first). As Genesis 34 presents the matter, these two full brothers of Dinah exploited the inability of the local men to fight while they recovered from the painful surgery. They "took their swords and came against the city unawares, and killed all the males. They killed Hamor and his son Shechem with the sword, and took Dinah out of Shechem's house, and went away" (34:25-26).[26] The other nine brothers then take all survivors and property as booty from the conquest of the town (34:27-29). In Jubilees the account is much shorter and all of the action is attributed to Simeon and Levi.[27] Genesis 34:25 says they "came against the city unawares [בטח]," perhaps meaning

---

22 Use of this designation for Dinah could lead one to think Jacob was one of the speakers.

23 The change is, of course, often noted in the literature. See, e.g., Charles, *Jubilees*, 179. This is one of the major differences between the rewriting of Genesis 34 in Jubilees and in the Aramaic Levi Document, where the circumcision offer appears in 1:3. According to the story in the Testament of Levi, Levi urged Jacob and Reuben to tell Hamor's people not to be circumcised (6:3), although there is some uncertainty about whether the negative is to be read (for reading the negative here, see Kugel, "Story of Dinah," 6-12). But 6:6 indicates that circumcision took place, something that displeased and sickened Jacob and led to his cursing of Levi and Simeon. Levi recognized that he and Simeon had sinned in some way, but God had pronounced a sentence on Shechem (see 6:6-8). It is surprising that Josephus, who generally and briefly retells the story of Genesis 34, also omits circumcision from his account (see *Ant*. 1.339-40). Omission of circumcision from L.A.B. 8:7-8 is less surprising since the story is told so briefly.

24 Addition of "acted in a crafty way" could be a reflection of the idea, found in *Tgs. Neof.* and *Onq.* Gen 34:13, that מרמה is to be understood as "wisdom" (see Kugel, *Traditions*, 409). In the Latin translation of Jubilees, only Simeon and Levi "mocked them in a crafty way" (see T. Levi 7:3). The text of the Aramaic Levi Document is broken in the relevant line, but it appears to have indicated how the brothers spoke to the Shechemites. Greenfield, Stone, and Eshel do not suggest a restoration (*Aramaic Levi Document*, 56, 112), but Drawnel reads and restores: "and we said to them with [*wisdom and* under]standing" (*Aramaic Wisdom Text*, 106).

25 In the Latin translation, Jacob and his sons are angry with the Shechemites, but only "Simeon and Levi mocked them in a crafty way, and Simeon and Levi resolved to destroy them." The men of Shechem, of course, had their own agenda—they wanted to acquire the property of Jacob and his family (Gen 34:23).

26 Though a different verb appears in the two verses, in Gen 34:17 the brothers had threatened to take their sister (actually called "our daughter") and leave if the Shechemites did not agree to circumcision, but here in v. 26 they take her and leave despite the fact that their victims had undergone circumcision.

27 Werman misses this point, claiming that Jubilees makes no distinction between Simeon and Levi on the one hand and the brothers on the other in the pillaging of Shechem (also pointing to v. 24)

the people of the city were oblivious of the imminent attack, while in Ethiopic Jubilees *gebta*[28] expresses more the idea of surprise, that is, the two brothers surprised them.[29] Simeon and Levi are the ones who executed the people as a punishment (note the idea of punishment in Gen 34:27: the other nine brothers "plundered the city, because their sister had been defiled [lit., who/because they had defiled their sister]." Jubilees underscores their killing of all the males (and more) by repeating it—they killed every man and left absolutely no one alive.[30] The idea that annihilating the population of Shechem was meant as a punishment also figures a second time ("because they had violated [*gammanu*] their sister Dinah"),[31] but in this instance the author adds that they killed them "in a painful way." In Genesis 34 the only pain mentioned is the suffering the newly circumcised men endured ("On the third day, when they were still in pain [כאבים]," v. 25). Since Jubilees fails to mention the entire incident of the circumcision, the writer has switched the pain to the manner in which Simeon and Levi killed their victims—something deserved because of what all of them had done to Dinah.[32]

5-10 There Is to Be No Such Defilement in Israel

Once he has reported that the brothers decimated the population of Shechem (v. 4), the writer drops the narrative until v. 24, where he will pick it up with words from Gen 34:26. In the intervening verses (30:5-23), the wider meaning of the story, the grave lesson it contains, becomes the focal point.

■ **5** Jubilees 30:5 begins and ends with expressions drawn from Gen 34:7. The first statement—"Nothing like this is to be done anymore from now on" reflects the end of Gen 34:7, where, after mention of Shechem's act of having sex with Jacob's daughter, the text reads: "for such a thing ought not to be done."[33] In Jubilees, the Angel of the Presence declares that an act of this kind is never to happen again, and the book stipulates that the ruling applies to any Israelite woman.[34] The Ethiopic text words the forbidden act as "to defile an Israelite woman" where the Latin has "that Israelite women should be defiled," with the plural subject making it clearer that the Dinah incident contains a general

---

("*Jubilees* 30," 8; cf. *Jubilees*, 411). Jubilees explicitly attributes all the action to Simeon and Levi. Testament of Levi 6:4-5 agrees with the division of labors given in Genesis.

28 Leslau, *Concise Dictionary*, 167: "suddenly, unexpectedly" (his first two equivalents).

29 *Genesis Rabbah* 80:10 understands the word as pointing to the confidence the two brothers felt in attacking the city; they felt confident because of Jacob's strength. "Now Jacob had not desired that his sons should act so, but when his sons did perpetrate that deed he said: 'Shall I let my sons fall into the hands of the heathens?' What did he do? He took his sword and bow and stood at the entrance to Shechem and exclaimed, 'If the heathens come to attack my sons, I will fight them.'" This was taken to be the incident to which Jacob referred in Gen 48:22. Josephus (*Ant.* 1.340) says Simeon and Levi attacked during a feast when the Shechemites were in no condition to defend themselves (as noted above, Josephus makes no reference to their becoming circumcised).

30 Testament of Levi 6:4-5 says that Levi killed Shechem, Simeon executed Hamor, and the other brothers dispatched all the remaining people with the sword. Kugel attaches the idea that each of the two killed one person to the singular form איש in Gen 49:6 ("Story of Dinah," 12-15), though see T. Levi 5:4.

31 Testament of Levi 6:8-11 claims the Shechemites tried to treat Sarah in the same way as they treated Dinah and that they violated the wives of strangers.

32 Halpern-Amaru sums up the situation in Jubilees in this way: "Gone also is any evidence of a break in the family, of an overt or even covert clash between Jacob and sons. Everyone is concerned about Dinah; everyone is angry; and there is no suggestion that circumcision and marriage could vitiate the offense and the outrage" (*Empowerment*, 129).

33 Kugel notes that some ancient expositors took the words "for such a thing ought not to be done" as "implied direct speech," with God being the speaker (this is made explicit in Jdt 9:2 ["for you (God) said, 'It shall not be done'"]) ("Story of Dinah," 25-28). As a result, the deity himself condemned the action of the Shechemites and justified punishing them for it.

34 Halpern-Amaru thinks that the identification of Dinah as the daughter of Jacob in v. 2 is significant: "Dinah, daughter of Jacob whose name will become

lesson. It should be emphasized that the writer used the same verb already in v. 2 so the nature of the act is not in doubt.[35] Just as the idea of punishment found expression in v. 4, it reappears here as the proper way in which to characterize what Simeon and Levi did. In v. 5 the author insists that the punishment was not just the reaction of brothers incensed at the abuse their sister had suffered: the sentence to slaughter all the people of Shechem had its origin in a heavenly decree. It was God's idea,[36] and, once more highlighting the guilt of all Shechemites, the deity issued the order "since they [the Shechemites][37] had done something shameful [ḥafrata[38]/ignominiam] in Israel." These words, besides echoing the idea of collective guilt from Gen 34:27, take up another clause from Gen 34:7: "because he [Shechem] had committed an outrage [נבלה] in Israel."[39] The language resembles the words of David's daughter Tamar when her brother Amnon tried to violate her: "She answered him, 'No, my brother, do not force me [תענני]; for such a thing is not done in Israel; do not do anything so vile [הנבלה הזאת]!'" (2 Sam 13:2). The actions of the Shechemites (all of them, not just the men) earned them the fate of annihilation.

■ **6** The next verse continues to deal with the situation of Genesis 34 and repeats some of the points made in v. 5.[40] It was the Lord himself who delivered the Shechemites to Jacob's sons—Simeon and Levi[41]—for execution and uprooting. The punishment of uprooting occurs frequently in contexts where the nations are under consideration (e.g., 10:30; 16:9; 20:4; 22:20; 24:31; 31:17, 20; 35:14) and/or where impurity is involved (6:12 [eating blood]; 20:4 [intermarriage with Canaanites]; 21:21 [impurity of humanity]; 22:20 [marrying a Canaanite]; 33:13, 17, 19 [Reuben and Bilhah]). The writer is insistent that nothing of the sort—this time, defiling an Israelite virgin—is to be done in Israel again. It is incompatible with the holiness of Israel (see v. 8 below).

■ **7** With v. 7 the author moves to a wider application of the Shechem-Dinah story,[42] although key vocabulary items (especially "defile") remain the same. The incident had involved sexual relations and a proposal of marriage between a member of Jacob's family and a foreigner, so the writer turns to the general category of cases in which an Israelite male wants (!)[43] or is

---

	Israel, is designed to represent every 'daughter of Israel,' 'בת ישראל,' the Hebrew designation for any Israelite woman" (*Empowerment*, 129).		B´ The Lord handed them over to Jacob's sons for them to uproot them with the sword and to effect punishment against them
35	"Defile" occurs in vv. 2, 3, 5-10, 15, 16—ten times, while it figures three times in Genesis 34.		A´ so that there should not again be something like this within Israel—defiling an Israelite virgin
36	See T. Levi 6:8, where Levi says, "God's sentence upon Shechem was for evil" (trans. Harm W. Hollander and Marinus de Jonge, *The Testaments of the Twelve Patriarchs: A Commentary* [SVTP 8; Leiden: Brill, 1985] 146).	41	It is difficult to believe that so soon after v. 4 the writer should mean any more than Simeon and Levi by the designation "Jacob's sons," but Werman thinks he purposely uses the general expression to show there was unity in Jacob's group (*Jubilees*, 411). She finds evidence for her claim by contrasting Gen 34:25 (it mentions Simeon and Levi) with this verse in Jubilees, but it is not the parallel to Jub 30:6.
37	Syriac Gen 34:7 also reads a plural verb.		
38	For the noun Leslau lists "shame, blush, ignominy, disgrace, dishonor" (*Concise Dictionary*, 118). Eth. Gen 34:7 uses the same term.		
39	Of the thirteen times the noun occurs in the HB, eight involve sexual misconduct (e.g., Deut 22:21; Hamilton, *Genesis 18–50*, 357).	42	On the section, see Endres, *Biblical Interpretation*, 133–42. He calls intermarriage, not rape, "the real crime."
40	Werman (*Jubilees*, 411) shows how vv. 5-6 take chiastic form: A Nothing like this is to be done anymore from now on—to defile an Israelite woman B For the punishment had been decreed against them in heaven that they were to annihilate all the Shechemites with sword C since they had done something shameful in Israel	43	One could read Gen 34:8-12, 15-16 as saying that Jacob and his sons thought seriously of giving Dinah away to a foreign man. They did not reject the suggestion out of hand—at least Jacob did not. Or one could infer that nine of Jacob's sons were sincere in their suggestion about circumcision but only Simeon and Levi were deceptive about it (see Kugel, *Traditions*, 421–22, for texts expressing this

about to[44] give a daughter or sister to a non-Israelite in marriage. As he takes up the larger legal issue, of which the Dinah–Shechem episode was an example, it becomes apparent that legislation in Leviticus 18 and 20 underlies the presentation. Those passages are filled with laws about marriage and sexual relations and are the only ones in the Pentateuch that resort to the word Molech—one that the author will use in 30:10. A number of passages in the Torah link exogamy with an increased danger of idolatry. For example, in Exod 34:16 the Lord predicts to Moses when speaking about relations with the peoples in Canaan: "And you will take wives from among their daughters for your sons, and their daughters who prostitute themselves to their gods will make your sons also prostitute themselves to their gods." Or, in Deut 7:3-4a, he commands: "Do not intermarry with them, giving your daughters to their sons or taking their daughters for your sons, for that would turn away your children from following me, to serve other gods" (see Judg 3:6 for an example that includes Hivites). The perception that the two subjects—intermarriage and idolatry—were tightly intertwined lies behind a reading of the Molech passages in Lev 18:21 and 20:2-5 as referring to sexual relations and marriage with non-Israelites. Jubilees provides the earliest attestation of this interpretation, which figures in several later sources.[45] A clear statement of it occurs in *Tg. Ps.-J.* Lev 18:21:

---

view). A goodly number of the Ethiopic copies add after the conditional "If there is a man in Israel who wishes to give his daughter or" a second condition: "there is one who has given his daughter" (followed by "or his sister"); that is, they refer to a case in which he has carried out the act, not just contemplated it. The plus is meant to alleviate the extreme statement that even the thought of marrying a female family member to a non-Israelite is punishable by death (see the textual note; and VanderKam, *Jubilees* 2:193). For Albeck, the text did not mean a male merely thought about giving a female in marriage to a non-Israelite; he wrote that the sequel shows the writer meant a male who actually carried out the deed (*Jubiläen*, 28). The sequel does show he also included men who committed the infraction, but v. 7 talks about the intention. In fact, Werman says that in vv. 7-10 "voluntary defilement is now the heart of the matter" ("Jubilees 30," 11; cf. *Jubilees*, 411–12). For reasons not to accept Segal's ("Shechem and Dinah," 235–38) suggestion that somehow MS. 38ᵗ alone (it lacks the words "or his sister") has preserved the original form of the condition, when it disagrees with all other Ethiopic copies and with the Latin translation, see the textual note.

44 For this possible rendering of *faqada* (= בקש), see Segal, "Shechem and Dinah," 238–39.

45 For those sources, see Singer, *Jubiläen*, 200–202; Charles, *Jubilees*, 181; Finkelstein, "Rabbinic Halaka," 57; Geza Vermes, "Leviticus 18:21 in Ancient Jewish Bible Exegesis," in Jacob J. Petuchowski and Ezra Fleischer, eds., *Studies in Aggadah, Targum and Jewish Liturgy in Memory of Joseph Heinemann* (Jerusalem: Magnes/Hebrew Union College Press, 1981) 108–24. Vermes refers to this interpretation of Molech as "exegesis no. 2" and deals with Jub 30:7-10 on pp. 119–22, in connection with his attempt to date this understanding of the Molech verses. Exegesis no. 2 usually takes the form of a Jew who marries a foreign woman, but Jubilees forbids giving a daughter or sister in marriage to a non-Israelite. Regarding this difference, Vermes writes: "But this is, I submit, no more than a dialectical twist. The author of *Jubilees* sought support for his reshaped *Genesis* story, which was about a proposed union between a Gentile and a Jewish woman, and found it in the sexual interpretation of Lev. 18:21. But we may be certain that he did not exclude the Jewish man/Gentile woman relation, for in the subsequent verses he treats both types of mixed marriage as equally reprehensible (30:12-14)" (p. 120). Kugel also cites a series of texts with the sexual interpretation of Molech (*Traditions*, 425-27). Cf. Endres, *Biblical Interpretation*, 135–37; Werman, "Jubilees 30," 17–21; Frevel, "Intermarriage," 242–48 (his suggestion that the author knew the Greek rendering of Molech as αρχων and understood it as applying to Hamor is most implausible [pp. 248–49]). A number of these scholars refer to *m. Meg.* 4:9, suggesting it forbids this interpretation of Lev 18:21: "If a man says *And thou shalt not give any of thy seed to make them pass through [the fire] to Molech* [means] 'and thou shalt not give of thy seed to make it pass to heathendom,' they put him to silence with a rebuke." Y. Ta-Shema suggests more plausibly that the passage is to be read in light of *m. Meg.* 4:10, which indicates that the Sages are discussing passages that are not to be translated in public ("On the Interpretation of a Section of the Book of Jubilees," *Bet Miqra* 11 [1966] 99–101).

Leviticus 18:21	Targum Pseudo-Jonathan Leviticus 18:21
You shall not give any of your offspring to sacrifice them to Molech,	You shall not give any of your offspring to *have sexual intercourse with a pagan woman, impregnating her to the benefit of* idolatry,
and so profane the name of your God; I am the LORD.	and you shall not profane the name of your God. I am the Lord.[46]

It appears that the word זרע (translated "offspring" above) was taken in the sense of "seed = sperm," as interpreters attempted to understand the unusual expression.[47]

The references to Molech in Lev 18:21 and 20:2-5 appear in different contexts. Chapter 18 contains a series of laws dealing with sexual relations; the fact that v. 21 is located among them implies a related meaning for it.[48] The penalty for committing any of the violations enumerated in the chapter is to be "cut off from their people" (18:29). However, in chap. 20, which contains a number of parallel laws, the Molech unit may have to do with a forbidden form of worship;[49] it is not set among the laws on sexual topics (they begin at v. 10). Furthermore, the penalty for giving offspring to Molech is death at the hands of "the people of the land" (vv. 2, 4, "cutting off" is also mentioned). The writer of Jubilees read both 18:21 and 20:2-5 as referring to mixed marriages—attaching the meaning of 18:21 to 20:2-5—and thus associated the death penalty with 18:21 too, as will be seen below.[50]

In a situation in which an Israelite male intends or is about to give a female relative to a non-Israelite in marriage (Jub 30:7), the penalty is death by stoning. This is the sentence prescribed by Lev 20:2 for those who actually carry out the deed of "giving any of their offspring to Molech": "Any of the people of Israel, or of the aliens who reside in Israel, who give any of their offspring to Molech shall be put to death; the people of the land shall stone them to death."[51] In Jubilees, even the plan to bring about such a marriage is punishable by death. To the law of Leviticus the writer adds a reason for the harsh sentence: the man has committed a shameful act in Israel—using the term found in v. 5 for Shechem's act (see Gen 34:7 [נבלה]).

The woman involved in the Israelite–non-Israelite marriage, though she may seem only a passive partner in the transaction, is to be burned to death "because she has defiled the reputation [= name] of her father's house."[52] The language here is reminiscent of Lev 21:9: "When the daughter of a priest profanes herself through prostitution, she profanes her father; she shall be burned to death." The cases seem clearly distinguished from each other (Lev 21:9 speaks of a priest's daughter), but it should be observed that Lev 20:5 uses the expression "prostituting themselves to Molech," so the writer of Jubilees may have connected the two verses. One could speculate that he placed the woman in the category of people mentioned in the preceding verse in Leviticus 20—those who "close their eyes" when offspring are given to Molech (v. 4; for a reference to this verse, see Jub 30:15), that is, they do not object and respond properly to such behavior, and therefore the woman, who presumably accepted the marriage arrangement, was likewise guilty of the Molech sin and deserving of death by burning.[53] But it is also possible that the writer

---

46   The translators in the Aramaic Bible series italicize passages not in the Hebrew text, but some confusion seems to have led to mistakes with it in this verse. They are altered in the version given above.

47   See, e.g., Vermes, "Leviticus 18:21," 113.

48   Cohen explains the reasoning of early exegetes like the author of Jubilees this way: "They concluded that the verse must prohibit some sexual offense which could be equated with idolatry (Lev 20:5 speaks of those who 'go whoring after Molek'), and since the chapter otherwise omits intermarriage, the obvious conclusion was that Lev 18:21 prohibits sexual intercourse with idolaters" ("Intermarriage," 34).

49   Milgrom, *Leviticus*, 2:1728-29.

50   See Ta-Shema, "Interpretation," 100-101.

51   Albeck, *Jubiläen*, 28.

52   Ibid., 28-29: "Ebensowenig lässt sich der Feuertod für 'ein Weib,' das einen Heiden heiratet, aus der Thora belegen und halachisch rechtfertigen" (p. 28).

53   This is the way Kugel explains the association (*Traditions*, 426-27). As Charles noted, Judah demands that Tamar be burned for becoming pregnant through prostitution in Gen 38:24 (*Jubilees*, 180). In Jub 41:17 Judah justifies the punishment with the charge that "she has done something impure [*rekwsa/inmunditiam*; the Syriac has *ṭnpwt'*] in Israel."

in fact applies a law regarding a priest's daughter to any Israelite woman since Israel was holy, a "priestly kingdom" (Exod 19:6; cf. Jub 22:12; 33:20).[54] However that may be, he does not make this explicit and simply lists the penalty. The sentence also recalls Abraham's words to his sons: "If any woman or girl among you commits a sexual offense, burn her in fire; they are not to commit sexual offenses (by) following their eyes and their hearts so that they take wives for themselves from the Canaanite women because the descendants of Canaan will be uprooted from the earth" (20:4). The writer accuses her of defiling the name or reputation of her father's house,[55] a charge that also recalls the one lodged against the daughter of a priest who turns to prostitution. He goes on to say that "she is to be uprooted from Israel" (cf. Lev 18:29; 20:3, 5). Uprooting in Jubilees, frequently related to the nations, is also a possibility for Israelites (2:27 [someone who works on the Sabbath]; 6:12, 14 [one who consumes blood]; 15:14, 26, 28, 34 [the male who remains uncircumcised on the eighth day or leaves his sons uncircumcised]; 21:22 [one who imitates the deeds of humanity]; 33:13, 17, 19 [those who act like Reuben with Bilhah]; 49:9 [one who fails to celebrate Passover properly]).

■ 8 The passage continues to deal with the woman of v. 7 and what she has done. She is a prostitute[56] and she has caused defilement.[57] As in v. 7, so here the Holiness Code shines through the text. The writer, in calling the woman a prostitute, indicates that he regarded even her more passive role in the situation as participating in what Lev 20:5 calls "prostituting themselves to Molech."[58] The woman's act led to the defiling of the name of her father's house (the man's act also causes defilement; see the end of v. 8), and no defilement is to be present in Israel—"for Israel is holy to the Lord."[59] These words echo the insistence of the Holiness Code regarding Israel, "You shall be holy, for I the Lord your God am holy" (Lev 19:2; see also 20:7: "Consecrate yourselves therefore, and be holy" and 20:26: "You shall be holy to me; for I the Lord am holy, and I have separated you from the other peoples to be mine"). Lest one think that only the woman is guilty, the writer adds that any man/person who brings about such defilement in Israel[60] is to be executed by stoning (as in Lev 20:2).

■ 9 The writer keeps his focus on the legislation in Leviticus 20 and relates it to the theme of the heavenly tablets. Using his typical two-verb pattern (ordained and written) he asserts that the law he has just enunciated is part of the vast record in that celestial resource. His wording suggests he is quoting from that text, and it is apparent that the penalty he cited at the end of v. 8 is the text in question. Leviticus 20:2 refers, literally, to "any man/person from the sons of Israel who gives of his seed to Molech"; the parallel in Jubilees is (literally) "any seed (or any of the seed) of Israel who defiles."[61] The wording of the penalty in the texts is as follows:

---

54 Christine E. Hayes, "Intermarriage and Impurity in Ancient Jewish Sources," *HTR* 92 (1999) 3–36, here 17–18. Berger (*Jubiläen*, 471 n. g to v. 7) and Endres (*Biblical Interpretation*, 139–47) had earlier made a similar proposal; cf. also Frevel, "Intermarriage," 235–36.

55 In the HB there is no parallel passage. Ezekiel 43:7 talks of defiling God's holy name, but there are no references to defiling a human's name.

56 In VanderKam, *Jubilees* 2, the term *zammā* was interpreted as masculine (= adulterer; the verb of which it is the subject is masculine singular), though the Latin translation has the feminine *fornicaria* ("prostitute"). Kugel has correctly objected to the translation of *zammā* as adulterer (*Walk through Jubilees*, 144–45 n. 263), although his inference about the gender of the Ethiopic verbal form and the work of his interpolator here is to be rejected. On this, see below.

57 The best reading in the Ethiopic copies is *rekus*, which is either a masculine singular adjective (= an impure man, as it is rendered in VanderKam, *Jubilees* 2) or an alternate spelling of the noun *rekws*, "filth, impurity, defilement, pollution, abomination, anything unclean or vile" (Leslau, *Concise Dictionary*, 61; for the alternate spellings, see Dillmann, *Lexicon*, 301). The Latin translation uses *abominatio*. Regarding *rekus* as a noun seems preferable in the context. Goldmann translates with טמאה, which has the advantage of using a cognate of the verb "to defile."

58 Cf. Loader, *Sexuality*, 170.

59 For other references in Jubilees to Israel as holy or sanctified, see 2:19-21, 23-24; 15:27, 31; 16:26; 22:12, 27, 29; 25:12, 18; 33:20.

60 The Ethiopic text lacks a direct object in "Any man who has defiled (it)," but Latin reads *eum*, likely referring to Israel.

61 Here, as in v. 8, the preferred reading among the Ethiopic copies is a verb without an object suffix,

Leviticus 20:2 (MT SP):	môt yûmāt 'am hā'āreṣ yirgĕmūhû bā'āben
Jubilees 30:9 (Ethiopic):	mota la-yemut wa-ba-'eben yewgerewwo
Jubilees 30:9 (Latin):	mortem morietur et lapidibus lapidabitur

The wording is the same apart from Ethiopic Jubilees' indefinite plural (lit., "they are to stone him") to replace "the people of the land"[62] and the reversal of the verb and prepositional phrase in the second clause (separated from the first clause by a conjunction).[63]

■ **10** The author resorts to one of his fixed expressions regarding a law—it has no temporal limits (for other instances, see 6:14 [prohibition of consuming blood]; 13:26 [tithe to be given to the Lord]; 16:30 [celebrating the Festival of Tabernacles]; 32:10 [giving a tithe a second time; also on the heavenly tablets]). He declares it a law that is absolute in the sense that one who violates it cannot be forgiven—a statement he also made in connection with those Israelites who leave their sons uncircumcised (15:34) and those who, after the relevant law was revealed, repeat the sin of Reuben against Bilhah (33:17; here too he says, "There is no time when this law will be at an end"). Clearly the law is of fundamental importance for him, and to make his point he restates the legislation. Taking the parts of the law in the order in which he expresses them, they are:

Is to be eradicated (*yeššarraw/ut exterminetur*): the verb appears to be the equivalent of יכרת—the penalty in Lev 20:3, 5 (Eth. Lev 17:4; 19:8 attest a form of the same verb where the MT has a form of כרת).

The one who has defiled his daughter. Shechem had defiled Dinah, the daughter of Jacob (Gen 34:7); no Israelite father was to cause such defilement through giving his daughter to a non-Israelite.

Because he has given one of his descendants/from his seed to Molech (*'esma 'em-westa zar'u wahabo la-molok/ quoniam ab omni semine eius dedit alienigena*[64]). This is a quotation from Lev 20:3: "because they have given of their [text: he has given of his] offspring/seed to Molech.

And has sinned by defiling it (that is, the seed). Leviticus 20:3 is probably the base text here as well because the next clause in it speaks of defiling (למען טמא), but the object defiled there is "my sanctuary" (see Jub 30:15, 16 where this phrase appears), not, as in the present case, a daughter in Israel. Defilement of the sanctuary does result from acts of the sort treated in the chapter (see vv. 15-16 below), but the statement of the point is quite different in Jubilees.

Werman, who finds a chiastic structure in vv. 7-10—Molech (though the term is not actually mentioned in v. 7), generic prohibition (v. 8), generic prohibition (v. 9), Molech (v. 10)—summarizes the teaching in this section as follows:

> According to *Jubilees*, fornication and impurity are any kind of illicit sexual congress. . . . The inclusion of intermarriage within this framework of "fornication and impurity" reveals the book's extreme aversion to such unions. For *Jubilees*, intermarriage resembles these other transgressions [in Leviticus 18] that, according to the Bible, cause "impurity" and pollute the entire nation. Not only does the author of *Jubilees* follow the line of Leviticus 20 in demanding punishment for offenders, but, in accord with Leviticus 18, he also assesses the deed of marrying a daughter to a foreigner as an act that defiles the nation.[65]

---

though mss. 12 17 20 read a masculine singular suffix (it/him) and 58 has a feminine singular suffix (it/her). In this instance the Latin has no object pronoun.

62 Note that the Latin translation has a third person singular passive form of the verb.

63 García Martínez can classify v. 9 under the heading "Heavenly Tablets: New Halakot" because, while it reflects a law in Leviticus, it interprets the term Molech as meaning marriage to foreigners and, unlike any passage in the HB, attaches the death penalty to those guilty of such marriages ("Heavenly Tablets," 257).

64 The Latin translation—*alienigena* ("foreigner") expresses the way in which the writer understood *Molech*, while the Ethiopic version transliterates the Hebrew noun/name.

65 Werman, "*Jubilees* 30," 14; for the chiastic arrangement of vv. 7-10, see pp. 12-13. As she indicates (pp. 14-15), the charge that the act defiles the entire nation shows that the author does not view impurity as depending on physical contact with

11-16 No Marriage with Non-Israelites

■ **11** The authorial device of having the Angel of the Presence mention Moses by name introduces the next paragraph. In the preceding section (vv. 7-10) he had, without naming Moses, dealt with the issue of defiling an Israelite woman and the penalties for a man and woman who engaged in such behavior. Now he takes up the still more encompassing law that prohibits either marrying an Israelite woman to a non-Israelite or taking a foreign woman as a spouse for an Israelite man.[66] That law, influenced by Deut 7:3 ("Do not intermarry with them, giving your daughters to their sons or taking their daughters for your sons"; cf. Josh 23:12; Judg 3:6), Moses is to command and testify to the Israelites, and the reason for the law, says the angel, is "because it [the act] is despicable [*mennun*[67]/*abominatio*] before the Lord." The significance of the term will become clearer in v. 12.

■ **12** The angel now tells Moses about what he wrote in "the words of the law" (see also v. 21 below). This is a second direct reference to a part of the Pentateuch as a composition by the Angel of the Presence (6:22 is the other), and he proceeds to indicate exactly which passage he has in mind. He says he had written for Moses "everything that the Shechemites [note the plural] did to Dinah and how Jacob's sons said, 'We will not give our daughter to a man who has a foreskin because for us that would be a disgraceful thing.'" That is, he first refers to the story in Genesis 34, one greatly abbreviated in Jubilees 30, and in effect tells Moses that the narrative is there for him to consult, though its many details were not required for the point he wishes to make in this context.[68] The second part of his statement makes explicit that the author, as the reader would expect, knows about the role circumcision plays in Genesis 34. His words are a quotation from Gen 34:14b (the introductions to the words of Dinah's brothers differ in Genesis and Jubilees and are not cited here).

Genesis 34:14b (MT): lā-tēt 'et-'ăḥōtēnû lĕ'îš 'ăšer lô 'orlâ kî ḥerpâ hî' lānû

Jubilees 30:12 (Eth.): nehub walattana la-sab' za-bo qwelfata 'esma ṣe'lat we'etu lana

Jubilees 30:12 (Lat.): dabimus filiam nostram homini qui habet praeputium obprobrium enim est nobis.

The only surprise is that in both versions of Jubilees the brothers refer to Dinah as their daughter (as if Jacob were speaking) rather than their sister as in Genesis. A simple explanation is to posit influence from Gen 34:17, where the brothers say (after calling Dinah their sister in v. 15): "But if you will not listen to us and be circumcised, then we will take our daughter and be gone."[69] Segal, who acknowledges the possible effect of Gen 34:17 on Jub 30:12, finds greater significance in the reading "our daughter" in v. 12. For him the verse expresses a veiled criticism of Jacob as portrayed in Genesis 34, where he is willing to marry Dinah to Shechem. He was not opposed to the union, but the brothers were; by refusing to acquiesce in the marriage of their sister, they acted according to the law in Lev 20:2. Moreover, Levi is the one who receives the praise, not Jacob. For Segal, this is another instance in which a halakic section

---

the source of the defilement—a point that becomes clearer in vv. 13-16. See below on those verses. Werman also maintains that v. 16a should follow directly on v. 10, since it speaks in the singular about the impossibility of purification from the defilement caused by mixed marriages; in addition, beginning with v. 11 the writer moves to the effect of the act on the entire people (*Jubilees*, 408 n. 16). The change in location is unwarranted, since v. 16a uses the singular to refer either to the one mentioned in v. 15 ("If one does this") or to the nation (a noun singular in number). It seems quite at home in its present context. The same penalty applies in this instance as in v. 10.

66 David Rothstein concludes from v. 11 (and v. 14) that for the author there was no distinction between "a singular act of sexual congress with a foreigner and marriage to him/her; both constitute a violation of pentateuchal law, in consequence of which the offenders are to be executed" ("Sexual Union and Sexual Offences in *Jubilees*," *JSJ* 35 [2004] 363-84, here 382-84; quotation from 383). Thus sexual unions of this kind and marriage are the same.

67 Leslau, *Concise Dictionary*, 38: "despicable, abominable, ignoble, contemptible, vile, worthless, useless."

68 See VanderKam, "Moses," 36-37.

69 In v. 16 they refer to giving "our daughters" and taking "your daughters," and this too probably affected the wording in v. 17.

in Jubilees conflicts with the rewritten story to which it is attached. In the rewritten story (vv. 1-4), Jacob and his sons together are enraged at the Shechemites and deal shrewdly with them; in the legal part Jacob's sons are the ones who object to the marriage and Jacob is not mentioned.[70] Segal admits, however, that his case is not strong. Since the angel is quoting from Genesis, the brothers are the ones who speak here, and the term they use for their sister is the one they employ in Gen 34:17.[71] The word that interests the angel is חרפה (rendered ṣeʿlat[72]/obprobrium in Jubilees; see 2 Sam 13:13), which he takes as an appropriate label for marital relations with a non-Israelite (see v. 13). It appears to be in the same category as the word translated "despicable" in v. 11.[73]

■ **13-15** The Angel of the Presence expands on the nature of the transgression involved. In explaining the passage cited in v. 12, he makes the principle encompass giving an Israelite woman to a foreigner (circumcised or not) and an Israelite male wedding a foreign woman.[74] He characterizes the action as disgraceful (repeating ṣeʿlat/obprobrium), impure (rekus/abominatio [see v. 8]), and despicable (mennun/inmunditia [see v. 11])—all three of the Ethiopic and two of the Latin words were used earlier in the chapter (this is the first occurrence of inmunditia in chap. 30). They resemble closely the language that Abraham employed when giving final instructions to Jacob regarding other peoples:

> Separate from the nations,
> and do not eat with them.
> Do not act as they do,
> and do not become their companion,
> for their actions are something that is impure,
> and all their ways are defiled and something
> abominable and detestable. (22:16; cf. 20:5; 33:19)

The horrible condition that results when a foreign wife is present in Israel or an Israelite woman has been given to a non-Israelite husband is such that it cannot be removed until the non-Israelite spouse disappears. In fact, a rich diversity of punishments will befall the violators; they recall ones mentioned in chap. 23 when speaking about the time of great evil:

> because (there will be) blow upon blow, trouble upon trouble, distress upon distress, bad news upon bad news, disease upon disease, and every (kind of) bad punishment like this.... All of this will happen to the evil generation that makes the earth commit sin through sexual impurity, contamination, and their detestable actions. (23:13-14)

The situation about which the angel speaks in chap. 30 matches the circumstances in the time of the evil generation in chap. 23.[75]

The writer shows in v. 15 that Leviticus 20 continues to affect his rhetoric. He refers not only to one who commits the reprehensible act but also to an individual who, while not actually causing or engaging in marriage with a foreign person, ignores the perpetrators or fails to protest against them ("shuts his eyes to those who do impure things"). The source for the statement is Lev 20:4: "And if the people of the land should ever close their eyes to them." The word "them" refers to people who commit the faults mentioned in 20:3, and Jubilees cites it next.

---

70 "Shechem and Dinah," 238–40. Segal's text-critical argument for the short reading in v. 7–"If there is a man in Israel who wishes to give his daughter" (i.e., lacking "or his sister")—was found unconvincing above. He takes it to be more evidence for finding a criticism of Jacob in the halakic section (he would be the one who wished or was about to give his daughter to a foreign man). Since, however, the only likely reading in v. 7 includes "or his sister," Segal's case is further weakened.

71 Halpern-Amaru explains "our daughter" in v. 12 in a different way: it is understandable "for the unwed and childless Dinah becomes a woman of consequence only as a metaphoric 'every daughter of Israel'" (*Empowerment*, 132).

72 Ethiopic Gen 34:14 uses the same word.

73 The story about Amnon and Tamar also shares this word with the present passage (2 Sam 13:13): she says to him, "where could I carry my shame [חרפתי]?"

74 Werman, *Jubilees*, 413.

75 See Loader, *Sexuality*, 171–72.

Leviticus 20:3	Jubilees 30:15
... defiling my sanctuary and profaning my holy name.	... who defile the Lord's sanctuary and to those who profane his holy name

Impurity defiles what is holy, and two prominent examples of holiness are noted here.[76] The angel charges that the whole nation of Israel, if it allows such marriages to take place, will suffer condemnation because of the resulting impurity and contamination (*rekws* and *gemmānē*; Latin has just one noun, *abominationibus*). Everyone is responsible for avoiding exogamy and also for not tolerating it in others.[77] His inclusion of all Israel in the guilt makes one think of Ezra's response to mixed marriages: "You have trespassed and married foreign women, and so increased the guilt of Israel. Now make confession to the Lord the God of your ancestors, and do his will; separate yourselves from the peoples of the land and from the foreign wives" (Ezra 10:10-11).

■ **16** The unit concludes with a verse regarding consequences flowing from the impurity and contamination mentioned at the end of v. 15. It provides a sequence of expressions and terms for Israel's special status and for the sacrificial system through which the nation removes impurities and the like. There will be no "lifting of his face," that is, "no favoritism"—a phrase that echoes in a negative sense the one from the priestly blessing in Num 6:26: "[may] the Lord lift up his countenance upon you." The second and synonymous expression is less certain textually: Ethiopic has "accepting the face/causing the face to be pleasing," that is, "showing partiality/favoritism."[78] Latin lacks an equivalent but could be haplographic in a context where the verb *accipi-* occurs several times (see the textual note). The Ethiopic text follows with a list of five items regularly presented to the Lord that he will not accept (literally, he will not take from his hand):[79] fruit, sacrifices, offerings, fat, and pleasant aromas (Latin has: sacrifice, burnt offering, pleasant fragrance). "Fruit" occurs in some sacrificial contexts (Deut 26:2, 10), and the two kinds of offerings and the appealing aroma listed in both Ethiopic and Latin reflect the language of anticultic rhetoric in the Prophets. For example, see Amos 5:22: "Even though you offer me your burnt offerings and grain offerings, / I will not accept them; / and the offerings of well-being of your fatted animals / I will not look upon." Or Jeremiah quotes the Lord as saying, "Your burnt offerings are not acceptable, / nor are your sacrifices pleasing to me" (6:20; cf. Ps 40:6; Isa 1:12). Leviticus 26:31 cites the Lord's rejection of the scent of sacrifices: "I will not smell your pleasing odor." Fat (חלב; Latin lacks an equivalent) is also referenced frequently in sacrificial contexts (many times, for instance, in Leviticus 3; note v. 16: "All the fat is the Lord's"). So the passage is saying that if the impurity caused by exogamy exists in Israel, the sacrificial system will not be effective; the Lord himself will reject both the offerings made to him and the people who bring them.

The primary basis for v. 16 appears to be Mal 2:11-12:

Judah has been faithless, and abomination has been committed in Israel and Jerusalem; for Judah has profaned the sanctuary of the Lord, which he loves, and has married the daughter of a foreign god. May the Lord cut off from the tents of Jacob anyone who does this—any to witness or answer or to bring an offering to the Lord of hosts.

---

76 Mal 2:11, part of a context that was influential in forming the picture of Levi in Jubilees, also connects marriage with a non-Israelite woman to profaning or defiling the sanctuary. See below and Ta-Shema, "Interpretation," 101; VanderKam, "*Jubilees* and the Priestly Messiah of Qumran," *RevQ* 13 (1988) 353–65, here 361–62 (= *From Revelation to Canon*, 471–72). For defiling the temple, see also Werman, "*Jubilees* 30," 15–16.

77 In this sense there is a parallel between the guilt of all the Shechemites for the sin with Dinah and of all Israel for its incorrect approach to mixed marriages (Werman, *Jubilees*, 414).

78 Leslau, *Concise Dictionary*, 191.

79 For the expression, see Mal 1:10 (the divine response to sacrifices of defective animals): "Try presenting that to your governor; will he be pleased with you or show you favor? says the Lord of hosts"; and 1:13: "You bring what has been taken by violence or is lame or sick, and this you bring as your offering! Shall I accept that from your hand? says the Lord."

Like Jubilees 30, the prophetic passage combines mixed marriage and profaning the temple, and as punishment it lists cutting off the malefactor from Israel and any sacrifice he may bring to the sanctuary.[80]

Defiling of the sanctuary through impurity is recognized in pentateuchal legislation, where provision to remove it is also found. Leviticus 16:16 describes one of the acts of Aaron on the Day of Atonement: "Thus he shall make atonement for the sanctuary, because of the uncleannesses [טמאת] of the people of Israel, and because of their transgressions, all their sins; and so he shall do for the tent of meeting, which remains with them in the midst of their uncleannesses [טמאתם]."[81] Himmelfarb has pointed out that, through its assertion about the resulting defilement of the temple, "[e]ven ordinary Jews are thus given a sort of priestly power. Only if they observe God's commandments regarding sexual relations will sacrifices, the priestly work *par excellence*, be acceptable."[82]

The use made in Jubilees 30 of the terms *impure/impurity* and *defilement* has elicited discussion about their meaning. Werman, in contrasting the author's views with those of the Sages, wrote: "While asserting that Israelites who marry foreigners incur impurity through physical contact (a view partially consistent with Jacob's viewpoint in Genesis 34), *Jubilees* also believes that such unions pollute the entire nation as well as the sanctuary, an evaluation that follows from the biblical notions (of H and P)."[83] Hayes examined the chapter in light of the larger debate about whether there existed at the time of the author a view that non-Jews possessed an inherent ritual impurity.[84] She appeals to the distinction between ritual and moral impurity and correctly notes that Jubilees does not attribute ritual impurity to gentiles so that, through physical contact with them, the Israelite becomes impure.[85] She finds the teaching that Israel is a holy seed, a holy nation, to be essential for understanding the author's approach.[86] He bases it on Exod 19:5-6: "Now therefore, if you obey my voice and keep my covenant, you shall be my treasured possession out of all the peoples. Indeed, the whole earth is mine, but you shall be for me a priestly kingdom and a holy nation." Hayes maintains that from these verses "*Jubilees* concludes that the entire nation of Israel is categorically distinct from other peoples, that all Israel are holy priests. The application of priestly standards of ritual and marital purity to all Israel is the next logical step."[87] Jubilees does, of course, consider Israel holy and absolutely distinct from the nations (cf. Ezra 9 and the reference to "the holy seed" in v. 2), and it vehemently prohibits intermarriage between these separate entities. In chap. 30 the teaching that Israel is holy is explicit in v. 8: "for Israel is holy to the Lord."[88] Defilement and impurity from intermarriage affect the whole population along with the temple; intermarriage involves crossing a boundary that should never be bridged. Jonathan Klawans, who has done much to clarify the distinction between ritual and moral impurity, explains the situation in these words:

> As in Ezra and Nehemiah, the moral impurity of Gentiles is deemed to be inherent, and therefore intermarriage is prohibited (30:7). Indeed, not only is intermarriage prohibited, but it appears to have become a source of moral defilement in its own right, presumably because of the fear that it leads to idolatry (30:8-9, 13-14). And Jubilees does not stop with intermarriage: All Jewish–Gentile interaction is to be shunned (22:16). It is often suggested that ritual impurity is the concern of these passages, and that Jubilees considered Gentiles to be a source of ritual defilement. Yet the concern here is not that Gentile

---

80 Ta-Shema, "Interpretation," 101–2.
81 Cf. Milgrom, *Leviticus*, 1:229–31, 1033–35.
82 Himmelfarb, "Sexual Relations and Purity in the Temple Scroll and the Book of Jubilees," *DSD* 6 (1999) 11–36, here 31; cf. also her essay, "Levi, Phinehas," 13–14.
83 Werman, "*Jubilees* 30," 16; cf. *Jubilees*, 413–14.
84 Hayes, "Intermarriage and Impurity," 15–25.
85 Frevel ("Intermarriage," 236–42), although citing Hayes, agrees more with Werman. On p. 242 he speaks about the Canaanites' "constitutional impurity," but the texts he references (Jub 20:3; 21:21, 23; 22:14, 16, 19) do not attribute such impurity to them; they speak, rather, of the impurity of their actions.
86 Note the references to Jacob's descendants as holy in Jub 25:3, 18, and to Jacob as holy in v. 12.
87 Hayes, "Intermarriage and Impurity," 17.
88 See Loader, *Sexuality*, 169.

persons are ritually defiling, but that Gentile behavior is morally abominable, because Gentiles practice idolatry (22:17-22) and perform sexual transgressions (20:3-7). For this reason, Abraham urges his descendants to remain separate from them—even to refrain from eating with them. Jubilees's use of purity language in these and similar passages thus reflects not the ritual purity laws of Leviticus 11–15, but the moral impurity prohibitions applied to all Israel in the biblical traditions quoted in chapter 1 [of Klawans's book; examples are Leviticus 18 and 20]. Indeed, ritual purity surfaces only now and then in the book of Jubilees. Moral impurity, however, is one of Jubilees's central themes.[89]

17-23 The Example of Simeon and Levi

The writer has, then, issued a strong condemnation of both the kind of defilement involved in giving an Israelite woman to a non-Israelite man (vv. 5-10) and in any intermarriage between the line of Jacob and foreigners (vv. 11-16). For him, Simeon and Levi, in contrast to their ambiguous role in Genesis 34, were heroes because they had savagely dispatched the people who had defiled Jacob's daughter, thus preventing intermarriage with non-Israelites. The favorable assessment of the two, however, encountered roadblocks in Genesis itself. First, Jacob was not at all pleased with the behavior of Simeon and Levi and feared death for himself and his household as a result of their brutality (Gen 34:30; see Jub 30:25). Second, and more decisively, Jacob later cursed their violence (Gen 49:5-7):

> Simeon and Levi are brothers;
>   weapons of violence are their swords.
> May I never come into their council;
>   may I not be joined to their company—
> for in their anger they killed men,
>   and at their whim they hamstrung oxen.
> Cursed be their anger, for it is fierce,
>   and their wrath, for it is cruel!

> I will divide them in Jacob,
>   and scatter them in Israel.

The writer of Jubilees faced a more difficult challenge in the case of Levi, the ancestor of the priestly tribe, because he claims that the massacre at Shechem won him not simply accolades but the priesthood. In vv. 17-23 he makes an attempt to cope with the troublesome evaluations of the act in Genesis (he will continue to enhance Levi's résumé in other ways in chaps. 31–32).

■ **17** The angel again addresses Moses as he did in v. 11 but this time without using his name. He has a specific message that he commands Moses to present to Israel—a message that he terms a "testimony" or perhaps here a "warning." The two verbs (order/command and testify) occurred in v. 11, where he spoke directly to Moses (they are imperatives). The reader is led to think that the angel will tell Moses exactly what he was to say to Israel, that is, that the text will contain a quotation (within the larger quotation that constitutes chaps. 2–50). Dillmann and Charles placed opening quotation marks before "Proclaim," and this is the way in which Schodde, Wintermute, Caquot, and VanderKam represent it. However, neither Dillmann nor Charles indicated where they thought the quotation ended (in this vicinity there are no closing quotation marks in their translations). Caquot also does not signal where it ends, whereas Schodde, Wintermute, and VanderKam conclude it with the final word in v. 17. This latter approach receives some support from the fact that the angel shifts to the first-person plural beginning in v. 18 (and continuing through v. 20).

The testimony or warning that Moses is to deliver to the Israelites has to do with evaluating the deed performed by Simeon and Levi. The fate of the Shechemites, all of whom were deserving of punishment since all were involved in defiling Dinah, is to serve as a lesson about what happens to those who cause or tolerate such defilement in Israel. The angel, referring to both the Shechemites and their children, says "they were handed over to Jacob's two sons." This is another way of expressing the claim he made in v. 6: "The Lord

---

89   Jonathan Klawans, *Impurity and Sin in Ancient Judaism* (Oxford/New York: Oxford University Press, 2000) 48.

handed them over to Jacob's sons" to effect the punishment decreed against them in heaven. He also reiterates what he said in v. 4: "They killed everyone in a painful way." As a result, the correct assessment of their behavior was to call it an act of justice (ṣedqa)—a fact recorded in their favor, presumably on the heavenly tablets (see v. 19). The Ethiopic text says that "it was/became a just act for them" where the wording of the Latin (conputatum est illis in veritate) reminds one more of Gen 15:6, where Abram's belief that God would keep his promise was considered a righteous act for him (LXX: ελογισθη αυτω εις δικαιοσυνην). It is no accident, however, that the expression appears in this context where Simeon and Levi anticipate the zeal of Phinehas (see below). In Ps 106:31, in a context regarding the Baal of Peor incident (vv. 28-31), the poet says about Phinehas's deed: "And that has been reckoned to him as righteousness/from generation to generation forever."[90]

■ **18**[91] The angel's attention now turns to Levi alone, though Simeon had also participated in the righteous slaughter of Shechemites. In fact, Simeon's name does not appear again in Jubilees 30, though he is included in "Jacob's sons" and the pronouns referring to the two of them in vv. 23-25. It is understandable that the focus would fall on Levi, the younger of the protagonists, because of the role he plays in subsequent parts of the HB.[92] He became the ancestor of the tribe named after him; all males of that tribe were Levites (in both a biological and vocational sense) and one group within it, Aaron and his male descendants, served as priests (as, e.g., in Numbers 18). The Pentateuch provides no explanation for or justification of why Levi attained this honor. Of all Jacob's sons, most of whom are nondescript in Genesis, only four receive much consideration: Reuben, Levi, Judah, and Joseph. Both Reuben (Gen 35:22) and Judah (Genesis 38) were guilty of sexual sins (Jacob had some harsh words about Reuben for this in Gen 49:3-4, even charging him with "defiling" his father's bed), and Levi helped kill the residents of a city. Reuben somewhat distinguished himself in dealing with his younger brother Joseph (Gen 37:21-22, 29-30; cf. 42:22), but Judah was the one who came up with the idea to sell him to the Ishmaelites (Gen 37:26-27; he thought this would be preferable to killing him). Both made something of a recovery in their dealings with him and his brother Benjamin when Joseph was in Egypt (Reuben, 42:37; Judah, 43:8-10; 44:14-34), but Levi does nothing positive. He must have been among the brothers who sold Joseph and was not a leader in the negotiations with him and the discussions with Jacob. Finally, he with Simeon received Jacob's curse for the wrath they showed at Shechem. Why should this negative character be the ancestor of the priests?

Excursus: Source Texts

Commentators on Jubilees and on the Levi literature often point to a series of texts that contributed to the image of Levi and/or place him in a different light.[93] The first is Exod 32:25-29, part of the story about the golden calf. After Moses pulverized and burned the offending object and interrogated Aaron (a descendant of Levi and the one responsible for making the golden calf), he asked who was on the Lord's side.

---

90 Hayes, "Intermarriage and Impurity," 22–24.
91 On Levi in vv. 18–20, see VanderKam, "Jubilees' Exegetical Creation of Levi the Priest," *RevQ* 17/65–68 (1996) 359–73, here 361–62 (= *From Revelation to Canon*, 547–48).
92 The author does not explain why Simeon, the older of the two, failed to receive a similar reward. Genesis 46:10 // Exod 6:15 implies that he had a Canaanite wife, as his son Shaul is said to be "the son of a Canaanite woman"—surely an awkward situation for the zealous man of Genesis 34 (see Jub 34:20; 44:13; according to 34:20 her name was Adebaa; Simeon subsequently changed his mind and "married another woman from Mesopotamia" [v. 21]). Simeon was the brother whom Joseph imprisoned to ensure that his brothers would return to Egypt with Benjamin (Gen 42:24, 36; 43:23; Jub 42:6, 9-10, 22). Zimri, the man whom Phinehas executed with the Midianite woman Cozbi, was from the tribe of Simeon (Num 25:14). The tribe did not play a distinguished part in Israel's biblical history; in fact, it seems to have disappeared into Judah. Nevertheless, Judith appeals to the example of her forefather: "O Lord God of my ancestor Simeon, to whom you gave a sword to take revenge on those strangers who had torn off a virgin's clothing to defile her, and exposed her thighs to put her to shame, and polluted her womb to disgrace her; for you said, 'It shall not be done'—yet they did it" (9:2).
93 E.g., Endres, *Biblical Interpretation*, 147–51; Kugler, *From Patriarch to Priest*, 9–22.

"And all the sons of Levi gathered around him" (v. 26). Moses ordered them to kill "your brother, your friend, and your neighbor" (v. 27), and they complied by slaughtering about three thousand of them (v. 28). "Moses said, 'Today you have ordained yourselves for the service of the Lord, each one at the cost of a son or a brother, and so have brought a blessing on yourselves this day'" (v. 29). According to this story, "all the sons of Levi" ordained themselves to divine service by their zealous punishment of idolaters. This explains why they served,[94] but, apart from providing a precedent for pairing violence and appointment to sacred office, it says nothing about any virtue their ancestor Levi might have had.[95]

A second passage in this category is Num 25:1-14, the story about Israelites having sexual relations with Midianites and worshiping the Baal of Peor. When an Israelite named Zimri "brought a Midianite woman into his family" in the sight of all (v. 6),

> Phinehas son of Eleazar, son of Aaron the priest, saw it, he got up and left the congregation. Taking a spear in his hand, he went after the Israelite man into the tent, and pierced the two of them, the Israelite and the woman, through the belly. So the plague was stopped among the people of Israel. (Num 25:7-8)

Twenty-four thousand had died by this time (v. 9). This act of violence by another of Levi's descendants led to a reward for Phinehas: "Therefore say, 'I hereby grant him my covenant of peace. It shall be for him and for his descendants after him a covenant of perpetual priesthood, because he was zealous for his God, and made atonement for the Israelites'" (Num 25:12-13). More bloodshed (and prevention of improper sexual relations between Israelites and Midianites) thus led to selecting Phinehas's family to the priesthood. He earned the "perpetual priesthood," but again Levi or any qualities he may have had play no part in the choice of this line. The parallel between Phinehas's and Levi's zealous, bloody suppression of sexual misconduct with foreigners was, however, suggestive to ancient readers like the author of Jubilees.[96]

Deuteronomy 33:8-11 can more readily be viewed as connecting Levi the person and appointment to the priesthood.

> And of Levi he said:
> Give to Levi your Thummim,
>   and your Urim to your loyal one [לאיש חסידך],
> whom you tested at Massah,
>   with whom you contended at the waters of Meribah;
> who said of his father and mother,
>   "I regard them not";
> he ignored his kin,
>   and did not acknowledge his children.
> For they observed your word,
>   and kept your covenant.
> They teach Jacob your ordinances,
>   and Israel your law;
> they place incense before you,
>   and whole burnt offerings on your altar.
> Bless, O Lord, his substance,
>   and accept the work of his hands;
> crush the loins of his adversaries [קמיו],
>   of those that hate him, so that they do not rise again.

Verses 8-9a are phrased in the singular, referring to Levi himself, it seems. Only when his children appear does the rhetoric switch to the plural, with a return to the singular in v. 11. As a result, "only this passage brings together Levi the individual, a violent passion for purity, and a consequent elevation to the priesthood."[97]

Another passage putting the man Levi in a favorable light is Mal 2:4-7, where the prophet conveys a report about him that has no parallel in Genesis.[98] As the Lord criticizes the priests for not properly carrying out their roles, he adds:

---

94 See Houtman, *Exodus*, 3:670: "In short, 32:26-29 relates how the tribe of Levi acquired its unique position, its separation unto the service of YHWH."

95 Kugler, *From Patriarch to Priest*, 14. He adds that the appointment of the Levites to their position comes from Moses, not the Lord.

96 See Kugler, *From Patriarch to Priest*, 14-16. As Himmelfarb comments regarding Levi in the Aramaic Levi Document and Jubilees: "Levi becomes another Phinehas, and his violence against the Shechemites becomes the very first instance of priestly zeal in defense of endogamy" ("Levi, Phinehas," 2).

97 Kugler, *From Patriarch to Priest*, 16. Kugler (p. 17) surveys the variant readings in the witnesses (including 4QTestimonia 14–20) regarding whether the verbs in vv. 9b-11 are plural, as in the MT, or singular, as in 4QDeut^h frgs. 11–15 3–4. The reading in this manuscript from Qumran makes the entire passage refer to Levi so that he is the one who "observed your word and kept your covenant," etc.

98 Modern commentators often interpret the passage as referring to the Levites in general, but since the name Levi is used it could be read as referring to the patriarch.

Know, then, that I have sent this command to you, that my covenant with Levi may hold, says the Lord of hosts. My covenant with him was a covenant of life and well-being, which I gave him; this called for reverence, and he revered me and stood in awe of my name. True instruction was in his mouth, and no wrong was found on his lips. He walked with me in integrity and uprightness, and he turned many from iniquity. For the lips of a priest should guard knowledge, and people should seek instruction from his mouth, for he is the messenger of the Lord of hosts. (Mal 2:4-7).

So Malachi attests to a tradition in which Levi was an extraordinarily pious man with whom the Lord made "a covenant of life and well-being" (v. 5; v. 8 also mentions the covenant of Levi).[99]

The author of Jubilees knew these passages and worked with them in chap. 30 (and in 31-32). He read the traits of Levi in Mal 2:4-7, for example, back into the Genesis narratives and showed how Levi was indeed an appropriate ancestor of the priestly and Levitical tribe. For example, he may have read the words "He walked before me in integrity and uprightness, and he turned many from iniquity" as alluding to the Shechem story. If so, the Lord through Malachi called his actions there upright, and his intervention prevented others from contracting marriages with non-Israelites and in this way "turned many from iniquity."[100] In Jubilees, Levi himself is selected from among Jacob's sons as the priest and functions as one. This meant that the author had to modify the negative impression left by Jacob about him in Gen 34:30 and in 49:5-7. He accomplished the first task in Jub 30:18-23 (with 31:13-17; 32:1-9) and handled the second by giving only the briefest summary of Jacob's "blessing" (Genesis 49) in 45:14 where nothing is said about Simeon and Levi.

In v. 18 the writer draws upon some of the language from Exod 32:25-29. The idea that Levi's descendants "were chosen for the priesthood and as Levites to serve before the Lord" is related to Moses's words that the Levites "have ordained yourselves for the service of the Lord" (v. 29). But inclusion of the priesthood and the fact that the service (cf. Deut 10:8) will be for all time could come from Num 25:13. At this juncture the angel speaks for himself and his colleagues, the angels of the presence, when he says that Levi's descendants will always serve before the Lord just as they do (see also 31:14, where Isaac includes in his blessing of Levi: "may he make you and your descendants [alone] out of all humanity approach him to serve in his temple like the angels of the presence and like the holy ones").

Language from the other passages cited above continues to influence the wording in the remainder of v. 18. The angel says that "Levi and his sons will be blessed forever"; he may be alluding to Exod 32:29, where Moses refers to the blessing the Levites acquired on that occasion; see also Deut 33:11 ("Bless, O Lord, his substance"). The reason for that eternal blessing was his zeal[101] in carrying out "justice, punishment, and revenge on all who rise against Israel." The immediate reference is to his attack on the Shechemites that the angel had characterized as an act of justice (v. 17). It may be as well that he is reflecting the language of Mal 2:6: "He walked with me in integrity and uprightness," though different words are used. "Punishment and revenge" are fitting descriptors of what Levi and Simeon did at Shechem according to the writer (see vv. 4-6, 23). The ones who rise against Israel seem, therefore, to be the people of Shechem, but the term may be another borrowing from Exodus 32, where v. 25 refers to Aaron's letting the people "run wild, to the derision of their enemies [lit., those who rise (against) them (קמיהם)]." See also the conclusion to the blessing of Levi in Deut 33:11: "Bless, O Lord, his substance, / and accept the works of his hands; / crush the loins of his adversaries [קמיו], / and of those that hate him, so that they do not rise again."

■ 19 The angel makes explicit what he implied in v. 17: Levi's violence at Shechem earned him a blessing and a favorable entry on the heavenly tablets as having carried out justice. He did this "before the God of all." The

---

99 For the relevance of this passage to the picture of Levi in Jubilees, see VanderKam, "Priestly Messiah," 361-63 (= *From Revelation to Canon*, 470-72); Kugel, "Levi's Elevation," 30-33; Kugler, *From Patriarch to Priest*, 18-21 (he argues that all of the passages cited above underlie Mal 2:4-7).

100 See Kugler, *From Patriarch to Priest*, 20-21.

101 The Ethiopic verb is *qan'a*, a cognate of the Hebrew verb translated "be zealous" in connection with Phinehas in Num 25:13.

title appears several times in Jubilees (22:10, 27; 31:13 in Isaac's blessing of Levi), and it signifies that this God has ultimate power and control.[102] Hence, there is no doubt about the blessing and justice credited to Levi on the heavenly tablets. On those tablets they serve "as a testimony," here apparently not in the sense of a warning but as a statement about his status noted in the verse.

■ 20 The angel again speaks for himself and his colleagues by claiming that they "remember the justice that the man performed during his lifetime at all times of the year." An interesting element here is that Levi's just behavior is not limited to the one incident recorded in this chapter. The justice he performed at Shechem was characteristic of him, something he did regularly throughout his life. In making such a remarkable claim for Levi, the writer seems to base himself on Malachi. The Lord said through the prophet that Levi revered him "and stood in awe of my name" (Mal 2:5), but the next clause may be the immediate inspiration for the way in which v. 20 describes Levi: "He walked with me in integrity and uprightness" (Mal 2:6). "He walked with me [הלך אתי]" conveys the idea that this was his normal, ongoing way of life, one that was appropriate in their covenantal relationship.[103] The next expression in v. 20 points to the notion of a very long time: "As far as 1000 generations [Latin: years]"[104] reminds one of the Decalogue where the Lord, a jealous God, shows "steadfast love to the thousandth generation of those who love me and keep my commandments" (Exod 20:6 in the interpretive translation of NRSV; see Deut 7:9, where God "maintains covenant loyalty with those who love him and keep his commandments, to a thousand generations"; cf. Exod 34:7). The following verb ("enter") is one regularly used for inserting information on the heavenly tablets.

Perhaps the idea is that the information about Levi will remain on the tablets for an exceedingly long time. The benefit won by Levi will accrue to him and his family in subsequent times. Numbers 25:13 supplies the source for the sentiment: "It shall be for him and for his descendants after him a covenant of perpetual priesthood." The final benefit for Levi is a notation on the celestial tablets that he is "a friend and a just man." Abraham was called a friend of God on the tablets of heaven (Jub 19:9 from Isa 41:8; cf. 2 Chr 20:7; CD iii:1-4), and that is likely to be the meaning here for Levi. He and Abraham are the only two individuals to merit the title in Jubilees (for Israel as a friend, see v. 21).[105] That he was a just man is an implication of the justice he executed at Shechem and, as the present verse indicates, he also exercised it throughout his life (see Deut 33:8; Mal 2:6).

■ 21 With v. 21 the writer expands the audience to all of Israel. The angel again (see v. 12) informs Moses that he wrote the account ("this entire message") for him, but this time he seems to be referring not to Genesis 34 (as in v. 12) but to the preceding material about intermarriage. If so, this would be an instance in which the surviving texts of Jubilees contain the result of a translator's not distinguishing the meanings of the qal ("to write") and hiphil ("to cause to write" = "to dictate") forms of the verb כתב.[106] That is, the angel may have said he has dictated the previous message to Moses and did so to convey a message to the nation. They were not to "transgress the statutes or violate the covenant" made with them so that they would obey it. The language used resembles the words of Lev 26:14-15, where they are expressed negatively: "But if you will not obey me, and do not observe all these commandments, if you spurn my statutes, and abhor my ordinances, so that you will

---

102 For the title and the several attestations of it, see VanderKam, "Isaac's Blessing," 503-4.
103 So David L. Petersen, *Zechariah 9–14 and Malachi* (OTL; Louisville: Westminster John Knox, 1995) 191.
104 The word may have entered the text under influence from *anni* at the end of the previous sentence (VanderKam, *Jubilees* 2:198).
105 Hayes comments on the fact that Abraham and Levi share not only the title of being God's friend but also the language of reckoning a deed of theirs as righteousness ("Intermarriage and Impurity," 22-24). Both, as she points out, are strong advocates of separation from the nations. She suggests "the transformation of Abraham into the original champion of strict endogamy is probably the result of an associative transference of the qualities of Phineas to the patriarch" (p. 23). This seems unnecessary, despite the association of the two, along with several other heroes, in 1 Macc 2:49-60.
106 VanderKam, "Putative Author," 214-17; "Moses," 37.

not observe all my commandments, and you break my covenant . . ." (see also Isa 24:5). Exhortations to obey statutes and keep the covenant are familiar enough, but the reason the angel gives for why they should behave in this way is unusual: it "was established for them so that they should perform it and be recorded as friends." The result of keeping the covenant would be that the Israelites, like Levi (v. 20) and Abraham (19:9), would have their names recorded on the heavenly tablets as "friends of God" (as the Latin reads).[107] The tablets are not mentioned, but the sequel suggests this is the meaning. The people of Israel are never called the friends of God in the HB, but the relationship of love between God and his people comes to expression in several places. Some verses in Deuteronomy 7 may lie behind the formulation. After Moses tells the Israelites that the divine election of them was not caused by their large numbers, he informs them (7:8-9): "It was because the Lord loved you and kept the oath that he swore to your ancestors, that the Lord has brought you out with a mighty hand. . . . Know therefore that the Lord your God is God, the faithful God who maintains covenant loyalty with those who love him and keep his commandments, to a thousand generations."[108]

■ 22 The angel next turns to the negative side of the subject: if Israel is disobedient (and here he adds "behave in any impure ways,"[109] making it particularly relevant to the context), they will indeed be recorded not as friends but as enemies. It is worth noting that even enemies are registered on the tablets, while other compositions or parts of the tablets also figure in the verse. There is a book of the living (see ALD 10:12-13, where the names of Levi and his descendants are entered in a memorial book of life)[110] from which their names will be deleted; there is also a book for the names of people who are going to suffer destruction and uprooting (see 36:10). The wording reminds one of the terms the writer uses for the fate of the nations. In all likelihood, Exod 32:32-33 provides at least some of the inspiration for the references to books. Near the end of the golden calf story, Moses says to the Lord, "'But now, if you will only forgive their sin—but if not, blot me out of the book that you have written.' But the Lord said to Moses, 'Whoever has sinned against me I will blot out of my book.'" The context suggests that the book is a record of the living, because Moses is pleading for the Israelites who survived the Levitical massacre. It is a book in which names are entered and from which they can be erased, but no book of those to be destroyed or uprooted is referenced in the context. Psalm 69:28 (Heb. 29) seems to speak of the same sort of document: "Let them be blotted out of the book of the living; / let them not be enrolled among the righteous" (see also Mal 3:16).[111] Other passages attest to the notion of a book holding the names of sinners and/or their evil deeds. Daniel 7:10 refers to "books" in its judgment scene; apparently they provide the information on the basis of which punishments on the wicked are determined. The point is clearer in the Animal Apocalypse, where Enoch, in his vision, sees a man (= an angel) documenting each person the shepherds destroyed. He also recorded "everything that they had done, and everything that each one of them had taken away, and everything that they had handed over to destruction" (1 Enoch 89:70; cf. v. 76). In 90:17 Enoch looks "until he opened the book of the destruction that those last twelve shepherds worked," and in vv. 20-27 the Lord levels judgment on all the sinners once he has opened the sealed books. The writer of Jubilees,

---

107 See Himmelfarb, "Sexual Relations," 31. As she notes, this promise reduces the division between Levi as priest and other Jews.
108 Malachi, the influence of which on chap. 30 has been noted in several places above, also speaks of God's love for Israel and Jacob (1:2).
109 See CD iii:17; viii:4-5; xix:17; 1QS iv:10; 1QpHab viii:12.
110 See Himmelfarb, "Levi, Phinehas," 14-16, 23. What Jubilees says about Israel, the Aramaic Levi Document says about Levi and his descendants. This is consistent with the theme in Jubilees that Israel is a kingdom of priests.
111 Leslie Baynes, *The Heavenly Book Motif in Judeo-Christian Apocalypses 200 B.C.E.-200 C.E.* (JSJSup 152; Leiden: Brill, 2012) 32-36, 74-75; Houtman, *Exodus*, 3:672-74. For the book of the living/life, see also Phil 4:3; Rev 3:5; 13:8; 20:15.

therefore, knows about two kinds of books—a book of the living and a book for those who are to be destroyed/uprooted. The language of uprooting is, of course, common in Jubilees as a punishment of the nations but also on individuals from the chosen line, should they prove unfaithful (see on vv. 6-7 above).[112]

■ **23** The unit concludes with another comment about writing in heaven. The celestial record-keeping system proves to be up-to-date because on the very day on which Levi and Simeon carried out their attack on Shechem an appropriate notice was placed in it. It recorded that the two brothers had acted virtuously—they exercised righteousness, justice, and revenge (see v. 18 where two of the three terms occur). The writer takes this opportunity to refer to the Shechemites as sinners (the Israelites guilty of the golden calf committed a "great sin" [Exod 32:21, 30-31], and sinners are the ones to be erased from God's book [32:33]). The final sentence in the verse adds that their action was entered as a blessing. It almost sounds as if the author is hinting at Gen 49:5-7—the part of Jacob's "blessing" in which he curses the anger of Simeon and Levi—and saying that the proper assessment of what they did is the opposite of what those verses say.[113]

24-26 The End of the Episode

The long interlude regarding the fuller meaning adhering to the sin of Shechem and the punishment that addressed it occupies vv. 5-23. At v. 24 the author returns to the narrative in Genesis 34, taking elements from Gen 34:26-29. Genesis 34:25-29 describes the military work of Simeon, Levi, and their brothers in Shechem.

Jubilees had already mentioned that Levi and Simeon killed everyone in Shechem (30:4), so there was no need to repeat this information related to Gen 34:25.

■ **24** They[114] removed Dinah[115] from Shechem's house (Gen 34:26) and, unlike in the account in Genesis, Levi and Simeon also plunder the city (the other nine brothers do this in Gen 34:27-28). The writer places in the first position the general category "(they) captured everything that was in Shechem" (a phrase resembling one in Gen 34:28) and then lists the various kinds of livestock (the flocks or sheep, herds or cattle, and the donkeys—all in Gen 34:28) and the other property (= "All their wealth" in 34:29). Where Gen 34:29 includes among the captured "all their little ones and their wives, all that was in the houses [MT reads a singular noun]," Jubilees has "and all their flock." That is, Simeon and Levi do not capture any human beings from Shechem. The thought of having Shechemite women with the family of Jacob probably struck the writer as most inappropriate and a source of temptation.[116] So he read them out of the story (note v. 4: "They left absolutely no one in it. They killed everyone"). All of the animals and the property Simeon and Levi accumulated from Shechem they brought to their father Jacob. Genesis says no such thing. It may be that the line serves as a transition to the following scene in Genesis 34, where in the very next verses (30-31) Jacob is speaking with the two brothers. The transition to their conversation is more natural in Jubilees than in Genesis, but bringing all the booty to their father proved that Simeon and Levi had not plundered the city for their own gain, and it demonstrated their loyalty to their father, no matter what he thought of their actions.[117]

---

112 García Martínez, who classifies the present reference under the rubric "Heavenly Tablets: Heavenly Register of Good and Evil," writes about vv. 19-22: "It is very interesting that in this case the inscription in the HT is made out of consideration of its motivational value. It ought to move its hearers to imitate Levi in the carrying out of the law and the covenant in order to also attain inscription as friends. The passage underlines, on the other hand, that inscription in the heavenly register will be made in any case. One might be inscribed in them as an enemy, that is there exists a double register" ("Heavenly Tablets," 247).

113 Werman suggests that one part of the message in vv. 20-23 to is answer the question why Simeon seemed left without a reward: he will gain it at the end of time when those who, like him, are entered in the book of life receive their just deserts.

114 The subjects of the verb should be Levi and Simeon, as they were in v. 4. Note too that in v. 25 Jacob speaks to "them" about killing the Shechemites; this was true only of Levi and Simeon, not all the brothers.

115 With Syr OL Eth. Gen 34:26 Jubilees adds "their sister" to Dinah's name.

116 See Segal, "Shechem and Dinah," 234 n. 20; Frevel, "Intermarriage," 241.

117 Endres thinks the presentation of the loot to their

■ **25** The verse rewrites Gen 34:30 and makes the encounter between Jacob and his two violent sons sound rather different than it does in Genesis. In Genesis, when he addresses his two sons, Jacob appears weak, not at all confident God will carry out his great promises to him: "You have brought trouble on me by making me odious to the inhabitants of the land, the Canaanites and the Perizzites; my numbers are few, and if they gather themselves against me and attack me, I shall be destroyed, both I and my household." He is as fearful as he was when meeting Laban (Genesis 31) and Esau (chaps. 32–33). He hardly sounds like a person who believes what God had said to him: "the land on which you lie I will give to you and to your offspring; and your offspring shall be like the dust of the earth, and you shall spread abroad to the west and to the east and to the north and to the south; and all the families of the earth shall be blessed in you and in your offspring. Know that I am with you and will keep you wherever you go" (Gen 28:13-15 // Jub 27:22-24). The author of Jubilees comments only that he spoke with[118] the young men about the Shechemite killings, and he admits that Jacob was afraid of the Canaanite and Perizzite residents of the land.[119] He does not reproduce Jacob's fearful words about death for him and his badly outnumbered family. In Genesis the brothers reply rather curtly to their father, as if he does not realize the main point of the whole story according to their assessment of it: "Should our sister be treated like a whore?" (34:31). Jubilees omits this line as well, probably because Jacob, unlike his neutral role in Genesis 34, was angry at the Shechemites and was involved in the deception practiced on them for defiling Dinah (see 30:3). Jubilees wanted to avoid leaving the impression that Jacob could tolerate what was done to Dinah. Besides, the story was about much more than treating Dinah as if she were a prostitute.

■ **26** The author of Jubilees moves ahead to the next chapter in Genesis and draws Gen 35:5 into the present context. In Genesis, Jacob's fear of the local peoples finds no response, but in Jubilees it has an immediate one. The "terror from God" in Gen 35:5 is related to the journey of Jacob's family toward Bethel, but in Jubilees it directly follows Jacob's admission of fear. The divine intervention could be seen as a vindication of what Simeon and Levi had done: God himself did not allow any retaliation from the neighbors of Shechem. The author adds to the end of the verse a phrase not in Gen 35:5: "because terror had fallen on them."[120] The passage says nothing about Jacob himself (in neither Genesis nor Jubilees was he involved in what happened to the people and property of Shechem), only about Jacob's sons, who were responsible for the destruction of the city and the death of its residents.

> **Excursus: An Interpolator?**
>
> Kugel maintains that an interpolator is responsible for much of chap. 30. One has to do a bit of hunting to find exactly which parts he attributes to the interpolator, but in the list of passages in his article he identifies vv. 8-17 and vv. 18-23,[121] so sixteen of the twenty-six verses in the chapter are not from the author. The interpolator, according to Kugel, added vv. 8-17 because he was concerned that the author addressed only the case of giving an Israelite woman to a foreign man and not the reverse—an Israelite man taking a foreign spouse. This led to his use of Lev 18:21 and his claim that it dealt with marriage in both directions. All of this went beyond what the story of Dinah communicated and the interpretation placed on it by the author of Jubilees.[122] Kugel's argu-

---

father could have been derived from Gen 34:30: "Jacob's reproach and the assumptions of the narrative would suggest that they had deposited their spoils in his vicinity, perhaps out of filial devotion" (*Biblical Interpretation*, 131). Segal's ("Shechem and Dinah," 234) suggestion—the action makes Jacob a participant, though a passive one, in the event—seems unlikely to be correct.

118 Charles's translation is "He reproached them," and he explains in a note (*Jubilees*, 184) that the Greek of Jubilees contained the wrong preposition after ελαλησε: the translator selected προς αυτους but should have used κατ' αυτων. It is difficult to see why one should accept the emendation, when Gen 34:30 uses את. Charles appeals to T. Levi 6:6, but that is a poor basis for a textual decision in Jubilees.

119 The LXX says "all those inhabiting the land," but Jubilees sides with the MT and SP in lacking "all."

120 Werman sees this as restoring balance with the peace mentioned in 30:1 ("*Jubilees* 30," 8).

121 Kugel "Interpolations," 250-53, 264; *Walk through Jubilees*, 144-48, 287; "Jubilees," 395-98.

122 Loader makes a related claim: "The transition is somewhat artificial, since the author must deal

ment is not convincing. As shown above, vv. 5-10 deal with the defilement found in Genesis 34, and Lev 18:21 and 20:2-5 were brought in to explain the point. The next section takes up the broader application of the teaching. This was a natural step because Genesis 34, contrary to what Kugel says, does deal with marriage both ways (see 34:9 [mentioned by the men of Shechem], 16 [repeated by the sons of Jacob]). The author had to deal with the issues actually raised in the text of Genesis. As he did this, he elaborated his point with the two texts from Leviticus where defiling the sanctuary and profaning the name figure.

As for vv. 18-23, Kugel makes the claim that the reason given for Levi's winning the priesthood (slaughter of the Shechemites) contradicts the explanations given by the author in chaps. 32-33 (e.g., Isaac blesses him with the priesthood in 31:14; cf. also 32:1-9).[123] It would be a contradiction if the text said slaughter of the Shechemites was the only way in which or reason why Levi gained the priesthood, but it says nothing of the sort. The killings at Shechem are one story about acquiring the priesthood; the others are examples of what Kugel has elsewhere called "overkill" and are hardly *contradictory* to the account in Jub 30:18-20. They are supplementary to it, not in conflict with it.

---

with an incomplete analogy, which will attack both parties, whereas in the original story Dinah is not portrayed as guilty" (*Sexuality*, 168). He, like Kugel, fails to see the halakic section as dealing with the suggestions in Genesis 34 of intermarriage in both directions; unlike Kugel, he does not have recourse to an interpolator to explain the situation.

123 Kugel's assessment of the four places in Jubilees where Levi receives the priesthood has changed since he wrote "Levi's Elevation." There he characterized the multiple traditions as "a classic case of 'overkill'" (6; see also 62–63) and attributes their combination to a single author.

31

Bethel (1): Jacob Sees His Parents and Isaac Blesses Levi and Judah

1/ On the first of the month Jacob told all the people of his household: "Purify yourselves and change your clothes; we are to set out and go up to Bethel where I made a vow, on the day[a] that I ran away from my brother Esau, to the one who has been with me and has brought me back safely to this land. Remove the foreign gods that are among you."[b] 2/ They *handed over*[a] the foreign gods, their earrings and their necklaces, and the idols that Rachel had stolen from her father Laban. She gave everything to Jacob, and he burned them, broke them into pieces, demolished them, and hid them beneath the oak that is in the land of[b] Shechem. 3/ On the first of the seventh month[a] he went up to Bethel. He built an altar at the place where he had slept and had set up a pillar.

He sent word to his father Isaac and to his mother Rebekah as well to come to him[b] to his sacrifice. 4/ Isaac said,[a] "Let my son Jacob come so that I can see him before I die." 5/ Jacob went to his father Isaac and his mother Rebekah in the house of[a] his father Abraham. He took two of his sons with him—Levi and Judah. He came to his father Isaac and his mother Rebekah. 6/ Rebekah went out of the tower into the tower gates[a] to kiss Jacob and hug him because she had revived at the time she heard[b] (the report): "Your son Jacob has now arrived."[c] She kissed him. 7/ When she saw his two sons, she recognized them. She said to him,[a] "Are[b] these your sons, my son?" She hugged them,[c] kissed them, and blessed them as follows: "Through you Abraham's descendants will become famous.[d] You will become a blessing on the earth."

8/ Jacob went in to his father Isaac, to his bedroom where he was lying down. His two children were with him. He took his father's hand, bent down, and kissed him. Isaac hung on his son[a] Jacob's neck and cried on his neck.[b] 9/ Then the shadow passed from Isaac's eyes and he saw Jacob's two sons—Levi and Judah—and said, "Are these your sons, my son, because they look like[a] you?" 10/ He told him that they were indeed his sons:[a] "You have noticed correctly, father,[b] that they are my sons." 11/ When they came up to him, he turned to them and hugged both[a] of them together. 12/ A spirit of prophecy descended[a] into his mouth.[b] He took Levi[c] by[d] his right hand[e] and Judah by his left hand.[f]

13/ He turned to Levi first and began to bless him first.[a] He said to him,[b] "May the Lord of everything—he is the Lord of all[c] ages—bless you[d] and your sons throughout all ages.

14/ May the Lord give you and your descendants greatness and honor;[a]
    may he make you[b] and your descendants (alone) out of all humanity approach him
    to serve[c] in his temple[d] like the angels of the presence and like the holy ones.
    The descendants of your sons will be like them in honor, greatness, and holiness.
    May he make them great[e] throughout all the ages.
15/ They will be princes, judges, and leaders[a] of all the descendants of Jacob's sons.[b]
They will declare the word of the Lord justly
and will justly judge all his verdicts.
They will tell my ways[c] to Jacob[d]
and my paths[e] to Israel.
The blessing of the Lord will be placed in their mouth,[f]
so that they may bless all the descendants[g] of the beloved.
16/ Your mother named you Levi,
and she has given you the right name.
You will become one who is joined to[a] the Lord
and a companion of all Jacob's sons.
His table[b] is to belong to you;
you and your sons are to eat (from) it.
May your table be filled throughout all history;
may your food not be lacking throughout all ages.
17/ May all who hate you fall before you,

843

and all your enemies be uprooted and perish.
May the one who blesses you be blessed,
and any[a] nation who curses you be cursed."[b]
18/ Then he said to Judah:
"May the Lord give you the power and strength to trample[a] on all who hate you.
Be[b] a prince—you and one of your sons—for Jacob's sons.
May your name and the name of your sons[c] be one
that goes and travels around[d] in the entire earth and the regions.
Then the nations will be frightened before you;
all the nations will be disturbed;
all peoples will be disturbed.
19/ May Jacob's help be in you;[a]
May Israel's safety be found[b] in you.
20/ At the time when you sit on the honorable throne that is rightly yours,
there will be great peace for[a] all the descendants of the beloved's sons.[b]
The one who blesses you will be blessed,
and all who hate and trouble you,
and those, too, who curse you[c]
will be uprooted[d] and destroyed from the earth
and are to be cursed."

21/ He turned,[a] kissed him again, and hugged him. He was very happy that he had seen the sons of his true son Jacob. 22/ He moved out from between his feet, fell down, and bowed to him. He then blessed them.[a] He rested there near his father Isaac that night. They ate and drank happily. 23/ He made Jacob's two sons sleep,[a] one on his right, and one on his left; and it was credited to him as something righteous.

24/ That night Jacob told his father everything—how the Lord had shown him great kindness, that he had directed all his ways favorably and had protected him from evil. 25/ Isaac blessed the God of his father Abraham who had not put an end to his mercy and faithfulness for the son[a] of his servant Isaac.[b] 26/ In the morning Jacob told his father Isaac the vow that he had made to the Lord, the vision that he had seen,[a] that he had built an altar and everything was ready for offering the sacrifice before the Lord as he had vowed, and that he had come[b] to put him on a donkey. 27/ But Isaac said to his son Jacob, "I am unable to come with you because[a] I am old and unable to put up with the trip. Go safely, my son, because I am 165 years[b] of age today. I am no longer able to travel. Put your mother on an animal and let her go with you. 28/ I know, my son, that it was on my account that you came. Blessed be this day on which you have seen me alive and I, too, have seen you, my son. 29/ Be successful[a] and carry out[b] the vow that you made. Do not delay (in carrying out) your vow[c] because you will be held accountable regarding the vow. Now hurry to perform it.[d] May the one who has made everything, to whom you made[e] the vow, be pleased (with it)." 30/ He said to Rebekah, "Go with your son Jacob."[a]
So Rebekah went with her son Jacob and Deborah[b] with her. They arrived[c] at Bethel. 31/ When Jacob[a] recalled the prayer[b] with which his father[c] had blessed him[d] and his two sons—Levi and Judah—he was very happy and blessed the God of his fathers Abraham and Isaac. 32/ He said,[a] "Now I know that I and my sons, too, have an eternal hope before the God of all." This is the way it is ordained regarding the two of them, and it is entered for them[b] as an eternal testimony on the heavenly tablets just as Isaac blessed them.

Textual Notes

1a   the day] om. 9 38 63.
b   among you] "from among you" 9 38ᶜ; "with them" 21.
2a   *handed over*] The Eth. MSS. read "melted," which seems wrong in this clause; MSS. 12 35 read an impv. form, also yielding an inappropriate sense. Ms. 38 reads "tore them away." Charles (*Ethiopic Version*, 115 n. 9; *Jubilees*, 185) emended from *masawewwomu* to *maṭawewwomu*, "gave up" (one consonant different). Cf. ויתנו in Gen 35:4. This is a reasonable and a simple change, but possibly already on the Heb. level נתן and נתך were confused, leading to the majority Eth. reading (VanderKam, *Jubilees* 2:201).
b   the land of] om. 17 35.
3a   the seventh month] "the month in the seventh" 20 25.
b   to him] om. 17.
4a   Isaac said] + "to her" 35.
5a   the house of] "the tower of" 21 (see v. 6).
6a   tower gates] "gates" 12 21.
b   she heard] "and they said to her" 63; + "and they said to her" 12; + "which they said to him" 58.
c   has now arrived] "is arriving" 9 17 21 38 44.
7a   to him] "to them" 42 48.
b   Are] Mss. 9 17 38 om. the interrogative particle, making it possible to read the sentence as a statement, not a question.
c   She hugged them] om. 21.
d   will become famous] "are to become famous" 21 25 38 39 42 47 48 58 63.
8a   his son] om. 21 35.
b   his neck] "the neck of his son" 12 21.
9a   like] Lat. *similis* should be *similes* (Rönsch, *Jubiläen*, 58; Charles, *Ethiopic Version*, 115 n. 6 to Lat.).
10a   that they were indeed his sons] Eth. presents the line as indirect speech, whereas Lat., reading *dicens* after *indicavit illi*, phrases it as a quotation and the possessive as first person: "they are indeed my sons." Possibly בניו + בני, in a context where the next letter is the conjunction *vav*, led to the difference (VanderKam, *Jubilees* 2:202).
b   father] so Lat. Eth. = "truly/indeed" (*ba-'amān*). Charles (*Ethiopic Version*, 115 n. 27) suggested the possibility that *'amān* (= the reading of 9 12 17 38 44 63, i.e., without the preceding *ba-* in the other copies) was an error for *'abbā*, "father." This makes good sense in a context where *'amān* is used two other times (VanderKam, *Jubilees* 2:203).
11a   both] = Lat. *utrosque*. Eth. *kwellomu* is probably a mistake for *kel'ēhomu*, "the two of them, both." So Dillmann in Rönsch, *Jubiläen*, 59 n. 2. This is the reading of MS. 63. See VanderKam, *Jubilees* 2:203.
12a   descended] "came" Lat.; + "upon him" 12.
b   his mouth] "the mouth of Isaac his father" 21; Lat. = "the mouth of Isaac."
c   He took Levi] "He took his hand" 12.
d   by] "of/which is" 12.
e   his right hand] "the right hand of Levi" 12.
f   his (left) hand] om. Lat. and MS. 12.
13a   (him) first] om. 21 38; *et primis* Lat., corrected to *in primis* by Rönsch, *Jubiläen*, 58; Charles, *Ethiopic Version*, 117 n. 1 to Lat.
b   He said to him] "He blessed Levi, saying" Lat. See VanderKam, *Jubilees* 2:203.
c   he is the Lord of all (om. Lat. 12 58)] om. 21 35 42 47; pr. "and" Lat.
d   you] Both translations read the pronoun, but Eth. repeats it after the lengthy description of God.
14a   greatness and honor] "great greatness for honor" Eth.; "(your) great (descendants) to know his honor" Lat. Eth.'s noun + cognate adj. looks questionable, although the term "greatness" is used elsewhere for Levi and his offspring—see the commentary. Lat. may give a better text, but the expression "to know his honor" is not attested (though cf. 4Q400 1 i:6: בינות כבודו). Priestly knowledge is a familiar theme. Charles preferred Lat. and proposed changes to conform Eth. to Lat. (*Ethiopic Version*, 116 n. 7; 117 nn. 3-4 to Lat.); Werman (*Jubilees*, 418–19 n. 9) also follows Lat. but changes it to read "an abundance of knowledge in his glory." The two versions share the words "great" and "honor" so they were parts of the text. In VanderKam, *Jubilees* 2:203 it was suggested: "It may be that, under the influence of the word 'greatness' (μεγαθος?), a scribe or translator misread μαθειν as μεγαν and thus gave rise to the Ethiopic adjective." Perhaps it is safest to conclude that the text speaks about two gifts from the Lord to Levi and his descendants: greatness and honor = the reading of MS. 21. See VanderKam, "Isaac's Blessing," 505–6 (cf. T. Levi 13:3, 8; 17:3).
b   you²] Lat. lacks.
c   to serve] Eth. lit., "that he/it (they in 9 38; cf. 47) may serve"; Lat.: "that you (pl.) may serve him." Ms. 21 reads: "that you (sg.) may serve."
d   temple] Lat. has a pl. noun = "sanctuary."
e   make (them) great] "sanctify" Lat. The verb in Lat. seems a mistake by attraction to the preceding *sanctificationem* (VanderKam, *Jubilees* 2:204). Mss. 12 25 read an indicative from of the verb.
15a   and leaders (*malā'ekta*)] Lat. lacks. The MSS. collated for the edition in *Jubilees* 1 offer only the variant lacking the termination (acc. ending) *-a*. For a discussion of Berger's alleged *'amālekta* ("kings"), see the commentary on v. 15. Lat. may have omitted from *et* to *et*.
b   sons] Lat. and MS. 17 lack.
c   my ways] Both versions support "my," though this makes the sentence sound as if God, not Isaac, is speaking. Mss. 17 63 read "his," and 21 has "your [sg.]." 39 58 preface "all" to the phrase.
d   to Jacob . . . to Israel] Lat. places *huius* before both

845

e	"Jacob" and "Israel." Rönsch (*Jubiläen*, 145) explained the two instances as translations of Gk. definite articles.
e	my paths] Again, both versions support "my." Several Eth. MSS. read a verb: *'asareya* became *'astar'aya*, "he appeared" (38 47 63; with "to him" in 39 42 48).
f	in their mouth] "to his seed" Lat. The Eth. is preferable, reflecting Mal 2:6. No reason for the Lat. suggests itself, except perhaps confusion between forms of στομα and σπερμα (suggested by Brandon Bruning).
g	the descendants [lit., "seed"] of the beloved] "beloved seed" Lat. Charles harmonized Lat. with Eth. by reading *dilecti* rather than *dilectum* (*Ethiopic Version*, 117 n. 8 to Lat.). Ms. 63 reads a noun *feqr*, "love, friendship"; MS. 21 reads "Jacob," as may 48ᶜ.
16a	one who is joined to] "for the adornment of God" Lat. Rönsch (*Jubiläen*, 145–46) and Charles (*Jubilees*, 188) explained the Lat. as a translation of לויה ("crown, garland"); Eth. relates the name Levi to the verb לוה.
b	His (table)] "Your" Lat. Apparently Lat. has confused *sua* and *tua* (Rönsch, *Jubiläen*, 58; Charles, *Ethiopic Version*, 117 n. 10 to Lat.).
17a	May the one who blesses you (those who bless you 38 42 47 48) . . . and any] Lat., as read by Ceriani, reads: *quia ut ille benedicit te . . . et si*, "For so the one (who) blesses you . . . also if." Charles (*Ethiopic Version*, 117 n. 12 to Lat.) emended *quia ut ille* to *et qui* = MSS. 25 35 39 42 44 47 48 58, but problems remain (see VanderKam, *Jubilees* 2:205). Since Ceriani marked two letters as uncertain, perhaps the Lat. actually reads *quicumque*, "whoever." For *et si*, the conjunction is expected, but *si* may be a remnant of *omnis*. If so, the versions would agree.
b	be cursed] "all (are to be cursed)" 25 35 39 42 44 47 48ᶜ 58. Lat. lacks "all."
18a	trample] "drive out" 21.
b	Be] "You will be" Lat.
c	for Jacob's sons. May your name and the name of your sons] Lat. om. by parablepsis: *filiorum tuorum–filiorum tuorum*.
d	travels around] Lat. *optinens*, "possess." Rönsch (*Jubiläen*, 146) wondered whether the difference was to be traced back to an interchange between περιεχομενον (= Lat.) and περιερχομενον (= Eth.).
19a	in you] om. 44.
b	be found] "you will find" 20.
20a	for] "in/among" 17.
b	of the beloved's sons] "of the sons of Jacob and the beloved" 12.
c	curse you] om. 25.
d	will be uprooted] "are to be uprooted" 9 21 38 39 58 (cf. 12 42 47 48 63).
21a	He turned] + "to him" 35 47.
22a	blessed them] "blessed him" 63.
23a	He made . . . sleep] He made . . . rise 21 39 42 47 48 58 63.
25a	the son] "the sons" 21 44.
b	Isaac] om. 58.
26a	that he had seen] om. 21.
b	had come] om. 21 39ᵗ.
27a	because] om. 38.
b	years] om. 20 25 35.
29a	Be successful] "You are to be successful" 9 21.
b	carry out] "you are to carry out" 21.
c	your vow] "what you vowed" 21.
d	it] om. 9 12 21 38 63.
e	you made (the vow)] "he vowed" 9 17 21 38 63; "he made" 12.
30a	Jacob] Lat. lacks.
b	Deborah] + "her nurse" Lat. See VanderKam, *Jubilees* 2:207. Werman (*Jubilees*, 419 n. 15) accepts the Lat. reading, despite recognizing that such specifying additions are typical of Lat.
c	arrived] + "with her" 20.
31a	Jacob] om. Lat. 21.
b	prayer] "blessing" Lat. Lat. gives the expected reading, but Eth. has the more difficult yet meaningful one. Isaac's blessing was in fact a prayer. Cf. VanderKam, *Jubilees* 2:208. Werman (*Jubilees*, 419 n.16) accepts Lat. and thinks Eth. was influenced by the presence of "vow" (another meaning of the Eth. word) in the preceding verses.
c	his father] + "Isaac" 35 58.
d	him] om. 12 20.
32a	He said] Lat. lacks (perhaps *et isac et dixit* became just *et isac* because of the repeated conjunction).
b	it is entered for them (for him 21)] "their share" Lat. Lat. seems wrong in the context and could be the result of confusion in the copying process: *portio* may have resulted from misreading a form of *porto* or *reporto* (a similar mixing of related words could have happened in Gk; see VanderKam, *Jubilees* 2:208).

Commentary

Jubilees 31 begins by reworking the opening verses of Genesis 35 (less almost all of v. 1), in which Jacob, after many years, returns to Bethel, the place where God had appeared to him as he began his flight from home. There Jacob had uttered a vow that, if God were with him and returned him to his father's house in peace, "then the LORD shall be my God, and this stone, which I have set up for a pillar, shall be God's house; and of all that you give me I will surely give one-tenth to you" (Gen 28:21-22 // Jub 27:27). The deity had abundantly blessed Jacob with family and wealth, and he had restored him to the land. Jacob had, however, neither returned to Bethel nor had he come to his father's house. Both occur in Jubilees 31. Yet the chapter only begins (vv. 1-3a) from the base in Genesis; the remainder consists of a long section not present in Genesis. In it Jacob returns to his father's house and sees his parents after Isaac requests his presence in Hebron (vv. 3b-4). In vv. 5-30 Jacob is joyfully reunited with Rebekah and Isaac, with a large amount of space given to the blessings that Isaac pronounces on Levi (vv. 13-17) and Judah (vv. 18-20) and the sequel to them (vv. 21-23). The next day Isaac urges Jacob to fulfill his vow at Bethel and sends him back there along with Rebekah and Deborah, Rebekah's nurse (vv. 24-30). Jacob was, of course, delighted with the words of blessing his father had spoken over Levi and Judah—blessings that were also recorded on the heavenly tablets (vv. 31-32).

The major units in chap. 31 are:
1-3a   Preparations and travel to Bethel
3b-30a Jacob, his parents, and his two sons Levi and Judah
    3b-7   Invitations, arrival with Levi and Judah, and meeting with Rebekah
    8-23   Meeting with Isaac and blessing of Levi and Judah
    24-30a Further conversation with Isaac
30b-32 Return to Bethel and joyful reflection on his father's blessings

The Ethiopic version offers the full text of the chapter, and the Latin translation is available for vv. 1 (first five words), 9 (end)-18, and 29-32.

1-3a Preparations and travel to Bethel[1]

Jubilees 31:1 draws expressions from Gen 35:1-3 but orders them differently.

■ 1 The author prefaces to the story the date for it—"the first of the month." The year should be the same as the last one mentioned, 2143 (30:1; 32:33, where it is still the same year). The month in 30:1 is the fourth month, but as the present action occurs on the first of the month a later month should be intended. It is possible he means the seventh month in this instance because 7/1 is the time for the trip to Bethel in 31:3. If he does, all the action in the chapter takes place in the early days of the seventh month.[2] In Genesis 35 the story is set in motion by the deity: "God said to Jacob, 'Arise, go up to Bethel, and settle there. Make an altar there to the God who appeared to you when you fled from your brother Esau'" (35:1). The writer of Jubilees bypasses the command and makes Jacob the instigator.[3] The only expression he takes from Gen 35:1 is "when you fled from your brother Esau," which he places in Jacob's mouth in the rewriting of Gen 35:3. Genesis 35:2-3 and Jub 31:1 read as follows:

Genesis 35:2-3	Jubilees 31:1
So Jacob said to his household and to all who were with him, "Put away the foreign gods that are among you, and purify yourselves, and change your clothes; then come, let us go up to Bethel, that I may make an altar there to the God who answered me in the day of my distress, and has been with me wherever I have gone."	. . . Jacob told all the people of his household: "Purify yourselves and change your clothes; we are to set out and go up to Bethel where I made a vow, on the day that I ran away from my brother Esau, to the one who has been with me and has brought me back safely to this land. Remove the foreign gods that are among you."

The expression in Genesis "and to all who were with him" (whoever they may have been) is absent from Jubilees, except the word "all" that is made to modify "his household." Jacob in Jubilees has no one with him apart from members of his household.[4] Genesis places the

---

1 On these verses, see Rapp, *Jakob in Bet-El*, 187-90.
2 Jubilees 27:19 implies that Jacob traveled from Beersheba to Bethel in one day. The journey to Bethel from his present location (apparently near Shechem [30:26 and v. 2 below]) would be shorter.
3 Rapp, *Jakob in Bet-El*, 189. Not reproducing God's command implies that the writer of Jubilees read the situation differently than the authorities cited in *Gen. Rab.* 81:1-2, who held that Jacob's failure to this point to pay his vow at Bethel was the reason God addressed him as he does in Gen 35:1.
4 One could easily infer that these were the women and children captured at Shechem (Gen 34:29). According to *Tg. Ps.-J.* Gen 35:2 Jacob tells his household members and those with him to get rid of the idols of the peoples that they had taken from the temple in Shechem. The author of Jubilees had said that Simeon and Levi killed everyone in Shechem (30:4); perhaps that is why he omitted "and to all who were with him" from his treatment of Gen 35:2.

command about discarding foreign gods at the beginning of his instructions, whereas Jubilees puts it at the end. In that way it stands immediately before the execution of the command in the next verse (as in Genesis, so in Jubilees removing the idols is Jacob's idea; God did not mention it [see Gen 35:1]). A more significant difference is that in Genesis Jacob speaks of making an altar in Bethel (as commanded by God in v. 1), but Jubilees has him refer to the vow he had made.[5] This is a clue to an important element in the Bethel story and traditional exegesis of it. As noted above, Jacob in Jubilees recalls his flight from Esau (from Gen 35:1) where the Jacob of Genesis speaks of "the day of my distress." The version in Jubilees has Jacob add that God has not only been with him but has also conducted him safely back to the land. By doing this, the writer brings Jacob's words into greater conformity with the vow in Gen 28:21 // Jub 27:27, though there he specified "to my father's house," not just to the land. At any rate, the time to carry out his vow had arrived, as Jacob saw the situation; God did not have to remind him of it as he does in Genesis.

■ **2** The following verse builds on Gen 35:4 but supplements it liberally.

Genesis 35:4	Jubilees 31:2
So they gave to Jacob all the foreign gods that they had, and the rings that were in their ears;	They *handed over* the foreign gods, their earrings and their necklaces, and the idols that Rachel had stolen from her father Laban. She gave everything to Jacob, and he burned them, broke them into pieces, demolished them,
and Jacob hid them under the oak that was near Shechem.	and hid them beneath the oak that is in the land[6] of Shechem.

Jubilees is more comprehensive in including neckwear besides earrings, but the addition of Rachel's idols is interesting because they did not figure in the place (chap. 29) that parallels the one where Genesis deals with them (Gen 31:19, she steals them; 31:30, Laban accuses Jacob of stealing them; 31:32-35, Laban's unsuccessful search for them). Here the writer shows he is aware of the motif that he had earlier omitted. He is thus able to offer a simple identification for the pagan gods that Jacob demands from his household.[7]

Jacob's treatment of the idols is decidedly more destructive than in Genesis.[8] It reminds one of what Moses did in Exodus 32: "He took the calf that they had made, burned it with fire, ground it to powder, scattered it on the water, and made the Israelites drink it" (Exod 32:20). Jacob also seems to be following the Lord's command to Moses in Deut 7:5 regarding how to handle the cultic paraphernalia of the seven Canaanite nations: "break down their altars, smash their pillars, hew down their sacred poles, and burn their idols with fire." The gods would be unusable to anyone who came upon the site in the future. Jacob, in burning the gods, imitated his grandfather Abraham, who had incinerated the temple of Ur with its idols (Jub 12:12).[9] It is interesting that the place where he hid the remains of the idols is under an oak in the region of Shechem, since much later Joshua would exhort the Israelites to "put away the foreign gods that are among you" when they gathered at Shechem (Josh 24:1, 23).

■ **3a** The journey and arrival at Bethel (see Gen 35:6-7) the writer dates to the first day in the seventh month—one of the four memorial or seasonal dates in the year (e.g., 6:26). The month number is consistent with the fact that in chap. 32 Jacob will celebrate the Festival of Tabernacles. Genesis calls the place by its former name,

---

5   Endres, *Biblical Interpretation*, 159.
6   The versions of Gen 35:4 do not attest "the land of," but *Targums Pseudo-Jonathan* and *Neofiti* read "near/in the vicinity of" where the MT and SP have עם. Josephus (*Ant.* 1.342) has: εν Σικιμοις εις γην υπο τινα δρυν (εις γην means "in the ground" here).
7   According to Josephus, "While he was purifying his company accordingly, he lit upon the gods of Laban, being unaware that Rachel had stolen them" (*Ant.* 1.342).
8   The LXX tradition reads at the end of v. 4: "and he destroyed them to the present day."
9   For the Abraham connection, see Halpern-Amaru, *Empowerment*, 94 (and pp. 93–95 on the presentation of Rachel and her handing over the idols). Rapp also calls attention to 2 Kgs 23:4-20, where Josiah thoroughly destroys cultic objects through crushing and burning, including the altar at Bethel (*Jakob in Bet-El*, 190 n. 122).

Luz, but Jubilees uses the one it acquired later. Genesis resorts to the name Luz because it has Jacob naming the city "El-bethel" on this occasion (see also 35:15); Jubilees dispenses with the naming (Jacob had named it "Bethel" the first time he visited it [28:19 // Jub 27:26] so it may have appeared superfluous to repeat the exercise).[10] Genesis 35:7 reports only that he built an altar there; Jubilees paraphrases and expands parts of 35:7 by saying that he constructed the altar "at the place where he had slept and had set up a pillar" (for the pillar, see Gen 28:18// Jub 27:26). Genesis alludes to the first time he visited Bethel only to explain the name Jacob now gives it: "because it was there that God had revealed himself to him when he fled from his brother" (35:7).

3b-30a Jacob, His Parents, and His Two Sons Levi and Judah

A long insertion into the Genesis narrative occurs at this point (it will continue to 32:16, 21-29). The writer of Jubilees transforms the Bethel story into a time when Jacob and his parents at last reunite and Levi is multiply confirmed as priest and ancestor of the priestly line.

3b-7 Invitations, Arrival with Levi and Judah, and Meeting with Rebekah

To his credit, Jacob, though he has not gone to see his parents in the years since returning from Haran, initiates their reunion.

■ **3b** Jacob, who had not seen his parents for twenty-eight years,[11] though he had cared for them by sending them supplies (29:15-20), now invites them[12] (they live in Hebron [29:19]) to attend the sacrificial rite he was about to perform in Bethel.[13] Genesis, as noted before, attributes no actions to Rebekah after Jacob left home (in 28:1-5); as for Isaac in this period, it reports only his death at 180 years (35:27-29). In Jubilees both parents have significant direct contact with Jacob after his return, beginning at the present time when he reaches their residence. The chronology implies that Isaac should have more than two decades to live after Jacob's arrival at Bethel. Jacob was born in 2046 (Jub 19:13), and the events of chap. 31 occur in 2143; therefore, Jacob was now ninety-seven. Since Isaac was sixty years of age when Rebekah gave birth to the twins, he would have been 157 at this time, leaving him twenty-three more years before his death (though he again thinks he is about to die).[14] One of the inconsistencies in the Jubilean chronology is that Isaac says in 31:27 his age is 165 years.

■ **4** In v. 4[15] Isaac does not explicitly turn down the invitation (he will in v. 27) but reverses it: he urges Jacob to visit him before he dies. Jacob was being dutiful in fulfilling what he had vowed to God at Bethel, but he was being much less dutiful to his elderly parents by still not seeing them face to face. Isaac understandably calls upon Jacob to make the journey to Hebron (for Hebron as their home at this time, see Jub 29:19) and thus to

---

10   The Bethel passage in Genesis 28 is generally assigned to the J source, the one in Genesis 35 to E.
11   He left home in 2115 (27:19), and the reunion with his parents now occurs in 2143.
12   It is perhaps significant that both parents receive his invitation in v. 3b, since some have concluded that Jacob himself was not a priest and thus needed Isaac to perform the sacrifice. For references, see the commentary on v. 26 below. That both parents were invited makes one doubt that Isaac's official priestly status was the point of requesting his presence in Bethel.
13   Davenport maintains that v. 3b "conflicts with the narrative in xxxi, 26-30 when vss. 4-25 are removed, for Jacob has not sent (vs. 3b) but gone for Isaac and Rebecca (vss. 26-30)" (*Eschatology*, 57 n. 1). It is puzzling why one should remove vv. 4-25 from the consistent context in which they appear. Verses 3b and 4 are not from Genesis but present no conflict between themselves or with vv. 26-30 (also not from Genesis). Davenport makes a stronger point in observing that Jacob's invitation to his father in v. 26 makes him seem "oblivious to the previously described condition of Isaac" (p. 57 n. 3), but the statement that Jacob has a donkey ready to carry him removes the force of the objection.
14   Syncellus wrote: "In Isaac's 153rd year, Jacob returned to him from Mesopotamia. When Isaac recovered his sight and saw the sons of Jacob, he blessed Levi as high priest and Judah as king and ruler" (124.1–3; Adler/Tuffin, *Chronography*, 155). Syncellus claims that the information comes from Josephus, but here again he confuses Josephus and Jubilees. As Adler and Tuffin remark, in Josephus's narrative Rebekah died before this (p. 155 n. 1).
15   Davenport finds vv. 3 and 4 to be contradictory: "Vs. 4 portrays Isaac as the initiator of Jacob's visit, whereas vs. 3 says that Jacob sent for Isaac and

complete the trip he had envisioned at Bethel ("so that I come again to my father's house in peace" [Gen 28:21 // Jub 27:27]). Isaac's words are richly ironic when one recalls the blessing scene of Genesis 27 // Jubilees 26: on that occasion he had also thought he was about to die and blessed the wrong son because he could not see well. Now he says, "Let my son Jacob come so that I can see him before I die."[16]

■ 5 Jacob complies with Isaac's request and finally visits his parents "in the house of his father Abraham," the place to which they had moved to distance themselves from Esau (Jub 29:17-19). The narrative stresses that he came to see both parents by naming them twice in v. 5, both times in the order Isaac-Rebekah. His arrival at his parents' residence proved the accuracy of Isaac's prediction when consoling Rebekah after Jacob had left: "For I well know that his ways will be directed favorably wherever he goes until he returns safely to us and we see that he is safe" (Jub 27:16). An unexpected notice in v. 5 is the news that Jacob arrived with his sons Levi (aged sixteen in the book's chronology) and Judah (aged fourteen).[17] The writer does not at this point reveal why Jacob selected his third and fourth oldest sons and not any of the other nine. After the events at Shechem, Levi is perhaps not a complete surprise, but why did he not choose Simeon, the other hero of the slaughter, along with Levi? A person familiar with the HB knows what the futures of the two who accompanied him will be, but the choice of Levi and Judah is unexplained in v. 5.

■ 6-7 Just as the reader might anticipate, Rebekah, who was more spry than her elderly husband, is the first to greet her long-absent son. When she got the news that Jacob had come, she went out to meet him before he even got inside the tower gates. The writer relates that she "revived [lit., her spirit lived; cf. 25:19]"[18] when she heard of his arrival. She showered affection on him as she had before (see 25:23)—the fact that she kissed him is said twice. She seems to have been as perceptive as ever because, as soon as she caught sight of Levi and Judah, she recognized them as Jacob's sons. Once she saw the family resemblance she asked the rhetorical question: "Are these your sons, my son?" This might seem to be just a warm motherly or grandmotherly touch in the story, but the reader would hardly be confident about Isaac's ability to recognize whether they really were Jacob's sons. Because Rebekah makes the identification, there is no room to doubt the identity of the two young men who were about to receive splendid blessings from Isaac. The tremendous standing that Rebekah enjoys in Jubilees comes to expression once more in this scene.[19] She not only anticipates Isaac in recognizing Levi and Judah and greeting them affectionately as she had just done to Jacob; she also precedes him in blessing the grandsons. It is through the two of them that Abraham will have a name, and they will prove to be a blessing on the earth (for the name blessing, see Gen 12:2 // Jub 12:23; both passages also mention being a blessing; see too Gen 48:16). The covenant promises will continue and come to fruition through them.[20] She had earlier prayed that she would "see your [Jacob's] blessed children during my lifetime" (25:18), and now she had.

Rebecca. Whoever joined them may have assumed that Isaac's words would sound like a response to Jacob" (*Eschatology*, 57 n. 1). How the two verses contradict each other is exceedingly difficult to see; they fit very smoothly and logically in the narrative sequence.

16 Werman draws attention to the parallel involving Jacob and Joseph in Gen 45:28 // Jub 43:24 (*Jubilees*, 421).

17 Genesis relates no encounter between Isaac and Rebekah and any of their grandchildren, but, as was the case with Abraham and his meetings with Jacob, the chronology provided ample time for meetings between them. Isaac (born apparently in 1987; see 16:15) would have been 149 years when Jacob returned to Canaan in 2136 with his eleven sons and one daughter. Isaac lived until the age of 180 (Gen 35:28 // Jub 36:18), so there were a few decades in which he could have met Jacob's children. See VanderKam, "Exegetical Creation," 364-65 (the claim on p. 365 that Jubilees does not list Isaac's age at death as 180 is incorrect).

18 As Charles observed, the phrase comes from Gen 45:27, where Jacob's spirit revives when he sees the goods Joseph had sent, proving that he was alive (*Jubilees*, 185). See also Gen 48:2, though the wording is different.

19 Cf. Endres, *Biblical Interpretation*, 159-60; Halpern-Amaru, *Empowerment*, 61-62.

20 Werman relates her blessing to Abraham's words in 19:20-24, where he speaks about Jacob's descendants (*Jubilees*, 421). As she understands the passage, Rebekah now identifies Levi and Judah as the seed of Jacob about which Abraham was speaking

8-23 Meeting with Isaac and Blessing of Levi and Judah

The reunion with Isaac follows the one with Rebekah, and his blessing of Levi and Judah also comes after her benediction on them.

■ **8** Bedridden at the time, Isaac was unable to come out of Abraham's tower to meet Jacob, so Jacob with the two young men went to his room. This is the first time there is open affection between Isaac and Jacob, the son whom he had favored less than Esau. In Gen 27:26-27 (// Jub 26:21) Jacob, at Isaac's command, kissed him, but Isaac thought he was Esau. Abraham and Jacob and Rebekah and Jacob had been physically affectionate; now Isaac and Jacob are as well. The scene is patterned in a number of respects on the story in Gen 47:28—48:20, where Joseph and Jacob are at last reunited, the son visits the bedridden and nearly blind father, and he brings along his two sons—Manasseh and Ephraim—whom the elderly man blesses (see below; in that passage Jacob kisses and embraces the two grandsons, not his son Joseph [v. 10]). The Joseph-Jacob unit is the third place in Genesis where the experience at Luz/Bethel receives attention (see 48:3-4).[21] There Joseph "bowed himself with his face to the earth" (v. 12); here Jacob takes his father's hand and leans over to kiss him. The affection between Isaac and Jacob is modeled on Joseph's reception of Jacob in Egypt: when he saw his father, "[h]e[22] presented himself to him, fell on his neck, and wept on his neck a good while" (Gen 46:29). The writer of Jubilees has crafted a scene of great importance according to the shape of one that Genesis ascribes to the next generation and in this way conveys the message that there were relations of genuine warmth in the previous generation as well. Isaac no longer loves Esau more than Jacob!

■ **9-10** Isaac, whose eyesight had remained poor over the years, experienced a sudden recovery from the malady—"the shadow passed from Isaac's eyes."[23] The wonderful improvement in his vision provides the reader with reassurance that in the ensuing section he knows exactly whom he is blessing, that there will be no mistaken identity this time. He, like Rebekah, even displays a keen eye because he notices that Levi and Judah look like their father; also, as Rebekah did, he asks about their identity so that Jacob can confirm it (see Gen 48:8, where Jacob asks, upon seeing Joseph's sons, "Who are these?"). Jacob does verify his father's statement; in fact, v. 10 both reports Jacob's words and quotes them. This time Isaac got it right.[24]

■ **11-12** The parallels with Genesis 48 become stronger as the scene develops. According to v. 11, when the sons approached Isaac he hugged them. The corresponding passage in Genesis 48 reads: "So Joseph brought them [his two sons] near him [Jacob]; and he kissed them and embraced them" (v. 10). Genesis 48 places in Jacob's mouth several predictions regarding Ephraim and Manasseh; Isaac in Jubilees 31 also speaks of the two sons' futures. For this reason the writer says in v. 12 "A spirit of prophecy descended into his mouth." Something similar happened to Rebekah when she blessed Jacob and his descendants in Jub 25:14: "the spirit of righteousness descended into her mouth" (for the phrase, see Rev 19:10; *Tg. J.* Isa 61:1). Isaac, like Abraham and Rebekah, spoke as a prophet (see Gen 20:7 for

---

and on whom the existence of heaven and earth depend (as in 19:25). But Abraham was dealing more generally with Jacob's descendants (note the reference to their great numbers in 19:21-22) and gave no indication that he meant only some of them.

21 On the parallels between the sections, see VanderKam, "Exegetical Creation," 370-71: "It appears that the writer of *Jubilees*, as he assembled into his large Levi addition as much material as possible from the Bethel sections of *Genesis*, noticed Jacob's last reference to the revelation at Luz/Bethel and exploited it as the framework for another of the scenes in which an authoritative figure appoints Levi to the priesthood. In this connection we should recall that his procedure was not arbitrary. The writer drew upon a passage in which Jacob adopted Joseph's two sons who became ancestors of the tribes which, in some biblical lists, provide the extra name that replaces the priestly and thus landless tribe of Levi" (p. 371).

22 The context implies that Joseph is the subject of the verbs, but this is not explicit. See also Gen 45:14-15: "Then he [Joseph] fell upon his brother Benjamin's neck and wept, while Benjamin wept upon his neck. And he kissed all his brothers and wept upon them; and after that his brothers talked with him."

23 See Tob 11:7-15 for restoration of Tobit's eyesight when his son Tobias "peeled off the white films from the corners of his eyes" (11:13). Cf. also Job 16:16.

24 VanderKam, "Isaac's Blessing," 497-98.

Abraham as a prophet). Isaac assumes the posture for blessing by taking Levi with his right hand and Judah with his left. The choice of hand indicates priority as the order of blessings in vv. 13-20 shows and as the parallel in Genesis 48 indicates.[25] When Joseph presents his two sons Manasseh and Ephraim (in that order, as Manasseh was the older [48:1]), Jacob reverses the names already in his speech in v. 5, but Joseph leads them forward in such a way that Jacob will place his right hand on Manasseh and his left on Ephraim when he blesses them. Jacob, however, insists on the opposite arrangement so that Ephraim would be the one to have precedence (48:13-20). In Jubilees 31 Isaac needed no switching of hands and Jacob offered no protest: Levi the older (Leah's third son) Isaac took with his right hand, and Judah the younger (Leah's fourth son) he took by the left. Levi the future priest has priority.

Verses 13-17[26] contain Isaac's blessing of Levi and his descendants. The writer of Jubilees may not have been the first to have Isaac bless Levi as priest (a word not mentioned in the blessing) because the same motif appears in the Aramaic Levi Document (and later in the Testament of Levi). In the Aramaic Levi Document, the specific situation described in Jubilees 31 occurs in 5:1: "And we [Levi is speaking] went to my father Isaac, and thus he [blessed] me." At this point, however, Levi does not quote the words of Isaac. In fact, when Isaac does speak to him, it is on a later occasion—after Jacob and his family returned to Bethel and subsequently traveled again to Abraham's house where Isaac was living. At that time Isaac instructed Levi in "the law of the priesthood" (5:8; the instructions occupy chaps. 6-9). These instructions do not resemble the wording of Isaac's blessing in Jub 31:13-17; rather, they align much more closely with Abraham's priestly instructions to Isaac in Jubilees 21 (see the commentary there for the parallels). Isaac continues to instruct Levi in Aramaic Levi Document 10, where Isaac says Levi is "a holy priest of the Lord, and all your seed will be priests" (vv. 1-2). Isaac was happy that Levi was "elected for the holy priesthood, and to offer sacrifice to the Most High Lord, to do as is proper, according to that instruction" (v. 4). Verses 11-14 sound more like the blessing in Jubilees though the wording is hardly the same.

> And now, beloved child, as I say to you, you are beloved of your father and holy to the Most High Lord. And you will be more beloved than all your brothers. And blessing shall be pronounced by your seed upon the earth and your seed shall be entered in the book of the memorial of life for all eternity. And your name and the name of your seed shall not be annihilated for eternity. And now, child, Levi, your seed shall be blessed upon the earth for all generations of eternity.

There are some parallels between Jub 31:13-17 and Levi's prayer in Aramaic Levi Document 3 (cf. also his vision in chap. 4, esp. v. 7: "the kingdom of priesthood is greater than the kingdom" [presumably the kingdom of the sword/royalty]; 4:11 he is greater and more loved than all).

The parallels in the Testament of Levi are also scattered. The situation is described in 9:1-2: "After two days I and Judah went up with our father to Isaac. And the

---

25 In connection with the parallel between Jubilees 31 and Genesis 48 regarding the gesture of taking one grandson by the right hand and the other by the left, Endres speaks of the author's "telescoping" events from the scriptures (*Biblical Interpretation*, 160).

26 On these verses, see Rapp, *Jakob in Bet-El*, 212-22. In his analysis, he is especially concerned to determine the relations between the contents of vv. 13-17 and material in the Aramaic Levi Document and the Testament of Levi. He notes (p. 221) that Jub 31:13-17 and T. Levi 2:1–5:8 have a high degree of correspondence, including verbal parallels. The similarities between Jubilees and the Testament of Levi here are closer than with the Aramaic Levi Document. Kugel, however, maintains that there really are no parallels with the section about the first vision in Testament of Levi 2-5 ("Levi's Elevation," 42-46)—a proposition difficult to accept, as the commentary will show. In the same essay (pp. 22-24), Kugel finds in the fact that Isaac blesses Levi with the priesthood—something that he did not do for his son Jacob in the two places where he blessed him—evidence that in Jubilees Jacob is not a priest. The priesthood jumps a generation from Isaac, whom Abraham instructed in the priesthood in chap. 21, to Levi. On this, see the commentary on Jub 32:4-9.

father of my father blessed me according to all the words of my visions which I had seen. And he did not want to come with us to Bethel."[27] In this text, too, Isaac's actual instructions (again "the law of the priesthood" [v. 7]) are separated from the blessing scene by a return to Bethel and then a move to Hebron (vv. 3-5). The instructions are, however, much abbreviated compared with the Aramaic Levi Document (they are in 9:6-14, where there are parallels with Jubilees 21). But Levi says in v. 2 that Isaac blessed him "according to all the words of my visions," and it is in the vision passages that the parallels with Jub 31:13-17 appear. In the first (2:5—4:6) an angel tells him he will "stand near the Lord and will be his minister and will declare his mysteries to men" (2:10). He also learns from him that in the sixth heaven the angels of the presence minister and offer a bloodless offering (3:5-6). Moreover, Levi will become for the Most High a "son and a servant and a minister of his presence. You will light up a bright light of knowledge in Jacob, and you will be as the sun to all the seed of Israel. And a blessing will be given to you and to all your seed" (4:2-4a). In 5:2 the angel tells him he has received "the blessings of the priesthood." In his second vision (chap. 8), seven men in white clothing adorn him with the priestly garb and say, "From now on become a priest of the Lord, you and your seed for ever" (8:3). They anoint, wash, clothe, and crown him with "a diadem of priesthood. And they filled my hands with incense that I might serve as priest to the Lord" (8:10; note also the three offices into which his seed will be divided in 8:11).

The author of Jubilees has gathered material from different sections in the Aramaic Levi Document (or the source they shared) and located them in the first meeting of Isaac and his grandsons. The blessings of Levi, Judah, and their descendants are introduced in v. 12, and the poetic words Isaac spoke begin in v. 13.

■ **13a** As if one might have missed the hint in v. 12 about Levi's precedence over Judah, the writer repeats it twice in v. 13a, where Isaac first turns to him and pronounces the initial blessing on him. The priesthood comes before the monarchy in this arrangement. Following the preface to the Levi section in v. 13a, the blessing itself falls into three parts:

vv. 13b-14a blessing on Levi and his descendants
vv. 14b-15   blessing on Levi's descendants
vv. 16-17   blessing on Levi (one reference to his sons in v. 16).[28]

■ **13b-14a**[29] The first words of the blessing are for both Levi and his offspring. Isaac asks that the "Lord of everything—he is the Lord of all ages" be the one to bless Levi and his line forever. Clearly the divine titles are well suited to an eternal benefit. The first, which has appeared in other blessings (see 22:10, 27; cf. 30:19),[30] points to God's power over the creation, while the second refers to the unending duration of his control. The Angel of the Presence had told Moses in Jub 30:18: "Levi's descendants were chosen for the priesthood and as Levites to serve before the Lord as we (do) for all time. Levi and his sons will be blessed forever because he was eager to carry out justice, punishment, and revenge on all who rise against Israel" (see also ALD 10:14). This God of all and all times will be able to grant Isaac's wishes. His more specific requests follow.

May the Lord give you and your descendants greatness[31] *and honor* (for the readings in the Ethiopic and Latin versions, see the textual note).[32] In ALD 4:11 the angels

---

27 Rapp asserts that the passage places the blessing on both Levi and Judah (*Jakob in Bet-El*, 207–8), but Levi relates only that Isaac blessed him and says nothing about a blessing for Judah.
28 VanderKam, "Isaac's Blessing," 502.
29 On these verses, see Kugler, *From Patriarch to Priest*, 162–63; VanderKam, "Isaac's Blessing," 505–7.
30 The title may appear twice in 11QPs[a] xxviii:7–8, and it is used in 4Q409 6 8; see VanderKam, "Isaac's Blessing," 503–4. To these instances one may add 5Q13 1 2 (frg. 2 6-9 refer to Jacob at Bethel and Levi and his sons).
31 Werman, who reads "knowledge" with the Latin translation, stresses its importance and comments that the priests' nearness to God makes it available to them (*Jubilees*, 422).
32 Davenport assigns v. 14 to his sanctuary-oriented redaction (the last of the three editions) (*Eschatology*, 15–16, 57–58, 60). About the verse he writes: "The addition of vs. 14 has heightened the more commonly conceived priestly role of the Levites" (pp. 57–58 n. 4). The statements in v. 14, however, draw on ones in the HB that speak of priests *and* Levites as approaching God and serving in his sanctuary. Though it mentions the temple, there is nothing problematic in the verse that would point to it as an addition to an earlier form of Jubilees.

tell Levi in a vision "how we gave you the anointing (or: greatness [רבות])³³ of eternal peace." The same text uses the word "glory/honor" (יקר) several times in connection with Levi (11:10, explaining the name Jochebed; especially in his speech about wisdom in chap. 13 [vv. 4-6, 9-10, 15-16]). The two nouns from this line in Jubilees occur in ALD 13:6 where Levi says, "Observe, my children, my brother Joseph [who] taught reading and writing and the teaching of wisdom, for glory [ליקר] and for majesty [ולרבו]." 1QSb iii:4 also refers to glory in connection with the eschatological priest and his offspring: "with [perpetual] glo[ry. May He] sanctify your descendants with glory [בכבוד] without end!" (trans. Wise, Abegg, and Cook, *DSSR* 5:429; see also v:18, where the text refers to the glory of Zadok's sons; Sir 45:26). In v. 14b Isaac will speak about the honor, greatness, and holiness of Levi's descendants.

May he make you and your descendants (alone) out of all humanity approach him. In the HB the Levites are separated from the other Israelite tribes in order to carry out their appointed functions, and some from that tribe—the priests—have the exclusive right to approach the altar to offer sacrifice on it (Num 18:1-7; cf. 1:50-53; 3:5-13). Exodus 32:29 has Moses say to the Levites, "Today you have ordained yourselves for the service of the LORD, and so have brought a blessing on yourselves this day." Or, Deut 18:5 declares, "For the LORD your God has chosen Levi [text: him] out of all your tribes, to stand and minister in the name of the LORD, him and his sons for all time" (see also v. 7). The language of approaching the deity occurs in Num 16:8-10:

> Then Moses said to Korah, "Hear now, you Levites! Is it too little for you that the God of Israel has separated you from the congregation of Israel, to allow you to approach him in order to perform the duties of the LORD's tabernacle, and to stand before the congregation and serve them? He has allowed you to approach him, and all your brother Levites with you; yet you seek the priesthood as well!" (cf. also Deut 33:10; Ezek 40:46; Sir 45:15-16; ALD 3:10).

So, "approaching" is not only a priestly privilege; it is one shared with the Levites.

To serve in his temple like the angels of the presence and like the holy ones. The verb "serve/minister" is a regular one in connection with priestly duties (e.g., Sir 45:15; ALD 3:10; T. Levi 2:10; 4:2); in fact, the priests are "the ministers of the Lord" (see Joel 1:9; 2:17). In describing the holy district, the angel tells Ezekiel that one part of it "shall be for the priests, who minister in the sanctuary and approach the Lord to minister to him"; another section "shall be for the Levites who minister at the temple" (45:4-5; cf. also Jer 33:21-22; 11QTᵃ lx:14). Isaac speaks of their serving in God's temple "like the angels of the presence and like the holy ones." These are the two highest classes of angels, according to Jub 2:2. The Angel of the Presence who is revealing the account to Moses had said in 30:18: "Levi's descendants were chosen for the priesthood and as Levites to serve before the Lord as we (do) for all time." Testament of Levi 3:5-6 relates that in a vision Levi saw seven heavens, in the sixth of which "are the angels of the presence of the Lord, those who minister and make propitiation to the Lord for all the sins of ignorance of the righteous, and they offer to the Lord a pleasant odour, a reasonable and bloodless offering."³⁴ An especially good parallel figures in the blessing on the sons of Zadok, the priests in 1QSb iv:24–26: "May you (abide forever) as an Angel of the Presence in the holy habitation, to the glory of the God of host[s. May you serve the Lord forever and b]e all around. May you serve in the temple of the kingdom of God, ordering destiny with the Angels of the Presence" (trans. Wise, Abegg, and Cook, *DSSR* 5:149).³⁵ The passage, like Isaac's blessing, expresses a correlation between the heavenly and the earthly priestly service.³⁶

---

33   See Drawnel, who correctly prefers the rendering "greatness" (*Aramaic Wisdom Text*, 115–16).

34   *Pirqe Rabbi Eliezer* 37 echoes the same thoughts: "And He put forth His right hand and blessed him, that the sons of Levi should minister on earth before Him, like the ministering angels in heaven" (Friedlander, 284). The text continues by dealing with the food given to Levi's descendants from the sacrifices. For this passage, see Kugel, "Levi's Elevation," 34–35.

35   The words "serve in the temple of" at the end of line 25 are added from their *The Dead Sea Scrolls: A New Translation*, 149; they were accidently omitted from the rendering in *DSSR* 5.

36   See VanderKam, "Isaac's Blessing," 506–7. Werman

14b-15 Blessing on Levi's Descendants

As he focuses his attention on Levi's offspring, Isaac continues the comparison with the high-ranking angels. He declares that they will be "like them in honor, greatness, and holiness. May he make them great throughout all the ages" (v. 14). "Honor" and "greatness" were the terms he used in v. 14a for both Levi and his descendants; now he adds "holiness" to them. Holiness is a trait that the HB ascribes to the clergy (Exod 29:21 [priests]; Lev 21:6-8 [priests]; 2 Chr 23:6 [priests and Levites]; 35:3 [Levites]; Sir 45:6 [Aaron]; 1QSb iv:27-28 [sons of Zadok]). As for magnifying them, a similar expression occurs in ALD 4:11, where angels, in a vision, say to Levi, "Now, see we have made you greater than all." In Sir 45:2 (Greek) the verb "magnify" has Moses as its object, and 45:6 says the Lord exalted Aaron. In the sentence in Jubilees, where the Ethiopic version has "May he make them great throughout all the ages" the Latin translation reads, "He will sanctify them throughout all the ages." The holiness of the clergy is a frequent theme (see above), but the verb *sanctificavit* (= *sanctificabit*) may be an error induced by *sanctificationem* directly before the clause in question.[37] At any rate, the Ethiopic is the more difficult and hence more likely reading.

The functions that Levi's posterity will perform are the subject of v. 15, where Isaac envisages an extraordinary future for them. Though they will indeed perform sacred tasks, he predicts that they will also be "princes, judges, and leaders of all the descendants of Jacob's sons."

Princes (Ethiopic: *makwānent*; Latin: *principes*). It is reasonable to think שרים was the term in Hebrew Jubilees. 1 Chronicles 24:5 applies it to Levites, and 1QSa i:22-24, which lists three offices for Levites, includes it (line 24).

Judges (Ethiopic: *masāfent*; Latin: *iudices*). The Levites played judicial roles (Deut 17:8-13; 1 Chr 23:4; 26:29; 2 Chr 19:8-11; Ezek 44:24), and 1QSa i:24 uses שופטים for them. In some passages (e.g., in Judges especially) the term encompasses broader leadership roles.

Leaders (Ethiopic: *malā'ekt*;[38] Latin lacks a third term). A likely equivalent is שוטרים (1 Chr 23:4; 26:29; 2 Chr 34:13), another of the three offices for Levites in 1QSa i:24 (supralinear).[39]

---

adduces the word מלאך for a priest in Mal 2:7 (*Jubilees*, 422).

37 VanderKam, *Jubilees* 2:204.
38 Berger oddly translates "und Könige" and explains that the Latin lacks an equivalent "weil es der Funktion Judas konkurriert" (*Jubiläen*, 478 n. a to v. 15). He seems to have confused *malā'ekt* with a form related to the root *malaka*—perhaps *'amlāk* (pl. *'amālekt*), though it means "God, gods" (Leslau, *Concise Dictionary*, 29-30), not "kings." His mistake has entered the literature. M. de Jonge and J. Tromp ("Jacob's Son Levi in the Old Testament Pseudepigrapha and Related Literature," in M. Stone and T. Bergren, eds., *Biblical Figures outside the Bible* [Harrisburg, PA: Trinity Press International, 1998] 211) write about priests as kings and add, "In his edition, VanderKam reads *malā'ᵉkt* ('messengers'), but translates the variant reading 'leaders' (*'amālᵉkt*), obviously because of the context" (n. 13). There is no such variant in the manuscripts collated for the edition; the translation "leaders" is an accurate rendition of *malā'ekt*. Schubert (*Tradition*, 159-60) finds Berger's translation preferable (also giving the nonexistent variant *'amālekta*) and thinks the Ethiopic reading "kings" derives from a Greek manuscript of Jubilees into which someone placed this pro-Hasmonean insertion. One can safely jettison the suggestion of a pro-Hasmonean addition, since there is no reading "kings," only the more modest "leaders," a term reflecting usage in the HB.
39 VanderKam, "Isaac's Blessing," 508. The Aramaic Levi Document and the Testament of Levi also speak about different offices or functions for Levi's descendants. Aramaic Levi Document 13:16 certainly mentions "heads and judges" (or heads and leaders [ראשין ושפטין]) and probably "judges" (ודא]נין); this is the reading of Kugler (*From Patriarch to Priest*, 119) and Drawnel (*Aramaic Wisdom Text*, 164), while Greenfield, Stone, and Eshel read the third word as ידע] (*Aramaic Levi Document*, 104). In T. Levi 8:11 seven men in white tell Levi that "his seed will be divided into three offices [αρχας]." Rapp suspects the offices of high priest, priests, and Levites were meant (*Jakob in Bet-El*, 218-19; he follows P. Grelot, "Notes sur le Testament Araméen de Lévi," *RB* 63 [1956] 391-406, here 395-96), yet the verses that follow (11b-15) are difficult and speak about three eras—they may be a Christian addition. In 8:17 they tell Levi his offspring will be "high priests and judges and scribes [αρχιερεις και κριται και γραμματεις]." For the first two terms

Isaac envisions these offices as being exercised over the entire nation of Israel ("all the descendants of Jacob's sons"), and the sources cited indicate this was a more common understanding of Levitical roles. The fact that all of the terms Isaac uses for Levi's seed are assigned to them in the HB renders highly unlikely Charles's suggestion that v. 15 refers to "the early Maccabean princes" who held both the highest civil and religious posts.[40]

They will declare the word of the Lord justly / and will justly judge all his verdicts.[41] The neatly parallel lines express the teaching and related judicial tasks of the priests and Levites. Instruction (that is, Torah) is regularly associated with the priests (e.g., Lev 10:11 [Aaron is to teach the statutes revealed through Moses]; Jer 18:18; Ezek 7:26; Hos 4:6; Hag 2:11; Mal 2:7). The point is well stated in Sir 45:17: "In his commandments he gave him [Aaron] authority and statutes and judgments, / to teach Jacob the testimonies, / and to enlighten Israel with his law." The Levites, too, assumed the role of teaching the divine law. Deuteronomy 33:10 says regarding Levi/Levites, "They teach Jacob your ordinances, / and Israel your law"; and Mal 2:6 declares of Levi, "True instruction was in his mouth, / and no wrong was found on his lips." 2 Chronicles 17:7-9 speaks of priests (two) and Levites (eight) with five other officials going through the cities of Judah teaching the book of the Lord's law, while in Neh 8:7-9 the Levites explain the law to the people (see also Deut 17:8-11, where the Levitical priests judge difficult cases at the central sanctuary).

They will tell my ways to Jacob / and my paths to Israel.[42] The prediction once more highlights the teaching role of the clergy.[43] The precise imagery of "ways/paths" does not occur in the HB passages dealing with sacerdotal functions, but it may derive from a text such as Isa 2:3 = Mic 4:2: "'Come, let us go up to the mountain of the LORD, / to the house of the God of Jacob; / that he may teach us his ways / and that we may walk in his paths.' / For out of Zion shall go forth instruction / and the word of the LORD from Jerusalem." The clergy would be the agents for communicating the divine instruction about his ways/paths.

The blessing of the Lord will be placed in their mouth, / so that they may bless all the descendants of the beloved. An important duty of priests was to pronounce blessings on the people of Israel. In Deut 10:8 (after the death of Aaron) Moses reports, "At that time the LORD set apart the tribe of Levi to carry the ark of the covenant of the LORD, to stand before the LORD, to minister to him, and to bless in his name, to this day." Deuteronomy 21:5 (cf. 1 Chr 23:13; 11QT^a lx:11; lxiii:3) reads similarly with regard to the priests: "Then the priests, the sons of Levi, shall come forward, for the LORD your God has chosen them to minister to him and to pronounce blessings in

---

in Jub 31:15, see the discussion of Davenport, *Eschatology*, 60–62; he notes various scriptural passages in which the terms occur and translates them "judges" and "princes." Werman takes *malā'ekt* to represent מלאכים but in its literal sense of a messenger sent by God to the people (*Jubilees*, 422).

40 Charles, *Jubilees*, 187. The three offices as presented in the Testament of Levi, he thought, pointed to John Hyrcanus (Charles did not make this claim for the terms here in Jubilees). As noted in VanderKam, *Textual*, 247–49, the same situation, with priests holding the top religious and governmental positions, seems to have prevailed during much of the Second Temple period (see also Davenport, who identifies the scriptural bases for ascribing these roles to the descendants of Levi [*Eschatology*, 62–63]). Halpern-Amaru thinks the three offices, like the double meaning of a child's name (according to her, Jubilees gives *Levi* a double meaning), connect the Hannah–Samuel story with the present one (*Empowerment*, 99–100), but the fact that the offices are mentioned in connection with the priests makes this unlikely. Also, the priests are not assigned a prophetic role in Jub 31:13-17.

41 For "word" and "verdicts" as poetic parallels, cf. Ps 119:16 and esp. 119:43; ALD 3:17.

42 The first-person possessive forms are interesting because they make the parallel lines sound as if God is speaking them, not Isaac (see Davenport, *Eschatology*, 62 n.1). Isaac would then be quoting a passage in which God speaks, but what passage that might be is not known. Possibly the suffix יו- on the nouns was miscopied so that the *vav* fell out; if it did, then the original would have been "his ways" and "his paths."

43 Endres emphasizes what he calls "the teaching and preaching responsibilities of these priests" in Isaac's blessing of Levi (*Biblical Interpretation*, 160–61).

the name of the Lord, and by their decision all cases of dispute and assault shall be settled." The most famous blessing in this category is the priestly benediction in Num 6:24-26. The image of placing the divine blessings in their mouths may be influenced by Mal 2:7 ("people should seek instruction from his mouth"), but teaching is under consideration in that verse. A closer parallel occurs in Sir 50:20 regarding the high priest Simon: "Then Simon came down and raised his hands over the whole congregation of the Israelites, to pronounce the blessing of the Lord with his lips." The expression "all the descendants of the beloved" (Ethiopic: lit., "all the seed to the beloved") is somewhat uncertain; the Latin reads *semen dilectum*, "beloved descendants/seed." Charles emended it to *semen dilecti*, the equivalent of the Ethiopic reading.[44] The Ethiopic manuscripts overwhelmingly support a noun followed by a prepositional phrase, not a noun with an adjective. Abraham, the friend of God (see Isa 41:8: זרע אברהם אהבי), could be meant,[45] although he has not figured to this point in the blessing; perhaps Jacob is the one intended,[46] since the priests are to bless the Israelites, the descendants of Jacob (see v. 20 below).

■ 16-17 Blessing on Levi

Isaac focuses his attention in vv. 16-17 on Levi himself with just one reference to his children in v. 16. The first topic he raises is his name.[47] When the author presented the birth notices about the children of Jacob and his wives he said nothing about the meaning of *Levi*, a name Jacob gave to his third son (28:14). In the present passage Isaac claims that his mother (Leah) gave him the name and the right name it was.[48] Genesis 29:34 said about the name, "Again she conceived and bore a son, and said, 'Now this time my husband will be joined to me because I have borne him three sons'; therefore he was named[49] Levi." Jacob seems to play with the name Levi in Gen 49:6: "may I not be joined to their company," though he uses a different verb; Num 18:2 employs the verb לוה and reflects the same reading of it: "So bring with you [Aaron] also your brothers of the tribe of Levi, your ancestral tribe, in order that they may be joined to you." Aramaic Levi Document and the Testament of Levi interpret it in the sense of "being close to" God (ALD 3:16; 6:5 ["near to the Lord and near to all his holy ones"]; T. Levi 2:10). Isaac adopts the meaning "joined to the Lord,"[50] more in keeping with the nuance in these latter two texts, though he offers a more literal interpretation. It may be that his being "a companion of all Jacob's sons" echoes ALD 6:5, where Levi is not only close to God but also "to all his holy ones." Whoever (angels?) or whatever (sacred objects?) "his holy ones" may be,[51] in Jubilees the Israelites occupy that position. Levi is thus to be joined to both God and his people.[52]

The second topic in v. 16 is the provision of food for Levi and his sons: "His table is to belong to you; / you and your sons are to eat (from) it." The table in connection with priests and Levites should be the altar at the sanctuary, where the priests present sacrifices from which they and the Levites receive their food. Since sacrifices were called the food of God (Lev 21:6, 8, 17, 21, 22), the altar was conceived of as his table (Ezek

---

44 Charles, *Ethiopic Version*, 117 n. 8 to Lat.
45 Berger adduces the passage in support of interpreting the "beloved" here as Abraham (the friend of the Lord in Jub 19:9) (*Jubiläen*, 478 n. g to v. 15).
46 So also Werman, *Jubilees*, 423.
47 Among others, see Charles, *Jubilees*, 187-88; Davenport, *Eschatology*, 63; Endres, *Biblical Interpretation*, 161.
48 Halpern-Amaru finds significance, not a contradiction, in the two statements in Jubilees about which parent named Levi: ". . . it serves as the basis for creating a link between Leah and the priesthood. Levi, like Benjamin, is named by both parents. Jacob assigns the name in the birth narrative (28:14). However, in the far more prestigious context of Isaac's blessing, the patriarch attributes the name to Leah" (*Empowerment*, 98; see also pp. 68-69 and the commentary above on Jub 28:14).
49 The MT reads a masculine singular verbal form, while the SP attaches a feminine singular ending.
50 Latin reads *ad decorum dei*, a phrase meaning "for the adornment of God" and presupposing the noun לויה. See Rönsch, *Jubiläen*, 145-46; Charles, *Jubilees*, 188; Berger, *Jubiläen*, 478 n. b to v. 16.
51 See Kugler, *From Patriarch to Priest*, 73 (he refers to Zech 3:1-10, where the high priest Joshua stands among angels); Greenfield, Stone, and Eshel, *Aramaic Levi Document*, 161; Drawnel, *Aramaic Wisdom Text*, 268. For priests among the holy ones (angels), see 1QSb iii:25-26; iv:23, 28.
52 Cf. Halpern-Amaru, *Empowerment*, 98-99.

44:16; Mal 1:7, 12). From those offerings given to God on the altar the priests and Levites could eat prescribed portions (Lev 10:12-15; Num 18:8-32; Deut 18:3-8; Ezek 44:15-31; Sir 45:20-21; ALD 4:9; T. Levi 2:12; etc.). The tithes too belonged to the Levites, who in turn tithed from them to the priests (e.g., Num 18:21-32); cf. Neh 12:44-47).[53] Those provisions were their eternal allotment because they received no land assignment in Israel. Testament of Levi 8:16 expresses the matter thus: "Every desirable thing in Israel will be for you and your seed; and you will eat everything beautiful to see, and your seed will divide among themselves the table of the Lord" (cf. T. Jud. 21:5). Consequently, Isaac prays that there would be eternal provision for Levi and his tribe, just as the matter would later be codified in the law and described elsewhere.

The final part of the blessing on Levi (v. 17) extends to him the wish that his enemies would enjoy no success against him. The passage seems dependent on Deut 33:11: "crush the loins of his adversaries, / of those that hate him, so that they do not rise again" (see also Sir 45:18-19, where God defeats the opposition to Aaron from Dathan, Abiram, and Korah). Destruction of their enemies recalls the violent episode of Levi at Shechem and of the Levites at the time of the golden calf. The final couplet in the verse in a sense extends the first one because it mentions opposition in the form of a nation that curses Levi. The antithetically parallel references to the one blessing him and the nation cursing him bring to mind similar blessings extended to Abram (Gen 12:3 // Jub 12:23) and to Jacob (Gen 27:29 // Jub 26:24).

Isaac's blessing of his grandson Levi and his descendants naturally centers on their future status and is not a full job description for them. In their study of the unit consisting of vv. 13-17, de Jonge and Tromp survey many of its sources in the HB and elsewhere and also make the observation that "the image of Levi in Isaac's blessing is largely a projection of the figure of the ideal priest onto Levi."[54] That image was perhaps available to the writer, not one he created. They add that atonement for the people, a central priestly function, does not appear in the blessing. "It seems that the author of *Jubilees* is primarily concerned with priestly *rights*, and is less interested in describing the benefits of priests' actions for others." It is true that the text barely mentions anything about sacrifice other than to speak about providing food for priests and Levites—in this respect it contrasts sharply with the Aramaic Levi Document—but it is not obvious that any important conclusions follow from this point. The writer offers a comprehensive picture of clerical prerogatives without entering into detail in connection with them. The picture is so general that Isaac makes no distinction between priests and Levites. In addition and on the positive side, the teaching and blessing functions of the Levitical line figure prominently in v. 15.

18-20 Isaac's Blessing of Judah[55]

The secondary position of Judah the writer established in vv. 12-13a, and placement of his blessing after that of Levi reinforces the point.[56] The blessing of Judah differs from the one Isaac pronounced on Levi in that, while he does to some extent mine the HB for royal references, there is for Judah no work comparable to the Aramaic Levi Document. The Greek Testament of Judah exhibits some parallels with Jub 31:18-20 but not as many as the Testament of Levi contains for Jub 31:13-17.

---

53   One of Nehemiah's reforms was to ensure that the tithes that the Judeans had failed to donate would indeed be brought to the sanctuary (13:10-14).

54   De Jonge and Tromp, "Jacob's Son Levi," 212. The next quotation in this paragraph is from the same page. See also pp. 213, 231-32.

55   In T. Jud. 17:5 Judah tells his sons, "And Abraham my father's father blessed me, to be king over Israel; and Isaac blessed me in like manner." As Hollander and de Jonge comment, tracing the blessing to Abraham is "somewhat strange" (*Testaments*, 216). Levi reports in his testament (9:1) that he and Judah visited Isaac and next tells how he blessed him, without mentioning the blessing of Judah.

56   According to T. Jud. 21:2-4a, Judah himself recognized the situation: "For to me the Lord gave the kingship and to him the priesthood, and he set the kingship beneath the priesthood. To me he gave the things upon the earth, to him the things in the heavens. As heaven is higher than the earth, so is the priesthood of God higher than the kingship on the earth" (cf. 25:1-2).

■ **18** *May the Lord give you the power and strength to trample on all who hate you.* Possibly Ps 89:23 is the immediate inspiration for the line: "I will crush his [the Davidic king's] foes before him / and strike down those who hate him." The language also partially resembles words from other blessings on Judah: Genesis 49:8 ("your hand shall be on the neck of your enemy") and Deut 33:7 ("and be a help against his adversaries"). *Genesis Rabbah* interprets the phrase "Judah is a lion's whelp" (Gen 49:9) as meaning: "This teaches that he gave him the strength of a lion and the boldness of his whelps" (*Gen. Rab.* 98:7). See also 2 Sam 22:17-20, 38-43 = Ps 18:16-19, 37-42; Isa 11:4; Pss. Sol. 17:22-25.

Be a prince [makwannen/princeps[57]]—you and one of your sons—for Jacob's sons. The command (Ethiopic) or prediction (Latin) that Judah will be a royal ruler over Israel echoes several phrases in Jacob's blessing of him in Gen 49:8, 10: "your father's sons shall bow down before you" (v. 8); "The scepter shall not depart from Judah, / nor the ruler's staff from between his feet" (v. 10; see T. Levi 17:6; 21:6). The Genesis passage (49:10) receives a commentary in 4Q252 (4QCommentary on Genesis A) v:1-4:

"*The sceptre*[58] *shall [n]ot depart from* the tribe of Judah" (49:10a). When Israel rules [*there will not*] *be cut off one who occupies the throne for David* (Jer 33:17). For "*the staff*" (49:10a) is the covenant of the kingship; the [thousa]nds of Israel are "the *standards*"[59] (Gen 49:10a) *vacat* until the coming of the messiah of righteousness, the shoot of David. For to him and his seed has been given the covenant of the kingship of his people for everlasting generations. (trans. G. Brooke, *DSSR* 2:111)

The phrase in Jub 31:18 "Be a prince—you and one of your sons" has sparked interest because some have spotted a messianic reference in it—especially in "and one of your sons." Charles, in a comment on vv. 18-19, argued that the idea of a messiah sprung from Judah's line underlies the text and that the words "'a prince ... thou and one of thy sons' admit most naturally of this interpretation."[60] François Martin echoed Charles's interpretation: the writer of Jubilees, who had to balance the prophetic teaching about a messiah from Judah and his preference for the priesthood, found a solution in a messiah from Judah who has no precise role in the kingdom.[61] This seems a rather forced interpretation. It is more likely that, as Testuz commented, the blessing envisages David, the ancestor of the royal dynasty.[62] It could also be read as indicating a monarchic principle: at any time only one of Judah's descendants would rule. Davenport finds in the words "one of" the result of editorial interference: "The present state of the text has been edited, however, perhaps as a glorification of one of the Maccabean warriors, perhaps under the influence of messianic expectations, or perhaps in an attempt to justify the church's teaching about Jesus by the addition of *one of*." The support for his conclusion is that "one of" ruins the parallelism in v. 18 where all of Judah's sons are under consideration in the other lines.[63] There is no textual evidence for assessing "one of" as an addition (both the Ethiopic and Latin versions have the expres-

---

57 The same equivalents are used for the first of the three titles attributed to Levi's descendants in v. 15. Davenport (*Eschatology*, 64), who implies that Charles translated the word as "judge" in v. 18 when he actually used "prince," suggested that it renders שופט ultimately, but it is more likely that the word שליט in Gen 49:10 (as read in 4Q252 v:1) lies behind it here.

58 The translation is wrong, as the text clearly reads שליט (LXX: αρχων), a term meaning "ruler" (Jastrow, 1583); it does not have שבט as in the MT. Cf. Kugel, *Traditions*, 491-93.

59 Reading דגליו (as does SP) where the MT has רגליו (his feet).

60 Charles, *Jubilees*, 188. He thought the writer assigned him no role in the "temporal messianic kingdom" that, according to Charles, was part of his eschatological expectation, but there is no clear indication in the book that the author anticipated such a kingdom. See also Charles, *Eschatology*, 236-37.

61 Martin, "Jubilés," 533. See also Bent Noack, "Qumran and the Book of Jubilees," *SEÅ* 22-23 (1957-58) 191-207, here 201.

62 Testuz, *Idées*, 68; see also John J. Collins, *The Scepter and the Star: The Messiahs of the Dead Sea Scrolls and Other Ancient Literature* (ABRL; New York: Doubleday, 1995) 86; Kugel, *Walk through* Jubilees, 151; "Jubilees," 402 (in both places he allows the possibility that a messianic king is intended).

63 Davenport, *Eschatology*, 65.

sion). As for damaging the parallelism, the point is not at all evident in this context where balance between lines is not precise—or at least not in the granddaughter translations.

May your name and the name of your sons be one / that goes and travels around in the entire earth and in the regions. The sequel mentions the fear he is to arouse among the peoples; this presupposes that they know about him and thus that his fame circulates internationally. The queen of Sheba spoke about Solomon's reputation that reached her distant land (1 Kgs 10:1-10); the remainder of 1 Kings 10 highlights the king's fame among the nations (note v. 24: "The whole earth sought the presence of Solomon to hear his wisdom"). Of more specific pertinence for this line is 1 Kgs 4:31 (Heb. 5:11): ". . . his fame [lit., his name] spread throughout all the surrounding nations" (cf. Pss. Sol. 17:30-31).

Then the nations will be frightened before you; / all the nations will be disturbed; / all peoples will be disturbed.[64] In the Testament of Judah, Judah relates battles he fought against various enemies and adds that they feared him after he defeated them (3:7; 7:11). But sentiments more in line with Isaac's wishes come to expression in 1QSb regarding the prince of the congregation:

Thus may you d[estroy peoples] by the might of your [mouth,] lay waste *vacat* the earth with your rod! *"With the breath of your lips may you kill the wicked!"* (cf. Isa 11:4) May he give [you a *"spirit of coun*]sel *and [may]*[65] *eternal might [rest upon you], the spirit of vacat knowledge and the fear of God"* (Isa 11:2). *"May righteousness be the belt [around your waist, and faithful]ness the belt around your loins"* (Isa 11:5). *"May he make your horns iron and your hoofs bronze!"* (Mic 4:13) May you gore like a bu[ll   May you trample the nati]ons like mud in the streets! For God has established you as the sceptre over the rulers; bef[ore you peoples shall come and bow down, and all nat]ions shall serve you. He shall make you mighty by His holy name. (v:24-28; trans. Wise, Abegg, and Cook, *DSSR* 5:433)

■ **19** *May Jacob's help be in you; / May Israel's safety be found in you.* The Lord, who had raised David to the throne to give deliverance to his people from their enemies (2 Sam 7:8-11), predicted through Jeremiah the rise of a righteous Branch for David: "In his days Judah will be saved and Israel will live in safety" (Jer 23:6 = Jer 33:16). See also T. Naph. 8:2: "Do you also, therefore, command your children that they unite with Levi and Judah, for through Judah salvation will arise unto Israel and by him Jacob will be blessed."[66]

■ **20** *At the time when you sit on the honorable throne that is rightly yours, / there will be great peace for all the descendants of the beloved's sons.* The language reminds one of the situation in 2 Samuel 7 where David is settled in his palace enjoying peace from his enemies; the Lord then promises him an eternal dynasty, a throne established forever. A concomitant of the provision for David is that the Lord "will appoint a place for my people Israel and will plant them, so that they may live in their own place, and be disturbed no more; and evildoers shall afflict them no more, as formerly, from the time that I appointed judges over my people Israel; and I will give you rest from all your enemies" (2 Sam 7:10-11). Isaiah too spoke of the conditions when the new ruler from David's line would reign: "His authority shall grow continually, / and there shall be endless peace / for the throne of David and his kingdom" (9:7a; see Jer 23:6; Jub 23:30). The commentary on Isa 11:1-5 in 4QpIsa[a] 8–10 17–21 mentions a throne of glory in the context of other themes that emerge in Isaac's blessing of Judah: "[Its interpretation concerns the Shoot of] David who will arise at the e[nd of days   ] his [ene]mies, and God will sustain him with [the] Law [th]rone of glory, a ho[ly] crown,

---

64 Charles bracketed "all the peoples will be disturbed," which he translated as "And all the peoples will quake," as a dittography (*Jubilees*, 189). His conclusion is understandable, as the verb is repeated from the previous line, though a singular form of the same subject appears in this line. However, the Latin text does have another clause beginning with *et omnes* (the text after these two words is not available) as in the Ethiopic copies. Only MS. 21 omits the phrase, presumably by haplography.

65 "May" is mistakenly omitted from the *DSSR* version and supplied from Wise, Abegg, and Cook, *Dead Sea Scrolls*, 150.

66 The passage could be one of the Christian insertions in the text (Hollander and de Jonge, *Testaments*, 316–17).

and garments of variegate[ed stuff   ] in his hand, and over the G[entile]s he will rule, and Magog [al]l the peoples shall his sword judge" (trans. Allegro with Gordon, *DSSR* 2:55). The emphasis on the righteousness of the Branch of David in Isa 11:1-5 could lie behind Isaac's reference to Judah's rightly holding the throne. "The descendants of the beloved's sons" should be the offspring of Jacob's children. The use of "the beloved" here makes it more likely that "the beloved" in v. 15 is also Jacob.[67]

Isaac concludes his words for Judah with ones resembling the conclusion of Levi's blessing: He contrasts the fate of the one who blesses Judah with those who hate, trouble, and curse him. Those in the latter category are to suffer the punishment of Levi's enemies—they will be uprooted, lose their lives, and themselves suffer a curse. Judah and the kingship may rank below Levi and the priesthood, but their opponents will meet the same end. Judah, like Levi, is protected with the very guarantees enjoyed by Abram and Jacob (Gen 12:3 // Jub 12:23; Gen 27:29 // Jub 26:24).[68]

■ **21** After the patriarch pronounced these weighty blessings upon Levi and Judah, the moving scene draws to a happy conclusion. The pronoun "He" at the beginning of v. 21 refers to Isaac, who, after blessing the two young men so grandly, turns his attention to Jacob. He kisses him again (note that Jacob was the only one of the three Isaac kissed, or rather Jacob kissed him [v. 8]; he merely hugged Levi and Judah [v. 11]) and embraces him. Isaac, like Rebekah, was overjoyed that he had the privilege of seeing these grandsons. Perhaps he had met Esau's sons, but the presence of Levi and Judah delighted him (compare Gen 48:11). The author identifies their father as "his true son Jacob." Isaac, who once preferred Esau to Jacob (19:15; 19:31: "Isaac loved Esau much more than Jacob"), now realizes that Jacob is (literally) "his son who is in righteousness [*waldu za-ba-ṣedq*]" (see 35:12, where Rebekah calls Jacob Isaac's "perfect and true son" [cf. 25:12]). At a later juncture (35:13) Isaac will speak more explicitly about his change of mind: "At first I did love Esau more than Jacob, after he was born; but now I love Jacob more than Esau."[69] Verse 21 shows that he had reversed his views about Esau and Jacob well before the occasion depicted in Jubilees 35.

■ **22** In v. 22 Jacob is the one who moves away from a position between his father's feet.[70] Nothing had been said in vv. 8-11 about Jacob occupying such a place, but the fact that "Isaac hung on his son Jacob's neck and cried on his neck" (v. 8) may imply it. He seems to have remained there all the time Isaac was blessing Levi and Judah. With the blessings complete, Jacob could now move a step or two back so that he could prostrate himself in front of his father whom he thus honored. It appears as if the writer is continuing to draw parallels with the scene in Genesis 48, although the situation is not identical. There, after Joseph had presented Ephraim and Manasseh to Jacob, "Joseph removed them from his father's [text: his] knees, and he bowed himself with his face to the earth." Westermann's comment about Gen 48:12, which precedes Jacob's blessings upon his grandsons, is interesting for the post-blessing location of v. 22 in Jubilees 31: "V. 12 clearly closes the narrative scene. Both sentences in v. 12 presuppose that Jacob has blessed Joseph's two sons. The procedure of blessing is over and so Joseph takes his sons away."[71] Once Jacob had bowed to Isaac, "[he] then blessed them." A likely

---

67 Charles thought "the beloved" was Abraham, both here and in v. 15 (*Jubilees*, 189), but the context hardly favors his view.

68 Berger (*Jubiläen*, 477-78 n. b to v. 12 and n. a to v. 15) follows Anders Hultgård (*L'eschatologie des Testaments des Douze Patriarches* [2 vols.; Acta Universitatis Upsaliensis, Historia Religionum 6-7; Uppsala: Almqvist & Wiksell, 1977, 1981] 1:58-72) in maintaining that the leadership roles Isaac mentions for Levi apply to the author's present but the titles for Judah refer to the past and future Davidic rule. The tenses used in both blessings make this an unlikely inference; Isaac's words predict great futures for the descendants of both Levi and Judah and do not distinguish the times in which they will be applicable to one or the other.

69 Isaac had indicated much earlier that he held an elevated view of Jacob when he said to Rebekah: "he is just in his way. He is perfect; he is a true man" (27:17).

70 Hartom thinks Judah is the subject ("Jubilees," 98). The blessing on him has just concluded, but it seems unlikely that he is being singled out for more attention than Levi receives.

71 Westermann, *Genesis 37-50*, 187.

suggestion for the meaning of "them" is the two boys, though possibly Jacob is included (see v. 31), but who pronounces the blessing this time? The context in the verse, where Jacob is the subject of the other verbs, implies that he is the one who blesses his sons after Isaac had done so.[72] If he did, his words of blessing are not cited. The words "He rested there near his father Isaac that night" remind the reader of the situation at the end of Abraham's life. After he had blessed Jacob, the two of them lay down in the same bed, Abraham felt joyful, and he again blessed Jacob and his future offspring (Jub 22:25-30; cf. 36:17-18). Jacob and Isaac have a similar relationship. The text does not say they shared a bed, only that Jacob rested near his father. Rather than sleep, they enjoyed a meal together (in Jub 22:4-6 Abraham and his family, including Jacob, did the same on the last day of his life).[73] This meal forms a distinctive contrast to the one Isaac had eaten before blessing the deceptive Jacob instead of Esau (Gen 27:25 // Jub 26:20).

■ **23** Wherever Jacob was resting, Isaac had his two sons, Levi and Judah, "sleep, one on his right, and one on his left." The blessing section in the chapter favors the conclusion that Levi would have been the one on his right and Judah the one on his left. This again reminds one of the Genesis scene in which the aged Jacob, while confined to his bed, took Ephraim by his right hand and Manasseh by his left (Gen 48:8-20). Isaac's parallel act of so taking his two grandsons "was credited to him as something righteous." That expression links him with his believing father Abram (Gen 15:6 // Jub 14:6; cf. Jub 30:17). The entire scene in chap. 31 greatly enhances the stature of Isaac, who before this hardly aroused admiration as a father and ancestor of the covenant people. He made a beginning at burnishing his reputation when he sent Jacob away and consoled Rebekah (Gen 28:1-5; Jub 27:9-18). Now he takes a major step forward and proves to be a worthy, prophetic conduit for passing along blessings to his son and grandsons.

24-30a Further Conversation with Isaac

After being away for twenty-eight years, gaining a family of four wives and twelve children, and acquiring great wealth, Jacob had much to tell Isaac.

■ **24** That very night, a night early in the seventh month (see v. 3), he brought his father up-to-date on his life, emphasizing how God had cared for him through many adventures and had guided him safely home. The wording of v. 24 takes up the language Isaac had used when consoling Rebekah just after Jacob left home long ago: "My sister, do not cry for my son Jacob because he will go safely and return safely. The Most High God will guard him from every evil[74] and will be with him because he will not abandon him throughout his entire lifetime. For I well know that his ways will be directed favorably wherever he goes until he returns safely to us and we see that he is safe" (27:14-16). What Isaac predicted then had now been realized with the return of Jacob to his parents.

■ **25** Isaac was understandably pleased and responded by blessing "the God of his father Abraham who had not put an end to his mercy and faithfulness for the son of his servant Isaac." The author chose these words carefully. They echo Gen 24:27, where Abraham's servant whom he had dispatched to find a wife for Isaac said: "Blessed be the LORD, the God of my master Abraham, who has not forsaken his steadfast love and his faithfulness toward my master."[75] The divine faithfulness to Abraham in his dealings with the Haran branch of the family had been repeated now in the experience of Isaac and Jacob. Isaac is looking more and more like Abraham.[76]

■ **26** The more immediate issue that occasioned the visit comes to the fore beginning in v. 26. Jacob waited until the following morning to mention the key elements involved in his first stay at Bethel, particularly the vow he had made. He must have retold the entire episode, including the visionary appearance of the Lord to him. The vow he had made at Bethel is noted twice in the verse, and the importance attached to it is what in fact triggers all the

---

72 Charles said about the sentence: "This clause seems out of place here" (*Jubilees*, 189). But there is no textual evidence for omitting or moving it (MS. 63: "he blessed him").

73 Rapp highlights the parallels with Jubilees 22 (and Jubilees 19) (*Jakob in Bet-El*, 209–10).

74 The reading in 27:15 is *'ekuy*, an adjective that could mean "the evil one" or "evil." In 31:24 the same form appears, though in VanderKam, *Jubilees* 2 (see the note on p. 206) it is rendered "the evil one." The word should be translated in the same way in the two passages, with "evil" probably being the intended sense (as Kugel [*Walk through* Jubilees, 151] rightly suggests).

75 Kugel, *Walk through* Jubilees, 151; "Jubilees," 402.

76 See VanderKam, *Book of Jubilees*, 111–12.

action in chap. 31 (and much of that in chap. 32). Jacob's vow at Bethel was a subject of great interest in the ancient comments on the scene and especially on the sequel in Jacob's life. That vow the author of Jubilees had reproduced almost verbatim from Gen 28:20-22.

Genesis 28:20-22	Jubilees 27:27
Then Jacob made a vow, saying,	Jacob vowed to the Lord:
"If God will be with me,	"If the Lord is with me
and will keep me in this way that I go,	and guards me on this road on which I am traveling
and will give me bread to eat and clothing to wear	and gives me food to eat and clothes to wear
so that I come again to my father's house in peace,	so that I return safely to my father's house,
then the LORD shall be my God,	then the Lord will be my God.
and this stone, which I have set up for a pillar,	Also, this stone that I have set up as a pillar for a marker in this place
shall be God's house;	is to become the house of the Lord.
and of all that you give me I will surely give one-tenth to you."	All that you have given me I will indeed tithe to you, my God."

Jacob had vowed not only that the Lord would be his God but also that the place would become the deity's house and that Jacob would tithe everything he received from him. Genesis describes Jacob's return to Bethel in 35:1-15, yet the passage says nothing about Jacob's building a sanctuary there (though he does construct an altar [35:7]) or about tithing his possessions. Did Jacob make a vow setting conditions for God to meet—all of which he had now met—and then not carry out his part of the agreement? Genesis provides no answer, but Jubilees and other ancient texts do.[77]

Jacob had not actually vowed to offer a sacrifice at Bethel, though the text refers to "offering the sacrifice before the Lord as he had vowed" (v. 26). Genesis 35:1, however, contains God's command to Jacob "to make an altar there to the God who appeared to you when you fled from your brother Esau." Jacob had constructed one (Gen 35:7 // Jub 31:3) and now wanted his father to join him for the offering related to the great event that had taken place twenty-eight years ago.[78] He realized his father could no longer walk from Hebron to Bethel so he planned to transport him on a donkey—he is solicitous about the welfare of his elderly father.

■ **27** At this point Isaac declines his son's attractive invitation, citing the infirmities of old age. As he had wished Jacob a safe journey in the past (Jub 27:11), now he does the same. Isaac supports his argument about his advanced age by claiming, "I am 165 years of age today" (v. 27).[79] In this case "today" does not mean the two were conversing on Isaac's birthday, since the time is the seventh month and he was born in the middle of the third month on the Festival of the Firstfruits of the harvest (Jub 16:13); rather, it means "at the present/now." Isaac urges him to have Rebekah accompany him to the sacrifice and to mount her on the animal—another indication that she was in better physical condition than Isaac (as she had demonstrated in v. 6).

■ **28** Isaac is, nevertheless, grateful for Jacob's desire that he attend, as he realized Jacob had made the journey from Bethel to Hebron for the very purpose of bringing his father (and Rebekah; see v. 3) back to Bethel with him. It was enough for Isaac to have seen his son again—a meeting that made the day blessed. His words resemble the exclamation Jacob made when he saw Joseph after so many years had passed: "I can die now, having seen for myself that you are still alive" (Gen 46:30; cf. 48:11).

■ **29-30a** Though Isaac was too infirm to accompany Jacob to Bethel, he was concerned about Jacob's fulfilling the vow he had made there. He uses several expressions in v. 29 to underscore the urgency of doing so without delay. Apparently from what Jacob had told

---

77 Kugel, "Levi's Elevation," 3-4.
78 Kugel, who thinks Jacob is not a priest in Jubilees (for the evidence regarding this point, see the commentary on Jub 32:4-9 below), argues that Jacob needed his father, who was a priest, to preside at the sacrifice in Bethel ("Levi's Elevation," 17-21; *Walk through* Jubilees, 149; "Jubilees," 402-3; so also Werman, *Jubilees*, 421, 425). As Rapp comments about Kugel's view, there is no suggestion in vv. 26-30 that this was Jacob's motivation for inviting him (*Jakob in Bet-El*, 210). See above on v. 3.
79 As noted in connection with 31:3 above, the chronology of Jacob's life implies that Isaac is 157 at this time; however, the overall chronology in Jubilees makes him 156 years of age. He was born in 1987 (Jub 16:13), while the action in chap. 31 takes place in 2143. He will die at the age of 180 (Gen 35:28 // Jub 36:18).

him, Isaac knew that his son was under obligation to carry out certain acts lest he renege on the promises he had made to God himself. The wise father is speaking in harmony with and partly echoing the words of Deut 23:21-23: "If you make a vow to the LORD your God, do not postpone fulfilling it; for the LORD your God will surely require it of you, and you would incur guilt. But if you refrain from vowing you will not incur guilt. Whatever your lips utter, you must diligently perform, just as you have freely vowed to the LORD your God with your own mouth" (see also Num 30:2; Eccl 5:4-6). Paying vows and sacrificing figure together in passages such as Ps 50:14: "Offer to God a sacrifice of thanksgiving, / and pay your vows to the Most High" (also in Ps 22:25 [Heb. 24] and elsewhere). Perhaps that association explains the connection between Jacob's vow and the need to sacrifice in Jubilees 31 (see 32:5). Isaac realizes the gravity of the situation and wants Jacob to please[80] the God to whom he made the vow. Isaac could not endure the trip, but he gave orders to Rebekah that she was to accompany Jacob. This time Isaac is the one in charge, whereas twenty-eight years earlier Rebekah had given commands to him (see Jub 27:7-9). There seems to be no special significance in the fact that Isaac refers to Jacob as Rebekah's son in his instructions, since earlier in the chapter Isaac called him "my son" (vv. 9, 27, 28).

30b-32 Return to Bethel and Joyful Reflection on His Father's Blessings

The writer of Jubilees continues to craft a narrative that he spliced between notices in Genesis in order to offer a fuller explanation of this stage in the life of Jacob's family.

■ **30b** Rebekah obeyed her husband and departed on the way with Jacob. But she, Jacob, and his two sons were not alone as they journeyed: traveling with them was a woman named Deborah, who has not been mentioned in the story to this juncture. According to Gen 35:8,[81] Deborah was Rebekah's nurse;[82] she died in Bethel, where she was buried beneath an oak tree that received its name from the mourning caused by her death (see Jub 32:30 for the parallel passage). The writer of Jubilees thus introduces her into the narrative before Genesis does. Kugel has shown that the mention of Deborah is no accident in this context in Jubilees; rather, the Deborah notice in Gen 35:8 allowed the author of Jubilees to create the visit of Jacob with his parents in the present chapter.[83] He must have been puzzled, as other readers were,[84] why Deborah was with Jacob at Bethel in Gen 35:8, when at the time Isaac and Rebekah, whom she served, were in Hebron. To explain her presence in Bethel he may have inferred that Jacob had actually gone to visit his parents in Hebron before this. He would have gone there and brought back with him to Bethel at least Deborah and probably Rebekah too, as Deborah was her nurse. A visit by Jacob to see his parents would ease somewhat the embarrassment about how long it took him to seek them out after returning to the land and it would explain the presence of Deborah at Bethel in Gen 35:8. Genesis said nothing about Isaac being in Bethel at this time; perhaps that implied he had stayed in Hebron when his wife and Deborah returned to Bethel with Jacob. The frailties of old age would have supplied a

---

80 This is, of course, a verb used regularly for God's acceptance of sacrifices and the like. In connection with vows, Qohelet says, "When you make a vow to God, do not delay fulfilling it; for he has no pleasure in fools. Fulfill what you vow" (5:4 [Heb. 3]).

81 This is the only place where Genesis mentions her name. In 24:59 Laban and his family send Rebekah and an unnamed nurse away with Abraham's servant to meet Rebekah's future husband Isaac.

82 Latin Jubilees reads *nutrix sua* after *debborra*; see VanderKam, *Jubilees* 2:207.

83 Kugel, "Levi's Elevation," 24-27; *Walk through* Jubilees, 149-50; "Jubilees," 400.

84 *Tg. Ps.-J.* Gen 35:8 and *Gen. Rab.* 81:5, through a different interpretation of the name of the tree under which Deborah was buried (Allon-bacuth = "another weeping," with "Allon" related to αλλον), read the text as saying that on this occasion Jacob received news of the death of his mother. Rashi thought that Rebekah had sent Deborah to fetch Jacob from Paddan-aram (see Gen 27:45) and that she died on the journey. Modern commentators, too, have had difficulty with the mention of her in 35:8. Skinner wrote: "How she could have come into Jacob's family is quite inexplicable; and the conjectures that have been advanced on this point are all puerile" (*Genesis*, 425). Cf. also Westermann, *Genesis 12-36*, 552.

reasonable excuse for him not to travel. Another implication of an earlier visit by Jacob to his parents' house (the one here in Jubilees 31; it lacks a parallel in Genesis) was that God had now met all the conditions Jacob had stated in his vow so that he was obligated to fulfill his side of the agreement.[85] The author of Jubilees, though in chap. 31 he crafted a scene not described in Genesis, told a story that the text of Genesis suggested to him.

The traveling party reached Bethel—oddly, only Jacob, Rebekah, and Deborah are mentioned, not Levi and Judah—where the story about Jacob's vow and the elevation of Levi to the priesthood will continue.

■ **31-32** Before it does there is a brief interlude. Presumably at Bethel Jacob paused to reflect on the momentous words uttered by his father. It is significant that Jacob refers to the blessings of Isaac as a prayer (Latin: blessing; see the textual note) and that he includes himself with his two sons as the beneficiaries of the blessings. Unless he is referring to the vague sentence "He then blessed them" (v. 22) as including himself (see above), he would mean that by blessing his sons and their offspring Isaac had also blessed him. The great gifts mentioned led Jacob to rejoice and in turn to bless the God of his ancestors Abraham and Isaac. Reference to the two patriarchs is most appropriate because the blessings given to them and to Jacob were now being passed on to future generations in Jacob's line. As he put the matter, he now knew that he and his sons had an unending future before "the God of all," a title used more often in blessings (e.g., 22:27; cf. 31:13). The future looked bright now for the man who had deceived his father into blessing him (in Genesis and Jubilees), fled from his brother (Genesis and Jubilees), feared Laban and Esau (Genesis), and failed to visit his parents for a long time after returning to the land (Genesis and Jubilees). At Bethel God had made wonderful promises to him, and to Bethel he had returned to fulfill his vow made there. Those blessings of Bethel, ones that included his descendants (Gen 28:13-14 // Jub 27:22-23), were now extended and concretized in Isaac's words to his two sons.

Lest anyone think that Isaac was merely engaging in wishful thinking in the blessings upon Levi and Judah recorded in vv. 13-20, the writer adds that they were ordained for the two young men and that they were entered on the heavenly tablets "as an eternal testimony."[86] Their presence in the celestial document guaranteed that they would both come into effect and endure through all time.[87] There could be no greater confirmation than this; there was no doubt that Isaac's words of blessing, like those of God, would find fulfillment.[88]

---

85 See also VanderKam, "Exegetical Creation," 365-66.
86 Endres writes: "Thus the prerogatives of the tribes of Judah and Levi, as reported by the author of Jubilees, derive from divine revelation and not from mere political analysis" (*Biblical Interpretation*, 162).
87 García Martínez includes this reference under the heading "The Book of Destiny," on the grounds "that the blessings are not related to the actions of Levi and Judah, but that the blessings predestine their future and the future of their descendants" ("Heavenly Tablets," 249-50, here 250).
88 Since v. 32 mentions the heavenly tablets, Kugel assigns it to his interpolator (in "Interpolations," 264, he lists vv. 31-32, but in the later version of the article in *Walk through* Jubilees, 287, he gives just v. 32). Here too, however, he fails to identify a plausible reason why someone would insert the reference. He writes: "the Interpolator felt it necessary to assert that these predictions were in fact already written in the Heavenly Tablets" ("Interpolations," 264 = *Walk through* Jubilees, 288). In the commentary portion of his book (p. 151) he says, "For the Interpolator, the fact that Isaac had blessed Levi and Judah 'down here' did not in itself affect their status 'up there.'" In "Jubilees," 403, his wording is: "For the Interpolator, the fact that Isaac had blessed Levi and Judah 'down here' was another act of human initiative that could not seem to stand on its own." None of this is convincing. The Angel of the Presence, following the Lord's orders given and described in 1:27-29, has been dictating to Moses from the heavenly tablets since 2:1. Hence, interpolating such a notice here would serve no helpful purpose. Moreover, to say that Isaac's blessing "was another act of human initiative" is to ignore what is said in v. 12—Isaac gave the blessings through a spirit of prophecy.

32

Bethel (2): Tithing, Temple-Building, and Departure

1/ That night he stayed^a at Bethel. Levi dreamed that^b he—he and his sons^c—was appointed and ordained^d to the priesthood^e of the Most High God forever. When he awakened, he blessed the Lord. 2/ Jacob got up early in the morning on the fourteenth day of this month and gave a tithe of all that had come^a with him—from people to animals,^b from money to all utensils and clothing. He gave a tithe of all. 3/ At that time Rachel was pregnant with her son Benjamin. Jacob counted his sons^a from him. He went up (the list), and it came down on Levi in the Lord's share.^b His father put priestly clothes on him and ordained him. 4/ On^a the fifteenth of this month he^b brought to the altar 14 young bulls from the cattle, 28 rams, 49 sheep, 7^c kids, and 21^d goats—as^e a burnt offering on the altar and^f as a pleasing offering for a pleasant aroma before God. 5/ This^a was his gift because of the vow^b which he had made that he would give a tithe along with their^c sacrifices and their libations. 6/ When the fire had consumed it, he would burn^a incense on the fire above it;^b and as a peace offering two young bulls, four rams, four sheep, four he-goats,^c two year-old sheep, and two goats. This is what^d he would do daily for the seven days. 7/ He^a was eating happily there^b—he, all his sons, and his men—for the seven days. He was blessing^c and praising the Lord who had freed him^d from all his difficulties and who^e had granted him his vow. 8/ He tithed all the clean animals^a and made an offering of them.^b He gave^c his son Levi the unclean animals and gave him all the persons of the people. 9/ Levi rather than^a his ten brothers served as priest in Bethel before his father Jacob. There he was a priest, and Jacob gave^b what he had vowed. In this way he again gave a tithe^c to the Lord. He sanctified it,^d and it became^e holy.

10/ For this reason it is ordained as a law on the heavenly tablets to tithe^a a second time, to eat it before the Lord—year by year—in the place that has been chosen (as the site) where his name will reside. This law has no temporal limits forever. 11/ That statute has been written down so that it should be carried out year by year—to eat the tithe a second time^a before the Lord in the place that has been chosen. One is not to leave any of it^b over from this year to the next year. 12/ For the seed is to be eaten in its year until the time for harvesting^a the seed of the year; the wine (will be drunk) until the time for wine; and the olive (will be used) until the proper time of its season.^b 13/ Any of it that is left over and grows old^a is to be (considered) contaminated; it is to be burned up because it has become impure. 14/ In this way they are to eat^a it at the same time^b in the sanctuary;^c they are not to let it grow old. 15/ The entire tithe of cattle and sheep is holy to the Lord, and^a is to belong to his priests who will eat (it) before him year by year, because this is the way it is ordained and inscribed on the heavenly tablets regarding the tithe.

16/ During the next night,^a on the twenty-second day of this month, Jacob decided to build up that place and to surround the courtyard with a wall, to sanctify it, and make it eternally holy for himself and for his children after him forever.^b 17/ The Lord appeared to him during the night. He blessed him and said to him, "You are not to be called Jacob only^a but you will (also) be named Israel." 18/ He said to him a second time, "I am the Lord^a who created heaven and <u>earth. I will increase your numbers</u> and multiply you very much. Kings will come from you, and they will rul<u>e wherever</u> humanity <u>has set foot</u>.^b 19/ I will give your descendants all of the land^a that is beneath the sky. They will <u>rule</u>^b <u>over all the</u> nations just as they wish.^c Afterwards, they will gain the entire earth, and they will possess it forever." 20/ When he had finished spea<u>king with him, he went up</u> from him, and Jacob kept watching^a until he had gone up^b into heaven. 21/ In a ni<u>ght</u> vision he saw^a <u>an angel</u>^b coming down from heaven with seven tablets^c in his hands.^d He gave (them)^e to Jacob, and he read them.^f He learned^g everything^h that was written in them—what would happen to him and his sons throughout all ages. 22/ After he had shown him everything^a that was written on the tablets, he said to him, "Do not build up this place, and do not make it an eternal temple. Do not live here because this is not^b the place. Go^c to the house^d of your father Abraham and live^e where^f your father Isaac is until the day of your father's^g death. 23/ For you will die peacefully in Egypt and be buried honorably in this land in the grave of your fathers^a—with^b Abraham and Isaac. 24/ Do not be afraid because everything will happen just as you have seen and read. Now you write down everything just as you have seen and read."^a 25/ Then Jacob said, "Lord,^a how shall I remember everything^b just as^c I have read and seen?" He said to him, "I will remind you of everything." 26/ When he had gone up from him,^a he awakened and remembered everything that he had read and seen. He wrote down^b all the things that he had read and seen. 27/ He celebrated one more^a day there. On it he sacrificed exactly as^b he had been sacrificing on the previous days. He named it Detaining because he was detained^c one day.^d He named the previous ones^e the Festival. 28/ This is the way it was revealed that it should be, and it is written on the heavenly tablets. For this reason^a it was revealed^b to him that he should celebrate it^c and add it^d to the seven days of the festival. 29/ It was called Detaining^a because of the fact that^b it is entered^c in the testimony^d of the festal days in accord with^e the number of days in the year.

30/ In the night, on the twenty-third of this month,^a Deborah, Rebekah's nurse, died. They buried her^b below the city, beneath the oak^c (near) the stream.^d He named^e that place^f the Stream of Deborah and the oak the Oak of Mourning for Deborah.^g

31/ Then Rebekah set out^a and returned home^b to his father Isaac. Through her Jacob sent rams, he-goats, and sheep^c to make his father a meal as he would wish.^d 32/ He followed his mother until he reached the country of Kabratan,^a and he remained there. 33/ During the night^a Rachel gave birth to a son. She^b named him Son of my Pain because she had difficulty when she was giving birth to him.^c But his father named him Benjamin on the eleventh of the eighth month, during the first year of the sixth week of this jubilee^d [2143]. 34/ Rachel died there^e and was buried in the country^b of Ephrathah, that is, Bethlehem. Jacob built a pillar at^c Rachel's grave—on the road above her grave.^d

Textual Notes

1a he stayed] "they stayed" Lat.
b that (he)] "as if/as it were" Lat.
c he and his sons] Lat. lacks. Cf. T. Levi 8:3 (where he and his descendants are included; Charles, *Jubilees*, 191).
d appointed and ordained] Lat. lacks "and ordained," perhaps by haplography (VanderKam, *Jubilees* 2:208). Where Eth. uses third person pl. verbs (lit., "they appointed him and they ordained him"), Lat. resorts to a passive, third person sg. form for "appointed."
e priesthood] "priest" Lat. (and MS. 12), perhaps since in it Levi is the subject of the verb of appointment. Cf. T. Levi 8:3 (priest).

2a had come] "he had brought" 35.
b animals] "every living thing and" Lat. (MS. 58 also reads the conjunction). *Animam* should, presumably, be *animal*.

3a his sons] "his son" Eth.; "his sons" Lat. The Lat. is obviously correct; the Eth. reading has resulted from a small error in spelling (VanderKam, *Jubilees* 2:208).
b came down on Levi in the Lord's share] Charles (*Ethiopic Version*, 119 n. 28; *Jubilees*, 191) thought the Lat. should be rendered "Levi fell to the portion of the Lord," but the two texts more likely reflect the same reading. See VanderKam, *Jubilees* 2:208.

4a On] The sentence begins with a conjunction in Eth. (only 20 om.), but Lat. lacks one, entailing that the date of 7/15 is attached to the investiture of Levi.
b he (brought)] Lat. reads a conjunction before the verbal form (see n. a).
c 7] This is the Lat. reading. Eth.: "60." Rönsch (*Jubiläen*, 147) uncovered the source of the variation: ξ' = 60 is a mistake for ζ' = 7. Charles (*Ethiopic Version*, 199 n. 36; *Jubilees*, 192) and Littmann ("Jubiläen") have also adopted this attractive, economical solution.
d 21] Eth. reads "29." Rönsch (*Jubiläen*, 147) has found the solution to this confusion as well: ενα = 1 was misread as εννεα = 9. So Charles, *Ethiopic Version*, 119 n. 38; *Jubilees*, 192; Littmann, "Jubiläen," 94 n. c.; Berger, *Jubiläen*, 481–82 n. a to v. 4.
e as] Lat. uses *haec* = "this/those" to sum up and introduce the next clause. Eth. simply places "offering" after the list of animals.

f   and (as)] Lat. (and MS. 12) lacks a conjunction before "a pleasing offering," so that it reads: "(on the altar) of pleasing offerings."
5a This] "Which" 9 12 63; pr. "And" 17 (Lat. *hoc*).
b   because of the vow] om. 20 (Lat. *a voto*).
c   their (sacrifices)] Lat. lacks, but the possessive *ipsorum* after *vino* may be intended to be read with both nouns (*sacrificiis*, *vino*).
6a it, he would burn] Lat. lacks, though the content favors reading the words (see Charles, *Ethiopic Version*, 121; Dillmann in Rönsch, *Jubiläen*, 63).
b   above it] "above" Lat. The pronoun "it" (masc.) could refer to the sacrifice or the altar. Werman (*Jubilees*, 426 n. 9) renders the Eth. suffix with a fem. pronoun (עליה) and thinks it refers to the offering by fire (אשה). She rejects the Eth. reading in favor of the Lat., which she considers more understandable (it means "above [the altar]"), but why she uses a fem. form is not clear.
c   four sheep, four he-goats] Lat. lacks, apparently by paraplepsis, *quattuor—quattuor* (Charles, *Ethiopic Version*, 121).
d   This is what] *et semel haec* Lat. *Semel* means "once," which seems wrong in the context. Since three of the letters in the word are uncertain, one wonders whether the reading should be *secus*, "according to, in proportion to," or a corruption of it.
7a He was—seven days] Lat. om. by paraplepsis: "seven days" (end of v. 6)—"seven days."
b   there] om. 21 38.
c   He was blessing] Lat. also reads a third person sg. form, but a number of Eth. MSS. make the verb pl. (9 12 17 38 63; also 21 [different form], 44 [another form]). The same MSS. make the verb "praise" pl., though Lat. also reads a sg. form for it.
d   him] om. 9 25 38 (*eum* Lat.).
e   who (had granted)] *quoniam* ("because") Lat. Perhaps *quoniam* is a corruption from *qui etiam* (see VanderKam, *Jubilees* 2:210).
8a the clean animals] "the choice and clean animals" 12; + "and the ones who were not clean" 35 58.
b   them] om. 9 12 38 39 42 47 48.
c   He gave] Charles (*Ethiopic Version*, 120; *Jubilees*, 193) inserted a negative before the verb, claiming that the text in the MSS. would incorrectly limit the tithe to clean animals (cf. T. Levi 9:4). See the commentary. Mss. 17 38 63 read ". . . unclean animals and he gave," separating the animals from Jacob's donation of people.
9a rather than] pr. "and" 9 17 21 38 39 42 48, though the conjunction does not seem to change the meaning. Ms. 63 reads "and" in place of "rather than" so that Levi serves as priest before Jacob and his ten brothers.
b   gave] + "to him" 21 35 38 44 47 58 63.
c   again (gave) a tithe] or: "a second tithe."
d   (sanctified) it] om. 9 12 20 25 35 63. The suffix "it/him" probably refers to the tithes but could stand for Levi (see VanderKam, *Jubilees* 2:211).
e   became] + "for him" 35 39 42 47 48 58.
10a to tithe (lit., "to tithe tithes")] Most MSS. place "tithes" in the non-acc. case, but MSS. 9 12 17 38 attached the acc. ending. In them the word *kāʿeba* could be an adj. = "a second tithe."
11a a second time] Mss. 12 17 read an acc. ending on *ʿašrat* so that the following word *dāgema* could mean "second" (as in v. 10 above).
b   of it] om. 20 25 35; they add the word after "the (next) year."
12a harvesting] Mss. 9 17 38 63 have the reading "has passed," possibly confusing words that share two consonants; MSS. 21 39ᶜ 42 47 48 have "first" (for "first seed"?), and MSS. 12 39ᵗ 58 om. See VanderKam, *Jubilees* 2:211.
b   the proper time of its season] For "the proper time" 9 12 20 38 have "its proper time." Ms. 21 has "olive." All of these MSS., except 20, then om. "of its season." Ms. 20 places a conjunction between "its proper time" and "its season."
13a grows old] "he eats" 17 58 (confusion of two verbs looking much alike).
14a are to eat] "will eat" 9 12 48.
b   at the same time] Another translation is "together." The context, however, deals with the time when various products may be eaten, so "at the same time" seems preferable. See VanderKam, *Jubilees* 2:212. Werman (*Jubilees*, 427, with n. 10) renders as אז ("then").
c   in the sanctuary] om. 20 25; "in the temple" 21 35 38 44.
15a and (is to belong)] om. 9 12 17 20 21 63.
16a the next night] "that day" 12 (?).
b   forever] om. 9 12 17 21 38 63.
17a only (*bāḥtito*)] "but" (*baḥtu*) 38. For the readings and the ways in which experts have translated them, see VanderKam, *Jubilees* 2:212.
18a the Lord] + "your God" 39 42 47 48 58.
b   humanity has set foot] Eth. and Lat. have several differences whose source is not clear.
    Eth. (lit.): "the footsteps of humanity have trod"
    Lat.: "they will make their footprint against humanity"
    Perhaps the meaning differs little (see VanderKam, *Jubilees* 2:213), but 4Q223–224 unit 1 i:2 shows that the original was in part:] כף מדרוך בכול = lit., "in every treading place of the sole." For the phrase, see Deut 2:5.
19a land] "blessings" Lat. Genesis 35:12, the base text, has "earth." Eth. is preferable in a context speaking of territory, while Lat. probably derives from other patriarchal blessings such as Gen 28:4. Charles (*Ethiopic Version*, 121 n. 45; *Jubilees*, 194) thought Lat. might be correct.

b rule] Lat. has a double reading: "rule and exercise power." The Heb. frg. lacks the extra conjunction and verb (DJD 13:100-101).

c just as they wish] Almost all Eth. MSS. read *faqadu*, "they wish(ed)"; Lat. has *voluntatem suam*. Lengthening the second vowel to -*ā*- in *faqadu* ("they wish[ed]") would yield the same reading (as in MS. 12).

20a kept watching] "watched" 21; Lat. "kept watching."

b gone up] + *ab eo* ("from him") Lat.

21a he saw] "he kept looking" 9 12 38 (see v. 20); Lat. *vidit*, "he saw."

b an angel] + "of God" Lat.

c tablets] + *buxeas* ("of boxwood") Lat. See Rönsch, *Jubiläen*, 147; VanderKam, *Jubilees* 2:213.

d hands] Several MSS. read a dual rather than a pl. form. Lat.: "hand." See VanderKam, *Jubilees* 2:213.

e gave (them)] Eth. uses an anticipatory suffix (third person masc. sg.) on the verb, which is resumed by *la-yāʿqob*. It thus lacks a direct object, though Lat. supplies one (*illas*).

f read them] Lat. lacks "them."

g He learned (= Lat.)] om. 12. Eth. is strange in repeating the verb "He read" at this point. It may be that it resulted from confusing ανεγνω and εγνω (see VanderKam, *Jubilees* 2:213).

h everything] Lat. lacks the word.

22a everything] Lat. lacks the word.

b not (the place)] Lat. lacks a negative; both Rönsch (*Jubiläen*, 62) and Charles (*Ethiopic Version*, 123 n. 3 to Lat.) supplied one in the Lat. text, as the context definitely requires it.

c Go] Lat. places *sed* ("but") before the verb; MSS. 17ᶜ 35 58 63 read *wa-*.

d house] Lat. = "the place, the tower." Cf. VanderKam, *Jubilees* 2:214.

e live] + "there" 21 35; most MSS. read the word after "your father Isaac." Lat. has it in neither place.

f where] "the house of" 20 25 39 42 44 47 48 58 63. Lat. *ad* "with"?

g your father's] om. 25 44.

23a in the grave of your fathers] Eth. uses a pl. "graves"; Lat. has a sg. fem. form. Lat. places a conjunction before "in" and a verb after "your fathers" to form a new clause: "and you will be put in the grave of your fathers."

b with] om. 25 35 44.

24a Now you write down everything just as you have seen and read] "all the things that have been written" Lat. The two versions share a word for writing and the term "all/everything/all things." Verses 25-26 show that the angel had issued a command to Jacob to write.

25a Lord] om. 9 12 17 21 38 39 42 47 48 63.

b everything] Lat. reads *universa* after "remember," but Eth. locates it after "seen."

c just as] Lat. "which" (= MS. 12 which reads *za-* rather than *zakama*).

26a When he had gone up from him] This is the reading of Eth. and Lat., but Werman (*Jubilees*, 428 n. 22) inserts at this point a clause she removed from v. 20 ("and Jacob kept watching until he had gone up into heaven") on the grounds that the author would not have had Jacob watch God ascend but would more likely have written this about an angel. At least there is no textual support for her bold change. There are similarities between vv. 20 and 26, but if she is right she would have to assume that at some point someone transferred the statement about Jacob's watching the angel to his following the ascent of God. Why would someone do this? In addition, space considerations in 4Q223-224 unit 1 i:4-5 make it very likely the clause belongs in v. 20 (DJD 13:100).

b wrote down] "hid" Lat. Rönsch (*Jubiläen*, 148) saw that the variant in Lat. came about through confusing εγραψε (= Eth.) and εκρυψε (= Lat.). Eth. seems more likely; in it Jacob does as the angel told him in v. 24.

27a more] Lat. and MSS. 38 44 om. The context favors reading the word.

b exactly as] "as much as" Lat. Perhaps the difference arose from the similarity between ככל אשר (= Eth.; so Goldmann) and כאשר (= Lat.; so Hartom).

c Detaining . . . detained (= Lat.)] Eth. = "Addition . . . added." Lat. *retentatio* (= *retentio*) embodies the etymological sense of עצר (BDB, 783) in the noun and the explanatory verb. The Eth. readings "Addition . . . added" are understandable in the context as the eighth day was indeed added to the previous seven of the holiday. Note that Lat. says the eighth day was added to the seven of the festival in v. 28. Rönsch (*Jubiläen*, 148) suggested the simplest, most economical way of explaining the readings in the two granddaughter versions: *retentatio/retentio* renders επισχεσις (used in some texts to translate עצרת), but Eth. translates επιθεσις (accepted by Büchler, "Studies," 265; Charles, *Jubilees*, 195; in *Ethiopic Version*, 122 nn. 21-22 to Lat., he had regarded Lat. as corrupt; Rapp, *Jakob in Bet-El*, 232). Once the confusion in the names occurred, the verb would have been leveled through in v. 27 to agree with it.

d day] + *ibi* ("there") Lat.

e ones] "days" Lat.

28a this reason] Lat. = "which reason." MSS. 12 38 agree with Lat.

b revealed] = Lat. MS. 20: "ordained."

c (celebrate) it] "that day" Lat.

d (add) it] Neither Lat. nor most Eth. MSS. read an object for the verb, but MSS. 9 12 17 38 47 58 do (= "it").

29a Detaining] Again Eth. has "Addition." See n. c in v. 27 above.

b   because of the fact that] Both versions support the reading. Charles (*Jubilees*, 196) thought it did not yield the correct sense because the sequel does not explain why the extra day received its name. He proposed that *propter quod* rendered διοτι = כי. The Heb. term means "when" in this context (= οτε). So it was given the name when it was entered on the tablets. But the latter part of the verse does seem to give the reason why the day acquired its name (see VanderKam, *Jubilees* 2:216).

c   it is entered] "it is added" Lat. Eth. uses the normal verb for recording data on the tablets, lit., "they will bring (it) up." The word translated "it" (for the indefinite pl. to indicate a passive sense), however, is sg. (*ye'eti*), whereas the verb is pl. Since the context deals with the heavenly tablets, Eth. seems preferable. Charles (*Ethiopic Version*, 122 n. 26) changed the verb to a G-stem sg. to make it agree with *ye'eti*. Several Eth. MSS. (21 39 42 47 48 58) read *bāti* ("in it") instead of *ye'eti*, and one reads both (35); MS. 20 reads neither. The reading "in it" is problematic because the referent of "it" (fem.) is not clear. It is simpler to read *ye'eta* (acc.) = "the day." The line then reads: "they make it go up," i.e., "it is entered." See VanderKam, *Jubilees* 2:216.

d   testimony] "days" Lat. Charles (*Ethiopic Version*, 122 n. 26) changed *ba-sem'a* to *ba-'elata* = Lat. But "testimony" is expected when speaking about the tablets, while Lat. *dies* could have resulted from the following *dierum*.

e   in accord with] = both versions. The idea is that the day is recorded in its appropriate, unchanging place in the days of the 364-day year (see Berger, *Jubiläen*, 485 n. c to v. 29). Charles (*Jubilees*, 196) thought an original ב was misread as כי. Only MS. 38 agrees with his suggestion, but it may be a mistake (*ba-* for *bakama*).

30a In the night, on the twenty-third of this month] Lat. has the same meaning, though it gives the date first and the reference to night second—the reverse of their order in Eth. However, the word *tertia* is in the wrong place so that Lat. reads: "On the twentieth day of this month, in the third night." The two are the same if *tertia* is moved after *vigensimo* and changed to *tertio* (Rönsch, *Jubiläen*, 64; Charles, *Ethiopic Version*, 123). Werman (*Jubilees*, 428 n. 24), again with no textual support, changes the date to the twenty-fourth, not the twenty-third. She assumes that the appearance of the angel came a night after God's appearance—something the text does not say. Verse 21 certainly leaves the impression that the angel appeared to Jacob in the same night as the Lord spoke to him. She does not regard the Lat. reading "in the third night" (Eth. "In the night") as a result of a misplaced ordinal but as the original reading (n. 25), a conclusion that results in a misreading of the chronology (then one would have to presuppose that Lat. referred to the twentieth of the month, which is clearly not correct in the context).

b   They buried her] "She buried her" 9 12 17 20 21 38 44 48°; "he buried her" 63.

c   beneath the oak] Rönsch (*Jubiläen*, 149) observed that Lat. must have translated a form of βαλανος, "acorn, oak tree." *Glans* = "acorn," which is the wrong word in the context.

d   (near) the stream] The Eth. text reads "of the stream." Lat. and MS. 44 have "in the stream," perhaps meaning "at the stream."

e   He named] Lat. "They named"; "She named" 20 25 35 39 42 44 48 58; cf. 47; om. 12.

f   that place] "that stream" 25 35 39 42 44 48 58; cf. 47; om. 12.

g   and the oak the Oak of Mourning for Deborah] om. Lat. (from *debborae—debborae*).

31a Rebekah set out] Lat. has "Jacob set out," a reading that can hardly be correct in context. Ms. 21: "Rebekah did not set out."

b   home (lit., "to the house")] "the tower" Lat. (see also 32:32). Mss. 9 38 63 read "her house."

c   he-goats, and sheep] Lat. and MS. 38 reverse the terms.

d   as he would wish] "as he would love" 20 25 35 44. Lat. (lit.): "according to his wish."

32a Kabratan] There are many spellings in the Eth. MSS. Lat. *dabratan* should be corrected to *cabratan* (see Rönsch, *Jubiläen*, 64; Charles, *Ethiopic Version*, 125 n. 1 to Lat.). The reading of כברת הארץ (Gen 35:16) as a place-name is found also in LXX. See VanderKam, *Jubilees* 2:217.

33a the night] "that night" Lat. (preferred by Werman, *Jubilees*, 428 n. 28).

b   She named him—named him] om. Lat. (parablepsis: *vocavit nomen eius—vocavit nomen eius*).

c   to him] om. 9 17 21 48.

d   on the eleventh—this jubilee] The two versions offer nearly the same date, but the order of the units in it is different in that Eth. puts the jubilee unit last and Lat. places it first. They differ on the exact date: eleventh in Eth., tenth in Lat., with MSS. 42 47 48 58 63. See VanderKam, *Jubilees* 2:217.

34a there] om. 39 42 58.

b   country] Both. Eth. and Lat. read a word for land/country where Gen 35:19 has "way."

c   at] "above" Lat.

d   on the road above her grave] "his/her pillar of her grave" Lat. The wording is strange (*titulum eius supulcri eius*). Rönsch (*Jubiläen*, 64, 149) suggested *secus [viam] supulcri eius* (so Charles, *Ethiopic Version*, 125 n. 4 to Lat.).

Commentary

Jubilees 32 constitutes the second major unit devoted to matters related to Bethel. Like Jubilees 31, the other Bethel chapter, it has limited parallels in Genesis 35:

Jubilees 32:17-20 // Genesis 35:9-13
Jubilees 32:30 // Genesis 35:8
Jubilees 32:32-34 // Genesis 35:16, 18-20.

Verses 1-29 largely deal with two topics that had arisen when Jacob made a vow during his first visit to Bethel: he had promised that the place would become the house of God and that he would give a tenth of all the deity provided for him. The chapter pictures Jacob paying the tithe—a subject that turns out to have connections with Levi as priest—and resolving to build a sanctuary at Bethel, though in the end he received instructions from on high not to proceed with the project. The time for paying the tithe was the fourteenth day of the seventh month, and Jacob followed that payment with elaborate sacrifices on the Festival of Tabernacles that began on the fifteenth. The sacrifices were a "gift because of the vow which he had made that he would give a tithe along with their sacrifices and their libations" (v. 5). Jacob's celebration of the holiday that his grandfather Abraham had inaugurated (16:20-31) preceded appearances to him by the Lord and then an angel and a decree that this day was to be added to the seven-day festival. The final verses of chap. 32 (vv. 30-34) draw the Bethel story to a close with everyone leaving the place. After Deborah dies, Rebekah returns to her home with the others accompanying her for a certain distance. At that time Rachel dies giving birth to Benjamin, her second son.

The chapter can be outlined as follows:

- 1-29 Bethel
  - 1   Levi's dream
  - 2-9   Jacob's tithes
  - 10-15 Tithes
  - 16-26 Night appearances to Jacob
  - 27-29 An extra day
- 30-34 Departure from Bethel
  - 30   Deborah's death
  - 31-32 Departure of Rebekah
  - 33-34 Rachel's Death

The textual witnesses for the chapter are the complete Ethiopic version and the Latin translation that is available for vv. 1-8 (first three words) and 18-34. In addition, 4Q223–224 unit 1 col. i:1-5 preserves remnants of vv. 18-21.

1-29 Bethel

Jacob had returned to Bethel from Hebron at the end of chap. 31 (v. 30) because, to carry out his vow, he planned to make an offering on the altar he had constructed at the site. The date in v. 2 (the fourteenth of month 7) implies that they had arrived back at Bethel on the thirteenth.

■ 1 Levi's dream[1]

The writer relates that Jacob remained in Bethel the night he and his traveling party arrived there. The sentence could be regarded as the end of chap. 31[2] or as a smooth transition to chap. 32 in which Levi's dream occurs in the same time period. During this night Levi, the recipient of Isaac's blessing that he and his descendants would eternally carry out sacerdotal functions (31:13-17), saw confirmation of Isaac's words in a dream. The text does not say who sent the dream to Levi; it reports only that he had one and in it he learned that[3] he "was appointed and ordained[4] to the priesthood of the Most High God forever." The Ethiopic text reads third-person plural verbs (here the equivalents of passives) and Latin has a passive singular form. Because of the

---

1   Armin Lange ("Divinatorische Träume und Apokalyptik im Jubiläenbuch," in Albani, *Studies in the Book of Jubilees*, 27–28) classifies Levi's dream and the one Jacob has in vv. 21-26 as "theorematische Träume," that is, ones that are understandable without any explanation being given. See also Rapp, *Jakob in Bet-El*, 222–23; he notes that, in Jubilees, dreams are secondary in importance to visions, with the only others identified by the term being Rebekah's (27:1) and Judah's (41:24).

2   So Davenport, *Eschatology*, 61 n. 2.

3   Ethiopic reads *kama* and Latin has *quasi*. The latter means "as, as it were, as if," making it even clearer that the appointment did not take place in actuality, only in a dream. See VanderKam, *Jubilees* 2:208. The earthly ordination takes place in v. 3.

4   The verb *rassaya* has a range of meanings: Dillmann ("Jubiläen") translated *verordnete* (= "ordained/established"); see also his *Lexicon*, 281–82. Leslau lists these senses: "put, place, set,

formulation, the reader does not learn who appointed and ordained Levi and his offspring to the priesthood.[5] The matter is left vague,[6] and the status of the dream appointment remains unclear (see below).

There is some material in the Aramaic Levi Document and the Testament of Levi resembling Levi's dream about being appointed to the priesthood. As they have pieced together what they call chap. 4 in the Aramaic Levi Document, Greenfield, Stone, and Eshel read in 4:4: "Then I was shown visions[7][. . .] in the vision of visions." In the sequel there is a reference to the priesthood and possibly to "the Most High God" (only a few letters of the words survive in 4:7),[8] while in 4:13 Levi reports that he awakened from sleep.[9] The closest parallel in the Testament of Levi is in chap. 8,[10] where Levi has his second vision, in which "seven men in white clothing" invest him with priestly garments. They say to him, "From now on become a priest of the Lord, you and your seed, for ever" (8:3; cf. v. 10). He awakens in v. 18.

Kugel agrees that the parallel is with Testament of Levi 8, a section he labels "Levi's Priestly Initiation." For him, this is an originally independent work that was incorporated into the Aramaic Levi Document (and eventually into the Testament of Levi). The author of Jubilees was aware of it and felt he had to acknowledge it, but it posed a problem for him. As Kugel sees the matter, he was especially interested in the motif of a chain of priests stretching from the ancient patriarchs through Abraham and Isaac. Since Jacob is not a priest in Jubilees, Isaac appointed his grandson Levi to the position (31:13-17). Appointment by heavenly figures in a dream—a dream in which Levi is actually appointed priest—hardly harmonized with this theme, so the writer reduced it to one line.[11] Kugel has correctly noted that the material in "Levi's Priestly Initiation" is downplayed in Jub 32:1.[12] Yet, as it appears in Jubilees, there is no conflict between it and Isaac's blessing which, contrary to Kugel, did not involve appointing Levi to the priesthood—chap. 31 contains only his predictions about Levi, not ordination of him.[13] Both Isaac's blessing and the dream appointment are parts of the overwhelming case the author makes for Levi as priest and for the roles of his descendants. Jubilees took various elements of Levi's vision in Aramaic Levi Document 4 and incorporated them at different points in chaps. 30–32. The redistribution suggests the writer did not wish to emphasize a visionary, dreamlike installation;[14] it adds to the Levi tradition in chaps. 31–32 but does not introduce a conflict into the account.

Verse 1 refers to "the priesthood of the Most High God [*'amlāk le'ul/dei excelsi*] forever" (as noted above, "the Most High God" may be present in ALD 4:7;[15] cf. T. Levi 4:2). The title figures a number of times in the HB from which it was probably drawn, but commentators

---

    set up, establish, institute, do, make, convert (into), arrange, treat, prepare, consider, regard something as, clothe, arm, equip" (*Concise Dictionary*, 58). Latin lacks an equivalent.

5 Cf. Rapp, *Jakob in Bet-El*, 223.

6 Davenport notes that "they" in the Ethiopic version occurs where T. Levi 8:2 speaks of "seven men in white clothing" (*Eschatology*, 61 n. 2). If "they" replaces "seven men in white clothing" (apparently angels) from a source, it may be another mark of how the writer de-emphasizes this experience.

7 The form חזיון should be rendered as singular (so J. T. Milik, "Le Testament de Lévi en araméen: Fragment de la Grotte 4 de Qumrân," *RB* 62 [1955] 394-406, here 400; Kugler, *From Patriarch to Priest*, 78; Drawnel, *Aramaic Wisdom Text*, 104).

8 Drawnel also reads the divine title here (*Aramaic Wisdom Text*, 111). The suggestion was originally Milik's (in D. Barthélemy and Milik, eds., *Qumran Cave 1* [DJD 1; Oxford: Clarendon, 1955] 88).

9 Kugler, *From Patriarch to Priest*, 87: "the mention in *Jub*. 32:1 that Levi was ordained a priest in a dream is surely a single-sentence summary of the material found in this vision."

10 Charles, *Jubilees*, 191.

11 Kugel, "Levi's Elevation," 47-52.

12 Ibid., 48-49.

13 Kugler, *From Patriarch to Priest*, 152 (referring to Kugel, "Levi's Elevation," 6). Kugel says that "here it is Isaac who designates Levi and his descendants to serve in the sanctuary forever" (p. 7; on p. 51 he uses "appointed"), but "designates" (or "appointed") is not the appropriate word for what Isaac does.

14 See Rapp, *Jakob in Bet-El*, 222-23.

15 It does occur in ALD 5:8 (Levi says he is "priest of the Most High God") and 8:6 (a pleasing fragrance "before the Most High God").

have found considerable importance in its presence here because it is used in some sources in connection with the Hasmonean high priesthood. If so, v. 1 could reflect the Maccabean background of the book. Charles wrote:

> This was the specific title chosen by the Maccabean priest-kings. Thus they are called *sacerdotes summi Dei* in Assumpt. Mos. vi. 1. . . . Hyrcanus II. is designated αρχιερευς θεου υψιστου by Joseph. (*Ant.* xvi. 6. 2), and the Rosh ha-Shanah 18*b* states that it used to be said: "In such a year of Johanan priest of the Most High God." This title, anciently borne by Melchizedek (Gen. xiv. 18), was revived by the new holders of the high priesthood. Our author has Gen. xiv. 18-20 before him; for in the next verse he adopts a clause from Gen. xiv. 20: "And he gave him a tenth of all."[16]

He may have been correct that the kings who are called or who call themselves *sacerdotes summi Dei* in As. Mos. 6:1 are Hasmoneans,[17] but the passage says nothing about whether this was an unusual rather than a more common way to refer to high priests. The reference in Josephus's *Antiquities* comes from an official document issued by Caesar Augustus in which in one place he refers to the Hyrcanus as "high priest of the Most High God" (16.163). The passage from the Babylonian Talmud is even more problematic. There the sages are discussing the statement in *Megillat Ta'anit* that on the third of the month Tishri mentioning God's name in legal documents was prohibited.

> For the Syrian government decreed that [the Israelites] could not mention the name of [God in] heaven. But when the Hasmonean kingdom grew strong and defeated them [that is, the Syrians], they ordained that [Israelites] should mention the name of heaven even in legal documents. And thus [people] would write: "In the such-and-such year of [the reign of] Yohanan the high priest of the almighty God [the text reads אל עליון]."

This use of the divine title has nothing specific to do with the Hasmonean high priests; they figure in the passage because they are the ones who defeated the Seleucids. For Charles's thesis to stand he needed to establish that adding "the Most High God" to the name of their office was a practice distinctive to the Hasmonean high priests (as he wrote, it was "the specific title chosen by the Maccabean priest-kings"); the passages he cited in support of it do not make the point. The evidence from Sir 50:1-21, the poem lauding the pre-Hasmonean high priest Simon, should give one pause. The readings are not secure in each place in the chapter, but in the Greek text forms of υψιστος for God occur in vv. 7, 14, 15-17, 19, and 21. The only Hebrew for the chapter is the medieval copy B, and it has various terms where Greek has υψιστος, including עליון in vv. 14, 16. Simon is not called "high priest of the Most High God," but the divine title seems to be associated with the temple and its liturgy.[18] It is surely significant that 1 and 2 Maccabees never call a Hasmonean "priest of the Most High God."[19] Moreover, it is a very frequent title for God in Jubilees (twenty-four times) and occurs often in blessings (e.g., 22:11, 19; 27:15).[20]

It is probably safer to say that Jub 32:1, in referring to the appointment of Levi and his sons to the priesthood of the Most High God, uses a title more generally employed for the priesthood, not for the Maccabean pontiffs alone.[21] It is, of course, the title used for Melchizedek in Gen 14:18, and the Melchizedek peri-

---

16 Charles, *Jubilees*, 191. As Charles indicates later in the same note, at his time some experts dated various Psalms to the Maccabean period, including Psalm 110 with its reference to Melchizedek. One piece of evidence was the supposed acrostic on the name Simon/Simeon in vv. 1-4.

17 See Johannes Tromp, *The Assumption of Moses: A Critical Edition with Commentary* (SVTP 10; Leiden: Brill, 1993) 198-99.

18 Cf. Westermann, *Genesis 12–36*, 204; Hultgård, *L'eschatologie*, 1:32, 35-36; Schubert, "'El 'Æljôn," 8-9.

19 Hultgård, *L'eschatologie*, 1:42. He thinks that since the title is used for Levi in the Aramaic Levi Document and in Jubilees and these two works drew on a common source, they attest to a pre-Maccabean use of it (1:41-43). So also Schubert, *Tradition*, 155-57.

20 Schubert, "'El 'Æljôn," 3.

21 See also Goldstein, "Date," 76-77.

cope is an important source for the present passage (see below). Levi reacts to the dream, the third time Jubilees relates the priesthood to him and his offspring (see 30:18; 31:13-17), by blessing the Lord—a fitting response to good news (see, e.g., 31:25).

Excursus: Levi, Levites, and the Levi Tradition

1. *Levi, the Levites, and the Hasmoneans*. Though the passages adduced to demonstrate a special connection between the title "the Most High God" and the Hasmonean high priests are inadequate to the task, R. Meyer has argued from another angle that there is a relationship between the Hasmoneans and the Levi of Jubilees (and of the Testaments of the Twelve Patriarchs).[22] After sketching the information about the Levites in the HB, concluding with their lofty position in Chronicles, he turns to the picture of Levi in Jubilees and the Testaments. While the *Tendenz* expressed in them could be explained as an assertion of priestly power so that Levi would be the *heros eponymos* of the priesthood, he finds this unconvincing because the picture of Levi does not match that of the postexilic priesthood; moreover, if they are priestly, it would be strange that these works fail to mention Aaron. He locates the key for understanding the situation in the apocalyptic survey in Testament of Levi 17-18. It predicts that an old priesthood will fall and a new dynasty will assume power; this is a reference to Jonathan and Simon, the first two Hasmonean high priests. In order to legitimate the assumption of the office by members of their family, their defenders resorted to a genealogical argument (see 1 Macc 2:1), but more was needed. An additional attempt at legitimizing them is the one found in Jubilees and the Testaments—the connection with Levi. The argument in these books is understandable if the Hasmoneans were Levites by birth. If one views them from a Hasmonean standpoint, the characteristics of Levi in Jubilees and the Testaments become clear: zeal for the law, cult, and freedom, and a willingness to fight for them not only against external foes but also against internal ones. The Hasmoneans thus embody the ideal situation of Levi's time, and this is the reason why Aaron is not mentioned. He would not fit in a framework of legitimating a Levitical dynasty of priests.[23] This line of defense for the Hasmonean usurpation also deflected the popular expectation of a Davidic messiah by moving it to the future and in this way leaving the present to the new dynasty. Meyer concludes his case by noting that the rise of the Hasmoneans had little effect on the Levitical class; that group, however, continued to strive for improvement in its status as indicated by Josephus (*Ant.* 20.216-18) and several rabbinic sources (e.g., *b. Yebam.* 86a-b).

Levites may indeed have striven to improve their standing relative to the priests, but there is no adequate basis for thinking those efforts had anything to do with the picture of Levi in Jubilees. The Hasmoneans, who were, of course, priests, would have had no closer connections with Levites than any other priestly clan; according to the genealogical picture in the HB, all of Levi's offspring were Levites, some of whom (Aaron and his male descendants) were priests. Another flaw in Meyer's case is the date he assumes for Jubilees and for the Levi tradition embodied in it; both very likely belong to times before the Hasmoneans assumed the high-priestly office in 152.

2. *Levi's title Priest of the Most High God and the circles responsible for Jubilees*. The epithet "Most High God" has played an important role in trying to identify the background of Jubilees, that is, the milieu out of which the book arose. Anders Hultgård used it in his argument that the Levi ideology found in the Aramaic Levi Document and Jubilees, both of which refer to him as priest of God Most High, took shape in the third century BCE and developed in the early second century into the form it assumes in the two works.[24] That is, the phenomenon is pre-Hasmonean and thus the title "priest of the Most High God" is not tied to this later dynasty. He drew attention to the fact that it occurs most frequently in the Psalms and that, of the seventeen psalms in which it figures, eight are associated with Levitical singers (Korahites and Asaphites). For him, the data did not point to specific Levitical associations but rather to priestly ones; the title was at home in the Jerusalem temple. Conservative Zadokite circles, who, far from opposing the Levites, believed they performed important functions alongside the priests, adopted this ancient epithet in their polemic against high-ranking, Hellenistically inclined priests who corrupted their office.

---

22 R. Meyer, "Levitische Emanzipationsbestrebungen in nachexilischer Zeit," *OLZ* 41 (1938) cols. 721-28.

23 Regarding the absence of Aaron, Hultgård makes the sensible point that it is due to the fictive setting of these books (*L'eschatologie*, 1:40 n. 2).

24 Hultgård, *L'eschatologie*, 1:31-45 (he refers to the Aramaic Levi Document as the Apocryphon of Levi). Endres (*Biblical Interpretation*, 164-65) also provides a summary of Hultgård's arguments.

These Zadokites did not reject the temple and its liturgy but sought to purify them.

Friedemann Schubert accepts much of what Hultgård wrote but reads the evidence as pointing to a Levitical rather than a priestly background or origin for the Levi ideology and thus for the two works.[25] The relative frequency with which "Most High God" recurs in psalms attributed to Levitical singers shows that they in particular used the title—a title staking a claim to legitimacy and orthodoxy. He agrees that the Levi ideology is pre-Hasmonean and thinks the powers attributed to Levi in Jubilees, including military capabilities, simply reflect developments of the high priestly office in the postexilic period. The close parallels between Deut 33:8-11 (Moses's blessing of Levi) and Jub 31:13-17 indicate that the traditional interests of Levitical groups lie behind the name "Levi" in Jubilees. In the blessing Isaac pronounces on Levi, the writer appeals to texts of Levitical provenience to give him responsibilities that are primarily Levitical. As a result, the evidence favors seeing the exaltation of Levi in Jubilees 30–32 as the expression of a Levitical tradition. The priestly focus of the Phinehas passage in Numbers 25 and the borrowings from Malachi 2, where the prophet is engaged in a dispute with priests, cause a problem for Schubert, but in the case of the Malachi material he holds that Levites, like the prophet, adopted a stance against corrupt priests. Use of the two passages does not negate the strong Levitical associations of the way in which Levi, including his title priest of the Most High God, is presented in Jubilees.

The positions adopted by Hultgård and Schubert are intriguing and perhaps do uncover important information about the circles in which the Aramaic Levi Document and Jubilees originated. But both rest on a rather fragile basis in the texts. Naturally, too little evidence has survived to be sure about the answer to the origins of these books in general and the Levi tradition in particular, but arguments such as a special Levitical association with the title "the Most High God" are hardly convincing. The title occurs most frequently in poetry and that poetry likely had connections with the temple in Jerusalem, but the title was used more widely (e.g., often in Sirach). It is one that stresses the uniqueness, the greatness of God.[26] The use of it in connection with Melchizedek reveals its associations: this "priest of God Most High" blesses Abram "by God Most High, maker of heaven and earth" (Gen 14:18, 19). Perhaps Levitical circles had something to do with Jubilees, but the conclusion would not follow from use of the title "Most High God" in connection with Levi.

2-9 Jacob's Tithes[27]

Jacob, perhaps unaware of Levi's dream, seized the first opportunity, once he was back in Bethel, to begin fulfilling the terms of his vow. He had promised: "All that you have given me I will indeed tithe to you, my God" (27:27 // Gen 28:22). Now he will do precisely that.

■ 2 The text says he rose early in the morning to do this, just as he did when he made the vow (Gen 28:18 // Jub 27:26). In the parallel passage in the Testament of Levi, the report differs about exactly who did what but otherwise agrees with Jub 32:2: "And when we came to Bethel, my father Jacob saw in a vision concerning me that I should be a priest for them to God. And after having risen early in the morning he paid tithes of all to the Lord through me" (9:3-4; these words immediately follow the mention of Isaac's blessing in 9:1-2). Aramaic Levi Document 5:2-3 is related (it too directly follows a reference to Isaac's blessing in 5:1): "Then, when Jacob [my father] tithed everything which he possessed, in accordance with his vow, [then]I was before <him>[28] at the head of the [priesth]ood" (5:2-3). In Jubilees, Jacob tithed "all that had come with him" (cf. Gen 14:16; the

---

25 Schubert, *Tradition*, 153–75. See also his "'El ʿÆljôn," 4–14.

26 See, e.g., H.-J. Zobel, "עליון *ʿelyôn*," *TDOT* 11:121–39, here 125–26, 135.

27 Davenport thinks that in this context "the immediate concern is the law of the tithe, not the origin of the priesthood" (*Eschatology*, 61 n. 2). That seems right for this context, although the larger context of chaps. 30–32 focuses on why Levi received the priesthood. He suggests further a strong connection between the first part of chap. 32 and Isaac's blessing of Levi in 31:13-17.

28 It is better to read "I was first" (Drawnel, *Aramaic Wisdom Text*, 114, 117). There is an inconsistency in the edition of Greenfield, Stone, and Eshel: in their translation they read "I was before <him>" (based on an emendation, *Aramaic Levi Document*, 71), but in their commentary they cite the lemma as "I was first" (p. 148).

writer repeats the thought at the end of the verse), just as he had vowed earlier at Bethel. In this respect he imitates his grandfather Abram who "gave a tithe of everything [מכל]"[29] to Melchizedek (Gen 14:20; cf. Jub 13:26), "the priest of God Most High" (14:18). The author is very specific about the categories[30] included in Jacob's action; he gave a tenth of:

people (*sab'/homine*)
animals
money (gold)
utensils
clothing

The scriptural laws regarding tithes refer to animals (e.g., Lev 27:32; Deut 12:17; 14:23), in addition to agricultural products, but the other categories in v. 2 are more difficult. The idea of tithing humans and the other kinds of possessions likely arose from Genesis 14. Abram tithes everything to Melchizedek (v. 20), but in the sequel he discusses both property and people with the king of Sodom—as if people were included in "everything."[31] The wording in *Tg. Ps.-J.* Gen 14:20-21 may suggest an awareness of this implication: "And he gave him a tithe of all that he had *brought back*. The King of Sodom said to Abram, 'Give me the *human* persons *of my people whom you brought back*, and the possessions take for yourself.'" Genesis 14:16, by defining what he brought back, furnishes the basis for thinking Abram's tithe was comprehensive: "Then he brought back all the goods, and also brought back his nephew Lot with his goods, and the women and the people." Besides Gen 14:20, the writer could also have been thinking about the wording of Jacob's vow—he would give a tenth of all God granted him. God had granted him family, animals, and other wealth, so he was obligated to offer a tithe of each category. Note too that in his vow Jacob had specifically mentioned clothing ("clothing to wear," Gen 28:20 // Jub 27:27).

■ **3** A specific instance of tithing humans is the subject of v. 3. It happens that Rachel was then pregnant with her second child (he will be named Benjamin when he arrives in the next month [see 32:33]), and Jacob, who somehow knew the child she carried was a boy, counted his sons but did so backwards—beginning with the as-yet-unborn Benjamin. The result was that Levi, the third oldest, was the tenth from Benjamin, a happy result in this tithing context.[32] The tenth is "the Lord's share," that is, the tithe, so that Levi becomes a human tithe to the Lord in accord with Lev 27:32 (the subject is tithes of animals): "every tenth one . . . shall be holy to the Lord." With this stunning confirmation of Levi's special status—the fourth time the priesthood is related to him—his father takes the decisive step and actually ordains him to the office. The priesthood thus seems to pass from father to son. In 30:18-20 the angel told Moses that, because of his zeal at Shechem, Levi's descendants were selected to be priests and Levites; in 31:13-17 Isaac prayed that Levi and his descendants would become the ones who enjoy sacerdotal privileges and carry out clerical functions, and in 32:1 Levi dreamed that he and his offspring were appointed and ordained to the priesthood. Now, Jacob officially installed Levi in the office through two actions: he clothed him in priestly vestments and "filled his hands." Exodus 28 furnishes a full description of the sacred clothing for Aaron and his sons, but the writer of Jubilees does not elaborate on the attire in this setting. The expression "filled his hands" is the idiom employed for ordaining Aaron and his sons: "You shall put them [the priestly vestments] on your brother Aaron, and on his sons with him, and shall anoint them and ordain them [ומלאת את ידם] and consecrate them so that they may serve me as priests" (Exod 28:41; see 29:9, etc.). Note that Jacob, who has the priestly garments in his possession, is the one ordaining Levi (see Exod 29:29-30). Isaac apparently did not

---

29 Ethiopic Jubilees uses the same expression: *'em-kwellu*.
30 Jubilees 13:26 stipulates that one is "to give a tenth of everything to the Lord—of seed, the vine, oil, cattle, and sheep"; 13:25 refers to it as "the tithe of the firstfruits for the Lord."
31 See Westermann, *Genesis 12–36*, 206.
32 The expression "it came down on" reflects the language of casting lots (VanderKam, *Jubilees* 2:209). Although the translators have recognized this and have posited a change in subject for the two verbs "went up/came down," it is not impossible to render the text: he (Jacob) went up and came down on Levi in the share of the Lord.

have custody of the vestments[33] and he certainly did not ordain Levi as priest.

Excursus: Levi as the Tenth

The theme of Levi as a human tithe, however strange it may seem, is more widespread in ancient literature, though the other attestations are much later in date than Jubilees.[34] Syncellus, whose account most nearly resembles the one in Jubilees 32, mentions it twice. "After offering a tithe of his own possessions, Jacob proclaimed Levi as high priest when he was 18 years of age,[35] since he was the tenth from the last, reckoning backwards" (122.14-15; Adler/Tuffin, *Chronography*, 152; Syncellus says he took the material from Africanus). Syncellus also explains that Reuben the firstborn lost the kingship and the priesthood because of his sin with Bilhah (he does not deal with why Jacob skipped over Simeon). In a later context he returns to the same subject: "And the high priesthood was given to Levi, because, as the tenth from the last of the sons of Jacob, he, along with all his father's property, was tithed to God, just as Jacob prayed, 'All that you give to me, I will offer a tenth of it'" (207.7-10; Adler/Tuffin, *Chronography*, 159).

In Jewish texts, the motif is present but with different methods of calculation to make Levi the tenth. Some of the sources attach it to the time when Jacob wrestled with the mysterious being at the Jabbok. *Targum Pseudo-Jonathan* Gen 32:25 reads:

> Jacob was left alone *beyond the Jabbok*. And *an angel in the form of* a man wrestled with him. *And he said, "Did you not promise to tithe all that would be yours? Now behold, you have twelve sons*[36] *and one daughter, and you have not tithed them."* Immediately he set aside the four first-born of the four mothers, and there remained eight. And he began to count from Simeon, and Levi happened to be the tenth. Michael spoke up and said, "Master of the world, this one is your lot." It was on account of these things that he tarried beyond the stream *until the column of* the dawn arose.

This text does not explain exactly how Levi was the tenth when the four firstborn sons were left out of consideration, leaving only eight to count. Although it connects Levi with Jacob's tithing, it presupposes the somewhat fuller explanation in passages such as the following.

Pirqe de Rabbi Eliezer 37 (Jacob and the Angel):[37]

> Jacob wished to cross the ford of the Jabbok, and he was detained there. The angel said to him: Did you not say—"Of all that you will give me I will surely give a tenth to you"? What did our father Jacob do? He took all the cattle in his possession which he had brought from Paddan-Aram, and he gave a tithe of them amounting to 550 (animals). From this you may learn that all the cattle in the possession of our father Jacob, which he had brought from Paddan-Aram, amounted to 5500 (animals). Again Jacob wished to cross the ford of the Jabbok, but he was hindered here. The angel said: Did you not say this—"*Of all* that you will give me I will surely give a tenth to you"? Now you have sons. You have not given a tithe of them. What did Jacob do? He put apart the four firstborn children of the four mothers, and eight children remained. He began (to count) from Simeon, and finished with Benjamin, who was still in his mother's womb. Again he began (to count) from Simeon, and he included Benjamin, and Levi was reckoned as the tithe, holy to God, as it is said, "The tenth shall be holy to the Lord" (Lev. xxvii.32). (Friedlander's translation modernized in several places)

The way in which this text makes Levi the tenth is the following:
There are twelve sons if Benjamin is included.
Subtract the firstborn of each of the four mothers, leaving eight, of whom Simeon would be the first (not Reuben, who was subtracted since he was Leah's firstborn).
If one counts from Simeon through Benjamin the total is eight.
One then begins again at the top of the list with Simeon (who is now number nine overall) and the next son is Levi who is number ten.

---

[33] Kugel says about Jacob's possession of the priestly clothing: "no doubt given to him by Isaac" (*Walk through* Jubilees, 152; "Jubilees," 404). Since the text says nothing about this, there is much room for doubt.

[34] For them, see, e.g., Charles, *Jubilees*, 191-92; Kugel, "Levi's Elevation," 13-17.

[35] In the chronology in Jubilees, he is sixteen years at this time.

[36] The text assumes that Benjamin counts in some way, though the crossing of the stream occurred well before his birth.

[37] Beer drew attention to this parallel (*Jubiläen*, 36-37).

Genesis Rabbah 70:7 attaches the motif to Gen 28:22 (where Jacob makes the vow at Bethel) but presents it in yet another way.

> A certain Cuthean asked R. Meir: "Do you not maintain that Jacob was truthful?" "Certainly," he replied. "And did he not say thus, AND OF ALL THAT YOU WILL GIVE ME I WILL SURELY GIVE THE TENTH TO YOU?" he went on. "Yes," he replied, "and so he separated [to God] the tribe of Levi, which is one in ten." "But why did he not separate a tenth of the two remaining tribes?" "Were there then only twelve tribes," he replied; "surely there were fourteen, for it says Ephraim and Manasseh, even as Reuben and Simeon, shall be mine" (Gen. XLVIII, 5). "Then the difficulty is all the greater," he exclaimed; "if you add water you must add flour." "Will you not admit that there were four matriarchs?" he said to him. "Yes," he replied. "Then deduct the four firstborn of the four matriarchs from these [fourteen], since the firstborn is holy, and what is holy does not exempt what is holy." (Freedman's translation, very slightly modernized; the Cuthean was greatly impressed with R. Meir's answer).

In this version, Levi would be one of ten remaining sons, but it is not evident how he rather than any of the others would have been regarded as the special tenth one, since he would have been second in the list.

All of the sources find some way to make Levi the tenth, and they include Benjamin in the count though he was not yet born (the sources attaching the "Levi as tithe" motif to Gen 28:22 or Gen 32:25 place Jacob's knowledge about Benjamin earlier than Jubilees does). Jubilees (and Syncellus, who presumably derived it from Jubilees through an intermediary or two) alone opts for a backward count up from Benjamin.

Kugel, in his 1993 article "Levi's Elevation," proposed tentatively that the motif "Jacob Counts Backwards" was not originally a part of Jubilees and indicated several reasons for regarding it as an interpolation. One is "ideological," that is, one purpose served by the motif was to explain why Simeon, who also won praise for the slaughter of Shechem, did not receive the priesthood as a reward: "It was nothing personal, and it had nothing to do with the previous conduct of either brother; it was simply a matter of blind arithmetic."[38] Another indication that the passage is an interpolation, he maintains, is that the words "At that time [lit., in those days]" are inappropriate in the context that speaks about Rachel's becoming pregnant. The phrase normally introduces a new unit in a text and does not function as a continuation of the previous one as it does in v. 3. The awkward phrase shows it was "artlessly" imported from elsewhere. In addition, Jacob's tithe "was the occasion of a great feast"—the Festival of Tabernacles—but Jubilees has another story about the origin of that festival (16:20-31) where the details about the animals to be sacrificed conflict with the ones for Jacob's offerings.[39]

Kugel's case is not convincing. In general, his statements about "random choice" versus determinism in Jubilees rest on a misunderstanding of the author's approach (see the Introduction), but his more specific arguments are also off target. The point regarding the inappropriateness of the words "In those days" at the beginning of v. 3 arises from a misreading of the text. The phrase means "at that time" and the verb signifies "was pregnant,"[40] so that the sentence is giving helpful background information. The context makes this transparent because Rachel would hardly have become pregnant in the middle of the seventh month and have given birth less than a month later to a child who survived (32:33). As for Jacob's celebration of the Festival of Tabernacles, see the commentary below.

---

38 Kugel, "Levi's Elevation," 15. Later in the essay he comments: "Moreover, the very idea that random choice had determined such an important thing as the hereditary priesthood would certainly have been anathema to an author obsessed with, among other things, the priestly line. This author would not, it seems to me, have included this last motif if he could help it" (p. 49). Exactly how "Jacob Counts Backwards" constitutes "random choice" he does not explain. In Jubilees nothing is attributed to random choice. The author surely would have believed that Levi's place as third son of twelve occurred through divine causation. Also, the author never overtly addresses the question why Simeon did not receive a reward like the one granted to Levi.

39 Kugel, "Levi's Elevation," 50-51. On these arguments, see the comments of Rapp, *Jakob in Bet-El*, 223-24 n. 269. For Rapp, there are places where the text is rough, but they are due to the author's use of existing material, not to an interpolator.

40 The Latin expresses this point: *Et in illo tempore rachel in utero habentem beniamin.*

■ **4** With v. 4 the text moves to the next day, the fifteenth of the seventh month,[41] the date for the beginning of the seven-day Festival of Tabernacles in the scriptural calendars (Lev 23:34, 39; Num 29:12). The name Festival of Tabernacles does not occur in chap. 32 (it is called "the Festival" in v. 27, as it is designated in 1 Kgs 8:2), but the fact that Jacob celebrates a holiday for seven days in month 7 (vv. 6-7) leaves no doubt about its identity.[42] The section devoted to the festival extends through v. 29. In Jub 16:20-31 Abraham was the first to celebrate the festival; there the name is used and it lasts seven days, but the precise starting date in the seventh month is not given.[43]

The first notice after the date concerns the number and nature of the offerings Jacob[44] brings to the altar (for the readings, see the textual notes), all of which constituted "a pleasing offering for a pleasant aroma before God."[45] The many victims are accompanied by grain and liquid offerings. The numbers are unusual, as is the way in which the writer presents them. The following chart compares the number of sacrificial animals for the Festival of Tabernacles in five lists: two from the HB, one from the Temple Scroll, and two from Jubilees. In the first four the numbers are explicitly for the offerings each day of the seven, with the number of bulls in columns 1 and 3 reduced by one every succeeding day; in the case of Jub 32:4 the numbers seem to be for one day.

	Numbers 29:13-34	Ezekiel 45:23-25	11QT^a xxviii:3–xxix:1	Jubilees 16:22	Jubilees 32:4
bulls	13-7	7	[13]-7	2	14
rams	2	7	2	2	28
lambs	14		14	7	49
goats	1	1	1	1	7

The figures in Jub 32:4 are different from those in the other four enumerations in every instance.[46] In comparing columns 4 and 5, a case could be made that Jub 16:22 lists the numbers for each day of the festival while Jub 32:4 gives the totals for the seven days; this would bring the numbers into agreement except for the rams (the number of them in 16:22 agrees with the figures in both Numbers and the Temple Scroll).[47] The Ethiopic tradition connects the date "On the fifteenth of this month" with the list of sacrifices; this makes it sound as if Jacob offered all of them on the fifteenth and thus, perhaps, on each of the following days. The Latin, however, attaches the date to Jacob's investiture of Levi as priest; consequently, the date would not be the one for the sacrifices and the number of animals offered

---

41 Judging from the placement of the conjunctions, the Latin translation attaches the date to Jacob's ordination of Levi in v. 3. Levi would therefore have become (high-)priest at the Festival of Tabernacles as the Hasmonean Jonathan did (1 Macc 10:21).

42 Rubenstein writes: "The author interpreted Gen 33:17, where Jacob builds sukkot for his animals, to imply that Jacob observed the festival" (*History of Sukkot*, 55). There is no hint about such an interpretation in Jubilees 32, though Rapp repeats it (*Jakob in Bet-El*, 250).

43 Though the two accounts of the festival in Jubilees share several features (see below), they also differ in a number of respects. For example, chap. 16 mentions booths/tents and a procession around the altar; neither appears in chap. 32 (for a list of differences, see Rapp, *Jakob in Bet-El*, 200–201. As he often does, he attributes some differences like these to the author's use of sources).

44 Jacob is the only logical subject here, despite Kugler's claim that Levi offers the sacrifices (*From Patriarch to Priest*, 149). This would make the next verses, where Jacob continues to be the subject (vv. 5-8), meaningless. The verse also shows that Jacob is indeed a priest in Jubilees. Kugel has denied that he was (e.g., "Levi's Elevation, 19–21), but Jacob certainly seems to act as one here. The passage conflicts with Kugel's claim that Jacob had invited his father to come to the sacrifice in Bethel (chap. 31) because Jacob, who was supposedly not a priest, needed one to officiate at his altar. Note that Jacob says nothing of the sort in chap. 31 where he invites both parents to Bethel. Moreover, Isaac does not mention the subject. Kugel thinks that Isaac made Levi a priest so that he could officiate at the altar in Bethel, but he does not make Levi a priest and again fails to say anything about Levi's assuming the duty in Bethel. See also Rapp, *Jakob in Bet-El*, 183.

45 To translate the phrase "a pleasing offering for a pleasant aroma" Goldmann uses familiar sacrificial language: לקרבן אשה ריח ניחוח.

46 Cf. Albeck, *Jubiläen*, 21.

47 This is the argument presented in VanderKam, "Temple Scroll," 229–31.

could then be viewed as the totals for the entire festival. A problem in the Latin translation is posed by the phrase *in ipso*: it seems as if it refers to *die* (day), so that the text would be saying he brought the offering on the day, but *die* is treated as feminine here. Rönsch thought *in ipso* referred to Levi, through whom Jacob made the offerings; Charles bracketed the phrase but explained "May be right; cf. Test. Levi 9 απεδεκατωσε παντα δι' εμου."[48] But Levi is there speaking about Jacob's presenting tithes through him (cf. Jub 32:8-9), not about the offerings for the Festival of Tabernacles. It could be that *in ipso* refers to the seventh month (*mensis* is masculine) and thus would be indicating not that Jacob offered all of the animals on day fifteen but that he offered them during that month, but this would be an odd statement.

■ 5 The explanation for the strange numbers of animals lies in 32:5: "This was his gift because of the vow which he had made that he would give a tithe along with their sacrifices and their libations." According to this verse, the sacrificial animals of v. 4 were not the ones prescribed for each day of the holiday or even for the entire seven-day celebration: they constitute payment of the vow he had made. Sacrifices as payments of vows are mentioned several times in the Pentateuch. In a section of Leviticus 22 prohibiting the offering of blemished animals, Moses is told, "Speak to Aaron and his sons and all the people of Israel and say to them: When anyone of the house of Israel or of the aliens residing in Israel presents an offering, whether in payment of a vow or as a freewill offering that is offered to the LORD as a burnt offering, to be acceptable in your behalf it shall be a male without blemish, of the cattle or the sheep or the goats" (22:18-19). Similar legislation covers the presentation of a well-being/peace offering (22:21; see also Deut 12:6). The language of "gift" in connection with the tithe appears in Num 18:24, which could be translated literally as: "because the tithe of the Israelites that they set apart/raise to the LORD as a contribution [תרומה] I have given to the Levites as their heritage." The Ethiopic version of Num 18:24 uses *mabā'* where תרומה stands, and *mabā'* is the word translated in Jub 32:5 as "gift." Jacob is giving the contribution or gift of a tithe that he promised in his vow. The unusual numbers of animals, given as sum totals, are his gift, his tithe. Note, too, that Num 29:39 provides for such additional offerings at festivals. After detailing all the sacrifices on festivals, the writer adds "These you shall offer to the LORD at your appointed festivals, in addition to your votive offerings and your freewill offerings, as your burnt offerings, your grain offerings, your drink offerings, and your offerings of well-being."[49]

There is a hint of such an interpretation of Jacob's sacrifices in the passage from *Pirqe de Rabbi Eliezer* 37 quoted above:

> Jacob wished to cross the ford of the Jabbok, and he was detained there. The angel said to him: Did you not say—"Of all that you will give me I will surely give a tenth to you"? What did our father Jacob do? He took all the cattle in his possession which he had brought from Paddan-Aram, and he gave a tithe of them amounting to 550 (animals). From this you may learn that all the cattle in the possession of our father Jacob, which he had brought from Paddan-Aram, amounted to 5500 (animals).

Friedlander comments in a note on the number of animals: "Jubilees xxxii. 4 refers to the separation of the tithe of Jacob's cattle, 119 animals being offered" (he then cites Jub 32:5).[50]

■ 6 Jacob did more than offer the many animals in payment of his vow. He used the fire to burn incense, and he presented a peace offering—as Abraham did at the inaugural celebration of the festival (Jub 16:23)—for which the writer again lists the animals (eighteen in all). The

---

48   For Rönsch, see *Jubiläen*, 147; for the quotation from Charles, see *Ethiopic Version*, 119 n. 9 to Lat.; in VanderKam, *Jubilees* 2:209, *in ipso* is taken to refer to *die* despite the gender clash.

49   See Levine, *Numbers 21–36*, 391–92. Ulfgard wonders whether the high number of animals arises from this being "not only a *sukkot* celebration, but also a festival of priestly investiture, on which Jacob has vowed to pay extra tithes" (*Story of Sukkot*, 171 n. 346). The text does not relate the sacrifices to the investiture but rather to the payment of tithes.

50   Friedlander, *Pirḳê de Rabbi Eliezer*, 283 n. 5.

number of sacrificial victims differs in the two accounts of a peace offering during the Festival of Tabernacles:

Jubilees 32:6	Jubilees 16:23
2 young bulls	
4 rams	7 rams
4 sheep	7 kids
4 he-goats	7 sheep
2 year-old sheep	7 he-goats
2 goats.	

Leviticus 3 (see Lev 7:16-18 for peace offerings in connection with vows), which provides the instructions for these sacrifices from which parts are offered to God and the rest eaten by the one presenting the offering, seems to imply that the peace/well-being sacrifice consists of a single animal, whether from the cattle, sheep, or goats. That may have been normal for an individual, but there were public peace offerings involving more animals. Jacob offers a goodly number but hardly approaches Solomonic abundance in this regard (1 Kgs 8:63-64). It may be that this is the only offering to which the writer adds the notice that he presented it each of the seven festal days.

■ 7 The peace offering is a social occasion in which the person sacrificing eats a part along with other people (e.g., Exod 32:6; Lev 7:16-18; 19:5-8; Deut 27:7; Deut 12:18 is explicit about this for votive offerings; Deut 14:26-27 mentions the practice with the tithe that has been exchanged for money to be spent at the sanctuary).[51] So Jacob includes the males in his household in his meal on the joyful occasion. The Lord is the one identified as the source of Jacob's happiness because, as Jacob mentioned in the conditions of his vow, he had been with him and kept him safe. He had faced many trials in the years between his two visits to Bethel, and now he was not only carrying out the terms of his vow but also giving thanks for deliverance.[52] The joy Jacob experiences while celebrating with his family and his gratitude to God for deliverance echo themes in the report about Abraham's Festival of Tabernacles (16:20, 25-27).[53]

■ 8 In v. 8, Jacob, still the protagonist in the scene,[54] is said to tithe "all the clean animals." This could be a reference to what he had done in v. 4, where he had offered the large number of animals listed and which v. 5 associates with his vow about giving a tithe, or it could be an additional tithe (see below). The scriptural legislation for sacrifices stipulates that animals offered should be without blemish; it also provides for sacrificing only clean animals (see Lev 27:11 regarding sacrificial animals in connection with vows), but no passage specifies that clean animals alone are included under the laws of tithing. Perhaps it is a natural inference from the sacrificial legislation: how could one pay the tithe with something unclean?[55] Whatever the source of the statement may

---

51   See Milgrom, *Leviticus 1–16*, 220.
52   Perhaps his peace offering fits in the category that would later be named שלמי שמחה.
53   Halpern-Amaru, "Joy as Piety," 191–96. Jubilees 16:29 reports that the heavenly tablets command Israel to celebrate the festival with joy (see Lev 23:40; Deut 16:14). Deuteronomy 27:7 legislates that peace offerings were to be eaten joyfully. On deliverance in connection with the festival, see also Werman and Shemesh, *Revealing*, 376–78; Werman, *Jubilees*, 431.
54   In commenting on vv. 2-9 and the innovations Jubilees shows here in what he calls the Levi priestly tradition, Kugler writes: "So, whereas the accounts of the vision and of Jacob's ordination of Levi in *Aramaic Levi* are focused almost entirely on Levi, this report pushes him to the periphery; it is principally interested in showing how Jacob brought to fruition the three 'prophecies' of the elevation [i.e., 30:18-20; 31:12-17; 32:1], how he was able to fulfill his tithe, and how the law of the second tithe came into existence" (*From Patriarch to Priest*, 166–67, here 166).
55   Kister sees evidence in v. 8 and the legal unit that follows (esp. v. 15) that the halakic section does not fit the narrative and thus existed independently ("Qumranic Halakhah," 586–88). He uses Wintermute's translation, in which the beginning of v. 9 reads: "And he gave a tithe of every clean animal and he made a burnt offering." If it was a burnt offering, Levi did not receive it. However, the term that Wintermute (with Dillmann, Littmann, Charles, and Berger) rendered "burnt offering [*ṣenḥaḥ*]" need not be equivalent in meaning to עולה. It can mean "burnt offering" but is also a more general term for a sacrifice (Leslau, *Concise Dictionary*, 228: "burnt offering, sacrifice, oblation, fumigation, incense"). As "burnt offering" would not make sense in the passage, the more general meaning is preferred (as noted by Albeck, *Jubiläen*, 57 n. 210; it is translated "an offering" in VanderKam, *Jubilees* 2). Kister also thinks the notion of giving a tithe a

be, Jacob hands the unclean animals in his possession to Levi and does the same for "the persons of the people" (cf. the king of Sodom's request in Gen 14:21).

Reference to unclean animals in the passage has sparked debate. Charles translated: "but the unclean animals he gave (not) to Levi his son, and he gave him all the souls of the men." He justified his insertion of the negative by pointing to T. Levi 9:4 ("he paid tithes of all to the Lord through me") and claimed that, in contrast, the writer of Jubilees was limiting Jacob's tithe to the clean animals.[56] Littmann disagreed with Charles and thought the text was correct if one understood it to be saying that Jacob gave Levi power over the unclean animals (and the persons of the people) in order eventually to destroy them.[57] Exactly what Jacob intended by ceding the unclean animals and the people to Levi the text does not say, but for the humans Charles hypothesized: "Levi was to exercise his priestly functions on behalf of these."[58]

Werman has made an attractive case that the writer of Jubilees fashioned the section about tithes (vv. 2-15) according to the structure of Leviticus 27 (see v. 9 below where he quotes Lev 27:30), a chapter mostly concerned with vows.[59] It treats: vows regarding the equivalent of a human being (vv. 2-8), clean animals (vv. 9-10), unclean animals (vv. 11-13), house (vv. 14-15), field (vv. 16-24), and things devoted (vv. 28-29). It concludes, however, with laws about tithes from produce and cattle. Jubilees 32 starts with the story about Jacob paying his vow, mentioning humans, as well as clean and unclean animals. Next he takes up the second tithe but also mentions the tithe of cattle (on vv. 10-14 [second tithe] and 15 [tithe of cattle], see below).

■ 9 The writer says that Levi, out of all the brothers, exercised the office of priest at Bethel. This is the first time he acts as a priest, since Jacob had just ordained him into the office. He performs his new role "before his father Jacob," that is, in his presence, in front of him. It seems as if this sentence as well as the next one—"There he was a priest, and Jacob gave what he had vowed"—are summaries of the actions just completed. Yet how the sentence "In this way he again gave a tithe to the Lord" fits into the context is not obvious on first glance.[60] How did he *again* give a tithe? Possibly something he provided in the previous verses is meant—and the sequel in vv. 10-15 indicates that v. 7 is the referent (see below). His action there becomes the subject of specific legislation in the next section.[61] As all tithes are holy to the Lord (Lev 27:30-33), the verse ends appropriately with verbs indicating that Jacob set these apart—he sanctified them—for the deity and in this way made them holy.

---

second time in v. 9 was added by an editor (so, too, Werman, "Levi and Levites in the Second Temple Period," *DSD* 4 [1997] 211-25, here 219), but see the commentary on the verse and on vv. 10-14.

56 Charles, *Jubilees*, 193. Wintermute also reads a negative, explaining that the manuscripts lack it "but the sense requires it" ("Jubilees," 117 n. b). Caquot reads the negative with no parentheses around it and no note explaining the change.

57 Littmann, "Jubiläen," 95 n. a. He did not indicate where the idea of destruction could be found.

58 Charles, *Jubilees*, 193. Albeck doubts the author meant to say that unclean animals, people, and vessels also needed to be tithed (*Jubiläen*, 57 n. 210). Rather, he argued, Jacob was simply acting according to his vow that he would tithe everything. 4Q251 (4QHalakha A) frg. 10 4, after mention of a tenth part in line 3 (apparently a measure), refers to unclean animals (also in line 5), but the text is too poorly preserved to be helpful in elucidating Jub 32:8. See Rapp, *Jakob in Bet-El*, 226.

59 Werman and Shemesh, *Revealing*, 390. As Werman sees the situation (pp. 390-97), Jacob fulfills his obligations as a participant in a pilgrimage festival; that is, he obeys the command not to appear before the Lord empty-handed. The text does refer to a journey to the site but does not allude to the command against appearing empty-handed.

60 One can certainly agree with Albeck (*Jubiläen*, 31) that the subject of the sentence is Jacob (the subject of the preceding clause) and not Levi. Finkelstein had argued that Levi here tithed from the tithe he received from Jacob—a tithe of the tithe in accord with Num 18:25-28 ("Rabbinic Halaka," 52).

61 Since the subject here and in the following legislation concerns what eventually went by the name "second tithe," Werman, who thinks it refers only to crops and not animals, tries to find a place in the story where Jacob engaged in agriculture

10-15[62] Tithes

The paragraph appeals to the heavenly tablets for the rules about tithes, and from the language adopted it is evident that Deuteronomic legislation lies behind vv. 10-14.

■ **10** Most of the expressions in v. 10 are standard ones in the author's statements about the heavenly tablets: a law ordained and valid forever. In rabbinic teaching, the second tithe is the one found in Deut 14:22-27, which requires a tithe of "all that is brought in yearly from the field" (v. 22) but also includes animals (v. 23): "In the presence of the Lord your God, in the place that he will choose as a dwelling for his name, you shall eat the tithe of your grain, your wine, and your oil, as well as the firstlings of your herd and flock." *Targum Neofiti* Deut 14:23 speaks about "the second tithe of your herds and of your flocks" where the MT refers to "the firstlings of your herd and flock." The passage also treats cases in which the distance between a person's home and the sanctuary is too great to make transport of the tithes feasible; in such instances the owner was to change the tithe into money, take it to the sanctuary, and there buy whatever he wished to eat and drink. "And you shall eat there, you and your household rejoicing together" (v. 26). This is what Jacob was doing in Jub 32:7 so that this verse becomes the basis for the section about legislation on the heavenly tablets in vv. 10-14. This connection also clarifies the notice in v. 9 that Jacob again, that is, for a second time, gave a tithe. In the present circumstances Jacob had no need to convert the tithe into money because he was already at the sanctuary, where he enjoyed a meal with the people of his household. Deuteronomy indicates that this second tithe was an annual tax (v. 22), just as Jub 32:10 stipulates.[63]

■ **11-14** From the fact that the tithe is an annual requirement the writer draws the inference that "[o]ne is not to leave any of it over from this year to the next year."[64] Mention of the subject provides an opportunity for him to explain the meaning of the ruling. He lists three agricultural products—the seed, wine, and the olive. Each of these crops is to be consumed in the period from one harvest to the harvest in the following year. They are not to be eaten after the cutoff point because the arrival of the new harvest season marks the old as contaminated and impure. The wording in this section is fairly clear, but the entire subject can now be viewed in a more complete light because of the remarkable parallel in the Temple Scroll xliii:3-17.[65]

3. [   ] and on the days of the first fruits of the grain, of the wi[ne and of the oil]
4. [and at the feast of the] wood [offering.] On these days it shall be eaten; and let [them] not leave
5. of it from one year to another year. For thus they shall eat it:
6. from the feast of the first fruits of the grain of wheat they shall eat the grain

---

(*Jubilees*, 431). There is no such report in Jubilees, but she suggests that the author wants the reader to think about Jacob's time in Succoth (she refers to Jub 29:13, where Jacob "lived in tents," which she understands to be Succoth [see p. 404]; farming is not mentioned). According to Gen 33:17, "Jacob journeyed to Succoth, and built himself a house, and made booths for his cattle; therefore the place is called Succoth." Why one should suppose Jacob farmed the area is not apparent, but Werman assumes this and adds that, as Succoth fell outside the three-day limit set in Qumran texts, beyond which one could exchange crops for money, Jacob used the money so raised to buy sacrifices in Bethel. None of this has a basis in the text of Genesis or Jubilees.

62 On these verses, see Rapp, *Jakob in Bet-El*, 227-33.
63 There is no explicit indication in Jubilees that in years 3 and 6 of a sabbatical cycle this tithe was replaced by a tithe for the poor (Deut 26:12), as in the rabbinic system of tithes (Albeck, *Jubiläen*, 31-32).
64 See Albeck, *Jubiläen*, 31. As Albeck and others (e.g., Baumgarten, "The First and Second Tithes in the *Temple Scroll*," in Ann Kort and Scott Morschauer, eds., *Biblical and Related Studies Presented to Samuel Iwry* [Winona Lake, IN: Eisenbrauns, 1985] 5-15, here 12) have indicated, this principle is opposed to rabbinic halakah, where there is no time limit on the eating of the second tithe (e.g., *b. Tem.* 21b).
65 As Baumgarten ("First and Second Tithes," 11) and Shemesh (Werman and Shemesh, *Revealing*, 192-93) have noted, the Temple Scroll, like Jubilees 32, deals with matters relating to the Festival of Tabernacles before this section elaborating on the tithe in Deuteronomy 14.

7. to the following year, until the feast of the first fruits; and the wine, from the day
8. of the feast of the wine, until the day of the feast
9. of the wine of the following year; and the oil, from the day of its feast to the following year,
10. until the feast, the day of offering of new oil on the altar. And all that
11. remains of their feasts shall be consecrated and burnt; it shall never again be eaten,
12. for it is holy. And those who dwell at a distance of a three-days' journey from the temple
13. shall bring whatever they can bring. And if they cannot
14. carry it, let them sell it for money and bring the money and buy with it grain,
15. wine and oil and cattle and sheep; and they shall eat it on the days of the feast. But they shall not
16. eat of it on the working days in their sorrows, for it is holy.
17. But on the holy days it shall be eaten, and it shall not be eaten on the working days.

(trans. Yadin, *DSSR* 3:179)[66]

The Temple Scroll appeals here to its system of firstfruits holidays, in which there is a period of seven weeks between the first and the second and the second and the third:

Festival of Weeks (the holiday of the firstfruits of the wheat harvest) on 3/15
Festival of New Wine on 5/3
Festival of Oil on 6/22.

Each of these marks the time when the new harvest can be eaten and the point at which the old harvest is no longer to be consumed. Jubilees does not refer to the latter two—new wine and oil—as festivals and hence does not specify dates for them, but the writer operates with the same firstfruits system, which he treats in connection with the second tithe. Both texts provide that the tithe be eaten at the sanctuary,[67] both deal with it in connection with the Festival of Tabernacles, and both stipulate that any of the tithe left over after the next harvest is to be burned.[68]

■ **15** With v. 15 the writer addresses a tithe of cattle and sheep. It must be a different tithe than the one in vv. 10-14 because in this case the owner does not consume it; it belongs to the priests (cf. 4QMMT B 63-64). The language of the verse reflects that of Lev 27:32; in fact, it quotes from it:

Jub 32:15   wa-kwellu 'āsrāta lāhm wa-'abāge' qeddus la-'egzi'abḥēr . . . yekun
Lev 27:32   wkl   m'śr bqr wṣ'n . . . yhyh qdš lyhwh.

The Leviticus passage does not deal with the question where the tithe may be eaten, but since it is for the Lord and thus for the priests—the words "and is to belong to his priests" in v. 15 are added to Lev 27:32—it is a natural inference that they would consume it at the sanctuary, or, as Jub 32:15 puts it, "before him [the Lord]."[69] 2 Chronicles 31:6-10 also describes a tithe of cattle and sheep donated by people who lived outside of Jerusalem; according to v. 10 the animals were brought to the house of the Lord and the priests, along with the Levites, ate them. In Tob 1:6-7 the protagonist says that he formerly transported various gifts, including the tithe of cattle, to Jerusalem, where he gave them to the priests, the sons of Aaron (see Jub 13:25-27).[70] In saying the tithe of v. 15 belongs to the priests, was the writer taking a stand on the issue whether this first tithe was for the Levites or the priests (see also 13:25-27)—something that became controversial in Second Temple times? Since the text is dealing with the patriarchal priest Levi and therefore with a time before the division between priests and

---

66 See also Yadin, *Temple Scroll*, 1:114-16.
67 Rubenstein suggests that, since the second tithe had to be eaten at the sanctuary, "Jubilees appropriately pronounces this law on Sukkot when most people could be expected to journey to Jerusalem" (*History of Sukkot*, 56).
68 Cf. Werman, *Jubilees*, 432. Shemesh proposes that the rule about burning the old derives from similar laws regarding several sacrifices in the HB (e.g., Exod 29:34) (Werman and Shemesh, *Revealing*, 193). For the similarities and differences between the passages in Jubilees and the Temple Scroll, see Rapp, *Jakob in Bet-El*, 231.
69 That Lev 27:30-33 refers to the first tithe is the view also of the Qumran legal texts, while the rabbinic position was that it deals with the second tithe. See Shemesh, in Werman and Shemesh, *Revealing*, 190, 202-3.
70 Albeck, *Jubiläen*, 30.

Levites existed, perhaps no conclusion should be drawn. There is reason to think, as Albeck maintained, that in Jubilees "priests" refers to both priests and Levites.[71]

16-26 Night Appearances to Jacob

The section contains a blend of material from Genesis and elsewhere.

■ 16 The verse sets the stage for the next part of the drama having to do with Bethel and the Festival of Tabernacles. Technically speaking, at this point the observance of the holiday should be completed because it lasts, according to Lev 23:34 and Num 29:12, seven days beginning with the fifteenth of the month (thus 7/15-21). The twenty-second should, therefore, be the day following the festival. The fact that the night after the end of the festival occurs on the twenty-second indicates that in Jubilees the day begins in the evening.[72] The sequel shows, however, that the festival continues to provide the context. In addition, concerns with Jacob's vow at Bethel remain to the fore. In 32:2-9 the writer described how Jacob fulfilled his vow to tithe all that God had given to him, but there was still an element in his vow that remained outstanding. Jacob had said after the vision at Bethel that if God were with him and brought him back safely to his father's house, "this stone, which I have set up for a pillar, shall be God's house" (Gen 28:22 // Jub 27:27). Consequently, Jacob now resolves to build a temple at Bethel.[73] The narrator does not use the word *temple* here (for the term, see v. 22), but from the description of Jacob's plans it is obvious that he intends a sanctuary. He wanted to construct a building and "surround the courtyard with a wall." The wall sounds like the one Ezekiel was shown, a wall that surrounds the entire temple complex (Ezekiel 42).[74] The building Jacob envisions has a single courtyard, and he plans to sanctify it for himself and for his offspring forever. It sounds as if Jacob, not Solomon, will be the one who constructs the temple of God, the place where he will be worshiped forever.

Jacob's vow to build a house of God in Bethel plays no part in Genesis after the patriarch makes the promise. There would be no temple of the Lord until the time of King Solomon centuries later (dedicated during the Festival of Tabernacles, 1 Kgs 8:2, 65), and that temple would be in Jerusalem. How, then, was one to handle Jacob's vow, especially in light of the fact that, after the time of Solomon, King Jeroboam of Israel built an idolatrous place of worship in Bethel? Jubilees will answer the question but not before the Lord first appears to Jacob and renews the patriarchal promises to him.

■ 17 Jubilees 32:17-20 rewrites Gen 35:9-13, the first time the writer has returned to the Genesis account since 31:1-2 (the arrival at Bethel to sacrifice).[75] At v. 17 // Gen 35:9 both narrators tie the event to the contexts in their own works. Genesis relates it to Jacob's arrival from Paddan-aram, while Jubilees dates it to the very night[76] in which he had resolved to erect a temple at Bethel. The context in Jubilees' reworking, therefore, suggests

---

71 Ibid. Baumgarten ("First and Second Tithes," 7), after pointing out that Levi is the ancestor of both priests and Levites, thought the situation in Jub 32:2-9 is to be explained from a statement in the Temple Scroll: "And to the Levites, one tenth of the grain and the wine and the oil which they have first [לראישונה] dedicated to me" (lx:6-7; trans. Yadin, *DSSR* 3:205). Unlike Yadin (*Temple Scroll*, 2:272), who took לראישונה as a reference to the first tithe, Baumgarten understood it to mean "formerly" and proposed that the Temple Scroll and Jubilees reconciled the various scriptural statements about the first tithe (Numbers 18, where it is for the Levites; Leviticus 27, where it is for the Lord, that is, the priests) through a developmental solution: it was at first given to the priests but is now donated to the Levites. Shemesh also prefers this interpretation (Werman and Shemesh, *Revealing*, 190-91). Cf. Schiffman, "Priestly and Levitical Gifts in the *Temple Scroll*," in his *Courtyards*, 541-56, here 549-50; he weighs the various options without deciding between them.

72 Baumgarten, "Beginning of the Day," 356.

73 Treatment of this problem may not be an element Jubilees took from the Aramaic Levi Document, where it is absent from the surviving sections. See J. Schwartz, "Jubilees, Bethel and the Temple of Jacob," *HUCA* 56 (1985) 63-85, here 66-69.

74 The Temple Scroll also provides for walls around the three courts: the inner court (xxxvii:9), the middle court (xxxviii:14-15), and the outer court (xl:9-10).

75 On these verses, see Rapp, *Jakob in Bet-El*, 191-95.

76 The LXX and Old Latin read "in Luza," where Jubilees has "in/during the night." That is, they presuppose בלוזה where Jubilees reflects בלילה.

a connection with Jacob's plans for Bethel. In both texts the deity blesses Jacob, who has now fulfilled his obligation to tithe. Following that, the first subject that God addresses is the name of the patriarch to whom he appears. This is the second time in Genesis that Jacob's name becomes Israel (see also 32:27-28), a duplication explained by modern commentators as arising from two sources: 32:27-28 is thought by many to derive from J, while 35:10 belongs to P. Jubilees, in its one-verse (29:13) retelling of the story about crossing the Jabbok and meeting Esau—the context for the first renaming—says nothing about the new name and in this way reserves the announcement for the current place.

Genesis 35:10	Jubilees 32:17
God said to him, "Your name is Jacob; no longer shall you be called Jacob, but Israel shall be your name." So he was called Israel.	... and said to him, "You are not to be called Jacob only but you will (also) be named Israel."

The rather full text of Gen 35:10 Jubilees reduces to the essentials (was it necessary for God to tell him that his name was Jacob?), but it also solves a difficulty entailed by it. According to Genesis, he was no longer to be called Jacob, but in subsequent passages he frequently goes by this name (this happens already in 35:14-15, directly after the theophany). The formulation in Jubilees leaves open the possibility that both names will be used. The Ethiopic copies of Jubilees offer strong support for the reading *baḥtito*, "only, alone," a word that appears where Genesis has כי אם, "but." Charles emended it to *baḥtu*, "but."[77] However, Dillmann, Goldmann, and Berger have all correctly rendered the form as above.[78]

■ 18 Commentators on Genesis often note the parallels between the appearance to Jacob in Gen 35:9-13 and the one to his grandfather in Genesis 17 (where, for example, his name was changed from Abram to Abraham).[79] The similarities with Genesis 17 are even more pronounced in Jubilees.

Genesis 35:11	Jubilees 32:18
God said to him, "I am God Almighty; be fruitful and multiply; a nation and a company of nations shall come from you, and kings shall spring from you." (See 35:12a.)	He said to him a second time, "I am the Lord who created heaven and earth. I will increase your numbers and multiply you very much.[80] Kings will come from you,[81] and they will rule wherever humanity has set foot."

Jubilees indicates that God spoke to Jacob a second time because it seemed awkward that both Gen 35:10 and 35:11 begin with "God said to him." The words "who created heaven and earth" may simply explain the meaning of שדי (for the same designation, see Gen 17:1), somewhat like the frequent rendering of the title in LXX Job as παντοκρατωρ.[82] By supplying the words "very much" after "increase/multiply" the writer is able to indicate a large number without reproducing the promise that Jacob would become a "company of nations." One could immediately suspect that the nationalistic author would balk at the idea that more than one nation would spring from Jacob, but it should be recalled that he retained the expression in the promise that Isaac made to Jacob when he first left home (Gen 28:3 // Jub 27:11). Jubilees phrases the sentence about multiplying as a promise made by God (as in the last part of the verse), whereas Genesis expresses it as an imperative. In this respect, Jubilees imitates Gen 17:6. Jubilees adds a strong statement to the end of the verse—a promise regarding the extent of the land controlled by the kings who would arise among his offspring. Here the writer borrows language from Deut 11:24 (= Josh 1:3), a promise regarding the borders of the land that will belong to Israel if the people would obey the Lord's command: "Every place on which you set foot [תדרך כף רגליכם][83] shall be yours; your territory shall extend from the wilderness to the Lebanon and from the River, the river Euphrates, to

---

77 Charles, *Ethiopic Version*, 121 n. 37.

78 See VanderKam, *Jubilees* 2:212 for references. Cf. also Rapp, *Jakob in Bet-El*, 192–93.

79 In Gen 17:5, unlike in 35:10, use of עוד, "(no) longer," is appropriate because after this verse the new name is always used and the old one discarded.

80 For "very much" with "be fruitful," see Gen 17:6. There is space for במאוד מאוד in 4Q223–224 unit 1 i:1, though this part of the text is lost (see DJD 13:100–101).

81 For this line (there is space for it as well in 4Q223–224 unit 1 i:1), see Gen 17:6.

82 *Targum Neofiti* standardly renders אל שדי as "the God of the heavens."

83 At Jub 32:18 4Q223–224 unit 1 i:2 preserves these words: וימש[לו בכול מדרוך כף.

the Western Sea." Where the HB passages speak of the places where the Israelites set foot, Jubilees claims that the kings from Jacob's line will rule wherever people have set foot, that is, the entire earth (see v. 19).[84]

■ **19** The expansion at the end of v. 18 resembles the one in v. 19.

Genesis 35:12	Jubilees 32:19
The land that I gave to Abraham and Isaac I will give to you, and I will give the land to your offspring after you.	I will give your descendants all of the land[85] that is beneath the sky. They will rule over all the nations just as they wish. Afterwards, they will gain the entire earth, and they will possess it forever.

The Genesis passage limits the land to the one allotted to Abraham and Isaac, but, as Charles commented, "Our author here forsakes Gen. xxxv. 12 and promises to Israel the possession of the whole earth."[86] Rule over the nations is a well-attested hope already in Genesis (e.g., 27:29 // Jub 26:23; Gen 49:10; cf. also Jub 30:18). The Davidic king receives such promises: "Ask of me, and I will make the nations your heritage, / and the ends of the earth your possession" (Ps 2:8; see also Pss. Sol. 17:24-25, 29-30, 34-35; 1QSb v:24–28). Jubilees introduces this notion into the promises God made to Jacob and in this way also confirms the ones for which Abraham had prayed in blessing his grandson (Jub 22:11-12, 14).[87]

■ **20** Genesis and Jubilees bring the theophanic scene to a close in related but different ways.

Genesis 35:13	Jubilees 32:20
Then God went up from him at the place where he had spoken with him.	When he had finished speaking with him, he went up from him, and Jacob kept watching until he had gone up into heaven.

Genesis does not report that the deity finished speaking, only that he ascended. A verb of speaking appears at the end of 35:13, and Jubilees, perhaps for a smoother transition, moves it to the beginning.[88] The extra lines at the end of v. 20 in Jubilees may be meant to indicate that Jacob wanted to verify that the speaker was God whose home is in the heavens, or perhaps he was just stunned by the whole experience.[89] It is also worthwhile to recall his reaction to the dream the first time he visited Bethel. After he acknowledged that it was the Lord's place, "He was afraid, and said, 'How awesome is this place! This is none other than the house of God, and this is the gate of heaven'" (Gen 28:17 // Jub 27:25). Now that God had again appeared to him in Bethel, he seems to have watched until he reentered heaven through its gate.[90] The author does not call this appearance a vision; the impression left is that God actually came down to Jacob.

■ **21** The second night appearance granted to Jacob on 7/22 occupies vv. 21-26, and it, unlike the first, is called a vision (v. 21). The story does not appear in Genesis, but it is not entirely divorced from it. According to Gen 35:14-15 (the immediate sequel to God's departure to heaven), "Jacob set up a pillar in the place where he had spoken with him, a pillar of stone; and he poured out a drink offering on it, and poured oil on it. So Jacob called the place where God had spoken with him Bethel." This is, of course, a duplicate of Gen 28:18-19, and, since he had presented the material when recounting Jacob's first visit to Bethel (27:26), the author of Jubilees may have bypassed it as redundant. But the passage does depict Jacob treating the place like a sanctuary, a thought that the writer may not have wished to underscore by repeating it. The bigger problem was, however, that Genesis did not respond to the vow Jacob had made to build a temple at Bethel. What was the implication of his promise in Gen 28:22 (// Jub 27:27), "this stone, which I have set up for a pillar, shall be God's house," read in light

---

84 See Halpern-Amaru, *Rewriting the Bible*, 40–41. *Tg. Neof.* Gen 35:11 renders "kings *who rule nations* shall come forth from your loins."

85 Latin reads "blessings," which seems strange in the context, though Charles (*Ethiopic Version*, 121 n. 45; *Jubilees*, 194) thought it might be the preferred reading. See VanderKam, *Jubilees* 2:213.

86 Charles, *Jubilees*, 194. For this expansion see Rapp, *Jakob in Bet-El*, 193–95.

87 Halpern-Amaru, *Rewriting the Bible*, 40–41.

88 4Q223–224 unit 1 i:4 preserves most of the expression as well as the following verb and in this way confirms the order of the sentence.

89 For Werman's removal of the clause from v. 20 and placement in v. 26, see the textual note to v. 26.

90 In Judges 13 the angel who appeared to Manoah and his wife "ascended in the flame of the altar while Manoah and his wife looked on; and they fell on their faces to the ground" (v. 20). See also Acts 1:9-11.

of what Jacob now does—he sets up a pillar and offers sacrifices (Gen 35:14-15)? Was he making the place of worship he had vowed to construct?[91] Whatever a reader might infer from the Genesis stories about Bethel, the author of Jubilees takes emphatic steps to avoid any unwanted conclusions by tackling the temple vow in vv. 21-22 especially.[92]

That the angel[93] appeared to Jacob during the same night in which God had revealed himself to him follows from two facts: some time later after awaking from sleep Jacob celebrates that day, which is added to the seven of the Festival of Tabernacles; and the next night is said to be the twenty-third (vv. 26-30). The angel who descends from heaven[94] in the vision carries seven tablets. They are not called the heavenly tablets—both the Ethiopic (*salēdāt*) and Latin (*tabulae buxeae*) translations use different terms for them than they do for the heavenly tablets[95]—but their contents are consistent with what is elsewhere said to be on the heavenly tablets.[96] He handed over those voluminous documents on which Jacob, who had learned to write at an early age (Jub 19:14), saw, read, and understood[97] the futures of himself

---

[91] Testuz attributes Jacob's resolve to build a temple at Bethel to his confidence that God would carry out the wonderful promises he had just made to him at this place (*Idées*, 67). But he had already made a vow to do this during his first visit, and Jubilees is concerned with making sure vows are effected (see Isaac's words in 31:29).

[92] Schwartz claims: "Just as there was no reason to construe Jacob's intended construction of the Temple as fulfillment of Genesis, thus there is no reason to assume that Jubilees 27 was understood as pertaining to a temple" ("Jubilees, Bethel," 69). The entire context makes the connection plain. Schwartz's contention is part of his case that this scene arises not from Genesis but from the author's historical situation (see below).

[93] The discussion in *Gen. Rab.* 82:2-3 regarding the words "God appeared to Jacob again" (Gen 35:9) includes an angel who was present at Bethel. The problem under consideration was that Jacob's name seems to be changed twice in Genesis. The first passage, after he wrestled with the mysterious being at the Jabbok, was explained as a prediction. The angel with whom he struggled (Hos 12:4 so identifies his opponent) said (according to R. Berekiah in the name of R. Levi): "The Holy One, blessed be He, will reveal Himself to you at Beth-el and change your name, and I too will be present there." The Hosea passage reads: "He strove with the angel and prevailed, / he wept and sought his favor; / he met him at Bethel, and there he spoke with us [NRSV follows LXX in translating 'with him']." This is taken to mean that at Bethel God confirmed the word of the angel in Gen 32:29 (about the name change). The discussants maintain that on both visits to Bethel God spoke to Jacob through an angel.

[94] Endres observes that the "author skillfully connected the two visions by suggesting that Jacob saw the angel descending from the sky because he was still gazing upwards after God's ascent (32:20)" (*Biblical Interpretation*, 167). The connection is there but the book calls only the second experience a vision.

[95] In v. 28 where the text mentions the tablets of heaven, both versions resort to their normal terms for them (*selāta samāy* and *tabulis caeli*).

[96] Apart from the frequency of the number in Jubilees, it is not known why the author says the angel was carrying precisely seven tablets. B. Z. Wacholder, after pointing out that elsewhere in the book one reads of just two tablets (he neglects to say that those two are not the heavenly tablets), wrote that perhaps "the two tablets may be divided into seven books: the Five Books of Moses, the Qumranic Torah [he means the Temple Scroll], and another book, possibly Enoch or even the Book of Jubilees itself" (*The Dawn of Qumran: The Sectarian Torah and the Teacher of Righteousness* [HUCM 8; Cincinnati, OH: Hebrew Union College Press, 1983] 61). There is surely too little said about them here to make such identifications plausible. For Rapp (*Jakob in Bet-El*, 236–41) the presence of an anonymous angel and the fact that seven tablets (not the heavenly tablets) are read point to the night vision as deriving from a source that the author of Jubilees incorporated into his account.

[97] The Ethiopic text uses the verb "read" twice ("he read them. He read everything"), but Latin has *legit et cognovit*, "he read and he knew/understood/learned." Charles thought the double use of "read" in Ethiopic, which he changed to agree with the Latin, was a dittography and that the two Latin verbs were "alternative renderings of ανεγνω, where the first is right" (*Jubilees*, xli-xlii, 194; quotation from p. xlii). Either the Ethiopic or the Latin reading could be defended, but in the translation the Latin is followed since it uses two distinct verbs rather than repeating the one.

and his offspring forever.⁹⁸ Naturally, in the theology of Jubilees, all of this was prerecorded.

■ **22** One thing Jacob might have noticed from his reading was an omission—the tablets would have said nothing about his building a temple at Bethel. However, the matter was not left for him to infer from the silence of the records; rather, the angel stated, "Do not build up this place, and do not make it an eternal temple." So, the reason why Jacob did not fulfill this part of his Bethel vow was that a heavenly angel forbade him to do so.⁹⁹ Moreover, the angel was simply giving an order consistent with the account on the tablets in which Jacob would not have been the temple builder.¹⁰⁰

After issuing his negative command, the angel adds that Jacob is to leave Bethel. Despite the great events that happened there, it was not to become his residence; rather, he was to move to the place where his parents lived. Genesis 35:27 reports that "Jacob came to his father Isaac at Mamre, or Kiriath-arba (that is, Hebron), where Abraham and Isaac had resided as aliens." The information is presented there as if the move was a continuation of Jacob's journey away from Bethel begun in vv. 16 and 21. In Jubilees he will make the trip in obedience to the angel's bidding. The angel says he is to go to "the house of your father Abraham and live where your father Isaac is" (v. 22); there he is to remain "until the day of your father's death." In Genesis this is the first and only time Jacob sees his father (Rebekah is not mentioned) after his return from Mesopotamia; he apparently sees him just before his death (35:28-29). The passage in Jubilees, as does the one in Genesis, associates Jacob with his grandfather and father.

■ **23** The angel elaborates on the point by predicting details about the end of Jacob's life—that even in death he will be together with his two ancestors.¹⁰¹ Though the tablets he had read related his own future, the

---

98   Kugel (*Walk through* Jubilees, 154 n. 278; "Jubilees," 462) draws attention to frg. B of the Prayer of Joseph, where Jacob says, "For I have read in the tablets of heaven all that shall befall you and your sons" (trans. J. Z. Smith, *OTP* 2:714). It is interesting that in this statement the tablets in Jub 32:21-26 have become "the tablets of heaven."

99   As Halpern-Amaru has noticed, this is one of the parallels between the present scene and the temple in the David–Solomon stories ("Joy as Piety," 195). Jacob, like David, is told that he is not the one to build the temple. For other points of contact with Solomon's dedication of the temple (it too took place during the Festival of Tabernacles), see below.

100 Cf. Kugel, *Walk through* Jubilees, 154; "Jubilees," 406. For Schwartz, Jacob's intent to build a temple at Bethel reflects events in the author's time ("Jubilees, Bethel," 69-85). When Judas the Maccabee in 162 BCE was forced to retreat to the area of Gophna near Bethel and Jerusalem was not accessible, the inhabitants of Bethel, Schwartz hypothesizes, attempted to reassert the ancient cultic status of the place (older than Jerusalem) but they were unsuccessful. Judas controlled the area for only a brief time in 162. Schwartz also thinks Jacob's "dawdling" about getting to Hebron from Bethel (he leaves Bethel early in the eighth month [32:31-33] and does not go to Hebron, as the angel ordered in v. 22, until the first of month ten [33:1]) is to be explained by the fact that Hebron was likely not under Jewish control at the time. He surveys the history, primarily the cultic history, of Bethel, but its undoubted importance provides a weak basis for locating Jubilees' Bethel story in the very short time Judas was in the area of the city. It is an unsupported assumption that residents of the city made any cultic claims for it and that the anti-temple-building theme in Jubilees is directed against their argument. It is much simpler to adhere to the text of Jubilees, which connects Jacob's intention with his vow at Bethel. It should be added that, contrary to what Schwartz says, the Temple Scroll (xxix:8-10) does not offer a reply to Bethel's pretensions but furnishes another indication that a temple was part of the story when Jacob was at Bethel. Endres entertains ideas about Bethel as a possible pilgrimage site but eventually concludes that the author, who has identified Abraham's "place" with Mount Zion (18:13) and used the title El Elyon, which was associated with Jerusalem, "reinterpreted biblical traditions in order to substantiate the legitimacy (if not the practice) of the priesthood and cultus in Jerusalem" (*Biblical Interpretation*, 167-68; quotation from p. 168).

101 On the expression "house of Abraham," see Rapp, *Jakob in Bet-El*, 241-46. He notes the difficulty in determining its exact location and the fact that after Jub 22:24, where it first occurs (there it refers to Abraham's household for all time), the place-name Hebron is still used but "house of Abraham" and "tower of Abraham" predominate. Being buried with his fathers is another parallel with

angel underscores the relevant parts of their contents by repeating them to Jacob. Jacob would have read on the tablets that he would die in Egypt, but he was not to be worried because he would eventually be buried with Abraham and Isaac (see Gen 49:29-33, where Jacob gives his dying instructions about where to bury him, and 50:4-14, where Joseph and his brothers complied with his orders; see also Jub 44:1-6, where he is concerned about going to Egypt, as he knows he will die there, and 45:15, where he is buried with his ancestors).

■ **24-26** After reassuring Jacob about his own place of burial at the side of Abraham and Isaac, the angel tells him not to fear because the future will transpire as recorded on the tablets he has just read. He also tells him to write all the information he had read—a sizable task indeed. When Jacob, who calls the angel "lord," expresses concern about remembering so much, the angel promises, "I will remind you of everything."[102] The angel's departure is described differently than God's ascent in v. 20, and nothing is said about Jacob's watching him. He simply went upward as part of Jacob's visionary experience. When Jacob awoke he did in fact remember all that he had read and was able to put the contents of the angel's tablets into an accessible, written form. Possession of such information would equip him to tell his sons "what will happen to you in days to come" (Gen 49:1; Jub 45:14).

Excursus: No Temple in Bethel

The angel vision in which Jacob receives an order not to construct a temple is unusual in that it is a part of the Bethel story in Jubilees not paralleled in either the Aramaic Levi Document or the Testament of Levi. Esther Eshel has surveyed several highly fragmentary Qumran texts that refer to Jacob, Bethel, and/or Levi.[103] An example is 5Q13 (Sectarian Rule) frg. 2 7-13. The section is part of what appears to be a historical survey that may mention Isaac and likely says "you made yourself known to Jacob at Bethel" in line 7. Levi is named in the next line; perhaps the next word is "you have separated," and this is followed by "and you appointed/gave him to bind [לאגוד]." It is not at all clear how one is to understand "to bind" in this broken context.[104] Berger referenced it in connection with Jub 32:8 (where Jacob gives Levi the unclean animals and the people),[105] but Eshel suggests it relates to binding the four species carried during the Festival of Tabernacles.[106] There is no way to check the suggestion, although the association with the festival is attractive. She also adduces 4Q177 (Catena A) frgs. 1-4, but it is far from clear that the section has any connection with the story of Jacob at Bethel.

More important for the present context is her proposal that 4Q537 (4QTestament of Jacob) frgs. 1-3 1-6 is a source for the unusual vision in Jub 32:21-26. Her translation of the passage (p. 34, with almost none of her restorations, and with a few corrections) reads:

1. your descendants. And all just men will survive and [the] upright [
2. debauchery, and absolutely no deceit is to be found [
3. and now, take the tablets and read everything [
4. and all my troubles and all that was to happen to [   ]' years of my life[   ] the tablet from my hands[
5. [I] took this tablet from his hands[   ] and I saw written in them that[
6. [ ]you will come out of it and on the day [ ]n exit empty-handed before[

The passage does resemble the angelic vision in Jubilees in that someone is told to take tablet(s)

---

the David story in 2 Samuel 7 (see v. 12; Werman, *Jubilees*, 435).

102 Charles noted the parallel with the role of the Paraclete in John 14:26: he will "remind you of all that I have said to you" (*Jubilees*, 195).

103 Esther Eshel, "*Jubilees* 32 and the Bethel Cult Traditions in Second Temple Literature," in Esther Chazon, David Satran, and Ruth Clements, eds., *Things Revealed: Studies in Early Jewish and Christian Literature in Honor of Michael E. Stone* (JSJSup 89; Leiden: Brill, 2004) 21-36. The translations cited below are hers.

104 M. Kister considers its use here "puzzling" and wonders whether it was selected as an etymology for Levi's name ("5Q13 and the *'Avodah*: A Historical Survey and Its Significance," *DSD* 8 [2004] 136-48, here 141). Eshel uses Kister's edition of the text in this essay, including his line numbers.

105 Berger, *Jubiläen*, 482 n. c to v. 8. His interpretation relates to his idea that Levi received authority over these categories of untithed animals and humans, but there is no hint about this as involving "binding."

106 Eshel, "*Jubilees* 32," 27 n. 14. As an example of the usage, she notes *m. Suk.* 3:1, 8.

from another's hands and read everything on them; and from them he learns his own future, with line 6 apparently speaking about the exodus. The editor of the text, É. Puech, inserted in the missing section at the end of line 5 a prohibition of building a temple at Bethel,[107] but Eshel rejects the suggestion. For her, though the text did not contain this order, it was, nevertheless, a source for Jubilees, whose author added the negative command regarding a sanctuary in Bethel. His purpose in doing so was to emphasize the importance of Jerusalem while also echoing the prophetic critique of Bethel during the period of the monarchy.[108]

Eshel properly rejects Schwartz's attempt to relate Jub 32:21-26 to conditions in 162 BCE, when Judas withdrew to Gophna near Bethel, but because 4Q537 is so fragmentary it is not advisable to draw larger conclusions from it either. It could have been a source for Jubilees, but perhaps it was not; moreover, it could have given the angel's command not to build a temple in Bethel, but maybe it did not. Possibly the command is original to the author of Jubilees, who, of course, knew of Jerusalem and mentions it as the place of the temple (see 1:10, 28-29). It would be hazardous to conclude that this broken text, with all its uncertainties, is a source for Jub 32:21-26.[109]

Excursus: The Angel Vision from Another Writer?

Kugel maintains that Jub 32:21-26 is only in part from the author of Jubilees.[110] The message of the angel that Jacob was not to build a sanctuary in Bethel is thoroughly at home in Jubilees, as Kugel recognizes. It is one of many instances in which the writer spots a problem in Genesis (Jacob's vow to build up Bethel and the absence of any indication he did) and provides a solution for it. For Kugel, the difficulty does not concern the angel's negative command about constructing a temple in Bethel but his next order—that Jacob is to go to Abraham's house until Isaac dies. This is followed by what he takes to be "almost a non-sequitur" (154)—that Jacob was to die peacefully in Egypt. The next clause—that he was to be buried honorably in this land (v. 23)—follows more naturally on the command to go to Hebron. The angel's exhortation that he not be afraid takes one back to the beginning of the section.

His argument, then, is that the angel's orders do not yield what Kugel regards as a reasonable sequence. He adds that the presence of two visions (i.e., the appearance of God and the angel vision) in the same night "suggests the second one is not the work of the original author" (155). His reason for this surprising claim is that the angel vision has no biblical "anchor." One could object that a lot of material in Jubilees has no biblical anchor, but Kugel explains his point this way: if the same person presented the theophany (from Gen 35:9-12) and the angel vision "he would have had no reason *not* to combine all their elements into a single vision so that the whole thing would seem to be anchored in the biblical text, being a more detailed version of Gen 35:9-12" (155). The phrasing "no reason *not* to combine" is peculiar, as is the implication that by not combining the two reports the impression left is that the second lacks an anchoring in the biblical text. The whole context of the book, following the order of Genesis, provides that. He gives no adequate reason why the writer should in this instance have fashioned the two experiences into one.

Another problem Kugel finds in the vision report is something he takes to be "on consideration, rather silly" (155). If Jacob read and memorized the futures of himself and his children, he would have known, for example, that Joseph was not killed by a wild animal and that his sons were misleading him about this. However, when he receives their lying report, he reacts with powerful emotions. Kugel writes: "*Jubilees'* author, a careful writer who thought long and hard about Scripture, would hardly have introduced this second vision and thereby spoiled everything he had labored to create" (155). Kugel seems not to have grasped how the writer's predestinarian system works. If everything is predetermined to happen in a

---

107 E. Puech, "537. 4QTestament de Jacob? ar," in his *Qumrân Grotte 4.XXII: Textes araméens première partie 4Q529–4Q549* (DJD 31; Oxford: Clarendon, 2001) 175–76. As the question mark in Puech's title for the text suggests, it is not certain that the text deals with Jacob.

108 Eshel, "*Jubilees* 32," 34–36.

109 Rapp had earlier brought the text into the discussion about the angelic vision; he concluded that 4Q537 and Jubilees depend on the same source (*Jakob in Bet-El*, 129–40). He, too, rejects Schwartz's thesis about claims made for Bethel in 162.

110 Kugel, *Walk through* Jubilees, 154–57; "Jubilees," 406, 462 nn. 212-13. Page numbers in the text are to the former.

certain way, even if one knows this in advance, it still has to happen in that way.[111]

So who was responsible for such non sequiturs and silly comments (to use Kugel's terms)? He thinks neither the author of the book nor his interpolator is likely to have fashioned the angel vision. The interpolator is improbable, he argues, because the tablets in the vision are not the heavenly tablets that he always references, the standard terms in heavenly-tablet contexts are not used, and the vision does not conform to the way the interpolator works, that is, by adding large chunks to the text (actually, some passages Kugel assigns to his interpolator hardly could be called large units, e.g., 31:32). Here someone has interwoven statements within an earlier text. Kugel reconstructs what he takes to be the original form of the passage.

1. In the work of the author of Jubilees there was only one vision. It includes 32:16-19, 22b-23 and reads: "During the next night, on the twenty-second day of this month, Jacob decided to build up that place and to surround the courtyard with a wall, to sanctify it, and make it eternally holy for himself and for his children after him forever. The Lord appeared to him during the night. He blessed him and said to him, 'You are not to be called Jacob only but you will (also) be named Israel.' He said to him a second time, 'I am the Lord who created heaven and earth. I will increase your numbers and multiply you very much. Kings will come from you, and they will rule wherever humanity has set foot. I will give your descendants all of the land that is beneath the sky. They will rule over all the nations just as they wish. Afterwards, they will gain the entire earth, and they will possess it forever.' . . . . he said to him, 'Do not build up this place, and do not make it an eternal temple. Do not live here because this is not the place. Go to the house of your father Abraham and live where your father Isaac is until the day of your father's death. **For you will die peacefully in Egypt** [these words are from writer #2; see below] and be buried honorably in this land in the grave of your fathers—with Abraham and Isaac.'"

2. A second writer inserted the contents of the angelic vision, starting with vv. 20 (actually, this is part of the appearance of God as described in Gen 35:13-22a and continuing in 24-26. This is the inserted material. "When he had finished speaking with him, he went up from him, and Jacob kept watching until he had gone up into heaven. In a night vision he saw an angel coming down from heaven with seven tablets in his hands. He gave (them) to Jacob, and he read them. He learned everything that was written in them—what would happen to him and his sons throughout all ages. 32:22 After he had shown him everything that was written on the tablets, **he said to him** . . .

32:24 'Do not be afraid because everything will happen just as you have seen and read. Now you write down everything just as you have seen and read.' Then Jacob said, 'Lord, how shall I remember everything just as I have read and seen?' He said to him, 'I will remind you of everything.' When he had gone up from him, he awakened and remembered everything that he had read and seen. He wrote down all the things that he had read and seen."

When writer #2 supplemented the original text, a problem remained: why should the angel tell Jacob at this time to go to Hebron after he had read about his death in Egypt since he would eventually be buried in Hebron? Because of this problem writer #2 inserted into v. 23 "For you will die peacefully in Egypt" though these words "interrupted and ran counter to the whole purpose of the original sentence" (156). How this is a problem, given the theological system of the book, is very difficult to see.

An obvious question is why anyone would add non sequiturs, silly things, and contradictions to a text. Kugel thinks the contributions of writer #2—the command that Jacob both memorize and write down what he saw—sound like "an etiology for some other text, a lengthy revelation of Israel's future" (157). To lend authenticity to that other text its author or a supporter inserted this reference to it into the text of Jubilees. This person paid no attention to the logical inconsistency of Jacob's behavior in the rest of the account about him in Jubilees if he had seen this vision of the future (he thinks 4Q537, the text noted above, is a candidate for that other work). In a footnote (p. 157 n. 281) he suggests that the same writer added what may be two more references to this vision—44:2; 45:4—neither of which fits well in its

---

[111] Genesis presents a similar situation. According to Gen 46:4, God assures Jacob that he will return him to the land, but in 47:27-31 Jacob takes pains to make Joseph swear he will not bury him in Egypt but in the family tomb in Canaan. If he already knew this was going to happen (God told him), why was he so concerned to make Joseph swear about this?

context. This would be a surprising way for an author of one text to advertise his work in another—a procedure for which Kugel cites no parallels.

His entire argument about the angel vision results from misunderstanding a key point about the nature of Jubilees—the author's predestinarian approach—and involves the introduction of yet another writer when there are no sound reasons for doing so.[112] From this misunderstanding he hypothesizes a text as he thinks it should have been written; and, by having to excise two other texts (44:2; 45:4) that could be understood as documenting how the angel vision section fits well in the book, he admits that his theory regarding this passage conflicts with other evidence in Jubilees.

27-29 An Extra Day

God appeared to Jacob, and Jacob received a vision in which an angel spoke with him during the night of 7/22, the day after the Festival of Tabernacles ended. That momentous following day is now to be appended to the previous seven days of the festival to create an eight-day holiday (7/15–22).

■ **27-28** This was not a decision Jacob made in the enthusiasm of the moment but one revealed to him (v. 28).[113] The supplemental day is recorded on the heavenly tablets—the writer uses his normal title for the comprehensive source. The author says that Jacob offered the same sacrifices on this day as he had on the previous seven and that he named day 8 "Detaining because he was detained there one day" (v. 27, following the Latin; see the textual note).

The extra day that Jacob celebrates as an extension of the Festival of Tabernacles is the one mentioned somewhat unexpectedly in Lev 23:36: "Seven days you shall present the LORD's offerings by fire; on the eighth day you shall observe a holy convocation and present the LORD's offerings by fire; it is a solemn assembly [עצרת];[114] you shall not work at your occupations"; and again in v. 39, in the second section of that chapter dealing with the holiday (vv. 39-43): "Now, the fifteenth day of the seventh month, when you have gathered in the produce of the land, you shall keep the festival of the LORD, lasting seven days; a complete rest on the first day, and a complete rest on the eighth day" (however in vv. 40-42 it is considered a seven-day festival). In Numbers 29, though it is still called a seven-day celebration (v. 12) and the sacrifices for each of the seven are detailed in vv. 13-34, the text adds: "On the eighth day you shall have a solemn assembly [עצרת]; you shall not work at your occupations" (v. 35). The following verses (36-38) describe sacrifices for day 8 that differ from the ones for all of the previous seven.[115] The legal sections, then, provide no motivation or explanation for an eighth day, but the story about

---

112 As noted above, Rapp accounts for unusual elements in the angelic vision by positing a source that *the author* of Jubilees placed into his book (*Jakob in Bet-El*, 236–41).

113 Rapp believes that v. 28 refers to the night vision but reinterprets it in a halakic direction—as revealing a calendrical point (*Jakob in Bet-El*, 240–41). He sees this as an example of a procedure that occurs more often in the book where apocalyptic material is reoriented. However, there is no compelling reason to think that the expression "it was revealed" (said twice in v. 28) alludes to the vision in vv. 21-26. It concerns the occasion for the night vision (the twenty-second of the seventh month), not the content of the vision. Werman thinks these words hark back to God's appearance to Jacob in vv. 17-20 and that, as a result, the themes of rule and power are associated with the extra day (in Werman and Shemesh, *Revealing*, 401; cf. *Jubilees*, 434), but nowhere in vv. 27-29 is there a link to the appearance in vv. 17-20 and certainly no overt linking of rule and power with celebration of the eighth day.

114 עצרת is related to the verb עצר, "restrain, detain" (BDB, 783); the noun is supposed to have the sense of "confined, held in" (ibid.) from which various meanings such as "solemn assembly" developed.

115 Deuteronomy 16:13-15 speaks only of a seven-day Festival of Tabernacles (though the chapter uses עצרת in connection with the last day of the Festival of Unleavened Bread in v. 8). See also Ezek 45:25. In Neh 8:13-18, however, there is reference to an eighth day: "They kept the festival seven days; and on the eighth day there was a solemn assembly [עצרת], according to the ordinance" (v. 18; so too Josephus, *Ant*. 3.245, 247). Regarding the eighth day, see Tabory, *Festivals*, 200–204 (where he treats the sources that debate whether the eighth day was a separate festival or a part of the Festival of Tabernacles). The Festival of Hanukkah, modeled in part on Tabernacles and, like it, associated with

Solomon's dedication of the temple furnishes some useful information. He gathered the people at the festival in the seventh month (1 Kgs 8:2), and after the ceremony and his lengthy prayer the king offered a vast number of animals as peace offerings (as Jacob did during the same festival). It is called a seven-day holiday in 8:65; on the eighth day Solomon sent them home (v. 66). The parallel passages in 2 Chronicles 5–7 locate the dedication on the same festival (5:3), but at the end, while they do celebrate for seven days (7:8), "On the eighth day they held a solemn assembly [עצרת]; for they had observed the dedication of the altar seven days and the festival seven days" (7:9). On the twenty-third the people depart (7:10). It is noteworthy that in these sections both histories refer to the seven-day Festival of Tabernacles as "the festival," just as Jub 32:27 does. The book thus offers a solution for the way in which the HB talks about a seven-day celebration and the extra day: the original seven days Jacob called "the Festival," and the eighth day he designated "Detaining."

■ 29 The wording of v. 29 has been a subject of dispute, due in part to differences between the Ethiopic and Latin versions. The former continues to call the day Addition and the latter Detaining, but the next clause, which seems to give the reason for the name, has some problematic readings. Oddly, the Latin translation says it was called Detaining because it was added among the festival days. Here the Ethiopic, in keeping with v. 28, employs vocabulary familiar in contexts dealing with the heavenly tablets ("it was entered," "testimony"). The details regarding the readings are treated in the textual notes, but at this point the Ethiopic has a greater claim to preserving a superior text. After it supplies the reason for the name given to day 8, it says that it is entered in the testimony of the festival days; that is, it is part of what the tablets record about the holidays in the 364-day calendar of the book.[116]

Excursus: An Interpolator in vv. 27-29?

Kugel thinks his interpolator makes another appearance in this section (note "the heavenly tablets" in v. 28).[117] As he assesses the situation, Jub 32:27 is from the author of the book (actually, the last sentence is from the interpolator; see p. 158.) It provides, says Kugel, "another bit of Torah legislation that began with something initiated spontaneously by one of the patriarchs on his own" (157). To repeat a point made many times, this is a mischaracterization, since all actions, according to the author of Jubilees, are predetermined; moreover, in this case the phrase "initiated spontaneously" is transparently inaccurate. But, for Kugel, such patriarchal spontaneity was unacceptable to the interpolator so he inserted vv. 28-29 to show that the extra day had always been recorded on the tablets.

Kugel thinks, however, that we do not have in the Ethiopic and Latin translations the original text of these verses. Rather, both of them (our only textual witnesses for the passage) embody different ways in which to solve the problem of why the festival day had two names (Detaining and Addition, 159–60). He reconstructs the history of the text in this way:

1. Latin preserves the original text for the most part. The festival day was called Detaining/Retention because Jacob was detained in Bethel another day. That is, human circumstance accounts for making it a holiday and its name.
2. The interpolator contradicts this and gives it the name Addition, as it is called on the heavenly tablets. The name Jacob gave to it was only a nickname (!) for the day whose real name was Addition (a name for it not found in any other source). Jacob also had given a nickname to the first seven days—the Festival—though its real name was the Festival of Tabernacles.
3. The interpolator, however, made a mistake. He says that Jacob named the other seven days "the Festival," but he forgot that the original author had called it "the Festival" in 16:27 (159–60). A quick look at 16:27 shows that Kugel is wrong about this; there Abraham names it "the Festival of the Lord [taken from Lev 23:39]—a joy accept-

---

temple dedication, lasted eight days (see, e.g., van Goudoever, *Biblical Calendars*, 32). Jubilees seems to say that Jacob repeated on day 8 the sacrifices he offered on each of the seven previous days, although Num 29:36-38 prescribes a different set for the eighth day. Repeating the sacrifices offered on days 1 through 7 suggests that the author of Jubilees views the eighth day (despite having its own name) not as a separate festival but as an extension of the Festival of Tabernacles.

116 See Berger, *Jubiläen*, 485 n. c to v. 29.
117 Kugel, *Walk through* Jubilees, 157–61 (page references in the text are to this work); "Jubilees," 406–7.

able to the Most High God." He does not name it "the Festival."

All of this subtlety was lost, Kugel continues, on the people who transmitted the text by copying and translating it (160–61). The two surviving forms of vv. 27-29 offer different solutions to the problem of two names for the same festival. The Latin, as noted above, retains most of the original text. The only change it introduced was altering the interpolator's name from Addition to Detaining/Retention, but Latin left the interpolator's justification for the name Addition untouched (because it was added), though it made no sense.

The Ethiopic translation shows the opposite approach. It uses "it is entered" (v. 29) and changes Detaining/Retention to Addition in v. 27 to make it consistent with the rest of the passage. It moved "because that day was added" to its present location from the last sentence in the paragraph. That left a problem in the last sentence—it would have repeated what was said earlier. So Ethiopic changed the last sentence to "it is entered"—a "somewhat lame non-sequitur" (161).

Here is how Kugel's version of vv. 27-29 reads, with the interpolator's contributions in italics (cited from p. 158):

And he [Jacob] celebrated there one [more] day and sacrificed on it as much as he had been sacrificing on the previous days; and he called its name "Retention" (עצרה) because he was held back (נעצר) there for a day. *And he called the previous days "The Festival"* (חהג).

And thus it was revealed that it should be, and it was written in the Heavenly Tablets, because of the fact that it was revealed to him [Jacob] to keep that same day and add it to the seven days of the festival. And its name is called "Addition," because it was added to the established time (תעודה) *of the days of the Festival in keeping with the number of days of the year.*

So Kugel has to recover what he thinks was the original text and to hypothesize that the two surviving versions differ in their readings because the traditions they represent are trying to explain why the festival day had two names. However, he says nothing about Rönsch's simple scribal explanation for variations between the Latin and the Ethiopic texts (see the textual notes). The confusion of two lookalike Greek words provides a more economical and convincing account of the textual evidence than a hypothetical interpolator and two subsequent attempts at explaining what was probably only a single name for the eighth day in the original text. There are two names because of an instance of confusion in transmission, not because an interpolator was inventing a name to counteract one that implied a "spontaneous" naming of the holiday.

30-34 Departure from Bethel

The remarkable Bethel pericope comes to a close when all of the principals depart from the place.

■ **30** The last event recorded for Jacob's stay there, dated to 7/23,[118] the day after the eighth day of the festival,[119] is one mentioned in Gen 35:8—the death of Rebekah's nurse Deborah. In the Genesis narrative, the notice separates the account of Jacob's altar building from the theophany in vv. 9-13; in Jubilees it follows two night appearances to Jacob and closes the Bethel story.[120] The writer quotes much of Gen 35:8 but offers expansions toward the end.

Genesis 35:8	Jubilees 32:30
And Deborah, Rebekah's nurse, died, and she was buried below Bethel under an oak.[121] So it was called Allon-bacuth.	. . . Deborah, Rebekah's nurse, died. They buried her below the city, beneath the oak (near) the stream. He named that place the Stream of Deborah and the oak the Oak of Mourning for Deborah.

Mention of the stream is not motivated by the text of Genesis, while the name for the oak is spelled out and explicitly connected with the time of mourning for Deborah.[122] It is possible that the writer was influenced by what is said about the other Deborah in the HB—the

---

118 For Werman's mistaken change of the date to 7/24 (*Jubilees*, 428 nn. 24-25, 435), see the textual note.
119 Oddly, Charles says she died on the eighth day of the festival, when the text places it on 7/23 (*Jubilees*, 196; Endres [*Biblical Interpretation*, 163] repeats the point).
120 On this, see Rapp, *Jakob in Bet-El*, 196.
121 The order of "below Bethel" and "under an oak" is switched in the NRSV, though they appear in this order in the Hebrew text.
122 By naming the tree "the Oak of Mourning for Deborah" the author shows none of the concerns that underlie the treatment of Gen 35:8 in targums *Onqelos* and *Pseudo-Jonathan*, where she is buried beneath the plain to avoid association with a tree that might have been involved in idolatry (Maher,

prophetess and judge in Judges 4–5. "She used to sit under the palm of Deborah between Ramah and Bethel in the hill country of Ephraim" (Judg 4:5). The judge Deborah was associated with a stream (Wadi Kishon, Judg 4:7, 13; 5:21), but it is not in the region of Bethel. Presumably the stream named after Rebekah's nurse was one of the wadis in the vicinity.[123]

■ **31-32** With the festival at Bethel completed and her nurse buried, Rebekah sets out for her home in the region of Hebron to be with her elderly husband Isaac (v. 31). Isaac had sent her to be present at the sacrifice in his stead (31:30); she had accomplished that assignment and now could leave. Jacob, ever the solicitous son in Jubilees, sends a gift to his father consisting of animals from his large herds. Earlier (29:15-20), the reader learned that Jacob had done this from time to time ever since he had returned to the land. The reason for dispatching the animals to Isaac is "to make his father a meal as he would wish." The expression reminds one of another time when Jacob, also with the assistance of Rebekah, fetched the ingredients for a dinner that would please Isaac—the time when he deceived his nearly blind father (Jub 26:2, 6, 10; see Gen 27:4, 9, 14, 17). Now his motivation is only positive—he wants to provide for his father, who had missed the festive meals in Bethel.

Rebekah's traveling from Bethel provides the occasion for the next part of the story. Verse 32 is related to Gen 35:16, where Jacob and his party are the ones on the move: "Then they journeyed from Bethel; and when they were still some distance from Ephrath [ויהי עוד כברת הארץ לבוא אפרתה] . . . ."[124] According to Jubilees, the dutiful Jacob accompanied his mother on her trip "until he reached the country of Kabratan [Latin: *dabrata*, an error for *cabrata*]." The writer interpreted כברת הארץ as the name of a land or region, just as the LXX (χαβραθα εις γην) did. It appears to be a term designating a stretch of land, with no certainty about the length; use of the phrase in 2 Kgs 5:19 (where Naaman goes just a short distance from Elisha's house), however, implies that it was not very long.[125] Whatever the meaning of the word, it caused uncertainty, and Jubilees shows one option some interpreters adopted. In the book, Kabratan is the name of an area between Bethel and Hebron. It marked the place to which Jacob accompanied his mother, so he did not escort her all the way home. For some reason he stayed in this locale.

■ **33-34** There it was that Rachel went into labor. The author, like the writer of Gen 35:18, says nothing about why the party decided to travel when her pregnancy was so advanced. Jubilees 32:33-34 rewrites Gen 35:16b, 18-20 (omitting the statement of the midwife in v. 17):

Genesis 35:16b, 18-20	Jubilees 32:33-34
. . . Rachel was in childbirth, and she had hard labor. As her soul was departing (for she died), she named him Ben-oni; but his father called him Benjamin.	During the night Rachel gave birth to a son. She named him Son of my Pain[126] because she had difficulty when she was giving birth to him. But his father named him Benjamin on the eleventh of the eighth month, during the first year of the sixth week of this jubilee [2143].
So Rachel died, and was buried on the way to Ephrath (that is, Bethlehem), and Jacob set up a pillar at her grave; it is the pillar of Rachel's tomb, which is there to this day.	Rachel died there and was buried in the country of Ephrathah, that is, Bethlehem.[127] Jacob built a pillar at Rachel's grave—on the road above her grave.

Targum Pseudo-Jonathan: Genesis, 120 n. 10). *Pseudo-Jonathan* and *Gen. Rab.* 81:5 also preserve the explanation deriving אלון from Greek (αλλον) so that the phrase means "another weeping." The additional mourning implied in "another weeping" was for Rebekah, of whose death Jacob is supposed to have heard at this time.

123 Büchler thought that "stream" and "oak" were double translations of אלון ("Studies," 262–63); he did not, however, supply any examples where the term is rendered as "stream."

124 Jubilees does not insert Gen 35:21 (MT SP) after the first clause of v. 16 as LXX does.

125 See BDB, 460, s.v. כבר.

126 The Ethiopic name *walda ḥemāmeya* reflects the interpretation of בן אוני given in the LXX: υιος οδυνης μου.

127 The author simply copies the gloss "that is, Bethlehem" from Gen 35:19 (see 48:7), despite the problems it causes for the location of Rachel's tomb. According to 1 Sam 10:2, it was "in the territory of Benjamin at Zelzah." Jeremiah 31:15 is also thought to be relevant because it refers to Rachel (now long dead) weeping for her children in Ramah, located north of Jerusalem. For an ancient discussion of the issue, see *Gen. Rab.* 82:10. Perhaps the existence

The author of Jubilees rearranges the material in Gen 35:16, presumably to create a smoother text. The naming of Benjamin is the first instance in which Jacob overrules a wife when she named a child; neither Genesis nor Jubilees explains why. In the case of Rachel's other son, Joseph, she had been the one to name him (28:24). In the Jacob cycle, Genesis supplies several instances in which one of the mothers named a child after her feelings or experiences (e.g., 29:32-35), but this is the only time it happens in Jubilees.[128] The writer of Jubilees, as is his practice, dates the birth but places it during the night of a date with no known significance (8/11), unlike the birthdays of Benjamin's older brothers Levi, Judah, and Joseph. For the second time in this context in Genesis Jacob erects a pillar to mark a special place (the same word is used in both passages): in 35:14 he put one at the spot in Bethel where God had spoken with him, and now he does the same at the place of Rachel's grave (35:20). Jubilees says nothing about a pillar at Bethel during this second visit to the site, but it does reproduce the notice about the marker for his wife's tomb. Where Genesis asserts it "is there to this day," however, Jubilees describes more precisely where he built the pillar—"on the road above her grave."[129] Jacob and his family are in transit, so they bury her along the way, and he erects a pillar so that he will know where the exact place is. Neither Genesis nor Jubilees says anything about Jacob's mourning for his favorite wife Rachel.[130]

---

of two places named אפרתה, one near Bethlehem (or אפרתה is another name for Bethlehem) and one farther north, encouraged confusion. By reading "in the country of Ephrathah" rather than "on the way to Ephrathah," the writer indicates that her tomb was at Bethlehem.

128 Halpern-Amaru considers this a second instance in which both Jacob and one of his wives name a child (*Empowerment*, 68-69). The first case involved Levi (in Jubilees both Jacob and Leah are credited with giving him the name [28:14, Jacob; 31:16, Leah]). However, Jacob and Leah gave their third son the same name, but for Rachel's second son they give different names and Jacob's choice overrides the one Rachel gave him (Benjamin is the only name used after this). It is not, therefore, an example of partnership between spouses. Werman conjectures that the name Benjamin (meaning, son of the right hand, that is, the south) was suggested by the command from the angel that Jacob travel to the south (to Hebron, v. 22) (*Jubilees*, 436).

129 Bradley Gregory suggests that by omitting "is there to this day" the writer of Jubilees subtly detracts from the importance of Rachel, while mention of Leah in the following verse (33:1) signals a change in Leah's status ("The Death and Legacy of Leah in Jubilees," *JSP* 17 [2008[99-120, here 105). This is part of the process of elevating Leah's stature in the book relative to the one she has in Genesis.

130 The word עלי in Gen 48:7 is often understood as an expression of sadness by Jacob when he recalls Rachel's death. The passage is lacking in Jubilees.

33

Reuben's Sin with Bilhah and Jacob's Move to the House of Abraham

1/ Jacob went and stayed to the south of the tower of Eder Ephrathah.ᵃ He went to his father Isaac—he and his wife Leah—on the first of the tenth month. 2/ When Reuben sawᵃ Bilhah, Rachel's maidᵇ—his father's concubine—bathing in water in a hidden place, he loved her. 3/ Heᵃ entered Bilhah's houseᵇ secretly at night and found her lying alone in her bed and sleepingᶜ in her tent.ᵈ 4/ After he had slept withᵃ her, she awakened and sawᵇ that Reuben was lyingᶜ with her in bed. She uncovered the edge of her (clothing),ᵈ took hold of him, shouted out, and realized that it was Reuben. 5/ She was ashamed because of him.ᵃ Once she had released her grip on him, he ran away.ᵇ 6/ She grieved terribly about this matter and told no oneᵃ at all.ᵇ 7/ When Jacob came and looked for her,ᵃ she said to him,ᵇ "I am not pure for you because I am contaminated from you,ᶜ since Reubenᵈ defiled me and slept with me at night.ᵉ I was sleeping and did not realize (it) until he uncovered the edge of my (garment) and lay with me." 8/ Jacob was very angry at Reuben because he had lain with Bilhah, since he had uncovered the covering of his father.ᵃ 9/ Jacob did not knowᵃ herᵇ again because Reuben had defiled her.

As for any man whoᶜ uncovers the covering of his father—his act is indeed very bad and it is indeedᵈ despicable before the Lord. 10/ For this reason it is written and ordained on the heavenly tabletsᵃ that a man is not to sleepᵇ with his father's wife and that he is not to uncover the covering of his father because it is impure. They are certainly to die together—the man who sleeps with his father's wife and the woman, too—because they have done something impure on the earth. 11/ There is to be nothing impure before our God within the nation that heᵃ has chosen as his own possession.ᵇ 12/ Again, it is wri<u>tt</u>en <u>a second time</u>: "Let the one who sleeps with <u>his father's</u> wife be cursed <u>because he has uncovered his father's covering</u>.ᵃ All of the Lord's holy onesᵇ said, 'So be <u>it, so be it</u>.'"

13/ <u>Now you</u>ᵃ <u>order the</u> Israel<u>ites</u> to observe thi<u>s</u> command <u>because it is a capital offense</u> and it is an <u>im</u>pure thing.ᵇ To eternity there is no expiation to ato<u>ne for the man</u>ᶜ <u>who does</u> this; but he is <u>to be put to death, to be ston</u>ed, and to be killed and uprootedᵈ from among the people of our God.ᵉ 14/ For any manᵃ wh<u>o commits it in Israel</u> <u>will not be allowed to live</u> a single dayᵇ on the earth because he is despicable and impure.ᶜ 15/ <u>They are</u> not to <u>say,</u> "<u>Reuben was allowed</u> to live and (have) forgiveness afterᵃ he had slept with the concub<u>ine</u>ᵇ <u>of his father</u> whileᶜ she had a husband and her husband—his father Jacob—was alive." 16/ For the statute, the punishment, and the lawᵃ had not been completely revealed to all but (only) in your timeᵇ asᶜ a law of itsᵈ particular time and as an eternal law for the history of eternity. 17/ There is no time when this law will be at an end,ᵃ nor is there anyᵇ forgiveness for it; rather both of themᶜ are to be uprooted amongᵈ the people. On the day in which they have done this they are to kill them.

18/ Now you, Moses, write for Israel so that they keep it and do not act like thisᵃ and do not stray into a capital offense; because the Lord ourᵇ God, whoᶜ shows no favoritism and takes no bribe,ᵈ is the judge. 19/ Tellᵃ them these words of the covenantᵇ so that they may listen, guard themselves,ᶜ be careful about them, and notᵈ be destroyed or uprooted from the earth. For all who commit itᵉ on the earth before the Lord are impure, something detestable, a blemishᶠ and something contaminated. 20/ Noᵃ sin is greater than the sexual impurity that they commitᵇ on the earth because Israel is a holy people for the Lord its God.ᶜ It is the nation that he possesses;ᵈ it is a priestly nation; it is a priestly kingdom; it is what he owns.ᵉ No such impurity will be seenᶠ among the holy people.

21/ During the third year of the sixthᵃ week [2145] Jacobᵇ and all his sons went and took up residence at the houseᶜ of Abraham near his father Isaac and his motherᵈ Rebekah. 22/ These are the names of Jacob's sons: Reuben, hisᵃ firstborn, Simeon, Levi, Judah, Issachar, Zebulun, were Leah's sons. Rachel's sons were Joseph and Benjamin. Bilhah's sons were Dan and Naphtali. And Zilpah's sons were Gad and Asher. Leah's daughter Dinah was Jacob's only daughter. 23/ After they had come, they bowed to Isaac and Rebekah. When they saw them,[a] they blessed[b] Jacob and all[c] his children. Isaac was extremely happy that he had seen the children of his younger son Jacob, and he blessed them.

Textual Notes

1a tower of Eder Ephrathah] See the commentary. Lat.: *magdala efratam*. The Eth. MSS. have a variety of spellings.

2a When Reuben saw] Eth. uses the form *re'eyo* ("When Reuben saw"), but many MSS. read the more frequent *re'ya*, "he saw" (17 21 35 42 47 58). Syr. Chr. introduces the verse with "One day" (lit., "One of these days"), but Eth. and Lat. have a conjunction.

b Rachel's maid] Syr. Chr. lacks these words.

3a He entered (Bilhah's house) secretly at night] This is the reading of Lat. and Syr. Chr. (but see the next note). The Eth. reading seems defective (so too Rochus Zuurmond, "De misdaad van Ruben volgens Jubileeën 33:1-9," *Amsterdamse Cahiers* 3 [1982] 107–16, here 111): "At night he hid. He entered Bilhah's house at night." It may be that the similarity between חבא and בא led to the repetition in the Eth. version. See Charles, *Ethiopic Version*, 124 n. 21; VanderKam, *Jubilees* 2:218.

b Bilhah's house] *mšknh* Syr. Chr.; Lat. uses a preposition ("to Bilhah"), lacking a reference to Bilhah's residence. Eth. adds a second reference to "at night" after "Bilhah's house." Syr. Chr. lacks the remainder of the verse.

c and sleeping] Lat. lacks. See VanderKam, *Jubilees* 2:218–19.

d in her tent] Eth. *bēta* would usually mean "her house," but Lat. reads *in tabernaculo suo*, suggesting that the original read אהלה. Eth. *bēt* can mean "tent" (Dillmann, *Lexicon*, 535). Zuurmond ("De misdaad," 111) suggests the original was משכן.

4a with her—with her] Syr. Chr. lacks, through parablepsis or the chronicler's desire to shorten the text.

b and saw] Lat. lacks; perhaps jumping from the first to the second conjunction in *et vidit et ecce* led to omission of the conjunction and verb. See VanderKam, *Jubilees* 2:219.

c lying] Lat. lacks; perhaps *cubans cum* proved confusing and led to omission of the participle.

d She uncovered the edge of her (clothing)] Syr. Chr. lacks (it om. other parts of the verse as well). Lat. lit., "removing the covering." Eth. *kenfā* = כנפה. Ms. 17 lacks the suffix (as in Lat.).

5a She was ashamed because of him] Eth. and Syr. Chr. read this way; Lat. reverses the pronouns: "he was confused by her."

b he ran away] Most Eth. MSS. read a masc. sg. form, while Lat. is ambiguous, and Syr. Chr. lacks the clause. Mss. 25 39 44 48 read a fem. sg. form ("she ran away"). Cf. the parallel in T. Reub. 3:14, where Reuben is the one who leaves; and VanderKam, *Jubilees* 2:219.

6a told no one] Lat. mistakenly omits the negative (*non*) so that Bilhah tells everyone.

b all] Lat. adds *quemadmodum veniret* ("how he came") beyond what the Eth. MSS. read. Syr. Chr. lacks the extra words as well. See Zuurmond, "De misdaad," 113.

7a and looked for her] Eth. and Syr. agree on the expression, but Lat. reads: "She told him." The verb in question—*indicavit*—was used near the end of the previous verse and may have been repeated mistakenly. *Inquisivit* would have been expected, followed by *illam*. Zuurmond ("De Misdaad," 113) thinks Lat.'s reading rests on a misunderstanding.

b to him] "to Jacob" Lat.; Eth., and Syr. Chr. agree on "to him."

c because I am contaminated from you] Syr. Chr. lacks the clause, perhaps jumping from "because" to "because/since" (the same word is used in both places by Eth. and Lat.). For being contaminated/defiled from someone, see 1QapGen xx:15 (noted by Rothstein, "Sexual Union," 373; Werman, *Jubilees*, 440).

d Reuben] Syr. Chr. adds "your son."

e at night] Syr. Chr. lacks.

8a since—father] Lat. omits the clause, but both Eth. and Syr. Chr. (written in the margin; see Tisserant, "Fragments," 216 n. 1) have it. Syr. Chr. introduces it, not with "since," but with "and" = MS. 21. At the end of this verse, Syr. Chr. cites from Gen 49:4.

9a know] = Lat. and Syr. Chr.; Eth. reads "approach." See VanderKam, *Jubilees* 2:220.

b her] "Bilhah" Syr. Chr.; 12 25 44 48 63 lack the pronominal suffix. After "Jacob did not know Bilhah again" Syr. Chr. has a statement about Reuben fasting that parallels the one in T. Reub. 1:10. Berger (*Jubiläen*, 488 n. a to v. 9) thinks Syr. Chr. did not draw the line from a Syriac translation of the Testaments of the Twelve Patriarchs but reproduces an old text of Jubilees or that it is a tradition put together with the text of Jubilees—one that is older than Jubilees. See the commentary.

c who] "because" 9 17 39 42 47 48 (see also the note on "indeed . . . indeed"); "if" 21.

d indeed . . . indeed] This is a rendering of both instances of *'esma* in the Eth. text of v. 9b; it is based on the assumption that it ultimately reflects כי, which can mean "surely, indeed" (BDB, 472; see VanderKam, *Jubilees* 2:221). If one translated *'esma* as "because" in both instances, the sentence would be strange: "And every man who has uncovered the covering of his father because his act is very bad and because it is despicable before the Lord." Charles (*Ethiopic Version*, 124; 125 n. 35) omitted the first of these uses of *'esma*; Werman (*Jubilees*, 438 n. 10) regards the second *'esma* as a dittography. Berger (*Jubiläen*, 488 n. b to v. 9) followed MSS. 9 17 63 (see also 39 42 47 48) that read *la-kwellu* rather than *wa-kwellu* at the beginning of the sentence. But the meaning would be surprising: it would be saying the act disqualified Bilhah for any (other) man—hardly the issue here (see VanderKam, *Jubilees* 2:221).

10a For this reason it is written and (om. written and 21) ordained on the heavenly tablets] "For this reason it is written in the law" Syr. Chr. After this it greatly abbreviates the line, saying only "that anyone who sleeps with his father's wife is to die." It lacks any reflection of vv. 11-15 and merely summarizes v. 16.
  b sleep] "uncover" 21.
11a he] "our God" 21.
  b as (his own) possession] om. 21 (so it reads: "the nation that he has chosen for himself").
12a covering] Eth. *ḥafrata*, "shame" (*kednata*, "covering" in 12 20), but 4Q221 frg. 4 2 reads כנף, from Deut 27:20 from which the verse cites. The Eth. version of Deut 27:20 also reads *ḥafrata*.
  b All of the Lord's holy ones] "his holy ones" 20.
13a you] The Eth. MSS. add "Moses," reflecting the expression used elsewhere by the angel when he directs to Moses a message specifically for Israel. 4Q221 frg. 4 2-3 read ואתה at the end of line 2 and צ at the beginning of line 3, leaving no place for the name.
  b an impure thing] In DJD 13:73 the suggested reading for 4Q221 frg. 4 4 is ונא]צה (all the visible letters have circlets over them); Werman (*Jubilees*, 438 n. 13) proposes ונד]ת. The reading is very difficult, but it is not evident why she thinks the Hebrew shows another word is needed after the one she reads, since she is responsible for placing a construct ending on it.
  c the man] "the wicked one" 21 (cf. MS. 58); MSS. 39 48 read "wicked" but place it in the acc. case—perhaps relating it to *zanta*, "this" (the object of the verb): "does this evil thing." Because 4Q221 frg. 4 5 would be several letters too short if the best attested Eth. readings are retroverted into Hebrew, it is suggested in DJD 13:73, 75 that הרעה הזאות appeared in the Heb. text ("the man who will d[o this evil"), though the inclusion of הרעה is uncertain. Mss. 42 47 actually have precisely this reading.
  d to be put to death . . . stoned . . . killed . . . uprooted] All of the forms are literally "to put him to death . . ." etc. The Eth. MSS. use four infinitives: "put to death, kill, stone, uproot." 4Q221 frg. 4 6 preserves the first (להמיתו) and a second: "to sto[ne him" (see Deut 22:21). That is, it places "to stone him" in the second position, while the Eth. MSS. put it in the third spot. One could argue that the Eth. tradition has added a verb synonymous with the first ("to kill him"), expanding a list of three verbs into four, but space considerations suggest that the Heb. fragment also had four verbs. Perhaps the second and third simply were reversed, though there is no evidence for this. See DJD 13:73, 75, where two verbs for "stoning" are used.
  e of our God] It may be that there is insufficient space for this word on 4Q221 frg. 4 6-7 (see DJD 13:74).
14a man] om. 20 25 58.
  b a single day] "a single hour" 20. 4Q221 frg. 4 7 reads ים at the left edge of the fragment; through these letters the scribe has drawn a line to delete them, perhaps because of the defective spelling. See DJD 13:75, where it is proposed that the scribe wrote אחד ים, deleted both words, and then wrote יום אחד. This longer reading would fill the available space on the line.
  c and impure] om. 25 35.
15a after] "when" 9 17 38 63; "because" 21 39 42 47 48 58.
  b concubine] 4Q221 frg. 4 10 appears to preserve the last letter in פילגש ("concubine"), while Eth. reads two words: *'eqebta be'sita*, "concubine wife" (om. *'eqebta* 12 35; om. *be'sita* 42 47 63).
  c while] "who" 12 20 (reading *'enta* rather than *'enza*).
16a the statute, the punishment, and the law] "the laws, the commandments, and the punishments" Syr. Chr.
  b time] pr. "all" 39 42 47 48.
  c as (*kama*)] "just, merely" (*kemma*) 20.
  d its] om. 9 21 (with a construct ending on "time"); 12 17 38 44 63 (without a construct ending).
17a an end (*tawdā'a*)] There are many spellings of a word related to the root *wadde'a*, "to finish, complete" (Leslau, *Comparative Dictionary*, 604). A number of MSS. read verbal forms that would not fit the context. Only 58 63 have forms not related to *wadde'a*.
  b nor is there any] The negative is carried over from the first clause, but 25 35 39 42 44 47 48 58 add one to make the point even clearer.
  c both of them] + "together" 39 42 47 48 58.
  d among] It seems the MSS. should read "from" rather than "in," but they unanimously support *ba-*, "in." See VanderKam, *Jubilees* 2:222.
18a do not act like this] Neither Dillmann nor Charles, both of whom read the negative in their editions, translated it, and Littmann and Hartom have followed their procedure. See VanderKam, *Jubilees* 2:222-23.
  b our (God)] om. 9 12 17 21 38; "your (God)" 63.
  c who] "this one" 35 38.
  d shows no favoritism and takes no bribe (lit., "lifts up no face and takes no bribe")] Lat. resumes here. The first three letters (*-nam*) Rönsch (*Jubiläen*, 66) and Charles (*Ethiopic Version*, 127) thought came from the end of

personam. If so, the object preceded the verb rather than following it as in Eth. Also, Lat. seems not to have repeated the verb "take/receive" before the second noun.

19a Tell] "He told" 17 63; Lat. has an impv. sg.
b these words of the covenant] "the words of this covenant" Lat.
c guard themselves] Lat. lacks (perhaps haplography in a series of three verbs, the last two preceded by "and"); "guard" 17 63.
d and not] "so as not" Lat. (perhaps *ut* is mistaken for *et*?).
e it] "them" Lat.
f blemish] *odium* Lat. For the suggestion that μυσερος and a form related to μισεω were interchanged, see VanderKam, *Jubilees* 2:223.

20a No] Lat. lacks a negative. It says, "It is a great sin on the earth," that is, Lat. also lacks the next clause.
b than the sexual impurity that they commit] Lat. lacks the words, perhaps through parablepsis on the Gk. level: απο της . . . επι της γης (see VanderKam, *Jubilees* 2:223).
c its God] "our God" 21 25 35 44; om. 39 42 47 48 58 (they add *la-'amlāku*, "for its God," after the word *rest*, "inheritance, possession").
d the nation that he possesses (lit., "people of inheritance")] Lat. = "the people of (his) share." The two versions probably are translations of κληρον, "lot, inheritance." See VanderKam, *Jubilees* 2:223.

e it is a priestly kingdom; it is what he owns] "a royal one of sanctification" (?) Lat. (*et regalis et sanctificationis*). See VanderKam, *Jubilees* 2:223–24. It is likely that Lat., with 12 58, lacks an equivalent for *wa-ṭerit we'etu*, "it is what he owns." The two adjectives separated by *et* (see Eth. MSS. 21 38 42 47) stand where Eth. has a construct: "a kingdom of [12 21 35 38 42 44 47 58 63 lack the construct ending] priesthood." It may be that Lat. *regalis* stands where a noun may once have been found. Several of the MSS. that lack a construct ending on "kingdom" omit "priesthood" (12 35 44 58). Werman (*Jubilees*, 439 n. 20) modifies the text on the basis of the fairly close parallel in 16:18, which, she thinks, offers a text nearer to what Lat. reads here.
f such (impurity) will be seen] Lat. lacks.

21a the sixth] "this sixth" Lat. = MSS. 39 42 47 48 58. But *ze* ("this") can easily be mistaken for *za* ("of" in this context), despite the fact that both Dillmann and Charles read *ze* in their editions.
b Jacob (= Lat.)] om. 9 12 17 21 38 63.
c house] "tower" Lat. (as in 29:19; 34:3).
d his mother Rebekah] Lat. and MS. 12 read "Rebekah his mother."

22a his] Lat. lacks.
23a they saw them (= Lat.)] "he saw them" 17 63.
b they blessed (also = Lat.)] "Isaac blessed" 17 63; they also om. "Jacob and."
c all (also = Lat.)] om. 20 25 35.

Commentary

As the chapter opens, Jacob and his party have placed some distance between themselves and Bethel. The narrative is quite simple in that it begins with a continuation of their journey (33:1) and ends with their arrival at the house of Abraham where Isaac and Rebekah lived (21-23). Most of the chapter, however, deals with an incident mentioned only briefly in Gen 35:22a—Reuben, Jacob's oldest son, had sex with Bilhah, one of Jacob's two concubines. Jubilees recounts the act in far more detail than Genesis does (vv. 2-9a) and attaches to it an address to Moses by the Angel of the Presence regarding the nature of the sin, the death penalty for it, and why Reuben avoided execution (vv. 9b-17). The writer also explains how such behavior is incompatible with Israel's character as a holy nation (vv. 18-20). The narrative then resumes with the actual move to the house of Abraham (v. 21; compare Gen 35:27), a list of Jacob's twelve sons and one daughter (v. 22 // Gen 35:22b-25), and a joyful meeting with Isaac and Rebekah (v. 23).

The chapter can be outlined in this way:
1-9a   Jacob and Leah's absence and Reuben's sin with Bilhah (Gen 35:21-22a; cf. v. 27)
9b-20 The angel's address to Moses
       9b-12 The law regarding the sin
       13-17 Commands for Israel and the special case of Reuben
       18-20 Israel as a holy nation
21-23 Jacob and his family move to the house of Abraham (Gen 35:22b-25, 27)

Several textual witnesses join the complete Ethiopic version for parts of the chapter.
Latin: vv. 1-9 (first three words), 18-23
Syriac: vv. 2-10, 16
Hebrew: vv. 12-15 (4Q221 frg. 4).

1-9a Jacob and Leah's Absence and Reuben's Sin with Bilhah (Gen 35:21-22a; cf. v. 27)

The author introduces the story by creating a context for it.

■ **1** Genesis 35:21 reports: "Jacob journeyed on, and pitched his tent beyond the tower of Eder." Ethiopic Jubilees has him go and stay[1] "to the south of *magdaladrā'ēf*. The first syllables transcribe the place-name מגדל עדר, and the last syllable may be the beginning of אפרתה (the term is actually present in MS. 44; 63 has "the land of Ephrathah"). The Latin transcription suggests as much: *magdale efratam*; in it the element Ephrathah is clear, while the word Eder seems to have left little trace. Charles drew attention to T. Reu. 3:13, where Reuben tells his sons about this very situation: "For while Jacob our father was absent (having gone) to Isaac his father, and we were in Gader, near to Ephratah [εν Γαδερ πλησιον Εφραθα]."[2] All of these names imply that the unknown Eder (Gk. Γαδερ) was not far from the spot where Rachel was buried.[3] Jubilees says that Jacob went "to the south of" where Genesis phrases it as "beyond" the place, but the meaning may be the same because their movement from Bethel in the north entails they would be south of Migdal Eder in Ephrathah if they had gone beyond it. Once the writer enters the travel notice, he redeploys the beginning of Gen 35:27 ("Jacob came to his father Isaac"), where Jacob goes to be with Isaac at the end of the elderly man's life. He applies the words to a preliminary trip that only he and Leah, his surviving wife, make to visit his parents, just as the angel had ordered him during the night vision in the preceding chapter (32:22). She had still not met Isaac, though she and Rebekah would have come into contact when the two of them were in Bethel. That she accompanies Jacob evidences her rise in importance, now that Rachel has died. The narrative function of the present trip, which occurs at an earlier time than the one in Genesis 35, is to explain that Reuben slept with Bilhah while Jacob and Leah were away (as in T. Reu. 3:13 quoted above)[4] and thus not present to curb his youthful passion.[5] The narrator dates their journey to the first of the tenth month, one of the memorial or seasonal days (Jub 6:23).

■ **2** The story about Reuben's sin with Bilhah occupies vv. 2-9a. Genesis strangely says almost nothing about Reuben's rape of Rachel's maid and Jacob's concubine: "While Israel lived in that land, Reuben went and lay with Bilhah, his father's concubine; and Israel heard of it." The brevity of the passage is astonishing. The reader might wonder how and why this happened and whether Reuben suffered any consequences for it. Genesis 35 says only that his father "heard of it."[6] But Gen 49:3-4, part of Jacob's last words to his sons, shows that he did more than just hear about the act:

> Reuben, you are my firstborn,
> > my might and the first fruits of my vigor,
> > excelling in rank and excelling in power.
> Unstable as water, you shall no longer excel
> > because you went up onto your father's bed;
> > then you defiled it—you went up onto my couch![7]

The subsequent history of the tribe descended from Jacob's eldest son also indicated a loss of status. As 1 Chr 5:1 says about Reuben, "He was the firstborn, but because he defiled his father's bed his birthright was given to the sons of Joseph son of Israel."[8] The writer of Jubilees was familiar with the various passages about

---

1   The Ethiopic manuscripts use *ḥadara*, "reside, dwell, lodge, inhabit, abide, stay overnight" (Leslau, *Concise Dictionary*, 116), where Latin reads *requievit*, "rest, stop, stay" (Lewis and Short, *Latin Dictionary*, 1574).
2   Charles, *Ethiopic Version*, 124 n. 14; *Jubilees*, 197.
3   In Mic 4:8 "tower of the flock [עדר]" is a poetic parallel to "hill of daughter Zion."
4   Halpern-Amaru characterizes the behavior of Reuben and of Jacob in this way: "The tale opens with Jacob and Leah off in Hebron visiting Isaac—an addition that both accounts for the absence of intervention and at the same time creates a contrast between Jacob, who piously cares for his father and Reuben, who violates the dignity of his own" (*Empowerment*, 109).
5   Or, as Zuurmond sees it, the trip by Jacob and Leah explains why Bilhah was not under supervision ("De misdaad,"110).
6   The LXX has a longer reading here: "and Israel heard, and it seemed evil in his sight."
7   The Syriac citation of this part of Jubilees quotes from Gen 49:4 at the end of its version of 33:8.
8   *Genesis Rabbah* 82:11 adduces this passage in treat-

Reuben himself and his descendants, and he rewrote Gen 35:22a with at least some of them in mind.

The author, as noted above, created a context for the story by having Jacob and Leah leave the family to visit Isaac and Rebekah. While they were absent, Reuben, now twenty-one years of age in the book's chronology (see 28:11), saw Bilhah bathing. The impetus to the sexual misdeed reminds one of King David who saw Bathsheba in the same circumstances and took her for himself at a time when her husband Uriah was away (he was campaigning with David's army, 2 Sam 11:1-7). The parallel with the David-Bathsheba story is transparent, but there may be a trigger in Gen 49:4 for the idea that Bilhah was taking a bath when Reuben developed a strong desire for her. Jacob said there that Reuben was "unstable as water." Following a hint in *Gen. Rab.* 98:4, Kugel proposes that this strange phrase may have given rise to the idea that, as with David and Bathsheba, water was involved.[9] But the writer is quick to assert Bilhah's innocence in the matter. She was in no way exhibiting herself but was bathing "in a private/hidden place."[10] She was being appropriately modest. The verb used for Reuben's emotion when he saw her naked is interesting: all three surviving versions read "he loved her." The original verb must have been a form of אהב (so Goldmann, Hartom, and Werman), but the nuance of it in the context is likely to have been the one it has in Gen 34:3 where Shechem "loved" Dinah or 2 Sam 13:1, 4, 15 where Amnon "loved" Tamar in the sense of "lusted for."[11]

■ 3 While Bilhah here and in the sequel is an innocent victim, Reuben is despicable. With his lust now aroused, he secretly entered Bilhah's residence (called both a house and a tent in v. 3), apparently that very night. He found her alone, asleep in her bed. The notion that she was in bed was indicated also in Gen 49:4, where Jacob charges Reuben with going up onto his father's bed/couch.[12] Once more she is totally innocent and not anticipating anything untoward.[13]

■ 4 The text leaves the clear impression that Reuben attacked her while she was asleep. Perhaps after he had finished raping her she awoke and discovered that Reuben was in bed with her—meaning she was aware that a man was with her, although the darkness made it difficult to recognize who he was.[14] Once she realized what was happening, she lifted her covering, grabbed him,

---

ing Gen 35:22a. See also Kugel, "Reuben's Sin with Bilhah in the Testament of Reuben," in David Wright, David N. Freedman, and Avi Hurvitz, eds., *Pomegranates and Golden Bells: Studies in Biblical, Jewish, and Near Eastern Ritual, Law, and Literature in Honor of Jacob Milgrom* (Winona Lake, IN: Eisenbrauns, 1995) 525-54, here 527-28.

9   Kugel, "Reuben's Sin," 528-31; *Traditions*, 466-67. The passage in *Gen. Rab.* 98:4, where "unstable as water" is under discussion, reads: "The Rabbis commented: You have sinned through water; then let him who was drawn from water [Moses] come and restore you to favor: *Let Reuben live, and not die* (Deut. xxxiii, 6)" (trans. Freedman, slightly modernized). The statement supplies good support for Kugel's suggestion, but his further proposal—that the difficult word פחז (translated "wanton") might have made readers think of חזה ("see") and thus that Reuben saw Bilhah in water—seems less likely. Note that none of the many playful meanings for פחז in *Gen. Rab.* 98:4 has to do with seeing (as Kugel admits). Segal doubts that even the bathing motif came from Gen 49:4 and believes it more likely arose from the David-Bathsheba story (*Jubilees*, 74 n. 4). For other similar bathing scenes in ancient literature, see Zuurmond, "De misdaad," 110-11.

10 The same is not said about Bathsheba's location in 2 Sam 11:2. Whereas 2 Sam 11:2 comments on Bathsheba's beauty, nothing is reported about Bilhah's appearance in Jubilees 33 (see Halpern-Amaru, "Bilhah and Naphtali," 9-10).

11 Halpern-Amaru (*Empowerment*, 110-11 n. 22) prefers the translation "desire" over the verb "love" in VanderKam, *Jubilees* 2 (Wintermute uses "desired"). She is correct that the verb has this connotation in v. 2, but it might not be the most accurate way to render it.

12 Kugel, *Traditions*, 467. He hypothesizes that an interpreter could infer more details of Jubilees' form of the story from Gen 49:4: if Reuben went up into Jacob's bed, Jacob must have been away, Bilhah would have already been there, and she would have been alone. See also his "Reuben's Sin," 535. For doubts about this, see Segal, *Jubilees*, 74 n. 6.

13 Testament of Reuben 3:13 presents Bilhah in a much less favorable light: "Bilhah lay uncovered in her chamber, drunk and sleeping."

14 Werman thinks that, as the second instance of the

and cried out. Only at this point did she know for sure her bedmate was Reuben. Kugel, following Rabin, thinks the text might make more sense if it read "*he* uncovered the edge of her (clothing), *he* took hold of her, and she shouted out,"[15] but the united witness of the versions is against the proposal (as is v. 5). The sense of the passage calls for Bilhah to be the subject of all the verbs because the first two clauses describe the process through which she discovered that Reuben was the one who had just accosted her.[16]

It turns out that Bilhah acts in the way Deuteronomy 22 requires. After the legislator deals with a case in which a man raped an engaged woman in a town and she did not cry out (vv. 23-24), he continues:

> But if the man meets the engaged woman in the open country, and the man seizes her and lies with her, then only the man who lay with her shall die. You shall do nothing to the young woman; the young woman has not committed an offense punishable by death, because this case is like that of someone who attacks and murders a neighbor. Since he found her in the open country, the engaged woman may have cried for help, but there was no one to rescue her. (Deut 22:25-27)

The fact that no one heard when Bilhah cried out—a sign she was not complicit in the act—could suggest that the location of Reuben's crime fell into the category described in Deut 22:27 (there was no one to hear her cry out). The innocence of Bilhah will be borne out in Jacob's reaction when he learns of the incident and in the legal section that follows.[17]

■ **5-7** In v. 5 the protagonists act in a way consistent with their characters to this point. Bilhah feels shame at what he had done. She had taken hold of him in v. 4; now she lets go of him, and he, released by the woman he had violated, runs away rather than taking responsibility for what he had done.[18] Verse 6 reports that she was terribly sad about the incident yet told no one about it. Her initial silence regarding the attack comes to an end in v. 7. She thought it was right not to tell others (was she protecting Reuben's reputation?)[19] or perhaps she was too ashamed to report the deed, but she decided that she had to tell Jacob when he returned from his journey and visited her. She told him the full story. For Kugel, her telling no one but eventually informing Jacob was an exegetical inference from the last words in Gen 35:22a: "and Israel heard of it" (the translator in NRSV adds "of it"). "*Jubilees* apparently interprets this phrase to mean that Jacob *alone* heard of it, that is, 'and Israel heard of it' but no one else did. In this way, an apparently pointless phrase acquired a certain sense."[20] Bilhah uses the language of impurity: Reuben had defiled her so that she was no longer pure as a sexual partner for him. The usage reflects the vocabulary of passages such as Leviticus 18, where illicit sexual relations are characterized as defiling (e.g., vv. 20, 24-30);[21] the term could also be another influence from Gen 49:4, where Jacob charges that Reuben "defiled [חללת]" his bed.[22] She makes sure

---

verb "lie" ("Reuben was lying with her in bed") does not have sexual connotations, the first instance (here translated "After he had slept with her") also does not (*Jubilees*, 440). This seems an unlikely way to read the sequence of actions in v. 4.

15 Rabin, "Jubilees," 102 n. 1; Kugel, *Traditions*, 467 n. 5; *Walk through* Jubilees, 162; "Jubilees," 409, 462 n. 216. Zuurmond thinks that Reuben is the subject of only "uncovered" (referencing v. 7 in support), not the other verb ("took hold of"), though he considers it possible ("De misdaad," 112-13). But, as he recognizes, this requires an emendation; in addition, the meaning of the expression in v. 7 is different (see the commentary there).

16 Zuurmond is reminded of Ruth 3:7-9, though the gender roles are reversed in the passage ("De misdaad, 111).

17 Zuurmond ("De misdaad," 111) and Segal (*Jubilees*, 74-75) list the ways in which the rewritten narrative defends the innocence of Bilhah.

18 In T. Reu. 3:14 he tells his sons, "And I, having entered and seen her nakedness, I did the impiety, and leaving her sleeping I went out." Bilhah is simply there in this version and does not react in the commendable way she does in Jubilees.

19 Halpern-Amaru, *Empowerment*, 110 ("the regard for peaceful family relationships implied in her remaining silent"); cf. Loader, *Sexuality*, 197.

20 Kugel, "Reuben's Sin," 536-38 (quotation from p. 537).

21 Himmelfarb, "Sexual Relations," 28-29.

22 Milgrom, "Impurity," 281. He deals with the evidence in the HB for ethical impurity (both Jubilees and the Temple Scroll confuse the categories חול and טמא [pp. 279-80]) and notes that the "most important area of impurity in *Jubilees* concerns

that Jacob knows about her innocence in the matter—she tells him she was asleep when it occurred so that she was not a partner to the crime. Reuben had already committed the act when she became aware of what was happening. The expression she uses—"he uncovered the edge of my (garment)"—does not imply that Reuben was the one who "uncovered the edge of her (clothing)" in v. 4; rather, in v. 7 it is the biblical expression for having sex with someone. An example of it pertinent to the case of Reuben and Bilhah is Deut 27:20: "Cursed be anyone who lies with his father's wife, because he has violated his father's rights [גלה כנף אביו, lit., uncovered the covering of his father]."

Halpern-Amaru has nicely documented how the rewritten story mirrors in reverse several elements from the episode involving Joseph and Potiphar's wife.

Multiple images in the created description call to mind the tale of the attempted seduction of Joseph by Potiphar's wife. Both narratives involve sexual intercourse with a proscribed woman. In each a seducer, driven by desire (33:2; 39:5), entraps the object of desire when she/he is most vulnerable (33:4; 39:9). In each there is a grasping (33:4; 39:9), an outcry (33:4; 39:10), a flight (33:5; 39:9), a point made about the woman informing her husband (33:6; 39:10), and an halakhic discourse involving the behavior of each son of Jacob (33:9-16; 39:6-7).

Such parallels prompt contrasting images. The innocent Bilhah grabs hold in error; the seductive wife of Potiphar grabs hold to entrap. The victimized wife lets forth a legitimate cry of protest; the villainous wife feigns such a cry. The grieving Bilhah keeps silent; the plotting wife of Potiphar is quick to confront her husband. Reuben and Joseph both flee; but one does so in order to escape confrontation after perpetrating a treacherous act; and the other to prevent the act from happening.[23]

■ **8-9a** Jacob's reaction also reflects the expression in Deut 27:20 noted above. When he heard what had happened (the only thing said about him in Gen 35:22a), he was very angry with Reuben "since he had uncovered the covering of his father."[24] By defiling his father's wife, Reuben had made himself liable to a curse and in fact to the death penalty. Deuteronomy 22:22 prescribes: "If a man is caught lying with the wife of another man, both of them shall die, the man who lay with the woman as well as the woman. So you shall purge evil from Israel." And, regarding the specific circumstances pertaining to the account of Reuben and Bilhah, Lev 20:11 stipulates: "The man who lies with his father's wife has uncovered his father's nakedness; both of them shall be put to death; their blood is upon them."[25] Bilhah, of course, did not deserve to be punished because of her innocence and her cry, as provided in Deut 22:25-27, but Reuben clearly had no grounds for avoiding capital punishment. Jacob does, however, make a decision regarding Bilhah: because Reuben had made her impure, defiled, he "did not know her again" (cf. T. Reu. 3:15).[26] The narrator implies it was not due to any fault on her part; rather, it was "because Reuben had defiled her." There is something of a parallel with the story about David's ten concubines whom he left in Jerusalem and with whom Absalom had sexual relations (2 Sam 15:16; 16:21-22). When David regained control of his kingdom, he "came to his house at Jerusalem; and the king took the ten concubines whom he had left to look after the house, and put them in a house under guard, and provided for them, but did not go in to them. So they were shut up until the day of their death, living as if in widowhood" (20:3).[27]

---

illicit unions." The first cause for impurity, he says, is incest. He treats the present passage in this context. The underlying concept is that Israel is holy (see Jub 33:20); thus Reuben's act constituted pollution.

23 Halpern-Amaru, *Empowerment*, 110-11.
24 In T. Reu. 3:15 an angel informs Jacob about Reuben's sin and he "mourned over me." For the variant readings here in Jub 33:8, see the textual notes.
25 For these two passages, see Endres, *Biblical Interpretation*, 169-70 and below on vv. 9b-12.
26 Loader compares Deut 24:1-4, the case of a woman divorced by her husband (*Sexuality*, 198). If she marries another man who also divorces her, the first husband is not allowed to take her back as his wife "after she has been defiled."
27 On these parallels, see Albeck, *Jubiläen*, 29; and especially Halpern-Amaru, "Bilhah and Naphtali," 9. As she points out, both Bilhah and the ten

Rothstein is correct in seeing here an instance of the principle that sexual union creates a new reality.

The upshot of this analysis is that *Jubilees* 33:9, along with 1QapGen 20:1, maintains that rape of a married woman renders her forbidden ("unclean") to her husband. On this view, no significance attaches to the question of a woman's passive or active role. The mere fact that she has been involved in extra-marital intercourse entails, as a matter of natural consequence, the wife becoming "defiled" (Deut 24:4), so that she and her husband may no longer engage in conjugal relations. The issue is, thus, not one of punishing the wife (or the husband), but the fact that a new ontological reality—involving violation of the marital bond—has been created.[28]

Jacob is not treating Bilhah as if she had done something wrong but does recognize the changed nature of the situation and for that reason refrains from sexual relations with her.[29]

9b-20 The Angel's Address to Moses

There follows a pause in the narrative to reflect on the significance of what Reuben had done. There is no such section in Genesis 35; it merely mentions the deed and does not expatiate on or criticize it. The expansion in Jub 33:9b-20 divides itself into three parts.

9b-12 The Law regarding the Sin

The first paragraph lacks an explicit indication that the angel is now engaging in one of his asides to Moses, but vv. 13 and 18 strongly suggest that such is the case here.

■ **9b** The Angel of the Presence takes up the expression used in v. 8—"uncovered the covering of his father"—and enunciates it as a law applying to all men (in Israel). In v. 9b he describes the act with two phrases: it is "very bad" and "despicable before the Lord." The latter classifies the act among those that are to be strongly rejected (see 30:11, 13), and the appeal to the heavenly tablets in the next verse directs attention to the legislation that applies to it.

---

women in 2 Samuel are called concubine-wives (cf. Jub 33:15; 2 Sam 20:3), and, after the sexual relations with a son of their husbands, they live in places separate from their spouses (see Jub 34:15). Halpern-Amaru thinks the writer of Jubilees deliberately set up the parallels. It seems questionable that the motif of Jacob having no more sexual relations with Bilhah relates to the statement "Now the sons of Jacob were twelve" that immediately follows in Gen 35:22b. Kugel argues that both Jubilees and the Testament of Reuben preserve an ancient tradition, reflected in the *pisqa be-'emṣa' pasuq* (the Masoretic notation separating the two halves of the verse yet allowing them to stand together as if they were related) ("Reuben's Sin," 538-40). According to that tradition, the juxtaposition of Gen 35:22a and b entailed that, as a result of the union between Reuben and Bilhah, Jacob had no more children. The number was fixed at twelve. Werman (*Jubilees*, 440) argues that Jubilees retains a certain proximity to this midrash in that the wives are not included in the list in vv. 21-22 (she takes this to mean his wives were not with Jacob; see the commentary below on those verses). Jubilees, however, makes no such statement and separates the notice about the termination of his sexual relations with Bilhah from the list of the twelve sons (and one daughter) by vv. 10-21 (and by two years; compare 32:33; 33:1 and 21). Further, it does not reproduce the number twelve from Gen 35:22b. Rothstein ("Sexual Union," 372-75) likewise rejects Kugel's inference. He adds the objection that Jacob was still married to Leah and Zilpah; there was no reason to end sexual relations with them after Reuben's act.

28 Rothstein, "Sexual Union," 375-76. He adds (p. 376 n. 37) that any further intercourse between Jacob and Bilhah would have rendered him defiled and any children born to them subsequent to Reuben's act would likewise have been "ontologically tainted." Cf. Zuurmond, "De misdaad,"114.

29 Anderson proposes that Bilhah had to be innocent in Jubilees because there was an existing law that applied to her case ("Torah before Sinai," 22-24). In Jub 20:4 Abraham told his sons and grandsons: "If any woman or girl among you commits a sexual offence, burn her in fire." So no one could claim that this law was unknown at the time; moreover, it is the one that Judah cites in 38:24 when he thinks Tamar has sinned sexually. Since Bilhah did not commit a sexual offense, the death penalty did not apply to her.

■ **10** In v. 10 the angel says that the tablets contain laws against sleeping with the wife of one's father and "uncovering the covering" belonging to him. The laws that the angel adduces and that were already implied in the narrative appear in Lev 20:11 (and see below in v. 12) and especially in Deut 27:20.[30] The former refers to a man who lies with his father's wife and thus uncovers his father's nakedness (the man and the woman are to be executed). The latter includes both of the expressions in Jub 33:10:

Deuteronomy 27:20	Jubilees 33:10
Cursed be anyone who lies with his father's wife, because he has uncovered the covering of his father.[31]	. . . that a man is not to sleep with his father's wife and that he is not to uncover the covering of his father

The writer quotes from the verse, but unlike in Deut 27:20, he adds a reason for the law: Jubilees characterizes the act as impure (*rekus*) and declares that both the man and the woman are to die "because they have done something impure [*rekusa*] on the earth." The idea that both individuals deserved the death penalty is stated in Lev 20:11: "The man who lies with his father's wife has uncovered his father's nakedness; both of them shall be put to death; their blood is upon them." Assessing the action as impure may draw on the language of Leviticus 18.[32] That chapter contains laws prohibiting a variety of sexual relations, including with a wife of one's father (vv. 7-8), and concludes with a general exhortation about them (vv. 24-30). Verse 24 reads: "Do not defile yourselves [תטמאו] in any of these ways, for by all these practices the nations I am casting out before you have defiled themselves [נטמאו]." Engaging in forbidden sexual relations brings the descendant of Jacob into the category of the nations. In Jub 22:16 Abraham told Jacob regarding the nations: "Do not act as they do, / and do not become their companion, / for their actions are something that is impure [*rekws*], / and all their ways are defiled [*gemmun*] and something abominable and detestable."[33] It may be that the concern with defiling the land through sexual sins in Lev 18:24-30 accounts for the phrase "on the earth" (it could be rendered "in the land") at the end of v. 10.

■ **11** The verse supplies the theological rationale for the prohibition. Impurity is incompatible with Israel's nature in that it is "the nation that he has chosen as his own possession" (see v. 20 below). Identifying Israel in this way calls to mind Ps 33:12: "Happy is the nation whose God is the LORD, / the people whom he has chosen as his own possession [לנחלה לו]" (see also 47:5 [Eng. v. 4]).[34] Leviticus 18 and 20 speak several times about how sins such as the one considered in this chapter defile the land; Jubilees says it defiles the people.[35]

■ **12** The writer placed a citation of the relevant legislation near the beginning of the paragraph (v. 10), and he closes it in the same way. The law in v. 10 was cited from Deut 27:20, and now in this second instance he reverts to the same verse (cf. also Lev 20:11).

Deuteronomy 27:20	Jubilees 33:12
Cursed be anyone who lies with his father's wife, because he has uncovered his father's covering.[36] All the people shall say, "Amen!"	Let the one who . . . be cursed . . . sleeps with his father's wife . . . because he has uncovered his father's covering. All of the Lord's holy ones said, "So be it, so be it."

Where Deuteronomy has the people agreeing to the curse, Jubilees refers to "the Lord's holy ones." "Holy ones" can be a designation for angels, but in the context it is more likely a term for Israel, the holy people (see v. 20).[37] The double "amen, amen = so be it, so be it" is a phrase familiar from various places in the HB (as in Psalm doxologies such as 41:13 and 72:19) and adds emphasis to what has just been said. A close parallel

---

30 See Loader, *Sexuality*, 198–99.
31 The expression is rendered literally, not as in the NRSV ("he has violated his father's rights").
32 Reuben characterizes his deed as impure/impurity frequently and admonishes his offspring on the subject in T. Reu. 1:6; 4:6-11; 5:1—6:4.
33 The noun *rekws* is related to the adjective *rekus* in 33:10, and *gemmun* is related to the verb *tagammanku* that Bilhah uses in 33:7 ("I am contaminated from you").
34 Both Goldmann and Hartom translate the term at the end of 33:11 as נחלה. On the word in Jubilees, see Schwarz, *Identität*, 94–95.
35 Werman, *Jubilees*, 443 (but see Lev 18:24, 30).
36 As for the citation of this line in v. 10, the text is rendered literally, not as in the NRSV ("because he has violated his father's rights").
37 Loader (*Sexuality*, 199) thinks they are angels, as does Kugel, *Walk through* Jubilees, 163; "Jubilees," 410.

is in Neh 8:6: "Then Ezra blessed the Lord, the great God, and all the people answered, 'Amen, Amen.'" The enveloping legal statements make clear the gravity of the offense: the two key scriptural laws place the man and woman under a curse (Deut 27:20) and require the death of both (Lev 20:11). As neither Reuben nor Bilhah suffered the penalty of execution after the act, the reader anticipates an explanation why this was so. It was not difficult to infer that these statements from Deuteronomy and Leviticus did not directly address the situation of Bilhah, but they certainly applied to Reuben.

13-17 Commands for Israel and the Special Case of Reuben
The eager reader has to wait a little while for the answer to his question because the author first underscores in several declarations how terribly wrong it is to have sex with the wife of one's father.

■ **13** The angel now addresses Moses (by name, in the Ethiopic tradition but not in 4Q221) and, as he has often done before, tells him to give orders to the Israelites about the subject under consideration. He reiterates points made before—the punishment of death for such incestuous relations (as in Lev 20:11) and the impurity that characterizes it (see vv. 11-12). In case anyone thought that some mitigating circumstance would allow a person to escape capital punishment after committing the sin, the angel insists there is none. He declares that there is no means through which the offender could atone for his transgression, to remove his guilt. In 5:17 the writer had said (speaking about the Day of Atonement without mentioning it by name [see v. 18]): "Regarding the Israelites it has been written and ordained: 'If they turn to him in the right way, he will forgive all their wickedness and will pardon all their sins.'" Though that option existed, there were circumstances under which it would not be applicable. So, for example, Israelites who neglect circumcision will have no opportunity to be forgiven: "For they have made themselves like the nations so as to be removed and uprooted from the earth. They will no longer have forgiveness or pardon so that they should be pardoned and forgiven for every sin, for (their) violation of this eternal (ordinance)" (15:34). The angelic address that deals with the sexual sin involved in the Dinah-Shechem episode touches on the same subject: "This law has no temporal end. There is no remission or any forgiveness; but rather the man who has defiled his daughter within all of Israel is to be eradicated because he has given one of his descendants to Molech and has sinned by defiling it" (30:10). The kind of sin committed by Reuben falls into the category of those for which there is no redress (cf. 30:16).

Denying any possibility of atoning for some sins finds an echo in the Rule of the Community. The writer, speaking of the person who refuses to enter the fellowship, denies him the ability to obtain forgiveness (1QS iii:1) and adds: "Ceremonies of atonement cannot restore his innocence, nor cultic waters his purity. He cannot be sanctified by baptism in oceans and rivers, nor purified by mere ritual bathing. Unclean, unclean shall he be, all the days that he rejects the laws of God, refusing to be disciplined in the *Yaḥad* of his society" (iii:4-6, trans. Wise, Abegg, Cook, *DSSR* 1:7; see also 5Q13 frg. 4 2-3).

The angel emphasizes his point by enumerating punishments that will befall a person who sinned as Reuben had. He first names being put to death. Death is the punishment stipulated in Lev 20:11. The other penalties in v. 13 consist of stoning (perhaps execution again; see the textual note) and cutting off/eradicating. None of the laws that deal with sexual relations between a man and his father's wife calls for stoning of the offender, but one law regarding sexual relations in Leviticus 20 (a chapter that does prohibit such unions) requires stoning as the punishment—giving offspring to Molech (v. 2; in Jubilees this refers to intermarriage with non-Israelites). However, the death penalty in Lev 20:11 is interpreted to mean death by stoning in *b. Sanh.* 54a through analogy with the case of the wizard or medium in Lev 20:27 (to be killed by stoning), as in both places the expression "their blood is upon them" is used. Deuteronomy 22:21 requires stoning for a woman who prostituted herself in her father's house, and v. 24 mandates it for the man who raped an engaged woman in a town and for the woman as well (see Ezek 16:38-40). In Jub 30:8-9 (see v. 7) anyone who defiles the Israelite "seed" is to die by stoning. The Mishnaic tractate *Sanhedrin* contains a list of those transgressors who are to suffer stoning; it begins with "he that has connexion with his mother, his father's wife, his daughter-in-law" (7:4, over a dozen more follow). The punishment of uprooting or cutting off from one's people (כרת) figures in the summary section in Leviticus

18, after the litany of sexual wrongs practiced by the nations Israel was to dispossess: "For whoever commits any of these abominations shall be cut off from their people" (v. 29). Jubilees 30 also refers to this punishment in contexts dealing with sexual misdeeds (e.g., 30:7, 10). Removal from the people of God means demotion to a category like that of the nations.

■ **14** There is also to be no delay in effecting capital punishment on the offender (repeated more clearly in v. 17: "On the day in which they have done this they are to kill them"). Verse 14 makes this statement in the context of again declaring the act despicable and impure (as in vv. 9-11).[38] The idea of execution on the very day a sin is committed is found already in Gen 2:17 ("in the day that you eat of it you shall die"), but it is not attested in the sections of the Torah that legislate regarding sexual relations. Rothstein has proposed that passages such as Deut 21:22-23 (a corpse hanged on a tree must be buried the same day) and Num 19:20 (seven-day period for cleansing from corpse impurity, with no delay of even one additional day implied) may have influenced the rule in Jubilees.

In short, while the Hebrew Bible does not explicitly prescribe same-day punishment for either capital or lesser offenses, it does offer unequivocal support for the notion of prompt removal of impurity and evil, a position further amplified in the writings uncovered at Qumran. While *Jubilees* does not address these specific issues, it is clear that the quintessential perception of impurity, of any sort, as a very real, ontological entity is common to Jubilees and the other works uncovered at Qumran.[39]

Immediate punishment is another way of focusing attention on the serious nature of the sin and the resulting impurity.

■ **15** Verses 15-16 provide the anticipated answer to why Reuben did not die for what he had done. The writer of Jubilees sets as one of his objectives in rewriting Genesis and the first half of Exodus to demonstrate that the ancients lived according to more laws than a casual reading of the narratives might imply. Those narratives refer to few specific laws; almost all of the pentateuchal legislation is revealed to Moses and Israel in the wilderness (from Exodus 25 to near the end of Deuteronomy). However, Genesis does offer a few hints that the patriarchs lived in obedience to revealed law. Abraham, for example, received the law of circumcision, and of him God said, he "obeyed my voice and kept my charge, my commandments, my statutes, and my laws" (Gen 26:5 // Jub 24:11). Jubilees crafts an account in which the ancient ancestors of Israel have more laws disclosed to them than in the HB and they transmit them to the next generations (as Noah does in 7:20-39). One of the subjects on which Abraham had instructed his offspring was sexual matters and the need to avoid impurity in them (Jub 20:3-6; 22:19-21; see also the words of Rebekah and Jacob in 25:1-10), although he had not addressed the particular issue of incest.

The case of Reuben and Bilhah in Genesis could, however, be used to counter the author's thesis about the patriarchs. He raped his father's wife but escaped punishment other than the harsh words his father uttered in Gen 49:3-4. If the patriarchs were supposed to live according the law, why did this happen? Surely Reuben would have known that violating his father's wife was wrong. The author states the issue in the form of a claim he places in the mouths of some anonymous debate partners in v. 15: "They are not to say: 'Reuben was allowed to live and (have) forgiveness after he had slept with the concubine [*'eqebta be'sita*] of his father while she had a husband[40] and her husband—his father Jacob—was

---

38 For the expression "not be allowed to live," see Exod 22:18: "You shall not permit a female sorcerer to live."

39 Rothstein, "Same-Day Testimony and Same-Day Punishment in the Damascus Document and Jubilees," *ZABR* 11 (2005) 12-26, here 12-20 (quotation from p. 17). Werman (*Jubilees*, 442 n. 32, 443) objects to Rothstein's explanation. She correctly points out that if prompt removal of impurity were the reason for the command, one would expect the same provision to occur in chap. 30, where it is lacking. For her stipulation that the violator be punished on the very day of the offense appears here in chap. 33 because the pertinent scriptural legislation makes no provision for divine intervention if Israel fails to punish the offender; the sin in chap. 30 is one for which Leviticus provides that God will cut off the guilty party if the people close their eyes to what has occurred (see Lev 20:4-5).

40 Segal, who thinks the legal sections in Jubilees

alive.'" The combination of the terms "concubine" and "husband" indicates that the case falls into the category of having sexual relations with another man's wife; it does not support the idea that Bilhah, as a concubine, was not a full wife and therefore not included in the legislation regarding violation of another's wife.[41] A new aspect is mention of the fact that Bilhah's husband was alive when the crime occurred. Albeck took this to entail that Reuben would not have had to pay the death penalty if Jacob had been dead when he slept with Bilhah.[42] At any rate, the opponents object that, despite what he did, Reuben remained alive and even experienced pardon (otherwise he would have been executed). The narrative about Reuben's sin (vv. 2b-9) says nothing about repentance on his part, a sorrow for his sin that could have led to pardon (this is an important theme in the Testament of Reuben; see 1:9 [he repented for seven years]; 2:1; 4:4).[43] The writer inferred that he was

---

stem from a different hand than the rewritten narratives, finds a conflict between 33:1-9a and the section in 33:9b-20 regarding Bilhah's legal status (*Jubilees*, 78–79). The narrative makes her entirely innocent, while in the legal section the law cited (particularly Lev 20:11) requires that both the man and the woman in the illicit sexual relationship are to die. That point is obvious enough, and the legal section makes abundantly clear that, once the law was revealed, such was the case. But Segal thinks v. 15 says that Bilhah too was to die although that did not happen. He follows the translation of Charles: "And let them not say: to Reuben was granted life and forgiveness after he had lain with his father's concubine, and to her also though she had a husband, and her husband Jacob, his father, was still alive." That is, the opponents would be saying that Bilhah too received life and forgiveness. He claims that the syntactical structure here is the same as in v. 10: "They are certainly to die together—the man who sleeps with his father's wife and the woman too." However, he fails to note that in v. 15 the name Reuben is preceded by the preposition *la-* ("to Reuben" [confirmed by 4Q221 frg. 4 9]) while the name Bilhah lacks a preposition paralleling the one with Reuben. This favors understanding the sentence in the way it is translated here: the latter part of the sentence indicates two conditions that characterized the situation. The legal section and the rewritten story are not in conflict on this point. See VanderKam, "One Author?" 511-12.

41 Rothstein comes to the opposite conclusion ("Sexual Union," 378–79). As he sees the situation, the author maintains that Reuben was not aware of what the laws encompassed: "*Jubilees*' point is that while it is true that it is the sexual union, per se, which is determinative in all matters of law—and, hence, there is no essential difference between a full wife and a concubine—Reuben was not aware of this fact; he believed, erroneously, that the law forbade sexual relations only with the full wife of one's father or another man" (p. 378). The text lacks any hint of Reuben's holding such a belief; also, Jacob is called her husband here, suggesting that their relationship was considered a marriage. It seems unlikely, in view of their relationship, that the writer was trying to "mitigate Reuben's offense" in 28:17, where, unlike for Zilpah in 28:20, he reports simply that she was given to Jacob, not that she was given to him "as a wife."

42 Albeck, *Jubiläen*, 29. He notes that this stand is contrary to *m. Sanh.* 7:4: "He that has connexion with his father's wife is thereby culpable both by virtue of the law of the father's wife and of another man's wife, whether in his father's lifetime or after his father's death." See also Hartom, "Jubilees," 103.

43 For the thesis that Jacob spoke the words of Deut 33:6 ("May Reuben live, and not die out, / even though his numbers are few"), see Kugel, "Reuben's Sin," 543. Taken in this way, the verse would fit well with T. Reu. 1:7, where Jacob prays for Reuben. This is not said in Jubilees, though the writer does mention that he was forgiven. Berger (*Jubiläen*, 488 n. a to v. 9) argues that the Syriac Chronicle preserves an original part of the text at Jub 33:9 (or at least an element older than Jubilees) where it reads: "Jacob did not know Bilhah again. Reuben proclaimed a fast for himself that he would not eat meat or drink wine because of his offence." The fasting theme has left no trace in the Ethiopic translation (the Latin breaks off after the first three words of v. 9), but it agrees with T. Reu. 1:10: "Wine and strong drink I did not drink / and meat did not enter into my mouth / and I did not taste any pleasant food, / mourning over my sin for it was great / and such a thing shall not happen in Israel." Since the words about fasting are present only in the Syriac Chronicle, a text that cites from Jubilees as well as from other works, it seems precarious to regard them as an original part of Jubilees. The extra line could indeed have been placed together with the text of Jubilees; this would not entail it was older than Jubilees (see VanderKam, *Jubilees* 2:220–21). Tisserant ("Fragments," 217–18) sensibly

forgiven because the penalty for what he did was not exacted. But why was he forgiven? It was not because pardon is an option for people who imitate Reuben.

■ **16** Rather, Reuben received forgiveness because the law regarding the act had not yet been revealed.[44] Verse 16 states the principle: "For the statute, the punishment, and the law had not been completely revealed to all[45] but (only) in your time as a law of its particular time and as an eternal law for the history of eternity." That is, God had not yet disclosed laws such as Lev 18:7-8; 20:11; and Deut 27:20 when Reuben slept with Bilhah. The author's teaching is that, while some laws (e.g., circumcision, festivals) had been revealed to the heroes of Genesis, not all of the legislation now in Exodus–Deuteronomy was disclosed in that earlier period. Reuben was not punished because God had yet to reveal the law that prohibited sexual relations with a wife of one's father.[46] As the apostle Paul later expressed the matter, "For the law brings wrath; but where there is no law, neither is there violation" (Rom 4:15).[47] Once God declared the law to Moses ("in your time") it became eternally valid, so that any future violation of it would trigger the death penalty.

■ **17** Verse 17 closes the paragraph by repeating several ideas already mentioned earlier in it. After God made the particular law covering such a case, it would remain in force for all time, and transgressors of this revealed law would meet their deaths. Both the man and woman involved in the illicit sexual union were to be uprooted/cut out from their people. This is the language of Lev 18:29, which calls for "cutting off" any who are involved in the abominable practices enumerated earlier in the chapter, including lying with a father's wife (vv. 7-8). The writer once more bases himself on Lev 20:11 in demanding that both the man and woman involved be executed, since among the laws governing rape of a father's wife it is the only one to stipulate capital punishment for both. And, as he said in v. 13, the executions are to take place on the very day of the crime.

---

proposed that the chronicler drew the material from T. Reu. 1:10.

44 It may be that several passages in the Rule of the Community express the same or a similar idea of revelations meant for certain time periods (i:9; iii:10; viii:15; ix:13).

45 The Ethiopic phrase *la-kwellu* is ambiguous: it could refer to people (to all people), circumstances, or times. Rabin ("Jubilees") translates "to cover every case," and Anderson ("Torah before Sinai," 21 n. 37, 23 n. 42) prefers his understanding of the phrase to the rendering "to all" in VanderKam, *Jubilees* 2. The suggestion is appealing, especially with the preceding word *feṣṣuma* ("complete, completely"), so that the meaning would be "complete for all (circumstances)." It is possible in this context, however, that the vague phrase refers to time, with the sequel making the point more explicit. Segal, in line with his view that according to the legal section both Reuben and Bilhah should have received punishment, thinks *la-kwellu* means "to all (people)" (*Jubilees*, 79–81). The law in question was known to Judah and to Joseph (see below for Jub 39:6 and 41:17), but not to Reuben and to Bilhah. A decision about the meaning of the phrase is difficult, but "to/for all (time)" seems appropriate in this setting.

46 See Anderson, "Torah before Sinai," 21–22. He indicates (p. 21 n. 38) that the author's stance on the point raises a problem in connection with the story about Joseph and Potiphar's wife. In Jubilees' retelling of the story, Joseph "remembered the Lord and what his father Jacob would read to him from the words of Abraham—that no one is to commit adultery with a woman who has a husband; that there is a death penalty that has been ordained for him in heaven before the Most High God" (39:6). Not only did Joseph know the anti-adultery law; Jacob read it to him from the words of Abraham. Hence, the law was known well before Reuben's time. How did Joseph know about it and not Reuben? Anderson thinks v. 16 claims the revelation was not complete in the sense that it covered every case. He also considers "the possibility that Reuben would have had a good suspicion that his behavior was wrong, but since it did not exactly coincide with the teaching he had learned from his father he opted for a lenient understanding of the law. Since he lived in the pre-Sinaitic period, his poor moral reasoning was forgiven him. On the other hand, Joseph opted to be more rigorous in these matters, and, in keeping with how he is generally portrayed in Second Temple Jewish sources, became a model of obedience to the commandments."

47 The parallel is frequently noted, e.g., by Charles, *Jubilees*, 199.

18-20 Israel as a Holy Nation

The wider context for understanding the gravity of the transgression now comes to the fore.

■ **18** For the second time in just a few verses (see v. 13), the Angel of the Presence addresses Moses more directly, this time by name. In v. 18, however, he does not tell him to command the Israelites (as in v. 13) but to write for them. It is hard to imagine that any significant difference underlies the change in wording because Moses is pictured as recording in Jubilees all the words the angel dictates to him. In this instance the writing he is to do seems to be more of an exhortation than a legal statement (note the verb "listen" in v. 19). He is to write for them so that they do not imitate Reuben and, because the law has now been revealed, suffer the consequence—death. To reinforce this point he adopts language he used in chap. 5 when describing the justice practiced by the Lord. There he said, "He is not one who shows favoritism nor one who takes a bribe" (5:16; cf. 30:16); in 33:18 he uses the very same expressions to describe him as the preeminently just judge. There will be no avoiding the consequences should anyone in the future act as Reuben had.

■ **19** The angel tells Moses to relay to Israel "these words of the covenant [Latin: the words of this covenant]." The expression in the Ethiopic copies strongly resembles one in Deut 28:69 (Eng. 29:1): "These are the words of the covenant that the Lord commanded Moses to make with Israel," and the Latin wording is like the one in 29:8 (Eng. v. 9): "Therefore diligently observe the words of this covenant, in order that you may succeed in everything that you do" (cf. 2 Kgs 23:3). Conveying the message to Israel is to serve several purposes: so that they listen, take special care to act precisely (compare Jub 20:3) in conformity with the instructions, and thus avoid the penalties of destruction and uprooting from the earth/land. A number of these elements are found in negative form in Jer 12:17: "But if any nation will not listen, then I will completely uproot it and destroy it, says the Lord." The Ethiopic version employs two verbs for watching carefully or being careful where Latin has just one. It is possible that the original Hebrew text used two forms of שמר. Israel is often exhorted to exercise care in obeying divine commands. For example, Deut 4:15-16 resorts to such an expression for keeping oneself from making idols, and Deut 4:9 makes double use of the verb שמר: "But take care and watch yourselves closely so as not to forget the things that your eyes have seen." Repetition emphasizes the importance of diligence in obeying the law in question. If one exercises due caution (Jub 7:31), he will escape destruction and uprooting (for both, see Jub 15:26)—punishments that are familiar in the HB and Jubilees (for perishing/destruction, see, e.g., Deut 4:26; 11:17; and Jub 23:18; 30:22; for being cut off, examples are Lev 18:29 and Jub 30:6, 7, 10).

The last sentence in v. 19 contains several of the author's favorite terms for characterizing evil people and/or their deeds. He charges that all who act as Reuben did are impure (a word met several times already in chap. 33 and, of course, frequently in Jubilees), something detestable or abominable (perhaps rendering תועבה; see 22:16; 23:14, 17), a blemish (*nekfat* = *neqfat/odium*; a new word of reproach),[48] and something contaminated (see 21:21; 23:14, 17; 30:15; 41:25; 50:5). The author exerts great effort to condemn the offense in the strongest terms.

■ **20** The paragraph in which Moses is named ends with an important statement about the author's view of sexual sins and of Israel's status. To this point in the book he has taken several opportunities to address issues of impropriety in sexual matters, including marriage with foreigners (e.g., 7:21; 16:5-9; 20:3-7; 22:20-21; 23:14; 25:1-9; 27:8-10), and the story about Shechem and Dinah motivated him to write at length about the subject (esp. 30:5-17). He will add more on the topic when speaking about Judah and Tamar (41:23-28), but here he declares that there is no greater sin than fornication (*zemmunā*). So it is as bad as or worse than, say, murder or idolatry. The reason why he makes the strong claim appears in the next sentences. Israel is a holy nation, and the impurity associated with sexual sins is incompatible with its character. The expressions he uses to describe Israel

---

48   Both Goldmann and Hartom render with תבל, itself a rare word in the HB but one that does appear in connection with sexual immorality (Lev 18:23; 20:12; NRSV uses "perversion" in both passages; the sense seems to be "confusion, violation of nature" [BDB, 117, s.v. בלל]).

in this verse draw on the Lord's words in Exod 19:5-6: "Now, therefore, if you obey my voice and keep my covenant, you shall be my treasured possession out of all the peoples. Indeed, the whole earth is mine, but you shall be for me a priestly kingdom and a holy nation." Israel as a holy nation is also a theme in the sections in Leviticus where sexual wrongs are treated (primarily chaps. 18 and 20)—units that are part of the Holiness Code. In Lev 19:1 the Lord commands Israel: "You shall be holy, for I the LORD your God am holy" (see also 20:26).

The author used the same language in 16:18 and 19:18. In the former, the angels tell Abraham that one of Isaac's sons would become "the share of the Most High. All his descendants had fallen into the (share) that God owns so that they would become a *treasured* people of the Lord out of all the nations; and that they would become a kingdom, a priesthood, and a holy people." Later, Abraham told Rebekah: "the Lord will choose him [Jacob] as his own people (who will be) more enduring than all who are on the surface of the earth" (19:18). In the latter he does not repeat the themes of being a kingdom and priesthood. In 33:20 the writer more nearly echoes what he said in 16:18, but he alters the message slightly by repeating that Israel is the Lord's own, his special possession both before and after he refers to it as a priestly nation and kingdom.[49] The expressions for Israel as the Lord's possession are worded differently in the Ethiopic text: "It is the nation that he possesses" renders *ḥezba rest we'etu*, and "it is what he owns" translates *ṭerit we'etu*. Dillmann proposed that the latter renders סגלה from Exod 19:5,[50] for the former he pointed to Isa 19:25 (ונחלתי ישראל; see also 63:17; Joel 4:2 [Eng., 3:2]; Sir 24:12).[51] All of these are terms forcefully characterizing the unique relationship between God and his people who are to reflect his holiness. Sexual sins fundamentally mar that covenantal bond by rendering the holy people impure (cf. 30:13-16, where intermarriage with people of the nations produces defiling impurity; 41:26).[52]

Excursus: An Interpolator in 33:10-20?

Kugel finds the work of his interpolator in 33:10-20, where the heavenly tablets occur in v. 10 and are alluded to in v. 12.[53] The issue in this instance, writes Kugel, is that the interpolator takes up something the author of Jubilees does not discuss: "the fact that Reuben's crime was not appropriately punished" (actually, in Jubilees Reuben is not punished at all). Kugel thinks that the text of 33:16 is corrupt[54] but that the original sense of it can be inferred. As he sees the situation, the angel meant to say that Reuben, who did lose the birthright, did not receive the full, fitting punishment for what he had done. As a matter of fact, Jubilees says nothing about Reuben's losing his birthright or being punished in any way. Kugel's rewriting of v. 16 shows only a loose relation with the wording and word order of the Ethiopic text and creates *ex nihilo* a decision by Jacob: he made a temporary ruling and disinherited Reuben, following the principle of fair warning. Our surviving textual evidence gives no support for importing the idea into the text and context. As noted in the commentary, the case of Reuben did not harmonize with the author's general thesis that the patriarchs lived in accord with more of the laws than Genesis indicates, so he maintained that this particular law had not yet been revealed. There is no need to assume the work of an interpolator here and certainly no reason to rewrite the text to make it say something it does not say.

---

49 See Schwarz, *Identität*, 93–94. As he notes, the vocabulary in v. 20 is close to Deut 7:6; 14:2, where Israel is a holy people and the Lord's "treasured possession [סגלה]."

50 Dillmann, *Lexicon*, 1221.

51 Dillmann, *Lexicon*, 897. On the expressions, see also Charles, *Jubilees*, 199; Schwarz, *Identität*, 94–95. The designation appears multiple times in Abraham's words to Jacob in chap. 22 (vv. 9, 10, 15, 29), as well as in vv. 11 and 20 here in chap. 33.

52 Endres speaks of the combination in vv. 10-20 of holiness and covenant theology (*Biblical Interpretation*, 170).

53 Kugel, "Interpolations," 265; *Walk through* Jubilees, 163–64, 288; "Jubilees," 409–11. He accepts Segal's claim that the narrative and legal sections of the chapter do not agree, a position rejected above.

54 He refers to the relevant note in VanderKam, *Jubilees* 2:222; there the emendations proposed by Charles and adopted by a couple of translators

21-23 Jacob and His Family Move to the House of Abraham (Gen 35:22b-25, 27)

Having completed his special message to Moses regarding the sin of Reuben, the angel returns to the narrative of Genesis.

■ **21** He situates the family's move chronologically by dating it to the year 2145—an unexpectedly long time after the previous episodes. Jacob and Leah had traveled to see Isaac and Rebekah at the beginning of month 10 in the year 2143 (see 33:1; 32:33). Not a word is said in v. 21 about why there was a delay of at least one year and three months, perhaps more, in carrying out in full the command of the angel in 32:22 to go to the house of Abraham and live with Isaac until his death. At any rate, the trip mentioned in Gen 35:27 (where only Jacob is said to have gone) now at last takes place. Jacob and his entire household (though only he and his sons/children are specified)[55] move to "the house of Abraham near his father Isaac and his mother Rebekah." In Gen 35:27 "Jacob came to his father Isaac at Mamre, or Kiriath-arba (that is, Hebron), where Abraham and Isaac had resided as aliens." The phrase "the house of Abraham" that the angel substitutes for the place-names in Gen 35:27 appeared in Jub 22:24 where, on the last day of his life, Abraham said to Jacob:

> This house I have built for myself to put my name on it upon the earth. It has been given to you and to your descendants forever. It will be called Abraham's house. It has been given to you and your descendants forever because you will build my house and will establish my name before God until eternity. Your descendants and your name will remain throughout all the history of the earth.

Use of "house of Abraham" to mean him and his descendants is related to Gen 17:23, where all the males of Abraham's house undergo circumcision. But it also serves as a place-name for a locale around Hebron/Kiriath-Arba, the site where Abraham lodged at the end of his life (Jub 19:1, 5; 22:3). To that site two names are applied: "house of Abraham" (31:5; 32:22; and here in 33:21) and "tower of Abraham" (29:16, 17, 19; 31:6 [twice]; 36:12, 20 [it becomes Jacob's home]; 37:14, 16, 17; 38:4, 5, 6, 7, 8).[56] So Isaac and Rebekah had returned to the tower of Abraham in the vicinity of Hebron (29:15-20). The fact that all three great patriarchs live at this place bearing a name resonant of the covenantal promise of descendants suggests the writer adopts it intentionally here where Jacob moves his own household to the dwelling where he will remain until he goes to Egypt. This is the thematically charged spot where he provides a listing of the names of his twelve sons and one daughter. All of them settle near Isaac and Rebekah since the latter two remain the occupants of the tower itself.

■ **22** The verse incorporates the list of Jacob's children in Gen 35:23-25. In the pertinent section of Genesis 35 the order of material is:

22a   Reuben's sin with Bilhah
22b   "Now the sons of Jacob were twelve."
23   The sons of Leah
24   The sons of Rachel
25   The sons of Bilhah
26   The sons of Zilpah
27   Jacob goes to his father Isaac.

The writer of Jubilees re-orders these elements and introduces other changes.

---

are surveyed and rejected as unnecessary on the grounds that the verse is clear as it stands.

55   Werman infers from the list that Jacob's surviving wives were not with him in this move to Hebron, since they are not mentioned (*Jubilees*, 444). Genesis 35:23-26 includes the wives' names, though Rachel had already died, but since it is an enumeration of Jacob's twelve sons (Gen 35:22), the writer of Jubilees may have felt no need to incorporate the names of the mothers. At any rate, the sequel shows that Leah is very much a part of Jacob's household.

56   See Rapp, *Jakob in Bet-El*, 241-46. He thinks that Jub 22:24 would have called to the reader's mind the reference to the house in 2 Samuel 7 and thus the temple. It seems more likely that it would have reminded the ancient reader of the other house in that chapter, the house of David.

33:1-9a   Reuben's sin with Bilhah
33:9b-20   The angel's address about the sin
33:21   Jacob and his household go to Isaac and Rebekah
33:22a   "These are the names of Jacob's sons" (the text does not say his sons were twelve in number)
33:22b-f   Leah's sons, Rachel's sons, Bilhah's sons, Zilpah's sons, and Leah's daughter Dinah.

The sentences in which the writer names the sons of each mother are also somewhat different in Genesis and Jubilees. In Genesis each of the lines begins with "the sons of [mother's name]" and then lists the sons; in Jubilees, the name of Leah appears at the end of the sentence naming her six sons. The names of the other three wives stand before the two sons born to each, and in the cases of Bilhah and Zilpah their titles as "Rachel's maid" and "Leah's maid" are absent from Jubilees. The writer, who often gives more attention to female characters, also adds the name of Leah's daughter Dinah, who does not figure in the list in Genesis 35. She too is among the ancestors of Israel.[57] In addition, he does not reproduce the line "These were the sons of Jacob who were born to him in Paddan-aram" at the end of Gen 35:26, probably because it was inaccurate in the case of Benjamin, who was born not in Paddan-aram but in the land just after Jacob and his party left Bethel and headed south. Placing the names of Jacob's children after the travel notice locates the entire family, the true descendants of Abraham, at the house of Abraham together with Isaac and Rebekah.

■ 23 The next notice in Genesis 35 is the death of Isaac. That event will not happen in Jubilees until 36:18, about three chapters later. The writer pictures the scene of Gen 35:27 much differently. When Jacob and his large family arrive, they pay the proper respect to the aged couple. Naturally, Isaac and Rebekah enjoyed the occasion, as this was their first chance to meet eleven of the children (they had become acquainted with Levi and Judah in chap. 31) as well as Bilhah, and Zilpah. Both of them blessed Jacob and his children,[58] but of Isaac alone is it said he "was extremely happy that he had seen the children of his younger son Jacob, and he blessed them" (note that Jacob is still his younger son). Isaac had been the one who unwittingly blessed Jacob with the words: "May all the blessings with which the Lord has blessed me and blessed my father Abraham / belong to you and your descendants forever" (26:24). He had sent Jacob off to Paddan-aram with another blessing, this time with full awareness of which son he was addressing: "May the God of Shaddai bless you; may he make you increase, become numerous, and be a throng of nations. May he give the blessings of my father Abraham to you and to your descendants after you so that you may possess the land where you wander as a foreigner—and all the land that the Lord gave to Abraham" (27:11 // Gen 28:3-4). Jacob not only had returned home permanently but had come with his three wives and thirteen children—a tremendous start toward fulfillment of the promise that he would "become numerous." Isaac and Rebekah had previously blessed Jacob when he sent them goods (29:20), and both had blessed Levi and Judah (Rebekah in 31:7; Isaac in 31:13-20 [and 22]). Now they bless the entire family, and on this occasion Levi and Judah are not singled out for special treatment. In Genesis neither Rebekah nor Isaac ever sees Jacob's children; in Jubilees they both see and bless them, thus more closely binding together the generations in the chosen line, the house of Abraham. Like the first great patriarch himself, Isaac and Rebekah were able to bless the next two generations of their family.

---

57   Gregory, "Death and Legacy of Leah," 112-13. On the designation of Dinah as Jacob's daughter (as in 30:1; 34:15), see Halpern-Amaru, *Empowerment*, 127-30.

58   This is a good example of their partnership in Jubilees but also of the much greater role Rebekah plays in the book (Halpern-Amaru, *Empowerment*, 61-62).

34

War with the Amorite Kings, Joseph and His Brothers, the Day of Atonement, and the Wives of Jacob's Sons

1/ During the sixth year of this[a] week of this forty-fourth jubilee [2148], Jacob sent his sons to tend his[b] sheep—his[c] servants were also with them—to the field of Shechem. 2/ Seven Amorite kings assembled against[a] them to kill them from their hiding place beneath the trees[b] and to take their animals[c] as booty. 3/ But Jacob,[a] Levi, Judah, and Joseph remained at home[b] with their father Isaac because he was distressed[c] and they[d] were unable to leave him. Benjamin was the youngest, and for this reason he stayed[e] with him.[f] 4/ Then came the kings[a] of Tafu,[b] the king of Ares, the king of Seragan, the king of Selo, the king of Gaaz, the king of Betoron, the king of Maanisakir, and all who were living on this[c] mountain, who[d] were living in the forest[e] in the land of Canaan. 5/ It was reported to Jacob:[a] "The Amorite kings have just surrounded your[b] sons and have carried off your flocks by force." 6/ He set out from his[a] house—he, his three sons, all his father's servants, and his servants—and went against[b] them with 6,000 men who carried swords. 7/ He[a] killed them in the field of Shechem, and they[b] pursued the ones who ran away. He[c] killed them with the blade of the sword. He killed Ares, Tafu, Saregan, Silo, Amanisakir, and Gagaas[d] 8/ and collected his[a] flocks. He got control of them and imposed tribute on them[b] so that they should give him as tribute one-fifth[c] of their land's products. He[d] built Robel and Tamnatares 9/ and returned safely. He made peace with them, and they became his servants until the day that he and his sons went down to Egypt.[a]

10/ During the seventh year of this week [2149] he sent Joseph from his house to the land of[a] Shechem to find out about his brothers' welfare. He found them in the land of Dothan. 11/ They acted in a treacherous way and made a plan against him[a] to kill him; but, after changing their minds, they sold him[b] to a traveling band of Ishmaelites. They brought him down to Egypt and sold him to Potiphar, Pharaoh's eunuch, the chief cook, and the priest of the city of Elew. 12/ Jacob's sons slaughtered a he-goat, stained Joseph's clothing by dipping it in its blood,[a] and sent (it) to their father[b] Jacob on the tenth of the seventh month. 13/ He[a] mourned all that night[b] because[c] they had brought it to him in the evening. He became feverish through mourning his death and said[d] that a wild animal had eaten Joseph. That day all the people of his household mourned with him. They continued to be distressed and to mourn with him all that day.[e] 14/ His sons and daughter[a] set about consoling him, but he was inconsolable for his son. 15/ That day Bilhah heard that Joseph had perished. While she was mourning for him,[a] she died. She had been living in Qafratefa. His daughter Dinah, too, died after Joseph had perished. These three (reasons for) mourning came to Israel[b] in one month. 16/ They buried Bilhah opposite Rachel's grave, and they buried his daughter Dinah there as well. 17/ He continued mourning for Joseph for one year and was not comforted but said, "May I go down[a] to the grave mourning for my son." 18/ For this reason, it has been ordained regarding the Israelites that they should be distressed on the tenth of the seventh month—on the day when (the news) that made (him) lament Joseph reached his father Jacob[a]—in order to make atonement for themselves on it with a kid—on the tenth of the seventh month, once a year—for their sins. For they had saddened their father's (feelings of) affection for his son Joseph. 19/ This day has been ordained so that they may be saddened on it[a] for their sins, all[b] their transgressions, and all[c] their errors; so that they may purify themselves on this day once a year.

20/ After Joseph had perished, Jacob's sons took wives for themselves.[a] The name of Reuben's wife was Oda; the name of Simeon's wife was Adebaa, the Canaanitess; the name of Levi's wife was Melcha, one of the daughters of Aram—one of the descendants of Terah's sons; the name of Judah's wife was Betasuel, the Canaanitess; the name of Issachar's wife was Hezaqa; the name of Zebulun's wife was [Neeman];[b] the name of Dan's wife was Egla; the name of Naphtali's wife was

Rasu'u of Mesopotamia; the name of Gad's wife was Maka; the name of Asher's wife was Iyona; the name of Joseph's wife was Asenath, the Egyptian, and the name of Benjamin's wife was Iyaska. 21/ Simeon, after changing his mind, married another woman from Mesopotamia like[e] his brothers.

Textual Notes

1a   of this] Lat. lacks "this."
b   his (sheep)] "their" 12 20 21 25 35. For "his," cf. v. 5.
c   his (servants)] "their" 12 21 44.
2a   against] Lat. lacks a preposition here, though one is needed (probably *in*; see Charles, *Ethiopic Version*, 129 n. 2 to Lat.).
b   to kill them from their hiding place beneath the trees] A literal translation of Eth. is: "in order that they, having hid under the trees, might kill them." Lat. reads "and waited in the woods in order that they might kill them." The verb for their hiding—*taḫabi'omu*—is, according to Charles (*Jubilees*, 200; *Ethiopic Version*, 128 n. 7) perhaps a mistake for *nabiromu*, the equivalent of Lat. *sederunt* (both = "sat," i.e., "waited"). It is the case, however, that no MS. contains *nabiromu*. Werman (*Jubilees*, 446 n. 4) opts for a blend of elements from the two versions: "hiding" from Eth., and "in the trees" from Lat.
c   their animals] Ceriani placed four dots after *oves ipsorum*, indicating that a short word was once present there. Mss. 39 42 47 48 58 read after "animals": "and their wives." Mss. 9 38 read "their wives" in place of "their animals." The two words *'ensesāhomu* ("their animals") and *'anestiyāhomu* ("their wives") could have been confused, but there may not be enough space in the Lat. MS. for *et mulieres*, which Rönsch (*Jubiläen*, 68) proposed.
3a   Jacob (= Lat.)] "the sons of Jacob" 35 58.
b   at home] om. 17; Lat., as elsewhere, reads "in the tower" where Eth. has "in the house."
c   he was distressed] Lit., "his spirit was sad for him." Lat. has *pusillianimis erat spiritus eius*, "his spirit was faint." Lat. may reflect קצר רוחו, while Eth. may represent עצב רוחו (see VanderKam, *Jubilees* 2:225).
d   they (= Lat.)] "he" 39 58.
e   he stayed (= Lat.)] "they stayed" 12 44.
f   with him] "with his father" = Lat. and MSS. 42 47.
4a   kings . . . king . . . king . . . king] In both Eth. and Lat. the first instance of the royal title is pl., perhaps intended to refer to all seven kings. In instances 2–4 Eth. continues to use a pl. form, while Lat. properly has the sg. It may be that the close resemblance between βασιλευς and βασιλεις (pl.) led to confusion.
b   Tafu] Lat. *saffo* seems a corrupt form of a name more like the one in Eth., which bears a closer resemblance to the spellings of the name in the other versions of the story. It is the biblical "Tappuah."
c   this] Lat. lacks, as do MSS. 21 58.
d   (mountain), who] Lat. and MSS. 21 35 58 read a conjunction before "who," leaving the impression that two groups are mentioned: those living on the mountain and those living in the forest.
e   forest] Lat. *locis* is a mistake for *lucis*, "forest" (so Rönsch, *Jubiläen*, 68).
5a   Jacob] Eth. follows with *'enza yebelu* = לאמור; Lat. lacks an equivalent.
b   your] Thus 4Q223-224 unit 2 i:5 and MS. 21; the other Eth. copies read "their."
6a   his (house)] om. 9 38 48.
b   against] "to" 12.
7a   He] "They" 9 38 39 42 47 48 58.
b   they] "he" 25 35 44.
c   He[2]] "They" 9 38.
d   Gagaas] + "and Betoron" 44 (thus adding the only name in v. 4 missing from this list).
8a   his (flocks)] "their" 38 42[c] 44.
b   on them] om. 21 58.
c   one-fifth] The form *ḫāmesta* has given rise to two translations: (1) Jacob imposed a tribute of five agricultural products (Charles, Berger, VanderKam); or (2) he imposed a tax of one-fifth the land's produce (Littmann, Goldmann, Hartom). The word could be parsed as a form of the number *five* with the first -*a*- lengthened under influence from the preceding guttural; several MSS. read the normal spelling of "five" (12 44) or the numeral "5" (20 38 39 42 47 48; so also 39 48). But *ḫāmesta* would also be the correct spelling of "fifth," though the masc. form would be expected. Reading "one-fifth," despite this problem, makes more sense (see the commentary).
d   He (built)] "They" 42 47.
9a   to Egypt] om. 20.
10a   the land of (Shechem)] om. 42 47.
11a   against him] om. 20 25 35.
b   and sold him] om. 12.
12a   its blood] "the blood" 9 12 17 21 38 63.
b   their father] om. 42 47.
13a   He] "They" 17 38 39 42.
b   night] "day" 9 12 17 21 38 39 42 47 48 58 63.

c   because] "until" 21 38 39 42 47 48 58. Since *'esma* ("because") has stronger support and fits better with the following words (note how the later MSS. 38 39 42 47 48 58 add a conjunction before "they brought" to handle this problem), Jacob is mourning at night because he got the bad news at night; he is not mourning that day until evening. The reading "day" rather than "night" probably arose through confusion of the words *lēlita* and *'elata*. Once the reading "day" entered the MSS., *'esma* was altered to the similar *'eska*. See VanderKam, *Jubilees* 2:228.

d   (he [subject understood from the previous verb]) said] "they said to him" 35 58.

e   that day] "that night" 44.

14a His sons and daughter] "They" 21 (though it reads "his sons" as the subject of "consoling" later in the verse).

15a for him] om. 12 21.

b   to Israel] The best reading is *bašhomu la-'esrā'ēl*, with "Israel" understood as pl. Mss. 21 35 38 39 42 44 47 48 58 read a sg. suffix, apparently understanding "Israel" to be "Jacob."

17a May I go down] "I will go down" 9 38 58.

18a reached his father Jacob] Without textual support, Werman (*Jubilees*, 446 n. 11) changes "reached" to "they brought," arguing that the reading "reached" breaks the sequence in which the brothers have been the subjects of the sentence. It is the case, nevertheless, that the verb appears in a parenthetical remark explaining the choice of the date, that is, in a unit of the sentence that intentionally disturbs the sequence.

19a on it] om. 9 21 38.

b   all (their transgressions)] om. 20 25.

c   all (their errors)] om. 39 42 47 48.

20a for themselves] om. 25 35; they add the expression later in the sentence.

     Mss. 39 42 47 48 58 use a number with each of the wives. Ms. 38 also numbers them but is off by one.

b   [Neeman]] The older MSS. 9 12 17 20 25, with 38 44 63, list no name for Zebulun's wife. Ms. 21 reads *'eska*; MS. 35 *tebēr*; MS. 39 *'a'amēn*; Mss. 42 47 48 *nē'ēmān* (*-mēn* in 48). The Syr. list has *'dny*, which has no match in the Eth. copies. *Neeman* is placed in brackets as the best attested spelling, though her name is not at all clear.

21a like] "from" 21.

Commentary

The thirty-fourth chapter of Jubilees takes up life in the family of Jacob, beginning three years after their move to the area of Hebron. Like many sections in the book, it builds on Genesis but alters it greatly, primarily through additions. The first section of the chapter (war with seven Amorite kings, vv. 1-9) has no extended parallel in Genesis, although it is related to Gen 48:22. The story of Joseph and his brothers, told briefly in Jub 34:10-12, 14, 17, draws material from Gen 37:13-14, 17-18, 28, 36, 31, 32, 35. The section regarding the Day of Atonement in vv. 12-19 is largely independent of Genesis, and vv. 20-21 (the wives of Jacob's sons) collect information from sundry passages but do not have an exact counterpart in Genesis, that is, it offers no such comprehensive list of their names.

The chapter can be outlined in this way:
1-9   War with seven Amorite kings
10-19 Joseph and his brothers (Gen 37:13-14, 17-18, 28, 36, 31, 32, 35)
   10   Joseph's mission to his brothers
   11   Their harsh treatment of Joseph
   12-19 Jacob's grief and the Day of Atonement
20-21 The wives of Jacob's sons.

The complete Ethiopic text is joined by a small amount of evidence from two other versions:
Hebrew: vv. 4-5 (4Q223–224 unit 2 col. i:4-5)
Latin: vv. 1-5.
The amount of extant textual material is actually larger than this short list suggests because the story about a war between Jacob and his sons and a coalition of Amorite kings is attested in a rather different form in Hebrew in Midrash Wayyissa'u, in Greek in the Testament of Judah 3–7, and again in Hebrew in the later midrashic collections entitled the Book of Jashar and the Chronicles of Jerahmeel. In addition, the Syriac text listing the wives of the patriarchs supplies the names of the women whom Jacob's sons married (vv. 20-21).

1-9 War with Seven Amorite Kings

Genesis 35 ends with Jacob visiting his father in Hebron and apparently staying there until Isaac died. Esau and Jacob then buried him. The text does not say that he remained there after his father died (see vv. 35-37), but Gen 37:1 provides a little more information: "Jacob settled in the land where his father had lived as an alien, the land of Canaan." Perhaps the author of Jubilees inferred from 37:1 that Jacob took up residence where his now-deceased father had lived, as both 35:27 and 37:1 refer to the land where Isaac lived as an alien. Genesis 37:14, where Jacob sends Joseph "from the valley of Hebron" to pay his brothers a visit, would have confirmed the inference.

The events of vv. 1-9 occur three years after Jacob and his family relocated to Hebron (compare v. 1 with 33:21).[1] In this context, the writer does not retell the stories about Joseph in Gen 37:2-11, where he brings a bad report regarding his brothers with whom he was working, receives special treatment and clothing from his father, has two portentous but annoying dreams, irritates his brothers further, and receives a rebuke from Jacob. If one were to read Jubilees without knowing the underlying story in Genesis, s/he would not know why Joseph's brothers disliked him so intensely. For whatever purpose, the writer chose not to include the stories that put Rachel's older son in an unfavorable light, and in this way he burnished the reputation of Joseph[2] but left his brothers looking hateful and arbitrary.

■ 1 According to the first verse in the chapter, Jacob was the one who sent his sons to the region where they formerly lived—the area of Shechem—to shepherd the family flocks. Genesis 37:12 formulates the matter differently: "Now his brothers went to pasture their father's flock near Shechem."[3] In Jubilees there is an added notice that Jacob's servants were with them—a hint that his holdings in the area of Shechem were large indeed and also a preparation for the story about war with the Amorite kings who might easily have overpowered just eight brothers (see v. 3 below). Jubilees locates their place of work in "the field of Shechem," while Midrash Wayyissa'u puts it in the "valley of Shechem" (line 2).[4] Joseph, when sent by Jacob to check on his brothers in the vicinity of Shechem, wandered in the field [שדה] in that area (Gen 37:15); perhaps the "the field of Shechem" in Jub 34:1 was influenced by this note (see also Gen 33:19 where Jacob purchases part of a field near Shechem; Josh 24:32 [it is the burial place of Joseph]).[5]

■ 2 The description of the war occupies vv. 2-9. While the sons of Jacob were tending their father's many animals in the area of Shechem, seven Amorite kings tried to kill them and take their animals. There is no mention of a military conflict in Genesis 37, but the writer knew of a notice in Gen 48:21-22: "Then Israel said to Joseph, 'I am about to die, but God will be with you and bring you again to the land of your ancestors. I now give to you one portion [שכם] more than to your brothers, the portion [שכם] that I took from the hand of the Amorites with my sword and with my bow.'"[6] The word translated

---

1 Atar Livneh ("With My Sword and Bow: Jacob as Warrior in *Jubilees*," in Devorah Dimant and Reinhard Kratz, eds., *Rewriting and Interpretation: The Biblical Patriarchs in Light of the Dead Sea Scrolls* [BZAW 439; Berlin: de Gruyter, 2013] 189–213, here 194) draws attention to the fact that there are several units of six in Jub 34:1-9: the date places the events in the sixth year of the sixth week (of jubilee 44), Jacob has 6,000 servants and kills six Amorite kings (v. 7). And there is a fraction of the number six, as Jacob rushes off to war with three of his sons.

2 See Susan Docherty, "Joseph the Patriarch: Representations of Joseph in Early Post-Biblical Literature," in Martin O'Kane, ed., *Borders, Boundaries and the Bible* (JSOTSup 313; Sheffield: Sheffield Academic Press, 2002) 210. In passing over negative material, the writer treats Joseph as he does the other heroes of his story.

3 Some of the Ethiopic copies of Jub 34:1 read "his sheep" (9 17 38 39 42 47 48 58 63) as in Gen 37:12 ("their father's flock"), while others have "their sheep" (12 20 25 35). The Latin translation is ambiguous about whose animals they were, but v. 5 favors "his [Jacob's] sheep."

4 References to Midrash Wayyissa'u are from Tamar Alexander and Yosef Dan, "The Complete *Midrash Va-yissa'u*," *Folklore Research Center Studies* 3 (1972) 67–76, with the line numbers they assign.

5 Livneh thinks the writer is drawing a connection with the earlier Shechem story (Genesis 34 // Jubilees 30, which included a battle) by this allusion and notes that the brothers were in that field when they received the news about the rape of Dinah (Gen 34:5, 7) ("*Jubilees* 34:1-9: Joseph, the 'House of Joseph,' and the Josephites' Portion," *JSJ* 43 [2012] 22–41, here 27–28). Jubilees had earlier omitted the reference to Jacob's purchasing the field near Shechem, perhaps to give the impression that Israel gained the land through conquest, not purchase.

6 The term שכם is interpreted as "portions/shares" in Jub 45:14, where Jacob "gave Joseph two shares in the land." For the significance of Gen 48:22 for Jub 34:1-9 (and the midrashim related to the passage), see already Beer, *Jubiläen*, 2–4.

"portion" is the same as the name for the city Shechem.[7] A reader might infer that Jacob was talking about the sack of Shechem after the rape of Dinah (Genesis 34), though it would be curious for him to claim he took the city when Simeon and Levi were responsible for the conquest—an effort for which he criticized them.[8] Furthermore, the people of Shechem are called Hivites, not Amorites, in Gen 34:2 // Jub 30:2. The conclusion drawn in the story in Jub 34:1-9 is that there was a separate occasion when Jacob conquered Shechem, and the references to Shechem in Gen 37:12-14 may have seemed to signal the circumstances in which it occurred.

While Jacob's sons were shepherding in the region of Shechem, the Amorites[9] saw their chance. Jubilees says they gathered together (נתכנסו in Midrash Wayyissa'u line 2 and נתקבצו in line 4) against them and attempted to take them by surprise.[10] Their strategy, which brands them as evil in contrast to the fully justified attack on Shechem by Jacob's sons when avenging their sister,[11] was to exploit the cover provided by the forest in the area:

Ethiopic (literally): having hidden beneath the trees
Latin: waited in the woods.

Midrash Wayyissa'u says only that they "came against them [ובאו עליהם]" in line 4, and the Testament of Judah also lacks the element of hiding or waiting among trees. The versions of Jubilees (Hebrew, Ethiopic, Latin) refer to the forest in v. 4, where it appears to be the dwelling place of the kings and their people.

Why does the author refer to seven Amorite kings? He knew of Gen 48:22, where Jacob takes something from the hand of the Amorite, where "Amorite" should be a collective (the gentilic is singular; the LXX reads a plural form). But that passage mentions neither kings nor the number seven, though it could make one recall the words of Jub 29:11 regarding these people: "The Amorites—evil and sinful—lived in their [the Rephaim's] place. Today there is no nation that has matched all their sins. They no longer have length of life on the earth." That passage would have established in the reader's mind a decidedly negative estimate of the people who are now attacking the sons of Jacob.

The idea that the patriarchs were heads of vast households and that they were able to fight with kings and even defeat them is familiar from Genesis 14, where Abram armed 318 household servants and routed four kings and their forces (Gen 14:13-16). Both Abraham and Isaac had dealings with Abimelech, king of the Philistines: Abraham made a covenant with him (Gen 21:22-34); Isaac became too powerful for the king and his people (Gen 26:16), and he as well concluded a pact with him (26:26-33). Two of Jacob's sons massacred an entire city (Genesis 34); afterwards no one dared to pursue the clan (Gen 35:5). Jacob's immediate family was far larger than the one of either of his ancestors, so presumably he could muster an even greater force if the need arose.

All this would have been familiar to the author, but there are hints in other texts that may have helped him shape the story first attested in Jub 34:2-9. The Bible mentions Amorite kings in several places. Among them are the stories about Sihon and Og, two kings in the Transjordan defeated by Israel (Num 21:21-35; both are called Amorite kings in Josh 9:10). The conquest stories in Joshua 9–10 may also have contributed. "Now when all the kings who were beyond the Jordan in the hill country and in the lowland all along the coast

---

7 *Targum Pseudo-Jonathan* Gen 48:22 supplies both interpretations: "As for me, *behold* I give you *the city of* Shechem, one *portion as a gift more* than your brothers, which I took from the hands of the Amorites *when you went into it, and I arose and assisted you with* my sword and with my bow."

8 *Genesis Rabbah* 80:10 assigns Jacob a military role in the defeat of Shechem (Genesis 34) on the basis of Gen 48:22.

9 They are Amorites in Midrash Wayyissa'u (line 2); T. Jud. 3:1 refers to two Canaanite kings, but in 7:2 the word Amorites is used (Judah and Dan pretend to be Amorites, the people against whom they are fighting) and in 7:11 mention is made of Canaanites (after they defeat the kings, the Canaanites fear Judah and his brothers). Jerahmeel also calls them Amorite kings (36:1, 10) and says Jacob and his sons made peace with the Amorites (36:12; here Gen 48:22 is cited).

10 This is one of a series of parallels with the battle account in Jubilees 37–38 and serves to present the nations in a negative light, while Jacob and family respond only when attacked (see Livneh, "With My Sword," 195–96).

11 Livneh, "*Jubilees* 34:1-9," 30.

of the Great Sea toward Lebanon—the Hittites, the Amorites, the Canaanites, the Perizzites, the Hivites, and the Jebusites—heard of this, they gathered together [ויתקבצו] with one accord to fight Joshua and Israel" (9:1-2). Later, the text refers to those who attacked Israel's new covenant partners, the Gibeonites: "Then the five kings of the Amorites—the king of Jerusalem, the king of Hebron, the king of Jarmuth, the king of Lachish, and the king of Eglon—gathered their forces, and went up with all their armies and camped against Gibeon, and made war against it" (10:5). The Gibeonites complain that "all the kings of the Amorites who live in the hill country are gathered against us" (10:6). Eventually Joshua executes the five Amorite kings (10:16-27; King Jabin of Hazor later gathers the kings of many peoples, among whom are Amorite monarchs; see 11:3). It is not impossible that the idea of seven Amorite kings was suggested to the writer by a combination of the two Moses defeated and the five Joshua conquered.[12]

■ 3 However he came upon the theme of an attack by seven Amorite kings, the writer of Jubilees claims they ambushed Jacob's sons with the intent to kill them and steal their flocks. It turns out that they are partially successful (see v. 5)—they gain possession of the animals and surround Jacob's sons. At this juncture the reader learns that only some of Jacob's sons were shepherding the animals in the area of Shechem. Jacob was, as always, much concerned about the welfare of his frail father Isaac, who required constant attention, so he remained in Hebron with him and kept four sons there as well. This is another occasion when Levi and Judah seem to receive special treatment. Nothing is said regarding why Jacob did not send them off to Shechem with the others (e.g., that they were bad at shepherding), but the reader knows the remarkable words said about Levi in 30:18-20; 31:13-17, his appointment to the priesthood in 32:2-4, 8-9, and the rich blessings pronounced on Judah in 31:18-20. The special status of Joseph becomes evident, as he remains behind with Levi and Judah. The case of Benjamin is different because he was too young to take on herding duties some distance from home. In the book's chronology he is just five years of age (see 32:33 and 34:1). Joseph is only fourteen years, but his tender age is not noted.[13] The four who remain behind are, therefore, the two sons who were uniquely blessed and the two sons of Rachel (cf. T. Jud. 25:1, where Levi is first, Judah second, Joseph third, and Benjamin fourth as chiefs of the tribes at the resurrection). Judah's absence from the place of the Amorite attack is striking (even apart from the military might Isaac predicted for him in 31:18); in the other versions of the story he is the hero of the fighting and the one who first engaged the enemy. In those accounts there is no suggestion that Jacob and some of his sons were anywhere other than the region of Shechem when the attack came. In fact, Midrash Wayyissa'u mentions that Jacob and his sons had moved back to Shechem, and their claim on the land incited the kings of the Amorites to fight them (lines 3-4).

■ 4 The names of the places ruled by each of the seven kings are given in all the versions of the story (they are presented as the names of the kings themselves in v. 7):[14]

---

12 This is just one possibility. Another is Livneh's suggestion that the number seven came from Josh 10:28-43 ("Jubilees 34:1-9," 29). Not all of the kings defeated in those verses are among the Amorite kings listed earlier in the chapter, though there is some overlap.

13 Livneh sees the presence of the brothers at home as an instance of honoring their parents ("With My Sword," 197; also "Jubilees 34:1-9," 31-32), but the point is clearer in the battle account in chaps. 37-38, where the eleven brothers comfort Jacob as he mourns for Leah. In the present context, Jacob was the one who sent the others to Shechem, so they could hardly be accused of not honoring their father; they were obeying him. In "Jubilees 34:1-9," 27, Livneh points out that Abram at age fourteen (Joseph's age in the present story) separated from the idolatry of his father and drove away the ravens (Jub 11:16-23).

14 For similar lists, see Wilhelm Bousset, "Die Testamente der zwölf Patriarchen," ZNW 1 (1900) 141-75, 187-209, here 203; Charles, Jubilees, 202; S. Klein, "Palästinisches im Jubiläenbuch," ZDPV 57 (1934) 7-27, here 9.

Jubilees	Testament of Judah	Midrash Wayyissa'u	Likely Name
Tafu (Latin: saffo)	ταφουε	תפוח	Tappuah
Ares	ασουρ (etc.)	חסר	Hazor[15]
Seragan	αρεταν	פרתן or סרטן	Pirathon
Selo	σιλωμ	שילה	Shiloh
Gaaz	γαας	געש	Gaash
Betoron	αχωρ	ארם	Beth-horon
Maanisakir	μαχηρ	מחנה שפיר	Mahaneh Sakir

Several of the places are mentioned in the HB and elsewhere:

Tappuah: Josh 16:8; 1 Macc 9:50 (located south of Shechem)

Hazor: Neh 11:33 (unless it is the more northerly Hazor mentioned in Josh 11:1-15 and elsewhere; the context favors the one near Shechem)[16]

Pirathon: Since the forms of the name in Jubilees and Midrash Wayyissa'u can be explained by a *peh/samek* confusion and the name פרתן appears in the latter (as does Pirathon, though it is the name of the king of Hazor),[17] the city is very likely the Pirathon mentioned in Judg 12:13-15 as the home and burial place of the judge Abdon located in "the land of Ephraim." So it too is in the same general area as the other cities in the list.

Shiloh: Judg 21:19
Gaash: Josh 24:30
Beth-horon: Josh 10:10
Mahaneh Sakir: cf. John 4:5-6.[18]

All of these places are within the general region of Shechem, and the kings of these relatively minor locales are heads of cities. The size of their combined armies is not stated in the account, but Jacob was able to muster six thousand men against them (v. 6).

The people led by the kings are "all who were living on this mountain, who were living in the forest in the land of Canaan." The reference to the forest leads to a passage in the book of Joshua in which the content if not the vocabulary of Gen 48:22 is reflected. In Josh 17:14 the tribe of Joseph, in whose area the places mentioned in Jub 34:4 are located, complained to Joshua about the land assigned to them: "Why have you given me one lot and one portion as an inheritance, since we are a numerous people, whom all along the LORD has blessed?" He tells them to "go up to the forest, and clear ground there for yourselves in the land of the Perizzites and the Rephaim, since the hill country [הר] of Ephraim is too narrow for you" (v. 15). When they answered that the mountainous area was insufficient, "Joshua said to the house of Joseph, to Ephraim and Manasseh, 'You are

---

15 Kugel recognizes correctly, as have others, that an older text of the Amorite war (and the one with Esau and his sons) existed before any of the surviving forms of it were written, but he thinks the older form may have been in Greek (*Walk through Jubilees*, 166; "Jubilees," 412). One piece of evidence is the spelling errors for city names, where, for example, חצור appears as חסר, and another is a resemblance of the fighting accounts in Midrash Wayyissa'u with ones in the Greek epic tradition (he does not give references). The argument from names, however, would be relevant only to the midrashic account, since the ones in Jubilees are transcribed from Greek spellings based on Hebrew originals, and the Testament of Judah, even if it rests on a Semitic original, is extant only in Greek. It is not easy to see how a name such as תפוח in the midrash arose from a Greek text.

16 For the interpretation of the name as Hazor, see Bousset, "Die Testamente der zwölf Patriarchen," 204; Charles, *Jubilees*, 202. Both, however, took it to be the northern Hazor of Joshua 11, a location that seems unlikely for this city. VanderKam identifies it with Adasa (*Textual*, 220-21), but that seems less convincing than Hazor.

17 See VanderKam, *Textual*, 221-22. Klein ("Palästinisches im Jubiläenbuch," 11-12) preferred to identify it with צרתן (see Josh 3:16).

18 For a detailed identification of the name, see VanderKam, *Textual*, 223-27. Both Bousset ("Die Testamente der zwölf Patriarchen," 203 n. 6) and Charles (*Jubilees*, 203) recognized that the name in the Ethiopic text consisted of two words—something that is explicit in Midrash Wayyissa'u. The second element *-sakir* appears in the midrash as the name of the king of מקנהי (line 26, variant: מחנה; this suggested to Bousset that Jubilees drew its information from a list of the names both of the kings and of their cities) and as part of the city's name: שפיר [variant: שכיר] מחנה (lines 46-48). Klein ("Palästinisches im Jubiläenbuch," 13) first recognized the Sychar of John 4:5 (see *m. Menaḥ.* 10:2) in this element.

indeed a numerous people, and have great power; you shall not have one lot only, but the hill country [הר] shall be yours, for though it is a forest, you shall clear it and possess it to its farthest borders; for you shall drive out the Canaanites, though they have chariots of iron, and though they are strong'" (17:17-18).[19] This passage, dealing with the same region, supplies, then, both features in the description of the area in Jub 34:4 (mountain, forest), speaks of driving out the local inhabitants, and echoes Gen 48:22.

■ 5 A parallel with Genesis 14[20] appears in v. 5, where Jacob receives the news about the ambush of his sons and theft of the animals. In Gen 14:13 an escapee from the conflict told Abram about the capture of his nephew Lot by the forces of four invading kings; ironically, at that time Abram was allied with Amorites (vv. 13, 24). The Hebrew fragment that preserves two words from v. 5 confirms that the messenger referred to "your [Jacob's] flocks" as the booty the Amorites had captured, not "their [the brothers'] flocks" as in all the Ethiopic manuscripts except 21 ("your flocks").

■ 6 Like his grandfather before him, Jacob marched forth at once with the males of his household in order to rescue the endangered family members.[21] Abram had no sons to join him but led 318 "trained men, born in his house" (Gen 14:14) to rescue his relative Lot. Jacob, who had three sons of military age (Benjamin was too young) at home with him, marched at the head of six thousand swordsmen. According to Jub 44:33 there were seventy members of Jacob's household when he went down to Egypt (wives, sons, grandsons). If so, he must have had a huge staff in his employ to be able to field an army of this size. The text refers to his servants and those of his father Isaac, so he drew soldiers from both households. Since servants of his were already present with the brothers in Shechem (v. 1), the six thousand in v. 6 should be in addition to them.

■ 7 The action during the battle and its aftermath are described as being done by Jacob (all the verbs are third masculine singular in form, except one).[22] The focus on him sharply separates the account in Jubilees from the versions in the other sources where Jacob's sons, primarily Judah, are active in the carnage along with their father. In those accounts Jacob is just one actor among many. The form of the story in Jubilees suggests that Jacob, as the military commander, received credit for the accomplishments much as Joshua was said to have conquered Canaan. Nothing is disclosed about the participation of his sons or the six thousand men who went with him apart from their role in the pursuit once the attackers fled the battleground, the "field of Shechem."[23] Six of the seven names that figured in v. 4 reappear in v. 7, where Jacob is said to have killed them (Beth-horon is not in this list). Here they are the names of individuals, very likely the kings of the Amorites—unless the writer meant to say he slaughtered the inhabitants of these places. The other versions of the story mention the names of kings, and they are not identical with the place-names.

As Livneh has shown, each of the three clauses in v. 7 in which Jacob is said to kill explains something in Gen 48:22: he kills opponents in the field of Shechem (the place), he kills with the edge of the sword (the means—

---

19 Livneh writes that "Jub. 34:4 is an evident allusion to Josh. 17:18" ("With My Sword," 194–95 n. 21). This is true, but the relations between Jub 34:1-9 and Josh 17:14-18 are more extensive, as she explains more fully in "*Jubilees* 34:1-9," 32-33.

20 There is an entire series of parallels between Genesis 14 and Jubilees 34. See below.

21 Livneh notes the family solidarity and refers to 20:2, where Abraham tells his sons and grandsons to band together against opponents ("With My Sword," 199). She also comments (p. 203) on Jacob as a "family man" in this passage, where he is both a caring son and solicitous father. Cf. also "*Jubilees* 34:1-9," 34-35.

22 See Livneh, "With My Sword," 205. She emphasizes that Jacob, who, according to 19:14, learned writing rather than warfare like his brother Esau, was also skilled at fighting when the occasion called for it.

23 In this respect Docherty ("Joseph the Patriarch," 209) goes beyond the evidence of Jubilees in writing that the story "serves the author as an early manifestation of Joseph's power, greatness and closeness to his father." He is close to his father, but where is his power? Livneh also thinks the writer makes this point by first presenting an "adult" Joseph and a "youthful warrior" in contrast to the way he enters the scene in the Bible ("*Jubilees* 34:1-9," 25-26). But note that in Gen 37:2 he is already shepherding his father's flocks with his brothers.

his sword is mentioned in Gen 48:22), and he kills the kings (the Amorites).[24]

■ **8-9** Once he has finished the account of how Jacob dispatched the kings (or their cities) with the blade of the sword, the writer concludes by supplying several elements that his version of the story partially shares with the others. Most of the ones in Jubilees have a counterpart in Midrash Wayyissa'u or the Testament of Judah or both, but the distinctive character of each text and the order in which they place the items emerge if one aligns them side by side (translations of the midrash by VanderKam).

Jubilees	Midrash Wayyissa'u	Testament of Judah
(8) (he) collected his flocks.	they restored to Jacob's sons all the flocks they had taken from them (63-64)	
He got control of them and imposed tribute on them so that they should give him as tribute one-fifth of their land's products.	and they gave them tribute (64)	
He built Robel and Tamnatares,	Jacob traveled to תמנה and Judah to ארבאל (65)	"And I built Thamna and my father Rambael" (7:9)[25]
(9) and returned safely. He made peace with them,	Then they made peace with them (62-63)	"and he made peace with them" (7:7)[26]
and they became his servants until the day that he and his sons went down to Egypt.		

The unique elements in Jubilees are Jacob's initiating the peace process, gaining control of either the flocks or the enemy, the tribute of one-fifth of the produce of the land, Jacob's safe return, his building both cities, and the servitude of the Amorites to Jacob until the descent into Egypt. The matter of having control over animals or people is a natural inference from Jacob's conquest but one not mentioned in the other two versions. Imposition of tribute is found in the three texts, but only Jubilees specifies the form it took: one-fifth of the land's produce (see the textual note). The fraction agrees with Joseph's edict in Gen 47:24-26, where he establishes the statute that Pharaoh should have one-fifth of the harvest.[27] In the Genesis passage, just before the notice about the statute the narrator reported that Joseph had enslaved the people of Egypt; once they were in that state he subjected them to the twenty-percent tax (vv. 21, 23). Servitude of an enemy until the descent to Egypt is one of the features shared by this story with the one in chaps. 37–38 (see 38:12-13).[28]

The two cities constructed at this time can be identified with a degree of certainty. The one named first in Jubilees—Robel—is probably Arbela, a city in Galilee noted in 1 Macc 9:2 (a placed where Bacchides pitched his camp), and the second is Timnath-heres, a site associated in Judg 2:9 with another name in the present list: "So they buried him [Joshua] within the bounds of his inheritance in Timnath-heres, in the hill country of Ephraim, north of Mount Gaash."[29] If Robel is Arbela, it produces a modest difficulty: it would be the only one of the cities not in the region of Shechem. Interestingly, Jacob builds the cities but does not move to them since

---

24 Livneh, "With My Sword," 191–92; "Jubilees 34:1-9," 37. The bow of Gen 48:22 will reappear in the battle with Esau and his sons (ibid.).
25 The order of the two cities is reversed in Jubilees in comparison with the sequence in both of the other texts.
26 Both Midrash Wayyissa'u and the Testament of Judah say that the enemy first sued for peace.
27 Livneh, "With My Sword," 197 n. 29; "Jubilees 34:1-9," 38.
28 See Livneh, "With My Sword," 206–7 (this fulfills the prediction in Gen 27:29 // Jub 26:23 that peoples would serve him); Kugel, *Walk through Jubilees*, 166.
29 See Josh 19:50; 24:30, where the second element of the name has the first and last consonants reversed (Timnath-serah). For identification of the two cities that Jacob built, see Charles, *Jubilees*, 203–4; VanderKam, *Textual*, 227. Bousset ("Die Testamente der zwölf Patriarchen," 204 n. 2) suggested that Robel was the Raphon of 1 Macc 5:37, but the forms of the city name in the three witnesses make the proposal unlikely. Also unlikely is Klein's thesis that עקרבת is meant ("Palästinisches im Jubiläenbuch,"15–16); the spellings of the name in the versions make this implausible, although it has the advantage of being a place nearer to Shechem.

he returns home to Hebron in safety. Presumably he still wants to care for his parents.[30]

Excursus: War with the Amorite Kings

As experts have noticed from the beginning of the modern study of Jubilees and as indicated in the commentary, the story in Jub 34:1-9 has analogs in several other texts.
1. Testament of Judah 3–7 (Greek)
2. Midrash Wayyissaʻu:[31] the composition contains three units
   a. War with the Sons of Nineveh
   b. War with the Amorite Kings
   c. War with Esau and his Sons
3. The Book of Jashar, the section וישלח 37–40
4. The Chronicles of Jerahmeel 36 (37 has the war with Esau and his sons).[32] This work contains the Book of Jashar and thus has the same story about the war.

Since only a few words of Jub 34:1-9 have survived in Hebrew and as texts 2, 3, and 4 are extant in Hebrew, they are at times helpful for recovering the original reading, for example, of names that so often become garbled in transmission.

While the versions in all of these texts deal with a war waged by Jacob and his sons against Amorite kings (sometimes called Canaanites) whose people in the end submitted to the patriarchal family with whom they subsequently lived in peace, they do not tell it in the same way. The following are areas of major differences primarily between Jubilees, on the one hand, and, on the other, Midrash Wayyissaʻu and the Testament of Judah, accounts that more nearly, though certainly not entirely, resemble each other.[33]

1. *The protagonist.* In Jubilees Jacob is the hero and his sons play subordinate roles. Naturally, the form of the account in Testament of Judah 3–7 has Judah as its lead character; there he tells the story to his children in autobiographical form. In Midrash Wayyissaʻu he is also the foremost actor in the succession of battles that make up the war (see below under #3). In Jubilees he is one of the three brothers who remain in Hebron with Jacob so they can tend to the elderly Isaac (v. 3; the five-year-old Benjamin also stayed home because he was too young to fight), and he is included in the group that goes with Jacob to fight after the other sons are attacked. In the descriptions of the fighting, only Jacob's exploits receive attention.

2. *The organization of the story.* The general arrangement of the accounts is different in Jubilees and the other two versions. The sequence in Jubilees offers no indication regarding the passage of time, whereas the other two versions do—chronology is the central structuring element in Midrash Wayyissaʻu. Perhaps in the form of the story underlying Midrash Wayyissaʻu and the Testament of Judah a six-day sequence ending in peace provided the organizing principle. It is present fully in the midrash: that day = day 1 (22, 30), second day (31), third day (42), fourth day (45), fifth day (49), and sixth day (61). The Testament of Judah provides some indication of a similar arrangement, though not all the specifics are present in the text: 5:1 refers to "The next day," and 6:3 says that the men of Makir attacked Judah and the others on "the fifth day," though no explicit references to days 1 through 4 precede the notice. 7:1 then mentions "the next day."[34] Perhaps as a function of the difference in organization, Jubilees presents the conflict as a single battle won by Jacob over the combined Amorite foes; the other two describe a series of battles against individual

---

30 Livneh, "*Jubilees* 34:1-9," 38–39.
31 Jellinek published the Hebrew text (*Bet ha-Midrasch*, 3:1–5). In his introduction he notes the parallel in Jubilees 34 and cites the entire text of the unit. The close relationship between the accounts in the midrash and Jubilees 34 and 37–38 gave Jellinek the opportunity to add comments about Jubilees, which he thought must have been written in Hebrew and was "eine essenische Tendenzschrift" directed against Pharisaic views about the calendar (ix–xiv; quotation from p. xi). More copies of the midrash were identified by Tamar Alexander and Yosef Dan and utilized for their edition "Complete *Midrash Va-yissaʻu.*" They located two manuscripts containing all three units (one in Hamburg and one in London) and five others with only the first unit (in full or in part). They use the London manuscript for the two parts that Jellinek had published.
32 Used here are Moses Gaster's introduction and translation in his *The Chronicles of Jerahmeel; or, The Hebrew Bible Historiale* (Prolegomenon by Haim Schwarzbaum; New York: Ktav, 1971; original ed., 1899).
33 The other two texts—the Book of Jashar and the Chronicles of Jerahmeel—will be left out of the comparison because the story in them is essentially the one in Midrash Wayyissaʻu.
34 Hollander and de Jonge, *Testaments*, 189. They add: "If we take into account geographical remarks and sentences clearly serving as conclusion we are still able to arrive at a number of seven episodes: 3,1-8; 4,1-3; 5,1-7; 6,1-2; 6,3-5; 7,1-3; 7,4-9."

kings, armies, and cities. Those accounts are more extended in time and geography, though the same place-names occur at some points in all three versions.

3. The roles of the brothers: While Jacob is the protagonist in Jubilees and the sons are merely mentioned, they, especially Judah, play a more prominent role in the other two versions, where Jacob is one of the combatants alongside them. In Midrash Wayyissa'u these are the characters with the line numbers and the total number of lines in which they figure:

Judah	4-19, 20, 22, 26-29, 53-61, 65	[32]
Levi	19, 35, 58-59	[4]
Jacob	20, 25-26, 55-57, 63, 65	[8]
Sons of Jacob	20-22, 22-25, 29-34, 36-53, 61-66	[37]
Naphtali	27-29, 35-36, 58	[6]
Gad	35	[1]
Simeon	35, 58-59	[3]
Reuben	35	[1]
Dan	35, 57	[2]
Issachar	35-36	[2]

The group "the sons of Jacob" appears most often, and in most of those references Judah is included. Among the brothers he figures far more often than any of the others, and he far outshines even his father. The sons not mentioned by name are Joseph and Benjamin with Asher (Zilpah's second son) and Zebulun (Leah's sixth son).

The references in the Testament of Judah are these:

Judah	3:1-6 (cf. v. 10); 4:1-2; 5:2; 6:1, 5; 7:2, 5-6, 9-11	[18]
Jacob	3:7 (cf. v. 9); 7:9	[3]
We/us (the sons)	3:8; 4:1, 3; 5:1, 3-7; 6:1-5; 7:1, 3-4, 7-8, 11	[20]
Gad	5:2	[1]
Reuben	5:2	[1]
Levi	5:2	[1]
Simeon	6:5	[1]
Dan	7:2, 6	[2]

Here the pattern is the same as in the midrash, where the brothers (in the we/us passages at least two of them are involved) are mentioned most frequently and Judah himself far more than any other (Judah is included in all the "we/us" references). Here only six brothers are named (the four oldest sons of Leah, Bilhah's first son Dan and Zilpah's first son Gad). Livneh has observed that Joseph appears as a combatant in neither Midrash Wayyissa'u or the Testament of Judah so that his military role (that is, he took part but without being named in the battle account) is unique to Jubilees.[35]

Jubilees tells a more restrained story that features Jacob and lacks much of the gory detail in the other accounts. Even though it agrees with the other two in reporting that the warring sides made peace in the end, Jubilees has Jacob impose it on his foes and exact tribute from them, while Midrash Wayyissa'u and Testament of Judah say the Amorites sued for peace and make no reference to servitude (the victors returned to the vanquished the goods they had captured from them).

The version of the story in Jubilees glorifies Jacob, who has vast holdings in the area of Shechem and who commanded six thousand fighting men. In this way it provides a more direct referent for Gen 48:22, which says that Jacob was the one who took a portion/Shechem from the Amorites with his sword and bow. The versions in the other two sources make it sound as if Judah was the one who conquered in this fashion.[36]

Excursus: Jubilees 34:1-9 and Hasmonean Sites

There is a venerable tradition of interpreting Jub 34:1-9 as reflecting places prominent in Maccabean battles with the Seleucids. A number of the city names in Jubilees recur in 1 Maccabees as it recounts those military struggles, leading several scholars to conclude that the resemblances were not accidental.

The initial hint about the topic came from Jellinek, who, in the introduction to his edition of Midrash Wayyissa'u, wrote that the midrash glorified Judah, the namesake of Judah the Maccabee.[37] Bousset, however, was the first to formulate a more detailed case for the position.[38] On his view, the story underlying the one in the various versions contained,

---

35 Livneh, "With My Sword," 200 n. 40.
36 It seems doubtful that Jubilees is sending a message about Joseph and the house of Joseph and their right to the land, as Livneh ("*Jubilees* 34:1-9," throughout) maintains. The message would be exceedingly subtle if it were there, as Joseph is mentioned only in v. 3 and as an unnamed part of a group in v. 6. Because of the area where the battle takes place, there are reminiscences of territory later held by the Joseph tribes, but that does not seem very important in the story.
37 Jellinek, *Bet Ha-Midrasch*, 3:ix.
38 Bousset, "Die Testamente der zwölf Patriarchen," 204–5.

in a confused way, reminiscences of great Maccabean battles. The facts of history have in this case been pressed into service to adorn the story. He noted that four of the city names in the story about the war with the Amorite kings corresponded with ones in the list of fortresses the Seleucid officer Bacchides set up in Judea (1 Macc 9:50). The four are Beth-horon, Tamnatha, Tephon = Tappuah, and Parathon. In addition to these overlaps, he pointed to a series of events in 1 Maccabees that resembled incidents in the form of the story in Midrash Wayyissa'u. So, for example, in 1 Macc 10:83-85 the Hasmonean Simon fought a Seleucid phalanx and defeated them. "They fled to Azotus and entered Beth-dagon, the temple of their idol, for safety. But Jonathan burned Azotus and the surrounding towns and plundered them; and the temple of Dagon, and those who had taken refuge in it, he burned with fire" (vv. 83-84). Bousset thought this sounded much like the way Midrash Wayyissa'u describes the defeat of Saretan, where two hundred died on the tower to which they had fled (see lines 31-39). He also compared 1 Macc 5:4-5, where Judah trapped the residents of Baean in towers and burned them to death.

These parallels led Bousset to conclude that the story of the war with the Amorite kings reflects Maccabean battles. Therefore, the story more than likely arose in the period of the Maccabees because at a later time the events of this golden age were forgotten. Charles spoke favorably of Bousset's view. When studying the date when Jubilees was written, he commented, along with a series of other arguments: "Again the Maccabean wars are adumbrated in the struggle of Jacob's sons with the Amorite kings in xxxiv.1-9. This is clearer in the completer narrative in Test. Judah 3-7. The cities Tappuah, Hazor, and Bethoron, which are mentioned here, are associated with notable victories and incidents in the Maccabean war."[39] In his notes to chap. 34 he wrote that the story "is probably here recast so as to call to mind some of the great victories of the Maccabees."[40]

In 1977 VanderKam defended the Bousset thesis in the sense that the story of the Amorite war is a "possible literary reflection of some of Judas' battles,"[41] especially the battle with Nicanor in 161 BCE (see 1 Macc 7:26-50). "That the present narrative may be based primarily upon the conflict with Nicanor can be deduced from the fact that nearly all of the cities over which the seven Amorite kings ruled are mentioned in the Maccabean sources either in connection with Judas' triumph over Nicanor or in the sequel to this account where they are noted in such a way that they may have played a part in the battle."[42] The nine cities (those of the seven kings, along with Arbela and Timnat-heres) as identified there[43] are north of Jerusalem, with several near Shechem and only one (Arbela) much farther north. "Six of the nine are mentioned in Maccabean sources, either in connection with Judas' victories in the north, or in 1 Mac. 9:50 . . . , where the cities which the Seleucids fortified after Judas' death are enumerated."[44] After discussing the evidence and possibilities, VanderKam concludes that this is only a possible explanation and not a very strong one.[45]

The Hasmonean approach advocated in *Textual* has aroused opposition in reviews[46] and particularly in two essays devoted to the topic of how to read Jubilees 34 and 37-38 (the battle with Esau and his sons). Jonathan Goldstein wondered why, if the author wished to reflect the reality behind a passage such as 1 Macc 9:50, he did not reproduce the entire list rather than just a few names from it.[47] Moreover, many of the place-names in question are familiar from the book of Joshua. He discusses the disputed identification of some of the city names in Jub 34:4, 7-8 (his explanation of Mahaneh Sakir would result in eight kings, not seven, and thus can hardly be correct), but whichever choice one makes about them his

---

39 Charles, *Jubilees*, lxii–lxiii.
40 Charles, *Jubilees*, 200. In comments regarding the individual cities he adduces references in 1 Maccabees for Tappuah, Aresa (Hazor), Beth-horon, Arbela, and Tamnatares (pp. 202–4). For other favorable though at times cautious reactions to this approach, see Martin, "Jubilés," 336; Berger, *Jubiläen*, 300; Wintermute, "Jubilees," 44; and Caquot, "Jubilés," 766–67. Klein accepted a Hasmonean interpretation of the passage but thought battles of John Hyrcanus were reflected in it, not those of Judah ("Palästinisches im Jubiläenbuch," 18–20). On his view, the writer of the story now present in Jubilees 34 was claiming that Hyrcanus's conquests were reasserting an ancient right to the territory won by Jacob and his sons.
41 VanderKam, *Textual*, 218. The arguments from Jub 34:2-9 are found on pp. 218–29.
42 Ibid., 219.
43 The only difference between VanderKam's lists in *Textual*, 227, and the present commentary is for the second city: it was there identified as Hadashah (Adasa, see pp. 220–21) but here as Hazor.
44 VanderKam, *Textual*, 228.
45 Ibid., 229.
46 An example is the review of *Textual* by G. W. E. Nickelsburg in *JAOS* 100 (1980) 83–84.
47 See Goldstein, "Date," esp. 82–86.

point is well taken: there are correspondences with Maccabean place-names (very few in his estimation) but more with locations in Joshua. Why would the ones in the Maccabean accounts be considered the more likely explanation for the toponyms in Jubilees? On Goldstein's view, someone probably added to the place-name Shechem sites mentioned in Joshua.

Robert Doran approached the problem from another angle. His thesis is that the account in Jubilees 34 (with 37-38 and also the apocalyptic survey in chap. 23) should be read as literature, not as reflections of Maccabean events. One should examine the functions these pericopes perform in Jubilees, not mine them for historical tidbits of information. Specifically regarding 34:1-9 he notes the close association in Jubilees between Abraham and Jacob and regards this passage as a case in point: Jacob in chap. 34 imitates his grandfather in chap. 13 (Genesis 14).[48]

> In the narrative of Abraham, after he settles at Hebron (Gen 13:18; Jub 13:22) comes the report of his pursuit and battle against five [sic] kings (Gen 14; Jub 13:22-29). After Jacob settles at Hebron at the house of Abraham comes the report of Jacob's pursuit and battle against seven Amorite kings (Jub 34:2-9). A similar structure underlies the two narratives.
> A. 1. Hero at home
>   2. Relation distant
> B. Attack against relation
> C. Message brought to hero
> D. Hero and household set out, defeat and pursue the enemies (This section missing at Jub 13:25.)
> E. Hero recovers lost possession[49]

This is another way in which the writer presents Jacob as Abraham's true son.

Doran has helpfully set forth the detailed parallels between the two accounts and tied them to an important theme in Jubilees. That is valuable, but it does not answer why the writer chose to mention the specific cities that he includes. In other words, the approach is beneficial but leaves some elements unexplained.

Among the negative responses to the thesis that battles of Judas lie behind the names of cities in the accounts of the Amorite war is a modified version of the Hasmonean interpretation. Doron Mendels finds that the toponyms do not fit the evidence for Judas's campaigns and proposes rather that they mirror the relations between John Hyrcanus and the Samaritans. He notes that the Samaritans lived in the traditional tribal regions of Ephraim and Manasseh (i.e., the Joseph tribes) west of the Jordan and proposes that "Hyrcanus acted against the Samaritans (in 129/8), conquered Shechem and destroyed Garizim, but he left the town of Samaria intact. As a consequence of this action, the Samaritans remained a regional political power, although a weak one. This is obviously reflected in 34:1-9, where the wars of John Hyrcanus with the Samaritans are transferred back into the war with the Emorite [sic] kings of Genesis 14 and 48:22, a popular topic in the second century B.C."[50] His view, besides implying an unlikely date of composition for the book, encounters the same problem as the attempt to relate the story to the time of Judas in that it does not explain the presence of all the city names.

The correspondences between place-names in Jub 34:4, 7-8 and 1 Maccabees (for any period it covers) are probably unintentional, and a more plausible motivation for the toponyms in Jubilees is their proximity to Shechem, with the writer's larger goal being to flesh out the brief givens of Gen 48:22. It could be the case that the story stakes an ancient claim to the area, but the author of Jubilees hardly needed one since Noah had given the entire land to their ancestor Shem just after the flood and God had already promised all of the territory to the patriarchs several times over.

10-19 Joseph and His Brothers (Gen 37:13-14, 17-18, 28, 36, 31, 32, 35)

After the war section with its slender basis in Genesis, the writer returns to the text of chap. 37 but summarizes the material and appends to it another unit absent from the first book in the Bible.

---

48 Several commentators have noted the parallels. See, e.g., Caquot, "Jubilés," 766; Werman, "Attitudes," 12-16 (and in *Jubilees*, 447-48), and especially Livneh, "With My Sword," 202-3; "Jubilees 34:1-9," 33-34. Livneh also advocates reading the text as a literary unit, though she does not entirely rule out some influence from the circumstances existing in the author's time (see "With My Sword," 209).
49 Doran, "Non-Dating," 3-4.
50 Mendels, *Land of Israel*, 70-72; quotation from p. 70.

■ 10 Joseph's Mission to His Brothers

The writer dates the next events to the year after the war with the Amorite kings, so that Joseph should now be fifteen years of age (he is seventeen in Gen 37:1). The base text is Gen 37:13-14, 17b: "And Israel said to Joseph, 'Are not your brothers pasturing the flock at Shechem? Come, I will send you to them.' He answered, 'Here I am.' So he said to him, 'Go, now, see if it is well with your brothers and with the flock; and bring word back to me.' So he sent him from the valley of Hebron. . . . So Joseph went after his brothers and found them at Dothan." The rather full text of Genesis—one that relates somewhat awkwardly to Gen 37:1, where Joseph works with his brothers[51]—becomes in Jubilees a brief report that Jacob sent Joseph from home to Shechem to check on his siblings' welfare and that he found them in Dothan. Jubilees also bypasses the verses about Joseph's losing his way and receiving assistance from an anonymous guide (Gen 37:15-17a).

■ 11 Their Harsh Treatment of Joseph

If v. 10 is distinguished by its brevity, v. 11 exceeds it in this regard. The unit in Gen 37:18-30 tells of the brothers' reaction to Joseph for whom they had earlier developed a strong dislike, their plans, counterplans, and eventual sale of him to Ishmaelites (or Midianites) who brought him to Egypt. Jubilees says only that they treacherously made a plan to kill him (from Gen 37:18b), but, after changing their minds, they sold him to Ishmaelites (37:28b) who carried him off to Egypt (37:28b). There is nothing about the role of Reuben, the pit into which they lowered Joseph, their meal, Judah's intervention, or the Midianite traders. In the space of one verse Joseph moves from being an important son in the land to a slave in Egypt. In Jubilees there is no motivation for the brothers' ill treatment of Joseph, who had fought with them against the Amorites just a few verses earlier. Why should the brothers want to execute Joseph? The reference to the brothers' change of mind summarizes much more material in Genesis. The puzzling variation between Ishmaelites and Midianites in Gen 37:25-28 is avoided by omitting the Midianites.[52] The writer also does this at the end of v. 11, where he reflects Gen 37:36:

Genesis 37:36	Jubilees 34:11 (end)
Meanwhile the Midianites[53] had sold him to Egypt to Potiphar,[55] one of Pharaoh's officials, the captain of the guard.	They [the Ishmaelites] brought him down[54] to Egypt and sold him to Potiphar, Pharaoh's eunuch, the chief cook,[56] and the priest of the city of Elew.[57]

The author not only introduces consistency into the narrative (only Ishmaelites are involved) but also, by adding to Gen 37:36 that he was the priest of On/Heliopolis, identifies Potiphar with "Potiphera, priest of On" in Gen 41:45, 50; 46:20, the father of Joseph's future wife Asenath. Identification of Potiphar and Potiphera is more widely attested in the interpretive tradition, including the LXX, which spells the names in the same way ($\pi\epsilon\nu\tau\epsilon\phi\rho\eta\varsigma$; see also *Gen. Rab.* 86:3).

12-19 Jacob's Grief and the Day of Atonement

The section rewrites Gen 37:31-35 (almost entirely omitting vv. 33-34) in a striking way.

■ **12** It begins by citing Gen 37:31-32a with a few variations.

---

51   In modern scholarship on Genesis, 37:1-2 is understood to be from P and the following material from J and E (or JE); see Skinner, *Genesis*, 442–43. Since Jubilees does not reproduce Gen 37:2, it lacks the possible implication that the brothers in it are only the sons of Bilhah and Zilpah.

52   Or, as Werman proposes, the writer identified the Ishmaelites and Midianites (*Jubilees*, 448). Midian was a son of Abraham and Keturah (Gen 25:2 // Jub 19:12), and Keturah's sons and Ishmael's family mixed together and were named Arabs and Ishmaelites (Jub 20:11-13).

53   The name is spelled differently in Gen 37:28 and 36.

54   The verb 'awradewwo ("they brought him down") corresponds with LXX $\kappa\alpha\tau\eta\gamma o\nu$ $\tau o\nu$ $\iota\omega\sigma\eta\phi$, with a pronoun replacing the name.

55   In Gen 39:1, Potiphar bought him from Ishmaelites who had transported Joseph to Egypt.

56   The rendering "the chief cook" is found in the LXX and dependent translations in Gen 37:36; 39:1; and in Josephus, *Ant.* 2.39. See VanderKam, *Jubilees* 2:228.

57   The text reflects $\eta\lambda\iota o\upsilon$ $\pi o\lambda\epsilon\omega\varsigma$ in Gen 41:45, 50. Jubilees translates the word for "city" but transliterates its name (VanderKam, *Jubilees* 2:228).

Genesis 37:31-32a	Jubilees 34:12
Then they took Joseph's robe, slaughtered a goat, and dipped the robe in the blood.	Jacob's sons slaughtered a he-goat, stained Joseph's clothing by dipping[58] it in its blood,
They had the long robe with sleeves taken to their father	and sent (it) to their father Jacob
	on the tenth of the seventh month.

The differing immediate contexts (Genesis is speaking about the brothers, but Jubilees has just noted that Potiphar bought Joseph from the Ishmaelites) required that the sons of Jacob be identified as the subject of the initial verb. The writer of Jubilees, who has not referred to Joseph's special coat (see Gen 37:3), speaks generally of his clothing where Genesis reports that it was "the long robe with sleeves" (the NRSV's interpretation of the difficult כתנת פסים) that the brothers dipped in the goat's blood. The brothers wanted to leave no doubt in Jacob's mind about whose garment was blood-stained; in Jubilees he has to recognize less distinctive garb. The most noticeable difference between Genesis and Jubilees is, of course, the timing of the event. Genesis does not say when it happened, but Jubilees assigns it to the date on which Leviticus and Numbers place the Day of Atonement. The major clue suggesting the connection was the slaughtering of a goat and manipulating its blood—key events in the solemn day as described in Leviticus 16 (see vv. 9, 15, 19).

■ 13 Verses 13-17 relate to Gen 37:32b-35 but, in presenting Jacob's response to the news, they modify the base text extensively and borrow only a few phrases from it. The author supplies no verbal report from the brothers to their father nor of course a line about recognizing the unusual coat he had given his favorite son (Gen 37:32b-33a). The first words taken from Genesis are that he mourned (Gen 37:34: "mourned for his son many days") and thought a wild animal had eaten Joseph (37:33: "A wild animal has devoured him; Joseph is without doubt torn to pieces"). Jacob's mourning in v. 13 is set in a temporal framework and expanded: Jacob "mourned all that night because they had brought it to him in the evening. He became feverish through mourning his death and said that a wild animal had eaten Joseph. That day all the people of his household mourned with him. They continued to be distressed and to mourn with him all that day." Besides the attention to Jacob's emotions, several reminders of the legislation for the Day of Atonement populate the verse.

Evening. Leviticus 23:32: "It shall be to you a sabbath of complete rest, and you shall deny yourselves; on the ninth day of the month at evening, from evening to evening you shall keep your sabbath."[59]

Distressed. The causative of *ḥamama* is the verb used to render forms of ענה in Lev 16:29, 31; 23:29, 32; Num 29:7. Leslau lists as meanings for the causative: bring suffering, inflict pain, afflict with illness, harm, grieve, make sorrowful, torment, distress. The Ethiopic text actually uses the G-stem of the verb, meaning "be in pain, suffer illness, be ill, have labor pains, be afflicted, suffer distress."[60] The distress the household of Jacob experiences along with him (the brothers should be included in "his household") seems related to mourning or grieving regarding what has taken place.

All that day. The phrase mirrors the language of Lev 23:29: "For anyone who does not practice self-denial during that entire day shall be cut off from the people"; and Lev 23:32 cited above ("from evening to evening").

■ 14 At this point the writer takes up Gen 37:35, skipping over almost all of v. 34, where Jacob's mourning rites are pictured: "Then Jacob tore his garments, and put sackcloth on his loins, and mourned for his son many days" (for "many days," see v. 17 below).[61]

---

58 For this meaning of *ṣanqaqa*, see Leslau, *Concise Dictionary*, 228: "pollute, contaminate or stain by dipping." The LXX's ἐμόλυναν has the same sense.

59 For debates the passage has engendered regarding when the day began, see Milgrom, *Leviticus*, 3:2025-27. In 34:12-19, Jubilees speaks only of the tenth day in the seventh month, not mentioning the ninth, as the day runs from evening to evening in it.

60 Leslau, *Concise Dictionary*, 15.

61 His feverish grief in v. 13 appears to replace the other outward signs of mourning in Genesis—tearing clothes and wearing sackcloth.

Genesis 37:35	Jubilees 34:14
All his sons and all his daughters sought to comfort him; but he refused to be comforted, ...	His sons and daughter set about consoling him,[62] but he was inconsolable for his son.

The author makes the obvious correction of the plural "daughters" in Genesis, since Jacob had just one (*Tg. Ps.-J.* Gen 37:35 has "all *his sons' wives*");[63] perhaps he left out "all" in recognition of the fact that only eleven sons mourned with him, not Joseph. Genesis says that Jacob refused to be comforted, but in Jubilees he simply was not comforted.

■ **15-16** These verses explain that Joseph's "death" was not the only catastrophe to strike Jacob's family at that time. Genesis, of course, mentions Bilhah on several occasions as one of Jacob's wives and the one Reuben raped (35:22); Dinah is named in the lists of Jacob's children and she too was raped (Genesis 34). But the book does not record when either of them died. In fact, it mentions the deaths of none of the women in Jacob's family—Rebekah, Leah, Bilhah, Zilpah, and Dinah—apart from Rachel. Jubilees claims that both Bilhah and Dinah, the two victims of male violence, died in the very month that Jacob received the report about Joseph's fate. These deaths only intensified the level of grief for Jacob and his household at that fateful time.

The details that the writer adds regarding Bilhah and Dinah convey a message worth examining. Bilhah, Rachel's maid, perhaps felt a special bond with Joseph, Rachel's first son. Though all the people in Jacob's household mourned for Joseph, only Bilhah, other than Jacob himself, is identified by name as grieving for him. Moreover, the writer may imply that she died on the day the news arrived (note "That day" in vv. 13 and 15), although the writer does not actually say her death occurred on the very day the terrible news came. It also turns out that she was not living where Jacob lived. Jacob was in Hebron, but she lived in *qafrātēfā*.[64] Exactly which Hebrew name these letters transcribe is uncertain. Littmann identified it as Kephirat Ephraim—כפירת אפרים[65] (see כפירה in Ezra 2:25 = Neh 7:29; and הכפירה in Josh 9:17; 18:26), with the first part of the name perhaps representing a construct form of כפירה. This could be significant because it would allow the author to use a name that would remind the reader of the occasion—the Day of Atonement.[66] Yet the second part of the name should be אפרתה. Charles suggested possibly Eder of Ephrath (Jub 33:1) but more likely Kabratan in 32:32 (see the commentary there).[67] Charles's proposal of Kabratan has the advantage that it was the place where Rachel died. Her burial in Ephrathah should have been near it, and Bilhah was buried "opposite Rachel's grave." No details are added regarding the death of Dinah except that it occurred "after Joseph had perished" but in the same month. The two women were accorded the honor of burial "opposite Rachel's grave." This would be understandable for Bilhah, given her relationship with Rachel; why Dinah should be buried in this place away from the ancestral tomb is not stated. More importantly, the writer of Jubilees once more shows greater interest than Genesis in the lives and deaths of women (see also the wives' names in v. 20).[68] The deaths of these two women, both of whom were childless after suffering defilement,

---

62 Both texts read literally: "arose to comfort/console him." The LXX and dependent translations have "gathered to comfort him."

63 *Genesis Rabbah* 84:21: "R. Judah said: The tribal ancestors married their sisters [see 82:8]; hence it is written, AND ALL HIS SONS AND ALL HIS DAUGHTERS ROSE UP, etc. R. Nehemiah said: Their wives were Canaanitish women. Now according to this view of R. Nehemiah, [how can you say], ALL HIS DAUGHTERS? How many daughters then did he have? One, and would that he had not known her! But the fact is that one does not refrain from calling his son-in-law, son, and his daughter-in-law, daughter." Though Jubilees corrects here to the singular, the fact that chap. 34 ends with a full list of Jacob's daughters-in-law may suggest that the writer also knew of this interpretation of "daughters" in Gen 37:35 (so Halpern-Amaru, *Empowerment*, 117).

64 As noted in the commentary on 33:9, separation from a husband after a concubine-wife was defiled is one of the parallels between the stories about Reuben–Bilhah and David and his ten concubines (Halpern-Amaru, *Empowerment*, 109).

65 Littmann, "Jubiläen," 98 n. i.

66 VanderKam, *Jubilees* 2:229.

67 Charles, *Jubilees*, 205.

68 Endres, *Biblical Interpretation*, 172. Cf. Halpern-Amaru, *Empowerment*, 127.

also entail that no contamination entered the family of Jacob through them.[69]

■ **17** Genesis 37:34 says that Jacob mourned for Joseph "many days." Jubilees interpreted the indefinite expression to mean "one year." The writer follows with a rewriting of the middle part of v. 35.

Genesis 37:35	Jubilees 34:17
. . . but he refused to be comforted, and said, "No, I shall go down to Sheol to my son, mourning."	. . . and was not comforted but said, "May I go down to the grave mourning for my son."

The word *Sheol* the writer interprets as meaning "grave," so that Jacob does not anticipate a journey to a place called Sheol but only to his tomb. He uses "Sheol" elsewhere as a designation for a location where sinners receive condemnation (7:29, for those who shed or eat blood; 22:22, for those who worship idols; 24:31, for the Philistines); such a place would hardly be one to which Jacob wishes to descend, so "grave" served as a more appropriate substitute. Also, Jacob does not say he will go down to his son because that language from Gen 37:35 does not fit his use of "grave" rather than "Sheol."[70] He would hardly be saying that Joseph was in his father's grave.

■ **18-19** Having described the remarkably cruel deeds of the brothers and the intense grief brought on first by the implied death of Joseph and then intensified by two actual deaths in the family, the author turns to the subject about which he has hinted several times in vv. 12-17—the Day of Atonement. He does not say that the holiday is inscribed on the heavenly tablets, but he uses a verb that he characteristically employs in places where he mentions them—ordained (*tašar'a[t]*)—in both v. 18 and v. 19. This occasion too is ordained for the Israelites. The commandments given in vv. 18-19 reproduce ones found primarily in Leviticus 16, the fullest scriptural description of the Day of Atonement.

The Israelites are to be distressed (*yeḥmamu*). See v. 13 above and the references there (e.g., Lev 16:29: תענו את נפשתיכם).

The tenth of the seventh month. Lev 16:29; 23:27; Num 29:7. It is the day when Jacob received the report that made him grieve for Joseph.

To make atonement for themselves. Aaron makes atonement for himself, his household, and all Israel (Lev 16:6, 11, 16-17, 20, 24, 30, 32-34; 23:28). Note 16:30: "For on this day atonement shall be made for you."

With a kid/goat. The ritual in Leviticus 16 calls for two goats. The one on which the lot for the Lord falls Aaron slaughters as a sin offering for the people (16:9, 15). This is, of course, the point of contact with the story about Joseph's brothers. Aaron sprinkles the blood of the goat inside the curtain of the sanctuary, whereas the brothers soaked Joseph's clothing in it.[71] This is the only place in which the Day of Atonement prescriptions in Jubilees have a connection with the temple ritual—the Israelites are to make atonement through the goat that is sacrificed and whose blood is sprinkled in the temple.[72]

Once a year (in vv. 18 and 19). The note seems redundant if the Day of Atonement is to be marked on the tenth day of the seventh month, but it appears in Lev 16:34: "This shall be an everlasting statute for you, to make atonement for the people of Israel once in the year for all their sins." There it concludes the section in the chapter prescribing that the ceremony was to occur every year, not just once or only during Aaron's time—or even several times in the year. For the phrase, see Jub 6:17, 20, 22, where it pertains to the Festival of Weeks, another one-day occasion.

For their sins. Leviticus 16 provides the background for this statement in several places. The goat for the Lord became a sin offering for the people, and in v. 16 Aaron makes atonement with its blood "for the sanctuary, because of the uncleannesses of the people of Israel, and because of their transgressions, all their sins." In v. 21 Aaron places his hands on the goat for Azazel and confesses "over it all the iniquities of the people of Israel, and all their transgressions, all their sins" (cf. v. 22). The list in Jub 34:19 ("their sins, all their transgressions, and

---

69 For Dinah, see Werman, *Jubilees*, 450.
70 Ethiopic Gen 37:35 also has Jacob say he will go down to the grave but it reproduces "to my son." The LXX renders Sheol with Hades.
71 Their handling of blood can scarcely have pleased the author of Jubilees, who provides such careful instructions for how it is to be treated—including blood on clothing (21:17). On this, see Dorman, "'Commit Injustice,'" 57-60.
72 Werman, in Werman and Shemesh, *Revealing*, 356.

all their errors") clearly reproduces the one in Lev 16:21. The focus on their sins relates to what the brothers had done: they had sinned in their treatment of Joseph and of their father, and the Day of Atonement was instituted to remove the guilt of wrongdoing.

To be saddened on it for their sins (see the comment on "For their sins" in v. 18 above). Something distinctive about Jubilees' conception of the Day of Atonement comes to expression here. The solemn festival marked the time when the brothers made their father extremely sad, and the entire household mourned with him. As a consequence, the Israelites were to be sad on it for their sins. Their sadness is supposed to mirror that of Jacob, but if the pattern were to hold, it should be the brothers, the sinners, who are remorseful for what they had done. For this reason, it is not unreasonable to think that, in the author's imagination, the brothers were already sad about their transgressions,[73] though their sadness did not make them tell Jacob the truth or inspire an effort by them to obtain Joseph's release.

Purify themselves [yānṣeḥu res'omu] *on this day once a year*. The purpose of atonement is to cleanse Israel from the sins committed that year. The expression draws on Lev 16:30: "For on this day atonement shall be made for you, to cleanse you; from all your sins you shall be clean before the LORD."[74]

Chapter 34:12-19 is the second unit in which the writer of Jubilees treats the Day of Atonement but the first time he calls it by its name and deals with its origin. In 5:17-18, after the angel told Moses about God's justice, he adds:

> Regarding the Israelites it has been written and ordained: "If they turn to him in the right way, he will forgive all their wickedness and will pardon all their sins." It has been written and ordained that he will have mercy on all who turn from all their errors once each year.

Both passages teach that the Day of Atonement is for the Israelites, and both emphasize sins and divine pardon for those who demonstrate the proper attitude toward the wrongs they have done. Jubilees 5:18-19 uses the language of appropriate "turning" from errors, while 34:18-19 speaks of sadness or distress about them.[75]

This is the place to comment on Kugel's argument that the presentations of the Day of Atonement in chaps. 5 and 34 come from his interpolator and the author respectively.[76] The evidence that they do not come from the same hand, apart from mention of the heavenly tablets in 5:13, is that there are supposedly two different etiologies and two differing explanations for the solemn occasion. According to 5:13-18 (all from the interpolator), it is a day for Israel to turn from sins in the proper way so that God will forgive them, whereas according to 34:15-19 (from the author) it is a day for Israel to be sad for their sins. There clearly are not two etiologies for the day: chap. 5 mentions the future institution of the Day

---

73 Werman, in Werman and Shemesh, *Revealing*, 357; *Jubilees*, 450.

74 For the two verbs translated "cleanse" and "be clean" Eth. Lev 16:30 uses forms of the verb Jubilees employs here: *yānṣeḥkemu* and *tenaṣṣeḥu*. Werman explains at some length that in Jubilees and the Qumran texts the focus shifts from the sanctuary to the individual (*Jubilees*, 448–50). While that seems right, Leviticus 16 does provide some support for the attention given to the sins of each Israelite. Moreover, as Dorman has commented, the setting of Jubilees in patriarchal times before there was a sanctuary contributes to how the day is described ("Commit Injustice," 56–57).

75 For related texts from Qumran, see Baumgarten, "Yom Kippur in the Qumran Scrolls and Second Temple Sources," *DSD* 6 (1999) 184–91, here 185–89. He notes the occurrences of יום התענית (CD vi:19), מועד תענית (e.g., 4Q508 2 3), and the like. Baumgarten thinks that for the Qumran texts, as for Jubilees, it is "a day of mourning and affliction" (p. 191), a conception of it that contrasts in some ways with the Pharisaic-rabbinic view in which there is both fasting and "the joy of moral purification" (ibid.).

76 Kugel, "Interpolations," 230–33; *Walk through Jubilees*, 56 and 167; "Jubilees," 414 It is not easy to understand how Kugel can write about 34:18-19: "There, the Day of Atonement has quite a different character: it is a day of mourning, but repentance plays no part in it" (*Walk through* Jubilees, 56). Do being distressed for their sins (v. 18) and being saddened for their sins so that they may purify themselves (v. 19) really have nothing to do with repentance?

of Atonement (note, it is for the Israelites, not all the post-flood generations) and the role of repentance; chap. 34 speaks about the origin of the day and remorse for wrongdoings. The example of the two passages regarding the Day of Atonement nicely illustrates how Kugel's telltale marker of an interpolator does not work. The expression "the heavenly tablets" appears in 5:13 but not in 34:12-19; nevertheless, chap. 34 uses "ordained," one of the standard verbs in heavenly tablet references: "For this reason, it has been ordained regarding the Israelites" (v. 18); and "this day has been ordained" (v. 19).[77] The writer speaks about the Day of Atonement twice and does so in a consistent fashion. There is no plausible evidence for an interpolator in 5:13-18, which, like 34:12-19, is from the author of the book.

20-21 The Wives of Jacob's Sons

The final section in the chapter offers a full roster of the women whom the sons of Jacob married. Genesis supplies no such list, though it mentions the spouses of Judah (Gen 38:2: בת שוע, Bath-shua)[78] and Joseph (Gen 41:45, 50; 46:20: Asenath) and refers, though not by name, to the Canaanite wife of Simeon (46:10; also Exod 6:15). Since Genesis contains an extended enumeration of the children fathered by Jacob's sons (46:8-27), the writer knows they were married (see the reference to "the wives of his sons" in 46:26). Although even a composition like the Testaments of the Twelve Patriarchs supplies only one more name beyond those Genesis records (Levi's wife Melcha), the author of Jubilees was deeply interested in the identity of all of them because of his great concern with the purity of the chosen line—a purity requiring qualified mothers. The sons of Jacob, the ancestors of the twelve tribes of Israel, had to marry acceptable women to ensure the genealogical purity of their descendants. It is no surprise, therefore, that the writer of Jubilees fashioned a complete list and took pains to explain that all of the wives were from appropriate ethnic backgrounds.

■ 20 The author says that the marriages occurred after the "death" of Joseph (he has referred to his "perishing" several times [vv. 13, 15 (twice)]). Genesis too says nothing about any marriages in the family before this time; the first notice about one (Judah's) will come in chap. 38, the chapter following the one in which the brothers sell Joseph. The names of the wives in the Ethiopic text and the Syriac list[79] are these:

Jacob's Son	Wives in 34:20-21	Syriac List
Reuben	Oda	Ada
Simeon	Adebaa the Canaanitess	Ya'aka'a the Canaanitess
Levi	Melcha (of Aram)	Malka (of Aram)[80]
Judah	Betasuel the Canaanitess	Bath-shua the Canaanitess
Issachar	Hezaqa	Azaqa
Zebulun	[Neeman][81]	Ednay
Dan	Egla	Tob-hagla
Naphtali	Rasu'u (of Mesopotamia)	Rusha (of Bet-naharin)
Gad	Maka	Ma'aqa
Asher	Iyona	Yona
Joseph	Asenath the Egyptian	Asnat
Benjamin	Iyaska	Asamana

Even the few names in Genesis presented problems for the author in that Judah, the ancestor of the kings, married a Canaanite woman in utter violation of Abraham's instructions to his children (Jub 20:4) and specifically to Jacob (22:21-22), Rebekah's commands to Jacob (25:1, 3), Jacob's assurances to his mother (25:4-9), his parents' orders (27:8-10), and the emphatic lesson of the Shechem–Dinah incident (chap. 30). According to Gen 38:12 Judah's wife died but not before bearing three sons.[82] This could have infused Judah's entire line with

---

77 Cf. Endres, *Biblical Interpretation*, 172–73.

78 This is apparently not her name in Gen 38:2, 12, where she is "the daughter of a certain Canaanite whose name was Shua" (v. 2) "Shua's daughter" (v. 12), but in 1 Chr 2:3 she is "the Canaanite woman Bath-shua." Cf. Jub 41:2. She is βησσουε in T. Jud. 8:2; 10:6; 13:3; 16:4; 17:1

79 The text offers just the consonants of the names; vowels are added here for the purpose of comparing them with the Ethiopic forms.

80 She is μελχα in T. Levi 11:1.

81 See the textual note for the absence of a name in the older Ethiopic copies. None of them has a name resembling *Ednay* in the Syriac list, but 42 47 48 read *Neeman*, while 39 and 58 have *Aamen/Amin*.

82 Werman believes the author located the list here to show how Judah could have mature sons by the time of the action in Genesis 38 // Jubilees 41 (*Jubilees*, 450).

contamination, so it was convenient for the author of Jubilees that Genesis 38, despite the other difficulties it raised (see the retelling in Jubilees 41), offered the assurance than none of the three sons of Judah and Bath-shua had any children (38:6-11).

■ **21** So Genesis—mercifully—allowed Bath-shua to be deleted from the list, but her absence left one other Canaanitess on it—Simeon's wife Adebaa. Surely Simeon should have known better after his experience at Shechem and its implications. It has plausibly been suggested that his bad decision was the factor that disqualified him from the priesthood—despite his zeal at Shechem—so that the office devolved on his younger brother Levi.[83] Genesis offered no help in erasing Adebaa, so the writer of Jubilees took on the task. He attributes a change of heart to Simeon—literally a turning from his previous action, the same sort of turning mentioned in Jub 5:17-18 when addressing what Israelites were to do regarding their sins on the Day of Atonement (the same verb is used in both places).[84] The author says that he took a wife from Mesopotamia as his brothers had done. The text does not claim that Simeon divorced Adebaa: that Simeon took another wife could mean that he now had two wives or that he replaced the first with the other one.[85]

The brothers Simeon imitated by taking a bride from Mesopotamia must be Levi and Naphtali. Levi married Melcha, "one of the daughters of Aram—one of the descendants of Terah's sons." Aram is a son of Kemuel, a son of Abraham's brother Nahor (Gen 23:20-21) who lived in Aram-naharaim (Gen 24:10). In the Aramaic Levi Document, Levi took a wife "from the family of Abraham, my father, Milka, daughter of Bethuel, son of Laban, my mother's brother" (11:1). Something is strange about this genealogical statement in comparison with the data in Genesis, where Bethuel, whose mother is named Milcah, is the father of Laban, the brother of Levi's grandmother Rebekah. However the confusion is to be explained,[86] the place of Levi's wife Melcha in the family of Abraham is secure,[87] though she came from a different branch of Nahor's family than Rebekah, Leah, and Rachel had. Naphtali's wife is said to be from Mesopotamia, though she is not linked directly to Terah's family;[88] perhaps this is implied. At any rate, there seems to have been no problem with marrying someone from Mesopotamia as Isaac and Jacob had done; it was the Canaanites against whom all the warnings had been issued.[89]

Asenath, Joseph's wife, is identified as an Egyptian; she is never actually given this gentilic in Genesis—she is always called "daughter of Potiphera, priest of On" (Gen 41:45, 50; 46:20)—but it is obviously what the text entails. The writer of Jubilees gives no indication that marrying a woman from Egypt was forbidden, so he makes no objection to the marriage of Abram with Hagar and Joseph with Asenath.[90] Again, his concern is that no one of the tribal ancestors should marry a Canaanite woman. After Simeon came to his senses, no Canaanitess remained on the list.

---

83   Halpern-Amaru, *Empowerment*, 96.
84   Charles translated "And Simeon repented."
85   As Halpern-Amaru points out, in Gen 46:10, where the six sons of Simeon are named, only the last one, Saul, is said to be a son of the Canaanite woman (*Empowerment*, 120). This seems to imply that the other five had a different mother.
86   See Drawnel, *Aramaic Wisdom Text*, 304-5. He suggests that the writer, to find a woman of appropriate age for Levi to marry from the clan of Abraham still in Haran, assumed the practice of papponymy and thus created the appropriate number of generations: Bethuel was Laban's father, and Laban had a son named Bethuel (Genesis does not name Laban's sons) who would have been Leah's brother; this Bethuel was the father of Levi's wife Milka.
87   Halpern-Amaru, *Empowerment*, 118.
88   The Testament of Naphtali in the Testaments of the Twelve Patriarchs does not name his wife. The concern there is with establishing the genealogy of Bilhah, his mother (1:6-12). Halpern-Amaru wonders whether something of the prominence Naphtali enjoys elsewhere (e.g., 4Q215 and the Hebrew Testament of Naphtali) is suggested here by the notation regarding his wife (*Empowerment*, 118-19).
89   Cf. Werman, "Attitude," 278.
90   Werman ("Attitude," 280-93) surveys the picture of Egypt in Jubilees and finds a softening in it of the anti-Egyptian sentiment in places in Genesis-Exodus (e.g., in 10:30 Mizraim [= Egypt] criticizes Canaan for stealing the land, leaving the curse of Ham on Canaan, not on all Ham's sons), though certainly not a completely positive view of the land and its inhabitants. Cf. Halpern-Amaru, *Empowerment*, 121-22.

35

The Last Instructions and Death of Rebekah

1/ During the first year of the first week in the forty-fifth jubilee [2157], Rebekah summoned her son Jacob and ordered him regarding his father and[a] brother that he[b] was to honor them throughout Jacob's[b] entire lifetime. 2/ Jacob said, "I will do everything just as[a] you ordered me because this matter will be something honorable and great for me; it will be a righteous act for me before the Lord that I should honor them. 3/ You, mother,[a] know[b] everything I have done and all my thoughts from the day I was born until today—that at all times I think[c] of doing good[d] for all. 4/ How shall I not do what[a] you have ordered me—that I should honor[b] my father and brother?[c] 5/ Tell me,[a] mother, what impropriety you have noticed in me and I will certainly turn away[b] from it and will experience[c] mercy."[d] 6/ She[a] said to him, "My son, throughout my entire lifetime[b] I have noticed no improper act in you but only proper one(s). However, I will tell you the truth,[c] my son: I will die during this year and will not make it alive[d] through this year because I have seen the day of my death in a dream[e]—that I will not live more than 155[f] years. Now[g] I have completed my entire[h] lifetime that I am to live."[i] 7/ Jacob laughed at what his mother was saying because his mother said to him that she would die,[a] but she was sitting in front of him in possession of her strength. She had lost none of her strength because she could come and go;[b] she could see[c] and her teeth were strong. No sickness[d] had touched[e] her throughout her entire lifetime.[f] 8/ Jacob said to her, "Mother,[a] I would be fortunate if my lifetime approached your lifetime[b] and (if) my strength would remain with me in the way your strength has. You are not going to die but rather have jokingly spoken idle nonsense with me about your death."[c]

9/ She[a] went in to Isaac and said to him, "I am making one request of you: make Esau swear[b] that he will not harm Jacob[c] and not pursue him in hatred.[d] For you know the inclination of Esau—that he has been malicious since his youth and[e] that he is devoid of virtue because he wishes to kill him[f] after your[g] death. 10/ You know everything[a] that he has done[b] from the day his brother Jacob went[c] to Haran until today—that he has wholeheartedly abandoned us. He has treated us badly; he has led away[d] your flocks and has taken all your possessions away from you by force.[e] 11/ When we would ask him in a pleading way[a] for what belongs to us, he would again do something treacherous[b] like someone[c] who was being charitable to us. 12/ He is embittered toward you[a] due to the fact that you blessed your perfect and true son Jacob since he has virtue only, no evil. From the time he came from Haran until today[b] he has not deprived us of anything but[c] he always brings us everything in its season. He is wholeheartedly happy when we accept (anything) from him, and he blesses us. He has not separated from us from the day he came from Haran until today. He has continually been living with us at home[d] (all the while) honoring us." 13/ Isaac said to her,[a] "I, too, know[b] and see the actions[c] of Jacob who is with us—that he wholeheartedly honors us and does our wishes.[d] At first I did love Esau much more[e] than Jacob, after he was born;[f] but now I love Jacob more than Esau because he has done so many bad things and lacks (the ability to do) what is right. For the entire way he acts is (characterized by) violence and wickedness and there is no[g] justice about him. 14/ Now my mind is disturbed about[a] his actions. Neither he nor his descendants are to be saved because they will be destroyed from the earth and uprooted from beneath the sky. For he has abandoned[b] the God of Abraham and has gone after the impurity of the women and after the error of the women.[c] 15/ You are saying[a] to me that I should make him[b] swear not to kill his brother[c] Jacob. If he does swear, he will not persevere[d] and will not do what is virtuous but rather what is evil. 16/ If he wishes to kill his brother[a] Jacob, he will be handed over[b] to Jacob and will not escape[c] from his control but will fall[d] into his control. 17/ Now you are not to be afraid[a] for Jacob because Jacob's guardian is greater and more powerful, glorious, and praiseworthy than Esau's guardian.[b] For like dust befor[e   ] all the guardians of Esau

936

Jubilees 35

before the God of [J]acob [my perfect and de]ar s[on.] But I lo[ve   do]es our wishes [   ] my sister in peace."

18/ Then Rebekah sent and summoned Esau. When he had come to her, she said to him: "I have a request that[a] I will make of you, my son; say[b] that you will do it,[c] my son." 19/ He said,[a] "I will do anything[b] you tell me;[c] I will not refuse your request." 20/ She said to him: "I ask of you that on the day I die you bring me and bury me near your father's mother Sarah; and that you and Jacob love one another,[a] and that the one not desire harm for his brother[b] but only[c] love for one another. Then you will be prosperous, my sons, and be honored[d] on[e] the earth. Your enemy will not be happy over you. You will become a blessing and an object of kindness in the view of all who love you."[f] 21/ He said,[a] "I will do everything that you say to me. I will bury you on the day of your death near my father's mother Sarah as you have desired that her bones be near[b] your bones. 22/ My brother Jacob I will love more[a] than all humanity. I have no brother on[b] the entire earth but him alone. This is no great thing for me if I love him because he is my brother. We were conceived together in your belly and we emerged together from your *womb*.[c] If I do not love my brother, whom shall I love? 23/ I myself[a] ask of you that you instruct Jacob about me and my sons because I know that he will indeed rule over me and my sons. For on the day when my father blessed him he made him the superior and me the inferior one. 24/ I swear to you that I will love him and that throughout my entire lifetime I will not desire harm[a] for him but only[b] what is good." He swore to her about this entire matter.

25/ She summoned Jacob in front of Esau and gave him orders in line with what she had discussed with Esau. 26/ He said,[a] "I will do what pleases you. Trust me[b] that nothing bad against Esau[c] will come from me or my sons. I will not be first except in love only."[d] 27/ She and her sons[a] ate and drank that night. She died that night at the age of three jubilees, one week, and one year[b] [= 155 years]. Her two sons Esau and Jacob buried her in the twofold[c] cave near their father's[d] mother Sarah.

Textual Notes

1a his father and] om. 21 (but it retains the pl. suffix on the verb = "honor them").

b Jacob's] The words *la-yāʿqob* may seem unnecessary (Charles [*Jubilees*, 207] regarded the phrase as a gloss), but they clarify the referent of the third person masc. sg. suffix on "lifetime."

2a just as (*zakama*)] "which/that" (*za-*) 21 38 58.

3a mother] "my mother" 17 38.

b know] + "me" 9 17; MS. 21 adds "me" and makes this a question. Lat., which is not yet legible here, may have read "me," since it places a conjunction before *universa opera mea*, which is the direct object of "know" in most Eth. MSS.

c think] Lat. is illegible here but must have read a verb like the Eth. one, since an inf. (*facere*) follows.

d of doing good] "what is good" Eth. The original may have read as Lat. does (*bona facere*). The Eth. inf. for "to do good" is *ʾašanneyo*, which was miscopied as the more common form *šannāya*—the present reading in Eth. See VanderKam, *Jubilees* 2:231.

4a what (lit., "the thing/matter")] Lat. and MS. 38 read "this" with the noun.

b honor] "do" Lat. Though Charles (*Ethiopic Version*, 131 n. 36) thought *ʾekber* might be a mistake for *ʾegbar* (= Lat.), it is more likely that *honorem* dropped from Lat. because it ends with the same letter as *faciam* (VanderKam, *Jubilees* 2:231).

c brother] "brothers" Lat. The pl. can hardly be correct here, though the blessing of Isaac included the words "Become lord of your brothers" (26:24 // Gen 27:29).

5a Tell me] "I ask. Tell me" Lat. Two Eth. MSS. 35 58 read *ʾesku*, "Let me ask," before "Tell me." Possibly it dropped from the other groups of MSS. because it begins with the same consonant as the last word in v. 4; it could be original.

b I will certainly turn away] The preferred Eth. reading is the equivalent of a Heb. inf. abs. + finite verb construction. Mss. 9 12 17 21 35 38 63 lack the inf., as does Lat.; Lat. reads *ut* (not *et*) with a subjunctive.

c will experience (lit., "there will be")] Lat. = "that it may be" (a subjunctive form like the previous verb).

937

d   mercy] + "of the Lord" Lat.
6a She] "*rebecca*" Lat.
b   lifetime (lit., "days")] Lat. lacks "days," though the context requires the word. The shared endings on *omnibus diebus* caused the omission.
c   the truth] "all the truth" Lat.
d   alive (lit., "in life")] "in my life" Lat. Ms. 12 also has the possessive—an easy scribal addition making the word into the more familiar expression (as at the end of the verse).
e   because – dream] Lat. lacks the clause, reading only *ego moriar*, which may stand where Eth. reads "the day of my death." Mss. 21 35 38 39 42 47 48 58 63 read "my dream."
f   155] Many Eth. mss. have 155, including all the older ones (9 12 17 20 21 25 35 38; also 44 58 63), but Lat. may have lacked *et quinque* (so Charles, *Ethiopic Version*, 131). This is suggested by space considerations for the gap after *amplius* (the text becomes illegible until *quinquaginta annorum* = "50 years"). Mss. 39 42ᵗ 47 48 also lack "five." But see v. 27, where her age is the equivalent of 155 years (expressed in jubilees, weeks, years).
g   Now] Lat. lacks.
h   entire] Lat. and ms. 21 om. Lat. is shorter also in lacking an equivalent for "days" ("my entire lifetime" is lit., "all the days of my life").
i   that I am to live] Lat. lacks (see VanderKam, *Jubilees* 2:232). The similarities between "my life" and "I am to live" probably triggered the omission in this rather full statement.
7a because his mother said to him that she would die] Lat. is mostly illegible here, though the word fragments fit ones that would be retrojected from Eth. It is questionable, however, whether there is space for all of the words reflected in Eth.
b   come and go] Lat. = "go and come."
c   she could see] Lat. lacks, perhaps omitting because *intrans* and *videns* end with the same letters. See VanderKam, *Jubilees* 2:232.
d   sickness] 4Q223–224 unit 2 i:45 reads דאוה ("sickness") where Eth. *ḥemām* and Lat. *infirmitas* have the same meaning.
e   touched] "harmed" (*contristavit*) Lat.; the equivalent of the Eth. would be *contrectavit*, to which Charles (*Ethiopic Version*, 131 n. 8; cf. n. 56) emended Lat. The two lookalike verbs were probably confused.
f   her entire lifetime (lit., "all the days of her life")] "all her days" Lat.; "his entire lifetime" 20.
8a Mother] om. Lat.; י[אמ 4Q223–224 unit 2 i:46; the reading is quite uncertain and the *yod* could be the final letter of אני or אנכי if the text, like Lat., lacks a reference to his mother. Space considerations, however, favor reading אמי here (DJD 13:104).
b   my lifetime . . . your lifetime] Both Eth. and Lat. read lit. "my days . . . your days," but 4Q223–224 unit 2 i:46 reads חי[י לשני שנ], "my years to the years of [your] life." Eth. and Lat. render idiomatically; Leslau (*Concise Dictionary*, 165) lists "period, era, time" as meanings for the term used here (*mawāʿel*).
c   your death] Both Heb. texts have the word for "your death," though they spell the suffix on it differently. 1Q18 frgs. 1-2 1 has a blank space after the word (the end of the verse), but there is no such gap after it in the Cave 4 copy.
9a She] There is a space after the verb in the Lat. ms.; Rönsch (*Jubiläen*, 70) inserted *rebecca*—a reasonable proposal.
b   make (Esau) swear] Lat. uses a purpose or result clause, while Eth. reads an impv. השבע in 1Q18 frgs. 1-2 2 confirms the Eth. reading.
c   Jacob] + "his brother" Lat.
d   in hatred] Lat. reads a clause "and not act in hatred against him." 1Q18 1-2 3 reads באיבה with the Eth.
e   and that he is devoid . . . death] Eth. contains these words, as does Lat. as far as it is legible. 4Q223–224 unit 2 i:49, where extant, confirms that the section appeared in the Heb. text. However, 1Q18 omitted it and thus has a defective text (see VanderKam, *Textual*, 84–87, where the Eth.-Lat. reading is preferred to the one in 1Q18, though 4Q223–224 was not yet available).
f   (kill) him] "his brother" Lat.
g   your (death)] "my" Lat. (though Ceriani read only ....*m meo*, perhaps for *mortem meam* [so Rönsch, *Jubiläen*, 70]).
10a everything] The Eth. mss., apart from 12, place "all" after the verb, while Lat. and ms. 12 locate it before the verb. If either of the Qumran copies read "all," it would have appeared before the verb. Mss. 21 39 42 47 48 58 have "all the days."
b   has done] + "with/to us" 4Q223–224 unit 2 i:50. Neither 1Q18 nor Eth. or Lat. reads the prepositional phrase. The same expression occurs later in the verse, where Eth., the only other version available, also has it.
c   went] Eth. has a past tense verb, while 1Q18 4 may have read an inf. cs. (though only the *lamed* of לכת survives) and 4Q223–224 unit 2 i:50 has the noun ה]ליכת.
d   led away] = 4Q223–224 unit 2 i:51 נהג, though the first two letters are difficult. Eth. = "gathered." It is ironic that נהג is the verb in Gen 31:18 where Jacob drives away his flocks from Haran, flocks that Laban claimed were his (31:43).
e   taken . . . by force] Most Eth. read a second person masc. sg. suffix on the verb (not 20 21 25 44). The phrase *ʾem-qedma gaṣṣeka* (lit., "from before your face") probably explains the suffix.
11a ask him in a pleading way] The Eth. mss. employ two finite verbs ("we plead we ask"); some mss. place a conjunction between them (21 35 42 47 48 58). Several of these copies then om. a conjunction before "he."
b   he would again do something treacherous] The Eth.

MSS. have *yerēsi*, "he would do/act"; 4Q223–224 unit 2 i:52 may preserve the final two consonants of "do/act" but continues with זמה ד[. The word ending with *d* is unknown, though עוד is suggested in DJD 13:102, 105–6 and is reflected in the translation here.

c someone] Eth. has "man, person" (*be'si*), but Lat. uses just the pronominal subject of *faciebat*. 4Q223–224 unit 2 i:52 agrees with Eth.

12a toward you (= Lat.)] "toward us" 9 12 17 21 38 48 63.

b today] 4Q223–224 unit 2 i:54 reads היום הזה, if the small frg. 4 belongs here (see DJD 13:106).

c but] om. 9 38.

d at home (lit., "in the house")] "in our house" 38 63.

13a to her] om. 17 63.

b know] + "him" 17 63.

c actions] + "which" 21 (therefore the actions are the ones Jacob does with his parents; see VanderKam, *Jubilees* 2:235).

d and does our wishes] This is the reading of 4Q223–224 unit 2 ii:4. No Eth. MS. reads an equivalent.

e first I did love Esau much more] The Heb. text, if it read a word for "first," placed it before "Esau," rather than after as in Eth.

f he was born] "they were born" 17.

g there is no] "any/every" 9 38. 4Q223–224 has ואין (unit 2 ii:6).

14a about] + "all" 9 12 21 35 38 39 42 47 48 58 63.

b he has abandoned] "they have abandoned" 12.

c after the impurity of the women and after error of the women] It is not clear how 4Q223–224 unit 2 ii:8 (see DJD 13:111) reads. The first letter traces are not at all obvious, except for final *mem*. "And after error" follows, and the next letter is *he* followed by a vertical stroke. As read in DJD 13 it is: "the wo]men and after the error of the wo[men." It is perhaps possible that the word ending in final *mem* is טומאותם. "And after error" would then stand where Eth. has "and after their errors." It may be that הנשים should be read at the end of the legible section, or Heb. may have lacked a suffix and the next word is הוא = *we'etu* = he. The Eth. text reads: "after his wives, after impurity, and after their errors (his desire 21)—he and his sons."

15a are saying] "said" 9 38.

b him] "Esau" 35.

c brother] "brothers" 9 12 17 63.

d persevere (lit., "stand")] So 4Q223–224 unit 2 ii:9. The Eth. MSS. have "be," that is, his oath would not happen. Mss. 35 58 supply "therefore," and MS. 38 adds "in his oath." Neither of these additions is in the Heb. text.

16a brother] "brothers" 9 17 63. The Heb. reading is "his brother."

b (will be) handed over (lit., "given into the hands of")] The Heb. frg. agrees with the reading, but the scribe left a space between ביד and יעקוב and wrote ינתן above the line at the word "Jacob"—where Eth. has the equivalent.

c will not escape] "is not to escape" 9.

d fall] The text reads "descend," which has the sense of "fall" in the expression "descend into his hands." Charles (*Jubilees*, 209), though he thought "will fall into his control" was a gloss, also suggested reading *yewaddeq* ("will fall" = MS. 58) but the change from *yewarred* is unnecessary.

17a you are not to be afraid] The Heb. frg. may contain the last letter of an unusual spelling of the second person fem. sg. pronoun אתי, though the reading is most uncertain. The *hiphil* form of דאג is surprising, as in the context the *qal* meaning is appropriate (it can mean "be afraid," just as Eth. reads).

b Esau's guardian] Between the end of v. 17 as it reads in Eth. (= line 12 in the Heb. frg.) and the beginning of Eth. v. 18 (= line 14 in 4Q223–224 unit 2 ii), the Heb. frg. has two lines of text absent from Eth. The surviving Heb. letters and words indicate that the extra lines evidence a scene like Jub 27:13-17, where Isaac consoled and reassured Rebekah after Jacob left for Haran. See the commentary, and DJD 13:112.

18a that] om. 17 25.

b say] Several MSS. (39 42 47 48 58) add *'oho*, "an expression of consent"; when used with a verb of speaking, as here, it means: "agree, obey, promise, submit" (Leslau, *Concise Dictionary*, 132).

c it] om. 21 39 42 44 47 48 58; instead, some of them (39 42 47 58) add: "what I say to you."

19a He said] "He said to me" 21 38.

b anything (lit., "all")] om. 20 38. If the small frg. 9 is correctly placed (it is uncertain), it too lacks "all."

c you tell me] "you command me" 20.

20a you and Jacob love one another] Ms. 21 places the verb after "you and Jacob," unlike the other MSS., which reverse them. 4Q223–224 unit 2 ii:18 is drawn from the small frg. 11, which preserves only the last three letters of "Jacob" followed by זה אוהבין. If the frg. is correctly located, the order of subject–verb would agree with MS. 21. The pl. ptc. has an Aram. ending (see DJD 13:112). Mss. 39 42 47 48 58 read "your brother" after "Jacob," but the Heb. frg. lacks the word.

b for his brother] The reading is literally "one to his brother," but MS. 12 has "one with his companion/friend."

c only] The word *kemma* has been confused with the more common *kama* by 9 17 21 35 38 39 42 44 47 48 58; most of these then omit the following conjunction. Their text as a result says, "so that you may be prosperous."

d be honored] Mss. 12 21 35 39 42 47 48 continue to read purpose clauses and thus have a subjunctive form.

e on (the earth)] Lit., "in the middle of/within." Ms. 21 has "on."

- f who love you] If the tiny frg. 12 belongs here, its reading או[הב would differ from the pl. suffixal form in the Eth. Because the location of the Heb. frg. is so uncertain, the Eth. text is translated.
- 21a He said] + "to her" 21 44.
- b near²] om. 20 35 44, though 35 44 add "near her bones" at the end of the verse: "your bones may be near her bones" (a more logical order).
- 22a I will love more] If frg. 13 belongs here, the preserved letters would agree with the Eth. text. The letter read as *mem* Milik took as an *aleph*; if so, it is not impossible that it supports the reading in 17 21 39 48 58 63, which place a suffix on the verb: "I will love him (אותו)." Milik suggested, however, that the frg. belonged in v. 20 (DJD 13:112).
- b on (the entire earth)] "from" 12.
- c womb] The most strongly attested reading is *meḥrateki*, "your mercy." Littmann ("Jubiläen," 100 n. a) perceived the cause of the mistaken reading: רחם means "womb," but רחמים means "compassion/mercy." Cf. Dillmann, *Lexicon*, 158; Charles, *Jubilees*, 210; Berger, *Jubiläen*, 500 n. a to v. 22. Some of the Eth. MSS. offer various corrections. See VanderKam, *Jubilees* 1:195; 2:236.
- 23a myself] The best reading seems to be *kemma*, "thus, also, even, nearly, almost, just, merely, alone, the same, yet" (Leslau, *Concise Dictionary*, 151; but see Dillmann, *Lexicon*, 830, and VanderKam, *Jubilees* 2:236, for the meaning suggested here.) It could be rendered "(I ask) only" (see Wintermute). Some MSS. (12 25 38 47 63) read *kama*, "thus" (similarly MS. 58), while others omit (21 39 44 48).
- 24a desire harm] Most MSS. read a reflexive form, not the G-stem used in the other instances of the expression. It is not likely, however, that any difference in meaning is being expressed (see Leslau, *Concise Dictionary*, 112; Dillmann, *Lexicon*, 585). MSS. 12 21 35 58 have the expected form.
- b only] om. 12 21 38.
- 26a He said] + "to her" 21 48.
- b Trust me] "So that you may stand as guarantor for me" 21 44.
- c Esau] + "my brother" 39 42 47 48 58.
- d only] om. 21 38.
- 27a her sons] + "with their sons" 39 48; "his sons" 63.
- b one year] om. 35. The text reads lit., "its one year."
- c twofold] om. 35 39 42 47 48.
- d their father's] "his father's" 9 12 17 38 63.

Commentary[1]

Rebekah, that redoubtable woman of Jubilees, dominates chap. 35, in which she reaches the end of her life. Ever the diligent wife and mother who left nothing to chance, she imparts vital instructions to the three men in her immediate family before she meets the death that she knew from a dream would come that very year (v. 6). The order in which she deals with them—Jacob, Isaac, Esau—is thoroughly consistent with the character evaluations the author has presented throughout the account of the family. In some ways the words and procedure of Rebekah in chap. 35 parallel what she said and did in chap. 25 and again in chap. 27, although at the end of the chapter she has her two sons with her and not Jacob alone as on the two previous occasions. Genesis does not narrate the death of Rebekah, though it mentions it at a later juncture (49:31). As noted several times before, it assigns her no role in the narratives after Jacob left home for Haran. Chapter 35, which has no basis in Genesis, provides the final installment in the author's extraordinary biography of Rebekah, Jacob's mother.

The chapter can be outlined as follows:

- 1-8 Conversation between Rebekah and Jacob
- 9-17 Conversation between Rebekah and Isaac
- 18-24 Conversation between Rebekah and Esau
- 25-26 Esau and Jacob with Rebekah
- 27 Esau and Jacob's final meal with Rebekah and her death

The textual basis for the chapter is, of course, provided by the Ethiopic version. The Latin translation is available for vv. 3-12, though the manuscript is illegible in places. There is also Hebrew evidence:

---

1 Endres calls the chapter "Rebekah's Testament of Peace" (*Biblical Interpretation*, 173-74), though as he notes it differs in some ways from other testaments in the book.

1Q18 frgs 1-2   vv. 8-10

4Q223-224 unit 2 col. i:45-54; col. ii:1-22   vv. 7 (last word)-22. The surviving letters and words appear on a series of small fragments, around which a large percentage of the text must be reconstructed. In some cases just a few letters from a verse survive, but at least one word or part of a word is extant for each verse from 7 through 22. An unusual feature is that the two Hebrew copies overlap and in places allow comparison of their readings.

1-8 Conversation between Rebekah and Jacob

As she had in chaps. 25 and 27, Rebekah summons her son Jacob and in this way sets in motion the next episode in the narrative. She has weighty words to tell the men of the family, and, as before, she begins with her younger son, not with Isaac and, naturally, not with Esau.[2]

■ **1** The story takes place eight years after the brothers sold Joseph into slavery (compare 34:10 and the present verse). The year of Rebekah's death happens to be a significant one in the overall chronology: the first year in the first week of a new jubilee (number 45). In chaps. 25 and 27 Rebekah had given Jacob instructions, and now she does so again. She no longer has to worry about the women her son would marry, as she had on those earlier occasions; now she turns to other family matters[3]—his relationship with his frail father and with his difficult brother. She orders him to show honor to them throughout his life. In her exhortation to Jacob she echoes the words of Noah to his offspring that they honor father and mother and love one another (7:20). Honoring a parent is commanded in the Decalogue (Exod 20:12 // Deut 5:16), and Jacob had repeatedly distinguished himself in his concern for both Isaac and Rebekah (26:7-8, 10; 27:6; 29:15-20; 31; 32:31-32; 33:21-23). He will continue to be a model son in the present chapter and the next, in contrast to his brother Esau, who, though he enjoys some good moments in them, had on his record that he had defied, defrauded, and abandoned his parents. Not for the first time he is the object of heavy criticism from them.

The theme of honoring a brother has special force in the present context because in the previous chapter Joseph's brothers had been such poor examples. Moreover, Rebekah had reason to be concerned about the relations between Jacob and Esau because they had been seriously strained (24:3-7; 26:24 [Jacob is to be lord of his brothers], 30, 35; 27:2, 4), though the two had become reconciled (29:13). Concern for relations between children has surfaced before in the book. Noah had ordered his offspring to love one another (7:20), and Abraham had done the same (20:2). Outside Jubilees, the Testaments of the Twelve Patriarchs contains exhortations about loving brothers (T. Reub. 6:9; T. Sim. 3:4; 4:7; T. Zeb. 8:5; T. Dan 5:3; T. Gad 6:1, 3; 7:7) but also about honoring them. The instances in which a patriarch tells his sons to honor Levi and Judah (e.g., T. Gad 8:1; T. Jos. 19:6) have a different nuance because of the special roles the two play in the book, but in T. Jos. 10:6 Joseph says he honored his brothers, and in 11:1; 17:2 he commands his sons to honor their brothers.[4] The Isaac of Jubilees will also speak to his sons about the matter in 36:4, 8-11, though he does not use the language of honor. Lambert suggests that the topic arose from an exegetical consideration: after all, Esau had threatened to kill Jacob (Gen 27:41).[5] One might add that Jubilees had heightened the tension because in it not only does Esau speak of killing Jacob, but Jacob also mentions the possibility of dispatching Esau (27:4).[6] Moreover, both parents remark in the sequel that Esau had shown none of the sort of virtue that they tried to inculcate in their sons (see

---

2   "The author clearly viewed Jacob as Rebekah's closest relative" (Endres, *Biblical Interpretation*, 174).

3   Halpern-Amaru writes: "Rebecca's primary function involves the immediate next generation, her sons, not the distant future. Her interests are familial; and in that context she is the more assertive partner" (*Empowerment*, 62-63).

4   Hollander and de Jonge, *Testaments*, 405: "In the Testaments, Joseph is the prototype of the man who loves his brothers or his neighbour in general."

5   Lambert, "Last Testaments," 100-101.

6   These considerations and parallels appear more pertinent than Werman's suggestion that the similarity in appearance between father and son (she refers to Jub 31:9; 38:1) is of relevance: since sons looked like their fathers, they too were to be honored (*Jubilees*, 454).

vv. 9-17). Rebekah grasps the true nature of the situation and addresses it forcefully before her death.

■ **2** Jacob, true to character, declares he is eager to carry out his mother's wishes. He had always been obedient to her, even when it involved deceiving his father to swipe the blessing meant for Esau (26:7-10). The command she was now giving him was far easier for him to obey than the one she expressed in that chapter (i.e., misleading Isaac): having the proper attitude toward Isaac and Esau "will be something honorable and great for me; it will be a righteous act for me before the Lord that I should honor them." In the Ethiopic text, he uses three nouns:

kebr: honor (used seven times in chap. 35)
'ebay: greatness
ṣedq: righteousness, right.

These terms appear, either alone or in tandem, at some critical junctures in Jubilees. The angels led Enoch into the Garden of Eden "for (his) greatness and honor" (4:23). When he blessed Levi, Isaac said: "May the Lord give you and your descendants greatness and honor [lit., greatness for honor]," and he prayed that the descendants of his sons would be like the angels "in honor, greatness, and holiness, / May he make them great throughout all the ages" (31:14). The quality of righteousness is related to the practice of brotherly love in other contexts where a father is exhorting his children. In a passage referenced several times above, Noah "testified to his sons that they should do what is right, cover the shame of their bodies, bless the one who had created them, honor father and mother, love one another" (7:20). Later he added, "Now listen, my children. Do what is just and right so that you may be rightly planted on the surface of the entire earth. Then your honor will be raised before my God who saved me from the floodwaters" (7:34). Abraham instructed his sons and grandsons "to keep the way of the Lord so that they would do what is right and that they should love one another; that they should be like this in every war so that they could go against each one *who rises* against them; and do what is just and right on the earth" (20:2; see v. 9).[7] Long before, Jacob himself had assured Rebekah "I will behave rightly and will never conduct myself corruptly" (25:10); now he makes a similar promise to his mother regarding her latest instructions.

■ **3-5** In the remainder of Jacob's response to Rebekah's admonition he points out what should have been obvious to her (and to the reader) throughout Jacob's life. That is, he expresses surprise that she feels the need to urge him to do what he always does anyway. Jacob acknowledges that Rebekah knows him better than anyone, an understanding that began the first moment of his life. Very early on she loved him more than Esau (19:16, 19, 31), and her early assessment of the boys had found repeated confirmation. With that in mind, Jacob reminds her "at all times I think of doing good for all" (v. 3). Esau might have disagreed with Jacob's confident assertion about himself because his brother had forced him to lose both the right of the firstborn and the blessing, and Laban could have harbored some reservations about the point, but Jacob is simply claiming for himself the sort of character traits Abraham, Isaac, and Rebekah had seen in him: Abraham immediately recognized him as his true descendant and pronounced lavish blessings on him in chaps. 19 and 22; Rebekah called him "a pure son and a holy offspring [lit., seed]" (25:12) and blessed him and his children (25:15-22); and Isaac said of him that he "is just in his way. He is perfect; he is a true man" (27:17; see v. 12 below where Rebekah echoes his sentiments) and blessed him (27:11). Perhaps in asserting he always intended to do good for all Jacob had in mind his relations with Abraham, Isaac, and Rebekah together with his wives and children. At any rate, he is almost offended that his mother reminds him about his duty (v. 4). When she spoke to him about marriage in chap. 25, he responded more gently than he does here (see 25:1-10). There he simply pointed out to her what his practice and intentions were; here he wonders how he could possibly do anything other than what she was urging him to do. However, since she knew him so well, he seems to leave open the possibility that he had failed in some way

---

7 For the influence of Gen 18:19 and Lev 19:18, see the examination of the phrases "What is Right" and "What is Just" by Lambert, "Last Testaments," 88–94.

and asks her to name his fault so that he could fix it and obtain the favor that would come with the improvement. He uses the language of "turning away" from something wrong and experiencing grace as a result. The thought, though not the vocabulary, is reminiscent of Jub 5:17-18 where divine mercy is promised to Israelites who turn from their errors in the right way.

■ **6** Rebekah acknowledges that Jacob was correct to be taken aback by her request. In fact, she makes as strong a statement about him as Jacob did about himself: she had never perceived any improper act in him. This is a remarkable claim, but it comes from his own mother, the one who knows Jacob best and furnishes an authoritative confirmation of his virtuous character (she will say the opposite about Esau in v. 9). But, after placing her imprimatur on his self-assessment, she discloses the real reason ("I will tell you the truth") why she had raised the subject at this time: Rebekah had learned that she was going to die in that very year. She makes the point at some length, with repetition perhaps reinforcing the gravity of her announcement (the Latin version is somewhat shorter). First, she announces that she will die in the present year ("I will die during this year and will not make it alive through this year"). The claim to know the very year of her death almost begged for an explanation, and she supplies one. She knew the timing of her end because she had seen it in a dream (Latin reads only: "I will die," lacking reference to the dream). Rebekah had been the recipient of revelations in the past. Genesis 25:22-23 records the occasion when the children she was carrying struggled in her womb: "So she went to inquire of the Lord. And the Lord said to her, 'Two nations are in your womb, / and two peoples born of you shall be divided; / the one shall be stronger than the other, / the elder shall serve the younger.'" Strangely, Jubilees passes over this remarkable incident in Rebekah's life (it would have appeared in the vicinity of 19:13), but it accords her other revelatory experiences.

25:13-14: Speaking of Jacob, she says, "'Bless him, Lord, and place a righteous blessing in my mouth so that I may bless him.' At that time the spirit of righteousness descended into her mouth" (the blessing follows in vv. 15-23).

27:1: "Rebekah was told in a dream what her older son Esau had said."

Now for the second time Rebekah learns otherwise inaccessible information through a dream, and, of course, the prediction proves accurate (v. 27).[8]

The oldest Ethiopic manuscripts support the reading "155 years" as her final age, but a few others and probably the Latin translation read "150 years" (see the textual note).[9] The year number, expressed here as (literally) "one hundred and fifty and five years," receives confirmation from 35:27, where her age at death is presented in terms of jubilees, weeks, and years. There, where no other textual evidence exists and the Ethiopic copies are in agreement, the numbers are: three jubilee periods = 147 years + one week of years = 7 years + one year = 155 years. It may be that the witnesses supporting the reading "150 years" reflect concern about the inconsistency that the number "155" produces. If she had attained the age of 155 in the year of the world 2157, she was born in 2002. Isaac, who was born in 1987, was therefore fifteen years her senior. However, if, according to 36:1, he died in the year 2162 when he had reached 180 years, he would have to have been twenty years her elder. Perhaps a chronologically attuned scribe thought he could erase the five-year discrepancy by reducing her life span by five years, but the dates in 35:1 and 36:1 frustrate the attempt. Either way, if Rebekah was 155 in the year 2157

---

8 Lambert suggests that Rebekah's words in Gen 27:6-9 (in which she instructs Jacob how to obtain the blessing from Isaac) lie behind aspects of what she says, including the dream revelation, honoring his parents by giving provisions to them (see v. 12), and reference to her death ("Last Testaments," 102). If one identifies the words she quotes from Isaac such that he said only "Bring me game, and prepare for me savory food to eat," and construes the next words as coming from her ("that I may bless you before the Lord before I die"), then she would have mentioned her death and the other features that arise in chaps. 35–36. Lambert's proposal is overly speculative, and he is able to adduce no indication that the passage was so divided by early readers. It is an unsuccessful part of his otherwise helpful concern to find exegetical reasons for topics covered in parents' testimonies to their children in Jubilees.

9 Berger claims the Latin translation reads "145 years," but the only legible number is "50 [*quinquaginta*]" (*Jubiläen*, 497 n. e to v. 6).

or 150 (that is, either fifteen or twenty years younger than her husband), Isaac's age would be 175 five years later, in 2162 (i.e., five years too few). As Werman has observed, the number of her years fits a pattern in that the wife lives fewer years than her husband.[10]

■ **7-8** Jacob's reaction is one of complete disbelief. He even laughed at his mother[11] because the news was so implausible. Judging from his emphatic words, Jacob was not convinced that, just because the information came through a dream, it was credible. The description of Rebekah's remarkable health is interesting: she maintained her physical dexterity as proven by the fact that she could go about her normal activities ("she could come and go"),[12] she retained her ability to see (unlike Isaac), and her teeth were healthy. Astonishingly, she had never been sick. The vocabulary is different, but the description of Rebekah reminds one of the way in which Deuteronomy describes Moses: "Moses was one hundred twenty years old when he died; his sight was unimpaired and his vigor had not abated" (Deut 34:7). Her son says that he himself would be fortunate to match her longevity and health. Jacob accuses her of not being serious in speaking as she had. The Ethiopic text (the only one surviving for this expression) uses two words for how, according to Jacob, Rebekah is speaking: *baka baṣaw*. The first means "in vain, uselessly, for nothing, fortuitously, without cause, for no purpose, in idleness, by mere chance." The second is related to a verb with the senses of "be sleepy" and the like and "rave, tell things that are not true"[13] though the exact form is not listed in the lexica (a related term is used in Eth. Prov 26:19, where the MT has משחק).[14] Whatever the original may have been,[15] Jacob accuses his mother of being anything but serious in speaking about her imminent death. Dream or no dream, the facts that Jacob saw with his own eyes convinced him otherwise.

9-17 Conversation between Rebekah and Isaac[16]

As she had done before when she could not convince Jacob (27:1-8), she went to Isaac. On the former occasion, when, as here, a dream and danger of violence between her two sons were involved, she urged Jacob to flee to Haran. When he would not leave without his father's permission, she turned to Isaac and prevailed upon him to give the desired order. There she spoke negatively about Esau in the sense that he had married Canaanite women and positively about Jacob whom she wanted to marry properly, within the clan. On this occasion, she sharpens the differences between Jacob and Esau, idealizing the former and demonizing the latter.

■ **9** As she did in chap. 27, she contrasts the character of her sons. Esau had not yet done the deed she condemns, but she is worried that he will kill Jacob once Isaac dies. This is another connection with chap. 27, where in a dream Rebekah learned the words of Esau: "The time of mourning for my father is now approaching. Then I will kill my brother Jacob" (26:35; see 27:1 [// Gen 27:41-42]). Rebekah still remembered the threat and wanted to thwart his murderous intent. In making her case—her one request—she cites Esau's יצר (= inclination, nature; the term appears in 1Q18 line 3),[17] the way he is. That evil nature he had exhibited repeatedly, leaving her with more reason to worry that he would carry out his earlier intention. She says about her own son "that he has been malicious since his youth and that he is devoid of virtue."

---

10 Werman, *Jubilees*, 454. So Abraham lived 175 years but Sarah 127; Isaac reached 180 years but Rebekah 155.

11 Kugel speaks of the text as becoming "strikingly novelistic" at this point (*A Walk through* Jubilees, 168).

12 BDB, 97, s.v. בוא (referring to Deut 28:6, 19; Ps 121:8; Zech 8:10). The phrase occurs in 1 Sam 2:30, 35 for priests going in and out of the Lord's presence, that is, serving before him, doing their normal duties. Berger refers to Acts 1:21, where it is said of Jesus (*Jubiläen*, 497 n. d to v. 7).

13 Leslau, *Concise Dictionary*, 101, 105.

14 Dillmann, *Lexicon*, 549.

15 See the discussion in DJD 13:104–5.

16 Syncellus was aware of this scene, though he erroneously attributed the information to Josephus: "Rebecca petitioned Isaac in his old age to counsel Esau and Jacob to love one another. And, after exhorting them [see chap. 36], he foretold that if Esau would rise up against Jacob, he would fall at his hands" (124.5-7; Adler/Tuffin, *Chronography*, 155).

17 See Lichtenberger, "Bedeutung von יצר," 3–6. As its meaning here he gives "Charakter, Grundausrichtung (des Denkens, Planens)" (p. 6).

The reconciliation between Jacob and Esau reported in Jub 29:13 seems not to be part of her memory. She feels a need, therefore, to remind Isaac about Esau's desire to murder his brother. Despite all she has just said about her older son, she still wants Isaac to make him swear an oath not to hurt Jacob or "pursue him in hatred." In effect, she wants him to swear that he will abide by the law of Lev 19:18 ("You shall not take vengeance or bear a grudge against any of your people") and 19:17 ("You shall not hate in your heart any of your kin").

■ **10** Rebekah documents her case against Esau by reviewing for the elderly Isaac the actions Esau had taken between the time of his threat ("from the day his brother Jacob went to Haran") and the present. Her charge is that he had abandoned his parents and stolen their property. She is recalling what the narrator had said in 29:17-18 when explaining why Isaac and Rebekah had moved from Beersheba to Abraham's tower:

> For Isaac had returned from the well of the oath, had gone up to the tower of his father Abraham, and had settled there away from his son Esau, because, at the time when Jacob went to Mesopotamia, Esau had married Mahalath, Ishmael's daughter. He had gathered all his father's flocks and his wives and had gone up and lived in Mount Seir. He had left his father Isaac alone at the well of the oath.

From her summary in v. 10, it appears that Rebekah thought Esau had taken all of Isaac's property, not just the flocks as in 29:18. Unlike Esau, who frightened his parents into moving farther away from him, Jacob sent provisions to them on a regular basis (29:15-16, 20).

■ **11** Rebekah further indicts Esau for the attitude he assumed toward his parents after relieving them of all their property—property that she refers to as "what belongs to us." Not only had their son stolen it from them, but they were reduced to begging him to give them an allowance from it. The Hebrew fragment indicates that her charge is even stronger than the one in the Ethiopic version: where the Ethiopic says "he would act like someone who was being charitable to us," the Hebrew seems to say "he would again do something treacherous like someone" who was being charitable to us (the fragment breaks off after "someone").[18] Rebekah minces no words about her older son, who was a duplicitous thief.

■ **12** One might think she had made her case by this point, but in v. 12 Rebekah clinches it by laying out comprehensively the gulf that divided the nature of their two sons. First she clarifies Esau's motive for behaving despicably toward them: he was bitter or jealous because Isaac blessed Jacob—the very event that inspired Esau's threat to kill Jacob. Rebekah says nothing about the underhanded way in which she and Jacob had acted on that occasion; she speaks only of how poorly Esau reacted to being cheated of the blessing. She faults Esau for his rage at the deception and acts as if the whole scheme was entirely in order.[19] The words she uses to describe Jacob are strong indeed: he is Isaac's "perfect and true son." Isaac himself had applied both adjectives to Jacob before this:[20]

Perfect (*feṣṣumāwi/perfectum*): "He is perfect [*feṣṣum/ perfectus*]" (27:17).

True (*rāteʿa/veracem*): "because he is just [*rāteʿ*/cf. *recta*] in his way . . . he is a true [*meʾman/verax*] man."

In contrast to Esau, who was "malicious [or: evil] since his youth" and "devoid of virtue" (v. 9), Jacob "has virtue only, no evil."

After condemning Esau and praising Jacob, Rebekah presents a personal view of her younger son's behavior since returning from Haran. She correctly recalls that he had provided for them from that time on. As soon as he crossed the Jordan River and settled on the west side of it, he began sending his parents "everything they needed" (29:20; see vv. 15-16). When Rebekah went back home after being a witness to Jacob's payment of his vow in Bethel, he sent "rams, he-goats, and sheep" for his father

---

18 See the textual note and DJD 13:105–6.
19 See van Boxel, "God of Rebekah," 16–17. He highlights the fact that the incident arose from Rebekah's love for Jacob; moreover, it was divinely directed (Jub 26:18).
20 Genesis 25:27 refers to Jacob as an איש תם (translated "a quiet man" in the NRSV).

to eat (32:31). Rebekah says that Jacob "always brings us everything in its season," apparently having in mind his practice of giving them provisions "four times per year—between the seasons of the months, between plowing and harvest, between autumn and the rain(y season), and between winter and spring" (29:16). In sharp contrast to Esau's begrudging them anything from their own property and his condescending attitude when he allowed them to have something, Jacob was delighted whenever his parents would accept a gift that came from his own goods. Esau acted as if he was supplying charity; Jacob blessed them when they accepted anything from him.

The last part of her paean to Jacob's virtue comes as a bit of a surprise: "He has not separated from us from the day he came from Haran until today." Jacob crossed to the west side of the Jordan in the year 2136 (29:14), but it was not until seven years later (2143 [30:1]) that he visited his parents (the reunion in chap. 31 occurs in the same year as the action of chap. 30). Adding these seven years to the twenty he had spent in Haran, he had not seen them for twenty-seven years. After the twenty-year absence in Haran, he did not make an effort to see them immediately upon his return. Rebekah's memory seems sharper and more comprehensive regarding Esau than Jacob, about whom she conveniently forgets damning details. Perhaps she meant only that he had remained in contact with them since arriving back in the land, although her phrasing does not say that. At the end of the long verse, she seems to be referring to the time after Jacob and his family moved to the Hebron area (33:21-23): from that time on he remained at home with them (not literally in their house) and showed honor to them. In honoring them, he obeyed the fifth commandment. Rebekah's words about Jacob and Esau in this chapter are interesting when read with *b. Qid.* 31b: "What is the form of honor [to a father] that is owing? The son should feed him, give him drink, dress him, cover him, bring him in and take him out" (cf. *Mek. Baḥodesh* 8.1). Jacob was living in true obedience to the commandment; Esau was not.

Isaac (vv. 13-17) too acts in accord with the precedent in chap. 27. There, when Rebekah had made her argument about Esau's bad marital decisions and demanded that Jacob not follow suit, Isaac agreed with her and sent Jacob to the home of Laban to find a wife (27:9-11). After blessing his younger son and sending him away, he highly praised Jacob and consoled Rebekah (27:14-17). On that earlier occasion, however, nothing was said explicitly about a change in Isaac's feelings toward his sons. Isaac, of course, loved Esau at first (19:15); in fact, he "loved Esau much more than Jacob" (19:31). In chap. 27 he called Jacob just, perfect, and true (27:17), but he did not deny having affection for Esau. In chap. 35 he remedies the situation.

■ 13 He indicates that he, too, has noted Jacob's presence with them and practice of honoring them—the two points with which Rebekah ended her words (v. 12). He even exceeds her praise of Jacob by declaring that he honors them wholeheartedly, sincerely. He admits that, after the twins were born, he loved Esau much more, "but now I love Jacob more than Esau because he has done so many bad things and lacks (the ability to do) what is right" (v. 13). So, Esau's disgusting behavior and in fact his very nature caused Isaac to switch his paternal preference; the evidence was so strong that even he saw the facts that Rebekah had discerned much earlier on. Isaac cites Esau's violence,[21] wickedness,[22] and lack of righteousness—all opposites of Jacob's traits. Each of these terms could be applied to the way he treated Isaac and Rebekah and to his actions and those of his sons in chaps. 37-38. Marriage to Canaanite women could be the substance behind the charges that he was wicked and lacked righteousness. Both parents pronounce Esau morally hopeless, a person incapable of doing what is right.

■ 14 Isaac's thoughts next turned to the future. He was disturbed about the results of Esau's evil actions and bad choices. The chosen line, as he now saw clearly, could not be traced through him because he and his descendants, rather than finding deliverance, were to be

---

[21] The Hebrew term seems to be חמס, though it is not easy to decipher (4Q223-224 unit 2 ii:6); Ethiopic *'ammaḍā* can mean "injustice, violence, oppression, iniquity, crime, lawlessness" (Leslau, *Concise Dictionary*, 171).

[22] The Hebrew word may be רשע though the reading is difficult (4Q223-224 unit 2 ii:6); Ethiopic *gefʿ* means "oppression, violence, wrongdoing, wrong, persecution, vexation, injustice" (Leslau, *Concise Dictionary*, 214).

destroyed and uprooted. These verbs have occurred in a number of contexts; prominent among them are cases in which the punishments of Canaan and his descendants (10:30; 20:4; 22:20, 21) and/or those guilty of sexual sins (20:6; 30:7, 22; 33:13, 17, 19; 41:27) are under consideration. Esau was culpable on both counts through marrying Canaanite wives (see the textual note), and therefore the verdicts Isaac envisages were appropriate for him and his offspring. Isaac charges him with abandoning Abraham's God. The narrative has not mentioned apostasy by Esau, but Isaac's point may be that his conduct demonstrated or flowed from his religious error. That the two went together is implied by Abraham's instructions to his sons and grandsons in 20:7 (after he had warned about Canaanite women and impurity): "I testify to you my sons: love the God of heaven and hold fast to all his commandments. Do not follow their idols and their uncleanness."[23] The reader is hardly surprised by this time to see the word "impurity" used in connection with Esau's wives (25:1, 7; cf. 20:3-6). A new point in Isaac's critique is that Esau's sons share his ways. This is the first mention of these characters, who will play a major and thoroughly negative role in chaps. 37–38.

■ 15 As if Esau's theological and sexual transgressions were not bad enough, his father assails his personal integrity as well. Rebekah had asked him to make Esau swear not to hurt Jacob (v. 9), though she criticized her older son severely. The fact that she made this single request of him implies that she believed forcing him to take an oath would still have the desired effect—that solemnly declaring something before God would make Esau behave properly. But Isaac had just noted that Esau did not fear God—he had turned away from or abandoned the God of Abraham; as a result, even swearing an oath before the deity would not produce the desired result. Esau would say the words, but he would then do as he wished.[24] Both parents realized that Esau lacked any integrity. He would not, therefore, keep his sworn word but would act in an evil way. Isaac is the only one in this chapter not to agree to what Rebekah demanded. This is another occasion when Isaac, unexpectedly, has more insight into one of their sons than Rebekah (see also 27:13-17).[25]

■ 16 Isaac expected only the worst from Esau and made his case emphatically in vv. 13-15. His words were liable, therefore, to have unsettled Rebekah all the more, so he next begins to reassure her that, despite Esau's character, she was not to fear that he would kill Jacob once his father died. His claim that Jacob would prove the stronger, should Esau try putting his plan in motion, would sound dubious to readers familiar only with the brothers of the Genesis stories. But the Jacob of Jubilees is far different than the timid character there. Jubilees did tell the story about Jacob's flight from his brother who was breathing murderous threats against him. At that time Rebekah had said to him "run away to my brother Laban" (27:3); but Jacob had replied to her: "I am not afraid. If he wishes to kill me, I will kill him" (v. 4). Also, the writer of Jubilees reduced the long account about the preparations for and meeting between Jacob and Esau to a single verse (29:13) that said nothing about his fears. The surprisingly insightful Isaac now tells his anxious wife that the opposite of what she dreads will take place: Esau would fall to Jacob if he attacked him. Isaac resorts to a passive verb (lit., "will be given into his hands") to suggest that God is the one who protects Jacob, a point he develops in v. 17. To some extent he echoes the sentiments he expressed to Esau when speaking to him after he mistakenly blessed Jacob: "You will live by your sword and will serve your brother. May it be that, if you become great and remove his yoke from your neck, then you will commit an offense fully worthy of death and your descendants will be eradicated from beneath the sky" (26:34).

■ 17 The final unit in Isaac's response to Rebekah contains his explanation of the true nature of the situation, the reason for his confidence. He refers to Jacob's guardian or keeper (שומר יעקוב in 4Q223–224 unit 2 ii:11). The expression comes from Ps 121:4, where it takes

---

23 See Berger, *Jubiläen*, 499 n. b to v. 14.
24 4Q223–224 unit 2 ii:9-10 uses two verbs (literally): he will not stand and he will not do. The first of these (יעמוד) has the sense of "endure, persist, persevere" (see BDB, 764) in the expression.
25 Halpern-Amaru says that Rebekah, unlike Isaac, "is blinded by parental love into believing that Esau will be faithful to a vow to keep peace with his brother" (*Empowerment*, 63).

the form: שומר ישראל. When Jacob left home for Laban's house, the Lord had said to him that he would "keep you wherever you go" (Gen 28:15 // Jub 27:24), and Jacob adduced that promise in his prayer (Gen 28:20 // Jub 27:27). Isaac appeals to that understanding of God[26] and can comfortably assert that "Jacob's guardian is greater and more powerful, glorious, and praiseworthy" than whatever idol(s) or spirits Esau might revere. All the attributes Isaac names are applied to God in the HB. Many passages refer to him as great and powerful: the two words on the Hebrew fragment—גדול and גבור—are used together for him in Deut 10:17; Neh 9:32; Jer 32:18. The other two are likewise attested adjectives for the deity: glorious (perhaps נכבד; see Deut 28:58, where it modifies "his name") and praiseworthy (perhaps מהולל; e.g., Ps 96:4, where "great" also occurs). With the God of Abraham on Jacob's side, Esau, who has abandoned this God for the ones of his wives, stood no chance—a prediction that will materialize in chaps. 37–38.

4Q223-224 unit 2 ii:12-14 demonstrates that the Hebrew was a full two lines longer than the Ethiopic text after the words "than Esau's guardian" (the end of v. 17 in the Ethiopic copies). The words and letters that survive on the Hebrew fragment can be translated:

12 (after the end of Ethiopic v. 17) For like dust befor[e   ] all the guardians of Esau before the God of
13   J]acob [my perfect and de]ar s[on.] But I lo[ve   do]es our wishes
14   ] my sister in peace (v. 18 of the Ethiopic version then begins).

Line 12 compares Esau's keepers (pl.) to dust, perhaps before the wind,[27] in contrast to the God of (Abraham?). A thought like this would be consistent with the mockery of idols found in several passages in Jubilees.[28] Little from the middle of line 13 has survived apart from Jacob's name. The next preserved letters could be a statement by Isaac about his love for Jacob.[29] At any rate, the phrase at the end of the line recalls the description of Jacob in v. 13 (line 4 in the fragment). The extant words on line 14 are reminiscent of the way in which Isaac referred to Rebekah in 27:14, 17 ("my sister"), and "in peace/safety" is the phrase used several times in that context regarding Jacob's safe return (27:14, 16: in both places the Ethiopic expression is the cognate *ba-salām*).

It is likely, therefore, that in the original text of Jubilees Isaac comforted Rebekah as he had in 27:13-17: he assured her that God would protect Jacob (in 27:15 he says God will guard him [*ya'aqqebo* and *'aqābi*, the word for "guardian," are associated with the same root]), describes Jacob in a positive way,[30] and ends with a term of endearment for her and a promise that Jacob would remain safe.

A note should be inserted about the oath Rebekah mentions to Isaac in v. 9. Rebekah told Isaac to make Esau swear not to harm Jacob, but the text of the chapter gives no indication that Isaac complied. He in effect tells her it is useless to have his older son take an oath because he would not abide by it.[31] In the sequel,

---

26 Charles thought the reference was to a guardian angel (*Jubilees*, 209). The passages noted above make it more likely that the Lord is Jacob's guardian or keeper (so also Hartom, "Jubilees," 109; Berger, *Jubiläen*, 499, n. a to v. 17, who points to 15:32, where the other nations are under spirits and angels but Israel is under God who guards them; Kugel, *Walk through* Jubilees, 169, who references Deut 32:8-9; Werman, *Jubilees*, 455–56).

27 This was Milik's suggestion, and it is incorporated into the reconstructed text in DJD 13:106, 112. The appearance of the term here, though it almost certainly means "dust" in the context, is interesting because the verb related to the root is the one used in Gen 32:25, 26 for Jacob's wrestling with the mysterious being at the Jabbok (see DJD 13:112).

28 Werman relates the image to the evil spirits associated with the nations (*Jubilees*, 456).

29 Milik understood אבל to mean "weeping." The masculine form entails that Isaac would be the one weeping, as Rebekah did in 27:13. See DJD 13:112. Above and in DJD 13 it is taken as "But."

30 The letters קר that are legible before "But" in line 13 may be from יקר, "dear, precious" (DJD 13:106, 110).

31 Endres finds in Isaac's reply to Rebekah evidence of his humility, an expression of doubt about his "effectiveness in trying to curb Esau's violence," but no one is effective in this regard (*Biblical Interpretation*, 175). Isaac is not being humble but realistic, fully aware of Esau's character.

Rebekah presents the matter to Esau as a request, and in chap. 36 Isaac will give orders regulating the relationship between the brothers. He will mention an oath in 36:7-11, but there is no statement that the brothers actually took it. In chap. 37 Esau will say his father made them swear such an oath (v. 4), but he promptly forgets it (v. 13). Jacob will then claim that Esau swore the oath to both his father and his mother, so apparently it was assumed that in his meetings with his parents in chaps. 35 and 36 Esau had indeed sworn not to harm Jacob. This is explicit in his meeting with Rebekah (35:24), but Isaac and Esau never converse in chap. 35 (yet see chap. 36).

18-24 Conversation between Rebekah and Esau

With the background provided in vv. 9-17 regarding the character of Esau, it seems that little good was likely to come from him, but Rebekah makes the effort nevertheless. It is what one would expect from a woman who was always so devoted to her son Jacob. Esau is the last man in the family to whom she turns, and he is definitely the lowest in her estimation. She and Isaac were convinced he would not live up to his word, but she made him give his word to behave anyway since she was afraid Jacob's life was at stake.

■ **18** As she did with Jacob in v. 1, she summoned Esau to come to her (she went to Isaac in v. 9), and he obeyed (presumably he had to travel from Edom). She began her words to him just as she started her speech to Isaac: she had a single request for him. In the case of Isaac, she then spelled out what that request was, but in speaking to Esau she first demanded (using an imperative form) that he agree to do whatever she asked of him before she explained the nature of her request. She does not trust him and does not want to give him a way out of doing as she wishes. Twice she calls him "my son" in this verse. Though she is aware of all his faults, she is still his mother.[32]

■ **19** Esau's response makes him sound like a dutiful son. He promises that whatever she asks of him he will do, and he phrases his answer both positively and negatively. Jacob had responded in a similarly positive way in v. 2 when she told him what her request was: "I will do everything just as you ordered me." Jacob did not raise the possibility of denying his mother's request as Esau does. The reader knows, however, that a promise from Esau did not mean he would carry it out (see v. 15).

■ **20** Rebekah's single request turns out to have multiple parts. It is interesting that she mentions the day of her death but does not disclose to Esau that it will fall within the current year. She asks only that, when the time arrives, he will transport her body to the place where Sarah was buried.[33] For her tomb Abraham had purchased a field containing the cave of Machpelah. Genesis 23:19 (see Jub 19:5-6) says of its location: "After this, Abraham buried Sarah his wife in the cave of the field of Machpelah facing Mamre (that is, Hebron) in the land of Canaan." Since Isaac and Rebekah now lived in that area, he would not have to carry her body very far. Esau with Jacob will fulfill her request in v. 27. In Genesis Jacob expresses a desire for burial with his ancestors (47:30; 49:29-32), but no matriarch does.

Her second request is that "you and Jacob love one another, and that the one not desire harm[34] for his brother but only loving one another" (see 36:4, 8-9, where Isaac will make a similar demand of his sons; cf. 37:4, 13). She does not tell him to honor his brother, as she had ordered Jacob in v. 1. Rather, she wants them to avoid injuring each other and to practice mutual love (see 7:20; 20:2). She is not asking anything unusual but is trying to ensure that no violence takes place between

---

32 Cf. Halpern-Amaru, *Empowerment*, 63.
33 In Gen 24:67 the two women were also in a sense united when Rebekah first joined the family: "Then Isaac brought her into his mother Sarah's tent. He took Rebekah, and she became his wife; and he loved her. So Isaac was comforted after his mother's death." See Halpern-Amaru, *Empowerment*, 63-64.
34 The Hebrew behind the Ethiopic phrase may have been בקש רעה (so Goldmann and Hartom). It appears in Num 35:23; 1 Sam 24:10; 25:26, etc. Livneh makes a strong case that desiring a brother's harm is the writer's interpretation of Lev 19:17: "You shall not hate in your heart anyone of your kin" ("'Love Your Fellow,'" 184-87). In Jubilees, especially as exemplified by Esau and Jacob, it has to do with intending to murder the other.

Esau and Jacob. Her particular formulation may, as Kugel suggests, reflect Lev 19:18 ("you shall love your neighbor as yourself") followed by a negative version of the golden rule.[35] *Targum Pseudo-Jonathan* Lev 19:18 is an example of this combination: "You shall not take revenge nor harbor *enmity* against your kinsmen. You shall love your neighbor, *so that what is hateful to you, you shall not do to him*." Great benefits would accrue to the two of them if they behaved as she urged: they would have success/prosperity, receive honor, and prove a blessing—that is, she places fulfillment of Lev 19:17-18 within a covenantal framework.[36] Rebekah takes Lev 19:18 to mean they are to live in mutual peace.[37] She also says they will be a *meḥrat*, literally a "compassion, pardon, mercy, pity, clemency,"[38] that is, they will be an object of mercy and will be treated in a kindly way. Not only would they get along well together; their relations with others would be cordial. According to the Ethiopic text, this is the treatment they will receive from those "who love you" (see the textual note). She seems to be saying they will be on good terms with their friends. Psalm 133:1 expresses the gist of what Rebekah says to her sons: "How very good and pleasant it is when kindred [אחים] live together in unity!"

Esau (vv. 21-24) gives a proper answer to his mother, once she has explained exactly what she wants from him.

■ **21-22** He repeats his reply from v. 19. Now that he knows her wishes, he agrees to them fully and enthusiastically. He has no inkling that the time of his mother's death is near, so he does not protest, as Jacob had, that she is too healthy to be entertaining morbid thoughts. He simply pledges to bury her, whenever the end arrives, at the honored place beside Sarah that she requested. That was a simple task, and one that a son should perform. The other exhortation was that he and Jacob be joined by brotherly love. Here Esau sounds like an ideal brother. Rebekah asked that the siblings love one another and not try to hurt each other; Esau promises that he will love Jacob more than any other person. He points out the obvious fact that Jacob was his only brother and that it was no great challenge to love him (though he once wanted to kill him). Rebekah already knew this, but Esau reminds her that the two were twins, conceived at the same time in her womb and born together. He asks a question that will soon have ominous meaning: "If I do not love my brother, whom shall I love?" Here he is supposed to be reassuring Rebekah, but his words will come to imply, after he attacks Jacob, that he loves no one. Despite appearances, Esau is incriminating himself as he paints a rosy picture of what his relationship with Jacob should be, a picture that reality will contradict.

■ **23-24** Esau turns the tables on his mother by presenting a request to her. In it he expresses concern about how Jacob will relate to him. Esau once again gives the appearance of a most understanding and agreeable son. When Jacob tricked his father into blessing him rather than Esau, the latter was furious and threatened to kill Jacob. The only impediment in the way of carrying out the threat was the presence of Isaac (Gen 27:41 // Jub 26:35). Once Isaac died, Esau was going to kill Jacob and become the only possible heir. Now he gives the impression that he entirely accepts the fact that his father blessed Jacob and made him ruler of his brother. Isaac had said, "Become lord of your brothers; / may the sons of your mother bow to you" (Jub 26:24 // Gen 27:29), and he had reiterated the matter a few verses later when Esau discovered what had happened: "I have just now designated him as your lord. I have given him all his brothers to be his servants" (Jub 26:31 // Gen 27:37). Even in the leftover blessing he conceded to Esau, Isaac gave voice to his subjection: you "will serve your brother" (Jub 26:34 // Gen 27:40).[39] Jubilees, unlike Genesis, has Isaac end his "blessing" of Esau with these words (after he removes his brother's yoke from his neck): "then you will commit an offense fully worthy of death and your

---

35 Kugel, *Walk through* Jubilees, 170.
36 See Livneh, "'Love Your Fellow,'" 188. In Jub 19:20 Abraham said that Jacob would prove to be a blessing.
37 Livneh, "'Love Your Fellow,'" 183–84. The same understanding is present in Noah's address to his children in chap. 7.
38 Leslau, *Concise Dictionary*, 31.
39 So Esau knows that Jacob will rule over him because that is what Isaac predicted. Kugel's suggestion (*Walk through* Jubilees, 170) that he knows it from the oracle to Rebekah in Gen 25:23 can hardly be correct, as Jubilees omits it.

descendants will be eradicated from beneath the sky" (26:34). Esau perhaps remembered that line or may have understood Isaac's plural form "brothers" to refer to him and his sons because he asks his mother to give instructions to[40] Jacob about him and his sons. Esau, reversing Rebekah's concern, seems to be asking for protection from Jacob, who will rule over him and his offspring. On his view, his father's blessing was a fact and would take effect; Esau was accepting of this and simply wanted his mother to urge Jacob to be considerate in that role. Is he serious? Has he not figured out that his mother knew about his intent to kill Jacob?

Esau concludes his response to Rebekah by taking the oath she wanted Isaac to make him swear. Though she had worded it as a request, he now swears to do as she asked: he would love Jacob and would never seek to harm him throughout his entire life. On the contrary, he would strive to do only what was good to his brother. By promising he would behave in this fashion throughout his life (see v. 1 where Rebekah tells Jacob to honor his father and brother during all his days), Esau was again incriminating himself. In fact, his own life will end with an attempt on Jacob's life. As if to augment the case he is building against Esau, the writer terminates the scene with the assertion: "He swore to her about this entire matter."[41] He made himself take the oath; neither of his parents did.[42]

25-26 Esau and Jacob with Rebekah

After speaking with the three men in the family, Rebekah for the first time brings the two principal players together, the future of the line, to make the necessary agreements. For the second time she summons Jacob, who comes to the place where she and his brother have been meeting. Esau had just taken an oath to love his brother and never seek his injury, and Jacob had agreed to honor his brother throughout his life. In the present scene Rebekah makes Jacob, with his brother as witness, pledge to follow her wishes, as Esau had vowed. The words "oath" and "swear" do not figure in these two verses. Perhaps Rebekah assumed that Jacob's word was good enough; an oath was not needed for him as it was for Esau. She had not said to Jacob in vv. 1-9 that he was to love Esau and avoid doing harm to him; she referred only to honoring him. Now she commands him to agree to those two orders and, judging from v. 27 below, also to bury her near Sarah. Jacob, of course, obeys; he always wants to do as his mother wishes. On this occasion he speaks for himself and for his sons, since Esau had mentioned his own sons when he asked Rebekah to instruct or exhort Jacob about his rule over them. Jacob promises that he and his sons will initiate nothing harmful against Esau. Of course, this does not address the possibility that Esau and his sons would instigate violence, but it leaves room for self-defense should that prove necessary, as it will. The only respect in which Jacob will be first or take the lead is to love his brother. So Rebekah achieved her purpose: both sons gave their word, Esau by oath, that they would love each other and never try to harm the other; and Esau acknowledged Jacob's primacy. All seems good at this moment, but Esau's terrible character casts a dark shadow over his mother's dying attempt to produce lasting harmony between her sons.

27 Esau and Jacob's Final Meal with Rebekah and Her Death[43]

The flurry of family meetings arranged by Rebekah was more urgent than one might have expected. The very night of the mutual assurances by the brothers, the three of them shared a meal. Perhaps it is no accident that Isaac was not a fellow diner on this solemn, heartwarm-

---

40 The verb *gaššaṣa* can also mean "admonish, exhort," etc. (Leslau, *Concise Dictionary*, 204).
41 Cf. Endres, *Biblical Interpretation*, 175.
42 Berger sees in Esau swearing an oath but not Jacob at least a latent rejection of taking an oath, as with the Essenes (*Jubiläen*, 500 n. a to v. 24). However, though Jacob is the sort of person who does not have to resort to oaths, in 29:7 he swears to one in his agreement with Laban, and the writer of Jubilees does not criticize him for it.
43 Endres lists the features that make the account of the end of Rebekah's life an example of the patterns he finds in farewell speeches in the book (*Biblical Interpretation*, 175), but for some reason he leaves chap. 35 out of his chart for such speeches in his Appendix 2 (p. 255).

ing occasion.[44] She had done all the planning with her sons while Isaac had not actually done what she asked, so now she celebrates with Esau and Jacob. That night proved to be the last one in her life (regarding her age at death, see the commentary on v. 6 above). The dream message she had shared with Jacob was accurate: she died at age 155. Her two sons honored her dying wish that she be buried near her mother-in-law, that is, in the cave of Machpelah.[45] In so doing, they carried out one of her last requests and seemed poised to act on the other two.

The Rebekah of Jubilees is remarkable in death as she was in life. The author of Jubilees has pictured her last day as a parallel with the end of Abraham's life and to some extent that of Isaac (see 36:17-18). On his last day, Abraham's two sons had come to celebrate the Festival of Weeks with him, and Rebekah and Jacob were involved in the meal he ate on that occasion (22:1-6). After he provided instructions for Jacob, through whom his line would be traced, he died, and Isaac and Ishmael "buried him in the cave of Machpelah near his wife Sarah" (23:7). So too Rebekah's twin sons had come to her, to them she gave instructions to ensure the continuation of the chosen line through Jacob, with them she shared a final meal, and they buried her in the same cave near Sarah. She and Abraham had been the first to recognize the sterling qualities of Jacob, and she had carried out his instructions to "take care of my son Jacob because he will occupy my place on the earth" (19:17). Abraham had added: "Increase your favor to him still more; may your eyes look at him lovingly because he will be a blessing for us on the earth from now and throughout all the history of the earth. May your hands be strong and your mind be happy with your son Jacob because I love him much more than all my sons; for he will be blessed forever and his descendants will fill the entire earth" (19:20-21). Jacob stood in Abraham's place as the one through whom the promises and blessings flowed; Rebekah stood in Abraham's place as the one who guaranteed the future of the chosen people.

---

44 Halpern-Amaru, *Empowermnt*, 64. She speculates that his absence may be due to his weakness or it could have resulted from the writer's desire to create a parallel scene with Isaac's death and burial in chap. 36. She also thinks the passive voice in Gen 49:31 ("there Isaac and his wife Rebekah were buried") could be an exegetical basis for excluding Isaac from the burial. However, the same passive is used for the burials of Abraham and Sarah, yet Genesis reports that Abraham buried Sarah.

45 Jacob records the place where Rebekah and others were buried in Gen 49:31 after he charged his sons to bury him in the cave of Machpelah: "There Abraham and his wife Sarah were buried; and there Isaac and his wife Rebekah were buried; and there I buried Leah."

Isaac's Last Day and the Death of Leah

36

1/ During the sixth year of this week [2162] Isaac summoned his two[a] sons Esau and Jacob. When they had come to him, he said to them: "My children, I am going the way of my fathers, to the eternal home where my fathers are. 2/ Bury me near[a] my father Abraham in the double cave in the field of Ephron the Hittite that Abraham acquired[b] to (have) a burial place there. There, in the grave that I dug for myself, bury me. 3/ This is what I am ordering you, my sons: that you do what is right and just on the earth so that the Lord may bring on you everything that the Lord said that he would do for Abraham[a] and his descendants.[b] 4/ Practice brotherly love[a] among yourselves, my sons, like a man who loves himself, with each one desiring what is good for his brother[b] and doing things together[c] on the earth. May they love one another as themselves.[d] 5/ Regarding the matter of idols, I[a] am instructing[b] you to reject them,[c] to be an enemy of them,[d] and not to love them[e] because they are full of errors for those who[f] worship them[g] and who bow to them.[h] 6/ My sons,[a] remember the Lord, the God of your father Abraham[b]—afterwards[c] I, too, worshiped and served him properly and[d] sincerely[e]—so that[f] he may make you numerous and increase your descendants in number like the stars of the sky and plant you in the earth as a righteous plant that will not be[g] uprooted throughout all the history of eternity. 7/ Now I will make you swear with[a] the great oath—because there is no oath which is greater than it, by the praiseworthy, glorious, and great, splendid, marvelous, powerful, <u>and great name</u>[b] which made the heavens and the earth <u>and everything together</u>—that you will continue to fear and worship <u>him</u>, 8/ as each loves his brother[a] kindly and <u>proper</u>ly. One is <u>not</u> to desire[b] harm for his brother <u>from now and forever</u>,[c] throughout your entire lifetime, so that you may be prosperous in <u>everything</u> that <u>you do and not</u> be destroyed. 9/ If <u>one</u> of you desires harm for his brother, be aware from now on that anyone who <u>desires harm for his fellow</u>[a] will fall <u>into</u> his <u>control</u> and will be uprooted from the land of <u>the living</u>, while his descendants will be destroyed from beneath the sky. 10/ On the day of <u>anger with raging wrath and fury</u>[a]—with a blazing fire that devours—he will burn his land, his <u>cities</u>, and everything that belongs to him <u>just as</u> he <u>burned</u> Sodom. He will be erased from the disciplinary book of humanity.[b] He will not be entered in the book of life but is one who[c] will be destroyed. He will pass over to an eternal[d] curse so that their punishment may always be renewed with denunciation and curse, with anger, pain, and wrath, and with blows and eternal sickness. 11/ I am reporting and testifying to you, my sons, in accord with the punishment that will come on the man who wishes[a] to do what is harmful[b] to his brother."[c]

12/ That day he divided[a] all the property that he owned between the two of them. He gave the larger part[b] to the man who was the first to be born[c] along with the tower,[d] every<u>thing</u>[e] <u>around</u> it, and everything[f] that Abraham had acquired at the well of the oath. 13/ He said, "I am making this[a] portion larger[b] <u>for the man</u> who was the first to be born." 14/ But Esau[a] said, "I sold (it)[b] to Jacob; I gave my[c] birthright to Jacob.[d] <u>It is</u>[e] <u>to be given</u> to him. I will say absolutely nothing about it because it belongs to him." 15/ Isaac then said, "May a blessing rest on you, my sons, and on your descendants today[a] because you have given me rest. My mind is not sad regarding the birthright[b]—lest you do[c] <u>something evil</u> about it. 16/ May the Most High Lord bless the man[a] who does what is right—him and his descendants[b] <u>forever</u>." 17/ When he had finished giving them or<u>ders and</u> blessing them, they ate and drank together in front of him. He was happy[a] because there was agreement <u>between them</u>. They le<u>ft</u> him, rested[b] that day, and fell asleep.[c] 18/ <u>That</u> day Isaac <u>was happy</u> as he fell asleep on his bed. <u>He fell asleep</u>[a] forever <u>and died</u> at the age of <u>180</u> years. He had completed[b] <u>25 weeks of years</u>[c] and five <u>years</u>. His two sons Esau and Jacob <u>b</u>uried him.

19/ <u>Esau</u> went[a] <u>to the land</u> of Mount <u>Seir</u>[b] <u>and lived there</u>, 20/ while Jacob lived on the mountain of[a] Hebron, in the tower <u>in the land of Canaan</u>,[b] <u>in the land</u> of his father A<u>braham</u>.[c] <u>He</u> worshiped the Lord wholeheartedly[d] and

953

in line with the revealed commands <u>according</u> to the divisions of[e] the <u>times</u>[f] <u>of</u> his generation.

21/ His[a] wife Leah died during the fourth year of the second week of the forty-fifth jubilee [2167]. <u>He</u>[b] <u>buried</u> her in the twofold cave near his mother Rebekah, on the left of her <u>grand</u>mother Sarah's grave.[c] 22/ All[a] her sons[b] and[c] his sons[d] <u>ca</u>me to mourn with him for his wife Leah[e] and to comfort him regarding her because he was lament<u>ing</u> her. 23/ For he loved her very much from the time when <u>her</u> sister Rachel died <u>because</u> she was <u>perfect</u> and right in all her <u>behavior</u>[a] and <u>honored</u>[b] Jacob. In[c] all the <u>time that she lived</u>[d] with him[e] he did not hear[f] a[g] harsh[h] word from her mouth because she was gentle and possessed (the virtues of) peace, truthfulness, and honor.[i] 24/ As he recalled all[a] the things that she had done in her lifetime, he greatly lamented her because[b] he loved her[c] with all his heart and with all[d] his person.

Textual Notes

1a two] om. 38.
2a near] + "Sarah, the tomb of" 21 48.
 b Abraham acquired] + "with his gold" 35.
3a Abraham] + "to him" 38.
 b his descendants (lit., "seed")] "his sons" 12.
4a brotherly love] The full phrase is unusual: "Be, my sons, among yourselves loving your brothers." The pl. "your brothers" does not fit the situation, as just Esau and Jacob are addressed. It is likely that the second person masc. pl. suffixes and verbs misled a translator into reading אחיך as pl., as the form could be either sg. or pl. See VanderKam, *Jubilees* 2:237–38.
 b his brother] "his brothers" 63 (see the previous note).
 c together] + "from the heart" 20 25 35 39 42 44 47 48 58.
 d themselves] + "they will become a blessing" 44.
5a I] + "am commanding you and" 12 17[c].
 b instructing] "commanding" 9 21 38 39 42 47 48 58.
 c them] "it" 9 21 39[t] 42 47; MS. 38 reads an indicative form of the preceding verb (= you will reject) and "it" as the suffix.
 d (be an enemy) of them] "of it" 21 38; MS. 38 also inserts a verb before this one: "loathe it and."
 e (love) them] "it" 21 38.
 f those who] + "love it and" 21.
 g (worship) them] "it" 21.
 h to them] "to it" 21.
6a My sons] om. 12.
 b Abraham] "Israel" 21.
 c afterwards] "for this reason" 21 39 48. Charles (*Ethiopic Version*, 135 n. 9) emended *wa-'em-ze* to *wa-kama*, which he translated "how" (*Jubilees*, 211). Littmann, Goldmann, and Hartom adopted the proposal. It is unnecessary, since Isaac is reporting that, after his father Abraham, he too worshiped the God of Abraham (VanderKam, *Jubilees* 2:238).

 d and (sincerely)] om. 21 39; "as/like" 42 47; + "as/like" 48.
 e sincerely] "happily" 12 21 39 42 47 48; "with a sincere heart" 35 44 (cf. 58).
 f so that] om. 42 47 48.
 g will not be] "is not to be" 21.
7a with] om. 21.
 b name] "his name" 21 35.
8a brother] "brothers" 9 12 38.
 b is (not) to desire] "will (not) desire" 9 20[t] 21 38 39 47 48 58 63.
 c forever] om. 21.
9a for his fellow] "against him" 12. The Heb. frg. 4Q223-224 unit 2 ii:51 has רעהו, while the other Eth. copies read "his brother."
10a anger with raging wrath and fury] The best Eth. reading is "turmoil and [Ms. 38 lacks the conjunction] curse, of anger and wrath." The translation follows the Heb. frg. (4Q223-224 unit 2 ii:52).
 b disciplinary book of humanity] Several MSS. lack the construct ending joining "book of" and "humanity" (12 21 38 39 44 48 63). It is not clear how this expression in them should be read. Ms. 12 om. "humanity," but 20 25 35 39 42 44 47 48 58 read "the sons of humanity."
 c is one who] So 42 47 58 63. The other copies read: "in the one that" (see the commentary).
 d eternal] om. 21.
11a wishes] om. 12.
 b what is harmful] "what is evil" 12.
 c his brother] "his companion/neighbor" 21; + "is to be cut off" 35 58 (58 places a conjunction before the verb).
12a divided] + "it" 25 63; "it" (fem.) 12.
 b the larger part] om. 21 38; "the double part" 21.
 c to be born] "to be fashioned/created" 17.
 d the tower] "his tower" 38 39 42 48.
 e everything] pr. "and" 20 21 25 35 42 44 47 58.

f   and everything] om. 35.
13a this] om. 25 35.
b   larger] "double" 21.
14a Esau] om. 20 25 (the subject is "He").
b   (it)] "everything" 12 21.
c   my (birthright)] "the" 9 17ᵗ 38 63.
d   to Jacob²] om. 20.
e   It is] pr. "and" 9 20 25 44 63.
15a today] om. 21 (added later in the sentence—after "you have given me rest").
b   the birthright] "your birthright" 21; "my birthright" 25 39 42 47 48 (44, with a different spelling).
c   lest you do] om. 21.
16a May the Most High Lord bless the man] "May the man bless the Most High Lord" 20 25 63.
b   his descendents] Ms. 38 reads an acc. form but without the suffix "his." The other MSS. read "his descendants" but place it in the nom. rather than in the acc. case (MS. 44 places la- before it, thus making the case correct). Only MS. 51 (not collated in VanderKam, *Jubilees* 1) has the correct word *zar'o*. It may be that the immediately preceding word *kiyāhu* influenced the form *zar'u*. See VanderKam, *Jubilees* 2:240.
17a He was happy] "They were happy" 9 17 38 44.
b   (they) rested] "(he) rested" 17 21.
c   and (they) fell asleep] om. 17 21 48; pr. "he being happy" 38.
18a He fell asleep] om. 21 (ויּישן 4Q223-224 unit 2 iii:10).
b   He had completed] The Eth. MSS. place the verb either after "180 years" (39 42 47 48 58) or after "25 weeks" (the others). As 4Q223-224 unit 2 iii:11 is reconstructed in DJD 13, the verb would have appeared after "180 years."
c   weeks of years] Where the Eth. copies have "weeks," 4Q223-224 unit 2 iii:11 reads "weeks of years."
19a went] 4Q223-224 unit 2 iii:12 uses לוא = לו, a standard prepositional phrase after a form of הלך. It is not realized in the Eth. version.
b   to the land of Mount Seir] This is the reading of 4Q223-224 unit 2 iii:12 ("to the land [of Mount] Seir"). There does not seem to be space for the Eth. reading "to the land of Edom—to Mount Seir," since after לארץ there may be space only for הר before the preserved name שעיר.
20a on the mountain of] "in the land of" 9 17 20 21 38 39 48 58 63.
b   in the land of Canaan] This is the reading of 4Q223-224 unit 2 iii:13. The prepositional phrase fell out of the Eth. MSS. tradition through parablepsis with the following one that also begins with בארץ. Cf. Gen 37:1.
c   in the land of his father Abraham] So 4Q223-224 unit 2 iii:13. The Eth. reading is, lit., "in the land of the sojourning of his father Abraham."
d   wholeheartedly] + "and with all his soul/person" = Lat. The expression could have been omitted by the Eth.

tradition, but it may equally be the result of adding an expected phrase (see VanderKam, *Jubilees* 2:240).
e   according to the divisions of] om. 20 25 35; om. "the divisions of" 39 42 47 48 58. For "divisions" Eth. reads a verbal form *falaṭa*, which should be *felṭata* (see VanderKam, *Jubilees* 2:241). Lat. has *divisionem*.
f   the times] In DJD 13:113 the letters ימי (all with circlets over them) were read at the point where Eth. has "days/times" in "the divisions of the times." It seems more likely that the bits of ink are from the first four letters of העתים (with thanks to Eugene Ulrich for his assistance with the reading).
21a His] "Jacob's" 35 = Lat.
b   He (buried)] "They" = Lat. 4Q223-224 unit 2 iii:16 reads] ויקברו but breaks off at this point so that one cannot determine the number of the verb. In view of v. 22, a pl. is implausible (his sons are not with him).
c   on the left of his grandmother Sarah's grave] Lat. lacks, perhaps through parablepsis: *matrem eius . . . patris eius*. 4Q223-224 unit 2 iii:16, if the small fragment belongs here, supports the longer reading of Eth. as it preserves the last word in it (אביהו; lit., "the mother of his father").
22a All] om. 12.
b   her sons] "the sons" 12 58 (with acc. ending); "his sons" 21.
c   and (his sons)] + "the sons of" 21.
d   his sons] Eth. uses the same word for the offspring of Leah and of Jacob, but Lat. has *filii* in the first instance and *pueri* in the second (= servants?). It is less likely that his servants would be mentioned here.
e   to mourn . . . for his wife Leah] The best-supported reading is an anticipatory suffix on the verb followed by "Leah" with the acc. ending where one would expect *la-leyyā*. Several MSS. do read *la-leyyā* (12 21 35 38 39 48; 44 has "regarding"), but only MSS. 21 and 38 remove the anticipatory suffix on the verb. Lat. reads the acc. *liam* as expected.
23a in all her behavior (lit., "ways")] om. 25.
b   honored] "loved" 20 25.
c   Jacob. In] By reading a conjunction after "Jacob," Eth. separates this statement from the next. Mss. 9 21 38 44 lack the conjunction, as does Lat. The result is: "She honored Jacob in all the time that she lived with him [Lat. = he lived with her]."
d   she lived] Eth. and 4Q223-224 unit 2 iii:19 read a noun: "(the days of her) life" (no suffix in Eth., except in 21 38), where Lat. has a verb: "she lived." The meaning is the same.
e   with him] "with her" Lat. = "he lived with her."
f   he did not hear] Lat. reads a conjunction before this clause.
g   a (harsh)] "any" Lat.
h   harsh] Lat. *nequam* has the sense of "bad, worthless, good for nothing."

i   peace, truthfulness, and honor] Eth. has nouns where Lat. has *pacifica erat* and then becomes illegible (*hono . . .* suggests that the text agreed with the terms of Eth. if not the grammatical forms). Mss. 35 58 agree on an adjectival form with Lat. for "peaceful." Ms. 35 also has an adjective where the other mss. read a noun ("truthfulness"). For a similar list of nouns Werman (*Jubilees*, 459 n. 10) refers to 1QS iv:2–6.

24a   all] om. 39 47 58.

b   he greatly lamented her because] Lat. lacks (except for "greatly," which it reads with "he loved her") due to the similarity between *lubebat* and *diligebat* (Rönsch, *Jubiläen*, 152). Lat. also reads *ideo*, "for this reason," which lacks an equivalent in Eth. (but note *'esma*, "because," without a preceding "and").

c   loved her] pr. "knew her and" 21; om. 35 but it adds it at the end of the verse; + "very much" (see Lat. *valde*) 39 42 47 48 58.

d   all (his person [lit., "soul"])] Lat. lacks.

Commentary

After Rebekah's death at the end of chap. 35, Isaac lived on as the single parent of Esau and Jacob. In chap. 36 the patriarch gives final instructions to them and then reaches the end of his own life. It seems he should have preceded Rebekah in death, since he spent an inordinate stretch of time thinking he was about to die. The author dates the occasion when Isaac believed he was blessing Esau to the year 2114 (26:1); he wanted to pass the blessing to him then because he anticipated his death would come soon. When Jacob invited him to Bethel in the year 2143 (twenty-nine years later), he replied: "Let my son Jacob come so that I can see him before I die" (31:4). Just after this, when Jacob encouraged him to accompany him back to Bethel, he declined saying, "I am old and unable to put up with the trip" (31:27). Rebekah went in his stead. Now, some forty-eight years after expecting his death in chap. 26 and nineteen years after feeling too feeble to travel, he does in fact arrive at his final age of 180 years. Esau and Jacob bury their father and then return to their separate homes. The chapter ends with an account of Leah's death followed by statements about her and about Jacob's strong feelings of affection for her.

The paragraph in Gen 35:27-29 reports the death of Isaac at 180 years and provides the occasion for the action in Jubilees 36. In Gen 35:27-29 Jacob visits Isaac, apparently for the first and only time after traveling back from Mesopotamia, Isaac passes away, and his two sons bury him. The three verses say nothing about any final words Isaac spoke to Esau and Jacob, so the address he makes to them in Jub 36:1-11 comes from elsewhere—from the writer himself and/or another source(s).

The sections in the chapter are these:

1-11   Isaac's instructions regarding his burial and his testament to Esau and Jacob

12-18   Isaac divides his estate, dies, and is buried

19-20   Esau and Jacob go to their homes

21-24   Jacob's beloved wife Leah dies.

There is textual evidence in three languages for the chapter. In addition to the Ethiopic version, the Latin translation is legible for most of vv. 20-24, and in 4Q223–224 unit 2 one can read words and letters from v. 7 to v. 23:

Column ii:48–54 = vv. 7-10

Column iii:1–19 = vv. 10-23.

In the two columns only small parts of the text have survived on assorted fragments. In col. iii, several of the lines have to be reconstructed in their entirety (6–7 and 15), but something from each of the verses is extant, apart from v. 11 for which nothing remains. There is space for it in the reconstructed column, but none of the fragments contains a single letter from it.[1]

---

[1] Milik (DJD 1:83, 84) suggested that 1Q18 frg. 3 came from 36:12. The small piece, which, as he recognized, may not belong to 1Q18, has five legible letters, three of which are פלג, "divide." However, this would not be the verb used for dividing property, and the preceding two letters (קה) also do not fit in 36:12 (see VanderKam, *Textual*, 99). Baillet (DJD 7:1-2) raised the possibility that 4Q482 frg. 2

1-11 Isaac's Instructions regarding His Burial and His Testament to Esau and Jacob[2]

Like his father Abraham, Isaac provides instructions and guidance for his sons before his death.

■ **1** The text dates Isaac's last day to the year of the world 2162 when, according to v. 18, he was 180 years of age (so Gen 35:28). This is another instance in which the dates in the overall chronology are inconsistent. Isaac was born in 1987 (16:15) so that in 2162 he should have been 175 years (his father's age at death).[3] Like Rebekah, he summoned his two sons who are named in their birth order—Esau and Jacob. The order is the first indication that Isaac will deal with them as if Esau, the elder, was the legitimate heir, the one owed the special rights connected with his position in the family. In Genesis, Isaac does not give instructions to Esau and Jacob, but in this chapter he waxes rather poetic as he announces his imminent death to them. He says that he is "going the way of my fathers," that is, he will proceed to the place where his deceased ancestors repose, a place he calls "the eternal home where my fathers are." The expression reminds one of Eccl 12:5, where Qohelet, speaking of death, says "all must go to their eternal home." Picturing death as joining the ancestors also echoes language Jacob employed in Genesis when he was nearing death. At that time he made Joseph promise: "Do not bury me in Egypt. When I lie down with my ancestors [אבתי], carry me out of Egypt and bury me in their burial place" (Gen 47:29-30). Then, just before his death, Jacob addressed all his sons: "I am about to be gathered to my people. Bury me with my ancestors [אבתי]" (Gen 49:29; see also v. 33). In Gen 25:8 Abraham is gathered to his people, and the same is said about Isaac in 35:29. For Isaac to claim that he will be joining his fathers is peculiar because he wants to be buried in the cave of Machpelah where only one father lay—Abraham (see v. 2). So the expression may refer more generally to joining the souls of those who have gone before.[4]

■ **2** The first command he issues is that his sons lay him to rest in the ancestral tomb—in the cave of Machpelah near Abraham. Isaac and Abraham are paired in Gen 35:27; it describes the former's home as the place "where Abraham and Isaac had resided as aliens." The Genesis passage does not say where the sons buried him, only that "he was gathered to his people" (v. 29). The expression is rather general (see above on v. 1), but Jacob in Gen 49:31 names Isaac's final resting place: the cave in the field of Machpelah where "Abraham and his wife Sarah were buried; there Isaac and his wife Rebekah were buried." It is worthy of note that Isaac does not request burial near Rebekah in the same cave; in death he is the son of Abraham. That the writer has the context of Gen 49:31 in mind is clear from how Isaac identifies the tomb. He uses the words Jacob employs for it when preparing for his own death: "Bury me with my ancestors—in the cave in the field of Ephron the Hittite, in the cave in the field at Machpelah, near Mamre, in the land of Canaan, in the field that Abraham bought from Ephron the Hittite as a burial site" (Gen 49:29-30). But his next statement is unexpected: Isaac refers to the grave that he dug for himself as the site where Esau and Jacob should inter his body. The expression parallels Gen 50:5, where Joseph says to Pharaoh, "My father made me swear an oath; he said, 'I am about to die. In the tomb that I hewed out for myself in the land of Canaan, there you shall bury me.'" However one relates the two passages in Genesis regarding the burial place of Jacob (49:31 [from P] and 50:5 [from J]), the author of Jubilees has drawn elements from these fuller statements to fashion a parallel account for Isaac.[5]

---

contained text from Jub 36:9 (in its three lines one can read the verb יחרוש, "devise," and the word "sky," but the verb would not be the one used in 36:9 (see VanderKam, "Manuscript Tradition," 7, and the Introduction above).

2   In a passage that he attributes to Josephus, Syncellus writes, "Rebecca petitioned Isaac in his old age to counsel Esau and Jacob to love one another. After exhorting them, he foretold that if Esau would rise up against Jacob, he would fall at his hands" (124.5-7; Adler/Tuffin, *Chronography*, 155). The citation mostly reflects the situation in Jubilees 35, but the words "After exhorting them" appear to presuppose the circumstances of chap. 36.

3   Wiesenberg lists a series of discrepancies in Jubilees relating to dates in Isaac's life ("Jubilee of Jubilees," 34-36).

4   Werman, *Jubilees*, 454.

5   He did something similar in crafting the blessing scene in chap. 31 from Jacob's blessing of Joseph's

Once he has communicated instructions for his burial (neither of his sons protested that he was too healthy to die, as Jacob did to Rebekah), Isaac delivers a testament to Esau and Jacob in vv. 3-11. The themes he enunciates have numerous parallels in Jubilees' other addresses by parents to their children and grandchildren, but they are also highly appropriate to the particular situation of chap. 36.

▪ 3 The first testamentary command—to "do what is just and right on the earth"—echoes Noah's exhortation in 7:20, 34 and Abraham's words in 20:2 and 22:10 (in 35:13 Isaac declared that Esau "lacks [the ability to do] what is right"). The result of behaving properly will be that God will "bring on you everything that the Lord said he would do for Abraham and his descendants." The mandate takes up some of the language in Gen 18:19, where the deity says about Abraham: "I have chosen [known] him, that he may charge his children and his household after him to keep the way of the Lord by doing righteousness and justice; so that the Lord may bring about for Abraham what he has promised him." Isaac phrases the consequence of right conduct (for righteousness, see also v. 16) in a way befitting his situation as the middle person in transmitting the blessings of his father to the next generation. Noah, of course, put the matter differently, since he lived before Abraham, but Abraham himself in blessing Jacob (and not mentioning Isaac) offered a closer parallel to Isaac's words "bring on you everything that the Lord said he would do for Abraham and his descendants" when, on more than one occasion, he prayed that the blessings accorded him and his ancestors be given to Jacob (see 19:23, 27; 22:13-15, 24).

▪ 4 The second command in the testament is that Esau and Jacob practice brotherly love (he will return to the subject in vv. 8-11).[6] Rebekah had also addressed them about the topic (35:20; cf. v. 22, 24, 26), and it is an element in the other speeches to children (7:20; 20:2). Isaac develops the notion of fraternal affection in ways showing unmistakably that he is applying Lev 19:17-18: "You shall not hate in your heart anyone of your kin [אחיך]; you shall reprove your neighbor, or you will incur guilt yourself. You shall not take vengeance or bear a grudge against any of your people, but you shall love your neighbor [רעך] as yourself: I am the Lord." Isaac twice mentions loving a brother as oneself, a reflection of "you shall love your neighbor as yourself," understanding "neighbor" to mean "brother."[7] Isaac reiterates Rebekah's instructions that the brothers desire or seek what is good for the other (35:20 [expressed negatively]; see v. 24). If the expression "not desire harm" (35:20) is an interpretation of "You shall not hate in your heart anyone of your kin," the positive formulation ("desiring what is good for his brother") is another way of stating the underlying principle.[8] Isaac also enjoins "doing things together on the earth." Noah had warned his offspring about the danger of separating from one another: "But now I am the first to see your actions—that you have not been conducting yourselves properly because you have begun to conduct yourselves in the way of destruction, to separate from one another, to be jealous of one another, and not to be together with one another, my sons" (7:26; see also 7:13-17; 11:2-6). Abraham seems to have had a similar goal of unity for his sons and grandsons—at least in military situations: "He ordered them to keep the way of the Lord so that they would do what is right and that they should love one another; that they

---

two sons in Genesis 48 (see the commentary on Jubilees 31). Werman notes that the phrase "I dug for myself" implies burial in the ground (*Jubilees*, 454, cf. 13-14).

6   The fact that Isaac says "Practice brotherly love among yourselves, my sons, like a man who loves himself" (36:4) has led Kugel (*Walk through* Jubilees, 171; cf. "Jubilees," 417) to suggest: "It seems that the phrase 'among yourselves' is intended to limit the scope of this commandment [Lev 19:18], much as the Qumran community and others sought to limit it: it did not necessarily mean loving all humanity, nor even all of Israel, but only some subsection thereof" (the entire statement is in parentheses). All of humanity are certainly not included, but in the context Isaac is addressing only his two sons so little can be extrapolated from the prepositional phrase.

7   See Livneh, "'Love Your Fellow,'" 175-76.

8   Livneh shows that in Jubilees the idea of not wishing or seeking harm for a brother (from Lev 19:17) has the sense of not intending to kill ("'Love Your Fellow,'" 184-86). Conversely, loving one's fellow means living together in peace (e.g., 183-84, 189).

should be like this in every war so that they could go against each one *who rises* against them; and do what is just and right on the earth" (20:2).

■ **5-6** Isaac, unlike Rebekah, takes up the subject of idols, the need to reject them, and the requirement to remember the God of Abraham alone.[9] These too are themes in the speeches of Abraham (Noah lived in the pre-image period). He had taken an anti-idol turn already as a young man and, as Isaac does in this verse, had labeled them an error (of the mind) for those who worship them (12:3, 5). Abraham admonished his children to love and serve God and not to make or follow idols so that his blessings would flow to them (20:7-10). He disclosed to Isaac that he hated idols and maintained exclusive devotion to God (21:3), and he warned him not to pursue "idols, statues, or molten images" (21:5). Jacob as well received instructions from Abraham about the worthlessness of idols and the benefits of serving God (22:18-19). Isaac, who transmits the Abrahamic tradition in this regard, issues to Esau and Jacob three directives about idols: they are to reject them, be hostile to them, and not love them because they are saturated with errors for those serving them. He makes sure his sons know that he, like his father (he mentions the "God of Abraham"), worshiped the Lord in the proper way (e.g., 24:23 // Gen 26:25) and that the promise of progeny as numerous as the stars (e.g., Jub 24:10 // Gen 26:4; Jub 25:16) would find fulfillment in them if they revered the ancestral God. This familiar patriarchal assurance he couples with another: so that he may "plant you in the earth as a righteous plant that will not be uprooted throughout all the history of eternity." The planting metaphor is the one Noah, the first to plant a vineyard (7:1), quite appropriately used for his offspring: "Now listen, my children. Do what is just and right so that you may be rightly planted on the surface of the entire earth" (7:34). Abraham had also employed it as he promised to Isaac: "He will bless you in all your actions. He will raise from you a righteous plant of truth in the earth throughout all the generations of the earth" (21:24; cf. 16:26). The permanence and growth suggested by the image stand in contrast to the message conveyed by the metaphor of being uprooted (as here) in passages announcing punishment on sinners.

The last part of Isaac's address (vv. 7-11) begins with a description of a tremendous oath; that oath will obligate the brothers to continue fearing and worshiping the one God and to practice brotherly love (see 7:20; 20:2; the latter topic receives expanded treatment in vv. 8-11).[10]

■ **7** In v. 7 Isaac speaks about the oath. It should be recalled that he had some experience with oaths. He swore one with King Abimelech and his officers at a time when there were disputes about wells and when a place received the name "the well of the oath" (Beersheba). Isaac felt he had committed himself under pressure and uttered a robust curse against the Philistines (24:25-32; cf. Gen 26:26-33). Rebekah asked him to make Esau swear not to harm Jacob (35:9), but Isaac

---

9   Ibid., 190: "Significantly, the reference to Lev 19:17-18 in relation to fraternal love in Isaac's testament (*Jub.* 36:4) is juxtaposed with an order regarding that which may *not* be loved, namely, foreign idols."

10 Isaac's two commands of fearing and worshiping God and loving one's brother indicate a combination of Deut 6:5 and Lev 19:18. David Flusser wrote: "Thus the book of Jubilees is the earliest document for the juxtaposition in Midrash fashion of two Torah commandments which start with the word *We'ahavta*, 'you shall love': i.e., you shall love him, your God (Deut. 6:5); and you shall love your neighbor (or fellow man—Lev. 19:18)" ("A New Sensitivity in Judaism and the Christian Message," in his *Judaism and the Origins of Christianity* [Jerusalem: Magnes, 1988] 474). Verses 7-8 are similar in some ways to the double command of love (love God above all and your neighbor as yourself) in Mark 12:28-34 and parallels. As John P. Meier comments, "Thus, in both the Dead Sea Scrolls and *Jubilees*, what we find is a certain 'seedbed' or intimation of what will come in Jesus' double command, but nothing more. Another type of foreshadowing that we see in these texts is the growing tendency to summarize the commandments of the Law in certain key obligations, with obedience to God and/or love for fellow members of the community (however narrowly defined) placed early on in the lists. Hence, while Jesus' double command is new in its formulation, conciseness, and insistence on the superiority of the two commandments of love to all other commandments, it is not entirely bereft of ancestors within Palestinian Judaism at the turn of the era." (*A Marginal Jew: Rethinking the Historical Jesus*, vol. 4, *Law and Love* [AYBRL; New Haven: Yale University Press, 2009], 507).

did not do as she requested because he believed Esau would renege on any oath he swore (35:15). In view of his strong skepticism about the effectiveness of a vow for Esau, it seems strange that he now decides his twin sons must take an oath, but he impresses upon them that it was an awesome oath and that taking it was an uncommonly solemn exercise. He calls the oath he has in mind one than which there is no greater. The reason why it is unsurpassed in greatness is that the person who takes it swears by the name of God.[11] Isaac resorts to six adjectives (actually seven, since "great" appears twice) to define that name. Four of the six are shared with Isaac's description of Jacob's guardian in 35:17 (see the commentary there).

The Name (36:7)	Jacob's Guardian (35:17)
Praiseworthy (*sebuḥ*)	Great
Glorious	Powerful
Great (twice)	Glorious
Splendid (*seruḥ*)	Praiseworthy (*'ekut*)
Marvelous (*manker*)	
Powerful	

Only "splendid" and "marvelous" are not shared by the two enumerations (synonyms are employed for "praiseworthy"). The two may reflect descriptions of God in Exodus. The glory of God that appears on Mount Sinai is designated with a noun related to the adjective *seruḥ*: *šarḥu la-'egzi'abḥēr* (= the glory of the Lord; Eth. Exod 24:16, 17), and Exod 15:11 uses a term rendered in the Ethiopic version by *manker*: "Who is like you, O Lord, among the gods? / Who is like you, majestic in holiness, / awesome [*manker*] in splendor, doing wonders?" The Lord or his name is presented with a series of descriptors in Exod 34:5-7, but none of them figures in the two lists above. The name, so grandly depicted in v. 7, is the one borne by the God who created "the heavens and the earth and everything together" (for inclusion of "everything" in summaries of his creative work, see also 2:25; 12:4, 19; 22:27; 31:29).[12] A parallel to the string of adjectives but describing God himself rather than his name appears in 4Q372 (4QNarrative and Poetic Composition[b]) frg. 1 29 ("For a God great, holy, mighty, and majestic; awesome and marvelous [," after which there is a reference to the heavens, not preserved, and the earth, line 30; trans. Schuller and Bernstein, *DSSR* 3:637).[13]

The oath about which Isaac speaks and the creative power of the God who sanctions it exhibit some parallels with 1 Enoch 69:13-25.[14] The text mentions "the name and the oath" that make people quake (v. 14). Through that oath the heavens were put in place, as were the earth, the sea, and the pillars of the deep (vv. 16-17). The sequel (vv. 20-24) indicates that the oath has to do with the way the universe was created to operate, and the oath is called "mighty" (v. 25; "powerful and strong" in v. 15). There are commonalities between the passages, but Isaac's oath, though it is to be taken in the name of the Creator, relates especially to worship and the relations between brothers, not to the order of the universe.

The first duty to which Isaac makes Esau and Jacob swear is to "continue to fear and worship him."[15] The fear of God, a frequent theme in wisdom literature, is connected with Isaac through the divine title "the fear

---

11 Flusser ("New Sensitivity," 475–76) maintains that Isaac's appeal to an oath here may be based on Deut 6:13 ("The Lord your God you shall fear; him you shall serve, and by his name alone you shall swear") and that "the author of this testament of Isaac was evidently familiar with the concept that the commandment of altruistic love was enforced by a divine oath (Lev. 19:18): 'You shall love your fellow man as yourself—I—the Lord!' The words 'I—the Lord' were understood to mean that God promulgated this law with the seal and oath of his divine name." He refers to such an interpretation in '*Abot de Rabbi Nathan* version A chap. 16. Livneh, however, thinks that since several other examples of parental instructions in Jubilees involve an oath (she lists 9:14; 10:30-32; 25:9) the one in this passage need not be taken as an interpretation of "I am the Lord" in Lev 19:18 as an oath ("'Love Your Fellow,'" 187–88). The Damascus Document (CD xv:1-5) prohibits swearing by the divine names Adonai and El(ohim); on the passage, see Ginzberg, *Unknown Jewish Sect*, 91–94.

12 The expression "and everything together" survives, except for the last two letters, on 4Q223–224 unit 2 ii:48.

13 Noted by Werman, *Jubilees*, 460.

14 On the passage, see Nickelsburg, *1 Enoch 2*, 304–10.

15 Werman points out that Isaac does not command them to love God (see the order not to love idols in v. 5), even though in 20:7 Abraham commands his sons to love God (*Jubilees*, 460). She attributes the absence of it to the context of an oath that Isaac is making his sons swear.

of Isaac" (Gen 31:42, 53); perhaps that phrase influenced the writer to include the imperative "fear" in his address to his sons, although the Hebrew verb normally used for fear of God (ירא) is not related to the one in the phrase "the fear [פחד] of Isaac." Worship of the one true God is, of course, a teaching throughout the instructions given by parents and in other passages (for the verb "worship," see 12:4; 20:9; and on v. 6 above).

■ **8** The second requirement enjoined by the oath is the practice of brotherly love. Proper fear and worship of God go hand in hand with appropriate relations between people. Isaac adds qualifiers to the fraternal love he wishes to guarantee: it is to be done in a kindly and just fashion (בצדקה in 4Q223-224 unit 2 ii:49). This appears to be another way to articulate the command to love one's fellow as one's self. As Rebekah had (35:20, 34), he invokes the negative side of the command to brotherly love—they were not to wish harm on each other. Rebekah had insisted that the promise extend throughout the lifetime of her sons (35:20, 24; see v. 1), and Isaac states the point more precisely. Virtuous relations would lead to success in all their actions and avoidance of destruction.[16] Success or prospering in one's actions is a result that Rebekah cited when speaking to Esau about not harming his brother and regarding fraternal love (35:20; cf. 20:9; 31:24). Destruction is a penalty meant for the nations, but the writer of Jubilees holds it out as a possibility for those in the chosen line who stray in fundamental ways (15:26; 20:6; 21:22; 30:22; 35:14 [where Isaac predicts that Esau and his descendants will be destroyed]). Isaac, again like Rebekah (35:1; cf. v. 24), stresses that proper attitudes are to prevail throughout the brothers' lives and prefaces the sentiment with the words "from now and forever." Esau had threatened to kill Jacob after Isaac died (Gen 27:41 // Jub 26:35); Isaac makes a forceful effort to thwart him from being able to carry out his threat once he departed the scene.

■ **9** The verse is a prediction about the consequences of reneging on the duty of brotherly love "from now on" (in v. 8). The person who does the opposite, who, rather than loving his brother, wishes harm for him, will suffer terribly for it: the victim of the hurtful intentions will gain control over the offender (see Isaac's prediction in 35:16 where Esau will be handed over to Jacob), and the punishments associated with the nations—uprooting and destruction—will befall him and his descendants. As Canaan and his progeny and the Philistines were to be uprooted and destroyed (10:30; 22:20-21; 24:30-31), so too will the one guilty of the great sin suffer annihilation along with his line. Isaac is preparing the reader for what will happen in chaps. 37-38, where Esau does the opposite of what he swore to do (see 37:13, 17-23). He and all his sons will die as a result.

■ **10** The nature of the punishment that the malefactors will suffer is made more graphic and explicit in v. 10—a passage that proves to be an important statement of the writer's eschatology. Isaac refers to a "day of anger with raging wrath and fury—with a blazing fire that devours."[17] The language reminds one of passages where writers heap up words for anger, such as Isa 13:9 (in an oracle against Babylon): "See, the day of the LORD comes, / cruel, with wrath and fierce anger, / to make the earth a desolation, / and to destroy its sinners from it."[18] Terms of anger appear together with fire imagery in Isa 30:30 (against Assyria): "And the LORD will cause his majestic voice to be heard and the descending blow of his arm to be seen, in furious anger [בזעף אף] and a flame of devouring fire, with a cloudburst and tempest and hailstones" (cf. 30:30; 1QpHab iii:12-13).[19] The Ethiopic text refers

---

16 Livneh points out that here, as Rebekah did in 35:20, Isaac places fulfillment of Lev 19:17-18 in a covenantal context ("'Love Your Fellow,'" 190-91).

17 For a parallel, Charles (*Jubilees*, 212) pointed to 1 Enoch 39:2: "In those days Enoch received books of jealous wrath and rage and books of trepidation and consternation."

18 In Jub 24:28 Isaac spoke of the Philistines as being "cursed from among all peoples at the day of anger and wrath."

19 See DJD 13:113. Werman refers to Obad 18 ("The house of Jacob shall be a fire, / the house of Joseph a flame, / and the house of Esau stubble; / they shall burn them and consume them, / and there shall be no survivor of the house of Esau; for the LORD has spoken"), where the vocabulary is not as similar as in the examples cited above but the reference is to Esau (*Jubilees*, 460).

to a "day of turmoil and curse," an expression possibly related to Isa 22:5: "For the LORD of hosts has a day of tumult [יום מהומה]."[20] "Curse" is not coupled with "day" in the HB, but the term with its context in Jubilees 36 could echo parts of the oracle against Edom in Jer 49:7-22 (an oath; note also "the time when I punish him [עת פקדתיו]" in v. 8), where v. 13 reads: "For by myself I have sworn, says the LORD, that Bozrah shall become an object of horror and ridicule, a waste, and an object of cursing; and all her towns shall be perpetual wastes." Further along in the oracle, as here in Jub 36:10, the doom of Sodom figures: "Edom shall become an object of horror; everyone who passes by it will be horrified and will hiss because of all its disasters. As when Sodom and Gomorrah and their neighbors were overthrown, says the LORD, no one shall live there, nor shall anyone settle in it" (49:17-18).

Isaac combines the vocabulary of wrath and fire with references to books that list names.

Maṣḥafa tagśāṣa sabʾ ("the disciplinary book of humanity"). Leslau lists for *tagśāṣ*: "rebuke, reproach, reproof, discipline, admonition, exhortation, correction, instruction, chastisement, punishment."[21] The book is a positive phenomenon, one in which it is good to have one's name recorded and from which it is bad to be removed. Although a book under this name is not attested elsewhere,[22] Berger takes it to mean that the ones recorded in it are those who receive reproof (or discipline/instruction) in their lives. Only later are their names entered into the book of life or death.[23] Perhaps he is correct, but the context offers little assistance in decoding the nature of this book.

Maṣḥafa ḥeywat ("the book of life"). This book is mentioned in Jub 30:22 (the book of the living; see Ps 69:29 [Eng. 28]: "Let them be blotted out of the book of the living; / let them not be enrolled among the righteous") and in a number of other passages.[24] The oath violator will not have his name entered into this record.

Za-yethaggwal (lit., "the one that will be destroyed"). It seems from the reading in the early copies (Ethiopic is the only surviving witness) as if this is another book: although the construct noun *maṣḥafa* is not placed before the relative clause, the preposition "in" is repeated with it as with the other two books. The best-supported Ethiopic text does not, however, yield a satisfactory sense. The translation follows the reading in MSS. 42 47 58 63: "because he (= *weʾetu* rather than *westa*, 'in,' which appears in the other copies) is one who will be destroyed."[25] In other words, this is not another book but an announcement of the violator's fate.

It appears as if Isaac can hardly emphasize enough the severity of the judgment. To removal from the book of life and to destruction he adds that the offender will experience an eternal curse (so do the Philistines in 24:32). There will never be forgiveness for the person guilty of breaking the oath. An eternal curse entails that the person or people affected will undergo continuous punishment; Isaac says it will "be renewed" with seven negative phenomena:

denunciation/disgrace/reproach (perhaps חרפה)
curse
anger
pain
wrath
blows
sickness

---

20 See Dillmann, *Lexicon*, 10. *Hakak* ("turmoil") is used three times in connection with Canaan in Jub 10:30 (Canaan too had violated an oath); it is a term for what the sinful nations will cause in Israel according to 23:23.

21 Leslau, *Concise Dictionary*, 204. It is the term used for the Proverbs of Solomon.

22 Kugel, after noting that such a book is found in no other text, wonders whether "the book of" came from the next phrase ("the book of life") (*Walk through* Jubilees, 171; "Jubilees," 418). The writer would then simply be referring to a disciplinary act on humanity, not to this unfamiliar book.

23 Berger, *Jubiläen*, 502 n. a to v. 10. Werman proposes that the original term was תולדות ("history/generations"), not תוכחות (presupposed by the Ethiopic term) (*Jubilees*, 460).

24 For a survey of attestations, see Baynes, *Heavenly Book Motif*, 65–81.

25 VanderKam, *Jubilees* 2:239. Werman, who objects that the Ethiopic reading makes it seem as if the book is to be destroyed, thinks the text would have read בזה לאשר יכרת, "in the one for the person who will be cut off" (*Jubilees*, 458 n. 2, 460).

Several of these nouns populate other "curse" passages such as Deuteronomy 28 (curse, anger, wrath, fever); Jub 23:13 (blows, disease) and Jub 24:28 (anger, wrath, and curse in Isaac's imprecation on the Philistines) shares several as well.[26] Accumulating negative nouns serves to reinforce the case Isaac is making regarding the terrible future that awaits the one who reneges on his oath. Somehow Esau will manage to forget all of this in the very next chapter.

The words of Isaac in v. 10 appear at first glance to envision a specific future time or day of universal judgment upon evildoers ("On the day of anger ..."). On closer examination, however, the picture is different. Elsewhere and at times using similar vocabulary, the author has written about judgment on individual peoples whose destruction had already occurred. A clear example is Sodom: that city and the surrounding towns and areas met their end when the Lord "burned them with fire and brimstone and annihilated them until the present" (16:5; see Gen 19:24-25). The experience of Sodom serves as an explicit precedent for the fate Isaac decreed upon the one who violates his oath. With fire the deity "will burn his land, his cities, and everything that belongs to him just as he burned Sodom." Isaac appears to anticipate at some point a time of judgmental destruction specifically for the violator of the oath and his descendants and in this context is not dealing with all nations. As Hanneken puts the matter: "Judgment is a rolling process for individual nations, rather than a single batch judgment deferred to a future time."[27] Hence, rather than speaking of a universal eschatological judgment, the verse may be speaking only about the punishment of Esau and his offspring.[28] That judgment shares traits with other instances in which the Lord punished peoples, but each of them seems to have its own date with destiny.

■ **11** Isaac sums up the essence of his testament in v. 11 by using two verbs to underscore the certainty with which he is predicting the fate that will afflict the one who, contrary to the oath, desires what is hurtful for his brother. He is not only telling them about it but is also testifying to them or warning them concerning the consequences of such disobedience. The verb "testify/warn" occurs in just a few places in Jubilees. In 1:12 the Lord says he will send witnesses to testify to or warn Israel but to no avail; Enoch is placed in the Garden of Eden "as a sign and to testify against all people in order to tell all the deeds of history until the day of judgment" (4:24); in 6:38 the angel says he is testifying to Moses so that he will testify to Israel about the correct annual calendar; in 7:31 Noah testifies to his offspring about the importance of treating blood properly; in 20:7 Abraham testifies to his sons and grandsons about loving God and obeying his commandments; and in 30:11 the angel orders Moses to testify to Israel about not intermarrying with foreigners. All of these are solemn contexts, ones in which key topics receive emphasis, and several of them are the speeches of parents to their descendants, passages with which Isaac's testament shares much. It should be recalled that Jubilees presents itself as a testimony (e.g., 1:8). It is, therefore, fitting that Isaac testifies or warns his sons about the punishment on the one who violates the oath (of course, this will be Esau) and in this way places the continuation of his line in jeopardy.

12-18 Isaac Divides His Estate, Dies, and Is Buried

Isaac, who this time correctly perceived that his death was near, delivered essential teachings to his sons Esau and Jacob in vv. 3-11. Once he completed his testament, he turned to the problem of dividing his property between the two heirs. The reader of Genesis and Jubilees knows that the identity of the firstborn in Isaac's family and therefore the heir to certain rights and the major share of the property had become complicated by two events. First, Esau had exchanged his right of firstborn for a helping of porridge (24:3-7 // Gen 25:29-34). The author of Jubilees appended a comment to that story: "So Jacob became the older one, but Esau was low-

---

26 The word pair "anger and wrath" occurs in Ezekiel's oracle against Edom (25:14).
27 Hanneken, *Subversion*, 164-65.
28 So too Davenport, *Eschatology*, 67-68. Martin ("Jubilés," 524) and Testuz (*Idées*, 170), however, think the passage fits into the picture of a universal time of judgment, while Werman (*Jubilees*, 460) thinks of it at the end of days.

ered from his prominent position" (v. 7; there is no parallel in Genesis 25). Second, Jacob had duped his father into giving him the blessing meant for Esau (chap. 26 // Genesis 27). That blessing included the words: "May all the blessings with which the Lord has blessed me and blessed my father Abraham / belong to you and your descendants forever" (26:24; the line is lacking in Genesis 27). Another complicating factor was that Esau had stolen his parents' property so that he already had a large part of any goods to be inherited (29:17-18; 35:10). Moreover, Isaac's feelings about his two sons had changed over the years: first he loved Esau more (19:15, 31), but later he turned that greater affection to Jacob (35:13). It would appear, therefore, that Isaac should now treat Jacob as his principal heir and give Esau what was left.

■ **12-13** Perhaps Isaac was just being cautious, not wishing to revive any bad feelings between his sons—especially after he had just made them swear to love each other. Then, too, he might have been testing Esau to see whether he still acknowledged Jacob's superior position as he had five years earlier to Rebekah (35:23). Whatever his motive may have been, he proceeded as if Esau retained the right of firstborn. "He gave the larger part to the man who was the first to be born."[29] The possessions Isaac was unevenly dividing between Esau and Jacob consisted of a building and land: the tower of Abraham where Isaac resided, the lot around it, and the territory Abraham had acquired in the area. The territory Abraham bought must be the field containing the cave of Machpelah (see Jub 19:6), as no other purchase in the area is credited to him. By twice referring to "the man who was the first to be born" Isaac is not trying to be clever—subtly meaning Jacob but sounding as if he had Esau in mind. He seems to be speaking literally and is so understood in v. 14. His initial step in dividing the property was, then, to give the majority of what he owned to Esau, the twin who emerged from Rebekah's womb shortly before Jacob did.

■ **14** Esau, the actual older brother, is the first to respond, and his answer agrees in character with the one he gave to his mother just before she died (35:23). But whereas there he referred to the blessing Isaac had given to Jacob instead of to him, here he bases his statement on the birthright story, no doubt because of the way Isaac had phrased the matter ("the man who was the first to be born") and because of the situation. He admits that he sold the right to Jacob and even says, "I gave my birthright to Jacob," using the verb "give" that appears in Jubilees' version of the story but not in the one in Genesis. In Jub 24:4 the oath Jacob made him swear reads: "I (hereby) give (it) to you." Since the transaction involving the right of primogeniture had taken place, and Esau had sworn his consent to it, Jacob was the one deserving the greater part of the inheritance that Isaac had just described. Esau even declares that he will not argue the point; for him it was a fact that the larger share, the one for the person born first, now belonged to Jacob. Here he remains true to his sworn word. As a result, Esau in both 35:23 and in 36:14 explicitly recognizes the new situation created by the two events in the past and promises not to dispute the matter. After he lost the blessing he had labeled that experience and the birthright incident as cases of cheating on Jacob's part (26:30 // Gen 27:36); now he accepts the results without question.

■ **15-16** Isaac, who before v. 14 had every right to be worried, is overjoyed by Esau's response. It is not easy to understand his reaction in light of what he had said in 35:13 (Esau is unable to do what is right), 14 (he and his descendants will be destroyed), and 15 (he would not keep his word even if he swore to something). Nevertheless, Esau's strong assertion that Jacob rightfully should receive the majority of the property sets his mind at ease. This time, unlike what he did in chap. 26 (Genesis 27), Isaac prays that a blessing will rest upon both sons and their children. It should be noted, however, that he adds "today" to the request—that a blessing befall them "today." He does not ask for an eternal blessing on them (see below on v. 16). He professes that he is at rest, at peace, and that he is not sad[30] anymore regarding the birthright. As he approaches death, a great load

---

29   Deut 21:17 says the firstborn should receive "a double portion."
30   The verb *ḥazana*, also used regarding Isaac in 34:3 (translated "was distressed"), has the senses of "be sad, be sorrowful, be grieved, be in mourning, be sorry for, sympathize" (Leslau, *Concise Dictionary*, 25). In 34:3 Isaac's spirit (*manfas*) was distressed; here his heart (*lebbeya*) is not distressed or sad.

has fallen from his shoulders. The last words in v. 15 are phrased in an interesting way: "lest you do [*tegbar*] something evil [הרעה in 4Q223-224 unit 2 iii:8][31] about it." Isaac employs a verb that is second person singular, referring to Esau.[32] The line betrays the fact that he had worried Esau would do something terrible regarding the birthright issue. Now, after Esau's hearty assurance, he no longer worries. It is good that Isaac did not live to see the events narrated in chaps. 37–38.

Isaac resorts to ambiguous language in v. 16. He calls upon the Most High, a title for God found frequently in blessings,[33] for an eternal blessing, not just for today as in v. 15, upon "the man who does what is right" and on his offspring. In the context, both sons seem, in Isaac's eyes, to have the potential to act properly, and so the blessing could come to fruition for both. But Isaac's cautiously worded prayer will apply only to Jacob and his descendants, since Esau, who is incapable of doing what is right (as Isaac said in 35:13), will not be able to live up to this standard of behavior. As a result, the dying Isaac in effect pronounces an eternal blessing on Jacob and his descendants; Esau and his children will prove unworthy of such benefits.

■ **17-18** With the conclusion of the testament and the full assent of Esau to his reduced status, the last events of Isaac's life transpire. Here the parallels with the last day in the lives of Abraham and Rebekah continue. They celebrated a meal with their sons just hours before they died (22:1-6; 35:27). Now Isaac does the same although there is a difference: the writer does not have Isaac participate in the meal. On Abraham's last day, Isaac "prepared a joyful feast in front of his brother Ishmael" (22:4). Rebekah and Jacob also contributed food, but Abraham is the only one who is said to have eaten and drunk in preparation for blessing Jacob (22:4-6). Of Rebekah the text reports, "She and her sons ate and drank that night" (35:27). Isaac, however, may simply be watching as Esau and Jacob share a meal: "they ate and drank together in front of him" (v. 17). The final meal in chap. 36 is one that fits the context well: the issue had been the relations between the brothers. All seemed peaceful between them, and they signaled their unity by breaking bread together. The sight of union between Esau and Jacob made the elderly patriarch's last moments ones of joy. They were together as he had urged in v. 4. With the meal completed, the brothers left Isaac and fell asleep for the night, as Abraham had gone to bed and Jacob fell asleep in his bosom on that final night (22:25; 23:1-2). The feeling of great happiness remained with Isaac as he fell asleep, never to awaken.[34] His happiness imitated that of his father, who died with feelings of much joy about Jacob (22:26, 28; nothing is said about what Rebekah felt as her life ended in 35:27).

Jubilees rejoins the text of Genesis in v. 18b, d (see Gen 35:28-29). With Genesis the writer gives Isaac's age at death as 180 years (see above on v. 1)[35] and expresses it both in numbers and in weeks of years (25 x 7 = 175) and years (5). As in the cases of Abraham (Jub 23:7 // Gen

---

31   Kugel says the Ethiopic term here means "left/left-handed" (*Walk through* Jubilees, 172 n. 308; "Jubilees," 463 n. 230), but he has confused two words that partially resemble each other: *ḍug* ("wickedness") and *ḍagām* ("left-handed").

32   Werman (*Jubilees*, 458 n. 5) appeals to the definite article on הרעה and changes the verb to a second person plural form: lest you do the evil thing (she misrepresents the Geʿez text as if it read a passive form). There is no support among the Ethiopic copies for a second person plural verb. If one objects to the singular form here where Isaac has been speaking to both of his sons, it would be simpler to suppose that the original read "lest the bad thing be done," in which expression the consonantal text would be the same as the one underlying the Ethiopic reading.

33   Those blessings regularly occur in a parent's words to children and grandchildren. See 20:9; 21:25; 22:11, 13, 19, 27; 25:3 (cf. v. 11).

34   Charles drew attention to the parallel expressions in three of the units in the Testaments of the Twelve Patriarchs (*Jubilees*, 213). Jubilees says literally, "he slept the sleep that is forever" (the verb and the first letter of "sleep" survive on 4Q223-224 unit 2 iii:10); the same wording occurs in T. Iss. 7:9; T. Dan 7:1; and T. Jos. 20:4. It is also attested in the HB in Jer 51:39, 57, and it is said of Abraham in Jub 23:1.

35   The versions of Gen 35:28 are consistent about the number, but Josephus credits him with 185 years (*Ant.* 1.346). He adopts the impression left by Genesis that Jacob and Isaac had only a short time together after he returned from Mesopotamia; he claims too that Rebekah was dead when he arrived back home. Of Isaac he says, "Isaac also died not

25:9) and Rebekah (35:27), his two[36] sons, still listed in their birth order as in Gen 35:29, buried him. With Genesis, Jubilees does not say they buried him near his wife Rebekah, though Gen 49:31 puts them in the same place.

The author has, therefore, fashioned parallel parting scenes for the two great patriarchs and for Rebekah—another indication of her stature in the book.[37] Genesis gives slight warrant for the parallels between Abraham and Isaac by saying both were buried by their two sons,[38] but the entire scene for Rebekah and the greatly enhanced ones for Abraham and Isaac derive from the writer or from sources on which he drew. As noted above, he also raided the stories about the final words and days of Jacob in Genesis as he crafted the scene for Isaac. Isaac outlived his greater father and proved a slight counterexample to the process of decreasing ages set forth in Jubilees 23.

19-20 Esau and Jacob Go to Their Homes

After briefly making contact with the text of Genesis in 36:18, the author again departs from it to insert an extended section that traces the relations between Jacob and Esau right to their tragic end (36:19—38:14). From Genesis a reader learns of no further contact between them after they interred their father Isaac. Genesis 36, the chapter that immediately follows the paragraph about the death of Isaac, lists Esau's family members and descendants as well as the clans and early kings of Edom, but it does not record his death. The only material Jubilees borrows at any length from Genesis 36 is the king list in vv. 31-39 (see Jub 38:15–24). After chap. 36 Esau's name never appears in Genesis; instead the story follows Jacob and his family, especially Joseph. The situation is very different in Jubilees.

■ **19** The writer reflects in this short verse some of the data in Gen 36:6-8:

> Then Esau took his wives, his sons, his daughters, and all the members of his household, his cattle, all his livestock, and all the property he had acquired in the land of Canaan; and he moved to a land some distance from his brother Jacob. For their possessions were too great for them to live together; the land where they were staying could not support them because of their livestock. So Esau settled in the hill country of [הר] Seir; Esau is Edom.

He could also draw on Gen 32:3, where Esau lived "in the land of Seir, the country of Edom" (cf. Jub 29:13) at the time when he and Jacob met. Prior to 32:3 Genesis said nothing about Esau's move to the area, and it is only in chap. 36 that the reason is given—the possessions of the two were so large and required so much territory to accommodate them that the two could not live close together. The reason is a logical one for his presence in Edom at some distance from Jacob and one that recalled the separation of Abram and Lot in Genesis 13. Jubilees had already given a tendentious twist to Esau's relocating to Edom. According to 29:18, Esau had moved there because, "at the time when Jacob went to Mesopotamia, Esau had married Mahalath, Ishmael's daughter. He had gathered all his father's flocks and his wives and had gone up and lived in Mount Seir. He had left his father Isaac alone at the well of the oath." So he went to Edom as a place where he could keep away from Isaac the flocks he stole from him, abandoning his parents in the process. This is Jubilees' explanation for the animals Esau acquired in Canaan and why his herds were so

---

long after the coming of his son; he was buried by his children beside his wife at Hebron in their ancestral tomb. Isaac was a man beloved of God and was deemed worthy of His special providence after his father Abraham; in longevity he even surpassed him, having completed one hundred and eighty-five years of a virtuous life when he died" (*Ant.* 1.345-46; Thackeray, LCL). In *Ant.* 1.234 Josephus placed a prediction that Isaac would "attain to extreme old age" in the words of God to Abraham directly after the binding of Isaac.

36 Jubilees uses the number "two," but it is lacking in the versions of Gen 35:29, apart from a few Greek minuscules.
37 Endres emphasizes the parallels with Rebekah in Jubilees 35 and the important role Rebekah plays in family matters (*Biblical Interpretation*, 176–77).
38 Genesis 25:7-8 and 35:28-29 contain a series of parallels: both indicate the age of the patriarch at death, that he breathed his last, died old and full of days, was gathered to his people, and was buried by his two sons.

large. In Jub 36:19 Esau, therefore, simply returns to his home after helping Jacob bury their father.[39]

■ **20** Jacob, however, remains at the ancestral home and does not separate from it. Here the author reflects some of the language of Gen 35:27: "Jacob came to his father at Mamre, or Kiriath-arba (that is, Hebron), where Abraham and Isaac had resided as aliens." Also, Gen 37:1, the first verse to mention Jacob after the burial of Isaac, says, "Jacob settled in the land where his father had lived as an alien,[40] the land of Canaan." Rather than calling it the place where both Abraham and Isaac sojourned, he makes the connection with Abraham: he went to the tower (the only tower in the area is the tower of Abraham)[41] "in the land of Canaan, in the land of his father Abraham."[42] Abraham had called Jacob his son a number of times (19:17 [in v. 21 he loves him more than his own sons], 27, 29; 22:10 [twice], 11, 16, 19, 20, 23 [twice], 28), and Jacob referred to him as father (23:3; 25:5, 7; cf. 31:31). The bond between them continues after Isaac's death.

Whereas Esau left the family home, Jacob remained there. His decision imitates the example set long before by Shem, the son of Noah, who built a city "next to his father" (7:16) when his brothers separated from him to build their cities elsewhere (7:13-17). Jacob seems to be obeying his dying father's wish that his sons be unified, that they act together (see 36:4), not go their separate ways. Esau, however, departs to the place to which he had moved with his regrettable wives in order to distance himself and his stolen goods from his parents. Jacob is at any rate carrying on the patriarchal tradition in Hebron; Esau definitely is not.

The last sentence in v. 20 deals with another matter in which Jacob puts Isaac's instructions into effect. The elderly man had said, "My sons, remember the Lord, the God of your father Abraham—afterwards I, too, worshiped and served him properly and sincerely" (v. 6). Jacob, the reader learns, did just as Isaac directed: he worshiped the Lord with his whole heart.[43] He served him not only in a sincere fashion but also "in line with the revealed commands according to the divisions of the times of his generation." The Latin translation reads *praecepta visibilia* ("the visible commands") where the Ethiopic version offers *te'zāzāt za-yāstare'i* ("the revealed/visible commands"). There have been three proposals about how to render and interpret the expression(s).

1. *Visible commands.* Rönsch argued that the phrase pointed to Jub 32:21-26, where an angel showed seven tablets to Jacob, who saw what was written on them and read them; that is, the contents were visible to him. Charles accepted the proposal as did VanderKam.[44] The seven tablets disclosed "what would happen to him [Jacob] and his sons throughout all ages" (32:21); Jub 36:20 refers to "the divisions of the times of his generation" and thus may echo the theme of 32:21. A difficulty with this interpretation is that the contents of the seven tablets can hardly be called "commands," since they deal with events that will happen, not legal matters.

2. *Revealed commands.* The rendering was suggested before the Qumran finds, but it has taken on a new cogency with the discoveries. Forms of גלה are frequent in the sense of revelation, for example, of the Torah (e.g., 1QS viii:1), and there are instances in which it figures in expressions indicating disclosures appropriate to each time. An example is 1QS viii:15: לעשות ככול הנגלות עת בעת, "do according to all that has been revealed from age to age." If this is the meaning of the words in Jub 36:20, the writer would be referring to the commands that Jacob had received through the ancestral tradition, especially through Abraham, Rebekah, and Isaac, and ones disclosed to him personally. As 33:16 indicates, not everything in the law had yet been revealed in patriarchal times.[45]

3. *Appropriate commands.* Littmann thought the original might have contained a plural form of ראוי whose meaning is: Jacob acted in harmony with the laws appro-

---

39 See Endres, *Biblical Interpretation*, 178.
40 The Ethiopic version of Jub 36:20 refers to "the land where his father Abraham had resided as a foreigner/alien."
41 Isaac tried to give it to Esau in v. 12 (Kugel, *Walk through* Jubilees, 172; "Jubilees," 419).
42 As Werman comments, while it is called "the land of Canaan," it is really "the land of his father Abraham" (*Jubilees*, 461).
43 Cf. Endres, *Biblical Interpretation*, 179.
44 Rönsch, *Jubiläen*, 152; Charles, *Jubilees*, 213; VanderKam, *Jubilees* 2:240-41.
45 "Revealed commands" or "commands that were

priate to his time.[46] He compared usages of the same Ethiopic verb in Jub 2:29 (the subject is doing something that is not appropriate on the Sabbath) and 3:15 (angels were teaching Adam everything appropriate for working in the Garden of Eden). This could be regarded as a variation of proposal #2 above. There are no exact parallels to this usage in the Qumran texts.

Option #2 appears to be the most likely interpretation of the phrase in its context. Jacob served God in the way that had been revealed from time to time throughout the course of the book of Jubilees to this point.[47]

"The divisions of the times of his generation"[48] is an expression that reminds one of the title of Jubilees ("the book of the divisions of the times") and in the present instance designates the age in which Jacob lived. He conducted himself in a way that accorded with the commandments revealed to his ancestors and to him up to this time; he could not be expected to live by laws whose disclosure lay in the future. The words constitute another formulation of the author's view that revelation was ongoing and that the heroes of his story were obedient to those parts of the law divulged by their time.

21-24 Jacob's Beloved Wife Leah Dies

Verses 21-24 deal with the death of Leah and the relationship between Jacob and his first wife, the mother of seven of his children. They present a remarkable portrait of her that goes far beyond the sparse givens of Genesis regarding her.

■ 21 The writer says that Leah died five years after Isaac. If she died in 2167, she and Jacob would had been married for forty-five years (see 28:2 for the year 2122 as the date of their wedding and v. 11 for the birth of her first child), with twenty-four of them coming after Rachel died (see 32:33).[49] Jacob, like Abraham before him, buried his wife. The sons were apparently not involved, as they were not at the family home when she died (see v. 22). The exact location of her burial is noted: Jacob placed her in the cave of Machpelah ("the twofold cave") "near his mother Rebekah, on the left of his grandmother Sarah's grave." Genesis does not record the occasion when Leah died, but Jacob refers to her burial when speaking with his sons about his own death: "Bury me with my ancestors—in the cave in the field of Ephron the Hittite, in the cave in the field at Machpelah, near Mamre, in the land of Canaan, in the field that Abraham bought from Ephron the Hittite as a burial site. There Abraham and his wife Sarah were buried; there Isaac and his wife Rebekah were buried; and there I buried Leah" (Gen 49:29-31).[50] So Leah, the daughter of a branch of the Abrahamic family, took her place among the great matriarchs through whom the chosen line was traced. Esau and Jacob had buried Rebekah "near their father's mother Sarah" (35:27), and now Jacob interred Leah "near his mother Rebekah." Leah, not Rachel who "was buried in the country of Ephrathah, that is, Bethlehem" (32:34), reposed in the ancestral tomb.[51]

---

revealed" are translations found in Goldmann, Rabin, Wintermute, Berger, and Caquot.

46   Littmann, "Jubiläen," 102 n. a (he translated as "sichtbaren Geboten" but mentioned this option in n. a). Paul Riessler ("Jubiläenbuch oder Kleine Genesis," in idem, *Altjüdisches Schrifttum ausserhalb der Bibel* [Augsburg: Filser, 1928; 2nd ed., Darmstadt: Wissenschaftliche Buchgesellschaft, 1966] 539–666) rendered as "den geziemenden Geboten," and Hartom ("Jubilees," 111) also referred to this sense but omitted the word from his translation.

47   So Kugel, *Walk through Jubilees*, 172; "Jubilees," 419; Werman, *Jubilees*, 461.

48   "His generation" translates *ledatu/generationum eius*. Though *ledatu* could mean "his birth" (so Rabin), that seems unlikely in the context (see Dillmann, *Lexicon*, 887–88).

49   Gregory ("Death and Legacy of Leah," 109–10) shows that the numbers reveal a certain symmetry: Jacob was married to Rachel and loved her more than Leah for a total of twenty-one years (see 32:33-34), a time when Leah desired his love; he was married to and loved Leah after Rachel's death for twenty-four years, three years longer. In addition, Jacob lived twenty-one years after Leah's death (see 45:13), during which time he greatly missed her love, thus paralleling the twenty-one years when the opposite situation prevailed.

50   Gregory thinks that interpreters may have inferred from Gen 49:31 that something had happened to change Jacob's attitude toward Leah in a more positive direction ("Death and Legacy of Leah," 107).

51   Ibid., 106. Werman combines the notices about the burials of family members in the cave of Mach-

Genesis presents Leah as a fertile but unloved wife of Jacob. Once the family returns to Canaan, she is never again mentioned except as Dinah's mother (34:1), in lists of names (35:23, 26; 46:15, 18), and in the burial notice quoted just above.[52] She was, of course, the mother of six tribes of Israel, including Levi and Judah, and thus a woman of tremendous importance in sacred history. The author of Jubilees attributes a somewhat larger and more positive role to Leah than Genesis does. Genesis 29:17 notes something about Leah's eyes as it contrasts her with the "graceful and beautiful" Rachel, and 29:30 is explicit that Jacob "loved Rachel more than Leah," who sensed she was unloved (v. 31) and expressed her feelings in the names she gave her first three sons (vv. 32-34). Of these passages, Jubilees rewrites only the first two: "For Jacob loved Rachel more than Leah because Leah's eyes were weak, though her figure was very lovely; but Rachel's eyes were beautiful, her figure was lovely, and she was very pretty" (28:5; see also v. 12). When Jacob summoned his two wives preparatory to leaving Laban's place, he simply spoke to them in Genesis, but he addressed them tenderly in Jubilees (Gen 31:4-5 // Jub 29:2).[53] In a passage not found in Genesis, Jacob and Leah visited Isaac (33:1).[54] But v. 21 here and especially vv. 22-24 form the unit that puts the brightest gloss on Leah's person.

■ 22 Not only did Jacob bury his wife in the ancestral tomb beside the bodies of her two predecessors as matriarchs; he also loved her deeply because of her character.[55] There is some variation in the textual evidence for who came to mourn her passing with Jacob. The reading with the strongest backing among the Ethiopic manuscripts is "her sons and his sons,"[56] a meaningful expression because Leah was the mother of six of Jacob's twelve sons; the reading claims that all of them, not just Leah's own sons, came to grieve with their father.[57] They came to offer consolation to Jacob "because he was lamenting her." When Sarah died, Abraham mourned (lit., "wept") for her (19:3); Jacob mourns and laments for Leah (neither verb is used for his response to Rachel's death in

---

pelah and infers this arrangement: Abraham and Sarah were at the center, the males (Isaac and later Jacob) were placed to his right in that order, and the females (Rebekah and Leah) were interred to Sarah's left in that order (*Jubilees*, 13-14).

52 For her portrait in Genesis, see Gregory, "Death and Legacy of Leah," 101-2.

53 Halpern-Amaru, *Empowerment*, 69-71. Jubilees omits Jacob's preparations for meeting Esau in Gen 33:1-3, where the relative places he assigned to the wives and their children reflected his feelings toward them: the concubines and their children would be the first to encounter Esau and his four hundred troops; Leah and her family come second; and Rachel and her child Joseph are last and thus farthest from danger.

54 Gregory ("Death and Legacy of Leah," 104), in agreement with Halpern-Amaru (e.g., *Empowerment*, 66-72), summarizes the situation in Jubilees prior to 36:21-24: "In the final analysis, it is evident that *Jubilees* maintains the biblical emphasis on the preference for Rachel, but also elevates Leah in order to reduce the gap between them. As the narrative progresses, the two appear to have more equal roles as the matriarchs who are the partners of Jacob in bringing about the twelve tribes of Israel. In other words, they both are viewed as crucial and significant contributors to God's covenantal plans."

55 That is, he loved her for more than her physical attractiveness noted in 28:5 (Hartom, "Jubilees," 111 n. to vv. 23-24; Endres, *Biblical Interpretation*, 179). As Halpern-Amaru observes, the writer of Jubilees "breaks apart the triad of associations—infertility, maternity to primary heir, and spousal love—that diminish Leah's status as a matriarch" in Genesis (*Empowerment*, 101). Livneh cites the relationship between Jacob and Leah, in contrast to the one between him and Rachel whose physical beauty attracted him, as illustrating the principle in the book that, to use her expressions, moral appeal is preferable to eye appeal ("Not at First Sight: Gender Love in *Jubilees*," *JSP* 23 [2013] 3-20, here 13-16). "In line with the portrayal of the 'virtuous wife' of Proverbs, the author of Jubilees implies that countenance is deceptive and beauty illusory; a woman is truly to be praised and valued for her righteousness" (p. 16).

56 For the second group the Latin manuscript reads: *pueri eius*. Possible translations are "his sons/boys" or "his servants" (see 24:16 for an example of the meaning "servants"), but when the author wanted to indicate the wider circle of those who came to mourn for Abraham at his death he makes the point clear by referring to the people of his household (see 23:6-7).

57 Hartom, "Jubilees," 111 n. to v. 22.

32:33-34 // Gen 35:16-20). So the writer has Jacob react strongly to Leah's passing and offers an explanation for his intense grief in the next lines.

■ **23** The first point he makes is that Jacob "loved her very much from the time when her sister Rachel died." Since both Genesis and Jubilees reported that Jacob loved Rachel more than Leah, one could have concluded, especially from Genesis, that his feelings remained unchanged after the premature death of Rachel. Jubilees forcefully denies the inference. After Rachel died, he loved Leah deeply;[58] she was surely not Jacob's unloved wife. It seems that Rachel remained the favorite as long as she lived, but after her death Jacob's love for her sister became much stronger.[59] To document why this happened, the author amasses the longest list of traits for any woman in Jubilees. Gregory has shown that the attributes of Leah can be paralleled from the Wisdom literature:

> ... the virtues listed evoke the sapiential background of the ideal wife and of Lady Wisdom. Leah is described as perfect (cf. Sir. 26.2; 40.19), right in behavior (cf. Prov. 3.17), one who honors her husband (cf. Sir. 26.26; Prov. 31.23), does not speak a harsh word (cf. Prov. 15.1; 31.26), is gentle (cf. Sir. 3.17; 36.23), and possesses peace (cf. Sir. 26.2; Prov. 12.20), truthfulness (cf. Prov. 12.22; 23.23), and honor (cf. Prov. 3.16; 11.16).[60]

While his point is correct, there is another dimension to her traits. The first adjective used for her—perfect—already reveals the source for the description: Jacob is called perfect in several passages: 19:13 (see Gen 25:27); 27:17; 35:12 (Abraham in 23:10).[61] Moreover, Leah was "right in all her behavior [lit., ways]," as was Jacob (see 27:17 for this descriptor; cf. 21:2 for Abraham). Leah showed honor to Jacob as he consistently honored his parents and brother (35:1, 4, 13). The Ethiopic adjective for the kind of speech that never emerged from Leah's mouth (*deruk*) is the word describing Esau in 19:13 and his actions in 19:14 (harsh), the antithesis of Jacob and his behavior, so that in this way too Leah resembled her husband. Her gentleness imitated the way in which Abraham had spoken to the Hittites as he tried to buy a burial plot for his wife (19:5). By being peaceful she was again the opposite of Esau (19:14), and in being true she bore another trait of Jacob (27:17; 35:12). As a result, the author pictures Leah as being like Jacob particularly but also like Abraham and completely unlike Esau. She was a most fitting wife for Jacob.

■ **24** When Jacob called all her goodness to mind,[62] he was terribly sad "because he loved her with all his heart and with all his person [soul]." This is the way in which Rebekah loved her son Jacob (Jub 19:31) and the way in which one was to love God (e.g., Deut 6:5).[63] Jacob must have loved Leah most sincerely. The mother of half the Israelite tribes was a truly impressive person. As chap. 37 will explain, it was during the intense mourning period for Leah that Jacob's brother Esau and his forces attacked him (vv. 14-17).

The writer of Jubilees has shown his interest in the female characters of Genesis on many occasions, and he demonstrates it powerfully in the sentences with which he ushers Leah off the stage of history. Halpern-Amaru describes the situation well: "The encomium completes the transformation of Leah in *Jubilees*. The matriarch acquires not only her husband's love, but a stature that places her, like her burial site, 'near his mother Rebekah, on the left of his grandmother Sarah's grave' (36:21)."[64] In Jubilees the domestic situation for Jacob is far more pleasant than Genesis implies, and there is harmony in the immediate family.

---

58 Livneh, who draws attention to the statements about Jacob's love for Leah at the beginning and end of the description of her in vv. 23-24, comments that Jacob loves Leah very much (v. 23) and with his whole being (v. 24), whereas he merely loved Rachel (28:5, 12) ("Not at First Sight," 15).
59 Cf. Halpern-Amaru, *Empowerment*, 66.
60 Gregory, "Death and Legacy of Leah," 108-9; cf. Livneh, "Not at First Sight," 14-15.
61 Berger says the attribute is used only for Jacob (*Jubiläen*, 504 n. b to v. 23), but he seems to have missed 23:10, where it describes Abraham.
62 Gregory writes that Leah did not change but Jacob's perception of her did ("Death and Legacy of Leah," 109).
63 On this last point, see ibid., 108.
64 Halpern-Amaru, *Empowerment*, 72. She adds that, for the author, the "lines of Israel's priests and kings must descend not only from a perfect mother, but also from an untroubled marriage" (ibid.).

Hostilities Break Out between Esau and Jacob

37

1/ On the day[a] that Isaac, the father of Jacob and Esau, died Esau's sons heard that Isaac had given the birthright[b] to his younger son Jacob. They became very angry. 2/ They quarreled with their father:[a] "Why is it that when you are the older[b] and Jacob the younger your father gave Jacob the birthright[c] and deposed you?"[d] 3/ He[a] said to them,[b] "Because I gave[c] the right of the firstborn[d] to Jacob[e] in exchange for a little lentil broth. The day my father sent me to hunt game[f] so that he could eat (it) and bless me, he came in a crafty way and brought in food and drink[g] to my father. My father[h] blessed him and put me under his control. 4/ Now our[a] father has made us[b]—me and him—swear that we will not seek harm,[c] the one against his brother,[d] and that we will continue in (a state of) mutual love[e] and peace, each[f] with his brother, so that we should not corrupt our behavior."[g] 5/ They[a] said to him, "We will not listen[b] to you by making peace with him because our strength is greater than his strength, and we are stronger[c] than he is. We will go against him, kill him, and destroy his sons.[d] If you do not go with us, we will harm you, too. 6/ Now[a] listen to us: let[b] us send[c] to Aram, Philistia, Moab, and Ammon;[d] and let us choose for ourselves select men[e] who are brave in battle. Then let us go against him, make war with him, and uproot[f] him from the earth before he gains strength." 7/ Their father[a] said to them, "Do not go and do not make war with him so that you may not fall before him."[b] 8/ They[a] said to him, "Is this not[b] the very[c] way you have acted from your youth until today. You are putting your neck beneath his yoke. We will not listen to what you are saying."[d]

9/ So they[a] sent to Aram and to their father's friend Aduram. Together with them[b] they hired for themselves 1,000 fighting men, select warriors.[c] 10/ There came to them from Moab and from the Ammonites 1,000 select men who[a] were hired; from the Philistines 1,000 select warriors; from Edom and the Horites 1,000 select fighters, and from the Kittim[b] strong warriors. 11/ They said to their father, "Go out;[a] lead them.[b] Otherwise we will kill you." 12/ He[a] was filled with anger and wrath when he saw that his sons were forcing[b] him to go in front in order to lead them[c] to his brother Jacob.[d] 13/ But[a] he remembered all[b] the bad things that were hidden in his mind[c] against his brother Jacob, and he did not remember the oath[d] that he had sworn to his father and mother not to seek harm[e] against Jacob[f] throughout his entire lifetime.[g]

14/ During all this time, Jacob was unaware that they were coming to him for battle.[a] He, for his part, was mourning for his wife[b] until they approached him near[c] the tower[d] with 4,000 warriors.[e] 15/ The people of Hebron sent word to him:[a] "Your brother has just now[b] come against you to fight you[c] with 4,000 men who have swords buckled on and are carrying shields and weapons."[d] They told him[e] because they loved Jacob more than Esau, since Jacob was a more generous and kind[f] man than Esau. 16/ But Jacob did not believe (it) until they[a] came near the tower.[b] 17/ Then he[a] closed the gates of the tower,[b] stood[c] on the top, and spoke with his brother Esau. He said,[d] "It is a fine[e] consolation that you have come to give me for my wife who has died. Is this the oath[f] that you swore to your father and your mother twice[g] before he died?[h] You have violated the oath and were condemned in the hour when you swore (it) to your father."[i]

18/ Then[a] Esau said in reply to him,[b] "Neither humankind nor serpents[c] have a true oath[d] that they, once they have sworn,[e] have sworn (it as valid) forever. Every day they desire harm for one another, how to kill[f] his[g] enemy and opponent. 19/ You hate me and my sons[a] forever. There is no[b] observing of brotherly ties[c] with you. 20/ Listen to what I have to say[a] to you. If[b] a pig changes its hide and makes its hair limp like wool;[c] and[d] horns like the horns of[e] a ram and sheep[f] go out on its head, then I will observe brotherly ties with you. The breasts have been separated from their mother, for you have not been a brother to me.[g] 21/ If wolves make peace with lambs so that[a] they do not eat them[a] or injure them; and if they have resolved to treat them well, then there will be peace in my mind for you.[b] 22/ If a lion becomes the friend of a bull and a confidant,[a] and if it

971

is harnessed together with it in a yoke[b] and plows (as) one yoke,[c] then[d] I will make peace with you. 23/ If[a] the ravens turn white[b] like a pelican,[c] then know that I love you[d] and will make peace with you.[e] (As for) you—be[f] uprooted and your children are being uprooted.[g] There is to be[h] no peace for you."[i]

24/ When Jacob saw that he was adversely inclined toward him from his mind[a] and his entire self so that he could kill him and (that) he was coming and bounding along[b] like a boar that comes upon the spear that pierces it and kills it but does not pull back from it, 25/ then he[a] told his sons[b] and his servants[c] to attack him[d] and all his companions.[e]

Textual Notes

1a day] "year" 21; "after" Syr. Chr.
b the birthright] Lat. seems to have had a longer expression: *maiorem . . . honorif. . . .* Rönsch (*Jubiläen*, 72) proposed to read: "the larger and more honored part." In v. 2 Lat. renders "birthright" as *maiorem portionem*.
2a their father] "Esau" Lat.; Syr. Chr. agrees with Eth.
b you are the older (Syr. Chr.: "you are older than Jacob")] Lat.: "Jacob is placed before you."
c the birthright] + "the greatness" Syr. Chr.
d deposed you] "made you inferior" Lat. Syr. Chr. is somewhat more paraphrastic here and lacks an equivalent.
3a He] "Esau" Lat. and Syr. Chr.; but see VanderKam, *Jubilees* 2:243.
b to them] "to his sons" Syr. Chr.
c gave] "sold" Eth. Since both Lat. and Syr. Chr. read "gave," the reading has strong support and reflects the word in Jub 24:4—the incident to which Esau is referring. However, the two readings would look similar in Gk.: Eth. = απεδομη; Lat. and Syr. Chr. = εδωσα. Cf. LXX Gen 25:33: απεδοτο.
d the right of the firstborn (= Lat.)] "my right of the firstborn" Eth.; Syr. Chr. again has a double expression: "the birthright and the greatness."
e Jacob] + "my brother" Syr. Chr.
f to hunt game] The Eth. mss. read three verbs: "to hunt and trap and to bring (something) to him." The three verbs appear in the original story (26:2, 4, 5) and are repeated in 26:28. Perhaps the Eth. tradition drew them from chap. 26. See Tisserant, "Fragments," 224; VanderKam, *Jubilees* 2:243.
g food and drink] "food" Syr. Chr.
h My father] "He" Syr. Chr.
4a our] "my" Syr. Chr. (= 12 21 38 44).
b us] "me" Syr. Chr. (= 12 44).
c seek harm] "harm" Syr. Chr.
d the one against his brother] "against his brother" Syr. Chr.
e mutual love] "love" Lat.; "tranquillity" Syr. Chr.
f each . . . behavior] Syr. Chr. lacks.
g corrupt our behavior (lit., "ways")] "practice what is wrong toward one another" Lat. Tisserant ("Fragments," 224) thought the two traditions represent independent completions of a truncated text; cf. Berger, *Jubiläen*, 506 n. d. to v. 4; VanderKam, *Jubilees* 2:243. How the differences arose is not evident.
5a They] "His sons" Syr. Chr.
b listen] "agree" Syr. Chr.
c stronger] "strong(er) men" Lat.
d destroy his sons] "destroy him and (his) sons" Lat. (the text breaks off after *filios*; hence *suos* is not preserved). Mss. 12 21 38 also read a suffix: "destroy him." Syr. Chr. lacks the verb but reads "and his sons" as the object of the preceding verb: "kill him and his sons." See VanderKam, *Jubilees* 2:244.
6a Now] The Eth. mss., except 42 47, read a conjunction at the beginning of the sentence; Syr. Chr. also lacks one.
b let us . . . against him] Syr. Chr. lacks.
c let us send] "we will send" 58.
d and Ammon] om. 21.
e select (om. 12 44) men] om. 21.
f uproot] "destroy" Syr. Chr.
7a father] + "Esau" Syr. Chr.
b before him] "into his control (lit., into his hands) and he destroy you" Syr. Chr. Berger (*Jubiläen*, 507 n. a to v. 7) entertains the idea that Syr. Chr. has the original reading; at least it has left no trace in the Eth. tradition.
8a They] "His sons" Syr. Chr.
b Is this not] The strongest reading is the demonstrative *ze-* to which an interrogative particle is suffixed. Mss. 21 35 38, each with a different form, lack the interrogative, while ms. 21 uses a different one (*-ma*).
c very] Eth. *kemma*, "thus, the same, nearly" (see Leslau, *Comparative Dictionary*, 285). Syr. makes this a declaration: "This is . . ."
d what you are saying (lit., "this word")] "to you" Syr. Chr. Mss. 25 35 read "this your word." Syr. Chr. adds a sentence indicating that at this time Jacob was mourning for his wife Leah.
9a they] "the sons of Esau" Syr. Chr.

b to Aram—with them (from them 42ᶜ 44)] Syr. Chr. lacks.
c 1,000 fighting men, select (pr. "and" 39 42 47 58 63) warriors] Syr. Chr. does not render the text but takes numbers from vv. 9-10, the total of which is 4,000. It identifies them as coming from Aram and Edom, whereas the Eth. text of these verses pictures them as coming from these and other neighboring peoples.
10a who] "because" (i.e., because they were hired) 35; om. 48.
b Kittim] The form is kēṭēwon (+ "1,000" ms. 20) which Dillmann, Littmann, Goldmann, and Hartom read as "Hittites"; Charles took them to be "Kittim" (cf. 24:28). Either seems possible.
11a Go out] pr. "Get up" Syr. Chr.; + "with them and" 12.
b lead them] Syr. Chr., rather than a verb, uses "at our head" after "Go out."
12a He] "Esau" Syr. Chr.
b forcing] If the Heb. ptc. מחז]יקים is read correctly in 4Q221 frg. 5 2, the meaning would be similar: "prevailing upon, encouraging."
c in front in order to lead them] Syr. Chr. lacks.
d Jacob] Syr. Chr. lacks.
13a But] Many Eth. mss. read "afterwards" after the opening conjunction (translated "But"); Syr. Chr. lacks an equivalent, and ms. 20 25 44 also do not read it. There may not be space for the expression in 4Q221 5 2.
b all] Syr. Chr., with mss. 21 35, om.; 4Q221 5 3 includes the word.
c in his mind] Syr. Chr. adds "from before."
d the oath] "his oath" 17 38 58, but neither the Heb. frg. nor the Syr. Chr. reads a suffix.
e seek harm] Syr. Chr. phrases as: "to harm."
f against Jacob] 4Q221 5 5 reads ליעקוב, without "his brother" added to the name; Eth. has "his brother Jacob" (ms. 38 lacks "his brother") and Syr. Chr. "his brother."
g throughout his entire lifetime] Syr. Chr. lacks. There is space for the expression in 4Q221 5 4.
14a that they were coming to him for battle] Syr. Chr. lacks. There is space for the expression in 4Q221 5 5.
b his wife] Eth. adds "Leah" as does Syr. 4Q221 5 6 lacks the name.
c him near] Syr. Chr. lacks, though there is space for the words in 4Q221 5 6. Mss. 12 21 38 om. "him."
d the tower] "his enclosure" Syr. Chr.
e warriors] 4Q221 5 7 reads "men for war," i.e., warriors. Syr. Chr. has only "men," but Eth. has two terms that have appeared in vv. 9, 10: "warriors, select fighting men." They may be alternative renderings ultimately of the same Heb. text.
15a to him] Syr. Chr. lacks, but 4Q221 5 7 may have the first letter of the preposition at the edge of the frg. Syr. Chr. adds "to Jacob" after the verb of speaking later in the verse.

b just now] Eth. nāhu is the equivalent of הנה; Syr. Chr. lacks it.
c to fight you] "for war" Syr. Chr.; "to kill you" 35; om. 38.
d with 4,000 men—weapons] Syr. Chr. lacks.
e They told him] Syr. Chr. lacks as do 25 44.
f more generous and kind] Syr. Chr. uses nouns, but the meaning is the same: he was a man of mercy and goodness/kindness.
16a they] "he" 9 17 38 63; mss. 39 42 47 48 use impf. tense forms, sg. in 42 47, pl. in 39 48. Syr. Chr. reads with the text given here.
b tower] "enclosure" Syr. Chr. Midrash Wayyissaʿu reads "tower."
17a Then he] "At once he hastily" Syr. Chr. Cf. Syncellus, 124.9-10; Adler/Tuffin, *Chronography*, 155.
b of the tower] "of the enclosure" Syr. Chr. Cf. v. 16 above.
c stood] pr. "went up" Syr. Chr. Ms. 9 has a pl. subject ("they").
d He said] + "to him" Syr. Chr. 35 44 63.
e It is a fine] "Is it a fine" 39 42 47 48 58 63; "How fine it is" Syr. Chr.
f Is this the oath] "Are those the oaths" Syr. Chr. (see v. 13).
g twice] Eth. reads kāʿeba, "again, a second time" (cf. Dillmann, *Lexicon*, 867). Syr. Chr. reads "two times." The reference is to the oaths he swore to Rebekah and Isaac. See VanderKam, *Jubilees* 2:246.
h he died] This is the more difficult reading after the reference to both parents. Syr. Chr. "their death" supports a pl., and mss. 9 20 39ᶜ 42 44 47 48 also make the adjustment to a pl. by reading "they died." Ms. 35 om. "before he died."
i and were condemned in the hour when you swore (it) to your father (om. to your father 12)] Syr. Chr. lacks.
18a Then] Syr. Chr. lacks.
b said in reply to him] "said in reply to Jacob" Syr. Chr.
c serpents] Eth. and Syr. Chr. use standard expressions for "animals" in general, but 4Q223-224 unit 2 iv:4 reads נחשים (the nun is restored), a word that can be translated by the expressions in Eth. and Syr. Chr. See DJD 13:123.
d oath] The Heb. frg. and Eth. read a sg. form, but Syr. Chr., as it does throughout this section, has a pl. form because the oaths sworn to Rebekah and Isaac are under discussion.
e once they have sworn] Syr. Chr. lacks.
f how to kill] Eth., other than 44, places a conjunction before this expression; there is no conjunction in the Heb. frg. The unusual form היככה corresponds in meaning to kama, though kama seems to introduce the jussive verb.
g his] om. 20 25 35; 39 42 47 48 have "an enemy his enemy," while 21 44 63 have "his enemy an enemy."

19a You hate me and my sons] "You and your sons are enemies of me and my sons" Syr. Chr.

b no] + "for me" Syr. Chr. Neither the Heb. frg. nor the Eth. texts read the plus.

c brotherly ties] "peace" Syr. Chr. (On the Syr. Chr. addition at the end of the verse, see the commentary. There is no space for it in 4Q223-224 unit 2 iv:6. See also DJD 13:123.)

20a Listen to what I have to say] The Eth. reads literally: "Hear this word of mine that I am speaking to you." Syr. Chr.: "Hear these (things) that I am saying to you"; that is, it has no word corresponding to "word."

b If (*'emma*—so also Syr. Chr.)] "When" (*'ama*) 17 20 25. Eth. reads a second "if" before "makes . . . limp."

c and makes its hair limp like wool] "to soft wool" Syr. Chr. Eth., that is, reads a second "if" clause regarding the pig's hair, but Syr. Chr. does not. It is not clear whether the Heb. frg. reads a verb or adjective ("make soft" or "soft"). It could support the shorter Syr. Chr. reading but there is space in the reconstructed line for "its bristles/hair" as in Eth.

d and] Eth. repeats "if" (om. "and if" 25 39 42 44 47 58) before the verb as does Syr. Chr., but the Heb. frg. has only a conjunction.

e horns like the horns of] So Heb. and Eth.; Syr. Chr.: "horns of a ram."

f and sheep] The Heb. reading is difficult, but the frg. may read the last letter of צאן and thus support the Eth. reading. Syr. Chr. lacks.

g The breasts have been separated from their mother, for you have not been a brother to me] Syr. Chr. lacks, but there is space for the sentence on 4Q223-224 unit 2 iv:8, and "you have [n]ot been a brother" has survived on it. The Eth. MSS. show several variant readings of and before the verb "have been separated"—the first word in the sentence. Several MSS. strangely read a sg. form (17 20 38 47 48 63); 44 has "we have been separated" followed by "from the breasts." Ms. 38 prefixes "and" to the verb, while 39ᶜ 42 47 58 prefix "and if" ("and when" 48); 44 prefixes "because." Werman (*Jubilees*, 463 n. 10) suggests several changes: adding יונקי before שדים and reading נפרדנו: we sucklings were separated. There is no textual support for the first change, and only very slight backing for the second (MS 44 has "we have been separated").

21a so that they do not eat them] Syr. Chr. lacks. 4Q223-224 unit 2 iv:9 seems to have a *lamed* before the text breaks off; if so, it would have been worded as in Eth. There is space on the line for the equivalent of the Eth. reading.

b and if they have resolved—for you] Syr. Chr. lacks, but 4Q223-224 unit 2 iv:9-10 has the longer reading of Eth. The Heb. frg. reads perhaps a prepositional phrase after the inf.: "to do well to them/treat them well," where Eth. has just the inf.

22a friend of a bull and a confidant] Unlike Eth. and Syr. Chr., 4Q223-224 unit 2 iv:10 places the word "friend" after "to a bull" (= "a friend of a bull"). Neither Eth. nor Syr. Chr. has an equivalent of "confidant." It is reasonable to think that the word was om. in a Heb. MS. because of the repeated letters in ומאמין ואם (see DJD 13:123-24); the shorter reading in the versions would have arisen from this mistake.

b and if it is harnessed together with it in a yoke] "and draws the yoke with it" Syr. Chr. Mss. 20 25 44 om. "with it."

c and plows (as) one yoke] "and plows with it" Eth. The Heb. reading is highly uncertain (see DJD 13:120), but it seems to have worded the line differently from Eth. Mss. 20 25 35 38 39 42 47 48 58 read "one" before "yoke," but "yoke" is in a different position in them.

d then] The Heb. frg. may have an *aleph* at this point, suggesting that אז appeared here, directly after the clause about plowing. The Eth. MSS. have an extra clause before "then": "and makes peace with it" (MSS. 42 47 om., but they do so by paraplepsis: *meslēhu–meslēhu*). There is not enough space on the Heb. frg. for the clause. See VanderKam, *Jubilees* 2:248.

23a If (*'emma*)] "When" (*'ama*) 20 21 35 63.

b the ravens turn white] Syr. Chr. uses pl. forms, and 4Q223-224 unit 2 iv:11 has a pl. subject = "the ravens" and therefore would also likely have had a pl. verb. Eth. uses a sg. verb (pl. in 12 17 42 47) and subject.

c pelican] Heb. reads קא[ת], "pelican," where Eth. has *rāzā*, a bird whose precise identity is unknown. See VanderKam, *Jubilees* 2:249.

d know that I love you] Syr. Chr. lacks these words. 4Q223-224 unit 2 iv:11-12 attests each of them, though some must be partially restored.

e with you] om. 9 38 63.

f be uprooted—for you] Syr. Chr. lacks. 4Q223-224 unit 2 iv:12 preserves several words from this sentence, each agreeing with the Eth. reading. The Eth. MSS. show variety in the verb: "be uprooted" (impv.) is well supported, but several have "you are to be uprooted" (9 39 48 63); "you will cause to be uprooted" (12); "you will be uprooted" 42 47; "you (pl.) will be uprooted" (58).

g are being uprooted] The Heb. frg. (line 12) reads a ptc.; the most strongly supported Eth. reading is "may (your children) be uprooted," but 42 47 58 read "will be uprooted" (cf. MS. 9).

h is to be] "will be" 42 47 58.

i for you] om. 9 38, but the Heb. frg. (line 12) probably preserves the last letter of the phrase.

24a from his mind (lit., "heart")] "from/with all his mind" Syr. Chr. (but it is used to express how he came against Jacob). Syr. Chr. has a rather abbreviated form of the entire verse: "When Jacob saw that Esau had come

against him with all his mind and all his intelligence so that he could kill him."
b   was coming and bounding along] The Heb. (iv:14) reads two ptcs. where Eth. has a perf. tense verb followed by a circumstantial clause, without a conjunction between them.
25a he] "Jacob" Syr. Chr., but Heb. and Eth. lack the name.
b   his sons] Eth. reads "(his) own/(his) people," but Heb. and Syr. Chr. have "his sons."
c   and his servants] Syr. Chr. lacks.
d   attack him] "go out against him" Syr. Chr.
e   and all his companions] Syr. Chr. lacks. Mss. 25 35 39 42 44 47 48 58: "all his own (people), his companions."

Commentary

Like Jubilees 36, chap. 37 offers an expansion on Genesis—one that does not end with the chapter but extends through 38:1-14. Chapter 37 depicts events leading to a war between Esau and Jacob, and 38:1-14 describes the war itself. The action begins on the same day as the events of 36:1-18—the day of Isaac's death. At that time Esau's sons (there are four of them; see 38:8; Gen 36:1-5 names five) berated him for losing the birthright to Jacob and for being unwilling to retrieve it by force (for the chronological problem caused by placing the scene on the day Isaac died see the commentary on v. 1 below). They assembled an army from the neighboring nations and, after Esau came over to their way of thinking, marched against Jacob who was mourning the death of Leah. After the two brothers spoke angrily with each other and reconciliation became impossible, Jacob gave the order for his own forces to fight against his brother and the 4,000 troops with him.

The contents of the chapter can be outlined in this way:

1-8   Esau's sons want to fight Jacob for the birthright but Esau opposes their plan
9-10   Esau's sons assemble an army from the neighboring nations
11-13 Esau changes his mind and agrees to attack Jacob
14-23 Jacob is surprised by the attack and has an unpleasant exchange with Esau
24-25 Jacob orders a counterattack against Esau and his army.

A war between Esau and Jacob is attested in several other sources, although Jubilees is the oldest work to contain a story about it.

Testament of Judah 9: Judah, on his deathbed, tells his sons about the war in a way that differs substantially from the one in Jubilees. The story is shorter and focuses on aspects of it that are not developed in Jubilees, particularly the role of Judah in the fighting.

Midrash Wayyissa'u: The third unit in the midrashic collection presents an account showing some parallels with Jub 37:1–38:14, just as the second unit exhibits similarities with Jub 34:1-9. While it contains many of the details found in Jub 37:1–38:14, it too devotes far more space to elements treated more briefly in Jubilees—especially the extended battle against the army that attacked Jacob and his sons. Judah is very prominent in this version as well.

Book of Jashar and the Chronicles of Jerahmeel: These later sources have the account in the form it takes in Midrash Wayyissa'u.

Textual evidence for Jubilees 37 comes in four languages. The full Ethiopic text can be compared with:

Latin   vv. 1-5
Syriac   for the entire chapter apart from v. 10
Hebrew   two manuscripts contain letters and words from segments of the chapter
         4Q221 frg. 5: vv. 11-15
         4Q223-224 unit 2 iv:2-15: vv. 17-25 (often very little of the text has survived on several small pieces)

1-8 Esau's Sons Want to Fight Jacob for the Birthright but Esau Opposes Their Plan

■ 1 Both the Ethiopic and Latin translations place the conversation between Esau and his sons (vv. 1-8) "[o]n the day that Isaac, the father of Jacob and Esau, died" (the Syriac citation merely summarizes with "after Isaac's death").[1] The statement of date is noteworthy for several reasons. A minor one is the order of the sons' names—Jacob is now first, and that simple fact constitutes the very issue Esau's sons raise in v. 2. The larger reason for dwelling on the beginning of v. 1 is the precise timing of the conversation: it happened on the day (*ba-ʿelata/in die*) of Isaac's death. Jubilees 36:1 assigns his death to the year 2162, and the date in v. 1 implies that the events of chap. 37 took place in that year on whatever day Isaac died. The sons of Esau and eventually Esau himself would then be guilty of violating his oath to Isaac within hours of the patriarch's death. Any breaking of an oath (especially the great one the brothers had sworn) would be a grave sin, but to time the transgression so poorly would only add to his (and their) guilt. This was likely the author's intent.

But the date is impossible. Jubilees 36:21 sets the death of Leah five years after Isaac's life ended. One could imagine chap. 37 as a flashback to a conflict that erupted five years before Leah died, even though the account of it happens to follow the one about her death. Yet 37:14 says that Jacob was caught off guard by the attack because he was mourning the death of Leah. So the war happened after Leah died and therefore could not have begun on the day Isaac died, if he had passed away five years before she did.

Interpreters have advanced different proposals to solve the chronological contradiction. Charles's solution was to separate the parts of the chapter: "The sons of Esau began their opposition to Jacob from the day of Isaac's death (2162 A.M.), but did not attack him until Leah died (2167 A.M.). See ver. 14."[2] His suggestion is not impossible, but the text implies that only a little time passed between the scene in vv. 1-8 and the attack later in the chapter—only enough time to form a coalition and to do so hastily (see the end of v. 6). Kugel, who rejects Charles's idea, approaches the difficulty in another way. As he rightly notes, the time directly after Isaac's death would have been a natural setting for the story; the scriptural trigger for it also favors the juxtaposition. In Gen 27:41 (// Jub 26:35) Esau threatened, "The days of mourning for my father are approaching; then I will kill my brother Jacob." Verse 1, as a result, arranges the events of chaps. 37–38 in a logical way—they follow immediately after Isaac's death, as Esau had long ago threatened. Kugel thinks that in the original form of the tradition (its pre-Jubilees form) Jacob was mourning for his father, not Leah, at the time of Esau's attempt on his life. In Jubilees, Esau is not an entirely negative character, so the author was not inclined to picture him as so impious as to assault Jacob when he was grieving for Isaac. Therefore he inserted the verses about the death of Leah to change the meaning of Jacob's ironic charge in v. 17 ("[i]t is a fine consolation that you have come to give me") so that it alludes to his mourning not for Isaac but for Leah. He thinks the author, after inserting "for my wife" in v. 17, did not notice the contradiction with the date in v. 1, though later writers did and solved the inconsistency by eliminating the first verse of the story.[3]

This is a more plausible explanation than the one Charles offered, but it does entail that the writer of Jubilees overlooked a blatant chronological contradiction within just a few verses. That is possible, but it

---

1   Since "[o]n the day that Isaac, the father of Jacob and Esau, died" appears in the Ethiopic and Latin translations, the reading would have been present at least in the Greek version of Jubilees.
2   Charles, *Jubilees*, 215.
3   Kugel, *Walk through Jubilees*, 174–75; "Jubilees," 463–64. Actually, the other sources do not so much eliminate the first verse as offer their own chronologies. Kugel mentions Midrash Wayyissaʿu, in which the war is more generally dated to "after a time" (74, line 3 of the story) but during the year *Leah* died (lines 4-5, 7-8). The Testament of Judah, also noted by Kugel but without discussing the details in it, offers exact dates. Judah says that Jacob and his sons lived at peace with Esau and his sons for eighteen years after their return from Mesopotamia. According to Jub 29:14 Jacob and his party crossed the Jordan back into the land in 2136. Adding eighteen years to that number yields 2154. Hollander and de Jonge (*Testaments*, 199) try to relate the eighteen years to the time after the war with the Amorites (2148 in Jub 34:1), but T. Jud. 9:1 does not count the eighteen years from that date (Judah was twenty at the time of the Amorite war [7:10] and he is forty [9:2] when the war with Esau breaks out). Jubilees 28:15 dates Judah's birth to 2129 (2128 is proposed in the commentary) so that he would have been forty years old in 2169, close but not identical to the date for Leah's death in Jubilees.

would be better if there were another way of handling the conflict between vv. 1 and 14. It will be recalled that the date for Isaac's death (2162) fell 175 years after his birth whereas 36:18 says he died at the age of 180, that is, the date of his death should be 2167—the same as the date for Leah's death. If so, then the deaths of Isaac and Leah would have occurred in the same year—2167—and therefore the events of chap. 37 could take place at the time Isaac died. A problem with this suggestion, apart from resorting to a textual emendation, is that the death of Leah seems to have taken place a little while after that of Isaac; at least 35:19-20 implies the passage of some time (Esau goes to Edom and Jacob pursues a pious life). Nothing is said about the two deaths happening on the same day, yet for the sake of the sequence of chap. 36 and 37:1 they would have to have fallen on the same date. In addition, if Isaac and Leah died on the same day, the reader might expect Jacob to include Isaac's name in vv. 14, 17 as at least one of those whose deaths Jacob was lamenting. As a result the chronological problem remains, with each of the proposed solutions suffering from some weakness. It would disappear if v. 1 said that the action commenced on the day or at the time when Leah died (much as in Midrash Wayyissaʻu, which puts it in the year she died),[4] but that would remove the immediacy of the birthright issue and the order implied by Gen 27:41 // Jub 26:35.

It may seem strange that Esau's sons did not hear about the birthright issue until the day Isaac died because Esau had in fact ceded it to Jacob many years earlier (in 2080 according to 24:2, that is, eighty-two years before Isaac died). But the text is explicit that they heard Isaac had actually given the larger share to Jacob—a grant made only on his final day. Isaac's deeding the major part of the property to Jacob made it official, and that act is the one that aroused the ire of Esau's sons; their inheritance was affected by the sanction Isaac, on the basis of Esau's emphatic assent, gave to the transfer his sons had negotiated years before. Chapter 37, like chaps. 35–36, relates an encounter between a parent and children, but in this case it is the children who instruct the father, not the reverse. Naturally, the results are awful.

■ **2** The sons quarrel or argue[5] with their father, hardly the proper attitude of respect they should have shown to him. Their question is simple: since Esau was older and Jacob younger, why did Isaac give the younger son the share belonging to the older. The versions differ on exactly what, according to Esau's sons, Isaac did to him: the Ethiopic reading is *ḥadaga*, "abandon, leave, leave behind, leave out, omit, give up, let go, dismiss, depose, ignore, renounce."[6] Latin has *inferiorem fecit*, "made the inferior one." The two, while not equivalents, are also not far apart in meaning, particularly if *ḥadaga* means "deposed" here. Whatever the nuance the author intended, the point made by Esau's sons is that Isaac moved or lowered their father from his rightful position.

■ **3** It seems as if Esau had not shared with them the story about forfeiting the birthright (perhaps he was too embarrassed to do so), so now at last he tells them the truth regarding the episode narrated in Jub 24:3-7. The wording in his version of the story is interesting because he admits to some regret. At the time when he gave Jacob the birthright, the narrator said, "Then Jacob gave the food and porridge to his brother Esau, and he ate until he was full" (24:6).[7] Here, however, Esau says he gave the birthright "in exchange for a little lentil broth." He seems to recognize at this late date that he made a poor trade. Yet, though his sons referred only to the birthright, Esau adds the other awkward story that also involved food—his loss of the blessing to Jacob. He mentions the day (chap. 26 // Genesis 27) when Isaac sent him on a hunting expedition, a first step in preparing a meal for him so that he could bless Esau. On that occasion, says Esau, Jacob "came in a crafty way" (see 26:30) and, before Esau could complete his assignment, brought food and drink to Isaac. Not only did Isaac then bless Jacob, but he also "put me under his control." He is referring to Isaac's words to Jacob: "Become lord of your brothers; / may the sons of your mother bow to you" (26:24). Later Isaac had repeated the thought to Esau: "I

---

4   See the commentary on v. 17 below, where the context of Leah's death is more important to the story than the death of Isaac.

5   For *tagāʼazu*, see Leslau, *Concise Dictionary*, 208.

6   Leslau, *Concise Dictionary*, 116–17 (a selection of the meanings listed). The Syriac citation is too paraphrastic here to be helpful.

7   Genesis 25:34: ". . . and he ate and drank, and rose and went his way."

have just now designated him as your lord. I have given him all his brothers to be his servants" (26:31). Esau seems to have accepted his casual loss of the birthright, but he still thinks Jacob stole the blessing (as he did in 26:30). His response to his sons has a different ring to it than the one he gave to his mother the day she died: "For on the day when my father blessed him he made him the superior and me the inferior one" (35:23). He had not called Jacob's action crafty or sly on that occasion but simply accepted the result.

■ **4** Further updating his sons on events in the family, Esau reports more of what transpired earlier on that day when Isaac met with him and Jacob before his death (chap. 36). He gives an acceptable summary of the oath Isaac caused them to take: they were not to desire harm for the other (36:4, 8-11); rather, they were to continue practicing brotherly love (36:4, 8) and peace. In that way they would not pursue an evil path in their conduct. Esau adds to Isaac's words the notion of being in peace, and he presumably inferred that, if they practiced the virtues Isaac inculcated, the brothers would not resort to bad behavior.

■ **5-6** Esau's sons reply to him in an astonishingly inappropriate way to answer a parent and in a manner thoroughly contrary to the teachings about family relations in chaps. 35–36. Their initial refusal has to do with living in peace with Jacob—the point their father had just made in his summary of the oath Isaac had them swear. Their attitude is one of might makes right.[8] They dismiss the fact that their father had agreed under oath to live in harmony with his brother. Their desire is to fight Jacob and his sons to regain what Esau had lost through his thoughtless decision and Jacob's cunning. They include Jacob's sons in their plans for military action because they were the heirs to the wealth he received from Isaac—wealth that Esau's sons thought they could procure for themselves by brute force. They

hope not only to defeat Jacob and his sons but also to kill them and thus end that branch of the family—the chosen line. Jacob and Esau had agreed not to inflict injury on the other, but now Esau's sons threaten to harm their father if he does not go along with their plan. They are assuredly not honoring their father and are behaving in a reprehensible fashion. The reader could conclude from the scene that if Esau was bad his sons were even worse.[9]

The strategy that they force upon Esau is to seek military reinforcements from four neighboring peoples: Aram,[10] Philistia, Moab, and Ammon (see the commentary on vv. 9-10 for these nations). They continue to reverse the proper relations between children and parents by saying to Esau, "Now listen to us." They demand that he be involved in the invitations to the four peoples from whom they wish to choose "select men who are brave in battle," that is, elite soldiers. With their assistance they intend to advance against Jacob and eradicate him from the earth. Isaac, who anticipated destruction and uprooting from the earth for Esau and his descendants, had ordered his sons, "Practice brotherly love among yourselves, my sons, like a man who loves himself, with each desiring what is good for his brother and doing things together on the earth. May they love one another as themselves" (36:4). The course of action that Esau's sons urge upon their father could hardly be farther from what Isaac had commanded Esau and Jacob. The four of them want to "uproot" Jacob and his sons—a punishment Isaac had predicted for the one who desired his brother's harm (36:9). Besides sending to the surrounding nations to assemble an army against Jacob, Esau's sons want to dispatch the message right away before Jacob can muster a counterforce. They want to seize the moment and not squander a chance to recover what their father had lost.

■ **7-8** The subsequent exchange between Esau and his four sons is enlightening. Esau shows, just as he

---

8   The reader knows that Jacob is actually far stronger than Esau and his sons, as Isaac had declared regarding the guardian or keeper of Jacob in 35:17 (Werman, *Jubilees*, 464).
9   See VanderKam, *Textual*, 232–33.
10 The name "Aram" is attested by all the Ethiopic copies and is mentioned in each listing of the foreign peoples who contributed troops to Esau's force. Nevertheless, Werman (*Jubilees*, 464) changes the name to "Amorite" because she finds it unlikely that Arameans, from whose ranks Leah and Rachel had come, would be included among the hostile neighboring peoples. This does not seem to be an adequate basis for a textual decision that is opposed by all copies in several places.

did when speaking with his mother and father in chaps. 35 and 36, that he heard what his parents had said and understood the situation. He had agreed to love Jacob and desire only good things for him, and he had acknowledged Jacob's superiority to him and affirmed that the birthright belonged to his younger brother. But he had also heard the weighty curse Isaac had pronounced on the one who desired injury for his brother: "If one of you desires harm for his brother, be aware from now on that anyone who desires harm for his fellow will fall into his control and will be uprooted from the land of the living, while his descendants will be destroyed from beneath the sky" (36:9; see also v. 10). Moreover, when he "blessed" Esau in chap. 26, he said to him, "You will live by your sword and will serve your brother. May it be that, if you become great and remove his yoke from your neck, then you will commit an offense fully worthy of death and your descendants will be eradicated from beneath the sky" (26:34).[11] That is, Isaac predicted for the one who violated the command of fraternal love the very fate that Esau's sons planned for Jacob and his offspring.[12] It is no wonder, then, that Esau tells his sons not to execute their martial plan lest they suffer a terrible defeat (as they will in 38:1-14). He knows the facts of the matter far better than his sons do and realizes the chance they will succeed is nil.

The sons, however, pay no attention to their father's wise counsel and again reverse the roles of sons and fathers. Rather than obeying their father, who wanted to honor the oath he swore to both parents, they criticize him as they had in v. 2 and refuse to listen to him as they had in v. 5. They regard his behavior in the present instance as objectionable yet typical of the way he had acted since his childhood. They find nothing worth respecting or honoring in their father Esau. The charge they make against him—"You are putting your neck beneath his yoke"—echoes the image Isaac used for Esau's subjection to Jacob. His sons now berate him for adopting the posture that Isaac had prescribed for him. Ironically, the sons will soon find themselves beneath that very yoke.

9-10: Esau's Sons Assemble an Army of Foreign Mercenaries

Without their father's consent,[13] Esau's sons set their plan in motion and recruit an army from the neighboring nations. The sons proposed in v. 6 that they hire troops from four of the surrounding countries: Aram, Philistia, Moab, and Ammon. They now carry out their scheme by sending messages to these peoples, although the lists in vv. 9-10 and chap. 38 are a little different from the one in v. 6.

Jubilees 37:6[14]	Jubilees 37:9-10	Jubilees 38
Aram	Aram and Aduram: 1,000 men	Aduram the Aramean (v. 3)
Philistia	Moab and Ammon: 1,000 men	Moab and Ammon (v. 6)
Moab	Philistines: 1,000 men	Philistines (v. 7)
Ammon	Edom and the Horites: 1,000 men Kittim: strong warriors.	Edom and Horites (v. 8)

---

11 The parallel in Gen 27:40 is significantly different: "By your sword you shall live, / and you shall serve your brother; / but when you break loose, / you shall break his yoke from your neck."
12 Esau would not have known it, but Isaac had said to Rebekah: "If he [Esau] wishes to kill his brother Jacob, he will be handed over to Jacob and will not escape from his control but will fall into his control" (35:16).
13 Neither the version in Testament of Judah 9 nor that in Midrash Wayyissa'u notes this circumstance. They say only that Esau came with a strong force against Jacob. The entire scene in which Esau's sons argue with their father and plan the attack is lacking from them.
14 Caquot draws attention to the similarities between this list and 2 Sam 8:1-12, where, according to v. 12, David dedicated spoil "from Edom, Moab, the Ammonites, the Philistines, Amalek, and from the spoil of King Hadadezer son of Rehob of Zobah" (Zobah was an Aramean kingdom; see below) ("Jubilés," 776, n. to v. 6). For hiring troops against Israel, Caquot (p. 777 n. to v. 9) referred to 2 Sam 10:6: "When the Ammonites saw that they had become odious to David, the Ammonites sent and hired the Arameans of Beth-rehob and the Arameans of Zobah, twenty thousand foot soldiers, as well as the king of Maacah, one thousand men, and the men of Tob twelve thousand men." Isaiah 11:14 speaks about a future conquest of Philistia, the people of the east, Edom, Moab, and Ammon.

Several questions arise from the lists, and neither Testament of Judah 9 nor Midrash Wayyissaʻu offers much assistance in clarifying them. Aduram, who is said to be Esau's friend in 37:9, is identified as an Aramean in 38:3. He plays no role in Testament of Judah 9, but in the midrash (line 15) he is the first one Jacob kills with an arrow (he is second to Esau in Jub 38:2-3), and there he is called an Edomite (האדומי; "the Aramean" would be הארמי). The midrash probably reads a mistaken form of the gentilic, while Jubilees preserves his correct affiliation with the Arameans, whom he seems to represent in 38:3. Adoram is a biblical name (e.g., 2 Sam 20:24; it is an alternate form of Adoniram), but the person with the scriptural name is not said to be an Aramean.[15] Aduram also resembles the name of a city near Hebron—Adoraim (2 Chr 11:9); note that in Jub 38:8 Esau died "on the hill that is in Adoraim"[16] (he fell there when attacking Jacob in Hebron).

The lists in Jub 37:9-10 and in chap. 38 group Moab and Ammon together as a unit but add to the nations enumerated in 37:6 "Edom and the Horites." Esau was the ancestor of the Edomites (see Gen 36:8-9, 19, 43), and the Horites, "the inhabitants of the land" (Gen 36:20; in Deut 2:12 the Horites are the original residents of Seir who were displaced by Esau's descendants), were interrelated with him: Seir the Horite was a grandfather of Oholibamah, one of Esau's wives (Gen 36:2, 20, 25). Naturally Esau's own people supplied recruits for his army above and beyond those hired from the other nationalities. Each national grouping contributes the round figure of one thousand warriors to the cause. A surprising entry in the list is, therefore, the Kittim, who appear only in 37:10.[17] Inclusion of them is peculiar not only because they figure in none of the other lists but also because there is no indication that they supplied one thousand troops as all the others did (only manuscript 20 adds the number). The number of four thousand soldiers[18] in the mercenary army is mentioned in 37:14 and probably in Midrash Wayyissaʻu line 6 (the reading 40,000 is likely a mistake for 4,000); since the total for the mercenaries from the other four groups is four thousand, there would be no place for more armed men from the Kittim. In the absence of other textual evidence for Jub 37:10, the Ethiopic reading cannot be verified or excluded, but it does seem strange.[19]

11-13: Esau Changes His Mind and Agrees to Attack Jacob

The sons, who had criticized their father so strongly in vv. 5, 8, continue to put pressure on him.

■ **11** They issue commands to him and threaten him with death if he fails to comply. The only measure of respect they show him is to order him to lead their army of elite fighters. They force their father into a hopeless situation: if he refuses to accompany them death awaits

---

15 See Littmann, who also mentions the possibility that the place-name Adoraim (see the comment above) may have been transferred to an individual ("Jubiläen," 102 n. e). Caquot thinks the name reminds one of Joram, son of Toi the king of Hamath (an Aramean place, according to Caquot) ("Jubilés," 777, n. to v. 9). However, since King Toi is there an ally of David, Caquot further believes that the author confused this Joram with another Aramean—Hadadezer in 2 Sam 10:5, an enemy of David as Aduram is an enemy of Jacob in Jubilees. But associating Aduram and Joram and attributing a confusion of characters to the author are claims too speculative to be convincing.

16 4Q223-224 unit 2 iv:27 (Jub 38:8) preserves the spelling אדורים where the Ethiopic spelling is ʼadurām and the Latin adurin. So Aduram seems to represent biblical Adoraim.

17 As Charles explained (*Jubilees*, 216), one could also interpret the form as "the Hittites" (so Dillmann, Littmann, Goldmann, Hartom), but he adds that a name spelled similarly appears in 24:28, where it has to mean "the Kittim." Rabin has "Kittim," as do Wintermute and Caquot. Werman considers the term an addition to the list, comparing 24:29, where they also appear and relating their appearance to the eschatological expectations of the author's community (*Jubilees*, 464).

18 The four thousand augment the four hundred men of Esau (Gen 32:6; 33:1) tenfold.

19 The Syriac citation for v. 9 reads: "Esau's sons sent and hired for themselves 4000 strong men from Aram and Edom." It reproduces nothing from v. 10 apart from adding up the troops listed in the Ethiopic version of vv. 9-10 (see Tisserant, "Fragments," 224; he thinks the chronicler was uninterested in the nations around Israel).

him from his own sons, but if he leads the troops with the aim of killing his brother and his family he would also lose his life, as Isaac had declared in no uncertain terms (36:9). The circumstances will eventually force Esau to reassess the oaths he had taken—in fact, to reassess oaths altogether (see v. 18).

■ **12** The dilemma in which he found himself forced Esau to reflect. His initial response was great anger at his sons for the way in which they were treating him. The terms for his emotion—*ma'āta wa-qweṭ'a* ("anger and wrath")—are the ones Isaac used in 36:10 when he predicted the fate that would befall the son who sought the harm of his brother: "On the day of anger with raging wrath and fury[20]—with a blazing fire that devours—he will burn his land, his cities, and everything that belongs to him just as he burned Sodom." The rage he feels is also the punishment he and his sons will receive. His sons were making him turn against his brother, and Esau was only too aware of the consequences.

■ **13** In his difficult situation, Esau made another fateful decision based on his old feelings about Jacob. Two facts presented themselves to him: he disliked Jacob, but he had sworn not to harm him. The force of the animosity he felt toward his brother now overpowered the feeling of obligation he incurred when he vowed to his parents that he would always love Jacob. The Ethiopic translation speaks about matters hidden in Esau's mind (lit., heart) against his brother; the Syriac citation talks of matters concealed in his heart "from before."[21] The line proves that, in spite of the assurances he gave his parents, Esau had not outgrown the emotions toward Jacob that long ago made him threaten his life. Those feelings were still present and, though he had suppressed them for a time, they now surged over him. As a result, he forgot what he had sworn to Rebekah and Isaac—that he was not to desire harm for his brother during his entire lifetime. To his mother he had said (35:24), "'I swear to you that I will love him and that throughout my entire lifetime I will not desire harm for him but only what is good.' He swore to her about this entire matter." The tremendous oath Isaac required of Esau and Jacob included similar language: "One is not to desire harm for his brother from now and forever, throughout your entire lifetime" (36:8). Somehow, Esau let his resentment toward Jacob erase the memory of these oaths from his mind. The one he made to his mother was now some five years in the past (if the episode in chaps. 37–38 belongs in the year 2162, ten years if it happened in 2167), but in the present chronology of the chapter he had hardly finished swearing the one to his father when he forgot it. Under intense pressure from his sons and confronted with the army they had hired, he obeyed their order. Verse 13 does not say this explicitly, but v. 15 indicates that he accompanied the four thousand mercenaries when they marched on Hebron.

The wording of v. 13, especially the report that Esau retained his old animosity toward Jacob, reminds one of Amos 1:11:

> Thus says the LORD:
> For three transgressions of Edom,
>   and for four, I will not revoke the punishment;
> because he pursued his brother with the sword
>   and cast off all pity;
> he maintained his anger [lit., his anger tore]
>   perpetually,
>   and kept his wrath forever.

This passage, the source for the word pair "anger and wrath" in Jub 37:12 (cf. also Isa 63:6), could be read as recalling a military attack on Jacob by Esau (= Edom, who "pursued his brother with the sword"), one motivated by Esau's unending hatred. Midrash Wayyissa'u cites the end of Amos 1:11 at the beginning of its version of the war between Esau and Jacob (line 3). The Amos passage points to nothing that occurred in Genesis, but Jubilees provides a basis for the prophecy of doom on Edom.

---

20 See the commentary and textual note on the passage. The Ethiopic text has "On the day of turmoil and curse, of anger and wrath. . . ."

21 Lines 2–3 in Midrash Wayyissa'u refer to the same idea: "he had not removed the jealously [הקנאה] from his heart" (part of a discussion of why Esau went to Edom and thus away from Jacob; the reason, according to some, was not that he had expelled any jealousy from his heart but that he had moved his property to Edom). This is the context for the citation from Amos 1:11 in the midrash (see below).

14-23: Jacob Is Surprised by the Attack and Has an Unpleasant Exchange with Esau

The scene now changes to the place where Jacob was living. Esau and his sons presumably hatched their plot in Mount Seir, that is, Edom, while Jacob and his family resided in the area of Hebron (see 36:19-20). The distance between the two locales would have made it possible for Esau's sons to gather an army and start marching toward Hebron without Jacob knowing what was happening.

■ **14** Geographical facts could explain why Jacob was unaware of the impending attack, yet the writer further incriminates Esau and his associates by explaining that Jacob was otherwise occupied: he was still in the period of mourning for his dear wife Leah (see Midrash Wayyissa'u 4-5, 8-9; for the chronological problem in Jubilees 37, see the commentary on v. 1 above). Where Jub 37:14 says that "Jacob was unaware [lit., did not know (the first two letters of ידע are legible on 4Q221 frg. 5 5)] that they were coming to him for battle," the midrash says about Jacob and those members of his household who arrived to comfort him: "it did not enter their minds [lit., heart] that anyone would come against them to fight with them" (line 9). It was only when the attacking force of four thousand men came close to the tower where Jacob lived that he learned about the invasion.

■ **15** Even then Jacob and his party did not notice the danger moving their way but heard of it only when the people of Hebron informed him. Their report left no doubt about the intentions of Esau and the men with him: the four thousand had "swords buckled on" and were "carrying shields and weapons."[22] The occasion provides another opportunity for the author to picture Jacob positively and Esau negatively. It was not only luminaries such as Abraham, Rebekah, and Isaac who recognized the superiority of Jacob to his brother but also common people like the Hebronites. They felt greater affection for him because they found Jacob to be "more generous and kind"[23] than Esau. Neither Testament of Judah 9 nor Midrash Wayyissa'u contains this element of character evaluation so that it probably comes from the writer of Jubilees—by this point in the story the reader expects flattering words about Jacob and critical ones about Esau. But one could ask how the inhabitants of Hebron knew about the nature of Esau since he did not live there. The text does not say, but Isaac and his family had lived in Hebron for a while. Abraham had resided there at the time when Sarah died, when a wife was found for Isaac, and when the twins were born (19:1). Isaac subsequently moved to Beersheba (see 22:1-2), though he visited his father in Hebron (22:3). Later still, Isaac was again at Hebron (see 24:1) but left, returning only when he and Rebekah moved away from Esau (29:17-19). So, in the narrative world of the story, people in Hebron could have known Esau for periods in his younger days, but they may have heard about his cruel, thoughtless ways from his parents when they relocated to the tower of Abraham.

■ **16** Jacob, who no doubt remembered well what Esau and he had promised their parents, simply could not believe what he heard. It was only when he saw the evidence for himself—when they approached the tower[24]—that he realized the people of Hebron had spoken the truth. His brother, who had offered such impressive assurances in chaps. 35 and 36, had completely reversed himself and was now poised to do what he had so solemnly declared he would never do.

■ **17** It is noteworthy that Jacob does not respond in kind. Rather than immediately resorting to arms to repulse the attack with his own forces, Jacob first speaks with his brother. This is the only extended conversation between them in the book of Jubilees. For the sake of safety he closed the gates of the tower—so little had

---

22 Midrash Wayyiss'u lines 5-6 has a very similar statement: Esau came against them with a large force (40,000 [4000]) wearing armor made of iron and bronze, all armed with shields, bows, and javelins. The Syriac citation lacks the information about armor and weapons, as does T. Jud. 9:2: "Esau, the brother of my father, came upon us with a mighty and strong people."

23 The word translated "kind" (*maḥāri*) is the first adjective to describe God in Eth. Exod 34:6 (רחום, "merciful").

24 Both the Ethiopic text of Jub 37:16 and Midrash Wayyissa'u mention the tower or fortress (בירה), while the Syriac citation uses a more general term—enclosure.

he expected an armed attack that the compound was hardly on military alert. The Ethiopic translation and the Syriac citation say that he stood "on the top,"[25] but Midrash Wayyissaʻu is more specific: "he stood on the wall of the tower" (line 12). From that high vantage point he addressed his brother and expressed astonishment at what he was doing. The first point he makes is sarcastic: "It is a fine consolation that you have come to give me for my wife who has died." Jacob's sons had come to comfort him on the sad occasion (36:22),[26] but his own brother, who at such a trying time should have supported his only sibling and perhaps joined the mourners, was exploiting a time of weakness as an opportunity for killing him and his family. That Jacob mentions the time of mourning for his wife first is a strong indication that the story, at least in its form in Jubilees, is tied to the time of Leah's death, not that of Isaac (see also v. 14).

The second point Jacob addresses is the matter of the oaths that Esau had sworn to his parents. Notice that he does not say that Isaac has just died and that he is mourning his death as Esau should also have been doing. He refers to Isaac's dying but only as the time before which Esau had sworn twice—once to Rebekah (35:21-24) and once to Isaac (36:7-11). He does not need to explain the details of the oaths; he just asks Esau whether he is acting in conformity with his sworn pledges to his parents. The question is rhetorical, since Esau was obviously contradicting his own promises in Jubilees 35 and 36. The last sentence in v. 17 is Jacob's way of telling his brother that at the very time when he made the vows to his parents, he incurred guilt—perhaps because his actions now showed the lack of sincerity in his assurances to Isaac. If Esau was guilty of breaking his oath, he and Jacob knew the consequences Isaac had specified—utter destruction of the violator, his family, and his land (36:9-10). At any rate, Jacob in just a couple of sentences sets out the case against his brother in unequivocal terms. Testament of Judah 9 records no speech for Jacob, and Midrash Wayyissaʻu contents itself with a summary: as the army and Esau approached, Jacob "was speaking words of peace, friendship, and brotherhood with his brother Esau" (lines 12-13).[27]

Esau's reply in vv. 18-23 is perversely emphatic but surprisingly eloquent—and found only in Jubilees among the ancient witnesses to the war between the brothers.[28] Verses 14-17 established Jacob's pure innocence and the enormity of what Esau was doing. Jacob acted responsibly by rebuking Esau for failing in his duties as a brother and violating oaths sworn to his dying parents (v. 17). In vv. 18-23 Esau further incriminates himself by denying the validity of oaths and the possibility of living as a brother with Jacob. His words, utterly opposed to what his parents taught, fall into two parts: vv. 18-19 and 20-23, both of which are prefaced by notices regarding speech ("Then Esau said in reply to him," v. 18; "Listen to what I have to say to you," v. 20). These markers precede animal references, and each ends with Esau speaking directly to Jacob, using the second person singular "you," (vv. 19, 23).[29] Note too the repetitive terms and statements by Esau throughout the speech and the absolute negative declarations near the beginning and at the end. Between them he sandwiches a series of apodoses also of a negative character:

Absolute statement: There is no observing of brotherly ties with you (v. 19).
    Apodosis: then I will observe brotherly ties with you (v. 20)

---

25   The Syriac citation prefaces "he went up" to the verb "he stood."

26   Midrash Wayyissaʻu lines 4-5: "Jacob and his sons were in mourning, and some of his sons were comforting them."

27   In lines 14-15 Judah asks Jacob how long he was going to speak "words of peace and love with him" when Esau was attacking them. The sentiments Jacob expresses in Jub 37:17 do not sound very much like words of peace, friendship, brotherhood, and love.

28   As it summarized Jacob's speech, so Midrash Wayyissaʻu says of Esau's response to Jacob's words: "he did not accept (them)" (line 13). For detailed studies of Jub 37:18-23, see Gershon Brin, "The Sources of the Saying of Esau in Jubilees 37 according to 4Q PapJubilees[h], unit 2, col. IV," in Rimmon Kasher and Moshe Sippor, eds., *Memorial Volume for Yehudah Qomlosh* (Studies in Bible and Exegesis 6; Ramat Gan: Bar-Ilan University Press, 2003) 17-24; and Livneh, "'Can the Boar Change Its Skin?' Esau's Speech in *Jubilees* 37:18-23," *Hen* 34 (2012) 75-94.

29   Livneh, "'Can the Boar Change Its Skin?,'" 78.

Apodosis: then there will be peace in my mind for you (v. 21)
Apodosis: then I will make peace with you (v. 22)
Apodosis: then know that I love you and will make peace with you (v. 23)
Absolute statement: There is to be no peace for you (v. 23).[30]

■ 18 The first point he makes is that "Neither humankind nor serpents have a true oath" that is valid for all time. His comment, of course, strikes at the core of his parents' provisions for ensuring harmony between their sons. The commitment of Jacob and Esau to living in fraternal peace was sealed by oaths, and now Esau denies that oaths have any enduring power. Jacob had asked whether he was abiding by those solemn assurances, and Esau denies that they had the force Jacob attributes to them.[31] 4Q223-224 unit 2 iv:4 shows that Esau claimed neither humans nor *serpents* (not "animals" in general, as in the Ethiopic and Syriac texts) had reliable oaths, ones that remained in force.[32] The reference to serpents makes one think of Eve's interlocutor in Genesis 3: the action attributed to it there is that it deceived or misled the woman with its words (Gen 3:13), and the punishment is unending enmity between the serpent and the seed of the woman (v. 15)—just as there is between Esau and Jacob.[33] Serpents and deceptive words are associated elsewhere in the HB. Psalm 58:3-4a says, "The wicked go astray from the womb; / they err from their birth, speaking lies. / They have venom like the venom of a serpent." Or Ps 140:3, while talking about evildoers who stir up wars, declares, "They make their tongue sharp as a snake's, / and under their lips is the venom of vipers."[34] As serpents are symbols of deception, of lying or misleading with words, so humans do not keep oaths. But also in direct opposition to what he swore to his parents, Esau asserts that people and snakes habitually desire harm for others[35] (cf. Gen 3:15) and even wish to kill their "enemy and opponent" (Judah will use almost the same two terms in reference to Esau in 38:1). It is a daily occurrence, and swearing oaths changes nothing. Esau, therefore, considers himself under no obligation to abide by what he had vowed to his parents.

■ 19 After declaring his view of oaths, Esau lays on Jacob the charge that he hates Esau and his sons unendingly and that one cannot observe fraternal ties with such a person. Resort to the verb "hate" in connection with Jacob and Esau reminds one of Mal 1:2-3: "I have loved you, says the Lord. But you say, 'How have you loved us?' Is not Esau Jacob's brother? Says the Lord. Yet I have loved Jacob but I have hated Esau; I have made his hill country a desolation and his heritage a desert for jackals." If Jacob hated Esau, he would be doing no more than what the Lord himself did. Yet in the narrative of Jubilees there is no evidence that Jacob hated Esau or his sons. True, he had threatened to kill Esau if he tried to dispatch him (27:4), but Jacob had maintained good relations with his brother (29:13) and had sworn to his mother: "Trust me that nothing bad against Esau will come from me or my sons. I will not be first except in love only" (35:26). He and Esau shared a meal with their mother and one in front of their father to show they were in agreement about practicing the brotherly love

---

30 Cf. Brin, "Sources," 21, where he notes the repetitions.
31 Livneh, "'Can the Boar Change Its Skin?,'" 78-79. She refers to Zech 8:17, where an antonym to "a reliable oath" appears—a false oath. Since Esau swore by the name of God (see 36:7), he violated Lev 19:12: "And you shall not swear falsely by my name, profaning the name of your God."
32 As Brin perceives, Esau does not deny that he swore oaths to his parents; his point is rather that despite the oaths there can be no peace with Jacob—the oaths did not change the situation ("Sources," 18). The following animal comparisons illustrate Esau's case. Brin (p. 20) considers the Hebrew reading "serpents" more original and holds that the variant "animals" arose to serve as an opening to the list of creatures that follows.
33 Brin, "Sources," 19-20 (see p. 24 for parallels).
34 Since in vv. 20-23, however, the Esau of Jubilees clearly uses animal imagery drawn from Isa 11:6-7 and 65:25 (see below), it is reasonable to think that the snake imagery in v. 18 also derives from these passage (11:8; 65:25). See Brin, "Sources," 20-21; and Livneh, "'Can the Boar Change Its Skin?,'" 80-81.
35 As Livneh comments, the expression relates elsewhere in Jubilees to the prohibition of hating one's kin (Lev 19:17) ("Can the Boar Change Its Skin?," 80).

both parents had enjoined upon them (35:27; 36:17). So Esau places the blame for the bad relations on Jacob when in fact he, by attacking Jacob, was the one guilty of breaking the oaths he had sworn.[36]

At the end of the opening salvo by Esau, the Syriac citation supplies words not present in the Ethiopic textual tradition: "Jacob said, 'Do not do (this), my brother. As for me, there is no evil in my mind against you; do not plan evil against me. Be aware that there is a God, and he sees secrets and repays each one in accord with what he has done. Calm your great anger and do nothing hastily. Then evil would come upon you.'" Tisserant thought the words were original in Jubilees and that they had fallen from the text represented in the Ethiopic manuscripts by homoioteleuton: from the phrase "with you" at the end of v. 19 to "upon you" at the end of Jacob's speech as preserved in the Syriac text.[37] His textual solution does not work ("with you" is not the last expression in v. 19 in the Ethiopic text; "brotherly ties" is and both Ethiopic and Syriac read a noun in this place). Berger argued for the originality of the section from the themes and vocabulary in Jacob's extra words—they agree with ones met elsewhere in Jubilees.[38] Neither argument is persuasive for deeming the reply original to Jubilees. Moreover, 4Q223–224 unit 2 iv:6 has insufficient space for the Syriac plus; the available space implies a text of the same length as the one in the Ethiopic copies.[39]

■ **20-23** The second section of Esau's speech (vv. 20-23) contains the elements noted above for the first section (vv. 18-19), and it is arranged chiastically. The first and fourth of the appeals to animals deal with implausible changes in them, and the middle two concern equally improbable relations between wild and domestic animals.[40]

Esau, as he begins the second part of his speech, issues a command to Jacob, summoning him to listen (the expanded Syriac text inserts before this: "Then Esau replied and said harshly"). He had referred to serpents in v. 18 and now reverts to animal imagery. Using conditional sentences, he makes reference to four kinds of creatures and cites highly unlikely circumstances for each. All of these are rhetorical means to underscore how unthinkable it is that Esau would live in peace and fraternal harmony with Jacob.[41]

1. *If a pig changes its hide and makes its hair limp like wool; and horns like the horns of a ram and sheep go out of its head (v. 20).* If such happened, says Esau, he would observe the bonds of brotherhood with Jacob. Charles noted that in the Animal Apocalypse Esau is represented as a wild boar (1 Enoch 89:12; see also vv. 43, 66). He also mentioned Ps 80:13 (Heb. 14), where a boar from the forest ruins the Lord's vineyard.[42] The author of Jubilees will compare Esau to a boar in 37:24.[43] Yet the point of the image here has to do with the nature of its hair: it is bristly and tough, the opposite of something soft like wool. The idea that a pig would have woolly hair[44] or that it would have horns is absurd; it does not

---

36 Livneh, "'Can the Boar Change Its Skin?,'" 81–82. Genesis 27:41 says that Esau hated Jacob after the blessing incident.

37 Tisserant, "Fragments," 224.

38 Berger, *Jubiläen*, 509 n. a to v. 19.

39 DJD 13:123; cf. VanderKam, *Jubilees* 2:247. This is not the only place where the Syriac citation is supplemented from a source other than Jubilees in the war section (see the ends of 38:1, 3).

40 Livneh, "'Can the Boar Change Its Skin?,'" 85. About the meaning she writes: "The frame (A/A´), which stresses the inconceivability of Esau changing his wicked nature and practicing brotherly love, explains why the everlasting animosity expressed in B/B´ will always prevail between Esau and Jacob." For the imagery, see Justin Strong, "Aristotle and Hippocrates in the Book of Jubilees," *JSJ* 48 (2017) 309–30.

41 Caquot ("Jubilés," 778 n. to v. 20) adduces Jer 13:23 for a similar rhetorical device: "Can Ethiopians change their skin / or leopards their spots? / Then also you can do good / who are accustomed to do evil." Brin also notes the parallel ("Sources," 21). After his study of Esau's entire speech, he wonders whether the author meant to say through it that it was impossible for Israel to live in true peace with the nations (p. 24).

42 Charles, *Jubilees*, 218.

43 Brin, "Sources," 21, 23. He refers to *Gen. Rab.* 65:1, where, in connection with Gen 26:34, two passages dealing with swine (Ps 80:14 and Deut 14:8) are applied to Esau/Rome. He also adduces Prov 11:22 for another absurdity regarding this kind of animal: "Like a gold ring in a pig's snout / is a beautiful woman without good sense."

44 Livneh ("'Can the Boar Change Its Skin?,'" 86) cites

happen in nature. In the same way, Esau cannot act as a brother to Jacob. It can hardly escape notice that Esau uses imagery (pig or boar) attested elsewhere for himself while "sheep/flock" is a metaphor used frequently for Israel in the HB; he employs them to express the idea of incompatibility between the two.

2. *If wolves make peace with lambs so that they do not eat them or injure them; and if they have resolved to treat them well (v. 21).*[45] The middle two conditional sentences, both related to imagery in Isaiah, appeal to the natural relations between certain animals: if a wild animal and its prey live in peace, so will Esau and Jacob. The wolf-lamb pairing is found in Isa 11:6, where it is part of the picture of the ideal future kingdom: "The wolf shall live with the lamb" (see v. 7 for the lion and ox). It also appears in Isa 65:25 along with the next pair in Jubilees: "The wolf and the lamb shall feed together, / the lion shall eat straw like the ox." The specific language Esau uses—not eating or harming but resolving to treat the domestic animal well—is reminiscent of the demand that a brother not seek the harm of the other.[46] He argues that this does not happen in the world—wolves harm and devour lambs—while Isaiah uses the image as an example of the reversals that will mark the new age of righteousness and peace.

3. *If a lion becomes the friend of a bull and a confidant, and it is harnessed together with it in a yoke and plows (as) one yoke* (v. 22). As noted above, the pairings appear in Isa 11:7; 65:25 and articulate the same idea as in (2).[47] A lion attacks a bull/ox and does not coexist with it. A somewhat similar image appears in Ahiqar 8:11 (Syriac): "My son, thou has been to me as an ox that was bound with a lion; and the lion turned and crushed him" (trans. Harris, *APOT* 2:770).[48] Esau develops this image further: he speaks of the two kinds of animals being yoked with each other and plowing in tandem. If those two natural enemies make a truce with each other, Esau will live in peace with Jacob. The theme of a yoke should recall Isaac's words to Esau: "You will live by your sword and will serve your brother. May it be that, if you become great and remove his yoke from your neck, then you will commit an offense fully worthy of death and your descendants will be eradicated from beneath the sky" (26:34; cf. Gen 27:40).[49]

4. *If the ravens turn white like a pelican (v. 23).*[50] 4Q223-224 unit 2 iv:11 supplies enough evidence to show that the bird being contrasted with ravens is a pelican (קאת).[51] The word occurs in Isa 34:11a in an oracle against Edom: "But the hawk [קאת = pelican] and the hedgehog shall possess it; / the owl and the raven shall live in it." A raven is black (see Cant 5:11: "His head is the finest gold; / his locks are wavy, / black as a raven"), and pelicans are white, so the contrasts continue. In this case Esau says that he will love Jacob as a brother and make peace with him if very black birds somehow turn white. It is not going to happen. He adds a hostile "you" statement directed toward Jacob: he and his children are to be uprooted/eradicated. This is the very punishment Isaac had promised for Esau and his descendants (35:14) and for the one who failed to practice brotherly love (36:9).

---

a saying from the Syriac version of Ahiqar: "even if the tail of the swine should grow to seven ells, he would never take the place of a horse; and even if his hair should become soft and woolly, he would never ride on the back of a free man" (8:7; trans. Harris in *APOT* 2:770). As Harris indicates in a note, the last clause sounds backwards and should say: a free man would never ride on his back.

45 See Brin, "Sources," 20–21, with parallels on 23.
46 Livneh, "'Can the Boar Change Its Skin?,'" 89; see also her "'Love Your Fellow,'" 184–86.
47 Werman (*Jubilees*, 465), who also summarizes the patterns in Esau's speech, draws attention to the likelihood that use of Isaiah 11 in this context was not accidental because later in the chapter the prophet speaks of a day when Judah and Ephraim will defeat, among others, the Philistines, Edom, Moab, and the Ammonites (Isa 11:14)—the peoples allied with Esau and his sons in Jubilees 37–38.
48 Livneh, "'Can the Boar Change Its Skin?,'" 90. She raises the question whether the image might also suggest the prohibition of mixing varied kinds of animals as in Deut 22:10: "You shall not plow with an ox and a donkey yoked together."
49 Livneh, "'Can the Boar Change Its Skin?,'" 90–91.
50 See Brin, "Sources," 21–22, 23. Cf. Ahiqar 2:62 (Syriac A): "My son, if the waters should stand up without earth, and the sparrow fly without wings, and the raven become white as snow, and the bitter become sweet as honey, then may the fool become wise" (trans. Harris, *APOT* 2:737). See Livneh, "'Can the Boar Change Its Skin?,'" 87–88.
51 The first two letters are legible, but the third must be supplied.

There could be no peace with such a person in Esau's opinion.

The only part of vv. 20-23 not involving a statement about animals and birds is the last line in v. 20: "The breasts have been separated from their mother, for you have not been a brother to me." The puzzling line has elicited comments of more than one kind. It is recognized to be a challenging expression to understand, with the cause of the difficulty perhaps being that it is idiomatic. Charles thought that, whatever it meant, it was in the wrong place. There is the obvious problem that it breaks the series of animal images in vv. 20-23. "Nor do the words as they stand form a distich. If they belong to the text at all, they are corrupt. It is not improbable that originally they followed immediately after ver. 19a 'thou dost hate me and my children for ever.'"[52] He also changed the word "breasts [*aṭbāt*]" to "twins [*aṭbuʿ*]"[53] to yield the sense: "And thou dost hate me and my children for ever; for thou hast not been a brother to me since the twins were separated from their mother. Yea, there is no observing the tie of brotherhood with thee." Berger, who considers the suggestions of Charles arbitrary, proposes that the words μητρός ("mother") and μήτρας ("womb") were interchanged and that the line should read: "The breasts have been separated from their womb. For you have not been a brother to me." The meaning would then be that breasts and the mother (or the womb), which belong together, have been torn apart, just as the two brothers have been separated.[54]

Kugel has drawn attention to the relation between the expression and Gen 25:23, where Rebekah receives a communication from the Lord: "Two nations are in your womb, / and two peoples born of you shall be divided [= separated]; / the one shall be stronger than the other, / the elder shall serve the younger." The verb "separated" links the two passages. "It would seem that Esau is evoking this oracle and saying something like: 'From the time *we were separated* from the womb, you have not been a brother to me.'" That is, for this interpretation he would accept Berger's proposal about "womb" instead of "mother" (as Kugel notes). But he also thinks Charles's understanding of the expression makes excellent sense, though perhaps "since we were separated at our mother's breasts" would fit better with the Hebrew fragment.[55] It is very likely that the oracle of Gen 25:23 was in the writer's mind as he composed the line, but 4Q223–224 unit 2 iv:8, while it has space for the expression, preserves only "you have [n]ot been a brother." The section about the birth of Esau and Jacob in Genesis 25 has another shared word with Jub 37:20. When Esau was born, "he came out red, all his body like a hairy mantle [lit., mantle of hair]" (v. 25); the word for "hair" in Eth. Gen 25:25 is the one Esau uses for the hair of the pig in his first "if" sentence (v. 20; see Jub 19:13 for Esau as a hairy man). Whatever the original wording of the line may have been, Esau asserts that the brothers lost their unity from the beginning. Perhaps the reader is supposed to remember what Rebekah said to Isaac regarding Jacob: "He has not separated from us from the day he came from Haran until today" (35:12), whereas Esau had abandoned them (35:9) and God (35:14). His words now sound much different than when he said

---

52 Charles, *Jubilees*, 218. 4Q223–224 unit 2 iv:8 shows that the expression is not misplaced in the Ethiopic version, since it preserves part of the line—"you have not been a brother"—where the Ethiopic manuscript tradition locates it. Consequently, during the first century CE (the date of the manuscript), the Hebrew line was in its present location.

53 The word does not mean "twins" but "males" (Leslau, *Concise Dictionary*, 108; Dillmann, *Lexicon*, 561). Wintermute ("Jubilees") translates: "And if sucklings separate themselves from their mother, you would not be a brother to me" and places the sentence inside brackets. In a note (p. 127 n. j) he explains, after referring to Charles, that "sucklings" stands where the text has "breasts" and thinks there is "obviously something wrong" with the words in brackets. Rabin ("Jubilees," 113 n. 7) leaves the line out of the text and gives Charles's revision of it in a note. Livneh ("'Can the Boar Change Its Skin?,'" 83–84) details the reasons for thinking the line would fit better in the first part of Esau's speech (vv. 18–19) and thinks it is misplaced, though she recognizes that this would have happened already in the Hebrew stage of transmitting the text.

54 Berger, *Jubiläen*, 510 n. f to v. 20.

55 Kugel, *Walk through* Jubilees, 177–78; "Jubilees," 422–23.

to Rebekah on the day of her death: "This is no great thing for me if I love him because he is my brother. We were conceived together in your belly and we emerged together from your *womb*. If I do not love my brother, whom shall I love?" (35:22).

24-25: Jacob Orders a Strike against Esau and His Army

When Jacob heard the poetic words of his brother and perceived the intractable determination he showed to ignore the oaths made to his parents, he saw there was no choice but to defend himself against the attack.

■ **24** Use of animal imagery continues in the narrator's description of the situation. Jacob sees that Esau is totally (heart and soul) committed to killing him—something Esau had long ago threatened to do. Rebekah knew he still wanted to carry out his menacing words (35:9), though Isaac had assured her he would fail (35:16). Esau had denied the possibility of peaceful coexistence by the brothers so that Jacob had to take emergency action. The writer compares Esau's unchangeable resolve to an attack by a wild animal[56] so obsessed that it ends up killing itself. He charged "like a boar that comes upon the spear that pierces it and kills it but does not pull back from it."[57] Esau is being compared to an irrational beast whose folly leads to its death. The image recalls the description of the young man whom the strange woman of Proverbs lures to his death: "Right away he follows her, / and goes like an ox to the slaughter, / or bounds like a stag toward the trap / until an arrow pierces its entrails. / He is like a bird rushing into a snare, / not knowing that it will cost him his life" (Prov 7:22-23). Esau is insanely bent on killing his brother. Isaac was right: even if he swore an oath not to seek Jacob's harm, it would do no good (35:15). All of this serves to justify the decision Jacob makes under these difficult circumstances.

■ **25** Only after he saw for himself the nature of the situation and that this man who, when he grew up, "learned (the art of) warfare, and everything that he did was harsh" (19:14), had stooped to the level of an animal in his murderous intent, did Jacob tell his sons and servants to counterattack Esau and his forces. Jacob is the leader, the one to give the decisive order that was forced upon him by a brother and his sons who had utterly rejected the wishes of Rebekah and Isaac that their sons live in unending peace with each other.[58] It should be noted that once again in the book defensive warfare is acceptable: one fights only when first attacked by an enemy (see the examples of Abram [Jub 13:22-25] against the eastern kings, and Jacob versus the Amorite kings [Jub 34:1-9]).[59]

---

56   In a seminar paper entitled "The Exegetical Background to the Battle between Jacob and Esau in *Jubilees*" (2010), David DeJong, a doctoral student at the University of Notre Dame, argued that this passage as well as the references to wild animals in Esau's speech are related to the verb טרף ("his anger tore perpetually") in Amos 1:11. The verb almost always has a wild animal as its subject.

57   See Brin, "Sources," 21–22 (noting the pig references near the beginning and end of the section), 23–24 (parallels).

58   Syncellus, who at the end of the relevant paragraph names the Little Genesis (= Jubilees) as his source, summarizes the material in chap. 37: "So after Isaac died, Esau, stirred to action by his sons, amassed his Gentile cohorts and came out for combat against Jacob and his sons. But Jacob closed the gates of the tower and admonished Esau to recall his father's injunctions. Now when he was not restrained, but was instead hurling insults and making reproaches"(124.7-11; Adler/Tuffin, *Chronography*, 155). The passage continues with a short summary of the material in Jub 38:1-14.

59   The attack on Shechem (Jubilees 30) presents a different kind of case. In it a violent crime precipitated the sack of the city and annihilation of its population by Jacob's sons. Jacob expresses some misgivings about killing the people of the city (30:25), but the angel refers to it as a just act (vv. 17-18).

38

War between Esau and Jacob and an Edomite King List

1/ After this[a] Judah spoke to his father Jacob and said to him,[b] "Draw your bow, father;[c] shoot your arrow;[d] strike the enemy; and kill the foe.[e] May you have the strength[f] because we will not kill your brother,[g] since he is your brother[h] and he is similar to you,[i] and, in our estimation,[j] he is like you[k] in honor."[l] 2/ Jacob then stretched his bow, shot an arrow,[a] struck[b] his brother Esau on his right breast,[c] and killed[d] him. 3/ He shot a second arrow[a] and hit Aduran the Aramean on his left breast; he drove him back[b] and killed him.[c] 4/ After this[a] Jacob's sons[b]—they and their[c] servants—went out,[d] dividing themselves to the four sides[e] of the tower. 5/ Judah[a] went out first.[b] Naphtali and Gad were with him, and 50 servants[c] were with them[d] on the south side of the tower. They killed everyone whom they found[e] in front of them. No one at all escaped[f] from them. 6[a]/ Levi, Dan, and Asher went out[b] on the east side of the tower, and 50 were with them. They killed the Moabite and Ammonite bands.[c] 7[a]/ Reuben,[b] Issachar, and Zebulun went out[c] on the north side of the tower,[d] and their 50 with them.[e] They too[f] killed the Philistine fighting men. 8/ Simeon,[a] Benjamin, and Enoch—Reuben's son—went out[b] on the west side of the tower, and their 50[c] with them. Of (the people of) Edom and the Horites they killed 400 strong[d] warriors, and 600 ran away.[e] Esau's[f] four sons ran away with them. They left their slain father[g] thrown[h] on the hill that is in Adoraim.[i] 9/ Jacob's sons pursued them as far as Mount Seir,[a] while Jacob buried his brother[b] on the hill that is in Adoraim[c] and then returned[d] to the tower.[e] 10/ Jacob's sons besieged[a] Esau's sons in Mount Seir. They bowed their neck[b] to become servants for Jacob's sons. 11/ They sent to their father[a] (to ask) whether they should make[b] peace with[c] them or kill them.[d] 12/ Jacob sent word to his sons to make peace.[a] So they made[b] peace with them and placed the yoke of servitude[c] on them so that they should pay tribute[d] to Jacob and his sons for all time. 13/ They continued paying tribute[a] to Jacob until the day that he went down[b] to Egypt. 14/ The Edomites have not extricated themselves[a] from the yoke of servitude[b] that Jacob's sons imposed[c] on them until today.

15/ These are the kings who ruled in Edom[a]—before a king[b] ruled the Israelites—until today in the land of Edom. 16[a]/ Balak[b], son of Be'or, became king in Edom.[c] The name of his city was Danaba. 17/ After Balak died, Yobab son of Zara who was from Bosir became king in his place. 18/ After Yobab[a] died, Asam who was from Mount Teman[b] became king in his place. 19/ After Asam died, Adat son of Bared who slaughtered Midian in the field of Moab became king in his place. The name of his city was Awutu. 20/ After Adat died, Saloman who was from Emaseqa became king in his place. 21/ After Saloman died, Saul who was from the river Raabot became king in his place. 22/ After Saul died, Baelunan son of Akbur became king in his place. 23/ After Baelunan son of Akbur[a] died, Adat became king in his place. His wife's name was Maytabit, daughter of Matrit, daughter of[b] Metabedezaab. 24/ These are the kings who ruled in the land of Edom.

Textual Notes

1a After this] Syr. Chr. lacks.
b and said to him] Syr. Chr. lacks. There seems to be space for the expression in 4Q223-224 unit 2 iv:16.
c Draw your bow, father] Syr. Chr. reads the command but later in the verse, after Judah explains why he and his brothers cannot kill Esau. At that point Syr. Chr. lacks "father."
d shoot your arrow] Syr. Chr. lacks. 4Q223-224 unit 2 iv:16 has the last letter of the verb and the words "your arrow." Mss. 12 21 25 38 39 58 read "your arrows."
e strike the enemy; and kill the foe] 4Q223-224 unit 2 iv:16 has the last two letters of "the foe." Syr. Chr., after the explanation why the brothers cannot kill Esau and after the command for Jacob to stretch his bow, reads: "slay your enemy; and kill your foe."
f May you have the strength] 4Q223-224 unit 2 iv:16 has the verb (at the end of the line), while the beginning of line 17 is not extant. Syr. Chr. = "We are not

989

	able to draw the sword before [lit., in the face of] your brother."			a very similar line at this place (124.13; Adler/Tuffin, *Chronography*, 155).
g	we will not kill your brother] Syr. Chr. lacks; there is space for it in 4Q223-224 unit 2 iv:17.	4a	After this] Syr. Chr. lacks, but Eth. and Lat. support the reading.
h	he is your brother] Syr. Chr. preserves the expression (but after "and kill your foe"), but 4Q223-224 unit 2 iv:17 has "he is your brother" at this point, that is, after "we will not kill your brother." The Eth. MSS. lack the words due to parablepsis: your brother . . . your brother. See DJD 13:124.	b	Jacob's sons] So Heb. Eth. Lat.; Syr. Chr. om.
		c	their (servants)] Mss. 20 25 35 44 read "his servants."
		d	went out] came 9 38; om. 35.
		e	the four sides] This seems to be the meaning of Eth. *marbeʿta* (for *marābeʿt* with this meaning, see Leslau, *Comparative Dictionary*, 460). Lat. suggests the Heb. original was ארבע רוחות (ארבע is preserved in 4Q223-224 unit 2 iv:20, but the next word at the beginning of line 21 is lost).
i	he is similar to you] Syr. Chr. lacks. The Eth. MSS. have "he is near to you," that is, *ḫabēka weʾetu*. The next, parallel line suggests the prepositional phrase has the sense of "like/similar to you" (see VanderKam, *Jubilees* 2:250).		
j	in our estimation] The Eth. reading is lit., "with us," while Syr. Chr. has "in our eyes." See VanderKam, *Jubilees* 2:250 for the opinions of the translators.	5a	Judah . . . tower] Syr. lacks the entire section.
		b	first] So Lat. and 4Q223-224 unit 2 iv:21. Eth. *feṣma* means "before, in front of, foremost" (Leslau, *Comparative Dictionary*, 169), so the meaning is similar if not exactly that of Lat. and Heb. Midrash Wayyissaʿu: "first" (line 17).
k	he is like you] 4Q223-224 unit 2 iv:17 preserves the reading, as do Syr. Chr. and Eth. (*mamseleka*); a number of MSS. perhaps read another noun for "likeness"—*mesl*—which became confused with the familiar preposition *mesla*, so that they read *meslēka*, "with you"; 17 21 25 44 47 63; 35 39 42 48 have the correct *mesleka*.		
		c	servants] So Eth. and Lat., but there may not be space for the word in the Heb. text (line 21). Note that "servants" is not used with the number "50" in the following verses.
		d	with them] 4Q223-224 unit 2 iv:21 may read a pl. suffix, but the noun to which it is attached is not preserved. Eth. and Lat. read "with him." Midrash Wayyissaʿu (line 18) and MSS. 12 20 44 have "with them."
l	in honor] Lat. reads, "in order that we may give him the honor." The verb is not reflected in Eth.; the place where the passage would have appeared in 4Q223-224 unit 2 iv:18 has not survived, but it is doubtful there is space for the extra verb and prepositional phrase. Cf. DJD 13:124.		
		e	they found] Syr. Chr. = "they were found."
		f	No one at all escaped] Syr. Chr. = "they did not escape." 4Q223-224 unit 2 iv:22 reads a sg. verb with Eth. and Lat.
2a	an arrow] "arrows" 17; "his arrow" 35 38 39 42 44 47 48 58. Lat. = "an arrow." For the possibility of "the first arrow" here, see DJD 13:125.	6a	Syr. Chr. lacks the verse.
		b	went out] "came" 9 38.
b	struck] So Syr. Chr. and Midrash Wayyissaʿu (line 16); cf. Syncellus, 124.12; Adler/Tuffin, *Chronography*, 155. Eth.: "pierced."	c	bands] This appears to be the reading of 4Q221 6 2; 4Q223-224 unit 2 iv:23 has only the first letter (*gimel*), which could be from "warriors" or "bands." Eth. and Lat. have "warriors."
c	on his right breast] Eth. omits, but Syr. Chr. and Lat. read the expression, and there is space for it in 4Q223-224 unit 2 iv:19. Midrash Wayyissaʿu also reads it (line 16).	7a	Syr. Chr. lacks the verse.
		b	Reuben] 4Q223-224 unit 2 iv:23 and Eth. (except MS. 38) read a conjunction at the beginning of the sentence, but Lat. lacks it.
d	killed] "caused to fall" Syr. Chr. and Syncellus. Perhaps a *hiphil* form of נפל appeared in the original—a verb that can be used for killing.		
		c	went out] 4Q223-224 unit 2 iv:23 uses a sg. form of the verb (with the sg. noun—Reuben—that follows); Eth. and Lat. have pl. forms.
3a	He shot a second arrow] The versions agree about the meaning, but Heb., Syr. Chr., and Lat. have "a second arrow," while Eth. has: "he again shot an arrow" (with slightly different formulations among the copies). Mss. 17 20 35 38 44 48 have "his arrow."		
		d	on the north side of the tower] om. Lat.
		e	their 50 with them] So 4Q223-224 unit 2 iv:24, probably 4Q221 6 3, and Lat.; Eth. = "50 with them."
b	he drove him back] Syr. Chr. lacks, though Eth. and Lat. agree on the reading for which there is space in 4Q223-224 unit 2 iv:20.	f	They too] *et ipsi* Lat.; without an equivalent, the Heb. text of 4Q223-224 unit 2 iv:24 would be a little short. Eth. lacks. See DJD 13:125.
c	killed him] + "when Jacob's sons saw that Esau was dead, they opened the gates of the enclosure" Syr. Chr. Neither Eth. nor Lat. has the plus; there is no space for it at 4Q223-224 unit 2 iv:20. Syncellus, however, has	8a	Simeon—and 600 ran away] om. Syr. Chr.
		b	went out] The form is pl. in Eth., but sg. in Lat. Midrash Wayyissaʿu has a pl.
		c	their 50] "50" Eth. Midrash Wayyissaʿu lacks "their."

d strong] Lat. lacks.
e ran away] Lat. lacks, but Midrash Wayyissaʻu has the necessary verb.
f Esau's] Syr. Chr. resumes at this point but connects the clause to its previous one ("None escaped from them") by inserting "except" before "Esau's sons."
g their slain father] Lat. reads "the body of their father," but Eth. and Syr. Chr. lack "the body of," as does Midrash Wayyissaʻu (see lines 52, 54). Lat. thus lacks "slain," which is present in Eth., Syr. Chr., and Midrash Wayyissaʻu (מת).
h thrown] Lat. *proiectum*, "thrown"; and Syr. Chr. is similar (it places a conjunction before the pass. ptc.). Midrash Wayyissaʻu probably preserves the correct reading: מוטל, "thrown." Eth. "as he fell" may be a paraphrase.
i on the hill that is in Adoraim] Syr. Chr. lacks; אדורים is the spelling in 4Q223-224 unit 2 iv:27.
9a Jacob's sons—Mount Seir] Syr. Chr. lacks.
b his brother] Lat. and Syr. Chr. add "Esau," with Lat. placing the name before "his brother," and Syr. Chr. after it.
c on the hill that is in Adoraim] Syr. Chr. lacks. Lat. lacks "in."
d returned] The verb is sg. in Eth. and Lat., referring to Jacob, but Syr. Chr. makes "he and his sons" the subject of a pl. form.
e the tower] Eth. = "his house." Both Lat. (*barin*) and Syr. Chr. (*drt'*) use their standard equivalents for tower/fortress. See DJD 13:126.
10a besieged] The Eth. reading is "harassed/pressed on" or the like (perhaps reflecting a form of צרר), while the Lat., when an easy correction is made (*cumsederunt* → *circumsederunt*), means "besieged," echoing a form of צור. Midrash Wayyissaʻu supports this reading (וצרו [line 56]). T. Jud. 9:4 also has "besieged." See VanderKam, *Jubilees* 2:253 for the views of the editors and translators.
b They bowed their neck] "They subjugated them" Lat. 4Q223-224 unit 2 iv:29 preserves "their neck," indicating that the Eth. more literally reflects the Heb. original.
11a their father] + "Jacob" Lat.
b whether they should make] "so that they might make" 38 44.
c with them—So they made peace with them (v. 12; see VanderKam, *Jubilees* 2:254)] Lat. om. by parablepsis. 4Q223-224 unit 2 iv:31 has space for the fuller Eth. text, and the two preserved letters from the last word of v. 11 in line 31 indicate that the word was "them" as in Eth.
12a peace] + "with them" 38 39ᶜ 58.
b they made] "he made" 21 63.
c servitude] Lat. reads "fear." Rönsch (*Jubiläen*, 156) suggested that the translator confused δουλειας ("servitude") and δειλιας ("fear") in his Gk. base text. Midrash Wayyissaʻu reads מס עובד (line 58).
d pay tribute] "give honor" Lat. Rönsch (*Jubiläen*, 156) thought the ambiguity of a word such as τιμη misled the translator. Its meaning is "honor," but it can also be used for "tribute," as in LXX Ezek 22:25. T. Jud. 9:7 refers to "tribute," as does Midrash Wayyissaʻu (line 58). See VanderKam, *Jubilees* 2:254. Yet *honor* can mean "fee, recompense." See v. 13.
13a paying tribute] Lat. again reads *honorem* where Eth. has an expression for tribute (see above on v. 12).
b he went down (= Lat.)] "Jacob went down" Eth. (MS. 12 = "he went down"). If frg. 30 belongs at this point, it preserves a form of ירד, but the suffix on it is very difficult to decipher (read as יורדם, "their going down" = "they went down" in DJD 13:126). Because of the uncertainty regarding the last letter of the Hebrew form (and placement of the fragment) the translation uses a sg. suffix as in Lat. and Eth. Lat. has a copyist's error of *defensionis* for *descensionis* (Rönsch, *Jubiläen*, 74).
14a extricated themselves] Eth. *natagu*, "they ceased, stopped, removed" (Leslau, *Comparative Dictionary*, 407), and Lat. *cessaverunt*, "they ceased." The two apparently agree in meaning and indicate that the Edomites have not stopped being under the yoke of Jacob's sons. Expressing the meaning in English is not easy, as saying "they have not stopped/ceased from the yoke" is not very idiomatic. The suggested translation is an attempt to express the meaning and be idiomatic. Another possibility is "stopped (being subject to) the yoke."
b servitude] Lat. again uses *timoris* as in v. 12. Mss. 25 39 42 47 48 om.
c imposed] So Lat. Eth. reads "twelve," which would leave the clause without a verb. Mss. 9 12 17 20 21 38 44 63 point the way toward the correct reading. For "ten and two," that is "twelve" (where the word for "ten" is *'ašartu*), they read *šar'u*, "they set/established/arranged/erected" (Leslau, *Comparative Dictionary*, 532). Perhaps this verb was original to Eth. Jubilees, but before "the sons of Israel" a scribe confused it with the number "10." That number was then expanded to "12" for the number of the sons of Israel—the reading in most MSS. Mss. 35 58 read this verb and the number 12; only MS. 44 has just the verb *šar'u*, as in Lat. See VanderKam, *Jubilees* 2:254-55. Note that the prepositional phrase "on them" presupposes a verb like this.
15a in Edom] "for Edom" 9 12 17 21 38 44 63. Jubilees, with LXX Gen 36:31, lacks "land of" before Edom. MT SP read "land of" here.
b king] "kingship" Lat. Perhaps the person who translated Jubilees into Lat. misread βασιλεα ("king") as βασιλεια ("kingship"). See VanderKam, *Jubilees* 2:255.
16a Lat. om. the first words of v. 16—"became king in Edom"—by parablepsis from the end of v. 15.

b   Balak] *barad* Lat. The Lat. spelling is unique (cf. "Bared" in v. 19), whereas the one in Eth. matches the name in many Gk. copies of Gen 36:32 and LXX 1 Chr 1:43.
c   Edom] "Sodom" 20 25.
18a Yobab] + "who was from Basir" 21 (see v. 17); + "the son of Zara" 39ᶜ 48 58 (see v. 17).
b   who was from Mount Teman] om. 12.
23a son of Akbur] om. 20 38 58.
b   Matrit, daughter of] om. 25 35.

Commentary

The first verses of chap. 38 are a direct continuation of the story about a military campaign in chap. 37, a part of the major expansion on the narratives in Genesis, where no such war appears. The hard feelings that were coming to a head at the end of Jubilees 37 now erupt into open warfare between the forces of Esau and Jacob. Jacob and his smaller contingent of troops, organized into four divisions led by his sons (and one grandson), win a crushing victory over the much larger army gathered by Esau's sons. Esau himself, a victim of his brother's arrow, dies in the conflict as do so many of those who came with him to fight Jacob and his family. Jacob spared the lives of Esau's sons, but his own sons imposed tribute on them. A list of kings who ruled in Edom, Esau's land, is appended to the war story; the list derives from Gen 36:31-39.

The chapter can, then, be outlined as consisting of two parts:

1-14   The war between the forces of Jacob and Esau
15-24 The kings who ruled in Edom (Gen 36:31-39)

Testament of Judah 9:3-8 supplies some parallels to the war section (vv. 1-14), and Midrash Wayyissaʻu furnishes more of them, including some helpful information about how certain items were phrased in Hebrew. The Book of Jashar and the Chronicles of Jerahmeel, as noted in the commentary on chap. 37, provide later attestations of the story.

The textual witnesses for the chapter are, as for chap. 37, more numerous than usual.

1. Latin   vv. 1 (end)-16
2. Syriac vv. 1-5, 8-9
3. Hebrew
   a. vv. 1-13 in 4Q223-224 unit 2 iv:15-33 (in many instances very little of a verse survives).
   b. vv. 6-8 in 4Q221 frg. 6 (just a few letters and words).

1-14[1] The War between the Forces of Jacob and Esau

By the end of chap. 37, Esau's rage had reached such a fever pitch that violence was inevitable. At that moment (v. 25) Jacob, having failed to mollify his only sibling with words, ordered his sons and servants to attack Esau and those with him, but he himself did not spring into action. It was only at the urging of his son Judah that he took up arms against his brother.[2] Judah was, of course, the natural leader in a war. Isaac had said about him: "May the Lord give you the power and strength to trample on all who hate you" (31:18); and "the nations will be frightened before you; / all the nations will be disturbed; / all peoples will be disturbed. / May Jacob's help be in you; / may Israel's safety be found in you" (31:18). The fact that Jacob hesitated to reach for a weapon, even faced with 4,000 hostile soldiers and a brother who sought his and his sons' lives (37:23), demonstrates his innocence and extraordinary forbearance. He took up arms against Esau only when there was no choice; his brother forced his hand.

---

1   Livneh has shown the many parallels between this account and the one in Jub 34:2-9, both of which, she argues, relate to Gen 48:22 ("With My Sword"). She arranges the parallels in ten categories, most of which will be noted throughout the commentary. One that is not treated below has to do with the location of the two battles: Shechem in chap. 34 (though Hebron is Jacob's residence) and Hebron in chap. 38. As Livneh indicates, these are the only two places that patriarchs purchase for a price in Genesis. For Hebron (where Machpelah is) see Gen 23:16, and for Shechem see Gen 33:19.

2   Livneh, "With My Sword," 206 (Jacob does not initiate conflicts but fights in self-defense).

■ **1** Judah, rather poetically (four balanced lines), directed his father to begin the counter offensive. Esau's position relative to the army that his sons assembled receives no clarification in the text, but he was a key figure in the campaign (in 37:11 his sons ordered him to lead the troops). Unlike the sons of Esau, who showed no respect for their father or for Jacob, Judah is much concerned with the dignity possessed by Esau as his father's brother. No matter how appalling Esau's behavior had been, he was still Jacob's brother and had to be treated with the proper deference.[3] Judah declares that he and the others will not kill Esau because, in their estimation, he shared the same stature as Jacob. The wording at the end of v. 1 is somewhat uncertain, but it seems as if Judah says twice that Esau is like Jacob[4] and thus deserving of respect ("similar to you" and "like you in honor"). Jacob had pledged to Rebekah that he would always honor his brother (35:1-4), and his son Judah now gives voice to that principle. Yet, while recognizing the inherent status possessed by Esau, the honor Judah accords him in this instance is that his father, Esau's equal, is the one to kill him. Jacob's sons do not have the right to do so, only their father has such standing. Judah, while being respectful regarding Esau, also leaves no doubt about the immediate danger in which they find themselves and the need to take action. He urges his father to shoot Esau with an arrow and calls Esau the enemy and the foe (Esau had used almost the exact terms in 37:18).[5] It appears he realizes how difficult this will be for Jacob even in the current situation and asks that he may have the strength to carry out the terrible deed.

4Q223-224 unit 2 iv:15-17 preserves enough of the text to show that the wording in the Ethiopic version is more reliable than the rather different presentation in the Syriac citation. The Syriac, which contains most of what the Ethiopic copies read, offers parts of the verse in a different order and adds to it at the end. It reads: "Judah said to his father Jacob: 'We are not able to draw the sword before your brother, since in our estimation he is equal to you. Draw your bow; slay your enemy; and kill your foe, because he is your brother. Leave the rest of the warriors to us. Do not ask any more questions.'"[6] The shorter version in the Ethiopic and Hebrew texts lacks the reference to the other fighters in Esau's army and the command to Jacob that the time for talk had ended.

■ **2** Jacob did as Judah told him—his response follows literally the four commands Judah expressed in v. 1. Jacob, under compulsion, shoots his own brother, and he does not miss. The Latin translation and the Syriac citation say that the fatal arrow shot by Jacob[7] struck Esau on the right breast; space considerations suggest that 4Q223-224 unit 2 iv:19 also contained the anatomical notice that is absent from the Ethiopic tradition. Pierced by the arrow, Esau perished. Jacob, the man of peace, killed his brother who had "learned (the art of) warfare" (19:14). Esau who, at least from the stories in Genesis, could have been deemed a rival to Jacob as heir of the patriarchal promises, was no more. Because of Esau's terrible behavior, the ideal of brotherly love, so strongly urged by their parents, was not realized.[8]

---

3 See Livneh, "With My Sword," 197-98, 204.
4 Werman believes Judah is referring in part to a physical resemblance between Esau and Jacob (*Jubilees*, 468), but that seems unlikely from the way the two were described in 19:13. Judah's point is the status of the two as brothers and, naturally, as senior in age to him and his siblings.
5 Isaac had indicated that the one who sought his brother's harm would fall into his hand (36:9; Werman, *Jubilees*, 468).
6 The Hebrew fragment (see lines 15-17) does not have space to contain the Syriac plus at the end of the verse.
7 Livneh makes a good case that the bow in this story derives from Gen 48:22, where Jacob says he took a portion from the Amorite "with my sword and with my bow" ("With My Sword," 191-92). The battle story in 34:2-9 depicts him using his sword (e.g., 34:7), while the one here in chap. 38 shows him using the bow. As she notes, *Gen. Rab.* 97:6 presents an opinion that "Amorite" in Gen 48:22 refers to Esau.
8 Cf. Doran, "Non-Dating," 5-7. He shows how this contrasts with the way in which the author presents the relations among Jacob's sons after they come into contact with Joseph in Egypt. See also Livneh, "With My Sword," 203-4, for Jacob as a family man who nevertheless must kill the one who violates the command to love one's fellow as oneself. As she also points out, the passage shows off Jacob's skill as a warrior (p. 205).

■ 3 Jacob's next act was to draw a second arrow and to shoot Esau's friend Aduram (for him see 37:9) in the left breast. Aduram staggered backward and fell dead. Perhaps he too was a leader of the invading forces—37:9 may imply he headed the Arameans among them—or perhaps, as a friend of Esau, he also deserved the peculiar privilege of dying at the hands of Jacob. With two arrows Jacob symmetrically and efficiently deprived the enemy of two senior leaders.

■ 4-8 The verses contain a highly structured account of the tactics Jacob's forces used and of how the battle itself transpired, once Jacob had killed Esau and Aduram. The writer sketches a counterattack in which three of Jacob's offspring fight on each of the four sides of the family fortress or tower—again illustrating their unity.[9] Largely the same descriptions appear in the four sections, with, in most cases, only the names of Jacob's children and those of the opponent changing. In no instance does the enemy, though they consisted of "select men" (see 37:6, 9-10), stand a chance fighting against the men of Jacob's household. They suffered an overwhelming defeat, according to the writer, but he furnishes almost no details about the fighting. He limits himself to saying that the sons of Jacob killed their opponents, with the exception of the fourth group from whom six hundred escaped. The section differs dramatically from the versions in T. Jud. 9:4-6 and Midrash Wayyissa'u 17-53 whose writers/compilers devote the largest amount of the narrative to the intense and, especially in Midrash Wayyissa'u, not always successful fighting by Jacob's army.

In Jubilees twelve descendants of Jacob and their servants array themselves in this way:[10]

South of the tower (v. 5). Judah first, Naphtali, and Gad with fifty servants—the enemy that they wiped out is not identified, though by default they should be the Arameans.[11] Whoever they were, no one of them escaped.

East[12] of the tower (v. 6). Levi, Dan, and Asher with fifty (servants)—they killed the Moabites and Ammonites.

North of the tower (v. 7). Reuben, Issachar, and Zebulun with fifty (servants)—they killed the Philistines.

West of the tower (v. 8). Simeon,[13] Benjamin, and Enoch (Reuben's oldest son) with fifty (servants)—they killed four hundred of the Edomites and Horites, with six hundred escaping.[14] Apparently Esau's four sons are among them.

The arrangement of the twelve is worth noting: the two major sons of Jacob, the recipients of Isaac's blessings in 31:13-20, command the first two trios, with sons from each of Jacob's two concubines as the other two members. Judah would naturally be the lead officer in a battle, so he heads the first group.[15] Only after the lines about Judah and Levi does Reuben, the firstborn

---

9 Livneh, "With My Sword," 197-98.
10 As various commentators have observed (e.g., Berger, *Jubiläen*, 511 n. a to chap. 38), there are in the HB somewhat similar arrangements with the twelve tribes divided into four groups and placed on the four sides of a structure: the tabernacle in Numbers 2, and the city in Ezek 48:31-34 (also cols. xxxix-xli in the Temple Scroll; cf. Rev 21:12-14). But in none of these passages are the details (e.g., which tribes make up each trio and the sides they occupy) the same as those in Jub 38:4-8.
11 Werman thinks the same, although, as in chap. 37, she has changed the name to Amorite(s) (*Jubilees*, 468). 4Q223-224 unit 2 iv:19 shows that Aduram at least was an Aramean.
12 The gate of Levi is on the east in the Temple Scroll (xxxix:12), but the gates on the northeast and southeast (that is, the ones on either side of his) are named after Simeon and Judah, not Dan and Asher.
13 Endres comments on how Levi and Simeon, as leaders in their two groups, continue their military careers that began at Shechem (*Biblical Interpretation*, 182).
14 The text takes up the sides of the tower in a counterclockwise direction: south, east, north, west. That much looks deliberate, but the writer did not put the enemy nations on the sides that correspond with their geographical locations. If the Arameans were on the south, it is the opposite of the direction from which they would have come, and the same is true for the Edomites and Horites, who are on the west. Only the Moabites and Ammonites (on the east) battle on the side from which they would have reached Hebron.
15 Caquot refers to Judah's military superiority and adds that his presence in the south may be conditioned by the fact that Edom lies in that direction ("Jubilés," 780 n. to vv. 5-8). But see the previous note.

brother, figure as the initial name in the third group of three, and the two brothers with him are also sons of Leah (the two youngest). Simeon, the second oldest after Reuben, is the first in the fourth group, and the other two are Rachel's son Benjamin (Joseph was not available [see 34:10-11]) and Enoch, Reuben's firstborn (see Gen 46:9 // Jub 44:12)—presumably the next oldest male in the family after the twelve sons of Jacob.[16] The fact that fifty servants accompany each of the four groups of three agrees with the notice in Midrash Wayyissaʻu 10 that the servants with Jacob and his sons numbered two hundred.[17]

Mention of Esau's four sons in v. 8 furnishes another opportunity to put them in a bad light. These men who had instigated the war continued to dishonor their father by leaving his body where he had fallen—on the hill in Adoraim. Of course, the occasion was hardly optimal for burying him since they were running for their lives; but once again they thought only of themselves in abandoning Esau. As the reader might expect, it was Jacob who honored his brother by burying his corpse at the spot where he lay,[18] struck by his arrow. The version in Jubilees is the only one to attribute this virtuous act to Jacob (see below).[19] After honoring the slain body of his brother, he returned to the tower while his sons pressed the attack on the six hundred who fled the battlefield.

It is instructive to compare major elements in the story of the war in Jubilees with the versions in the Testament of Judah 9 and in Midrash Wayyissaʻu. The one in the Testament of Judah is relatively short, but each form of the account has traits it shares with one or both of the others as well as distinctive elements.

1. *The role of Jacob.* In Jubilees Jacob kills Esau with an arrow to the right breast and then Aduram the Aramean with a second arrow to his left breast. In T. Jud. 9:3 Esau "fell by the bow of Jacob," and Aduram plays no role. In Midrash Wayyissaʻu "Jacob stretched his bow and killed Aduram the Edomite,[20] and he again stretched his bow and stuck Esau on the right shoulder" (15-16; the blow only wounded him). It is peculiar that Jacob would initially shoot Aduram, whereas Esau was the natural candidate for his first missile as in Jubilees. Since neither of the other two versions has the section about the argument between Jacob and Esau (Jub 37:17-23) that led up to the fighting, they contextualize the war story differently.

2. *The battle scene.* Jubilees offers a schematic, symmetrical picture of Jacob's offspring as they deployed on the four sides of the fortress. The Testament of Judah does not describe fighting at the tower; Midrash Wayyissaʻu begins as Jubilees does, but the pattern breaks down after describing what happened on sides one and two of the fortress.

Judah first, along with Naphtali and Gad, marches to the south side of the fortress with fifty servants (17-18; nothing is said about who their opponents were).

Reuben, Issachar, and Zebulun are on the north and fifty servants with them (18-19).

The midrash then stops listing the brothers and comments that Joseph was not present because he had already been sold (19);[21] the comment explains why one of the trios (Simeon, Benjamin, and Enoch) included a grandson of Jacob and presupposes, one would think, that these three names had just figured in the text.

---

16   Livneh, "With My Sword," 199-200 (mixing of sons from more than one mother in each group [other than the third] demonstrates their unity). For the roles of Levi and Judah in 34:2-9 (both were among those who had at first stayed home, v. 3) and 38:1-14, see her comments on pp. 200-201.

17   The number is surprisingly small compared with the "6,000 men who carried swords" during the war of Jacob and his sons against the Amorite kings (34:6). It is even smaller than Abram's force of 318 in Gen 14:14. The low figure is another indication of how little Jacob anticipated an attack and perhaps is also meant to suggest how insignificant was the power of the finest troops from the nations in comparison with the men of Jacob's household, none of whom was a professional fighter.

18   That is, he does not receive burial in the tomb of the patriarchs, the cave of Machpelah (Werman, *Jubilees*, 468).

19   Livneh, "With My Sword," 204.

20   It would be very easy, of course, to interchange Aramean (ארמי) and Edomite (אדמי).

21   The note is a clear indication that the midrash follows the order of events in Jubilees because in Genesis Joseph had not been sold at this time.

Jubilees, which lacks the note about Joseph, is the only version that supplies the name of the twelfth person in the list of Jacob's offspring. It appears, then, that the midrash should have had the listing of the fourth trio (and the third as well) but it does not. At least this is the case in the London manuscript that Alexander and Dan follow in their edition.[22] After listing the first two groups alone, it devotes a lengthy section to the difficult fighting endured by Judah, Naphtali, and Gad (19–37). Only in line 37 does Levi, the first of the second trio in Jubilees, make an appearance; the brothers with him are not named—only "those who were with him" figure here. In this context the manuscript mentions Reuben and those with him and Simeon, leader of the fourth trio in Jubilees, and those with him (37–38). All join to help Judah and his group who are encountering tough resistance.

The first names in all four groups of three (Judah, Levi, Reuben, and Simeon) thus participate in the fighting, but the full pattern survives only in Jubilees (and some copies of the midrash), where none of the groups has any difficulty defeating their opponents (the opponents of the groups are not named in Midrash Wayyissa'u). The fighting is so arduous in the midrash that Judah prays for divine assistance and receives it in the form of a storm wind that blows in the face of the enemy and blinds them while Judah and his army see clearly because the wind is at their back (40-46, 48-49). At this point, the story indicates that the sets of brothers fought on different sides of the fortress: there is mention of the south (46), and Reuben and Simeon defeated the enemies in front of them (46–47). In lines 47–48 Judah and his brothers kill those opposed to them, and line 49 says that Reuben and Levi, who were opposite Simeon, slew four hundred warriors,[23] while six hundred ran away (see Jub 38:8 for Simeon, Benjamin, and Enoch). These last totals (four hundred and six hundred) appear before a reference to Esau's four sons, as in Jub 38:8.[24]

3. Esau's sons and Esau's body. Jubilees claims that Esau's four sons left the corpse of their father where he died and that Jacob paid him the respect of burying him (38:8-9). The description appears to be tendentious when compared with the other two versions. The Testament of Judah is characteristically brief: "He fell by the bow of Jacob / and was taken up dead on Mount Seir; / and as he went he died above Eiramna" (9:3). The puzzling statement seems to incorporate some traditions embedded in Midrash Wayyissa'u. In it, after Jacob shot Esau, his sons put their wounded father on a donkey but he died there in Arodin. It adds, however, that others deny this (16-17). Later, when the victors are pursuing Esau's sons as far as the city Arodin, the latter dumped their father's body there and ran away to Mount Seir (52–53). Jacob's sons then buried their uncle out of respect for their father (54). Here again the text offers another opinion: "Some say that he did not die there but departed in his ailing condition from Arodin and fled with his sons to Mount Seir" (54–55).

The number of Esau's sons is interesting. Genesis 36:4-5 lists five of them: Eliphaz, Reuel,[25] Jeush, Jalam, and Korah. Jubilees and the midrash, however, both

---

22 Other editions (e.g., Jellinek, *Bet Ha-Midrasch,* 3:3-5) contain a text like that of Jubilees for all four groups. Since the notes about each of the groups ends in the same way ("with them"), there were ample opportunities for omissions. Even if the midrash did describe all four groups as Jubilees does, its account of the fighting remains very different and far longer.

23 This is the number of men Esau had with him when he met Jacob (Gen 32:6; 33:1).

24 Since there were four thousand soldiers in the army, it was reasonable to assume that one thousand fought on each of the four sides of the tower. Livneh has emphasized the role of multiples of the number four in 37:1–38:14 (six was the key number in 34:2-9) ("With My Sword," 194–95). Examples include the following: the battle takes place in year 4 of a week (36:21), Esau's four sons recruit four thousand soldiers while Jacob has only his twelve offspring (divided into four groups who fight on the four sides of the tower) and two hundred servants (four groups of fifty). The number four hundred is given for those killed on the west side of the tower.

25 Though there is no hint of it in the text, Werman suggests that Reuel (a son of Ishmael's daughter) is the one Jubilees omits because he was not born in Canaan (Esau moved to Mount Seir after he married Mahalat [she is called Basemath in Gen 36:3, 4, 10, 13]) and thus would have no claim on the tower in Hebron (*Jubilees,* 468). The latter point has no relevance because the issue in the text is whether Esau and his sons or Jacob and his would be the primary heirs of Isaac, with no consideration given to where they were born.

refer to four, although the latter also deals with the fifth son. The midrash singles out Eliphaz, Esau's oldest son (Gen 36:4, 15): it says that he did not wish to go with the other four because, according to one reading (the witnesses to the text vary): "our father Jacob was his teacher [his Rab]." When Jub 38:8 refers to Esau's four sons, it seems to presuppose that one was not involved in the invasion but does not offer the sort of explanation found in the midrash to account for the fifth son.[26]

■ **9-14** The verses deal with the conclusion to the war.[27] The writer does not explain why six hundred warriors survived on the west side of the fortress, the side on which the Edomite and Horite soldiers opposed Simeon, Benjamin, and Enoch. They alone of the four threesomes failed to dispatch all the fighters in their area.

■ **9** The survivors fled the scene, and all Jacob's sons chased them to their home territory of Mount Seir. Jacob, who had killed his brother Esau and Esau's friend Aduram, seems not to have participated in the fighting on the sides of the tower and certainly was not part of the pursuit. Rather, as noted above, he took the opportunity to bury his brother's body, once the fighting concluded and the remaining attackers ran away; he then returned to his residence. The battle itself and the pursuit of the survivors involved only the sons (and one grandson) of Israel, the ancestors of the nation. Moreover, the text is explicit that, while six hundred survived, the sons of Jacob pursued the sons of Esau, the ancestors of the Edomites. It sounds as if two future nations are now in view.

■ **10** The sons of Esau stood no chance as Jacob's offspring surrounded them in their homeland. The text uses the language of bending their necks to servitude, vocabulary that recalls the words of Isaac to Esau when he pleaded for a blessing: "You will live by your sword and will serve your brother. May it be that, if you become great and remove his yoke from your neck, then you will commit an offense fully worthy of death and your descendants will be eradicated from beneath the sky" (26:34).[28] Esau had tried living by the sword, but the result was that his sons became subject to the yoke of servitude that Jacob's sons imposed on them (see vv. 12, 14 below).

■ **11-13** Though he was not part of the contingent that pursued Esau's sons into Edom and encircled them there, Jacob remains the authority figure in the story.[29] His sons did not make their own decision about how to handle the captives but sent word to Jacob to ask him whether they should kill these men who had caused the war or make peace with them. It will be recalled that Jacob had promised Rebekah the day she died: "Trust me that nothing bad against Esau will come from me or my sons. I will not be first except in love only" (35:26). Isaac had threatened that the brother who sought the harm of his sibling would be destroyed with his descendants (36:9; see also v. 14). Jacob would have been justified, then, in ordering the execution of Esau's sons, but he magnanimously directed that his own sons were not to treat them as they deserved; they were to make peace with them.[30] Jacob's sons dutifully complied but imposed unending tribute on the sons of Esau. The tribute was to be delivered eternally,[31] yet the writer explains that they continued supplying it only until the time when Jacob descended to Egypt. The forces of Jacob could well have declared that the tribute was never to end, but reality overtook their ambitious intent. The war with the sons

---

26   Livneh comments on the references to only four sons of Esau but, rather than relating it to the midrash, sees a parallel with Jacob's sons from whom one is also missing (Joseph) ("With My Sword," 195).
27   See Livneh, "With My Sword," 206–7.
28   Kugel offers an argument that Gen 27:40 played a key role in the development of the story about a war between Esau and Jacob (*Traditions*, 370–72). He recognizes that Amos 1:11 was instrumental in its evolution, but he highlights the connection between the repeated yoke language here in Jubilees (37:8; 38:10, 12-14) and Isaac's words to Esau. He also suggests that the story offers an interpretation of the verb Isaac used in MT Gen 27:40 (תריד) as meaning "go down" (תרד), thus accounting for the note about going down to Egypt. He may be correct, although Isaac is speaking to Esau when he employs the verb.
29   See Livneh, "With My Sword," 202.
30   See Endres, *Biblical Interpretation*, 182; he contrasts the situation with the one at Shechem, where Jacob's sons, without his consent, slaughtered the population of the city.
31   David too forced servitude on the Edomites (2 Sam 8:13-14).

of Esau, therefore, ends as the battle against the Amorite kings did: the victors established peace but made the defeated enemy their servants and imposed tribute on them—a situation that lasted until the descent to Egypt (see 34:8-9). Unlike the end of the Amorite War account, however, here the writer adds that "the Edomites" have not extricated themselves from the yoke of servitude (tribute is not mentioned) to which Jacob's sons subjected them "until today" (see also v. 15).

The expression "until today" in vv. 14 and 15 raises problems. One is trying to determine the time meant by "today." In the narrative world of the book "today" should designate the time when the angel is speaking to Moses on Mount Sinai.[32] Elsewhere in the book there are similar usages indicating "until today" means until the time of the speaker:

22:8: Abraham says the enemy's sword has not subdued him "until today" (his last day).
35:3: Jacob refers to his behavior from the day he was born "until today" in speaking with his mother (her last day).
35:10, 12 (twice): Rebekah refers to the time from Jacob's departure to or return from Haran "until today" while talking with Isaac (her last day).
45:12: Joseph made a law for Egypt "until today" (// Gen 47:26).
45:16: Jacob gave books to Levi to preserve and renew for his sons "until today."
50:4: The angel refers to the time from Adam until today (when speaking to Moses).

In all of these cases, it is either the character in the text (Abraham, Jacob, Rebekah [22:8; 35:3, 10, 12]) or the angel (45:16; 50:4) who speaks about a literal day, the very day on which the person is speaking. The only exception may be 45:12, which is also the only instance in which the expression comes from Genesis.

If one infers, therefore, that "until today" in 38:14, 15 means until the time when the angel is speaking to Moses on Mount Sinai, another problem results. Is the text saying that the Edomites remained under the yoke of servitude to Jacob's family until the Sinai revelation and that the monarchs listed are those who reigned in Edom before the same date? That is a reasonable inference, but what would it mean for the Edomites to be subject to Jacob's family even during the long stay in Egypt? Possibly, the writer intends to say that, while they no longer paid tribute and had had no contact for a long time, they still in fact were subject to the descendants of Jacob. It is also possible that he thought the kings reigned in Edom at a very early period because he reproduces the notice from Genesis that they "reigned in the land of Edom, before any king reigned over the Israelites [lit., before ruling of a king for the sons of Israel]" (Gen 36:31 // Jub 38:15). Readers have interpreted these words in two senses: the line in Genesis says they reigned before there was an Israelite monarchy, or they reigned before an Israelite king ruled in Edom.[33] The writer of Jubilees may have read the temporal note as pointing to premonarchical times in Israel.[34] In fact, he may have thought that the pre-Sinai period was under consideration: the list names eight kings, and he may have understood the first as becoming king right after the war. There is no indication of the lengths of the reigns so that all of them could belong in time from Jacob to Moses—four generations (Exod 6:16-20). All of this is only a suggestion but one consistent with usage in the book.[35]

The accounts of the war's conclusion in Testament of Judah 9 and in Midrash Wayyissa'u bear some resemblance to the one in Jubilees. Testament of Judah 9:7-8 reports: "Then they asked from us terms of peace, and having taken counsel with our father, we received them

---

[32] Cf. Werman, *Jubilees*, 469. The Angel of the Presence uses "today" for the time when he is revealing Jubilees to Moses in 1:5, 7; 4:26 (29:11?); cf. 50:4.

[33] See, e.g., Hamilton, *Genesis 18–50*, 399–400. Westermann rejects the second explanation and thinks the notice points to a "simultaneous chronology" as in the ones for the kings of Israel and Judah (*Genesis 12–36*, 565).

[34] Werman thinks the wording "in Edom," not "over the Edomites," is decisive in favor of rule by an Israelite king over Edom (*Jubilees*, 469).

[35] Others have explained "until today" differently. Charles thought it pointed to the author's time (the time of John Hyrcanus) (*Jubilees*, lxii, 222; he bracketed the instance of it in v. 15; cf. Caquot, "Jubilés," 781; Hartom, "Jubilees," 115 n.). Kugel believes it was added by a "later writer or copyist" after Hyrcanus subdued the area (*Walk through Jubileees*, 179; "Jubilees," 424).

as tributaries. And they gave us two hundred cors of wheat, five hundred baths of oil, fifteen hundred measures of wine, until we went down to Egypt." In Midrash Wayyissaʿu, once Jacob's sons had surrounded Esau's sons in Mount Seir, "Esau's sons and all those men who had fled went out and fell before Jacob's sons and were slaughtered before them. They implored them for mercy until they made peace with them and subjected them to tribute of servitude" (57–58). Neither of these accounts adds the notice about subjection "until today."

Excursus: The War with Esau and His Sons and Maccabean History

As in the story about the Amorite War in Jubilees 34, so in the account in 37:1–38:14 a number of commentators have seen reflections of actual battles in Hasmonean times. Charles, for one, wrote:

> The legend of the conquests of Esau's sons by the sons of Jacob in xxxvii.–xxxviii., points very clearly to the complete conquest of Edom by Judah in the Maccabean wars. In these wars the Edomites had sided with the Syrians till they were made tributary by John Hyrcanus. This subjection of Edom is referred to in xxxviii. 14, "The sons of Edom have not got quit of the yoke of servitude . . . until this day" (*i.e.* the author's time).[36]

So, on his view, the story reflects events from two periods: the battles between Judas and the Edomites and Hyrcanus's final subjection of them nearly four decades later.

VanderKam subsequently compiled a series of arguments for a connection between Judas's campaign against the Edomites (not the efforts of John Hyrcanus), especially in 1 Maccabees 5, and the account in Jub 37:1–38:14.

1. In both a person named Judah/Judas leads his brothers and their forces against the Edomites (e.g., 1 Macc 5:3).
2. In both the surrounding nations banded together against the Jews, and the Edomite campaign follows (Edom, Moab, Ammon, and Philistia are involved in both sources [1 Macc 5:1-8, 58-60]).
3. Hebron is the site of the victory in Jubilees and of Judas's second victory over the Idumeans (1 Macc 5:65).
4. Judas divided his forces into three (1 Macc 5:17-18) and campaigned in four directions (throughout 1 Maccabees 5).

From these points he concluded:

> These parallels are far too substantial and precise to assign to coincidence. In both Jub. and the Maccabean sources, Judah (Judas), the leader, and his brothers fight the sons of Esau (this phrase occurs in 1 Mac. 5:3, 65/*Ant.* 12.8, 1 §328) who were joined in their opposition to Israel's sons by the surrounding peoples, namely Ammon, Moab, and Philistia. Even the site of the battle with Edom is the same. All of these similarities virtually require that one view Jub. 37:1–38:14 as a highly stylized account of Judas Maccabeus' wars against the surrounding nations in the year 163 BC.[37]

In this case, as with Jub 34:1-9, the Hasmonean hypothesis has experienced modification or outright opposition. As for modification, Mendels, who points out significant differences between the details of the Maccabean conflicts and the one in Jubilees 37–38, thinks the war with Esau reflects John Hyrcanus's final submission of the Edomites in the southern part of Israel in 125 BCE.[38] However, the differences between the story in Jubilees 37–38 and the accounts of the conquest by Hyrcanus are even larger than for the campaign by Judas. In particular, it is difficult to see much in common between the treatment of the Edomites in Jub 38:12-14 and Hyrcanus's requirement that the Edomites be circumcised. The author of Jubilees would have been adamantly opposed to having Edomites circumcised, and assimilating them

---

36 Charles, *Jubilees*, lxii. Bousset had drawn attention to parallels between the story in Jubilees 37–38 and conflicts with Edom in the times of Judas and John Hyrcanus (e.g., the city Adoraim is Adora) ("Die Testamente der zwölf Patriarchen," 205). See also his essay, "Neueste Forschungen auf dem Gebiet der religiösen Litteratur des Spätjudentums," *ThR* 3 (1900) 287-302, 327-35, 369-81, here 375-76.

37 VanderKam, *Textual*, 237-38; the arguments listed above come from pp. 234-37. The phrase "highly stylized" is worth emphasizing; the claim is not that there is an exact mirroring of events in Hasmonean times. See VanderKam, *Book of Jubilees*, 20, for a more tentative statement about the matter, and "Recent Scholarship on the Book of Jubilees," *CurBR* 6 (2008) 408, where the claim is deemed "problematic."

38 Mendels, *Land of Israel*, 77-82. In this he sides with Charles to a certain extent. See also Caquot, "Jubilés," 781 n. to v. 14.

to the Jewish way of life would hardly have appealed to him. Assimilation is not the same as rooting out the descendants of Esau, as Mendels claims. Also, the fighting in Jubilees continues into the area of Mount Seir, something that did not occur in Hyrcanus's (or Judas's) time.[39]

Among those who have written in opposition to the Hasmonean hypothesis is J. Goldstein, who listed in detail the differences between the accounts of Judas's war with the Edomites and the battle between Jacob and Esau. He is correct that a set of parallels offset by a larger array of differences fails to demonstrate a connection between the two, but he makes the more important point that the story in Jubilees serves to convey a message, not to reflect historical events. "Rather, it is a demonstration that the fulfilment of the promises in Amos 9:12, Isa 11:14, and Obadiah will merely reestablish the conquests of Jacob. Jacob's descendants have a right, not only from Isaac's blessing, but also through conquest in war, to rule over Edom."[40] Whether one agrees that these were the texts the writer had in mind or finds other scriptural bases for the account, it is the case that Jubilees tells the story of the conflict against a backdrop of scriptural passages regarding Esau and the Edomites. Moreover, the author crafts the account with an eye to themes in his own book. Doran has emphasized the latter in connection with Jubilees 37–38: the disastrous relations between brothers in the family of Isaac create tension for the reader regarding Jacob's family and the relations between his sons. The eventual reconciliation between Joseph and his brothers in Egypt will serve as a contrast to the situation in Isaac's family. Chapters 35–38 show what happened with Jacob and Esau. Just before these chapters, in a section moved intentionally by the author from its location in Genesis, one finds that the relations between Joseph and his brothers deteriorated so badly that they sold him into slavery (34:10-19; the list of the brothers' wives in 34:20-21 shows that Joseph is not in the family). Joseph will later test his brothers and learn that they are unified; they then live in harmony, unlike Esau and Jacob.[41]

Werman, who also thinks the story in Jubilees 37–38 does not mirror either Judas's or John Hyrcanus's conflicts with the Edomites, suggests that the writer concluded from Gen 36:6 that the separation between Jacob and Esau came about because of a battle.[42] That passage reads: "Then Esau took his wives, his sons, his daughters, and all the members of his household, his cattle, all his livestock, and all the property he had acquired in the land of Canaan; and he moved to a land some distance from [lit., from before] Jacob." As she indicates, Midrash Wayyissa'u cites the end of this passage (line 1) and offers different explanations for why Esau moved away from Jacob. Her argument is not very convincing because Genesis 36 does not speak about Esau's death and goes on to explain in the next verse that the extent of the brothers' possessions prevented them from living closer together. It seems more likely that the next passage the midrash quotes—part of Amos 1:11 (line 3)—proved more important in giving rise to a story about a war between the brothers. There the Lord says through the prophet regarding Edom: "because he pursued his brother with the sword / and cast off all pity." Then come the lines quoted in the midrash: "he maintained his anger perpetually, / and kept his wrath forever."

These sorts of considerations were surely more important in the creation of a story about a war between Jacob and Esau than a desire to rewrite events of the second century BCE. Whoever fashioned the story first, each writer who used it shaped it to meet the needs of his composition. In Jubilees the story demonstrates why there was such animosity between the sons of Jacob (Israel) and the sons of Esau (Edom) and why the latter should be subject to the former. The author could be inviting the reader to connect the story to circumstances in his time (perhaps the ongoing spread of Idumeans into formerly Judean territory) by using the expression "until today," though in the narrative world of Jubilees "today" is the time when the angel is speaking to Moses on Mount Sinai (see above). The story also adds to Jacob's stature—he wants to live in harmony with his brother, he did not start the conflict but took

---

39 For criticisms of the positions of VanderKam and of Mendels, see Werman, "Attitude," 22; *Jubilees*, 29–30, 45–46 (in the latter, she mentions the argument in VanderKam, *Textual*, but none of the later statements indicating a change of viewpoint).

40 Goldstein, "Date," 77. On pp. 77–82 he goes through VanderKam's arguments and highlights differences between the wars of Judas against Edom and the battle pitting Jacob against Esau.

41 Doran, "Non-Dating," 5–7. Thanks are due to David DeJong for his seminar paper "The Exegetical Background to the Battle between Jacob and Esau in *Jubilees*" (December 2010). In it he offers an insightful analysis of Amos 1:11 and relates the various terms in it to the situation in Jubilees 37–38.

42 Werman, "Attitude," 16 (she mistakenly writes 35:6). See also Kugel, *Traditions*, 372.

up arms out of necessity, and he still had the decency to bury his brother and spare his incorrigible sons. It also eliminates a potential rival to Jacob as heir of the promises, showing how Esau violated the oath to his parents and thus received the penalty of annihilation for him and his descendants. Jacob and his sons are now the unchallenged heirs of the promises, but there is little reason to believe at this point in the narrative that relations among his sons will be better than they were between Jacob and his brother. As Doran indicates, the story sets up tension as the reader looks to the next generation.

15-24 The Kings Who Ruled in Edom (Gen 36:31-39)

Once he has told the story of Esau's death at Jacob's hands and the defeat of his sons and their allies by Jacob's household, the writer returns to the text of Genesis by reproducing a list of eight Edomite kings from Gen 36:31-39.

The paragraph contains the names of eight monarchs with a small amount of information about each one. In the list below, the names of people and places follow the spellings in the NRSV; an X indicates that an element in the pattern of the list is present in Jubilees. The place-names are of unknown location other than Bosra and Teman.[43]

Name	Father's Name	City	In Place of Previous King	Died
Bela	Beor	Dinhabah		X
Jobab	Zera	Bosra	X	X
Husham		Land of the Temanites[44]	X	X
Hadad[45]	Bedad	Avith	X	X
Samlah		Masrekah	X	X
Shaul		Rehoboth on the Euphrates[46]	X	X
Baal-hanan	Achbor		X	X
Hadar[47]			X	

Why did the author of Jubilees, with his attitude toward Esau and the Edomites, include this passage when he felt free to exclude other sections of Genesis? One can ask a similar question about the presence of chap. 36 in Genesis. It furnishes a genealogy of Esau (vv. 1-8), with the same material reappearing in vv. 9-14 but with the addition of his grandsons' names, the clans of Esau's sons (vv. 15-19), the genealogy of Seir the Horite (vv. 20-30), the king list (vv. 31-39), and Esau's clans (vv. 40-43). Why would Genesis devote forty-three verses to such information?

There is a structural explanation for the presence of chap. 36 within the larger arrangement of Genesis. After the death of Abraham, the reader encounters a genealogical statement for Ishmael first (Gen 25:13-18) followed by one for Isaac second (25:19). That is, the compiler initially provides a *tôlĕdôt* section for the older son, through whom the promises are not transmitted, then for the younger one, who receives those promises. The pattern repeats itself in the case of Isaac's children: After his death (35:27-29), first there is a genealogical notice for Esau (see 36:1) and then one for Jacob (37:2).[48] Yet, if one can find an explanation for the presence of chap. 36 in Genesis, is there one for the king list in Jubilees as well?

Jubilees reproduces Gen 36:31-39 word for word, apart from three differences. First, in Jub 38:15 the writer gives the text of Gen 36:31 (and 1 Chr 1:43), but at the end he adds: "until today in the land of Edom" (the extra phrase is supported by both the Ethiopic and the Latin versions of Jubilees). Second, in 38:23 (Gen 36:39 // 1 Chr 1:50) Jubilees lacks "the name of his city being Pau."[49] And third, Jubilees, unlike Genesis, adds to the end of the section (v. 24) a summary statement "These are the kings who ruled in the land of Edom"—a line repeated from the beginning of the list (Jub 38:15

---

43 See Westermann, *Genesis 12–36*, 567.
44 He is from Mount Teman in Jub 38:18.
45 He is the only one in the list to whom the writer attributes a deed: "who slaughtered Midian in the field of Moab" (Jub 38:19 // Gen 36:35).
46 Genesis 36:37 says he was from "Rehoboth of the river" (// Jub 38:21).
47 His name is spelled Hadad (Adat in Jub 38:23 reflects this spelling) in 1 Chr 1:50 and in some versions of Gen 36:39. The unusual feature in his entry is that the names of his wife and her ancestors appear. This Hadad could be the one who was reigning when David stationed garrisons in Edom (2 Sam 8:13-14), when the monarchy would have ended. Note that the adversary of Solomon in Edom is named Hadad according to 1 Kgs 11:14 (see Westermann, *Genesis 12–36*, 565).
48 See Hamilton, *Genesis 18–50*, 391.
49 The Latin translation is not available for the verse. It is likely the words were omitted by parablepsis

// Gen 36:31a). Thus, the book has extra units near the beginning and at the end of the section, with one omission between them.

The first extra phrase—"until today in the land of Edom" (v. 15)—reminds one of the words "until today" in the immediately preceding verse. The connection made between vv. 1-14 and vv. 15-24 by means of "until today" raises the possibility that Jubilees intends for the two sections to be read together in a deeper sense than their simple juxtaposition would imply. Possibly the king list relates to the previous story in the following way. The reference in 38:8-9 to the four hundred Edomite and Horite warriors killed on the west side of the tower (the same number of men were with Esau in Gen 32:6; 33:1) and the six hundred who fled all the way to Mount Seir indicates that, though many died in the area of Hebron, there were survivors among these peoples beyond the four sons of Esau whom Jacob spared. They became subject to Jacob and his sons. The kings who ruled in Edom in the period before the monarchy in Israel (if that is how the author understood the notice in Gen 36:31), therefore, ruled over a reduced population. The only military exploit attributed to any of them is the defeat of Midian in Moab by Adat son of Bared (38:19 // Gen 36:35 [Hadad son of Bedad]). The context of the king list in Jubilees implies that the strength of Edom over which these monarchs ruled was insignificant.

In addition, the author makes it more evident than Genesis that no son of Esau became king in Edom.[50] His sons survived the battle with Jacob and his forces but only through Jacob's mercy. No one of the eight kings listed is among the sons or grandsons of Esau in Gen 36:1-14. The point may have been important to the author of Jubilees because of some earlier promises in the book. The Lord had said to Jacob that kings would come from his line (32:18 // Gen 35:11). Earlier, he had told Abraham that the son born to Sarah and him would become a nation and kings of nations would arise from him (15:17 // Gen 17:16). And, of course, Isaac had spoken of the throne that Jacob's son Judah would occupy (31:20). The only kings to arise in Isaac's family line were, therefore, to be traced to Jacob, not to his older but unworthy brother Esau. No sons of Esau became kings, and his line plays no further role in the story either in Genesis or Jubilees. Now the narrator can turn to developments in the family of Jacob, the heir of all the promises.

---

from ושם to ושם (or repetition of the equivalent words in Greek or Ethiopic).

50 See also Werman, *Jubilees*, 469.

39

The Humble Beginnings of Joseph's Career in Egypt

1/ Jacob lived[a] in the land[b] where his father had wandered as a foreigner—the land[c] of Canaan. 2/ This[a] is the history of Jacob. When Joseph was 17[b] years of age, they brought him down to Egypt.[c] Pharaoh's eunuch Potiphar, the chief cook,[d] bought him. 3/ He put Joseph in charge of his entire[a] house. The Lord's blessing was (present) in the Egyptian's house because of Joseph. The Lord made everything that he did succeed for him. 4/ The Egyptian placed[a] everything before Joseph[b] because he noticed[c] that the Lord[d] was with him and that God made everything that he did[e] succeed for him.[f]

5/ Now Joseph was well formed[a] and very handsome.[b] The wife of his master looked up at him,[c] saw Joseph, loved him, and pleaded with him to sleep with her. 6/ But he[a] did not surrender himself.[b] He remembered the Lord and what his father Jacob would read to him from[c] the words of Abraham—that[d] no one is to commit adultery with a woman who has a husband; that[e] there is a death penalty that has been ordained for him[f] in heaven before the Most High God. The sin will be entered regarding him[g] in the eternal books[h] forever before the Lord.[i] 7/ Joseph remembered what he had said[a] and refused[b] to sleep with her. 8/ She pleaded with him[a] for one year and a second,[b] but he refused to listen[c] to her. 9/ She *grasped* him[a] and held on to him in the house[b] to compel him[c] to sleep[d] with her. She closed the door[e] of the house and held on to him.[f] He left his clothes in her hands,[g] broke[h] the door, and ran away from her to the outside. 10/ When that woman saw that he would not sleep with her,[a] she accused him falsely[b] to[c] his master: "Your Hebrew slave whom you love[c] wanted[d] to force me so that he could sleep with me. When I shouted, he ran outside,[e] left his clothes in my hands when I grabbed him by his clothes, and broke the door."[f] 11/ When the Egyptian saw[a] Joseph's clothes and the broken door, he believed what his wife said. He put Joseph[b] in prison in the place where the prisoners of the king[c] were held.[d]

12/ While he[a] was there in prison,[b] the Lord gave Joseph[c] a favorable reception before the chief of the prison guards[d] and a kind reception before him because he saw that the Lord was with him and that the Lord[e] was making[f] everything that he[g] did succeed for him. 13/ He[a] left everything to him.[b] The chief of the prison guards[c] knew[d] nothing at all about his affairs[e] because Joseph would do everything[f] and the Lord would bring (it) to completion.[g] He remained there for two years.

14/ At that time Pharaoh, the king of Egypt, became angry at two of his eunuchs—the chief butler[a] and the chief baker. He put them in prison, in the house of the chief cook, in the prison where Joseph[b] was held. 15/ The chief of the prison guards[a] appointed Joseph to serve them. So he would serve in their presence.[b] 16/ Both of them[a]—the chief butler and the chief baker—had a dream[b] and told it[c] to Joseph. 17/ Things turned out[a] for them just as he[b] interpreted for them. Pharaoh restored the chief butler to his cupbearing,[c] but he hanged[d] the baker[e] as Joseph had interpreted[f] for him.[g] 18/ The chief butler forgot Joseph in prison although he had informed him (about) what would happen to him.[a] He did not remember to tell Pharaoh[b] what Joseph had told him[c] because he forgot.

Textual Notes

1a lived] "went" 21.
b in the land] om. 21 38.
c the land (of Canaan)] pr. "in" 21.
2a This] The Eth. MSS., except 38 (*ellu*, "these") and 63 (om.), read *'ella*, "who" (pl.). The meaning is not in doubt as the line reproduces "these are the generations of" from Gen 37:2. Somehow, *'ellu* or *'ellā* (fem. pl. demonstrative) became misspelled as *'ella* in most of the copies. See VanderKam, *Jubilees* 2:256.
b 17] "12" MS. 17.
c Egypt] + "and his brothers sold him" 35 58.
d cook] As in 34:11, Charles (*Ethiopic Version*, 143 n. 44) emended "cooks" (in the expression "the chief of the cooks") to "guards," but the reading of the Eth. MSS. reflects the interpretation of שר הטבחים as αρχιμαγειρος, as in LXX Gen 37:36.
3a entire] + "(all) his property and" 21 38 (21 lacks "and").

4a placed] 4Q221 7 1 very likely reads נתן where the Eth. mss. have ḫadaga, "left." Both verbs are attested in parallel passages in Genesis: "left" = עזב in Gen 39:6 and "placed" = נתן in Gen 39:4, 8.

b Joseph] There may not be enough space on 4Q221 7 1 to include the name (as Eth. does) so that "before him" may have been the Hebrew reading. See DJD 13:81.

c noticed] + "and perceived and knew" 12.

d the Lord] + "God" 12.

e he did] + "and thought in his heart" 12.

f for him] om. 9 (it reads a subjunctive verb) 17 63.

5a well formed (lit., "his form/appearance [was] beautiful")] Mss. 39 47 48 58 lack "his," agreeing with Gen 39:6 (see DJD 13:81 for the attestation of the suffix in the versions).

b and very handsome (lit., "and his form/appearance was very handsome")] Mss. 39 47 48 58 also lack "his" in this place. The mss. read "very," which is not present in Gen 39:6 (ms. 12 adds another word for "very, very much" to the "very" in the other copies). There may not be space for "very" and the two instances of "his" in 4Q221 7 2 (see DJD 13:81). Mss. 12 44 om. "his form/appearance."

c up at him] The Eth. mss. lack "at him." The reading is based on 4Q221 7 3 where an *aleph* and *lamed* are legible at the edge of the fragment. See DJD 13:81.

6a But he] Some mss. (39 42 47 48 58) add *we'etu-sa* to make "he" emphatic.

b himself] + "to her" 21 38 39 42 47 48 58.

c from] pr. "and" 9 38 44.

d that] pr. "and" 12.

e that (there)] pr. "and" 42 47 58.

f for him] "for them" 9 12 17 21 38 (cf. "in/against? him" 63).

g (regarding) him] "her" 17 63.

h books] "book" 21.

i the Lord] + "Most High" 12. (In DJD 13 the little frg. 7b is presented as preserving letters and words from v. 6 to v. 9. Since several of the small number of readings visible on the piece conflict with those of Eth. and/or Lat. and its placement is uncertain, the bits surviving are not underlined in the translation but are discussed in the notes. If the frg. belongs here, part of "heaven" and of "forever" are supported by it.)

7a what he had said (lit., "this utterance/speech")] this word and this utterance/speech 12.

b refused] + "very much" 12. On frg. 7b some letters of "refused to lie" survive.

8a with him] om. 21; + "yet again and kept pleading with him" 12.

b and a second] "complete" (hence = "for one complete year") 12. There are several variant readings (e.g., *kale'a* in 9 17 20 21 48) that appear to be corruptions of "second" (*kāle'a*) although they are forms of "refused."

c to listen] "and he heard/listened" 21; pr. "and" 39; + "to this word" 12; + "the word" 17ᶜ.

9a She *grasped* him (or: "She brought/conceived a plot against him")] Determining the correct reading here is difficult. If 4Q221 frg. 7b is properly placed and read, it offers two words מרמה עלו that lack equivalents in Eth. and Lat. Eth.*'aṭaqato* or *'aṭaqato* = "She constrained/forced/compelled him"; Lat. = "She approached him." There are variant forms of the unusual verb in Eth.: *'aṭayyaqato* = "she made sure to him/of him"; "she acknowledged (to) him" = 12 38 44 63 (35 58 add "without shame"). Milik attempted to explain how the Eth. and Lat. readings could have resulted from the text on the Heb. frg.: in Gk. the expression was ἐπιβουλη ἐπιλαμβανουσα: the repeated first element ἐπι- led to haplography: ἐπιλαμβανουσα became the entire reading. This would explain why there is no evidence of מרמה = ἐπιβουλη in the versions based on Gk. ἐπιλαμβανω = "to take hold of, grasp." The Testament of Joseph uses words with meanings like those of מרמה a few times in describing the scene (see T. Jos. 3:9; 4:1; 5:2; 7:1). The correct reading remains highly uncertain because of problems with all of the possibilities.

b in the house] om. 9 25.

c to compel him] "to cause him and to" 12; om. "him" 21.

d to sleep] "and (he would sleep)" = Lat. (confusing *ut* and *et*?). Rönsch (*Jubiläen*, 74) and Charles (*Ethiopic Version*, 145 n. 1 to Lat.) emended to *ut*.

e door] "doors" (but "door" later in the verse) Lat. 4Q221 7 11 (on frg. 7b) has שער, which would be a highly unusual word for a door in a private home.

f held on to him] "but he tore away from her hand" 39 42 47 48; + "openly" 35; + "openly, but he tore away from her hand" 58.

g in her hands] om. Lat. Gen 39:12 has "in her hands," as does 4Q223–224 unit 2 v:1 (the form is sg. "her hand").

h broke] "opened" Lat. The reason for the difference is not clear; Gen 39:12 lacks the expression. Charles (*Ethiopic Version*, 145 n. 3 to Lat.) altered *aperiens* to *frangens* to agree with Eth. The Heb. frg. breaks off just before the verb. In v. 10 the woman reports that he broke the door.

10a he would not sleep with her] 4Q223–224 unit 2 v:2 confirms the Eth. reading. Lat. = "he had defied her." See VanderKam, *Jubilees* 2:258.

b accused him falsely] Lat. adds: "to her husband"—a reading that seems redundant with the reference to his master that follows. Mss. 12 35 42 47 58 read an alternative spelling of the verb.

c whom you love] The phrase is confirmed by 4Q223–224 unit 2 v:3. Lat., which also reads it, places the relative clause five words after "your Hebrew slave" that it modifies. The Heb. עתה ("now") is likely a miswriting of the homophone אתה ("you") employed to emphasize the subject of the verb (DJD 13:131). The consonants of the Hebrew verb "to love"—אהב—are a rearrangement of הבא ("bring"), used in Gen 39:17. Mss. 20 25 om. "whom you love (wanted) to force me."

d   wanted] "tried" Lat. The two verbs with closely related meanings may translate ηθελε, whereas Gen 39:17 ("he came") would have been rendered as ηλθε in Gk. Jubilees (εισηλθεν in LXX Gen 39:17).

e   ran outside] om. Eth. (Gen 39:18 has "outside").

f   when I grabbed him by his clothes, and broke the door] 4Q223-224 unit 2 v:5 seems to require, for space considerations, a word such as בבגדו, but Eth. lacks an equivalent. Lat., though it is largely illegible in this context, does read *vestimenta sua* here. For the Lat., see Rönsch, *Jubiläen*, 76; Charles, *Ethiopic Version*, 145; VanderKam, *Jubilees* 2:258-59. The translation "door" is retained, though the Hebrew form מוצא as read in DJD 13:126 is unexpected (המנעול ["bolt"] may be better—so Werman, *Jubilees*, 480).

11a saw] + "that he left" 12 (= the clothing that Joseph left).

b   Joseph] "him in" 12.

c   the prisoners of the king] So Lat. (correcting *reges* to *regis*, Rönsch, *Jubiläen*, 76); Eth. has what appears to be a redundant or at least prolix reading: "where the imprisoned ones whom the king imprisoned."

d   were held] Eth. = "would stay."

12a he] "Joseph" 21 39^c 48.

b   prison] In v. 11 Eth. expressed "prison" as *beta moqeḥ*, an expression like בית הסהר in Gen 39:20. Here, however, the reading with the stronger backing is just *moqeḥ* = Lat. *vincula*, though Mss. 17^c 21 39 48 place *beta* before it. The Heb. frg. here has בית הסֹ].

c   Joseph] om. Lat., with LXX OL Gen 39:21.

d   prison guards] "prison" Lat. But LXX Gen 39:21: αρχιδεσμοφυλακος.

e   the Lord (was making)] "God" Lat.

f   making . . . succeed for him] "was directing" Lat. (see Vulgate Gen 39:23).

g   he (did)] "Joseph" Lat.

13a He] + "for that reason" Lat.

b   left (everything) to him] Lit., "left (everything) before him" (for "him" Ms. 35 reads "Joseph"). Lat. = "gave into his hands" (see v. 14), which is the expression in Gen 39:22. Charles (*Ethiopic Version*, 144 n. 28) emended the Eth. "before him" to agree with Lat., but the fact that Eth. differs from the versions of Genesis is an argument in favor of it. See VanderKam, *Jubilees* 2:259-60.

c   guards] Lat. again lacks an equivalent, as in v. 12.

d   knew] Eth. and Lat. agree with the interpretation in LXX Gen 39:23 (γιγνωσκων) where MT SP read ראה (saw).

e   about his affairs] Lit., "with him." See Gen 39:23 where LXX reads δι' αυτον (MT SP lack an equivalent). Lat. reads: "of what was done in the prison," which resembles a phrase from Gen 39:22, the previous verse. See Charles, *Ethiopic Version*, 144 n. 29; 145 n. 7 to Lat.

f   (do) everything] om. 20 25 35 44 (Lat. *universa*).

g   bring (it) to completion] Lat. reads "direct them" as in v. 12 and Gen 39:23. See VanderKam, *Jubilees* 2:260.

14a the chief butler] Lat. prefixes *idest* to the title but lacks an equivalent for "chief."

b   Joseph] + "too" Lat.

15a prison guards] Lat. lacks an equivalent for "guards." Genesis 40:4 has שר הטבחים, but a few Gk. witnesses attest a form that may underlie Eth. Jubilees here (αρχιδεσμοφυλαξ). See VanderKam, *Jubilees* 2:260-61.

b   in their presence] So Lat. and Mss. 12 20 39 58; other Eth. Mss. = "before him." The versions of Gen 40:4 agree with Lat. and with these Eth. copies. To the end of the verse Mss. 25 42 44 47 48 63 add: "and he was serving before them." See VanderKam, *Jubilees* 2:261.

16a Both of them] "the men" Lat. Charles (*Ethiopic Version*, 145 n. 36) thought Lat. *viri* could have arisen when αμφοτεροι ("both") was misread as ανθρωποι. However, it may be that in the Heb. lying behind the Lat. tradition שניהם ("both of them/the two of them") in Gen 40:5 was confused with אנשים. See VanderKam, *Jubilees* 2:261.

b   a dream] "dreams" Lat. Genesis 40:5 reads a sg. form.

c   it] "them" Lat. (see previous note).

17a turned out] Lat. seems to have reversed the order of *factum* and *et*. If one reads *factum et*, the text matches Eth.

b   he] "Joseph" Lat.

c   cupbearing] "place" Lat. Eth.: "his work/job." 4Q223-224 unit 2 v:15 may preserve the letters מש, the first two letters of משקהו ("his cupbearing") as in Gen 40:21. Ms. 21 reads "his house, to his job."

d   hanged] = Eth. and Lat. and Gen 40:22. However, Mss. 9 12 17 21 38 39 42^t 47 48 58 63 have "killed." Dillmann and Charles read "killed" in their editions, but *qatalo* ("he killed him") is a miscopying of *saqalo*.

e   the baker] "the chief baker" Lat. = Gen 40:22. Eth. may have omitted *liqa* ("chief of") after the preposition *la-*, but it does have the more difficult reading. See VanderKam, *Jubilees* 2:261.

f   interpreted] So Eth. and Gen 40:22; Lat. = "said."

g   for him] "for them" 9 12 17 21 38 39^c 42^t 47 48 58 63.

18a to him] om. 9 12 21 38 (Lat. = "to him").

b   to tell Pharaoh] "so that king Pharaoh could intervene" Lat. Some of the words in the Lat. text are uncertain at this point. See VanderKam, *Jubilees* 2:262.

c   what Joseph had told him, or: "as Joseph had told him"] Lat. again differs and is in part difficult to read: "and release Joseph." It may be that 4Q223-224 unit 2 v:17 presupposes that a direct obj. was involved ("what Joseph had told him"); see DJD 13:133.

Commentary

The chapter begins by reproducing the contents of Gen 37:1-2a, verses that immediately follow the Edomite chapter (Genesis 36) and lead into the Joseph story. In the middle of Gen 37:2, however, the writer of Jubilees shifts to the account in Genesis 39–40—Joseph's arrival in Egypt, his success in Potiphar's house, his encounter with his master's wife, his imprisonment, his success in prison, and his correct interpretation of the dreams seen by Pharaoh's butler and baker. The writer did not continue rewriting the text of Genesis 37 because he had already related its principal episodes—Joseph's brothers selling him to traders who brought him to Egypt and misleading their father regarding his fate (34:10-12; see Gen 37:12-36). Transposing the narrative of Joseph and his brothers to a place before Jubilees 35–38 must have been important to him because he had to disturb his overall chronology to do it (see the commentary on vv. 1-2a below). In addition, he postponed his treatment of Genesis 38 (Judah and Tamar) until chap. 41, that is, to a time after Joseph's rise to power in Egypt. In this way the author leaves the impression that throughout the period covered in Jubilees 35–38 Joseph was in Egypt. He is not explicit about it, but the placement of the story regarding how his brothers mistreated him implies it, as does the fact that Joseph is mentioned neither in the list of Jacob's sons and their wives (34:20-21—note "After Joseph had perished" in v. 20) nor as a participant in the war against Esau's army (38:4-8). So, as the book of Jubilees is structured, the story about disunity in Jacob's family (34:10-12) now precedes the one about the disastrous relations between Esau and Jacob.[1]

The chapter can be outlined in this fashion:

1-2ab Jacob in Canaan (Gen 37:1-2a)
2c-4   Joseph succeeds in Potiphar's house (Gen 39:1-6a)
5-11   Joseph and Potiphar's wife (Gen 39:6b-20)
12-13 Joseph succeeds in prison (Gen 39:21-23)
14-18 Joseph successfully interprets two dreams (Genesis 40)

The text for Jubilees 39 rests upon the complete Ethiopic version with partial support from:
1. Latin: vv. 9-18
2. Hebrew
   a. 4Q221 frg. 7 1-9: vv. 4-7, 9 (?)
   b. 4Q223-224 unit 2 v:1-18: vv. 9-12, 14, 17-18.[2]

There is also some comparable material in the Testament of Joseph.

1-2ab Jacob in Canaan (Gen 37:1-2a)

The passage is a verbatim reproduction of the Genesis passage in which the compiler of Genesis locates Jacob at the site where his ancestors lived as aliens (he, with Genesis, calls it Canaan) and supplies the structural *tôlĕdôt* statement for Jacob in order to introduce the story of his family (see Jub 36:20 for a related text). Once the writer of Genesis has recorded Joseph's age of seventeen years, he supplies stories to illustrate his penchant for annoying his older brothers and relates his disastrous trip to visit them. The author of Jubilees, since he had already told the story about their horrible violation of brotherly love, redeployed the material in Gen 37:1-2a as an introduction to the narrative about Joseph in Egypt.

The chronological picture that emerges from the text is unusual. According to Gen 37:2, Joseph was seventeen years of age when the fateful events of the chapter unfolded. Among those events is the episode that led to his forced journey to Egypt, so the text implies that Joseph was seventeen when he arrived in Egypt. These are the dates for Joseph's youth in Jubilees:

2134   His birth (28:24)
2149   His brothers sell him (so he would have been fifteen years of age, 34:10)
2151   Arrival in Egypt at age seventeen (39:2).[3]

---

1 See Doran, "Non-Dating," 5-7.
2 In DJD 13 the verses for 4Q221 frg. 7 are listed as 39:4-9 and for 4Q223-224 unit 2 v as 39:9-18 (continuing in 40:1-7). The verse numbers given above identify those for which something is actually preserved on the fragments. In the reconstructions of both manuscripts there is space for the other verses included in the DJD 13 listing, but they must be entirely restored.
3 There is no explanation for the two-year gap between when his brothers sold him and when he reached Egypt.

The material between Jub 34:10 (when the brothers sold Joseph) and 39:2 (when Joseph went down to Egypt) contains a series of dated events that present a surprise regarding the larger chronology in Jubilees. Rebekah's death occurred in 2157 (35:1), when Joseph would have been twenty-three years; Isaac died in 2162 (36:1), when Joseph would have been twenty-eight years (see 40:11-12 where Isaac dies in the year that Joseph, at age thirty, gained his high position with Pharaoh, that is, 2164). Leah's death, dated to 2167 (36:31), the writer recounts just after that of Isaac.

All of these numbers show that at the beginning of chap. 39 the writer steps back in time from the point he had reached at the end of the previous chapters to resume the story of Joseph where he had dropped it in 34:10-12. He chose first to narrate events that happened in the land and in this way to conclude the story about Rebekah, Isaac, and the relations between their sons Jacob and Esau. He then backtracked to bring the reader up to date regarding Joseph. Later, in 40:11-12 he will synchronize events in the two places through the notice about Joseph's age when Isaac died.

2c-4 Joseph Succeeds in Potiphar's House (Gen 39:1-6a)

■ **2c** Rather than completing the sentence about the seventeen-year-old Joseph (on which, see above) as Genesis 37 does, the writer employs it to form a segue to the next unit.

Genesis 37:2	Jubilees 39:2
Joseph, being seventeen years old, was shepherding the flock with his brothers....	When Joseph was 17 years of age, they brought him down to Egypt.

The second part of the sentence in Jub 39:2 ("they brought him down to Egypt") and the next clause resume what the author had said in 34:11.

Jubilees 34:11	Jubilees 39:2
They brought him down to Egypt and sold him to Potiphar, Pharaoh's eunuch, the chief cook, and the priest of the city of Elew.	they brought him down to Egypt. Pharaoh's eunuch[4] Potiphar, the chief cook, bought him.

Both passages reflect Gen 37:28b, 36; and (skipping over chap. 38) 39:1. That is, both Genesis 39 and Jubilees 39 resume the Joseph story at the point they had left it. Genesis separates the two units about Joseph by inserting the lengthy chap. 38 (about Judah and Tamar), while Jubilees positions four chapters (35–38) between them. So the writer of Jubilees transports the reader to a time earlier than the years covered in chaps. 35–38 and to a different place—Egypt—the central stage for the following scenes.[5] Here, as in 34:11, the text identifies Potiphar, Pharaoh's officer, with Potiphera, the priest of On (the title appears only with the person of this name in Gen 41:45; it is not used with the one named Potiphar) and father of Joseph's future wife Asenath (Gen 41:45, 50).

■ **3-4** Verses 3-4 summarize and rearrange material in Gen 39:3-6.

Jubilees 39:3-4	Source in Genesis 39:3-6
He put Joseph in charge of his entire house	v. 4: . . . he made him overseer of his house
The Lord's blessing was (present) in the Egyptian's house because of Joseph.	v. 5: . . . the Lord blessed the Egyptian's house for Joseph's sake. . . .
The Lord made everything that he did succeed for him.	v. 3: . . . the Lord caused all that he did to prosper in his hands.
The Egyptian placed everything before Joseph	v. 6: . . . so he left all that he had in Joseph's charge

---

4 The term *eunuch* for Potiphar in Genesis 39 and Jubilees 39 is especially interesting because he is married. Moreover, since Jubilees, with other ancient sources, identifies Potiphar, Pharaoh's official, with Potiphera, the father of Asenath, Joseph's wife (see the commentary on Jub 34:11), he was a parent. The author of Jubilees does not clarify how a eunuch could be a father, but *Gen. Rab.* 86:3 does. There it is said that the two—Potiphar and Potiphera—were the same and explanations of both names are offered. It also includes a suggestion that because Potiphar bought Joseph for sodomy the Lord emasculated the Egyptian (Ps 37:28 is cited in this connection). The targums translate סריס in Gen 37:36 and 39:1 as "officer," not as "eunuch," and modern translators and commentators tend to follow suit.

5 Hamilton comments about Gen 39:1 (and his words would fit Jub 39:2, apart from the reference to the Midianites): "This verse resumes the narrative of Joseph from 37:36. At the end of ch. 37 Joseph is 'sold' . . . , and here he is *purchased*. . . . This semantic shift reinforces the shift in the story from the brothers and the Midianites to Joseph and Potiphar" (*Genesis 18–50*, 458).

| because he noticed [saw] that the Lord was with him and that God made everything that he did succeed for him. | v. 3: His master saw that the Lord was with him, and that the Lord caused all that he did to prosper in his hands. |

In his rewriting, the author removes some of the repetition from Genesis, although he uses the last clause of Gen 39:3 twice. It is a bit strange that he did not place the first sentence of Gen 39:2 at the beginning of the paragraph: "The Lord was with Joseph, and he became a successful man." Those words motivate the Egyptian's appointment of him to his lofty position. In Jubilees, the master simply puts Joseph over his household (v. 3) and the Lord brings about a good result, but the reader does not learn why the master appointed him in the first place. Joseph exercises his talents and the Lord ensures successful results; subsequently, the Egyptian notices this and leaves everything to Joseph. One other expression that the author fails to reproduce from Genesis is the end of v. 6: "and, with him there, he had no concern for anything but the food that he ate." The line might seem to conflict with Joseph's report to Potiphar's wife about the limits on his authority in Gen 39:9: "He [his master] is not greater in this house than I am, nor has he kept back anything from me except yourself, because you are his wife."[6] Possibly for this reason it was omitted.

The message arising from the passage in Genesis and Jubilees is, however, largely the same. The Lord is with Joseph and that fact makes him remarkably successful[7]—so successful that the Egyptian perceives what is happening and discerns in it a divine presence with his slave. These verses introduce the fundamental theme of the Lord prospering Joseph, a theme that will recur in vv. 12-13 when Joseph is in prison.[8] Despite his circumstances, the presence of the Lord with him, even in Egypt, provides hope for success in the end.

5-11 Joseph and Potiphar's Wife (Gen 39:6b-20)

The writer reworks the seduction scene according to the teaching he wishes to convey through it; as a result, it contains a legal element and proof of Joseph's complete innocence. Genesis describes the episode in more detail and has the two characters speak with each other. The author of Jubilees includes no quotations either from the woman or from Joseph. The only words anyone says are the ones she directs to her husband after her attempts failed and Joseph fled (v. 10).

■ **5** In describing Joseph, Jubilees echoes the words of Gen 39:6b, though the Ethiopic text uses the same noun (rā'y)[9] twice where the versions of Genesis employ two words (form/appearance). The first statement about him (he was "well formed") reproduces one used for his mother Rachel in Jub 28:5 (// Gen 29:17; see *Gen. Rab.* 86:6). His physical appeal is what draws the attention of Potiphar's wife;[10] nothing is said about any admiration she may have had for, say, his success in running the household.[11]

Initially Jubilees expands the Genesis account in describing what the woman did.

---

6   *Genesis Rabbah* 86:6 interprets "the food that he ate" as a euphemism, apparently referring to Potiphar's wife. The explanation could arise from comparing vv. 6 and 9. The same understanding appears in *Tg. Ps.-J.* Gen 39:6 and elsewhere.

7   The extent of his success is expressed through the frequent repetition of "all/entire" in both Gen 39:3-6 and Jub 39:3-4. Cf. Hamilton, *Genesis 18-50*, 461.

8   See Westermann, *Genesis 37-50*, 61-62.

9   It can mean "vision, image, likeness, form, appearance" (some of the equivalents listed by Leslau, *Concise Dictionary*, 61). See VanderKam, *Jubilees* 2:256-57.

10 See Kugel, *Traditions*, 443-46, for other references to and elaborations on Joseph's physical beauty. He devotes the third chapter in his *In Potiphar's House* to the subject (*In Potiphar's House: The Interpretive Life of Biblical Texts* [San Francisco: HarperSanFrancisco, 1990] 66-93).

11 Josephus (*Ant.* 2.41-42) presents the matter somewhat differently, although he too suggests she was looking more at the surface than the substance of Joseph: "For his master's wife, by reason both of his comely appearance and his dexterity in affairs [την τας πραξεις αυτου δεξιοτητα], became enamoured of him. She thought that if she disclosed this passion to him, she would easily persuade him to have intercourse with her, since he would deem it a stroke of fortune to be solicited by his mistress: she was looking but at the outward guise of his present servitude, but not at his character, which notwithstanding his change of fortune stood firm" (Thackeray, LCL).

Genesis 39:7	Jubilees 39:5
After a time his master's wife cast her eyes on Joseph and said, "Lie with me."	The wife of his master looked up at him, saw Joseph, loved him, and pleaded with him to sleep with her.

The present verse is another instance in which the verb "love" carries the sense of "lust" (see, e.g., Jub 33:2, where Reuben "loved" Bilhah when he saw her bathing). In Genesis it does not seem as if the woman is *pleading* for Joseph to sleep with her—she uses an imperative as one might to a servant (introduced by "[she] said"); she takes a different, more humble approach in Jubilees.

■ **6-7** Joseph, of course, rejects her advances in both books, but in Gen 39:8-9 he defends his refusal by citing the orders his master gave about his role in the household. There he concludes by saying to her: "He is not greater in this house than I am, nor has he kept back anything from me except yourself, because you are his wife. How then could I do this great wickedness, and sin against God?" (v. 9). In Jubilees he refuses to surrender himself to her lusts, not because Potiphar had ruled his wife off limits to Joseph. On the contrary, Joseph, apparently clarifying what Genesis meant by "do this great wickedness, and sin against God," recalled his religious training and the law he had learned from Jacob. "He remembered the Lord and what his father Jacob would read to him from the words of Abraham—that no one is to commit adultery with a woman who has a husband; that there is a death penalty that has been ordained for him in heaven before the Most High God. The sin will be entered regarding him in the eternal books [*maṣāḥeft za-la-ʿālam*] forever before the Lord" (v. 6). The law itself is located between two (outer) statements that Joseph refused the woman's entreaties (vv. 6, 8) and within two (inner) ones that Joseph remembered (vv. 6, 7); in this way the writer highlights it as the focus of the unit.[12]

Thus, the bases for Joseph's resistance to Potiphar's wife are two: he brought to his mind the Lord himself—recalling what he knew about God was an important impetus for his action[13]—and he remembered the ancestral law applicable to the situation.[14] The first of these (the Lord) is mentioned and not further explained—perhaps the writer thought it was clear enough; but the second undergoes some elaboration. Joseph recalled what his father Jacob used to read to him when he shared the written words of Abraham with his son. Jacob here is credited with a pedagogical role that is not visible elsewhere in Jubilees. The text pictures him as a dutiful father who passed along the legal tradition from his ancestors to his son(s). What were the words of Abraham that he read, and are they documented elsewhere in Jubilees?

The writer explains that the words of Abraham prohibited "adultery with a woman who has a husband." Abraham receives much attention in Jubilees, but the work does not record an instance in which he passes along his books to a representative of the next generation as Noah (10:14) did and as Jacob will do (45:16). The Lord instructed the angel to teach Abram the Hebrew language that had fallen into disuse (12:25-26), and, once he learned it, he "took his fathers' books—they were written in Hebrew—and copied them. From that time he began to study them, while I [the Angel of the Presence] was telling him everything that he was unable (to understand). He studied them throughout the six rainy months" (12:27). He was, therefore, a copyist of his ancestors' books, but there is no story about Abraham

---

12   Livneh shows that the section is chiastically organized so as to place the statement of the law in the middle of the structure and thus to emphasize it ("Not at First Sight," 11–13). The present scene is one of the three she analyzes as illustrating the notion of attraction between a woman and a man based on sight (the others are Jacob and Rachel and Reuben and Bilhah). A relationship beginning in this way leads to violation of law (pp. 5–13). Cf. also Endres, *Biblical Interpretation*, 184; and Loader, *Sexuality*, 201.

13   In T. Jos. 2:2 he says, "And I struggled against a shameless woman, urging me to transgress with her; / but the God of Israel my father guarded me from the burning flame."

14   For references to the incident, see Kugel, *Traditions*, 442–43. Among the passages he adduces is 1 Macc 2:52-53, which, in a list of heroes to be emulated, associates Abraham and Joseph and refers to a "commandment": "Was not Abraham found faithful when tested, and it was reckoned to him as righteousness? Joseph in the time of his distress kept the commandment, and became lord of Egypt." See also Philo, *Jos.* 42–44.

writing his own volumes, though 39:6 implies that he had been an author. There are, however, frequent references to the teachings of Abraham. Among the subjects that he taught his offspring was the need to avoid sexual impurity. He mentioned it several times in his final addresses to them. Clear examples occur in chap. 20 where he is speaking to all of his sons and grandsons, including Isaac and Jacob (see v. 1). There they learn "that we should keep ourselves from all sexual impurity [zemmut] and uncleanness [rekws]; and that we should dismiss all uncleanness [rekws] and sexual impurity [zemmut] from among us" (20:3; see also v. 4, where verbal forms related to the noun zemmut occur twice; and v. 6, where he warns his sons and grandsons about sexual impurity). Consequently, Abraham had taught Isaac and Jacob about the subject, and Jacob referenced his grandfather's teachings when speaking with his mother in chap. 25. There he tells her that Abraham ordered him not to marry a Canaanite woman (v. 5) and adds: "For this reason I have kept myself from sinning and becoming corrupted in any ways during my entire lifetime because father Abraham gave me many orders about lewdness [mer'āt] and sexual impurity [zemmut]" (v. 7).[15] The prohibition Joseph cites—"no one is to commit adultery"—uses the verb yezēmu, just as Abraham did in 20:4 (although there it applies to a woman).[16] So, the reader is supposed to imagine that Abraham or his descendants recorded his instructions in order to preserve and transmit them to their children, as Jacob did to Joseph in the instance referenced in Jub 39:6.

The book of Jubilees is not the only work that claims Joseph remembered his father in the time of temptation.[17] Joseph tells his children in T. Jos. 3:3: "I, then, remembered the words of my father Jacob, / and going into my chamber I prayed to the Lord." The writer of Joseph and Aseneth describes Joseph's reaction to all the Egyptian women who propositioned him:

> Joseph said, "I will not sin before (the) Lord God of my father Israel nor in the face of my father Jacob." And the face of his father Jacob, Joseph always had before his eyes, and he remembered his father's commandments. For Jacob would say to his son Joseph and all his sons, "My children, guard strongly against associating with a strange woman, for association (with) her is destruction and corruption." (7:5–6)

It is possible that *Tg. Ps.-J.* Gen 49:24 provides something of an exegetical basis for the idea that Jacob's teaching saved Joseph from sinning with Potiphar's wife. Genesis 49:24 itself (part of Jacob's blessing of Joseph) reads: "Yet his bow remained taut, / and his arms [lit., the arms of his hands] were made agile / by the hands of the Mighty One of Jacob [אביר יעקב], / by the name of the Shepherd, the Rock of Israel." The targum presents the passage as:

> *The strength of his member returned to its former state, so that he might not have intercourse with his mistress, and his hands were withheld from voluptuous thoughts. And he subdued his inclination because of the* strict *instruction he had received from* Jacob. *Thus he was found worthy of becoming administrator and of having his name engraved with theirs on the stones of Israel* [that is, on the stones of the high priest's ephod].[18]

---

15 For these passages, see Charles, *Jubilees*, 223. He and Hartom ("Jubilees," 117) refer to *b. Soṭah* 36b, where it is said that the visage of Jacob appeared to Joseph reminding him that his brothers and he were destined to have their names inscribed on the stones of the ephod and that to sin on this occasion would jeopardize that privilege. Cf. also *Gen. Rab.* 87:7. Loader writes about Jub 39:7: "*Jubilees* offers no such teaching on the lips of Abraham, but it is to be understood as one of those 'mortal sins' like incest (33:13) of which he spoke in 21:22 without specifying adultery, in particular, and is to be assumed also under his other warnings about impurity" (*Sexuality*, 201). As the above references show, Abraham was more specific than Loader suggests.

16 Werman thinks that this is the reason why the death penalty mentioned in 39:6 is in heaven, not one carried out by humans (*Jubilees*, 482). The one against the adulterous woman in 20:4 is a punishment (burning) executed by people, but men will not escape either. See below, however, on the death penalty in 39:6.

17 See Kugel, *Traditions*, 447–48, for the ones that follow and others. Cf. also his *In Potiphar's House*, 98–101.

18 For understanding "Rock of Israel" as "the stones of Israel," see *b. Soṭah* 36b.

The words "the strict instruction he had received from Jacob" may have arisen by reading אביר ("the Mighty One" in the NRSV, a name for God) as אביו ("his father"); as a result, the text could be understood as pointing to the assistance Joseph received from his father Jacob.[19]

The death penalty that would befall the one who transgressed the command against adultery is not explicit in Abraham's testament in chap. 20, but it is an easy inference from the sequel, where he mentions the fates suffered by the giants and the people of Sodom for their deeds of sexual impurity (20:5-6; see also 41:28 [the law of Abraham requires burning for an adulteress]).[20] Capital punishment for an adulterer is said to be "ordained for him in heaven before the Most High God" (39:6). It is noteworthy that the writer does not use the expression "the heavenly tablets" here. He employs a verb frequently associated with them ("ordained") but not in combination with another verb as often happens in tablet references. It is not clear how this sort of heavenly record would differ from the tablets on which punishments are recorded.[21] The present passage may be another indication that the author refers to the heavenly writing in more than one way—tablets (1:29; 32:21-22), heavenly tablets (in many passages), and "eternal books" (here in 39:6). At any rate, the sin is permanently inscribed in "the eternal books." It will therefore never be erased or forgotten. Joseph had the presence of mind to remember all of this as the Egyptian woman tempted him, and for that reason he rejected her advances. It is interesting that the instruction Joseph calls to mind contains nothing about sexual contact with a foreign woman, when the subject is such a large issue in Jubilees. These verses join other units in Jubilees in which Egyptians are treated more favorably than Canaanites. Joseph will eventually marry Asenath, an Egyptian woman, and the author will not criticize the union (see 40:10).[22]

■ 8 Potiphar's wife refused to take no for an answer. According to Jubilees, she continued her attempts to seduce Joseph over a considerable length of time. Genesis 39:10 is vague about the matter: "day after day [יום יום]," but Jub 39:9 is more specific although there is a textual problem in it. The Ethiopic version, the only one surviving for the expression, offers these options: (1) "She pleaded with him for one year[23] and a second [wa-kāle'a], but he refused to listen to her"; or (2) "She pleaded with him for one year, but he refused [wa-kal'a] and refused to/would not listen to her." Both readings have strong manuscript support, and both make sense in the context. There is nothing in the chronology of Joseph's life in Jubilees that would preclude a two-year time of temptation in Potiphar's house (see 46:3, where he is said to have been a slave for ten years),[24] and there

---

19   On the exegesis here, see Kugel, *Walk through Jubilees*, 179–80; "Jubilees," 425.

20   Leviticus 20:10 mandates the death penalty for adultery: "If a man commits adultery with the wife of his neighbor, both the adulterer and the adulteress shall be put to death." However, identifying the woman as "the wife of his neighbor" can be understood to restrict the law to an Israelite (see Milgrom, *Leviticus*, 2:1747–48) so that it would not be applicable to a case like that of Joseph and the Egyptian woman.

21   Livneh quite understandably assumes that the reference is to the heavenly tablets without use of the actual term ("Not at First Sight," 12 n. 30); Maren Niehoff does the same (*The Figure of Joseph in Post-Biblical Jewish Literature* [AGJU 16; Leiden: Brill, 1992] 44). Werman refers to 30:22 for a similar provision (*Jubilees*, 482). Kugel, however, thinks the reference is not to the heavenly tablets, since the language indicates that the passage is from the author, not from an interpolator who, on his view, is the one who appeals to the heavenly tablets (*Walk through* Jubilees, 180; "Jubilees," 425). See also Baynes (*Heavenly Book Motif*, 92–93), who considers this reference under the rubric of "the heavenly book of deeds."

22   Abram married an Egyptian—Hagar. On the Egyptians in Jubilees, see Werman, "Attitude," 280–93.

23   Kugel, who prefers the reading "for one whole year" ("whole" is attested only in MS. 12), suggests that this is a midrashic inference from Esth 3:7, where "from day to day and from month to the twelfth month" is taken to mean a full year, from month 1 to month 12 (*Walk through* Jubilees, 180; "Jubilees," 464 n. 239). He adduces Midrash Tanhuma on the passage as a source for this understanding.

24   If, as in the present translation, the temptation extended over two years and if Joseph remained a slave for ten years, then the woman began propositioning him after Joseph had been in Potiphar's house for eight years (Werman, *Jubilees*, 482). According to Werman, this fact serves to

is no objection to reading two synonymous but not identical expressions to emphasize Joseph's absolute opposition to the Egyptian woman's importunities.[25] The verse makes clear, whichever reading one chooses, that her seductions lasted a long time and that Joseph always fended them off. She continued to beg, though she was the lady of the house; he steadfastly resisted, though he was a slave.

■ 9 When her constant pleas proved ineffectual, Potiphar's wife became more forceful. Here again there is a textual issue. The superior reading among the Ethiopic manuscripts is *'aṭaqato*. The verb means "gird, gird oneself, put around the waist, fasten, restrain." A well-supported alternative reading is *'aṭayyaqato*: this causative verbal form means "make sure, assure, make certain, ascertain, inform, make known, affirm," and so on.[26] Neither reading seems very satisfactory in the context with an object suffix referring to a person. The Latin translation reads quite differently: *adgressa est eum*, "she approached him." It makes good sense but hardly one related to the Ethiopic readings.

The translators have favored a sense such as "embraced" (so Charles, Goldmann, Hartom, Wintermute, Caquot) or "pressed" (Berger), while VanderKam rendered as "drew him close." The meaning "drew him close" rests on the supposition that the original text read ותקרב. The textual tradition behind the Ethiopic reading understood the form to be causative (she caused to come near), while the one behind the Latin read it as a *qal* (she approached). Testament of Joseph 8:2 offers a sense parallel to this understanding of the Ethiopic reading: "At last, then, she laid hold of my clothes, / forcibly drawing me to have intercourse with her." A problem with the suggestion is that it would have been strange for a translator to render the Hebrew form as a *qal* if a direct object followed (as in the Ethiopic text). Another possibility—the one adopted in the translation—is that the Ethiopic forms represent inner-Ge'ez corruptions of another verb sharing the same consonants, *ṭa'aqa*, "enclose, clasp around, tighten, put in straits" (the causative can have the same meaning).[27] The actions attributed to her, then, would be grabbing hold of and hanging on to him. So desperate was she that she tried physically to compel a grown man to have sex with her.[28] To ensure they would not be disturbed, she closed the door. With the two of them confined indoors, she would not let go of him. Genesis 39:11-12a is somewhat more tame: "One day, however, when he went into the house to do his work, and while no one else was in the house, she caught hold of his garment, saying, 'Lie with me!'" It does not explain why no one else was in the house, and it says nothing about shutting the door.

This is the textual situation as represented in the Ethiopic and Latin translations, but 4Q221 7 10 introduces a further complication. It reads: עלו מרמה ("against him a deceitful plan"). These words occur at the beginning of a line on a four-line fragment (7b) that Milik proposed locating here. If so, it is thoroughly different from the two granddaughter translations. Milik attempted to account for the readings in Ethiopic and Latin through a corruption on the Greek level (see the textual note), but the placement of the fragment is problematic. In fact, if it belongs at this point in the text, two of its four short lines clash with the readings in the versions. That is not impossible, but when dealing with a small fragment whose location is uncertain, the number of disagreements with the existing texts raises doubts about whether it actually belongs in chap. 39. Furthermore, Potiphar's wife does not seem to be fashioning a deceptive plan; she simply grabs Joseph after closing the

---

enhance the image of the woman, but it is not easy to see how this is the case. She also believes that Joseph's situation in Egypt is elevated in Jubilees relative to the picture in Genesis, and that is true. But note that, even for the time he was over Potiphar's household, the writer designates his status as that of a slave.

25 Cf. VanderKam, *Jubilees* 2:257.
26 The definitions for both verbs are from Leslau, *Concise Dictionary*, 180 and 221, respectively. See also *Comparative Dictionary*, 76, 600.
27 Leslau, *Concise Dictionary*, 220; *Comparative Dictionary*, 584. The Latin reading would have to be explained differently if a form of *ṭa'aqa* points to the Hebrew original.
28 Philo (*Jos.* 41) deals with the incongruity by writing: "She caught hold of his outer garment and powerfully drew him to her bed by superior force, since passion which often braces even the weakest gave her new vigor" (Colson, LCL).

door.[29] As a result, the Ethiopic text forms the basis for the translation at this point.[30]

Joseph's response was swift and decisive in Genesis and Jubilees, although the two are not the same.

Genesis 39:12b	Jubilees 39:9c
But he left his garment in her hand, and fled and ran outside.	He left his clothes in her hands, broke the door, and ran away from her to the outside.

Since Genesis had reported she grabbed hold of his clothing in v. 12a, the succeeding description deals with his garment and his flight outside the house in which only the two of them were present. The writer of Jubilees had not said that the woman held on to Joseph's clothing (only that she grabbed him), but he follows the text of Genesis by referencing the garment here. In both texts, therefore, she is left with tangible evidence in her possession. In Genesis there are two verbs for his escape: he "fled and ran outside." In Jubilees there are also two, but the first takes up the earlier reference to the door the woman had closed: Joseph, in his haste to escape, broke it down[31] and thus fled outside the house. Kugel suggests that the expansion of Genesis in this regard arose from the presence of the two verbs: "Since the second verb specifies 'outside,' the first seems to suggest that there was some obstacle to be overcome before Joseph could go outside."[32] The door scene also demonstrates his zeal for getting away from her.[33] Jubilees says not only that he fled outside as Genesis does but adds "from her" to remove any doubt about his purpose.[34]

■ 10 As one would expect, Joseph's energetic response to her forceful ploy convinced the Egyptian woman that she had failed despite her best efforts. At this point she turned from her unsuccessful approach and tried a new one: "she accused him falsely to his master." The word "falsely" does not figure in Genesis 39 (but see 40:15), where she first calls out to the members of her household (apparently they had returned after being away in v. 11). Speaking to them, she accused Joseph of attempted rape while also managing to criticize her husband for bringing such a contemptuous person to them (39:14-15). She then kept Joseph's garment until Potiphar came home, at which time she repeated the charge to him (39:16-18). The author of Jubilees bypasses her accusation to the people of the household[35] and reproduces only the scene where she speaks to her husband.

Genesis 39:17b-18	Jubilees 39:10b
The Hebrew servant, whom you have brought among us, came in to me to insult me; but as soon as I raised my voice and cried out, he left his garment beside me, and fled outside.	Your Hebrew slave whom you[36] love wanted to force me so that he could sleep with me. When I shouted,[37] he ran outside, left his clothes in my hands when I grabbed him by his clothes, and broke the door.

Though she had been so powerfully attracted to Joseph, he is now "your slave" (he is only "the Hebrew servant" in Genesis)[38] and, in contrast to her loving Joseph in v. 5, Joseph is now the slave "whom you love." The verb in Hebrew Jubilees is preserved in 4Q223–224 unit 2 v:3, and, as the Ethiopic and Latin would lead one to expect, it is אהב]תה. The verb has the same consonants as the one in Gen 39:17 (הבאת, "you have brought") but in a different order. The meaning "brought" is attested in all the

---

29 For Werman (*Jubilees*, 482), closing the door was her plan, but that seems an overly generous assessment of her simple act.

30 Several passages in the Testament of Joseph refer to her guile/deceit (3:9; 4:1; 5:2; cf. 7:1), but in it her approach to Joseph is much more considered and elaborate than it is in Jubilees.

31 In the Latin translation he merely opens the door. If 4Q221 frg. 7b 11 does contain text from this passage, it has an unexpected word for door—שער. Perhaps this is another reason to question the placement of the fragment.

32 Kugel, *Walk through* Jubilees, 180; "Jubilees," 425.

33 Cf. Werman, "Attitudes," 288; *Jubilees*, 482.

34 According to *b. Soṭah* 36b, some understood the presence of only the woman and Joseph in the house as implying that both intended to sleep together. There is no such implication in Jubilees.

35 Werman regards this change too as improving the woman's image (*Jubilees*, 482). It could, however, be a simple omission of largely repetitive material.

36 4Q223–224 unit 2 v:3 very clearly reads עתה, "now," but it is unexpected. It does not seem as if the woman is talking about a recent development in Potiphar's feelings toward Joseph. The word may be a mistake for אתה, "you," as proposed in DJD 13:131.

37 Like Genesis, the text reads literally, "When I raised my voice." Jubilees does not reproduce "and cried out."

38 She called him "a Hebrew man" when speaking to the household in v. 14.

ancient versions of Gen 39:17, so the change in Jubilees seems intentional.[39] It nicely expresses the sharp reversal from the attitude of Potiphar's wife in v. 5.[40] The commentators on Genesis debate the meaning and significance of the verb translated "to insult me [לצחק in 39:14, 17]."[41] Jubilees (both Ethiopic and Latin) offers its own interpretation: "to force me." Whereas in Genesis she accuses him of leaving his clothing "beside me" (vv. 15, 18), in Jubilees she more nearly reproduces the language of Gen 39:12, 13 (where her latching onto his clothing is described) by saying he left it in her hands (as in Syr and *Tg. Neof.* Gen 39:18). Both formulations clearly incriminate Joseph, though the one in Genesis suggests he had already removed his garment before running away. In Jubilees she adds that he left the garment in her hands when she seized it (as in Gen 39:12, where she does this to pull him to her) and that he "broke the door [perhaps המוצא in 4Q223–224 unit 2 v:5,[42] though several letters are difficult to read]."

■ 11 The episode ends with the decision made by Potiphar. Genesis makes him seem a gullible judge, but Jubilees somewhat softens the negative image.

Genesis 39:19	Jubilees 39:11
When his master heard the words that his wife spoke to him, saying, "This is the way your servant treated me," he became enraged.	When the Egyptian saw Joseph's clothes and the broken door, he believed[43] what his wife said.

The Potiphar of Genesis simply accepts what his wife tells him and does not investigate the matter further—not even Joseph's garment receives mention. The Egyptian of Jubilees, however, deals with two pieces of evidence beyond the story of his wife: the abandoned clothing[44] and the shattered door. Philo was concerned with the injustice perpetrated by Potiphar in Genesis:

> Joseph's master, believing this [his wife's story] to be true, ordered him to be carried away to prison, and in this he committed two great errors. First he gave him no opportunity of defence, and convicted unheard this entirely innocent person as guilty of the greatest misconduct. Secondly, the raiment which his wife produced as left by the youth was a proof of violence not employed by him but suffered at her hands. For if force were used by him he would retain his mistress's robe, if against him he would lose his own. But his master may perhaps be pardoned for his gross ignorance, since his days were spent in a kitchen. (*Jos.* 52–53 [Colson, LCL])[45]

The writer of Jubilees, for whatever reason, presents Potiphar as considering the facts of the case, though he did not attempt to determine whether his wife was telling the truth. Perhaps the identification of Potiphar as the father of Joseph's future wife led the author to present him more favorably.[46] The real culprit is Potiphar's wife, not Potiphar.

Halpern-Amaru has shown the parallels and contrasts between the Joseph–Potiphar's wife story and the one

---

39 Perhaps it is relevant that his master will become Joseph's father-in-law (see below) so that he is pictured as having positive feelings toward Joseph.

40 Kugel thinks it is a mistake, even though it is documented in the Hebrew copy of Jubilees (*Walk through* Jubilees, 180; "Jubilees," 426). The explanation given above seems more likely.

41 See, e.g., Hamilton, *Genesis 18–50*, 468.

42 Note that this is a different term than the one in 4Q221 frg. 7b 11 (v. 9), if the fragment belongs at that point. Werman reads המנעול, "lock, bolt," marking the first four letters as visible in some way on the fragment (*Jubilees*, 480). It is exceedingly difficult to interpret the letters after *mem*. Her reading may be correct (on an enhanced photograph the letter following *mem* does look more like a *nun* than a *waw*), but the resulting word would also be one not used in the context in Genesis. Both Ethiopic (*māʾdo*) and Latin (*ostium*) have words for "door" here and in vv. 9, 11, although *māʾdo* can also have the sense of "bolt" (Leslau, *Comparative Dictionary*, 75).

43 Literally, "he heard" (both Ethiopic and Latin).

44 This is the second time Joseph's clothing is misused and misinterpreted (the brothers too had deceived Jacob with his garment [Gen 37:31-33 // Jub 34:12]).

45 In Philo's Bible, Potiphar was the chief cook, not the captain of the guard (Gen 37:36; 39:1); see Jub 39:2.

46 So Halpern-Amaru, *Empowerment*, 122. Her point regarding the more positive portrayal of Potiphar is correct, but her claim that in Jubilees the woman is "a less conniving and manipulative wife than she appears to be in the biblical story" is debatable (though Loader [*Sexuality*, 202] cites it with approval).

about Reuben and Bilhah in Jub 33:1-9 (see the commentary there).

Both narratives involve sexual intercourse with a proscribed woman. In each a seducer, driven by desire (33:2; 39:5), entraps the object of desire when she/he is most vulnerable (33:3; 39:9). In each there is a grasping (33:4; 39:9), an outcry (33:4; 39:10), a flight (33:5; 39:9), a point made about the woman informing her husband (33:6; 39:10), and an halakhic discourse involving the behavior of each son of Jacob (33:9-16; 39:6-7).

Such parallels prompt contrasting images. The innocent Bilhah grabs hold in error; the seductive wife of Potiphar grabs hold to entrap. The victimized wife lets forth a legitimate cry of protest; the villainess wife feigns such a cry. The grieving Bilhah keeps silent; the plotting wife of Potiphar is quick to confront her husband. Reuben and Joseph both flee; but one does so in order to escape confrontation after perpetrating a treacherous act; and the other, to prevent the act from happening.[47]

She adds that Reuben sinned through his ignorance of the law, while Joseph's knowledge of Abraham's commandment kept him from sinning. When compared with his older brother Reuben, Joseph is a shining example of obedience to the law[48] whereas Reuben is a failure saved only by the limited amount of law revealed by the time of his sin.

The result of the encounter between Joseph and the Egyptian woman is the same in Genesis and Jubilees: Potiphar sends Joseph to the prison where the king of Egypt detained those who had fallen from his favor. Potiphar must have been a high officer of Pharaoh, if he had the right to send a person to the royal prison, but the fact that he imprisoned rather than executed Joseph may be a hint that he was not convinced of Joseph's guilt.[49] However that may be, the place for his imprisonment proves to be vital for the next episode in the story when Joseph encounters officials of the monarch in the same place (see also v. 14 below).

12-13 Joseph Succeeds in Prison (Gen 39:21-23)

The prison phase of Joseph's career mirrors his experience in Potiphar's house but with a vastly different ending.

■ **12** Verse 12 begins by reproducing the last line of Gen 39:20 ("he remained there in prison"), but it and v. 13 continue by summarizing and rearranging elements in Gen 39:21-23. In Genesis the first statement in v. 21 is that "the LORD was with Joseph," just as the section about Joseph in Potiphar's house began in v. 2; the next sentence in v. 22 expresses through two nouns (חסד, "steadfast love," and חן, "favor") the gracious reception God gave him before the chief jailer. In Jubilees the two elements appear but in reverse order. Initially the writer expresses twice, as in Genesis, the favor Joseph received from the chief of the prison guards;[50] only then does he mention that the Lord was with him, not as a direct statement of fact, but as something the official noticed. This parallels Gen 39:3 // Jub 39:4, where Potiphar observed that the Lord was with Joseph. Another item the chief of the prison guards noted was that the Lord made everything Joseph did succeed. This is the last

---

47 Halpern-Amaru, *Empowerment*, 110-11. The contrast between Reuben and Joseph in Jubilees she sees as replacing the one in Genesis between Judah and Joseph. A comparison between Judah and Joseph is suggested by the juxtaposition of Genesis 38 and 39. In Jubilees the Judah-Tamar story is postponed until chap. 41, some distance after the Joseph–Potiphar's wife incident here in chap. 39 (see pp. 111-12).

48 Docherty ("Joseph the Patriarch," 210-12) treats the present story as illustrative of how the "representation of Joseph in *Jubilees* is, then, entirely positive" (p. 212), with any element that might imply something negative about him deleted from the account. See also Niehoff, *Figure of Joseph*, 46.

49 See Westermann, *Genesis 37–50*, 67 (where he adds Potiphar's failure to investigate the charges against Joseph more aggressively); Hamilton, *Genesis 18–50*, 471. Cf. also Kugel, *Traditions*, 456.

50 These are rendered as "a favorable reception [*mogasa/gratiam*]" and "a kind reception [*meḥrata/misericordiam*]" in the translation. The title of the official—"the chief of the prison guards"—echoes the LXX understanding of שר בית הסהר as ἀρχιδεσμοφύλαξ.

point in Gen 39:23, where the narrator declares it and does not present it more indirectly as something the prison official saw. Jubilees will reproduce it there (v. 13) as well, this time as a direct statement.[51]

■ **13** Genesis 39:22 says that he committed all the prisoners to Joseph; Jubilees lacks the element but agrees with Gen 39:22-23 that, like Potiphar in his house, the prison chief placed full responsibility for the institution in Joseph's hands. Jubilees alone adds here that Joseph remained in the prison for two years (see Gen 41:1 for the number, and compare Jub 40:1). The sentence "He remained there for two years" need not be taken as marking the full duration of his stay in prison. It more likely refers to the period from when Potiphar incarcerated him until the butler and baker arrived there (see v. 14), since Jub 46:3 assigns three years to his time in prison. Both texts make abundantly clear that Joseph succeeded so marvelously because the Lord was with him. His imprisonment turns out to be more positive than expected, and his presence there situates him for the next scene.

14-18 Joseph Successfully Interprets Two Dreams (Genesis 40)

The final four verses in Jubilees 39 offer a greatly condensed version of Genesis 40. In Genesis the narrator devotes much space to describing the dreams experienced by the chief butler and chief baker and to Joseph's interaction with the two men when he interpreted their dreams (vv. 9-19). In Jubilees the reader never learns what they dreamed and only indirectly about the interpretations Joseph supplied. Apparently the author thought he could convey the desired message without the details regarding the dreams and their explanations. By writing so tersely, he sacrificed much of the artistic craft manifest in the longer Genesis version. Jubilees' story about Joseph and the two officials relates to Genesis 40 in this way:

Jubilees 39:14 = Genesis 40:2-3
Jubilees 39:15 = Genesis 40:4
Jubilees 39:16 = Genesis 40:5
Jubilees 39:17 = Genesis 40:21-22
Jubilees 39:18 = Genesis 40:23

The section containing the dreams and their interpretation (Gen 40:6-20) constitutes most of what Jubilees leaves out of the chapter.

■ **14** The writer skips over the vague explanation for Pharaoh's imprisonment of the chief butler and chief baker in Gen 40:1 (they offended him) and begins the scene with the information that in his anger the king consigned them to the prison where Joseph was (Gen 40:2-3). Both Genesis and Jubilees give an interesting description of which prison was meant:

Genesis 40:3	Jubilees 39:14
and he put them in custody in the house of the captain of the guard, in the prison where Joseph was confined.	He put them in prison, in the house of the chief cook, in the prison where Joseph was held.

The intriguing feature is that the corrections official is identified differently than in the previous section about Joseph's imprisonment (Gen 39:21-23 // Jub 39:12-13): there he was "the chief jailer" ("[t]he chief of the prison guards" in Jubilees), but here he is "the captain of the guard" or, in Jubilees, "the chief cook." This is the title borne by Potiphar in Gen 39:1 // Jub 39:2 (see also Gen 37:36 // Jub 34:11; cf. Gen 40:7). The texts, therefore, indicate that the chief butler and chief baker are in a prison associated with Potiphar and that Joseph was in the same place.[52]

■ **15** The expected title for the official in charge of the prison appears in v. 15 (// Gen 40:4)—"[t]he chief of the prison guards"—the one employed in the previous section. At this point Genesis (v. 4) again uses Potiphar's title ("The captain of the guard"). The writer of Jubilees thus seems to identify the officials in the two passages as the same person, whereas Genesis appears to intend two different individuals. Genesis 39:22 had

---

51 Where the versions of Genesis read "made it prosper," Jub 39:13 has "would bring (it) to completion" (Ethiopic) and "would direct them" (Latin).

52 For explanations of the situation as arising from the combination of sources, see Skinner, *Genesis*, 460. According to Hamilton (*Genesis 18–50*, 475), the text implies that Potiphar is the one called "the captain of the guard" (40:3 [his translation is "chief steward"]): "The prison in which the chief butler and baker are detained would be a room attached to Potiphar's house (40:3, which specifically identifies the place of detention as 'the house of the chief steward')."

stated, "The chief jailer committed to Joseph's care all the prisoners who were in the prison"; Jubilees omitted the statement in vv. 12-13, but in v. 15 the author has the same official give Joseph the task of "serving" the two new inmates—the butler and the baker. Verse 15 uses the verb "serve" twice—in the report about the appointment and in a statement that Joseph carried out the assignment—whereas Gen 40:4 resorts to it only once—to relate that "he waited on them," as the NRSV translates the verb. Neither Jubilees nor Genesis discusses how such service to the butler and baker relates to the lofty position Joseph had attained in 39:12-13 (// Gen 39:21-23),[53] but the key point is that Joseph has close contact with Pharaoh's two highly ranked but now disgraced servants.

■ **16** The verse summarizes in one sentence the story about the dreams and their interpretation in Gen 40:5-19. The Genesis account has these elements:

The butler and baker have dreams that distress them (v. 5).
Joseph learns about this and their need for an interpreter (vv. 6-8).
The butler relates his dream, Joseph interprets it, and asks to be remembered to Pharaoh (vv. 9-15).
The baker relates his dream and Joseph interprets it (vv. 16-19).

About most of this the writer of Jubilees says, "Both of them—the chief butler and the chief baker—had a dream and told it to Joseph."[54] He will do something similar in chap. 40, where he notes that Pharaoh had two dreams but does not reproduce their content (compare Jub 40:1-2 with Gen 41:1-8, 17-24). Joseph's interpretations of the butler's and baker's dreams play no part in this short summary; they will receive brief mention in v. 17 but only in connection with the fates of the two men. The author, therefore, did not copy the details in these symbolic or allegorical dreams and referred to them only insofar as they advanced the story line.[55]

■ **17** Even Joseph's interpretations of the dreams merit only the briefest mention: "Things turned out for them just as he interpreted for them." The writer omits his specific statements about the symbols in each of the dreams: "This is its interpretation: the three branches are three days" (Gen 40:12); and "This is its interpretation: the three baskets are three days" (Gen 40:18). Though Genesis takes pains to have Joseph acknowledge God as the real interpreter of dreams ("And Joseph said to them, 'Do not interpretations belong to God? Please tell them to me'" [40:8]), Jubilees omits all the features of such dreams—their symbols that demanded professional analysis—and merely notes that the dreams occurred and Joseph interpreted them correctly. Doing just this much entails that the writer thought dreams could predict what would occur, but he seems to say as little about them as possible. When he relates what happened to each of Pharaoh's officers afterward, the author returns to the text of Genesis by citing the relevant clauses from Gen 40:21, 22: the monarch restored the butler to his

---

53 The tension regarding Joseph's status has functioned as an argument for distinguishing sources behind the two passages. Hamilton, however, thinks the role of Joseph in the two chapters is consistent (*Genesis 18–50*, 475–76).

54 Werman regards omission of Joseph's complaints about his prison circumstances (Gen 40:14-15) as part of a larger pattern in Jubilees that Joseph does not suffer in Egypt ("Attitude," 288). Further evidence comes from omitting Joseph's explanation for his son Ephraim's name (Gen 41:52: "For God has made me fruitful in the land of my misfortunes"). The same could be said for leaving out the interpretation of Manasseh's name where he refers to "all my hardship," although the reference to forgetting his father's house would not have served the author of Jubilees' purposes.

55 See Lange, "Divinatorische Träume," 28–30, 35. He relates the writer's rejection of allegorical dreams to his critical distance from the apocalyptic movement that saw great value in them. As Lange shows, Jubilees does not take a stance against all dreams—it even adds some to the text of Genesis; the problem is with allegorical dreams. See also Hanneken, *Subversion*, 252–57. Endres thinks the author's omission of the dream descriptions in the passage "suggests that their content (concerning the fate of these two Egyptian officials) would not further his program: would their 'Egyptian' referents distract his audience rather than teaching or consoling them?" (*Biblical Interpretation*, 183). That seems less likely than Lange's thesis.

cupbearing/butlership[56] but he hanged the baker "as Joseph had interpreted[57] for him." That was all the information needed.

■ **18** In spite of Joseph's success as a dream interpreter, his plea to the butler proved ineffective. As he summarized the dreams section of Genesis 40, the author of Jubilees included nothing about Joseph's conversation with this official. Yet after explaining the dream to him, Joseph had said, "But remember me when it is well with you; please do me the kindness to make mention of me to Pharaoh, and so get me out of this place. For in fact I was stolen out of the land of the Hebrews; and here also I have done nothing that they should have put me into the dungeon" (Gen 40:14-15). In Jubilees it is perhaps assumed that the reader knows this, though the writer did not record it in his more positive picture of Joseph's experience in Egypt. Verse 18 is based on Gen 40:23 but, unlike the other parts of the chapter, it expands the base text:

Genesis 40:23	Jubilees 39:18
Yet the chief cupbearer did not remember Joseph,	The chief butler forgot Joseph in prison although he had informed him (about) what would happen to him. He did not remember to tell Pharaoh what Joseph had told him
but forgot him.	because he forgot.

In this case the writer sensed a need to fill out the sparse text of Genesis, perhaps to explain that the cupbearer was not guilty of simply forgetting about Joseph; rather, he was guilty of not remembering his debt to Joseph and the specific request he had made of him. Joseph had predicted that the monarch would restore the butler to his former post—a job that would bring him into direct contact with Pharaoh, who would be in a position to release Joseph from his imprisonment. Perhaps Joseph thought there was no hope of Potiphar releasing him, or possibly he figured Pharaoh could overrule Potiphar. Whatever his thoughts may have been, he asked the chief butler, who should have felt deep gratitude to him, to remember him to Pharaoh, and, amazingly enough, he failed to do as requested. The formulation in Jubilees makes clearer exactly what it was the butler forgot and why it was such a serious omission on his part.

---

56 This appears to be the reading of 4Q223-224 unit 2 v:15, although only the first two letters of the word are preserved and neither is read with certainty. The Ethiopic text has *gebru*, "his work, occupation" (Leslau, *Concise Dictionary*, 206); the Ethiopic translation follows the approach in LXX Gen 40:21 (αρχην αυτου) rather than the more specific משקהו ("his cupbearing") in MT SP and the Hebrew fragment of Jubilees. The Latin translation of Jubilees reads *locum suum* ("his position"), as does the Vulgate Gen 40:21.

57 The Ethiopic text has "interpreted [*fakkara*]" in agreement with the versions of Gen 40:22, while Latin Jubilees has "said [*dixit*]," as does Josephus (*Ant.* 2.73). Earlier in v. 17 the Latin did refer to interpreting (*interpraetatus est*).

40

Joseph Interprets Pharaoh's Dreams and Becomes Ruler of Egypt

1/ At that time Pharaoh h<u>ad t</u>wo dreams in <u>o</u>ne night about the subject of^a the famine that would co<u>me on</u> the <u>who</u>le land.^b When he awakened, he summoned all the dream interpreters who were in Egypt^c and the enchanters. <u>He told</u> them his two dreams,^d but they were unable to interpret them.^e 2/ Then the chief butler remembered Joseph. After he had <u>told</u> the king^a <u>about</u> him, he was brought from prison and he related the^b <u>dreams</u>^c in his presence. 3/ He interpre<u>ted them</u>^a in Pharaoh's <u>presence</u>^b—that his^c two dreams were one. He said to him,^d "Seven years are coming^e (in which there will be) abundance i<u>n the entire land</u> of Egypt, but a<u>fter</u>wards^f there will be a seven-year famine, the like of which^g has never been in the entire <u>land</u>. 4/ <u>So now let</u> Pharaoh appoint of<u>ficers</u>^a throughout the entire land of Egypt and^b let them collect^c each city's^d food in the <u>city</u> during the period of the years of abundance.^e Then there will <u>be food</u>^f for the seven years of famine, and the land will not perish because of the famine, since it will be very severe."^g 5/ <u>God</u> gave Joseph a favorable and kind reception <u>before</u>^a <u>Pharaoh</u>. Pharaoh said to his servants,^b "We will not find^c a ma<u>n</u> as <u>wise</u> and knowledgeable^d as this man,^e for the spirit of God is with him."^f 6/ He appointed him as the second^a (in command) in his entire kingdom, gave him authority <u>over all the land of Egypt,</u>^b and <u>allowed him to ride</u>^c on Pharaoh's second <u>chariot</u>.^d 7/ He dressed <u>him</u> with <u>clothing</u> made of linen and put a gold chain on his neck. He made a proclamation^a before him^b and said, "Il il and abirer." <u>He put the</u> signet ring on his hand and made him ruler over his entire household. He made him great and said to him,^c "I will not be greater than <u>you except</u> with regard to the throne^d only."

8/ So Joseph became ruler over the entire land of Egypt. All of Pharaoh's princes, all of^a his servants, and all who were doing the king's work loved him because he conducted himself in a just way. He was not arrogant, proud, or partial, nor did he accept bribes because he was ruling all the people of the land in a just way. 9/ The land of Egypt lived in harmony before Pharaoh because of Joseph for the Lord was with him. He gave him a favorable and kind reception for all his family before all who knew him and who heard reports about him.^a Pharaoh's rule was just, and there was no satan or any evil one. 10/ The king named Joseph Sefantifanes and gave Joseph as a wife the daughter of Potiphar, the daughter of the priest of Heliopolis—the chief cook. 11^a/ On the day when Joseph took up his position with Pharaoh he was 30 years of age when he took up his position with Pharaoh. 12/ (Isaac died that year^a). Things turned out just as Joseph had reported^b about the interpretation of^c his^d two^e dreams, just as he had reported to him.^f There were seven years of abundance in the whole land of Egypt. The land of Egypt was most productive: one measure (would produce) 1800^g measures. 13/ Joseph collected (each) city's food in the city^a until^b it was so full of wheat that it was impossible to count or measure it^c because of its quantity.

Textual Notes

1a the subject of] om. Lat. Mss. 35 58 add: "plenty and about the subject of."

b the whole land] So Eth. and 4Q223-224 unit 2 v:19. Lat. om. "whole" though there is space for *omnem* where, at this point, Ceriani placed seven dots to mark the spot as illegible.

c Egypt] "in his kingdom" Lat. Eth. agrees with Gen 41:8.

d his two dreams] "his dreams" Lat.; Gen 41:8 also lacks "two." It is not clear that there is space for "two" in 4Q223-224 unit 2 v:20, though the text here is not preserved (DJD 13:133).

e to interpret them] The suffix on the verb is sg. because the word translated "dreams" (see previous note) is actually sg. in form, though "two" is read with it. Lat. = "to interpret his dreams for him". Eth. reads "understand," but Lat.'s verb "interpret" agrees with Gen 41:8. Reading a pronoun "them" (= Gen 41:8) seems preferable to Lat.'s "his dreams." For the reconstructed reading in DJD 13:127, the verb דעת with no suffix is proposed, but פתר may be better.

2a the king] Lit., "to the king." Mss. 25 35 39 42 44 47 48

1019

58 read *ḫaba*, suggesting the idea of "in the presence of." Lat. which places "king" in the dat. case adds "Pharaoh."

b the (dreams)] If frg. 35 is correctly placed, 4Q223–224 unit 2 v:22 lacks the suffix "his"; Lat. is illegible.

c dreams] Both Lat. and Eth. read "two" before "dreams," but there may not be space for it in 4Q223–224 unit 2 v:22. See DJD 13:133, where it is noted that space considerations are not very weighty in this context.

3a interpreted them] "interpreted" Lat.; "said" Eth. 4Q223–224 unit 2 v:22 is unclear: only a tip of the second-to-last letter and a final *mem* remain where the verb should be (see DJD 13:129 for the difficulty of reading the letter before final *mem*). Milik thought the *mem* was from אותם referring to the dreams. The proposed reading in DJD 13 is ויפת[רם, which, apart from the suffix, would agree with Lat. Genesis 41:25 reads as in Eth. (= "said").

b in Pharaoh's presence] 4Q223–224 unit 2 v:22 and Eth. agree that "before/in the presence of" belongs here; there is an illegible gap in the Lat. until the word "two."

c his] Lat. lacks.

d He said to him] Lat. reads *autem*, "but." Genesis 41:29 הנה. Mss. 21 63 omit "to him."

e are coming] See Gen 41:29. Lat. = "successive (years)," though the reading Ceriani marks as uncertain.

f afterwards] Lat. lacks, but 4Q223–224 unit 2 v:24 has most of "after," showing it had the expression (as in Gen 41:30).

g the like of which] Lat. *sic erit*, "so it will be" (cf. MS. 35: "will come")/"in the same way it will be." Eth., except 9 38 58, reads another instance of "famine" after this expression, but there may not have been space for it in 4Q223–224 unit 2 v:24. Mss. 17 20 omit from the first to the second instance of "famine."

4a officers] The reading of 4Q223–224 unit 2 v:25, though uncertain, verifies that Jubilees read as does Gen 41:34 פקדים. Lat. *speculators*, "overseers," seems a reasonable representation of the Heb. noun, but the Eth. reading is a puzzle. All the MSS. have a form related to the root *k-y-d*, "trample, tread" (Leslau, *Comparative Dictionary*, 301), and none of them seems correct in the context. Several explanations have been offered to account for Eth.: that words for an officer and the place for the officer's kind of work have been confused (Rönsch, *Jubiläen*, 157–58; Charles, *Ethiopic Version*, 146 n. 26; see *Jubilees*, 225). Charles emended to *mekwannena*. In addition to offering a puzzling word, the Eth. version also places it in an unusual position—after "throughout the entire land of Egypt" rather than before it as in the Heb. and Lat. See VanderKam, *Jubilees* 2:263–64.

b and] "who" Lat. Cf. Gen 41:35, which reads a conjunction.

c collect] The verbs in the two versions can both mean "collect," contrary to VanderKam, *Jubilees* 2:263–64.

d each city's] Lit. (Eth.), "for a city in a city" (MSS. 12 35 38 lack "in a city"); Lat.: "the individual cities." Cf. Gen 41:35 and v. 13 below.

e during the period of the years of abundance] "and store it during the seven years of abundance" Lat. Both versions speak about the years of abundance (Eth. lacks "seven"). How the difference arose is not clear.

f Then there will be food] "as food that will be" Lat. 4Q223–224 unit 2 v:26 may support the Eth. reading. Eth. and Lat. reflect different phrases in Gen 41:36. See VanderKam, *Jubilees* 2:264.

g severe] Lat. adds: "over the entire land." There is no basis for this in Gen 41:31, and there probably is not space for it in 4Q223–224 unit 2 v:27. In fact, the Heb. may also have lacked "very" (DJD 13:134).

5a before] So Lat. and 4Q223–224 unit 2 v:27; Eth. = "before the eyes of."

b to his servants] pr. "to his people and" 21 39 48.

c We will not find] "Will we be able to find" Lat. The verse rewrites Gen 41:38, which phrases Pharaoh's words as a question as in Lat. See VanderKam, *Jubilees* 2:264; DJD 13:127, 130 (where "Will we find" is proposed).

d as wise and knowledgeable] Lat. uses comparative forms as in LXX Gen 41:39.

e this man] Lat. lacks "man," as does MS. 12.

f with him] "upon him" 9 21 38 (= Eth. Gen 41:38).

6a second] + "to himself" Lat.

b the land of Egypt] So 4Q223–224 unit 2 v:29 and Lat. (and Gen 41:43); Eth. om. "the land of," other than 39ᵗ.

c allowed him to ride] Or: "caused him to ride." Lat. = "put him."

d second chariot] Eth. places a suffix "his" on "chariot," but it seems superfluous with, lit., "of Pharaoh" at the end of the verse. Lat. lacks it, and if the letter *he* is correctly read in 4Q223–224 unit 2 v:29, and it is the definite article, the following noun "chariot" would not have had a suffix.

7a He made a proclamation] "They made a proclamation" Lat. It is likely that the pl. in Lat. resulted when εκηρυξεν and εκηρυξαν were confused. See Littmann, "Jubiläen," 106 n. d; VanderKam, *Jubilees* 2:265. In Gen 41:43, MT reads a pl. "they," but SP LXX have the sg.

b before him] + "and said" Eth. No version of Gen 41:43 has the plus except the Fragment Targum.

c (and said) to him] Lat. lacks.

d the throne] "my throne" Lat. No version of Gen 41:40 reads a possessive, though a few LXX witnesses (and Eth. Jub. MS. 35) do. See Charles, *Ethiopic Version*, 148 n. 3.

8a all of (his servants)] Lat. lacks.

9a about him] lit., "with him."

11a For whether the last clause "when he took up his posi-

12a	that year] "that day/time and year" 38; "that day/time" 63.	e	two] om. 42 47.
b	had reported] + "to him" 9 38.	f	(reported) to him] om. 25 35 44.
c	the interpretation of] om. 21; "two interpretations" 17 (which om. mention of the dreams).	g	1800] The number is expressed as 10 and 8 hundred; mss. 20 21 35 38 lack "hundred."
d	his] om. 12.	13a	in the city] om. 20 25 38 44.
		b	until] om. 21; "because" 38.
		c	count or measure it] The suffix "it" is actually attached to the first infinitive (the suffix is omitted by 20 25 35).

Commentary

Chapter 39 ended with the royal butler restored to his lofty position in Pharaoh's court and Joseph, who predicted his restoration, forgotten in prison. Chapter 40 swiftly traces his ascent from the depths of confinement to the heights of power in Egypt, where ideal conditions resulted from his just administration. The account is a rewriting of Genesis 41, which the author drastically condensed, reducing the first forty-six verses to just thirteen.

Jubilees 40 falls into two major parts:
1-7 Pharaoh's dreams and Joseph's appointment as second ruler in Egypt
8-13 Joseph's just rule over Egypt

The texts for Jubilees 40, apart from the full Ethiopic version are two:
Hebrew: 4Q223-224 unit 2 v:18-32: vv. 1-7
Latin: vv. 1-8.

1-7 Pharaoh's Dreams and Joseph's Appointment as Second Ruler in Egypt

The writer's procedure in this section resembles the way he handled the dreams of the butler and baker in chap. 39: he leaves out the lengthy descriptions of Pharaoh's two dreams, both where the narrator relates them in Gen 41:1-7 (with the king's reaction in v. 8) and where Pharaoh tells them to Joseph in vv. 17-24. The omission constitutes more than just an exercise in eliminating duplication; the rewriter erases virtually everything. In fact, of the first twenty-four verses in Genesis 41, apart from a few summary words, he reproduces only the part of v. 8 regarding the inability of the Egyptian experts to interpret the dreams (Jub 40:1b).

■ 1 As implied by Genesis, Jubilees reports that Pharaoh had two dreams in one night. The author passes over the chronological note "After two whole years" at the beginning of Gen 41:1. He had already indicated that Joseph remained in prison for two years before the butler and baker joined him (39:13), so he seems to have thought the notice referred to that period of time since he introduces the chapter with "At that time." It did not define the interval between restoration of the butler and Pharaoh's two dreams as Genesis suggests.[1] So little interest does the writer show in the two symbolic dreams seen by Pharaoh that he never mentions their contents and says concerning them only that they were "about the subject of the famine that would come on the whole land"[2] (v. 1; see Gen 41:27, 30-31, 36)—thus removing any dramatic tension from the narrative. In v. 1 he notes no more than that the ruler had the two dreams in one night (see Gen 41:5 and 22 [LXX]), their real subject (the famine), and the failure of the dream interpreters and enchanters to understand them after hearing them recounted by Pharaoh (see Gen 41:8). Where Gen 41:8 refers to two kinds of dream experts—"magicians" and "wise men"—Jubilees speaks of "dream interpreters [*mafaqqerāna*[3] *ḥelm/interpraetes somniorum*]" and "enchanters [*raqāyt/praecantatores*]."

■ 2 Genesis 41:9-24 contains the story about how the chief butler, upon seeing what was happening, remembered Joseph and his successful interpretations of the dreams he and the chief baker had seen. Pharaoh then summoned Joseph from the dungeon. Joseph, after

---

1 See Hamilton, *Genesis 18-50*, 486.
2 The words translated "land"—*medr/terra*—could also mean "earth."
3 Ethiopic Gen 41:8 uses the same word but not with a following *ḥelm*.

tidying himself up to be presentable to the ruler, entered his presence and informed him that God was the real interpreter of dreams. Thereupon Pharaoh divulged the two dreams to him and the failure of the magicians to explain them. All of this the writer of Jubilees condenses into v. 2: "The chief butler remembered Joseph [see Gen 41:9]. After he had told the king about him [Gen 41:10-13], he was brought from prison [Gen 41:14] and he related the dreams in his presence [Gen 41:17-24a]." The heavy abbreviation in this instance could be attributed to a literary desire not to repeat material, but the reduction of the Genesis story is more extreme than that. For example, when Joseph, after shaving and changing his clothes,[4] was ushered into the monarch's presence, a conversation ensued: "And Pharaoh said to Joseph, 'I have had a dream, and there is no one who can interpret it. I have heard it said of you that when you hear a dream you can interpret it.' Joseph answered Pharaoh, 'It is not I; God will give Pharaoh a favorable answer'" (41:15-16). Why would the author bypass a theologically congenial[5] passage like this—just as he omitted the parallel one in Gen 40:8? The answer could be related to his discomfort with symbolic dreams: attributing interpretations to the Lord would entail that he was involved with decoding such dreams. From Jubilees one gains the impression that the deity communicates more clearly than through symbols or allegories. As Hanneken puts the matter,

> Dramatically different from the apocalypses, and even compared to the base text of Genesis, Jubilees disambiguates revelation. Jubilees avoids allegorical symbolism and potentially ambiguous visions. Jubilees does not communicate in code, does not read Genesis as if a code, and downplays codes that do appear in Genesis. Jubilees introduces angelic teachers not as interpretive guides of fantastic visions but as tutors for language and memory skills, guaranteeing the clarity and accuracy of the laws and testimony.[6]

The symbols, therefore, could be jettisoned; only the heart of the message was needed—the dreams presaged the great famine that would soon strike the land (or earth). Almost all of the other details in this part of Genesis 41 were not germane to the writer's purposes and could be omitted. Just a few words convey Joseph's rise from prison to Pharaoh's presence.

■ **3** For the interpretation of the two dreams (though in Gen 41:15, 24, 25 mention is made of just one) the writer follows much of the text in Gen 41:25, 29-30. As in Genesis, Joseph tells Pharaoh that the two dreams are in fact one (Genesis says this twice—41:25 and 26) and informs him that there will be seven years of plenty followed by seven years of an unprecedented famine. The author does not select all features of v. 25—he leaves out "God has revealed to Pharaoh what he is about to do" (he also omits v. 28, which largely repeats these words). But he completely omits the two verses (26 and 27) in which Joseph explains the specific meaning of the seven good cows/good ears and the seven bad cows/bad ears (e.g., "The seven good cows are seven years, and the seven good ears are seven years" [v. 26]). The writer leaves no trace of the passages in which Joseph decodes mysterious symbols. Joseph, who does not use the word "great" to describe the abundance of the good years as in Gen 41:29, also explains the unique gravity of the coming famine in a briefer way than in the base text. In Genesis, Joseph tells

---

4 Werman suggests that the process of improving his appearance was not needed in Jubilees because he was a free person in prison (*Jubilees*, 485).

5 It may be that the writer was concerned about Joseph's claim "God will give Pharaoh a favorable answer," when the interpretation included a heavily negative side (the seven-year famine). The meaning of the expression is not entirely clear. It reads literally, "God will answer the peace/welfare of Pharaoh." Westermann rather generously paraphrases it as saying, "Even though I have to interpret tidings of misfortune to you, what God has to say to you will ultimately result in prosperity" (*Genesis 37–50*, 89).

6 Hanneken, *Subversion*, 252-53. Specifically regarding the passages in Jubilees 39 and 40, he comments, "Jubilees is not trying to replace Genesis or polemicizing against the legitimacy of allegorical dreams in Genesis, but Jubilees does present its own revelation according to its 'no nonsense' view of revelation. Whatever complex and ambiguous stories may have been received by Israel, the bottom line of covenantal fidelity, the law, and the testimony is completely unambiguous" (p. 254). See also Lange, "Divinatorische Träume," 27-30, 35.

Pharaoh, "all the plenty will be forgotten in the land of Egypt; the famine will consume the land. The plenty will no longer be known in the land because of the famine that will follow, for it will be very grievous" (41:30b-31). This becomes in Jub 40:3 "a seven-year famine, the like of which has never been in the entire land." The author also saw fit not to copy Gen 41:32 with its divinatory implications: "And the doubling of Pharaoh's dream means that the thing is fixed by God, and God will shortly bring it about." The Joseph of Jubilees deals with the facts—especially the famine—and discards any words that suggest the Lord communicates through mantic media. The author so thoroughly truncates the text of Genesis that one could read his entire story about Pharaoh's dreams and never learn that God sent them. That information comes later.

■ **4** Joseph not only interprets Pharaoh's dream but also offers a plan of action for coping with the two seven-year periods he has just predicted were to transpire. He describes his proposal to the monarch in Gen 41:33-36, and the writer of Jubilees again trims his words to a single verse. Placing the two units side by side illustrates the nature of the rewriting in Jubilees.

Genesis 41:33-36 (with v. 31)	Jubilees 40:4
Now therefore let Pharaoh select a man who is discerning and wise, and set him over the land of Egypt.	So now let Pharaoh
Let Pharaoh proceed to appoint overseers over the land, and take one-fifth of the produce of the land of Egypt during the seven plenteous years. Let them gather all the food of these good years that are coming, and lay up grain under the authority of Pharaoh for food in the cities, and let them keep it.	appoint officers throughout the entire land of Egypt

and let them collect each city's food in the city during the period of the years of abundance. |
| That food shall be a reserve for the land against the seven years of famine that are to befall the land of Egypt, so that the land may not perish through the famine. (v. 31 ... for it will be very grievous.) | Then there will be food for the seven years of famine, and the land will not perish because of the famine, since it will be very severe. |

The first and most glaring difference, aside from the brevity of Jubilees, is that Joseph does not suggest choosing "a man who is discerning and wise, and set him over the land of Egypt." He calls only for the appointment of officers/overseers throughout the land. In addition, he does not say these officers should "take one-fifth of the produce of the land of Egypt during the seven plenteous years" or that they should "gather all the food of these good years that are coming." The only task he envisages for them is collecting "each city's food in the city," and even that assignment is to be done by them and not (at least not explicitly), "under the authority of Pharaoh." Joseph's program will ensure that there will be food during the famine years rather than mass starvation under the extreme conditions anticipated. In Jubilees he envisages less intrusion by the central government (no one-fifth tax, no countrywide gathering of food) and focuses more on the local level. Each city will have its own food collected there to save up for the bad years that are coming. This last policy is, nevertheless, drawn from Genesis but from a different location (41:48).

■ **5** The interpretation involved in the rewriting becomes evident again when the relevant passages from Genesis are compared with v. 5.

Genesis 41:37-39	Jubilees 40:5
The proposal pleased Pharaoh and all his servants.	God gave Joseph a favorable and kind reception before Pharaoh.
Pharaoh said to his servants, "Can we find anyone else like this—one in whom is the spirit of God?" So Pharaoh said to Joseph, "Since God has shown you all this, there is no one so discerning and wise as you."	Pharaoh said to his servants, "We will not find a man as wise and knowledgeable as this man,[7] for the spirit of God is with him."[8]

The writer of Jubilees begins the verse by giving the reason why Joseph's proposal appealed to Pharaoh: it

---

[7] The Latin translation of Jubilees phrases this sentence as a rhetorical question, and Gen 41:38 (quoted above) does as well. LXX Gen 41:38 makes it part of a question anticipating a negative answer: "Surely we shall not [μή] find such a person, who has a divine spirit within [sic]?" The Ethiopic version of Jubilees seems to have rendered an expression like the one in LXX as a declarative sentence. See VanderKam, *Jubilees* 2:264. In DJD 13:127 (4Q223-224 unit 2 v:28) הנמצא is proposed in a gap, but the reading is, of course, uncertain.

[8] It is not clear how Werman ("Attitude," 290) can

was because of the pleasing qualities with which God endowed Joseph. In this way he makes the present scene parallel the one in the prison where he used the same words (39:12). It is also similar to Joseph's experience in Potiphar's house, although there the vocabulary is different (39:3-4). The Lord's presence with Joseph continues to manifest itself wherever he goes, whether it is a good place or a bad one. The fact that God envelops Joseph with his favor and thus induces his audience to admire him is what leads the ruler to address his servants; it was not just the quality of Joseph's proposed plan.

Pharaoh perceives in Joseph a very wise and knowledgeable man. These adjectives derive from the beginning of Joseph's proposal in Genesis where he urged the monarch to "select a man who is discerning and wise, and set him over the land of Egypt" (41:33). Jubilees lacks the line, but Pharaoh repeated the two words in speaking to Joseph in 41:39: "Since God has shown you all this, there is no one so discerning and wise as you." In Jubilees it is the monarch who perceives the character of Joseph; Joseph does not call for the appointment of a person with these traits and certainly did not hint to Pharaoh that he name him to the crucial position. He appears more humble in Jubilees, where he never calls for Pharaoh to designate one person over the preparations for the famine years. Pharaoh's reason for wanting Joseph to head up the project is worded differently in Genesis and Jubilees. In Genesis he gives as his reason, "Since God has shown you all this," where "all this" refers to the message of his dreams. He is pointing to the special information God gave Joseph so he could decode the symbols that disturbed Pharaoh's sleep. The author of Jubilees expunges all of that from the record and sees the spirit of the Lord in him because of the favor the Lord gave him before Pharaoh; with the direction provided by the divine spirit, his idea for dealing with the coming catastrophe could only be brilliant. It has nothing to do with divinatory skills.

■ **6-7** As a result, though Joseph had not included himself in the blueprint for Egypt's survival, Pharaoh appoints the freed prisoner to the position he described in Gen 41:33. The writer summarizes and rearranges material in Gen 41:41-44 (with borrowings from v. 40) in vv. 6-7.

Genesis 41:41-44	Jubilees 40:6-7
And Pharaoh said to Joseph, "See, I have set you over all the land of Egypt." Removing his signet ring from his hand, Pharaoh put it on Joseph's hand; he arrayed him in garments of fine linen, and put a gold chain around his neck. He had him ride in the chariot of his second-in-command; and they cried out in front of him, "Bow the knee!" Thus he set him over all the land of Egypt. Moreover, Pharaoh said to Joseph, "I am Pharaoh, and without your consent no one shall lift up hand or foot in all the land of Egypt."	He appointed him as the second (in command) in his entire kingdom, gave him authority over all the land of Egypt, and allowed him to ride on Pharaoh's second chariot.[9] He dressed him with clothing made of linen and put a gold chain on his neck. He made a proclamation before him and said, "Il il and abirer." He put the signet ring on his hand and made him ruler over his entire household. He made him great and said to him, "I will not be greater than you except with regard to the throne only."

The author uses the elements in Gen 41:41-44 but at times presents them in a different order and with slightly different content.

First, both units begin with statements about Joseph's rule over Egypt. Genesis mentions this twice in these verses (41, 43), but Jubilees brings them together at the beginning (second in command, authority over the whole country). In addition, Jubilees moves the notice about the chariot, a symbol of his status as second only to Pharaoh in Egypt, to this point, possibly because the writer thought it was a more logical place for it, given its relation to the lines regarding his position in the Egyptian hierarchy.

Second, the ruler endows Joseph with symbols of authority and wealth.[10] The order of the items is not the same:

---

claim that, in Jubilees, Pharaoh does not mention God's name, since he does so here in v. 5 in a quotation (not from the narrator), just as in Genesis (four of the six letters of אלהים can be read on 4Q223-224 unit 2 v:28.

9 The expressions in Gen 41:43//Jub 40:6 are the same, except that in Jubilees "Pharaoh's" replaces "his" in Genesis.

10 Werman overstates the case regarding the difference between Genesis and Jubilees at this point ("Attitude," 289-90). She says that in Genesis Pharaoh gives Joseph his power (citing 41:44), while

Genesis	Jubilees
Signet ring	Linen clothing
Linen garments	Gold chain
Gold chain	Proclamation
Chariot	Signet ring
Proclamation	

The Genesis sequence chariot + proclamation is reasonable because the proclamation would likely be made when Joseph rode on this vehicle, but since Jubilees had attached the chariot notice to the general statements about ruling the land it does not repeat it in this list. The signet ring the writer moved to a position just before the concluding items (see *Third* below), perhaps because he thought it more naturally went with those statements about Joseph's authority and status. Anyone who has read through the Joseph stories from the beginning will be struck by another instance in which clothing figures at a major turning point in his career. As his brothers soaked his coat in blood when they sold him into slavery (34:12) and Potiphar's wife used his garment as evidence leading to his imprisonment (39:10-11), so now the monarch dresses him in linen to mark his ascent to power over Egypt.

The proclamations made before Joseph are interesting to compare. Genesis 41:43 reads a curious word, אברך, that has, naturally, attracted various interpretations. Some modern scholars have related it to Egyptian terms,[11] but the ancient expositors proceeded with the evidence they had. One option was to associate it with the Hebrew root ברך that concerns the knees in some way and to explain the proclamation as a summons for people to bow to Joseph. Another was to split the word in two: the first two consonants אב mean "father" and the second two are an Aramaic word for "king" (רכה); the proclamation, therefore, designates Joseph the father of the king (so all the targums[12] to the passage). Proponents of this derivation could appeal to Gen 45:8, where Joseph tells his brothers God had made him a father to Pharaoh. The Greek translation of Genesis reads κηρυξ ("herald"), that is, it says simply that a herald called out (something) in front of him. The versions of Jubilees offer words that appear to be transcriptions of Hebrew terms.

Ethiopic: 'il 'il[13] wa-'abirer
Latin: elel et habirel

'il 'il/elel should be the word אל ("god") repeated, while 'abir-/habir- could be transcriptions of אביר, the epithet for God in Gen 49:24 (part of Jacob's blessing of Joseph);[14] the last letters may again represent אל (note the letter *l* at the end of the Latin form). The expression would then mean: God, God, the mighty one of God. Though an Egyptian is the one who orders that these words be said before Joseph, for the author אל אל may have had the more modest sense of "hero, hero."[15]

---

in Jubilees (she refers to 40:9) it comes from God. However, Pharaoh is the subject of the verbs used for appointing and honoring Joseph, and Pharaoh does say he will be greater than Joseph on the throne. Moreover, it is not true that in Jubilees, unlike Genesis, it is Joseph who rules, not Pharaoh, and that therefore the governance was just. Note that Jub 40:9 says it is Pharaoh's rule that is just.

11 See the summary of views in Hamilton, *Genesis 18–50*, 506 (one suggestion relates it to an Egyptian word meaning "do homage").
12 All of them except Onqelos add that he was great in wisdom but tender/young (an interpretation of the last two consonants, רך) in years. See also *Gen. Rab.* 90:3.
13 These two words are spelled *'ēl 'ēl* in MSS. 12 21 35 38 42 44.
14 Berger thinks that the description of Joseph in Gen 49:22 lies behind the proclamation (*Jubiläen*, 519 n. b to v. 7). He follows those who find reference to a bull (שור) in that verse (vocalized in MT as the word sharing the same consonants but meaning "wall"), and, as he claims, the word אביר can also mean "bull" (see *DCH* 1:106). There are too many uncertainties in his proposal (see Westermann [*Genesis 37–50*, 237] for a rejection of the animal interpretation of Gen 49:22), and a simpler one is available (see below).
15 This is the way in which Rönsch explained the words called out before Joseph (*Jubiläen*, 158–59). Regarding the meaning of the title for a monotheistic writer, he suggested, "God is (and remains) God, and Joseph is a hero on whom God has bestowed strength" or, better, "Hero [= a possible meaning of אל], Hero, mighty Hero." He was able to cite a text—the History of Aseneth—in which Joseph is called "the mighty one of God" (see also Charles, *Jubilees*, 226). To Rönsch's citations from this later text, one can add that the title figures several times in Joseph and Aseneth: in 4:7

Third, Genesis and Jubilees add (a) a statement about ruling, and (b) a statement about the relationship between Pharaoh and Joseph. In the statement about ruling, Genesis repeats the idea that Pharaoh set Joseph over all the land, but Jubilees says he "made him ruler over his entire household." The reference to the king's household comes from Gen 41:40 (see 45:8). So, rather than repeat the notion of ruling that both texts mentioned at the beginning of this unit, the writer of Jubilees uses an alternate formulation from a verse just before it. In doing that, however, he reminds the reader of another household over which Joseph held sway—that of Potiphar (Gen 39:4-5; Jub 39:3). There too he controlled the entire establishment with one exception. That exception comes to expression in the next line in Jubilees.

In speaking about the relationship between the two men, Pharaoh says in Gen 41:44, "I am Pharaoh, and without your consent no one shall lift up hand or foot in all the land of Egypt." In Jubilees he makes Joseph great and declares, "I will not be greater than you except with regard to the throne only." The writer has taken the statement from Gen 41:40 to make the point that there is a limit on Joseph's authority in the palace, just as there was in Potiphar's household where only his wife was not under Joseph's control (39:9). So, for a second time the rank Joseph held with Pharaoh parallels his status in Potiphar's house.[16]

8-13 Joseph's Just Rule over Egypt

Though the unit Jub 40:1-7 constitutes a drastic shortening of the account in Gen 41:1-45, the section still pursues the same story line; but in vv. 8-13 the writer operates more independently of the base text. Jubilees 40:8, 10-11, 13 are connected with Gen 41:44c, 45-46, 50, but other parts of the section delineate a picture of Joseph's ideal rule over the land of Egypt. The depiction is not inconsistent with Genesis's words regarding his governance, but it moves well beyond them to make points important to the author.

■ 8[17] The verse draws the previous episode to a close as it introduces the next one—now Joseph is indeed "ruler over the entire land of Egypt." The idea derives from the

---

Pentephres (Potiphar) calls Joseph "the Powerful One of God" (in 8:9 Joseph appeals to the deity as "the Powerful one of Jacob"); cf. 11:7, 9; 18:1; 21:21. Rönsch also adduced the comments of Jerome about the title: "Instead of what Aquila translated as: *And he called for the bowing of the knee before him*, Symmachus takes up the Hebrew word itself and says: *And he called before him abrech*. Consequently, it seems to me that neither 'crier' nor 'bowing the knee', which can be taken as a greeting or entreating of Joseph, should be understood, so much as what the Hebrews hand on by tradition when they say that from this word *tender father* is in fact to be translated. For *ab* means 'father', and *rech* 'soft' or 'most tender'; and the Scripture indicates that he was indeed father of all in respect of sound judgement, but a very tender young man, even a boy in respect of his age" (trans. Hayward, *Jerome's Hebrew Questions*, 77–78; see also p. 226). Kugel considers the possibility that Jubilees derives the title from אבירך (your Mighty One) (*Walk through Jubilees*, 181). In that case, the meaning would be "God, God is your [i.e., Joseph's] Mighty One," though Kugel calls this "only a guess."

16 Cf. Hamilton, *Genesis 18–50*, 503–4 (commenting on Gen 41:39-40).

17 Niehoff thinks the description in vv. 8-9 replaces Genesis's picture of his harsh rule (*Figure of Joseph*, 45–46), but 45:8-12 is the parallel to the section about his harsh rule in Gen 47:13-26. Jubilees 40:8-9 deals with material in Genesis 41. She correctly sees, however, that "the most important items, namely uprightness, modesty and the absence of evil and Satan, are typical features of *Jub*'s religious views and certainly not identifiably Greek" (p. 46; see below for these themes in these verses). In this statement she is reacting negatively to Büchler ("Traces," 329–30), who claimed that the picture in 40:8-9—praise of Joseph as governor and judge in Egypt and general recognition of his personality and services to Egypt—was meant in the first place to impress the non-Jewish reader in Egypt with what the ancestor of the Jews had done in the country where Jews were publicly attacked. Docherty also sees contemporary relevance in the description of Joseph as ruler in these verses ("Joseph the Patriarch," 211–12), though she does not assign the book to Egypt and acknowledges that, according to many experts, the author had a more positive view of the Hasmonean rulers of his time.

end of Gen 41:45: "Thus Joseph gained authority over the land of Egypt,"[18] though the language is closer to other statements about his role (e.g., 41:41, 43; 45:8, 26). Like Potiphar and the chief of the prison guards before him, Pharaoh placed everything in his jurisdiction under Joseph's control. Once the author has made this general remark about the status Joseph had suddenly attained, he fleshes out the nature of Joseph's rule in a way quite unlike the presentation in Genesis.[19]

He begins by reporting that "All of Pharaoh's princes [see Gen 12:15 for the phrase], all of his servants, and all who were doing the king's work loved him." There are several references in the Joseph stories in Genesis to Pharaoh's servants (41:37, 38; 45:16; 50:7) but none to the other categories of officials, and in no passage in Genesis does one read that any of Pharaoh's servants loved Joseph. The information in Genesis about the reaction to Joseph's rule in Egypt is sparse, but the few lines that do address the subject could lead one to suspect it might not have been as favorable as Jubilees makes it seem. True, Joseph himself says to his brothers, "You must tell my father how greatly I am honored in Egypt" (45:13), but his administration during the famine years seems harsh and even exploitative. Genesis 47:13-26 describes how Joseph first took all the money of people in Egypt and Canaan in exchange for food; once he had transferred all their money to the royal coffers, he demanded and received their livestock as the price for additional food; and when that source of exchange was exhausted he purchased their land and persons—that is, he made slaves of them—and demanded one-fifth of the crops they raised with the seed he provided for them. In the end, however, they accepted these conditions because "You have saved our lives" (47:25).[20]

For the author of Jubilees there were good reasons why the royal officials loved Joseph:

He was not arrogant or proud. According to *Exod. Rab.* 1:7 (commenting on the note in Exod 1:5 about Joseph's presence in Egypt): "although Joseph had attained royal office, he was not haughty towards his brothers and his father's family; but just as he was humble in his own eyes when he was at first only a slave in Egypt, so was he still humble even after he became vice-regent."[21]

He was not partial (lit., did not lift the face).

He did not take bribes.

He ruled all the people of the land in a just way.[22] Werman wishes to connect the statement with Gen 41:57

---

18   A literal translation is: "And Joseph went out over the land of Egypt." *Targum Pseudo-Jonathan* Gen 41:45 renders it as "And Joseph went forth *as ruler* over the land of Egypt," and *Targum Onqelos* translates as "Thus Joseph emerged as ruler over the land of Egypt." According to Werman, the writer of Jubilees places this statement at an earlier point than Genesis to show that Joseph was more than just an ad hoc ruler for the two periods of seven years (Genesis implies this more limited role for him) (*Jubilees*, 486).

19   Philo attaches a short statement about Joseph's governance to his rendering of Gen 41:45 (and 46): "Joseph, thus appointed viceroy to the king and promoted to the superintendence of Egypt, took a journey to make himself known to all the people of the country. He visited the nomes, as they are called, city by city, and made his presence very welcome to those who saw him, not only through the benefits which they received from him, but through the remarkable and exceptional charm of his appearance and his general deportment" (*Jos.* 157 [Colson, LCL]).

20   According to Josephus (*Ant.* 2.192-93), after the famine Joseph returned the land to its former owners permanently, though it still belonged to the king; they were to pay the king a tax of one-fifth their crops. Naturally, this strengthened Joseph's reputation and the people's loyalty to Pharaoh. On the significance of Joseph's action for Josephus, see Niehoff, *Figure of Joseph*, 108-9.

21   The translator, S. M. Lehrman, comments that the line "Joseph was in Egypt" is taken in the sense that "he was still the same Joseph in Egypt" (*Midrash Rabbah Exodus*, 8 n. 4; NRSV translates as "Joseph was already in Egypt"). See Hartom, "Jubilees," 118 n. to v. 8.

22   See T. Jos. 20:5-6: "And all Israel mourned for him [Joseph] and all Egypt with a great mourning. For he also had sympathy with the Egyptians as with his own members and showed them kindness, aiding them in every work and counsel and matter." Cf. Josephus, *Ant.* 2.94 (once the famine begins): "Nor did he open the market to the natives only; strangers also were permitted to buy, for Joseph held that all men, in virtue of their kinship, should receive succour from those in prosperity" (Thackeray, LCL). Later, after recounting Joseph's

("Moreover, all the world came to Joseph in Egypt to buy grain, because the famine became severe throughout the world") and thinks the writer turns the nations of the world into servants of Joseph,[23] but the line more likely refers to the Egyptians in Gen 41:55-56.

■ **9** The results were that

The land of Egypt lived in harmony before Pharaoh because of Joseph for the Lord was with him. For harmony, see 46:1; for the Lord being with Joseph, see 39:4 (in Potiphar's house); 39:12 (in prison); 40:5 (Pharaoh says the spirit of God is with him)

He gave him a favorable and kind reception for all his family.[24] This is the third time Jubilees uses the expression "a favorable and kind reception" in connection with Joseph: 39:12 (in prison); 40:5 (before Pharaoh). The Lord arranged the highly positive reactions to Joseph not only from people who had direct acquaintance with him but also from anyone who even heard about him.[25] Even the rumor mill was favorable to Joseph.

Pharaoh's rule was just.
There was no satan or any evil one.

The last characteristic reminds one of those other passages in the book in which the absence of a satan is noted; all of them speak of ideal times. The occurrence in 46:2 parallels the present one because "There was no satan or any evil one throughout all of Joseph's lifetime that he lived after his father Jacob because all the Egyptians were honoring the children of Israel for all of Joseph's lifetime." The passage follows a verse in which the narrator says the Israelites were numerous and unified and they loved and helped one another. The expression recurs in eschatological contexts. One is in Jub 23:29, part of the depiction of the new age when people will be numerous and live lives of antediluvian length in peace and joy: "There will be neither a satan nor any evil one who will destroy. For their entire lifetimes will be times of blessing and healing." The final occurrence is in the last chapter where the angel predicts that Israel will become pure of evil and live confidently in the land: "They will no longer have any satan or any evil one. The land will be pure from that time until eternity" (50:5). The implication is that the way in which Joseph governed the country produced conditions matching those anticipated in eschatological times.

Berger maintains that the writer presents Joseph's rule as an ideal time of deliverance and that it has a messianic character. He notes the connection between the absence of a satan and an evil one (or evil) as a characteristic of the final age; he adds that the other traits attributed to Joseph (he is a just judge, beloved, there is peace, God is with him, and the kingdom is properly ordered) are typical of a broadly attested tradition regarding earthly-messianic expectations for salvation.[26] It seems unhelpful to use the term "messianic" in connection with the picture in Jub 40:8-9, but there is no doubting the relation between the two eschatological passages in chaps. 23 and 50 and the present one (with 46:1-2). Endres, building on Berger's insights, also speaks about the eschatological imagery joining Jub

---

death, the historian writes: "a man of admirable virtue, who directed all affairs by the dictates of reason and made but sparing use of his authority; to which fact he owed that great prosperity of his among the Egyptians, albeit he had come as a stranger and in such pitiable circumstances as we have previously described" (2.198). Artapanus (frg. 2) pictures Joseph as introducing land reforms in Egypt and as beloved by the Egyptians for his achievements.

23 Werman, *Jubilees*, 486.
24 For *zamad* Leslau lists "kin, family, related, relative, race, tribe, species" (*Concise Dictionary*, 184). The referent is unclear, as Joseph has no family with him at this time. Perhaps it refers proleptically to the time when they would be in Egypt or to Joseph's wife, children (see v. 10; 44:24), and descendants.
25 Werman cautiously suggests that Gen 45:16 ("Pharaoh and his servants were pleased"—when they heard Joseph's brothers had arrived) has been transferred to this point and applied to Joseph to show how highly he was regarded by those mentioned here (*Jubilees*, 486).
26 Berger, *Jubiläen*, 518 n. a to chap. 40.

40:8-9 with Jubilees 23. He places in parallel columns these two units:

Jubilees 40:8-9	Jubilees 23:23, 29
So Joseph became ruler over the entire land of Egypt. All of Pharaoh's princes, all of his servants, and all who were doing the king's work loved him because he conducted himself in a just way. He was not arrogant, proud, or partial, nor did he accept bribes because he was ruling all the people of the land in a just way.	He will arouse against them the sinful nations who will have no mercy or kindness for them and who will show partiality to no one, whether old or young, or anyone at all....
The land of Egypt lived in harmony before Pharaoh because of Joseph for the Lord was with him. He gave him a favorable and kind reception for all his family before all who knew him and who heard reports about him. Pharaoh's rule was just, and there was no satan or any evil one.	They will complete and live their entire lifetimes peacefully and joyfully. There will be neither a satan nor any evil one who will destroy. For their entire lifetimes will be times of blessing and healing.

The overlaps between 40:8 and 23:23 mostly provide a contrast between the best and worst of times, while those between 40:9 and 23:29 concern only the best. Endres concludes from the evidence: "Joseph's stewardship in Egypt, then, presented the Jubilees community with a glimpse of the end-times promised by God for those who adhere to the commands of the covenant, and especially those revealed from the heavens."[27]

Besides the parallels Berger and Endres noticed, there are important ones in the descriptions of God himself as righteous judge. The qualities practiced by Joseph as ideal ruler match those exercised by God as he weighs human actions:

Jubilees 5:16	Jubilees 40:8
He is not one who shows favoritism nor one who takes a bribe, if he says he will execute judgment against everyone. If someone gave everything on earth he would not show favoritism nor would he accept (it) from him because he is the righteous judge.	... loved him because he conducted himself in a just way. He was not arrogant, proud, or partial,[28] nor did he accept bribes because he was ruling all the people of the land in a just way.

Abraham described the Lord in similar terms in his testament to Isaac: "For he is the living God. He is more holy, faithful, and just than anyone. With him there is no favoritism nor does he accept bribes because he is a just God and one who exercises judgment against all who transgress his commands and despise his covenant" (21:4; cf. vv. 19, 20). And the angel tells Moses after the Reuben-Bilhah episode that no one was to act in this way "because the Lord our God, who shows no favoritism and takes no bribe, is the judge" (33:18).[29] It causes little wonder, then, that Joseph proved to be an astonishingly adept governor if he imitated the character and practices of the deity.

■ 10 To mark his new status, Pharaoh bestowed a name on Joseph and provided him with a wife of sufficient rank. Genesis 41:45 is the source for both Joseph's special name and for the identity and family connections of his spouse. Joseph's name in Genesis is Zaphenath-paneah (MT צפנת פענח); Jubilees transcribes it, and the spellings in the Ethiopic manuscripts vary. One that enjoys some support is *sefānṭifānes*, where the vowel *i* is like the one in SP Gen 41:45 (it spells the first part of the name as צפנתי). The unusual words have spawned many attempts at interpretation, both ancient and modern. One modern proposal that has found wide acceptance encourages a comparison with Joseph who rules (the verbal form *yekwēnen* [end of v. 8] is related to *makwannen*) justly.

---

27 Endres, *Biblical Interpretation*, 185.
28 The expression is the same as the one translated "show/s favoritism" in 5:16: literally, he does not lift the face. The translations differ because of the contexts. Berger refers to 5:16 but does nothing more with the passage (*Jubiläen*, 519 n. e to v. 8).
29 Both here and in 5:16 the word *makwannen* is translated "judge" because of the judicial context, but it is also a word for ruler, prince, high official (Leslau, *Concise Dictionary*, 155)—a fact that

is that of G. Steindorff: "the god [god name] speaks, and he/she lives."[30] Ancient expositors, who looked for Hebrew explanations, tried to relate the name to Joseph's experiences. Several of these appear in *Gen. Rab.* 90:4:

> R. Johanan said: The name connotes: He reveals things that are hidden[31] and easily declares them. Hezekiah interpreted the name: With his knowledge he reveals things that are hidden and sets the mind of people at ease. The Rabbis said: [The name is an abbreviation and stands for]: *Zofeh* (seer), *podeh* (redeemer), *nabi* (prophet), *tomek* (supporter), *pother* (interpreter), *'arom* (skilled), *nabon* (understanding), and *ḥozeh* (seer).

Whatever the author of Jubilees thought it meant, he does not report; he simply transcribes the strange-sounding name and moves on with the story—just as Genesis does.

The wife given to Joseph by Pharaoh—Asenath in Gen 41:45, 50—is not named in this passage nor are their two sons (see 34:20 for "Asenath"), but she is identified by reference to her father: "the daughter of Potiphar, the daughter of the priest of Heliopolis—the chief cook."[32] The last words "the chief cook" (that is, "the captain of the guard") are not present in MT SP Gen 41:45 because in them this man is not identical with the Potiphar of Genesis 39. However, Jubilees identifies Joseph's owner in chap. 39 with his new father-in-law and thus assigns his wife's father a title borne by Potiphar in chap. 39. Conversely, in Jubilees 39 the writer attributed to Potiphar the title of Potiphera—the priest of On (= Heliopolis). The writer has, of course, drawn the information about Joseph's wife from Genesis, but it is noteworthy that he offers no criticism of the union that produced ancestors of two central tribes in ancient Israel (Manasseh and Ephraim).[33] The marriage is another in a series of examples demonstrating that, in the author's eyes, Egyptians were better than Canaanites. Marriages to the latter were banned absolutely, while unions with Egyptians were permitted (e.g., Abraham and Hagar).[34]

■ **11-12a** The next topic consists of chronological information regarding Joseph at the time when he assumed his high office. Genesis 41:46a is the source for his age of thirty years "when he entered the service of Pharaoh king of Egypt." If he was thirty at this time and had been seventeen when his brothers sold him (Gen 37:2; see Jub 34:10 and 45:13), the periods when Joseph was in Potiphar's house and in prison lasted a total of thirteen years. Jubilees 46:3 says he spent seventeen years in Canaan, ten as a slave, and three in prison (see 39:13, where he spends two years in prison, apparently before the royal officials arrived). The text states his age of thirty years but does not date it within the full chronological system of jubilees, weeks, and years at this juncture. The unusual feature of v. 11 compared with Gen 41:46a is that the writer synchronizes Joseph's elevation with the year Isaac died. The latter event occurred, according to 36:1, in the year 2162 (for the difficulties

---

30   George Steindorff, "Der Name Josephs *Saphenat-Pa'neach* Genesis Kapitel 41, 45," *Zeitschrift für Ägyptische Sprache und Altertumskunde* 27 (1889) 41–42; Westermann, *Genesis 37–50*, 96; Hamilton, *Genesis 18–50*, 507–8 (he cites several other proposals as well).

31   *Targums Neofiti* and *Pseudo-Jonathan* explain it similarly, as does Josephus (*Ant.* 2.91: "Discoverer of Secrets"). These suggestions find the notion of "hidden things" in the first three consonants (צפן).

32   Recall that "the chief cook" is the interpretation that appears in the LXX where MT SP Gen 37:36; 39:1, etc., use "the captain of the guard." The author of Jubilees provides further information about Joseph's wife in 44:24 (part of a long list of the members of Jacob's family who descended to Egypt): "Before his father came to Egypt children, to whom Asenath—the daughter of Potiphar, the priest of Heliopolis—gave birth for him, were born to Joseph in Egypt: Manasseh and Ephraim—three." See Gen 41:50-52; 46:20.

33   In T. Jos. 18:3 he tells his sons, "For, look, you see that because of (my) patience I even took as my wife the daughter of my masters, and a hundred talents of gold were given me with her; for the Lord made them my servants." *Targum Pseudo-Jonathan* Gen 41:45 expresses a more widespread view: "And he gave him as wife Asenath, *whom Dinah had borne to Shechem*, and whom the *wife of* Potiphera, *chief of Tanis, had reared*." In that way Asenath had a proper mother. See also *Pirqe R. El.* 36 and 38.

34   Cf. Halpern-Amaru, *Empowerment*, 121–22; Loader, *Sexuality*, 178, 292.

the number poses, see the commentary there). Jubilees 28:24 dates the birth/naming of Joseph to the year 2134, and 34:10 places his descent to Egypt in 2149 (so, he was just fifteen; but see 39:2 where he is seventeen when taken to Egypt). If one adds the thirteen years of slavery and imprisonment to 2149, the year for assuming office was 2162—the year Isaac died in 36:1. Joseph will reign over Egypt for eighty years (Jub 46:3) and will die in 2242 (46:8), the number reached if one adds 2162 + 80.[35]

The reference to the death of Isaac in v. 12a is a deft literary touch that serves two ends: to remind readers who might have been enamored by Joseph's new splendor that he still had a family in the land, and to bring the two stories together. The author will soon return to the family back home for the story about Judah and Tamar in chap. 41 and the clan's response to the famine and their eventual move to Egypt in chaps. 42–44, but at this point he simply inserts a note, not found in Genesis, to synchronize the accounts. The fractured family is brought together chronologically.[36]

Jubilees sounds redundant in v. 11: "On the day when Joseph took up his position with Pharaoh he was 30 years of age when he took up his position with Pharaoh." Charles bracketed the last clause as a dittography, and Wintermute and Rabin agree. It certainly has a repetitious ring, but it is the reading of the manuscripts and follows the punctuation in them. One wonders, however, whether "when he took up his position with Pharaoh" should be read with "and in that year Isaac died," though the intervening conjunction does not favor realigning the clauses.[37]

■ **12b-13** The writer brings the chapter about Joseph's meteoric rise to a close by depicting briefly the abundance produced in the first seven-year period. The initial point he makes, however, is to say: "Things turned out just as Joseph had reported about the interpretation of his two dreams, just as he had reported to him" (v. 12).[38] The nearest parallel in Genesis is 41:53-54: "The seven years of plenty that prevailed in the land of Egypt came to an end; and the seven years of famine began to come, just as Joseph had said." The placement of the notice in Jubilees makes it refer only to the years of plenty; the writer will not take up the famine years until chap. 42. In Genesis the statement about how events comported with Joseph's prediction are connected with the fact that the one seven-year period issued directly into the other.

The units describing the good years read in this way.

Genesis 41:47-49	Jubilees 40:12 (end)-13
During the seven plenteous years the earth produced abundantly. He gathered up all the food of the seven years when there was plenty in the land of Egypt, and stored up food in the cities; he stored up in every city the food from the the fields around it. So Joseph stored up grain in such abundance—like the sand of the sea—that he stopped measuring it; it was beyond measure.	There were seven years of abundance in the whole land of Egypt. The land of Egypt was most productive: one measure (would produce) 1800 measures. Joseph collected (each) city's food in the city until it was so full of wheat that it was impossible to count or measure it because of its quantity.[39]

Both texts obviously highlight the limitless amounts of grain stored up during the first seven-year period—at

---

35 If he was born in 2134 (28:24), he would have been only 108 in the year 2242, not the 110 years of Gen 50:22, 26; Jub 46:3. The two mystery years (was he fifteen or seventeen when taken to Egypt?) continue to upset the chronology to the end of his life.

36 Halpern-Amaru thinks the author "pointedly" indicates that Joseph was already in Egypt when Isaac died (*Empowerment*, 95). He was not involved in any special way in the stories about continuity in the family while Rebekah and Isaac are still alive, part of the feature in the book that neither of Rachel's children "has a special status as a leader among the heads of the tribes." It seems simpler to take the synchronism of dates as a reminder of his birth family, not a pointedly thematic jibe against Joseph, who seems to be doing well and will eventually be the savior of his whole family.

37 Cf. VanderKam, *Jubilees* 2:266.

38 This is another case where the last words could perhaps more easily be read with the following clause: Just as he reported to him there were seven years of abundance. However, as in the other case just above, a conjunction before "there" casts doubt on the suggestion.

39 With the last expression in the verse, compare *Tg. Neof.* Gen 41:49 (end): "because there was no *sum total for such a quantity.*"

this point Genesis is more concerned than it was in vv. 34-36 with local harvests and storage—but Jubilees adds specific numbers: one measure would multiply 1800 times. *Targum Pseudo-Jonathan* Gen 41:47 reads, "The earth was *so fertile* during the seven years of plenty that *every ear* produced *two full* handfuls *until all the granaries were filled*." In Gen 26:12-13a "Isaac sowed seed in the land, and in the same year reaped a hundredfold. The Lord blessed him, and the man became rich." A hundredfold is understood to be a huge crop—so large that, with his other holdings, the Philistines envied Isaac. In the NT parable of the sower, the highest level of production is a hundredfold (Matt 13:8 // Mark 4:8 // Luke 8:8). If a hundredfold was a large yield, the 1800-fold productivity of Egypt becomes miraculous, though not without parallel. In Sib. Or. 3:261-64 the earth yields from one to a hundredfold; 1 Enoch 10:19 refers to a thousandfold, and 2 Bar 29:5 mentions a yield of ten thousandfold (the context is eschatological).[40] Joseph's wise policies ensure that enough of the gigantic supply is saved for a time of need. The image fits well in the utopian picture of Joseph's dominion. Genesis uses a phrase familiar for describing the many descendants of the patriarchs—"like the sand of the sea" (v. 49); the author of Jubilees does not repeat it but employs numerical language to express the hyper-productivity of Egyptian soil at the time.

---

[40] These references come from Joel Marcus, *The Mystery of the Kingdom of God* (SBLDS 90; Atlanta: Scholars Press, 1986) 42-43.

Judah and Tamar

41

1/ In the forty-fifth jubilee, the second week[a] during the[b] second year [2165], Judah took as a wife for his firstborn Er one of the Aramean women whose name was Tamar. 2/ He hated (her)[a] and did not sleep with her because his mother was a Canaanite woman and he wanted to marry someone from his mother's tribe. But his father Judah did not allow[b] him.[c] 3/ This Er,[a] Judah's firstborn, was evil, and the Lord killed him. 4/ Then Judah said to his brother[a] Onan,[b] "Go in to your brother's wife,[c] perform the[d] levirate duty for her, and produce descendants for your brother."[e] 5/ Onan[a] knew that the descendants would not be his but his brother's, so he entered the house of his brother's wife[b] and poured out the semen[c] on the ground.[d] In the Lord's estimation[e] it was an evil act,[f] and he killed him. 6/ So Judah said to his daughter-in-law[a] Tamar, "Remain in your father's house as a widow until my son Selom[b] grows up. Then I will give you to him as a wife."[c] 7/ He[a] grew up, but Judah's wife[b] Bedsuel did not allow her son Selom[c] to marry her.[d] Judah's wife Bedsuel died during the fifth year of this week[e] [2168].

8/ In its[a] sixth year [2169] Judah went up to shear[b] his sheep in Timnah. Tamar was told, "Your father-in-law is now going up to shear his sheep in Timnah."[c] 9/ Then she put aside her[a] widow's clothing from herself,[b] put on a veil,[c] beautified herself, and sat down at the gate near[d] the road to Timnah. 10/ As Judah was going along,[a] he found her[b] and supposed that she was a prostitute. He said to her, "Let me come in[c] to you." She said to him, "Come in." So he came in.[d] 11/ She said to him, "Give me my fee."[a] He said to her,[b] "I have nothing with me[c] except the ring on my finger,[d] my neck chain,[e] and my staff that is in my hand."[f] 12/ She said to him,[a] "Give them[b] to me until you send me[c] my fee." He said to her,[d] "I will send you a kid." He gave them to her.[e] After he was with her,[f] she became pregnant by him.

13/ Then Judah went[a] to his[b] sheep, but she went to her father's house.[c] 14/ He[a] sent[b] the kid[c] through his Adullamite shepherd,[d] but he did not find her.[e] He asked the men of the area, "Where[f] is the prostitute who was here?"[g] They said to him, "There is no prostitute here, nor do we have any prostitute with us."[h] 15/ He returned[a] and told him,[b] "I did not find her,[c] and when I asked[d] the men of the area[e] they said to me,[f] 'There is no prostitute here.'"[g] Judah said,[h] "Let her keep them[i] so that we may not become the object of mockery."[j]

16/ When she reached three months,[a] she was visibly pregnant.[b] Judah was told, "Your daughter-in-law Tamar has now become pregnant through prostitution."[c] 17/ Judah went to her father's house[a] and said to her father and brothers,[b] "Bring her out and let her be burned[c] because she has done something impure in Israel." 18/ When she was brought out to be burned, she sent the ring, the neck chain, and the staff[a] to her father-in-law and said, "Recognize whose these are because[b] I am pregnant by him." 19/ Judah recognized them[a] and said, "Tamar has been more just than I; therefore,[b] do not burn her." 20/ For this reason she was not given to Selom,[a] and he did not approach[b] her again. 21/ Afterwards she was pregnant[a] and gave birth[b] to two boys[c]—Perez and Zerah—during the seventh year of this second week[d] [2170]. 22[a]/ Following this the seven years[b] of copious harvest (about) which Joseph had told Pharaoh were completed.

23/ Judah knew that what he had done was evil because he had lain with his daughter-in-law. In his own view he considered it evil, and he knew that he had done wrong and erred,[a] for[b] he had uncovered his son's covering. He began to lament[c] and plead before the Lord because of his[d] sin. 24/ We told him[a] in a dream[b] that it would be forgiven for him because he had pleaded very much and because he had lamented[c] and did not do (it) again.[d] 25/ He had forgiveness because he turned[a] from his sin and from his ignorance,[b] for the sin was a great one before our God. Anyone who acts[c] in this way—anyone[d] who sleeps with his daughter-in-law[e]—is to be burned in fire so that he burns in it because impurity and contamination have come on them. They are to be burned.

1033

26/ Now you[a] order the Israelites that there is to be no impurity among them, for anyone who lies with his daughter-in-law or his mother-in-law[b] has done something that is impure. They are to burn the man who lay[c] with her and the woman. Then anger and punishment will cease[d] from Israel. 27/ We told Judah that his two sons had not lain with her. For this reason his descendants were established for another generation and would not be uprooted.[a] 28/ For in his integrity[a] he had gone and demanded punishment because Judah had wanted to burn her on the basis of the law that Abraham had commanded his children.

Textual Notes

1a the second week] There is a conjunction before the expression in most MSS., but 25 omits it. Mss. 20 21 42 47 read "in" before it, and MSS. 35 38 44 have "and in." Mss. 39 42 47 48 58 add "and."

b the (second year)] "its" 17 21.

2a (her)] Several later MSS. (42 47 58, and, with a different spelling, 63) add the suffix "her."

b did (not) allow] "would (not) allow" 21 42 47 48 63.

c him] om. 17 58.

3a Er] om. 42 47.

4a his brother] "his son" 39 42 47 48[t] 58.

b Onan] "Shelah" Syr. Chr. (see also v. 5).

c your brother's wife] pr. "Tamar" Syr. Chr.

d the (levirate duty)] "your" 21 35[c] 39 42 47 48 58. Syr. Chr. lacks an equivalent of "perform the levirate duty for her."

e for your brother] "so that it [i.e., seed = descendants] may be for your brother" 12.

5a Onan] "Shelah" Syr. Chr. (see v. 4 above).

b so he entered the house of his brother's wife] The Eth. reading reflects Gen 38:9, though Genesis does not mention her house. The Syr. Chr. citation reads: "so, when he was joined with her." Mss. 44 58: "he entered to his brother's wife."

c the semen] "his semen" Syr. Chr. Mss. 9 21 agree with Syr. Chr.

d the ground] + "so that he would not have sons" Syr. Chr. Cf. Gen 38:9.

e In the Lord's estimation (lit., "before the eyes of the Lord" as in MT SP Gen 38:10)] "before God" Syr. Chr., as in Syr LXX Gen 38:10.

f it was an evil act] The text could be translated: "he was evil," and the Syr. Chr. wording ("In this he did something evil") may favor this interpretation. Genesis 38:10 is ambiguous about the subject.

6a his daughter-in-law] om. Syr. Chr.

b Selom] "Awnan/Onan" Syr. Chr. (see above, vv. 4-5).

c Then—wife] "Then he will become your husband" Syr. Chr.

7a He] "Awnan/Onan" Syr. Chr.

b Judah's wife] om. Syr. Chr.

c her son Selom] "Awnan/Onan" Syr. Chr.

d her] So Lat. Eth. lacks a direct object, and Syr. Chr. supplies "Tamar."

e during—week] om. Syr. Chr. Mss. 38 44 om. "this."

8a its] Lat. represents the suffix with a demonstrative; MSS. 20 25 35 44 58 lack the suffix. The Syr. Chr. citation expresses the time statement more generally: "After some time."

b to shear] + "to Timnah" Syr. Chr. (it reads the same expression again after "his sheep"). See Gen 38:13.

c Timnah–Timnah] Many Eth. MSS. om. from the first instance of the name to the second (9 12 17 21 38 42 47 63). See VanderKam, *Jubilees* 2:268.

9a her] Syr. Chr. lacks, as does MS. 12.

b from herself] So Lat. and Syr. Chr.; Eth. and Eth. Gen 38:14 lack the phrase. The word 'emennēhā may have fallen from the text because a scribe omitted from one instance of the suffix –hā ("her") in "her widow's clothing" to the one on "from herself."

c veil] So Eth. and Syr. Chr., but Lat. has "the best clothes." See VanderKam, *Jubilees* 2:269.

d the gate near] om. Syr. Chr.

10a was going along] This is the tense of the Eth. expression; Lat. and Syr. Chr. indicate a past tense action. Syr. Chr. adds "to that place."

b he found her] "he saw her" Syr. Chr. = Gen 38:15. Mss. 9 12 25 63 lack "her."

c Let me come in] + "to your house and" 44.

d She said to him: "Come in." So he came in] om. Syr. Chr. Note that "She said to him" at the beginning of v. 11 could have triggered the omission. Lat. lacks "to him." At the end, Lat., with Gen 38:18, reads "to her."

11a my fee] "fee" Syr. Chr.

b to her] This is the reading of Eth. and Syr. Chr., but Lat. has *ille* ("he"), though it may be a mistake for *illi* ("to her").

c I have nothing with me] Eth. and Lat. read a negative + "in my hand(s)." Syr. Chr. has a negative and "with me." The sense of the three versions is the same.

d the ring on my finger] Syr. Chr. mentions just "the ring," while Lat. makes a clause: "the ring that I have on my finger."] Eth. = "the ring [MSS. 9 12 17 38 39 42 44 47 58 63 have "my ring"] of my finger."

e   my neck chain] Neither Lat. nor Syr. Chr. reads "my" (cf. LXX Gen 38:18). The Syr. Chr. term here is "staff," the third item in Eth. and Lat.

f   my staff that is in my hand] So Eth. and Lat. (though Lat. with MS. 21 lacks "my" with LXX Gen 38:18). Syr. Chr. has "robe," as in Syr. Gen 38:18, and om. "that is in my hand."

12a   to him] "to Judah" Syr. Chr.
b   them] "it" 9 12 17 21 38 44 63.
c   (send) me] Neither Lat. nor Syr. Chr. reads the indirect object.
d   He said to her] So Eth. and Syr. Chr.; Lat. = "Judah said."
e   He gave them to her] Syr. Chr. om. Mss. 12 21 om. "to her," as does 38 but with a different verb form. Ms. 21: "He gave it."
f   After he was with her] This is the reading of Lat. and Syr. Chr. It has dropped from the Eth. tradition, possibly when in its Gk. base a scribe's eye skipped from αυτη to αυτη ("to her . . . with her"). See VanderKam, *Jubilees* 2:270 for Charles's misguided attempt to change the Lat. and for how the translators have handled the issue.

13a   Judah went] "She went and Judah too went" 58.
b   his] om. Lat.
c   but she went to her father's house] Lat. and Syr. Chr. lack the clause. As Berger (*Jubiläen*, 523 n. b to v. 13) explained, the line is absent from Gen 38:19 but presupposed by Jub 41:17 (attested also in Lat. and Syr. Chr.) so it would have been present on the Gk. level. Perhaps the similarity of αυτου ("*his* sheep") and αυτης ("*her* father") led to the omission. See VanderKam, *Jubilees* 2:271.

14a   He (so Lat. and Syr. Chr.)] "Judah" Eth. Genesis 38:20 also reads "Judah."
b   sent] + "to her" Lat.
c   the kid] Both Lat. and Syr. Chr. repeat the term(s) for the animal they used in v. 12, but Eth. uses only *maḥse'a* rather than the expected *maḥse'a ṭali* as in v. 12 (MSS. 38 39 42 47 48 58 add *ṭali*). The meaning, however, appears to be the same. See VanderKam, *Jubilees* 2:271.
d   his (om. 21 47) Adullamite shepherd] Eth. and Lat. presuppose רעהו in Gen 38:20 (as in LXX), not רֵעֵהוּ ("friend") as in MT. Syr. Chr. reads with MT (and Syr. Gen 38:20). See Charles, *Ethiopic Version*, 150 n. 10. Lat. may read the gentilic as the man's name (*adollam*).
e   did not find her] So Lat., Syr. Chr., and Gen 38:20. Eth. uses a verb "failed to find" with no direct object. See VanderKam, *Jubilees* 2:271 (the difference involves only the length of the last vowel on the verb: *ḥaṭ'a*, "he failed to find"; *ḥaṭ'ā*, "he failed to find her").
f   Where] The versions agree on an introductory word before the quotations but MSS. 25 35 39 42 44 47 48 58 have "and said to them"; MS. 21 om. any word of speaking.

g   who was here] om. 25 35.
h   There is no prostitute (om. 25 35 44) . . . with us] Only Eth. reads the clause; Lat. has just "with us" and Syr. Chr. lacks it altogether. Eth. may have expanded, but the shorter answer could have been conditioned by the one in Gen 38:21 (also v. 22), or the repetition of "prostitute" could have caused problems. See VanderKam, *Jubilees* 2:271–72.

15a   returned] + "to Judah" Syr. Chr.
b   told him] "told Judah" Lat.; "said to him" Syr. Chr. (see Gen 38:22).
c   I did not find her] Lat., Syr. Chr., and Gen 38:22 phrase his words as a direct quotation, while Eth. uses an indirect statement: "that he had failed to find, and said to him." The difference probably arose when ουχ ευρον ("I did not find") and ουχ ευρεν ("he did not find") were confused. In the textual tradition attested in Eth., once the mistake was made, the copyist or translator would have inserted another verb of speaking before the next words, which definitely are a quotation. See VanderKam, *Jubilees* 2:272.
d   and when I asked] "I also asked" Lat.; Syr. Chr. reads a conjunction before the verb but, because of its different reading in the preceding clause, Eth. lacks one.
e   the area] Lat. again, as in v. 14, uses a demonstrative—"that place/area"—but neither Eth. nor Syr. Chr. reads one.
f   to me] Lat. lacks. See the next note.
g   There is no prostitute here] This is the reading of Eth. and Syr. Chr. Lat. phrases as indirect discourse: "that there was no prostitute in that area."
h   Judah said] So Lat. and Syr. Chr.; Eth. lacks "Judah," perhaps losing the name because of its similarity in appearance to the verb.
i   Let her keep them] So Lat. Syr. Chr. om., but Eth. reads: *tanše'*, "rise." Charles (*Ethiopic Version*, 151 n. 22; *Jubilees*, 230) solved the problem with the Eth. text: two forms were confused. The correct *tenšā'* ("let her take/keep") became *tanše'*. See Gen 38:23. Some Eth. copies reveal scribal attempts to correct the problem, once it occurred. Mss. 42 47 read: "rise; let's go"; MS. 44 has: "arise and let's go." Lat. alone supplies "them."
j   so that we may not become the object of mockery] Eth. and Lat. read a negative purpose clause, whereas Syr. Chr. introduces it with "why." Eth., Syr. Chr., and Gen 38:23 read "we," but Lat. has a third sg. verb: "so that she does not mock us." See VanderKam, *Jubilees* 2:272–73.

16a   When she reached three months] So Eth. The other versions also relate the passage of three months but in different ways: Lat. = "When three months were completed for her"; Syr. Chr. = "After three months" (see Gen 38:24: ויהי כמשלש חדשים).

b she was visibly pregnant] Lit.. "she became known/was recognized as pregnant." This is the reading of Eth. (MSS. 20 25 35 44 = "her pregnancy was known") and Syr. Chr. Lat. is ambiguous: "it was apparent" or "she appeared." See VanderKam, *Jubilees* 2:273.

c through prostitution] So Eth., Syr. Chr., and Gen 38:24; Lat. om.

17a her father's house] "to her father and her brothers" Syr. Chr.

b said to her father and brothers] "said to them" Syr. Chr. Mss. 39 42 47 48 58 = "said to her father, her mother, and her brothers."

c and let her be burned] Mss. 39 42 47 48 58 om. "and." Eth. reads lit., "Let them burn her"; Lat. and Syr. Chr. = "let her be burned." These latter two add "with fire" (= MSS. 35 44).

18a the neck chain, and the staff] So Eth., Lat., and Gen 38:25. Syr. Chr. places "the staff" in second position, and, as in v. 11, reads "the robe" in the third place (it is the second item in Syr. Gen. 38:25).

b because] om. Lat.

19a them] So Syr. Chr. Eth. and Gen 38:26 lack an object for the verb.

b therefore] Syr. lacks.

20a For this reason she was not given to Selom] om. Syr. Chr. Cf. Gen 38:26, which contains similar words but as part of direct speech by Judah.

b approach] Syr. Chr. = "know," which agrees with Gen 38:26. Eth. Gen 38:26 has the same verb as Jubilees; see T. Jud. 12:8 (ηγγισα).

21a Afterwards she was pregnant] Syr. Chr. om., as do most translators, though the clause has strong support. For "Afterwards," MS. 35 reads "For this reason." Mss. 21 35 42 47 lack "she was pregnant and."

b gave birth] + "to/for him" Syr. Chr.

c two boys] Syr. Chr. adds: "twins."

d during the seventh year of this second week] om. Syr. Chr.

22a Syr. Chr. reproduces nothing from this verse.

b years] om. 25 38.

23a In his own view he considered it evil, and he knew that he had done wrong and erred] om. Syr. Chr.

b for] "and" Syr. Chr. (but it om. the clauses just before this).

c He began to lament] "He was longing" Syr. Chr.

d his (sin)] "this" Syr. Chr.; om. 9 12 17 21 38 63 (MS. 9 seems to read a verb: "he sinned").

24a We told him] "It was told to him" Syr. Chr.

b dream] "vision" Syr. Chr.

c that it would be forgiven ("he would forgive" 12 21 35 38 39 44 48 63) for him because he had pleaded very much and because he had lamented] "It has been forgiven to/for you because you have prayed and pleaded" Syr. Chr.

d and did not do (it) again] "He received pardon because he had lamented very much about the matter" Syr. Chr. Mss. 21 35 38 add a second word meaning "again."

25a because he turned] om. 20 25 35 58. So, in these MSS. he had forgiveness from his sins (not: "because he turned from his sin"), although MS. 58 adds these words after "sin," and the others add them after "ignorance."

b and from (om. 20) his ignorance] om. 35.

c acts] has acted 12.

d anyone] pr. "and" 21 42 47 48 58.

e daughter-in-law] Mss. 20 21 35 58 use *mar'āt*, a word for "daughter-in-law," while the more widely supported reading has the noun *ḥamāt* ("mother-in-law"). For the issue, see the commentary. Werman (*Jubilees*, 492 n. 35) proposes reading both nouns in this place (see v. 26).

26a you] + "Moses" 20 38.

b mother-in-law] Here, used with *mar'āt* ("daughter-in-law"), the term must mean "mother-in-law."

c lay] "lies" 9 21 38 39 42 47 48 58.

d anger and punishment will cease] Many MSS. read acc. endings on the nouns, but 20 21 25 44 58 place them in the nom. case (MS. 9 does this for "punishment" only, since it reads the two nouns in a construct phrase). The verb is sg.; perhaps the number of the first noun governs it.

27a would not be uprooted] "was not uprooted" 21 35.

28a his integrity (lit., "the innocence of his eyes")] For "eyes," MSS. 20 21 35 58 read "heart."

Commentary

The story about Judah and Tamar is in part a quotation from and in part a strong rewriting of the version in Genesis 38. The author dealt with sexual misdeeds on several occasions before this (the Watchers, Sodom, Lot and his daughters, Shechem and Dinah, Reuben and Bilhah, and Joseph and Potiphar's wife), and, as in those other instances, he here treats a disturbing account in Genesis in light of his strong convictions about sexual behavior and about the patriarchs. Chapter 41 is unusual in Jubilees in that it breaks the sequence of Genesis. There the story follows directly on the "death" of Joseph when his brothers sold him and misled their father regarding his fate. In the narrative about their terrible mistreatment of Joseph, Judah acts far from nobly (though a little better than his brothers)—he advocates selling Joseph to Ishmaelite traders rather than killing him (Gen 37:26-27; his motive for scaling back the enormity of their plan was that "he is our brother, our own flesh" [v. 27]). Then comes the Judah–Tamar story in Genesis 38. His sinful conduct serves as a foil for Joseph's more laudable behavior when Potiphar's wife tried to seduce him (Genesis 39). Jubilees, however, transfers the story to a point after Joseph's successful resistance to her advances and his rise to power in Egypt. So the example of his obedience to the ancestral law and consequent success is fresh in the reader's mind when encountering Jubilees' version of the Judah–Tamar story. The way in which the writer of Jubilees grapples with the result of Judah's act (there is no punishment for him in Genesis 38), which led to the next generation in the line that would produce Israel's kings, forms a part of his rewriting; there is no similar paragraph in Genesis 38. He had expended much effort in chaps. 30–32 to make Levi a more worthy ancestor of the priests than he is in Genesis; now he labors once more to burnish the image of Judah as ancestor of the Davidic kings. He does not, however, completely efface the blemishes on his record. At the end, Judah stood in need of forgiveness.

The chapter can be outlined in this way:
1-7   Judah's sons and Tamar (Gen 38:6-12a)
8-21   Judah and Tamar (Gen 38:12b-26)
    8-12   Tamar misleads Judah (Gen 38:12b-18)
    13-15   Tamar disappears (Gen 38:19-23)
    16-21   The truth emerges and twins are born (Gen 38:24-30)
22   The seven years of abundance end (Gen 41:53)
23-28   Legal issues
    23-25   Judah's remorse and pardon
    26-28   The law for Israel

The textual evidence for the chapter consists of the full Ethiopic version and
Syriac   vv. 4-21, 23-24
Latin   vv. 6-19 (first word)
Hebrew (4Q223–224 unit 3 ii:1-3)
    vv. 7-10 (v. 9 must be reconstructed), 28?
    (see frg. 41)[1]

The story attracted the attention of many ancient writers. One can read a version of it in, for example, Testament of Judah 10–12 and frequent comments on it elsewhere.[2]

1-7 Judah's sons and Tamar (Gen 38:6-12a)

■ 1-3 The narrative about Judah and Tamar opens with a date—2165—and it will conclude with another—2170 (v. 21)—that is synchronized with the end of the seven plentiful years in Egypt (in 42:1 the famine begins the following year). The story in the chapter therefore fits in the chronological sequence of Jubilees (Joseph became second in command over Egypt in 2162 [40:11]). Genesis 38, which contains no dates or synchronisms, begins with an account of how it came about that Judah married a daughter of a Canaanite (vv. 1-2). The woman is not named, but her father is called Shua. Since she is the daughter (*bat*) of Shua, she acquired the name Bathshua in some retellings (so already in 1 Chr 2:3). Jubilees reported in 34:20 (see also v. 7 below): "the name of Judah's wife was Betasuel, the Canaanitess." *Betasuel* (with variations in the Ethiopic manuscripts; Latin: *bethsuae*) is an attempt at transcribing *Bathshua*. Genesis 38:3-5 recount the births of the three sons of Judah and the Canaanite woman: Er, Onan, and Shelah. The writer of Jubilees, who most emphatically disapproves of marriages with Canaanites, does not even summarize the verses regarding Judah's marriage and the births of his sons but picks up the story with Gen 38:6, where the marriage of Er, the eldest son, is the subject.[3] The

---

1   Milik placed it at 4Q223–224 unit 2 iii:1, but the only word on the fragment (ממשפ) does not agree with the Ethiopic text; the word could come from 41:28 but there is no certainty about its location (see DJD 13:116).

2   Yair Zakovitch and Avigdor Shinan document some seven hundred ancient references to or comments on the story from the translations of Genesis through the early *piyyutim* (*The Story of Judah and Tamar: Genesis 38 in the Bible, the Old Versions and the Ancient Jewish Literature* [Research Projects of the Institute of Jewish Studies Monograph Series 15; Jerusalem: Hebrew University, 1992] 1–206).

3   Cf. Halpern-Amaru, *Empowerment*, 113–14 (the

differences between the two versions of the episode are instructive.

Genesis 39:6-7	Jubilees 41:1b-3
Judah took a wife for Er his firstborn; her name was Tamar.	. . . Judah took as a wife for his firstborn Er one of the Aramean women whose name was Tamar. He hated (her) and did not sleep with her because his mother was a Canaanite woman and he wanted to marry someone from his mother's tribe. But his father Judah did not allow him.
But Er, Judah's firstborn, was wicked in the sight of the LORD, and the LORD put him to death.	This Er, Judah's firstborn, was evil, and the Lord killed him.

Tamar, destined to become the mother through whom the royal line of Judah would be traced by way of her son Perez (see Ruth 4:18-22; cf. Num 26:19-22), is identified as an Aramean woman. A similar statement occurs in T. Jud. 10:1: "After these things my son Er took to wife Thamar from Mesopotamia, a daughter of Aram" (note that Er, not Judah, takes her).[4] Genesis does not define her ethnicity, but it may be that the author of Jubilees took it by analogy from her namesake, Tamar, the daughter of David and Maacah who was the daughter of the king of Geshur (2 Sam 3:3; this was Absalom's mother, and Tamar was his sister [2 Sam 13:1]). Maacah also appears to be the name of an Aramean kingdom (note Aram-maacah in 1 Chr 19:6; in the entire context in the remainder of that chapter, the troops from it are included among the Arameans).[5] Whatever the source for the claim about Tamar's people, it is important in the rewriting in Jubilees because marriage with Arameans is acceptable.[6] Genesis 22:24 lists Maacah as a son of Abraham's brother Nahor and his concubine Reumah.[7] These people, then, were descendants of Abraham's family, the same branch of the family that produced Rebekah, Leah, and Rachel. Thus, already at the place where he introduces Tamar into the story, the writer provides crucial background information for contextualizing what happens in the chapter and for the future of Judah's line. Because of Judah's preemptive action in securing an Aramean wife for Er, the royal genealogy will not run through a Canaanitess.

If one reads the account in Genesis, the reason for the death of Er, apart from the wordplay, is too vague: Er (ער) was wicked (רע) in the Lord's sight. What did he do to merit the death penalty?[8] Jubilees is more forthcoming. The writer says that Er hated Tamar, not, apparently, for any fault of hers but because she did not come from a Canaanite tribe as his mother did. He wished to do what one should never do in Jubilees—marry a Canaanite woman (no wonder the Lord killed him). Judah, who is short on virtue in Genesis 38, does the proper thing in Jubilees by overruling Er's intent to take a wife from his mother's tribe. The writer is careful to add another important detail: because of his hatred for her, Er did not have sexual relations with Tamar.

"disasters" in the family are due to this unfortunate marriage); Anderson, "Torah before Sinai," 24–26; Kugel, *Walk through* Jubilees, 182.

4   Zakovitch and Shinan, *Judah and Tamar*, 43–44.
5   See Gary N. Knoppers, *1 Chronicles 10–29: A New Translation with Introduction and Commentary* (AB 12A; New York: Doubleday, 2004) 720.
6   In Jub 34:20 Levi marries "Melcha, one of the daughters of Aram—one of the descendants of Terah's sons." Simeon, who married a Canaanitess (Adebaa), later had a change of heart and "married another woman from Mesopotamia like his brothers" (34:21). Endres believes the writer has Judah arrange "an endogamous marriage for his eldest son, Er, in order to right his own wrong" of having married a Canaanite woman (*Biblical Interpretation*, 186).
7   J. Emerton deals with Tamar's ancestry in Jubilees 41, the possible connections with Tamar in 2 Samuel 13, and the genealogy in Gen 22:24 ("An Examination of a Recent Structuralist Interpretation of Genesis XXXVIII," *VT* 26 [1976] 79–98, esp. 91–93). He also refers to Deut 26:5 with its confession by an Israelite "a wandering Aramean was my ancestor."
8   *Targums Neofiti* and *Pseudo-Jonathan* use parallel expressions for Er and Onan to give some justification for the execution of Er. *B. Yebamot* 34b probably gives the reasoning behind the parallel: "There is no problem in explaining what Onan did wrong" (it quotes Gen 38:9). "But what about Er?" Said R. Nahman bar Isaac, 'And he slew him too' (Gen. 38:10)—he died by the same mode of the death penalty [hence for the same sin]." So the word גם ("too") in v. 10 suggested the same fault was involved. See also Hartom, "Jubilees," 119 n. to v. 3; Zakovitch and Shinan, *Judah and Tamar*, 49, 52.

She remained a virgin, despite being married to him. Genesis suggests nothing of the sort: 38:7 could be read to say that, before the Lord executed him, Er and Tamar had normal marital relations.[9] For the author of Jubilees their dysfunctional marriage will prove immensely helpful (see below, v. 27).

■ **4-5** The lines about the second brother Onan follow the text of Genesis more closely than for Er. Jubilees 41:4 quotes Gen 38:8, where Judah orders Onan to perform the duty of a brother-in-law to raise up an heir (seed) for his deceased brother. The text presupposes that this is the normal practice, though the legislation for levirate marriage appears in the HB only in the time of Moses (see Deut 25:5-10). The Deuteronomic law prescribes that, when a man dies without a son, his brother is to become a surrogate husband; the first son born to the union of the widow and her brother-in-law would perpetuate the name of the deceased in Israel. If the brother did not wish to assume this role, he had to appear before the elders at the gate to reaffirm his decision; the woman, neglected in this fashion, was to remove his sandal and spit in his face to shame him. The case in Genesis 38 and Jubilees 41 is not the same as the one in Deuteronomy 25. Judah does not order Onan to marry Tamar—only to have sex with her so that she could bear a son. What happens next is not precisely the same in the two texts:

Genesis 38:9-10
But since Onan knew that the offspring would not be his, he spilled his semen on the ground whenever he went in to his brother's wife, so that he would not give offspring to his brother. What he did was displeasing in the sight of the Lord, and he put him to death also.

Jubilees 41:5
Onan knew that the descendants would not be his but his brother's, so he entered the house of his brother's wife and poured out the semen on the ground.
In the Lord's estimation it was an evil act, and he killed him.

According to both texts, Onan decides not to carry out his father's command, and nothing is said about a ceremony shaming him for his failure to perform his fraternal duty. Yet where Genesis indicates that Onan destroyed[10] his semen "whenever he went in to his brother's wife,"[11] Jubilees pictures this as a one-time act, not something he did repeatedly. Moreover, the one occurrence happened when Onan visited her house;[12] the two lived in separate places. That is, he replaces the expression (literally) "he would go in to her" in Gen 38:9 with "he entered her house."[13] The writer is deeply concerned to show that Tamar had no sexual relations with either of the two brothers. Genesis leaves the impression of regular intimate contact between Onan and Tamar, but Jubilees limits it to one instance so that there could be no question about Tamar's virginity.[14] With Onan's death, Judah's first two sons are eliminated from the scene, and neither ever had intercourse with Tamar.[15]

---

9 In T. Jud. 10:3 "he had not known her on account of the craftiness of his mother, for he did not want to have children by her." In this text (v. 2) an angel of the Lord kills Er "in the night of the third day" (apparently of the wedding feast; see v. 4).

10 According to BDB, 1008, s.v. שחת, the meaning of the expression ושחת ארצה is that he "*spoiled* (it) *upon the ground*, made it ineffective." In LXX Gen 38:9 the verb used means "poured out" and Jub 41:5 offers the same interpretation.

11 See GKC §159 o, where this expression is referenced as exemplifying the "perfect frequentative."

12 No ancient version of Gen 38:9 mentions her house. The Syriac citation of Jubilees is different here: where the Ethiopic manuscripts read "so he entered the house of his brother's wife," it says, "so, when he was joined with her."

13 Halpern-Amaru, *Empowerment*, 114; Zakovitch and Shinan, *Judah and Tamar*, 63. Rothstein, while correctly noting how the reference to the house functions in the passage, makes the mistake of thinking Jubilees too pictures this as a repeated act ("Sexual Union," 364). This is not the case, since the text uses only a perfect-tense verb, not the compound expression that indicates repetition in MT SP Gen 38:9.

14 A similar message emerges from T. Jud. 10:4-5: "In the days of the wedding-feast I gave Onan to her in levirate marriage; and he also, in wickedness, did not know her, though he spent with her a year. And when I threatened him, he went in unto her, but spilled the seed on the ground, according to his mother's command; and he also died in wickedness." Judah's wife does not direct Onan's actions in Jubilees.

15 Dimant properly observes that the emphasis on Tamar's virginity serves not to mitigate Judah's sin later in the chapter but to legitimate her sons (see also below on vv. 23-28) ("Judah and Tamar in Jubilees 41," in Mason et al., *Teacher for All Generations*,

■ 6 The death of Onan left Judah with just one son, Shelah, to whom he could pass the seemingly powerless Tamar. He was too young to perform the duty of the brother-in-law for her, so Judah ordered her to live in her father's house as a widow while waiting for Shelah to mature. She was in fact Er's widow but had never been married to Onan. Jubilees ends the section about Shelah and Tamar differently than Genesis does.

Genesis 38:11	Jubilees 41:6
"... until my son Shelah grows up"— for he feared that he too would die, like his brothers.	"... until my son Selom grows up. Then I will give you to him as a wife."

The Judah of Jubilees is explicit that he will have Selom (= Shelah) marry Tamar, unlike the situation with Onan.[16] But the fear for Shelah's life felt by Judah in Genesis is not part of the retelling. Perhaps the reader is to conclude that Judah was not worried about the life of his only remaining son because of the blessing Isaac had given (31:18-20), assuring him of royal progeny. Based on Isaac's words, he did not have to fear that his line would end with him, and he could confidently tell Tamar that she and Shelah would marry. He had, of course, not received assurance of a kingly progeny to this point in Genesis. Genesis 38:11 ends with a notice that Tamar went to her father's house; it is lacking in Jubilees, though, as the story continues, that is where she is (41:13, 17).

■ 7 More of the specific concerns motivating the author of Jubilees emerge at this juncture in the narrative.

Genesis 38:12a	Jubilees 41:7
In the course of time the wife of Judah, Shua's daughter, died. When Judah's time of mourning was over,[18] ...	He [Selah/Selom] grew up, but Judah's wife Bedsuel did not allow her son Selom to marry her.[17] Judah's wife Bedsuel died during the fifth year of this week.

Genesis does not indicate here that Judah failed to keep his promise to Tamar. It reports the death of his wife and the comfort he received after the sad event. Only later, at end of the story, does Judah acknowledge that he erred in not giving Tamar to Shelah (38:26). The author of Jubilees sensed the need to say something about the subject here but also saw an opportunity to defend Judah. The one responsible for not giving Tamar to Shelah was his mother Bedsuel. This woman refused to allow her son to marry Tamar. The fault lay with her, not with Judah.[19] Judah's admission of wrongdoing will apply to a different fault in Jub 41:19, where nothing is said about forgetting to marry her to Shelah at an earlier time (see also v. 20). In Jubilees, Judah's wife, who is again named, dies, as in Genesis, and even the date is given; but there is no mention of any comfort he received on the occasion. The writer gives no hint that Judah grieved the loss of his Canaanite wife (or of his sons through her; Genesis also does not mention grief concerning the deaths of Er and Onan). He does, however, indicate that the events narrated in 41:1-7 took

---

783-97, here 790-92). A similar point was made in a Notre Dame seminar paper by Sarah Schreiber, "Is a Halakhic Redactor Necessary? A Closer Look at Jubilees 41" (December 10, 2010).

16 Zakovitch and Shinan, *Judah and Tamar*, 74.
17 In T. Jud. 11:3 Judah says that his wife actually took a Canaanite wife for Shelah while Judah was away. He then cursed her and she died (11:4-5). For Zakovitch and Shinan, juxtaposition of the two events in Jubilees suggests that in it too there is evidence of the tradition that her death was a punishment for her refusal to give Shelah to Tamar (*Judah and Tamar*, 81).
18 The text says literally "and Judah was comforted"; see the note to the NRSV rendering of 38:12.
19 The reader may conclude, however, that Judah was at fault for allowing his wife to negate the promise he made to Tamar in v. 6. Segal (*Jubilees*, 59-72),

who thinks that most of the changes the writer makes to the story in Genesis 38 were intended "to mitigate Judah's guilt throughout the narrative" (p. 60), cites the present instance as a case in point. "This change improves Judah's image in two respects: first, Judah is not responsible for preventing the marriage of Shelah and Tamar. Second, Judah did not lie to or mislead Tamar when he sent her to her parents' home. He intended to fulfill his promise [something that may not be true in Gen 38:11; on this point, see Zakovitch and Shinan, *Judah and Tamar*, 210-11, etc.]" (p. 61). His points are valid, but Judah is still a weak head of his household because he does not overrule the wishes of his Canaanite wife.

place over a three-year period (2165–2168). Judah is an unmarried man in the next episode.

8-21 Judah and Tamar (Gen 38:12b-26)

The familiar story of Tamar's skill at driving events in a different direction and the eventual birth of twins from the union of father-in-law with daughter-in-law occupies all the remaining space in Genesis 38 and most of it in Jubilees 41. Once again, however, the author of Jubilees subjects the account to a significant recasting.

8-12 Tamar Misleads Judah (Gen 38:12b-18)

The next stage in the family story transpires the following year (2169).

■ **8** According to Genesis, Judah went up to his sheep-shearers, while in Jubilees he goes up to do the work of shearing his sheep (this is what people tell Tamar in the next line in Genesis) in the year after Bathshua/Bedsuel died.[20] In both he goes to a place called Timnah, where his herds were located. Tamar received the news about his travel from unnamed informants who refer to Judah as her father-in-law.[21] Since the writer had bypassed Gen 38:1-5, the reader receives little help in learning where the action takes place. Judah's friend Hirah, with whom he was associated years earlier in Genesis—at the time when Judah originally laid eyes on the woman who became his wife—and with whom he now travels in Genesis (38:12), was an Adullamite (see 38:1). Adullam was, it is likely, located west of a line from Bethlehem to Hebron. Timnah seems to have been a few miles to the northeast of Adullam.[22] By going to Timnah, Judah must have been passing near the place where Tamar was staying in her father's house[23] because the news that he was traveling that route galvanized her into action. In Jubilees he travels alone, while Genesis suggests that he and Hirah were making the journey together.[24]

■ **9** Neither Genesis nor Jubilees says that Tamar had worked out a detailed plan of action to accomplish her purpose. The texts simply describe what she did after hearing that her father-in-law would be walking along a certain road. Her first action was to change her clothing from what must have been the recognizable garb of a widow. Judah had ordered her to live at her father's house as a widow until his third son came of age, and she had done precisely that. In fact, one could say that she was no longer obligated to live under such conditions, since Shelah had in fact reached maturity (Jub 41:7).[25] Jubilees noted this before the present verse, but Genesis does so only much later in the story (v. 26; in v. 14 Tamar is aware that Shelah was grown). Tamar, therefore, was within her rights to lay aside her widow's cloth-

---

20 T. Jud. 12:1 dates the journey two years later. Both Jubilees and the Testament of Judah lend specificity to the vague "In the course of time [וירבו הימים]" in Gen 38:12 (with reference to the death of Bathshua that was followed by the period of mourning and his visiting the sheepshearers).

21 There are three passages in the section about Judah and Tamar (that is, in vv. 8-21) in which their continuing in-law relationship is mentioned (vv. 8, 16, 18) and two in the legal section (that is, in vv. 23-28)—vv. 23, 26. This fact shows that Kugel, speaking about the point in the story when Tamar decides to act as a prostitute (*Walk through* Jubilees, 182), misstates the case in referring to Judah as her "ex-father-in-law." Both the narrative and the legal section present them as in-laws throughout. This becomes important in analyzing the legal section and is missed by Kugel and Segal, both of whom attribute part of the legal section to another writer (see below on these verses).

22 See Hamilton, *Genesis 18–50*, 432–33, 439.

23 This makes one wonder whether the author would have agreed with T. Jud. 10:1 that she was from Mesopotamia. If so, the family later moved to the Shephelah. Zakovitch and Shinan (*Judah and Tamar*, 44) cite *Bereshit Rabbati* in which there is a tradition that Judah took her from Aram-naharaim (= Mesopotamia) with her father, mother, and three brothers. He did not allow them to return to Aram-naharaim but built a city for them in the land where they settled.

24 Werman, *Jubilees*, 493.

25 Esther Menn, *Judah and Tamar (Genesis 38) in Ancient Jewish Exegesis: Studies in Literary Form and Hermeneutics* (JSJSup 51; Leiden: Brill, 1997) 32. Though Menn does not include Jubilees 41 among the later texts she studies in detail (she deals with the story in *Targum Neofiti*, Testament of Judah, and *Genesis Rabbah*), her book offers much of value for analyzing the one in Jubilees (she provides a list of unique agreements between the Testament of Judah and Jubilees 41 on p. 164). See also Hamilton, *Genesis 18–50*, 441.

ing, but her more radical step was to don a very different kind of apparel. There is some uncertainty about exactly what she does in Gen 38:14 after putting on a veil: she either covers herself or puts on perfume.[26] She then took a seat "at the entrance to Enaim, which is on the road to Timnah" (Gen 38:14). There are intriguing possibilities for translating "the entrance to Enaim," which could be rendered as "the opening of the eyes."[27] In Jubilees she put on a veil and "beautified herself"[28] before she "sat down at the gate near the road to Timnah." The writer saw no place-name in Gen 38:14 or ignored it; as he tells the story, she simply sat at some gate on the way to Timnah where Judah was bound to pass. Judah had failed to do as he promised; Tamar now seizes the initiative, obviously not to ensure she will be given as a wife to Shelah but to fashion events in a way that seemed better to her.

■ **10a** If "the entrance to Enaim" hints at the meaning "opening of the eyes," it would be ironic because Judah sees her but does not recognize her: "When Judah saw her,[29] he thought her to be a prostitute, for she had covered her face" (Gen 38:15). Apparently the veil itself did not signify that she was a prostitute; Judah did not recognize Tamar because the veil obscured her face,[30] and he drew a conclusion about the kind of woman she was from the place where she was sitting.[31] Judah and his brothers had duped their father with a piece of clothing (Joseph's robe); now he himself is fooled by an item of dress.[32] In Jubilees Judah "finds" rather than "sees" her and makes the same inference about her character.

■ **10b-12** The encounter between Judah and the "prostitute" occupies the next several verses.

Genesis 38:16-19	Jubilees 41:10b-12
He went over to her at the roadside,[33] and said, "Come, let me come in to you," for he did not know she was his daughter-in-law. She said, "What will you give me, that you may come in to me?" He answered, "I will send you a kid from the flock." And she said, "Only if you give me a pledge, until you send it." He said, "What pledge shall I give you?" She replied, "Your signet and your cord, and the staff that is in your hand." So he gave them to her, and went in to her, and she conceived by him.	He said to her, "Let me come in to you." She said to him, "Come in." So he came in. She said to him, "Give me my fee." He said to her, "I have nothing with me except the ring on my finger,[34] my neck chain,[35] and my staff that is in my hand."[36] She said to him, "Give them to me until you send my fee." He said to her, "I will send you a kid." He gave them to her. After he was with her,[37] she became pregnant by him.

---

26 *DCH* 6:430, s.v. עלף lists both possibilities. Hamilton (*Genesis 18–50*, 438 n. 4) prefers "perfumed herself."

27 E.g., Hamilton, *Genesis 18–50*, 440. *Targum Pseudo-Jonathan* Gen 38:14 reads: "She sat at the *crossroads* on the way to Timnah, *where all eyes look*." Kugel suggests that the author may have omitted the name because he thought it signified that the act was committed "in the sight of everyone" (*A Walk through* Jubilees, 182 n. 330). Ira Robinson quickly summarizes some of the possibilities and suggests, "She sat, invitingly,/at Enaim, which is by the way to Timna" ("*bĕpetaḥ 'ênayim* in Genesis 38:14," *JBL* 96 [1977] 569). Robinson thinks the phrase is to be contrasted with "covering of eyes" in Gen 20:16, where it has to do with freeing Sarah from the suspicion that Abimelech had committed adultery with her ("exoneration" in NRSV). Yet if the phrase in Gen 20:16 has the opposite sense of the one here, one should, for the sake of consistency, translate the words in Gen 38:14 without a place-name, with the two terms together suggesting the idea of openness.

28 Leslau, *Concise Dictionary*, 52. LXX Gen 38:14 understands the verb in the same way.

29 Genesis 38:2 mentions another instance of his seeing: "Judah saw the daughter of a certain Canaanite," who became his wife (the daughter of Shua).

30 This is the likely meaning of the text, though Hartom claims that Jubilees does not say the veil was for covering ("Jubilees," 119–20 n. to v. 9). Putting on the veil did not, however, signal that she was a prostitute; it did prevent Judah from recognizing her.

31 Zakovitch and Shinan, *Judah and Tamar*, 213; Hamilton, *Genesis 18–50*, 441–43; see also Menn, *Judah and Tamar*, 72–73. The Testament of Judah explains the situation differently: "she adorned herself in bridal array, and sat in the city of Enan by the gate. –For it was a law of the Amorites that she who was about to marry should sit in impurity by the gate for seven days" (12:1b-2). Judah did not recognize her because he was drunk (v. 3; wine and drunkenness are major topics in the Testament of Judah).

32 Zakovitch and Shinan, *Judah and Tamar*, 212; Menn, *Judah and Tamar*, 76. This is just one of the several

Both versions tell a similar story about requesting a prostitute's services, bargaining over the price, the sexual act, and the resulting pregnancy, but the order of events is not the same and some words assigned to one character in Genesis are assigned to the other in Jubilees. Both texts begin the interchange with Judah's proposition to the woman he takes to be a prostitute. In Genesis negotiations about the fee precede Judah's "going in" to her. In Jubilees it appears as if they first have sex together (after she invites him—something she never does in Genesis)[38] and then discuss payment. Genesis alone repeats that Judah was ignorant of the woman's identity. In Genesis, she asks what he will pay her if they go ahead with the act, and Judah promises her a goat. However, in Jubilees, after their union she demands payment.[39] Judah, perhaps traveling lightly, claimed he had nothing with him except his ring, chain, and staff. She accepts them as a pledge until he sends her proper payment. So he is the one who first mentions these three items. In Genesis, Tamar is the one who names the three objects that she would keep until he paid her with the animal. The kid appears in the conversation in Jubilees after the pledge is defined by Tamar and given by Judah. Only then does the assignation take place in Genesis followed by a notice of her pregnancy. Jubilees refers back to their intercourse that had occurred earlier and also notes the pregnancy. Tamar seems to be a stronger, more self-assured character in Jubilees. She performs as a prostitute before agreeing on the payment, and she is the one who determines what the pledge will be after Judah admitted that the three items were all he had in his possession.

13-15 Tamar Disappears (Gen 38:19-23)

Genesis and Jubilees relate the way in which Judah, who tried to pay his debt quietly, failed and called off the search—ironically, out of concern for his reputation.

■ **13** Genesis transitions from the previous scene by telling what Tamar did next: "Then she got up and went away, and taking off her veil she put on the garments of her widowhood" (38:19). Jubilees reports what both characters did: "Then Judah went to shear his sheep, but she went to her father's house." Judah, of course, needed access to his flock in order to fulfill the agreement with

---

33 Jubilees lacks an equivalent for the clause, but at the beginning of v. 10 it reads (unlike Genesis): "As Judah was going along."

34 "On my finger" is not present in the ancient versions of Gen 38:18 but is supported by both the Ethiopic and Latin versions of Jubilees. The Syriac citation of the passage lacks it.

35 See Leslau, *Concise Dictionary*, 191. LXX Gen 38:18 also has a word for a necklace. The cord in the Hebrew text apparently refers to something from which to hang one's signet ring (see Skinner, *Genesis*, 454; Charles, *Jubilees*, 229).

36 Testament of Judah 12:4 identifies the three items as "my staff and my girdle and the diadem of kingship" and in this way relates the incident to Judah's royal status. See also 15:3; *Gen. Rab.* 85:9; and Menn, *Judah and Tamar*, 154-55.

37 "After he was with her" has fallen from the Ethiopic manuscript tradition, but it is present in the Latin translation and the Syriac citation. It seems to refer to what had already occurred, since all three versions mention already in v. 10 that they had sex together. The Latin and Syriac readings are not, therefore, parallel to the order of events in Genesis

interconnections between the chapters that these writers and others have noticed.

38, as Charles implies (*Jubilees*, 229) and Zakovitch and Shinan (*Judah and Tamar*, e.g., 116, 120) repeat. Werman thinks the line indicates that their sexual union occurred after their bargaining over the fee (*Jubilees*, 493).

38 Kugel (*Walk through Jubilees*, 182; "Jubilees," 428) says that Judah's proposition to Tamar, which in Genesis could be taken as crude, is modified in Jubilees so that he asks to come into her house (Werman [*Jubilees*, 491 n. 17, 493] also thinks they are speaking about a house). Since Judah says the same words in both versions—let me come in to you—it is difficult to see any modification of the kind Kugel finds here. No house is mentioned in this verse.

39 Halpern-Amaru thinks that Tamar, who is a virgin at the beginning of the scene with Judah, does not have as her intention to lead Judah into impurity (*Empowerment*, 114-15). In this way, she "disengages the sexual union from the feigned harlotry" (p. 115). She assumes the role of a prostitute only when, after the act, she wants payment. The public place where she sat argues against Halpern-Amaru's assessment.

Tamar. Genesis assumes he continued on his way so that in the verses that follow he will be able to send her the promised compensation. While Genesis fails to specify where she goes, the writer of Jubilees says that Tamar went to her father's house; he does not say that she resumed wearing widow's clothing. She no longer had to do that, since Shelah had come of age; by now her days of widowhood should have ended.

■ **14-15** Judah's attempt at payment comes next.

Genesis 38:20-23	Jubilees 41:14-15
When Judah sent the kid by his friend the Adullamite, to recover the pledge from the woman, he could not find her. He asked the townspeople, "Where is the temple prostitute who was at Enaim by the wayside?" But they said, "No prostitute has been here." So he returned to Judah, and said, "I have not found her; moreover the townspeople said, 'No prostitute has been here.'" Judah replied, "Let her keep the things as her own, otherwise we will be laughed at; you see, I sent this kid, and you could not find her."	He sent the kid through his Adullamite shepherd, but he did not find her. He asked the men of the area, "Where is the prostitute who was here?" They said to him, "There is no prostitute here, nor do we have any prostitute with us." He returned and told him, "I did not find her, and when I asked the men of the area, they said to me, 'There is no prostitute here.'" Judah said, "Let her keep them so that we may not become the object of mockery."

Judah is at least true to his word, but he does not transport the payment to the "prostitute" himself. Rather, he sends someone who had appeared at the beginning of Genesis 38 (v. 1), while he figures here for the first time in Jubilees' retelling. The MT refers to him as Judah's friend, while in Jubilees he is his shepherd (as in LXX)—two well-attested readings of the same consonants (רעהו).[40] The reason why he sends this Hirah (for the name see Gen 38:1) is, of course, to deliver the goat,[41] but by doing so he was also to recover the items he had left with her as a pledge. Jubilees says nothing about the possibility of recovering them; Tamar had them firmly in her possession to be used at a later time. The Adullamite questions the local folk about how to find the person Judah took to be a prostitute—using a different term than the one in Gen 38:15 (hence "temple prostitute" in NRSV);[42] with the LXX interpretive tradition, the writer of Jubilees uses the same term for prostitute throughout this section. When specifying the place where she had been, the Adullamite refers to "Enaim by the wayside," but in Jubilees the location is simply "here." The locals are a little more helpful in Jubilees than in Genesis: they denied a prostitute was present and insisted they had no prostitute with them. Their town was not that kind of place.[43] So, in both versions of the episode, Tamar, by disappearing from the scene, retains the evidence from her encounter with her father-in-law (as Potiphar's wife retained Joseph's garment as proof of their contact). Judah in Genesis seems to excuse himself of wrongdoing by declaring that he had indeed forwarded the payment, but his messenger was unable to find the person to whom he, in good faith, had sent it. The writer of Jubilees does not reproduce the end of Judah's reply to the Adullamite.[44] Neither Genesis nor Jubilees suggests that Judah thought it odd that the woman could not be found[45] and that there might be more to the situation

---

40   See the textual note. Kugel, after noting the two possibilities for reading רעהו, writes, "*Jubilees*' author, with his horror of close ties with non-Jews, would obviously prefer 'his shepherd'" ("Jubilees," 428).

41   For the role of the goat here as a parallel to the one in Gen 37:31, see *Gen. Rab.* 85:9, where God says to Judah: "You deceived your father with a goat kid; by your life, Tamar will deceive you with a goat kid" (Freedman's translation modified).

42   Hamilton (*Genesis 18–50*, 447) thinks Hirah was trying to be polite and so used a euphemism. As he comments, there is no indication that Tamar was near or at a sanctuary. See also Menn, *Judah and Tamar*, 68–73 (whatever the precise meaning intended, the term קדשה provides a link with Deut 23:18 and Hos 4:14).

43   Cf. Zakovitch and Shinan, *Judah and Tamar*, 140. Werman finds more suggested by the double statement: the first ("There is no prostitute here") refers to the city gate, and the second ("nor do we have any prostitute with us") points to the city (*Jubilees*, 493). She includes her rather specific understanding of the two clauses in her argument that in v. 10 the several references to coming in mean coming in to her house. In the context of a conversation between a man and someone he took to be a prostitute, another explanation is more likely.

44   This is an instance in which Jubilees omits an element that could mitigate Judah's guilt—contrary to the tendency Segal finds throughout the retelling (see *Jubilees*, 59–72).

45   As Jubilees phrased it in v. 10, Judah "found her" when traveling and took her to be a prostitute.

than he suspected. Also, neither has Judah indulge in any self-reflection about visiting someone he thought was a prostitute. He simply moves on with his life after trying to limit the awkwardness. The recipient of Isaac's ringing blessing is not an impressive character. His marriage to a Canaanite woman had been a predictable disaster, two of his sons and his wife were dead, he lacked a married male heir, he failed to keep his word regarding his third son (allowing his miserable wife to cancel out his promise to Tamar), and he was now guilty of sexual misconduct.[46]

16-21 The Truth Emerges and Twins Are Born (Gen 38:24-30)

The high point of the drama comes in the section in which Judah finally does recognize the nature of the situation and his own failings in it. Once more the retelling in Jubilees follows the story line in Genesis but alters it in several ways.

Genesis 38:24-26	Jubilees 41:16-20
About three months later Judah was told, "Your daughter-in-law Tamar has played the whore; moreover she is pregnant as a result of whoredom." And Judah said, "Bring her out, and let her be burned."	When she reached three months, she was visibly pregnant. Judah was told, "Your daughter-in-law Tamar has now become pregnant through prostitution." Judah went to her father's house and said to her father and brothers, "Bring her out and let her be burned because she has done something impure in Israel."
As she was being brought out, she sent word to her father-in-law, "It was the owner of these who made me pregnant." And she said, "Take note, please, whose these are, the signet and the cord and the staff." Then Judah acknowledged them and said, "She is more in the right than I since I did not give her to my son Shelah." And he did not lie with her again.	When she was brought out to be burned, she sent the ring, the neck chain, and the staff to her father-in-law and said, "Recognize whose these are because I am pregnant by him." Judah recognized them and said, "Tamar has been more just than I; therefore, do not burn her." For this reason she was not given to Selom, and he did not approach her again.

■ **16** Genesis mentions an interval of approximately three months,[47] at which time Judah received an anonymous report—the second anonymous report in the chapter (see v. 13). The writer of Jubilees speaks of the passage of three months, at which time it became public knowledge that Tamar was pregnant because she was already showing. Genesis does not explain how people knew of her condition. The anonymous report in Genesis consists of two clauses: Tamar had become a prostitute, and moreover she had become pregnant because of her activity. In Jubilees the informants speak more tersely: she was pregnant through prostitution.

■ **17** A more telling difference appears in the next lines. According to Genesis, Judah simply announces that she is to be executed by fire; to whom he announced this (the verbal form is plural) and why burning was the penalty is not said. Jubilees makes a more formal occasion of it: Judah goes to her house and gives the order for burning her to the male heads of the family—her father and brothers.[48] He demands that Tamar be brought forth and burned, but, unlike Genesis, he furnishes a reason: "because she has done something impure [*rekwsa*/ *inmunditiam*/Syriac *ṭnpwt*'] in Israel."[49] The prohibition of impurity is, of course, a fundamental one in Jubilees, one enunciated by Noah (see 7:20), Abraham (20:3-6),

---

46 This description of Judah in Jubilees 41 seems more accurate than Segal's general claim: "In sum, *Jub.* 41:1-21, 27-28, presents a story in which Judah erred in the choice of a Canaanite wife, but from that point on, he neither made any mistakes nor did he sin" (*Jubilees*, 65). Judah has in fact allowed his wife to keep him from fulfilling his promise to Tamar, and he had slept with someone he thought was a prostitute but who, though she proved not to be a prostitute, was his daughter-in-law (Judah is called her father-in-law in 41:8, 18 and she is his daughter-in-law in 41:16). In other words, he both made mistakes and sinned.

47 As Zakovitch and Shinan (*Judah and Tamar*, 151) note, L.A.B. 9:5 refers to this notice: in Egypt, Amram tells his fellow Israelites that, like Tamar, the pregnancies of their wives will not be visible for three months (this figured into his plan to defy the king's orders about male Hebrew babies).

48 So the formulation in Jubilees serves to explain the plural verb in Genesis (Zakovitch and Shinan, *Judah and Tamar*, 150-51).

49 Zakovitch and Shinan take the Hebrew original to have been נבלה and relate it to other passages in which the term occurs (e.g., Gen 34:7; Judg 20:10; 2 Sam 13:12) (*Judah and Tamar*, 150-51).

and Rebekah (25:1) and one addressed by the angel (see 30:10, 13; 33:19, 20). There was to be no impurity in Israel, and Abraham had commanded all of his children: "If any woman or girl among you commits a sexual offense, burn her in fire" (20:4). The Angel of the Presence tells Moses (after the passage about Reuben's sin with Bilhah): "No sin is greater than the sexual impurity that they commit on the earth because Israel is a holy people for the Lord its God. It is the nation that he possesses; it is a priestly nation; it is a priestly kingdom; it is what he owns. No such impurity [rekws/inmunditia] will be seen among the holy people" (33:20). Judah, feeling a need to enforce the prohibition of impurity in Israel that he had ignored, demands that the law Abraham taught be applied to Tamar. In so doing, he was unwittingly indicting himself for the sin of sexual impurity.[50]

The penalty named by Judah—one that has no basis in Genesis—has been the subject of much interest. Several issues arise in connection with it. First, Judah addresses his words to Tamar's father and brothers. They are the ones who must bring her out and burn her. Fathers certainly were responsible for their unmarried daughters when they were living at home, but brothers too played a role. In Genesis 34 Hamor and Shechem speak to Jacob and his sons about giving Dinah to Shechem (vv. 8-17)—another occasion when an impermissible sexual act had been committed "in Israel" (Gen 34:7). So Judah calls upon these guardians of his daughter-in-law Tamar who too had "done something impure in Israel" (Jub 41:17) to carry out their responsibility.

Second, he claims that the appropriate punishment for her crime was death by fire. As many have noted, the only time in the HB when a daughter is to be burned for prostitution is Lev 21:9: "When the daughter of a priest profanes herself through prostitution, she profanes her father; she shall be burned to death."[51] The passage prescribes death by burning for a daughter guilty of prostitution, as in Jubilees 41, but the law applies only to a priest's daughter, not to daughters in non-priestly families, who, rather, suffer stoning for prostitution. Deuteronomy 22:20-21, which also shares some language with Judah's demand, speaks to such cases: "If, however, this charge is true, that evidence of the young woman's virginity was not found [when she married], then they shall bring the young woman out to the entrance of her father's house and the men of her town shall stone her to death, because she committed a disgraceful act in Israel by prostituting herself in her father's house. So you shall purge the evil from your midst." According to this law, Tamar should, therefore, have met execution by a different method—stoning—not by burning.

In the history of interpretation, one way in which to account for the death penalty by burning has been to find a priestly ancestry for Tamar. *Targum Pseudo-Jonathan* Gen 38:6 provides an example: "Judah took a wife for Er his first-born, *the daughter of Shem the Great*, whose name was Tamar." In v. 24 it continues in the same vein: "Now, after *a period of* three months *it became known that she was pregnant*; and Judah was told, as follows: 'Your daughter-in-law Tamar has played the harlot; and moreover, behold, she is pregnant because of (her) harlotry.' And Judah said, '*Is she not the daughter of a priest?* Bring her out and let her be burned.'"[52] Shem was regarded as a priest because he was identified with Melchizedek (instances are found in the targums to Gen 14:18).[53] If, then, Tamar was in some sense a daughter of Shem, she belonged to a priestly family and the law of Lev 21:9 would apply to her.

Jubilees, however, does not identify Shem as Melchizedek nor does it refer to Tamar as a daughter of Shem.[54] Shem is the son to whom Noah, who acted as a priest, passed all of his books (Jub 10:14), but even if the author of Jubilees thought Shem was a priest he does not call Tamar his daughter. It has been pointed out that Aram

---

50 Segal (*Jubilees*, 64) deals only with how 20:4 applies to Tamar but not with how 20:6 (addressed to Abraham's sons and grandsons) applies to Judah: "Now you keep yourselves from all sexual impurity and uncleanness." Judah too was guilty of violating Abraham's instructions and thus sinned in having sex with his daughter-in-law. He is not free of sin in the narrative.

51 See, e.g., Albeck, *Jubiläen*, 26–27.

52 The same identification occurs in *Gen. Rab.* 85:10, where Lev 21:9 is quoted. See Beer, *Jubiläen*, 52; Charles, *Jubilees*, 230; Zakovitch and Shinan, *Judah and Tamar*, 149, 152–54.

53 Cf., e.g., Menn, *Judah and Tamar*, 346–47.

54 See, e.g., Finkelstein, "Rabbinic Halaka," 56.

was a descendant of Shem (Gen 10:22; see Jub 7:18; 9:5), and Tamar is an Aramean in Jubilees (41:1),[55] but the writer attaches no priestly claims to this ethnic label.[56] He does, however, indicate clearly the source of Judah's verdict: Abraham (and the Angel of the Presence) dealt with sexual transgressions of this sort, and Judah was simply applying the ancestral law to the situation. The author makes this very point in 41:28: "For in his integrity he had gone and demanded punishment because Judah had wanted to burn her on the basis of the law that Abraham had commanded his children." Judah would have known the law from Jacob and possibly Isaac, both of whom were present when Abraham expressed it in chap. 20 (see v. 1).

■ **18** Tamar seems remarkably calm and collected as the men of her family bring her out to suffer a painful form of execution. Genesis again, as with the speech of the unknown informants in v. 24, divides her words into two parts: in her first sentence—directed to Judah—she declares that the owner of the objects she has in her possession made her pregnant; in the second she urges him to take note of the one to whom the signet, cord, and staff belong. In Jubilees she first sends Judah the three named items and then tells him to determine whose they are, as the owner is the one responsible for her pregnancy.[57] The passage reveals how clever she had been not only to demand the pledges but also to prevent Judah from recovering the distinctive, identifiable objects.

■ **19** When the charge of prostitution was made against Tamar, Judah did not investigate; her pregnancy was proof enough for him. Now when she declares the owner of the ring, chain, and staff to be the father, he again accepts the verdict without question.[58] In the story as told in Genesis and Jubilees, the key point is that Judah recognizes his own possessions and is forced to recall the occasion when he last had them. He had no choice but to acknowledge they were his and that he indeed was the person who impregnated her. In both texts he also realizes that Tamar was more righteous, more in the right, than he was.[59] In Genesis this relative judg-

---

55 Cf. Hartom, "Jubilees," 119 n. to v. 1.
56 Halpern-Amaru is surely correct when she writes: "The *Jubilees* concern with the sexual purity is an expression of this conception of the Israelite nation as a sanctified, or 'priest-like' community. Hence, in the halakha of *Jubilees* the violated woman (Bilhah) (33:10-12), the harlot (Tamar) (41:25-26), the Israelite woman given in marriage to a foreigner (Dinah and every future בת ישראל) (30:7), indeed, any female descendant of Abraham who commits a sexual offense (20:4), is to be treated as the daughter of a priest who has engaged in harlotry (Lev 21:9)" (*Empowerment*, 151). Several of the passages in Jubilees most pertinent to understanding the teaching in chap. 41 (30:7-8; 33:20) emphasize the holiness of Israel, but it does not entail that the writer in chap. 41 is claiming that Judah was appealing to Lev 21:9 to justify the sentence of burning for Tamar. The text is explicit that he was applying Abraham's law.
57 Genesis 38:25 uses the very words employed by Joseph's brothers when they asked Jacob to determine whether the cloak was Joseph's (37:32). The parallel regarding the two pieces of clothing was recognized long ago. It is found in the targums and elsewhere, as in *Gen. Rab.* 84:19, where, commenting on Gen 37:22, "R. Johanan said: The Holy One, blessed be He, said to Judah: 'You said to your father, KNOW NOW; as you live, you too will hear [the challenge], *Know now, whose are these?*' (Gen. xxxviii, 25)" (Freedman's translation modernized). What Judah (and the others) did to their father now happens to him.
58 His immediate acknowledgement contrasts with his report in the Testament of Judah where he says, "And not knowing what she had done I wanted to kill her; but she privately sent the pledges and put me to shame. And when I called her I heard also the secret words that I spoke in my drunkenness while sleeping with her. And I could not kill her, for it was from the Lord. But I said: Perhaps she did it deceitfully, having received the pledge from another woman" (12:5-7). Judah in the Testament does not admit that Tamar was more righteous than he. See Menn, *Judah and Tamar*, 155-56.
59 Christine Hayes distinguishes two meanings for "right/righteous" here, neither of which excludes the other: it could refer to ethical righteousness or to being right in a cause or contest (say, in a court case) ("The Midrashic Career of the Confession of Judah [Genesis xxxviii 26], Part I: The Extra-Canonical Texts, Targums and Other Versions," *VT* 45 [1995] 62-81, here 65-66). She then proceeds to show the ways in which these meanings played out in the ancient translations and other texts, such as Jub 41:19-20. The expression "She is more in the right than I" (two Hebrew words [צדקה ממני])

ment has to do with Judah's failure to keep his promise to Tamar about becoming Shelah's wife when he grew up. He was the one who was in the wrong, and in that specific regard Tamar was more just than he. But obvious questions remain unanswered, for example: as both were guilty of an illegal sexual union between father-in-law and daughter-in-law, why should both of them not be punished for this?

Jubilees formulates the matter differently. The writer does not claim that Judah was in the wrong because he forgot about carrying through on the levirate marriage arrangement. Judah publicly (her father and brothers are present) declares her more righteous than he—period; he had done something wrong and she acted more properly.[60] He withdraws the legal sentence he had pronounced on her so that she was not to be burned. But what does this mean? Was he saying that the two of them had not engaged in illicit sex and thus had not brought impurity into Israel? The sequel makes that an unlikely implication to draw from the scene.

■ 20 According to Gen 38:26 Judah saw his guilt in the fact that he did not give Tamar to Shelah. That option was now apparently no longer available because he does not tell Tamar he will make the arrangements for her to marry his third son right away.[61] In addition, the narrator reports that Judah never again had sex with Tamar. There is no suggestion that the encounter between them was wrong, and the thought of punishing Judah for anything he had done in the chapter never arises. In Jubilees Judah apparently is the one who makes a decision about his son Shelah: because of the events that had transpired in the chapter, he did not give Tamar to Shelah.[62] He, of course, was not the one primarily responsible for preventing the marriage; his wife had blocked it (41:7). So his guilt regarding the marriage that did not happen was mitigated to some extent, although he had not kept his promise. And now the marriage would have been inappropriate, since Judah and Tamar were apparently considered married and were expecting a child.[63] Shelah was no longer needed to produce a male heir for his brother Er, so there would be no question of another levirate marriage. The Judah of Jubilees also refrains from further sexual relations with Tamar: the Ethiopic text says he did not approach her again, while the Syriac citation agrees with most versions of Gen 38:26 by saying he did not know her again.[64]

---

was at times punctuated as two sentences: "she is just [צדקה]" and "it is from me [ממני]," with the latter meaning that Judah acknowledged the pregnancy was from him (e.g., *Tgs. Onq., Neof.*, and *Ps.-J.* Gen 38:26) or that the deity was saying the whole course of events had been orchestrated by him (e.g., *Gen. Rab.* 85:12). See below on v. 27. Judah's confession is not divided in any of these ways in Jub 41:19.

60 Anderson makes an interesting case that "she is more just than I" means that Tamar, unlike Judah, had not intermarried with Canaanites ("Torah before Sinai," 27–29). Judah married the Canaanitess Bathshua, so their sons were destined for uprooting according to Abraham's words in 20:4 (all the descendants of Canaan were to meet this fate). Tamar was more righteous than he in that she remained a virgin despite her marriage to Er and being given to Onan (both were half-Canaanite) and chose to have sexual relations with the non-Canaanite Judah. The next expression ("For this reason she was not given to Selom"), which the writer of Jubilees rewords as coming from the narrator rather than Judah (as it is in Gen 38:26 "'since I did not give her to my son Shelah'"), shows that it was foreordained that she not be given to Shelah and thus not marry a Canaanite. Anderson's point involves reading much into vv. 19-20, but is very helpful in understanding the teachings in v. 27 (see the commentary there). Hayes ("Midrashic Career," 67–68) also discusses how in Jubilees the "therefore" expression in Gen 38:26 "becomes a clause of consequence" and comes from the narrator, not from Judah. On the basis of v. 23, she takes Judah's meaning in confessing that Tamar was more in the right than he that Judah was confessing a sexual sin—sleeping with his daughter-in-law. He is more guilty of "sexual impropriety" than Tamar is. Cf. also Zakovitch and Shinan, *Judah and Tamar*, 172.

61 See Kugel, *Walk through Jubilees*, 183; "Jubilees," 429: this would have introduced another form of impurity.

62 See David Rothstein, "Why Was Shelah Not Given to Tamar? Jubilees 41:20," *Hen* 27 (2005) 120–22. He argues that the marriage would have been a violation of biblical law as the author understood it (e.g., having sex with the wife of one's father; Judah and Tamar had established a marital bond through intercourse and thus she could not be given to another man).

63 Cf. Loader, *Sexuality*, 182.

64 This is a case where Ethiopic Genesis and Ethiopic Jubilees agree on a distinctive reading, as the

■ **21** Genesis 38:27-30 next tells the entertaining story about the birth of twins—a story that has elements reminding one of the account regarding what happened when Esau and Jacob emerged from Rebekah's womb (Gen 25:24-26). A midwife is involved and the two boys receive names related to their actions and appearance. The author of Jubilees, as he did for the earlier twins (see 19:13), reduces the pleasant paragraph to one sentence reporting only the essentials: the births, the names of the two, and the date.[65] Perez and Zerah arrived in 2170, the year following the one in which Judah had gone on his fateful journey to shear his sheep (41:8). The date, besides situating the event in the overall chronology, provides proof—if more evidence were needed—that neither Er nor Onan could be the father of the children since they had died by the year 2168 (see v. 7). According to Gen 38:27-30, Perez was the first to emerge, though Zerah had extended his hand outside the womb before his brother was born. Jubilees gives their names in birth order, just as Gen 38:29-30 do. Perez becomes an ancestor of David (see Ruth 4:18-22).

22 The Seven Years of Abundance End (Gen 41:53)

For the second time the writer synchronizes events in the land with ones in Egypt. In 40:11-12 he noted that Isaac died in the year when the thirty-year-old Joseph rose to power in Egypt (2162). In the present instance he correlates the births of the twins with the end of the seven-year period of plenty that Joseph had predicted to Pharaoh when interpreting his dreams. So the years of abundance should have run from 2164 to 2170; that is, they began the second year after Joseph took office. Through the synchronisms the author of Jubilees takes care that the reader remember what was happening in Jacob's family in both places, though at this point the events could seem unrelated.[66] In the Testament of Judah something similar occurs, but it involves a different event: immediately after completing (in 12:10) his version of the story regarding Tamar and himself, he says, "And after this we came to Egypt, to Joseph, because of the famine" (12:11).[67]

23-28 Legal Issues[68]

The remainder of the chapter lacks a textual basis in Genesis. The writer takes up some of the questions a reader might have after reading the story in Genesis 38, and he handles them in ways that harmonize with his manner of reading the narratives about the patriarchs. Verses 23-25 deal with Judah's subsequent actions and the result that followed from them, while vv. 26-28 draw out the implications for Israel, with speaking interventions by the angel(s) in both parts.[69]

---

former too says that Judah did not approach her again. There could be influence from Ethiopic Genesis on Jubilees here, but the reading is more widely attested, as it is present also in T. Jud. 12:8: "But I did not again come near her until my death, because I had done this abomination in all Israel." For "approaching" in this sense, see also Jub 33:9, where Jacob does not again come near Bilhah.

65 See Halpern-Amaru, *Empowerment*, 116.
66 This more modest conclusion seems likelier than Berger's thesis that the sequence of vv. 22 and 23 (where Judah is penitent) leads to the conclusion that ending of the plentiful years was punishment for Judah's sin (*Jubiläen*, 520 n. a to chap. 41). Endres (*Biblical Interpretation*, 186), however, endorses Berger's idea, as does Loader (*Sexuality*, 182).
67 In Jub 42:1 the famine begins in 2171, and this is apparently the year in which the brothers first travel to Egypt to buy food. Judah was born in 2129 (Jub 28:15) so that he would have been forty-two years of age in that year. In T. Jud. 12:12 he is forty-six.
68 Menn has a helpful analysis of the legal questions raised by the story in Genesis 38 (*Judah and Tamar*, 49–73); her study is also relevant, naturally, to Jubilees 41, with some nuances.
69 This appears to be the natural way in which to divide vv. 23-28. Segal, however, thinks only vv. 23-26 constitute the legal section and vv. 27-28 continue the narrative (*Jubilees*, 59–72). That can hardly be the case, as Kugel has rightly noted, since all of vv. 23-28 are legal in nature (*Walk through* Jubilees, 288 n. 88 = "Interpolations," 265). Kugel, however, assigns vv. 23-26 to his interpolator (though the phrase "heavenly tablets" does not occur in it) and considers vv. 27-28 part of the author's text (e.g., *Walk through* Jubilees, 288–89 = "Interpolations," 265). See below for evaluations

23-25 Judah's Remorse and Pardon

The Genesis version of the story about Judah and Tamar is troubling for several reasons, not least because Judah receives no punishment for what he did. In fact, the subject never arises. He is eager to impose a penalty on Tamar but seems to hold himself to more relaxed standards. One could also ask whether Tamar still deserved punishment for her actions. Genesis leaves the reader wondering.

To his credit, the author of Jubilees addresses the larger issue of Judah's guilt and the lack of punishment for his violation of a law regarding sexual behavior. Naturally, he was not the only ancient writer to expand on the text in this fashion.

▪ **23** Judah himself recognizes that he has sinned, and he identifies the nature of his transgression: he unwittingly had sexual relations with his daughter-in-law. Thus, he does not claim she really was not his daughter-in-law because of the death of her husband Er (and Onan, though they did not marry); she remained his daughter-in-law to the present (see vv. 8, 16, 18).[70] The writer employs several terms to emphasize that Judah regarded his action as deeply wicked (evil [twice], wrong, erred, sin—all occur in v. 23). Judah definitely had done something bad. In asserting this, the passage is consistent with the narrative. The language used to describe the act—"he had uncovered his son's covering"—leads one to pentateuchal legislation regarding improper sexual relations, although the specific phrase does not occur in the two seemingly most relevant passages:

Leviticus 18:15: You shall not uncover the nakedness of your daughter-in-law: she is your son's wife; you shall not uncover her nakedness.

Leviticus 20:12: If a man lies with his daughter-in-law, both of them shall be put to death; they have committed perversion [תבל], their blood is upon them.

Another passage that is relevant, if one assumes the understanding stated in CD v:9–10 that while scriptural laws regarding sex are written for men they also apply to women, is Lev 20:14: "If a man takes a wife and her mother also, it is a depravity [זמה]; they shall be burned to death, both he and they, that there may be no depravity [זמה] among you." If that law were formulated for women, it would refer to a female who marries both a son and his father—the situation of Tamar in this story.[71] It would also account for the penalty that all parties involved be subjected to death by fire.

Judah's action, therefore, in impregnating Tamar would have been illegal by Mosaic law and both he and Tamar should have died, but was it illegal by the laws revealed to this time in Jubilees? The answer is yes, though the exact category of sleeping with one's daughter-in-law has not been mentioned before chap. 41. It would have been included under the more general rubric of sexual violations prohibited so strongly by Abraham in Jub 20:3-7 (the same term for sexual wrongdoing is used here).[72] Abraham's offspring were to keep themselves "from all sexual impurity and uncleanness and from all the contamination of sin so that you do not make our name into a curse, your entire lives into

---

of the contrasts they see between vv. 23-26 and the narrative.

70 Menn (*Judah and Tamar*, 61–62) correctly concludes, after considering the suggestion that once his two sons had died the in-law relationship between Judah and Tamar no longer existed, that the position is "untenable" in view of the several references to Judah as father-in-law and Tamar as daughter-in-law after the two deaths (Gen 38:11, 13, 16, 24, 25). The same is the case for Jubilees.

71 So Shemesh in Werman and Shemesh, *Revealing*, 169–70; Werman, *Jubilees*, 490, 494–95. The passage is reflected in vv. 25 and 26 below.

72 Segal (*Jubilees*, 65–66) elaborates an argument to the effect that the legal passage in the chapter, which he takes to be vv. 23-26, presents a "completely different evaluation of Judah's actions"

(p. 65) than the narrative does. As he understands it, the legal section does not mitigate Judah's guilt as the narrative seeks to do (but see above; the narrative is more concerned to establish Tamar's virginity than Judah's innocence; see also Dimant, "Judah and Tamar," 783–97; Schreiber, "Halakhic Redactor,"; Loader, *Sexuality*, 185 n. 472). Rather, it charges him with having illicit sex with his daughter-in-law (using the idiom "uncovered his son's covering"). The fact that she had not engaged in intercourse with Er and Onan does not help. That Judah needed forgiveness for his act shows it was a sin. He thinks that in the narrative Judah was not guilty of a sin (violating Lev 18:15 and 20:12; on these passages, see below) because Tamar had no relations with her first two husbands. So the one (the narrative) says it was not a sin, but the other

a (reason for) hissing and all your children into something that is destroyed by the sword. Then you will be accursed like Sodom, and all who remain of you like the people of Gomorrah" (20:6). In the case of Judah, the consequences for his children would be of much greater concern because the kings were to arise from him.

When Judah realized that what he did was wrong, "He began to lament and plead before the Lord because of his sin." He engages in penitential exercises much as his great descendant David would when his child with Bathsheba, another illicit union, was struggling for his life. "David therefore pleaded with God for the child; David fasted, and went in and lay all night on the ground" (2 Sam 12:16). Unlike the child of Bathsheba and David, the twins born to Tamar and Judah were allowed to live (see v. 27).

■ 24 At this juncture another dream appears in Jubilees. As in other instances, it is a dream in which a character—Judah, in this case—receives clear, straightforward information from a heavenly and thus utterly unimpeachable source. The Angel of the Presence, whose more direct speech continues to the end of the chapter, says that he and his colleagues ("We") disclosed to Judah that he would be forgiven (see v. 27 for another disclosure from them to Judah). The reasons they state are: the pleading and lamenting he had done and the fact that he never repeated the act (see v. 20). His behavior showed the sincerity with which he turned from his sin (cf. T. Jud. 15:4; 19:2–4).[73]

■ 25 The angel continues to explain why Judah received pardon for violation of a fundamental law.[74] Again he mentions Judah's refraining from repeating his action, but this time he adds that he turned "from his ignorance."[75] There certainly was an element of ignorance in Judah's behavior. In v. 10 he mistook Tamar for a prostitute (he obviously did not think she was Tamar),

---

73   One of Segal's reasons for thinking there is a conflict between the narrative and legal sections is what he takes to be two interpretations of Gen 38:26: one in the narrative (vv. 19 and 20b) and one in the legal paragraph (vv. 23-24) (*Jubilees*, 70–71). It is true that Jub 41:19 and 20b offer a rewritten version of Gen 38:26, but why one should think vv. 23-24 offer a second and different one is puzzling. The first element (v. 23) he pairs with Gen 38:26 because both say "Judah knew," but they are talking about different objects that Judah knew or recognized (the legal section) says it was. He concludes that Jubilees 41 is a case in which the narrative and legal sections are in conflict, showing they do not come from the same writer. His characterization of the narrative, however, ignores the fact that Judah and Tamar are called in-laws throughout and that their sexual union violated the prohibition stated by Abraham. Judah is guilty of sin in both the narrative and in vv. 23-26. The same point holds against Kugel, who thinks the author of the narrative was not interested in questions of guilt or innocence; he was concerned rather to show that Judah's descendants—the Jews—were not the offspring of an illicit union. Apart from the likelihood that the author was more concerned about the royal line than all the Jews, the contrast that Kugel finds between the work of the author (vv. 1-21, 27-28) and the interpolator results from a misinterpretation of both (see below).

nized (his three possessions in v. 19 and his guilt of sleeping with his daughter-in-law in v. 23); the second element (she is more just than I) does not match with the supposed corresponding feature in 41:23 ("He began to lament and plead"). The only correspondence is the fact that Jubilees, in discussing Judah's penitence, repeats that he did not sleep with her again. One does not have two differing interpretations of Gen 38:26 here; there is only a reference back to his appropriate response of not repeating his error.

74   Werman argues that the first sentence of v. 25 in Ethiopic is an addition because it repeats what is said in v. 24 and because the Syriac Chronicle lacks it (*Jubilees*, 492 n. 34). The first point is not accurate, since the line adds some new information, and the second is confusing since the Syriac citation ends with v. 24 and contains nothing from the rest of the chapter.

75   Charles suspected something was wrong with the text and thought it should read: "received forgiveness because of his ignorance and because he turned from his sin" (*Jubilees*, 231). The manuscripts offer two readings: (1) most have "He had forgiveness because he turned from his sin and from his ignorance"; (2) 20 25 35 have "He had forgiveness from his sin and from [MS. 20 om. "from"] his ignorance." So neither of the readings supports the change Charles wanted to make. It is not so clear that the text as present in the manuscripts

and he did not know he was responsible for her pregnancy and thus demanded death by burning for her (see v. 28).[76] The idea that Judah acted in ignorance occurs also in T. Jud. 19:3. After mentioning his repentance and the prayers of Jacob on his behalf (v. 2), he says, "But the God of my fathers, the compassionate and merciful, forgave me, because I did it in ignorance" (see also v. 4).

The angel hastens to add that the sin was a weighty one—perhaps he was concerned a reader might infer that he could imitate Judah and like him receive forgiveness. He alludes to Lev 20:14 as support for the notion that burning was the appropriate punishment—one that will befall anyone who acts in this way. The passage from Leviticus reads: "If a man takes a wife and her mother also, it is depravity; they shall be burned to death, both he and they, that there may be no depravity among you." It is likely that the writer is applying, as noted above (on v. 23), the principle stated in CD v:9–10 that laws written regarding males were also in force for females so that the passage fits the circumstances of Tamar and Judah (she was married to both a son and his father). Hence both should suffer burning.[77]

The wording in Jub 41:25, however, yields a sense that makes the law appear strange in its context: "Anyone who acts in this way—anyone who sleeps with ḥamātu [the word would most naturally be translated "his mother-in-law"]—is to be burned in fire so that he burns in it because impurity and contamination have come on them. They are to be burned." It is possible that in v. 25 the writer is talking more generally about sexual relations with a female in-law and forbidding them, and v. 26 indicates that this is the intention. Reference to the ḥamāt, however, seems peculiar, when the case under consideration involved a father-in-law sleeping with his daughter-in-law. As a result, some translators (Littmann, Goldmann, and Hartom)[78] have emended the text to read "daughter-in-law." Berger has taken a different approach: he adopts the reading "and anyone" (MSS. 21 42 47 48 58) so that the legal sentence begins: "Anyone who acts in this way and anyone who lies with his mother-in-law." For him, the writer is talking about two offenses as he does in v. 26: sex with a daughter-in-law, and sex with a mother-in-law.[79] However, neither an emendation nor adopting a reading found mostly in later manuscripts may be necessary, since the word ḥamātu introduces another potentially confusing element into the mix. The lexicographers say it can mean both mother-in-law and daughter-in-law,[80] and MSS. 20 21 35 58 read mar'ātu, "bride, spouse, daughter-in-law."[81] So the law in Lev 20:14 that deals with a forbidden in-law relationship is applied in Jub 41:25 to the specific instance described in the chapter; that law called for burning both the male and female(s) to death as punishment.

Segal suggests another way of arriving at a similar result. There is no need to change 41:25 from "mother-in-law" to "daughter-in-law" because of the midrash halakah operating here. Leviticus 20:12, which deals with the case of sleeping with a daughter-in-law, does not specify the method of punishment, but Lev 20:14 does—death by fire for the man and the two women involved (his wife and her mother). "*Jub.* 41:26 draws an analogy between the cases of intercourse with a daughter-in-law and with a mother-in-law, applying the method of punishment explicitly described in the latter case to the

---

76 means anything other than what Charles thought it should express.

76 Kugel, who attributes vv. 23-26 to an interpolator, thinks the approach to forgiveness in vv. 23-25 is like the one in the section about the Day of Atonement (5:17-19), which he also attributes to the interpolator (*Walk through* Jubilees, 184; "Jubilees," 429–30). He takes the reference in 5:18 to turning from "errors" to be a turning from unintentional sins like the one Judah committed. It is true that his ignorance of who the "prostitute" was moved his act into the category of unintentional and therefore less serious sins, ones for which penitence is appropriate and effective (cf. Dimant, "Judah and Tamar," 293-94), but the passage about the Day of Atonement concerns a once-per-year occasion, not the kind of situation pictured in 41:23-25 for Judah's process of repentance. For sins of ignorance, see Jub 22:14.

77 Werman, *Jubilees*, 490, 494–95.

78 Kugel also prefers "daughter-in-law" (*Walk through* Jubilees, 184; "Jubilees," 430).

79 Berger, *Jubiläen*, 524 n. e to v. 25. See VanderKam, *Jubilees* 2:275.

80 Dillmann, *Lexicon*, 77 (he refers to the present passage for the meaning *nurus*, "daughter-in-law"); Leslau, *Concise Dictionary*, 15.

81 Leslau, *Concise Dictionary*, 33.

82 Segal, *Jubilees*, 67 (see also pp. 68–69); cf. Loader, *Sexuality*, 183.

former."[82] But Segal's conclusion that this is "an alternative halakhic explanation for Tamar's punishment than that offered in the rewritten narrative"[83] is wide of the mark. He may have correctly retraced the writer's legal thinking, but he is guilty of confusing two matters: Why Judah wanted to punish Tamar in the story (he thought she was a prostitute) and the author's consideration of what actually happened—an illegal in-law relationship. There is no conflict here, since the story makes clear that Judah had sinned. In the narrative section, the writer indicates several times that in-laws were involved, and such unions were included under the category of sexual impurity. Kugel's suggestion that the author of vv. 1-21, 27-28 did not deal with questions of guilt or innocence likewise does not fit the evidence.[84] Exactly where the tension between the narrative and vv. 23-26 lies is not easy to see: Judah acknowledged that he had sinned in the narrative, and vv. 23-25 show why this man, this wrongdoer, received pardon. The two are consistent with each other.[85]

26-28 The Law for Israel

The second part of the legal section takes the familiar form of a direct address by the Angel of the Presence to Moses, though most manuscripts read just "you" in v. 26 and do not add "Moses." Kugel, as noted above, includes this verse in the section he thinks comes from an interpolator (vv. 23-26); if so, it is different from most other passages he assigns to this reviser in that it does not mention the heavenly tablets and the angel does not address Moses by name. Only form and content would be the identifying factors, but the form joins it with the preceding material (vv. 24-28 are a single angelic statement), and the content shows that it is consistent with all of chap. 41.[86]

■ **26** Now the Angel of the Presence tells Moses to give to the Israelites a law related to the story just narrated. Verse 26 casts helpful light on the law cited in v. 25—Lev 20:14. The angel mentions the basic principle that "there is to be no impurity among them"—a teaching that Abraham had conveyed to his children in 20:3, 6.[87] In this particular instance the prohibition takes the form of lying with one's daughter-in-law or mother-in-law, the two cases from Lev 20:12 and 20:14 that the writer may have associated with each other in v. 25. The law for Israel requires, therefore, that in cases like the one involving Judah and Tamar, both the man and the woman suffer death through burning so that such impurity can be literally purged from Israel (cf. 30:22; 33:11 for other statements about removal of impurity), with the terms "anger and punishment" suggesting that God is the one who actually does the punishing.[88] Once the offenders and the offense have been removed, that "anger and punishment" from him will also disappear. The reader is not to conclude that like Judah he would receive forgiveness if he imitated the patriarch in his dealings with Tamar.

■ **27** In v. 26 the writer established that both the man and woman involved in in-law sexual relations were to die, but, of course, neither Judah nor Tamar suffered that fate. In fact, once Judah was identified as the man who made her pregnant, there was no further thought about any punishment for Tamar. In this difficult verse the writer may be addressing that issue because Tamar

---

83 Segal, *Jubilees*, 67.
84 Kugel, *Walk through* Jubilees, 184-85; "Jubilees," 430.
85 Dimant, "Judah and Tamar," 791-92: the difference between the narrative and the unit in vv. 23-26 arises "not because it stems from a different source, as Segal argues, but because it deals with a different problem, namely Judah's crime." So also Schreiber, "Halakhic Redactor."
86 So Schreiber, "Halakhic Redactor"; and Dimant, "Judah and Tamar," 795-97. Regarding content or theme, Dimant indicates that v. 25 speaks of atonement for Judah's sin and v. 27 shows the result of the atonement—his offspring with Tamar survive for another generation. She finds a parallel with the material regarding Bilhah and Reuben in Jubilees 33, where Bilhah's ignorance and sorrow for what had happened form part of the same unit (as Segal also maintains), but both elements are, with the legal section, part of a consistent story.
87 Note that, according to Kugel, chap. 20 is by the author of the book.
88 Werman, *Jubilees*, 495.

now becomes the center of attention. He reverts to a point that he had emphasized in several ways early in the chapter: the Angel of the Presence and his fellow angels reveal to Judah that Tamar did not have sexual relations with either Er, her husband, or Onan, the reluctant levir.[89] It follows from this situation that Er and Tamar did not have a male heir, and Onan, who did not want to raise up seed for his brother, also did not. As a result, the line of Er came to an end; there was no succeeding generation for him. The person who was the progenitor of the next generation was Judah via Tamar—with no Canaanite involved.[90] Judah had received forgiveness in vv. 23-25, so now the angel and his colleagues tell him that the children born from the illegal union with Tamar were to survive and form another generation or family.

The term used for the other or future entity is *nagad*: "tribe, clan, kin, kindred, progeny, lineage, family."[91] The line or family will thus be traced from Judah/Tamar through their twin sons Perez and Zerah. This is in fact the situation in some of the genealogies of Judah. In Gen 46:12 Judah has five sons: Er, Onan, Shelah, Perez, and Zerah. The text then records that Er and Onan died in Canaan and proceeds to mention in the next generation only the sons of Perez. In Num 26:19-22, once the deaths of Er and Onan are noted, the writer refers to the clans of Shelah, Perez, and Zerah, and details the next generation only for Perez. The situation in 1 Chronicles is also pertinent. In 1 Chr 2:3-4 the genealogist names the five sons of Judah—the three with "the Canaanite woman Bath-shua" and the two with "[h]is daughter-in-law Tamar." He notes that the Lord killed the wicked Er and, upon turning his attention to the children of the twins, he devotes most of the chapter to tracing Judah's line through Perez. Finally, in 1 Chr 4:1 the sons of Judah are said to be: Perez, Hezron, Carmi, Hur, and Shobal.[92] The genealogies, therefore, bear out the contention in Jub 41:27 that Judah was the progenitor of another line, one that through Perez eventually produced King David. This line replaced the one that would normally have been continued through Judah's first son born of a Canaanite woman. The writer does not mention forgiveness for Tamar, but the fact that the children she had with Judah were established as another family suggests that she too was pardoned when Judah received forgiveness.[93]

---

89   Cf. Rothstein, "Sexual Union," 364; see also his conclusion: "In sum, whatever the precise meaning of the opaque formulation of 41:27, there can be no doubt that the author of *Jubilees* viewed the physical bond as determinative with regard to the legal status of individuals and the purity of their offspring" (p. 370). In other retellings of the story (see above on v. 19), a *bat qol* reveals to Judah important information. For example, *Tg. Ps.-J.* Gen 38:26 explains: "Then Judah acknowledged (them) and said, '*Tamar is* innocent; *she is pregnant* by me.' Then a heavenly voice came down from heaven and said, 'The matter has come from before me.' So both of them were delivered from judgment." In such reworkings, the comparative disappears and the preposition of that comparison (ממני) is rendered separately from "right/innocent" with two meanings: Judah confesses the pregnancy is "from me," so that Tamar is innocent; and the *bat qol* declares "the matter is from me," with the result that both Judah and Tamar are innocent. A similar rendering appears in *Targum Neofiti*.

90   See Anderson, "Torah before Sinai," 27-29 (cf. the summary of his view above on v. 19).

91   Leslau, *Concise Dictionary*, 128.

92   Only in v. 21 does Shelah put in an appearance. There he is called the son of Judah and he is the father, interestingly enough, of a son named Er. His descendants formed a guild of linen workers.

93   Segal (*Jubilees*, 62–64) considers different explanations of the word *nagad* (= family, for him): (1) the parallels between vv. 27 and 4 suggest that Judah performed the role of a levir for his sons and that "this offspring is for a different family, that of Er" (p. 62), though this would mean he violated the law prohibiting sleeping with his daughter-in-law. On this view, Segal thinks Jubilees implies that the laws of Leviticus are inapplicable when a marriage involving a son and daughter-in-law was not consummated. (2) v. 27 does not refer to levirate marriage. Since the sons did not have sex with Tamar she was not, in legal terms, his daughter-in-law. As a result, Judah did not violate Lev 18:15; 20:12. "Another family" refers to Judah's offspring in Numbers 26, where Shelah, Perez, and Zerah are the families descended from him. The first option seems unlikely, as there is no hint Judah is raising up a family for Er. The second tends more in the correct direction, but to say that "in legal terms"

■ **28** The punishment Judah had demanded for Tamar was the appropriate one, according to the angel. He emphasizes that Judah, at least in this instance, acted with integrity in sentencing her to death by fire because that was the law Abraham enunciated in Jub 20:4. The angel not only references the legislation by name ("the law that Abraham had commanded his children") but also draws language from it. He mentions the penalty of uprooting that Abraham names in 20:4 (he is speaking there about taking Canaanites for wives). Anyone who commits deeds of sexual impurity is to be uprooted (30:22; 33:13, 17, 19). The meaning is that the person is to lack descendants—to be removed from future existence on the earth. Judah and Tamar were forgiven for their offense and thus permitted to establish their new, totally non-Canaanite line upon the earth.

Tamar was no longer his daughter-in-law goes against the fact, noted several times above, that the writer calls her by that title throughout.

Joseph's Brothers Travel to Egypt

42

1/ During the first year of the third week of the forty-fifth[a] jubilee [2171], the famine began to come to the land. The rain refused to be given to the earth because there was nothing that was coming down. 2/ The earth became unproductive, but in the land of Egypt there was food because Joseph had gathered[a] the grain in the land[b] during the seven years of copious harvest and kept it.[c] 3/ When the Egyptians came to Joseph so that he would give them food, he opened the storehouses where the grain was. He gave (it) to them to eat in the first year[a] and[b] sold (it) to the people of the land[c] in exchange for money.[d]

4/ But the famine was very severe in the land of Canaan.[a] Jacob heard[b] that there was food in Egypt, so he sent his ten sons to get food for him in Egypt.[c] But he did not send Benjamin.[d] They arrived with those who were coming to Egypt.[e] 5/ Joseph recognized them, but they did not recognize him. He spoke with them, asked them questions,[a] and said to them, "Are you not spies?[b] You have come to investigate the paths of the land."[c] He then imprisoned them. 6/ Afterwards[a] he sent again[b] and summoned them.[c] He detained only Simeon[d] and sent his nine brothers away. 7/ He filled their sacks with grain[a] and returned their money to them[b] in their sacks. But they did not know (this).[c] 8/ He ordered them to bring their youngest brother because they had told him that their father was alive and their youngest brother (also).[a] 9/ They[a] went up from the land of Egypt and came to the land of Canaan. They told their father everything that had happened to them and how the ruler of the country[b] had spoken harshly with them and was holding Simeon until they should bring[c] Benjamin. 10/ Jacob said, "You have deprived me of children. Joseph does not exist nor does Simeon exist, and you are going to take Benjamin.[a] Your wickedness has come upon me."[b] 11/ He said, "My son will not go with you. Perhaps[a] he would become ill.[b] For their mother gave birth to two;[c] one has died and this one, too, you will take from me.[d] Perhaps he would catch a fever[e] on the way. Then you would bring down my old age[f] in sorrow to Sheol."[g] 12/ For he saw[a] that their money[b] was returned—each one in his purse[c]—and he was afraid to send him for this reason.[d]

13/ Now the famine grew increasingly severe[a] in the land of Canaan and in every land except the land of Egypt[b] because many Egyptians had kept[c] their seed in storage places[d] after[e] they saw[f] Joseph collecting grain,[g] placing it in storehouses, and keeping (it) for the years of the famine. 14/ The Egyptians[a] fed themselves with it during the first year of the famine.[b]

15/ When Israel saw that the famine was very severe in the land and (that) there was no relief, he said to his sons, "Go, return, and get us (some) food so that we may not die." 16/ But they said,[a] "We will not go. If our youngest brother does not come with us, we will not go."[b] 17/ Israel saw that[a] if he did not send him with them they would all die because of the famine. 18/ Then Reuben said,[a] "Put him under my control. If I do not bring him back to you, kill my two sons for his life." But he said to him, "He will not go with you."[b] 19/ Then Judah approached[a] and said,[b] "Send him with us.[c] If I do not bring him back to you, then let me be guilty[d] before you throughout my entire lifetime." 20/ So he sent him with them[a] during the second year of this week [2172], on the first of the month.[b] They arrived in the country of Egypt with all who were going (there) and (had) their gifts[c] in their hands: stacte, almonds, terebinth nuts, and honeycombs.[d]

21/ They arrived and stood in front of Joseph. When he saw his brother Benjamin, he recognized him[a] and said to them, "Is this your youngest brother?" They said to him, "He is."[b] He said, "May God be gracious to you, my son." 22/ He sent him[a] into his house and brought Simeon out to them.[b] He prepared[c] a dinner for them. They presented him with his gifts[d] that they had brought[e] in their hands. 23/ They ate in front of him. He gave portions to all of them, but Benjamin's share was seven times larger than the share of any of them. 24/ They ate and drank. Then they got up and stayed[a] with their donkeys. 25/ Joseph conceived of a plan by which he would know their thoughts—whether there were peaceful thoughts

Jubilees 42

between them.[a] He said to the man who was in charge of[b] his house, "Fill all their sacks with food for them and return their money to them in their containers; put the cup[c] with which I drink[d] in the sack of the youngest[e]—the silver cup—and send them away."[f]

Textual Notes

1a forty-fifth] "forty-fourth" 20 25 35 39 42 47 48. See 41:1.
2a gathered] + "in order to give them food and (because 58) Joseph gathered" 25 47 48ᶜ 58. The plus is lacking from almost all of the earlier MSS. and from Lat., so it is probably an addition to the text (see VanderKam, *Jubilees* 2:276).
b the grain in the land] "the grain of the land" Lat.
c (kept) it] om. 9 38 63.
3a the grain was. He gave (it) to them to eat in the first year] = Lat.; Eth. "the grain of the first year." There is no trace of the extra words of Lat. in the Eth. copies or in Gen 41:56. Charles (*Ethiopic Version*, 153 n. 1 to Lat.) thought they were corrupt. Cf. VanderKam, *Jubilees* 2:276. Possibly one could explain the difference between the two versions of Jubilees by positing an omission in the textual tradition represented by Eth.: if the Hebrew text read אכל where the versions have "grain" and the longer reading ended with לאכל, a scribe could have skipped from one to the other, leaving only the time designation. אכל would not, however, be a likely reading in the line, though the word is used fairly often in the context in Genesis (e.g., 41:35, 36). Werman (*Jubilees*, 496 n. 1) conflates the two versions: where the grain was, in the first year, and sold (it) to the people of the land in exchange for money.
b and (sold)] "because" Lat. Gen 41:56 has "and."
c to the people of the land (or: "people of the earth")] "to them" Lat. Gen 41:56: "to the Egyptians."
d in exchange for money] Lat. and Gen 41:56 lack these words.
4a But the famine was very severe in the land of Canaan] Eth. lacks the sentence, but it is present in Lat., and similar ones appear in Gen 41:56, where it applies to Egypt, and in 41:57, where the statement lacks a place-name. A sentence like this provides some context for Jacob's hearing about food in Egypt; otherwise, the reader is not aware there was a problem unless the general comment at the beginning of 42:2 sufficed. See also Gen 42:5. Charles considered it original and placed the equivalent words in his critical text of the Eth. version (*Ethiopic Version*, 152 n. 18; *Jubilees*, 232), and Hartom and Berger include it in their translations (Berger puts it in parentheses). See VanderKam, *Jubilees* 2:277.
b heard] Both Eth. and Lat. read "heard," where Gen 42:1 has "saw." Among the versions, only Eth. Gen 42:1 has "heard," but the reading must have been present in Jubilees already on the Gk. level if it is in both translations made from it, so the reading did not enter Eth. Jubilees from Eth. Gen. See Gen 42:2.
c (for him) in Egypt] Lat. lacks, while Gen 42:3 has "from Egypt."
d Benjamin] + "with them" Lat. Gen 42:4 lacks the extra words.
e They arrived with those who were coming to Egypt] "Jacob's ten sons arrived in Egypt" Lat. Gen 42:5: "Thus the sons of Israel were among the other people who came to buy grain." Both versions of Jubilees may have taken a short base text (e.g., "they arrived in Egypt") and expanded it. Note that Eth. actually reads a sg. form "with the one who was coming/going," whereas Gen 42:5 reads a plural.
5a He spoke with them, asked them questions] "Joseph addressed [*appellavit*] them harshly" Lat. Gen 42:7: "[he] spoke harshly to them." The noteworthy difference between Eth. and Lat. is the Eth. reading "he asked them questions/he questioned them" where Lat., with Gen 42:7, has "harshly." See Jub 42:9, where "harshly" occurs in the brothers' report about this incident. Charles preferred the Lat. reading (*Ethiopic Version*, 153 n. 26), but Littmann ("Jubiläen," 109 n. c) considered it possible that Lat.'s "harshly" entered the text here under the influence of Jub 42:9. In *Jubilees*, Charles translated the reading in the Eth. text. See VanderKam, *Jubilees* 2:277. The Eth. reading does prepare for the questions Joseph poses to them; in Lat. he simply makes an assertion. Werman (*Jubilees*, 497 n. 8; and see n. 9) offers a more complicated hypothesis for how, in her opinion, the differing readings arose. With Eth. she accepts that there were two verbs here, but where Eth. now has "asked them questions" the text earlier read "acted as a stranger to them" = a form of *tanakara* rather than the present *tanāgara*. The two similar-looking verbs became confused in the course of copying the text. But when *tanāgara* entered the text, it was noticed that there were two adjacent verbs of speaking with much the same meaning. A scribe then changed the second one to "questioned them" to make

1057

it read differently than the first verb. The latter step she posits seems rather unlikely; it is simpler to think that "asked them questions" is original since it prepares for what follows, while Lat. can be explained as assimilating to a reading from Genesis (and Jubilees).

- b Are you not spies] om. Lat., but Gen 42:9 has the equivalent, though it is not phrased as a question.
- c the paths of the land] "the land" Lat. Eth. Jubilees follows the interpretation found in LXX (ἴχνη, "footprints"), and OL (*vestigia*, "footprints") where the Heb. versions of Gen 42:9 have ערות (lit., "nakedness, exposed part"). Eth. '*asar*, "path, trace, track, sole of foot, footprint, sign, mark" (Leslau, *Comparative Dictionary*, 45, where it is spelled '*ašar* as in MSS. 17 20 39 44 58). See VanderKam, *Jubilees* 2:278.
- 6a Afterwards] Lat. lacks.
- b he sent again] The reading follows MS. 21; MSS. 9 12 17 38^c 44 48 63 support "again" but with the other Eth. MSS. lack "he sent." Lat. = *mittens* ("sending"), but it lacks "again."
- c summoned them] So Lat.; Eth. = "released them." The variation may rest on confusion of ἐξέλυσε ("he released") and ἐκάλεσε ("he summoned"). See VanderKam, *Jubilees* 2:278.
- d He detained only Simeon] "when he had taken Simeon from them, he bound him" Lat. The Lat. reading closely resembles Gen 42:24 and thus may be dependent on it.
- 7a with grain] Lat. lacks, but the words are present in Gen 42:25.
- b returned (their money) to them] So Lat. and Gen 42:25; Eth. = "put" (agreeing with Eth. Gen 42:25).
- c in their sacks. But they did not know (this)] om. Lat. Cf. Gen 42:25 and especially 43:22 (where the brothers report on this incident).
- 8a because they had told him that their father was alive and their youngest brother (also)] om. Lat., probably by parablepsis from "youngest brother" to "youngest brother." This could have happened if one assumes the more natural word order in Eth. with the verb "to bring" first in the previous clause, not last as in Lat.
- 9a They] "Jacob's sons" Lat. Gen 42:29 = "they."
- b country] Eth. reads *beḥēr*, which, while it can mean "country" (Leslau, *Comparative Dictionary*, 91), is not the word that usually stands where Genesis reads הארץ as here (Gen 42:30). Lat. = "country."
- c they should bring] "we should present our brother" Lat. Gen 42:34 also words as a quotation, but it is part of a much longer speech by the brothers.
- 10a and you are going to take Benjamin] "if you take Benjamin" Lat. Gen 42:36: "and now you would take Benjamin." See VanderKam, *Jubilees* 2:279.
- b Your wickedness has come upon me] "You are also making your evil full on me" Lat. For the notion of "full," see Syr. Gen 42:36 (Charles, *Ethiopic Version*, 155 n. 1 to Lat.). The versions of Gen 42:36 lack mention of "your wickedness/evil" other than the Vulgate.
- 11a Perhaps] Lat. (lit.) = "lest ever." See Rönsch, *Jubiläen*, 160; VanderKam, *Jubilees* 2:279.
- b ill] + "on the way" Lat. This phrase appears later in the verse (after "fever") where Gen 42:38 reads it. Lat. therefore seems to have expanded the text.
- c two] "these two" Lat., where the demonstrative may translate a Gk. definite article.
- d you will take from me] Lat., as it did in v. 10, reads: "if you take." It lacks an equivalent of "from me."
- e Perhaps he would catch a fever] Lat. includes this clause in the condition begun in its previous clause (*et* + a subjunctive). It also uses the general noun *infirmitas* (see LXX OL Gen 42:38) where Eth. is more specific.
- f my old age (*res'eya*)] "my head" (*re'seya*) 9 21 25 38.
- g Sheol] So Gen 42:38; Eth. = "death"; Lat. = "the depths." Both are interpretations of the original Heb. term.
- 12a he saw] "they said to him" Lat. Eth. represents ειδεν, and Lat. ειπον to which "to him" was added. Either could be correct, but Eth. seems better in the context. Ms. 38: "they saw."
- b their money] Lat. reads a conjunction before the phrase (= also) and adds "to them."
- c each one in his purse] Lat. lacks an equivalent for "each one," and it reads "their" with "containers." For the reading, see VanderKam, *Jubilees* 2:280.
- d he was afraid to send him for this reason] "Jacob was afraid to send him with them" Lat. "With them" in Lat. and "for this reason" in Eth. may be differing interpretations of the same Gk. text (VanderKam, *Jubilees* 2:280-81, but see Werman, *Jubilees*, 498 n. 27).
- 13a grew increasingly severe] Eth. lit., "became great/increased (would increase 9 12 17 21 38 63) and strong"; Lat. lit., "was going and becoming strong." The meaning of the two is the same. Cf. Gen 43:1.
- b Canaan—Egypt] om. Lat. See VanderKam, *Jubilees* 2:281.
- c kept] Lat.; Eth. "stored."
- d storage places] Lat. Eth. "for food" probably reflects an original לשבר, while Lat. would render לשמר.
- e after] "when" 9 17 38 63. Lat. adds *tamen*, "that is."
- f saw] "would see" 17 63.
- g grain] "seed" Eth. (see 42:2 for another pairing of the same two words).
- 14a The Egyptians] Eth. lit., "the people of Egypt." Lat. lacks an equivalent for "the people of," and MS. 17 also lacks it.
- b the famine] "their famine" 9 12 17 21 38 39 42 47 48 63.
- 16a they said] + "to him" 21.
- b we will not go²] om. 20 48.

17a that] om. 39 42 44 47 58.
18a said] + "to him" 20 44.
  b with you (sg.)] "with you" (pl.) 12 (= Gen 42:38).
19a approached] + "(to) him" 17 (cf. 63).
  b said] + "to him" 21 38.
  c with us] "with me" 9 21 35 38 39 42 47 48 58 (so Gen 43:8).
  d let me be guilty] "I will be guilty" 9 63.
20a with them] "with him" 21.
  b month] "tenth month" 58.
  c gifts] + "with them and" 35 58.
  d honeycombs] See Leslau, *Comparative Dictionary*, 562. As he indicates ṣaqāweʿ = "honey dropped from the comb, honeycomb"; and, as it is here, when combined with maʿār (another word for "honey, honeycomb," ibid., 326), the resulting meaning is also "honeycomb." Cf. Gen 43:11.

21a him] "them" 21 47.
  b He is] + "indeed/certainly" 17ᶜ 21 38 58.
22a him] "them" 17 39 42 47 48 58; om. 44.
  b to them] "to him" 12.
  c He prepared] "They prepared" 9 12 17 39 42 47 48 63; "They brought near/presented" 20.
  d his gifts] "the gifts" 25 35 44.
  e had brought] "had presented" 20 25 44.
24a and stayed] "and went (to)" 20 48; om. 63.
25a between them] "and whether there was no hostility/hatred" 21 35 58.
  b in charge of (lit., "over")] "in" 21 35.
  c the cup] "my cup" 20 25 42 47 58.
  d with which I drink] om. 20 25.
  e the youngest] "Benjamin" 20 25 44.
  f send them away] "he sent them away" 17 47 48 58 63; + "so they would go" 38 58.

Commentary

After the events involving Judah and Tamar—actions that were concurrent with most of the years of plenty in Egypt—the narrative returns to the situation in Egypt. Jubilees 42 overlaps with material in a much longer section of Genesis: it reduces Gen 41:54—44:2 to just twenty-five verses. At the conclusion of the seven plentiful years, the next part of Joseph's prediction to Pharaoh began to come true. A famine replaced the time of abundance, and, because the harsh conditions extended throughout the entire region, they affected the family of Jacob in the land. Their desperate need for food becomes the trigger that brings the two parts of Jacob's family together after they were separated years earlier when the brothers sold Joseph.

The story in Jubilees is part of a larger whole that deals with relations within the family of Jacob. His own family had been torn apart by hatred, just as the family of Isaac and Rebekah had been. The encounters between Joseph and his brothers serve not only to address the family's immediate need for food but also to determine the quality of the relations obtaining among the brothers.[1]

The chapter can be outlined into five parts:

1-3 The famine begins (Gen 41:54, 56)
4-12 The brothers make their first trip to Egypt, encounter a harsh Joseph, and return home (Gen 42:1, 3-5, 8, 7, 9, 17, 25, 29, 30, 36, 38)
13-14 The famine grows more severe and the Egyptians cope by imitating Joseph (Gen 43:1)
15-20 Jacob agrees to send Benjamin with his brothers on their second trip to Egypt (Gen 43:1-2; 42:37-38; 43:8-9, 11)
21-25 The brothers meet Joseph, who devises a plan to test them (Gen 43:15, 29, 23, 26, 34; 44:1-2).

The Ethiopic version continues to offer the complete text, and the Latin translation is available from v. 2 to the beginning of v. 14.

1-3 The Famine Begins (Gen 41:54, 56)

Genesis 41 takes up the inception of the famine directly after the brief overview of the abundant years, the information about Joseph's wife and sons, and the notice that the seven years of plenty came to an end (41:46-53). Jubilees places it immediately after the story about Judah and Tamar and the continuation of his line through

---

1 See Doran, "Non-Dating," 5-6.

their twins. Judah will reappear in the travel stories as an important figure, though not in connection with the first journey to Egypt.

■ 1 The author of Jubilees, as is his wont, dates the occasion in his overall chronology. The year 2170 was the last in the "seven years of copious harvest" (41:22), and now the second period predicted by Joseph begins to materialize in the ensuing year, 2171. In v. 1 he rewords the beginning of Gen 41:54—the famine begins to grip the earth/land—though here he does not call it a seven-year famine as Genesis does (he did in 40:3-4). The author, having dated the event, leaves the text of Genesis, possibly to describe conditions in places outside Egypt (in v. 2 he contrasts the situation in Egypt). The Ethiopic text, the only one extant here, twice uses the word *medr* ("land/earth") in the expressions "the famine began to come to the land" and "The rain refused to be given to the earth." In these instances "land/earth" may refer to Canaan[2] (as it does, e.g., in Gen 43:1) or non-Egyptian areas more broadly. If the author were not talking about Egypt, it would make sense for him to attribute the famine to the absence of rainfall. The description would be less appropriate for Egypt, where the flooding of the Nile produces conditions necessary for agriculture, but in Israel and lands around it the rains were more essential. The water of the Nile had to come from somewhere, however, and the writer later indicates that the Nile itself was affected in the time of the famine (it did not overflow, 45:10), so it is quite possible that he is here referring to Egypt.[3] The expression "The rain refused to be given to the earth" is a way of saying that there was no rainfall at all. The conditions were like those in the days of Elijah when the rains failed for years and a famine resulted (1 Kgs 17–18).

■ 2 The circumstances in Egypt, however, were different—not because crops were growing (although see v. 13 below) but because Joseph had made careful preparations. At this point in v. 2 the writer again picks up words from Gen 41:54. Jubilees does not say with Genesis that "There was famine in every country" (see also v. 57), but it does declare that the earth produced no crops. Both texts, however, contrast the situation elsewhere with the one in Egypt. Genesis 41:55-57 tells how the people came to Pharaoh, who directed them to Joseph. Joseph opened the storehouses (?) that he had filled (see 41:35-36, 48-49) "and sold to the Egyptians, for the famine was severe in the land of Egypt" (41:56). Jubilees presents the matter somewhat differently at first: there was food in Egypt "because Joseph had gathered the grain in the land during the seven years of copious harvest and kept it" (v. 2). The Ethiopic manuscripts say that Joseph gathered seed during the seven years—making it sound as if the writer is drawing on Gen 47:23-25, where Joseph gives out seeds after acquiring all the Egyptians and their property. The Latin translation, however, has "grain," which seems more likely to be correct in the context (see also v. 13). Joseph was doing something in connection with the harvests, as the next words indicate. The Latin joins "grain" with "land" in a genitival construction: "the grain of the land." That is, Joseph had gathered and kept (for the verb "keep," see Gen 41:35) some of the bounty that the land had produced so that it was now available for the many needing food.

■ 3 The Egyptians, acting on their own initiative and not on instructions from Pharaoh (in Gen 41:55 he sends them to Joseph), approached Joseph, whose wise plan had called for storing the excess in the years with bumper crops in order to guarantee a supply of food for the time of famine. It appears from the Ethiopic text of v. 3 that Joseph had so organized the grain collection program that an amount sufficient for the first year was located in certain designated storehouses. The Latin version words the verse so that "the first year" refers to the time when they were to eat the food Joseph made available to them.

Ethiopic: the storehouses where the grain of the first year was

Latin: the storehouses in which the grain was and gave (it) to them to eat during the first year

The Ethiopic version presupposes something not said earlier—Joseph put food for a specific year in a special place; the Latin wording does not make that assumption. The Latin reading suffers from the fact that it makes the

---

2   Cf. Hartom, "Jubilees," 121 n. to v. 1.
3   See Werman, *Jubilees*, 498.

line conform to the reason why the people came, but it does make good sense.

With several ancient versions of Gen 41:56 (Syriac along with LXX and daughter translations), Jubilees reads "storehouses" where the MT and SP have "all that was in them" (SP adds "grain" after the phrase as do most of the ancient versions along with the Ethiopic and Latin translations of Jubilees). Joseph does not give the grain to the populace free of charge; he sells[4] it to them "in exchange for money." The recipients of the grain are called "the people of the land" where Gen 41:56 labels them "the Egyptians." The two may mean the same thing, or Jubilees could be implying a wider distribution of the life-saving goods ("the people of the earth"?).

4-12 The Brothers Make Their First Trip to Egypt, Encounter a Harsh Joseph, and Return Home (Gen 42:1, 3-5, 8, 7, 9, 17, 25, 29, 30, 36, 38)

Jubilees severely abbreviates the longer presentation in its base text so that the action covered in Genesis 42 (thirty-eight verses) occupies just nine verses in it. One major way in which the writer reduces the length is by omitting much of the direct speech, including the dialogue between the ten brothers and Joseph that fills so much of Genesis 42. In this way the story loses some of its dramatic power, and only the important facts figure in the retelling. By removing a substantial portion of the quoted words, the author of Jubilees makes the brothers less chatty and self-incriminating than they are in Genesis.

■ **4** The verse offers a short summary of the action and words in Gen 42:1-5. It begins with a sentence preserved only in the Latin version: "But the famine was very severe in the land of Canaan";[5] it somewhat resembles Gen 42:5b: "for the famine had reached the land of Canaan" (cf. 41:56, 57).

Genesis 42:1-5
When Jacob learned that there was grain in Egypt, he said to his sons, "Why do you keep looking at one another? I have heard," he said, "that there is grain in Egypt; go down and buy grain for us there that we may live and not die." So ten of Joseph's brothers went down to buy grain in Egypt. But Jacob did not send Joseph's brother Benjamin with his brothers, for he feared that harm might come to him.[6] Thus the sons of Israel were among the other people who came to buy grain, for the famine had reached the land of Canaan.

Jubilees 42:4
Jacob heard that there was food in Egypt,

so he sent his ten sons to get food for him in Egypt. But he did not send Benjamin.

They arrived with those who were coming to Egypt.

Genesis keeps the name of Joseph before the reader by mentioning it twice; Jubilees does not refer to him here. In Genesis, Jacob berates his sons for their indecision;[7] he is the one in charge, and he takes the initiative in addressing the calamity that has struck his family. In Jubilees the sons receive no criticism from their father; he simply dispatches them to Egypt to purchase food supplies. Genesis explains why Jacob did not send Benjamin with his older brothers (literally): for he said: Lest something bad happen to him. The reason is not Benjamin's tender youth (unlike 34:3); in the chronology of Jubilees he was born in 2143 (32:33) so that at this time he was twenty-eight years of age. Jacob's reasoning may have been problematic for the author of Jubilees because it could imply that he did not trust the ten brothers to take adequate care of Benjamin—and perhaps that he cared more about the well-being of Benjamin than about theirs. At any rate, one could read the explanation in a negative way, as a reflection of ongoing problems in the family of Jacob.[8] A person familiar with what they had

---

4   MT SP (some manuscripts) Gen 41:56 read "bought," as if Joseph purchased the grain for the Egyptians. It seems as if a *hiphil* form ("caused to buy," i.e., "sold") should have been used rather than the *qal* form (see *DCH* 8:252, s.v. שבר).
5   See the textual note.
6   This is in fact a quotation in Gen 42:4 ("for he said: 'Lest something bad happen to him'"), despite the way in which the NRSV renders it.
7   Exactly what תתראו means (NRSV: "you keep looking at one another") is debated, but commentators and translators often give meanings such as the one in NRSV. The LXX read a verb meaning "idle," and Syr "afraid." None of the suggested senses qualifies as a compliment to Jacob's sons.
8   See Westermann, *Genesis 37–50*, 105; Hamilton, *Genesis 18–50*, 516.

done to Joseph could also harbor some doubts about what the brothers might do with Rachel's remaining son. The same sorts of suspicions would not follow from Jubilees, where Jacob furnishes no reason for keeping Benjamin at home. Both texts conclude the section by indicating that, as a result of their father's command, ten of Joseph's brothers were among the many people streaming into Egypt to purchase food.

■ 5 Once again a single verse in Jubilees covers the material in a longer stretch of Genesis—42:6-17. The paragraph in Genesis begins by identifying Joseph as governor of the land and as the one who sold provisions to the people—information the reader already knows. The author of Jubilees does not reproduce these details, and the text also lacks the sentence at the end of Gen 42:6: "And Joseph's brothers came and bowed themselves before him with their faces to the ground." Their prostration, of course, fulfills Joseph's predictions from his dreams in Gen 37:5-11, where the brothers' sheaves kneel before Joseph's and the sun, moon, and eleven stars "bow to the ground" (Gen 37:10) before him. Not surprisingly, Joseph, who recognized his brothers, recalled his dreams when he saw them kneeling in front of him (Gen 42:9). All of this is lacking from Jubilees, where the way in which the brothers presented themselves to Joseph goes unmentioned. The author had not included the section about Joseph's dreams when retelling Genesis 37 (see Jubilees 34) and thus could hardly depict the present scene as the one they foretold. He simply repeats the words of Gen 42:8—Joseph recognized them, but they did not know who he was.

The most striking difference between Genesis and Jubilees concerns the conversation between Joseph and his brothers. From Gen 42:7 through v. 16 they carry on a dialogue: Joseph speaks four times (vv. 7, 9, 12, 14-16) and they respond to each of his first three statements (vv. 7, 10-11, 13). After he initially inquires about their country of origin and they tell him (v. 7), he charges them several times with coming to Egypt on a spying mission (v. 9, cf. vv. 12, 14; see also v. 16). As they react to the shocking accusation, they disclose more about their family situation than was wise under the circumstances. Among their revelations is that they had a younger brother who remained home with his father and that another brother "is no more" (v. 13). Their words lead Joseph to concoct a plan whereby he could test their veracity: if they failed the test, they would convince him that they were indeed spies. He threatened at first that he would keep all but one of them imprisoned and send that one back to their home to fetch their youngest brother. Producing that brother would prove them truthful and that they were not spies.

Jubilees truncates the paragraph. The writer reports that Joseph spoke with and questioned them, but the only quoted words are Joseph's accusation in Gen 42:9, the first part of which reads as a question:

Genesis 42:9	Jubilees 42:5
"You are spies; you have come to see nakedness[9] of the land!"	"Are you not spies? You have come to investigate the paths of the land."

So, the brothers, who say nothing in Jubilees, do not divulge too much about their family—although in v. 8 the narrator discloses that they had told him their father and youngest brother were alive. Here Joseph lodges an accusation against them and imprisons them; nothing is said about testing the truth of their insistence that they were not spies, since they had made no such claim. Joseph imprisons them in Jubilees; there is no indication about the length of the confinement, unlike in Genesis, where it lasts three days (Gen 42:17, 18).

■ 6 Consistent with his practice to this juncture, the writer again bypasses a significant part of the story in Genesis where Joseph releases his brothers on the third day and says he will incarcerate only one of them while the other nine are to go home with grain for their families. Later they were to return with their youngest brother and in this way verify their claim of innocence and avoid a sentence of death. Joseph explains his more lenient treatment—originally he was going to jail nine of them—by declaring "for I fear God" (v. 18). His test relates ostensibly only to the truth of their declaration that they were not spies. The brothers then, thinking

---

9   The unusual expression led to varied attempts to clarify what Joseph meant: e.g., *Targum Neofiti*: "the entrances," *Targum Onqelos*: "the vulnerable part." The rendering "paths" in Jubilees aligns with the interpretation found in LXX ($\iota\chi\nu\eta$).

the Egyptian official could not understand their words, acknowledge to one another that they were suffering the due penalty for what they had done to Joseph. Years ago they had ignored his anguish when he pleaded with them, and "That is why this anguish has come upon us" (Gen 42:21).[10] The thoughts the brothers share with one another reveal not only their sense of guilt for selling Joseph but also a measure of discord among them. They are not a unified family. Reuben upbraids the others for not listening to him at that fateful time: "Did I not tell you not to wrong the boy? But you would not listen. So now there comes a reckoning for his blood" (v. 22). Their words moved Joseph to tears (v. 24). For some unexplained reason, he singled out Simeon for imprisonment (v. 24).[11] All this Jubilees summarizes by saying that Joseph called them from prison, detained Simeon alone, and sent the other nine away. In Genesis he hears about the lesson his brothers have learned as they recognized their guilt,[12] and he witnesses the lack of unity among them; in Jubilees he hears and witnesses nothing of the sort.

■ 7 The verse is closely related to Gen 42:25.

Genesis 42:25	Jubilees 42:7
Joseph then gave orders to fill their bags with grain, to return every man's money to his sack, and to give them provisions for their journey. This was done for them.	He filled their sacks with grain and returned their money to them in their sacks. But they did not know (this).

Joseph acts like a high-ranking official in Genesis: he gives a command and others carry it out. Among his orders is that the brothers receive what they need for the long trip home in addition to filling their sacks with grain and returning their money. Joseph acts more like a caring brother in Jubilees, where he is the one who fills the sacks with grain and places their money in them, although one has to imagine that he also gave them provisions for the trip since the text does not mention it. Where Genesis reports that unnamed others gave the brothers what Joseph had ordered, Jubilees says that the nine were unaware that he had returned their money (presumably they knew about the grain, since it was the purpose of their journey to Egypt). The note about their ignorance regarding the money probably comes from Gen 43:22, where they tell Joseph's steward on their second visit to Egypt: "'Moreover we have brought down with us additional money to buy food. We do not know who put our money in our sacks.'"

■ 8 In the verse the writer takes the opportunity to fill in a few items he had left out of his abbreviated account. Only at this point, after the imprisonment of Simeon and dismissal of the other nine with their food and money, does he report Joseph's instructions regarding the condition under which they could return to Egypt: they were to bring along with them their youngest brother. The note required that the author also disclose how Joseph knew they had a younger brother: the ten had told him that their father and younger brother were alive. Obviously the rewriter knew about the dialogue between Joseph and his brothers but chose not to reproduce it in v. 5 (the information is implied in Gen 42:13 ["the youngest, however, is now with our father"], one of their replies to Joseph's accusations about spying).

---

10 Genesis does not explain why their current bind made the brothers think about their mistreatment of Joseph years before. The description of the situation is also more detailed than in Genesis 37, where there is no indication that Joseph pleaded with his brothers.

11 One suggestion is that Reuben had just vindicated himself regarding the treatment of Joseph and placed the blame on his brothers. As a result, Joseph did not bind his oldest brother but Simeon, the next in line (see, e.g., Hamilton, *Genesis 18–50*, 528). In *Gen. Rab.* 91:6 the reason is that Simeon was the one who had pushed Joseph into the pit; also, Joseph wanted to separate him from Levi lest the two plot against him (as they did against Shechem). In *Tg. Ps.-J.* Gen 42:24 Simeon is the one *"who had counseled to kill him"* (in Genesis 37).

12 Werman thinks that the author may have figured the brothers had done their repenting in 34:13 after they reported Joseph's fate to Jacob ("That day all the people of his household mourned with him. They continued to be distressed and to mourn with him all that day") (*Jubilees*, 499). While the brothers may be included in those lines (they should be part of his household), the point is not made explicit in 34:13. It appears more likely that here in v. 6 the writer of Jubilees preferred to delete family discord from the record.

■ **9** Yet again the author abbreviates the text of Genesis by omitting the direct speech that fills it. Genesis 42:26-34 describes the return trip home by the nine brothers, the discovery by one that his money was in his sack, and their lengthy report to Jacob about their experiences in Egypt (vv. 30-34 are a quotation of their report). They conclude their speech by quoting Joseph's order: "Bring your youngest brother to me, and I shall know that you are not spies but honest men. Then I will release your brother to you, and you may trade in the land." The writer of Jubilees avoids the duplication involved in their rather full disclosure to Jacob. He omits the chance discovery of the money by one brother while on the journey (Gen 42:27-28), and, rather than quoting their words in vv. 30-34, he writes only that they told Jacob everything that happened to them in Egypt, the harsh words of the ruler, and the imprisonment of Simeon as a hostage until they should bring Benjamin with them. They do not mention that Joseph was testing whether they were honest about not being spies.

■ **10-12** The author of Jubilees changes his procedure when dealing with Jacob's response to the disturbing account his nine sons gave. Here he adheres much more closely to the text of Genesis (42:35-38) than he did in describing the journey, although he makes some significant alterations in it. In Gen 42:35 all the brothers, upon opening their sacks, find their money refunded. "When they and their father saw their bundles of money, they were dismayed." In the rewriting, Jubilees moves this item to the end of the section—v. 12—and merely notes here that Jacob saw their money had been returned. The writer understands this as a reason why Jacob feared sending Benjamin back to Egypt with his older brothers. A second change he makes is that he removes Reuben's rash intervention in Jacob's speech and for that reason has to present Jacob's words as two quotations with only "He said" intervening between them.

Genesis 42:36-38	Jubilees 42:10-11
And their father Jacob said to them, "I am the one you have bereaved of children: Joseph is no more, and Simeon is no more, and now you would take Benjamin. All this has happened to me!"	Jacob said, "You have deprived me of children. Joseph does not exist nor does Simeon exist, and you are going to take Benjamin. Your wickedness has come upon me."
Then Reuben said to his father, "You may kill my two sons if I do not bring him back to you." But he said, "My son shall not go down with you,	
	He said, "My son will not go with you. Perhaps he would become ill. For their mother gave birth to two;
for his brother is dead, and he alone is left. If harm should come to him on the journey that you are to make, you would bring down my old age in sorrow to Sheol."	one has died and this one, too, you will take from me. Perhaps he would catch a fever on the way. Then you would bring down my old age with sorrow to Sheol."[13]

Reuben's speech is strange and apparently not very helpful for Jacob.[14] How would the deaths of his two sons make the situation better, if Benjamin did not survive the trip? It would be quite understandable for the author of Jubilees to leave out his awkward statement and its negative reflection on an ancestor of Israel. He had erased any signs of discord between the brothers when they were discussing what they had done to Joseph (Gen 42:21-22); now he would be deleting another reason to think less of one of them—the only one who seemed to be virtuous in the Joseph incident according to his perhaps self-serving recollection (see Gen 42:22). Nevertheless, such conclusions are invalid because the writer of Jubilees did not expunge Reuben's speech in Gen 42:37 but moved it to Jub 42:18, where its new context may somewhat ameliorate the seeming foolishness of his offer (see the commentary on v. 18, below).

Jacob's lament that the nine had deprived him of children may imply that he suspected them of complicity

---

13   For "Sheol" (from Gen 42:38), see the textual note. For uses of the word in Jubilees, see 5:14; 7:29; 22:22; 24:31.

14   "Reuben's offer of his two sons if he fails to bring back Benjamin from Egypt is hardly therapeutic" (Hamilton, *Genesis 18–50*, 536). Zakovitch and Shinan relate Reuben's offer to the deaths of Judah's two sons in Genesis 38: Judah's two sons died as a punishment for his not returning Joseph to his father (Genesis 37), so Reuben's two sons would die as a punishment for his not returning Benjamin to him (*Judah and Tamar*, 47). At least there is a verbal link (involving *hiphil* forms of שוב) between Genesis 37 (in v. 22 Reuben plans to "return" Joseph to Jacob) and 42 (in v. 37 Reuben plans to return Benjamin to Jacob).

in the "death" of Joseph since he is the first one he lists among the three lost or in danger of being lost. Where Jacob speaks vaguely in Gen 42:36—"All this has happened to me"—in Jub 42:10 he refers to their wickedness that has impacted him so heavily. Exactly what he means he does not explain further, but once more it could be his way of saying he believed they bore guilt in the disappearance of Joseph.[15] The Jacob of Jubilees expresses his concern about Benjamin's welfare in more detail than he does in Genesis: in the latter he worries, just as he had in Gen 42:4, that harm will befall Benjamin; in the former he fears he will get sick or catch a fever (his youth is not a factor in either text).[16] The reference to his mother who bore two sons explains what Jacob meant by "his brother is dead, and he alone is left." Benjamin was, of course, not his only surviving son; Jubilees clarifies that he was talking only about Rachel's children (cf. Judah's words to Joseph in Gen 44:20 and Jacob's [cited by Judah] in 44:27-28). Both texts make clear that Jacob believed the loss of Benjamin would hasten the end of his life and would be the fault of his remaining sons.

13-14 The Famine Grows More Severe and the Egyptians Cope by Imitating Joseph (Gen 43:1)

The story will shortly continue when the famine tightens its grip and Jacob's family again exhausts their food supply. Genesis 43 begins with a brief comment on the situation: "Now the famine was severe in the land." Jubilees repeats and clarifies it by saying that it grew increasingly strong, and the writer specifies that the word "land" in Gen 43:1 means "the land of Canaan." To this he adds information that goes beyond the text of Genesis 43.

The famine was harsh in every land except Egypt—a reference back to Gen 41:54, 57. The next words may also be related to the end of Genesis 41. The author here explains why the Egyptians had enough food. Naturally, it had to do with Joseph, but this time he is the model imitated by the Egyptians. The wording of the two versions of Jubilees is somewhat different:

Ethiopic Jubilees 42:13	Latin Jubilees 42:13
. . . because many Egyptians had stored their seed for food[17] after they saw Joseph collecting seed, placing it in storehouses, and keeping (it) for the years of the famine.	. . . because many Egyptians kept their seed in storage place(s), that is, after they saw Joseph collecting grain and placing (it) in storehouses so that it would be kept for the years of the famine.

The two agree that the Egyptians saved seed from the years of plenty for use during the years of want. But the Ethiopic has the odd claim that they "stored their seed for food," where Latin says they kept it in storage places. This is also the second passage (see 42:2) in which the two versions offer the variants "seed" (Ethiopic) and "grain" (Latin). Here, too, "grain" makes more sense, though it is unclear how the reference to "seed" earlier in the verse fits into the report.[18] The reason for thinking v. 13 is speaking about grain is that v. 14 says, "The Egyptians fed themselves with it during the first year of the famine." So, v. 13 does not appear to be talking about seeds that could be planted to yield a crop that would be eaten later that year. However the text should read and whatever it means, the writer of Jubilees emphasizes more than Genesis that the Egyptians had food to eat and that Joseph was the one responsible for their more favorable situation.

---

15 Cf. Hamilton, *Genesis 18–50*, 535–36.
16 On the word אסון in Gen 42:4, 38 (NRSV: "harm"), see Kugel, *Traditions*, 693–95 (where he discusses it in connection with its occurrence in Exod 21:22-23); and *Walk through* Jubilees, 185; "Jubilees," 431. As he indicates, the exact meaning of the term posed problems for ancient readers. LXX Gen 42:4, 38 render the word as μαλακια (NETS: "sickness") and μαλακισθηναι ("becomes sick") respectively. This is the interpretation underlying "catch a fever" in Jub 42:11.
17 See the textual note.
18 Rightly noted by Kugel, *Walk through* Jubilees, 185–86: "In fact, this verse is apparently an interpretation of Gen 41:55, 'Pharaoh said to the Egyptians, "Go to Joseph; whatever he tells you, you shall do."' If all the Egyptians wished was to purchase grain, why did Joseph have to tell them *what to do?* Jubilees' author thus understood that Joseph instituted self-rationing among the people at the same time that he himself began storing grain for the government; that is why the famine was severe everywhere except in the land of Egypt" (186; so "Jubilees," 432). Cf. also Hartom, "Jubilees," 122 n. to v. 13.

15-20 Jacob Agrees to Send Benjamin with His Brothers on Their Second Trip to Egypt (Gen 43:1-2; 42:37-38; 43:8-9, 11)

The section in Jubilees, as expected, abbreviates a longer one in Genesis but also rearranges some of the parts.

■ **15** The verse corresponds with Gen 43:1-2.

Genesis 43:1-2	Jubilees 42:15
Now the famine was severe in the land. And when they had eaten up the grain that they had brought from Egypt, their father said to them, "Go again, buy us a little more food."	When Israel saw that the famine was very severe in the land and (that) there was no relief,[19] he said to his sons, "Go, return,[20] and get us (some) food so that we may not die."

The narrator in Genesis supplies the statement about the famine, but Jubilees presents it as something Jacob, here called Israel (as he is later, in Gen 43:6, 8, 11), observed. He saw the severity of the situation and also perceived no sign that it would end any time soon. Under such duress, he told his sons to make a second trip to procure food (Gen 43:2 indicates they had used up the supply from the first journey). He adds to his command a statement of purpose: "so that we may not die"—words that resemble the ones Jacob used as he dispatched his sons on the previous mission: "that we may live and not die" (Gen 42:2). Jubilees did not reproduce them at that point (Jub 42:4), but by moving them to v. 15 they heighten the impression of urgency at this later time (see also Gen 43:8).

■ **16** The next verses in Genesis 43 (vv. 3-5) contain the first of two responses that Judah makes to Jacob. He reminds him about the condition stipulated by "the man" in Egypt: if they did not bring Benjamin with them, they would not gain access to the official and would therefore not be able to purchase food from him. He sets out the options: either Benjamin accompanies them or they do not go. Israel replies with words critical of all those who had made the first trip: "Why did you treat me so badly as to tell the man that you had another brother?" (Gen 43:6) All of the brothers then counter that there was no way they could have anticipated from the man's questions that he would order them to bring their brother to Egypt (v. 7). Jubilees shortens and modifies this bit of familial unpleasantness by presenting all the brothers as responding to their father and explaining that if Benjamin did not travel with them, they would stay home. In this respect, the verse reflects Gen 44:26, where Judah attributes the statement to all of them, not just to himself. The situation is bad, but the brothers act together.

■ **17** There is no passage in Genesis 43 corresponding to v. 17. As the author of Jubilees presents the matter, Jacob, after hearing what all of his sons said, realized that he had no choice. If he did not allow his youngest son to accompany the other nine to Egypt, the famine would cause all of them to die. Genesis speaks about Israel's coming to grips with the unpleasant necessity only after Judah's second speech (Gen 43:8-10; Israel reluctantly consents in v. 11). The united testimony of the nine brothers is enough to make the situation clear to Jacob in Jubilees, but he has not yet fully agreed to send Benjamin.

■ **18** At this juncture, the writer introduces a unit (with several modifications, especially in word order) that he had omitted earlier when abbreviating parts of Genesis 42. There, when Jacob blamed his nine sons for the loss of his children, Reuben made what appeared to be a poor response—offering Jacob the right to kill his two sons if he, Reuben, failed to return Benjamin to him (Gen 42:36-37). The absence of Reuben's outburst from that context (Jub 42:10-11) was awkward—Jacob's words are still divided into two statements, despite the absence of Reuben's offer that responded to the first and motivated the second—but understandable if the author of Jubilees was interested in defending the reputation of the patriarchs. However, he moves Reuben's words to 42:18 where, at least in intent, they may not seem so foolhardy: the eldest son is sincerely trying to reassure his father, who has just realized the true nature of the situation. Reuben is no more successful in the new context than he was in Gen 42:36-38, but he wanted to be helpful. The appearance of Reuben's offer in Gen 42:37 locates it in a context where the discussion was more theoretical—the brothers had just returned from Egypt

---

19 Leslau (*Concise Dictionary*, 196) defines *deḥin* as "deliverance, salvation."

20 Most translators of Jubilees have understood the second imperative as reflecting the iterative use of שוב ("Go again"), but its position after "Go" rather

with a full supply of food; it was not a time to think seriously about a second trek. There is nothing theoretical about the new context in Jubilees, where the famine is exceptionally harsh, the food supply has been depleted, and there is no relief in sight. Reuben may have sensed he had to do something radical to get his father to agree to send Benjamin, and he proposed something really radical. He ordered Jacob: "kill [imperative, where Genesis has an imperfect/jussive form][21] my two sons for his [Benjamin's] life" (this prepositional phrase is not in Gen 42:37). Happily, as he did in Gen 42:38, Jacob rejected the bloody offer. The author of Jubilees reproduces only the beginning of Jacob's answer from that earlier context, since he had already used material from the latter part of Gen 42:38 in 42:11. In Genesis, Jacob said that Benjamin will not go "with you [plural]," but in Jubilees he uses the singular form of the suffix, meaning "with Reuben."

■ **19** At this point the writer introduces what is the second response of Judah to his father in Genesis 43 (vv. 8-10). There it follows the defensive speech by his brothers in reaction to Israel's criticism of them, but in Jubilees it comes after Reuben's offer and Jacob's outright rejection of it.

Genesis 43:8-9[22]	Jubilees 42:19
Then Judah said to his father Israel, "Send the boy with me, and let us be on our way, so that we may live and not die—you and we and also our little ones. I myself will be surety for him; you can hold me accountable for him. If I do not bring him back to you and set him before you, then let me bear the blame forever."	Then Judah approached and said, "Send him with us. If I do not bring him back to you, then let me be guilty before you throughout my entire lifetime."

Jubilees pictures Judah as stepping forward to make his proposal after Reuben's failure (see Gen 44:18, where he steps forward to speak with Joseph); in Genesis he simply speaks. He employs an imperative form "Send" and thus commands his father to release the young man to their care. It seems significant that where Judah in Genesis says, "Send the boy with me," in Jubilees he phrases it as "Send him with us." In some way the entire group assumes responsibility for Benjamin's safety, not Judah alone, though Judah does take on himself a higher level of obligation. In Jubilees he omits the positive side of the offer—to stand surety—and repeats only the negative aspect: if he does not restore Benjamin to Jacob, he will be guilty "throughout my entire lifetime" (a phrase drawn from the parallel in Gen 44:32, where Judah is relating the story to Joseph). His offer, while it is a strong statement of assurance and even a promise to his father, involves no additional loss of life—except perhaps Benjamin's[23]—should he fail. Judah, whose reputation is here making a comeback after his dubious performance in chap. 41, looks much better than Reuben, and Jacob responds accordingly. He accepts Judah's proposal, after he had dismissed Reuben's.

■ **20** The last verse of the section bears a relationship to Gen 43:11-15, where Jacob consents to the second trip with its crucial condition regarding his youngest son, tells the brothers to "take some of the choice fruits of the land" and double the money, and sends Benjamin with them accompanied by a prayer for the safe return of him and of Simeon (vv. 11-14). In the very next verse (15) the ten arrive before Joseph. Jubilees curtails and rearranges the text and also imports words from parallel passages. The writer notes that Jacob dispatched them on their mission and supplies a date for the trip—2172, the year after the brothers first traveled to Egypt. The date formula is incomplete: it designates the year and says the date of their journey was the first of the month, without naming the month. Where Gen 43:15 reads, "Then they went on their way down to Egypt, and stood before Joseph," v. 20 has: "They arrived in the country of Egypt with all who were going (there)." The last phrase

---

than before it suggests that is not the case (see VanderKam, *Jubilees* 2:281).
21 See VanderKam, *Jubilees* 2:282.
22 The writer of Jubilees leaves out the end of Judah's speech in 43:10, where he says with some exasperation: "If we had not delayed, we would now have returned twice."
23 Judah had, of course, already lost two sons and does not, like Reuben, offer two more.

derives from Gen 42:5 // Jub 42:4—verses dealing with their first journey—not from Genesis 43. Genesis presents the list of "the choice fruits of the land" the brothers carried with them as part of Jacob's direct speech (v. 11) and names six of them,[24] four of which appear in Jubilees:

Genesis 43:11	Jubilees 42:20
Balm	Stacte (= Resin)
Honey	Almonds
Gum	Terebinth nuts (= Pistachio nuts)
Resin	Honeycombs
Pistachio nuts	
Almonds	

So, Jubilees includes four of the six in Genesis and arranges them in the order 4, 6, 5, 2 (the equivalents in parentheses above are based on the terms in Eth. Gen 43:11). In Jubilees these are said to be the gifts they carried in their hands, with no indication that Jacob told them to bring them as a gift for "the man"; the writer also does not refer to their carrying twice as much money as the first time. Neither Genesis nor Jubilees explains why items such as honey, pistachio nuts, and almonds were available and expendable as gifts during a severe famine.

21-25 The Brothers Meet Joseph, Who Devises a Plan to Test Them (Gen 43:15, 29, 23, 26, 34; 44:1-2)

The author saw fit to shorten (twenty-two verses are reduced to five) and rearrange elements of the parallel section in Gen 43:15b—44:2. He opens the paragraph by paraphrasing the end of Gen 43:15: "They arrived and stood in front of Joseph." The reader might expect that for Joseph seeing and greeting Benjamin would be the first order of business, because he had told his brothers that they would not see him if they did not bring him along on their return journey. They had now done as he stipulated. In Genesis, however, though he immediately sees Benjamin with the other nine (43:16), Joseph waits another thirteen verses before interacting with him (43:29). In Jubilees he speaks to him immediately upon their arrival in v. 21.

■ 21 The verse corresponds with Gen 43:29 but does not reproduce the immediate sequel in v. 30.

Genesis 43:29-30	Jubilees 42:21
Then he looked up and saw his brother Benjamin, his mother's son, and said, "Is this your youngest brother, of whom you spoke to me? God be gracious to you, my son!" With that, Joseph hurried out, because he was overcome with affection for his brother, and he was about to weep. So he went into a private room and wept there.	They arrived and stood in front of Joseph. When he saw his brother Benjamin, he recognized him and said to them, "Is this your youngest brother?" They said to him, "He is." He said, "May God[25] be gracious to you, my son."

The author makes explicit that Joseph recognized Benjamin, whereas in Genesis he merely sees him; he also omits the reference to Benjamin as the son of the same mother. Genesis gives the brothers no chance to answer Joseph's question, which did not really require an answer, but in Jubilees they reply in the affirmative. As he blesses him, Joseph maintains the appearance of having no special relationship with Benjamin; so he calls him "my son" in both texts. Joseph's emotional reaction to seeing Benjamin (Gen 43:30) plays no part in Jubilees at this point, just as his earlier weeping (Gen 42:24) was absent from the rewriting.

After noting their initial appearance before Joseph (back in 43:15-16), Genesis inserted several units that either figure not at all or receive only summary notice in Jubilees. (1) In vv. 16-17 Joseph ordered his steward to prepare a meal for him and these men, and the steward led them to Joseph's house. (2) In vv. 18-23 the brothers became frightened that he was bringing them to Joseph's house because their money had been

---

24   In Gen 37:25 the Ishmaelite traders who are on their way from Gilead to Egypt carry three of these products: gum, balm, resin.

25   This is a case in which the Ethiopic text uses *'egzi'abḥēr*, a designation for the deity translated in this commentary as "the Lord." In the present context, however, it seems more likely to mean "God/god," since Joseph is speaking in the role of an Egyptian administrator. Most of the ancient versions of Gen 43:29 read a word for "God," although Eth. Genesis has *'egzi'abḥēr* and the targums read the Tetragrammaton. The brothers probably would have been quite surprised had Joseph used it.

refunded, so they explained the situation to the officer, who assured them he had received the payment. (3) In vv. 24-25 the brothers prepared to dine with Joseph. (4) In vv. 26-34 the meal took place, during which Joseph inquired about their father and then asked about Benjamin (see above); the brothers were amazed to be seated in birth order, and Joseph, who ate alone because of Egyptian sensibilities, provided portions for each of the brothers but five times as much for Benjamin. And (5) in 44:1-2 he gives instructions to his steward regarding the items he was to put in the brothers' sacks, including his silver cup in Benjamin's.

■ **22** In one short verse the writer covers the material in Gen 43:17-26. Genesis 43:17 says that the steward brought all nine of Joseph's brothers to his house. In Jubilees, however, Joseph himself and not the steward sends only one (presumably Benjamin) to his house, though in the next clause all the others are present there as well. Benjamin receives preferential treatment already at this stage. The scene—in which the brothers suspect they were brought to Joseph's house regarding the money "so that he may have an opportunity to fall upon us, to make slaves of us and take our donkeys" (Gen 43:18) and they discuss the matter with the steward—drops completely from the rewritten account. The reason for the omission may have been no more than a desire to abbreviate, but the brothers do not look very impressive in the Genesis story. They totally misread the purpose for the invitation to eat at Joseph's home and are fearful for their welfare. The section also contains a line in which the steward seems careless with the truth: "He replied, 'Rest assured, do not be afraid; your God and the God of your father must have put treasure in your sacks for you; I received your money'" (Gen 43:23).[26] The author of Jubilees takes from the section in Genesis the presence of the brothers at Joseph's house and apparently understands Joseph to be the one who brings Simeon out to the others (Gen 43:23) and prepares a meal for them (compare 42:7, where he, not the steward, filled their sacks and returned their money). Genesis attributes these actions to the steward. From Gen 43:26 he takes the note that the brothers gave Joseph the gifts they had carried with them. Genesis again (see 42:6) has them bow to Joseph (twice, vv. 26, 28); their prostration to him is absent from Jubilees as it was earlier (see 42:5).[27]

■ **23-24** The intriguing dinner scene in Genesis[28] should have made the brothers suspect that something unusual was happening, especially the fact that Joseph had them seated in their birth order, though they had not divulged their relative ages to him. They might also have wondered why Joseph had to excuse himself after blessing Benjamin. The writer of Jubilees reproduces a few of the features in the episode that should have made the brothers realize something special was taking place, but he also leaves out parts that might have been problematic in some way. For example, Joseph asks about Jacob: "Is your father well, the old man of whom you spoke? Is he still alive?" (Gen 43:27). The brothers assure him "your servant, our father, is well; he is still alive" (v. 28). He had already used the section where Joseph asks about Benjamin (v. 29; see Jub 42:21) so he does not repeat it here, but the explanation for why Joseph ate alone might have made the writer uncomfortable: "They served him by himself, and them by themselves, and the Egyptians who ate with him by themselves, because the Egyptians could not eat with the Hebrews, for that is an abomination to the Egyptians" (Gen 43:32). The brothers might have concluded from the seating arrangement that Joseph was a Hebrew, not an Egyptian, but of course they do not (they may not have known the way the Egyptians viewed eating with Hebrews). There is no segregated seating arrangement at the dinner in Jubilees. The only

---

26 It may be that his theology is actually very good: "Even if this perhaps is a way of covering over the facts, in the broader context of the Joseph story the steward is expressing what has really happened: God, the God of your father, has taken care of you; be at peace!" (Westermann, *Genesis 37–50*, 124).

27 Werman attributes the deletion to the author's intent to reduce the importance of Joseph (*Jubilees*, 502), but is his stature really reduced, given his role in handling the famine and saving the lives of his family members?

28 This is the first time the brothers eat together since Gen 37:25. At that time they had just thrown Joseph into a pit; now his position, also separate from the others, has undergone a remarkable change.

part of the meal pericope that Jubilees reproduces in any detail is the end of it:

Genesis 43:33-34	Jubilees 42:23-24
When they were seated before him, the firstborn according to his birthright and the youngest according to his youth, the men looked at one another in amazement.	They ate in front of him.
Portions were taken to them from Joseph's table,[29] but Benjamin's portion was five times as much as any of theirs. So they drank and were merry with him.	He gave portions to all of them, but Benjamin's share was seven times larger than the share of any of them. They ate and drank. Then they got up and stayed with their donkeys.

Even here, where he adheres more tightly to the Genesis text, the writer introduces important changes. For one, he continues to abbreviate the earlier account, most strikingly in this instance by omitting the line about the seating arrangement for Joseph's brothers and the amazement it produced among them. It is one of the hints that might have made the ten suspicious—something was unusual about their host—but it only surprises them. As usual in these stories, Jubilees leaves out statements about the reactions of the brothers (see Gen 42:28, 35; 43:18). A second change is that the writer remains consistent with the pattern established in the chapter that Joseph is the one who performs tasks that an underling carries out in Genesis. He is the one who gives shares of food to his brothers (the source of the food is not noted).[30] A third difference has to do with the proportional size of Benjamin's food: five times that of his brothers in Genesis, seven times in Jubilees. Favoritism among the patriarchs is the normal pattern in Genesis. Jubilees, rather than deleting it, elevates the level of it in this case, and in the process the writer indulges his fondness for sevens.[31] Finally, the ways in which the meal is described are worth noting. In Genesis there is no reference to any eating by the brothers (or Joseph): they drink and "were merry" (וישכרו, "they got drunk") with him. In Jubilees they do the expected eating (mentioned twice) and drinking with no suggestion it was to excess. Once Joseph's brothers get up from the table, they go to their donkeys. The line is probably influenced by Gen 44:3, where, as soon as it was light the next morning, Jacob's sons were sent away on their donkeys.

■ 25 The final verse in the chapter lays the groundwork for the next episodes in the drama (Genesis 44–45; Jubilees 43). It should be compared with the base in Genesis:

Genesis 44:1-2	Jubilees 42:25
	Joseph conceived of a plan by which he would know their thoughts—whether there were peaceful thoughts between them.
Then he commanded the steward of his house,[32] "Fill the men's sacks with food, as much as they can carry, and put each man's money in the top of his sack. Put my cup, the silver cup, in the the top of the sack of the youngest, with his money for the grain." And he did as Joseph told him.[33]	He said to the man who was in charge of his house, "Fill all their sacks with food for them and return their money to them in their containers; put the cup with which I drink in the sack of the youngest— the silver cup—and send them away."

---

29 The rendering in the NRSV is rather interpretive, since the text says, "He took portions from before him." It could be saying that Joseph was the one who took the portions (so Hamilton, *Genesis 18–50*, 553: "He passed a portion from what was before him").

30 So also *Tg. Neof.* Gen 43:34. It may be that MT Gen 43:34 is to be understood in the same sense, as the verb "take" is *qal* singular converted imperfect in form.

31 Kugel (*Traditions*, 479–80) calls attention to frag. 2 14 of Demetrius the Chronographer, where possibly Joseph gives Benjamin five portions and takes two for himself, totaling seven. As he notes, however, there are problems with the numbers in the manuscripts. In *Walk through* Jubilees, 186 and "Jubilees," 432, he thinks the person who translated Jubilees into Greek may have introduced "seven times," since one LXX manuscript attests the reading (see VanderKam, *Jubilees* 2:283), but that seems less likely than attributing it to the writer's fondness for the number seven. Other sources attempt to relieve the awkwardness Genesis pictures by assigning the five parts to different people. In *Tg. Ps.-J.* Gen 43:34 one is Benjamin's, one is Joseph's, and the other three are for his wife and two sons. *Genesis Rabbah* 92:5 makes clear that the wife and sons in question are those of Joseph.

32 The expression regularly translated "steward" in NRSV is, literally, "the one over his house," as here in Jubilees.

33 The last sentence corresponds to the beginning of Jub 43:1.

In Genesis Joseph had devised a plan or test for determining whether his brothers were honest men—a ruse to force them to bring Benjamin when they came back (see 42:15-16, 20). His siblings had now passed that test. The writer of Jubilees did not employ the language of testing in describing their encounter with Joseph during trip number 1 (see 42:5), but now he introduces similar vocabulary to serve another purpose: he wants to investigate whether "there were peaceful thoughts between them." He wants there to be peace among them, but he is still not convinced that harmony reigns. The trial will take the form of testing their feelings for Benjamin—whether they would be willing to consign him to slavery for stealing Joseph's special cup in exchange for their freedom.[34] Did they feel toward Benjamin as they had felt toward him? Would they abandon him as they had earlier abandoned him? Do rivalry and jealousy still characterize the siblings as they did years ago? To achieve his purpose, the wise Joseph, the man who had orchestrated the survival of so many during the famine, gives the steward the same orders as in Genesis: food and money in everyone's sack, and his silver cup in Benjamin's container. Here and again in chap. 43 the writer is careful to say that Joseph drinks with the cup—no more. He avoids any suggestion that Joseph uses it to practice divination (see Gen 44:15).

---

[34] See Kugel, *Traditions*, 461-62. For interpreting what Joseph does as a trial, he also refers to Philo, *Jos.* 232-35; and Josephus, *Ant.* 2.125. The motif of the test seems intended to soften the harshness of the way in which Joseph treats his brothers (Niehoff, *Figure of Joseph*, 43-44; Endres, *Biblical Interpretation*, 188; Docherty, "Joseph the Patriarch," 209-10).

43

Joseph Tests His Brothers and Reveals His Identity

1/ He did as Joseph told him. He filled their sacks completely with food for them and placed their money in their sacks. He put[a] the cup[b] in Benjamin's sack. 2/ Early in the morning they went (off). But when they had left that place, Joseph said to the man of his house, "Pursue them. Run and reprimand them as follows: 'You have repaid me[a] with evil instead of good. You have stolen from me[b] the silver cup with which my master drinks.' Bring their youngest brother back to me and bring him[c] quickly, before I go out[d] to the place where I rule." 3/ He ran after them and spoke to them in line with[a] this message. 4/ They said to him, "Heaven forbid that your servants should do such a thing and should steal any container from the house of your master. Your servants[a] have brought back[b] from the land of Canaan the money that we found in our sacks the first time. 5/ How, then, should we steal any container? We and our sacks are here.[a] Make a search, and anyone of us in whose sack[b] you find the cup is to be killed, while we and our donkeys are to serve your master." 6/ He said to them, "(That) is not the way it will be. I will take[a] as a servant only the man with whom I find it,[b] and you may go[c] safely to your home." 7/ As he was searching among their containers, he began with the oldest and ended with the youngest. It was found[a] in Benjamin's[b] sack. 8/ They[a] tore their clothing, loaded their donkeys, and returned to the city. When they arrived at Joseph's house, all of them bowed to him with their faces to the ground. 9/ Joseph[a] said to them, "You have done an evil thing." They said,[b] "What are we to say and what shall we say in our defense? Our master[c] has discovered the crime of his servants.[d] We ourselves and our donkeys, too, are our master's servants." 10/ Joseph said to them, "As for me, I fear God. As for you, go to your houses, but your brother[a] is to be enslaved because you have done something evil.[b] Do you not know that a man takes pleasure in his cup as I do[c] in this cup? And you stole it from me."[d] 11/ Then Judah said, "**Please**,[a] master, allow me, your servant,[b] to say something[c] in my master's hearing. His mother gave birth to two brothers for your servant our father. One has gone away and been lost; no one has found him.[d] He alone is left of his mother('s children). And your servant our father loves him and his life is tied together with the life of this one.[e] 12/ If[a] we go to your servant our father and if[b] the young man is not with us, then he would die and we would bring our father down[c] in sorrow to death. 13/ Rather, I your servant will remain[a] in place of the child[b] as a servant of my master. Let the young man go[c] with his brothers because I took responsibility for him from your servant our father. If I do not bring him back, your servant will be guilty to our father forever." 14/ When Joseph saw that the minds of all of them were in harmony one with the other for good (ends), he was unable to control himself, and he told them that he was Joseph. 15/ He[a] spoke with them in the Hebrew language. He wrapped his arms around their necks and cried. But they did not recognize him and began[b] to cry. 16/ Then he said to them, "Do not cry about me. Quickly bring my father to me and[a] let **him**[b] see **me**[c] before he[d] dies, while my brother Benjamin also looks on.[e] 17/ For this is now the second year of the famine and there are still five more years without harvest, without fruit (growing on) trees, and without plowing. 18/ You and your households come down quickly so that you may not die in the famine. Do not worry about your property because the Lord sent me first before you to arrange matters so that many people may remain alive. 19/ Tell my father that I am still alive. You now see that the Lord has made me like a father to Pharaoh and to rule in his household and over the entire land of Egypt. 20/ Tell my father about all my splendor and all the wealth and splendor that the Lord has given me."

21/ By personal command of Pharaoh he gave them wagons and provisions for the trip, and he gave all of[a] them colored clothing and silver. 22/ To their[a] father he sent clothing, silver, and donkeys that were carrying grain. Then he sent them away. 23/ They went up and told their father that Joseph

1072

was alive and that he was having grain distributed[a] to all the peoples of the earth and ruling over[b] the entire land of Egypt. 24/ Their father did not believe (it) because he was disturbed in[a] his thoughts. But after he saw the wagons that Joseph had sent, his spirit revived and he said, "It is enough for me that[b] Joseph is alive. Let me go down and see him before I die."

Textual Notes

1a put] om. 21 42 47 48ᵗ.
b the cup] "the silver cup" 21 35.
2a (repaid) me] om. 35.
b from me] om. 9 17 38.
c (bring) him] om. 9 12 17 38.
d go out] "enter" 9 38.
3a in line with] "regarding/concerning" 39. See LXX Gen 44:6 (κατα).
4a Your servants] om. 25 35.
b have brought back] "have not sold" 21 25 63 (cf. 12).
5a here] The particle *nāhu* (traditionally "behold") seems the best reading, but some MSS. read a similar word (*nā-*) but with different suffixes: "here I am" 9 (and "here we are"?); "here we are" 17 44; "here are all of us" 38; om. 21. The similarity of some of these forms to the previous word—*newāya*, "container"—has led to repetition of it: "our container" 63; "vessels" 12 (?).
b sack] om. 20 25 35 44 (= "anyone of us with whom you find ...").
6a take] + "and make him into" 35 58.
b (find) it] om. 21 35 58; "you (pl.) find it" 44.
c may go] "go" (impv.) 38 39 42 47 58 (cf. 9 48).
7a It was found] "He found" 9 20 38.
b Benjamin's (lit., "of Benjamin")] + "the youngest" 39 42 47 48 58.
8a They] pr. "They were terrified/dismayed/confounded and" 39 42 47 48 58.
9a Joseph] "He" 9 12 17 21 38 63.
b They said] + "to him" 20 38.
c Our master] Mss. 20 25 35 39 42 47 48 58 prefix *za-* to the word; perhaps the text then reads "the crime of his servants which/that our master has found."
d his servants] "your servants" 9 21 38 39 42 47 48 58.
10a brother] "youngest brother" 21 35 38.
b you have done something evil] "he has done something evil like this" 58.
c as I (+ "and drink" 39 42 47 48 58) do] "because I do" 44.
d from me] om. 9 12.
11a Please] Eth. *lā'lēya* ("upon me") is, as Charles (*Ethiopic Version*, 156 n. 27) observed, a literal but erroneous translation of ב, "please," in Gen 44:18. Mss. 21 35 om.; MS. 38 places an interrogative marker on "upon us."
b your servant] om. 42 47.
c something (lit., "a word")] om. 38 44.
d found him] "found" 25 47; "was (not) found" 9 20 21 35 38 44 63.
e this one] + "his son" (= "of this his son") 35 58.
12a If] "After" 21.
b if] om. 12.
c bring (our father) down] "kill" 39 42 47 48 58.
13a I your servant will remain] "let me your servant remain" 39 42 47 48.
b the child] "this child" 35.
c Let (the young man) go] "(The young man) will go" 9.
15a He] "Joseph" 17.
b began] pr. "they too" 39 42 47 48 58 (42 47 lack the preceding "and").
16a and (let)] om. 20 21 44.
b him] "me" MSS. (except "my father" 42 47 48).
c me] "him" MSS.
d he] "I" MSS. (except "we" 25).
e while my brother Benjamin also looks on] "let my brother Benjamin also look on" 12 20 21 38. For the problems with this and the preceding lemma, see the commentary and VanderKam, *Jubilees* 2:287.
21a all of] om. 42 47 48.
22a their] "his" 21 35 58.
23a having grain distributed] "meting out/measuring out" 12 39 42 44 47 48 58.
b over] "in" 17.
24a in] om. 39 58 (making "his thoughts" the subject of the verb as in Gen 45:26).
b (for me) that] "if" 12.

Commentary

Jubilees 43:1 begins by reproducing the last sentence in Gen 44:2. The remainder of the chapter then tells in fairly brief form the story about the placement and discovery of Joseph's cup in Benjamin's sack, the return of the ten brothers to an angry Joseph, Judah's moving speech on behalf of Benjamin, Joseph's disclosure of his identity, and the brothers' conveying of the good news to Jacob. The twenty-four verses of Jubilees 43 correspond with the action related in Genesis 44 (thirty-four verses) and 45 (twenty-eight verses). That is, twenty-four verses in Jubilees deal with events handled in the course of sixty-two verses in Genesis. Here again, then, the author's penchant for abbreviating stories in the latter parts of Genesis is on display.

One way of outlining the chapter is to divide it into three main sections.

- 1-13 The cup as an instrument for testing relations between the brothers (Genesis 44)
  - 1-8a Placing and finding the cup in Benjamin's sack (Gen 44:1-13)
  - 8b-10 Confrontation with Joseph (Gen 44:14-17)
  - 11-13 Judah's speech (Gen 44:18-34)
- 14-20 Joseph reveals his identity (Gen 45:1-20)
- 21-24: The return trip and announcement of the good news to Jacob (Gen 45:21-28).

The Ethiopic manuscripts are the only witnesses to the text of Jubilees 43.

1-13 The Cup as an Instrument for Testing Relations between the Brothers (Genesis 44)[1]

Joseph had settled on the idea of planting his silver cup in the sack of Benjamin in order to determine "whether there were peaceful thoughts between" his brothers (42:25). Now the official to whom he had given the orders carries them out.

1-8a Placing and Finding the Cup in Benjamin's Sack (Gen 44:1-13)

This time the official, not Joseph (see 42:7), filled the sacks of the ten with food,[2] refunded their money into the same containers, and put the cup in the sack of Joseph's full brother Benjamin.

■ 1 Jubilees reports that he performed these tasks after the general statement about his compliance with Joseph's commands (the writer had also included Joseph's orders about them in 42:25); in Gen 44:1-2 Joseph lists them in his command and the text does not repeat them when the steward obeys. His brothers were, therefore, prepared to go home after what appeared to be a remarkably successful trip: they had not only secured the necessary grain but had also recovered Simeon and protected Benjamin. All seemed in order—if one forgot about a terrible deed some twenty years in the past.

■ 2-3 But the situation soon changes dramatically.

Genesis 44:3-6	Jubilees 43:2-3
As soon as the morning was light, the men were sent away with their donkeys. When they had gone only a short distance from the city, Joseph said to his steward, "Go, follow after the men; and when you overtake them, say to them, 'Why have you returned evil for good? Why have you stolen my silver cup?[3] Is it not from this that my lord drinks? Does he not indeed use it for divination? You have done wrong in doing this.'"	Early in the morning they went (off). But when they had left that place, Joseph said to the man of his house, "Pursue them. Run and reprimand them as follows: 'You have repaid me with evil instead of good. You have stolen from me the silver cup with which my master drinks.'
	Bring their youngest brother back to me and bring him quickly, before I go out to the place where I rule."
When he overtook them, he repeated these words to them.	He ran after them and spoke to them in line with this message.

---

1 For Philo and Josephus as other sources that interpret Joseph's treatment of his brothers as a test, see Kugel, *Traditions*, 461–62.

2 Jubilees lacks "as much as they can carry" from Gen 44:1. The word *kwello* that is located after "He filled their sacks" means "entirely" (so Dillmann and Littmann; see Leslau, *Comparative Dictionary*, 281); if it appeared before the noun, it would mean "all their sacks" (as rendered in Charles, Rabin, Wintermute, Berger, VanderKam).

3 This question is not in the MT and SP but appears in LXX Gen 44:4 and dependent translations.

While generally the same story is told in the two works, some differences separate the formulations. Unknown dispatchers send out Jacob's brothers in Genesis ("the men were sent away"); in Jubilees they go on their own. Genesis says that the eleven had traveled only a short distance from the city, though the writer has referenced no city in the text to this point.[4] Of course, it is reasonable to think that a high official like Joseph would have a house in an important city, and both texts will mention the city later (Gen 44:13 // Jub 43:8). The writer of Jubilees contents himself with a less specific reference—they left "that place [lit., from there]"—and dispenses with the note about the short distance they had covered. The instructions to the man in charge of his house are similar, but Jubilees adds the verb "Run" (see also v. 3), which implies the men had not proceeded too far down the road. Joseph dictates the very words that his servant was to direct to the brothers. In Genesis he tells him to *say* them to the eleven, but in Jubilees he is to *reprimand* them with the charges. Charles wanted to change the form in the manuscripts—*tagāʾazomu* ("reprimand them")—to *taʾaḥazomu* ("seize them"), which he took to be equivalent to the verb in Gen 44:4. It would match the reading of the LXX and its daughter translations but not the one in MT SP Gen 44:4.[5] Since the change lacks manuscript support in Jubilees, it should be rejected.

The charges that the official was to level against the brothers take the form of questions in Genesis while in Jubilees they are declarative statements (see also v. 9) that are appropriate after the verb "reprimand." He accuses all the brothers of behaving dreadfully after Joseph had shown them such lavish hospitality and had restored Simeon to them. He had done much good for them, and they had responded by swiping a valuable item from his house. In Genesis, Joseph instructs the steward to refer to the cup as the silver one from which his master drinks, but he also is to identify it by its divinatory function. The author of Jubilees has a low view of divination, as seen, for instance, in his failure to reproduce Joseph's divinatory interpretations of Pharaoh's dreams in chap. 40 (cf. also 8:1-4) and consequently omits Joseph's words "Does he not use it for divination" from the directions he gives to the man.[6] In the place of this sentence Jubilees includes a command, not found in Genesis, that centers on Benjamin: the official is to bring back the youngest brother and to do so quickly, before Joseph leaves home to "go out to the place where I rule" (v. 2).[7] He wants to complete the test before that time, while he is still at his house (from which the cup presumably disappeared). As Kugel explains, the writer is interpreting a note a little later in the chapter, Gen 44:14, where all the brothers arrive at "Joseph's house while he was still there."[8] Joseph was going to settle matters before he left for work and included words to that effect in his instructions to the steward. The test will drag out no longer than is necessary. Of course, the servant carried out Joseph's orders precisely as he gave them.

■ 4-5 The ten brothers, who were hardly started on the trek back to the land, expected neither the pursuer nor the message he brought. They responded in predictable fashion.

Genesis 44:7-9	Jubilees 43:4-5
They said to him, "Why does my lord speak such words as these? Far be it from your servants that they should do such a thing! Look, the money that we found at the top of our sacks, we brought back to you from the land of Canaan; why then would	They said to him, "Heaven forbid that your servants should do such a thing and steal any container from the house of your master. Your servants have brought back from the land of Canaan the money that we found in our sacks the first time. How, then, should

---

The Hebrew texts, with no reference to the cup before the question "Is it not from this that my lord drinks?," are laconic indeed and at least qualify as the more difficult reading.

4 According to Gen 41:47-48 Joseph stored food from the surrounding fields in each city (see also v. 35). A city would, therefore, be the place to which Jacob's sons would journey to buy food.

5 Charles, *Ethiopic Version*, 155 n. 12; see VanderKam, *Jubilees* 2:283. Charles translated "seize them" in *Jubilees* without indicating it was based on an emended text.

6 Cf. Kugel, who refers to passages in the HB forbidding divination (*Walk through* Jubilees, 187; "Jubilees," 433).

7 The term is *mekwennān*, "court of justice, tribunal, governorship," etc. (Leslau, *Concise Dictionary*, 155). Both Goldmann and Hartom translate בית משפטי, with Hartom explaining that it was the place where Joseph dealt with matters having to do with the kingdom ("Jubilees," 123 n. to v. 2).

8 Kugel, *Walk through* Jubilees, 187; "Jubilees," 433.

we steal silver or gold from your lord's house? Should it be found with any one of your servants, let him die; moreover the rest of us will become my lord's slaves."

we steal any container? We and our sacks are here. Make a search, and anyone of us in whose sack you find the cup is to be killed, while we and our donkeys are to serve your master."

The author of Jubilees jettisons the first question by the brothers—"Why does my lord speak such words as these?"—for good reason. They really are not important and contain the odd first-person form "my lord," as if just one of the brothers is speaking to the steward, despite the fact that the verse opens with "They said to him" (Judah does not speak for all of them until the search of their bags is complete). The writer begins their reply with an oathlike statement as in Genesis (the form *ḥasa* ["heaven forbid, far be in from"][9] in Jubilees is the one used in Eth. Gen 44:7, where MT SP have חלילה). The brothers in Genesis refer to their doing "such a thing," as in Jubilees, but in it they add an explanation of what "such a thing is"—stealing "any container from the house of your master." That was, of course, the issue, and the writer of Jubilees makes it explicit (as he did in v. 2 // Gen 44:4-5, where the MT and SP do not use the word "cup"). The mention of Joseph's house as the place where the theft would have occurred is moved from Gen 44:8, where the brothers wonder why they should steal gold or silver from his house. They establish their reputation as financially honest men by recalling how they returned the money that perhaps mistakenly had found its way back into their sacks when they left Egypt on the first trip. Jubilees specifically mentions that they were alluding to their initial visit ("the first time"), as does *Tg. Neof.* Gen 44:8. Would people who had just acted so responsibly with money turn around and steal from Joseph's house? The brothers in Genesis speak of various valuable objects—"silver or gold"—but Jubilees reads "any container/vessel," since no one had mentioned the theft of gold.

In Genesis the brothers really do not quite invite the steward to search their sacks (though that is what he soon does). It seems as if they could be offering to look through them for themselves and not have him do it. But the author of Jubilees does not leave open that possibility: the brothers present themselves and their bags and tell him to look through them. They make strong offers to him in both texts: the death[10] of the person in whose sack the cup was hidden, and servitude for the others. They elevate their offer in Jubilees by adding that their donkeys too will enter Joseph's service.[11] It should not go unnoticed that the brothers articulate a form of corporate solidarity: all of them will receive punishment if one of them should prove to be the thief. The extreme terms they name show that they did not suspect that any of them actually had the cup. Death for the guilty party, should Benjamin be the one, would have posed a big problem for all of them, especially Judah, because of the responsibility they had assumed for his safety.

■ **6-8a** The scene that Joseph staged to test the relations between his brothers reaches its climax in the stunning discovery of the missing object.

Genesis 44:10-13
He said, "Even so; in accordance with your words, let it be: he with whom it is found shall become my slave, but the rest of you shall go free." Then each one quickly lowered his sack to the ground, and each opened his sack.
He searched, beginning with the eldest and ending with the youngest; and the cup was found in Benjamin's sack. At this they tore their clothes. Then each one loaded his donkey, and they returned to the city.

Jubilees 43:6-8a
He said to them, "(That) is not the way it will be. I will take as a servant only the man with whom I find it, and you may go safely to your home."

As he was searching among their containers, he began with the oldest and ended with the youngest. It was found in Benjamin's sack. They tore their clothing, loaded their donkeys, and returned to the city.

There is something strange about the first words in the steward's reply in Gen 44:10: it sounds as though he is accepting their proposal, but as he continues to speak he makes fundamental modifications in it. The writer of Jubilees noticed this and introduced a negative term that is unique among the ancient wordings of the line ("[That] is not the way it will be"): the steward was

---

9   Leslau, *Concise Dictionary*, 18.
10 Jubilees uses a passive form ("is to be killed"); see SP Gen 44:9 (יומת).
11 The brothers' donkeys figure in the text twice, whereas they are absent from Genesis (see also v. 9 below). Werman wonders whether the references to donkeys is meant to indicate that these were their only animals and that they were not shepherds (see Gen 46:32-34, where this is an issue; cf. Jub 44:10).

not accepting the sentences they had pronounced on themselves, should one of them prove guilty.[12] Rather unexpectedly, he ameliorated the severity of their terms: the guilty one would become a slave,[13] and the others would suffer no penalty. In Genesis they "shall go free [lit., will be clean/innocent]," but in Jubilees he gives them the right to "go safely to your home." The writer has taken these words from Gen 44:17, where Joseph tells all his brothers except Benjamin that they could "go up in peace to your father" (the words translated "safely" in Jub 43:6 are literally "in peace"). Once the steward states the conditions, the discussion ends. His intent (dictated by Joseph) is to test the solidarity the brothers had expressed in their proposal by leaving an easy way out for all but the thief.

In Gen 44:11 the brothers, who had not expressly invited the steward to search their bags, help him by lowering their containers and opening them so that he could inspect them. In Jubilees, the brothers had said in v. 5, "We and our sacks are here. Make a search." As a result, they had apparently already presented the containers to him and did not have to do it again; the writer, therefore, at this point skips the sentence about lowering and opening the bags. The steward, perhaps logically, began his search with the oldest (he knew their birth order from the meal) and worked down the list. Naturally, this draws out the scene and heightens the drama. When the man over Joseph's house reached the last bag, the one of the youngest, Benjamin, he found the cup. Joseph had sprung the trap, and now, under these sudden and horrible circumstances, he would be able to discern whether harmony or selfishness prevailed among his brothers. All of them were free to resume their journey to Jacob, and only Benjamin had to stay behind as a servant. Which way would the ten travel—home or back to Joseph's house? The response is immediate and unified: all of them expressed their dismay by tearing their clothing,[14] and all mounted their donkeys and returned to the city where Joseph lived. All eleven brothers acted together. That was positive, but little else seems to be at this stage in the story.

8b-10 Confrontation with Joseph (Gen 44:14-17)

Joseph must have been gratified to see that all his brothers returned to his house, not just one of them, but he was not finished with the trial through which he was making them pass.

Genesis 44:14-17	Jubilees 43:8b-10
Judah and his brothers came to Joseph's house while he was still there; and they fell to the ground before him. Joseph said to them, "What deed is this that you have done? Do you not know that one such as I can practice divination?"	When they arrived at Joseph's house, all of them bowed to him with their faces to the ground. Joseph said to them, "You have done an evil thing."
And Judah said, "What can we say to my lord? What can we speak? How can we clear ourselves? God has found out the guilt[15] of your servants; here we are then, my lord's slaves, both we and also the one in whose possession the cup has been found." But he said, "Far be it from me that I should do so! Only the one in whose possession the cup was found shall be my slave; but as for you, go up in peace to your father."	They said, "What are we to say and what shall we say in our defense? Our master has discovered the crime of his servants. We ourselves and our donkeys, too, are our master's servants." Joseph said to them, "As for me, I fear God. As for you, go to your houses, but your brother is to be enslaved because you have done something evil. Do you not know that a man takes pleasure in his cup as I do in this cup? And you stole it from me."

---

12 *Genesis Rabbah* 92:8 deals with this issue. There the steward says, "your words are indeed correct, for when one of a company of ten is discovered to be a thief, are not all liable to be imprisoned? Yet I will not do so." He is understood as saying that the legal principle is correct, but he is going to be kinder than the law demands.

13 Jubilees adds "only/alone" to emphasize that the steward would take just one of them, not the whole group. In not agreeing to the execution of the one who had the cup, the servant may have been exercising caution lest he be obligated to subject Benjamin to the death penalty the brothers had stipulated—something that would ruin Joseph's plan (see Hamilton, *Genesis 18–50*, 563).

14 Clothing is, of course, an important topic in the Joseph stories. In this case rending their garments recalls what Jacob did when he received the proof of Joseph's "death" (Gen 37:34; see Hamilton, *Genesis 18–50*, 564). Joseph will give all of them new clothing after he reveals himself to them (see below on v. 21 // Gen 45:22).

15 "Guilt" does not seem a good translation of עון; it means "sin, crime" as in this place in Jubilees.

For the first time in Jubilees' version of the Joseph stories, the brothers bow to him. They had not done so on their first (unlike Gen 42:6) or second (unlike Gen 43:26, 28) visit, but under the current conditions it was the right thing for them to do. Once again (see above, 43:2 // Gen 44:4), Genesis formulates something as a question ("What deed is this that you have done?") that appears as a statement in Jubilees: "You have done an evil thing" (repeated in v. 10). The Joseph of Genesis includes a question that the writer of Jubilees omitted: "Do you not know that one such as I can practice divination" (44:15). The deletion is consistent with his practice in 43:2 (see Gen 44:5) and elsewhere. In Jubilees the silver cup is for drinking, not for divinatory ends. The use for the cup is moved down to Jub 43:10 (the statement in v. 10 is a revision of one in Gen 44:15) where Joseph asks, "Do you not know that a man takes pleasure in his cup as I do in this cup?"[16]

A more telling difference occurs in vv. 8b and 9 (// Gen 44:14, 16) regarding the ways in which the brothers are identified and who speaks. Genesis refers to them as "Judah and his brothers," while Jubilees uses a pronoun ("they"), that is, the author does not single out Judah from the others. After Joseph makes his initial accusations against them, in Genesis Judah is the one who replies for the group; in Jubilees, however, all of them speak. All of them realize that there is really nothing they can say in their defense. The writer in this way underscores the fact that the brothers are functioning as a unified body, and they consider each member of their group guilty, not just one of them. They look more cohesive than they do in Genesis.

Judah says to Joseph in Gen 44:16 that God has found out the sin of the brothers. The statement is striking because, while it recognizes a certain liability all of them had, it appears to be saying that there really was something bad that they had done and that God himself was responsible for uncovering it. The writer of Jubilees reformulates the statement so that it is Joseph ("Our master")[17] who has discovered their very recent crime. This would seem to be what is being acknowledged, although in Genesis Judah could be referring to a past transgression on the part of the brothers.[18] The sequel in Genesis suggests that Judah is not in fact confessing the wrong he mentions: rather than saying that Benjamin was a thief, he describes him less critically as "the one in whose possession the cup has been found" (the expression is not in Jubilees).

As the speech progresses, Judah (in Genesis) and all the brothers (in Jubilees) maintain their united front. Whatever may have transpired, all of them, not just Benjamin, will become slaves to Joseph. The brothers will not be separated from one another; they are all in it together. Again in Jubilees (see v. 5 above) they include their donkeys in their pledge to become Joseph's servants.

Joseph in Gen 44:17 refuses to accept Judah's proposal that all become his slaves and employs an oathlike statement as the brothers had in v. 7 ("Far be it from me"). The brothers had declared to the steward that it was impossible they would do such a thing as steal the cup; now Joseph asserts most emphatically that it is impossible for him to do as Judah proposed. He also echoes Judah's way of referring to the guilty person—"the one in whose possession the cup was found"—as he insists that only the thief will be subjected to slavery; the other ten were free to return unpunished to their father. In Jubilees, Joseph does not repeat the earlier statements

---

16   Unlike Jubilees, whose author removes the notion that Joseph practiced divination with the cup, some other sources say he was able to arrange Reuben and Benjamin in their appropriate places in the order of the brothers at the meal he hosted by learning the information through striking his mantic cup. See Kugel, *Traditions*, 480–82.

17   This is more likely than Hartom's suggestion that in the first instance in the verse (the present one) "Our master" means "the Lord," and in the second instance it refers to Joseph ("our master's servants") ("Jubilees," 124 n. to v. 9). Use of the same form twice in one verse makes it more reasonable to think it has the same meaning in both.

18   Commentators on Genesis often relate the statement to their sense of guilt for what they had done to Joseph much earlier, not to the present circumstance (e.g., Westermann, *Genesis 37–50*, 133–34; Hamilton, *Genesis 18–50*, 565–66). If one applied the statement to its immediate context, it would seem as if Judah is saying that Joseph's knowledge of what had happened came to him from a divine source that he could access through his divining powers.

of the brothers and Judah; rather, he identifies himself as one who fears God. The writer has transplanted this description from Gen 42:18 where, once he had released the ten from imprisonment, he explained the conditions under which they would prove their honesty: "Do this and you will live, for I fear God." The writer of Jubilees did not use the expression at that point (42:6) but found it appropriate to insert it here in 43:10.[19] Joseph ends his speech quite differently than in Genesis: he tells the brothers they may return to their houses (not to their father, as in Genesis), repeats that they have committed a crime (the pronoun "you" in "you have done something evil" is plural), asks in effect how they could have taken a cup that he so enjoys, and adds "And you [pl.] stole it from me." His words conclude more harshly and accusatorily than they do in Genesis. He really gives the impression of being angry with all of them. He is trying to frighten the majority to determine whether they will abandon their youngest brother in order to save themselves from slavery to an enraged lord. He carries out his act superbly and succeeds in eliciting the answer he wanted.

11-13 Judah's Speech (Gen 44:18-34)

The reply of Judah should be the highlight of the drama in that what he has to say finally induces Joseph to end his pretense and disclose to them what is really going on. The narrator in Genesis assigns seventeen verses to his emotional outpouring before Joseph; these become just three verses in Jubilees. The writer of Jubilees leaves out most of the section in which his older brother rehearses the previous encounters between the Egyptian official (Joseph) and the brothers and the discussions with Jacob about sending Benjamin with them on the return trip to Egypt. He largely omits Gen 44:19-29 (using one line from v. 20 and some words from vv. 27-28), and then reproduces more of Gen 44:30-33 but nothing from v. 34.

■ **11** The two sections begin in a related way.

Genesis 44:18	Jubilees 43:11
Then Judah stepped up to him and said, "O my lord, let your servant please speak a word in my lord's ears, and do not be angry with your servant; for you are like Pharaoh himself."	Then Judah said, "*Please*,[20] master, allow me, your servant, to say something in my master's hearing."

Where Genesis has Judah stepping forward to address Joseph (cf. Jub 42:19), Jubilees has him merely begin speaking. In Genesis, Judah had just spoken on behalf of the group and Joseph had rejected his offer. Perhaps we are to imagine that he had stepped back after speaking or that Joseph's sharply negative response made him fall back. Whatever may be the case, in Jubilees, although he has not yet spoken, he does not have to advance toward Joseph to speak with him. The shorter text of Jubilees results primarily from omitting the second part of Judah's address here to Joseph. The Judah of Jubilees does not ask Joseph, who already appears to be exceedingly angry in the preceding verse, to withhold his wrath while he speaks and he does not flatter him by comparing him to Pharaoh. Judah is very polite to the high official in Jubilees, but he is not obsequious to him.

The remaining parts of v. 11 draw words from Gen 44:27-28, 20, and 30 (since the writer does not use them in order, they are placed in the right-hand column below at the appropriate places).

Jubilees 43:11	Genesis 44
His mother gave birth to two brothers for your servant our father.	27 You know that my wife bore me two sons [words Judah cites from Jacob];
One has gone away and been lost; no one has found him.	28 one left me, and I said, Surely he has been torn to pieces; and I have never seen him since.
He alone is left of his mother('s children).	20 he alone is left of his mother's children [cf. 42:38],
And your servant our father loves him	and his father loves him.

---

19 This is another case in which *'egzi'abḥēr* must means "god/God," not "the Lord" as it is usually rendered here (see Kugel, *Walk through* Jubilees, 187). While *'egzi'abḥēr* often appears where the HB uses the Tetragrammaton (LXX ο κυριος), it can also figure where "God" (LXX ο θεος) appears. If Joseph had used the Tetragrammaton with his brothers, he would have given himself away a bit too soon.

20 See the textual note for the emendation here.

and his life is tied together with the life of this one.	30 his life is bound up in the boy's life.

So, Jubilees takes some essential lines from Judah's speech in which he adduces the facts of the case; the writer apparently saw no reason to repeat the material that he had summarized in chap. 42. Judah emphasizes to Joseph the special status the boy occupied and the intimate bond joining him with his father. There is favoritism here, but it does not seem to offend the other brothers.

■ **12** In v. 12 the speech of Judah is related more closely to Gen 44:30-31.

Genesis 44:30-31	Jubilees 43:12
. . . when I come to your servant my father and the boy is not with us, then, as his life is bound up in the boy's life, when he sees that the boy is not with us, he will die; and your servants will bring down the gray hairs of our father with sorrow to Sheol.	If we go to your servant our father and if the young man is not with us, then he would die and we would bring our father down in sorrow to death.

It is noteworthy that Judah in Jubilees continues to represent the group ("If we go," "our father") whereas in Genesis he refers to himself ("when I come," "my father"). The author had used the line about Jacob's life being attached to Benjamin's above in v. 11, so he leaves it out of v. 12. The presence of the expression in Gen 44:30 leads to repetition on either side of it: "the boy is not with us" and "when he sees that the boy is not with us"; Jubilees uses only the first instance. In both texts Judah then maintains that the brothers would be responsible for their father's death. Jubilees lacks the reference to his gray hairs and uses the word "death" where Genesis mentions "Sheol."[21]

■ **13** Verse 13 then picks up expressions from Gen 44:32-33 but reworks and reorders them.

Genesis 44:32-33	Jubilees 43:13
33 Now therefore, please let your servant remain as a slave to my lord in place of the boy; and let the boy go back with his brothers. 32 For your servant became surety for the boy to my father,	Rather, I your servant will remain in place of the child as a servant of my master. Let the young man go with his brothers because I took responsibility for him from your servant our father.
saying, "If I do not bring him back to you, then I will bear the blame in the sight of my father all my life."	If I do bring him back, your servant will be guilty to our father forever.

Judah refers to Benjamin as a boy or young man (הנער) in Genesis, but Jubilees varies its terms as if to emphasize with the first one how unspeakable it would be for Joseph to enslave one so young and separate him from his family. In the first instance the word is *ḥeḍān*, "infant, young child" ("child" above); in the second case it is *warēzā*, "young, young man, youth, adolescent" ("young man" above).[22] According to the chronology in Jubilees, in the second year of the famine (2172; cf. 42:1) Benjamin would have been twenty-nine years old (he was born in 2143; 32:33), hardly an "infant" or "young child." But, for the sake of the story, he is presented as very young. The author had not used the language of surety in 42:19 when Judah convinced his father to send Benjamin; here he speaks of being responsible for Benjamin. In both texts Judah notes that he would be guilty to Jacob for the duration of his life if he failed to bring his youngest son back: here Jubilees has him say "forever," where Genesis uses "all my life." Oddly enough, the readings were reversed when Judah first made the guarantee: there Jubilees used "my entire lifetime" (42:19) and Genesis had "forever" (43:10). In Genesis and Jubilees, Judah, faced with the prospect of freedom for himself and nine of his brothers, offers to take Benjamin's place when he contemplates what the effect on his elderly father will be. He realizes the loss of Benjamin will kill Jacob. The Judah of Genesis uses more flowery language in predicting that all of them will bring their father's gray hair to Sheol in sadness, while in Jubilees he says they will bring him down to death grieving the loss of his youngest son. Note that in two more cases Judah speaks for all the brothers in Jubilees ("our father" twice where Genesis has "my father"). Judah himself, of course, would be more to blame than the others because he had assumed the duty of assuring safe travel for Benjamin. Perhaps the writer of Jubilees omitted Gen 44:34 because it uses more evocative, emotional language: Judah does not

---

21　None of the ancient versions of Gen 44:31 reads "death" at this point. In some other passages the term Sheol survives in the Ethiopic text (e.g., 5:14; 7:29; 22:22; 24:31; cf. 42:11).

22　See Leslau, *Concise Dictionary*, 27, 161. Ethiopic Genesis consistently uses *ḥeḍān* in this section.

know how he could look on his father's suffering if he did not restore the boy to him. He had already made his point that Jacob would die without Benjamin; no more needed to be said.

14-20: Joseph Reveals His Identity (Gen 45:1-20)

Judah's stirring words about family relations were sufficient to bring the test Joseph was administering to a close. The author of Jubilees is more explicit about this than the narrator in Genesis.

■ **14** The verse opens with a clause that lacks a parallel in Genesis. There it seems as if Joseph's decision to identify himself to his brothers is an emotional reaction to what Judah has just said; in Jubilees the presence of all the brothers before him, their solidarity with one another, and the offer of Judah to be enslaved rather than Benjamin prove to Joseph "that the minds of all of them were in harmony one with the other for good (ends)." In 42:25, as his brothers ate in his presence, he had "conceived of a plan by which he would know their thoughts—whether there were peaceful thoughts between them." Now he knows and it becomes appropriate to remove the veil of secrecy that had prevented them from recognizing him.[23] Yet it was not entirely a cold, calculated decision to reveal who he was, because the writer repeats from Gen 45:1 that Joseph "was unable to control himself." The reader does not learn more about his reaction in Jubilees because the author, not atypically, plays down the emotions—in this case the loud weeping by Joseph that is the subject of Gen 45:1b-2. In Genesis various Egyptians are also present, and Joseph orders them out before he tells the news about himself to his brothers. In Jubilees there appear to be no bystanders; the only ones mentioned are Joseph and the eleven. Having skipped over Gen 45:1b-2, the writer reports the disclosure of his identity to his brothers, while Gen 45:3 quotes it. He does not reproduce Joseph's question whether his father was still alive (Judah's words had made that clear); he also does not cite Gen 45:3b: "But his brothers could not answer him, so dismayed[24] were they at his presence."

■ **15** Jubilees reports that Joseph spoke with his brothers in the Hebrew language. The writer may have inferred that Hebrew was the medium through which they communicated from the fact that Joseph converses with his brothers without an interpreter present (he had sent everyone else away when he revealed himself—Gen 45:1b).[25] Also, in Gen 45:12 Joseph said to them, "And now your eyes and the eyes of my brother Benjamin see that it is my own mouth that speaks to you" (cf. the end of Gen 45:15).[26] Hebrew as the special language is

---

23   Cf. Niehoff, *Figure of Joseph*, 43–44; Endres, *Biblical Interpretation*, 189. Endres cites Josephus, *Ant.* 2.161, where Joseph also uses the language of testing: "I commend you for your virtue and that affection for our brother and find you better men than I had expected from your plots against me; for all this that I have done was to test your brotherly love." Livneh ("'Love Your Fellow,'" 192–95) shows how the test and the proof that there were thoughts of peace between them reveal that they were obeying the law of brotherly love in Lev 19:17-18. "Other details in the reworked story also indicate that the author of *Jubilees* took pains to present the relations between Jacob's sons—i.e., the Israelites—in a positive light. Firstly, Joseph's brothers never hated nor were jealous of him, Joseph, for his part, never bringing a bad report of them to their father (but cf. Gen 37:1-11). Secondly, the narrative concerning the brothers' conspiracy is extremely abbreviated (cf. *Jub.* 34:11 vis-à-vis Gen [37:]18-28). Also greatly truncated are the two reports of Joseph's harsh words to his brothers on their first visit to Egypt (*Jub.* 42:5, 9 vis-à-vis Gen 42:9-20, 29-34). By these literary means, the Jubilean author highlights the importance of fraternal love within Jacob's family, thereby stressing his conception of the proper relations the Israelites should practice amongst themselves—namely, fraternal love" (pp. 194–95). See also Docherty, "Joseph the Patriarch," 209–10; she stresses that the test is one of several ways in which the author demonstrates that Joseph is "an entirely virtuous character" (p. 210).

24   "Dismayed" seems unlikely to be the meaning intended by נבהלו; it is more plausible that the brothers were terrified or, perhaps better yet, "stunned" (so Hamilton, *Genesis 18–50*, 571).

25   According to Gen 42:23 Joseph spoke with his brothers through an interpreter.

26   *Genesis Rabbah* 93:10 makes the same point in connection with Gen 45:12—Joseph was speaking Hebrew. In *Tgs. Neof.* and *Ps.-J.* Gen 45:12 he spoke "in the language of the sanctuary," while in *Tg. Onq.* Gen 45:12 he speaks "in your language" (see B. Grossfeld's n. 12 in his translation of Onqelos

an important theme in Jubilees (see particularly 12:25-27, where it is the revealed language, the language of creation, and the one in which the ancestral books were composed). The writer, therefore, takes the opportunity furnished by the text of Genesis to state that Joseph spoke Hebrew to communicate with his brothers.

The writer of Jubilees assembled the remaining parts of v. 15 from different contexts in Genesis 45. The statement "He wrapped his arms around their necks and cried" probably reflects the contents of Gen 45:14-15: "Then he fell upon his brother Benjamin's neck and wept, while Benjamin wept upon his neck. And he kissed all his brothers and wept upon them." That his brothers did not recognize him even after he told them he was Joseph may be an allusion to Gen 45:4: "But his brothers could not answer him, so dismayed [stunned] were they at his presence." In Jubilees the brothers cry; in Genesis they do not.[27] They are just flabbergasted.

■ 16 Because the writer said that Joseph's brothers also broke out in tears, he has Joseph comfort them at the beginning of v. 16: "Do not cry about me." There is no direct parallel in Genesis, where the brothers do not weep, but the words may be meant to recall Joseph's reassuring words, after identifying himself as "your brother, Joseph, whom you sold into Egypt" (Gen 45:4). There Joseph continues, "And now do not be distressed, or angry with yourselves, because you sold me here" (45:5). There are two places in Genesis 45 in which Joseph urges his brothers to bring his father to Egypt as soon as possible: "Hurry and bring my father down here" (45:13); and "Hurry and go up to my father ... come down to me, do not delay" (45:9). In Jubilees he gives the order about his father just once ("Quickly bring my father to me"). After this clause, the preferred reading in the manuscripts is: "and let me see him before I die." The wish is strange in context since Joseph should be just thirty-eight years of age (see 28:24; 42:20), and the words are in fact ones that Jacob spoke after his sons convinced him Joseph was still alive (see Gen 45:28 // Jub 43:24; cf. Gen 46:30). It is possible that the rewriting of the Genesis account caused confusion regarding the person of the verb and object: the fact that Joseph tells his brothers to bring Jacob "to me" seems to have induced someone (author, copyist, translator?) to continue with first-person verbal forms, whereas the original would have said, "and let him see me before he dies." The translation has been emended to reflect this explanation.[28] To this statement Joseph adds, "while my brother Benjamin also looks on"—a sentiment that looks to a happy reunion of the father and his two sons by Rachel. The thought of Benjamin's looking on is indebted to Gen 45:12 (though with a different object observed), where Joseph says, "And now your eyes and the eyes of my brother Benjamin see that it is my own mouth that speaks to you."

■ 17 Joseph was, of course, terribly anxious to see Jacob again, but he was also concerned for the welfare of his entire family. He knew what lay in store for the residents of Canaan and Egypt throughout the remainder of the famine period, so he explains the situation to his brothers who would have had no idea how long the difficult times would last. Verse 17 is based upon Gen 45:6:

Genesis 45:6	Jubilees 43:17
For the famine has been in the land these two years; and there are five more years in which there will be neither plowing nor harvest.	For this is now the second year of the famine and there are still five more years without harvest, without fruit (growing on) trees, and without plowing.

[Targum Onqelos to Genesis, 149] for references to various midrashim that make the same identification). Cf. also Berger, Jubiläen, 530 n. a to v. 15; Endres, Biblical Interpretation, 189.

27 They do weep in 50:18, where they cry and fall in front of Joseph after the death of Jacob when they feared Joseph would finally take revenge on them.

28 See Goldmann, "Jubilees," 303 n. to v. 16; VanderKam, Jubilees 2:287, where there is also a review of the ways in which translators have handled the problem. Charles (Ethiopic Version, 157 n. 9; Jubilees, 237) emended more drastically so that the text reads more like Gen 45:12: "and ye see that it is my mouth that speaketh, and the eyes of my brother Benjamin see." Caquot ("Jubilés," 791 n. to v. 16) considers the first part of the expression in the manuscripts to be correct ("pour que je le voie avant mourir < > [so that I may see him before dying < >]") but regards the remainder of the line to be mutilated where it indicated whose death was intended.

For reasons that are not clear, the writer of Jubilees uses the order harvest/plowing against all ancient versions of the verse, and he uniquely adds the reference to fruit trees—perhaps to underscore that the famine would be complete. Absolutely nothing would be producing food so that immediate and drastic action was in order.

■ **18** The verse begins with instructions Joseph gave to his brothers: they and their households were to make a swift move to Egypt to avoid death due to the famine. Joseph never gives them such orders in Genesis 45; the brothers and their families are simply included in the more general summons given to Jacob that he and his household were to descend to Egypt so that Joseph could provide for them (see Gen 45:9-11; cf. Pharaoh's instructions in 45:18-19). Joseph also urged his brothers not to worry about their property that they would be leaving behind in the land of Canaan—another recommendation he does not make in Genesis 45. In fact, Pharaoh is the one who does: "Give no thought to your possessions [lit., your vessels], for the best of all the land of Egypt is yours" (45:20).[29] The author of Jubilees omits Gen 45:16-20, where it is learned in the palace that Joseph's brothers had arrived and where the monarch makes generous provisions for them, including giving them the "best of all the land of Egypt." The writer does, however, transfer some of Pharaoh's words to Joseph.[30]

Concern about his brothers and about their families is the immediate context for Joseph to mention the divine providence that sent him before them to Egypt. The precise sequence of subjects is distinct from the ones with the rich theological statements in Genesis 45—statements that should have interested the author of Jubilees but ones that he treats only briefly. In Genesis 45 Joseph recalls that his brothers had sold him years earlier (he does this three times, in vv. 4, 5, 8 [only an allusion to it]), but, rather than being bitter and vengeful, he encompasses their heinous act within God's larger guidance of events. For example, in Gen 45:5 he explains to his astonished brothers whose wicked treatment of him he has just mentioned, "for God sent me before you to preserve life." This clause is the basis for Jub 43:18: "because the Lord sent me first before you to arrange matters so that many people may remain alive." The phrase "to arrange matters" is added to the base text: the infinitive *šariʿ* perhaps has no more significance than "arrange, set in order," but it is the verbal root related to the term *šerʿat* ("law, precept, constitution, covenant") that is so important in Jubilees.[31] God sent Joseph to put things in proper order, to establish them as they should be. In this chapter Joseph will say nothing more about the providential direction that brought good out of evil. In Genesis, however, he reiterates the point in vv. 7-8, where he adds that it was God, not they, who caused him to go to Egypt (see also his later assurances to his brothers in Gen 50:19-21). So Jubilees in one verse ties the providential way in which God had orchestrated events to Joseph's concern for his brothers and their families, whereas Genesis three times connects it with the wrong they had done to him in chap. 37. The Joseph of Jubilees 43 never refers to how his brothers had once abused him. The author had bypassed their recollection of it on their first visit to Egypt in Gen 42:21-22, and now he does the same with Joseph's references. They are all one big happy family, with the past conveniently left in the past. Brotherly unity was the point the writer was seeking to make. The family of Joseph at last enjoyed harmonious relations after a period of separation.

---

29   It seems as if the ruler is talking about property they would have to leave behind, but in Gen 46:6, 32; 47:1 they bring their possessions with them to Egypt.

30   The text of Genesis 45–47 raises questions about who assigned Goshen to Jacob's family and when: was it Joseph (Gen 45:10) or Pharaoh (45:18, 20, though he does not at this point mention Goshen by name)? If Pharaoh, did he grant it to them in 45:18, 20 or in 47:1-6, after they had already moved there (46:28-34)? The overlap between what Joseph and Pharaoh said about Goshen may have provided the impetus for the writer of Jubilees to place the monarch's words about their possessions in Joseph's mouth as well.

31   See Leslau, *Concise Dictionary*, 50. Verbal and noun forms occur regularly with laws (e.g., Jub 3:13), calendar (6:23, etc.), festivals (e.g., 6:24), circumcision (15:25), and so on.

■ **19** Joseph now gives an order to his brothers about what they are to tell Jacob. First, they were to tell him the most important fact—that he was still alive (contrary to what Jacob thought in 42:36; 44:28, etc.). Joseph never actually tells them to say this in Genesis 45, but it was essential information and it was the first thing the brothers said when they returned to Jacob (45:26). To this Joseph adds words from Gen 45:8, where the brothers were to tell their father about his current status:

Genesis 45:8	Jubilees 43:19
. . . he has made me a father to Pharaoh, and lord of all his house and ruler over all the land of Egypt.	You now see that the Lord has made me like a father to Pharaoh and to rule in his household and over the entire land of Egypt.

Unlike any of the early versions of Genesis, Jubilees says only that Joseph was "like" a father to Pharaoh; he, of course, was not really his father. The powers to which he refers echo the language used by Pharaoh when bestowing them on Joseph after he interpreted his dreams (Gen 41:40-41 // Jub 40:6-7).

■ **20** The final verse of the section concludes the message Joseph dictates to his brothers. This time the writer draws on Gen 45:13 but introduces modifications into it.

Genesis 45:13	Jubilees 43:20
You must tell my father how greatly I am honored in Egypt, and all that you have seen.	Tell my father about all my splendor[32] and all the wealth and splendor that the Lord has given me.

Joseph sounds boastful at this juncture in Genesis, but the writer of Jubilees has appended these words to the previous message they were to give Jacob (they are separated by four verses in Genesis). In v. 19 Joseph credited the Lord with exalting him to his lofty position; now in the sequel of the dictated message Jubilees continues to have him give proper credit to God for all the good that had come his way.[33] Genesis limits his honor to Egypt; Jubilees does not.

21-24 The Return Trip and Announcement of the Good News to Jacob (Gen 45:21-28)

The author uses much of the material in Gen 45:21-28 regarding provisions for the journey back to Canaan, the exuberant report to Jacob about Joseph, and Jacob's resolve to make the difficult trip to Egypt to see Joseph before the elderly man died. The thought of Joseph traveling to Canaan to spare his father the rigors of the road is not a consideration in either text. The situation was so grave that only a move to Egypt and its food supply would save the chosen family from death.

■ **21** One of the themes in the Joseph stories in Jubilees emerges clearly in v. 21.

Genesis 45:21-22	Jubilees 43:21
Joseph gave them wagons according to the instruction of Pharaoh, and he gave them provisions for the journey. To each one he gave a set of garments, but to Benjamin he gave three hundred pieces of silver and five sets of garments.	By personal command of Pharaoh he gave them wagons and provisions for the trip, and he gave all of them colored clothing and silver.

The point the author makes by omitting the supersized outlay for Benjamin is obvious: rather than reproducing yet another manifestation of favoritism in Genesis, he wishes to present the twelve as a unity, living in harmony. He had, it will be recalled, mentioned the extra portions for Benjamin at the dinner table—even raising the number from five to seven times that of the share for each brother (see 42:23)—but in this new context there is no place for such disproportions or goads to discord. The only surviving hint of the line regarding the gifts for Benjamin is the word "silver," and in this case all eleven receive it from Joseph, not just Benjamin. Another difference between the two texts concerns the items of clothing Joseph gives to his brothers. Genesis uses general terms for these changes of clothing, but Jubilees speaks of "colored clothing" for all of them. The term in question—*ḥebr*—means "colored, of diverse colors, variegated, decorated with colors" and cannot fail to remind a reader of Joseph's special garment in Gen 37:3, 23, 32: whatever the Hebrew פסים means,[34] it was understood in the LXX tradition to mean "variegated, of different colors." Ethiopic Gen 37:3 uses the word found here in Jubilees as part of its description of Joseph's coat, although it is combined with *kabd* to produce the

---

32   The word *kebr*, used twice in the sentence, could also be rendered "honor, glory, magnificence" (Leslau, *Concise Dictionary*, 153).

33   Hartom, "Jubilees," 124 n. to v. 20.

34   For some suggestions among early interpreters, see Kugel, *Traditions*, 452.

meaning "purple."³⁵ By speaking of colored clothing, the text seems to be reminding the reader of the event in Genesis 37 where Joseph's special robe was a sign of his father's stronger love for him than for his brothers; now Joseph gives further expression to the unity and value of all by assigning them clothing like the kind he had received in Genesis 37.

■ **22** Jubilees also provides its own formulation of the lines regarding Joseph's gifts to Jacob.

Genesis 45:23-24a	Jubilees 43:22
To his father he sent the following: ten donkeys loaded with the good things of Egypt, and ten female donkeys loaded with grain, bread, and provision for his father on the journey. Then he sent his brothers on their way.	To their father he sent clothing, silver, and donkeys that were carrying grain. Then he sent them away.

Only Jubilees among the versions of this text mentions clothing and silver for Jacob, apparently explaining what the text meant by "the good things of Egypt." But it should not escape notice that the combination of clothing and silver is what, according to Gen 45:22, Joseph gave uniquely to Benjamin. In Jubilees all the males in the family receive items of clothing and money. Jubilees, which gives no number for the donkeys and does not distinguish their genders, abbreviates the section describing what the animals carried; the grain would supply the food to support Jacob on the arduous trip to Egypt. Naturally he and his family would have plenty of grain once they arrived in Egypt, where Joseph would provide for them.

■ **23** Neither Genesis nor Jubilees provides any details about the presumably challenging journey back to Canaan. The important point was that the long-suffering Jacob hear the news that his son Joseph was still alive. Again, Jubilees is a bit more matter-of-fact than Genesis, but the writer does not entirely overlook the emotional side of the joyous occasion. It is noteworthy that Jubilees omits Joseph's parting words to his eleven brothers: "Do not quarrel along the way" (Gen 45:24 [end]). As they were now in harmony with one another, there was no reason to warn them about fighting.³⁶

Genesis 45:25	Jubilees 43:23
So they went up out of Egypt and came to their father in the land of Canaan. And they told him, "Joseph is still alive! He is even ruler over all the land of Egypt."	They went up and told their father that Joseph was alive and that he was having grain distributed to all the peoples of the earth and ruling over the entire land of Egypt.

Jubilees abbreviates the report about the trip (their itinerary was obvious enough). This is another case in which Jubilees relates in the third person words that characters speak in Genesis. The report expands the brief sentence about Joseph as ruler over all Egypt by adding that he was in charge of dispersing grain to peoples from everywhere—a function evident throughout the previous chapters and explicit in places such as Gen 41:57; 42:6. It would have been helpful information for Jacob to have because food was now essential for survival, even to allow him to reach Egypt and see his son.

■ **24** The stories in Genesis and Jubilees end in very similar ways. Verse 24 includes material from Gen 45:26b-28:

Genesis 45:26b-28	Jubilees 43:24
He was stunned; he could not believe them.	Their father did not believe (it) because he was disturbed in his thoughts.
But when they told him all the words of Joseph that he had said to them, and when he saw the wagons that Joseph had sent to carry him, the spirit of their father Jacob revived. Israel said, "Enough! My son Joseph is still alive. I must go and see him before I die."	But after he saw the wagons that Joseph had sent, his spirit revived and he said, "It is enough for me that Joseph is alive. Let me go down and see him before I die."

The writer of Jubilees switches the first two clauses around and links them as cause and effect. "He was

---

35 Leslau, *Concise Dictionary*, 21.
36 This seems to be the meaning of the verb in v. 24. Note the translation of *Tg. Ps.-J.* Gen 45:24: "Do not quarrel about my sale, *lest those who make the journey (with you) become angry with you.*" According to *Gen. Rab.* 94:2, the meaning is: "Take no long strides, he bade them, do not refrain from religious study, and enter the city by day." However, in *b. Ta'an.* 10b R. Eleazar says the meaning is that the brothers were not to become involved in studying the law since that could lead to quarreling.

disturbed in his thoughts [lit., heart]" is an interpretation of the Hebrew expression which is literally "his heart grew numb." The almost impossible news with which his sons greeted him naturally jolted him and made him skeptical about its veracity. In Genesis two pieces of information convince him that his sons are telling the truth: Joseph's communications with them (perhaps meaning that he had proved who he was by all he knew about them and their father) and the physical evidence of the wagons with which they returned (perhaps Egyptian-style vehicles). Jubilees lacks the statement about Joseph's words and leaves the impression that Jacob believed only the proof offered by the wagons from Egypt (it does not say Joseph sent them to transport Jacob). Once he saw them, his mind cleared and he accepted the totally unexpected news that Joseph had not been torn to pieces by a wild animal but was now extraordinarily important in Egypt and was summoning him there. Neither Genesis nor Jubilees tells the reader anything about a possible awkward conversation between Jacob and his other sons when he learned what they had done to Joseph and to him years earlier. This is a time of joy, and Jacob resolves to make the trip to Egypt before he dies (see the emended form of Jub 43:16).

44

The Descent to Egypt by Jacob and His Family

1/ Israel set out from *Hebron*,[a] from his house, on the first of the third[b] month. He went by way of the well of the oath and offered a sacrifice to the God of his father[c] Isaac on the seventh of this month. 2/ When Jacob remembered the dream that he had seen[a] in Bethel, he was afraid to go down to Egypt. 3/ But as he was thinking about sending word to Joseph that he should come to him and that he would not go down, he remained there for seven days on the chance that he would see a vision (about) whether he should remain or go down. 4/ He celebrated the harvest festival—the firstfruits[a] of grain[b]—with old grain because in all the land[c] of Canaan there was not even a handful of seed in the land since the famine affected all the animals,[d] the cattle, the birds, and humanity as well.

5/ On the sixteenth the Lord appeared to him and said to him, "Jacob, Jacob." He said, "Yes?" He said to him, "I am the God of your fathers—the God of[a] Abraham and[b] Isaac. Do not be afraid to go down to Egypt because I will make you into[c] a great nation there. 6/ I will go down with you and will lead you (back). You will be buried in this land,[a] and Joseph[b] will place his hands on your eyes. Do not be afraid; go down to Egypt."

7/ His[a] sons and grandsons set about loading their father and their property on the wagons. 8/ Israel set out from the well of the oath on the sixteenth day of this third month and went to the land of Egypt. 9/ Israel sent his son Judah in front of him to Joseph to examine the land of Goshen because Joseph had told his brothers to come there in order to live there so that they would be his neighbors.[a] 10/ It was the best (place) in the land of Egypt and (it was) near him for each one and their cattle.[a]

11/ These are the names of Jacob's children who went to Egypt with their father Jacob. 12/ Reuben, Israel's firstborn, and these are the names of his sons:[a] Hanoch, Pallu, Hezron, and Carmi—five; 13/ Simeon and his sons,[a] and these are the names of his sons: Jemuel, Jamin, Ohad, Jachin, Zohar, and Shaul, the son of the Phoenician[b] woman—seven; 14/ Levi and his sons,[a] and these are the names of his sons:[b] Gershon, Kohath, and Merari—four; 15/ Judah and his sons,[a] and these are the names of his sons:[b] Shelah, Perez, and Zerah—four; 16/ Issachar and his sons, and these are the names of his sons:[a] Tola, Puvah, Jashub, and Shimron—five; 17/ Zebulun and his sons, and these are the names of his sons:[a] Sered, Elon, and Jahleel—four; 18/ These are Jacob's sons and their sons to whom Leah gave birth for Jacob in Mesopotamia—six and their one sister Dinah. All of the persons of Leah's sons and their sons who went with their father Jacob to[a] Egypt were twenty-nine. And, as their father[b] Jacob was with them, they were thirty.

19/ The sons of Zilpah, the maid of Jacob's wife Leah, to whom she gave birth for Jacob were Gad and Asher. 20/ These are the names of their sons who went with him[a] into Egypt. Gad's sons: Ziphion, Haggi, Shuni, Ezbon, [Eri],[b] Areli, and Arodi—eight. 21/ The children of Asher: Imnah, Ishvah, [Ishvi],[a] Beriah, and their one sister Serah—*six*. 22/ All the persons[a] were fourteen, and all those of Leah were forty-four.

23/ The sons of Rachel who was Jacob's wife were Joseph and Benjamin. 24/ Before his father came to Egypt[a] children, to whom Asenath—the daughter of Potiphar, the priest[b] of Heliopolis—gave birth for him, were born to Joseph in Egypt: Manasseh and Ephraim—three. 25/ The sons of Benjamin were: Bela, Becher,[a] Ashbel, Gera, Naaman, Ehi, Rosh, Muppim, Huppim, and Ard—eleven. 26/ All the persons of Rachel[a] were fourteen.

27/ The sons of Bilhah, the maid of Jacob's wife Rachel, to whom she gave birth[a] for Jacob[b] were Dan and Naphtali. 28/ These are the names of their sons[a] who went with them[b] to Egypt. The sons of Dan were Hushim, Samon, Asudi, Iyaka, and Salomon—six. 29/ They died in Egypt during the year in which they came (there). Only Hushim was left to Dan.[a] 30/ These are the names of Naphtali's sons: Jahzeel, Guni, Jezer, Shillem, and Ev.[a] 31/ Ev, who was born after the years of the famine, died in Egypt.[a] 32/ All those of[a] Rachel were twenty-six.

33/ All the persons of Jacob who entered Egypt were seventy persons. So all of these sons and grandsons of his were seventy, and five who died in Egypt before they married.[a] They had no children. 34/ Judah's two sons Er and

1087

Onan had died in the land of Canaan. They had no children. The sons of Israel buried those who died, and they were placed[a] among the seventy nations.

Textual Notes

1a *Hebron*] Though Haran (*kārān*) is the reading of the MSS., it is a mistake for *Hebron* (*kēbron*). Dillmann ("Jubiläen," 72 n. 74) noted this in the initial translation of Jubilees, and all others have followed his lead. That Jacob was living in Hebron follows from Gen 37:14 and Jub 44:6 (compared with 46:9-10 // Gen 50:13; see Charles, *Jubilees*, 238). The confusion could have occurred easily in the Heb., Gk., or Eth. See VanderKam, *Jubilees* 2:288.

b third] "second" 21.

c his father] "his fathers Abraham and" 35 58.

2a seen] "dreamed" 9 21 38 39 42 47 48 58.

4a the firstfruits] pr. "in/on" 21 58.

b of grain] om. 21 35 38 58; MS. 25 om. "firstfruits of grain."

c all (om. 38 58) the land] om. 20.

d all the animals] Mss. 20 25 35 move the expression to the end of the verse.

5a your fathers—the God of (om. 21 42 47 48)] om. 38 58.

b and (Isaac)] om. 12 21 48 63; + "the God of" 20.

c make you into] One could translate "establish you as." That is, the preferred reading is *'ešarre'aka*. Dillmann's and Charles's editions read *'erēseyaka* (Eth. Gen 46:3 reads the same form) = "I will make/establish/constitute you" (so MSS. 39 42 47 48 58). Both mean the same and appear to be alternate renderings ultimately of אשימך in Gen 46:3, although Charles (*Ethiopic Version*, 158 n. 11) thought *'erēseyaka* more nearly corresponded in meaning to the verb in Genesis.

6a land] + "and in it (lit., 'this')" 39ᶜ 48; + "and in this land" 58.

b Joseph] + "there" 39 58.

7a His] pr. "Jacob and" 21 35 58 (see Gen 46:5, where "Israel" is the one who sets out [the name "Israel" figures in Jub 46:8]).

9a his neighbors] The preferred and perhaps more unusual reading is the pl. adj. *qerubāna*; MSS. 9 12 17 38 39 42 47 48 63 read the more common *qeruba*, "near." Both Dillmann and Charles read the latter.

10a for each one and their cattle] The end of the verse is problematic in the Eth. manuscript tradition. The likely meaning is that the area of Goshen was near Joseph for all the family of Jacob and for their animals. The content of Gen 45:10 may underlie it. There Joseph is telling his brothers what they should say to Jacob: "You shall settle in the land of Goshen, and you shall be near me, you and your children and your children's children, as well as your flocks, your herds, and all that you have." Possibly the end of the line in Jubilees here is truncated into "for each one and their cattle." See VanderKam, *Jubilees* 2:290, for a slightly different proposal. At the end MS. 17 adds: "Jacob came and all his cattle to Egypt and all his sons."

12 a his sons] "the sons" 9 17 21 58.

13a his sons] "the sons" 9 17.

b Phoenician] *sifnawāt* 20 25 35 44; cf. 42 47. This form involves transposing consonants in "Phoenician" (= *fenisawāt*) and is thus unlikely to be the proper reading, despite Charles's claim (*Jubilees*, 240). "Phoenician" is a modernized term for "Canaanite" (see Gen 46:10).

14a his sons] "his brothers" 9 12 17 25 38ᵗ 48 63. This curious variant is conditioned by the fact that "brothers" is a way of referring to Levites (Num 16:10; 18:2, 6, etc.).

b his sons] "the sons" 9 17.

15a his sons] "the sons" 12.

b of his sons] "of the sons" 9 17 63; om. 48.

16a of his sons] "of the sons" 9 17; om. 25.

17a of his sons] "of the sons" 9 17 63; om. 25 44.

18a to (Egypt)] "to the land of" 25 35 44.

b their father] pr. "with" 39 42 47 48.

20a with him] "with them" 9 21 38ᵗ 39 42 47 48 58; om. 38ᶜ.

b [Eri]] The name has fallen from this list; see the commentary for the restored name to make the total eight as the verse specifies.

21a [Ishvi]] A name must have dropped from this list as well; the verse says there are five, but six are needed to meet the total in v. 22.

22a the persons] + "of Zilpah" 21 35; om. 48.

24a Egypt] pr. "the land of" 25 35 44.

b the priest] om. 39ᵗ 42 47.

25a Becher] om. 21 39 42 47 48 58.

26a Rachel] + "his wife" 39 58.

27a to whom she gave birth] om. 20.

b for Jacob] om. 21.

28a of their sons] om. 12 20 25; "the sons" 35.

b with them] "with him" 20.

29a to Dan] om. 21.

30a Ev] + "—six" 42 47.

31a in Egypt] om. 39ᵗ 42 47; + "—three" 39 48.

32a of] "from" 39 42 47 48 58.

33a they married (= *yāwsebu*)] "Joseph" 25 39ᶜ 42 47 48, but *yosēf* may be a corruption of the verb, though Charles (*Ethiopic Version*, 160 n. 19; *Jubilees*, 241) considered the name the preferred reading.

34a they were placed] "he was placed" 21; "they were named" 12.

Commentary

Jubilees 44 corresponds with Genesis 46, the text that deals with the migration by Jacob and his offspring to Egypt. While Jubilees adheres quite closely to the base text in Genesis, it introduces some changes that are characteristic of the writer. He dates the stages of the journey and also has Jacob celebrate the Festival of Weeks while partway on the road to the south. The verse regarding the celebration (v. 4) is one of the passages in the book that allow one to determine that the third month, the fifteenth day, is the date for the holiday in the writer's festal calendar. Much of the chapter (vv. 11-34 // Gen 46:8-27) is filled with the names of the seventy members of Jacob's household who went down to Egypt to escape the famine in Canaan. Their arrival in Egypt (not actually reported until 45:1) ends the centuries-long sojourn of the patriarchal clan in the promised land and introduces the Egyptian era, which, many years later, will eventuate in the exodus. In the author's chronology, Abram entered the land in 1953 or 1954 (see 12:28; 13:8); Jacob leaves it in 2172 (see 45:1), that is, either 218 or 219 years after his grandfather reached the area.[1] The Israelites will depart from Egypt in 2410 (48:1; 50:4), some 238 years after Jacob led his family there.

As with chap. 43, the Ethiopic copies contain the only version of Jubilees 44 that has survived.

The chapter divides into three major sections:
1-6   From Hebron to the well of the oath (Gen 46:1-4)
7-10 From the well of the oath toward Goshen (Gen 46:5, 6, 28)
11-34 The seventy who descended to Egypt (Gen 46:8-27)

1-6 From Hebron to the Well of the Oath (Gen 46:1-4)

In Gen 46:1 Jacob begins the trip to Egypt and arrives at Beersheba (translated the well of the oath in Jubilees) where he offers sacrifices.

■ 1 The writer of Jubilees expands the verse in Genesis and then introduces new lines after it (vv. 2-4).

Genesis 46:1	Jubilees 44:1
When Israel set out on his journey with all that he had	Israel set out from *Hebron*, from his house, on the first of the third month.
and came to Beersheba, he offered sacrifices to the God of his father Isaac.	He went by way of the well of the oath and offered a sacrifice to the God of his father Isaac on the seventh of this month.

Genesis has at times used the name Israel for Jacob in the Joseph stories (see 43:11 and Jub 42:15; Gen 45:21, 28); here, as in 42:15, the writer of Jubilees resorts to the alternate name Jacob had acquired at Bethel (see Jub 32:17).[2] Unlike Genesis, Jubilees names the place from which Jacob departed. Jacob had resided in Hebron (for the name see the textual note) since his father died (36:20), and it was there that Esau and his sons had attacked him (see 37:15; see Gen 35:27; 37:14). The writer uses this information to fill a gap in the text of Genesis and to show that Jacob had continued to reside in the ancestral home. The additional note that he left from his house reinforces the fact that Hebron was his home (for his house, usually called a tower, see 34:3, 6, 10; 36:12-16, 20; 37:14-17; 38:4-8). The author also inserts the date for embarking on the trip—the first of the third month. This would be the first day of the week and thus an appropriate one on which to begin a time-consuming journey. The date appears in the text where Genesis refers to Jacob's baggage—"all that he had." There may be a good reason why the author of Jubilees replaced this notice: Joseph had told his brothers not to "worry about your property" when they moved to Egypt" (Jub 43:18) because he had made preparations for them in their new home. Pharaoh had given similar instructions in Gen 45:20, so it might seem as if Jacob is not following orders by moving all his possession to Egypt. At any rate, the words about baggage are absent from Jub 44:1 (but see v. 7).

Why does the writer date the trip to the third month? The timing was probably suggested to him by

---

1   The descent to Egypt has been mentioned before as the time when relations with two conquered nations would change: in Jub 34:9 the Amorites remained the servants of Jacob until this point, and in 38:13 the Edomites paid tribute to him until he left for Egypt.

2   In Genesis, Jacob gains the name Israel twice (32:28 [Heb. 29]; 35:10), with the former assigned to J and the latter to P.

the reference to Beersheba/the well of the oath, since "oath" (שבועה) reminds one of the name for the Festival of Weeks (שבועות).[3] He will exploit this connection in v. 4. He also dates the time when Jacob made an offering to the God of Isaac at this place—the seventh of the month, which should be a Sabbath (see 50:10-11 on Sabbath sacrifices). He uses a singular form for *sacrifice* as do Syr LXX Gen 46:1, unlike the MT and SP, which read a plural, though the difference does not seem to be significant. The scene pictured in Genesis and Jubilees expresses a strong sense of piety and continuity: "A father on his way to see his son pauses to worship the God of his own father. It was at the same site that God appeared to Isaac and reminded him that he was the 'God of his father Abraham' (26:23-25)."[4] Jacob does not travel very far during the first week on the road, but he performs a religious rite at a significant locale in patriarchal history.

■ **2-4** The verses are an addition to the text of Genesis. While he is on the way to Egypt and tarrying at Beersheba, Jacob recalls an event depicted in Jub 32:21-26 but not found in Genesis. The event was the night vision he experienced at Bethel in which an angel gave Jacob seven tablets to read. Those tablets related "what would happen to him and his sons throughout all ages" (32:21). More specifically, Jacob learned from the angel that he was to live where Isaac resided (= Hebron) until he died (v. 22) and that "you will die peacefully in Egypt and be buried honorably in this land in the grave of your fathers—with Abraham and Isaac" (32:23).[5] Jacob, therefore, knew he was to die in Egypt and, as a result, was not eager to go there. In fact, the great patriarch feared to travel to the place where his life would end, though that was where he would see his dear son Joseph. Jacob considered an alternative: let Joseph come to him in Canaan so that Jacob could frustrate the cold hand of death. He obviously thought hard about plan B because he hesitated for another seven days.

The seven-day delay had a purpose: Jacob was hoping to receive a vision in which he would obtain a definitive answer to the question that was troubling him.[6] The wait provides a context for the vision that Jacob eventually sees in Genesis and in Jubilees. In the "visions of the night" that Jacob experiences in the former (Gen 46:2) God addresses an issue that had not arisen to this point in Genesis: he tells Jacob not to be afraid to go down to Egypt, though the reader does not know before this that he was anything but excited to make the trip. Jubilees is able to explain the situation more fully by appealing to the revelatory tablets in chap. 32 and the transparent reason they gave for his fear.[7]

---

3   VanderKam, *Book of Jubilees*, 124.
4   Hamilton, *Genesis 18–50*, 589. The parallel passage to Gen 26:23-25 is Jub 24:21-23.
5   The passage offers evidence that the vision of the angel with the tablets in chap. 32 was an original part of the book, not an addition (after the work of his interpolator) as Kugel thinks (*Walk through Jubilees*, 156–57; "Jubilees," 406–7).
6   The situation reminds one of Hab 2:1-2, where the prophet says he will "station myself on the rampart" (v. 1) as he awaits a response from God to his question. He then receives God's reply in a vision.
7   It is not surprising that Jacob's unexplained fear in Genesis received various interpretations. Josephus (*Ant.* 2.170–71) mentions several ideas that troubled the patriarch: "and fearing that by reason of the prosperity prevalent in Egypt his sons would become so enamoured of settling there, that their descendants would never more return to Canaan to take possession of it, as God had promised; and furthermore that having taken this departure into Egypt without God's sanction his race might be annihilated; yet terrified withal that he might quit this life before setting eyes on Joseph—these were the thoughts which he was revolving in his mind when he sank to sleep" (Thackeray, LCL). In *Pirqe R. El.* 39 Jacob asks himself: "Can I forsake the land of my fathers, the land where the Shekhinah of the Holy One, blessed be He, is in its midst, and shall I go to an unclean land in their midst, for there is no fear of heaven therein" (Friedlander). In *Tg. Ps.-J.* Gen 46:3 his fear is connected with the prediction to Abram that his descendants would be enslaved in Egypt for four hundred years (Gen 15:13). It is surprising that some interpreters think such explanations of Jacob's fear are also applicable to Jubilees when the night vision in chap. 32 supplies such a simple and convincing explanation for it. For example, Hartom ("Jubilees," 125 n. to v. 2)

As v. 1 related, Jacob reached the well of the oath on the seventh of the third month. He then waited another seven days in the hope of seeing a vision that would resolve his quandary. At this point, almost certainly on the next day, the fifteenth (see v. 5, which talks about the sixteenth), Jacob "celebrated the harvest festival—the firstfruits of grain." The harvest festival is the Festival of Weeks (see 16:13; 22:1) that Jubilees customarily dates to "the middle of the third month" (14:10; 15:1; 16:13). The present passage shows, as 1:1 also implies, that the date in question is the fifteenth.[8] The idea that Jacob celebrated the holiday at this time was suggested, as noted above, by the place-name the well of the oath, and the two preceding references to seven (שבעת)-day periods also play with the name. Naturally, Jacob, like his ancestors, followed the festival calendar revealed to them long before the time of Moses. Jacob had been present with Isaac, who was born at Beersheba/the well of the oath on the festival (16:12-13), when Abraham celebrated it on the day of his death (22:1-6). The unusual feature of the celebration for Jacob, besides the fact that he was in transit, was that there was no new grain/wheat with which to observe it because of the famine conditions in Canaan. The comprehensive extent of the famine is expressed in language reminding one of the all-embracing destruction caused by the flood: "there was not even a handful of seed (grain?)[9] in the land since the famine affected all the animals, the cattle, the birds, and humanity as well" (v. 4; for the flood, see 5:2, 20). The festival marked the season when the first of the wheat was harvested, but that proved impossible on this occasion as there was nothing to harvest.[10]

■ **5-6** The vision for which Jacob hoped came on the next day, the sixteenth. At this point the writer of Jubilees reverts to the text of Genesis 46.

Genesis 46:2-4	Jubilees 44:5-6
God spoke to Israel in visions of the night, and said, "Jacob, Jacob." And he said, "Here I am." Then he said, "I am God, the God of your father; do not be afraid to go down to Egypt, for I will make of you a great nation there. I myself will go down with you to Egypt, and I will also bring you up again; and Joseph's own hand shall close your eyes."	On the sixteenth the Lord appeared to him and said to him, "Jacob, Jacob." He said, "Yes?"[11] He said to him, "I am the God of your fathers—the God of Abraham and Isaac. Do not be afraid to go down to Egypt because I will make you into a great nation there. I will go down with you and will lead you (back). You will be buried in this land, and Joseph will place his hands on your eyes. Do not be afraid; go down to Egypt."

The vision for which he had waited patiently came to Jacob (Israel in Gen 46:2) on the day after the Festival of Weeks, the sixteenth of the third month. Genesis speaks of "visions[12] of the night" where Jubilees simply reports that the Lord appeared to him. In Genesis, the revealing deity identifies himself as "God, the God of your father," while in Jubilees he is "the God of your fathers."[13] It

---

thinks Jacob was afraid because he was worried about losing the land promised to him and his descendants in Gen 28:13. Endres, however, considers both explanations—fearing loss of the land and fearing death—to be acceptable (*Biblical Interpretation*, 189-90). The account given above fits Jubilees, however one explains Genesis.

8   See Jaubert, *Date of the Last Supper*, 22, 148 n. 11; VanderKam, *Book of Jubilees*, 123-25.

9   The Ethiopic copies read "seed," but it seems as if the narrator is talking about grain. In other instances where the Ethiopic reading is "seed," the Latin translation read "grain" (see 42:2, 13). This may have happened here as well, but since the Latin translation for this section is not available the point cannot be demonstrated. Werman thinks the writer is presenting Jacob as someone who tills the soil in this context and not as a nomad (*Jubilees*, 511), but see v. 10.

10 Finkelstein ("Rabbinic Halaka," 51) wrote: "Now the question of whether in case of an emergency old grain may or may not be used for the offering is a matter of dispute among the rabbis. The Mishna [*m. Menaḥ*. 8:1, which mentions the two loaves of Lev 23:17] insists that only new grain may be used; a baraita quoted in the Talmud [*b. Menaḥ*. 83b] permits the old grain."

11 The Ethiopic expression *nayya 'ana* is a literal equivalent of MT SP הנני; somehow, "here I am" does not seem to be a very helpful translation of the Hebrew idiom. See VanderKam, *Jubilees* 2:289. LXX reads "What is it?"

12 The form מראת is vocalized as plural in MT Gen 46:2, but it could be singular, as the LXX read. The experience to which Jub 44:2 alludes is termed "a night vision" in Jub 32:21.

13 The LXX and dependent translations also read "fathers" and lack the first occurrence of "God."

may be that the singular "father" in Genesis (MT SP) is carried over from the reference to "the God of his father Isaac" in v. 1, but Jubilees uses the plural form at the patriarchal location called the well of the oath, a place associated closely with both Abraham and Isaac. God is about to reiterate a central covenantal promise made to both Jacob's grandfather and father so that the plural is appropriate. The writer adds the names "Abraham and Isaac" to make clear whom he means; no ancient version of Genesis gives either name here. God had appeared to Jacob at Bethel as the God of his fathers Abraham and Isaac (Gen 28:13 // Jub 27:22) and had promised he would have many descendants. He does the same on this occasion.

The scene is also strongly reminiscent of the ones pictured in Genesis 26 and Jubilees 24 but with a surprising twist. In Gen 26:23-25 // Jub 24:21-23 Isaac traveled to Beersheba/the well of the oath, where the Lord appeared to him at night and identified himself as "the God of your father Abraham; do not be afraid." He also promises that Isaac's offspring will become numerous. Isaac then builds an altar and calls on the Lord's name (Jub 24:23 adds that he sacrifices on the altar). All of these items parallel the ones in Genesis 46 and Jubilees 44, but an earlier passage in the chapter about Isaac, Gen 26:1-4 // Jub 24:8-11, also should be compared. There, when there was a famine, Isaac started traveling toward Egypt, but when he was in the area of Gerar the Lord appeared to him and said:

> Do not go down to Egypt; settle in the land that I shall show you. Reside in this land as an alien, and I will be with you, and will bless you; for to you and your descendants I will give all these lands, and I will fulfill the oath that I swore to your father Abraham. I will make your offspring as numerous as the stars of heaven, and will give to your offspring all these lands; and all the nations of the earth shall gain blessing for themselves through your offspring. (Gen 26:2-4 // Jub 24:9-11a)

Amid all the parallels, the divine directive to Jacob to go down to Egypt on this occasion is the opposite of what God told Isaac at the earlier time. In both cases the Lord repeated the promise about many descendants.

What God denied Isaac he permits for Jacob. For Isaac Egypt was off-limits. For Jacob Egypt is the land in which God will bless Jacob and his progeny, and form them into a nation. Thus the sojourn of Jacob and his family to Egypt is not in fundamental opposition to God's purposes. Rather, the sojourn is part of the development of God's plan for this chosen family, first articulated to Abraham in 12:1ff.[14]

In both Genesis and Jubilees the deity promises to accompany Jacob on the road to Egypt, where he will become a large nation—in other words, this will not be a short-term visit. He also guarantees a return trip. MT SP Gen 46:4 use a strong expression for the future move from Egypt back to Canaan, literally, "I will surely also bring you [sg.] up." A problem posed by the text is that, while Jacob would indeed return to the land, he would go back there as a corpse (Gen 50:7-14; Jub 45:15)—hardly a parallel expression with the first clause about God's accompanying him to Egypt. Modern commentators tend to connect the clause to the exodus, as if "you" in "I will surely also bring you up" refers to the great nation that will emerge in Egypt.[15] That would be a sudden, surprising shift in the meaning of the pronoun "you" that designated Jacob in the previous clause, and perhaps a claim regarding the return by his descendants would not have been all that reassuring to Jacob at the moment. The ancient versions of Genesis betray some attempts to deal with the problem. In the LXX God says that he will bring him up "at last" (so also OL; Eth = in

---

14   Hamilton, *Genesis 18–50*, 590–91; cf. Berger, *Jubiläen*, 531 n. a to chap. 44.

15   So Skinner, *Genesis*, 492; Westermann, *Genesis 37–50*, 156; Hamilton, *Genesis 18–50*, 592. There are much earlier attestations of the same interpretation. The translation in *Tg. Ps.-J.* Gen 46:4 is an example: "*It is* I who *in my Memra* will go down with you to Egypt. *I will look upon the misery of your children, but my Memra will exalt you there*; I will also bring *your children up from there.*

perpetuity). The tradition represented by Jubilees reads a different verb: "I will lead/bring/conduct you." The less specific wording leaves open how that would occur, and in the very next clause in Jubilees the Lord refers to his being buried in the land. That line is absent from Genesis, so the writer of Jubilees has the Lord offering a fuller disclosure to Jacob than he does in MT SP Genesis. Genesis and Jubilees share the words that Joseph will set[16] his hands on Jacob's eyes (cf. 50:1), apparently an expression meaning that Joseph would be there when he died, perhaps also that he would close Jacob's eyes.[17]

That is the end of the divine message in Genesis, but in Jubilees God repeats the command that Jacob is not to be afraid and adds another: "go down to Egypt." As noted earlier, the second is the opposite of the command he gave Isaac in Gen 26:2 // Jub 24:9. The two imperatives represent a rephrasing of the order in v. 5 (// Gen 46:3): "Do not be afraid to go down to Egypt" as two separate ones. So Jacob had his question answered by a revealed and unequivocal message. The aged patriarch would not be sending for Joseph to come to him but would himself journey to Egypt in obedience to the command of God; there he would inaugurate the next stage in the history of his people.

7-10 From the Well of the Oath toward Goshen (Gen 46:5, 6, 28)

Both Genesis and Jubilees report that, when the vision(s) ended, Jacob went on his way from Beersheba/the well of the oath to Egypt, but the two texts arrange the material in different ways. Genesis 46:5-6 supplies the travel information, with v. 7 introducing the long list of Jacob's fellow travelers that extends from v. 8 to v. 27. After the list, a detail from the trip emerges: Jacob sends Judah ahead to Joseph so he could show them the way to the land of Goshen, a place to which all of them then come (46:28). Jubilees pulls the travel material together in one place before the list of names and reorders it somewhat in vv. 7-10 (for their actual arrival in Egypt, see 45:1).

■ **7** The verse revises words from Gen 46:5b:

Genesis 46:5b	Jubilees 44:7
... and the sons of Israel carried their father Jacob, their little ones, and their wives, in the wagons that Pharaoh had sent to carry him.	His sons and grandsons set about loading their father and their property on the wagons.

The author of Jubilees never said that Pharaoh had sent the wagons to transport Jacob, but Pharaoh himself had ordered in Gen 45:19: "take wagons from the land of Egypt for your little ones and for your wives, and bring your father, and come." In 45:27 Jacob saw "the wagons that Joseph had sent to carry him." Genesis 46:5b picks up on these passages and has Jacob's sons take charge of the loading process. In Jubilees both his sons and grandsons participate; mention of the latter arises from Gen 46:7, where one learns that both Jacob's sons and their sons were part of the move to Egypt. They are also included in the list of the seventy individuals who make the trek. Both texts agree that Jacob was placed on a wagon, but where Genesis mentions that the smaller children and the wives of Jacob's sons also rode on them, in Jubilees only "their property" has the privilege. The reading reflects in part the interpretive tradition present in the LXX and dependent translations, where the sons of Jacob (he is not called Israel here) load their baggage (and their wives). This reflects words from Gen 46:6, where they take "their livestock and all the goods that they had acquired in the land of Canaan." So both texts in this instance indicate that the clan, despite the reassurances of Pharaoh (Gen 45:20), follow the advice of Joseph, who told them to settle in Goshen where "you shall be near me, you and your children and your children's children, as well as your flocks, your herds, and all that you have" (45:10). It is curious that Jubilees fails to mention "their wives," but it is true that they are not a part of the list of seventy travelers later in the chapter—in either Genesis or Jubilees. In fact, Genesis explicitly excludes them from the count (46:26).

■ **8** The following verse in Jubilees again takes parts of more than one verse in Genesis in order to present events in what the writer took to be their proper order. Genesis first reports that Jacob started out on the trip

---

16   The NRSV rendering "shall close your eyes" is interpretive rather than literal.
17   Westermann, *Genesis 37–50*, 156.

and then says that his sons and grandsons loaded the wagons with people and property. In Jubilees the loading comes first and then the notice about travel.

Genesis 46:5a, 6b	Jubilees 44:8
Then Jacob set out from Beersheba	Israel set out from the well of the oath on the sixteenth day of this third month and went to the land of Egypt.
. . . and they came into Egypt, Jacob and all his offspring with him.	

For *Israel* setting out, see Gen 46:1.[18] The date for the departure—3/16—is the same as the one on which Jacob saw the vision telling him to go to Egypt. So he immediately obeys the order to go, once everyone and everything is reloaded onto the wagons sent from Egypt. With the notice in Gen 46:6b that Jacob and his offspring reached Egypt, Genesis introduces the list of all their names in v. 7 (the list itself is in vv. 8-27). The writer of Jubilees apparently thought that the story would read more smoothly if the travel-related information came first, followed by the list of names; as a result, he departs from the order in Genesis in the next verses.

■ **9** To complete the travel section, the writer temporarily skips over the name list and draws upon Gen 46:28.

Genesis 46:28	Jubilees 44:9
Israel sent Judah ahead to Joseph to lead the way before him into Goshen	Israel sent his son Judah in front of him to Joseph to examine the land of Goshen because Joseph had told his brothers to come there in order to live there so that they would be his neighbors.

Both texts designate the patriarch as Israel, and both refer to the role of Judah as the advance scout for the clan. The exact role he carries out is expressed differently in the versions. MT Genesis 46:28 reads a verb meaning "to teach," perhaps here meaning "point out, show" (להורת),[19] but the SP has a passive form of the verb "see" (להראות, "appear") and the LXX and dependent translations have "meet" (perhaps reflecting להקרות).[20] The verb in Jubilees (*yāstaḥāyeṣ*) is intriguing because it is a form of the one Joseph used when accusing his brothers of spying out the land. He made the charge one time in Jubilees, in 42:5: "Are you not spies? You have come to investigate [*tāstaḥāyeṣu*] the paths of the land." At the parallel, Gen 42:9 reads לראות, an infinitive of "to see." At least in Jubilees, then, there seems to be a conscious wordplay: Joseph had accused his brothers of coming to spy out the land; that proved to be false, but now Judah speeds ahead of the others to do that very thing in a positive sense and in obedience to his father's orders. Jubilees refers to "the land of Goshen," but in the Hebrew texts of Gen 46:28 there is only the name Goshen with a directional suffix (not preceded by "the land of"), and in the LXX tradition the place is "Heroonpolis in the land of Ramesses" (see Gen 47:11 where Goshen is called "the land of Rameses").

The additional words of explanation at the end of Jub 44:9 lack a parallel in Gen 46:28 but are related to Gen 45:10, where, as Jubilees indicates here (v. 9), Joseph told his brothers: "You shall settle in the land of Goshen, and you shall be near me." The word translated "neighbors" is really a plural adjective meaning they were to be "ones near" him.

■ **10** There is no parallel in Genesis 46 for the words of Jub 44:10; they are drawn from other passages in the surrounding chapters. Jubilees here identifies Goshen as the best (place) in the land of Egypt. In Gen 45:18, 20, Pharaoh wanted to give Jacob and his sons "the best of (+ "all" in v. 20) the land of Egypt," and in the same chapter Joseph referred to Goshen as the place where they could reside near him (see Jub 44:9). In Gen 47:6, Pharaoh tells Joseph, "The land of Egypt is before you; settle your father and your brothers in the best part of the land; let them live in the land of Goshen." A similar

---

[18] Werman (*Jubilees*, 511–12) suggests that in vv. 7-8 the writer solves an exegetical problem raised by Gen 46:5: who was dependent on whom? Did Jacob depend on his sons ("the sons of Israel carried their father Jacob") or did they depend on him ("Then Jacob set out"; cf. 46:7: "all his offspring he brought with him into Egypt")? But Jubilees reflects both kinds of expressions in vv. 7-8 and does not opt for a picture of Jacob as dependent on his children (Werman thinks "Israel set out [lit., arose]" in Jub 44:8 is figurative, but it does not seem to be). Note that in v. 9 Jacob is the one who sends his son Judah ahead to examine the land of Goshen.

[19] BDB, 435, s.v. ירה.

[20] See the discussion in Hamilton, *Genesis 18–50*, 600.

thought appears in 46:11, where Joseph gives them "the best part of the land." The writer adds that the place was near Joseph "for each one and their cattle." Despite difficulties in understanding the expression translated "each one,"[21] it may refer to the entire family of Jacob, all of whom would live close to Joseph. Mention of the cattle points one to Gen 46:31-34, where Joseph instructs his relatives to tell Pharaoh they, like their ancestors, are herdsmen, and 47:1-6, where they carry out his instructions when speaking with the monarch. They request that they be allowed to live in Goshen with their flocks. The author of Jubilees does not reproduce the aside at the end of Gen 46:34: "because all shepherds are abhorrent to the Egyptians" (for a similar passage, also omitted by Jubilees, about Egyptian ways, see Gen 43:32).

11-34 The Seventy Who Descended to Egypt (Gen 46:8-27)[22]

The remainder of Jubilees 44 offers a list of the seventy members of the family who traveled to Egypt followed by a few summary notes. Both Genesis and Jubilees provide a sentence prefacing the section about the names.

Genesis 46:8	Jubilees 44:11
Now these are the names of the Israelites,[23] Jacob and his offspring, who came to Egypt.	These are the names of Jacob's children who went to Egypt with their father Jacob.

The headings over the lists mention not only Jacob and his children (a term that includes grandchildren) but also Jacob himself. As the following sections will show, there is a problem in the list as it is presented in the MT and SP, where, if Jacob is not included, the number in the list reaches only sixty-nine, not seventy. The list itself in Genesis 46 does not include him, though the words "Jacob and his offspring" here in v. 8 incorporate him. The formulation in Jubilees—"with their father Jacob"— already indicates that he will be part of the total number designated at the end of the list (see v. 18).

In the sections below, all the names in Genesis and Jubilees are placed side by side for ease of comparison. It will be especially useful to compare the patterns and numbers in the two lists and the ends served by them.

The patterns or structures of the lists in Genesis and Jubilees are related but not identical.

First, in both texts the list itself consists of four parts, one for each of Jacob's four wives, though the wives are not included in the count of those who went to Egypt with Jacob. Genesis has noted only the death of Rachel (35:18), but Jubilees has recorded the deaths of Leah (36:21), Rachel (32:34), and Bilhah (34:15). Presumably Zilpah too was no longer alive. If so, the wives of Jacob would not belong in the list. The order is Leah Gen 46:8[end]-15 // Jub 44:12-18), her maid Zilpah (Gen 46:16-18 // Jub 44:19-22), Rachel (Gen 46:19-22 // Jub 44:23-26), and her maid Bilhah (Gen 46:23-25 // Jub 44:27-32).

Second, in Genesis the names of the sons (and grandsons) figure first, and once the last one occurs, the mother's name is entered (Gen 46:15, 18, 22, 25). There is one exception: in the case of Rachel, her name appears both before (Gen 46:19) and after (v. 22) the list of her two sons and their children. In addition, in the Rachel section the names of her two sons are given and then repeated with those of their children. The author of Jubilees arranges the units differently: in each of the four sections, he places the mother's name before the list of her sons and grandsons (44:19, 23, 27) except in the case of Leah, whose name comes after them (44:18)— exactly where it occurs in Gen 46:15. For the three mothers who had two children each (Zilpah, Rachel, and Bilhah), the names of the two sons follow that of the mother and then are repeated with their children (as in the Rachel paragraph in Genesis).

---

21 See the textual note.
22 A parallel list appears in Num 26:45-51, where it records "The Israelites who came out of the land of Egypt" (v. 4, although see vv. 64-65). Many of the names appear in the lists in 1 Chronicles 2 and 4–8 as well.
23 This seems an unfortunate rendering of the phrase "the sons/children of Israel," since the following list gives their names, while "Israelites" suggests something else. The order of phrases in Genesis and Jubilees is the same, as in the Hebrew text of the former the expression "Jacob and his offspring [sons]" comes after "Egypt," just as it does in Jubilees.

Third, at the end of the section for each of the four mothers, Genesis 46 gives the total for the sons and grandsons (for Leah in v. 15; for Zilpah in v. 18; for Rachel in v. 22; and for Bilhah in v. 25). At the end of the entire list the four numbers are combined and explained. The author of Jubilees also supplies the number of sons and grandsons for each mother at the end of the section devoted to her with the exception of Bilhah (44:18, 22, 26), but a distinctive feature in Jubilees is that, while the writer sums up all the numbers at the end and explains them, along the way he provides subtotals for both mother + maid pairs: Leah + Zilpah (v. 22) and Rachel + Bilhah (v. 32). Moreover, after the list of each of Jacob's twelve sons, the writer gives the total for that son (the son + the grandsons = x).

These are the four sections, the names of the descendants, and the totals furnished in Genesis and Jubilees.

Section 1

Genesis 46:8-15	Jubilees 44:12-18[24]
Leah	Leah
Reuben	Reuben
Hanoch	Hanoch
Pallu	Pallu
Hezron	Hezron
Carmi	Carmi (= 5)
Simeon	Simeon
Jemuel	Jemuel
Jamin	Jamin
Ohad	Ohad
Jachin	Jachin
Zohar	Zohar
Shaul	Shaul[25] (= 7)
Levi	Levi
Gershon	Gershon
Kohath	Kohath
Merari	Merari (= 4)
Judah	Judah
Er	
Onan[26]	
Shelah	Shelah
Perez	Perez
Hezron	
Hamul	
Zerah	Zerah (= 4)
Issachar	Issachar
Tolah	Tola
Puvah	Puvah
Jashub	Jashub[27]
Shimron	Shimron (= 5)
Zebulun	Zebulun
Sered	Sered
Elon	Elon
Jahleel	Jahleel (= 4)

At the end of the list for Leah, the two writers pause to provide comments and to indicate the total of Jacob's offspring through her.

Genesis 46:15[28]	Jubilees 44:18
(these are the sons of Leah, whom she bore to Jacob in Paddan-aram, together with his daughter Dinah; in all his sons and his daughters numbered thirty-three).	These are Jacob's sons and their sons to whom Leah gave birth for Jacob in Mesopotamia—six and their one sister Dinah. All of the persons of Leah's sons and their sons who went with their father Jacob to Egypt were twenty-nine. And, as their father Jacob was with them, they were thirty.

---

24 The spellings of the names in all four sections in Jubilees listed here are those of the NRSV. Though they take many forms in the various Ethiopic copies, they are recognizable as the same names. For details about the spellings and comparisons with the forms in the ancient versions of Gen 46:8-27, see VanderKam, *Jubilees* 2:291-94.

25 Genesis 46:10 // Jub 44:13 add that he was the son of "the Canaanite woman" ("the Phoenician woman" in Jubilees; see the textual note for the gentilic and also for the confusion Rönsch and Charles have introduced into the interpretation of it by adopting a corrupt reading). In Jub 34:20 she is called a Canaanitess. In 34:21 Simeon changes his mind about his Canaanite wife and marries a woman from Mesopotamia. The list may imply, therefore, that the other five sons were the children of Simeon and the wife from Mesopotamia. Shaul occupies the last spot in the list, though he would have been the oldest, because he had a different mother (but this is not the procedure in the section about Judah; cf. Halpern-Amaru, *Empowerment*, 120).

26 The writer of the list in Genesis explains here (v. 12) that "Er and Onan died in the land of Canaan"—that is, they did not go down to Egypt with Jacob, though they are included in the totals for Leah (see below).

27 In MT Gen 46:13 the name is spelled יוב, but SP reads ישוב, and LXX reflects this spelling as do MT SP Num 26:24 (cf. MT 1 Chr 7:1).

28 The NRSV places the summary statements about each mother in parentheses, though it is not

The first statement in Genesis is strange, as the list contains more than just the sons of Leah; Jubilees rephrases to make it conform to the fact that the list also contains the names of Leah's grandsons. The information that Leah bore the six sons and one daughter Dinah to Jacob in Paddan-aram = Mesopotamia derives from Gen 29:31-35; 30:17-21 // Jub 28:11-15, 22-23 (for the name Paddan-aram in Genesis represented as Mesopotamia in Jubilees, see Gen 28:2 // Jub 27:10).[29] When Genesis sums up the list to this point by saying that it includes "all his sons and his daughters," it comes as a surprise because only one daughter appears in the list (Dinah). Jubilees does not mention any daughters in the parallel line (that is, her name appears in v. 18, but Dinah is not in the list): the writer states that the total includes only males—sons and grandsons. By saying this, he avoids the problem with the reading "his daughters" in Genesis; moreover, for him Dinah could not be a participant in the move to Egypt with Jacob because she was already dead by this time (Jub 34:15-16; she died when the news of Joseph's "death" reached Jacob).

The totals for Leah's offspring differ in the two texts: thirty-three in Genesis, twenty-nine in Jubilees. Genesis reaches the number thirty-three by counting not only Judah's five sons but also the two sons of Perez (Judah's grandsons). Including all seven of Judah's sons and grandsons is a dubious strategy because two of them, as Gen 46:12 points out, were dead (Er and Onan; see Gen 38:7, 10) and thus could not have journeyed with Jacob to Egypt in chap. 46. The author of Jubilees sensibly leaves those two names out of his list[30]—here he does not even mention that they had died (see v. 34, where he deals with them). As peculiarly, Genesis includes two sons of Judah's son Perez (Hezron and Hamul), neither of whom appears in the list in Jubilees. Their presence here in Genesis among those who descended to Egypt with Jacob raises a much-debated chronological issue—how could Perez have become the father of two children by the time Jacob and his family descended to Egypt?

Genesis provides just enough chronological information to suggest how improbable it would have been for Hezron and Hamul to have been among the seventy who entered Egypt with Jacob. In Gen 37:2, Joseph is seventeen years of age when his brothers sell him (an event narrated later in the chapter). Genesis 38, the story of Judah and Tamar, then follows, with the birth of Perez and Zerah at the end. Genesis 41:46 says that Joseph was thirty years when he began his service to Pharaoh, so he had been in Egypt thirteen years by this time. The seven years of plenty that occur when he is Pharaoh's officer ensue after his elevation; they end in Gen 41:53, when the famine years begin. The time when Joseph reveals himself to his brothers is the second year of the famine because five more were yet to come (Gen 45:6), and Jacob's family migrates to Egypt as soon as the sons deliver the word about Joseph to their father. There was no time to lose because they were escaping the famine in Canaan that threatened their lives. It appears, then, that twenty-two years elapsed from the time when Joseph was sold into Egyptian slavery to the point when the descent to Egypt occurred: thirteen years until Pharaoh appointed Joseph, the seven years of plenty, and the two of famine.[31] The claim in Genesis seems to be that two sons of Perez participated in that journey. The question is, then, would these twenty-two years be enough time to allow the following events to take place:

Judah leaves his brothers and gets married; he and his wife have three sons (Gen 38:1-5).

Two of their sons, Er and Onan, reach marriageable age (Er marries Tamar, and she is later given to Onan); both sons die (Gen 38:6-10).

There is a delay for an unspecified amount of time (see Gen 38:12) while the third son Shelah grows to maturity so that he could marry Tamar; even though he reaches a sufficient age Judah fails to give him to Tamar, who continues living as a widow at her father's house (Gen 38:14).

---

evident why this is done. The lines about the mothers are hardly parenthetical to the lists.

29 In this verse, where the place-name occurs in the list, LXX has Μεσοποταμια της Συριας.

30 Josephus does the same (*Ant.* 2.178).

31 These twenty-two years, when Joseph was absent from the family home, are symmetrical with the twenty-two that Jacob was separated from his father.

Judah and Tamar have sexual relations, Tamar becomes pregnant, and she eventually gives birth to twins, Perez and Zerah (Gen 38:18, 27-30). Perez becomes old enough to marry and father two sons. Could all of this have happened within the space of twenty-two years?

Ancient interpreters proposed various solutions to the problem (e.g., claiming astonishingly early ages for the males at the time of their marriages),[32] but the chronological issue disappears in Jubilees because the writer lists only the three surviving sons of Judah and says nothing about Judah's grandsons. It may be that the compiler of the list in Genesis included two of Judah's grandsons to replace his two sons who had died, but the presence of their names led to the hopeless chronological problem detailed above. Jubilees, which of course has many more dates than Genesis,[33] places the birth of Perez and Zerah in the year 2170 and the trip to Egypt in 2172. Obviously there would not have been time for Perez to father two children by the time he was two years of age. In this line, by not including Hezron and Hamul, the author of Jubilees removes another problem from the list in Genesis.

If one adds up the names in each list (or the subtotals in Jubilees), there are thirty-three names of males in Genesis (Dinah, then, would not be included), and there are twenty-nine in Jubilees. The Genesis list includes the two deceased sons of Judah, but, if the notice about their deaths (46:12) means they are to be subtracted, then just thirty-one males are left. It is likely, given the wording of Gen 46:15, that Dinah is part of the total in Genesis, but that would raise the number to thirty-two, leaving the list one short. An obvious candidate for the remaining slot is Jacob himself, though the text does not actually say this. The writer of Jubilees seems to be aware of the inconsistency in Genesis because he explicitly includes Jacob to raise the total: Leah's twenty-nine sons and grandsons and her husband Jacob make up the number thirty.

Section 2

Genesis 46:16-18	Jubilees 44:19-22
Zilpah	Zilpah
Gad	Gad
Ziphion	Ziphion
Haggi	Haggi
Shuni	Shuni
Ezbon	Ezbon
Eri	[Eri]
Arodi	Areli
Areli	Arodi (= 8)
Asher	Asher
Imnah	Imnah
Ishvah	Ishvah
Ishvi	[Ishvi]
Beriah	Beriah
Heber	
Malchiel	
Serah (sister)	Serah (sister) (= 6)

At the end of the Zilpah paragraph the two writers sum up matters in this way.

Genesis 46:18	Jubilees 44:22
(these are the children of Zilpah, whom Laban gave to his daughter Leah; and these she bore to Jacob—sixteen persons).	(see v. 19: The sons of Zilpah, the maid of Jacob's wife Leah, to whom she gave birth for Jacob . . .) All the persons were fourteen, and all those of Leah were forty-four.

The list of Zilpah's[34] sons, grandsons, and granddaughter adds up to just fourteen, so two sons of Beriah are included to reach sixteen (the second time Genesis resorts to great-grandsons); Jubilees leaves out the two

---

[32] For a short summary, see Zakovitch and Shinan, *Judah and Tamar*, 247-48. One possibility was to locate the Judah-Tamar account before the selling of Joseph (e.g., Ibn Ezra). *Seder Olam* is able to make all the events listed above fit within a twenty-two year period by positing marriages at the age of seven for Er and for Perez (who becomes a father at age eight). See Milikowsky, *Seder Olam*, 2:40-44, with a helpful chart on p. 41.

[33] The writer of Jubilees calculates very nearly the same twenty-two-year span of time between when Joseph was sold (2149; see Jub 34:10) and Jacob's descent (2172).

[34] Where Genesis recalls for both Zilpah and Bilhah that Laban gave them to his two daughters, Jubilees simply supplies their names and status with no reference to Laban.

sons of Beriah,[35] as it omitted the two sons of Perez above. The Ethiopic copies of Jubilees list six sons for Gad, yet they claim that he and his six sons add up to eight in all. Obviously a name is missing from the list, and, as a comparison with Gen 46:16 shows, the name is Eri. It was probably skipped over by a Greek copyist or by the person who translated the text from Greek to Ethiopic, because in Greek there are three consecutive names beginning with *alpha* at the end of the list; note too that Jubilees uniquely transposes the last two names—perhaps another hint of some disturbance in the text. Something similar happened with the list of Asher's sons and one daughter in Jubilees: though the manuscripts give the total for him and his five children as *five*, the number must be changed to *six* because the total for Zilpah, with the eight from Gad, is fourteen. The missing name can easily be explained: *Ishvi* dropped out because of its similarity to the preceding name (only one letter is different [וישוה וישוי]).[36] As Jubilees indicates, the totals for Leah (Zilpah was her maid) came to thirty + fourteen = forty-four.

Section 3

Genesis 46:19-22	Jubilees 44:23-26
Rachel	Rachel
Joseph	Joseph
Manasseh	Manasseh
Ephraim	Ephraim (= 3)
Benjamin	Benjamin
Bela	Bela
Becher	Becher
Ashbel	Ashbel
Gera	Gera
Naaman	Naaman
Ehi	Ehi
Rosh	Rosh
Muppim	Muppim
Huppim	Huppim
Ard	Ard (= 11)[37]

The concluding lines regarding Rachel's family are:

Genesis 46:22	Jubilees 44:26
(these are the children of Rachel, who were born to Jacob—fourteen persons in all).	All the persons of Rachel were fourteen.

The two lists agree as do the totals. Rachel, therefore, produces as many members of the clan as Zilpah did in Jubilees. Both writers add a note about Joseph, who, of course, is unexpected in the list because neither he nor his sons went down to Egypt with Jacob—they were already there when the rest of the family arrived. Genesis and Jubilees mentioned Joseph's wife and her father when Pharaoh gave her to him (Gen 41:45 // Jub 40:10; Jubilees does not name her here but did in 34:20), but Gen 41:50-52 named her and her father again when reporting that she and Joseph had two sons, Manasseh and Ephraim (it also gives etymologies for their names). The writer of Jubilees has not referred to Joseph's sons until this occasion. He also records the fact, not repeated here in Genesis (but see v. 27), that they were born before Jacob came to Egypt. A very surprising feature of the section is that by this time Benjamin has more sons than any of his brothers—ten. The number sits uncomfortably with the narrative in the previous chapter (occurring in the same year as the descent to Egypt in both Genesis and Jubilees), where he seems to be young and tender, his father is most reluctant to send him to Egypt, and his older brother Judah must take responsibility for him. In Jubilees Benjamin is twenty-nine years of age at this point; it would not have been impossible for him to have ten sons at age twenty-nine but it is unexpected. Neither text offers a comment on this curious situation.

---

35 Josephus turns them into sons of Asher (*Ant.* 2.183).
36 The same omission occurred in the parallel list in Numbers 26, where, in v. 44, the SP lacks the same name.
37 The spellings of Benjamin's sixth, eighth, and tenth sons vary considerably in the Ethiopic copies. See Charles, *Jubilees*, 241; VanderKam, *Jubilees* 2:293.

Section 4

Genesis 46:23-25		Jubilees 44:27-32	
Bilhah		Bilhah	
	Dan		Dan
	Hashum		Hashum
			Samon[38]
			Asudi
			Iyaka
			Salomon (= 6)
	Naphtali		Naphtali
	Jahzeel		Jahzeel
	Guni		Guni
	Jezer		Jezer
	Shillem		Shillem
			Ev

At the end of the list for Bilhah Gen 46:25 summarizes: "(these are the children of Bilhah, whom Laban gave to his daughter Rachel, and these she bore to Jacob—seven persons in all)." The book of Jubilees provides no conclusion like those in the previous three units. It does, however, offer a summary for Rachel and her maid Bilhah: "All those of Rachel were twenty-six" (44:32). From the total it follows that Bilhah had twelve offspring, as both Dan and Naphtali are the father of five sons.

The paragraphs for Bilhah in the two texts contain major differences. First, Dan has just one son in Genesis but five in Jubilees. It would be surprising in the passage for a son of Jacob to be father of just one son (Dan directly follows Benjamin, who has the largest number), though Joseph has only two; but Gen 46:23 prefaces this line with "These are the *children* [lit., sons] of Dan" and then mentions just one.[39] Whatever the explanation for the single son of Dan, the writer of Jubilees credits him with four additional ones, none of whom is mentioned in any of the parallel lists in the HB. But he renders the extra names less puzzling when he appends a comment to the listing of Dan's sons: "They died in Egypt during the year in which they came (there). Only Hushim was left to Dan" (Jub 44:29). That is, the four extra names belong among the seventy, but they died within a year of reaching Egypt, leaving Dan with only the one son named in Genesis (see below on Naphtali's fifth son). In this way the writer was able to explain the reading "the children of Dan" in Gen 46:23 when just one is named.[40]

Second, Naphtali has a fifth son where Genesis and the parallel lists assign four to him. As he did for Dan's four additional sons, the author adds an explanation: "Ev, who was born after the years of the famine, died in Egypt" (44:31). It seems odd, in light of the explanation, that his name would figure among those who descended to Egypt with Jacob, since he could not have done that—his birth would have occurred more than five years after the family arrived (five years of famine remained when they came). On him, see below.

In Jubilees, then, there are six names in excess over the lists in Genesis (Jacob, Dan's four extra sons, Ev), and Genesis includes seven not present in Jubilees (Er, Onan, Hezron, Hamul, Dinah, Heber, and Malchiel).[41]

---

38 Since the names for sons 2–5 are not present in Genesis, the spellings given here do not come from the NRSV but are those in the Ethiopic copies of the passage in Jubilees. The same is the case for Naphtali's fifth son, Ev.

39 The Testament of Dan uses a plural form "sons" for those to whom he delivers his last words (T. Dan 1:1-2 and throughout). Sensing something peculiar in Dan's having just one son after the reader has been led to expect a plural number, *Tg. Ps.-J.* Gen 46:23 reads: "The sons of Dan, *alert men and traders, whose number is beyond counting.*" There the name Hushum (Hashim in Hebrew) is related to a verb meaning "hurry" to arrive at the translation "alert men and traders" (see Maher, *Targum Pseudo-Jonathan: Genesis*, 150 n. 21). See also Charles, *Jubilees*, 241.

40 Hartom, "Jubilees," 126 n. to vv. 28-29.

41 Büchler, who thought Greek was the original language of Jubilees, uses the discrepancies between the lists in Genesis and Jubilees as an example demonstrating that the author of Jubilees was a Hellenistic writer who lived in Egypt or one of the Hellenistic cities in Palestine ("Traces," 331–34). He made arbitrary changes in the scriptural list (Büchler assumed that the MT was *the* text of the HB) to remove difficulties from it so non-Jewish critics could not use these improbable elements to discredit the history of the Jews. The author of Jubilees certainly tried to remove problems from the list, but there is no need to claim that the audience for the changes consisted of non-Jewish readers who pored through the Pentateuch to spot implausible claims. The history of exegesis shows that Jewish writers tried to solve the difficulties for Jewish readers who were familiar with and perhaps concerned about them.

Some of the discrepancies and surprises in the lists are sorted out in the conclusions Genesis and Jubilees append to them.

Genesis 46:26-27
All the persons belonging to Jacob who came into Egypt, who were his own offspring, not including the wives of his sons, were sixty-six persons in all. The children of Joseph who were born to him in Egypt, were two; all the persons of the house of Jacob who came into Egypt were seventy.

Jubilees 44:33-34
All the persons of Jacob who entered Egypt were seventy persons. So all of these sons and grandsons of his were seventy,

and five who died in Egypt before they married.[42] They had no children. Judah's two sons Er and Onan had died in the land of Canaan. They had no children. The sons of Israel buried those who died, and they were placed among the seventy nations.

It appears reasonable to think that Genesis arrives at the total sixty-six by subtracting Er and Onan (two of Judah's sons who died in Canaan) and Manasseh and Ephraim (Joseph's sons who were born in Egypt) from the number seventy (which is the sum of the numbers given for each of the mothers: Leah thirty-three, Zilpah sixteen, Rachel fourteen, Bilhah seven).[43] However, the very next line refers to the two sons of Joseph born in Egypt—as if the compiler is now adding them and Joseph to the total of sixty-six that he had just obtained by subtracting them along with Judah's deceased sons.[44]

The text of Jubilees likewise offers some confusing numbers. The writer reaches the total of seventy by adding up the sums he has supplied throughout the list. In their simplest form they are: Leah thirty (including Jacob), Zilpah fourteen (the total for Leah is forty-four), Rachel fourteen, and Bilhah twelve (the total for Rachel is twenty-six); all told, they are seventy. However, the writer then takes up the cases of five individuals who died in Egypt: Dan's four extra sons (Samon, Asudi, Iyaka, Salomon) and Naphtali's fifth son Ev. The names belong in the total of seventy for the entire list, so the author is not excluding them from it. He had already reported that those four sons of Dan died the year they entered Egypt, so they legitimately belong among those who entered with Jacob. Ev, however, is problematic: though he is necessary to the list if the total is to be seventy, he could not have accompanied Jacob into Egypt because he would not be born for at least another five years. So why include him among the seventy? The manuscripts suggest no attempt at even trying to solve the problem raised by v. 31 ("Ev, who was born after the years of the famine, died in Egypt"). The difficult words are "who was born"; if they were not in the verse,[45] Ev would join four of Dan's sons as the five who died in Egypt, though they were born in Canaan. In context, it is reasonable to suppose that the original text claimed that he, like the four others, was born in Canaan but died in Egypt.

The writer introduces the relevant information about Er and Onan in the summary words at the end of the list. He had not even mentioned them among Judah's sons in 44:15, where they really did not belong, despite the fact that Genesis puts them there along with a line about their deaths in Canaan (46:12). Jubilees does

---

42 See the textual note and VanderKam, *Jubilees* 2:294, regarding the alternate reading "before Joseph" that Dillmann placed in his first translation (but not in his edition of the Ethiopic text) and Charles adopted in his edition and translation (it is present also in the translations of Riessler, Hartom, Wintermute, Caquot, and Rabin). "Joseph" is very unlikely to be the correct reading.

43 LXX Gen 46:27 gives the number seventy-five for the total; the extra five appear in the list of Joseph's offspring: his son Manasseh has a son and grandson, and his son Ephraim has two sons and one grandson.

44 Genesis 46:26-27 can easily give the impression that, for the writer, 66 + 3 = 70, and so the text was understood by some ancient expositors. See Kugel, *Traditions*, 482–84; *Walk through* Jubilees, 189, for some of the sources and solutions.

45 What happened to produce the existing text is unknown, but possibly the note "who was born" was mistakenly taken from the verse about Joseph's sons who were born in Egypt. Another suggestion is that "in Canaan" fell from the text after "who was born," so that the verse would be distinguishing the land of his birth from that of his death.

not repeat the information about Joseph and his sons; Genesis does, as the writer tries to explain how there were seventy descendants of Jacob in Egypt though only sixty-six arrived there with him. The concern in Jubilees is with the five who died: their deaths preceded any marriage for them so that their lines died out. Though they entered Egypt with Jacob, no later Israelites could trace their ancestry to them. In effect, their deaths removed them from the family line that led to Israel so that they were considered like the nations[46]—another group totaling seventy in number: as there were seventy members of Jacob's family, so there were seventy nations of the world.

Though it may seem that the long list of names interrupts the story, it makes a telling contribution to the message: the family of Jacob has multiplied far beyond those of Abraham and Isaac, and all seventy of them form a unity that now includes Joseph and his family.

---

46 See Hartom, "Jubilees," 127 n. to v. 34. See also Werman, *Jubilees*, 514, though the text does not say enough to indicate whether the writer was making a point about burial in the land, as she thinks possible.

Reunion of the Family and Death of Jacob

45

1/ Israel went into the land of Egypt, into the land of Goshen, on the first of the fourth month during the second year of the third week of the forty-fifth[a] jubilee [2172]. 2/ When Joseph came to meet his father Jacob in the land of Goshen, he wrapped his arms around his father's neck and cried. 3/ Israel said to Joseph, "Now[a] let me die after[b] I have seen you. Now may the Lord, the God of Israel, the God of Abraham, and the God of Isaac[c]—who has not withheld his kindness and his mercy from his servant Jacob—be blessed. 4/ It is enough for me that I have seen your face while I am[a] alive, because the vision that I saw in Bethel was certainly true. May the Lord my God be blessed forever and ever and may his name be blessed." 5/ Joseph and his brothers ate food and drank wine in front of their father. Jacob was extremely happy because in front of him[a] he saw Joseph eating and drinking with his brothers. He blessed the Creator of all who had preserved him and[b] preserved his[c] twelve sons for him.

6/ As a gift Joseph gave his father and his brothers (the right) to live in the land of Goshen, that is,[a] in Rameses; and (he gave) them all its districts that they[b] would rule in Pharaoh's presence. Israel and his sons lived in the land of Goshen, the best part of the land of Egypt. Israel was 130[c] years of age when he came into Egypt. 7/ Joseph provided as much food for his father, his brothers, and also for their livestock as would be sufficient for them for the seven years of famine.

8/ As the land of Egypt suffered from the famine, Joseph gained the whole land of Egypt for Pharaoh in exchange for food. He acquired the people, their cattle, and everything for Pharaoh.[a] 9/ When the years[a] of the famine were completed, Joseph gave seed and food to the peoples[b] who were in the land[c] so that they could sow seed[d] in the eighth year because the river had overflowed the entire land of Egypt. 10/ For during the seven years of the famine it had irrigated only a few places at the riverbank, but now it overflowed.[a] The Egyptians seeded the land,[b] and it yielded[c] good produce[d] that year. 11/ That[a] was the first year of the fourth[b] week of the forty-fifth jubilee [2178]. 12/ Joseph took the king's fifth part[a] of all[b] that had been sown,[c] and he left[d] four parts[e] for them for food and seed. Joseph made it[f] a law for the land[g] of Egypt until today.

13/ Israel lived for 17 years in the land of Egypt. All of the time that he lived[a] was three jubilees[b]—147 years. He died[c] during[d] the fourth year of the fifth week of the forty-fifth jubilee [2188]. 14/ Israel blessed his sons[a] before he died. He told them everything that would[b] happen to them in the land of Egypt; and[c] he informed them (about) what would happen to them[d] at the end of time. He blessed them and gave[e] Joseph two shares[f] in the land. 15/ He slept with his fathers and was buried near his father Abraham in the double cave in the land of Canaan—in the grave that he had dug for himself in the double cave in the land of Hebron.[a] 16/ He gave all his books and the books of his fathers[a] to his son Levi so that he could preserve them and renew them for his sons[b] until today.

Textual Notes

1a (forty-)fifth] "-fourth" 20.
3a Now] pr. "From" 21 35 38 44.
 b after] "as" 9 17 38† 63; "because" 39 42 47 48 58 (so LXX Gen 46:30).
 c Isaac] + "and Jacob" 38.
4a I am] This is the reading of the mss., but Gen 46:30 has "you are." Charles (*Jubilees*, 242) suspected 'ana ("I") was a mistake for 'anta ("you"), but there is no support for 'anta in the mss.
5a (in front of) him] "them" 9 38 44.
 b preserved him and] om. 9 38.
 c his (twelve)] om. 38 58.
6a that is, (in Rameses)] om. 17 63 and Gen 47:11.
 b they (would rule)] "he" 12 38.
 c 130] "134" 35.
8a He acquired the people, their cattle, and everything

1103

9a for Pharaoh] The Eth. version makes Pharaoh the subject of the verb (only MSS. 42ᶜ 44 47ᵗ have Joseph acquiring everything "for" Pharaoh). If one reads with Lat. and with these latter MSS., the text yields the proper sense (see Charles, *Ethiopic Version*, 161 n. 16; *Jubilees*, 243). The Eth. reading may have arisen on the Gk. level because the nom. and dat. forms of "Pharaoh" are the same (Φαραω). See VanderKam, *Jubilees* 2:296.
9a years] "seven years" Lat. (see v. 10).
b peoples] "people" 38.
c land] + "of Egypt" 21 35 38 58.
d seed] pr. "the land (with)" Lat.
10a it had irrigated only a few places at the riverbank, but now it overflowed] "it had not overflowed and had irrigated only a few places at the riverbank" Lat. The difference between the two versions is the placement of the statement about overflowing (whether it is positive or negative depends on where it occurs in the sentence). Ms. 38 has a reading much like the Lat. The translation is based on Eth., but it is difficult to determine which is preferable. See VanderKam, *Jubilees* 2:297.
b seeded the land] "seeded their land during the eighth year" Lat. (see v. 9 for seeding the land in the eighth year; Lat. could have added it under the influence of v. 9).
c it yielded] "(they) gathered" Lat. Charles (*Ethiopic Version*, 161 n. 26; *Jubilees*, 243) emended Eth. to agree with Lat., reading *'araru* instead of *farayat*. As the two Eth. verbs are not similar graphically, the difference in reading may have originated in Gk., where the verb could have been a form of καρπoω: the Eth. reading represents an active form of it and the Lat. a middle form.
d good produce] "much good" Eth. Where many Eth. MSS. read *šannaya*, "good," some have *sernāya*, "wheat" (listed under *šernāy* in Leslau, *Comparative Dictionary*, 534)—so MSS. 9 12 20 35 38 39 42 47 48 58. Both Dillmann and Charles selected this reading in their editions. However, *fructus* translates καρπος, and καρπος in turn is an acceptable rendering of Heb. בר, "grain, corn" (its consonants are the reverse of רב, which would ultimately underlie "much" in Eth.). So, rather than "much," "grain/produce" probably appeared in the original and the letters of the noun got reversed in the process of transmission. See VanderKam, *Jubilees* 2:297.
11a That (was the first year)] om. 17ᵗ 38 44 63.
b fourth] "fifth" Lat., which is inconsistent with the date in 45:1 (Eth. only). Perhaps the next word (*quinto*) misled a scribe into writing "fifth" instead of "fourth."

12a king's (fifth) part] So Lat.; Eth. = "the kings' fifth." Mss. 39ᵗ 48 58 read "portion" before lit., "to the king."
b fifth part of all] Eth., which refers to "fifth" a little later, reads at this point: "of/from the food." The word "food" stands where Lat. has "all." Charles (*Ethiopic Version*, 162 n. 4) correctly noted that כל and אכל lay behind the variation. Eth. may have read "a fifth part" (*ḥāmesta 'eda*) before *'em-'ekl*, with the shared first letter of *'eda* and *'em-* perhaps leading to omission of *'eda*. A scribe could then have moved "fifth" to what seemed a more natural spot before "the king's."
c sown] "produced" Lat. Littmann ("Jubiläen," 113 n. f) wondered whether Lat. *natum* was an error for *satum* = the Eth. reading. Berger (*Jubiläen*, 535 n. a to v. 12) thinks γενναω is behind the two readings: it can be used for giving birth to children and for producing crops. Lat. adds: "in the land of Egypt."
d left] "gave" Lat. Both may reflect נתן.
e four parts] So Lat.; Eth. = "a fourth part."
f made it] + "for all the Egyptians" Lat.
g (for) the land] "the entire land" Lat.
13a All of the time (lit., "days") that he lived] "All the years of his life that he lived" Lat. Genesis 47:8 is the source for both: "the days of Jacob, the years of his life."
b three jubilees] "in the third jubilee" Lat.—an obvious mistake.
c He died] "Departing, he died" Lat.
d during] As it does elsewhere with such dates, Lat. prefixes a conjunction to the date, making it seem as if it is separated from the information just given.
14a his sons] "all of them" 21; "all his sons" 35.
b that would (*za-kona*)] "as/how" (*zakama*) 9 12 17 21 38 39 42 47 48 58; "that" 63; Lat. = lit., "would be coming."
c and (he informed)] Lat. and 21 35 63 om., but the conjunction is needed for the sense. Otherwise, it sounds as if they will still be in Egypt during the last days.
d he informed them (about) what would happen to them] om. Lat. After "to them" MSS. 39 42 47 48 58 add: "and all."
e gave] Lat. repeats "blessed."
f two shares] "doubly" Lat.
15a in the double cave in the land of Hebron] "in Hebron" Lat. It lacks "the land of" before "Hebron," while omission of "in the double cave" resulted from writing only one instance of "in."
16a fathers] "father" Lat.
b for his sons] om. 25.

Commentary

The chapter leads from the time Jacob arrives in Egypt to the end of his life seventeen years later. The parallel material is found in Gen 46:28–50:14 so that the chapter brings the account almost to the end of Genesis. The only stories remaining after this material in Genesis concern peace between the brothers, the death of Joseph, and provision for his ultimate burial in the land (see Jub 46:1-6a [cf. v. 8] and Gen 50:15-26). The proclivity of the author to abbreviate in the Joseph stories is very much in evidence here: he devotes sixteen verses to episodes that require one hundred and seven in Genesis.

The emotional meeting between Jacob and Joseph leads off the narrative in chap. 45. Once his family was in Egypt, Joseph provided them with the land of Goshen and made generous arrangements for their welfare while he continued to oversee the distribution of food throughout the land. Before his death, Jacob blessed his sons and gave his books to Levi. He died in Egypt, but he was, as predicted, buried in Canaan. With his burial the writer of Jubilees brings his long story about Jacob, the main character in the book, to a close. From his birth in 19:13 to his death in 45:13-16, Jacob dominates the book to an even greater extent than his grandfather Abraham had (birth in 11:15, death in 23:1-7).

In chap. 45, the author does indeed move swiftly to the close of the patriarchal period, but, in accord with his custom, he takes the time to insert into his short narrative the dates when events happened in order to situate them in the grand narrative of the book. Also, when he sees a need, he furnishes additional background to make a story more comprehensible (see on vv. 8-12).

The contents of the chapter can be outlined in four parts:

1-5   The Reunion of Jacob and Joseph (Gen 46:28-30)
6-7   Joseph's provisions for his father and brothers (Gen 46:31–47:12)
8-12 Joseph's supervision of the famine relief (Gen 47:13-26)
13-16 Jacob's last days (Gen 47:28–50:14)

Besides the Ethiopic version in which the entire chapter survives, the Latin translation is available for vv. 8-16.

1-5 The Reunion of Jacob and Joseph (Gen 46:28-30)

The writer opens the chapter by reporting Jacob's actual entry into Egypt. The previous chapter described the beginning of his travels there but ended with the long list of his family members who accompanied him and without mentioning the completion of the trip.

■ **1** It seems most appropriate that the first verse refers to the patriarch as *Israel* since the entire clan has just been named. The writer uses a singular verb with Israel as subject ("Israel went"; SP Gen 46:28 also reads a singular form), while MT reads a plural ("they came"). Genesis does not name Egypt as the goal of the journey but uses the more specific "the land of Goshen." Since Goshen was a part of Egypt, Jubilees places the two names in apposition: "into the land of Egypt, into the land of Goshen."[1] The date for the momentous event, the beginning of the Egyptian sojourn, is spelled out in full form: the year is still the one in which the brothers made their second trip to purchase food in Egypt (2172; see 42:20), and the date of 4/1 for the arrival indicates that it took the family sixteen days to reach Goshen from the well of the oath (they left it on 3/16 [44:8]). All told, the move from Hebron to Goshen lasted one month (Jacob left Hebron on 3/1 [44:1]). The first of the fourth month is the date for one of the festivals instituted by Noah (6:23, 26) and thus in itself an important occasion, but the fact that Israel reached Goshen on this very date is doubly significant because it was also Joseph's birthday (28:24). The timing was perfect.

---

1   The two instances of "the land of" render different words in the Ethiopic text: *beḥēr* (among the meanings Leslau [*Concise Dictionary*, 96] records are "region, district, country, land") is frequently used before "Egypt," while the more general *medr* is here placed before "Goshen."

■ **2-3a** To describe the first meeting between father and son in twenty-two years the author rewrites Gen 46:29-30.

Genesis 46:29-30	Jubilees 45:2-3a
Joseph made ready his chariot and went up to meet his father Israel in Goshen. He presented himself to him, fell on his neck, and wept on his neck a good while. Israel said to Joseph, "I can die now, having seen for myself that you are alive."	When Joseph came to meet his father Jacob in the land of Goshen, he wrapped his arms around his father's neck and cried. Israel said to Joseph, "Now let me die after I have seen you."

Genesis pictures Joseph acting as the great ruler he was—he rides his chariot[2] to meet his father (for Joseph's chariot, see Gen 41:43 // Jub 40:6). That element goes missing in Jubilees, where Joseph's splendor receives less emphasis than in Genesis (although it is certainly present, e.g., in 43:19-20 // Gen 45:8, 13). Genesis uses the more dramatic image of Joseph's falling on his father's neck and weeping for some time; in Jubilees he embraces him and cries, with no indication how long the loving actions lasted. The Joseph of Genesis cries on several occasions in the stories involving his brothers (42:24 [first visit]; 43:30 [he nearly cries upon seeing Benjamin]; 45:14-15 [with Benjamin, then with the other brothers after revealing his identity]); of these Jubilees reflects only 45:14-15, where the verb "cry" appears once rather than twice as in Genesis. In the present passage Joseph greets Jacob in the way he reacted to his brothers in Jub 43:15, where he hugged them and cried. It may be significant that the writer of Jubilees does not reproduce "He presented himself to him," where the verbal form (וירא) is vocalized in the MT as a niphal: he appeared (to him). Genesis elsewhere employs the expression for manifestations of God to humans (Gen 12:7; 17:1; 18:1; 26:2, 24; 35:9); this is the lone instance in which it is used for a meeting between people. The verbal form followed by the preposition אל could suggest that Joseph was a superior manifesting himself to someone of a lower rank;[3] if that were the implication, it would be inappropriate in a general context, where the author of Jubilees is underscoring family unity. Leaving out both this clause and the one about the chariot seems to serve his larger purpose.

Jacob's words to Joseph (Gen 46:30 // Jub 45:3a) are nearly identical in the two texts and in Genesis are the only ones exchanged between them when they meet. A slight difference is that Jubilees, with SP LXX Gen 46:30, reads a perfect tense verb, "I have seen," where the MT has an infinitive (rendered by NRSV as "having seen"). Jubilees also reads a pronoun as the object of the verb ("I have seen you") where the versions of Genesis have literally, "I have seen/having seen your face" and add a statement about Joseph's still being alive (see below, Jub 45:4). Here Jacob speaks briefly and fervently to indicate that his great desire has been achieved; despite his advanced age, he was allowed to see his long-lost son (see Gen 45:28 // Jub 43:24). He will live seventeen more years in Egypt, but his strong assertion makes clear how important the reunion with Joseph was.[4] When Joseph had disappeared years before, Jacob had said, "May I go down to the grave mourning for my son" (34:17 // Gen 37:35). Now the ending of his life looks to be far happier than he once anticipated.

■ **3b-4** At this point the narrative in Genesis shifts to a visit with Pharaoh that Joseph arranges for his brothers and for Jacob. In Jubilees, however, Jacob continues to speak in order to mark the extraordinary nature of the reunion with Joseph. Jacob blesses God using a very full title for him: "the Lord, the God of Israel, the God of Abraham, and the God of Isaac." The appellation is most fitting because it draws together the three generations of the patriarchs who have served this deity.

---

2   The text says, however, that he hitched it up himself.

3   See Hamilton, *Genesis 18–50*, 602, though he thinks it does not convey a sense of superiority in this passage. One suggestion has been that it emphasizes the solemnity of the meeting (see Westermann, *Genesis 37–50*, 162–63, for a survey of this and other opinions).

4   Werman maintains that Jubilees does not replicate the implication from Genesis that by seeing Joseph Jacob has reached the goal of his life (*Jubilees*, 517). But it does seem as if Jacob says as much in vv. 3a and 4a. Nevertheless, it is true, as Werman notes, that a larger theme in Jubilees is family unity (see below).

There are some approximations to the title in Genesis. For instance, when Jacob is frightened at the prospect of meeting Esau and his army, he prays, "O God of my father Abraham and God of my father Isaac, O Lord . . ." (Gen 32:9). Or, as Jacob blesses Joseph and his sons, he begins, "The God before whom my ancestors Abraham and Isaac walked, the God who has been my shepherd" (48:15). And at Bethel, the deity identified himself to Jacob: "I am the Lord, the God of Abraham your father and the God of Isaac" (28:13; later in the passage Jacob talks of the Lord becoming his God [v. 21]).[5]

Though there are similar ways of naming God in Genesis, Jubilees brings the three generations together in another manner pointing to the future now unfolding itself before the patriarch at prayer. The wording that Jacob uses—"who has not withheld his kindness and his mercy from his servant Jacob"—recalls what Abraham's servant said when Rebekah's gracious reception of him marked her as the future wife of Isaac: "Blessed be the Lord, the God of my master Abraham, who has not forsaken his steadfast love and faithfulness toward my master" (Gen 24:27; the passage is not in Jubilees). The sentiment expressed by Abraham's servant is echoed in Jubilees' stories about Isaac when he first sees Jacob (and his sons Levi and Judah) after a long absence: "Isaac blessed the God of his father Abraham who had not put an end to his mercy and faithfulness for the son of his servant Isaac" (31:25).[6] Jacob now completes the patriarchal triad by borrowing these words to bless the God of his ancestors on the happy occasion of seeing Joseph. As the servant had blessed the Lord, the God of Abraham, and Isaac had done the same, so now Jacob blesses the God of Abraham and Isaac—his God—for not withdrawing his mercy from him because he now sees Joseph and his whole fruitful family together.[7]

Jacob's enthusiastic speech continues in v. 4 to reflect other passages. He first repeats what he said after becoming convinced that Joseph had not died: "Enough! My son Joseph is still alive. I must go and see him before I die" (Gen 45:28 // Jub 43:24). In Jubilees, Jacob employs a fuller form of the words to Joseph than he had used in v. 3: now he talks about seeing "your face while I ['ana = Jacob] am alive" (compare Gen 46:30, where Jacob sees Joseph's face while "you [the Ethiopic would be 'anta = Joseph] are still alive"). That is, in the Ethiopic text he switches the emphasis from Joseph's survival to his own (see the textual note, and 43:16, where a similar problem with personal pronouns occurs). A more interesting comment by Jacob follows this one: "because the vision that I saw in Bethel was certainly true." There are several instances when Jacob receives revelations at Bethel in Jubilees (the first two are also in Genesis): when he fled Esau's anger (27:21-25; it is presented as a dream, but it is termed a vision in 31:26); in connection with his return to Bethel (32:17-19: "The Lord appeared to him during the night" [v. 17]); and directly after that experience when an angel spoke with him (32:21-26 ["In a night vision" v. 21]). Only the last of these is called a vision in the passage where it occurs, and here in v. 4 Jacob refers to "the vision that I saw in Bethel." So the designation "vision" for the experience favors the thesis that the last revelation was the one Jacob was referencing.[8] It is also the only one of the Bethel disclosures that predicted his present circumstances. At that time the angel said to him that he was to live at Isaac's house until Isaac died and that "you will die peacefully in Egypt" (32:23). Jacob was now in Egypt as the angel said he would be—and he was there also in obedience to the revealed instructions accorded to him at the well of the oath (44:5-6). Jacob thus becomes more deeply aware that his ways have been directed by God and that the divine plans for him were coming to fruition, whatever unexpected turn they had taken. Therefore he blesses his God and his name eternally. The line about the blessing sounds very much

---

5 Identifying the Lord as the God of the three patriarchs is, of course, well attested elsewhere (e.g., Exod 3:15, 16).

6 In another parallel with the present passage Isaac told Jacob to come to him so he could see him before he died (31:4).

7 Hartom ("Jubilees," 127) notes that this addition to the text of Genesis serves to accent that Jacob too attributes to God all the good that has come to him.

8 See also Berger, *Jubiläen*, 534 n. a to v. 4; Kugel, *Walk through Jubilees*, 190; "Jubilees," 437; Werman, *Jubilees*, 517.

like the one his mother Rebekah used when speaking of the deity who had given her a son so wonderful as Jacob: "May the Lord God be blessed, and may his name be blessed forever and ever" (Jub 25:12).

■ 5 The scene in Jubilees concludes with a meal eaten by Joseph and his brothers in the presence of a beaming Jacob. Joyful meals mark special family occasions in the book, including ones at the end of a parent's life. Abraham was joyful that his sons Ishmael and Isaac (with Jacob) joined him for a meal on the Festival of Weeks—the last day of his life (22:1-6); Isaac rejoiced when Jacob (with his sons Levi and Judah) ate with him after their long separation (31:22). Later Rebekah shared a meal with her sons Esau and Jacob the last night of her life (35:27), and Isaac was happy when Esau and Jacob ate and drank together before him on the final day of his life (36:17). As Isaac had celebrated a meal with Jacob following their twenty-two year separation, so now Jacob is overjoyed when he sees Joseph and his brothers eating and drinking in front of him after the family had been apart for so long. There is unity among all as they break bread together.[9] Like his grandfather Abraham and his father Isaac, Jacob uttered a blessing to the Creator God on the occasion (see 22:6, 27; 31:13; 36:7). Jacob was grateful that God had preserved not only him but also his twelve sons. Not long before, he was convinced he had lost Joseph and Simeon and that he was likely to lose Benjamin as well (42:10-11). Now his sons were restored to their full number of twelve (see 25:16, where Rebekah prayed that he might have as many sons as there were months in a year).

6-7 Joseph's Provisions for His Father and Brothers (Gen 46:31—47:12)

The next sections in Genesis and Jubilees differ considerably, primarily because Jubilees abbreviates drastically. In Genesis, Joseph arranges for his brothers and father to appear before Pharaoh and to ask him for the land of Goshen since they were shepherds (46:31-34). He selects five of them for the royal audience (47:1-6), at the end of which Pharaoh tells Joseph, "The land of Egypt is before you; settle your father and your brothers in the best part of the land; let them live in the land of Goshen" (47:6). Next Joseph presents Jacob to the monarch, who wanted to know how old he was; the elderly man told him he was one hundred thirty years of age, a total far lower than the age his ancestors had attained (47:7-10). Finally, Joseph carries out Pharaoh's instructions by settling his family in "the land of Rameses" (v. 11) and provides food for them (47:11-12).

In Jubilees, the reader encounters nothing about a meeting with Pharaoh—neither for Joseph nor for other members of the family including Jacob. The author vaults over the sections in Gen 46:31—47:10 in which his brothers explain their great need and the monarch graciously grants their request to settle apart in Goshen so that they will not offend the Egyptians "because all shepherds are abhorrent to the Egyptians" (46:34). The only item he retains from those sections is Jacob's age of one hundred thirty years when he arrived in Egypt (see Gen 47:9).

■ 6 Instead of reproducing the encounters with Pharaoh, he moves to the final two verses in the pericope—Gen 47:11-12—where Joseph, not Pharaoh, makes a donation of territory.

Genesis 47:11	Jubilees 45:6
Joseph settled his father and his brothers, and granted them a holding in the land of Egypt, in the best part of the land, in the land of Rameses, as Pharaoh had instructed.	As a gift Joseph gave his father and his brothers (the right) to live in the land of Goshen, that is, in Rameses;
	and (he gave) them all its districts that they would rule[10] in Pharaoh's presence. Israel and his sons lived in the land of Goshen, the best part of the land of Egypt. Israel was 130 years of age when he came into Egypt.

---

9   See Berger, *Jubiläen*, 534 n. a to v. 5; Endres, *Biblical Interpretation*, 192.

10 The verb for "ruling" (*kwannana*) is a form of the one used for Joseph's governance of Egypt in Jub 40:6 (see the comment on the verb below).

In Genesis, Joseph, acting on Pharaoh's orders, places his family in a superior location in Egypt, but in Jubilees there is no mention of settling them by Pharaoh's command. It begins to cite the verse at the point where Genesis uses the expression "granted them a holding," which in Jubilees becomes Joseph's gift to them of living in Goshen. In v. 11 Genesis puts that "holding" in Egypt and refers to it as "the best part of the land"—words that have earlier described Goshen (see the combination of Gen 45:10, 18, and 20 and especially 47:6, where Pharaoh employs the phrase for Goshen), though the place-name does not occur here. The writer of Jubilees names not only Goshen but also Rameses, which in Genesis is described as "the best part of the land" (47:11), that is, just as Goshen is depicted in Gen 47:6. Unlike all the ancient versions of Gen 47:11, Jubilees places a conjunction before "Rameses" as if it were another district. It may be that the conjunction here has the sense of "even, namely, that is."[11] Elsewhere in the HB, Rameses is a city, not a district.

The surprising feature in this context is the addition Jubilees inserts between the end of its citation of Gen 47:11 and the beginning of its quotation from v. 12. Joseph gave his family districts in the area (Goshen and Rameses) to "rule in Pharaoh's presence." Genesis does not attribute a governing function to Jacob's family, but the claim may have arisen from Gen 47:6, where Pharaoh says to Joseph, "if you know that there are capable men [אנשי חיל] among them [his father and brothers] put them in charge of my livestock [שרי מקנה על אשר לי]." It appears that he wants to appoint any qualified member of Joseph's family over his own cattle, but Jubilees takes his words in a broader sense to denote a right to govern before Pharaoh. *Targum Neofiti* Gen 47:6 seems to take them in a similar sense: "And if you know that there be among them warriors, valiant men, you shall place them as masters of *our* flocks, over *all* that belongs to me." It may be that the writer of Jubilees understood מקנה in its wider sense of "property" and inferred that Pharaoh was inviting them to control all of his holdings on his behalf, not just the cattle.[12] What in Genesis is a suggestion by the monarch becomes a fact in Jubilees: they actually did rule, as Joseph ruled over a broader area (see 40:6).[13]

After the somewhat confusing statements about where Jacob's family was to live—the introduction of Rameses here is unexpected—the writer clarifies matters by declaring that they lived in Goshen, again termed the best part of Egypt. At this juncture he adds the note about Jacob's age, the only bit of the text from Gen 46:31—47:10 to make its way into Jubilees 45. This is yet another place where Jubilees reproduces a year number from Genesis that proves inconsistent with the larger chronology in the book. According to Jub 19:13 Jacob was born in 2046; as the present year is 2172 (45:1), he would be 126 or 127, not 130.

■ **7** At v. 7 the author returns to the text of Genesis.

Genesis 47:12	Jubilees 45:7
And Joseph provided his father, his brothers, and all his father's household with food, according to the number of their dependents.	Joseph provided as much food for his father, his brothers, and also for their livestock as would be sufficient[14] for them for the seven years of famine.

Despite the different arrangement of the sentence in the two English translations above, the word order is the same through the word "food." However, where Genesis mentions "all his father's household," Jubilees has "their livestock." The term *ṭerit* means "possessions, wealth, goods, property" but in the context should refer to property that needs food, namely animals.[15] Perhaps the

---

11 See *DCH* 2:597 s.v. ו.
12 See Jastrow, 831, s.v. מקנה. Genesis 47:1 uses the phrase "all that they possess [וכל אשר להם]" to refer to their property over and above cattle, the various types of which are listed before it.
13 Werman, *Jubilees*, 517–18.
14 The verb is *yaʾakkelomu*, "it would be enough for them." Charles (*Ethiopic Version*, 161 n. 8), observing that the LXX rendered לפי הטף ("according to their dependents") as κατα σωμα ("per person"), suggested emending the Ethiopic form to *ʾakālomu* ("their body, person" [Leslau, *Concise Dictionary*, 144]), a literal equivalent of the Greek term. By the time he wrote *Jubilees*, he seems to have changed his mind because he translated the verbal form in the text, though he mentioned the emendation in a note (243). See VanderKam, *Jubilees* 2:296. There is no manuscript support for changing the verb to a noun.
15 For the definitions of the word, see Leslau, *Comparative Dictionary*, 597. For the suggestion that it refers to "livestock" here, see VanderKam, *Jubilees* 2:296.

writer assumed that by supplying food to his father and brothers their households would be included; he also knew that they brought their cattle with them and that they too would have to be fed (see Gen 46:6, 32; 47:1; cf. Jub 44:7). A larger difference concerns the amount of food Joseph made available. In Genesis he divided it by the number of people involved (Benjamin's large household would have required more, Dan's small one less); in Jubilees he gave all—people and animals—enough to eat until the end of the famine years. It is odd that "seven" is used, as only five years of the seven-year famine remained. If one wished to defend the author's number, one could say that Joseph did in fact give them food sufficient for the seven years: he had already provided free of charge the amounts for the first two years; now he was donating what was required for the remaining five.

8-12: Joseph's Supervision of the Famine Relief (Gen 47:13-26)

The tendency to abbreviate dominates the present section as well as the previous one. Genesis begins by noting the effect of the famine on Egypt and Canaan (47:13) as the background for the negotiations represented in the remainder of the paragraph. The narrator describes how Joseph systematically demanded payment for the food he had stored and eventually acquired all of Egypt for Pharaoh. First the people bought food with their money (v. 14, silver); once they had exhausted their funds, they paid him with their cattle (vv. 15-17); finally, after losing all their livestock they handed over their bodies and land (vv. 18-21). All of this was worked out through conversations between Joseph and the Egyptians (not the Canaanites after v. 15). In this way Joseph acquired all of the land for Pharaoh, except the land held by the priests, and he enslaved the whole population (vv. 20-21,[16] 25). Moreover, he gave seeds to the Egyptians (after they begged for them in exchange for their freedom, v. 19) at the end of the process so that in the following year they would be able to plant their own crops and raise food for themselves. Joseph established a law, valid until the author's time, that one-fifth of the crop was to belong to Pharaoh, and the people could keep the remaining four-fifths for themselves (vv. 23-25). Throughout the unit Joseph, in stark contrast to the way he treated his family, appears to be a calculating, even cruel official who holds an essential commodity and exploits it to the advantage of his employer. The people acknowledge that he saved their lives, but he offered no bargains—he extorted the highest price possible. "Thus by a bold stroke of statesmanship private property in land (except in the case of the priests) is abolished throughout Egypt, and the entire population reduced to the position of serfs, paying a land-tax of 20 per cent. *per annum* to the king."[17] The passage, with its reference to seeds for planting, is the nearest the narrative in Genesis comes to implying the end of the famine years.

■ **8** Jubilees eliminates any dialogue from the paragraph in Genesis and simply summarizes the verbal exchanges by noting what Joseph acquired for Pharaoh as the price for food. He refers to the suffering[18] through which the land of Egypt was passing, with no mention of Canaan (it was no longer relevant to the story). The order in which he lists Joseph's acquisitions for Pharaoh reverses the one in Genesis, with the last one first—all the land—and after it "the people, their cattle, and everything." "Everything" stands where Genesis speaks about their money—"money/silver" is absent from Jubilees. Joseph may appear in a little more favorable light in Jubilees, where he is a remarkably successful agent of Pharaoh; at least he is not depicted as a ruthless official who, when the populace admits to having lost all their money and cattle and to be in danger of dying, wrests even more from them.

■ **9-10** Unlike Genesis, the author of Jubilees actually says that the famine ended and indicates exactly when it occurred. Genesis 47:13-19, where two different years are mentioned (vv. 17-18), indicates the passage of some

---

16 In v. 21 the MT says that he transferred the people to the cities; the SP and LXX read that he enslaved them. Words that look much alike in Hebrew are the cause of the different meanings.

17 Skinner, *Genesis*, 499.

18 In the Ethiopic text the land "suffers" (Leslau, *Comparative Dictionary*, 233), while the verb in the Latin version is only partially preserved (reconstructed as *labora*]vit by Rönsch, *Jubiläen*, 84 = "suffered"). Genesis 47:13 reads ותלה, "languished"; LXX εξελιπεν, "failed."

time, and v. 23 looks ahead to the next harvest season: "Then Joseph said to the people, 'Now that I have this day bought you and your land for Pharaoh, here is seed for you; sow the land.'" But the passage leaves a number of questions, and there is no suggestion that all five remaining years had elapsed. The only hint about the end of the famine is that Joseph expects the seed he provides for the people to yield crops for them in due time. In Jubilees there is an effort to clarify the situation. The writer specifically dates the donation of seed to a point after the seven-year period—to the eighth year. It is noteworthy that in Jubilees Joseph gives the people not only seed but also food to last them until the harvest (contrast Gen 47:23-24). Obviously there would have been no crops in the seventh year so rations would again have been necessary for the Egyptians to manage until the earth once again produced its bounty after the Egyptians planted seeds in the eighth year.

Though Joseph gives seeds to the people to plant, Genesis explains neither when nor why he adopted the new policy. The author of Jubilees says that he gave the seeds in the year after the famine ended and explains that conditions in Egypt had changed: "the river had overflowed the entire land of Egypt." Since the Nile's flooding furnished the necessary irrigation for the soil, agriculture was again possible. Presumably the return of Nile flooding signaled visibly that the time of no crops had ended. The writer goes on to give details about the anomalous situation during the seven years and how the river now resumed its accustomed ways. He claims the famine years coincided with an unusual pattern for the Nile: "it had irrigated only a few places at the riverbank, but now it overflowed."[19] Apparently not enough water coursed through Egypt to produce the normal amount of flooding, and the result was a lack of crops and thus the famine. So the writer adopts a natural explanation for famine conditions that are never so explained in Genesis.

The renewed, full flooding of the river made it reasonable for Joseph to give seeds to the people of Egypt to restart the agricultural cycle. Joseph's seed-distribution program, which lacks context in Genesis, has a very reasonable one in Jubilees. The writer adds that the planting proved successful and produced an excellent crop (see the textual note); Genesis mentions neither their obeying Joseph's order nor the result of the planting.

■ **11-12** Only after giving the background information about the Nile in vv. 9-10 does the author provide a precise date for the beginning of the post-famine period. The date 2178 is consistent with the ones he supplied earlier for the years of plenty and the years of want:
Years of plenty: end 2170 (41:21), therefore they began in 2164
Years of Famine: begin 2171 (42:1), 2172 is the second year (42:20), 2178 is the year after they ended (45:11), so they ended in 2177.
In the eighth year after the inception of the famine, Joseph made his donation of seed to the Egyptians. The gift in turn became the context for the tax that Joseph made into a permanent law in Egypt: 20 percent of the food produced from the seeds that he provided Joseph took on behalf of the monarch. The remaining 80 percent belonged to the farmer, certainly for food for him and his family but also to give a supply of seeds for the following year—the latter is a note added to the Genesis account. The writer reproduces from Genesis that the statute remained in effect in Egypt "until today."[20] As he presents the situation, Joseph simply gave the seeds to the people in the year after the famine ended. They did not have to beg for them and he did not demand payment for them. He was just being a wise overseer who was loyal to the king and concerned about the welfare of the many needy people in Egypt.[21] The tax-exempt status of priestly lands and their allowance from the royal coffers play no part in Jubilees (see Gen 47:22, 26).

---

19 Josephus (*Ant.* 2.191) also mentions that the river overflowed and the land resumed producing crops.
20 Josephus (*Ant.* 2.193) says the "law imposing payment of the fifth of the produce remained in force under the later kings" (Thackeray, LCL). In Jub 38:15 the expression "until today" appears where Gen 36:31 lacks it, and the same is the case in Jub 45:16 (see below).
21 The picture in this section makes unlikely Kugel's suggestion that the writer in vv. 1-7 and 8-12 leaves out contact with foreigners because it was contaminating (*Walk through* Jubilees, 189–90; "Jubilees," 438). Joseph had had contact with these supposedly contaminating foreigners before (e.g., chaps. 39–40) where the author showed no scruples about such intermingling. The reasons for leaving

13-16: Jacob's Last Days (Gen 47:28—50:14)

Genesis has an elaborate, multipart account of the end of Jacob's life. Beginning in 47:28 with a chronological note (he lived for seventeen years in Egypt; adding these years to his age of 130 when he arrived [see 47:9], he lived a total of 147 years), the story continues for several chapters. Jacob made Joseph promise to bury him in Canaan with his ancestors (47:29-31), blessed Joseph's sons Manasseh and Ephraim in reverse order (48:1-20), gave Joseph a portion above the one his brothers received (48:21-22), told his twelve sons "what will happen to you in days to come" (49:1-28; the quotation is from v. 1), made arrangements for his burial in the cave of Machpelah (49:29-32), and died (49:33). The mourning for and embalming of Jacob in Egypt, the funerary journey to Canaan, the weeping that took place there, the interment of his body in the cave of Machpelah, and the return to Egypt occupy Gen 50:1-14. The author of Jubilees condenses the end of Jacob's life into four verses. He had borrowed some of the Genesis material to fill in earlier stories,[22] but he still severely curtails the account about his hero's final days.

■ 13 The verse, which rewrites Gen 47:28, is devoted to chronological information. The numbers in Genesis and Jubilees agree, but in the latter his age of 147 years at death is also expressed in jubilees: 147 is exactly three jubilee periods. This may have struck the writer as remarkable and suggestive: of all the patriarchs, only Jacob (called Israel,[23] unlike in Gen 47:28 where he is Jacob) lived an exact number of jubilees, with no weeks or years left over.[24] It was as if his life fit perfectly in the chronology of the world, just as his place in the genealogy from Adam corresponded with the structure of creation (see 2:19-25). His death came in the year of the world 2188. Jubilees 19:13 placed his and Esau's birth in the year 2046. Subtracting 2046 from 2188 yields 142 (or 143), not 147 years for Jacob's life.[25] The numbers for his stay in Egypt are, however, consistent: he arrived in 2172 (45:1), lived there for seventeen years, and died in 2188. In Gen 47:9 Jacob told Pharaoh his age was far lower than "the years of the life of my ancestors," and he was correct: Abraham lived 175 years (Gen 25:7 // Jub 23:8) and Isaac 180 (Gen 35:28 // Jub 36:18).

■ 14 The long narrative between Gen 47:29 and 49:32 is trimmed down to just one verse in Jubilees. Gone are Jacob's conversation with Joseph about his burial and the blessing of Ephraim and Manasseh. The writer largely skips over Genesis 48 and focuses his attention on chap. 49. In saying that "Israel blessed his sons" he adopts the language of Gen 49:28, the verse that follows the poetic words Jacob spoke to each of his twelve sons in vv. 3-27: "All these are the twelve tribes of Israel and this is what their father said to them when he blessed them, blessing each one of them with a suitable blessing." Commentators, ancient and modern, have remarked that "blessing" may not be the best word to describe what Jacob says to at least some of his sons (e.g., he is critical of the first three, Reuben, Simeon, and Levi), and the word "blessing" does not occur in the chapter until the section regarding Joseph (vv. 22-26; see also 48:15-16).[26] The next two clauses likewise, it would seem, relate to what Jacob says to his sons in Genesis 49, but the first one is problematic. The author claims that

---

out much of the Genesis material seem rather to be a desire to abbreviate and to polish Joseph's image.

22 See, for example, the commentary on the blessings Isaac bestowed on Levi and Judah in 31:13-20 (a scene fashioned on Jacob's blessing of Ephraim and Manasseh in Genesis 48) and on the story of Reuben and Bilhah in 33:1-17 (where material from the "blessing" of Reuben [Gen 49:3-4] is employed).

23 Both the Ethiopic and Latin versions agree for the name Israel.

24 VanderKam, *Book of Jubilees*, 81. Abraham lived exactly twenty-five weeks of years (= 175; Jub 23:8 divides the years into three jubilees and four weeks of years); see VanderKam, "Chronology," 534–35.

25 Cf. Charles, *Jubilees*, 244.

26 Gerhard von Rad wrote about the title "Jacob's blessing": "But this designation is not quite apposite, for the twelve are not really blessed; the aphorisms have no generally common feature at all. Some are prophecies of the future, some contain censure or curse regarding what has happened, some describe current affairs" (*Genesis: A Commentary* [OTL; Philadelphia: Westminster, 1961] 416). In his commentary on Gen 49:28, Rashi also deals with the issue.

Jacob "told them everything that would happen to them in the land of Egypt." Exactly what he could mean by this is puzzling because Jacob does not talk about the subject either in Genesis or in Jubilees. Kugel[27] adduces similar language in Josephus's retelling of the event: "His sons were present at his end, and he offered prayers that they might attain to felicity and foretold to them in prophetic words how each of their descendants was destined to find a habitation in Canaan, as in fact long after came to pass" (*Ant.* 2.194 [Thackeray, LCL]). Placement of the words "offered prayers that they might attain to felicity" before relating what Jacob predicted may parallel the twofold structure in Jubilees, that is, his prayers for their "felicity" may correspond with Jubilees' "everything that would happen to them in the land of Egypt." The "blessings" of the sons in Genesis 49 refer to some events that had already occurred (the sin with Bilhah for Reuben, the slaughter of Shechem for Simeon and Levi are examples), but none of them deals specifically with what will happen to them while they remain in Egypt. Genesis 47:27, speaking about the period Israel (= Jacob's family) lived in Egypt, says "they gained possession of it [Goshen], and were fruitful and multiplied exceedingly" and very similar words appear in Exod 1:7 regarding the time after Joseph and his brothers died (see v. 6): "But the Israelites were fruitful and prolific; they multiplied and grew exceedingly strong, so that the land was filled with them." Though the two texts taken together could imply that such conditions characterized the entire generation of the brothers and beyond, both are narrative reports, not predictions. Possibly the writer of Jubilees believed Jacob told his sons what would happen to them in Egypt on the basis of the revelation given him by the angel in 32:21: on the seven tablets the angel gave to Jacob he read "what would happen to him and his sons throughout all ages" (in v. 26 he writes the information). But see below for another hypothesis.

The second clause says "he informed them (about) what would happen to them at the end of time." The base text is Gen 49:1, where Jacob, having assembled his sons, tells them "what will happen to you in days to come [באחרית הימים]." Jubilees has a literal representation of the phrase "in days to come": *ba-daḫāri*[28] *mawāʿel* (Eth Gen 49:1 uses the same words). It refers to the future, perhaps even a more distant future in the HB;[29] in later literature it took on an eschatological meaning.[30] Several of the sections about his sons (e.g., Judah) are future-oriented, and to these the writer refers by alluding to Gen 49:1.

A suggestion can be offered regarding why, in Jubilees, Jacob speaks of the two topics—what will happen to them in Egypt and what will befall them in the time to come. The poetic first verses of Genesis 49 place the line about the days to come in parallel with another: "Assemble and hear, O sons of Jacob; listen to Israel your father" (v. 2). It is conceivable that the writer of Jubilees took the parallel lines to be identifying two subjects on which he would address them, or perhaps he understood the various poetic lines in vv. 1-2 to mean that he predicted the entire future, near (events in Egypt) and far (the time to come/end of days).

Besides pointing to Genesis 49 and repeating that Jacob blessed his sons, the author also makes mention of Jacob's treatment of Joseph. Genesis 48:22 quotes the patriarch as saying to him, "I now give to you one portion more than to your brothers, the portion that I took from the hand of the Amorites with my sword and with my bow." In context, the passage may be dealing with the fact that Joseph's descendants through his sons Ephraim and Manasseh whom Jacob had just blessed

---

27 Kugel, *Traditions*, 468–69.
28 Leslau, *Concise Dictionary*, 196: "last, latter, posterior, rear, latest, hindmost."
29 See Westermann, *Genesis 37–50*, 223. Other pentateuchal uses of it are in Num 24:14 and Deut 31:29. The latter passage, which is important in Jubilees 1 and relates to the purpose of the book, places it in the mouth of Moses. In the context he speaks about the law as a witness against the people (v. 26), and he declares in v. 29: "For I know that after my death you will surely act corruptly, turning aside from the way that I have commanded you. *In time to come* trouble will befall you."
30 Annette Steudel, "אחרית הימים in the Texts from Qumran," *RevQ* 16/62 (1993) 225–46; she suggests that the best translation of the phrase in the Qumran texts is "the final period of history" (p. 231), one that for the writers of the texts had already begun.

(48:8-20) would become two tribes. With their father obtaining two portions, the two tribes from Joseph would each have one, just like the ancestors of the other tribes.[31] The extra portion for Joseph in Jubilees, where the blessings on Ephraim and Manasseh are omitted, takes the form of "two shares in the land" for Joseph. Joseph is privileged in Jubilees as he is in Genesis.

■ 15 The death of Jacob is the subject of Gen 49:33. Jubilees does not rewrite that verse in particular but draws on several others in the context to report the death and burial of the great man. In describing his death, Genesis says, "When Jacob ended his charge to his sons, he drew up his feet into the bed, breathed his last, and was gathered to his people" (49:33; compare Abraham in Gen 25:8 and Isaac in 35:29). The writer of Jubilees resorts to different but familiar language for the event: "He slept with his fathers."[32] Jacob had instructed Joseph about his coming death in Gen 47:30 ("When I lie down with my ancestors [lit., fathers]"), and in 49:29 he commanded his sons, "Bury me with my ancestors." The author draws on these passages to describe Jacob's death. Most of v. 15 in Jubilees gives specific information about where Jacob was buried. He himself left no doubt that he was to be buried in Canaan, and he named the cave of Machpelah as the site (Gen 49:29-32; cf. 47:30); it was there that Joseph and his brothers interred him (50:13). In Jubilees he is, of course, buried in the same place (with Machpelah, as usual, translated as "the double cave"—used twice in v. 15). The writer, though he said that Jacob "slept with his fathers," reports that he was "buried near his father Abraham," with no mention of his actual father Isaac (Jacob refers to Isaac and Rebekah in Gen 49:31). It is one more reminder that Jacob was, in a fundamental sense, the true son and heir of Abraham beside whom he now lies forever. The second description of the burial place refers to "the grave that he had dug for himself in the double cave in the land of Hebron." The line is related to Gen 50:5, where Joseph, when asking for permission to bury his father in Canaan, says, "My father made me swear an oath; he said, 'I am about to die. In the tomb that I hewed out for myself in the land of Canaan, there you shall bury me.'" The writer carefully identifies this hewn tomb as being in the cave of Machpelah in the area of Hebron (it is near Mamre in Gen 49:30).[33] Whatever the meaning of Gen 50:5,[34] it becomes part of the description of Jacob's grave. Completely absent from the account in Jubilees is any mention of foreign connections with the cave. In Genesis, Jacob included in his final instructions (49:29-32) two references to the fact that the former owner of the burial site was Ephron the Hittite and adds that it was purchased from the Hittites.

■ 16 The last act of Jacob, introduced into the text after the notice about his death and burial, was disposing of the patriarchal library. Jacob, not surprisingly, was in possession of the books of his ancestors. Throughout Jubilees the author has scattered notes about who in the chosen line had the ability to write and who wrote and transmitted books. Enoch was the first writer and composed a number of books on scientific, moral, and eschatological topics (4:17-19, 21; cf. also 4:23-24). The next[35] was Noah, who possessed a book regarding the division of the earth (8:11-12) and recorded teachings about medicines (10:13). "He gave all the books that he had written to his oldest son Shem because he loved him much more than all his sons" (10:14). Abram's father Terah taught him to write (11:16), and later, after the angel tutored him in the Hebrew language, he "took his fathers' books—they were written in Hebrew—and copied them. From that time he began to study them, while I [the Angel of the Presence] was telling him everything that he was unable (to understand). He studied them throughout the six rainy months" (12:27). When speaking with Isaac about sacrificial matters, Abraham referred to "the book of my ancestors, in the words of Enoch and the words of Noah" (21:10). Jacob learned to

---

31 Cf. Hartom, "Jubilees," 128.
32 He utilizes similar language for Abraham in 23:1 (he "was gathered to his ancestors [fathers]").
33 See also Jub 36:2, where Isaac tells his sons to bury him in "the grave that I dug for myself."
34 Cf. Westermann, *Genesis 37-50*, 200; Hamilton, *Genesis 18-50*, 693.
35 In Jub 8:1-4 Arpachshad taught his son Kainan to write, but he recorded illicit information and therefore is not part of the list of sanctioned writers.

write (19:14, with no indication who taught him). When an angel in a vision revealed seven tablets to him, Jacob read what was on them (32:21) and "wrote down all the things that he had read and seen" (32:26). Joseph, when propositioned by Potiphar's wife, recalled "what his father Jacob would read to him from the words of Abraham—that no one is to commit adultery..." (39:6; see 20:3-6; 41:28). Jacob as the true heir of Abraham not only possessed the books of his ancestors and his own writings (and carted them with him to Egypt), but now also passed them to his son Levi, who served as the priest in his generation (31:13-17; 32:1-9).

In Jubilees, all of the individuals in this litany of writers carried out priestly functions in their times—that is, they offered sacrifices and the like:[36]

Enoch: 4:25 (in Eden)
Noah: 6:1-4; 7:3-5
Abra(ha)m: 13:4, 9, 16; 14:11-12, 19; 15:2; 16:20-24; 18:5-8, 12 (he instructs Isaac regarding sacrificial procedures in 21:7-18)
Isaac: 22:3-4; 24:23
Jacob: 31:3, 26 (though actually carrying out the sacrifice is not described in v. 26); 32:4-6, 27; 44:1.

So the ancestral literature was passed along in the priestly line, and that practice will now continue with Levi, the progenitor of the priests. It is intriguing that Levi has played almost no role at all in the narrative since he became a priest in chap. 32. In 34:3 he remained behind with those who were with the elderly Isaac and who later participated with the other brothers in the war with the Amorites (v. 6); in 34:20 his marriage to Melcha of Aram is recorded. He led one of the four contingents fighting Esau and his forces (38:6), and he and his sons are listed among the seventy who descended to Egypt (44:14). He must have been among those who sold Joseph and lied to their father about it, and he was one of the brothers who made both trips to Egypt, though he plays no part in any of the scenes. Now suddenly the reader is reminded of his importance.[37]

Levi received the books and two assignments for what to do with them: he was "to preserve them" and to "renew them for his sons until today." The books containing the teachings of the ancestors Levi must now guard and maintain as the latest link in the chain of priests stretching back to earliest times. For the verb "guard," see Deut 33:9 (regarding Levi/the Levites): "For they observed [שמרו] your word, / and kept [ינצרו] your covenant." It was now his responsibility to ensure they were not lost or destroyed. But he was also to "renew them." The verb could be read in more than one way: perhaps he was to make fresh copies of them (as Abram did for the books of his fathers, 12:27), or, more likely, he was to keep them up-to-date as new revelations and situations arose, much as the covenant was renewed annually (6:17) and updated with new laws from time to time. If so, then the passage presupposes scribal capabilities for Levi[38] and perhaps also a duty to teach the tradition he is preserving and renewing. Note too that he was to "renew them for his sons [descendants] until today." This is the second time in the chapter that the writer has used "until today" (see 45:12, for Joseph's law in Egypt), but, whereas in the first instance it seems to be a cliché, in this case it is very likely that the writer means to say this function continues into his own time (the second century BCE).[39]

---

36 Adam too was a priest (3:27), but he is not called a writer.

37 There is no doubting the importance of the statement that Levi received the ancestral books to guard and renew, and Levi is clearly very prominent in certain parts of Jubilees (esp. chaps. 30–32), but this does not entail that he is exalted over Joseph or that Joseph's role in the book is reduced to influence in the political, not the family, sphere, as Halpern-Amaru ("Burying the Fathers: Exegetical Strategies and Source Traditions in *Jubilees* 46," in Esther Chazon, Devorah Dimant, and Ruth Clements, eds., *Reworking the Bible: Apocryphal and Related Texts at Qumran* [STDJ 58; Leiden: Brill, 2005] 135–52) argues. The point will receive further treatment in the commentary on Jubilees 46.

38 2 Chronicles 34:13 refers to some Levites who were scribes (cf. 1 Chr 24:6).

39 In Deut 10:8 the expression is used in connection with Levites and their duties: "At that time the LORD set apart the tribe of Levi to carry the ark of the covenant of the LORD, to stand before the LORD to minister to him, and to bless in his name, to this day."

Since writing and teaching are documented Levitical tasks, the verse has served as a basis for a conclusion about the social location of the author of Jubilees. For Charles, "It is reasonable to infer that our author who gave them [the ancestral traditions] to the world was a descendant of Levi, and probably a priest."[40] Schubert, however, has formulated an extended argument that the writer was specifically a Levite, not a priest; he bases it on material in the HB regarding Levitical functions that match well with what Levi is to do in Jubilees.[41] For example, in Deut 33:10, besides the preserving functions cited just above from v. 9, "They teach Jacob your ordinances, / and Israel your law"[42] (see also 2 Chr 17:7-9; 35:3; Neh 8:9 on Levites and teaching; for Levites and the law, see Deut 17:8-13; 2 Chr 19:8-11; 31:4; Neh 8:7-8). The topic is treated in more detail in the Introduction to the commentary,[43] but it is unlikely that there is enough evidence in 45:16 or elsewhere in the book to determine that the writer was a Levite rather than a priest (Levi is obviously a priest in Jubilees). The emphasis in the present passage is the ancient, revealed tradition: it has been written down and those contents are fixed; it now passes into the hands of a most reliable tradent who will guard it, update it, and make it available to his descendants.

The writer of Jubilees was not the only one to speak about a written deposit passed along in the priestly line. In 4Q542 (Testament of Qahat [= Kohath, a son of Levi; see Exod 6:16; Jub 44:14 // Gen 46:11]), Kohath[44] speaks to his sons and warns them:

be careful with the inheritance that has been entrusted to you, and which your ancestors have bequeathed to you. Do not give your inheritance away.... So hold firm to the command of Jacob your ancestor, grasp tightly the judgements of Abraham and the good deeds [צדקת] of Levi and myself.... And you will give me a good name among yourselves, happiness[45] to Levi, joy to Jacob, celebration to Isaac, and praise to Abraham,[46] because you have kept and passed on the inheritance that your ancestors left. (4Q542 1 i:4-5, 7-8, 10-12; trans. Cook, *DSSR* 3:567)

Later, in a more broken context, he tells his son Amram:

Now, to you, Amram my son, I command [a heritage that has been transmitted (to me) and which you receive] and to your chil[dren], and to their descendants I command[all the sacred writings that our fathers received/wrote] and gave to my father Levi, and that my father Levi [gave] to me [and which I Qohath give to you, my son, and to your sons] all my writings as a testimony, that you should take warning from them. (4Q542 1 ii:9-12; trans. Cook *DSSR* 3:569)[47]

So, in Jubilees 45 Jacob dies but not before he passes along his legacy and that of his ancestors to his son Levi, through whom it will pass to his descendants "until today."

---

40 Charles, *Jubilees*, 244. In his "The Book of Jubilees" in *APOT* 2:76 he phrased the point as: "Our author, who published these traditions, was probably himself a priest." Cf. Endres, *Biblical Interpretation*, 193-94.

41 Schubert, *Tradition und Erneuerung*, esp. 177-266.

42 It should be noted, however, that the very next lines deal with sacrificing at the altar—a priestly, not a Levitical, function in the period under consideration.

43 See also the Excursus: Levi, the Levites, and the Hasmoneans (in the commentary on chap. 32).

44 Though Kohath was the second son of Levi, his father discerned that he would obtain the high priesthood according to ALD 11:5-6; his oldest son Gershom he foresaw would not have the high priesthood (11:3; cf. T. Levi 11:2-6).

45 Cook inadvertently omitted the word "happiness" from his translation.

46 Tracing the line through Abraham, Isaac, Jacob, and Levi is attested in 4Q225 2 ii:12.

47 The text Visions of Amram (4Q543-549) identifies itself as a copy of the book that apparently contains what he told his sons on the day he died (see 4Q543 1 1-2). In ALD 13:4-5 Levi urges his sons to instruct their children in "reading and writing and teaching <of> wisdom" and points to the example of Joseph (13:6). In 13:15-16, though the text is damaged, he claims he had learned these subjects, and he speaks of his sons' inheritance that may include books. See also T. Levi 13:2.

From Harmony to Oppression

46

1/ After the death of Jacob, the children of Israel became numerous in the land of Egypt. They became a populous nation, and all of them[a] were of the same mind so that each one loved the other[b] and each one helped the other.[c] They became numerous and increased[d] very much—even[e] for ten weeks of years [= 70 years]—for all of Joseph's lifetime. 2/ There was no satan or any evil one throughout all of Joseph's lifetime that he lived after his father[a] Jacob because all the Egyptians were honoring[b] the children of Israel for all of Joseph's lifetime. 3/ Joseph died when he was 110[a] years of age. He had lived for 17 years in the land of Canaan; for ten years he remained enslaved; he was in prison for three[b] years; and for 80 years he was ruling the entire[c] land of Egypt under Pharaoh. 4/ He died[a] and all his brothers and all of that generation. 5/ Before he[a] died he ordered the Israelites to take his bones along at the time when they would leave the land of[b] Egypt. 6/ He made them swear[a] about his bones because he knew that the Egyptians would surely not allow him to be brought out[b] and be buried in the land of Canaan on the day of his death,[c] since Makamaron, the king of Canaan—while he was living in the land of Asur[d]—fought[e] in the valley[f] with the king of Egypt and killed him there.[g] He pursued the Egyptians as far as the borders of Egypt.[h] 7/ He[a] was unable to enter[b] because another new king ruled[c] Egypt. He was stronger than he, so he returned to the land of Canaan[d] and the gates of Egypt were closed with no one entering or leaving[e] Egypt.

8/ Joseph died in the forty-sixth jubilee, in the sixth week, during its second year[a] [2242]. He was buried in the land of Egypt,[b] and all his brothers died after him. 9/ Then[a] the king of Egypt went out to fight with the king of Canaan in the[b] forty-seventh jubilee, in the second week, during its second year [2263]. The Israelites[c] brought out all the bones of Jacob's sons[d] except Joseph's bones. They buried them[e] in the field of[f] the double cave[g] in the mountain. 10/ Many returned to Egypt but a few of them remained on the mountain of Hebron. Your[a] father Amram[b] remained with them.[c]

11/ The king of Canaan conquered the king of Egypt and closed[a] the gates of Egypt. 12/ He[a] conceived an evil plan against the Israelites[b] in order to make them suffer. He said to the Egyptians:[c] 13/ "The nation of the Israelites has now increased[a] and become more numerous than we are. Come on,[b] let us outwit them[c] before they multiply. Let us make them suffer[d] in slavery[e] before[f] war comes our way and they, too, fight[g] against us. Otherwise they will unite with the enemy[h] and leave our land because their mind(s) and face(s look) toward the land of Canaan." 14/ He[a] appointed taskmasters[b] over them to make them suffer in slavery.[c] They built[d] fortified cities for Pharaoh—Pithom and Rameses.[e] They built every wall and all the fortifications[f] that had fallen down[g] in the cities of Egypt. 15/ They were enslaving them by force, but however much they would make them suffer[a] the more they would multiply and the more they would increase.[b] 16/ The Egyptians considered the Israelites detestable.

Textual Notes

1a all of them] Lat. (and MS. 21) om., perhaps when the similarity between *universi* and the next word—*unianimes*—led to haplography.
 b each one loved the other] The forms are sg. in Eth., pl. in Lat.
 c each one helped the other] Eth. phrases as a second result clause, but Lat. has an imperfect tense verb. The verb in Lat.—*adiungebat*—means "joined," where Eth. reads "helped." It may be that a form of *adjuvo* ("to help") has been miscopied (see VanderKam, *Jubilees* 2:300). For the two nouns, Eth. phrases with "a man ... his brother," and Lat. as "a brother ... his neighbor."
 d and increased] Reading a verbal form is preferable to the more common *fadfāda* (without a prefixed conjunction) of 12 17 20 21 39 42 47 48 58; MSS. 12 39 42 47 48 58 add "and became numerous" after *fadfāda*.
 e even] Almost all Eth. MSS. read a conjunction before "for ten" (35 58 lack one), though the clause it introduces is strange in the context: and ten weeks of years (were) all the days of Joseph's life (with several

1117

incorrect case endings). Rendering the conjunction as "even" may be the best way to handle it (see VanderKam, *Jubilees* 2:300); no other versional evidence is available here.

2a his father] pr. "the death of" 35.

b were honoring] 2Q20 3 uses the expression "were giving honor" (verb + noun) where Eth. expresses the same continuous action through a causative verbal form without a noun following.

3a 110] "108" 12; "130" 17 21 38; "140" 63.

b three] "2" 17.

c entire] om. 17.

4a He died] om. 20 21 25; "(they) died" 38.

5a he] "Joseph" 21 35.

b the land of] om. 17 21 38 39 42 47 48 58.

6a He made them swear] The Gk. catena citation begins here; since the citation lacks the preceding context, it names Joseph as the subject of the verb and "his brothers" as the object.

b would surely not allow him to be brought out] So Gk. Eth. = "would not again bring him out." The difference involves "allow" (a form of ἐπιτρέφω) in Gk. and "again" (a form of ἐπιστρέφω lies behind it) in Eth., two verbs that look very much alike.

c and be buried in the land of Canaan on the day of his death] The best Eth. reading is: "to bury him on the day in the land of Canaan." The reading is suspect because "on the day" should be followed by information identifying which one the day was. Only MS. 39 transposes to read "and on the day to bury him." The Gk. lacks mention of burying but reads "in the land of Canaan on the day of his death." "And bury him" may be original to the text (and om. by Gk.), but "the day of his death" in Gk. seems the more likely reading.

d while he was living in the land of Asur] The Gk. citation lacks these words, but they may be meaningful in the context (see the commentary).

e fought] "was killed" 12 25 (cf. 63); "were killed" 21; "(they) fought" 38 42 47.

f in the valley] The Gk. lacks these words in this place in the text (but see below).

g there] + "in the valley" = Gk.

h the borders of Egypt] So the Gk. Eth. = "the gates of Ermon" (apparently a city name). See VanderKam, "Another Citation," 383–84. Werman (*Jubilees*, 526 n. 30) thinks the Eth. reading resulted from a corruption of ορων, but that would not explain the full expression.

7a He] Gk. supplies the name *Machmarōn*.

b to enter] + "into Egypt" = Gk.

c ruled] "arose" = Gk. (as in Exod 1:8).

d so he returned to the land of Canaan] Gk. lacks.

e entering or leaving] So Gk. and MSS. 20 25 38 58; the other Eth. copies reverse "entering" and "leaving." The preposition "in/into" read by Gk. and Eth. (not realized in the translation) seems strange, however, after "leaving."

8a in the (this 12 44 63) forty-sixth jubilee, in the sixth week, during its (om. 12 17 21 38ᵗ 39 42 47 48 58 63) second year] Gk. lacks this date formula (as it does in 47:1).

b in the land of (om. 44) Egypt] "in the coffin in Egypt" = Gk. (see Gen 50:26).

9a Then the king—its second year] This sentence is lacking in Gk. The catena citation leaves out Jubilees' date formulas; in this case the first clause, apparently presupposed by v. 11 below, was omitted with it. Note that the beginning of this sentence (the verb "went out") and of the next one ("brought out") are similar and could have caused the omission.

b the (forty-seventh)] "this" 12 44.

c The Israelites (lit., "The sons of Israel")] "The sons of Jacob" = Gk.

d Jacob's sons] "Israel's sons" = Gk. Eth. seems preferable here and in the preceding reading because it was the Israelites who brought out the bones of the actual sons of Jacob.

e (buried) them] The pl. object is expressed in Gk.; Eth., which must have the same meaning, reads a sg. object (except MS. 38).

f of (the double cave)] So Gk.; Eth. reads "in."

g cave] + "in Hebron" = Gk. Note that Hebron is mentioned in the next verse.

10a Your] Since the angel is telling Moses about his family, "your" is appropriate. The Gk. citation adapts the quotation to another context by substituting "of Moses."

b Amram] So Gk. Eth. has confused the name with Abram. See VanderKam, *Jubilees* 2:302.

c them] "him" Gk., but its referent is not apparent.

11a and closed] "the king of Egypt closed" = Gk. (= MSS. 35 58, though they read "the king of Egypt" at an earlier point in the clause). Possibly "the king of Egypt," which Gk. reads at the end of the verse, was lost from the Eth. tradition by parablepsis with the preceding "of Egypt," but the words may be an addition to clarify which king closed the gates of Egypt. See VanderKam, "Another Citation," 387.

12a He] "The king of Canaan" Lat., but this can hardly be correct, as the king of Egypt is speaking to his subjects. The sequel makes this transparent. Berger (*Jubiläen*, 539 n. a to v. 12) and Kugel (*Walk through* Jubilees, 192; "Jubilees," 440), however, accept the Lat. reading. See Charles, *Ethiopic Version*, 164 n. 14.

b against the Israelites] om. Lat., but both Gk. and Eth. read it.

c He said to the Egyptians] The Gk. citation ends with "to make them suffer," so only Eth. and Lat. remain. Lat. prefixes "At that time," which is present neither

in Eth. nor in Exod 1:9. Lat. also has the Egyptians speaking, not the king addressing the people of Egypt. Perhaps ειπεν αιγυπτοις became ειπον αιγυπτοι under the influence of the reading "the king of Canaan" at the beginning of the verse. See VanderKam, *Jubilees* 2:302.
13a increased] + "greatly" Lat.
b Come on] + "therefore" Lat. (so LXX Exod 1:10).
c let us outwit them] "let us make them suffer" Lat. (see the next sentence).
d make them suffer] "humble them" Lat.
e in slavery] "through their works" Lat. (see LXX Exod 1:11). Either reading is defensible.
f before (war)] "so that . . . not" Lat.
g they, too, fight (lit., "they, too, before they fight")] "then they too will fight" Lat.
h Otherwise they will unite with the enemy] Lat. om. but has "our enemies" (so also MSS. 21 39 58), which seems a remnant of a longer reading. Perhaps Lat. omitted by parablepsis (*super . . . super*?). See VanderKam, *Jubilees* 2:303.

14a He] "The king" Lat.
b taskmasters] "those who carry out tasks/work" Lat.; both seem to have about the same meaning. See VanderKam, *Jubilees* 2:303–4.
c in slavery] Lat., as it did in v. 13, reads "through their works."
d They built] pr. "They commanded them and" 39 42 47 48 58.
e Rameses] + "Oon" Lat. (so LXX Exod 1:11).
f and all the fortifications] om. Lat. (from "all—all").
g had fallen down] "had been destroyed" Lat. The two meanings are close together.
15a make them suffer] So MT SP Exod 1:12; Lat. "humble them" renders LXX Exod 1:12.
b and the more they would increase] om. Lat. Mss. 21 35 42 47 om. "the more," and MS. 20 om. "they would increase."

Commentary

Jubilees 46 presents the segment of sacred history stretching from the lives of Joseph and his brothers after Jacob's death to the beginning of the Egyptian bondage. Roughly parallel material is found in Gen 50:15–Exod 1:14, that is, the narrative in the chapter bridges the divide between Genesis and Exodus with no indication of a break. Throughout the years that remained in Joseph's life ideal conditions prevailed in Egypt: in the era of his wise leadership, his family and the Egyptians prospered and enjoyed positive relationships with one another. Once Joseph and his brothers reached the end of their days, the issue of burying them arose. Naturally, they should have been interred with their ancestors, and Joseph in particular ordered that his bones were to repose in Canaan. However, the international situation proved an obstacle to travel between the two places. It turns out that war raged between Canaan and Egypt; the dangerous situation forced a delay in transferring the bones of Joseph's brothers and set in motion an even longer delay in removing Joseph's remains. Eventually, during a lull in the fighting, their families were able to bury the eleven brothers in Canaan but, oddly, not Joseph, whose body remained entombed in Egypt.

The difficult military situation of Egypt serves as the context for initiating the oppression of the Israelites. The new king of Egypt who had temporarily prevailed over the Canaanite king only to suffer defeat at his hands was the one who conceived the plan of enslaving the Israelites lest these refugees from Canaan join forces with the king of Canaan and fight against the Egyptians who had hosted them for years.

An interesting feature of the chapter is that the angel who is revealing the story to Moses reaches the stage where Exodus talks about Moses's time. As a result, with the words "Your father Amram" (v. 10) he begins telling Moses about his immediate family and in the next chapters will remind him of events in his own life.

The chapter can be outlined as follows:
1-2   Harmonious relations in Egypt
3-11 Deaths of the twelve brothers with burials delayed by warfare
12-16 The Egyptian king initiates oppressive measures against the Israelites.

Evidence in three other languages joins the complete Ethiopic version in attesting parts of the chapter.

Latin   vv. 1, 12-16
Hebrew (2Q20 frg. 1)   vv. 1-3
Greek   vv. 6-12[1]

1-2 Harmonious Relations in Egypt

The author depicts a time of utopian conditions after the death of Jacob and before that of Joseph.

■ **1** During the many years of Joseph's rule in Egypt, the relations between the members of Jacob's family were exactly the way they were supposed to be, and they prospered while the situation lasted. Genesis does not describe this sort of circumstance, but the writer found something of a basis for his words in Gen 47:27 (set before Jacob's death): "Thus Israel settled in the land of Egypt, in the region of Goshen; and they gained possession in it, and were fruitful and multiplied exceedingly." The fecundity that is a significant part of the creation mandate (Gen 1:22, 28) and the post-flood command to humanity (9:1, 7) and that figures in divine blessings of or instructions to patriarchs (see 35:11; cf. 17:1-6; 26:22) is here related to Israel and signals a fulfillment of the ancient promise. The same kind of statement is made in Exod 1:7 regarding the time after Joseph and his brothers died: "But the Israelites were fruitful and prolific; they multiplied and grew exceedingly strong so that the land was filled with them." Perhaps inferring that if Jacob's descendants were fertile both before (Gen 47:27) and after the period in question (Exod 1:7) they were in the interval between as well, the writer of Jubilees takes up elements from both verses and applies them to the time between Jacob's death and the deaths of his sons (see also Gen 50:20). The first part of v. 1 may be influenced by Exod 1:7, where their multiplying in the land of Egypt is mentioned, but the reference to becoming a "populous/great nation [*hezba bezuḫa/gentem magnam*]" reflects Gen 50:20, where Joseph is reassuring his brothers that he will not take revenge on them: "Even though you intended to do harm to me, God intended it for good, in order to preserve a numerous people [עם רב], as he is doing today." This verse from Genesis supplies helpful information: Israel became a great nation while Joseph and his brothers were still alive. The double expression "became numerous and increased very much" reproduces the one in Gen 47:27.[2] So, in one verse of Jubilees there are four ways of saying that the population of Jacob's descendants mushroomed.[3] For Jubilees as for Genesis, the age of the nation has begun.

These four assertions about Israelite numbers—two on each side—enfold clauses that are not present in Genesis but are thematic in Jubilees: "all of them were of the same mind so that each one loved the other and each one helped the other." Both statements about the nature of the harmony Jacob's offspring enjoyed are expressions of how the author understood the commandment about brotherly love in Lev 19:17-18; they also articulate the theme of family unity that he has emphasized several times. The words "all of them were of the same mind" read literally, "all of them were the same in their heart(s)".[4] A similar line occurs in 43:14 (cf. 36:17) where Joseph observes the result of the test he administered to his brothers: "When Joseph saw that the minds of all of them were in harmony . . ." (lit., "that the heart of them all was the same"). That spirit continued to characterize the brothers and their families throughout the days of Joseph after Jacob was no longer on the scene.[5] It is no wonder that the writer chose not to reproduce the scene in which Joseph's brothers worried that, after Jacob was

---

1   The passage comes from the Catena to Genesis and is cited from F. Petit, *La chaîne sur la Genèse*, 4:453-54 (#2270, lines 1-21 [lines 22-23 correspond with Jub 47:1]). See also the study in VanderKam, "Another Citation."

2   Van Ruiten thinks the theme of multiplication in Jub 46:1-2 is taken from Exod 1:7 and that the author of Jubilees reverses Exod 1:6 (the deaths of Joseph, his brothers, and their generation) and 1:7 ("Between Jacob's Death and Moses' Birth," 473, 470, 474). That does not seem fully accurate, as the writer draws on the three passages discussed above and hence does not actually reverse Exod 1:6 and 7.

3   In Gen 41:52 Joseph explained the name of his son Ephraim as meaning: "For God has made me fruitful in the land of my misfortune" (see also 48:19-20 and the blessing Jacob pronounced on Joseph in Gen 49:22, 25-26). None of these passages appears in Jubilees.

4   Latin lacks "all of them." Ethiopic has a singular form "heart," where Latin reads a plural, but the meaning is the same.

5   Although Genesis contains no passage corresponding closely with Jub 46:1-2, Gen 50:21 might have suggested the positive relations lauded in Jubilees: "In this way he [Joseph] reassured

no longer available to act as a check on him, he would repay them in kind for their cruelty to him (Gen 50:15-21). The Genesis section suggested disunity and may have involved another lie by the brothers—that Jacob had told them to ask Joseph's forgiveness for what they had done. In Jubilees the children of Israel are unified, of the same mind. This seems to be the reason for the omission of Gen 50:15-21 by the author of Jubilees rather than a desire to downplay Joseph's role at the time.[6]

Livneh helpfully describes how the lines offer the writer's understanding of the teachings in Lev 19:17-18 as they applied on a national level:

> This expression [about having the same mind] refers to "intent," constituting an interpretation of the injunction "You shall not hate your kinsman in your heart" (Lev 19:17a). Secondly, the good intentions facilitated a situation in which "each one loved the other and each one helped the other." The first of the sentences clearly alludes to the commandment to "Love your fellow as yourself," which . . . denotes living together in peace. The second—"each one helped the other" recalls Isa 41:6: "Each one helped the other. . . ."[7]

Livneh does not claim that "each one helped the other" comes from Isa 41:6 but merely that the verbs "love" and "help" function as parallels in some contexts (e.g., 2 Chr 19:2): the command to love entails not only a feeling but actions as well.[8]

In Jubilees the dramatic growth in the Israelite population continued while Joseph remained alive, a period that lasted ten weeks of years, that is, seventy years. The details for the several phases in Joseph's life are given below in v. 3, but the figure of seventy years for the segment of his biography after the death of Jacob follows from these data:

Joseph was thirty years of age when he entered
 Pharaoh's service (Gen 41:46 // Jub 40:11)
Years of plenty: seven (Gen 41:47, 53; Jub 40:12)
Years of famine until the family arrives in Egypt: two
 (Gen 45:6 // Jub 43:17)
Joseph dies at age 110 (Gen 50:22 // Jub 46:3)

If one subtracts 39 (that is, 30 + 7 + 2) from 110, the result is 71. The writer rounds that number off to make it correspond with a multiple of his base-seven chronological system. The period of burgeoning numbers, then, includes not only the time after Jacob died (Joseph survived him by fifty-four or fifty-five years) but also the seventeen years the elderly patriarch lived in Egypt.[9]

■ 2 The description of the remarkable situation in Egypt continues in v. 2, where the author resorts to an expression he has already used two times in connection with ideal periods and will employ once more (see 50:5): "There was no satan[10] or any evil one" throughout

---

them, speaking kindly to them." *Targum Neofiti* Gen 50:21 reads: "And he consoled them and spoke to their hearts *words of peace*."

6 For the thesis that the writer reduces Joseph's "spiritual authority," see Halpern-Amaru, "Burying the Fathers," 138–39; it is doubtful that her interpretation comports fully with Jub 46:1-2 and other elements in the Joseph story. For family unity as the more salient point, see van Ruiten, "Between Jacob's Death and Moses' Birth," 471–72. For the role of Joseph and the transfer of elements from the blessings on Ephraim and Manasseh in Genesis 48 to Levi and Judah in Jubilees, making Levi, Judah, and Joseph the primary heirs in Jubilees, see Pauline P. Buisch, "The Absence and Influence of Genesis 48 (the Blessing of Ephraim and Manasseh) in the *Book of Jubilees*," *JSP* 26 (2017) 255–73.

7 Livneh, "Love Your Fellow,'" 195; cf. Halpern-Amaru, "Burying the Fathers," 137–38. For fraternal harmony, see also T. Jos. 17:2-3.

8 Livneh, "'Love Your Fellow,'" 195–96. She suggests the help in question may refer to fighting together against a common enemy (see 20:2).

9 It is true, as Halpern-Amaru observes, that placement of the great surge in population at this earlier time contrasts with Exod 1:7, but it fits with the notice in Gen 47:27 (as she also points out) and thus does not offer a new chronology vis-à-vis Genesis and replace a family story with a national one—it is during Joseph's life that good times prevail ("Burying the Fathers," 136–37). See also van Ruiten ("Between Jacob's Death and Moses' Birth," 474–75) for a similar critique of Halpern-Amaru.

10 In Gen 50:15 the brothers wonder whether Joseph "still bears a grudge against us [ישטמנו]," using a verb that seems to have some association with the word "satan" (e.g., BDB, 966, s.v. שטם).

Joseph's remaining years.[11] In the apocalyptic section of chap. 23, when the angel is describing the new age after "the children will begin to study the laws" (v. 26) and their numbers increase as well as their life spans (vv. 27-28), he predicts: "There will be neither a satan nor any evil one" (v. 29). The next use of it comes in the section regarding Joseph's exemplary leadership of Egypt on behalf of the monarch: "Pharaoh's rule was just, and there was no satan or any evil one" (40:9). Now the writer applies the same language to the era from the death of Jacob to the death of Joseph. The language is related to the way that Solomon, another wise ruler, characterized the peaceful conditions prevailing in the early days of his reign in contrast to those of his father: "But now the LORD my God has given me rest on every side; there is neither adversary [שטן] nor misfortune" (1 Kgs 5:4 [Heb., v. 18]).[12] The context in 1 Kings reports that "Israel and Judah were as numerous as the sand by the sea; they ate and drank and were happy" (1 Kgs 4:20). The family descended from Jacob follows the divine law mandated for them (fraternal harmony), and the result of their obedience is the removal of those beings—satan and evil one—whose purpose is to disrupt proper relations and make people sin (cf. 10:5, 8; 15:31).

The extraordinary nature of the time was due to the blessing of God upon the obedient Israelites, but the writer adds that the Egyptians also played their part: "all the Egyptians were honoring the children of Israel for all of Joseph's lifetime."[13] As Livneh points out, the wording reminds one of what Rebekah predicted would happen if Esau and his brother Jacob loved each other: "Then you will be prosperous, my sons, and be honored on the earth. Your enemy will not be happy over you. You will become a blessing and an object of kindness in the view of all who love you" (Jub 35:20).[14] When Joseph began ruling Egypt, "All of Pharaoh's princes, all of his servants, and all who were doing the king's work loved him because he conducted himself in a just way" (40:8). On two earlier occasions the writer chose not to copy statements from Genesis indicating an Egyptian distaste for Hebrews (43:32) or for people who, like them, were shepherds (46:34). The honors accorded by the Egyptians will end swiftly after Joseph's death, but the host nation received remarkable blessings because of Joseph's guidance and reciprocated with gratitude. Their honoring Jacob's family serves as a fulfillment of the promise repeated to the patriarchs that the nations would be blessed or would bless themselves through them (see Gen 12:3; 18:18; 22:18; 26:24; 28:14; Jub 12:22-23; 20:10; 21:25; 24:11; 27:23). This was most directly the case for the Egyptians,[15] but in a sense it was true for other peoples as well since they too came to Egypt to procure food and received it because of Joseph (Gen 41:54-57; Jub 43:23). It is truly remarkable that the conditions pictured in Jub 46:1-2 occur in Egypt, not in the land promised to the patriarchs.

3-11 Deaths of the Twelve Brothers with Burials Delayed by Warfare

Since the situation depicted in vv. 1-2 obtained while Joseph was alive, the writer turns next to the chronology for the major events in his life.

■ **3** Most of the numbers for Joseph derive from Genesis or can be inferred from it, but the author adds a few specifications.

Seventeen years in Canaan: Gen 37:2; cf. Jub 34:10 (the year is 2149). Since Joseph was born/named in 2134 (see Jub 28:24), he would have been fifteen (or sixteen) when Jacob sent him to his brothers. Jubilees 39:2, however, gives his age as seventeen when he was brought to Egypt.

Ten years as a slave: In the story itself, Genesis does not state how long Joseph served in Potiphar's house; there are only vague time indicators in Genesis 39 (vv. 7,

---

11 It is difficult to believe that the reference to the end of Joseph's life here is meant only to define the end of an era rather than to reflect his standing as head of the family—as Werman (*Jubilees*, 527) claims—or that it indicates only his influence in the public arena, not the spiritual one—as Halpern-Amaru ("Burying the Fathers," 136-39) maintains.

12 Livneh, "'Love Your Fellow,'" 196-97; cf. Halpern-Amaru, "Burying the Fathers," 137-38.

13 See Gen 45:13, where Joseph mentions how much he is honored in Egypt, and T. Jos. 20:6. Josephus (*Ant.* 2.199) refers to the happy time the brothers spent in Egypt throughout this period.

14 Livneh, "'Love Your Fellow,'" 197.

15 See, e.g., Hamilton, *Genesis 1-17*, 375-76.

10), and in Jub 39:8 there is reference to "one year and a second" (but see the commentary on the passage).[16]

Three years a prisoner: Again Genesis does not give the duration of the sentence. In the context Gen 41:1 dates Pharaoh's dreams two years after his officers were removed from the royal penitentiary; as a result, Joseph would have been there at least a little longer than two years. Jubilees 39:13 says that Joseph "remained there for two years," although the notice precedes the imprisonment of the officers and Pharaoh's dreams so it probably does not state the full time he spent in the prison (see the commentary on the passage).

Eighty years as ruler of Egypt: Genesis never mentions the length of Joseph's reign, but the number of years was an easy inference from his age at death—110 (Gen 50:22, 26). Since he began ruling for Pharaoh at age thirty (Gen 41:46 // Jub 40:11) and he apparently remained in his high office the remainder of his life, he reigned eighty years (110 – 30 = 80).

Exactly the same numbers figure in a passage from Procopius of Gaza (c. 475–c. 538), who compiled a catena on the Octateuch. It may not be a citation of Jubilees since the order of clauses and the verbs he uses are in part different but the data agree with those in Jub 46:3: "Joseph spent seventeen years in Canaan, for ten years he endured slavery, three years he spent in prison, and for eighty years he was second to the king and exercised authority in the entire land of Egypt. He died at one hundred ten years."[17]

■ **4** The verse reports the deaths of the twelve brothers and all those belonging to that generation. It is an exact reproduction of Exod 1:6, apart from lacking the name Joseph as the first subject (replaced by "He" since he was the subject of the preceding sentence, though his name occurs just before the line in Exod 1:6 as well).[18] Neither text explicitly indicates a sequence in their deaths, and in fact one never learns the final ages reached by any of Joseph's eleven brothers (v. 8, however, says that Joseph died first). The only point the writers of Exodus and Jubilees make is that the fourth generation in patriarchal history has now passed from the scene, after which time a very different situation arises. Of all the brothers, Genesis notes the death only of Joseph (50:26); Exodus then repeats the information. The writer of Jubilees records Joseph's passing in three places (vv. 3, 4, and 8), but in the latter two cases adds the deaths of his brothers as well.

■ **5** After entering the notes about the deaths of the brothers' generation, the writer returns to the end of Genesis to rewrite Joseph's instructions for handling his bones. In Genesis he waxes rather theological in telling his brothers what is to be done: "'I am about to die; but God will surely come to [visit] you, and bring you up out of this land to the land that he swore to Abraham, to Isaac, and to Jacob.' So Joseph made the Israelites swear, saying, 'When God comes to [visit] you, you shall carry up my bones from here'" (Gen 50:24-25).[19] The theological language drops out of the parallel in Jubilees: "Before he died he ordered the Israelites to take his bones along at the time when they would leave the land of Egypt" (a rewriting of Gen 50:25).[20] In Genesis, Joseph speaks to his brothers (v. 24) but then addresses his orders to "the Israelites" (= the sons of Israel, v. 25); in Jubilees his words are directed to all (literally) "the sons of Israel," perhaps because his brothers would not be the ones to transport his bones. The line in Jubilees says nothing about a divine visitation (stressed twice in

---

16 In T. Jos. 4:4 he fasts seven years while a slave, but the sequel (through chap. 7) may suggest that more time was spent in servitude (cf. also 11:8; 15:1). He remains with Potiphar fourteen years in L.A.B. 8:9, but as the text does not speak of a period in prison the number covers the years from Joseph's arrival in Egypt to his elevation by Pharaoh.

17 The text is #2268 in Petit, *La chaîne sur la Genèse*, 4:452 (translation by VanderKam). In the Catena itself, the passage is attributed to Eusebius. Note also Codex Athos Koutloumous 178 11v, lines 5-7, cited by Denis, *Fragmenta*, 99: all of the numbers in it are the same as those in v. 3 except the three years it assigns to his time as a slave (cf. VanderKam, *Jubilees* 2:301).

18 As van Ruiten explains, the writer bypasses Exod 1:1-5 (the names of Jacob's sons and the number of people in Jacob's family) because the verses add no new information to the earlier list (Jub 44:11-34) ("Between Jacob's Death and Moses' Birth," 472).

19 Unlike his father (Gen 47:29-31; 49:29-33), Joseph does not specify where in the land they were to bring his bones. The Israelites will eventually bury them in Shechem (Josh 24:32), not Hebron.

20 See van Ruiten, "Between Jacob's Death and Moses' Birth," 478-79.

Genesis) and God's leading in the exodus. It sounds as if Joseph simply figures they will depart from Egypt at some unknown point.[21] After all, the famine had ended years before, meaning there was no need for the brothers and their families to remain in Egypt. Why should they not return to Canaan, their homeland and the land promised to their ancestors?

■ 6 Genesis 50:25 has Joseph make "the Israelites" (though he is talking to his brothers in the preceding verse) swear to remove his remains from Egypt when God would come to them. The interchange of addressees is interesting: "his brothers" (v. 24) and "the Israelites" (v. 25, lit., the sons of Israel) may refer to the same people or the latter may have a broader reference.[22] If the eleven brothers are the ones he places under obligation, the claim could raise questions for someone who remembers the whole story about Joseph and his brothers. Why did Joseph feel the need to make his brothers swear an oath? Was there a problem? Did he still not trust them[23] (and perhaps their families) or did he fear they and their offspring would forget about his corpse when they returned home? Why would the brothers or the next generations not transport his bones to Canaan? Genesis does not furnish the reason why he exacted a sworn agreement from them, but Jubilees supplies one.

At this point the author departs from the text of Genesis to insert additional information clarifying the need for an oath from the sons of Israel[24] and addressing other questions as well. As it turns out, it was not that he distrusted his kinsmen (this would hardly be consistent with vv. 1-2 above); rather, Joseph was aware that the Egyptians would not allow reburial of his body in Canaan because fighting had broken out between the Canaanites and the Egyptians making travel between the two lands impossible. That is, Joseph did not anticipate the prompt burial in Canaan that his father received (Gen 50:1-14; Jub 45:15),[25] but it was not a sign of family disharmony—the Egyptians and their foreign relations were the problem. In Jubilees' chronology, Joseph died fifty-four or fifty-five years after Jacob (45:13 and 46:8). At some juncture between the deaths of Jacob (2188) and Joseph (2242) the Canaan–Egypt war broke out.

Though such a war is not mentioned in Genesis–Exodus, it is an important literary element in the larger context in Jubilees for understanding events related at the end of Genesis and the beginning of Exodus. The writer intersperses details about the conflict throughout his narrative regarding the death and burial of Joseph and his brothers and the beginning of Israelite slavery in Egypt.

Verse 6 introduces the war as the reason for the oath Joseph required in Gen 50:25. The king of Canaan,[26] whose name is Makamaron,[27] and who lived "in the land

---

[21] Halpern-Amaru finds further evidence here for her thesis about the diminution of Joseph's spiritual role in Jubilees compared with Genesis: "The words attributed to him in *Jubilees* imply nothing that would suggest a mediating role between the patriarchal past and the Israelite future; all that would imply a transmission of covenant has been deleted. Only a certain prescience remains in Joseph's prediction of future political events in Egypt (*Jub.* 46:6)" ("Burying the Fathers," 140). Much of what she says is true, but Joseph's role is still larger than that of the brothers. In addition, the writer's concern to document family unity and solidarity is the more important influence on the rewriting.

[22] Skinner, *Genesis*, 540: "*his brethren* are here the Israelites as a whole." Westermann comments: "This can only mean he has his brothers take the oath as representatives of the later generation of the Israelites of the exodus" (*Genesis 37–50*, 209). In *Tg. Ps.-J.* Gen 50:25 Joseph makes the sons of Israel swear to tell their children to bring up his bones from Egypt at the time appointed by God.

[23] See Hamilton, *Genesis 18–50*, 711.

[24] See the textual note for the variant regarding whom Joseph subjected to the oath: "them" (Ethiopic) referring to the Israelites (lit., the sons of Israel) in v. 5; "his brothers" (Greek), presumably supplied from Gen 50:24. See VanderKam, "Another Citation," 380–81.

[25] The Greek citation shows (see the textual note) that the proper reading is not "on the day" as in the Ethiopic version but "on the day of his death." The meaning is "at the general time of his death," since he would likely have received extended honors on his death as Jacob did (Gen 50:1-3).

[26] This is the title borne by Jabin of Hazor in Judg 4:2, 23-24.

[27] The name is known only from the story about the war and in this one verse (the Greek citation repeats it in v. 7). It is spelled *mākamāron* (*mamkaron* or *memkaron* in 39 42 47 48) in the Ethiopic tradition and μαχμαρων in Greek. For attempts to identify the monarch, see the excursus below.

of Asur,"[28] fought with the king of Egypt in an unnamed valley[29] and killed him. He followed up his victory on the field of battle by pursing the defeated Egyptians to "the borders of Egypt."[30]

■ **7** Makamaron and his forces would have invaded Egypt itself, but a new[31] king (see Exod 1:8) who replaced the slain Egyptian monarch succeeded in turning the tide of the war. Because he and his army somehow became the stronger side, they forced the Canaanite king to retreat to his own land. Nevertheless, concern for security dictated that the "gates," that is, the approaches[32] to Egypt be closed—no one entered or left because of the dangerous situation (see Josh 6:1).[33] It appears from the sequence in the text that the military movements described in vv. 6-7 started around the time Joseph died in 2242, though no precise date for them is given.[34] With the gates closed, bringing Joseph's bones to Canaan was no longer an option.

■ **8** Though he had already mentioned it in vv. 3 and 4, the writer now records the death of Joseph and assigns it to the year 2242.

Genesis 50:26	Jubilees 46:8
And Joseph died, being one hundred ten years old; he was embalmed and placed in a coffin in Egypt.	Joseph died in the forty-sixth jubilee, in the sixth week, during its second year [2242]. He was buried in the land of Egypt, and all his brothers died after him.

As happens regularly, the writer translates a date or number in Genesis into his jubilee/week/year formula and pegs it into his chronology of the world. Once again, the chronology yields an inconsistency, this time a slight one: Joseph was born in 2134 (28:24) and died in 2242, a total of 108 or 109, not the 110 of Jub 46:3. The ancient versions of Gen 50:26 preserve no final age for Joseph apart from 110 years. Jubilees lacks the reference to embalming, just as it did for Jacob (Gen 50:2-3 is not reproduced in Jub 45:15-16), but both texts mention that he, unlike his father, was buried in Egypt (Eth. Jubilees lacks the coffin, while the Greek citation has it). The notice of his burial there, not in Canaan, is an item crying out for explanation. Also unlike Genesis, the writer adds that Joseph's brothers died and specifies that their deaths were later than his (as implied by Gen 50:24; see *Gen. Rab.* 100:3). The deaths of the twelve are noted in Exod 1:6; perhaps the order of the presentation in that verse suggested that Joseph died first: "Then Joseph died, and all his brothers." It was so understood in *Tg. Ps.-J.* Exod 1:6: "Joseph died, and *after him* all his brothers *died*, and all that generation." So the lives of the eleven came to an end at various times between 2242 (Joseph's death) and 2263 (the year of their burials; see v. 9 below).

■ **9** Subsequently, in the year 2263 (twenty-one or twenty-two years after Joseph's death), the new Egyptian king set out to fight the king of Canaan (the place is not identified). Although the text does not mention it, the Egyptian offensive seems to have opened the gates of Egypt[35] because it was the occasion when the "Israelites brought out all the bones of Jacob's sons except Joseph's bones. They buried them in the field of the double

---

28	The Greek citation lacks the prepositional phrase. The name 'asur occurs one other time in Eth. Jubilees—13:1—where it probably represents Hazor (see Zuurmond, "Asshur in Jubilees 13.1?" *JSP* 4 [1989] 87-89). If the place where Makamaron lived was in the land of Hazor, it would provide another link with the context of Judges 4 and Joshua 11. See also VanderKam, "Another Citation," 382.
29	Both the Ethiopic version and the Greek citation locate the battle "in the valley" but place the phrase at different spots in the line.
30	The Greek citation reads "the borders of Egypt," where the Ethiopic texts have the curious "the gates of Ermon." For attempts to identify "Ermon," see VanderKam, *Jubilees* 2:301; "Another Citation," 383-84. Both the Ethiopic and Greek texts refer to "the gates of Egypt" in vv. 7 and 11.
31	The Ethiopic and Greek texts called him "another new king." The Hebrew versions of Exod 1:8 use the adjective "new" (חדש) for him, while LXX has "another" (ετερος). In Jubilees both adjectives are used.
32	It is unusual to refer to the gates of something other than a city or a building, but there are a few examples in the HB. Jeremiah 15:7 reads "the gates of the land," and in Nah 3:13 the prophet declares, "The gates of your land are wide open to your foes; fire has devoured the bars of your gates."
33	For the parallel expression in Josh 6:1, see Halpern-Amaru, "Burying the Fathers," 151.
34	Ibid., 141-42. Whether the new king began reigning in Joseph's lifetime is not clear, but Halpern-Amaru thinks he did.
35	Halpern-Amaru writes: "the Egyptian king reopens the conflict and, as a consequence, also the gates" ("Burying the Fathers," 143).

cave in the mountain." Neither Genesis nor Exodus (or any other book in the HB) reports about the burials of Joseph's brothers, but, since they must have been interred somewhere, other sources fill the gap. Genesis supplies one hint about the place in a prediction made by Jacob to Joseph: "I am about to die, but God will be with you [pl.] and will bring you [pl.] again to the land of your ancestors" (Gen 48:21). The plural pronoun could have suggested that the remains of Joseph and his brothers would return to Canaan. There are, however, variants of the story that ends Genesis, and in them their burials play a part. For example, Stephen in Acts 7:15-16 indicates that all twelve were laid to rest in Shechem: "He himself [Jacob] died there as well as our ancestors [the twelve], and their bodies were brought back to Shechem and laid in the tomb that Abraham had bought for a sum of silver from the sons of Hamor in Shechem."[36] The idea that the brothers were buried in Hebron is known from other sources, including all of the individual units in the Testaments of the Twelve Patriarchs except the Testament of Joseph (but see 20:2). They end with a notice about burial in the cave/in Hebron (T. Reu. 7:2; T. Sim. 8:2; T. Levi 19:5; T. Jud. 26:4; T. Iss. 7:8; T. Zeb. 10:6-7; T. Dan 7:2; T. Naph. 9:1, 3; T. Gad 8:2, 5; T. Ash. 8:1-2; and T. Benj. 12:1-4).[37]

So the tradition regarding burial of the eleven in the cave of Machpelah in Hebron is more widely attested. Moreover, two of the testaments in the Testaments of the Twelve Patriarchs connect the burials with a war between Egypt and Canaan. Simeon's children "laid him in a coffin of incorruptible (acacia-)wood to carry up his bones to Hebron; and they brought them up secretly during the war with the Egyptians" (8:2). And the family of Benjamin, in the ninety-first year of Israel's arrival in Egypt,[38] transported his bones to Hebron "secretly during the war of Canaan" (12:3) and afterward returned to Egypt until the exodus (12:4). While Jubilees shares with these sources the theme of burying the brothers in Hebron, it lacks the element of secrecy in the Testaments of Simeon and Benjamin.

The description of the place where the Israelites interred the eleven brothers picks up some words that occur in references to the cave of Machpelah at the end of Genesis. When Jacob explains where he is to be buried, he says it is to be "in the cave in the field of Ephron the Hittite, in the cave in the field at Machpelah" (Gen 49:29-30; see "the field and the cave" in v. 32; 50:13: "the cave of the field at Machpelah"; cf. 23:9, 11, 17, 19-20; 25:9). The Greek citation of Jubilees adds "in Hebron" although the phrase could have been influenced by Gen 23:19 (and Hebron is mentioned in Jub 46:10 in both Ethiopic and Greek).

The writer is explicit, however, that the Israelites did not carry Joseph's bones with them on the expedition to the ancestral burial grounds in Canaan. Genesis 50:26 reports that he, after being embalmed, was placed in a coffin and buried in Egypt, not in the cave of Machpelah. In the case of Joseph the author of Jubilees had to contend with a different situation than the one met in the case of his brothers. There is no information about their final resting places in the HB, but there are two references to the fate of Joseph's bones, and these could hardly be ignored. Exodus 13:19, which quotes Gen 50:25, says, "And Moses took with him the bones of Joseph who had required a solemn oath of the Israelites, saying, 'God will surely take notice of you, and then you must carry my bones with you[39] from here.'" And, following the conquest and division of Canaan, the Israelites, according to Josh 24:32, buried Joseph's remains in the plot of land Jacob had purchased in Shechem, not the

---

36 For the confusion here between the lands purchased by Abraham and by Jacob and thus the mistaken name for the place where Jacob and eleven of his sons were buried, see Fitzmyer, *Acts of the Apostles*, 374.

37 See Josephus, *Ant.* 2.199: "His brethren also died after sojourning happily in Egypt. Their bodies were carried some time afterwards by their descendants [and their sons] to Hebron and buried there" (Thackeray, LCL). For the passages adduced above, see VanderKam, "*Jubilees* 46:6–47:1," 145–46.

38 The number fits in the chronology of Jubilees: Jacob reached Egypt in 2172 (45:1), and the burials occurred in 2263 (46:9; 2263 − 2172 = 91).

39 The word "you" is plural, presumably referring to the Israelites. However, *Gen. Rab.* 100:11 says regarding it, "And how do we know that the bones of the tribal ancestors too were taken up with him? Because it says, '*with you.*'" So the plural form was related to the brothers' remains.

place where his ancestors reposed. The writer of Jubilees could not, therefore, have the Israelites include the bones of Joseph with those of his brothers when they buried the latter in the cave of Machpelah. His remains were removed from Egypt much later and eventually interred in a different place—Shechem where Jacob had given him a double portion (Gen 48:22 // Jub 45:14).

It has to be said, nevertheless, that the author does not really explain the situation regarding Joseph in a very satisfactory way in 46:9, where he does not refer to a future removal of his bones and does not adduce the givens in Exod 13:19 and Josh 24:32. Instead, he leaves some questions unresolved. Possibly the reader is to assume that Joseph's special status in Egypt dictated that his bones were to remain there even after those of his siblings were transported to Hebron.[40]

■ 10 A puzzling feature of the stories at the end of Genesis is the fact that Jacob's family remained in Egypt well after the seven-year famine ended. The first five years they were there would have brought them to the end of the bad years, at which point the cause of their displacement to Egypt no longer existed. Twelve years then remained in Jacob's life during which time it would have made sense to return home (in Gen 46:4 God promised to bring him up from Egypt).[41] When he died, Joseph and his brothers, who left their families and flocks behind in Goshen (50:8), traveled with an Egyptian escort to bury him in Canaan, but, rather than staying there, "Joseph returned to Egypt with his brothers and all who had gone up with him to bury his father" (50:14)—just as he had promised Pharaoh (Gen 50:5).[42] In his final conversation with his relatives, Joseph expressed confidence that God would someday lead them back to the land of their ancestors, but there is no indication it would happen soon. No one in the chosen family seems very eager to resume life in the promised land.[43]

The issue arises in Jubilees to a limited extent. The angel tells Moses that while many returned to Egypt (cf. T. Benj. 12:4) a minority did not: "a few of them remained on the mountain of Hebron. Your father Amram remained with them." Moses's father Amram (see Exod 6:20) was part of the burial party (he would have been included among the household of Jacob mentioned in Gen 50:8), and he and a few others, for reasons unexplained, stayed "on the mountain of Hebron,"[44] the patriarchal home where the eleven had been buried,

---

40   Other explanations figure in later sources. One is in T. Sim. 8:3-4: "For the Egyptians guarded the bones of Joseph in the treasure-house of the palace. For the sorcerers had told them that on the departure of the bones of Joseph there would be darkness and gloom in the whole land of Egypt and a very great plague to the Egyptians, so that (even) with a lamp no one would recognize his brother." Kugel cites the relevant texts and assesses the exegetical treatments of the problem (*In Potiphar's House*, 128–55; cf. *Traditions*, 602–3). He finds the solution in Jubilees to be the oldest but also rather inadequate for explaining why his bones remained in Egypt longer than those of his brothers; as a result, other solutions had to be found (*In Potiphar's House*, 144). See also VanderKam, "*Jubilees* 46:6–47:1," 147–48.

41   In the parallel in Jub 44:6, however, the Lord adds that he will die in Egypt.

42   The Egyptian escort would have been for defensive purposes but may also have come along to ensure that Joseph and the others returned (see Hamilton, *Genesis 18–50*, 698).

43   *Targum Pseudo-Jonathan* Gen 50:25 touches on the problem: "Then Joseph made the sons of Israel swear that they would say *to their children, 'Behold, you will be enslaved in Egypt, but do not make plans to go up out of Egypt until the time that two deliverers come and say to you, "The Lord surely remembers you," and at the time that you go up* you shall bring up my bones from here.'" The reference is to Moses and Aaron; their appearance will mark the time when, as Joseph put it twice and Exod 13:19 repeats, God will visit them.

44   As Halpern-Amaru notes, in the only other places in Jubilees in which this phrase occurs the author uses it to refer to the dwelling place of Isaac (29:19) and Jacob (36:19; he also designates it as the home of Abraham in both passages) ("Burying the Fathers," 144–45). She concludes from this, as part of her argument that Jubilees "deconstructs" the characterization of Joseph in Genesis: "So, at the next historical juncture, the shift from freedom to enslavement in Egypt, Amram's residence on the mountain of Hebron provides a Levite, rather than Joseph-informed, connection between eras" (p. 145). Since Amram is not said to be a Levite here, the writer may not be highlighting a Levitical connection; instead, the reference draws a connection between the family of Moses and the three great patriarchs.

after the other members of the large contingent made their way back to Egypt. The brief reference to a group who stayed in the land comes without a context to clarify its meaning. However, another text that mentions the Canaan-Egypt war, the Aramaic work called Visions of Amram (4Q543-549),[45] provides more detail that may have been present in a source on which the author of Jubilees drew.

The Visions of Amram naturally focuses on the character named in the title. Its perspective is, therefore, different from the one in Jubilees, where, in the context of Egyptian-Canaanite conflict, he figures far less prominently—he is mentioned by name here in v. 10 (as one of those who remained in Canaan) and referenced as "your father" in 47:1 (when he returned to Egypt). A genealogy in Exodus 6 relates that Levi was the father of Kohath, one of whose sons was Amram; Amram and his wife Jochebed became the parents of Aaron and Moses (Exod 6:16-20). Amram, consequently, is two generations removed from the twelve patriarchs, with Levi being his grandfather. In the part of the war story narrated in the Visions of Amram, he is already married and at work with many others building the tombs of the patriarchs in Canaan. A reconstruction of the relevant part of the text on the basis of all the fragmentarily preserved copies that attest it yields the following first-person narrative:[46]

1. in this land and I went up to stay in the land of Canaan[   ]
2. to bury our fathers and I went up [and my father] Kohath [also went up] there
3. to remain and to live and to build [the] t[ombs of our fathers, and] many [men went up with us]
4. from the sons of my uncles together[every] man and from
5. our servants, very many, [until] (the) dead [would be bu]ried. [In] the first year of [my] authority, [when there was]
6. a frightening rumor of war, our [gro]up returned to the land of E[gyp]t and I went up to bury [them]
7. quickly, but they had not built the tombs of their fathers, and my father Koha[th and my wife Jochebed] left me [to stay]
8. and to build and to take to them all their needs from the land of Canaan. [And we lived in Hebron] while
9. we were building; and there was the war between Philistia and [E]gypt and [Philistia and Canaan] defeated [Egypt].
10. And the b[orders] of Egypt were closed and it was not possible [for my wife Jochebed to] come [to Canaan
11. forty-one years and we were not able to return to Egypt [   ]
12. Therefore n[ot   war] between Egypt and Canaan and Philistia.
13. During all this Jochebed [my] wi[fe was far away from me in the land of Egypt and   ]
14. my charge?[for with me] she was not. [But] I [did not] take another wife [for myself][47]

In this text, Amram says that he was among the large party of people, including his father and wife, who were in Canaan "to build [the] t[ombs of our fathers]" (line 3), who must be the brothers of Joseph. This was clearly no small project as it involved many workers and took some time. While they were in Canaan they heard "a

---

45 For the publication, see É. Puech, in DJD 31:283-405, with pls. XVI-XXII.

46 The text is cited from VanderKam, "Jubilees 46:6-47:1," 151-52, where a fifteen-line Aramaic unit (the one word from the fifteenth line in Aramaic is incorporated into the translation of line 14) is compiled from the five copies that preserve parts of the war section: 4Q543 frgs. 3-4; 544 frg. 1 1-8; 545 frg. 1a-b ii:11-19; 546 frg. 2 1-4; 547 frgs. 1-2 iii:1-8. Apart from a few small differences (e.g., in spelling), the texts agree word for word in overlapping sections. The restorations of missing text follow Puech's suggestions. Halpern-Amaru also offers a composite version of the text but distributed over nine lines ("Burying the Fathers," 146-47). She thinks that the lines reading "our [gro]up returned to the land of E[gyp]t and I went up to bury [them] quickly" (6-7 in the translation here) indicate that Amram first returned with the others to Egypt and then went back to Canaan, but it is not so clear that this is the case. He may not be including himself in "our [gro]up," and "I went up" need not mean a return to Canaan—something that, at any rate, seems unlikely in a context of imminent war. For a comparison of the two texts, see also van Ruiten, "Between Jacob's Death and Moses' Birth," 482-84.

47 The translation is modified from the ones given for the several copies by E. Cook in DSSR 3:412-43.

frightening rumor of war" (line 6) that induced many of the group to flee to Egypt for safety, leaving the tombs unfinished. His father Kohath and wife Jochebed were included with those who departed, but Amram and others (note "while *we* were building" [8-9]) remained behind in Canaan to continue the large construction project. War did in fact break out—one involving not only Canaan and Egypt but Philistia as well—and the borders of Egypt were closed. The war separated Amram and Jochebed from each other for the next forty-one years.

The author of Jubilees, who seems not to have used the version of the war story in the Visions of Amram as a direct source,[48] probably knew a fuller form of it that included the information about Amram's remaining in Canaan after most of Jacob's family members returned to Egypt. It accounts for the circumstances that the angel notes only very succinctly in Jub 46:10. The notice about "Your father Amram" is the first narrative indicator in the text that the story has reached the era of Moses.

■ **11** The final phase of the war set forth in Jubilees is the one that separates Amram and Jochebed in the Visions of Amram. The writer claims that, despite the window of opportunity opened by the Egyptian counteroffensive in which the family members could travel to Canaan to bury the eleven brothers, the king of Canaan subsequently "conquered the king of Egypt and closed the gates of Egypt."[49] The result was that Amram would have had no opportunity to return to his kin in Egypt as he remained in Hebron, but this detail is not an explicit part of the story in Jubilees (see, however, 47:1 and the commentary there), though it is significant in the Visions of Amram.

In summary, the war story as related by the Angel of the Presence to Moses consists of four stages

1. Canaanite victory, death of Egyptian king, Canaanite forces at the Egyptian border.
2. Egyptian response under a new king forcing the Canaanite army to return to their land; the entrances to Egypt are closed. Joseph's bones therefore must stay in Egypt.
3. Years later the Egyptians attack the Canaanites, and the offensive provides an opportunity for the Israelites to bury Joseph's eleven brothers in the cave of Machpelah.
4. Canaanite victory over the Egyptians leading to further closure of Egypt's gates (implying, though it is not mentioned in Jubilees, that Amram could not return to Egypt [for his later return, see 47:1]).

Throughout all four stages of the war, the bones of Joseph remained in Egypt.

The story as formulated in Jubilees achieves certain ends for the author. Most importantly, the military account provides answers to questions one might have in reading the end of Genesis and the beginning of Exodus. The first has to do with a delay anticipated by Joseph in the final disposal of his body: why did he not receive immediate burial in Canaan as Jacob did (unlike Jacob, he was buried in Egypt [50:26])? The partial response is that the conditions of war ruled out any journey to Canaan for burying him. A second and related puzzle is why he made the Israelites swear to remove his bones when they would eventually leave Egypt. The first stages of the war—victory by Canaan, pursuit to the borders of Egypt, and eventual withdrawal to Canaan—directly follow the notice that Joseph put the Israelites under oath regarding his corpse. According to the text, he insisted on the oath because he knew the Egyptians, in view of the war, would not permit that his bones be treated as Jacob's were.[50] There would be a delay of unspecified duration, but he wanted to make sure, however long it was, that his remains would eventually reach their proper resting place. He was eager to have his bones interred in Canaan, but circumstances dictated that he be buried at least temporarily in Egypt.[51]

Another question an inquiring reader might raise has to do with the remains of Joseph's eleven brothers. What

---

48 So Halpern-Amaru, "Burying the Fathers," 148–51; VanderKam, "*Jubilees* 46:6–47:1," 153–58.
49 The Greek citation has the king of Egypt closing the gates. See the textual note.
50 Note that in Gen 50:7-8 not only Jacob's family but also "the servants of Pharaoh, the elders of his household, and all the elders of the land of Egypt" accompanied Joseph on the burial mission; v. 9 adds that "chariots and charioteers went up with him." So Egyptian involvement was significant, and the entire journey was enabled by the monarch's permission (50:6).
51 Cf. van Ruiten, "Between Jacob's Death and Moses' Birth," 479; Kugel, *Walk through* Jubilees, 191; "Jubilees," 440.

happened to them, the ancestors of most of the Israelite tribes, and why are their corpses not mentioned when Moses removed Joseph's bones from Egypt (Exod 13:19) or when the Israelites buried his remains (Josh 24:32)? The account in Jubilees claims their families interred them in the cave of Machpelah as soon as there was a favorable opportunity when Egypt counterattacked Canaan.[52]

12-16[53] The Egyptian King Initiates Oppressive Measures against the Israelites

One other end achieved by introducing the war story into the narrative is a minor one and, it seems, hardly necessary: it explains how it came about that there was a new king in Egypt "who did not know Joseph" (Exod 1:8).[54] Joseph had died in 2242 and the new king may have come to the throne at about the same time, since he replaced his fallen predecessor at an early point in the conflict (see v. 7). He continued to reign for some time because he went to fight the Canaanites in 2263, twenty-one years later. That king (note that Jubilees does not call him "new" in this context), on the heels of a defeat at the hands of the Canaanite monarch, now adopts a new policy. Possibly this is how the author of Jubilees understood the relative clause "who did not know Joseph" (words he does not reproduce): he rejects the former favorable treatment granted to Joseph's family and now proposes to treat them harshly. This is a well-attested interpretation of the descriptor in early sources. *Targums Pseudo-Jonathan* and *Neofiti* render it literally and add that he did not conduct himself in line with Joseph's ways, while *Tg. Onq.* Exod 1:8 reads "Now there arose a new king over Egypt *who did not implement the law of Joseph.*" Other sources preserve a debate about the king as both "new" and not knowing Joseph.

When the Egyptians saw this, they promulgated new decrees against them; this is what is implied by AND THERE AROSE A NEW KING. Rab and Samuel explained this differently. One said it means a new king actually, and the other, merely that new decrees were issued by him, in that he made new decrees and tribulations for them. The reason of the one who maintains that it was a new king actually is because it says New; and the reason of him who thinks it means only that the decrees were renewed, is because it does not say "and he died, and there reigned." (*Exod. Rab.* 1:8; see also *b. Erub.* 53a)

The war context is what drove the Egyptian monarch to institute harsh treatment of the Israelites after the long period during which the Egyptians honored them.

The first chapter of Exodus is important for ascertaining where the motif of an Egyptian–Canaanite war originated, a conflict that in Jub 46:12-16 continues to provide context for the narrative. It arose in part from a desire to account for the curious delay in the burial of Joseph in Canaan and the omission of any notice about the brothers' burials. But there are clearer triggers in the scriptural text that would have given an interpreter warrant for assuming there were hostile relations between the two areas. Joseph sold grain to the inhabitants of Canaan as well as to the Egyptians; the last one hears about the Canaanites is that they spent all their money in the process (Gen 47:5). The most explicit indicator, however, is in Exod 1:8-10: "Now a new king arose over Egypt, who did not know Joseph. He said to his people, 'Look, the Israelite people are more numerous and more powerful than we. Come, let us deal shrewdly with them, or they will increase and, in the event of war, join our enemies and fight against us and escape [ועלה] from the land.'" The ruler was worried that the large foreign element in the population had deeper loyalties than their attachment to Egypt. He does not say where those loyalties lay, but an easy inference would be that it was to their former home, Canaan. In fact, the very verb he uses (עלה) is the standard one for going to Canaan from Egypt. So, the new king feared what would happen if war broke out with Canaan; if it did, the Israelites might

---

52 Cf. Kugel, *Walk through* Jubilees, 191–92; "Jubileees," 440.

53 The Greek citation lacks Jub 46:12b-16, probably because the section fairly closely reproduces Exod 1:9-13 and therefore the text of Jubilees was not needed here (VanderKam, "Another Citation," 379, 388).

54 See van Ruiten, "Between Jacob's Death and Moses' Birth," 479–80.

support the residents of their homeland.[55] War had in fact broken out, according to Jubilees, and the Israelites had seized the first available chance during it to bury their dead in Canaan. They remembered their roots, as the new king suspected. One other note that could have suggested a military backdrop was the term used for the cities on which the Israelite slaves worked: the precise sense of מסכנות (Exod 1:11) is debated,[56] but a common interpretation of it was "fortified" (so LXX, *Targums Pseudo-Jonathan* and *Neofiti*, etc.). The writer of Jubilees took it in a military sense (see v. 14).

Excursus: The War between Egypt and Canaan

As with the cases of other war accounts present in Jubilees but absent from Genesis-Exodus, some experts have attempted to find a reflection of history in the Canaanite-Egyptian war of Jub 46:6–47:1. Charles confessed his inability to identify Makamaron (the king of Canaan according to Jub 46:6), but he noted that, while Merneptah fought against Palestine around the time presupposed in Jubilees, "our text, which emphasises the weakness of Egypt, points rather to the period of the successors of Rameses III. when Egypt lost her Syrian dependencies."[57] Berger thinks the account of the war, like the ones in chaps. 13, 34, and 38, echoes disputes in the second century BCE. If the report in v. 6 is accurate, it would indicate that an Egyptian (i.e., Ptolemaic) king died after a conflict with a Canaanite (i.e., Seleucid) monarch. The only candidate who fits the description is Ptolemy VI Philometor who died in 145 BCE from wounds suffered in a battle that likewise saw the death of the latest Seleucid king Alexander Balas. Berger also wonders whether the success enjoyed by the Canaanite king in v. 11 points to Ptolemy VIII.[58]

Both Charles and Berger assume that the account reflects historical circumstances but disagree emphatically on the identity of those circumstances. Against Charles, one could object that nothing in the early period to which he points is at all similar to the events depicted in Jub 46:6–47:1, and the same can be said about Berger's identification. What, apart from the fact that Ptolemy VI, a monarch from Egypt, died from wounds received in battle while supporting one claimant to the Seleucid throne against another, reminds one of the war account in Jubilees or the Visions of Amram? That he was the only Ptolemaic monarch to die in a war with the Seleucids seems a poor basis for finding the death of Ptolemy VI as the historical referent of the Egyptian king who, in Jub 46:6, dies in a battle with the ruler of Canaan.

Werman finds a different kind of backdrop for the introduction of the war account into the version of the story in Jubilees 46.[59] She suggests that by means of it the author of Jubilees responded to the narratives regarding Jewish departure from Egypt that Josephus attributes to Manetho. She turns to these negative portrayals of the exodus because of some features in Jubilees 46 that serve no function in it and are otherwise unexplained: the reference to Amram who stayed in Canaan; mention of a group who remained there with him (both in v. 10); and the report that the Egyptians regarded the Israelites as impure (v. 16). These are the two accounts of Manetho as Josephus presents them.

1. The first story Josephus considers authentic and helpful proof that Jewish people came to Egypt from another place and that they were ancient because the events recounted occurred almost a thousand years before the Trojan War (*Ap.* 1.103-5). He claims to be quoting from Manetho (*Ap.* 1.75-90), who related the following: A people from the east called the Hyksos, whom Josephus understands to be the Jews' ancestors, invaded Egypt, conquered it, set up their own king, and strengthened the country against the Assyrians. The king also rebuilt and fortified the city of Avaris. The Hyksos (the word means "king-shepherds") badly mistreated Egypt and its people during their 511-year rule. Eventually various Egyptian rulers united and drove the Hyksos out. After a siege of Avaris, the Egyptians agreed to let the Hyksos leave Egypt; 240,000 of them then went to Judea where they built Jerusalem.

2. The second story, in which Josephus thinks Manetho is writing falsehoods, he relates in *Ap.*

---

55 In view of the terribly negative opinion the writer of Jubilees had of Canaanites, the fear seems strange.
56 BDB, 698, s.v. סכן; Houtman, *Exodus*, 1:244.
57 Charles, *Jubilees*, 245-46. He also adduces Josephus's story about a war between Egypt and Cush (Ethiopia) at the time of Moses.
58 Berger, *Jubiläen*, 537 n. a to chap. 46. In Berger's opinion, the date of Ptolemy VI's death serves as the *terminus post quem* for when Jubilees was written (see p. 300).
59 Werman, *Jubilees*, 523-25, 529. In the fifth appendix to her book (pp. 572-77) she makes a case that elements of the double story about a Jewish departure from Egypt were known in the land at the time the author of Jubilees wrote his book.

1.227-52 (for Josephus's refutation of it, see 1.252-87). According to it, a certain King Amenophis wanted to have a vision of the gods and was advised that to attain his goal he should purge Egypt of lepers and other polluted people. He then collected some eighty thousand maimed individuals and made them work in stone quarries away from other Egyptians. Among the people segregated in this way were priests suffering from leprosy. (As it turns out, the ancestors of the Jews were also supposed to be among them.) After they had suffered for a long time in the quarries, the king agreed to their request to settle in Avaris. There they appointed as their leader Osarsiph, who promulgated a law that these mistreated people were not to worship the Egyptian gods, that they were to eat the meat of sacred animals, and were to have no connection with anyone outside their group. (Osarsiph eventually took the name of Moses). He also ordered them to repair the city walls and to prepare to battle against Amenophis. They sent to the shepherds (the Hyksos) in Jerusalem to join them in Avaris (their former city) and to ally with them in their fight against Egypt. Some two hundred thousand of the shepherds accepted the invitation. After a military confrontation, the king of Egypt withdrew to Ethiopia, while the Egyptians suffered at the hands of their new masters. Thirteen years later the king of Egypt returned, defeated the combined forces of the people from Jerusalem and their allies, killed many of them, and drove the others to the borders of Syria.

To these stories, according to Werman, Jubilees responds by working the Canaanite-Egyptian war account into the narrative at the end of Genesis and the beginning of Exodus. She believes the stories attributed to Manetho by Josephus and the account in Jubilees yield a rather similar plot as she details in a chart.

Manetho in Josephus	Jubilees
A foreign ruler in Egypt	A foreign ruler in Egypt (Joseph)
Departure of his people from Egypt amid a struggle	Departure of his people from Egypt at a time of war
A stay in Canaan (building Jerusalem)	A stay in Canaan (Mount Hebron)
Banishing of the lepers	Banishing of the Israelites
Rebuilding by the lepers of Avaris that was destroyed in war with the foreigners from Canaan	Rebuilding by the Israelites of the fortified cities destroyed in the war with the king of Canaan
The inhabitants of Canaan return from Canaan to Egypt	The inhabitants of Canaan return from Canaan to Egypt
A connection between those who returned and those ostracized in Egypt.	A connection of those who returned with the ostracized
Sequel: brutality of the returnees and the ostracized in Egypt	Sequel: the plagues that the God of the returnees and ostracized brings down on Egypt
Departure of the returnees and the ostracized	Departure of the returnees and the ostracized

Werman argues that the unexplained details in Jubilees' story become clear against this background: Amram and his group in Canaan parallel the Hyksos (both groups came from Egypt and both return to it, joining with ones who remained there); and the Egyptian view that the Israelites were impure echoes the theme of the lepers and other impure people whom the Egyptian king purged from his land. Perhaps by saying that the story in Jubilees responds to the ones attributed to Manetho Werman means that the former sets the latter straight, but the parallels she finds between them are usually, on closer inspection, so dissimilar that they bear no weight. It seems forced, for example, to say that the rebuilding of cities is parallel in Manetho's version and in Jubilees. In the second story of Manetho the rebuilding is done by people who are fortifying the place for their own safety while in Jubilees (and Exodus) the Israelites, under compulsion, fortify them for Pharaoh, their oppressor. The same objection could be leveled against the suggestions that the stay of the Hyksos in Canaan in Manetho's first account is parallel to the brief sojourn of the burial party, including Amram, in Jubilees or that the return of the Hyksos to Avaris in the second story parallels the return of the burial party to Egypt. It seems improbable that the writer of Jubilees had these stories directly in mind as he wrote his version of the war story.

The war between Egypt and Canaan, like the other supplementary battle accounts in Jubilees, is more easily explained as arising from literary needs, a Jewish source, and textual triggers than as reflecting historical events. The name Makamaron may just possibly be an indicator of how the story came about. No king known from history bore the name, but he is said to have lived in Asur = Hazor (if the phrase belongs in the text), and Jabin of Hazor is called "the king of Canaan in Judg 4:2, 23, 24 (see the commentary on v. 6 above). There are, therefore, two points of contact between this king and the story in Jubilees: the king's city and his title (both mentioned in Judg 4:2). With the greatest hesitation it may be hazarded that the writer who fashioned the war story drew the name Makamaron from the other context that mentions Jabin of Hazor: in Josh 11:1 one of Jabin's allies is the "king of Madon (MT), but he is "king of Marron" in the LXX. The Hebrew behind the title attested in the LXX would be: מלך מרון, and it would supply all the consonants of Makamaron if the *lamed* of מלך happened to drop out. This is only a guess (perhaps a wild one), but the more significant point is that the story itself has the earmarks of having been created for literary and exegetical reasons, not to mirror historical events in Pharaonic times or in the second century, none of which it reflects at all closely. It is also unlikely to be a direct response to negative portrayals of the Exodus found in non-Jewish sources from the Hellenistic period. For it Jubilees drew on the kind of story contained in the Visions of Amram (this explains the mention of Moses's father and those with him), and the Egyptian verdict that the Israelites were impure is a documented interpretation of a term in Exod 1:12b (see the commentary below on v. 16).

■ **12** Because of the tendency to abbreviate that dominates the latter part of the book, an ambiguity arises about the subject of the verbs in v. 12. The king of Canaan was the subject of both verbs in v. 11,[60] and v. 12 uses a pronoun for the subject ("he"). Is "he" the king of Canaan or the king of Egypt? The sequel makes it transparent that the king of Egypt is the subject: he speaks to the Egyptian people, identifies with them ("more numerous than we are," "let us outwit them," "leave our land," etc.), and is concerned about the threat posed by Canaan—all thoroughly implausible for the Canaanite ruler. The Latin translation of Jubilees strangely reads *rex chanaam* as the subject in v. 12—an identification that can scarcely be correct, though Berger and Kugel adopt it.[61] The Greek citation sides with the Ethiopic in reading a pronoun as the subject.

In Jubilees the Egyptian monarch "conceived an evil plan against the Israelites,"[62] a statement not found in Exodus and apparently related to the author's understanding of "who did not know Joseph" (see above)—a phrase signifying a complete reversal of Egyptian policy toward the sons of Israel. The notion of making them suffer comes from the report about the work of the taskmasters in Exod 1:11 // Jub 46:14; the writer presents it here first, repeats it in Pharaoh's speech (unlike Exod 1:10), and includes it in v. 14 to place emphasis on it.[63] With the strongly negative statement preceding it in Jubilees, the reader is not optimistic about what the king will say when he outlines his plan to the populace. In Exodus, the reason for the altered policy is not thoroughly explained (see below on v. 13 // Exod 1:9-10), but in Jubilees the ongoing hostilities between Canaan and Egypt and the fact that the Egyptians were confined within their own borders provide a reasonable context for the king's plan.[64]

■ **13** The king's announcement reads somewhat differently in the two texts.

Exodus 1:9-10
Look, the Israelite people are more numerous and more powerful than we are. Come let us deal shrewdly with them, or they will increase and, in the event of war, join our enemies and fight against us and escape from the land.

Jubilees 46:13
The nation of the Israelites has now increased and become more numerous than we are. Come on, let us outwit them before they multiply. Let us make them suffer in slavery before war comes our way and they, too, fight against us. Otherwise they will unite with the enemy and leave our land because their mind(s) and face(s look) toward the land of Canaan.

---

60 The Greek citation names the king of Egypt as the subject of the second verb ("the king of Egypt closed the gates of Egypt"), apparently to remove any ambiguity. See the textual note.

61 Berger, *Jubiläen*, 539 n. a to v. 12; 537 n. a to chap. 46 (where he says the king who did not know Joseph is identified with a Syrian monarch who then turns the Egyptians against the Israelites); Kugel, *Walk through* Jubilees, 192; "Jubilees," 440. Strange results come from reading "The king of Canaan" as the subject of the verbs in v. 12 (see vv. 13-14 for instance—why would the Canaanite king want the fortresses of Egypt rebuilt—and rebuilt "for Pharaoh"?). Kugel thinks this king was worried the Israelites would go to Canaan and conquer it, though the text never even hints at such an idea. The assignments given to the Israelite slaves make sense in the war context of Jubilees if they are meant to strengthen Egypt against an enemy with whom the Egyptians are at war and whom, the Egyptian king fears, they will join. See also Werman, *Jubilees*, 526 n. 33, 529 (she too recognizes the king of Egypt is under consideration).

62 In Jub 34:11, Joseph's brothers make a plan against him that leads to his enslavement, as the Egyptian king's plan leads to slavery for the Israelites. For the expression "conceived an evil plan," compare Ezek 38:10; Nah 1:11; 1 Macc 11:8.

63 Van Ruiten, "Between Jacob's Death and Moses' Birth," 487.

64 See Halpern-Amaru, "Burying the Fathers," 142-44. She thinks the burial expedition to Canaan during a war and the fact that some Israelites remained there are part of the author's explanation

The author expresses the idea of a burgeoning population in two ways, just as LXX Exod 1:9 does (MT SP have only one), but, against the versions of Exod 1:9, Jubilees lacks "more powerful."[65] The king's intent is to outwit the Israelites before[66] their numbers grow even larger than they already are. For the second time the writer of Jubilees inserts into the account a statement about making the Israelites suffer, this time adding "in slavery" (taken from Exod 1:11, which is not part of the king's speech). The monarch's deeper concern clearly arises from what might happen if fighting should break out with an enemy. In Exod 1:10 he does not clarify who the enemy might be, but, as noted above, the verb עלה (curiously rendered as "escape" in the NRSV)[67] is the standard one for going up from Egypt to Canaan (e.g., Gen 50:5-7, 9). Jubilees makes the reference to Canaan explicit: the monarch realizes that the Israelites have a historic connection with Canaan, and, if Canaan should attack Egypt, he feared that the huge Israelite population would prove to be a fifth column. He identifies their deeper loyalty to their Canaanite home by claiming that (literally) "their heart and face are in the land of Canaan." The ruler realizes that they have hopes of returning to the homeland, and he fears the consequences if they seized the opportunity presented by warfare with Canaan to fulfill their desire. In Jubilees, where Egypt and Canaan have been at war for years, his fears are thoroughly understandable. Unless drastic steps were taken, Egypt would be plunged into an even worse situation than was presently the case. Israel had been an asset, but now the war context coupled with their surging population made them into a serious liability; the king reversed his policy toward them accordingly.

■ **14** The specific form the king's "evil plan" took comes in a report about what happened as a result of his address to the nation:

Exodus 1:11
Therefore they set taskmasters over them to oppress them with forced labor. They built supply cities, Pithom and Rameses, for Pharaoh.

Jubilees 46:14
He appointed taskmasters over them to make them suffer in slavery. They built fortified cities for Pharaoh—Pithom and Rameses.
They built every wall and all the fortifications that had fallen down in the cities of Egypt.

This is the first time Exodus mentions oppressing the Israelites/making them suffer, whereas it is the third time it occurs in Jubilees (see vv. 12 and 13). Genesis has a group ("they") imposing taskmasters on the Israelites (though the labor they perform is for Pharaoh), but Jubilees charges just the king with doing so.[68] The cities on which the newly enslaved Israelites toiled are called "fortified cities" as in the LXX tradition and *Targums Pseudo-Jonathan* and *Neofiti* (see the excursus above). So the slaves work to strengthen Egypt's defenses against the kind of attack Pharaoh fears. The military nature of the forced labor performed by the Israelites continues in the addition Jubilees places at the end of v. 13: Egypt's military preparedness was in a bad state, so the Israelite slaves received the assignment to work in various places in Egypt to make it ready to withstand an attack. Their efforts were far more widespread than work on just two cities would suggest. The king was taking no chances.

■ **15** The verse draws on and reverses two passages in Exodus: 1:13 and 1:12:

Exodus 1:13, 12
13 The Egyptians became ruthless in imposing tasks on the Israelites
12 But the more they were oppressed, the more they multiplied and spread.

Jubilees 46:15
They were enslaving them by force,
but however much they would make them suffer the more they would multiply and the more they would increase.

A more literal rendering of Exod 1:13 is: The Egyptians enslaved the Israelites with harshness/severity (see BDB,

---

for the change in Egyptian policy toward the Israelites (so also van Ruiten, "Between Jacob's Death and Moses' Birth," 481). Perhaps they were, but the king focuses on their numbers and their attachment to Canaan as causes.

65 עצום can mean either "mighty" or "numerous" (BDB, 783). The ancient versions understood it as "mighty," suggesting that the ruler saw the growth in the Israelite population as posing a security threat; his next words confirm the interpretation of the term.

66 The reading is similar to the one in the Peshitta and *Targums Pseudo-Jonathan* and *Neofiti*; the other versions read "lest/so that not."

67 In Jubilees the verb used here means "leave" as in the LXX tradition (so it is understood as referring to an exodus).

68 See Werman, *Jubilees*, 522-23, 529.

827, s.v. פרך). LXX Exod 1:13 took the last expression (בפרך) to mean "by force [βια]," and Jubilees reflects that interpretation. The forced labor, while it served to strengthen Egypt's defenses, was meant primarily to limit the Israelite population explosion—the root problem identified by Pharaoh—but it was having the opposite effect. Where MT SP Exod 1:12 use "spread" as the second verb regarding the growing population, Jubilees has a verb meaning "to be many/increase" and the LXX tradition and the targums read words for becoming strong (cf. Exod 1:9).

■ 16 The result of the new royal policy toward the Israelites was to ruin relations between the two peoples. During Joseph's lifetime the Egyptians honored the Israelites (46:2) despite the vast growth in their population (46:1). Now the numbers of the Israelites had become too large to ignore, leading the Egyptians to subject them to slavery. The writer sums up the situation by citing Exod 1:12b.

Exodus 1:12b	Jubilees 46:16
the Egyptians came to dread the Israelites.	The Egyptians considered the Israelites detestable.

The verb in Jubilees (both Ethiopic [yāstarākwesewwomu] and Latin [abominabantur]), which suggests something impure, offers a different nuance than the Hebrew verb (ויקצו), which articulates a loathing, abhorrence (BDB, 880-81, s.v. קוץ);[69] but both indicate a strong distaste and express forcefully that the Egyptians' feelings toward the Israelites, under the pressures of war and the ever-growing number of this foreign element, had completely reversed themselves. The era of Joseph has decisively ended.[70]

---

69   Neither the Hebrew nor the Ethiopic version of Gen 43:32 uses exactly the same expression in the earlier statement that the Egyptians could not eat with the Hebrews "for that is an abomination to the Egyptians." Cf. also Gen 46:34.

70   Note that in Jubilees at this point the passage about the midwives and about throwing Israelite boys into the river do not figure in the text. The reason may be the process of abbreviation in this part of Jubilees, but the drowning of Israelite boys in the Nile is mentioned in 47:2-3, just before the story about Moses in the little boat.

47

From Moses's Birth to His Escape from Egypt

1/ During the seventh week, in the[a] seventh year, in the forty-seventh jubilee [2303], your father[b] came from the land of Canaan. You were born[c] during the fourth week, in its sixth year, in the forty-eighth jubilee [2330]. This was[d] the time of distress for the Israelites. 2/ Pharaoh, the king of Egypt, had given orders[a] regarding them that they were to throw their sons—every male who was born[b]—into the river. 3/ They continued throwing (them in) for seven months until the time[a] when you were born. Your mother hid you for three months. Then they told about her.[b] 4/ She[a] made a box for you,[b] covered it with pitch and asphalt,[c] and put it in the grass[d] at the riverbank. She put you in it for seven days. Your mother would come at night and nurse you, and[e] during the day your sister Miriam would protect you from the birds. 5/ At that time Tarmuth, Pharaoh's daughter, went out to bathe in the river and heard you crying. She told her slaves[a] to bring you,[b] so they brought you to her.[c] 6/ She took you out of the box and pitied you. 7/ Then your sister said to her, "Should I go[a] and summon for you one of the Hebrew women[b] who will care for and nurse this infant for you?"[c] She said to her, "Go."[d] 8/ She went[a] and summoned your[b] mother Jochebed. She gave her[c] wages[d] and she took care of you.

9/ Afterwards, when you had grown up, you were brought[a] to Pharaoh's daughter[b] and became her child.[c] Your father Amram taught you (the art of) writing. After[d] you had completed three weeks [= 21 years], he brought[e] you into the royal court. 10/ You remained in the court for three weeks of years [= 21 years] until the time when you went from the royal court and saw the Egyptian beating your kinsman[a] who was one of the Israelites.[b] You killed[c] him and hid him[d] in the sand. 11/ The next day[a] you found two of the Israelites fighting. You said to the one who was mistreating (the other):[b] "Why are you beating your brother?" 12/ He became angry and indignant[a] and said,[b] "Who appointed you as ruler and judge over us? Do you want to kill me as you killed the Egyptian?"[c] Then you were afraid[d] and ran away because of this matter.

Textual Notes

1a the (seventh year)] "its" Lat.
b your father] Αμβραμ (= Ambram, the LXX spelling of Amram) Gk.; "his father" Lat. The Catena lacks both date formulas in the verse (as in 46:8, 9), and words it in the third person, contrary to the pattern in the book. Oddly, Lat. does here as well.
c You were born] "He was born" Lat.; "He bore Moses" Gk. See the previous note.
d This was] So Gk. and Lat. Eth. *za* ("which"); it may be a mistake for *ze* ("this," read by 21 35 38).
2a orders] "his orders" 25 44.
b every male who was born] "all males who were born to them" Lat. Exodus 1:22 reads sg. forms. Lat.'s "to them" resembles "to the Hebrews" in SP LXX Exod 1:22; the Eth. reading without these words agrees with the MT.
3a the time] Eth. reads literally "the day" where Lat. has a relative pronoun; 20 25 35 39c read "you" (*'anta* [added by 44]) where one might have expected the form *'enta* (relative pronoun) read by 42 47 48. The meaning with these readings is the same.

b about her] So Eth. and Lat., but 20 has "about him" and 38 "about you."
4a She] + "being afraid" Lat. The words are not present in Exod 2:3.
b for you] Lat. om., probably because the words *tibi tibin* ("for you in a box") were so similar that one was skipped.
c pitch and asphalt] Lat. reverses the two nouns. Mss. 17 21 38 39 48 om. the conjunction between them, thus placing them in a construct relationship—the reading Berger prefers (*Jubiläen*, 540 n. c. to v. 4).
d in the grass] om. Lat.; cf. Exod 2:3.
e and (during)] om. Lat.
5a slaves] Eth. reads "her Hebrews" (fem.), where Lat. has "her slave" (fem.). Exodus 2:5 (אמתה) offers the equivalent of the Lat. reading. The Eth. form represents, as Dillmann ("Jubiläen," 72 n. 80) recognized, a misunderstanding of the Gk. form αβραις ("maidservants") as a rendering of עבריות (= εβραιαις, "Hebrew women"). Dillmann's explanation has been widely accepted. See VanderKam, *Jubilees* 2:306. The pl. in the Eth. text is related to the number of the verbs that follow.
b to bring you] The Eth. verb (the text has a finite form)

c   appears to be masc. sg. but is probably to be interpreted as fem. pl. (the difference is only the length of the *a-* vowel before the suffix; see VanderKam, *Jubilees* 2:306). Lat. continues to read a sg. form here, and, rather than "you," it has "the baby to her."

c   they brought you to her] See the preceding note for the Eth. verbal form; Lat. has a pl. verb and lacks "to her."

7a   Should I go] Eth. marks Miriam's words as a question, but Lat. does not. After the next verb and prepositional phrase, it reads "if you wish" as in LXX Exod 2:7. MT SP Exod 2:7 read a question, but LXX indicates this only by punctuation.

b   one of the Hebrew women] So Eth. and Exod 2:7; Lat. = "a Hebrew woman."

c   care for and nurse this infant for you] So Eth., and see Exod 2:7, where two forms of the verb "nurse" appear. Lat. lacks "care for and" and, rather than "this infant" (see Exod 2:7), reads "him."

d   She said to her, "Go"] So Lat. and Exod 2:8; all Eth. MSS. om., except 38, which reads "She said: 'Go.'" Note that v. 8 begins with "She went," so it is likely paraplepsis occurred (as it did in Lat., which om. the verb at the beginning of v. 8). See VanderKam, *Jubilees* 2:307.

8a   She went] om. Lat. (see previous note).

b   your] pr. "his and" Lat. Exodus 2:8 also lacks the extra words.

c   gave her] "gave that woman" Lat.

d   wages] After the suffix on the verb "gave" = "gave (to) her," MSS. 17 21 39 44 47 48 58 63 add what appears to be a superfluous "her" = "gave her her wages."

9a   you were brought (lit., "they brought you")] "she brought you" 17 (as in Exod 2:10: "she brought him"); "he brought you" 58.

b   *daughter*] "the house of" Eth. As Charles (*Ethiopic Version*, 166 n. 27) indicated, the incorrect text resulted from confusing בית ("house") and בת ("daughter"). Exodus 2:10 reads "daughter." See VanderKam, *Jubilees* 2:307.

c   her child] The best Eth. reading is *weludā* 12 17; it is a passive participial form with a third person fem. sg. suffix. It is, however, spelled the same way as the word meaning "her sons/children," and this has caused some confusion in the manuscripts, where 21 48 read "his sons" or "his son" and 25 39 "sons" (or perhaps: "son"). Ms. 20 = "her son"; 35 42 44 47 = "his son" (also 38 with a nominative form); 58 63 "son."

d   After] "When" Lat. A number of Eth. MSS. read "After this" (20 35 42ᶜ 44 47 58), and several have "When" (38 39 42ᵗ 48 63).

e   he brought] Lat., though it is partially illegible, preserves a pl. verbal ending ("they . . ."); MS. 12 also reads a pl. form.

10a   your kinsman] "your companion" Eth.; "your brother" Lat. Both are attempts at rendering the meaning of אחיו ("[one of] his brothers") in Exod 2:11, where the form does not designate a biological brother. Mss. 12 17 = "his companion." See v. 11.

b   who was one of the Israelites] om. Lat.

c   killed] "struck" Lat.—perhaps ultimately from a form of הכה (ויך in Exod 2:12), which can mean "kill." Mss. 12 21 38 read "interceded," and 17 = "fought."

d   and hid him] "covered/buried him" Lat. See Exod 2:12. Lat. places before this verb "you dug into the ground" (not in Exod 2:12).

11a   day] So Eth. and Lat., but 20 25 35 44 om.

b   mistreating (the other)] See Exod 2:13. Lat. = "beating his fellow." That is, it repeats the verb from v. 10 and from the end of this verse. "His fellow" is not present in Exod 2:13.

12a   angry and indignant] "angry with indignation" Lat. Ms. 20 om. "and indignant."

b   said] "they said to you" 35; "he said to you" 58.

c   Egyptian] + "yesterday" Lat. (= 12 38). "Yesterday" is present in LXX Exod 2:14.

d   afraid] + "of him" 17 47 58 63.

Commentary

Jubilees 47 rewrites much of the material in Exod 2:1-15a (with 1:22), the story about Moses's birth, his life in the royal court, and the events that forced him to flee Egypt. The first verse ties the narrative to the war account in chap. 46 by reporting the return of Moses's father to Egypt from Canaan, where the hostilities had stranded him for forty-one years. Amram and his wife Jochebed became the parents of Moses twenty-eight years later. During all this time the Egyptian policy of oppressing the Israelites was in force, but a new and cruel application of it required that Israelite male babies be drowned in the river (Exod 1:22). Moses was born into these trying circumstances, and his life was spared only when the Egyptian princess Tarmuth rescued him and eventually, after Jochebed cared for and Amram educated him at home for his first twenty-one years, adopted him so that he spent his second twenty-one years in the royal palace. At the end of that period he killed an Egyptian who was beating an Israelite; the news got out, and he had to leave Egypt to avoid punishment for his act of violence. The chapter takes the form of a report by the Angel of the Presence telling Moses what happened during the first forty-two years of his life; he phrases it, therefore, in the second person singular.

The short chapter can be outlined into three parts:

1-8 Moses's birth and rescue by Pharaoh's daughter (Exod 1:22; 2:1-9)
9-10a Life at home and in the royal court (Exod 2:10)
10b-12 Danger and flight from Egypt (Exod 2:11-15a)

There is textual evidence for the chapter in three languages. Both the Ethiopic and Latin translations are available for all of Jubilees 47, though the Latin is illegible in places at the end of v. 8 and the beginning of v. 9. The Greek citation that supplied text for Jub 46:6-12 concludes with parts of 47:1.[1]

1-8 Moses's Birth and Rescue by Pharaoh's Daughter (Exod 1:22; 2:1-9)

The first event to receive attention is the return of Moses's father Amram to Egypt from Canaan.

■ **1** It is likely that the initial verb in Exod 2:1 ("Now a man of the house of Levi went [וילך] and married a Levite woman") in some sense lies behind the idea that Moses's father traveled to Egypt from elsewhere.[2] He had been in Canaan since 2263, the year of the burial expedition to the cave of Machpelah (46:9); Amram was one of those who stayed in Canaan when the majority returned to Egypt (46:10). The conditions that kept him there must now have eased so that he could rejoin his wife, who had been in Egypt all this time. Jubilees places his return in the year 2303. If he had been in Canaan since 2263, he had been away for forty or forty-one years—exactly the amount of time that the Visions of Amram assigns to this period (see line 11 in the text given in the commentary on chap. 46; the number "forty-one" is preserved in full in 4Q544 1 6).[3] So, on this point the two texts agree chronologically. They do not, however, put the information to the same use. In the Visions of Amram, the hero comments on the fact that, though he and Jochebed were separated for forty-one years, he did not take a wife from among the Canaanite women (4Q544 1 8-9 [lines 13-14 in the translation in the commentary on chap. 46]; significant parts of the text must be filled in at this juncture). The point would have been valuable, one might think, to the writer of Jubilees, but he does not mention it and merely records the dates for the beginning and end of the period.[4]

It is of interest that in Jubilees there is no marriage notice for Amram and Jochebed, despite the presence of one in Exod 2:1 (and in Exod 6:20; cf. Num 26:59).[5] Exodus 2:1 says nothing about the marriage partners apart from their membership in the family of Levi, but Exod 6:20 is more explicit: "Amram married Jochebed his father's sister and she bore him Aaron and Moses" (see also Num 26:59, where Jochebed is presented in the same way but Miriam is added to the list of their children). The verse confirms the Levitical lineage of both, but the problem is that Amram married his aunt, and marriage to one's aunt is forbidden in the Torah: "You shall not uncover the nakedness of your mother's sister or your father's sister, for that is to lay bare one's own flesh; they shall be subject to punishment" (Lev 20:19; so also 18:12; cf. 11QT[a] lxvi:14-15). There is no doubt that this problem exercised early exegetes. Several versions of Exod 6:20 (LXX, Peshitta, *Targum Neofiti*) make Jochebed not the aunt of Amram but "the daughter of

---

1 See Petit, *La chaîne sur la Genèse*, 4:453-54 (#2270, lines 22-23]).
2 Halpern-Amaru, "Burying the Fathers," 150; van Ruiten, "Moses and His Parents: The Intertextual Relationship between Exodus 1:22–2:10 and Jubilees 47:1-9," in Antti Laato and Jacques van Ruiten, eds., *Rewritten Bible Reconsidered: Proceedings of the Conference in Karkku, Finland, August 24–26, 2006* (Studies in Rewritten Bible 1; Turku: Åbo Akademi University; Winona Lake, IN: Eisenbrauns, 2008) 43-78, here 60-62.
3 VanderKam, "*Jubilees* 46:6–47:1," 153-54.
4 Ibid., 157-58 (it is one of several reasons for concluding that the author of Jubilees did not use the Visions of Amram as a source).
5 Van Ruiten, "Moses and His Parents," 62-71. In ALD 11:10-11 Levi speaks about the birth of his daughter Jochebed when he was sixty-four years of age and after the family had entered Egypt; in 12:3-5 he mentions Amram's marriage to Jochebed (the two were born on the same day) when he (Levi) was ninety-four years of age.

the brother of his father," that is, his cousin—a permitted union.[6] Jubilees opts for neither this nor any other explanation and simply omits a marriage announcement, thus avoiding any implication that Moses was the child of an illicit union.[7]

Although Amram and his wife had been separated for forty-one years, his arrival in Egypt did not lead at any time soon to pregnancy for Jochebed and the birth of a child. The writer assigns the birth of Moses to the year 2330, twenty-eight years after his father returned to Egypt. At this point he says nothing about Moses's two older siblings. His sister Miriam figures in v. 4, but Aaron (three years his senior [Exod 7:7]) is never mentioned in Jubilees. There is no special significance to the fact that Aaron is absent from the story at this juncture— he is not a character in Exodus 2 either, and the writer is reworking the text of chap. 2.

The period when Moses was born is called "the[8] time of distress [θλιψεως/mendābē/tribulationis] for the Israelites." The designation characterizes the period when the Egyptians were oppressing the Israelites (for the situation, see Exod 3:9; 4:31), so the birth of Moses occurs at a dark time in the people's history. The difficult situation is, however, about to get worse.

■ 2 The writer at this stage in the story departs from the order in Exodus and inserts information from 1:22 regarding a new population control measure mandated by the king.

Exodus 1:22	Jubilees 47:2
Then Pharaoh commanded all his people, "Every boy that is born [ ][9] you shall throw into the Nile, but you shall let every girl live."	Pharaoh, the king of Egypt, had given orders regarding them that they were to throw their sons—every male who was born—into the river.[10]

The author again avoids direct speech and reports about rather than quotes the monarch's instructions, which may well have been given before this time (hence the rendering "had given orders").[11] Both texts use two terms for the victims of the new oppressive measure: a word for sons and a term for a male who is born. In Exodus, girls are specifically exempted from drowning, while in Jubilees the reader must infer this, as girls are not mentioned. So Moses enters the world at a time when his people are suffering from oppression and when baby boys are to die in the river. The situation looks hopeless for the child Amram and Jochebed have just brought into the world.

■ 3 Though Exodus does not indicate how long the policy of throwing boys into the Nile was in effect, the author of Jubilees claims it had been going on for seven months by the time Moses was born ("for seven months until the time when you were born"). His mother then hid the child[12] for three months (from Exod 2:2), yielding a total of ten months from the inception of the drowning practice to the time when his mother placed Moses in the box.[13] The text may suggest that the executions by water ended at this point; it is not explicit

---

6   This view is noted in *b. Sanh.* 58b, but the solution there seems to be that, since Jochebed was an aunt on the father's side, she was permitted to Amram before the Sinai revelation (with a discussion of Abram's marrying Sarai his sister, the daughter of his father but not of his mother [Gen 20:12]); cf. *Gen. Rab.* 18:5. See also Maori, *Peshitta Version*, 139–40.

7   Halpern-Amaru, *Empowerment*, 122–23; van Ruiten, "Moses and His Parents," 62–63 (the reference both make to *b. Soṭah* 58b should be to *b. Sanh.* 58b).

8   The Greek text uses a definite article with the noun.

9   The NRSV adds "to the Hebrews," a reading found in SP LXX Exod 1:22 and reflected in the targums, which have "to the Jews." The Ethiopic translation of Jubilees lacks the extra words, while the Latin, after "every male who was born," reads "to them." See the textual note. The words "to the Hebrews" clarify that Pharaoh's order applied only to them, not to the Egyptians as well (see Kugel, *Traditions*, 523; *Walk through* Jubilees, 193).

10 There is no doubt about which river is meant, but the Ethiopic and Latin versions of Jubilees, with LXX and the targums, read "river" rather than "Nile" as in MT SP Exod 1:22. The word ποταμος is the standard LXX translation of יאר in this section of Exodus, so Jubilees and the versions do not reflect a Hebrew reading different from the one in MT SP.

11 Cf. Hartom, "Jubilees," 131 n. to v. 2.

12 The Hebrew versions of Exod 2:2 have the mother hide the child; in the LXX tradition "they" (Amram and Jochebed) serve as the subjects of the verb.

13 As a way of arriving at nearly the same number of months, *Tg. Ps.-J.* Exod 2:2 reads: "The woman conceived and bore a son *at the end of six months*. When she saw that he *was viable*, she hid him for three months, *which gives a total of nine.*" The targumic rendering, which is meant to explain "and when she saw that he was a fine baby [lit., that he was good], she hid him for three months" (Exod

about it.[14] The note "They continued throwing (them in) for seven months" could be intended to address a problem with the sequence of events in Exodus: in 1:22 Pharaoh issues the decree about drowning Israelite male babies, and 2:1-2 reports the marriage of the Levite man and woman and the birth of their son. Why would an Israelite couple bring a son into the world when he was doomed to death as soon as he was born? Would it not be wiser to refrain altogether from having children in that "time of distress"?[15] If Moses's mother gave birth to him after the drowning policy was in effect for seven months, it may imply that she became pregnant with him two months before Pharaoh gave the command. Hence, the author of Jubilees would be saying, his parents conceived him when no death penalty hung over Israelite baby boys.[16] *Ten* as the number of months (that is, seven before his birth and three after) may be significant in connection with Jub 48:14, where one million Egyptian men die as revenge for one thousand Israelite infant boys who were drowned. Perhaps the Egyptians threw one hundred boys into the river each month for ten months (see the commentary on 48:14). The Byzantine historian Cedrenus, who says he based his statement on Jubilees ("the Little Genesis"), claims that the ten plagues corresponded to the ten months in which the Egyptians were casting Hebrew males into the river.[17]

Van Ruiten argues that the seven-month period of drowning baby boys before Moses's birth seems to imply that there is a relationship, whatever it may be, between the commandment of Pharaoh to kill every male newborn, and the anticipation of the birth of Moses. The rearrangement of the decree and the conception in Jubilees not only clears Amram and Jochebed of the accusation that they had intercourse in a time when the decree was already proclaimed, it also makes a connection between the decree and the birth of Moses. Possibly, according to the author of Jubilees, the decree was issued at the conception of Moses. In this case, too, "seven months" then implies that Moses was born too early.[18]

But there is no indication that the decree and the conception coincided. The seven months may not echo the tradition that Moses was born prematurely; yet they could simply indicate that his parents were not reckless in having a child in such awful times.

Exodus 2:3 refers to a point when Moses's mother "could hide him no longer." It does not say what changed so that it became impossible to shield her son from detection and death. Jubilees provides a reason but not a very specific one: "Then they told about her." It does not identify the informants, reporting only that word about the child got out. The same sort of note appears in various sources, e.g., *Tg. Ps.-J.* Exod 2:3: "It was no longer possible for her to hide him, *because the Egyptians had noticed her.*"[19]

2:2), indicates that Jochebed gave birth to Moses prematurely.

14 The failure of the text to address the issue directly should make one cautious about accepting Werman's hypothesis (*Jubilees*, 531) that the birth of Moses is a turning point similar to the one marked by the death of Joseph: until Joseph died there was no satan or evil one (46:2), and with Moses's birth the persecution ended.

15 Several sources claim that the Israelite men, including Amram, decided not to approach their wives—or even divorced them—so as not to have any more children (see Kugel, *Traditions*, 524–26, where he cites *b. Soṭah* 12a and L.A.B. 9:2, 4). In *Exod. Rab.* 1:13, 20, Amram divorces his wife when she is three months pregnant; Moses is born six months after Amram took Jochebed back (cf. *Tg. Ps.-J.* Exod 2:1-2).

16 Werman thinks the writer was aware of the tradition that Moses was born prematurely and rejected it (*Jubilees*, 531). That may be true, but it need not follow from the references to months that can be interpreted as above. She also thinks the author knew the idea that throwing baby boys into the river commenced at the time Moses was conceived by Jochebed and rejected it as well. Perhaps he did know that latter tradition, but it does not follow from anything explicit in the text. See also the views of van Ruiten cited below.

17 For the text, see Denis, *Fragmenta*, 99; Rönsch, *Jubiläen*, 164; and Charles, *Jubilees*, 248.

18 Van Ruiten, "Moses and His Parents," 73.

19 In *b. Soṭah* 12a and *Exod. Rab.* 1:20, the Egyptians were able to discover Hebrew male infants by bringing an Egyptian baby to a suspect Israelite house, making the Egyptian child cry, and thus causing the Israelite infant to wail in response.

■ 4 The texts describe what Moses's mother did to protect her infant son after hiding him was no longer feasible.

Exodus 2:3	Jubilees 47:4
... she got a papyrus basket for him, and plastered it with bitumen and pitch; she put the child in it and placed it among the reeds on the bank of the river.	She made a box[20] for you, covered it with pitch and asphalt, and put it in the grass at the riverbank. She put you in it for seven days. Your mother would come at night and nurse you, and during the day your sister Miriam would protect you from the birds.

Exodus implies she took an existing container, while in Jubilees she actually constructs the box (both parents make it in Josephus, *Ant.* 2.220). The texts reverse the words for the two substances with which she made the container watertight. In Exodus the mother first puts Moses into it and then sets it among the reeds, whereas in Jubilees it seems that her initial action was to place the box among the plants[21] on the edge of the river and then to lay the baby in it. [22]

The writer of Jubilees alone adds several clauses to the end of Exod 2:3. In the first he states that the child remained in the box for seven days (note the "sevens" in the date formula in v. 1 and the seven months in v. 3); no other version of Exod 2:3 specifies how long Moses spent in it. He also explains how it was that the child could survive that long. "Your mother would come at night and nurse you" is a clause that may draw upon the later mention of her nursing the child on behalf of Pharaoh's daughter (Exod 2:7-9; Jub 47:7-8). Because she wanted to keep the baby's presence a secret, she fed him under the cover of darkness.[23] The second additional clause relates how Moses was protected from natural dangers. In Exod 2:4, "His sister stood at a distance, to see what would happen to him," but in Jubilees she is named and is more active: "during the day your sister Miriam would protect you from the birds." Since the box had to have an opening, the child was subject to attack from whatever creatures happened to be around. Birds would naturally be a problem, so the young Miriam, like Abram (Jub 11:11-24; 14:12; or Rizpah in 2 Sam 21:10), was able to drive these winged creatures off. Mastema was the one who sent birds to destroy crops when Abram was born; perhaps this was a means by which he could attack the infant Moses (he will try again in 48:2-4).[24] The baby receives around-the-clock care from the two women in his family.

■ 5-6 Exodus 2:5 gives no indication of when Pharaoh's daughter went down to bathe in the river, but the text of Jubilees speaks generally of "At that time [*ba-we'etu mawā'el/in tempore illo*]," that is, when Moses was in the box. After that notice, vv. 5-6 relate quite closely to Exod 2:5-6:

Exodus 2:5-6	Jubilees 47:5-6
The daughter of Pharaoh came down to bathe at the river, while her attendants walked beside the river. She saw the basket among the reeds and sent her maid to bring it. When she opened it, she saw the child. He was crying, and she took pity on him. "This must be one of the Hebrews' children," she said.	Tarmuth, Pharaoh's daughter, went out to bathe in the river and heard you crying. She told her slaves to bring you, so they brought you to her. She took you out of the box and pitied you.

---

20 *Nafq* means "box, chest, ark," etc. (Leslau, *Comparative Dictionary*, 389) and is the term employed in Eth. Exod 2:3 as well. With the LXX tradition, Jubilees lacks a reference to papyrus as the material of which the basket was made.

21 The Ethiopic noun (Latin omits the prepositional phrase) *šā'r* means "herb, herbage, grass, vegetation, straw" and "meadow, grassland" (Leslau, *Comparative Dictionary*, 525). It is not the word used at this point in Eth. Exod 2:3 (*mā'dot*, "bank [of the river]"; that is, it lacks a term for the kind of plants among which she set the container); it seems closer to LXX which has ἕλος, "marsh, meadow," and *Tg. Neof.* Exod 2:3.

22 See van Ruiten, "Moses and His Parents," 73–74.

23 According to Halpern-Amaru (*Empowerment*, 123), the writer of Jubilees, who had to omit the details of Jochebed's family connections, "focuses on presenting her as a nurturing mother to her son" and leaves out any hint of hesitation about saving him suggested by the note in Exod 2:2, "when she saw that he was a fine baby."

24 Cf. Halpern-Amaru, *Empowerment*, 123 n. 52, and "Protection from Birds in the *Book of Jubilees*," in Aren Maeir, Jodi Magness, and Lawrence Schiffman, eds., *'Go Out and Study the Land' (Judges 18:2): Archaeological, Historical and Textual Studies in Honor of Hanan Eshel* (JSJSup 148; Leiden: Brill, 2012) 59–67, here 64–67; van Ruiten, "Moses and His Parents," 74.

Exodus 2:5 does not supply Pharaoh's daughter with a name, but Jubilees does (*tarmut/termot*). The Syriac list of patriarchal wives as recorded in Jubilees spells the name *trmwty*, and Josephus (*Ant.* 2.224) attests it as well ($\theta\epsilon\rho\mu o\nu\theta\iota s$).[25] John Day comments that the name "appears to be derived from that of Thermuthis (= (Ta)Renenutet), the Egyptian goddess of fertility and (appropriately) child nursing."[26] Since Moses will become the adopted son of this woman (see Jub 47:9), it is fitting that she have a name, as do the other mothers of significant characters in Jubilees.

A number of other small differences distinguish the two accounts. In Jubilees the princess does not go down to the river but out to it. Possibly the verb was influenced by Exod 2:11, where Moses goes out (from the palace), as she presumably does here. The writer then omits the information about her retinue. In Exodus she sees the basket among the reeds, suggesting this was not all that good a hiding place; in Jubilees she becomes aware of the box because she hears the baby crying (his crying is mentioned in Exod 2:6 but after she opens the container). Though she had a group of maids with her, she sends just one of them to fetch the basket according to Exod 2:5. The textual situation is a bit more complicated in Jubilees.

Ethiopic: She told her Hebrew women (*la-'ebrāwiyātihā*)
Latin: She said to her maid (*puellae suae* = Exod 2:5)

Dillmann noticed that the Ethiopic form *'ebrāwiyātihā* represented a misunderstanding of a Greek reading $\tau\alpha\iota s\ \alpha\beta\rho\alpha\iota s\ \alpha\nu\tau\eta s$ ("her maidservants") as $\tau\alpha\iota s\ \epsilon\beta\rho\alpha\iota\alpha\iota s\ \alpha\nu\tau\eta s$ ("her Hebrew women"; see Exod 2:7 // Jub 47:7, where "Hebrew women" appears).[27] The Ge'ez version, then, presupposes a plural form (maidservants), not a singular noun as in the Latin translation and Exod 2:5. It appears as if the Ethiopic text, with the plural noun, continued with plural verbal forms (bring . . . brought); Latin places the first verb in the singular (with "her maid" as the subject) but the second in the plural ("they brought").[28] It seems in this reading as if Tarmuth ordered one maid to fetch the box and several of them then carried it to her. Exodus does not report that the maid(s) did as she said, but she obviously got the basket because in the next sentence she (possibly but less likely her maid) opens it.

According to Exod 2:6 the princess (probably) opened the basket, but the text says nothing about taking the baby in her arms; in Jubilees she removes Moses from the box. The infant's crying is what moves her to pity in Exodus, whereas in Jubilees, in which she had first noticed the basket when he cried, she pities him as she takes him out of the box. She generally adopts a warmer, more motherly approach to the child in Jubilees. The writer also drops her identification of Moses as a Hebrew child and thus avoids having to explain how she discerned his ethnic origin and why she violated her father's orders about what to do with Hebrew baby boys.[29] From Jubilees one would not know Tarmuth was aware she had rescued a Hebrew child.

■ **7-8** Miriam, who is never named in Exodus 2, now springs into action and suggests a clever plan.

Exodus 2:7-9	Jubilees 47:7-8
Then his sister said to Pharaoh's daughter, "Shall I go and get a nurse from the Hebrew women to nurse the child?"	Then your sister said to her, "Should I go and summon for you one of the Hebrew women who will care for and nurse this infant for you?"
Pharaoh's daughter said to her, "Yes."[30]	She said to her, "Go."
So the girl went and called the child's mother.	She went and summoned your mother Jochebed.

---

25 In some rabbinic sources she is Bithiah, on the basis of 1 Chr 4:18, where a woman with this name is said to be Pharaoh's daughter (possibly she has a daughter named Miriam in v. 17). For the name, see *b. Meg.* 13a; *Lev. Rab.* 1:3; and Hartom, "Jubilees," 131. The same name appears in *Tg. Ps.-J.* Exod 2:5.

26 John Day, "The Pharaoh of the Exodus, Josephus and Jubilees," *VT* 45 (1995) 377–78, here 377. He rejects any suggestion that Josephus and Jubilees had access to historical knowledge or ancient tradition (e.g., that Rameses II had a daughter by this name [377–78]).

27 Dillmann, "Jubiläen," 72 n. 80. Cf. the textual note and see VanderKam, *Jubilees* 2:306, for references to others who have accepted Dillmann's explanation.

28 See VanderKam, *Jubilees* 2:306.

29 There are suggestions about these questions in the early exegetical literature. See, e.g., *b. Soṭah* 12b, where the maidservants raise the question about violating her father's command and where she knows he is a Hebrew boy because he is circumcised.

30 Exodus 2:8 says literally, "Go."

Pharaoh's daughter said to her, "Take[31] this child and nurse it for me, and I will give you your wages." So the woman took the child and nursed it.

She gave her wages and she took care of you.

Miriam offers to find a wet-nurse for Moses, but where in Exod 2:7 she suggests getting "a nurse . . . to nurse the child," in Jub 47:7 she has a wider kind of service in mind. She wonders whether the princess would like to have a Hebrew woman who would care for the child and nurse him. The verb translated "will care for" is *taḥaḏḏeno*; it has a range of meanings: "hold in the lap, nurse, nourish, suckle, feed, rear, bring up, train, educate, foster, take care of (one's young),"[32] but the fact that it is followed by another verb with the narrower sense of "nurse [*tāṭabbewo*]" suggests its meaning lies in the area of rearing, caring for (it is used again at the end of v. 8).[33] The verb chosen seems to be an interpretation of the verb הילכי (or whatever spelling may have occurred in the Hebrew text of Jubilees) in Exod 2:9.[34] The point is important because in v. 9 the writer makes clear that Moses grew up in the family home under the guidance of his parents, not in the palace. His mother both nurses and raises him, and his father instructs him (see v. 9).

The author of Jubilees bypasses the conversation between the princess and Moses's mother and records only the results. Those results are, however, different from the ones in Exod 2:9: in v. 8 she actually takes the wages (never noted in Exodus), and once more the verb meaning "take care of/rear" is used. Moses's mother Jochebed is more than a hired nurse for Pharaoh's daughter. She is the one who rears the child and receives pay for what she as a mother would naturally have done.

9-10a Life at Home and in the Royal Court (Exod 2:10)

Neither Exodus nor Jubilees says very much about the time Moses spent as the adopted son of Pharaoh's daughter, but their presentations are quite different.

Exodus 2:10
When the child grew up, she brought him to Pharaoh's daughter, and she took him as her son.

Jubilees 47:9-10a
Afterwards, when you had grown up, you were brought to Pharaoh's *daughter* and became her child.
Your father Amram taught you (the art of) writing. After you had completed three weeks [= 21 years], he brought you into the royal court. You remained in the court for three weeks of years [= 21 years].

She named him Moses, "because," she said, "I drew him out of the water."

It is impossible to tell from the sparse givens in Exodus how long Moses remained in his mother's care (his father is not part of the story here). One learns only that he grew up and that at some time she delivered him to the princess, who "took him as her son [lit., he became her son]." Since the mother's role was to be a wet-nurse, it would be safe to assume that once the child was weaned[35] she brought him to Pharaoh's daughter. The writer of Jubilees largely reproduces the text of Exod 2:10a, though he phrases it in the second person since the angel is telling Moses about the events. One difference concerns who brought Moses to the princess. The Hebrew texts of Exod 2:10 use a third person feminine singular form of the verb "bring," indicating that Moses's mother conducted him there. In Jubilees, the verb is third person plural,

---

31 The form הילכי (SP הליכי; 4QExod^b frgs. 3 i–4 8 may attest the spelling הולכי, though the reading is very uncertain) has been explained in various ways, one of which (understanding it as a hiphil imperative) is adopted in the NRSV. See Houtman, *Exodus*, 1:286. The response of Moses's mother "So the woman took" offers support for this understanding of the word. The LXX rendered with "watch/take care of [διατήρησον]" as Jubilees does (see below). McNamara translates איבילי as "*rear*" in *Tg. Neof.* Exod 2:9, though perhaps it means "bring, carry, take." For the interpretation הא שליכי ("Behold, what is your own"), see *b. Soṭah* 12b; *Exod. Rab.* 1:25.

32 Leslau, *Comparative Dictionary*, 226.

33 Goldmann renders with תגדל; Hartom omits the verb in both vv. 7 and 8. The Latin translation lacks it in v. 7

34 This explanation is different from the one offered in VanderKam, *Jubilees* 2:307, where it is suggested that use of both "care for" and "nurse" reflects the two uses of "nurse" in Exod 2:7.

35 Some commentators on Exod 2:10 have proposed reading ויגמל ("he was weaned") instead of ויגדל ("he grew up"); see Houtman, *Exodus*, 1:287–88.

"they brought," a form that could imply that his parents brought him to her or it may express a passive sense ("you were brought"; for the emendation of "house" [*bēta* = בית] in the Ge'ez text to "daughter [*walatta* = בת]," see the textual note). The sequel names the one who brought him to the royal court.

The expression rendered by the NRSV as "she took him as her son" attracted the attention of ancient readers. What was implied in the statement? Was this an official adoption?

Targum Pseudo-Jonathan Exodus 2:10 translates: "he was *as dear* to her *as* a son."

Exodus Rabbah 1:26 explains: "Pharaoh's daughter used to kiss and hug him, loved him as if he were her own son and would not allow him out of the royal palace" (Pharaoh too kissed and hugged him, and Moses would even remove the king's crown and place it on his own head).

In Jubilees the implications are not elaborated in this place; the text is simply reproduced but in the second person. It may be, however, that the continuation of the verse is meant to clear up any uncertainties in this regard. The author of Jubilees omits the naming section of Exod 2:10—he, of course, is called *Moses* in Jubilees, but it may have seemed odd that the name came from an Egyptian princess and was given to him when he was twenty-one years old. Did his parents not give him a Hebrew name when he was an infant?[36] The writer ignores the issue and diverts attention from Pharaoh's daughter to Moses's father Amram. Kugel suggests that the "author saw two stages here: the child is brought to Pharaoh's daughter after weaning, perhaps to be officially 'adopted' by her. . . . But later, he is returned to his father Amram for education."[37] So, the writer explains that, far from spending most of his early years in the royal court and being surrounded by its influences, Amram served as Moses's teacher and, like a good father in Jubilees, he instructed him in writing. The father–son pair Amram and Moses repeat the practice attested for Terah and Abram (11:16), and Moses joins the line of illustrious ancestors who were literate and passed on as well as contributed to a written tradition: Enoch (4:17-18), Noah (10:13-14), Abraham (11:16; 12:25-27; 21:10), and Jacob (19:14; 32:24-26; 45:16). It was after twenty-one years—not after he was weaned—that Amram brought Moses to the court for a more lasting stay; as a result Moses's upbringing and education came from his own family, not from Tarmuth or any other Egyptian.[38] He was a mature and fully educated man when he arrived in Tarmuth's world. Moses then spent the next twenty-one-years in the palace.

In the chronology for Moses's life in Jubilees, he was forty-two years of age when he left Pharaoh's court: he had spent twenty-one years in his home and twenty-one in the palace. The numbers of years for the various periods in his life are given partially in Exodus and Deuteronomy. He was eighty years old when he and his brother Aaron spoke with Pharaoh (Exod 7:7), and he died at age 120 (Deut 31:2; 34:7) after the forty years in the wilderness (see Deut 1:3). There is, however, no indication of his age when he fled Egypt or of how long he remained

---

36 Some sources claim Moses's parents gave him a different name. Syncellus writes: "After he passed his early years and reached manhood, Pharaoh's daughter renamed him Moses. For she said, 'I took him from the water,' whereas he had previously been named Melchias by his parents" (139.3-5; Adler/Tuffin, *Chronography*, 173). Kugel points to *Lev. Rab.* 1:3, where he has ten names, including Moses; most of them derive from 1 Chr 4:17-18, the passage that mentions "Bithiah, daughter of Pharaoh," whom some understood as the princess in Exod 2:5-10 (*Traditions*, 530). The Visions of Amram already attests the name מלאכיה for Moses (4Q545 1a i:9). On the subject, see further R. Duke, "Moses' Hebrew Name: Evidence of the Vision of Amram," *DSD* 14 (2007) 34-48; Kister, "Ancient Material in *Pirqe de-Rabbi Eli'ezer*: Basilides, Qumran, the *Book of Jubilees*," in Aren M. Maeir, Jodi Magness, and Lawrence Schiffman, eds., *'Go Out and Study the Land' (Judges 18:2): Archaeological, Historical and Textual Studies in Honor of Hanan Eshel* (JSJSup 148; Leiden: Brill, 2012) 69–93, here 84–89.

37 Kugel, *Walk through* Jubilees, 194; "Jubilees," 442.

38 As Berger comments, the emphasis in Jubilees shows that the author does not adopt the position expressed by some writers—e.g., Philo, *Moses* 1.23-24; Acts 7:22—that Moses was educated in Egyptian wisdom (*Jubiläen*, 539-40 n. a to chap. 47). See also Halpern-Amaru, *Empowerment*, 123–24; van Ruiten, "Moses and His Parents," 75-78.

away in Midian. *Exodus Rabbah* 1:27 (commenting on Exod 2:11 and the end of the first Egyptian phase of his life) says, "Moses was twenty years old at the time; some say forty" (see also 1:30 on Exod 2:14). Stephen in Acts 7:23 puts his age at forty when he "visited his relatives" and soon after had to flee the country and in 7:30 credits forty years to his sojourn in Midian, so that his 120 years consisted of three forty-year periods (see v. 36 for the forty wilderness years). The same division is attested in *Gen. Rab.* 100:10: "Moses spent forty years in Pharaoh's palace, forty years in Midian, and served Israel forty years." The writer of Jubilees comes very close to the system of three forty-year units but modifies it slightly so that the first period consists of twenty-one plus twenty-one years, perhaps because of his fondness for sevens but especially from the need to give him a proper Israelite upbringing. This will leave only thirty-eight years for his time in Midian (see 48:1 and the commentary there).

10b-12 Danger and Flight from Egypt (Exod 2:11-15a)

The events that bring Moses's time in the palace to a close and eventuate in his first exodus from Egypt are the subject of Exod 2:11-12 and Jub 47:10b.

■ **10b** After giving the twin periods of time for the first forty-two years of Moses's life, the angel continues the story:

Exodus 2:11-12	Jubilees 47:10b
One day, after Moses had grown up, he went out to his people and saw their forced labor.	. . . until the time when you went from the royal court
He saw an Egyptian beating a Hebrew, one of his kinsfolk.	and saw the Egyptian beating your kinsman who was one of the Israelites.
He looked this way and that, and seeing no one he killed the Egyptian and hid him in the sand.	You killed him and hid him in the sand.

Exodus repeats that Moses had grown up (see v. 10), though this time it must mean he was much farther along in the maturing process than in 2:9; Jubilees had no need to make the comment because it had just given his age (forty-two [twenty-one plus twenty-one]). In Exodus his attachment to his fellow Hebrews comes strongly to the fore as he goes out (it is not said from where): he proceeds to his kin and witnesses their oppression. None of this appears in Jubilees; Moses simply exits the palace. Yet it would not be fair to say that the Moses of Jubilees lacks a sense of identity with his own people, as the next line shows. In both texts Moses comes across an Egyptian who was mistreating one of his people—a Hebrew from among his brothers/kinsfolk in Exodus, his companion/kin[39] (Latin: brother) from among the Israelites[40] in Jubilees. As Werman has noted, by replacing "Hebrew" in Exod 2:11 with "kinsman" the writer also avoids the implication that, from Moses's point of view, the person was a foreigner.[41] Moses does not act spontaneously in Exodus but clearly contemplates what he is going to do: by looking all around, he makes sure no one is present to witness his response to the abuse and then kills the Egyptian. In Jubilees he just kills him. In both texts he buries the body to hide the evidence of his deed.

■ **11** A second episode that compelled Moses to leave Egypt takes place the very next day.

Exodus 2:13	Jubilees 47:11
When he went out the next day, he saw two Hebrews fighting; and he said to the one who was in the wrong,	The next day you found[42] two of the Israelites fighting. You said to the one who was mistreating (the other):

---

39 See the textual note. *Kāleʾ* has the meanings "other, another, anyone else, second, successor, companion, friend, neighbor" (Leslau, *Comparative Dictionary*, 282). Werman prefers "your brother" because, for the author, the connection of blood Moses has with these people is the principal point.

40 Peshitta and LXX Exod 2:11 also refer to the Israelites to clarify the meaning of אחיו (lit., his brothers).

41 Werman, *Jubilees*, 532. In the HB, "Hebrew" is placed in the mouth of a foreigner or is used by an Israelite in speaking to a foreigner.

42 Where MT SP Exod 2:13 read the particle הנה instead of a verb, a number of the versions use a verb of seeing (LXX, *Targum Pseudo-Jonathan*; Peshitta has both "saw" and the particle), and Eth. Exod 2:13 has "found," just as Ethiopic Jubilees does. However, the fact that Latin Jubilees also reads "found" indicates that the verb appeared already in the Greek version of Jubilees and that Ethiopic Jubilees was, therefore, not influenced by Ethiopic Exodus at this point.

Exodus 2:13b	Jubilees 47:11b
"Why do you strike your fellow Hebrew?"[43]	"Why are you beating your brother?"

Again Jubilees, which lacks an equivalent for "went out," avoids the designation "Hebrews," preferring "Israelites" to it. Otherwise the two versions largely agree in the way in which they present Moses encountering the men who were fighting, with the expression "mistreating (the other)" clarifying the adjective רשע ("the one who was in the wrong") in Exod 2:13. Since the conflict involved two fellow Israelites, Moses might have thought he could more easily resolve it than the incident the previous day.[44]

■ **12** The surprising response of the wrongdoer to Moses's intervention proves fateful for the next major portion of his life.

Exodus 2:14-15a	Jubilees 47:12
	He became angry and indignant and
He answered, "Who made you a ruler and judge over us? Do you mean to kill me as you killed the Egyptian?" Then Moses was afraid and thought, "Surely the thing is known." When Pharaoh heard of it, he sought to kill Moses. But Moses fled from Pharaoh.	said, "Who appointed you as ruler and judge over us? Do you want to kill me as you killed the Egyptian?" Then you were afraid
	and ran away because of this matter.

Though he tends to abbreviate the accounts in Exodus, the writer here prefaces two verbs to the quoted words of the guilty person. They are found in no ancient version of Exodus but are present in both the Ethiopic and Latin translations of Jubilees and make explicit the tone in which he spoke (this will hardly be the only time in the Pentateuch that Israelites become angry at Moses). The first question posed by the speaker concerns positions Moses appears to be assuming without due process of appointment,[45] and he clearly does not think Moses has the authority to settle the matter. But in neither Exodus nor Jubilees does the issue of official functions for Moses become the point of emphasis; rather, the man's second question, which proves that Moses had failed in his attempt to keep his execution of the Egyptian secret, determines Moses's response. The man categorizes Moses's act of the previous day as killing or murder,[46] not an act meant to help his own people. Both texts report that Moses became afraid, but Exodus adds the words Moses spoke to himself and also that Pharaoh became involved in the situation. In this instance as in others, Exodus does not speak about a family relationship between the monarch and his daughter's adopted son. Why would he want to kill Moses for having executed an abusive Egyptian? In Jubilees the king has no role in the present circumstances. Moses, when he recognizes the situation, decides to flee; he does not run away because Pharaoh had pronounced a death sentence on him. He flees Egypt because the Israelite knows about how he killed an Egyptian.[47] He does not run away from Pharaoh.

---

43 The translator in the NRSV has added the word "Hebrew."

44 Acts 7:25-26 says, directly after reporting the killing of the Egyptian: "He supposed that his kinsfolk would understand that God through him was rescuing them, but they did not understand. The next day he came to some of them as they were quarreling and tried to reconcile them, saying, 'Men, you are brothers; why do you wrong each other?'"

45 Some readers of Exodus inferred that the two Hebrew men were the Dathan and Abiram who would later challenge the right of Moses and Aaron to hold the positions they claimed—they charged them with exalting themselves over the other Israelites (Num 16:3). Besides the parallel of their questioning Moses's right to the office of leadership, the verb for their opposing Moses in Num 26:9 is a form of the one used for the fighting of the two Hebrews in Exod 2:14, and Dathan and Abiram are called "evil" in Num 26:26 just as the wrongdoer is in 2:14. For these connections, see, e.g., Maher, *Targum Pseudo-Jonathan: Exodus*, 165 n. 20.

46 Houtman, *Exodus*, 1.293.

47 Stephen, in Acts 7:29, presents the situation in a similar, abbreviated way: "When he heard this, Moses fled."

48

Moses's Return to Egypt, the Plagues, and the Exodus

1/ During the sixth year of the third week of the forty-ninth jubilee [2372], you went and lived there[a] for five[b] weeks and one year [= 36 years]. Then you returned to Egypt in the second[c] week, during the second year in the fiftieth jubilee [2410]. 2/ You know who spoke[a] to you at[b] Mount Sinai and what the prince of[c] Mastema wanted to do to you[d] while you were returning to Egypt—on the way at the shady fir tree.[e] 3/ Did he not wish with all his strength to kill you and to save[a] the Egyptians from your power because[b] he saw that you were sent to carry out punishment and revenge on the Egyptians? 4/ I rescued you from his power. You performed the signs and miracles that[a] you were sent to perform in Egypt[b] against Pharaoh, all his house, his servants,[c] and his nation.[d] 5/ The Lord effected a great revenge against them[a] on account of Israel. He struck them and killed them[b] with blood, frogs, gnats, dog flies, bad sores that break out in boils;[c] (and he struck) their cattle with death; and with hailstones—with these[d] he annihilated everything that was growing for them; with locusts that ate[e] whatever was left for them[f] from the hail; with darkness; (and with the death of) their firstborn[g] of men and cattle. The Lord took revenge on all their gods[h] and burned them up. 6/ Everything was sent through you, before it was done, so that you should do (it).[a] You were speaking with the king of Egypt and in front of all his servants and his people.[b] 7/ Everything happened by your word. Ten great and severe punishments came to the land of Egypt so that you could take revenge on it for Israel. 8/ The Lord did everything for the sake of Israel and in accord with[a] his covenant that he made with Abraham to take revenge on them[b] just as they were enslaving them with force. 9/ The prince of Mastema would stand up against you and wish to make you fall into Pharaoh's power. He would help the Egyptian magicians and they would oppose (you)[a] and perform in front of you. 10/ We permitted them to do evil things, but we would not allow healings to be performed by them. 11/ When the Lord struck them with bad sores, they were unable[a] to oppose (you) because we deprived them of (their ability) to perform any sign at all.[b] 12/ Despite all the signs and miracles, the prince of[a] Mastema was not shamed until he gained strength[b] and cried out to the Egyptians to pursue you[c] with all the Egyptian army—with their chariots, their horses—and with all the throng of the Egyptian people.

13/ I[a] stood between you, the Egyptians, and the Israelites.[b] We rescued the Israelites from his power[c] and from the power of the people.[d] The Lord brought them out through the middle of the sea as if on dry ground. 14/ All of the people whom he brought out to pursue the Israelites the Lord our God threw into the sea—to the depths of the abyss—in place of the Israelites, just as the Egyptians had thrown their sons into the river. He took revenge on 1,000,000 of them, 1,000 strong men and also officers eager for battle,[a] perished for one infant of your people whom they had thrown into the river.

15/ On the fourteenth day, the fifteenth, the sixteenth, the seventeenth, and the eighteenth the prince of[a] Mastema was bound and locked up behind the Israelites so that he could not accuse them. 16/ On the nineteenth day we released them[a] so that they could help[b] the Egyptians and pursue the Israelites. 17/ He hardened their hearts[a] and made them strong. They were made strong[b] by the Lord our God so that he could strike the Egyptians and throw them[c] into the sea. 18/ On the fourteenth[a] day we bound him so that he[b] could not accuse the Israelites on the day when they were requesting utensils and clothing from the Egyptians—utensils of silver, utensils of gold, and utensils of bronze; and so that they could plunder the Egyptians in return for the fact that they were made to work[c] when they enslaved them by force. 19/ We did not bring[a] the Israelites out of Egypt empty-handed.[b]

Textual Notes

1a there] om. 20 42 47. Lat. = "in the land of Mid[ian]" ("mad" is legible; see Exod 2:15). Charles (*Ethiopic Version*, 167 n. 48) emended Eth. to agree with Lat. Berger (*Jubiläen*, 542 n. a to v. 1), however, prefers the Eth. reading and says Lat. loves clarifications of this kind. It is difficult to grasp why one would change "in the land of Midian" to "there" but easy to understand why someone would do the reverse. See VanderKam, *Jubilees* 2:309. Werman (*Jubilees*, 533 n. 2) thinks the word "there" is original to the text, but that "the land of Midian" must also have been present because "there" alone does not make sense. So she arranges it differently: you went to the land of Midian and you stayed there. Her proposal, though it lacks textual support, is appealing, but it is not evident how such a reading would have produced what is now in Eth. and Lat.

b five] So Eth. and Lat., but MSS. 39 42 47 (with 44ᵗ 48ᵗ 58) read "sixth."

c second] "its second" Lat.

2a who spoke] "that which was said" 20 25 35.

b at] *sub* ("under") Lat., a term that could have its literal meaning here or could mean "at."

c the prince of] Mss. 12 20 35 38 42 44 47 58 lack the construct ending, so that the meaning is "Prince Mastema."

d to you] om. 25.

e at the shady fir tree] The Eth. reading is: "in/at the fir of the tabernacle/shady place/shelter/both (for *'alāṭē*, see the word that Leslau spells as *'ilāṭe/'eleṭe* in *Comparative Dictionary*, 21). As Leslau indicates, the word he lists is a transcription of ελατη (see also Berger, *Jubiläen*, 542 n. c to v. 2). In some copies this word was spelled *'ālāta*, which, with the prefixed preposition *ba-*, resembles the word for "festival" so that the entire expression looks like the name for the Festival of Tabernacles (so Dillmann, "Jubiläen"). Berger suggested that the reading originated when καταλυμα (the word for "inn" in LXX Exod 4:24) was taken in the sense of "the shade of a tree." The Lat. reading is: "you passed him at the lodging place/inn." While Lat. refers to the "inn," as does LXX Exod 4:24 (in Hebrew, מלון), the Eth. reading could reflect אלון (though it means "oak"—see VanderKam, *Jubilees* 2:310 where other proposals for revisions of Eth. can be found).

3a and to save] Lat. lacks a conjunction but repeats *ut* before the second subjunctive verb. *Ut* could be a mistake for *et* or the combination *te et ut* could have led to omission of "and." The Lat. verb "save" is third pers. pl. "that they might save," but it is not clear who "they" are. Both Rönsch (*Jubiläen*, 88) and Charles (*Ethiopic Version*, 169 n. 3 to Lat.) changed the pl. to a sg. form to agree with Eth.

b because (*'esma*)] "when" 12 17 21 38 42 44 47 48 63 (*'ama*).

4a that] So Lat. Eth. *ba-za* ("in which") or *la-za* ("for which") do not fit the context well. Possibly *ba-za* is a mistake for *bo-za* ("someone, something")—an indefinite pronoun (see Dillmann, *Lexicon*, 481; Leslau, *Comparative Dictionary*, 83; VanderKam, *Jubilees* 2:310).

b in Egypt] + "and" Lat. The Lat. version, by using *in* before "Egypt" and *et in* before all the remaining nouns in the verse, yields the meaning: against Egypt, Pharaoh, all his house, etc. In Eth. "in Egypt" simply designates the place, and the signs and wonders are *against* the remaining entities.

c his servants] Lat. om. Charles (*Ethiopic Version*, 168 n. 14) suggested that the similarity between *domum* ("house") and *domesticos* ("servants") led to omission of the latter from the list.

d his nation] "all his nation" Lat. (so MS. 21).

5a against them] Lat. is partially lost, but if the letters Ceriani read are correct (*in pa . . .*), it may have differed from Eth. Rönsch (*Jubiläen*, 90) proposed *in pa[lam]* and Charles (*Ethiopic Version*, 169 n. 4 to Lat.) read *eos* = Eth., but those letters do not fit the ones Ceriani read.

b and killed them] Lat. om., perhaps from *eos . . . eos*. Charles, Littmann, Goldmann, and Hartom have left the words out of their translations, but Berger retains them. Though הכה ("strike") can mean "kill," it is reasonable to include both verbs to denote two things that the plagues did to people. Werman (*Jubilees*, 534 n. 8, 536) objects that "and killed them" is inappropriate since the plagues involved did not kill people; also, where the plagues led to death the writer makes the point explicit (as with the death of cattle mentioned later in the verse [and, of course, with the tenth]). However, the author of Jubilees may have had the seventh plague in mind, which, according to Exod 9:19, 25, brought about the deaths of animals and people, though, as Werman observes, Jubilees mentions destruction only of what was growing.

c bad sores that break out in boils] Lat. agrees with Eth. for the first three words but is uncertain for the end of the expression. The fact that Ceriani read . . . *vento*, where the expression ended has led to interesting proposals. Rönsch (*Jubiläen*, 167) thought the *wind* played a part in the plague: Moses took ashes and threw them upward. The wind spread the ashes that produced boils on the Egyptians (see Exod 9:8-12 = the sixth plague). However, if *vento* (which Rönsch changed to *venti*) is correctly read, it could be the end of another word, not a complete word (VanderKam, *Jubilees* 2:311).

d with these] om. Lat.

e locusts that ate] "locusts ate" Lat.

f (left) for them] Lat. lacks, as do 42 47.

g (and with the death of) their firstborn] Rönsch

1148

	(*Jubiläen*, 90) correctly proposed adding the words in parentheses because "firstborn" is in the gen. case in the Lat. text and thus presupposes a noun before it. It may also be that the short expression came about because the author was copying the names of the plagues from a list (see Berger, *Jubiläen*, 543 n. j to v. 5).
h	all their gods] "all the gods of the Egyptians" Lat.
6a	(it)] "revenge" 20.
b	his people] pr. "all" 38.
8a	in accord with] "concerning/because of" 20.
b	on them] "because of them/for their sake" 21 35.
9a	they would oppose (you)] "you would oppose them" 21 35; "he could oppose them" 25 39 42ᵗ 44 47 48 58; "he would oppose you" 38; "they would oppose you" 42ᶜ.
11a	they were unable] "so that they were not able" 20 25 44.
b	any sign at all] "any work/deed of a sign at all" 20 25 35.
12a	prince of] A number of MSS. lack the construct ending so that they read "Prince Mastema" (20 35 38 42 44 47 58).
b	gained strength (ḥayyala)] Many MSS. read ḥallaya, "consider, think"; it resulted when the consonants of ḥayyala were switched around.
c	(pursue) you] "them" 20 58; "before you" 63.
13a	I] "We" 39; "They" 44; "You" 48.
b	between you, the Egyptians, and the Israelites] The MSS. strongly support reading all three substantives. Charles (*Ethiopic Version*, 169 n. 16; *Jubilees*, 251–52) omitted "you" so that the angel stood between the Egyptians and the Israelites. Littmann ("Jubiläen," 116 n. c) agreed, though for him either "you" or "Israel" could be a gloss. Berger (*Jubiläen*, 545 n. a to v. 13) retains all three.
c	his power] "their power" 20 25 35 38 39 42 44 47 48 58.
d	the people] "his people" 12; "the peoples" 44.
14a	strong men and also officers eager for battle] The text says literally: "strong men and those who also were energetic three" (in the acc. case; om. 12 21 38). Berger suggested that "three" is an incorrect translation of the prefix τριο- which intensifies the adjective to which it is prefixed (*Jubiläen*, 545 n. c to v. 14). It could, therefore, be translated "*very*" (so VanderKam, *Jubilees* 2:314). The phrase probably continues describing the 1,000 men—they were strong and also very energetic. See the citation from Cedrenus, who refers to 1,000 strong men; there is not a second group of 1,000 (see Littmann, Charles, and Goldmann, and the discussion in VanderKam, *Jubilees* 2:314). Werman (*Jubilees*, 534 n. 13), however, has found a better solution to the problematic word "three." She points out that the term שלשם ("officers") occurs in Exod 14:7, where it designates a group that accompanied Pharaoh in pursuit of the Israelites (she also mentions 1QM xi:10, which refers to the same group). She posits that the word was transliterated into Greek, not translated, and was then misunderstood. With her explanation the expression makes good sense, although the accusative ending on "three" is unexpected.
15a	prince of] "Prince" 20 35 38 42 44 47 58.
16a	them] "him" 42ᶜ 58. The overwhelming preponderance of manuscript evidence favors "them," that is, Mastema and his forces (see 49:2), although they have not been mentioned in chap. 48. Segal (*Jubilees*, 219 n. 45) and Werman (*Jubilees*, 534 n. 14) counter, however, that even with so little support, the reading "him" is to be preferred because the writer, in this context, must be referring to Mastema. The pl. is surprising but hardly impossible, and it does have the textual evidence on its side.
b	they could help] "he could help" 42ᶜ 58.
17a	He hardened their hearts (lit., "He strengthened their hearts")] "Their hearts became firm" 20 25 38 (cf. 21).
b	They were made strong] "He was made strong" 38; "when he was mindful of" 20 25; "when he became strong" 39ᶜ 44 48 (see 42 47); om. 39ᵗ 63.
c	(throw) them] "him" 20.
18a	fourteenth] "seventeenth" 12 17 21 38 39 48 63; "fifteenth" 42ᵗ 47.
b	he] "they" 38.
c	were made to work] om. 17; "when they were made to work" 39 42 44 48 58 63 (both Dillmann and Charles read this form found only in later MSS.).
19a	We did not bring] "We brought" 12 17 20 25 38 63.
b	empty-handed] Mss. 42 47 place it directly after the verb.

Commentary

The chapter continues the personal story of Moses as he reaches the land of Midian, returns to Egypt, performs the ten plagues, and leads the Israelites out of Egypt to the sea while God and his angels overpower Mastema and his forces. It is remarkable for the brevity with which it treats Moses's time in Midian but especially for how it abbreviates the divine encounter with Moses and the revelation of the Lord's special name, which occupies Exodus 3. The writer devotes one clause to it and does not even mention the burning bush or disclosure of the divine name other than indirectly. He seems much more concerned to show that God through Moses took revenge on the Egyptians and their gods through the plagues—another narrative drastically shortened—and to describe the unsuccessful attempts made by Mastema to thwart the divine purpose. Even the departure from Egypt receives only an allusion (see v. 19; cf. 49:23); more to the fore is the punishment of the Egyptians in the sea and the heavenly manipulation of Mastema so that, despite his intent to oppose God by helping the Egyptians and destroying the Israelites, he utterly fails and even hastens the death of the Egyptians.

It is not easy to divide the chapter into discrete sections, but the following is a workable outline:

1-3   Moses to Midian and back (Exod 2:15b—4:31)
4-8   Revenge through ten plagues (Exod 5:1—11:10; 12:29-32)
9-19 Defeat of Mastema and the Egyptians (Exod 12:33-36; 14).

The complete Ethiopic version of the chapter is joined by the Latin translation for vv. 1-5, while a passage from Cedrenus corresponds with a part of v. 14.

1-3 Moses to Midian and Back (Exod 2:15b—4:31)

The section opens with an allusion to Exod 2:15b prefaced by a typical date formula.

■ **4** The writer dates Moses's arrival in Midian to the year 2372 (forty-two years after his birth in 2330; see 47:1, 9) and says he remained there "for five weeks and one year [= 36 years]." The only words related to Exod 2:15b have to do with his settling in the foreign land, although even here there is a difference:

Exodus 2:15b: He settled in the land of Midian
Ethiopic Jubilees 48:1: you went and lived there
Latin Jubilees 48:1: you went and lived in the land of Mid[ian].

The Ethiopic "there" is definitely the more difficult reading (it seems as if "Midian" should have been mentioned earlier so that "there" would make sense), but it has a decent claim to being original in Jubilees since the Latin could be a correction from the vague adverb to the more specific "the land of Midian" under the influence of Exod 2:15. At any rate, while the place to which Moses fled is not in question, its name may not have been part of the text.[1] The author of Jubilees does not retell the stories about Moses meeting and marrying the Midianitess Zipporah, the birth of their son Gershom, and working as a shepherd for his father-in-law Jethro.[2] He simply elides the specifics and replaces them with the bland "you went and lived there." It is possible that the encounter with the Lord at Mount Sinai does not belong to this segment of Moses's life but takes place on the trip back to Egypt (see v. 2).

Exodus does not say how long he remained in Midian, although in 4:18-19 Moses tells his father-in-law that he wants to see whether his kinsfolk in Egypt are still alive and learns from God that those who wanted to kill him were no longer living (see also 2:23: "After a long time the king of Egypt died"). The impression left is that a lengthy but undefined span of time has elapsed; Jubilees defines it as thirty-six years. It is somewhat surprising, then, to read that, after spending thirty-six years in Midian, Moses returned to Egypt (see Exod 4:20) thirty-eight years after leaving (both the Ethiopic and the Latin versions have the same date). What happened during the other two years?[3] Perhaps the reader is to imagine that all the preparations for the journey and the journey itself took the remaining time. Moses arrives back in Egypt in the year of the world 2410 when he is eighty years of age (see Exod

---

1   Caquot ("Jubilés," 801 n. 1 to chap. 48) draws attention to the fact that the Angel of the Presence is speaking to Moses about Midian while the two are on Mount Sinai, which is in Midian. Perhaps the putative situation of the narrator influenced the way he referred to the place (in his translation Caquot renders the Ethiopic but inserts the Latin reading in brackets).

2   Hartom, "Jubilees," 132 n. to v. 1; Halpern-Amaru, *Empowerment*, 124. As for the scene at the well where Moses meets his future wife (Exod 2:15b-20), it joins the parallels in Gen 24:10-33 and 29:1-14 in being omitted by the writer of Jubilees. All three appealing stories about meeting a future spouse at a well fall victim to his abbreviating tendency, but in the case of Zipporah he would have had more incentive to bypass it because she was a foreign woman.

3   Charles thought that "one year" in the phrase "five weeks and one year" was a mistake for "three years" so that the two year numbers in the verse would be the same (*Jubilees*, 249).

7:7); the exodus will occur in the same year (see Jub 50:4). A surprising chronological implication arises from assigning his return to Egypt and the exodus to the same year: since the exodus coincided with the first Passover and Passover takes place on the fourteenth of the first month (see 49:1-6), Moses's arrival in Egypt, his encounters with Pharaoh, and the plagues occurred within a two-week period (see the note at the end of the commentary on this chapter).

■ **2** The author is not explicit about it, but one could infer from v. 2 that both the Sinai revelation (see Exodus 3) and the dangerous encounter with Mastema (cf. Exod 4:24-26) happened while Moses was traveling back to Egypt. However that may be ("while you were returning to Egypt" is connected directly only to the Mastema incident), the great theophany at the bush/Sinai during which God identified himself as the deity of the patriarchs, disclosed that he had seen the suffering of his people in Egypt, revealed his name Yahweh, and commissioned Moses to lead the Israelites to that mountain and eventually to a land flowing with milk and honey receives no more attention than these words: "You know who spoke to you at Mount Sinai."[4] In Exodus 3 the identity of the one who addressed Moses is obviously central to the revelatory experience, and Moses voiced some uncertainty about the matter. The Lord said that the people's future worshiping on Sinai would be "the sign for you that it is I who have sent you" (v. 12), but Moses still wondered what he should say to the Israelites when they asked for the name of the God who had sent him (v. 13). The name is then disclosed in vv. 14-15:

> God said to Moses, "I AM WHO I AM." He said further, "Thus you shall say to the Israelites, 'I AM has sent me to you.'" God also said to Moses, "Thus you shall say to the Israelites, 'The LORD, the God of your ancestors, the God of Abraham, the God of Isaac, and the God of Jacob, has sent me to you'; This is my name forever, and this is my title for all generations."

The angel's words "You know who spoke to you at Mount Sinai," however brief, do home in on the heart of the disclosure in Exodus 3.[5]

The report about the second incident mentioned in the verse is a remarkable example of rewriting. The reference is to the strange episode related in Exod 4:24-26:

> On the way, at a place where they spent the night, the LORD met him and tried to kill him. But Zipporah took a flint and cut off her son's foreskin, and touched Moses' [text: his] feet with it, and said, "Truly you are a bridegroom of blood to me!" So he let him alone. It was then she said, "A bridegroom of blood by circumcision."

The text seems to be saying that the Lord himself, who had just sent Moses back to Egypt to lead the exodus in response to the cry of his people, now wants to kill him. Moses's wife Zipporah circumcises their son Gershom and touches someone's feet with the foreskin. Moses appears to be the one at whose feet she places it because she refers to the person involved as a bridegroom, hardly an appropriate term for their son. In the downsized Jubilees version of the story, there is no reference to circumcising or circumcision, and the one who wants to kill Moses is Mastema, who makes his first appearance in the text since 19:28 and takes up his first active role in the narrative since 17:16; 18:9, 12 (the near-sacrifice of Isaac). Now, in the crucial time when the exodus is looming, he redoubles his efforts to frustrate the plans of God, and his initial ploy is to block Moses's return to wreak vengeance on Egypt.

The book of Jubilees is not the only source that credits the strange action of the Lord in Exod 4:24-26—specifically his attempt to slay Moses—to another agent.[6] The LXX tradition for the pericope and all the

---

4   See the textual note for the reading "what was said to you," which Kugel (*Walk through* Jubilees, 195; "Jubilees," 442) prefers, as does Werman (*Jubilees*, 533 n. 3). The textual evidence and the explanation above favor the reading adopted here.

5   This seems to fit the evidence from Exodus 3 better than the suggestion (mentioned but rejected by Kugel, *Walk through* Jubilees, 195; "Jubilees," 442) that the reading "who spoke to you at Sinai" is directed at the confusion about who talked with Moses from the burning bush, an angel (Exod 3:2) or the Lord/God (3:4).

6   See Charles, *Jubilees*, 250: "We have in this verse another instance (cf. also ver. 17) where our author

targums introduce another character or characters into the account.[7]

Exodus 4:24 (MT SP Peshitta): the LORD met him and tried to kill him
- LXX (and dependent translations): an angel of the Lord met him and was seeking to kill him
- Targums
  - *Onqelos*: an angel of the Lord met him and sought to kill him
  - *Neofiti*: *an angel from before* the Lord overtook him and sought to kill him
  - *Pseudo-Jonathan*: *the angel of* the Lord met him and sought to kill him

Exodus 4:25: and touched Moses's [text: his] feet with it
- *Fragment Targum*: and presented it at the feet of the destroyer . . . to save the bridegroom from the hands of the angel of death (trans. VanderKam)
- *Targum Neofiti*: and brought it near the feet of the *destroyer*
- *Targum Pseudo-Jonathan*: and brought *the circumcised foreskin* to the feet of *the Destroying Angel*

Exodus 4:26: So he let him alone . . . A bridegroom of blood by circumcision
- *Fragment Targum*: When the destroyer let him go . . . saved this bridegroom from the hands of the angel of death (trans. VanderKam)
- *Targum Neofiti*: And *the angel* let him go from him . . . *that has delivered this* bridegroom *from the hand of the angel of death*
- *Targum Pseudo-Jonathan*: And the *Destroying Angel* left him alone . . . *that saved* the bridegroom *from the hands of the Destroying Angel*.

By shortening the story as he does, the author of Jubilees makes only one reference to an evil being, who is also a destroyer,[8] and does not have to deal with the awkward facts that Moses had not circumcised his son and that his foreign wife saved the day (and Moses) by performing the task herself. The angel gives Moses only a brief reminder of the whole embarrassing situation and transforms the event into an attack by Mastema, who wants to stop Moses from carrying out his divine commission.[9]

Segal explains how the rewriting of the passage in Jubilees responds to one exegetical and two theological questions raised by Exod 4:24-26. The exegetical issue is: why would God want to kill Moses after having just commanded (see Exod 4:19) him to return to Egypt? The answer of Jubilees is that it was not God who wanted Moses dead but rather Mastema. The first theological problem is whether God is unjust in the Exodus passage since he wanted to kill someone (and Moses at that) without an explicit motive. The answer in Jubilees is that the theodicy question is irrelevant because God was not the one desiring to kill Moses without a reason. And the second theological problem is: if God wanted to kill Moses how could he not succeed? Is God not omnipotent? The reply is, of course, that God was not the one who failed.[10]

The location where Mastema made his attempt on Moses's life is an inn—a place to spend the night—

---

has followed the example of the Chronicler in 1 Chron. xxi. 1, where he assigns to Satan the action that in 2 Sam. xxiv. 1 is ascribed to Yahweh." One of the parallels between the Exodus stories in Jubilees and its version of the Aqedah is ascribing a puzzling action of God to Mastema.

[7] Vermes (*Scripture and Tradition*, 178-90) surveys these and other sources that deal with Exod 4:24-26, although his interest is more in the theme of circumcision in the passage itself and in the interpretations of it. Houtman (*Exodus*, 1:439-49) devotes a section to the passage and the ways in which writers ancient and modern have viewed it.

[8] The term used for the being who attacks Moses—destroyer (destroying angel)—in the targums to Exod 4:25-26 reminds one of the passages in Jubilees where Mastema is associated with destroying and destruction (10:1, 3, 5, 8; 11:5, 11). Segal sees a two-step process at work here (*Jubilees*, 208-10). First there was an interchange of God/the Lord with an angel, something that happens more often in the Bible (e.g., Exod 3:2); second, and this is a radical step, replacing an angel of the Lord with Mastema.

[9] Halpern-Amaru, *Empowerment*, 124-25. She comments: "The excision of Zipporah, and of her father, Jethro, as well, stands in sharp contrast to the biblical presentation of their positive and influential roles in the life of Moses. Indeed, their absence reflects the extent to which the concern with genealogy and exogamy influence the treatment of wives and mothers" (p. 125). In some texts, Zipporah receives a Hebrew pedigree by identifying her father Jethro (he is also called Reuel

according to Exod 4:24. Latin Jubilees agrees (*in refectione*), but the Ethiopic reading is *ba-'alātē meslāl*: in the fir tree ['*alātē* = a transcription of ελατη] of the shady place/shelter/booth/tabernacle (see the textual note).[11] How this reading arose when the entire textual tradition of Exodus reads "at the inn [Eth. Exod 4:24: *ba-westa māḥdar*]"[12] is not known, although it is just possible that the Hebrew of Jubilees read אלון where the MT and SP have מלון.[13]

■ 3 More important than the place where Mastema and Moses had their encounter is the purpose the evil being had in mind. The Angel of the Presence, who is speaking to Moses, depicts Mastema as the defender of the Egyptians. Somehow Mastema had learned that the Lord sent Moses "to carry out punishment and revenge on the Egyptians," and he wanted to do everything in his power to prevent execution of God's plan. The story about the plagues and the exodus is one of the few Jubilees narratives in which Mastema plays a major part. As in another one of them, the binding of Isaac, he aims to foil the realization of divine promises.[14]

The purpose for which the Lord sent Moses back to Egypt—to punish and take vengeance on the Egyptians—puts the focus on the negative side (what happens to the Egyptians), whereas in Exodus 3 the emphasis lies more on delivering the Israelites from their miserable situation (e.g., 3:7-12, 16-17). The statement of intent points, of course, to Moses's role in the stories about the ten plagues, but it may also echo a passage such as Exod 4:21: "And the LORD said to Moses, 'When you go back to Egypt, see that you perform before Pharaoh all the wonders that I have put in your power [lit., your hand]. . . .'" A number of verses refer to the plagues as punishments or judgments (Exod 6:6; 7:4; 12:12; see Gen 15:14 // Jub 14:14), but the idea of revenge is not explicit in the Hebrew text. In the LXX tradition, however, both Exod 7:4 and 12:12 read "vengeance" (forms of εκδικησις), where the Hebrew texts mention "judgments." In other words, there is early evidence that readers interpreted the plagues as revenge. The writer of Jubilees, presumably aware of this meaning, sees an important element of retaliation in the story about the plagues and the exodus (see vv. 5, 7-8, 14). In Jubilees, God not only saw the suffering of his people but also repaid the Egyptians for the oppression they had forced upon them; Moses was the human agent for carrying out the acts of revenge (cf. 4Q225 frg. 1 8).[15]

4-8 Revenge through Ten Plagues (Exod 5:1—11:10; 12:29-32)

After briefly tying in the sequel with what it has just related, the text moves directly to the plagues.

■ 4 The angel informs Moses that he was the one

---

      in Exod 2:18) as one descended from the marriage of Abraham and Keturah (LXX Gen 25:3 lists a person with the name Reuel as a great-grandson of Abraham). See Kugel, *Traditions*, 533-34.
10   Segal, *Jubilees*, 204-7.
11   For the two nouns, see Leslau, *Comparative Dictionary*, 21, 555. Both he (p. 21) and Berger (*Jubiläen*, 542 n. c. to v. 2) have noted that '*alātē* is an Ethiopic transcription of Greek ελατη. Dillmann, whose manuscript read *ba'ala meslāl*, rendered the phrase as "on the Festival of Tabernacles," and Goldmann with "when you were in the tent." See VanderKam, *Jubilees* 2:309-10.
12   Moses is even chided in some texts because of his association with an inn (e.g., *b. Ned.* 31b-32a).
13   For this suggestion, see VanderKam, *Jubilees* 2:309-10; Kugel (*Walk through* Jubilees, 195; cf. "Jubilees," 465 n. 260) and Werman (*Jubilees*, 533 n. 4) accept it.
14   Esther Eshel maintains that Maslj (1276-1786), on which a few letters from two columns survive, relates the scene where Mastema tries to kill Moses ("Mastema's Attempt on Moses' Life in the 'Pseudo-Jubilees' Text from Masada," *DSD* 10 [2003] 359-64). "Prince Mastema" appears on i:5, and "Midian" may be mentioned in ii:4. Eshel suggests that i:6, where part of the number has to be restored, reads "sev]enty years," possibly the end of a longer number—seventy-eight—which is Moses's age when he returns to Egypt (he is actually eighty according to Jub 48:1). The fragmentary text may relate to the incident here in Jub 48:2, but it is so badly preserved that little can be said about it.
15   Josephus (*Ant.* 2.276), after describing the miraculous powers God gave to Moses and the revelation of the ineffable name, writes about both aspects: "from all which tokens he came to trust more firmly in the oracle from the fire, to believe that God would be his gracious protector, and to hope to be able to deliver his people and to bring disaster on the Egyptians" (Thackeray, LCL).

responsible for rescuing him from Mastema. Exodus 4:26 speaks vaguely about Moses being spared after Zipporah circumcised their son: "So he let him alone," with "he" seemingly being the Lord and "him" standing for Moses.[16] If the Lord is the subject, then the present verse is another instance in which the angel (with or without his colleagues) does something attributed to God in Genesis–Exodus (e.g., Jub 3:1, 4, 9; 4:2, 23; 12:22; 14:20; 16:1, 2, 4; etc.). So the Angel of the Presence is an opponent of Mastema: he rescues Moses from him and will assist in saving the Israelites, while Mastema wants to kill Moses and save the Egyptians.

The angel also introduces the next subject—the plagues (they are listed in v. 5)—with a general rubric regarding the "signs and miracles [wonders] that you were sent to perform in Egypt." He declares that Moses did indeed accomplish the task for which he was sent, and again the emphasis falls on punishment for Pharaoh and his Egyptian subjects. The topic of signs and/or wonders is an important one in Exodus 3–12, but in those chapters several entities are so designated. The first time one of the terms appears ("sign") it refers to Moses's future leading of the people to Mount Sinai to signify that God had sent him (3:20). The next series of references to signs deals with the miracles Moses was empowered to enact in order to convince the Israelites that the Lord had actually appeared to him: the staff turning into a snake and back again, the hand becoming leprous and then healthy, and, if needed, transforming some Nile water into blood (Exod 4:1-3, 17, 28, 30). These can hardly be the signs and wonders to which the angel refers in v. 4 because, apart from the fact that he does not mention them, they were for the Israelites and were not directed against Egypt. The Nile water-to-blood miracle, however, overlaps with the first plague and hints at the use of sign/wonder language for the plagues. Such usage is possibly found in Exod 4:21,

where God ordered Moses: "When you go back to Egypt, see that you perform before Pharaoh all the wonders that I have put in your power," although the command could point to Exod 7:8-13, where Moses and Aaron perform the staff/snake wonder. A clearer reference to the plagues as signs/wonders comes in Exod 7:3, where the Lord threatens, "I will multiply my signs and wonders in the land of Egypt," and in 11:9-10, where, after nine plagues and a warning about the tenth, the text reports, "The LORD said to Moses, 'Pharaoh will not listen to you, in order that my wonders may be multiplied in the land of Egypt.' Moses and Aaron performed all these wonders before Pharaoh" (see also Exod 8:23; 10:1; Ps 105:27; Acts 7:36).[17] These wonders and signs Moses (with Aaron) did perform, and they affected Pharaoh, his house, his servants, and his people as Exodus 7–12 explains in detail and Jub 48:4 declares briefly. In Jubilees, Aaron has no role in bringing about the plagues.

■ 5 Like Exodus, Jubilees names ten plagues, but it does not package them as elements in a lengthy narrative the way Exodus does. So, for example, the writer leaves out the meetings with Pharaoh, the various roles of Moses and Aaron in bringing about the individual plagues, the constant vacillating by Pharaoh, and most of the material about the devastating results of the miracles. He simply lists them as the objects of the words "He [= the Lord] struck them and killed them with." For the verb "strike" (hiphil forms of נכה) used with "plagues," see Exod 3:20; 7:25; 9:15; Pss 78:51; 105:33; 136:10. "Killing" appears in Exodus in connection with the fifth plague (disease of animals [Exod 9:3, 6]), the seventh (hail that killed animals and people in the fields [9:19, 25]), and, of course, the tenth (death of the Egyptian firstborn [11:5; 12:29-30]).

As they are identified in Exodus and Jubilees, these are the ten plagues:

---

[16] SP reads "her [= Zipporah]" in this place. 4QGen-Exod[a] frgs. 24-25 i:1 has "him," though the reading is uncertain. Werman thinks the writer learned about the Angel of the Presence's involvement in the episode from the verb ויפגשהו in v. 24 (*Jubilees*, 535). The subject according to the author is the angel (the subject is the Lord in Exodus). Her suggestion is certainly possible, but it would require a swift change of subject because Mastema would be the subject of the very next verb—"and tried (to kill him)."

[17] In Exod 12:13 the blood on the doorposts and lintel is called a sign for the Israelites.

Exodus	Jubilees
Blood	Blood
Frogs	Frogs
Gnats	Gnats
Flies[18]	Dog flies[19]
Pestilence on livestock	Sores[20]
Boils	Death for cattle
Thunder and hail	Hailstones[21]
Locusts	Locusts[22]
Darkness	Darkness
Firstborn	Firstborn

The lists are the same except for the order of plagues 5 and 6: Exodus places the cattle disease before the boils, and Jubilees has them in reverse order. There are various early enumerations of the plagues, with none of them yielding the order of either Exodus or Jubilees (see Pss 78:42-51; 105:26-36; Josephus, *Ant.* 2.293-314 [he does not mention the plague on livestock]; Philo, *Moses* 1.96-139).[23]

These ten plagues the writer of Jubilees understood as vengeance that the Lord wreaked on the gods of Egypt. The theme of repaying the gods of Egypt comes from Exod 12:12 (see Num 33:4), where the Lord says to Moses regarding the tenth plague: "For I will pass through the land of Egypt that night, and I will strike down every firstborn in the land of Egypt, both human beings and animals; on all the gods of Egypt I will execute judgments: I am the LORD."[24] This is one of the passages (see above; it also happens in Num 33:4) in which LXX renders "I will execute judgments" as "I will execute vengeance [ποιησω την εκδικησιν]."[25] A prediction by the Lord in Exodus becomes a report of something accomplished in Jubilees. As for burning the gods of Egypt (i.e., their idols), the note may be an early witness to a way of understanding God's revenge or judgment on the Egyptian deities as absolutely thorough. *Targum Pseudo-Jonathan* Exod 12:12 (end) reads: "I will execute *four* judgments on all the *idols* of Egypt: *the molten idols will be melted, the idols of stone will be smashed, the idols of clay will be reduced to sherds, and the idols of wood will be reduced to ashes, that the Egyptians may know that* I am the Lord."[26]

---

18   While the NRSV and other versions translate ערב as "flies," it is not clear exactly what the swarm includes. Some ancient sources understood it to mean a lot of wild animals. See *Exod. Rab.* 11:3; *Tg. Ps.-J.* Exod 8:17, 20, 25, 27; Josephus, *Ant.* 2.303; L.A.B. 10:1. Cf. also Kugel, *Traditions*, 563-65.

19   Eth. Jubilees and Eth. Exod 8:16-28 (English, 8:20-32) use the same terms for the flies—flies of dogs; they reflect the noun used in the LXX for this plague—κυνομυιαν. The Latin of Jubilees too has a noun *flies* modified by an adjective meaning "pertaining to dogs [*caninas*]."

20   For the explanatory words "that break out in boils," see Exod 9:9, 10 ("cause[d] festering boils").

21   For the added words "with these he annihilated everything that was growing for them," see Exod 9:25.

22   For the expression "that ate whatever was left for them from the hail," see Exod 10:5, 12, 15.

23   Philo's order of the plagues differs because he groups them by the agent who carried them out: three by Aaron (plagues belonging to the denser elements earth and water), three by Moses (plagues belonging to air and fire), one by Aaron and Moses; the remaining three by God himself (*Mos.* 1.97). Several of the plagues also figure in Wisdom of Solomon 11-19. Ezekiel the Tragedian (*Exagoge* 132-51) may record ten plagues, but they are decidedly not in the same order as in Exodus; while Pseudo-Philo (L.A.B. 10:1), who refers to ten plagues, lists nine in a different order and without the plague of boils.

24   Segal concludes from the writer's use of Exod 12:12, in which the Lord is the subject of all the verbs, that God performed the plagues himself with no need of assistance (*Jubilees*, 214). The inference is dubious and will be addressed in the commentary on 49:2-6. Employing Exod 12:12 does not entail that the deity used no help.

25   Eth. Exod 12:12 uses the same verb and noun as Jubilees does here. It may be, as Segal maintains (*Jubilees*, 212 n. 26), that the Ge'ez rendering (for *baqal*, see Leslau, *Comparative Dictionary*, 100: "revenge") reflects the expression in Exod 12:12—a form of עשה with משפטים, but this was understood as revenge in at least part of the exegetical tradition, as the LXX shows.

26   *Mekilta de-Rabbi Ishmael, Pisḥa* 7 (trans. Lauterbach, 1:55): "They became soft, they became hollow, they were chopped down, they were burned." For these and other references, see Berger, *Jubiläen*, 543-44 n. k. to v. 5. Abram burned the temple of the idols in Jub 12:12-13, and Jacob burned the gods Rachel had stolen from Laban in 31:2. Burning the idols of the nations is what Deut 7:5 prescribes regarding the seven Canaanite peoples (so the Egyptians do

■ **6-7** The angel continues his report to Moses by reminding him of his role in the plagues. He does not say that Moses was ultimately the authority or power behind the plagues; vv. 5 and 8 state expressly that God was the one who made the plagues happen and accomplish their purpose. Moses, however, was the agent for them. The angel puts the point well: "Everything was sent through you, before it was done, so that you should do (it)." The first part of the sentence has to do with the fact that Moses was instrumental in sending all of the plagues because in every case he was the one to whom God made known what the plague would be and who then announced it (1-2, 4-5, 7-8, 10), ordered that Aaron carry it out (3), or received instructions from the Lord about effecting it without first announcing it to the monarch (6, 9). Aaron participates in various ways in all of the plague accounts except in plagues 5 and 9, but he is decidedly the junior partner in the entire exercise. The writer of Jubilees eliminates Aaron entirely from the plague section—something that may be significant, although his tendency to abbreviate is extreme in these stories.

That the agency of Moses in bringing the plagues is under consideration follows from the angel's further words that Moses spoke with Pharaoh and before his servants and people. For plagues 1-2, 4-5, 7-8, and 10 he did speak to the king (he and Aaron do so after plague 9 as well). In several cases royal "officials" (as the NRSV translates the word meaning "servants") and/or the people are mentioned (Exod 7:20; 8:4, 9, 11, 21, 29, 31; 9:14, 20, 30, 34; 10:6, 7; 11:1, 8; 12:30), and Exod 11:3 says, "Moreover, Moses himself was a man of great importance in the land of Egypt, in the sight of Pharaoh's officials and in the sight of all the people." There was nothing hidden about what Moses did and said; the entire population of Egypt knew about it.[27]

The angel reinforces the point in v. 7, where he highlights the fact that every plague took place at the time when Moses announced it or performed the action that brought it about (see Exod 7:19; 8:5, 16, 20; 9:1, 8, 22; 10:3, 21; 11:1); cf. 6:29: "tell Pharaoh king of Egypt all that I am speaking to you."[28] Exodus does not number the plagues visited upon Egypt, but the angel refers to "Ten great and severe punishments." For the plagues as punishments on the Egyptians, see 48:3, where the angel refers to them in this way. The language of punishment recalls Exod 6:6 ("mighty [lit., great] acts of judgment"), 7:4 ("great acts of judgment"), and 12:12 ("judgments"). The adjective "severe" is not used to describe the plagues in Exodus, though it is a most appropriate term for several of them. It is noteworthy that the Angel of the Presence says not only that the punishments struck Egypt but also that "you [Moses] could take revenge on it for Israel." Revenge is what the Lord effected according to v. 5, but in v. 3 Mastema tried to kill Moses because he was on his way to Egypt "to carry out punishment and revenge on the Egyptians." Moses's role in exacting vengeance takes the same form as his role in the plagues: he is the agent through whom the Lord sent the plagues and thus repaid the Egyptians for what they had done to the Israelites.

■ **8** The role of the deity in the action leading up to the departure from Egypt is the subject of v. 8. The Lord sent the ten severe punishments or plagues on Egypt for the benefit of his people Israel and did this because of his covenant promise to Abraham. The reference is to the covenant between the pieces (Genesis 15 // Jub 14:1-20), where there is a clearer connection between the

---

not figure there). Segal also adduces Ezek 30:14-19 and Jer 43:12-13, the latter of which refers to burning the temples of Egyptian gods (*Jubilees*, 212); he adds 1QM xiv:1, which speaks of God's wrath against the idols of Egypt. Cf. also Werman, *Jubilees*, 536.

27 Werman thinks the writer took the first part of v. 6 from Exod 4:21, which he detached from its context and read as referring to the ten plagues presented in miniature before Pharaoh (*Jubilees*, 536). Her hypothesis seems unnecessary in light of the passages adduced above as the basis for v. 6.

28 Werman alters the text at "by your word [*ba-qāleka*]" because, she thinks, it would make God the agent of Moses (*Jubilees*, 537). Moses would announce a plague and the Lord would obediently carry out his word. The proper reading for her is "according to your word." The change is not needed because the writer is conveying the message that Moses, as God's agent, declared the warnings to Pharaoh and events transpired in line with the divine message he brought.

Egyptians' mistreating Israel and God's punishing them for it than there is in Exodus. The passage from Genesis and its parallel in Jubilees speak of Abram's descendants suffering oppression and serving as slaves in a foreign land. They add the divine promise that "I will judge the nation whom they serve. Afterwards, they will leave from there with many possessions" (Jub 14:14 // Gen 15:14). As interpreted here in Jubilees, the plagues were the way in which God carried out his promise to Abram to judge the oppressing nation for what they did to Abram's descendants. The Egyptians enslaved the Israelites with force (see Jub 46:14-15; Exod 1:11, 13-14); God's judgment repaid them for abusing his people. It was his act of revenge[29] on their behalf for the terrible treatment they had suffered in Egypt.

The notions of punishment and revenge are certainly significant in the author's understanding of the plagues. He could take the theme of punishment from the references to God's judging[30] the Egyptians (Exod 6:6; 7:4; 12:12; Num 33:4), but in Exodus the plagues play the role of convincing Pharaoh to allow the Israelites to leave (e.g., 7:14), in some passages for just a three-day trip to worship their God (8:27 [Heb. 8:23] is one) or to prove that the Lord is supreme (7:5, 17; 8:10, 22 [Heb. 7:6, 18]; 9:14, 16, 30).[31] The plagues are not said to be punishments for how the Egyptians had mistreated the Hebrews (but see Neh 9:9). Genesis 15:14 probably was the source for connecting divine judgment or punishment with the oppression that preceded it. It may also have been suggested by Exod 4:22-23: "Then you shall say to Pharaoh, 'Thus says the LORD: Israel is my first-born son. I said to you, "Let my son go that he may worship me." But you refused to let him go; now I will kill your firstborn son.'"[32] So the tenth plague was a punishment for Pharaoh's refusal to let God's firstborn, Israel, go—a punishment in kind.[33] It perhaps was not a long step from this understanding of the plagues as punishment to relating them with the oppression the Israelites endured and thus, as LXX Exod 7:4 and 12:12 show, to the thought that they were repaying, taking revenge on the Egyptians, especially Pharaoh, for making Egypt a house of bondage for them.

9-19 Defeat of Mastema and the Egyptians (Exod 12:33-36; 14)

The remainder of the chapter focuses on the role of Mastema (he was mentioned above in vv. 2-4) and his forces during the time of the plagues and afterwards when the Egyptians pursued the Israelites to the sea.

■ **9-11** The verses explain several references in the plague narratives indicating that Moses and Aaron were not the only ones doing signs and wonders at the time. In Exod 7:8-12, Aaron, on Moses's instructions, throws down his staff and it turns into a snake. "Then Pharaoh summoned the wise men and the sorcerers; and they also, the magicians of Egypt, did the same by their secret arts. Each one threw down his staff, and they became snakes; but Aaron's staff swallowed up theirs" (7:11-12). After the first plague, "the magicians of Egypt did the same by their secret arts" (7:22), and they repeated their dubious success by bringing even more frogs on Egypt

---

29 In *Tg. Neof.* Gen 15:14 the idea of revenge arises: "I, however, will *be avenged* of the nations that will *enslave* them." According to *Tg. Ps.-J.* Gen 15:14 the passage means: "But the people whom they shall serve I will judge *with two hundred and fifty plagues.*" See *Exod. Rab.* 23:9. Exodus 2:24-25 says that God, in response to the groaning of Israel, recalled his covenant with Abraham, Isaac, and Jacob (cf. 6:5).

30 The verb used in Gen 15:14 (דן) can have the meanings "judge" and "execute judgment" (BDB, 192), with the latter close in nuance to "punish."

31 Pharaoh had made the mistake of asking, "Who is the LORD, that I should heed him and let Israel go? I do not know the LORD, and I will not let Israel go" (Exod 5:2). The plagues, therefore, serve as a harsh theological education for the king.

32 See Wis 18:5: "When they had resolved to kill the infants of your holy ones, / and one child had been abandoned and rescued, / you in punishment took away a multitude of their children; / and you destroyed them altogether by a mighty flood." The last line points to drowning the Egyptians at the sea, a natural candidate for a measure-for-measure approach to the drowning of Hebrew boys (see below, v. 14).

33 For Wisdom of Solomon 11–19 several of the plagues were measure-for-measure repayments of the Egyptians, although there the sage relates some of them to Egyptian worship of animals and others to events during the wilderness wanderings. An example confined to the plague stories is that the first (turning the water of the Nile into blood) requited them for drowning Israelite boys (11:6-7).

at the time of the second plague (8:7 [Heb. 8:3]). By the third plague (gnats), however, they had reached the limits of their expertise: "The magicians tried to produce gnats by their secret arts, but they could not" (8:18; in v. 19 they realize the plague was "the finger of God" [Heb. 8:14, 15]). In the sixth plague, "The magicians could not stand before Moses because of the boils, for the boils afflicted the magicians as well as all the Egyptians" (9:11). The successes enjoyed by Pharaoh's experts in mimicking miraculous actions done by Moses and Aaron the writer of Jubilees explains as due to the power of Mastema, but their failures resulted from the limits imposed on them by the angels of God and the Lord himself.

Mastema, in his role of opposing Moses, "would stand up against"[34] him in these scenes to make him fail and thus, rather than punishing Pharaoh, become his victim. His tactic was to "help the Egyptian magicians and they would oppose (you)[35] and perform in front of you" (v. 9). Presumably this refers to the three instances in which they matched the miracles of Moses and Aaron (once before the plagues, and during plagues 1 and 2). So it was not the power inherent in the magical exercises of the Egyptian experts that allowed them to do amazing things; the supernatural Mastema was helping them so that the plagues would not accomplish their purpose. These episodes left the impression that Moses possessed no greater power than Mastema brought to bear on the situation and that the God who had sent Moses had yet to demonstrate his superiority. In the plague stories in Exodus, it does not appear that Moses is in danger of falling into Pharaoh's hands (however bluntly he speaks to him),[36] but the king did say after the ninth plague: "Get away from me! Take care that you do not see my face again, for on the day you see my face you shall die" (10:28).

■ **10-11** While there may seem to have been a balance of power at this point, with Moses and the magicians able to do the same wonders, the true situation becomes clear in vv. 10-11. The apparent success of the magicians, empowered by Mastema, came about only by the permission of God's angels. The Angel of the Presence and his colleagues, who are Mastema's opponents (see below, vv. 13, 16, 18-19), allowed Mastema his little triumphs but set limits on their extent.[37] They permitted the magicians to do "evil things." Apparently these words mean their ability to imitate the first two plagues—displays of power that only made bad situations worse (more water into blood and more frogs). That is, the angels of the presence allowed the magicians to increase the damage to Egypt, but they did not permit them to do anything positive. The fabled power of the magicians resulted in nothing that would help their own people; they could only add to their misery. The good angels ruled out any healing miracles for the Egyptian experts. As v. 11 shows, this refers to the second case in which they could not imitate a miracle of Moses and Aaron: there was nothing they could do to heal the Egyptians or even themselves from the boils that broke out on all of them (Exod 9:11).[38] When the Lord struck them with the sores (for the term, see v. 5), they were unable to match the miracle God sent through Moses and thus could not oppose him as they had on the earlier occasions. Mastema, true to his nature, was very helpful when it came to doing harm (see Jub 10:8; 11:5, 11); he was powerless when it came to doing good. Preventing Mastema or his allies from performing cures recalls the story in Jub 10:1-13 in which the angels of the presence revealed to Noah medicines for counteracting the diseases and deceptions caused by Mastema and his evil spirits. Healing did not belong in his portfolio.

---

34 In Zech 3:4 the satan stands at the right hand of the high priest Joshua to accuse him. 4Q225 frg. 1 8 may refer to Mastemah (only the last letter is preserved) standing; it follows by saying Moses took vengeance (as in Jub 48:3, 7). On the passage, see Milik and VanderKam, DJD 13:145.

35 See the textual note for the variants in the manuscripts regarding who opposed whom.

36 Werman interprets "wish to make you fall into Pharaoh's power" as referring to the attempt to make the magical ability of the magicians (supported by Mastema) greater than or equal to that of God (through Moses) (*Jubilees*, 537).

37 In Jub 18:9 the Angel of the Presence stood between Abraham and Mastema to prevent the sacrifice of Isaac that Mastema clearly wanted.

38 Segal comments that in Exodus boils hinder the magicians from reproducing the miracle, whereas in Jubilees the angels of the presence thwarted them (*Jubilees*, 215).

■ **12** Mastema was, however, a slow learner or at least willing to try anything at this desperate juncture when it looked as if God's plans were moving forward. Despite the limits placed on his agents, the Egyptian magicians, and thus his failure to nullify the effects of the plagues, he kept trying to impose his will throughout the time of the plagues until he, for the second time in Jubilees (see 18:12), was ashamed or put to shame.[39] Plagues 1–10 did not convince him that his cause was lost; only what happened at the sea, after the Israelites left Egypt, made the point unmistakable.

The story in Exodus gives the strong impression that the Egyptians, including Pharaoh, were only too happy to see the Israelites go. After Moses had issued the threat about the coming of plague 8 (locusts), "Pharaoh's officials said to him, 'How long shall this fellow be a snare to us? Let the people go, so that they may worship the LORD their God; do you not yet understand that Egypt is ruined?'" (10:7). After the ninth plague Pharaoh never wanted to see Moses again (10:28). When it was time for the tenth plague, the Lord told Moses that it would make Pharaoh drive them away (11:1),[40] and Moses predicted that the king's officials would request respectfully that they depart (11:8). When that last, horrible blow struck, Pharaoh ordered Moses and Aaron, "Rise up, go away from my people, both you and the Israelites! Go, worship the LORD, as you said. Take your flocks and your herds, as you said, and be gone" (12:31-32). The Egyptians were terribly eager to see the exodus take place: "The Egyptians urged the people to hasten their departure from the land, for they said, 'We shall all be dead'" (12:33)—a prediction that will soon come true. They wanted the Israelites to go so badly that they gave them whatever they requested even before the last plague (11:2-3; 12:35-36; cf. v. 39; Ps 105:37-38; see below on vv. 18-19). Under these circumstances, why would the Egyptians almost immediately change their minds and rush after the Israelites?

The implausible decision is credited in Exod 14:4 (see also vv. 5, 8) to a familiar cause: "I will harden Pharaoh's heart, and he will pursue them, so that I will gain glory for myself over Pharaoh and all his army; and the Egyptians shall know that I am the LORD." The battle between the Lord and Pharaoh did not end with the plagues; there remained in it one last phase that would teach the lesson intended (see also Exod 14:17-18). Jubilees attributes the Egyptian decision to pursue the departing Israelites to the misleading work of Mastema, who convinced them to make this supremely foolish and suicidal choice. The author understood him to be the means through which God hardened Pharaoh's heart:[41] he urged the Egyptians—the army and the people together—to chase Moses (the word "you" after "pursue" is singular); see also v. 17. Since Moses was leading the Israelites, the pursuit was aimed at the whole nation. It may be that the passive phrasing of Exod 14:5 contributed to the kind of explanation offered in Jubilees: "When the king of Egypt was told that the people had fled, the minds of Pharaoh and his officials *were changed* toward the people, and they said, 'What have we done, letting Israel leave our service?'" If their minds "were changed," someone (or something) must have done the changing for them, and in Jubilees Mastema was responsible for their about-face. Hence, this demonic character, who does not know how the episode will end, continues to oppose God's plan for the redemption of his people.[42]

---

39 In 18:12 the form is passive (*taḥafra*), while here it is the base stem (*ḥafara*, "be ashamed, embarrassed, disgraced" [Leslau, *Comparative Dictionary*, 259]).

40 The word כלה in the verse has been taken by some to mean "totality," perhaps in the sense that Pharaoh would expel them "without exception" (see Houtman, *Exodus*, 2:129–31); it is rendered as "with everything" in the LXX and as "in all haste" in *Targum Neofiti* ("complete destruction" for Pharaoh in *Targum Pseudo-Jonathan*).

41 Cf. Caquot, "Jubilés," 802 n. to v. 12.

42 Segal, *Jubilees*, 216. In the same place he infers more from the passage: "The rewriting in *Jub.* 48:12 assumes that God has no interest that Egypt chase after Israel, and clears him of any direct responsibility for Pharaoh's decision. The replacement of YHWH with Mastema is the result of the general tendency in ch. 48: Mastema is Egypt's heavenly representative, in opposition to YHWH and the angel of the presence." Why one should conclude that God has no interest in the Egyptian pursuit is not easy to see. Segal's inference conflicts with the theme of measure-for-measure revenge that the Lord takes for the

The angel, in saying "until he gained strength," indicates that once Mastema recovered from the situation that will be described in vv. 15-18 (he was restrained for several days) he immediately resumed his baleful ways. The last part of the verse reflects Exod 14:9: "The Egyptians pursued them, all Pharaoh's horses and chariots, his chariot drivers and his army." For "all the throng of the Egyptian people" as part of the pursuers, see Exod 14:6, where Pharaoh also takes with him "his people" (עמו),[43] a term that means "his army" (so NRSV) but that was perhaps understood by the author of Jubilees as meaning the entire population.

■ **13-14** The short summary of the drama at the sea picks up several themes in Jubilees. When he introduced the Angel of the Presence into his book, the author described him with words drawn from Exod 14:19: "The Angel of the Presence, who was going along in front of the Israelite camp" (Jub 1:29). He now reverts to the same passage and has the angel apply it to himself:[44]

Exodus 14:19-20	Jubilees 48:13
The angel of God who was going before the Israelite army moved and went behind them; and the pillar of cloud moved from in front of them and took its place between them. It came between the army of Egypt and the army of Israel.	I stood between you, the Egyptians, and the Israelites.[45]

The Angel of the Presence sees himself in this passage in Exodus, and he is the one who performs the task accomplished there by the pillar of cloud (see Exod 23:20 where the angel guards Israel along the way).[46] The angel intervenes between Moses and the Israelites on the one side and Mastema and his Egyptians allies on the other. In so doing, the angel claims, he and the others of his group ("We") "rescued the Israelites" from the attack of their enemies. In a limited sense it is true that they did save Israel through separating them from their foes, but the angel is careful to say that God was the one responsible for pitching the Egyptians into the sea and thus getting revenge on them (vv. 14, 17). The action of the Lord in saving Israel comes to expression in the last sentence in v. 13, where he leads them "out through the middle of the sea as if on dry ground." The words translated "as if" (kama 'enta) do not come from the Exodus passages that refer to the crossing (14:22, 27; 15:19) but agree with the wording in Heb 11:29 ($ως$ $δια$ $ξηρας$ $γης$).[47] It almost sounds as if the writer is suggesting that the seabed may not have been completely dry.

The revenge that the Lord executes on the Egyptians for their mistreatment of the Israelites receives exceedingly strong articulation in v. 14. The text uses the language of God's tossing the pursuing Egyptians into the sea—an image drawn from Exod 14:27; 15:1, 4, 21. Though different Hebrew verbs are used in these verses (only 15:1 and 21 share the same verb), the idea of throwing people into water naturally recalls what Pharaoh had commanded in Exod 1:22:[48] "Every boy that is born to the Hebrews you shall throw into the Nile." The Lord now pays them back for that crime, as the writer makes explicit: he threw them into the sea "just as the Egyptians had thrown their sons into the river."[49] In the expression "whom they had thrown into the river"

---

drowning of the Israelite boys (48:13-14) and the Lord's part in encouraging the Egyptians to chase the Israelites (v. 17, on which see below). In addition, Mastema is not the patron of Egypt. He is rather the opponent of God who uses the Egyptians for his immediate purpose. See the commentary on 49:2-6.

43 Werman, *Jubilees*, 537.
44 VanderKam, "Angel of the Presence," 392.
45 See the textual note for the seemingly excessive number of "betweens" in the verse.
46 Cf. Hartom, "Jubilees," 133 n. to v. 13.
47 Cf. Hartom, "Jubilees," 133 n. to v. 13. Philo uses a similar formulation in *Mos.* 2.254: "the nation makes its passage, marching safely through the sea, as on a dry path [$ως$ $επι$ $ξηρας$ $ατραπου$] or a stone-paved causeway; for the sand is crisped, and its scattered particles grow together into a unity." In *Contempl.* 86 he talks about the people crossing on a dry highway but says the water on either side "had the semblance of [$οια$] solid walls." I am grateful to Professor Carl Mosser for his assistance with the reading of Hebrews and the references in Philo's writings.
48 In the LXX, the same verb appears in Exod 1:22 as in 15:1, 4, 21.
49 Segal comments on the chiasm in vv. 13-14a: A the angels rescue Israel; B the Lord brought them out through the sea as if on dry ground; B¹ all the people whom he (Mastema) brought out; A¹ the Lord threw into the sea (*Jubilees*, 218).

at the end of the verse the Ethiopic text uses the same verb (a form of *gadafa*) as the one employed in 47:2, 3 for pitching Israelite boys into the river. Jubilees is quite graphic about where the deity pitched the Egyptians: "to the depths of the abyss [*qalāy*]." The language draws from the poetic imagery in Exodus 15, where there are expressions such as "they went down into the depths[50] like a stone" (v. 5) and "the deeps congealed in the heart of the sea" (v. 8; see also Neh 9:11: "you threw their pursuers into the depths"; Wis 10:19: "cast them up from the depth of the sea"). In referring to the exposed seabed, Pseudo-Philo says "*the depths* of the earth were visible, and the foundations of the world were laid bare" (10:5; trans. Harrington, *OTP* 2:317).

The Jubilees passage even supplies numbers: one million Egyptian men suffered a watery death in repayment for one thousand Israelite infants drowned in the Nile. The rate was one thousand to one.[51] A similar notion appears in Wis 18:5 but without the specificity of Jubilees: "When they had resolved to kill the infants of your holy ones, / and one child had been abandoned and rescued, / you in punishment took away a multitude of their children; / and you destroyed them altogether by a mighty flood."[52] In *Mekilta de-Rabbi Ishmael* one finds a similar set of associations in a comment on Exod 14:26: "Let the wheel turn against them and bring back upon them their own violence. For with the same device with which they planned to destroy Israel, I am going to punish them. They planned to destroy My children by water, so I will likewise punish them only by water" (*Beshallaḥ* 7).[53]

The Byzantine historian Cedrenus echoes a part of Jub 48:14 but also introduces another comparison into his reworking of the verse: "For this reason ten plagues were given to the Egyptians in ten months, and finally they were destroyed in the sea in the manner in which the babies of the Hebrews were drowned in the river. 1000 strong men of the Egyptians were drowned in place of one Israelite baby."[54] That the plagues occurred over a ten-month period would be impossible in Jubilees' chronology that puts all of them within a two-week stretch,[55] but the number of Egyptian men who drowned in place of each Israelite boy is the same as in v. 14.

■ 15 The reader now learns more about the limits placed by the angels of the presence (see v. 18) on Mastema and his forces (see v. 16). It turns out that Mastema was in some way bound so that he could not carry out his normal functions. The writer plays on his name by saying, "so that he could not accuse them" (see 4Q225 frg. 2 i:9-10, where both his title "prince Mastema" and the verb וישטם, "accused," are used). The writer does not indicate what accusations he might have made, were he free to do so, until v. 18. The days when Mastema and his agents were made prisoners are the five days beginning with the date of Passover (the fourteenth) and continuing through the eighteenth; of these, days 15 through 18 would fall into the time for the Festival of Unleavened Bread (1/15-21). The purpose for restraining Mastema and the others is in part (see v. 18) so that the Israelites could place some distance between themselves and the Egyptians.

The book of Exodus is not generous with dates in chaps. 12–15. The tenth plague struck at the time when the Israelites were celebrating the first Passover (the night of 1/14-15); that very night Pharaoh ordered Moses and Aaron to lead the people with their possessions from Egypt (12:31). The Israelites then exited Egypt quickly, before the dough for their bread could

---

50 In Eth. Exod 15:5 the word *qalāy* is used to translate "depths."

51 It is possible that Jub 47:3, which implies that the drownings continued for ten months, is related to these multiples of ten: perhaps one hundred babies died in this way each month. See below on the citation from Cedrenus.

52 On the passage, see David Winston, *The Wisdom of Solomon: A New Translation with Introduction and Commentary* (AB 43; Garden City, NY: Doubleday, 1979) 314-15.

53 Lauterbach, *Mekilta de-Rabbi Ishmael*, 1:243-44; cf. Kugel, *Traditions*, 507-8.

54 Translation (slightly modified) by VanderKam in *Jubilees* 2:367. For the text, see *Jubilees* 1:299.

55 Possibly Cedrenus's ten months for the plagues is related to the note in Jubilees (47:3) that the drownings occurred over a ten-month period. The plagues could then be a response in kind—ten months of Egyptian suffering in repayment for ten months of Israelite suffering.

rise (12:34, 39, 51). There is no time indicator for how long it took them to reach the sea; only their stopping places are noted. When they were at the sea, the Lord drove it back at night and by the time of the next morning watch the Egyptians were dead (14:21, 24). Jubilees adds some details to this modest base. The Israelites traveled from the fifteenth through the eighteenth and were unhindered by any mischief the forces of evil might have mustered against them. In chap. 49 (vv. 22-23) the Israelites will complete the seven-day Festival of Unleavened Bread on the seashore—apparently after they had crossed "as if on dry ground"—at which time they could finish the celebration with joy. The pursuit of the Israelites began on the nineteenth of the first month when the Angel of the Presence and his friends released Mastema and his allies so that they could make the Egyptians chase the Israelites. The sea crossing must have occurred on the twentieth or even the twenty-first.[56]

■ **17** The writer refers back to v. 12, where he had explained that Mastema was the one who changed the minds of Pharaoh and his people so that they decided to go after the Israelites. This time, however, he uses an expression, frequent in Exodus but absent to this point from Jubilees, that a hardening of hearts was the immediate impetus for the Egyptian decision.[57] It is most likely that the first part of the verse has Mastema as the subject: he stiffened or hardened the hearts of the Egyptians (employing the same verb and object as the ones in Eth. Exod 4:21, for example, where God hardens Pharaoh's heart). Mastema took the Egyptians who had survived the horrors of the ten plagues and infused them with determination and strength so that they could defeat the Israelites. But the second part of the verse makes the Lord himself responsible for the invigorated state of the Egyptians. The verse shows a variation not unlike the fluidity in Exodus itself, where Pharaoh at times hardens his heart and at others God hardens it for him.[58] Here, however, the writer makes the point that God was behind the actions of Mastema: that evil being thought he was frustrating God's plan by strengthening the Egyptians, but it turns out that God was allowing him to do this so that he could "strike the Egyptians and throw them into the sea."[59] "Striking" appears to be a word for a plague, although it is not used

---

56 Hartom puts the crossing on the twenty-first, with the Egyptian pursuit therefore on the twentieth, the day after Mastema urged them to overtake the Israelites ("Jubilees," 134 n. to v. 16).

57 Since Jubilees merely lists the plagues, the element of hardening Pharaoh's heart is absent. In Exodus there are different formulations: the Lord hardens Pharaoh's heart (4:21; 7:3; 9:12; 10:1, 20, 27; 11:10 (with 14:4, 8); Pharaoh's heart is hardened (7:13, 14, 22; 8:19 [Heb. v. 15]; 9:7, 35); or Pharaoh hardens his own heart (8:15, 32 [Heb. vv. 11, 28]; 9:34). For Werman (*Jubilees*, 538), there may be more to the omission of the several instances in which God hardens Pharaoh's heart. For her the more likely explanation is that the way in which the theme figures in Exodus did not fit the writer's notion of determinism that he imposes on the Bible. In Exodus the repeated hardening of Pharaoh's heart leaves the impression of a chain of unexpected events and that the deity's responses are ad hoc. The author strives to avoid giving such an impression; for him the plagues were part of God's ordered plan. The case of hardening the Egyptians' hearts in the present verse is different from the ones during the plagues because in this instance the hardening is not a result of Egyptian stubbornness; it is rather an act of Mastema. Werman's explanation is reasonable if speculative. Yet one wonders whether the severe shortening of the account is the reason for not reproducing the hardening episodes.

58 In Exodus there is no reference to God's hardening the hearts of all the Egyptians. Besides Pharaoh, he hardened the hearts of Pharaoh's servants/officials (10:1; in 9:34 both Pharaoh and his servants/officials harden their hearts). Pseudo-Philo (L.A.B. 10:2, 6) refers to the Egyptians' hearts being hardened on this occasion (v. 2) and to God's hardening their perception (v. 6).

59 Segal argues a some length that v. 17b (where the Lord is the one who strengthens the Egyptians to pursue Israel) contradicts vv. 12-14 and the immediate context in vv. 15-17 (*Jubilees*, 218–22). Regarding the contradiction he sees with vv. 12-14 he writes, "Verse 17b does not seem concerned with the notion that God hardened Egypt's heart, and therefore contradicts vv. 12-14, both in its identification of who was responsible for the hardening of the heart, and regarding its treatment of the theological problem raised by

for them in Eth. Exodus; "throwing" refers to God's way of executing the Egyptians in the sea (using the same verb as in v. 14).

■ **18-19** The final episode in the chapter is the despoiling of the Egyptians. To describe it, the author returns to day 14, when the angels of the presence imprisoned Mastema so that he could not carry out his accusing function when the Israelites were requesting goods from the Egyptians. By placing the request on the fourteenth, the writer shows how he has read the three references to the despoiling in Exodus: in 3:21-22 the Lord predicts it will happen, in 11:2-3 before the tenth plague Moses receives orders to tell the Israelites to make the request, and in 12:35-36 the narrator refers back to it after the tenth plague. In Jubilees the Israelites asked for and received the goods on the fourteenth, and they began celebrating the first Passover that evening.

The good relations between the two peoples that permitted the exchange were perhaps a hint to the writer of Jubilees that Mastema was somehow temporarily out of the picture. In Exodus the donations result from the favor the Lord gave the Israelites with the Egyptians (see Exod 3:21; 11:3; 12:36). The plundering motif arises in places: besides the three in Exodus, there is one in Genesis (15:14) and one in the Psalms (105:37). Several of these passages mention items of silver and gold (Exod 3:22; 11:2; 12:35; cf. Ps 105:37), as Jubilees does, but none of them refers to utensils of bronze.[60] For clothing, see Exod 3:22; 12:35. The reason for asking the Egyptians to supply these items is not given in Exodus, but the writer of Jubilees sees in it another instance of repayment. He uses the word *plunder* that appears in Exod 3:22; 12:36. *Plunder* seems a rather strong term for obtaining a gift of goods from a group that regards the recipients with favor; it is just the right term in Jubilees because it is the way the Egyptians repaid the Israelites for the slave labor, extracted "by force" (see Exod 1:13), they had supplied. Despoiling as repayment is a theme in other texts as well. Genesis 15:14, where God predicts the Israelites will come out of Egypt with great possessions after he judged their oppressors, might have suggested the idea, but it is explicit in Wis 10:17 (wisdom "gave to holy people the reward of their labors") and particularly in Philo's *Moses* 141 (see also 142):

> for they took out with them much spoil, which they carried partly on their backs, partly laid on their beasts of burden. And they did this not in avarice, or, as their accusers might say, in covetousness of what belonged to others. No, indeed. In the first place, they were but receiving a bare wage for all their time of service; secondly, they were retaliating, not on an

---

the biblical story" (p. 219). His appears to be a misstatement of the case. The writer, with the biblical narrative of the plagues, sees two sides to the event of hardening (as in vv. 13-14) that at times he attributes to God and at times to another force. In Exodus, God in some passages hardens Pharaoh's heart and in other places Pharaoh does the hardening. Segal correctly sees that Mastema is the one who hardens the hearts of the Egyptians in v. 17a. He believes this contradicts v. 17b, where God is said to be the one who does so. This claim is as unconvincing as the one he makes for a contradiction with vv. 12-14 because it encounters the same difficulty. Segal suggests there are two solutions to account for the contradiction he finds. First, v. 17a is, through the author's negligence, "a vestige of the biblical text that survived in the rewritten text" as it agrees with Exodus. He rejects this option because the writer is not closely rewriting the scriptural text in chap. 48. A second solution is that v. 17b was "added at a later stage to Jubilees" (p. 221). But in these circumstances it is unlikely someone added v. 17b (even to parallel the treatment of Exod 4:24-26 in Jub 48:2-4, an instance that is different from the present one because there Mastema replaces God). There are indeed two approaches to the hardening of hearts in Jubilees and to other actions in chap. 49, but they represent the author's view that God worked through an agent.

60 As Kugel explains (*Traditions*, 556 n. 13), bronze may be added in Jubilees because some parts of the tabernacle were made of bronze. One explanation for how the Israelites in the desert had goodly amounts of gold, silver, and bronze for the tabernacle was that they came from the Egyptians. Yet, since Jubilees does not deal with construction of the tabernacle, it seems strange that the writer would have taken the addition from a source that did treat the tabernacle (the author mentions setting up the tabernacle in the land in 49:18; cf. 49:21).

equal but on a lesser scale, for their enslavement. (Colson, LCL)[61]

It was only fair that the Egyptians at least in a small way compensated the Israelite slaves for their long labors.[62]

The chapter ends by taking up the wording of Exod 3:21: "I will bring this people into such favor with the Egyptians that, when you go, you will not go empty-handed." The angel attributes to himself and to his fellow angels an action that the people of Israel seem to perform for themselves in Exodus. Possibly the statement reflects the odd claim Moses makes in his message to the king of Edom: "You know all the adversity that has befallen us; how our ancestors went down to Egypt, and we lived in Egypt a long time; and the Egyptians oppressed us and our ancestors; and when we cried to the LORD, he heard our voice, and sent an angel and brought us out of Egypt" (Num 20:14b-16a).[63]

A Note on Chronology. Since Moses returned to Egypt in the year in which the exodus occurred, the author of Jubilees implies that Moses spent no more than two weeks in Egypt from the time he arrived until Israel marched out under his leadership on 1/15. Exodus tends to use time indicators such as "in the morning" or "tomorrow" in the plague narratives, but even these notes and the few more specific ones show that a longer time than fourteen days was involved. The data in Exodus are these:

4:29	Moses is back in Egypt.
5:6	Pharaoh issues work-related commands the day he speaks with Moses and Aaron, and there are at least a few days of work under the new rules (5:14 "yesterday and today").
7:15	Moses is instructed to go to Pharaoh early in the morning to announce plague 1.
7:25	Seven days pass after the Lord strikes the Nile with plague 1.
8:10 (Heb. v. 6)	Tomorrow is the time when the frogs (plague 2) are removed.
8:20 (Heb. v. 16)	Moses is to rise early in the morning to announce plague 4, which will occur the next day (v. 23 [Heb. v. 19]); the plague ends the following day (v. 29 [Heb. v. 25]).
9:5-6	Fifth plague on the next day.
9:13	Moses is to rise early in the morning to announce plague 7, which comes the next day (v. 18).
10:4	Plague 8 will come tomorrow; all that day and night and in the morning the locusts come (v. 13).
10:22-23	Darkness lasts three days.
11:4	About midnight the firstborn will die and Israel will leave Egypt when it becomes light.

However one counts all the instances of "in the morning" and "tomorrow," the notices suggest that the number of days would probably be closer to twenty-one. Wiesenberg, who does not include all of the relevant texts, wrote, "The explicit references to time intervals—in *Exodus* 7, 15. 25; 8, 6. 16. 25; 9, 13. 18—presuppose, in fact, no less than a minimum of 16 clear days from Moses' first audience with Pharaoh till his message to Israel on the 10th of the 1st month (*ibidem* 12, 3)."[64] His mention of the tenth of the first month has to do with the command that the Israelites were to select the lamb for Passover on this date, although it is not obvious from Exod 12:3 that the narrator is claiming this happened before the initial Passover; it could be read as legislation for the future.[65] Wiesenberg uses the evidence to support his argument that the year of the exodus and revelation of Jubilees was 2411, not 2410.[66] By positing that, contrary to what Jubilees itself says (see 50:4), Moses

---

61 For these parallels and others (e.g., Ezekiel the Tragedian, *Exagoge* 162-66), see Kugel, *Traditions*, 555-56.
62 See Kugel, *Walk through* Jubilees, 197; "Jubilees," 445.
63 Cf. Kugel, *Traditions*, 584, 735-36.
64 Wiesenberg, "Jubilee of Jubilees," 7 n. 20.
65 According to *b. Pesaḥ.* 96a, however, the selection of the lamb on 1/10 took place in Egypt, but it would not in subsequent generations after they left Egypt.
66 Wiesenberg, "Jubilee of Jubilees," 4-17.

arrived back in Egypt sometime during the year prior to the exodus, he is able to relieve the problem with the cramped chronology in the book. However, that seems a dubious procedure, since the writer of Jubilees does not reproduce the time indicators from this section of Exodus, as Wiesenberg himself observes. It is preferable to accept that in Jubilees all these events occurred over a two-week period than to rewrite the chronology of the book. The year in question, year of the world 2410, also turns out to be very important to the message conveyed by the full chronological presentation in Jubilees (see the commentary on chap. 50).

The First Passover and the Laws of Passover

49

1/ Remember the commandments[a] that the Lord gave you regarding the Passover so that you may celebrate it[b] at its time on the fourteenth of the first month, that you may sacrifice it[c] before evening, and so that they may eat it at night on[d] the evening of the fifteenth[e] from the time of sunset. 2/ For on this night[a]—it was the beginning of the festival and the beginning[b] of joy—you were eating the Passover in Egypt when all the forces[c] of Mastema were sent[d] to kill every firstborn in the land of Egypt—from Pharaoh's firstborn to the firstborn of the captive slave girl at the millstone and to the cattle as well. 3/ This is the sign that the Lord gave[a] them: into each house on whose[b] door they saw the blood of a year-old lamb, they were not to enter that house to kill but were to pass over (it) in order that all who were in the house would be spared because the sign of the blood was on its door. 4/ The Lord's forces did everything that the Lord ordered them. They[a] passed over all the Israelites. The plague[b] did not come on them to destroy any of them—from cattle to humans to dogs. 5/ The plague on Egypt was very great. There was no house in Egypt[a] in which there was not a dead person, crying, and mourning. 6/ All Israel was eating the paschal meat, drinking the wine, and glorifying, blessing, and praising the Lord God[a] of their fathers. They were ready to leave the Egyptian yoke[b] and evil slavery.[c]

7/ Now you remember this day throughout all your lifetime. Celebrate it[a] from year to year[b] throughout all your lifetime,[c] once a year on its day[d] in accord with all[e] of its law. Then you will not pass over a day from the day[f] or from month to month. 8/ For it is an eternal statute[a] and it is engraved[b] on the heavenly tablets regarding the Israelites[c] that they are to celebrate it[d] each and every year on its day, once a year, throughout their entire history.[e] There is no temporal limit because it is ordained forever. 9/ The man who is pure but does not come[a] to celebrate it[b] on its prescribed day—to bring a sacrifice that is pleasing before the Lord[c] and[d] to eat and drink before the Lord on the day of his festival—that man who is pure and nearby is to be uprooted[e] because he did not bring the Lord's sacrifice at its time. That man will bear responsibility for his own sin. 10/ The Israelites are to come and[a] celebrate the Passover on its specific day[b]—on the fourteenth of the first month—between the evenings,[c] from the third part of the day[d] until the third part of the night. For[e] two parts of the day have been given[f] for light and its third part[g] for the evening. 11/ This is what the Lord commanded you[a]—to celebrate it[b] between the evenings.[c] 12/ It is not to be sacrificed[a] at any hour of the daylight[b] but in the hour of the boundary of[c] the evening. They will eat[d] it during the evening hour(s) until[e] the third part of the night. Any of its[f] meat that is left over from the third part of the night and beyond[g] is to be burned. 13/ They are not to boil it in water nor eat[a] it raw but roasted on a fire, cooked with care on a fire[b]—the head[c] with its[d] internal parts and its feet. They are to roast it[e] on a fire. There will be no breaking of any bone[f] in it because no bone of the Israelites will be broken.[g]

14/ Therefore the Lord ordered the Israelites to celebrate[a] the Passover on its specific day. No bone of it is to be broken[b] because it is a festal day and a day that has been commanded. From it there is to be no passing over a day from the day or a month from the month[c] because it is to be celebrated[d] on its festal day.

15/ Now you order[a] the Israelites[b] to celebrate the Passover each year during their generations,[c] once a year on its specific day. Then a pleasing memorial will come[d] before the Lord and no plague will come upon them[e] to kill[f] and to strike (them)[g] during that year when they have celebrated[h] the Passover at its time in every respect as it was commanded.[i]

16/ It is not therefore to be eaten[a] outside of the Lord's sanctuary but before the Lord's sanctuary.[b] All the people of the Israelite congregation[c] are to celebrate[d] it at its time. 17/ Every man who has come on its day,[a] who is 20 years of age and above,[b] is to eat[c] it in the sanctuary of your God[d] before the Lord, because this is the way it has been written and ordained[e]—that they are to eat it in the Lord's[f] sanctuary.

18/ Whenᵃ the Israelites enter the land that they will possessᵇ—the land of Canaan—and set upᶜ the Lord's tabernacle in the middle of the land in one of their tribes,ᵈ until the time when the Lord's temple will be built in the land, they are to come and celebrate the Passover inᵉ the Lord's tabernacle and sacrifice it before the Lordᶠ from year to year. 19/ At the time when the house is builtᵃ in the Lord's name in the land that they will possess, they are to go there and sacrificeᵇ the Passover in the eveningᶜ when the sun sets, in the third part of the day. 20/ They will offerᵃ itsᵇ blood on the baseᶜ of the altar. They are to placeᵈ the fat on the fire that is aboveᵉ the altar and are to eat its meatᶠ roasted on a fire in the courtyard of the sanctuaryᵍ in the name of the Lord. 21/ They will not be ableᵃ to celebrate the Passover in their cities orᵇ in any placesᶜ except before the Lord's tabernacle or otherwiseᵈ before the houseᵉ in which his name has resided. Then they will not go astrayᶠ from the Lord.

22/ Now you, Moses, order the Israelites to keep the statute of the Passover as it was commanded to youᵃ so that you may tellᵇ them its year each year,ᶜ the time of the days,ᵈ and the Festivalᵉ of Unleavened Bread so that they may eat unleavened bread for seven days to celebrateᶠ its festival, to bringᵍ itsʰ sacrifice before the Lord on the altar of your God each day during thoseⁱ seven joyful days. 23/ For you celebrated this festival hastily when you were leaving Egypt until the time you were crossingᵃ the seaᵇ into the wilderness of Shur, because you completed it on the seashore.

Textual Notes

1a the commandments (actually sg.)] "his commandment(s)" 58; om. 17.
b celebrate it] The object is not expressed but implied by most copies; MSS. 12 17 44 supply "it."
c (sacrifice) it] om. 12 35 58 (and they read a subjective form of the verb).
d on (the evening)] "from" 25 38 ('em for 'ama).
e the fifteenth] "its fifteenth" 21.
2a night] "day" 42 47.
b and the beginning] om. 25 35.
c forces] "force" 44 58.
d were sent] + "to him" 47.
3a the sign that the Lord gave] The original text probably included these words, though all of them are attested only in 35 39 42 44 (it places "that [the Lord] gave" one word later") 47 48. Mss. 20 25 lack "that (the Lord) gave." Some copies om. "the sign" (12 17 21 38 63); possibly the similarity between the two words זאת האות led to loss of the latter. See VanderKam, *Jubilees* 2:315, where "the sign" is not included in the text. Werman (*Jubilees*, 543 n. 10) also leaves it out.
b whose] "the" 38 47 58.
4a They (passed over)] "He" 25 35 58.
b The plague] "It" 25.
5a in Egypt] om. 42 47.
6a God] "our God" 21; om. 44.
b yoke] + "of slavery and from" (followed by "Egypt" = "from the yoke of slavery and from Egypt") 39 42 47 48 58.
c and (evil) slavery] om. 39 42 47 48 58 (so that "evil" modifies "Egypt").
7a it] om. Lat.
b year to year] "from eternity to eternity" 12 17ᶜ 35 42ᵗ 47 (for the second "year" 39 48 58 also read "eternity"); Lat. = "each year."
c throughout all your lifetime²] om. Lat.
d its day] "its days" Lat.; MSS. 12 17 21 63 = "them"; "all those days" 38.
e all (of its law)] om. Lat.
f Then you will not pass over a day from the day] The best attested form in the Eth. MSS. is *tāstaḥalef*, "you will make pass over each other/cross/transfer" (Leslau, *Comparative Dictionary*, 260). Another form, in 12 (?) 21 25, is spelled with a short -*a* after the guttural = "make pass, put off, leave out." The Lat. verb is *praeteribit*, "will pass by." Perhaps there is a play on words—in the context of the Passover one is not to pass over from day to day. Where Eth. has "day from the day," Lat. has "and it will (not) be from its days." Rönsch (*Jubiläen*, 90) thought one should read a verb ("transfer"), and Charles (*Ethiopic Version*, 171 n. 1 to Lat.) also inserted one ("go by/pass by"). Neither suggestion yields a text resembling the Eth. version. The Lat. *et erit* could be a dittography from the end of the preceding word (*prateribit*). If this is so, *illud*, "it," would stand in the place where Eth. has "day." Possibly an original *illum diem* became *illum* by homoioteleuton. The two versions would, then, have been similar before mistakes occurred in Lat. See VanderKam, *Jubilees* 2:316-17.
8a an eternal statute] "its eternal statute" 17.

b   engraved] "written" Lat.
c   the Israelites] "all the Israelites" Lat.
d   (celebrate) it] *ea* ("them," neuter pl.) Lat. Later in the verse, Lat. uses a sg. form to refer to Passover.
e   their entire history] om. "entire" Lat.
9a   does not come] "does not know how" Lat. Berger (*Jubiläen*, 548 n. a to v. 9) observed that ηδει (= Lat.) and ηκει (= Eth.) were confused. He preferred the Lat. reading, but see v. 10 and Num 9:13.
b   (celebrate) it] om. 17 21 38 39 48 58.
c   Lord] + "on the day of his festival" 47 58.
d   and (to eat)] om. Lat. and MSS. 20 44.
e   that man who is pure and nearby is to be uprooted] Lat. with MSS. 42 47 58 lacks a conjunction before the verb (the one in Eth. is not realized in the translation). Lat. has *et* ("and") after the verb (could it represent δε?). It could be a conjunction meaning "namely" (as in VanderKam, *Jubilees* 2:367), but Rönsch (*Jubiläen*, 90) and Charles (*Ethiopic Version*, 173 n. 2 to Lat.) altered it to *ille*, "that man." Lat. *inmundus* ("impure") must be an error for *mundus* ("pure"). For "is to be uprooted," MSS. 21 38 have "they are to uproot him."
10a come and] om. 21.
b   on its specific day (lit., "on the day of its time")] "at its time" Lat.
c   between the evenings (sg. = MSS. 12 20 39 42 44 47 48 58)] This is a literal translation of the phrase in Exod 12:6, but LXX rendered it with προς εσπεραν ("toward evening"), which underlies *ad vesperam* here in Lat.
d   third part of the day] "third part of it" Lat. It also reads *autem* within this phrase, possibly signifying a continuation of the previous clause. See VanderKam, *Jubilees* 2:318.
e   For] "Until" 25 35; om. 42 47.
f   have been given] Lat. lacks a verb.
g   its third part] This seems to be the meaning, assuming the suffix on "third part" is a possessive and not an anticipation of "to the evening" (= third part of the evening). Lat. and MSS. 17 63 lack a possessive, as do 25 35 but with a different form of "third."
11a you] om. 42 44 47.
b   it] om. 17 21 39 42 47 58 63.
c   between the evenings (sg. 12 20 63)] Eth. is again a more literal rendering of the original; Lat. = "in the evening."
12a It is not to be sacrificed] Lat. is similar in meaning but worded a bit differently: "One is not to sacrifice."
b   any hour of the daylight] Some MSS. read: "any (time) in the hours of daylight" = 12 17 21 38 44 63.
c   in the hour (or: time) of the boundary of] Lat. reads only "in." Charles (*Jubilees*, 255) referred to Deut 16:6 ("in the evening at sunset") to explain what was meant by this expression.
d   They will eat] "One is to eat" Lat. Mss. 12 38 44 58 also read a subjunctive form.

e   until] Lat. strangely lacks an equivalent.
f   its (meat)] om. Lat.
g   and beyond] "this" (*hoc*) Lat. See Exod 12:10. Lat. may have resulted when הלאה was misunderstood as הלזה ("this") or הלה ("that one"). See VanderKam, *Jubilees* 2:319. Mss. 42 47 read "again."
13a nor eat] "nor will they eat" 25 63.
b   cooked with care on a fire (om. "on a fire" 20 25)] Lat. = "you will eat it carefully." The place where they disagree is at "cooked" and "on a fire." Charles (*Ethiopic Version*, 172 n. 24; *Jubilees*, 255), who thought Eth. *besula* was meaningless, proposed reading *yeble'ewwo*, "they are to eat it"; however, Lat.'s form is second pers. sg. Goldmann ("Jubilees," 311 n. to v. 13) thinks that the Eth. rendering is an interpretation of צלי in Exod 12:9.
c   the head] "its head" Lat.; so also 12 35 39 42 44 48 58 (and 21, with a different form).
d   its (internal parts)] om. Lat.
e   They are to roast it] "You will roast" Lat.; "They will roast it" 12 25.
f   bone] "its bone" 17 25.
g   because no bone of the Israelites will be broken] "there is to be no distress among the Israelites on this day" Lat. Charles (see *Ethiopic Version*, 172 n. 31; but esp. *Jubilees*, 255-56) maintained that the difference arose when the phrase בעצם היום הזה, "on that day" (= Lat.), lost the last two words and בעצם became עצם, "bone." He also thought the Eth. verb "broken/crushed" used here should be taken "metaphorically." His case seems unlikely to be true. One could argue that Lat. *tribulatio* ("distress") resulted when forms of, or ones related to, συνθλιβω ("press upon") and συντριβω ("break, crush") were confused. See VanderKam, *Jubilees* 2:320. Werman (*Jubilees*, 544 n. 27) rewrites the latter parts of v. 13 in ways that lack support from either Eth. or Lat. She introduces "all the congregation of Israel" as the subject of the verb here translated "They are to roast it" and thinks the idea of a threat would not be in place after it. She thus reads "on that day" after the roasting verb (and after "at its time," for which there is also no evidence) so that there is no reference to breaking a bone at this point. The end of the verse in her version then reproduces "There will be no breaking of any bone in it," a clause that is not at the end of the verse in either translation. It is curious that she reads "on that day" at a point where neither of the versions attests it rather than where Lat. has it—at the end of the verse.
14a to celebrate] om. 21.
b   broken] + "on it" Lat., although see VanderKam, *Jubilees* 2:320. Werman (*Jubilees*, 544 n. 28) replaces this instance of "No bone of it is to be broken" with "on that day" (see n. g to v. 13), again with no support in the versions, because she thinks it unlikely the author

would have returned to this subject in v. 14, where the concern is with the time of the festival.
c a day from the day or a month from the month] Eth. and Lat. probably mean about the same thing, but they express it differently. Eth. reads just before the entire expression "from it [masc. (fem. in MS. 20)]" but Lat. lacks an equivalent. After this the two versions literally read this way:

Eth.: a day from a day and from a month (to) a month
Lat.: from a day into a day, from a month and a month.

d it is to be celebrated] om. Lat.
15a order] + "O Moses" 35.
b the Israelites] So Eth. and Lat., but MSS. 12 17 read "your children," and 63 has "his children."
c their generations] So Lat. = Exod 12:14 ("your generations"). Eth. reads "your days" = "your times," just as Eth. Exod 12:14 does.
d a pleasing memorial will come] "it will be an acceptable/pleasing testimony" Lat. See Exod 12:14 for "it will be," but the same verse uses "remembrance/memorial." Some MSS. have "is to come"—21 44 47 58.
e upon them] "from him" Lat. See Exod 12:13 for the pl.
f to kill] Lat. = "to destroy," as in Exod 12:13.
g to strike (them)] Lat. supplies the object. It is not present in Exod 12:13.
h have celebrated] "will celebrate" Lat., with 21 35.
i in every respect as it was commanded] "in accordance with all its commands" Lat. Mss. 12 and 38 read "its command" where the other copies read the related verb. Perhaps the Lat. is superior, as *ta'azzaza* and *te'zāzo* (= Lat.) could easily be confused.
16a It is not therefore (om. 42 47) to be eaten] "It will not be eaten" Lat.
b before the Lord's sanctuary] "at the Lord's tabernacle" Lat. Though *tabernacle* would be fitting in the setting and both versions mention it in v. 18, "sanctuary" may have been used to provide variety in vocabulary. Mss. 20 25 add "in front of" somewhat redundantly directly before "sanctuary."
c people of the Israelite congregation] "Israelite throng" Lat.
d are to celebrate] "will celebrate" Lat. (so also 20 25 47 63).
17a has come on its day] "passes in the census" Lat. The reference later in the verse to those twenty years and above may have led someone to introduce the idea of the census here, perhaps under the influence of a passage such as Exod 30:14. See VanderKam, *Jubilees* 2:322. Mss. 25 35 read a future form ("will come") like Lat. For "on its day," MS. 20 reads "on the day of its time"; MSS. 21 35 have "at its time and on its day"; 38 63 have just "on the day." Werman (*Jubilees*, 545 n. 34) defends the Lat. reading and thinks the word "day" in Eth. suggests the reading was more composite, but the reading is not "day" but "its day."

b above] "above it" 21 35 38 39 42 44 47 48 58.
c is to eat] Lat. lacks a main verb and reads an infinitive here. Some MSS. read an imperative—"eat it" (12 20 21 35)—and others read an imperfect (25 38 39).
d your God] Lat. "our God" seems to be an error. Mss. 17 58 read "their God," and 35 has "God." Ms. 21 places "the Lord" before "your God."
e written and ordained] Lat. transposes the verbal forms, as do 20 48.
f Lord's] "his" Lat.
18a When] "How" Lat. Rönsch (*Jubiläen*, 168) saw that the Heb. preposition ־כ or the Gk. ὡς (both mean "as" or "when" or "how") lies behind the two readings and that the Lat. translator chose the wrong sense.
b they will possess] pr. "they will enter and" 12.
c set up] "live in" Lat. This seems wrong. Charles (*Ethiopic Version*, 174 n. 22) proposed an underlying confusion between two Gk. verbs, but they do not explain the situation (VanderKam, *Jubilees* 2:323). Mss. 20 48 read a subjunctive (= "are to set up").
d their tribes] Eth. reads a pl., while Lat. has a sg. form. For the Eth. term *šarāw*, see Leslau, *Comparative Dictionary*, 535.
e in (the Lord's tabernacle)] "before" Lat.
f and sacrifice it before the Lord] Lat. om. by parablepsis.
19a is built] Eth. reads a perfect form, Lat. a future form.
b they are to go there and sacrifice (will sacrifice 35 38 63)] The best Eth. readings are two subjunctive verbs; Lat. has a participle and future form that mean "offer and sacrifice." The difference in meaning of the first pair—Eth. = "go," Lat. = "offer"—may be based on an original text that read יעלי which could mean "go up" (qal) or "offer" (hiphil). See VanderKam, *Jubilees* 2:323.
c in the evening] "until evening" Lat. The difference may be explained by positing ὡς behind Eth. and ἕως behind Lat.
20a They will offer] MSS. 20 58 read a subjunctive form = "they are to offer."
b its (blood)] "the" 35 38 44.
c the base] "the bases" 20 25.
d They are to place] "They will offer" Lat. For the same verbs, see 21:8.
e that is above] "of" Lat.
f its meat] "the meat" Lat.
g courtyard of the sanctuary] See 11QT[a] xvii:8–9. Both Eth. and Lat. read lit., "the house of holiness" for the sanctuary; the reading is preferable to "the house that was sanctified" 12 17 39[c] 44 48 63.
21a They will not be able] "It is not to be" 21 35 58.
b (cities) or (lit., "and")] om. Lat.
c places] "place" Lat.
d or otherwise] "and" Lat.
e the house] "the house of the Lord" 12; "his house" 17 39 42 47 48 58 63.

f	will not go astray] "are not to go astray" 17 20 35 39 42 47 48. Mss. 38 63 have a perfect tense form that does not fit the context.	f	to celebrate] Lat. places "and" before the expression.
22a	as it was commanded to you] Lat. prefaces a conjunction to the phrase.	g	to bring] Lat. also places "and" before this expression (so 12 44 58).
b	so that you may tell] Rather than a purpose clause, Lat. reads an imperative ("tell"). Many Eth. mss. read "so that you may do/perform/celebrate" 12 17 21 38 39 42 47 48 58 63.	h	its (sacrifice)] om. Lat. Mss. 35 44 = "their."
		i	those] om. Lat.
		23a	you were crossing] "you crossed" 25 58 (cf. 48 63). For some reason Charles (*Ethiopic Version*, 174) read "were entering," which is attested in no ms. He translated "entered" in *Jubilees*.
c	its year each year] "a year each year" 17 21 39 42 47 48. Lat. = "throughout each and every year."		
d	the time of the days] "at the time of its days" Lat.	b	the sea] "the Red Sea and until you were returning/will return" 35.
e	the Festival] Lat. places *per* ("throughout") before the word.		

Commentary

The narrative portion of Jubilees largely ends with chap. 48. In 49:2-6 the writer summarizes what happened on the night of the first Passover, but he devotes the remainder of the chapter to the legislation for proper celebration of the holiday throughout the generations (vv. 1, 7-21) and of the Festival of Unleavened Bread (vv. 22-23). In chap. 50 there are two brief notices about the angel's revelation of Sabbath laws to Moses in the wilderness of Sin and at Mount Sinai (vv. 1-2), but there is no narrative in it. Jubilees 50:3-13 supplies information about the meaning of the chronology in the book (the subject is introduced in v. 2 and elaborated in vv. 3-5) and more legislation for the Sabbath day (vv. 6-13). As the author has arranged his book, it ends with a heavy dose of legal material regarding several of his favorite topics: festivals, sabbatical chronology, and Sabbath.

Chapter 49 draws on Exodus 12–13 for much of the information about Passover and the Festival of Unleavened Bread, but it also taps into Passover-related texts located elsewhere in the HB.[1] Passover and the Festival of Unleavened Bread posed an interesting problem for the author because, while he reads the other great festivals (Weeks, Tabernacles) back into the Genesis narratives, he could not do the same for Passover and Unleavened Bread, since they were inextricably tied to post-Genesis events. His solution was to find a prefiguring of Passover in the attempted sacrifice of Isaac and of the Festival of Unleavened Bread in the seven-day journey of Abraham to and from the mountain (chap. 18). In his retelling of the Aqedah the writer did not use the words Passover and Unleavened Bread because they would not have been appropriate to that situation. Now in chap. 49 he names both of them in the proper narrative context.

The divisions of the chapter seem to be:

1	The timing of Passover
2-6	The first Passover
7-15	The proper time for celebrating Passover
16-21	The proper place for celebrating Passover
22-23	The Festival of Unleavened Bread

The Ethiopic manuscripts preserve the entire chapter, and the Latin translation is available from v. 7 to v. 22, where the parts of the manuscript Ceriani could decipher come to an end. For the Latin translation of Jubilees, there is, then, material stretching from 13:10 to 49:22 with many gaps between those outer limits.

1 The Timing of Passover

The angel, as he often does in legal sections, speaks to Moses more directly. In the present instance he orders him to "Remember the commandments that the Lord

---

1 Halpern-Amaru, "The Use of Bible in *Jubilees* 49: The Time and Date of the Pesaḥ Celebration," *Meghillot* 5-6 (2007) *81-*100, here *82.

gave you [sg.] regarding the Passover." The two characters are on Mount Sinai, according to the setting of the book, and the Angel of the Presence is referring back to the legislation revealed to Moses and Aaron in Exodus 12. That chapter is the only place where there is a detailed presentation of the laws governing the celebration of the festival prior to Sinai. In the Sinai legislation itself, Passover is mentioned only briefly in Lev 23:5 and Num 9:1-5,[2] so it is appropriate that the revealing angel tell Moses to recall what he had already learned about the way the celebration was to take place.

The chief concern in v. 1 is with the correct time for Passover (see also vv. 7-15, where there is a fuller explanation)—"so that you may celebrate it at its time." The expressions for celebrating (lit., "do") and "at its time" reflect the vocabulary of Num 9:2 ("Let the Israelites keep the Passover at its appointed time [במועדו]").[3] The fourteenth day of the first month is the date mandated for it in the festival rosters of the HB.[4] In Exod 12:6 the Lord stipulates that the lamb, selected on the tenth day (not mentioned in Jubilees 49),[5] is to be slaughtered on the fourteenth "at twilight," which is the way the NRSV renders the words that mean literally "between the two evenings [בין הערבים]." The Israelites were then to "eat the lamb that same night" (v. 8). Leviticus 23:5 uses the expression "between the two evenings" for the timing of the Passover offering on the fourteenth day of the first month (see also Num 9:3, 5; 28:16; cf. 2 Chr 35:1; Ezek 45:21). The author of Jubilees words the continuation of the law by saying that the Israelites were to "sacrifice it before evening" and "eat it at night on the evening of the fifteenth from the time of sunset." The meaning is that the sacrifice must occur before the fifteenth day of the month begins, since the events of Passover start on the fourteenth (see below on vv. 10-12). The actual eating continues into the night of the fifteenth (12:8)—a statement that provides one of the clear indications that for the writer of Jubilees the day begins in the evening.[6] The words "on the evening of the fifteenth from the time of sunset" echo the prescription in Deut 16:6: "offer the Passover sacrifice, in the evening at sunset," although there it relates to the sacrifice, not specifically to the time of eating. As will become apparent in vv. 10-12 in Jubilees 49, the word "evening" is used in more than one sense in the various statements about the time for the Passover.

2-6 The First Passover

Exodus 12 contains detailed instructions for how and when to observe Passover, but it never describes the actual celebration of it the last night in Egypt. The closest the chapter comes to doing so is in v. 28 when "[t]he Israelites went and did just as the LORD had commanded Moses and Aaron." In Jubilees 49 their eating of the meal is mentioned in vv. 2 and 6.

■ **2** The notice in v. 2 introduces the narrative section that details what happened that night as the tenth plague struck the Egyptians—it occurred while the Israelites were eating the paschal meal. Directly after the instructions for eating the meal during the night after they slaughtered the lamb "at twilight," the Lord told Moses in Exod 12:12: "For I will pass through the land of Egypt that night, and I will strike down every firstborn in the land of Egypt." The contrast between what was happening simultaneously to the Egyptians and among the Israelites is dramatic indeed: the Egyptians lost all their firstborn children, while for the Israelites, the Lord's firstborn (Exod 4:22-23), the night was "the beginning of the festival and the beginning of joy." The meal was in fact the start of the holiday, although the expression "the beginning of the festival" might be taken to refer to the onset of the longer period during which unleavened bread was to be eaten (that is, 1/14-21 [see Exod 12:18]). As for "the beginning of joy," there is no reference to joy in Exodus 12, but the writer intro-

---

2 The settings for Num 28:15 and Deut 16:1-8 are after the revelations on Mount Sinai.
3 Halpern-Amaru, "Use of Bible," *82.
4 This is the approach in texts assigned to the P source—Leviticus 23 and Numbers 28–29. In Deut 16:1-8 Passover seems to be the first day of the Festival of Unleavened Bread, and there is no mention of the fourteenth day of the first month (see, e.g., Driver, *Deuteronomy*, 190).
5 See Tabory, *Festivals*, 85. According to *m. Pesaḥ.* 9:5 and *b. Pesaḥ.* 96a, this requirement applied only to the Passover of Egypt, not to subsequent ones.
6 Baumgarten, "Beginning of the Day," 357.

duces it into the account as he does in describing other celebrations of holidays. Halpern-Amaru identifies two sources for the theme:

> In Num 10:10 "day of your joy" (יום שמחתכם) refers to all occasions when celebrants would offer well-being sacrifices, which are associated with occasions of thanksgiving. In addition, facets of the description recall the delayed Passover celebration decreed by Hezekiah in 2 Chr. 30:21-26. In that account the Chronicler not only repeatedly refers to rejoicing (2 Chr. 30:21, 23, 25-26), but also presents praising of God (2 Chr. 30:21) and sacrificial feasting (2 Chr. 30:22) as ritual expressions of joy.[7]

The account of what happened to the Egyptians that night resembles the one in Exod 12:29 although it blends into it an element from the parallel in Exod 11:5 (Moses's announcement of the final plague).

Exodus 12:29	Jubilees 49:2
... the LORD struck down all the firstborn in the land of Egypt, from the firstborn of Pharaoh who sat on his throne to the firstborn of the prisoner who was in the dungeon, and all the firstborn of the livestock.	... all the forces of Mastema were sent to kill[8] every firstborn in the land of Egypt—from Pharaoh's firstborn to the firstborn of the captive slave girl at the millstone and to the cattle as well.

The phrase chosen for the least fortunate in societal standing among the parents of a dead child ("the firstborn of the captive slave girl at the millstone") is taken from Exod 11:5 ("the firstborn of the female slave who is behind the handmill"). One could regard 11:5 as the base for all of the material here in Jubilees, but it formulates the beginning of the line in a different way ("Every firstborn in the land of Egypt shall die"). At that point Exod 12:29 and Jub 49:2 name the entity responsible for "striking/killing" the Egyptian firstborn: the Lord in Exodus, the forces of Mastema in Jubilees.[9] Here, not for the first time, a negative action, a cruel deed because it involves the execution of many innocent people, performed by God in Genesis–Exodus is laid to the charge of Mastema in Jubilees. His minions are the ones who carry out the tenth plague (see also on v. 4 below). In attributing the murderous deeds to the "forces of Mastema," the writer is consistent with his statement in 48:15 that Mastema himself was locked up on the fourteenth and fifteenth; it was, therefore, not Mastema himself but his forces that carried out the tenth plague.[10]

■ 3 The writer then explains that a sign hindered the destroying force from spreading the carnage to the Israelites as well. The Ethiopic copies differ about the reading at the beginning of the verse, but it is likely that the word "sign" appeared in the text here as well as near the end of the verse (see the textual note). In four verses in Exodus 12 there are instructions for daubing blood around the door of Israelite houses to mark them as places where the plague of killing the firstborn was not to strike. In vv. 7 and 22 the orders are simply given, but in vv. 13 and 23 there are more details about what will happen in view of the fact that the blood of a lamb marks those doors.

Exodus 12:13: The blood shall be a sign for you on the houses where you live: when I see the blood, I will pass over you, and no plague shall destroy you when I strike the land of Egypt.

Exodus 12:23: For the LORD will pass through to strike down the Egyptians; when he sees the blood on the lintel and on the two doorposts, the LORD will pass over that door and will not allow the destroyer to enter your houses to strike you down.

The author of Jubilees takes the term "sign" from v. 13, but then he has to deal with the fact that the unit Exodus 11–12 in some places has the Lord himself delivering

---

7   Halpern-Amaru, "Joy as Piety," 189.
8   The original text of Jubilees probably read a form of the verb MT SP Exodus has here (הכה); it can mean both "strike" and "kill" (BDB, 645–46, s.v. נכה).
9   Segal thinks the base text is 11:5 (*Jubilees*, e.g., 223), but the important difference noted above points toward 12:29 instead. Charles, after indicating that *Tg. Ps.-J.* Exod 12:29 says the Word of the Lord killed the Egyptian children, comments: "Here again (cf. xvii. 16, xlviii. 2, 17) our author interprets after his manner the statement in Exod. xii. 29 that 'Yahweh smote all the firstborn'" (*Jubilees*, 253).
10 See Halpern-Amaru, "The Festivals of Pesaḥ and Massot in the Book of Jubilees," in Boccaccini and Ibba, *Mosaic Torah*, 309–22, here 313.

the tenth plague and thus killing the Egyptian firstborn (11:1, 4-5; 12:12, 27, 29), but in other places he gives the impression that he was not the immediate cause of death. So, in Exod 12:13 the Lord says "when I see the blood, I will pass over you, and no plague shall destroy [נגף למשחית] you when I strike the land of Egypt." And in Exod 12:23 the Lord passes over the properly marked door "and will not allow the destroyer [המשחית] to enter your houses to strike you down." These two verses (v. 23 is clearer about the point) report that there was another destructive being involved, "the one who destroys."[11] In Jub 49:2 the writer had identified the slayers as the forces of Mastema, where the parallel in Exod 12:29 says the Lord "struck down all the firstborn in the land of Egypt."

In Jub 49:3 the verbs "saw," "enter," and "pass over" are plural, whereas Exodus consistently employs singular forms because the Lord is the subject (in 12:13, 23). Hence Jubilees replaces those instances in which Exodus has the Lord seeing the blood and thus not entering the house with expressions in which a plural entity sees the blood and does not go in. The ones who see, do not enter, and pass over the houses are not, however, an independent force. The Lord was the one who gave the Israelites the sign of the lamb's blood, and that sign from him was what dictated the actions of the potentially lethal body. The destroyers were under the Lord's control.

■ 4 The fact of the Lord's control over the actions of the executors that night comes to expression at the beginning of v. 4. Here, quite appropriately, the ones called "the forces of Mastema" in v. 2 are termed the Lord's forces because they do his bidding. They kill the firstborn in every home not marked with blood on its doors. They bypass the Israelite houses whose residents, as a result, remain completely safe. The author takes words from Exod 12:13 when he says, "The plague did not come on them to destroy any of them" (see also 49:15 below). The immunity granted extended not only to the people in the houses but also to cattle and dogs. The Lord had told Moses that when he passed through the land of Egypt that night he would "strike down every firstborn in the land of Egypt, both human beings and animals" (Exod 12:12; cf. 11:5). Then, when he carried out his prediction, he killed not only the firstborn children but also "all the firstborn of the livestock" (12:29). The reference to "dogs" may come from Exod 11:7: "But not a dog shall growl at any of the Israelites—not at people, not at animals—so that you may know that the Lord makes a distinction between Egypt and Israel."[12]

Excursus: The Agent of the Tenth Plague

As explained in the commentary above, the writer of Jubilees attributes to the forces of Mastema the actual execution of the tenth plague. He may have had various motives for making the assignment, but a factor in the decision was the ambiguity left by Exodus 12, where in some verses (12, 27, 29) the Lord carries out the destructive plague and in others (vv. 13, 23 [v. 23 is the clearer of the two]) someone termed "the destroyer" performs it.[13] The identity of "the destroyer" (המשחית in v. 23; in v. 13 the form, as vocalized in MT, lacks the definite article) naturally attracted interest in the exegetical tradition. Jubilees understands it to refer to the forces of Mastema, a being who is associated with destruction in the book. The rendering of Exod 12:13 in *Targum Pseudo-Jonathan* echoes the kind of reading found in Jubilees:

---

11   Segal (*Jubilees*, 212-14) accepts the view of some commentators on Exodus 12 that vv. 12-13 rewrite v. 23 and thus remove the destroyer as the agent of the tenth plague (obviously such a rewriting would not remove the destroyer from v. 23, since this hypothetical rewriter left the verse in the text). Source critics of Exodus 12 analyze the text in varied ways (for a quick overview, see Houtman, *Exodus*, 2:147-49), but the more relevant point for Jubilees is how ancient readers may have understood the passages. For that point, see below. The form משחית in 12:13 may be a noun meaning "destruction" (so BDB, 1008, s.v. שחת), but at least some early expositors took it to be a participle as in v. 23.

12   See also Segal, *Jubilees*, 224.

13   See *Exod. Rab.* 17: "Some say, through the medium of an angel; and others, the Holy One, blessed be He, Himself."

Exodus 12:13
... and no plague shall destroy you when I strike the land of Egypt.

Targum Pseudo-Jonathan Exodus 12:13
... and *the Angel of Death, to whom authority to destroy has been given*, will *have no power* over you when I slay in the land of Egypt.[14]

In Exod 12:23 *Pseudo-Jonathan* renders "the destroyer [המשחית]" with "the Destroying *Angel*," a term it had also used in Exod 4:25-26 for the one at whose feet Zipporah lay the foreskin of her son and for the one who left Moses alone after that. Jubilees attributed that attack on Moses to Mastema (48:2).

It is understandable that writers would be hesitant to ascribe to God the killing of the Egyptian firstborn,[15] but there is scriptural warrant for finding destructive angelic beings in the tenth plague. Psalm 78:49-51, after references to several of the plagues, reads:

> He let loose on them his fierce anger,
> wrath, indignation, and distress,
> a company of destroying angels.
> He made a path for his anger;
> he did not spare them from death,
> but gave their lives over to the plague.
> He struck all the firstborn in Egypt,
> the first issue of their strength in the tents of Ham.[16]

There are other passages that may have favored the sort of reading found in Jubilees. The familiar case of 2 Sam 24:1, where the Lord incites David to count the people, becomes in its parallel 1 Chr 21:1 an occasion when Satan moves him to take the census.[17] Later in the same passages, the Lord sends a pestilence on the people, and a destroying angel is the one who carries it out (2 Sam 24:16-17; 1 Chr 21:15-16). The sacrifice David brought, like the blood around the doors in Exodus 12, averted a plague from Israel (2 Sam 24:25; see 1 Chr 21:22).

Segal finds in the presentation of Mastema in Jubilees 48-49 more evidence for his thesis that the rewritten stories in Jubilees and the legal passages derive from different sources. By rewritten story in this instance he means chap. 48, and by legal material he means chap. 49 (vv. 1-6)—a curious division in that both are rewritings of texts in Exodus and both are narrative in character. The term "legal" for the passages in which Mastema appears in chap. 49 is a misnomer.[18]

He explains his thesis in these words:

> The transcendental nature of God in *Jub*. 49 emphasizes the glaring contradiction between chs. 48 and 49 regarding the plague of the firstborn. As we saw above, *Jub*. 48 emphasizes that the Lord himself killed the Egyptian firstborn (in addition to all the other plagues that he brought; see 48:5-8 . . .). In contrast, chap. 49 asserts that God sent "the forces of Mastema" to fulfill this mission (49:2-5). One who wants to resolve the contradiction between the two chapters is likely to suggest that ch. 48, which describes how God brought the plagues, actually meant that he sent his agents on his behalf. However, it is difficult to accept this kind of harmonization in light of the fundamentally different descriptions as to the nature of Mastema. In ch. 48, Mastema is an independent entity with his own aims, even if God and the angel of the presence can thwart his specific plans. He decided to attack Moses when he was returning to Egypt from Midian, and he encouraged the Egyptians to pursue the children of Israel. Mastema therefore cannot be God's envoy,

---

14   Ezekiel the Tragedian calls him "the fearsome angel" (*Exagoge* 159).

15   Philo (*QE* 1.23) wrote about the destroyer in Exod 12:23: "It weaves into the whole legislation the faithful and worthy sentiment that we are not to make the Deity the cause of any evil. For when it says that He will not suffer the destroyer, it makes plain that corruption and destruction are brought about through certain others as ministers but not through the sovereign King. There you have the literal meaning" (Marcus, LCL).

16   Segal (*Jubilees*, 225-26) also refers to the passage but adds that the reference to the destroying angels is "not specifically next to the firstborn plague" (p. 226). It clearly is "next to the firstborn plague."

17   Segal (*Jubilees*, 209 n. 19) observes that "Satan" in 1 Chr 21:1 replaces not "the Lord" in 2 Sam 24:1 but "the anger of the Lord" and that the Chronicler could have interpreted "the anger" as "an evil, divine entity" (see Ps 78:49). That may be the case, but it could also be a simple replacement of the Lord with Satan (whatever "Satan" means in the context).

18   Segal admits as much but dismisses the fact that vv. 2-6 are narrative in nature by writing: "Similar to the other examples of the juxtaposition of rewritten stories and legal passages, here too the legal passage first presents a short summary of the story (49:1-6) that contradicts the rewritten narrative (ch. 48)" (*Jubilees*, 228 n. 63). But the example is not the same as the other passages to which he points, and 49:1-6, as argued here, does not contradict the narrative in chap. 48.

but rather often works against him. He is Egypt's patron, in contrast to the Lord and the angel of the presence who are responsible for Israel. It is difficult to imagine that Mastema or his forces would knowingly work against Egypt's best interests. The picture is completely different in *Jub.* 49. The "forces of Mastema" (v. 2) are identified as the "forces of the Lord" (v. 4). God sent them and commanded them to kill the Egyptian firstborn. They are not the heavenly patrons of the Egyptians, but God's special forces for performing "dirty" operations on earth. God is responsible for their actions, because they function under his command; they are an integral part of the way God runs the world. The inclusion of Mastema in ch. 48 is to distance God from evil actions, while the goal of ch. 49 is to distance him from direct involvement in the world at all.[19]

Here it should be noted that Kugel, from a different angle, agrees with Segal that there is a contradiction between what chap. 48 reports about Mastema and his role in 49:2-5. As he phrases it, in chap. 48 "Mastema does everything in his power to foil God's plan to free the Israelites. He actually has to be held in restraints for five days."[20] But, in chap. 49 the "forces of Mastema were sent to kill every firstborn in the land of Egypt" (49:2). Kugel argues from these passages: "Here there is a clear about-face: instead of trying to frustrate God's plans, Mastema's legions actually become God's agents, carrying out the tenth plague instead of opposing it."[21]

There is much in Segal's statement and in Kugel's comments that is debatable, but at the heart of it all is misrepresenting how both narrative sections (chaps. 48 and 49) depict Mastema and indeed how the book describes him. Mastema is not the heavenly patron of Egypt. He is the leading opponent of God and his plans, and he does what he can to prevent those plans from reaching fruition. If he supports the Egyptians, as he does most of the time in both of these chapters, it is not because of any special attachment he has for them. He uses them in his war against God. When he made his first appearance in the book as "the leader of the [evil] spirits," he said he wanted to exercise his authority on people through those spirits who "are meant for (the purposes of) destroying and misleading before my punishment because the evil of humanity is great" (10:8). After the time of Noah, "Prince Mastema was exerting his power in effecting all these actions [the sins listed in 11:2, 4] and, by means of the spirits, he was sending to those who were placed under his control (the ability) to commit every (kind of) error and sin and every (kind of) transgression; to corrupt, to destroy, and to shed blood on the earth" (11:5). That is his nature in Jubilees—a misleader, a destroyer, one who incites people to oppose God and his will. He engages in anti-God campaigns by his very nature.

The author of Jubilees does not present conflicting pictures about the roles of Mastema in chaps. 48 and 49 and, by extension, regarding God's relation to the world. He does echo the ambiguity in Exodus regarding who executed the tenth plague, but he consistently pictures Mastema as a destroyer who contends against God in any way he can but who is always under God's firm control. And God may use him if he chooses to do so. The picture of Mastema in chaps. 48 and 49 aligns with his roles elsewhere in the book.
1. He works to ruin conditions among people so that they fail to do what God desires of them.
2. He replaces God in those passages where other expositors too felt God himself would not have done what the text attributes to him (the Aqedah, the attempt on Moses's life). This seems to be the case with plague 10 and the pursuit to the sea.
3. He is read into the text where it mentions that a destroyer and the Lord carried out the same action, as in Exod 12:23.

Claiming there is a contradiction between the pictures of Mastema in chaps. 48 and 49 is to misrepresent what Jubilees reports elsewhere about Mastema and God's control over him and his forces. For Kugel's division of the chapter between the author and his interpolator, see below on v. 17.

■ **5-6** As he continues to describe the events of that night, the writer, speaking about the extent of the plague among the Egyptians, provides his own summary statement and supplements it with words from Exod 12:30 (see also 11:6).

---

19 Segal, *Jubilees*, 226–27.
20 Kugel, *Walk through* Jubilees, 229; cf. "Jubilees," 445–46. This is one of the "contradictions" in the book that he takes from Segal.
21 Kugel, *Walk through* Jubilees, 229.

Exodus 12:30	Jubilees 49:5
... there was a loud cry in Egypt, for there was not a house without someone dead.	The plague on Egypt was very great. There was no house in Egypt in which there was not a dead person, crying, and mourning.

The severity of the blow that befell Egypt is also the subject in other reworkings of the Passover story. For instance, Wis 18:10-12 relates (directly following mention of singing by the Israelites):

> But the discordant cry of their enemies echoed back,
>   and their piteous lament for their children was spread abroad.
> The slave was punished with the same penalty as the master,
> and the commoner suffered the same loss as the king;
> and they all together, by the one form of death,
>   had corpses too many to count.
> For the living were not sufficient even to bury them,
> since in one instant their most valued children had been destroyed.

The contrast between what was occurring in Egyptian houses and in those of the Israelites becomes evident when v. 5 is compared with v. 6: all was sadness for the Egyptian families, all was joy for the Israelite households. Exodus 12 does not describe what the Israelites did that night since it contains only the legislation for celebrating Passover, so the picture in v. 6 comes from the author of Jubilees. That Israel was dining on the paschal meat serves as an enactment of the law in Exod 12:8, where they are ordered to eat the lamb on the night of the fifteenth; at this point Jubilees, unlike the sequel in Exodus (v. 9), does not adduce any information about how it was to be prepared but saves the instructions for v. 13. The writer adds that they were drinking wine "and glorifying, blessing, and praising the Lord God of their fathers." As various commentators have observed, this is the earliest mention of drinking wine and offering praise (cf. Wis 18:9) during the Passover meal.[22]

It is noteworthy that they were "praising the Lord God of their fathers." The designation for the deity is the one Moses was told to use in identifying him for the Israelites, after he asked the Lord at the burning bush for his name (Exod 3:15): "God also said to Moses, 'Thus you shall say to the Israelites, "The Lord, the God of your ancestors, the God of Abraham, the God of Isaac, and the God of Jacob, has sent me to you." . . .'" In the continuation of that passage Moses received a message to deliver to the Israelite elders: the Lord, the God of the ancestors, had heard them and had seen what was happening to them in Egypt. God adds, "I declare that I will bring you up out of the misery of Egypt" (3:17). He also predicted that he would "strike Egypt with all my wonders" (3:20). Though the writer of Jubilees had not reproduced those verses in his abbreviated account, he now indicates that the predictions were fulfilled so that Israel appropriately praised God by the name he had given to Moses in preparation for the deliverance from Egypt.

The story about the first Passover ends with a notice about the Israelites' readiness to leave Egypt—an allusion to their eating the meal with "your loins girded, your sandals on your feet, and your staff in your hand" in Exod 12:11. The situation from which they were preparing to leave is characterized as "the Egyptian yoke." The image could have been influenced by Lev 26:13: "I am the Lord your God who brought you out of the land of Egypt, to be their slaves no more; I have broken the bars of your yoke and made you walk erect." There are frequent references to Israel's servitude in Egypt, but "evil slavery" may be based on the harsh labor/servitude of Exod 1:14; 6:9; Deut 26:6.

7-15 The Proper Time for Celebrating Passover

The author had introduced the subject in v. 1 before he described what happened the night of Passover. In this section he deals in more detail with the legislation

---

[22] See, e.g., Albeck, *Jubiläen*, 15. The practices of drinking wine and praising (the Hallel) figure in the Synoptic Gospels (Matt 26:27-30 // Mark 14:23-26 // Luke 22:17, 20 [the song is not mentioned]) and the Mishnah (*m. Mo'ed* 10 prescribes the four cups and reciting of the Hallel psalms). As Albeck pointed out (48 n. 106), the writer of Jubilees says that Abraham (16:31) and Jacob (32:7) praised and thanked God during the Festival of Tabernacles so that these are regular features of holiday celebrations in the book. See also Charles, *Jubilees*, 254; and Werman, *Jubilees*, 547.

that pertains to the timing of Passover throughout the generations.

■ **7-8** He begins by using language for the correct timing of the celebration along with expressions he had adopted earlier in connection with other festivals. The angel orders Moses to remember the day throughout his lifetime (lit., "all the days of your life"). The vocabulary in the first part of v. 7 resembles Deut 16:3: "so that all the days of your [sg.] life you may remember the day of your [sg.] departure from Egypt" (cf. Exod 13:3). That passage is speaking about the first day of the Festival of Unleavened Bread,[23] but it does use the verb "remember" (see Exod 12:14: "This day shall be a day of remembrance for you") and "the days of your life." Exodus elsewhere commands that the holiday be celebrated "throughout your generations" (12:14, 42).[24] Observing the holiday "in accord with all its law" echoes the commands in Num 9:3: "according to all its statutes and all its regulations you shall keep it."[25] That the occasion should be marked once per year (also v. 8) would seem to follow from the fact that the Israelites were to celebrate it on the fourteenth of the first month, but Jubilees is explicit about the point. When giving the legislation for the Festival of Weeks, the writer employed such phrases several times:[26]

6:17: "during this month—once a year"
6:20: "one day in the year, during this month, they are to celebrate the festival"
6:22: "at each of its times one day in a year . . . during this month—one day each year."

He did the same for the Festival of Tabernacles ("in each and every year" [16:29]) and the Day of Atonement (34:18 "once a year" and 34:19 "on this day once a year"). The nearest expression in the festival calendars is "at its appointed time" in Num 9:2, 3 (see Lev 23:4).[27]

It may be that the author used a wordplay at the end of v. 7 (see the textual note).[28] The Ethiopic verb could be translated as "pass over each other, cross, transfer, adjourn,"[29] while the Latin *praeteribit* means "will pass by, pass over." The sense of the statement seems to be that if one celebrates the festival at its ordained time one will not pass over from one (correct) day and month to another (incorrect) day or month. The angel was insistent in chap. 6, when describing the year of 364 days, that if one used another calendar arrangement for the year one would "make a day of testimony something worthless and a profane day a festival. Everyone will join together both holy days with the profane and the profane day with the holy day, for they will err regarding the months, the Sabbaths, the festivals, and the jubilee" (6:37). The day for Passover in the pattern created by God is a sacred unit, and if a person somehow moved the celebration to another day (say, by following a luni-solar calendar) he would disturb this eternal design and mix the holy with the ordinary (see v. 14 below). It should be added that the statement about not moving the time for Passover to the wrong day probably says nothing about the possibility of a second Passover (see Num 9:6-14); it is speaking only about Passover itself.

---

23 As noted above, Deuteronomy does not draw a clear distinction between Passover and Unleavened Bread.
24 Halpern-Amaru thinks that "from year to year" in v. 7 is related to Exod 13:10 ("Use of Bible," *89), but the Exodus passage uses, literally, "from days to days" and was rendered in just that way in the LXX and related translations and in the targums.
25 See VanderKam, "Pentateuchal Legislation," 192. Halpern-Amaru ("Use of Bible," *90; "Festivals," 314, 316) thinks that the author of Jubilees used the singular "all of its law" whereas the noun is plural in Num 9:3 "to access Num. 9:14, where the similar phrasing, וכמשפטו, appears in the context of a pericope dealing with Pesah Sheni and the participation of the resident alien in the pesah celebration, neither of which does the author wish to include in his legislation." There is no basis for thinking he objected to the second Passover, since he never mentions it and never implies it would be invalid (see below).
26 Charles, *Jubilees*, 254.
27 Levine, *Numbers 1-20*, 296: "The point of the statement is that this rite must be observed in its designated date to start with."
28 Goldmann, who rendered the verb with תעבר, made the suggestion that the original reading was a form of פסח ("Jubilees," 310 n. to vv. 6-7).
29 Leslau, *Comparative Dictionary*, 260. Charles rendered with "adjourn"; Littmann, "leave out"; Wintermute, "delay"; and Caquot, "defer."

In v. 8 the writer again takes up language from Exodus 12. He calls the keeping of Passover at its time "an eternal statute," which is a phrase from Exod 12:14 (חקת עולם); see 12:24. The eternal statute is, of course, engraved on the tablets of heaven (see 6:28-31, 35; 16:29; 18:19 for other dates so inscribed). The date and the fact that the Israelites were to keep the festival annually, once per year, are etched unchangeably on the tablets; also recorded on them is that there is to be no end to the time span during which it is to be an annual celebration. On this occasion, to express the duration of celebrating Passover, the author resorts to the phrase "throughout your generations" from Exod 12:14, 42 (Ethiopic *tewleddomu* means literally "their generations" [cf. Latin *generationibus ipsorum*], but the general practice in the translation for the present commentary is to render it as "their history"). To these indications he adds, "There is no temporal limit because it is ordained forever," like the sentence he used in connection with the Festival of Tabernacles in 16:30.

■ 9 The angel continues to address the issue of the time for the celebration but also deals with the person who is obligated to observe it at exactly the right time. He enumerates two conditions: the "man who is pure" and "nearby" must celebrate Passover. He first mentions only the purity regulation, but later in the verse references both it and the one about proximity. Neither of these qualifications appears in the legislation of Exodus 12, but they do figure in the explanation for the second Passover in Num 9:1-14. When it was time to celebrate Passover in the second year after the exodus, some Israelites were impure through corpse contamination yet wanted to observe the festival. Moses presented their case to the Lord, who ruled, "Anyone of you or your descendants who is unclean through touching a corpse, or is away on a journey, shall still keep the passover to the Lord" (Num 9:10). The provision for celebrating on month 2, day 14 is then revealed. Since there were only two legitimate reasons for not celebrating Passover at its time on 1/14, it follows, as Jubilees states, that anyone who is both pure and nearby (not on a journey)[30] was obligated to mark the occasion at its normal time. The author does not concern himself with the second Passover because it appears in a part of the Torah that he does not reach in his rewriting, but he obviously knows the regulations in Numbers 9.[31]

The obligation of the Israelite male was "to bring a sacrifice that is pleasing before the Lord and to eat and drink before the Lord on the day of his[32] festival." These words like the ones earlier in the verse are a near-citation of Num 9:13:[33]

---

[30] The writer does no more than mention the conditions from Numbers 9 and therefore does not clarify what constituted not being nearby. In *m. Pesaḥ*. 9:2 the distance is "Beyond Modiith, or a like distance in any direction. So R. Akiba. R. Eliezer says: Beyond the threshold of the Temple Court." In the discussion of this passage in *b. Pesaḥ*. 93b-94b, a distance of fifteen miles is determined as the meaning of "Beyond Modiith," but the thesis of R. Eliezer is also considered.

[31] VanderKam, "Pentateuchal Legislation," 197-98. It seems reasonable to suggest that the writer of Jubilees, in naming the two conditions, implies that if a person was not pure or nearby he should not celebrate Passover. A further implication could be that such a person would have opportunity to keep the festival on the second Passover, though, as noted, Jubilees does not deal with the topic. Stéphane Saulnier ("Jub 49:14 and the [Absent] Second Passover: How [and Why] to Do Away With an Unwanted Festival," *Hen* 31 [2009] 42-47) rightly highlights the parallels between Numbers 9 and Jubilees 49 but fails to deal with the conditions mentioned in Jub 49:9. He argues that the prohibition of changing Passover from its day shows that the author did not accept a second Passover. Yet that law is applicable to Passover itself and need be saying nothing about the possibility of a Passover for those not pure or nearby on 1/14. The Qumran festival lists include the second Passover (e.g., 4Q320 frg. 4 iii:4; 4 iv:9; 4 v:3, 12).

[32] The suffix should refer to the Lord. According to Lev 23:2, 4, 37, 44 all the holidays listed in the chapter, including Passover, are called the festivals of the Lord; for Passover, see v. 5.

[33] Halpern-Amaru, "Use of Bible," *91-*92; VanderKam, "Pentateuchal Legislation," 192.

Numbers 9:13	Jubilees 49:9
But anyone who is clean and is not on a journey, and yet refrains from keeping the passover, shall be cut off from the people for not presenting the Lord's offering at its appointed time; such a one shall bear the consequences for the[34] sin.	The man who is pure but does not come to celebrate it on its prescribed day—to bring a sacrifice that is pleasing before the Lord and to eat and drink before the Lord on the day of his festival—that man who is pure and nearby is to be uprooted because he did not bring the Lord's sacrifice at its time. That man will bear responsibility for his own sin.

Because the writer resorts to two statements about the man's qualifications, the order of the sentence is different in Jubilees; he also twice mentions the stipulated time—"to celebrate it on its prescribed day" and "at its time," while Numbers uses a similar term only in the second case (with the sacrifice). However, where the passage in Numbers speaks in specifics only about bringing the prescribed offering as the way of celebrating the festival, the author of Jubilees adds to it the duties of eating and drinking before the Lord. Eating the Passover meal is part of the legislation in Exodus 12 and Numbers 9 (see v. 11 for the second Passover: "they shall eat it with unleavened bread and bitter herbs"), but the legislator in Num 9:13 noted only the sacrifice. Jubilees thus inserts the other requirement of eating and his addition of drinking (see v. 6) to the base text in Num 9:13. As he often does, the writer expresses removal of a person through the verb "uproot/eradicate [Latin: *exterminabitur*],"[35] where the MT and SP have "cut off." Thus, v. 9 is a solid example of how he incorporates legislation from relevant passages besides Exodus 12 into his presentation.

■ **10** The emphasis on the precise time for Passover continues with a repetition of the date—the fourteenth of the first month (Exod 12:6; Lev 23:5; Num 9:3; 28:16)—but also a further delimiting of the time frame in which the celebration is to occur. Exodus 12:6, Lev 23:5, and Num 9:3 use the term "between the two evenings [NRSV: at twilight]" to define the designated time; in Exod 12:6 it is the time to slaughter the lamb, and the same is the case in Lev 23:5; but in Num 9:3, as here in Jubilees, "between the two evenings" marks the time for celebrating Passover with all the word includes. The pentateuchal texts do not explain what "between the two evenings" means,[36] but the writer of Jubilees does. The time for the celebration is "from the third part of the day until the third part of the night." That is, according to the author, the day consists of three parts as does the night.[37] Rashi commented on the phrase in Exod 12:6: "those hours between the evening of the day and the evening of the night. The evening of the day is at the beginning of the seventh hour, from when 'the shadows of evening lengthen' [Jer 6:4], and the evening of the night is at the beginning of the night."[38] So the sacrifice took place at some point toward the end of the fourteenth and before the very beginning of the fifteenth. The last line in v. 10 explains that the day falls into three parts, with the first two occurring in the light portion and the last of the three being termed "the evening." As the night has three parts, the celebration could continue to the very last part of the night (see v. 12). The parallel "the third part of the day" and "the third part of the night" suggests that the latter also designates not the first part of the night (that is, a third part of the night) but the third and last division of the night.

■ **11-12** The angel further explains to Moses that the details in v. 10 were what the Lord meant when he used the phrase "between the two evenings" (Exod 12:6). Verse 12 deals with the sacrifice of the lamb and declares that it must not take place during those first two parts of the day mentioned in v. 10 ("two parts of

---

34 There is a suffix "his" on "sin," so that the MT and SP read just as Jubilees does here, though the NRSV omits the possessive.
35 The verb is spelled *exterminavitur* in the manuscript.
36 Rather than "between the two evenings," Deut 16:6 prescribes that the offering be made "in the evening at sunset." In the Temple Scroll (11QT^a xvii:7), the sacrifice occurs before the "offering of the evening," a term Yadin (*Temple Scroll*, 2:74) understood as meaning the evening *tamid* offering.
37 See Tabory, *Festivals*, 87.
38 Translation of VanderKam from the text in A. Ben Isaiah and B. Scharfman, eds., *The Pentateuch and Rashi's Commentary: Exodus* (Brooklyn, NY: S.S. & R., 1950) 102. See also VanderKam, "Pentateuchal Legislation," 196.

the day have been given for light"). Rather, its time is "in the hour of the boundary [*wasana*]³⁹ of the evening." This appears to be another way of formulating the idea that the sacrifice of the lamb is to take place in the last segment of the fourteenth day so that the meat can be prepared for the meal that is enjoyed that night.⁴⁰ The meal itself proceeds throughout the evening (of the night); this accords with Exod 12:8: "They shall eat the lamb that same night." It may continue throughout the other two parts of the night ("until the third part of the night").⁴¹ At that point the meat of the sacrificed lamb is no longer permitted for eating and must be burned. Exodus 12:10 supplies the law reflected here: "You shall let none of it remain until the morning; anything that remains until the morning you shall burn" (see also Num 9:12).

■ **13** Only after all the preceding details about when the celebration is to occur does the writer take up the topic of how the meat is to be prepared. Exodus 12:8-9 prescribes: "they shall eat it roasted over the fire with unleavened bread and bitter herbs. Do not eat any of it raw or boiled [ובשל מבשל] in water, but roasted over the fire, with its head, legs, and inner organs." Jubilees reproduces the various parts of the verse except "with unleavened bread and bitter herbs,"⁴² though it puts some items in a different sequence. The command that

---

39 Leslau, *Comparative Dictionary*, 620: "boundary, limit, border." The Latin translation of Jubilees reads only "in the evening."

40 Halpern-Amaru ("Use of Bible," *82-*87; also in her "Festivals," 311-12) thinks the writer of Jubilees interprets the expressions "on the evening" (Deut 16:4), "in the evening at sunset" (16:6), and "between the two evenings" as "time designators for the stages of the pesaḥ celebration" (*87, not unlike the interpretation in *b. Ber.* 9a), stretching from the fourteenth to the fifteenth of the first month. It is not so clear that the writer proceeded in this fashion (i.e., by taking "in the evening" in Deut 16:4, 6 to refer to times for slaughter and for eating), while the phrase "between the two evenings" and the word "night" in Exod 12:6, 8 were obviously crucial for the specifics of the legislation for the time of the sacrifice and the meal.

41 The designation "until the third part of the night" is ambiguous: does it mean the first third of the night (so Charles, *Jubilees*, 255; Kugel, *Walk through* Jubilees, 199-200; Lawrence H. Schiffman "The Book of Jubilees and the Temple Scroll," in Boccaccini and Ibba, *Mosaic Torah*, 99-115, here 112) or does it refer to the third of the three parts of the night (so Albeck, *Jubiläen*, 13)? It seems more likely that the text means the third of the three parts of the night (as Schiffman notes, the Temple Scroll mentions no limit on the time for eating). In the Mishnah (*m. Pesaḥ.* 10:9; cf. *m. Zebaḥ.* 5:8), the ruling is: "After midnight the Passover-offering renders the hands unclean." However, *m. Ber.* 1:1 indicates that the cutoff time of midnight was given only to prevent the danger of actually transgressing the command in Exod 12:8 (see the end of the paragraph). In the same passage, Rabban Gamaliel tells his sons: "Moreover, wheresoever the Sages prescribe 'Until midnight' the duty of fulfilment lasts until the rise of dawn." If so, the writer of Jubilees would be in agreement with the Sages on this point. *Targum Pseudo-Jonathan* Exod 12:8 reads: "They shall eat the flesh that night *of the fifteenth of Nisan until midnight*." Werman (in Shemesh and Werman, *Revealing*, 302-5; cf. *Jubilees*, 540-41, 548) thinks Jubilees, like a number of rabbinic texts that she adduces (for instance, the view of Rabbi Eliezer in *Mek. Pisḥa* 6), confines the time for the meal to the first third of the night, but it is at least as likely that the formulation in Jubilees permits eating throughout the night.

42 Werman thinks the omission is intentional because the writer of Jubilees bases his instructions for Passover not on the Passover of Egypt (Exod 12:1-24) but on the law of Passover in vv. 43-50 (Passover for the generations) (in Shemesh and Werman, *Revealing*, 300 and elsewhere in her discussion of Passover on pp. 296-306). Since eating with unleavened bread and bitter herbs is not mentioned in vv. 43-50, the writer does not include the practice. She may be correct on this particular point (as she indicates, perhaps the sectarian view was that unleavened bread and bitter herbs were consumed only at the second Passover [they are mentioned in Num 9:11]), but there are several indications that Jubilees also models its Passover legislation on the celebration in Egypt. Note these items (there are more), none of which appears in vv. 43-50 but all of which Jubilees took from the first part of Exodus 12: v. 1, the date of the fourteenth of month 1 (Exod 12:6); v. 6, eat prepared to leave (Exod 12:11); v. 8, eternal statute (Exod 12:14); between the two evenings (Exod 12:6); v. 12, eat it that night (Exod 12:8); not to leave any until morning (Exod 12:10).

the meat be roasted and the prohibition of boiling it in water contrast with Deut 16:7, which uses the verb בשל in a positive command (though without the addition of "in water"). The NRSV renders it there as "cook it," and perhaps that is what it means. However, as S. R. Driver wrote, "it is in any case remarkable that the term employed in Dt. is the one which is used in P (Ex. 12⁹) to denote the process that is not to be applied to the paschal sacrifice."[43] In its formulation of the law, Jubilees states the negative part as "They are not to boil it [*yābselewwo*] in water," using a cognate of the Hebrew verb in Exod 12:9, but in the positive expression "cooked [*besula*] with care on a fire" it uses a passive form of the same verb. The Ethiopic verb has the meaning "to cook" in the causative stem, and this is a possible meaning for בשל in the piel conjugation.[44] If one takes the verb in Jub 49:13 in the sense of "cook" (note, there is no reference to water after *besula*), then it seems as if the writer is combining Exod 12:8-9 and Deut 16:7.[45] The expression "with care" appears to be an interpretation of בחפזון ("hurriedly") in Exod 12:11.[46]

The final stipulation regarding the lamb is that there is to be no breaking of its bones.[47] Exodus 12:46 (also LXX Exod 12:10) rules that "you shall not break any of its bones," and Num 9:3 says "nor break a bone of it." The two pentateuchal passages simply declare the law but do not explain its rationale. The Ethiopic version of Jubilees says that no bone of the lamb is to be fractured "because no bone of the Israelites will be broken."[48] Houtman concludes regarding the ruling in Exod 12:46:

In the current context, an interpretation based on the link between wholeness of the animal = wholeness of the community is the most acceptable: breaking of the bones would be tantamount to breaking the wholeness of the community and constitute an assault on the protective power surrounding it (cf. 12:9). For an early interpretation in this spirit see Jub. 49:13.[49]

■ 14-15 The verses offer a summary of some of the preceding laws and in so doing emphasize the importance of celebrating Passover on the correct day. In v. 14 the

---

43 Driver, *Deuteronomy*, 194.
44 Leslau, *Comparative Dictionary*, 109; BDB, 143.
45 It is often suggested that 2 Chr 35:13 offers a compromise between Exod 12:8-9 and Deut 16:7: "They roasted the passover lamb with fire according to the ordinance; and they boiled the holy offerings in pots." Goldmann ("Jubilees," 311 n. to v. 13) suggested the reading in Jubilees "cooked with care on a fire" was an interpretation of צלי in Exod 12:9, but it is more likely to be a borrowing from Deut 16:7. See the textual note for Charles's view.
46 VanderKam, *Jubilees* 2:319. If this interpretation is correct, then Werman (in Shemesh and Werman, *Revealing*, 307) is mistaken that Jubilees does not use בחפזון in describing the Passover of Egypt. In the Latin translation of Jubilees the verb and object "you will eat it" appear before *diligenter* ("carefully"), just as in Exod 12:11.
47 See Werman (in Shemesh and Werman, *Revealing*, 299-300; cf. *Jubilees*, 548) for the suggestion that the law, which comes from the legislation in Exod 12:43-50, is for Jubilees a brief way of expressing what is found in Exod 12:9.
48 Consult the textual note for Charles's attempt to support the Latin reading "There is to be no stress among the Israelites on this day." Werman (in Shemesh and Werman, *Revealing*, 301 n. 66) argues that the Ethiopic reading should not simply be preferred to the Latin text, since the Ethiopic reading contradicts the tendency in the chapter to separate between the Passover of Egypt and that of the generations; however, as noted above, that distinction does not prevail throughout Jubilees 49. In John 19:36, Exod 12:10 and Num 9:3 are applied to Jesus, who, when he was crucified, did not have his legs broken: "These things occurred so that the scripture might be fulfilled, 'None of his bones shall be broken.'" The passage reflects the ones from the Pentateuch, but Ps 34:20 ("He keeps all their bones; not one of them will be broken"—lines said about the righteous) may also have influenced it (see Raymond E. Brown, *The Gospel according to John: Introduction, Translation, and Notes* [2 vols.; AB 29, 29A; Garden City, NY: Doubleday, 1966, 1970] 2:937-38). Berger (*Jubiläen*, 549 n. g to v. 13) speaks about a "Talionsschema" here in Jubilees, as in v. 15.
49 Houtman, *Exodus*, 2:208. In *Tg. Ps.-J.* Exod 12:46, the relevant part reads, "And you shall not break a bone of it, *to eat what is within it.*" See also *b. Pesaḥ.* 84b-85a.

writer connects the commandment about the specific date to the one prohibiting the breaking of the animal's bones by saying that the festal nature of the day, the fact that the day is one that the Lord has identified by command, entails that no bone was to be broken. The sacred character of the day designated by the Lord applied to that particular period of time; as a result, there could be no passing over from that day to another that lacked its holy nature (see v. 7). The Passover is to be an annual celebration on the precise date that he had ordered—the fourteenth of the first month. Moreover, Israel is to continue marking it every year "during their generations [Ethiopic, lit., days]," that is, throughout their history (note the Latin reading "in their generations").[50] The result is that "a pleasing memorial [Latin: testimony] will come before the Lord." The continuation of v. 15 draws upon Exod 12:13: "and no plague shall destroy you when I strike the land of Egypt." As a result, it seems as if the reference to a memorial comes from the same context. Exodus 12:13 calls the blood on the doors "a sign for you," and v. 14 says, "This day shall be a day of remembrance [זכרון] for you." In *Tg. Neof.* Exod 12:14 it is "a good memorial."[51] The term "pleasing" or "acceptable" (a niphal form of רצה) is commonly used with sacrifices (e.g., Lev 7:18). In the same way as sacrifices, if offered properly—according to the legislation for them—are acceptable to the Lord, so the Passover celebration, if carried out "in every respect as it was commanded," will be pleasing to him.

The notion of remembrance and what is associated with it may also be tied to Exod 13:9-10: "It shall serve you as a sign on your hand and as a reminder [זכרון] on your forehead, so that the teaching of the LORD may be on your lips; for with a strong hand the LORD brought you out of Egypt. You shall keep this ordinance at its proper time from year to year." Here too properly observing a festival and remembrance are combined. The language of Jub 49:15 in some ways also echoes the story about the covenant with Noah. After smelling the pleasing aroma of Noah's post-flood sacrifice, God made a covenant with him marked by a sign—the rainbow—that was to remind the deity of the covenant and of the promise that the waters would "never again become a flood to destroy all flesh" (Gen 9:15). In Jub 49:15 the pleasing memorial that will arise before the Lord when Israel celebrates the festival in exactly the right way will also prevent destruction: "no plague will come upon them to kill and to strike (them)[52] during that year." Each year the festival will, in some way, resemble the one in Egypt when the Lord made the Israelite homes immune to the tenth plague. In the future they will enjoy the same safety for the year in which they celebrate Passover as the Lord commanded them. The holiday occurs in the first month of the year and sets the course of the year for the people of Israel. That is, the future situation at Passover will not involve the specific danger that threatened that night in Egypt; the danger, of whatever kind, will be warded off for the coming year if the Israelites celebrate it in the right way.[53] It may be that the prohibition of breaking the lamb's bones "because no bone of the Israelites will be broken" (v. 13) is also related to the idea that Israel will enjoy safety from a destructive plague in the year in which they keep Passover as God commanded.

---

50 The line is reminiscent of the rabbinic distinction between the Passover of Egypt and the Passover of the generations (mentioned in *Tg. Ps.-J.* Exod 12:3, 11), with some different prescriptions applying to the latter (see, e.g., *m. Pesaḥ.* 9:5; *t. Pisḥa* 8:11–22 has a detailed list of differences and similarities).

51 R. Hayward, in the notes to McNamara's translation of *Neofiti* Exodus, comments that "good memorial," used more often in this targum, contrasts it with the memorial of wrongdoing mentioned in Num 5:15, 18. He refers to Jub 49:15 in the note (*Targum Neofiti 1: Exodus* [ArBib2; Collegeville, MN: Liturgical Press, 1994] 48 n. 12).

52 The combination of killing and striking reminds one of the words (in reverse order) that introduce the plague list in Jub 48:5.

53 See the comments of Werman (in Shemesh and Werman, *Revealing*, 308). She properly observes that, in this regard, the situation in the Passover of the generations is different from the one in Egypt. Baruch Bokser referred to this as "an added emphasis on the apotropaic effect of the celebration" and "a kind of preventive health care" (*The Origins of the Seder: The Passover Rite and Early Rabbinic Judaism* [Berkeley: University of California Press, 1984] 20).

16-21 The Proper Place for Celebrating Passover

Correct celebration of Passover in the future also involves keeping it at the right location, but the designated place was to change in the course of the nation's history.

■ **16** The initial rule is that the Passover is a festival that is to be observed at the sanctuary.[54] The first Passover took place in the Israelite houses at a time when they had no tabernacle or temple, but that procedure was unique to the celebration in Egypt. The writer of Jubilees is here dealing with Deut 16:5-7:

> You are not permitted to offer the passover sacrifice within any of your towns that the LORD your God is giving you. But at the place that the LORD your God will choose as a dwelling for his name, only there shall you offer the passover sacrifice, in the evening at sunset, the time of day when you departed from Egypt. You shall cook it and eat it at the place that the LORD your God will choose; the next morning you may go back to your tents.

Josiah kept the festival in Jerusalem (2 Kgs 23:21-23) as, apparently, the returned exiles did after completion of the Second Temple (Ezra 6:19-22). The expression used for the precise location in Eth. Jubilees is *ba-'anṣara*, "opposite, facing, across from, against, over against, toward, in front of" the sanctuary, while the Latin translation has *secus*, "by, beside."[55] Since only priests could enter the sanctuary itself, the lay Israelites would have to remain outside of the building proper. The prepositions express the notion of proximity to it that Deuteronomy words as "at" (using either אל or ב).[56] The stipulation regarding the centralized celebration includes one designating who are to observe the festival—"All the people of the Israelite congregation." The Ethiopic version uses *māḥbar* = association, multitude, congregation,[57] where Latin has *multitudo*. It is likely that a passage such as Exod 12:3 lies behind the designation: "Tell the whole congregation [עדת] of Israel that on the tenth of this month they are to take a lamb for each family" (see also vv. 6, 19). Other verses likewise imply that the entire nation participated in the festivities (e.g., vv. 21, 24). The full community is to keep the Passover "at its time."

■ **17** The subject continues to be the identity of the ones who celebrate Passover. Exodus 12 makes no statement about the age of the persons involved, but Jubilees and the Temple Scroll do: both stipulate that those twenty years of age and above are to celebrate it (11QT^a vii:8). Charles and Albeck noted that the age derives from other places in the Torah that suggest the time from which one became responsible for the commandments was twenty years. Exodus 30:14 orders that each person twenty years and above give the half-sheqel offering; Num 1:3 includes everyone in this age category in the census, as does Num 26:2.[58] Yadin pointed out that there is a word association between these passages and Exod 12:6: "The analogy is obvious, since the one text has 'the whole assembly of the congregation of Israel shall kill it' (Ex. xii:6), while the other has 'Take a census of all the congregation of the people of Israel' (Num. i:2)."[59] The

---

54 The translation in VanderKam, *Jubilees* 2 reads "It is no longer ['enka] to be eaten outside of the Lord's sanctuary." Upon further reflection, this appears to be an inaccurate rendering in context. The term *'enka* can have the meanings "so, then!, therefore, wherefore, now, then, forthwith, yet, and so" (Leslau, *Comparative Dictionary*, 29). As Kugel has noted (*Walk through* Jubilees, 201), the rendering "no longer" "would seem to presume the prior existence of a sanctuary" and this would not fit the perspective of the author who sets the revelation of Jubilees on Mount Sinai before there was a sanctuary (he thinks the passage is from his interpolator; cf. Kugel, "Interpolations," 255 n. 56 = *Walk through* Jubilees, 264 n. 49). Since the point of v. 16 is to insist that the Israelites eat the Passover sacrifice at the tabernacle or temple, it is more likely that *'enka* conveys the nuance of "therefore," tying this statement to the preceding one about celebrating the festival "in every respect as it was commanded" (v. 15, end). Latin lacks an equivalent for *'enka*.

55 Leslau, *Comparative Dictionary*, 406; Lewis and Short, *Latin Dictionary*, 1657.

56 Kugel (*Walk through* Jubilees, 201; cf. "Jubilees," 447) prefers the Latin reading and thinks it presupposes אצל, but the language of Deuteronomy 16 seems a more likely base.

57 Leslau, *Comparative Dictionary*, 256.

58 Charles, *Jubilees*, 256-57; Albeck, *Jubiläen*, 14-15.

59 Yadin, *Temple Scroll*, 1:97.

Temple Scroll requires that those twenty and above are, literally, "to do it," that is, celebrate it, and they are to eat it at night; Jubilees mentions only eating the sacrificial animal. According to Jubilees, they are to eat it "in the sanctuary of your God before the Lord," while the Temple Scroll stipulates that the eating take place in "the courtyards" of the sanctuary (xvii:9)—the place Jubilees mentions in v. 20. Both texts lend some specificity to the vague command of Deut 16:6-7, and both contrast with the practice attested elsewhere that the Passover could be eaten in any part of Jerusalem.[60]

Since v. 16 gives the impression that the entire Israelite congregation is to celebrate the festival, it raises the question of what is meant by the restriction to those twenty and above. In Jubilees they are the ones who are to eat the Passover sacrifice in the sanctuary on the correct day; in the Temple Scroll they are to celebrate the holiday and eat the sacrifice in the temple courtyards. Do these texts mean that what happened at the sanctuary pertained only to those of sufficient age, while all those below the age of twenty participated only in a more limited sense in the holiday?

The wording of v. 17 and of the parallel in the Temple Scroll surfaces a further issue in connection with who could eat the Passover sacrifice in the sanctuary: was it everyone twenty and above or was it just males in that age bracket?[61] The Ethiopic text uses the noun *sab'* and the Latin employs *homo*; both terms could be translated "man" or "person," so that they are ambiguous in this regard. The problem has arisen anew since the publication of 4Q265 (Miscellaneous Rules). In frg. 3 line 3, as read and reconstructed by its editor J. Baumgarten, the text says, "[Let no] young lad nor a woman partake [of] the paschal [sacri]fice."[62] If his reading is correct, it would lend support to the thesis that in Jubilees and the Temple Scroll women and children were not to eat the Passover sacrifice in the temple area. Baumgarten restored the negative word in the law in brackets at the beginning of the line so that there is uncertainty whether it is actually there. He defends his reading of the line by noting that, once Passover was transformed into a temple holiday, issues of purity became central. Moreover, in the section regarding the second Passover in Numbers 9, it appears that those for whom it was instituted were men—the term for the ones who were impure at the time is masculine (see vv. 6-7, 10)—and the description of those to whom the Passover offerings were given in Josiah's time (2 Chr 35:13) could be taken as limited to males. Baumgarten thinks Jub 49:17 and 11QT[a] xvii:8-9 are explicit in limiting the eating of the meat at the sanctuary to males. He continues:

> The implied exclusion of women and minors from partaking of the paschal offering was a sectarian stringency, later perpetuated in Karaite exegesis. The practice prevalent in the late Second Temple period was evidently more lenient, as one gathers from the description of Josephus. He states that each offering was eaten by a fraternity of between ten to twenty people, from which were excluded "those afflicted with leprosy or gonorrhea, or menstruous women . . . , or persons otherwise defiled" (*J.W.* 6.426). This is in accordance with tannaitic halakha, such as *m. Pesaḥ* 8.1, which allows a woman to partake of the paschal lamb offered by either her father or her husband.[63]

It seems reasonable to conclude, therefore, that all three texts—Jubilees, the Temple Scroll, and 4Q265—restrict the right of eating the paschal sacrifice at the temple to males who have reached the age of twenty.[64] Women and

---

60 E.g., Tabory, *Festivals*, 85-86; Albeck, *Jubiläen*, 14; Yadin, *Temple Scroll*, 1:97. These experts refer to *m. Zebaḥ*. 5:8, but whether it is explicit on this point is debatable; however, cf. *m. Mak*. 3:3. The Last Supper in the Synoptic Gospels is an example of eating the Passover in Jerusalem but not at the temple.

61 If one follows E. Qimron's plausible restoration at the end of 11QT[a] xvii:7 (he adds כול זכר after יובחוהו), then the Temple Scroll explicitly limits the sacrifice and eating in the temple courtyards to males. See Qimron, *The Temple Scroll: A Critical Edition with Extensive Reconstructions* (Beersheba and Jerusalem: Ben-Gurion University of the Negev Press and Israel Exploration Society, 1996) 27.

62 Joseph Baumgarten, "265. 4QMiscellaneous Rules," in DJD 35:63.

63 Ibid., 63-64.

64 See also Schiffman, "Jubilees and the Temple Scroll," 112. Werman thinks limiting the rights only

minors would still have taken part in the festivities of Passover (see v. 16) but in some other ways not further specified in any of these texts.

The author has the angel say "it has been written and ordained—that they are to eat it in the Lord's sanctuary." The legislation sounds somewhat like the law in Deut 16:7 that they were to eat the Passover in "the place the Lord your God will choose." It may be, too, that the reference to the deity in "the sanctuary of your God before the Lord" reflects the Deuteronomic phrase "the Lord your God."

Excursus: The Heavenly Tablets Reference in 49:8

Since 49:8 mentions the heavenly tablets, Kugel includes material from this chapter in the contributions he attributes to his interpolator. As he divides the chapter, the interpolator added vv. 2-17 and 22-23. Since the tablets figure only in v. 8 (and see the phrase "written and ordained" in v. 17), one naturally wonders how he determined the extent of the supplementary material. He maintains that vv. 18-21 were meant to be the immediate sequel to v. 1. If so, the original text would have read:

> 1 Remember the commandments that the Lord gave you regarding the Passover so that you may celebrate it at its time on the fourteenth of the first month, that you may sacrifice it before evening, and so that they may eat it at night on the evening of the fifteenth from the time of sunset. 18 When the Israelites enter the land that they will possess—the land of Canaan—and set up the Lord's tabernacle in the middle of the land in one of their tribes, until the time when the Lord's temple will be built in the land, they are to come and celebrate the Passover in the Lord's tabernacle and sacrifice it before the Lord from year to year. 19 At the time when the house is built in the Lord's name in the land that they will possess, they are to go there and sacrifice the Passover in the evening when the sun sets, in the third part of the day. 20 They will offer its blood on the base of the altar. They are to place the fat on the fire that is above the altar and are to eat its meat roasted on a fire in the courtyard of the sanctuary in the name of the Lord. 21 They will not be able to celebrate the Passover in their cities or in any places except before the Lord's tabernacle or otherwise before the house in which his name has resided. Then they will not go astray from the Lord.

The sequence is possible, but a reader might wonder why, when v. 1 deals with the time for the events of Passover, v. 18 suddenly switches to the locations where the celebration will take place after entry into the land. The matter of timing surfaces in v. 19, where there is a repetition of the reference to sunset from v. 1 and one explanatory phrase. Verse 20 takes up the sacrificial procedure and the manner of preparing the meat with more information about the place.

There is, then, the problem of a change of topic between vv. 1 and 18-21, but there is also a textual connection between vv. 1 and 2 (v. 2 begins: "For on this night . . .") that makes their juxtaposition very reasonable. In addition, the writer had not mentioned Passover in chap. 48 (where the plagues occupied his attention) so it was only natural that he take up the subject of Israel celebrating it in Egypt at the beginning of chap. 49.

In trying to defend his source division, Kugel in effect admits how problematic it is although even in doing so he misinterprets the text. He notes that some topics are treated more than once in chap. 49—the time and place of the sacrifice and the eating of it—and in ways that are consistent with each other.

> Given the fact that the Interpolator basically agreed with the original author on the laws of Passover, why did he even bother inserting the long passage of vv. 1-17 [he forgets from time to time that he assigned v. 1 to the author; see the next reference as well]? In part . . . it was to cover items omitted by the original author—the first Passover in Egypt (vv. 1-6), the calendrical exhortation (vv. 7-8), and the warning about the 'Second Passover' (v. 9).[65]

Of course, he can say the author omitted these items only after he has first excised them from the text. There are no stylistic or vocabulary reasons for deny-

---

to males twenty and above is related to Exod 12:48-49 where participants have the status of being a citizen ("native of the land" in NRSV) or, in the case of an "alien who resides with you," become like a citizen through being circumcised (in Shemesh and Werman, *Revealing*, 299-300). It was an easy move from this rule to limit sacrificing and eating Passover at the temple to males twenty years and older, the age of being a citizen responsible for the laws.

65 Kugel, *Walk through* Jubilees, 267; "Jubilees," 445, 448; 465 nn. 268-69.

ing these passages to the author. A second defense for the source division is similarly unconvincing: "But if he [the interpolator] went on to cover once more the proper time and place of the slaughter and eating of the Passover sacrifice, it was probably because . . . these issues were hotly disputed in his day; his emphatic formulations were designed specifically to deny the interpretations of the founders of rabbinic Judaism."[66] But does this explain why the author could not have contributed these passages? Obviously it does not. Why not say that the writer emphasized these points that are treated more than once in the chapter because they were debated at his time? Kugel's explanation provides no evidence that these sections come from a different hand.

The various sections of the chapter as outlined in the present commentary show that the writer of Jubilees takes up major topics regarding the Passover in a reasonable progression. After the heading to the chapter in v. 1, he describes the first Passover (vv. 2-6), devotes a section to a fuller explanation for the timing of Passover rites in the future (7-15), and follows them with a paragraph about the place for the celebration since that will change over time (vv. 16-21). After treating these subjects, he, as does the text of Exodus, takes up the Festival of Unleavened Bread (vv. 22-23). The repetition Kugel finds is not there;[67] each of the sections has its own topic and in each the author gives his understanding of points that, in some cases, were disputed by others.[68]

■ 18 The angel next addresses the fact that during Israel's future time in the land the sanctuary will take different forms. First, once they reach Canaan (he continues to use this name for the land, although according to 10:27-34 it is a misnomer) they will set up the tabernacle (it was mentioned also in 1:10). The Ethiopic version uses a verb meaning "to pitch (a tent)," but Latin has them inhabiting the tabernacle (see the textual note)—a reading that is unlikely to be correct. That tent shrine they will pitch in "the middle of the land in one of their tribes." He probably has in mind the placement of the tabernacle (or tent of meeting) in Shiloh, a very centrally located city where Joshua divided parts of the land among the tribes (Josh 18:1; Judg 18:31; for designating the sanctuary as the Lord's tabernacle, see Josh 22:19; cf. v. 29) and where later Eli and Samuel were to serve (1 Samuel 1–3). The phrasing "in the middle of the land" reminds one of the way in which the angel had described two other holy places: "Mount Sinai is in the middle of the desert; and (that) Mount Zion is in the middle of the navel of the earth" (8:19). The angel adds that the tabernacle will be a temporary sanctuary and will be the place for Passover only until the time that the temple is built. Nevertheless, the Deuteronomic regulation that festivals be celebrated at the one place where the Lord makes his name dwell means that it is the only location in the pre-temple period where one may annually keep the festival and offer the sacrifice in his presence.[69]

There are some hints in the narrative books of the HB that Passover was observed in pre-temple times. Joshua 5:10 refers to celebration of it at Gilgal just after entry into the land. 2 Kings 23:22 says of Josiah's Passover: "No such passover had been kept since the days of the judges who judged Israel, even during all the days of the kings of Israel and of the kings of Judah." The text could imply that Passover had been celebrated in the time of the judges but in a different way (say, in homes). The parallel in 2 Chr 35:18 reads somewhat differently: "No passover like it had been kept in Israel since the days of the prophet Samuel; none of the kings of Israel

---

66 Kugel, *Walk through* Jubilees, 267 (the passage is the direct continuation of the one quoted just above); cf. "Jubilees," 465 n. 269.

67 The only point about the time for Passover found in v. 1 (from the author) and in vv. 10-15 (supposedly from an interpolator) is the date of 1/14 for the sacrifice. Otherwise, the information about timing in vv. 10-15 represents a development. The real repetition is found in material that Kugel attributes to an interpolator—references to celebrating it on its specific day are in vv. 10, 14, and 15 (see also v. 7), and "between the evenings" occurs in vv. 10 and 11.

68 For arguments regarding the contradiction he, following Segal, finds between the ways in which chaps. 48 and 49 present Mastema, see above on v. 4.

69 Halpern-Amaru thinks the phrase "from year to year" is an allusion to Deut 15:20, where שנה בשנה is used in a law about eating the firstling of the flock at the central sanctuary ("Use of Bible," *94). The suggestion seems unlikely to be right as the phrase is not the same as the one in Jub 49:18 and the topic in Deut 15:20 is different.

had kept such a passover as was kept by Josiah." The formulation in 2 Chronicles "since the days of the prophet Samuel" would allow for celebration of the festival at the sanctuary throughout almost all the days of the judges.

■ **19** As the angel explains the matter, celebration of the festival at the tabernacle would end when "the house is built in the Lord's name in the land that they will possess." Associating the Lord's name with the house echoes the expression met frequently in those parts of the Deuteronomistic History that deal with construction of the temple. The Lord promised David that his son "shall build a house for my name" (2 Sam 7:13), and Solomon later mentioned that promise and his own intent to build "a house for the name of the LORD my God" (1 Kgs 5:5). Similar references appear several times in Solomon's dedicatory prayer for the temple (1 Kgs 8:19, 20, 29, 43, 48; see also 9:3, 7). When the temple stands in the land Israel will possess, the Israelites will have to travel to it to make the paschal sacrifice. The rule that there was only one locale for the holiday comes, of course, from Deuteronomy, and the author betrays his debt to that book when he quotes it regarding the time for the sacrifice: "in the evening when the sun sets." The passage that lies behind this statement and the one about offering the sacrifice only at the Lord's temple is Deut 16:5-6: "You are not permitted to offer the passover sacrifice within any of your towns that the LORD your God is giving you. But at the place that the LORD your God will choose as a dwelling for his name, only there shall you offer the passover sacrifice, in the evening at sunset." To this specification the writer of Jubilees adds "in the third part of the day," a phrase he had used in v. 10 for the beginning of the celebration, that is, the sacrifice (see v. 12).

■ **20** The offering of the paschal sacrifice that he mentioned near the end of the preceding verse now receives attention. The instructions for sacrificing the animal begin with the handling of the blood. The subject of the verb is not specified but the action is: "They will offer its blood on the base of the altar." The only Passover offering described at length in the HB is the one Josiah celebrated as depicted in 2 Chr 35:1-19 (2 Kgs 23:21-23 is much briefer). In that ceremony "the priests dashed the blood" as priests alone could (cf. 2 Chr 30:16). Nothing is said there about tossing the blood on the altar base, but the procedure for animal sacrifices, including the "offerings of well-being" (Lev 3:8) with which the paschal sacrifice shares some traits,[70] was to throw the blood on the sides of the altar. The base of the altar receives mention in several sacrificial contexts (e.g., Exod 29:12) but especially in connection with sin offerings (five times in Leviticus 4). Offering the fat parts of the animal is mentioned in 2 Chr 35:14, but putting them on the fire that burned on the altar reflects the instructions in a passage such as Leviticus 3 regarding the well-being offerings (vv. 3-5, 9-11, 14-16). Once he has treated the sacrificial procedure, the angel tells Moses that the meat is to be "roasted on a fire"—the phrase from Exod 12:8, 9. The place where the meal is enjoyed is "the courtyard[71] of the sanctuary in the name of the Lord" (the Temple Scroll [11QT^a xvii:9] mentions "the courtyards" of the sanctuary as the place [see above, vv. 16-17]).[72] Although the phrase "in the name of the Lord" seems odd at the end of the verse, it may refer to the temple as the place where his name resides, a temple for his name.

■ **21** The section closes by partially reiterating the instructions already given. The language again draws on Deut 16:5-6: "You are not permitted to offer the passover sacrifice within any of your towns. . . . But at the place that the LORD your God will choose as a dwelling for his name, only there shall you offer the passover sacrifice." The angel adjusts the Deuteronomic legislation to the historical sketch he has just given by applying it to both the tabernacle and then to the temple. In reference to the temple, he uses Deuteronomy's description—"the house in which his name has resided." Observing the

---

70 See also Werman, *Jubilees*, 549.
71 Both versions use a singular form (*'aṣada*/atrium), unlike the plural in the Temple Scroll.
72 Werman presents an appealing case for the thesis that the tabernacle/temple becomes the equivalent of the "one house" in Exod 12:46 where one must eat the Passover meal (in Shemesh and Werman, *Revealing*, 300; see also *Jubilees*, 549). The same verse adds that a celebrant is not to take any of the meal (the animal) outside the house; this would provide the basis for the ruling that one is not to eat the Passover sacrifice outside the sanctuary.

Passover in the correct place will keep the Israelites from going "astray from the Lord." For the expression, see, e.g., 2 Chr 34:33.

22-23 The Festival of Unleavened Bread

The final unit of the chapter opens with one of the angel's commands to Moses to pass along legislation to the Israelites when he eventually goes down from Mount Sinai. In this case, of course, he is to give them orders about keeping the statute or law of the Passover—the legislation he has given in the preceding verses (7-21)—"as it was commanded to you." Exactly what Moses is to relate to the Israelites is less than clear.

> Ethiopic (literally): its year every year and its day for the days
>
> Latin (literally): through each of the years in the time of their days

Perhaps the message he is to tell them is to celebrate the festival annually on the right day,[73] but the phrases are difficult.

It is much clearer that Moses is also to inform them about the Festival of Unleavened Bread. Exodus (13:3-10) offers legislation regarding the holiday directly after the Passover story in chap. 12. The connection is logical because the single day of Passover and the seven days of the succeeding holiday share the feature that no leaven was to be eaten (13:3, 6-7). In Jubilees, therefore, they also figure in the same general context. The writer mentions eating unleavened bread for seven days, as in Exod 13:6; Lev 23:6; Num 28:17; Deut 16:3, 8; Ezek 45:21. The notice applies to the Festival of Unleavened Bread and does not include the day of Passover, since altogether there are eight days without leaven in those passages that distinguish between Passover and the Festival of Unleavened Bread (see, e.g., Exod 12:18).[74] He also refers to bringing daily sacrifices during the week of the holiday now under consideration. Leviticus 23:8 mandates presenting offerings for the seven days, and Num 28:19-24 provides details about them (cf. Ezek 45:23-24; 11QT^a xvii:10–16). Once again the writer introduces the notion of joy into his description of a festival. Halpern-Amaru has observed that the phrase ending v. 22 ("seven joyful days") reproduces one in 2 Chr 30:23 (שבעת ימי שמחה), part of the passage about King Hezekiah's unusual celebration of the Festival of Unleavened Bread in the second rather than the first month and for an additional seven days beyond the prescribed week for the festival. 2 Chronicles 30:21 reports that the people celebrated the holiday "seven days with great gladness." "[T]he command in Jubilees decrees that when future commemorators of the redemption bring the prescribed daily sacrifice, they are to celebrate with an intensity of joy/gratitude comparable to that of celebrants who would extend the festival an additional seven days."[75] When the festival was first revealed to Abraham, he was told to celebrate it "for seven days with festal happiness" (18:19).

■ 23[76] As noted earlier in connection with the story about Moses's return to Egypt and the ten plagues, Exodus pays little attention to dates. The same is the case for the account of the departure from Egypt, the arrival at the sea, and the crossing of it. There is an element of haste in their leaving Egypt, as indicated by how the Egyptians urged them to depart and how they took their dough before it was leavened (Exod 12:33, 34, 39), but the source for the words "you celebrated this festival hastily when you were leaving Egypt" seems to be Deut 16:3: "For seven days you shall eat unleavened bread

---

73 Dillmann rendered with "annually on its day" and Charles with "every year and the day of its days." He was uncertain about the second phrase and thought that, with Latin, one should translate "during its days" (*Jubilees*, 257). See VanderKam, *Jubilees* 2:324. Halpern-Amaru thinks "its day for the days/in the time of their days" in the two versions of v. 22 is the writer's way of indicating there were two days involved, the fourteenth (for the sacrifice) and the fifteenth (for the meal) ("Use of Bible," *95; "Festivals," 319, with n. 27). She may be right about the plural "days," but the expression remains obscure.

74 Josephus (*Ant.* 2.317) refers to an eight-day festival, but he may mean that the Festival of Unleavened Bread itself lasts eight days.

75 Halpern-Amaru, "Joy as Piety," 189.

76 Berger points out that the chapter is framed by references to the historical occasion behind each of the festivals treated in it (*Jubiläen*, 546 n. a to chap. 49).

with it—the bread of affliction—because you came out of the land of Egypt in great haste."[77] Once they are on the move, there is reference to their camping at Etham (Exod 13:20), and at the sea there is mention of a night and the following morning (Exod 14:20-21, 24, 27). After they had crossed the water, they entered the wilderness of Shur a three-day journey (Exod 15:22). Nothing is said about observing a festival during this swift exit from Egypt. In fact, Exod 13:5 leads one to think the holiday was to be observed only in the future: "When the LORD brings you into the land . . . which he swore to your ancestors to give to you, a land flowing with milk and honey, you shall keep this observance in this month." That is, Israel will celebrate the holiday once they reach the land of promise.

Numbers 33, a chapter that lists the places where Israel encamped during their wilderness sojourn, provides the kind of data that would have been more useful to the author of Jubilees as he calculated the time that lapsed from leaving Egypt to reaching the sea. The sequence there is:

1/15 (v. 3): left Egypt (from Rameses)
    camped at Succoth (v. 5)
    camped at Etham (v. 6)
    camped before Migdol after turning back
      to Pi-hahiroth (v. 7; see Exod 14:2)
    from Pi-hahiroth they passed through the
      sea and made a three-day journey in the
      wilderness (v. 8).

If one counts one day for each of the three encampments, allows a similar stretch of time for the Egyptian forces to reach the sea, and adds the day for the crossing (a night and morning), the total is seven days from the time Israel left Egypt until their safe arrival on the far shore of the sea. The listing in Numbers, however, refers neither to the Egyptian pursuit nor to how long it might have taken, just as Exodus gives no explicit indication about the days involved in the Egyptian campaign.

Jubilees leaves a different impression about the seven-day festival and offers something of a chronology for the time from the exodus to the miracle at the sea. According to the writer, the Israelites actually celebrated the holiday as they raced out of Egypt "until the time you were crossing the sea into the wilderness of Shur, because you completed it on the seashore." He does not explain exactly how many days it took Israel to reach the sea and how long they remained on the opposite shore, but it was apparently after they crossed the sea that the seven days of the festival came to an end. Jubilees provides an explanation for why the holiday is to last seven days (Exodus gives no such account): the first national observance of the Festival of Unleavened Bread happened during and recalls the momentous days of the time they fled Egypt until they were safely across the unnamed body of water.[78] Since they concluded the celebration on the shore, the three-day march into the wilderness of Shur had not yet begun.

Ezekiel the Tragedian has left a chronology that sounds somewhat like the one in Jubilees. God says to Moses (167-71, trans. Robertson in *OTP* 2):

But when at last you enter your own land,
take heed that from the morn on which you fled
from Egypt and did journey seven days,
from that same morn, so many days each year
you shall eat unleavened bread and serve your God.

For Ezekiel, the Israelites traveled seven days, whereas the writer of Jubilees is not explicit that all the days were occupied in journeying. More significantly, Ezekiel echoes the instruction in Exod 13:5-7 that the festival would be kept when they entered the land.

A seven-day chronology from the exodus to the other side of the sea—a period during which Israel celebrated the holiday—is attested in various sources, including *Seder Olam* 5. There the listing in Num 33:3-7 is taken to be a three-day period, with each encampment marking one day. On the fourth day, Pharaoh heard that the Israelites had fled (see Exod 14:5), the Egyptians chased after them on the fifth and sixth days (cf. Exod 14:6-9),

---

77 Werman, in Shemesh and Werman, *Revealing*, 307.
78 In *b. Meg.* 31a, the lectionary section for the last day of Passover (i.e., of Unleavened Bread) is the passage about crossing the sea (the section *Beshallaḥ*, beginning at Exod 13:17). See also Kugel, *Traditions*, 568; Werman, in Shemesh and Werman, *Revealing*, 306.

and they caught up with Israel at the sea (Exod 14:9). The seventh day was the one when the Israelites entered the sea at night (see 14:20) and in the morning of that seventh day emerged from it while the Egyptians were drowning (cf. Exod 14:27-29). The chronologist ends the section by saying that this seventh day (a Thursday) was the last day of Passover, that is, of the sequence Passover–Unleavened Bread.[79]

A related yet somewhat different account can be found in the *Mekilta, Beshallaḥ* 2-3. It takes up the encampments in Numbers 33 and explains that the Israelites began the trip on the day before the Sabbath, continued on the Sabbath, and also traveled the next day. On the fourth day they gave the impression they were going even farther—something that aroused the attention of Egyptian guards, who reminded them they had requested only a three-day journey into the wilderness (quoting Exod 8:23). Later there is reference to a trip of one and one-half days by the guards to overtake the Israelites and of one day for Pharaoh to arrive. With the night and day of the crossing, one apparently arrives at or near the end of seven days.[80]

The Festival of Unleavened Bread is tied securely to the exodus from Egypt in the Bible. As a result, the author of Jubilees could not advance an origin for a festival by this name to commemorate an event in the patriarchal age as he did for the Festival of Weeks, the Day of Atonement, and the Festival of Tabernacles. He does, nevertheless, attach the holiday to an event in the life of Abraham and Isaac, although only indirectly. The same problem faced him in connection with Passover—also unbreakably attached to a post-patriarchal event. The solution he adopted was to prefigure both Passover and the Festival of Unleavened Bread in his story about the near sacrifice of Isaac. The subject was discussed above in the commentary on chap. 18. Here only a summary of the evidence need be adduced.[81]

In the chronology of Jubilees for the attempted sacrifice of Isaac (see the commentary there), Abraham and Isaac set out for the mountain (in Jerusalem) on 1/12 and arrive at the mountain and follow the Lord's command to offer Isaac late in the day of 1/14. The timing of Abraham's effort to sacrifice Isaac, his firstborn son, late on 1/14 corresponds with the time for offering the Passover sacrifice—late in the day on 1/14 (before sunset, in the evening of the day). Jubilees provides early evidence for a connection between the two events that is developed in later sources, both Jewish and Christian. The parallels between the two, as the stories appear in Jubilees, were transparent: in both cases the son (Isaac, or Israel as God's firstborn son) was delivered from death through the blood of an animal (either a lamb or a goat) at the same time on the same date. In both cases, Mastema was the one from whose attack the son was saved. And in both cases the Angel of the Presence was an opponent of Mastema (18:9-12; 48:9-10, 15-18; cf. 48:4).

In the case of the Festival of Unleavened Bread, the situation is similar though with a distinction. Jubilees 18:18-19 report that Abraham, after returning from the trip to sacrifice Isaac, celebrated "this festival joyfully for seven days during all the years. He named it the Festival of the Lord in accord with the seven days during which he went and returned safely. This is the way it is ordained and written on the heavenly tablets regarding Israel and his descendants: (they are) to celebrate this festival for seven days with festal happiness." A seven-day festival in the first month would seem to be the Festival of Unleavened Bread, but Abraham's holiday is associated with the seven days of his journey—1/12 to 1/18—whereas the Festival of Unleavened Bread extends from 1/15 to 1/21. However, as noted in the commentary on chap. 18, the text of Jub 18:18 says only that the days are "in accord with the seven days during which

---

79 On the section and other sources attesting the chronology, see the comments of Milikowsky, *Seder Olam*, 2:101-2.

80 Van Goudoever thinks that, according to this text, they crossed the sea the night after the seventh day of Unleavened Bread (*Biblical Calendars*, 124-25).

81 See van Goudoever, *Biblical Calendars*, 68-69 (though he mistakenly claims that the writer gives two sets of dates for the Festival of Unleavened Bread, 1/12-1/18 and 1/15-1/21; in Jubilees only that latter set is correct); Le Déaut, *La nuit pascale*, 179-84; VanderKam, "*Aqedah*," 241-57; Halpern-Amaru, "Festivals," 309-22; and Huizenga, "Battle for Isaac," esp. 41-46, 51-58.

he went and returned safely." So the seven-day period is associated with the holiday and no dates are given for it. The associations between the description of this festival in 18:18-19 and the Festival of Unleavened Bread in 49:22-23 are clear. The author connects the seven days of the festival with the seven-day journey of the Israelites from Egypt to the other side of the sea. It too is a period of seven days to be marked with festal joy. And in both cases Mastema is put to shame (18:12; 48:12).

Sabbaths, Weeks, and Jubilees

50

1/ After this law, I informed you about the Sabbath days in the wilderness of *Sin*[a] that is between Elim and Sinai. **2/** On Mount Sinai I told you about the Sabbaths of the land and the years of jubilees[a] in the Sabbaths of the years, but its year we have not told you until the time when you enter[b] the land that you will possess. **3/** The land will observe its Sabbaths when they live on it, and they are to know[a] the year of jubilee. **4/** For this reason I have arranged for you the weeks of years and jubilees[a]—49 jubilees from the time of Adam until today, and one week and two years. It is still 40 years off for learning the Lord's commandments until the time when he leads (them)[b] across to the land of Canaan, after they have crossed the Jordan to the west of it. **5/** The jubilees will pass by[a] until Israel is pure of every sexual evil,[b] impurity, contamination, sin, and error. Then they will live[c] confidently in the entire land. They will no longer have any satan or any evil one. The land will be pure from that time until eternity.

6/ I have now written for you the Sabbath commandments and all the statutes of its laws. **7/** You will work[a] for six days, but on the seventh day is the Sabbath of the Lord your God. Do not do any work on it—you, your children, your male and female servants, all your cattle, or the foreigner who is with you.[b] **8/** The person who does any work on it is to die. Any man who desecrates[a] this day;[b] who sleeps with a woman;[c] who says anything about work[d] on it—that he is to set out on a trip on it, or about any selling or buying; who on it[e] draws water that he had not prepared for himself on the sixth day; or who lifts[f] a load to bring (it)[g] outside his tent or his house is to die. **9/** On the Sabbath day do not do any work that you have not prepared for yourself[a] on the sixth day so that you may eat, drink, rest, keep Sabbath on this day from all work, and bless the Lord your God who has given you a festal day and a holy day. This day among their days[b] is to be the day of the holy kingdom for all Israel throughout all time. **10/** For great is the honor that the Lord has given Israel to eat, drink, and be filled on this[a] festal day; and to rest on it from any work that belongs to the work of humanity except to burn incense and to bring before the Lord offerings and[b] sacrifices for the days and Sabbaths. **11/** Only this (kind of) work is to be done on the Sabbath days in the sanctuary of the Lord your God[a] in order that they may atone continuously for Israel with offerings from day to day as a memorial that is acceptable before the Lord; and in order that he may receive them forever, day by day,[b] as you were ordered.[c]

12/ Any person who does work: who goes on a trip; who works farmland[a] whether at his home or in any (other) place; who lights a fire; who rides any animal; who travels[b] the sea by ship; any person who beats or kills anything; who slits the throat of an animal or bird; who catches either a wild animal, a bird, or a fish; who fasts and makes war on the Sabbath day—**13/** a person who does any of[a] these things on the Sabbath day is to die,[b] so that the Israelites may continue observing the Sabbath in accord with the commandments[c] for the Sabbaths of the land as it was written[d] in the tablets[e] that he placed in my hands so that I could write for you the laws[f] of each specific time in each division of its times.

Postscript[a] Here[b] the words[c] regarding[d] the divisions of the times[e] are completed.

Textual Notes

1a   *Sin*] The MSS. read "Sinai," a similarly spelled name that occurs a few words later. Here, Exod 16:1 is the base text, and it refers to the wilderness of Sin. See Charles, *Jubilees*, 258.

2a   jubilees] + "I told you" 12.

b   you enter] "you are to enter" 17 63.

3a   they are to know] "they will know" 12 21 (cf. 35 38 58).

4a   jubilees] pr. "the years of" 25.

b   he leads (them)] "they cross" 17 21 47; "he crosses" 35 39 44 48 58 63. All translators (except VanderKam, *Jubilees* 2 and Werman, *Jubilees*, 551) have chosen "they cross."

1192

5a	will pass by] "are to pass by" 21 39 48; "have passed by" 35.	b	day by day] om. 20.	
b	sexual evil] "evil of the land and fornication" 20; "fornication and evil" 39 42 47 48 58.	c	you were ordered] "your command/order" 12 20 21 25 42 58 63; "I commanded you" 38. Werman (*Jubilees*, 552 and n. 9), who places "I commanded you" in her text, claims it is the reading in the best copies, but it clearly is not (MS. 38, the only one to support her reading, is among the worst copies).	
c	will live] "are to live" 12 38; "he will cause to live" 25.			
7a	work (lit., "do work")] "you are to do your work" 21 35 44 58 63.			
b	with you] "You" is and should be pl. in this context, but MSS. 12 21 39ᵗ 42 47 58 63 read a sg. "you."	12a	farmland] pr. "his" 39 42 47 48 58.	
		b	travels] "goes" 21.	
8a	desecrates] pr. "does on it something that" 20.	13a	of (these)] "like" 20 (and 63 with a different form).	
b	this day] + "will surely die" 21 35 58; + "is to die and" 44.	b	is to die] om. 21; "will surely die" 35 63.	
c	a woman] "his wife" 38 58.	c	commandments] "commandment" 38 58.	
d	work²] "(what) he is to do" 12 17 21 38 39 42 47 48 63.	d	it was written] "it is to be written" 20 25.	
e	on it (draws)] om. 39 42 47 48 58.	e	tablets] + "of heaven" 35 39 42 47 48 58.	
f	lifts] + "any/all" 25 35.	f	laws] "law" 38.	
g	(it)] Mss. 25 58 supply the object.			
9a	for yourself] om. 12 39ᵗ.	Postscript		
b	among their days] "among your (pl.) days" 17 38.	a	om. postscript] 20 25 63.	
10a	(on) this] "the" 20.	b	Here] om. 35.	
b	and (sacrifices)] om. 25 35 48.	c	the words] "the book" 35 58.	
11a	your God] "their God" 20 25ᶜ(?).	d	regarding (lit., "of")] om. 21 35 38 44.	
		e	of the times] om. 35 38.	

Commentary

The final chapter in the book of Jubilees reverts to topics that have been central to the author's concerns since the beginning of his narrative in chap. 2. The travels of the Israelites as they moved from the sea and into the wilderness of Shur (Exod 15:22; arrival there is noted in Jub 49:23), to Marah (15:23),[1] Elim (15:27), and the wilderness of Sin (16:1) find no place in the text. The wilderness of Sin gets a brief notice (Jub 50:1) only because there the Lord revealed Sabbath laws (16:22-30) in connection with the schedule by which he provided manna for the people. From there Israel marched to Rephidim (17:1). Their complaints about a lack of water with the divine response (17:1-7), the subsequent attack by Amalek (17:8-16), and the visit by Jethro (chap. 18; it seems to have occurred at Sinai [18:5])—events that occupy two chapters in Exodus (17–18)—likewise play no part in Jubilees. Even the presence of Israel at Mount Sinai receives notice (Jub 50:2) only because of the sabbatical revelations that occurred there. Virtually all that the writer draws from the material after the exodus and until Sinai concerns the Sabbath. In dealing with the Sabbath in relation to creation (Jubilees 2) and the exodus (Jubilees 50), he echoes the formulations of the Sabbath law in Exod 20:10 and Deut 5:14.[2] The Angel of the Presence, by mentioning their encounter on Sinai, brings the story full circle: it began there with Moses's ascent and God's command that the angel reveal to Moses what was on the heavenly tablets (chap. 1); it ends with the two of them still on the mountain and the angel informing Moses about Sabbath laws as he had at the end of the creation story (2:17-33).

The fiftieth chapter speaks primarily about regulations governing the Sabbath (vv. 1, 6-13) but also deals with the sabbatical years and jubilees in the chronologi-

---

[1] It is noteworthy that the writer inserts no laws at this point, in spite of the report in Exod 15:25 that at Marah the Lord "made for them a statute and an ordinance" (see also v. 26). A number of rabbinic sources trace the disclosure of certain laws to the occasion (e.g., *Seder Olam* 5; *b. Sanh.* 56b).

[2] Doering, "Concept of the Sabbath," 183.

cal system of the book and the goal toward which the entire system was moving (vv. 2-5). The chapter can be outlined in this way:

1   Sabbath laws in the wilderness of Sin
2-5 Sabbaths of years, jubilees, and the chronological system
6-13 Sabbath laws.

The Ethiopic version alone has preserved Jubilees 50 (the legible parts of the Latin translation ended at 49:22).

1 Sabbath Laws in the Wilderness of Sin

The angel alludes to chap. 49 with his words "After this law." Now that he has disclosed to Moses the regulations governing future Passovers (and the related Festival of Unleavened Bread), he refers to a revelation that preceded the Israelites' arrival at Mount Sinai. The place where the disclosure occurred is identified in the Ethiopic copies as *Sinai*, but the name is a scribal error as the other geographical notices indicate.

Exodus 16:1	Jubilees 50:1
The whole congregation of the Israelites set out from Elim; and Israel came to the wilderness of Sin [סין], which is between Elim and Sinai [סיני].[3]	in the wilderness of *Sin* that is between Elim and Sinai.

The nearly lookalike names *Sin* and *Sinai* became confused, and the confusion may have been aided by the presence of the better-known *Sinai* at the end of v. 1 and the beginning of v. 2. The angel reminds Moses that he informed him there "about the Sabbath days." The time the Israelites spent in the wilderness of Sin began with their complaints against Moses and Aaron that they had no food (Exod 16:1-3). The Lord responded to their discontent by sending manna (vv. 4-21). Since the manna appeared only on the first six days of the week and not on the seventh, it was a fitting occasion for imparting Sabbath laws. Already in Exod 16:5 the Lord told Moses the people were to gather twice as much on the sixth day, but more specific instructions appear in 16:22-26.

On the sixth day they gathered twice as much food, two omers apiece. When all the leaders of the congregation came and told Moses, he said to them, "This is what the LORD has commanded: 'Tomorrow is a day of solemn rest, a holy sabbath to the LORD; bake what you want to bake and boil what you want to boil, and all that is left over put aside to be kept until morning.'" So they put it aside until morning, as Moses commanded them; and it did not become foul, and there were no worms in it. Moses said, "Eat it today, for today is a sabbath to the LORD; today you will not find it in the field. Six days you shall gather it; but on the seventh day, which is a sabbath, there will be none."

Later he supplemented these instructions with more words about the Sabbath: "See! The LORD has given you the sabbath, therefore on the sixth day he gives you food for two days; each of you stay where you are; do not leave your place on the seventh day" (16:29). According to Exodus, these are rules regarding the Sabbath that the Lord revealed to Moses who in turn transmitted them to the people; in Jubilees, they are instructions from the Angel of the Presence, who relayed them to Moses. The writer of Jubilees does not elaborate here regarding specific Sabbath regulations; they will come in vv. 6-13, where there are multiple indications that the manna story has left its influence (see esp. vv. 8, 9, and 12).

2-5 Sabbaths of Years, Jubilees, and the Chronological System

The angel next refers to what he told Moses on Sinai (their encounter is still continuing at this point),[4] but, rather than saying he disclosed the basic Sabbath command there (in the Decalogue, Exod 20:8-11), he draws

---

[3] Jubilees does not reproduce the date that Exod 16:1 assigns to the arrival in the wilderness of Sin—"on the fifteenth day of the second month after they had departed from the land of Egypt." This date played an important role in rabbinic calculations of the chronology from the exodus to the giving of the Ten Commandments on Mount Sinai (see Milikowsky, *Seder Olam*, 2:116–21).

[4] Wiesenberg suggests that, by having the angel refer to Mount Sinai and not to "this mountain," the writer "falls out of his role" ("Jubilee of Jubilees," 5 n. 13).

attention to the larger units in the sabbatical chronology.

■ **2** He calls them "the Sabbaths of the land and the years of jubilees in the Sabbaths of the years." He is referring to the legislation in Exod 23:10-11; Leviticus 25–26 (cf. Deuteronomy 15 [although it is post-Sinai]), both of which are included in the revelations given to Moses while he was at Mount Sinai for his first forty-day sojourn there.[5] The Sabbaths or weeks of years and jubilee cycles are, of course, the building blocks of the entire chronological system in the book. That they are used for the pre-Sinai period is an indication they were on the tablets from the beginning, although Moses first learned about them on Mount Sinai.[6]

The pentateuchal legislation prescribes a seven-year unit as a period that parallels the week:[7] for six years the Israelites were to plant their crops and harvest them, while in the seventh the land was to rest. The seventh year in one of these cycles is appropriately termed a "Sabbath of the land" (e.g., Lev 25:4, 6; 26:34, 43; 2 Chr 36:21). In the prescriptions regarding a jubilee, Lev 25:8 orders, "You shall count off seven weeks [lit., Sabbaths] of years, seven times seven years, so that the period of seven weeks [Sabbaths] of years gives forty-nine years." The year after these forty-nine—the fiftieth year—is termed the year of jubilee (see, e.g., Lev 25:13). These related units—sabbatical and jubilee cycles—were pressed into chronological service most famously in Dan 9:24-27, where the seventy-year prophecy of Jeremiah, interpreted in light of the sevenfold principle enunciated in Leviticus 26 (e.g., v. 18), is explained as meaning seventy weeks of years, that is, 490 years.[8] The author of Jubilees applied this sort of system—weeks of years and jubilees of years—to the period from creation to the entry into the land—and anticipated that the system would continue to be operative long after the Israelites settled there (see v. 5).

In v. 2 the angel, after mentioning the basic elements in the book's chronology, reminds Moses "but its year we have not told you until the time when you [pl.] enter the land that you [pl.] will possess."[9] He has in mind the very time when the Israelites will cross into Canaan and after which the sabbatical and jubilee cycles will run their course into an indefinite future.[10] So at this point he

---

5   The unit Leviticus 25–26, in which sabbatical and jubilee years are prominent (particularly in chap. 25), is unusual in that it is the only place in the book, apart from 7:38 (the end of the section on sacrifices) and 27:34 (the last verse in the book) where the writer makes a point of locating the revelation at Mount Sinai (see 25:1 and 26:46, the first and last verses of the unit). The unnecessary reference to Sinai in 25:1 drew the attention of the commentator in *Sifra* Behar 1 (see, e.g., Wacholder, "Date of the Eschaton," 93), but others concluded that it indicated that the passage actually belonged between Exodus 20 and 24 (for references, see Milgrom, *Leviticus*, 3:2151), in which case the angel in Jubilees could indeed claim he had told Moses about the sabbatical years and jubilees. On this, see VanderKam, "End of the Matter?," 278–80.

6   Werman, *Jubilees*, 552–53.

7   The two appear together in Exod 23:10-12.

8   For other texts that employ these units in their chronologies, see VanderKam, "Chronology," 524–28; and "Sabbatical Chronologies in the Dead Sea Scrolls and Related Literature," in Timothy Lim, ed., *The Dead Sea Scrolls in Their Historical Context* (Edinburgh: T&T Clark, 2000) 158–78; John Bergsma, *The Jubilee from Leviticus to Qumran: A History of Interpretation* (VTSup 115; Leiden: Brill, 2007) 233–94.

9   Although the negative in the expression "we have not told you" is attested by all the Ethiopic copies, Werman has made an intriguing case that it should be omitted so that the angel is informing Moses that he had told him the year in question (*Jubilees*, 553; cf. 552 n. 7). She bases her argument on Exod 16:35 (she mistakenly writes 16:30), which is part of the manna section that heavily influenced the author of Jubilees in 50:6-13 and to which he refers in v. 1: "The Israelites ate manna forty years, until they came to a habitable land; they ate manna, until they came to the border of the land of Canaan." Since the verse indicates that forty years will pass until the entry into Canaan, the writer of Jubilees could hardly have the angel maintain that he had not told Moses the year. But if the meaning of "its year" is as explained above, the year when the system of sabbatical cycles goes into effect in Canaan (as in v. 3), then the angel could be saying he had not told Moses the year and the reading of all the manuscripts could be retained.

10 Cf. Berger, *Jubiläen*, 552 n. c to v. 2.

discloses to Moses when Israel will receive its land and in so doing reveals the meaning or pattern of the system by which he has been dating the events since creation.

■ **3** The expression "The land will observe its Sabbaths when they live on it" recalls Lev 25:2: "When you enter the land that I am giving you, the land shall observe a sabbath for the Lord" (cf. Lev 26:34, 43; 2 Chr 36:21). From Lev 25:2 it sounds as if the weeks/jubilees cycles will begin to operate once the nation enters the land promised to them, but in Jubilees they are used for chronological purposes regarding both the time preceding that event and for the time after it (with an indirect reference here in v. 3 to its agricultural significance). When the people reside in the land, the land will enjoy its Sabbaths, and the people will know "the year of jubilee [ʿāmato la-ʾiyobēl]." The Angel of the Presence may be saying that, once they occupy the land, the nation will know which year constitutes the jubilee year and thus the basis for the chronology that will date their residence in the land. They would be unaware of this as Moses himself was learning about it from the angel only at Sinai. Knowing that year would also indicate when the entire cycle commences at the time Israel occupies the land. With such a thought in mind, the angel proceeds to explain in v. 4 exactly which year that will be. It is important to note that here he refers to "the year of jubilee," whereas in the overall chronology in the book to this point a jubilee has meant a period of forty-nine years.

■ **4** In order to specify when the cycles begin for the time Israel dwells in the land, the angel explains how the chronology has worked out to this juncture. He declares that he has arranged (šarāʿku) for Moses the "weeks of years and jubilees"—nothing is left to chance in this system—so that, from the days of Adam, there have been forty-nine jubilee periods ($49 \times 49 = 2401$ years) and an additional one week (seven years) and two years ($2401 + 7 + 2 = 2410$). This year of the exodus (see 48:1) precedes the entry into the land by forty years (see Num 14:33-34, where the forty years in the wilderness correspond with the forty days in which the spies were examining the land; Deut 1:3; 34:7; etc.). Adding those years to 2410 yields 2450.[11] That total allows one to see the pattern and meaning of the chronology in the book of Jubilees.

Two thousand four hundred fifty years is exactly fifty units of 49 years, that is, fifty jubilee periods. The exodus from Egypt (2410), therefore, occurred fairly early in the fiftieth jubilee period (the period includes the years 2402-2450). At the end of the forty years in the wilderness, the Israelites would reach the land that had been granted to them through their ancestor Shem after the flood (Jub 8:12-21; 9:2-6). Noah's grandson Canaan, contrary to the oath he had sworn, stole the land that was subsequently named after him, and his descendants illegally occupied it from that time to the present (Jub 9:14-15; 10:27-34). As a result, when Israel entered Canaan, they were not conquering territory rightly held by others; they were merely retaking the land given to them centuries earlier and repeatedly promised by God to their ancestors. This theme in Jubilees seems to be a response to the claim that Israel usurped the land of Canaan from its rightful owners.[12]

Two great events for Israel, then, are associated with the fiftieth jubilee period—freedom from slavery in Egypt and return to their ancestral land. Both of these themes in relation to individual Israelites come to expression in Lev 25:10: "And you shall hallow the fiftieth year and you shall proclaim liberty throughout the land to all its inhabitants. It shall be a jubilee for you: you shall return, every one of you, to your property and every one of you to your family." In the legislation regarding the jubilee year—the fiftieth year—Leviticus provides that two events occur in it: all were to return to their ancestral property (25:10, 13) if they had lost it in some way, and every Hebrew who had become enslaved was to be set free (25:39-43, 47-55). Those two

---

[11] For the same period (creation to the death of Moses) T. Mos. 1:2 gives 2500 years. Johannes Tromp notes that the figure is parallel to the one in Jub 50:4 if the writer of the Testament of Moses (= the Assumption of Moses) used jubilee periods of fifty years rather than the forty-nine year units in Jubilees (*The Assumption of Moses: A Critical Edition with Commentary* [SVTP 10; Leiden: Brill, 1993] 133). As he indicates, however, the author does not use a jubilee system of chronology elsewhere in his book.

[12] See VanderKam, "Their Place," 66–69, for the sources, dating from a later time, containing the charge that Joshua and the Israelites stole the land.

occurrences that applied to the individual Israelite in the fiftieth (jubilee) year happen to the nation of Israel in the fiftieth jubilee period in Jubilees: freedom from Egyptian slavery, and return to their ancestral land.[13]

The writer mentions the remaining forty years before entry into the land not only to clarify the pattern that history has followed to this point but also to explain the purpose for these forty years: "It is still 40 years off for learning the Lord's commandments."[14] Before the nation is fully prepared to enter the land, it must learn the covenantal laws that will guide their life there.[15] In this respect they imitate their ancestor Abram who, before he went to the land that the Lord would show him, "took his fathers' books—they were written in Hebrew—and copied them. From that time he began to study them, while I [the Angel of the Presence] was telling him everything he was unable (to understand)" (12:27).[16]

The passage makes the point that the many dates contained in the narrative of Jubilees were not isolated notices with no larger significance. All of them contributed to and belonged within a larger structure that demonstrated once more God's guidance of history, a long chronological progression that was moving in the direction preordained for it. Events happened when they did, not spontaneously or haphazardly, but by a grand design directed from heaven. As it had prevailed in the past, Israel could be confident it would continue in the future.[17]

The forty years in the wilderness when Israel learns the commandments will come to an end at "the time when he [God] leads (them) across to the land of Canaan, after they have crossed the Jordan to the west of it," that is, to the west of the Jordan.[18] The actual entry into the land, therefore, will directly follow the end of the fiftieth jubilee period.

■ **5** Leviticus 25 indicates that the sabbatical and jubilee cycles will be set in motion once the Israelites live in their land (25:2). Since the two related systems presupposed possession (and perhaps loss) of land and the practice of agriculture on it, it made sense that they would start once Israel settled in Canaan. The writer of Jubilees, who used the sabbatical system as a chronological measure for the pre-conquest period of sacred history, shows that he also knows about its application to the time in the land. He anticipates that the jubilee periods will continue until the time when Israel has attained a state of purity in every respect—a period that is to last forever. The impurities from which they will be liberated are familiar types from other passages in the book in which people are charged with such defilements (e.g., 9:15; 11:5; 20:7; 21:21, 23; 22:16, 19; 23:14, 17; 30:15; 41:25) or are warned to avoid them (e.g., 7:20; 20:3-6; cf. 22:14), including—prominently—sexual impurity (see 30:7-16; 41:24-26). In Jubilees 1, Moses prayed that God would not allow his people to conduct themselves "in the error of their minds" (v. 19) and asked that he would "Create for them a pure mind" (v. 21). God promised that after they acknowledged their sins and turned from their evil ways he would "create a holy spirit for them" and would "purify them in order that they may not turn

---

13 Wiesenberg, "Jubilee of Jubilees," 29; VanderKam, "Chronology," 540-43.
14 The reference seems clear enough—the forty years are those the Israelites were to spend in the wilderness—but some scholars have seen an eschatological sense in it (e.g., Testuz, *Idées*, 173-74; Davenport, *Eschatology*, 69-70). See below on v. 5.
15 Kugel observes that the positive reason for the forty years contrasts with the negative explanation (punishment because of the spies episode) given in Numbers 13-14 (*Walk through* Jubilees, 203; "Jubilees," 449). Cf. also Werman, *Jubilees*, 553 n. 11.
16 That event is dated to the year of the world 1951 (12:16), five hundred years before Israel entered the land. Abram himself, however, is said to have traveled to Canaan two years later (12:28).
17 Kugel, *Walk through* Jubilees, 203-4; "Jubilees," 449.
18 Scott argues that "to the west of it" means that the Jordan River is to the west of the land of Canaan; the expression shows that in Jubilees the territory on the east of the Jordan is part of the land (*On Earth as in Heaven*, 204-5). That the author thought the territory east of the Jordan belonged to the area promised to Israel is fair enough, but the line in Jubilees can hardly mean what Scott proposes. Apart from the general improbability of his reading, the suffix on "west" in the phrase "to the west of it" is masculine in gender and refers to the Jordan, whereas "land" is more likely to be treated as a feminine noun.

away from me from that time forever" (v. 23). Jubilees 50:5 speaks in similar terms about Israel's future purity from all kinds of contamination.[19]

Verse 5 is consistent with—in fact, probably discloses—the meaning of passages in chap. 1 that speak about the future and the range of material revealed to Moses on the mountain. For example, the Lord orders Moses: "Now you write all these words that I tell you on this mountain: what is first and what is last and what is to come during all the divisions of the times that are for the law and for the testimony and for the weeks of their jubilees until eternity" (1:26; see also 1:27-29). He does not define, in terms of weeks of years and jubilee periods, how long the era that begins after entry into the land will extend. It will go on and on into the future.

This conclusion about the indefinite period predicted in v. 5 runs counter to the thesis defended by several commentators that the writer of Jubilees does in fact disclose how long that future period will be. Testuz offered some speculation on the matter but recognized that the length of the future was unknown. Yet he thought one might be able to calculate the beginning of the eschatological era as coming at the start of the twenty-first or twenty-second jubilee after the exodus.[20] Wacholder believed that Jub 49:22—50:5, when read in an eschatological fashion, provided the key. He noted that CD xvi:2-3 identified Jubilees as the book that gives a precise interpretation of the times for Israel's blindness and thought the word "time(s)" referred to the eschaton. He helpfully noted the series of sevens present in 49:22—50:5, where the days of Unleavened Bread, Sabbaths, Sabbaths of years, and jubilees are discussed, but he takes some notices in these verses in a strange way, as if they were speaking about the end. In particular, he interprets the year for crossing of the Jordan in 50:4 as meaning the end of days rather than the event in the time of Joshua. His conclusion is directly opposed to what the context implies—it happens forty years after the Sinai disclosures. Nevertheless, Wacholder maintained that the purpose for mentioning the 2450 years in v. 4 was to imply that the time after the entry into Canaan would last a corresponding 2450 years. He relates this idea to Lev 26:34, which says the land will enjoy its Sabbaths to make up for the ones that Israel had failed to provide for it. As the land of Israel, in the period from creation to entry into the land, had not enjoyed its Sabbaths, so it would enjoy exactly the same number of them—fifty forty-nine-year units—once they were on the land.[21]

Scott has defended a more detailed and in some ways more plausible sketch of what he takes to be Jubilees' teachings about the future.[22] He maintains that the author calculated 980 years for the preexilic and exilic periods (490 for each of them); this period would be followed by another 2450 years that correspond with the era covered in the chronology of the book. He appeals to the picture in Jubilees 23, in which the long period of decline in people's ages after the antediluvian patriarchs is matched by an era of increasing lifetimes until they reach (and even exceed) the great ages of Adam and his immediate descendants. This symmetry, Scott believes, is evident also for the future after the exilic period. His thesis about the preexilic and exilic periods does not find much support in Jubilees, and the idea of a symmetrical period at some point after the 2450 years mentioned in 50:4, while not impossible, is hardly indicated in a clear way in any text in Jubilees.[23] The writer seems rather to be content with his account of the first 2450

---

19   See also Werman, *Jubilees*, 553. She adds that, as chap. 1 shows, the purification will come after exile and that, according to Lev 26:34-35, 43, failure to keep the sabbatical cycles would make the land vomit its residents from it.

20   Testuz, *Idées*, esp. 172-77. He gets the idea for twenty-two jubilees from the references to twenty-two in 2:15, 23 (twenty-two generations until Jacob, paralleling the Sabbath after twenty-two works of creation), but why one should think the references to twenty-two in chap. 2 hold some clue to eschatology is not easy to see. Davenport (*Eschatology*, 69–70), however, thinks Testuz has argued convincingly for his case. Davenport assigns 50:5 to his first redactor.

21   The above is a summary of Wacholder, "Date of the Eschaton," 87–97. In the remainder of the article he maintains in a thoroughly speculative way that the 390 + 20 years of CD i:1–10 presuppose the date for the eschaton that Jubilees allegedly gives.

22   Scott, *On Earth as in Heaven*, 73–158.

23   See the review of Scott's book by VanderKam in *JSP* 15 (2006) 233–37.

years and to be vague about the amount of time that will follow before a new era begins.

In v. 5, for the final time in the book, the angel addresses the more distant future. He begins by predicting that, once in the land, the nation will live upon it in a secure fashion. The basis for the statement is again Leviticus 25, this time vv. 18-19: "You shall observe my statutes and faithfully keep my ordinances, so that you may live on the land securely [לבטח]. The land will yield its fruit, and you will eat your fill and live on it securely [לבטח]." Note that Jubilees adds that they will live confidently "in the *entire* land."[24] In order to describe the conditions further the angel says, "They will no longer have any satan or any evil one." The absence of a satan and an evil one was predicted in 23:29, also in an eschatological context: "They will complete and live their entire lifetimes peacefully and joyfully. There will be neither a satan nor any evil one who will destroy. For their entire lifetimes will be times of blessing and healing." As seen earlier, the same expression is used to characterize the ideal conditions prevailing in Egypt when Joseph took over the rule of the land for Pharaoh and ensured that the monarch's administration would be just (40:9), and it features in the description of the utopian relations prevailing in Egypt after Jacob died: "There was no satan or any evil one throughout all of Joseph's lifetime that he lived after his father Jacob because all the Egyptians were honoring the children of Israel for all of Joseph's lifetime" (46:2; in v. 1 all the Israelites "were of the same mind so that each one loved the other and each one helped the other").

The elevated rhetoric of v. 5 as it looks to the indefinite future has led several commentators to regard it as the original conclusion to the book.[25] There is no mistaking that it would be a good ending, but it is also the case that there is no textual evidence or any formal considerations that would identify it as the last verse of Jubilees. In fact, 50:13 contains a more fitting end (see the commentary on v. 13 and the excursus that follows it).

Excursus: The Chronology in the Book of Jubilees

As explained above, Jub 50:2-4 supplies important information about the chronology that is such a visible feature of the book. The many dates that the author records, some of which seem to have suffered corruption as the text was transmitted, nevertheless fit into a pattern or system that conveys a theological message: what happens to the individual Israelite in the fiftieth year (the year of the jubilee) is experienced by the entire nation of Israel during the fiftieth jubilee period (the fiftieth forty-nine-year unit). Wiesenberg insightfully perceived this message in his study of the book's chronology, but he made other claims about it that are less likely. He thought the entire system pointed to the year 2451 as the time for the event of "paramount significance," the entry into the land.[26] He labeled this year "the jubilee of jubilees," a phrase that serves as the title of his article. He correctly identified the year when Israel entered the land, as implied by Jubilees' chronology, but he did so for the wrong reasons and misnamed the year.

He arrives at the year 2451 for the entry into Canaan principally by arguing that there is a one-year mistake in the date in 48:2, where Moses's return to Egypt is placed in the same year as the exodus (2410). He finds it absurd that Moses would return and that all the events between that time and the exodus would occur within fourteen days.[27] There is no doubt that the dates in the book compress the efforts of Moses and the ten plagues into a narrow time frame (see the commentary on 48:2), but Wiesenberg took the problematic result to be warrant for denying that Moses's return to Egypt and the exodus transpired in the same year. Rather, Moses had reached Egypt many months before the exodus. He returned in 2410 (as Jub 48:2 indicates),

---

24 Werman claims that "the entire land" here means "the entire earth" (*Jubilees*, 553). This seems implausible, not only in the context but also because of the basis of the promise in Lev 25:19; 26:5.

25 Davenport, *Eschatology*, e.g., 15, 68–69, though he assigns v. 5 to his first redactor and vv. 6–13 less certainly to the second; Ravid, "The Sabbath Laws in Jubilees 50:6-13," *Tarbiz* 69 (2000) 151–66, here 161; Kugel, *Walk through* Jubilees, 203–4; "Jubilees," 450.

26 He thought the original version of the book placed the exodus in the year 2451, not the entry into the land; a more politically inclined reviser put the entry into the land in 2451 ("Jubilee of Jubilees," 27–40).

27 Wiesenberg, "Jubilee of Jubilees," 7.

and Israel left Egypt the next year, 2411. The problem is that Jub 50:4 gives the date for Israel at Sinai as the year 2410, not 2411. Wiesenberg explained the verse in this way:

> The corrected date thus arrived at, is in no way contrary to the statement in Jubilees 50, 4, "there are 49 jubilees from the days of Adam until this day and 1 week and 2 years". The natural meaning of that statement is that from the creation until the chronological year of the exodus and of the legislation at Sinai there had elapsed 2410 *full* years—disregarding the additional four months or so—and had led to the year 2411 AM.[28]

Adding forty years to that number yields 2451 as the year for crossing the Jordan (dated to the first month, the tenth day in Josh 4:19).

It is exceedingly unlikely that Wiesenberg has given "the natural meaning" of 50:4, in which there is no hint that the angel is speaking about years already completed (and ignoring the extra months) rather than identifying the current year as 2410. Also, there has been no mention of a new year after 48:2, when Moses reached Egypt. Wiesenberg referred to the year 2451—the year after the fiftieth forty-nine-year period—as "the jubilee of jubilees," the year toward which the system was pointing, or, as he put it:

> The *Book of Jubilees*' ubiquitous chronological trappings are but a contrivance designed to give the air of plausibility to the preconceived notion that the Jubilee of Jubilees was marked by an event of paramount significance. That notion, in turn, is the result of *midrashic* speculation upon a parallel between the jubilee year on the individual level and the Jubilee of Jubilees on the national level.[29]

Or, as he expresses the point earlier in the essay:

> The climax of that cycle [of fifty jubilee periods]—and, at the same time, also the climax of all the jubilee years—is the 50th jubilee year = 2451 AM.

It is the JUBILEE OF JUBILEES, a kind of *annus mirabilis*, the year chosen by divine design to be marked by the most momentous event in the national epic of Israel. That event, according to the extant text of the Book of Jubilees, is Israel's entry into the land of Canaan.[30]

The writer of Jubilees very clearly places the exodus and the return to the ancestral land in the same jubilee period. Those are the events of the fiftieth jubilee. Though he did so for the wrong reasons, Wiesenberg nevertheless correctly observed that the crossing of the Jordan into Canaan would have occurred in the year 2451, the first year of the new jubilee period. The fiftieth jubilee period would have ended with Israel poised to ford the Jordan River, but, as Josh 4:19 indicates, the crossing itself occurred at the beginning of the next year (1/10). With the new year, the fifty-first jubilee cycle would have begun. Support for this interpretation comes from 4Q379 (4QapocJosh[b]) frg. 12 1-6:

3] they [cr]ossed over on dry ground in the [fir]st month
4 of the forty-f[irst] year of the exodus from the lan[d]
5 of Egypt. That was the year of the jubilees when they began to enter the land of
6 Canaan.[31]

If so, then the writer of Jubilees did not subscribe to the view that the sabbatical and jubilee cycles began only after the conquest and distribution of the land.[32] His was another interpretation of Lev 25:2: "When you enter the land that I am giving you, the land shall observe a sabbath for the LORD," that is, the system of sabbatical years would commence immediately.

Bergsma has also argued that for the writer of Jubilees the implied date for entering Canaan is the year 2451, not 2450. He writes that, while in the book the term "jubilee" normally designates a forty-nine-year unit, in 50:4 the writer refers to "the year of jubilee" and shows in the overall chronology that he

---

28 Ibid., 15.
29 Ibid., 29.
30 Ibid., 17.
31 Trans. Newsom, *DSSR* 3:327. As Newsom writes in the official edition ("379. 4QApocryphon of Joshua[b]," in DJD 22:271), Deut 1:3 dates Moses's farewell speech to the first of the eleventh month in the fortieth year of the exodus. Once he died, the Israelites mourned for him for thirty days (34:8). They then crossed the river on the tenth of the first month in the next year (Josh 4:19). Newsom, who notes the parallel with Jub 50:4, adds about line 4: "I have no explanation, however, for the author's preference for the plural, 'year of the jubilees,' rather than the singular." Perhaps the meaning is that this particular year is the one from which the jubilee cycles in the land begin, just as the chronology of Jubilees implies.
32 This is a widely attested view in rabbinic literature. An example is *Seder Olam* 11 (see Milikowsky, *Seder Olam*, 2:200–203).

is aware of the significance borne by the fiftieth unit. How is one to reconcile the two notions of a jubilee? Bergsma appeals to the view attributed to Rabbi Judah in *b. Ned.* 61a that the jubilee year was both the fiftieth year of the old cycle and the first year of the new jubilee cycle.[33] In this respect the method of counting is the same as for the pentecontad festivals in the Temple Scroll. Bergsma also suggests that the 2450 years of Jub 50:4 should be added to the point from which the chronology begins, that is, the year 1 (not a year 0), so that the result would be the year 2451, but it is doubtful that such a reading is consistent with the text. Rather, the implication seems to be that during the fiftieth jubilee period (years 2402-2450) the Israelites left Egypt and returned to Canaan, though the end of the period found them ready to cross the Jordan but not yet west of it. They would then have crossed the river at the beginning of the new year.

6-13 Sabbath Laws

The final section in Jubilees offers a series of specific laws concerning how to observe the Sabbath as well as some explanatory statements. This is the second place in the book where the reader meets such a unit. The first, in 2:26-33 (though, in a broader sense, the section on the Sabbath begins already in v. 17), elaborates on the mention of God's cessation from labor on the seventh day (Gen 2:1-3; cf. Jub 2:16-18). In chap. 50, the section about the Sabbath follows quite naturally on the preceding unit that referenced Sabbaths (v. 1), sabbatical years and jubilees (v. 2), and their significance for the structure of sacred history (vv. 3-5). For an analysis of the place occupied by vv. 6-13 in the chapter and book, see below.

■ **6** The angel opens the unit by addressing Moses directly (without using his name) and claiming that he had "now written for you the Sabbath commandments and all the statutes of its laws." Since vv. 6-13 contain some Sabbath legislation not found in the Sinai sections of Exodus–Numbers or anywhere else in the HB, this is one of the passages in which the Angel of the Presence, in the Ethiopic version, asserts that he has written a section of Jubilees for Moses. This instance, like the others in which one encounters such a statement from the angel, probably read in the Hebrew version of Jubilees: "I have now dictated to you the Sabbath commandments and all the statutes of its laws."[34] Those regulations were inscribed on the heavenly tablets from which the angel was reading to Moses, who in turn recorded them for Israel (see 1:27). The phrases "the Sabbath commandments" and "all the statutes of its laws" give the impression of being a heading for a section that lists specifics, and this indeed happens in the following verses.[35]

■ **7** The angel begins the section containing detailed legislation by citing the Sabbath law from the Ten Commandments. The version that he dictates to Moses is a slightly variant form of Exod 20:9-10 (cf. Deut 5:13-14). After v. 6, there was no need for the writer to provide the introduction to the Sabbath command in Exod 20:8 ("Remember the sabbath day, and keep it holy"), so he moves immediately to the fundamental law itself.[36]

Exodus 20:9-10	Jubilees 50:7
Six days you shall labor and do all your work. But the seventh day is a sabbath to the LORD your God; you shall not do any work—you, your son or your daughter, your male or female slave, your livestock, or the alien resident in your towns.	You will work for six days, but on the seventh day is the Sabbath of the Lord your God. Do not do work on it—you, your children, your male and female servants, all[37] your cattle, or the foreigner[38] who is with you.

---

33 Bergsma, "Once Again, the Jubilee, Every 49 or 50 Years?" *VT* 55 (2005) 121-25; and *Jubilee*, 236-37; see also Baumgarten, "The Calendars of the Book of Jubilees and the Temple Scroll," *VT* 37 (1987) 71-78, here 73; VanderKam, "Chronology," 524-25.

34 VanderKam, "Putative Author," 215-16.

35 Note the heading in CD x:14: על השבת לשמרה כמשפטה.

36 On the wording of the commandment in v. 7 and in the various sources, see Doering, "*Jub.* 50:6-13 als Schlussabschnitt des Jubiläenbuchs: Nachtrag aus Qumran oder ursprünglicher Bestandteil des Werks," *RevQ* 20/79 (2002) 359-87, here 372-75. As he comments, the version to some extent harmonizes different formulations of the fourth commandment—a feature well documented in various texts (e.g., 4QDeut^n).

37 MT SP Deut 5:14 reads "all" but MT SP Exod 20:10 lacks it (LXX Exod 20:10 has "all").

38 The term is *nakir*, whereas Eth. Exod 20:10 uses *falāsi* ("exile, stranger, sojourner" [Leslau, *Comparative Dictionary*, 160]). On the significance of the use of *nakir*, see below.

In the formulation in Jub 50:7, the angel begins with a singular verbal form that is appropriate to the setting in which he is speaking with Moses alone ("You" in "You will work" is singular, as in Exod 20:9), but in the remainder of the verse the pronouns are plural ("your God," "you, your children,[39] your male and female servants, all your cattle, or the foreigner who is with you"). In all of these cases Exod 20:10 uses singular forms (see Jer 17:19-27 for several plurals). Moses's message is for the nation so that the plural pronoun and suffixes are fitting. The author, faithful to his model, reproduces the mention of the stranger or sojourner.[40] The point is one of the factors that led Ravid to argue that the present section—vv. 6-13—in places contradicts other sabbatical legislation in Jubilees where the Sabbath is meant only for Israel (see 2:31).[41] The argument is not convincing because the "stranger/foreigner" is a person integrated into the nation (though still a foreigner) and thus included in the command[42] (as is the case regarding circumcision for foreigners in an Israelite household [see 15:23-34]). Halpern-Amaru has, however, used the presence of the word *nakir* ("foreigner") where the command in Exod 20:10 // Deut 5:14 reads גר (Eth. Exod 20:10 *falāsi*; Eth. Deut 5:14 *geyyur* ["stranger, alien"])[43] to claim that the author is making a polemical point against those who accepted proselyte conversion.

That substitution brings the polemic into the halachah of the Sabbath. Although the non-Jew who resides in the midst of Israel must observe the Sabbath, the requirement reflects no change of status. The non-Jew remains the נכרי, the total outsider. Acknowledged only as a foreigner, he achieves the status neither of an acculturated sojourner nor that of an accepted proselyte.[44]

It is true that in Jubilees there is no reference to conversion of non-Israelites to the religion of Israel, but to maintain that the author has deliberately substituted נכרי in the fourth commandment to make this case seems unjustified. The Ethiopic text of Jubilees regularly differs in readings with the Ethiopic version of the Bible, so that a disagreement in the wording of a text is not surprising. The word *nakir* likely renders αλλοτριος; it regularly translates forms of נכר but it could be a translation of προσηλυτος, which can mean, besides the specific "proselyte," the more general "stranger." It seems unlikely that the author, writing in Hebrew, would have substituted a different word in a very familiar text in order to state his opposition to a practice he does not mention.[45]

■ 8 After the fundamental prohibition of any work on the Sabbath day (v. 7), the angel names the penalty for one who nevertheless performs labor on it: "The person who does any work on it is to die" (see 2:25, 27). Capital punishment for Sabbath violations comes from Exod 31:14-15: "everyone who profanes it shall be put to death; whoever does any work on it shall be cut off from among the people.[46] Six days shall work be done, but the seventh day is a sabbath of solemn rest, holy to the

---

39 Where Exod 20:10 mentions both a son and a daughter, the Ethiopic text reads only one word—*weludekemu*, which could mean "your sons" or, more likely here, "your children." In the line "Do not do any work on it," the prepositional phrase does not occur in MT SP Exod 20:10 (it is in LXX and Ethiopic), but they read it in Exod 31:14; 35:2. It also appears in SP LXX Deut 5:14.

40 Exodus 20:10 reads, literally, "the stranger who is in your gates [NRSV: the alien resident in your towns]," but the Ethiopic text of Jubilees words as "the foreigner who is with you." The prepositional phrase reflects the interpretation of שעריך in LXX Eth. Exod 20:10 (εν σοι/*ḥabēka* [Jub 50:7 uses the same preposition]).

41 Ravid, "Sabbath Laws," 161–66.

42 See Doering, *Schabbat*, 65; "*Jub.* 50:6-13," 375–82. In his earlier essay, "Concept of the Sabbath," 189–91, he had explained the *nakir* as a proselyte. For the originality of 50:6-13 in Jubilees, see the excursus below.

43 Leslau, *Comparative Dictionary*, 208.

44 Halpern-Amaru, *Empowerment*, 157.

45 See Doering, "*Jub.* 50:6-13," 372–84. Werman (*Jubilees*, 554), against Doering, thinks the writer avoided the word גר but bases her view only on the Ethiopic *nakir*. On her view the writer here expresses the position stated in Qumran texts that one was not allowed to send a foreigner to do work for him on the Sabbath (CD xi:2). There is no hint of such a prohibition in the Sabbath section here in chap. 50.

46 The mention of death for Sabbath violation and cutting off from one's people as well led to discussions about the meaning of the two penalties. See, e.g., *Mek. Shabbata* 1. Finkelstein ("Rabbinic

LORD; whoever does any work on the sabbath day shall be put to death" (see also 35:2; Num 15:32-36 relates an incident in which the penalty was enforced).[47] That basic principle the angel then applies to the different ways in which one might desecrate/profane the day and thus incur a death sentence.[48] The cases relate to one who:

sleeps with a woman:[49] There is no such law in the HB, though Lev 15:18 says that a couple who engage in intercourse become impure.[50] In his comment on the passage, Albeck noted that Qaraites and Samaritans also practiced this prohibition.[51] Tchernowitz and Doering suggest that the ruling shows a particular understanding of what it means to hallow the Sabbath: it was accomplished through carrying out the stipulation in Exod 19:14-15 that the Israelites, as they prepared for the appearance of the Lord on the third day, refrain from sex. One was to keep from defiling the Sabbath by avoiding ritual impurity (cf. Lev 15:18; CD xii:1-2 prohibits sex in the holy city lest one make it unclean but does not mention the Sabbath).[52]

says anything about work on it—that he is to set out on a trip on it, or about any selling or buying: The prohibition has to do with speaking on the Sabbath about work one intends to do once the Sabbath ends. This is a better way of understanding the text than Charles's translation suggests: "whoever says he will do something on it."[53] Finkelstein quite rightly objected to the implication arising from Charles's rendering: "That our author should condemn a man to death for merely saying he will desecrate the sabbath is inconceivable."[54] Behind the prohibition against work-related talk on the Sabbath lies Isa 58:13:

> If you refrain from trampling the sabbath,
>   from pursuing your own interests on my holy day;
> if you call the sabbath a delight
>   and the holy day of the LORD honorable;
> if you honor it, not going your own ways,
>   serving your own interests, or pursuing your own affairs [ודבר דבר] . . . ."

The last words (lit., speaking a word) are reflected in CD x:19 (from the section on Sabbath laws) in a context that resembles the one in Jubilees: "He shall say nothing about work or labour to be done on the morrow

---

Halaka," 46) thought that the author of Jubilees understood the punishment of death to refer to this life and cutting off to the next life, citing 2:27, which mentions dying eternally (and being cut off [see the commentary there]). Cf. also Doering, "Concept of the Sabbath," 199-200.

47   The death penalty applies, according to *Mek.* Shabbata 1, to a person who deliberately does work when others tell him not to break the commandment. See also Rashi's commentary on Exod 31:14.

48   Tchernowitz, *History of Hebrew Law*, 4:361-62; Doering, "Concept of the Sabbath," 195-96.

49   In a lengthy note on the command, Charles speaks of this as a "severer usage" that gave way to more lenient rules (*Jubilees*, 259). He refers to many of the pertinent passages in rabbinic literature.

50   In his chart of passages taken up in the Sabbath sections of Jubilees, Doering (*Schabbat*, 582) lists Lev 15:18 among the ones that were formative materially but not literally (see below).

51   Albeck, *Jubiläen*, 9. For the positive rabbinic view about sex on the Sabbath, he refers to *b. Ned.* 82a (it is done on Friday nights). Beer had already noted the rabbinic evidence in his 1856 monograph (*Jubiläen*, 53-54). Both Beer and Albeck called attention to *b. Ned.* 38a-b, where there is reference to the ancient pious men who had intercourse with their wives only on Wednesday so that, given the number of days in a pregnancy (apparently a nearly fixed number, on their view), their wives would not defile the Sabbath by giving birth on it (there is also reference in the passage to "from the fourth day on" rather than just on the fourth day of the week). That practice, however, would have been different from the one Jubilees prohibits because the people in question thought the circumstances involved in giving birth on the Sabbath were the violation, not having intercourse then. The passage Finkelstein mentions (*b. Ketub.* 3a) also seems to discuss a different kind of practice ("Rabbinic Halaka," 48, esp. n. 30; it mentions avoidance of sex on the first Sabbath after a couple married). For an overview of the rabbinic texts, see Doering, *Schabbat*, 80-83.

52   Tchernowitz, *History of Hebrew Law*, 4:365; Doering, *Schabbat*, 79-80.

53   He based his translation on an inferior form of the text: *wa-za-ni yetnāgar nagara yegbar bāti*; a better reading is: *wa-za-ni yetnāgar nagara megbār bāti*.

54   Finkelstein, "Rabbinic Halaka," 48.

[למשכים]" (trans. Vermes). In this respect the prescription in Jubilees appears to be similar to the one in, say, *b. Šabb.* 150a: "your affairs are what is forbidden, affairs of Heaven are permitted." It is likely there would have been differences between the author of Jubilees and other experts of his time when it came to defining exactly which kinds of speech were allowed and forbidden, though he does not elaborate on the matter.[55]

The remainder of the line lists several kinds of topics, discussion of which is forbidden on the Sabbath.

The first has to do with journeying on it (note that Sabbath travel arises in v. 12 as well, though in a different way). With the prepositional phrase "on it," it sounds as if the prohibition here has to do with talking on the Sabbath about traveling on the Sabbath and perhaps beginning a trip on it. The word *gēsa* means "be early, do things early in the morning,"[56] but in the context the notion of "journeying" (note the noun *gays*, "journey") recommends itself. At any rate, one is not to talk about a Sabbath journey on the Sabbath.

The second forbidden topic is "about any selling or buying."[57] The discussion of commercial transactions is not a permitted topic on the Sabbath (cf. Amos 8:5). This prohibition may also be influenced by Isa 58:13 (pursuing one's own interests). Speaking about business activities on the Sabbath is not to be done, just as carrying out those actions on the Sabbath is forbidden.[58]

A new kind of regulation follows near the end of v. 8: on it one is not to draw "water that he had not prepared for himself on the sixth day" (see 2:29; CD xi:1-2).[59] Charles wrote regarding the words "that he had not prepared for himself on the sixth day": "This clause comes in awkwardly. A command against 'eating or drinking anything' may have originally preceded this clause in our text."[60] Finkelstein, however, objected to Charles's concern: "But if we bear in mind the rabbinic law, we see that we have here nothing more than the author's customary extension of the Pharisaic law. In the Talmud it is forbidden to use anything on the sabbath which at the coming of the holy day, that is, at nightfall on Friday, was not 'prepared' for use."[61] This appears to be in line with Exod 16:22-26 (note the preparations involving baking and boiling on the sixth day) in which the Israelites gathered manna on the sixth day for consumption on it and also on the seventh day. The ruling prohibits drawing water from a well or the like; that would have to be done on the sixth day and the water would have to be placed in a container in the dwelling for use on the seventh.[62] Albeck argued that the line in Jubilees (and the next one) meant not that water could be drawn on the Sabbath if it had been prepared on the sixth day but that drawing water itself was prohibited on the Sabbath and that therefore everything had to be readied in an appropriate way on the sixth day. In rabbinic law, however, drawing water per se was not a forbidden labor on the Sabbath.[63]

The final prohibition in v. 8 concerns carrying "any load to bring (it) outside his tent or his house" (see 2:29, where carrying items in and out of gates is under consideration, and 2:30, where houses are the places mentioned; cf. CD xi:7-9).[64] Nehemiah 13:19 opposes bringing burdens in through the city gates on the Sabbath, and Jer 17:21-22 states, "Thus says the LORD: For the sake of your lives, take care that you do not bear a

---

55 On this Sabbath prohibition in Jubilees, see Finkelstein, "Rabbinic Halaka," 48-49; Albeck, *Jubiläen*, 9; Doering, *Schabbat*, 83-87. All of these commentators point to Isa 58:13 and understand the prohibition as explained above (speaking on the Sabbath about doing work after the Sabbath). Doering, in addition to mentioning CD xi:17-19, refers to 4Q264a i:5-8 // 4Q421 13 3-4 as passages that appear to be addressing the issue.

56 Dillmann, *Lexicon*, 1196; Leslau, *Comparative Dictionary*, 208. The superior reading here appears to be an infinitive form (*gayiso* or *gayeso*). See VanderKam, *Jubilees* 1:253.

57 Several translators, perhaps following Charles, link this prohibition with the preceding one, e.g., Wintermute: "so that he might make a journey on it for any buying or selling." However, the manuscripts place a conjunction before "about/for" and thus separate it from the preceding unit.

58 Cf. Doering, *Schabbat*, 86.

59 The regulation in the Damascus Document, however, appears to relate to a person who is standing in a body of water (Ginzberg, *Unknown Jewish Sect*, 61-62).

60 Charles, *Jubilees*, 260.

61 Finkelstein, "Rabbinic Halaka," 49.

62 Tchernowitz, *History of Hebrew Law*, 4:367.

63 Albeck, *Jubiläen*, 8.

64 On the passage in the Damascus Document, see Ginzberg, *Unknown Jewish Sect*, 65-66.

burden on the sabbath day or bring it in by the gates of Jerusalem. And do not carry a burden out of your houses on the sabbath or do any work, but keep the sabbath day holy, as I commanded your ancestors." The reference to tents in connection with this prohibition may come from Exod 16:16, 30, where the Israelites are told not to leave their places (their tents) on the Sabbath. Carrying something from one domain to another is the last of the thirty-nine kinds of work prohibited in *m. Šabb.* 7:2 (cf. 1:1).[65]

■ 9 After the list of prohibited kinds of work in v. 8, the writer turns to some principles regarding the Sabbath before he provides another specific listing of prohibitions in v. 12. In v. 9 he provides a perspective on the statement regarding preparation on the sixth day. No work for which preparation was not made on the sixth day was to be done on the seventh so as to make the day entirely available for its positive purposes: Israel was to eat and drink on it, rest from all work, and bless the God who had given it to them. The passage builds upon some themes enunciated in Jubilees 2, where God tells the angels that he will choose Israel and give them the Sabbath to rest from all work on it (2:20). Moreover, "In this way he made a sign on it by which they, too, would keep Sabbath with us on the seventh day to eat, drink, and bless the Creator of all as he had blessed them and sanctified them for himself as a treasured people out of all the nations; and to be keeping Sabbath together with us" (2:21; cf. v. 30). The writer in 50:9 emphasizes the holiness of the Sabbath, as he had in chap. 2 (e.g., vv. 23-28), and he calls it "a festal day" as he had in 2:25 (it is included among the festivals in Leviticus 23).[66]

A new expression is: "This day among their days is to be the day of the holy kingdom for all Israel throughout all time."[67] In 2:31 the Lord sanctified Israel alone—none of the nations of the world—to keep Sabbath, but in other passages the language of kingdom, a term derived from Exod 19:6, served to express the relationship between God and his people. In Exodus 19, the Lord gave Moses a message for Israel and included in it an announcement that Israel, if they were obedient to the covenant, would be "my treasured possession out of all the peoples" (v. 5). To this he added the declaration: "but you shall be for me a priestly kingdom and a holy nation." The writer of Jubilees echoed the passage when the angels told Abraham that one of Isaac's sons

> would become a holy progeny and would not be numbered among the nations, for he would become the share of the Most High. All his descendants had fallen into the (share) that God owns so that they would become a *treasured* people of the Lord out of all the nations; and that they would become a kingdom, a priesthood, and a holy people. (16:17-18)

After Reuben's sin with Bilhah, the angel gave Moses a message for the Israelites, including: "No sin is greater than the sexual impurity that they commit on the earth because Israel is a holy people for the Lord its God. It is the nation that he possesses; it is a priestly nation; it is a priestly kingdom; it is what he owns. No such impurity will be seen among the holy people" (33:20). A crucial trait of Israel as God's holy people is the right to enjoy the Sabbath with him and his great angels;[68] it is an essential mark of Israel, separating them from the nations and joining them with God forever.[69] The writer says the Sabbath is "the day of the holy kingdom for all Israel throughout all time." There is no sectarian con-

---

65 Albeck, *Jubiläen*, 8. Finkelstein thought the prohibition had to do with the intent to transport something ("Rabbinic Halaka," 49), but the text says nothing about intent, as the law does not belong to the rules forbidding speaking about certain topics on the Sabbath. Tchernowitz believed the prohibition referred to carrying heavy burdens, as transporting of that kind is an activity belonging to the secular sphere of the six days of work (*History of Hebrew Law*, 4:366).

66 See Doering, "Concept of the Sabbath," 192-93; *Schabbat*, 65-68.

67 Kugel comments: "That it is a day of the holy kingdom sounds a bit like the rabbinic phrase 'kingdom of heaven,' which refers to God's sole mastery over all creation; presumably it is this divine mastery that is enacted every sabbath" (*Walk through* Jubilees, 204; "Jubilees," 450).

68 Doering, "Concept of the Sabbath," 194-95.

69 As Werman comments, the purpose of the statement is to compare the experience of the Sabbath with the last times, an experience of those times in the present (*Jubilees*, 555).

sciousness here; the entire nation keeps the Sabbath and must do so forever.

■ **10** The author underscores the privilege that belongs to Israel through God's gift of the Sabbath to them. By graciously allowing them to eat, drink, be filled, and rest on this festal day (see v. 9 and 2:20-21, 25, 31 for these expressions) he "honors" Israel. The honor he accords to them is the right to celebrate the Sabbath. According to 2:31, "The Creator of all blessed but did not sanctify any people(s) and nations to keep Sabbath on it except Israel alone. To it alone did he give (the right) to eat, drink, and keep Sabbath on it upon the earth." The idea of the Lord honoring human beings (in the future) occurs in Isa 30:19: "I will make them many, and they shall not be few; / I will make them honored, and they shall not be disdained" (see also 1 Sam 2:30; Ps 91:15). In Jubilees he honors them in the present as well through the gift of the Sabbath day.[70]

The Sabbath laws, of course, required the cessation of all work on the holy day so that it could be a time for the pleasures it offered. Verse 10 speaks about resting from any kind of human labor ("any work that belongs to the work of humanity"), but the author adds at the end of v. 10 and in v. 11 that one category of labor is permitted: burning incense and presenting offerings "for the days and Sabbaths." He knew from passages in the Pentateuch that certain actions in the sanctuary were to be done every day, thus including the Sabbath.[71] The first—burning incense—comes from Exod 30:1-10. The instructions for offering incense mandate that Aaron offer it every morning and evening when he tends to the lamps (vv. 7-8), and v. 8 refers to it as "a regular [תמיד] incense offering." The ruling regarding "days and Sabbaths" has to do with the two daily offerings and the special Sabbath sacrifices. The two daily offerings (Exod 29:38-46), one in the morning and one in the evening, also have the term תמיד applied to them (v. 38; see v. 42: "It shall be a regular [תמיד] burnt offering throughout your generations"; Num 28:3-8). Numbers 28:9-10 describes the Sabbath sacrifices and says of them: "this is the burnt offering for every sabbath, in addition to the regular burnt offering and its drink offering," that is, in addition to the daily תמיד offerings. The Torah, therefore, commanded that these three kinds of offerings and sacrifices be presented, the first two kinds every single day without exception and the third on all Sabbaths. Although they required work by the priests, they were necessary on the Sabbath.

A related law appears in CD xi:17-18, where the legislator also supplies the warrant from the HB: "No man on the Sabbath shall offer anything on the altar except the Sabbath burnt-offering; for it is written thus: *Except your Sabbath offerings* (Lev. xxiii, 38)" (trans. Vermes). The issue might seem to have been whether the daily offerings for festivals that fell on the Sabbath are under discussion, but in the calendar of Jubilees (and presumably of the Damascus Document) festivals cannot fall on the Sabbath so that is not the issue. It could deal with the daily offerings for festivals that included a Sabbath in them (that is, the two week-long holidays, the Festival of Unleavened Bread and the Festival of Booths). Possibly the Damascus Document intends to limit the Sabbath offerings to the ones mandated in Num 28:9-10 and to exclude the daily offerings, but the point is disputed.[72] For Jubilees, it is obvious that the permitted labors on the Sabbath involved the three kinds of offerings: incense, the *tamid* sacrifices, and the Sabbath offerings.[73]

■ **11** The author reinforces these points in v. 11. The offerings he mentioned in v. 10 are to be presented in God's sanctuary that has yet to be built, and the purpose

---

70 Finkelstein held that in Jubilees "only the joy of the Sabbath is forbidden to gentiles, nothing is said of abstention from work; but to the rabbis it seemed objectionable that the gentile should observe the Sabbath even in abstaining from work" ("Rabbinic Halaka," 46–47, here 47; cf. *Exod. Rab.* 25:11). Where Jubilees makes this distinction is not apparent (it is not in 2:31). In the book the Sabbath is for Israel pure and simple, and nothing is said about non-Israelites participating in any aspect of it. See also Albeck, *Jubiläen*, 10–11.

71 Doering, "Concept of the Sabbath," 197–98; *Schabbat*, 68.

72 See the survey of views in Doering, "Concept of the Sabbath," 198; *Schabbat*, 205–10.

73 The author would, therefore, have understood מלבד in Lev 23:38 to mean "besides," not "except," as in CD xi:18.

they serve is to make atonement continuously. If these sacrifices ceased on the Sabbath, the process of making atonement would also stop temporarily with dangerous consequences for the people of Israel who stood in constant need of it. The Sabbath and *tamid* offerings the Torah labels "burnt offerings" (Exod 29:42 for the *tamid* offerings; Num 28:10 for both types), and Lev 1:4 associates atonement with burnt offerings. The writer of Jubilees, though he mentions the sanctuary, does not say that priests are the ones who atone for Israel; he resorts to the indefinite "they," perhaps as a substitute for the passive ("that atonement may be made"). Additional sacrificial language occupies the latter part of the verse. The term "memorial" does occur in cultic contexts. For example, Lev 2:2 refers to a memorial (אזכרה, translated "token portion" in NRSV) in connection with incinerating the flour, oil, and frankincense from the grain offering, and Lev 24:5-9 does so in connection with the twelve loaves of bread to be placed on the golden table in the tabernacle—at those times frankincense is to serve as the memorial (v. 7). This may be significant for the present context in Jubilees because Aaron was to set fresh loaves in place every Sabbath. An association of terms similar to the ones in this passage in Jubilees figures in 4Q512 (4QpapRitual of Purification) 29–32 vii:10: ". . . and the blood of the burnt offering that You desire, a soothi[ng] memorial" (trans. Wise, Abegg, Cook, with Gordon, *DSSR* 5:465; in that same column, lines 8-9 mention atonement in relation to the burnt offering, and line 11 refers to incense). Calling an offering properly performed "acceptable [or: pleasing] before the Lord" is typical sacrificial language (e.g., Lev 1:3). The verb also appears in the blessing of Levi in Deut 33:10-11, where several terms from this context in Jubilees occur: "they place incense before you, / and whole burnt offerings on your altar. / Bless, O LORD, his substance, / and accept the work of his hands." The Lord is to receive the sacrifices day by day without exception, just as he told Moses in the passages mandating the daily incense offering, the *tamid* sacrifices, and the Sabbath holocausts.

■ **12** The second set of specific Sabbath regulations in this section appears in v. 12 (for the first, see v. 8). The list begins with a general rubric ("Any person who does work") and then breaks it down into several categories of forbidden activities. The verse seems to be systematically structured by means of repeating opening formulas for each part of the list, but the overall design seems odd. The general heading begins with *wa-kwellu sab'*, "Anyone," and it precedes five subclauses each of which begins with *wa-za-hi* (translated as "who"). But what appears to be the sixth subclause (having to do with someone who beats an animal, etc.) also begins with *wa-kwellu sab'*, "anyone." It is followed by three instances of *wa-za-hi*, only the first two of which seem to belong with the category introduced by the second *wa-kwellu sab'*, while the remaining one (introducing both fasting and war) constitutes a different type.

The initial "Anyone [translated 'Any person'] who does work" stands before these specific cases.

1. "who goes on a trip." The prohibition is worded completely differently than the one in v. 8. The verb used here is a standard one for going (*yaḥawwer*), and the object of the verb is the general noun *mangada* (acc. case), for which Leslau gives the meanings "road, journey, way, traveling, setting out, trip, pilgrimage."[74] The law in v. 8 concerned itself with one who was talking about a trip on the Sabbath; this one deals with the actual act of travel on the seventh day.[75] The statement is brief and does not deal with questions that naturally arise, such as the length of a forbidden trip and the location of it. Albeck believed it forbade movement from one's residence, while Doering thinks it likely that the proscription prohibits travel outside one's settlement. One reason pointing toward this conclusion is that two of the laws later in the verse deal with moving about in open spaces (riding an animal, sea travel). This rule, therefore, might be limiting movement in one's immediate environment as in Exod 16:29: "do not leave your place on the seventh

---

74   Leslau, *Comparative Dictionary*, 391. As Berger (*Jubiläen*, 553 n. f to v. 8) and Doering (*Schabbat*, 89) note, it is the term in Eth. Acts 1:12 for a Sabbath day's journey.

75   Albeck suggested that, besides the law about not discussing work, this and the next ruling (travel on a boat) are related to Isa 58:13 ("If you refrain from trampling the sabbath [אם תשיב משבת רגלך]," and "from pursuing your own interests [מעשות דרכיך]") (*Jubiläen*, 9).

1207

day").[76] The author makes no mention of the Sabbath limit known from CD xi:5–6; *m. Soṭah* 5:3, etc.

2. "who works farmland whether at his home or in any (other) place." The category of agricultural labor figures in one of the formulations of the Sabbath law in Exodus: "Six days you shall work, but on the seventh day you shall rest; even in plowing time and in harvest time you shall rest" (34:21). It also occupies a prominent position in the list of thirty-nine prohibited labors in *m. Šabb.* 7:2, where "sowing, ploughing, reaping, binding sheaves, threshing, winnowing, cleansing crops" are seven of the kinds (cf. 12:2). The mishnaic passage provides specific directions regarding what constitutes forbidden labor in this area, but the wording in Jubilees is again brief and short on specifics, although it does insist that one may not do such work either at home or in another's field.[77]

3. "who lights a fire." This is another of the categories forbidden in Exodus (35:3: "You shall kindle no fire in all your dwellings on the sabbath day");[78] it is also prohibited in *m. Šabb.* 7:2 ("lighting a fire"—"putting out a fire" directly precedes it). The terse prohibition in Jubilees does not take up an issue such as whether one may allow a fire kindled on the preceding day to burn on the Sabbath.[79]

4. "who rides[80] any animal." The commands regarding the Sabbath include animals in the prohibition of labor: "But the seventh day is a sabbath to the Lord your God; you shall not do any work—you, your son or your daughter, your male or female slave, your livestock, or the resident alien in your towns" (Exod 20:10 ["all your cattle" in v. 7 above]). In *m. Beṣah* 5:2 riding a beast on the Sabbath is included in a list of prohibitions (cf. the story in *b. Sanh.* 46a).[81] It may be that the prohibition is a way of preventing a person from interpreting the interdiction of Sabbath travel as applying only to journeying on foot.

5. "who travels the sea by ship." The law is another specification of the anti-travel regulation and may refer to setting out on a sea voyage that would continue over a Sabbath.[82] As Doering notes, the law presupposes a kind of open sea travel in which the person on a journey might not have access to a harbor.[83] One was not to make a trip in this manner according to Jubilees, while a number of rabbinic experts permitted spending the Sabbath on board a ship but debated the circumstances in which it was allowable.

The second "Anyone" heading (translated "any person") stands before a fairly detailed statement about the treatment of animals. The main clause addresses anyone

---

76 Albeck, *Jubiläen*, 9–10; Doering, *Schabbat*, 87–94. Tchernowitz also relates the ruling to Exod 16:29 and understands it to forbid movement outside one's house (*History of Hebrew Law*, 4:367). According to CD x:21 one is not to go outside his city more than one thousand cubits (cf. xi:5–6).

77 Doering, *Schabbat*, 94–95. CD x:20 prohibits going about in one's field to do the work one wishes. Charles commented about "at his home or in any (other) place," that "[t]hese words seem to be in their wrong place. They would give good sense if they were read immediately after 'every man who does any work thereon'" (*Jubilees*, 260). They certainly seem to "give good sense" in their present setting.

78 Presumably the man executed for gathering sticks on the Sabbath in Num 15:32–36 was doing so to light a fire (Levine, *Numbers 1–20*, 398–99).

79 Charles, *Jubilees*, 260; Doering, *Schabbat*, 96–97. Doering doubts the author would have permitted a fire, previously lit, to burn on the Sabbath. The Mishnah, however, deals at some length with the Sabbath lamp (e.g., *Šabb.* 2:1–7).

80 The verb *yeṣṣēʾan* means "ride" (Leslau, *Comparative Dictionary*, 543), but Berger, Rabin, and Caquot took it to mean "load, put a burden on." That, however, is the meaning of a different form of the root (the simple or causative stem). Albeck considered the notion of "load" but seems to have decided "ride" was the sense intended and referred to the relevant rabbinic passages (*Jubiläen*, 12). Tchernowitz also was aware of the different ways in which the text was read; as he commented, riding an animal is a form of placing a burden on it (*History of Hebrew Law*, 4:365).

81 Finkelstein, "Rabbinic Halaka," 50; Doering, *Schabbat*, 97–98.

82 Tchernowitz, *History of Hebrew Law*, 4:363. As he indicates, a rabbinic rule was that one was not to embark on such a trip fewer than three days before the Sabbath.

83 Doering, *Schabbat*, 99. For the rabbinic texts, see Finkelstein, "Rabbinic Halaka," 50; Albeck, *Jubiläen*, 10; Doering, *Schabbat*, 100.

"who beats [or: whips][84] or kills anything." *Mishnah Šabb.* 7:2 prohibits slaughtering an animal on the Sabbath (using the example of a gazelle). For striking an animal, see CD xi:6.[85] Though the object of the verbs here in Jubilees is the vague "anything [*menta-hi*]," the context indicates that animals are intended. Here again the author does not go into particulars about the kinds of animals covered by the legislation—whether dangerous ones were included,[86] for example, or unpleasant ones. The latter kinds of questions are discussed in some rabbinic sources.[87]

The two subheadings directly after this prohibition are clearly related to it.[88]

1. "who slits the throat of an animal or bird." Note "slaughtering or flaying or salting it [= a gazelle] or curing its skin, scraping it or cutting it up" (*m. Šabb.* 7:2).
2. "who catches either a wild animal, a bird, or a fish." *Mishnah Šabb.* 7:2 covers the category with "hunting a gazelle." See also 13:5-7; 14:1. The law is a subcategory of the general prohibition of killing a creature on the Sabbath.

At this juncture one would expect another "Anyone" statement, but the writer continues with a final, seemingly subordinate clause that consists of two rather different prohibitions: "who fasts and makes war on the Sabbath day." The rule forbidding fasting makes good sense in a work that stresses, as Jubilees does, that the Sabbath is to include eating and drinking. It also accords with Isa 58:13: ". . . if you call the sabbath a delight [ענג]."[89] The Israelites in the wilderness could not gather manna on the seventh day, but they were expected to eat it on the Sabbath (Exod 16:25: "Moses said, 'Eat it today, for today is a sabbath to the Lord; today you will not find it in the field'"). Judith 8:6 provides an interesting illustration of the importance of eating on the Sabbath and the kind of day it was deemed to be: "She fasted all the days of her widowhood, except the day before the sabbath and the sabbath itself, the day before the new moon and the day of the new moon, and the festivals and days of rejoicing of the house of Israel." There are references in rabbinic texts to the need to eat three meals on the Sabbath.[90]

The line forbidding warfare on the Sabbath is of special interest because there is written evidence that the subject was debated around the time Jubilees was written. It is formulated somewhat strangely in v. 12 because there is no relative clause (*wa-za-hi*) separating it from the previous prohibition (of fasting), but it is almost certain that the law does not mean to say that a person who both fasts and makes war on the Sabbath is liable to the death penalty. It should be a distinct ruling, not part of the previous one. The text forbids warfare on the Sabbath and makes no distinction between offensive and defensive fighting. That issue arose in the scene described in 1 Macc 2:29-41, where opponents of King Antiochus's edicts fled to the wilderness. Troops enforcing those edicts "attacked them on the sabbath, and they died, with their wives and children and livestock, to the number of a thousand persons" (1 Macc 2:38; cf. 2 Macc

---

84   Leslau, *Comparative Dictionary*, 631.
85   Ginzberg relates the prohibition of striking an animal with one's fist to the Sabbath command in Exod 20:10 (including animals in the Sabbath rest) (*Unknown Jewish Sect*, 65). He also thought that a small mistake had crept into the law in Jub 50:12: "I have a suspicion, I must admit, that in the Hebrew original of the Book of Jubilees there appeared the expression והכה ומת 'struck fatally,' which in the translation became 'to strike and kill.'" There is really no way to check whether his suspicion was correct, as only a translation has survived (see Doering, *Schabbat*, 102).
86   Harmful ones could be killed according to *b. Šabb.* 121b (Tchernowitz, *History of Hebrew Law*, 4:364).
87   See the analysis in Tchernowitz, *History of Hebrew Law*, 4:364; Doering, *Schabbat*, 101-3.
88   See Albeck, *Jubiläen*, 11-12.
89   Tchernowitz noted that the Isaiah passage does not make this a capital case and that Exod 16:23 is the source for the positive command (*History of Hebrew Law*, 4:367-68). See also Doering, *Schabbat*, 105-6. He documents the fact that a prohibition of Sabbath fasting is a more widespread practice (e.g., *b. Ber.* 31b). See, however, Finkelstein, "Rabbinic Halaka," 50-51; he indicated that under certain circumstances it was considered justified.
90   Albeck, *Jubiläen*, 10; Doering, *Schabbat*, 105-7. For the three meals and the Sabbath as a delight, see *b. Šabb.* 117b-118b.

8:26). Mattathias and his followers then determined: "Let us fight against anyone who comes to attack us on the sabbath day; let us not all die as our kindred died in their hiding places" (v. 41).[91] At least for Mattathias's group, the decision was an innovation vis-à-vis an older practice of avoiding warfare altogether on the Sabbath—the practice mandated in Jubilees.

Excursus: The Number of Prohibited Kinds of Labor

Two writers have maintained that Jubilees lists twenty-two kinds of labor prohibited on the Sabbath. This is supposed to be another indication of the close link between creation and Sabbath: as there were twenty-two kinds of works that God made during the first six days and before the Sabbath (and twenty-two generations until Jacob), so God forbade twenty-two kinds of work on the Sabbath. Tchernowitz provided a list of the twenty-two that he found in the two Sabbath sections in Jubilees (2:26-31; 50:6-13).

1. Doing what one wishes
2. Preparing food and drink
3. Drawing water
4. Taking out to the public domain
5. Bringing in from the public domain
6. Taking out from house to house
7. Bringing in from house to house
8. Having sex
9. Speaking about doing and traveling
10. Conducting business
11. Lifting a burden to bring it from a tent
12. Doing work (perhaps carrying vessels)
13. Going on a trip
14. Working the soil
15. Lighting a fire
16. Riding or putting a burden on an animal
17. Boarding a ship
18. Striking/killing a person
19. Slaughtering an animal or bird
20. Hunting an animal or bird
21. Fasting
22. Making war.

Tchernowitz even thought there were parallels between some prohibited kinds of labor and the creative acts of God. For example, lighting a fire was like the creation of light, and drawing water like the creation of water.[92] Sidney Hoenig thought that Jubilees specifically gives the number of forbidden labors as twenty-two, although he does not point out where the book says this; he goes on to discuss the reasons why the mishnaic total of labors not permitted on the Sabbath was thirty-nine whereas the earlier one in Jubilees was twenty-two.[93]

Ravid also drew up a list of the prohibited types of labor; for her the number is fifteen (the first three are shared between chaps. 2 and 50).[94]

1. Preparation of food and drink
2. Drawing water
3. Bringing/taking from house to house
4. Sexual relations
5. Conducting business
6. Setting out on a trip
7. Going on a trip
8. Working the soil
9. Lighting a fire
10. Lifting a burden onto an animal
11. Boarding a ship
12. Striking and killing
13. Slaughtering an animal or bird
14. Fasting
15. Going out to war

Ravid gives the references where she finds the specific rulings whereas Tchernowitz did not.

There are different ways to enumerate the types (for example, does the statement about saying something regarding work qualify as one or two commandments? How many prohibitions of carrying from one place to another are there?), but Tchernowitz's list is inflated (note nos. 4–7, 11) and includes the basic prohibition of work (no. 12). Ravid's is more accurate and demonstrates sufficiently that the author of Jubilees does not fashion a list of twenty-two prohibited labors to match the number of creative acts by God. The parallels between the acts of creation and the forbidden kinds of labor that Tchernowitz found have little plausibility.

---

91 Charles, *Jubilees*, 261; Albeck, *Jubiläen*, 11; Tchernowitz, *History of Hebrew Law*, 4:364; Doering, *Schabbat*, 107–8. Finkelstein ("Rabbinic Halaka," 51) thought the author of Jubilees was protesting the decision taken by Mattathias and his friends, but Doering rightly contends that there is nothing polemical about the way in which Jubilees formulates the prohibition.

92 His list is in *History of Hebrew Law*, 4:362, and he mentions parallels with the acts of creation on pp. 362–363. At times he reflects a different text of the prohibitions than the translation given in this commentary.

93 Sidney B. Hoenig, "The Designated Number of Kinds of Labor Prohibited on the Sabbath," *JQR* 68 (1978) 193–217, here 193–208. For his claim about the specific number in Jubilees, see p. 200.

94 Ravid, "Sabbath Laws," 165.

■ **13** The final verse in the section and in the entire book begins with a resumptive statement that anyone guilty of committing any of the actions prohibited on the Sabbath and listed above was to die (see v. 8). Israel must continue to keep the Sabbath in the prescribed way in the future (see v. 5). The phrasing of the line regarding the need for the Israelites to keep the Sabbath raises a problem: "so that the Israelites may continue observing the Sabbath in accord with the commandments for the Sabbaths of the land." One would have expected that, after the material in vv. 6-12, the text would say, "in accord with the commandments for the Sabbaths." The phrase "Sabbaths of the land" most naturally refers to sabbatical years or the seven-year units they conclude and would relate to vv. 2-4 or 2-5. Kister has appealed to the two different meanings of *Sabbath* in the passage (for weekly Sabbaths and seven-year Sabbaths) to question whether the laws in 50:6-13a were inserted secondarily into a text that originally moved from v. 5 to v. 13b.[95] It is understandable that he would raise the issue, but Kister himself listed so many arguments for why vv. 6-13 belong in Jubilees (see the excursus below) that it would be an extreme step to dismiss these verses—ones that are integral to the setting—because of a problematic reading in one place in v. 13. It may be that the difficulty resulted when a longer text was shortened through a scribal lapse. The original may have read, "so that the Israelites may continue observing the Sabbath in accord with the commandments for the *Sabbaths and for the Sabbaths* of the land." The statement would then include the two sabbatical topics treated in chap. 50. A scribe (working in Hebrew, Greek, or Ge'ez) could have skipped from the first instance of *Sabbaths* to the second, yielding the present text.[96] In the land, Israel is to obey the Sabbath laws and those of the sabbatical cycle.

The Angel of the Presence says that he has revealed the legislation to Moses "as it was written in the tablets that he placed in my hands so that I could write for you." The passive formulation ("it was written") indicates that the angel himself had not recorded the laws on the tablets; presumably God did that. Those tablets, already inscribed, the deity then placed in the angel's hands. The tablets in question should be the heavenly tablets from which he has been reading to Moses throughout the book, though the term "heavenly" does not accompany "tablets" in this verse. Through this reference, he is bringing the story full circle from chap. 1. In 1:29 one reads: "The Angel of the Presence, who was going along in front of the Israelite camp, took the tablets[97] (that told) of the divisions of the years."[98] The angel is never associated with "the two stone tablets, the law and the commandment" (1:1; see also the Prologue) that God gave to Moses. The next phrase "so that I could write for you" is another instance in which the Ethiopic text of Jubilees has the angel writing something for Moses. It is a case in which it becomes especially clear that the original text would have read "so that I could dictate to you," since he has just mentioned that the tablets were already inscribed (by God) when he received them from him and he does not give Moses a written text (see also v. 6).[99]

---

95 See Segal, *Jubilees*, 20, for the argument that Kister communicated to him orally (Segal concludes that 6-13 were tacked on to the text). Kugel, who thinks that someone added vv. 6-13 to the author's work, believes the statement "is an awkward attempt to return to the subject that preceded his insertion, the sabbaths of the land. With that, rather abruptly, the work ends—a sure sign that these sabbath laws were added later" (*Walk through* Jubilees, 205; "Jubilees," 451). A simpler explanation is available as explained above.

96 Among the texts collated for the edition in VanderKam, *Jubilees* 1, only MS. 38 offers a variant: it omits the word *medr* ("of the land"). The composition entitled *Te'āza Sanbat*, which nearly cites the list of Sabbath laws in Jub 50:6-13, reads in the part corresponding to v. 13: "He who does any manner of work on my Sabbath shall die. Thus shall the children of Israel be holy and celebrate the Sabbath according to the commandments as they are written in the tables which God gave to me that I might write down the law for thee from now on and throughout the generations" (trans. Leslau, *Falasha Anthology* [Yale Judaica Series 6; New Haven: Yale University Press, 1951] 20–21). In this text there is no reference to the Sabbaths of the land; however, since it does not reproduce the verse from Jubilees verbatim, it is not a reliable basis for determining the disputed reading in Jub 50:13.

97 The word "heavenly" is not used in this instance either, just as it is not in 50:13.

98 See Berger, *Jubiläen*, 556 n. c to v. 13; Doering, "Jub. 50:6-13," 367.

99 VanderKam, "Putative Author," 211–17.

The Angel of the Presence concludes his long address to Moses by defining what he has revealed to him: "the laws of each specific time [ḥegaga gizē wa-gizē] in each division of its times [ba-ba kufālē mawāʿelihu]." The idea is evident throughout the book, with the festivals being good examples of regulations revealed at specific times and then being incumbent upon future generations. But he had explained more explicitly on other occasions that the laws were revealed progressively—the ones for each period in their own time. One is in the section about Reuben's sin with Bilhah, where the problem of why Reuben was not executed arises. The angel explained on that occasion, using the same words as in 50:13, that he escaped the death penalty because "the statute, the punishment, and the law had not been completely revealed to all but (only) in your [Moses's] time as a law of its particular time [ḥegga gizē ba-mawāʿelihu]" (33:16). Since to this point the rule against such actions had not been disclosed, Reuben could not be held responsible for obeying it or be punished for violating it. Another example comes from the description of Jacob's way of life in the area of Hebron after Isaac died: "He worshiped the Lord wholeheartedly and in line with the revealed commands according to the divisions of the times of his generation" (36:20). Jacob lived in obedience to the laws revealed by the moment under consideration.

The last line of the book—"Here the words regarding the divisions of the times [nagar za-kufālē mawāʿel] are completed"—is not part of the angel's address to Moses but a conclusion from the pen of the author. It nicely rounds off the book by recalling the ways in which he had designated the composition in the Prologue and in chap. 1.[100]

Prologue: the words regarding the divisions of the times
1:4: the divisions of the times
1:26: the divisions of the times
1:29: the divisions of the years from the time.

The book of Jubilees, understandably known as "Divisions [kufālē]" in Geʿez, ends as it began by highlighting the importance of the historical periods that it covers and the laws that were disclosed in each segment of time. By distributing many of the laws now gathered in the Pentateuch throughout the generations of the ancestors, the writer in a sense subtracts from the centrality of the Sinai revelations and covenant but in another sense adds to it by making the claim that the laws now located at Sinai in Exodus 20–Numbers 10 were actually obeyed at earlier times by the ancestors of the people of Israel, just as the nation now pledges to abide by them.

Excursus: Is the Unit 50:6-13 Part of the Original Text?[101]

Verses 6-13 are situated somewhat unexpectedly in chap. 50 and, according to some, rather awkwardly in the book itself. Verse 1 refers to the Sabbath laws revealed in the wilderness of Sin, but, rather than listing them there, the writer moves to the related yet different topics of the sabbatical years and jubilee periods. Only after finishing with those subjects does he revert to Sabbath legislation and with it the book draws to a close.

The unusual location of the Sabbath laws in vv. 6-13 is worth noting, but it is more taxing to determine whether it constitutes evidence that the section is not from the author—that another hand inserted it into his text and at this particular location in it. Nevertheless, several scholars have concluded that there is enough information to regard the section as supplementary. Davenport tentatively assigned vv. 6-13 to his second redactor,[102] but Ravid has formulated a more detailed case for the secondary character of these verses.[103] Her arguments are as follows.

First, the author habitually attaches legal sections to places where the narrative in Genesis–Exodus suggests the topics. This does not happen in 50:6-13 where laws dating back to creation are explained. No event in the patriarchal history suggests the insertion of this set of laws at the end of chap. 50.

Second, the Sabbath as presented in 50:6-13 applies to servants, sojourners, and animals (see v. 7),

---

100 See, e.g., Kister, "Two Formulae," 297 n. 47; Doering, "*Jub.* 50:6-13," 362–67 (where he notes these correspondences and adduces evidence in other works for giving the title at the beginning and end of a text).

101 For this excursus, see VanderKam, "End of the Matter?," 270–84.

102 Davenport, *Eschatology*, 68–69, 75 (v. 5 is from his first redactor).

103 Ravid, "Sabbath Laws," 161–66.

but the laws in 2:15-33 limit celebration of the Sabbath to God, the highest classes of angels, and Israel. Naturally, Ravid recognizes that the writer of the section in chap. 2 was familiar with the fourth commandment and its references to servants, sojourners, and animals; on her view, he chose to ignore their presence in the commandment so that he could limit the Sabbath to God, the angels, and Israel.

Third, aspects of vv. 6-13 are in harmony with practices evident in other works that have undergone editorial expansion. A way in which editors could add a new law to a completed text was to include in the new law allusions to the older work and thus make it seem part of the original composition. Another technique was to add new material to the end of an older text. The person who supplemented Jubilees 50 with vv. 6-13 used such methods to modify the end of the book. He apparently thought that the Sabbath laws in chap. 2 were not sufficiently detailed so he rewrote them, placed allusions to the original section in the new one (on her count, chap. 50 contains three of the fifteen Sabbath laws present in chap. 2),[104] and situated the new unit at the end of the book. She thinks the person responsible for attaching vv. 6-13 to the end of Jubilees may have been a member of the Qumran sect, since Jubilees was used and copied at Qumran.

Doering wrote a detailed response to Ravid's proposal and showed the weaknesses in her arguments.[105] Her contention that the unit 50:6-13 does not conform to the author's practice of attaching a legal section to an appropriate event in the narrative is off base because the text relates it to the events of Exodus 16.[106] Doering also showed at length that her claim about a conflict between chaps. 2 and 50 regarding those to whom the Sabbath applies is invalid because the writer understands "the foreigner" to be a non-Israelite who became integrated into the nation of Israel. He has also demonstrated that vv. 6-13 fit well with the rest of the book. For example, the concluding statement ("Here the words regarding the divisions of the times are completed") sounds similar to the lines in the Prologue and chap. 1 (vv. 4, 26, 29 [see the commentary on v. 13]) that name and define the book; and topics such as the tablets and weeks of Sabbaths are also at home in it. The unit Jub 50:6-13, appropriately found at the end of the book, defines how the nation of Israel is to live in the land (just as 50:2-5 do). Doering also thinks it unlikely that a member of the Qumran group would have written the laws in vv. 6-13 because there are some differences between Sabbath legislation in Jubilees and the Qumran Sabbath codes.

In a lengthy footnote, Kister also commented on Ravid's arguments regarding the concluding section of Jubilees.[107] He drew attention to a couple of connections between these verses and earlier ones in chap. 50: v. 13c (the Sabbaths of the land as written on the tablets) relates to v. 5, and, without v. 6, 50:1 is left with nothing specifying its contents. As for a narrative trigger for the Sabbath laws, he agrees that Jubilees does not reproduce the story about gathering manna, but many (not all) of the laws in vv. 6-13 could be derived from Exodus 16 (several of these appear in the commentary above).[108] That makes it all the more puzzling why the book does not reproduce more of the manna story in v. 1. Kister does note, however, that the writer hurries through the Exodus narratives at the end of the book.

The arguments about editorial procedures are too weak to stand as serious objections to considering vv. 6-13 an original part of Jubilees. If editors at times added new laws to codes but included elements from the original text to make it seem as if they belonged to the unit to which the editor attached them, it would make it very difficult to discern whether they were from the author or from another. And, if at times editors added material to the end of a composition, one would still need additional evidence to distinguish such cases from works that end just as their authors intended. And should one believe that the person who composed the section about the Sabbath in chap. 2 ignored the explicit statement of the fourth commandment in

---

104 See her chart, "Sabbath Laws," 165.
105 Doering, "*Jub.* 50:6-13," 359-87.
106 Ravid ("Sabbath Laws," 162) states that Jubilees rewrites Genesis 1-Exodus 12—not an accurate delineation of the book's coverage. Cf. Doering "Concept of the Sabbath," 181: "Thus, by taking up the sabbath issue at the beginning and at the end of the book the author follows the structure of the biblical *Vorlage* that does not give any sabbath text 'between' Genesis 2 and Exodus 16."
107 Kister, "Two Formulae," 297 n. 47.
108 He mentions the issue of preparations for the Sabbath in 50:8-9 as possibly arising from Exod 16:23; the several travel restrictions in 50:8, 12 as related to Exod 16:24; and the duty of eating, not fasting, on the Sabbath in 50:9-10 as derivable from Exod 16:25. He does raise the possibility that the correspondences with Exodus 16 are accidental—a very unlikely thesis, given the extent of the overlaps.

the Decalogue regarding sojourners, servants, and animals? It is more likely that the author did not see fit to make the point explicit in the creation context in Jubilees 2 and that he considered chap. 50 the more appropriate place to quote the commandment about the Sabbath given at Sinai. It is not clear why the author refrained from saying more about the manna story at the beginning of chap. 50 (though he does reproduce several words from Exod 16:1 in 50:1), but he has left clues aplenty that Exodus 16 played an important part in his formulation of the laws in vv. 6-13. The Sabbath section, with its counterpart in 2:17-33, bookends the narrative in Jubilees. Sabbath was an absolutely essential element of Israel's life as the people of God, and the author of the book has highlighted that fact by devoting a section to it at the beginning and end of his rewriting of Genesis 1–Exodus 24.[109]

---

109 VanderKam, *Book of Jubilees*, 100–102; "End of the Matter?," 278.

Bibliography

1. English Translations

Biblical quotations
New Revised Standard Version

Septuagint
Albert Pietersma and Benjamin C. Wright, eds., *A New English Translation of the Septuagint and the Other Greek Translations Traditionally Included under That Title* (New York: Oxford University Press, 2007).

1 Enoch
George W. E. Nickelsburg and James C. VanderKam, *1 Enoch: The Hermeneia Translation* (Minneapolis: Fortress Press, 2012).

Aramaic Levi Document
Jonas C. Greenfield, Michael E. Stone and Esther Eshel, *The Aramaic Levi Document: Edition, Translation, Commentary* (SVTP 19; Leiden: Brill, 2004; their chapter and verse divisions are adopted).

Babylonian Talmud
Jacob Neusner, *The Babylonian Talmud: A Translation and Commentary* (1994–99; repr., 22 vols.; Peabody, MA: Hendrickson Publishers, 2005).

Mekhilta deRabbi Ishmael
Jacob Z. Lauterbach, *Mekhilta deRabbi Ishmael* (3 vols.; Philadelphia: Jewish Publication Society of America, 1933).

Midrash Rabbah
Harry Freedman and Maurice Simon, eds., *Midrash Rabbah: Translated into English with Notes, Glossary and Indices* (3rd ed.; 10 vols.; London: Soncino, 1983; original, 1938).

Mishnah
Herbert Danby, *The Mishnah: Translated from the Hebrew with Introduction and Brief Explanatory Notes* (Oxford: Oxford University Press, 1933).

Syncellus
Greek text: A. A. Mosshammer, ed., Georgius Syncellus, *Ecloga Chronographica* (Bibliotheca Scriptorum Graecorum et Romanorum Teubneriana; Leipzig: Teubner, 1984).
William Adler and Paul Tuffin, *The Chronography of George Synkellos: A Byzantine Chronicle of Universal History from the Creation* (Oxford: Oxford University Press, 2002).
References to the location of the text in the Mosshammer edition are given first; then the page number(s) in the translation of Adler/Tuffin.

Targums: Volumes from The Aramaic Bible series. Note in particular:
Martin M. McNamara, *Targum Neofiti 1: Genesis* (ArBib 1A; Collegeville, MN: Liturgical Press, 1992).
Michael Maher, *Targum Pseudo-Jonathan: Genesis* (ArBib 1B; Collegeville, MN: Liturgical Press, 1992).
Martin McNamara and Robert Hayward, *Targum Neofiti 1: Exodus*; Michael Maher, *Targum Pseudo-Jonathan: Exodus* (ArBib 2; Collegeville, MN: Liturgical Press, 1994).
Bernard Grossfeld, *The Targum Onqelos to Genesis* (ArBib 6; Wilmington, DE: Michael Glazier, 1988).
Bernard Grossfeld, *The Targum Onqelos to Exodus* (ArBib 7; Wilmington, DE: Michael Glazier, 1988).

Testaments of the Twelve Patriarchs
H. W. Hollander and M. de Jonge, *The Testaments of the Twelve Patriarchs: A Commentary* (SVTP 8; Leiden: Brill, 1985).

Tosefta
Jacob Neusner, *The Tosefta: Translated from the Hebrew with a New Introduction* (2 vols.; 1977–86; repr., Peabody, MA: Hendrickson Publishers, 2002).

2. Texts, Translations, and Commentaries (listed in order of their publication)

Dillmann, August
"Das Buch der Jubiläen oder die kleine Genesis," *Jahrbücher der Biblischen Wissenschaft* 2 (1850) 230–56; 3 (1851) 1–96.

Idem
Maṣḥafa Kufālē sive Liber Jubilaeorum (Kiel: C. G. L. van Maack and London: Williams & Norgate, 1859).

Schodde, George H.
The Book of Jubilees: Translated from the Ethiopic (Oberlin, OH: E. J. Goodrich, 1888).

Charles, Robert Henry
Maṣḥafa Kufālē or the Ethiopic Version of the Hebrew Book of Jubilees (Anecdota Oxoniensia; Oxford: Clarendon Press, 1895).

Littmann, Enno
"Das Buch der Jubiläen," in Emil Kautsch, ed., *Die Apokryphen und Pseudepigraphen des Alten Testaments*, vol. 2: *Die Pseudepigraphen des Alten Testaments* (Tübingen: Greiburg i. B.; Leipzig: J. C. B. Mohr [Paul Siebeck], 1900) 31–119.

Charles, Robert Henry
The Book of Jubilees, or The Little Genesis (London: Adam & Charles Black, 1902).
[*The Apocrypha and Pseudepigrapha of the Old Testament*, vol. 2: *Pseudepigrapha* (Oxford: Clarendon, 1913) 1–82. This is a shorter version of the above.

The Book of Jubilees, or The Little Genesis (Translations of Early Documents, Series 1: Palestinian Jewish Texts [Pre-rabbinic] 4; London: Society for Promoting Christian Knowledge; New York: Macmillan, 1917). [This volume contains just the translation from the 1902 book.]

Riessler, Paul
"Jubiläenbuch oder Kleine Genesis," in idem, *Alt-jüdisches Schrifttum ausserhalb der Bibel* (Augsburg: Filser, 1928; 2nd ed., Darmstadt: Wissenschaftliche Buchgesellschaft, 1966) 539–666.

Goldmann, Moshe
"The Book of Jubilees," in Avraham Kahana, ed., *The Apocryphal Books* (2 vols.; 1956; repr., Jerusalem: Maqor, 1970) 1:216–313.

Hartom, Eliyahu S.
"The Book of Jubilees," in *The Apocryphal Literature* (7 vols.; 3rd ed.; Tel Aviv: Yavneh, 1969) 5b.7–147.

Berger, Klaus
Das Buch der Jubiläen (JSHRZ 2.3; Gütersloh: Gütersloher Verlagshaus Gerd Mohn, 1981).

Rabin, Chaim
"Jubilees," in H. F. D. Sparks, ed., *The Apocryphal Old Testament* (Oxford: Clarendon, 1984) 1–139 [a revision of Charles's translation].

Wintermute, O. S.
"Jubilees," in James Charlesworth, ed., *The Old Testament Pseudepigrapha*, vol. 2: *Expansions of the "Old Testament" and Legends, Wisdom and Philosophical Literature, Prayers, Psalms, and Odes, Fragments of Lost Judeo-Hellenistic Works* (Garden City, NY: Doubleday, 1985) 35–142.

Caquot, André
"Jubilés," in André Dupont-Sommer and Marc Philonenko, eds., *La Bible: Écrits Intertestamentaires* (Paris: Gallimard, 1987) 627–810.

VanderKam, James C.
The Book of Jubilees (2 vols.; CSCO 510–11; Scriptores Aethiopici 87–88; Louvain: E. Peeters, 1989), volume 1 (text), volume 2 (translation).

VanderKam, James C.
The Book of Jubilees (Guides to Apocrypha and Pseudepigrapha; Sheffield: Sheffield Academic Press, 2001).

Kugel, James L.
A Walk through Jubilees: Studies in the Book of Jubilees and the World of Its Creation (JSJSup 156; Leiden: Brill, 2012).

[Kugel, James
"Jubilees," in *Outside the Bible: Ancient Jewish Writings Related to Scripture*, ed. Louis H. Feldman, James L. Kugel, and Lawrence H. Schiffman (3 vols.; Philadelphia: Jewish Publication Society, 2013) 1:272–465. The translation is different but the notes of explanation are related to those in the above volume.]

Werman, Cana
The Book of Jubilees: Introduction, Translation, and Interpretation (Between Bible and Mishnah; Jerusalem: Yishaq ben-Zvi, 2015).

3. Books, Monographs, and Articles (Alphabetically by author and title)

Aalen, Sverre
Heilsverlangen und Heilsverwirklichung: Studien zur Erwartung des Heils in der apokalyptischen Literatur des antiken Judentums und im ältesten Christentum (ALGHJ 21; Leiden: Brill, 1990).

Abel, Félix-Marie
Les Livres des Maccabées (EBib; Paris: Librairie LeCoffre, 1949).

Idem
Géographie de la Palestine (2 vols.; Paris: Librairie LeCoffre, 1933–38).

Idem
"Topographie des campagnes machabéenes," *RB* 32 (1923) 495–521; 33 (1924) 201–17; 34 (1925) 194–216; 35 (1926) 510–33.

Adler, William
"Abraham and the Burning of the Temple of Idols: Jubilees Traditions in Christian Chronography," *JQR* 77 (1986–87) 95–117.

Idem
"Jacob of Edessa and the Jewish Pseudepigrapha in Syriac Chronography," in John C. Reeves, ed., *Tracing the Threads: Studies in the Vitality of Jewish Pseudepigrapha* (SBLEJL 6; Atlanta: Scholars Press, 1994) 143–71.

Idem
"The Origins of the Proto-Heresies: Fragments from a Chronicle in the First Book of Epiphanius' Panarion," *JTS* 41 (1990) 472–501.

Idem
"The Reception History of the *Book of Jubilees*" (unpublished paper).

Idem
Time Immemorial: Archaic History and Its Sources in Christian Chronography from Julius Africanus to George Syncellus (Dumbarton Oaks Studies 26; Washington, DC: Dumbarton Oaks Research Library and Collection, 1989).

Adler, William, and Paul Tuffin
The Chronography of George Synkellos: A Byzantine Chronicle of Universal History from the Creation (Oxford: Oxford University Press, 2002).

Agouridis, S.
"The Book of Jubilees," *Theologika* 43 (1972) 550–83.

Idem
"Notes on the Books of Jubilees and Enoch," *Theologika* 45 (1974) 786–839.

Aharoni, Yohanan, and Michael Avi-Yonah
The Macmillan Bible Atlas (3rd rev. ed. by Anson Rainey and Ze'ev Safrai; New York: Macmillan, 1993).

Albani, Matthias
Astronomie und Schöpfungsglaube: Untersuchungen zum astronomischen Henochbuch (WMANT 68; Neukirchen-Vluyn: Neukirchener Verlag, 1994).

Idem
"Zur Rekonstruktion eines verdrängten Konzepts: Der 364-Tage-Kalender in der gegenwärtigen Forschung," in Matthias Albani, Jörg Frey, and Armin Lange, eds., *Studies in the Book of Jubilees* (TSAJ 65; Tübingen: Mohr Siebeck, 1997) 79–125.

Albani, Matthias, Jörg Frey, and Armin Lange, eds.
Studies in the Book of Jubilees (TSAJ 65; Tübingen: Mohr Siebeck, 1997).

Albeck, Chanoch
Das Buch der Jubiläen und die Halacha (Sieben und vierziger Bericht der Hochschule für die Wissenschaft des Judentums in Berlin; Berlin-Schöneberg: Siegfried Scholem, 1930).

Albright, William Foxwell
From the Stone Age to Christianity: Monotheism and the Historical Process (2nd ed.; Garden City, NY: Doubleday, 1957).

Alehegne, Mersha
The Ethiopian Commentary on the Book of Genesis: Critical Edition and Translation (Aethiopische Forschungen 73; Wiesbaden: Harrassowitz, 2011).

Alexander, Loveday
The Preface to Luke's Gospel: Literary Convention and Social Context in Luke 1.1-4 and Acts 1.1 (SNTSMS 78; Cambridge: Cambridge University Press, 1993).

Alexander, Philip
"Geography and the Bible (Early Jewish)," *ABD* 2:977–88.

Idem
"Jerusalem as the Omphalos of the World: On the History of a Geographical Concept," *Jud* 46 (1997) 148–63.

Idem
"Notes on the 'Imago Mundi' of the Book of Jubilees," *JJS* 33 (1982) 197–213.

Alexander, Tamar, and Yosef Dan
"The Complete *Midrash Va-yissa'u*," *Folklore Research Center Studies* 3 (1972) 67–76.

Allegro, John
Qumran Cave 4.I (4Q 158–4Q186) (DJD 5; Oxford: Clarendon, 1968).

Anderson, Gary
"Celibacy or Consummation in the Garden? Reflections on Early Jewish and Christian Interpretations of the Garden of Eden," *HTR* 82 (1989) 121–48.

Idem
"Sacrifice and Sacrificial Offerings (OT)," *ABD* 5:870–86.

Idem
"The Status of the Torah before Sinai: The Retelling of the Bible in the Damascus Covenant and the Book of Jubilees," *DSD* 1 (1994) 1–29.

Idem
"The Status of the Torah in the Pre-Sinaitic Period: St. Paul's Epistle to the Romans," in Michael Stone and Esther Chazon, eds., *Biblical Perspectives: Early Use and Interpretation of the Bible in Light of the Dead Sea Scrolls. Proceedings of the First International Symposium of the Orion Center, 12–14 May 1996* (STDJ 28; Leiden: Brill, 1998) 1–23.

Anderson, Gary, and Michael Stone
A Synopsis of the Books of Adam and Eve (2nd rev. ed.; SBLEJL 17; Atlanta: Scholars Press, 1999).

Andrei, Osvalda
"The 430 Years of Ex. 12:40, from Demetrius to Julius Africanus: A Study in Jewish and Christian Chronography," *Hen* 18 (1996) 9–67.

Aptowitzer, Victor
Kain und Abel in der Agada, den Apokryphen, der hellenistischen, christlichen und muhammedanischen Literatur (Vienna: Kohut Mem. Found., 1922).

Aune, David
Revelation (3 vols.; WBC 52A–C; Nashville: Thomas Nelson, 1997-98).

Avigad, Nahman, and Yigael Yadin
A Genesis Apocryphon: A Scroll from the Wilderness of Judaea (trans. Sulamith Schwartz Nardi; Jerusalem: Magnes Press, 1956).

Avi-Yonah, Michael
The Macmillan Bible Atlas (New York: Macmillan, 1968).

Baars, Willem, and Rochus Zuurmond
"The Project for a New Edition of the Ethiopic Book of Jubilees," *JSS* 9 (1964) 67–74.

Bacon, Benjamin Wisner
"The Calendar of Enoch and Jubilees," *Hebraica* 8 (1891–92) 124–31.

Baillet, Maurice
"Remarques sur le manuscrit du Livre des Jubilés de la grotte 3 de Qumrân," *RevQ* 5/19 (1964–66) 423–33.

Idem
"Le travail d'édition des fragments manuscrits de Qumrân," *RB* 63 (1956) 49–67.

Baillet, Maurice, Joseph Milik, and Roland DeVaux
Les 'petites grottes' de Qumrân (DJD 3; Oxford: Clarendon, 1962).

Baltzer, Klaus
The Covenant Formulary in Old Testament, Jewish, and Early Christian Writings (trans. David E. Green; Philadelphia: Fortress Press, 1971; German original, 1957).

Barth, J.
Review of Robert Henry Charles, *The Ethiopic Version of the Hebrew Book of Jubilees, Deutsche Litteraturzeitung* 34 (1895) 1062–63.

Barthélemy, Dominique
"Notes en marge de publications récentes sur les manuscrits de Qumrân," *RB* 59 (1952) 187–218.

Barthélemy, Dominique, and Joseph T. Milik
Qumran Cave I (*DJD* 1; Oxford: Clarendon, 1955).

Barton, George Aaron
"The Origin of the Names of Angels and Demons in the Extra-canonical Apocalyptic Literature to 100 A.D," *JBL* 31 (1912) 156-67.

Baumgarten, Joseph
"265. 4QMiscellaneous Rules," in *Qumran Cave 4 XXV: Halakhic Texts* (DJD 35; Oxford: Clarendon, 1999) 57-78.

Idem
"4Q502, Marriage or Golden Age Ritual?," *JJS* 34 (1983) 125-35.

Idem
"4QHalakhah, the Law of Ḥadash, and the Pentecontal Calendar," *JJS* 27 (1976) 36-46.

Idem
"4Q503 (Daily Prayers) and the Lunar Calendar," *RevQ* 12 (1986) 399-407.

Idem
"The Beginning of the Day in the Calendar of Jubilees," *JBL* 77 (1958) 355-60.

Idem
"The Calendar of the Book of Jubilees and the Bible," *Tarbiz* 32 (1962-63) 317-28.

Idem
"The Calendars of the Book of Jubilees and the Temple Scroll," *VT* 37 (1987) 71-78.

Idem
"The First and Second Tithes in the *Temple Scroll*," in Ann Kort and Scott Morschauer, eds., *Biblical and Related Studies Presented to Samuel Iwry* (Winona Lake, IN: Eisenbrauns, 1985) 5-15.

Idem
"The Laws of 'Orlah and First Fruits in the Light of Jubilees, the Qumran Writings, and Targum Ps. Jonathan," *JJS* 38 (1987) 195-202.

Idem
"Purification after Childbirth and the Sacred Garden in 4Q265 and Jubilees," in George Brooke and Florentino García Martínez, eds., *New Qumran Texts and Studies* (STDJ 15; Leiden: Brill, 1994) 3-10.

Idem
"Some Problems of the Jubilees Calendar in Current Research," *VT* 32 (1982) 485-89.

Idem
Studies in Qumran Law (SJLA 24; Leiden: Brill, 1977).

Idem
"Yom Kippur in the Qumran Scrolls and Second Temple Sources," *DSD* 6 (1999) 184-91.

Baumgarten, Joseph, and Daniel Schwartz
"Damascus Document (CD)," in James Charlesworth, ed., *Damascus Document, War Scroll, and Related Documents* (PTSDSSP 2; Tübingen: Mohr Siebeck; Louisville: Westminster John Knox, 1995) 4-57.

Bautch, Kelley Coblentz
"Amplified Roles, Idealized Depictions: Women in the Book of Jubilees," in Gabriele Boccaccini and Giovanni Ibba, eds., *Enoch and the Mosaic Torah: The Evidence of Jubilees* (Grand Rapids: Eerdmans, 2009) 338-52.

Bautch, Richard
"Afterlife in Jubilees: Through a Covenantal Prism," in Tobias Nicklas, Friedrich Reiterer, and Jozef Verheyden, eds., *The Human Body in Death and Resurrection* (Deuterocanonical and Cognate Literature Yearbook 2009; Berlin: de Gruyter, 2009) 205-19.

Baynes, Leslie
"Enoch and Jubilees in the Canon of the Ethiopic Orthodox Church," in Eric F. Mason, Kelley Coblentz Bautch, Angela Kim Harkins, and Daniel A. Machiela, eds., *A Teacher for All Generations: Essays in Honor of James C. VanderKam* (2 vols.; JSJSup 153/I-II; Leiden: Brill, 2012) 799-818.

Idem
The Heavenly Book Motif in Judeo-Christian Apocalypses 200 BCE-200 CE (JSJSup 152; Leiden: Brill, 2012).

Becker, Jürgen
Die Testamente der zwölf Patriarchen (JSHRZ 3; Gütersloh: Gütersloher Verlagshaus Gerd Mohn, 1974).

Idem
Untersuchungen zur Entstehungsgeschichte der Testamente der zwölf Patriarchen (AGJU 8; Leiden: Brill, 1969).

Beckwith, Roger
"The Essene Calendar and the Moon: A Reconsideration," *RevQ* 15 (1991) 457-66.

Idem
"The Modern Attempt to Reconcile the Qumran Calendar with the True Solar Year," *RevQ* 7 (1969-71) 379-96.

Idem
The Old Testament Canon of the New Testament Church and Its Background in Early Judaism (Grand Rapids: Eerdmans, 1985).

Idem
"The Qumran Calendar and the Sacrifices of the Essenes," *RevQ* 7 (1971) 587-91.

Idem
"The Significance of the Calendar for Interpreting Essene Chronology and Eschatology," *RevQ* 10 (1980) 167-202.

Bedenbender, Andreas
The Book of *Jubilees*—An Example of 'Rewritten Torah,'?" *Hen* 31 (2009) 72-78.

Beer, Bernhard
Das Buch der Jubiläen und sein Verhältniss zu den Midraschim (Leipzig: Wolfgang Gerhard, 1856).

Idem
"Noch ein Wort über das Buch der Jubiläen," *MGWJ* 6 (1857) 1-23.

Begg, Christopher
"Jacob's Descent into Egypt (Gen 45,25–46,7), according to Josephus, Philo and *Jubilees*," *EThL* 84 (2008) 499–518.

Idem
"Jacob's Escape from Laban in Josephus and Jubilees," *Hermen* 9 (2009) 3–38.

Idem
"Rereadings of the 'Animal Rite' of Genesis 15 in Early Jewish Narratives," *CBQ* 50 (1988) 36–46.

Ben-Dov, Jonathan
"319. 4QOtot," in Shemaryahu Talmon, Jonathan Ben-Dov, and Uwe Glessmer, eds., *Qumran Cave 4.XVI: Calendrical Texts* (DJD 21; Oxford: Clarendon, 2001) 195–244.

Idem
Head of All Years: Astronomy and Calendars at Qumran in Their Ancient Context (STDJ 78; Leiden: Brill, 2008).

Idem
"Jubilean Chronology and the 364-Day Year" [Hebrew], *Meghillot* 5–6 (2007) 49–59.

Idem
"Tradition and Innovation in the Calendar of Jubilees," in Gabriele Boccaccini and Giovanni Ibba, eds., *Enoch and the Mosaic Torah: The Evidence of Jubilees* (Grand Rapids: Eerdmans, 2009) 276–93.

Berger, Klaus
Das Buch der Jubiläen (JSHRZ 2.3; Gütersloh: Gütersloher Verlagshaus Gerd Mohn, 1981).

Bergsma, John
The Jubilee from Leviticus to Qumran: A History of Interpretation (VTSup 115; Leiden: Brill, 2007).

Idem
"Once Again, the Jubilee, Every 49 or 50 Years?" *VT* 55 (2005) 121–25.

Idem
"The Relationship between Jubilees and the Early Enochic Books (Astronomical Book and Book of the Watchers)," in Gabriele Boccaccini and Giovanni Ibba, eds., *Enoch and the Mosaic Torah: The Evidence of Jubilees* (Grand Rapids: Eerdmans, 2009) 36–51.

Berner, Christoph
"50 Jubilees and Beyond? Some Observations on the Chronological Structure of the *Book of Jubilees*," *Hen* 31 (2009) 17–23.

Idem
Jahre, Jahrwochen und Jubiläen: Heptadische Geschichtskonzeptionen im Antiken Judentum (BZAW 363; Berlin: de Gruyter, 2006).

Bernstein, Moshe
"4Q252: From Rewritten Bible to Biblical Commentary," *JJS* 45 (1994) 1–27.

Idem
"4Q252 i 2 לא ידור רוחי באדם לעולם: Biblical Text or Biblical Interpretation?," *RevQ* 16/63 (1993–94) 421–27.

Idem
"Angels at the Aqedah: A Study in the Development of a Midrashic Motif," *DSD* 7 (2000) 263–91.

Idem
"Noah and the Flood at Qumran," in Donald Parry and Eugene Ulrich, eds., *The Provo International Conference on the Dead Sea Scrolls: Technological Innovations, New Texts, and Reformulated Issues* (STDJ 30; Leiden: Brill, 1999) 199–231.

Idem
"'Walking in the Festivals of the Gentiles': 4QpHosea^a 2.15–17 and *Jubilees* 6.34–38," *JSP* 9 (1991) 21–34.

Bhayro, Siam
"The Use of *Jubilees* in Medieval Chronicles to Supplement Enoch: The Case for the 'Shorter' Reading," *Hen* 31 (2009) 10–17.

Billen, A. V.
The Old Latin Texts of the Heptateuch (Cambridge: University Press, 1927).

Black, Matthew
The Scrolls and Christian Origins (New York: Charles Scribner's Sons, 1961).

Blenkinsopp, Joseph
Ezra-Nehemiah: A Commentary (OTL; Philadephia: Westminster, 1988).

Idem
"Interpretation and the Tendency to Sectarianism: An Aspect of Second Temple History," in Ed Sanders, Albert Baumgarten, and Alan Mendelson, eds., *Jewish and Christian Self-Definition*, vol. 2: *Aspects of Judaism in the Graeco-Roman Period* (Philadelphia: Fortress Press, 1981) 1–26, 299–309.

Idem
Isaiah 1–39: A New Translation with Introduction and Commentary (AB 19; New York: Doubleday, 2000).

Idem
Isaiah 55–66: A New Translation with Introduction and Commentary (AB 19B; New York: Doubleday, 2003).

Block, Daniel
The Book of Ezekiel: Chapters 25–48 (NICOT; Grand Rapids: Eerdmans, 1998).

Boccaccini, Gabriele
"From a Movement of Dissent to a Distinct Form of Judaism: The Heavenly Tablets in Jubilees as the Foundation of a Competing Halakah," in Gabriele Boccaccini and Giovanni Ibba, eds., *Enoch and the Mosaic Torah: The Evidence of Jubilees* (Grand Rapids: Eerdmans, 2009).

Boccaccini, Gabriele, and Giovanni Ibba, eds.
Enoch and the Mosaic Torah: The Evidence of Jubilees (Grand Rapids: Eerdmans, 2009).

Boccaccini, Gabriele, et al., eds.
Enoch and Qumran Origins: New Light on a Forgotten Connection (Grand Rapids: Eerdmans, 2005).

Bockmuehl, Markus
"Natural Law in Second Temple Judaism," *VT* 45 (1995) 17–44.

Idem
"The Noachide Commandments and New Testament Ethics with Special Reference to Acts 15 and Pauline Halakhah," *RB* 102 (1995) 72–101.

Bohn, Friedrich
"Die Bedeutung des Buches der Jubiläen: Zum 50 jährigen Jubiläen der ersten, deutschen Übersetzung," *ThStK* 73 (1900) 167–84.

Bokser, Baruch
The Origins of the Seder: The Passover Rite and Early Rabbinic Judaism (Berkeley: University of California Press, 1984).

Bonneau, Guy, and Jean Duhaime
"Angélogie et légitimation socio-religieuse dans le livre des Jubilés," *Église et Théologie* 27 (1996) 335–49.

Borchardt, Paul
"Das Erdbild der Juden nach dem Buche der Jubiläen—ein Handelsstrassenproblem," *Petermanns Mitteilungen aus Justus Perthes' Geographischer Anstalt* 71 (1925) 244–50.

Borgonovo, Gianantonio
"Jubilees' Rapprochement between Henochic and Mosaic Tradition," *Hen* 31 (2009) 29–35.

Böttrich, Christfried
"Gottesprädikationen im Jubiläenbuch," in Matthias Albani, Jörg Frey, and Armin Lange, eds., *Studies in the Book of Jubilees* (TSAJ 65; Tübingen: Mohr Siebeck, 1997) 221–41.

Bousset, Wilhelm
"Neueste Forschungen auf dem Gebiet der religiösen Litteratur des Spätjudentums," *ThR* 3 (1900) 287–302, 327–35, 369–81.

Idem
"Die Testamente der zwölf Patriarchen," *ZNW* 1 (1900) 141–75, 187–209.

Bousset, Wilhelm, and Hugo Gressmann
Die Religion des Judentums im späthellenistischen Zeitalter (Berlin: Reuther & Reichard, 1903).

Bowley, James
"Moses in the Dead Sea Scrolls: Living in the Shadow of God's Anointed," in Peter Flint and T'ae-hun Kim, eds., *The Bible at Qumran: Text, Shape, and Interpretation* (Grand Rapids: Eerdmans, 2001) 159–81.

Boxel, Piet van
"The God of Rebekah," *SIDIC* 9 (1976) 14–18.

Boyd, James Oscar
The Text of the Ethiopic Version of the Octateuch, with Special Reference to the Age and Value of the Haverford Manuscript (Bibliotheca Abessinica 2; Leiden: Brill; Princeton: University Library, 1905).

Brady, Monica
"Prophetic Traditions at Qumran: A Study of 4Q383–391" (PhD diss., University of Notre Dame, 2000).

Brandt, Peter
"Bible Canon," in Siegbert Uhlig, ed., *Encyclopaedia Aethiopica* (Wiesbaden: Harrassowitz, 2003) 1:571–73.

Brin, Gershon
"Regarding the Connection between the Temple Scroll and the Book of Jubilees," *JBL* 112 (1993) 108–9.

Idem
"The Sources of the Saying of Esau in Jubilees 37 according to 4Q PapJubilees[h], unit 2, col. IV," in Rimmon Kasher and Moshe Sippor, eds., *Memorial Volume for Yehudah Qomlosh* (Studies in Bible and Exegesis 6; Ramat-Gan: University of Bar-Ilan, 2003) 17–24.

Brock, Sebastian
"Abraham and the Ravens: A Syriac Counterpart to Jubilees 11–12 and Its Implications," *JSJ* 9 (1978) 135–52.

Idem
"Genesis 12: Where Was Sarah?," *ExpT* 96 (1984) 14–17.

Brooke, George J.
"Exegetical Strategies in Jubilees 1–2: New Light from 4QJubilees[a]," in Matthias Albani, Jörg Frey, and Armin Lange, eds., *Studies in the Book of Jubilees* (TSAJ 65; Tübingen: Mohr Siebeck, 1997) 39–57.

Broshi, Magen, ed.
The Damascus Document Reconsidered (Jerusalem: Israel Exploration Society and Shrine of the Book, 1992).

Brown, Raymond E.
The Gospel according to John: Introduction, Translation, and Notes (2 vols.; AB 29, 29A; Garden City, NY: Doubleday, 1966, 1970).

Brownlee, William Hugh
"Light on the Manual of Discipline (DSD) from the Book of Jubilees," *BASOR* 123 (1951) 30–32.

Büchler, Adolph
"La fête des cabanes chez Plutarque et Tacite," *REJ* 37 (1898) 181–202.

Idem
"Studies in the Book of Jubilees," *REJ* 82 (1926) 253–74.

Idem
"Traces des idées et des coutumes hellénistiques dans le Livre des Jubilés," *REJ* 89 (1930) 321–48.

Buisch, Pauline P.
"The Absence and Influence of Genesis 48 (the Blessing of Ephraim and Manasseh) in the *Book of Jubilees*," *JSP* 26 (2017) 255–73.

Byron, John
Cain and Abel in Text and Tradition: Jewish and Christian Interpretations of the First Sibling Rivalry (TBN 14; Leiden: Brill, 2011).

Idem
"Cain's Rejected Offering: Interpretive Approaches to a Theological Problem," *JSP* 18 (2008) 4–7.

Calvert-Koyzis, Nancy
Paul, Monotheism and the People of God: The Significance of Abraham Traditions for Early Judaism and Christianity (JSNTSup 273; London: T&T Clark, 2004).

Caquot, André
"Deux notes sur la géographie des Jubilés," in Gérard Nahon and Charles Touati, eds., *Hommages à Georges Vajda: Études d'histoire et de pensée juives* (Louvain: Peeters, 1980) 37–42.

Idem
"Eléments aggadiques dans le livre des 'Jubilés'," in Andre Caquot, ed., *La littérature intertestamentaire. Colloque de Strasbourg (17–19 Octobre 1983)* (Bibliothéque des Centres d'Etudes supérieurs specialisés; Paris: Presses Universitaires de France, 1985) 57–68.

Idem
"Les enfants aux cheveux blancs (Remarques sur *Jubilés*, XXIII, 25)," *RHR* 177 (1970) 131–32.

Idem
"Jubilés," in André Dupont-Sommer and Marc Philonenko, eds., *La Bible: Écrits Intertestamentaires* (Paris: Gallimard, 1987) 627–810.

Idem
"Le Livre des Jubilés, Melkisedeq et les dîmes," *JJS* 33 (1982) 257–64.

Idem
"'Loi' et 'Témoignage' dans le Livre des Jubilés," in Christian Robin, ed., *Mélanges linguistiques offerts à Maxime Rodinson par ses élèves, ses collègues et ses amis* (Comptes rendus du Groupe linguistique d'études chamito-sémitiques, supplément 12; Paris: Geuthner, 1985) 137–45.

Idem
"Les protecteurs des tribus d'Israël: Notes d'angelologie à propos de *Testament de Juda* 25, 2," in *La vie de la parole: De l'Ancien au Nouveau Testament*: Études d'exégèse et d'herméneutique bibliques offert à Pierre Grelot professeur à l'*Institut Catholique de Paris* (Paris: Desclée, 1987) 49–59.

Carmichael, Calum
"Law and Narrative in Jubilees: The Biblical Precedent," *Hen* 31 (2009) 78–83.

Idem
"The Story of Joseph and the Book of Jubilees," in Timothy H. Lim, ed., *The Dead Sea Scrolls in Their Historical Context* (Edinburgh: T&T Clark, 2000) 143–58.

Cavallin, Hans Clemens
Life after Death: Paul's Argument for the Resurrection of the Dead in 1 Cor. 15 (ConBNT 7.1; Lund: Gleerup, 1974).

Cazelles, Henri
"Sur les origenes du calendrier des Jubilés," *Bib* 43 (1962) 202–12.

Ceriani, Antonio Maria
Monumenta Sacra et Profana (2 vols.; Milan: Bibliotheca Ambrosiana, 1861–63).

Chabot, I. B.
Chronicon ad annum Christi 1234 pertinens 1 (CSCO 81, Scriptores Syri 36; Louvain: Imprimerie Orientaliste L. Durbeq, 1953).

Charles, Robert Henry, ed.
The Apocrypha and Pseudepigrapha of the Old Testament (2 vols.; Oxford: Clarendon Press, 1913).

Idem
The Book of Enoch, or, 1 Enoch: Translated from the Editor's Ethiopic Text (Oxford: Clarendon, 1912).

Idem
The Book of Jubilees or the Little Genesis (London: Adam & Charles Black, 1902).

Idem
The Book of Jubilees or the Little Genesis (Translation of Early Documents, Series I; London: Society for Promoting Christian Knowledge; New York: Macmillan, 1917).

Idem
"The Book of Jubilees, Translated from a Text Based on Two Hitherto Uncollated Ethiopic MSS," *JQR* 5 (1893) 703–8; 6 (1894) 184–217, 710–45; 7 (1895) 297–328.

Idem
Eschatology: The Doctrine of a Future Life in Israel, Judaism, and Christianity: A Critical History (New York: Schocken Books, 1963; original, 1899; 2nd ed., 1913).

Idem
The Greek Versions of the Testaments of the Twelve Patriarchs (Oxford: Oxford University Press, 1908).

Idem
Maṣḥafa Kufālē or the Ethiopic Version of the Hebrew Book of Jubilees (Anecdota Oxoniensia; Oxford: Clarendon, 1895).

Charlesworth, James H.
"The Date of Jubilees and of the Temple Scroll," *SBLASP* 24 (1985) 193–204.

Chazon, Esther
"Psalms, Hymns, and Prayers," in Lawrence Schiffman and James C. VanderKam, eds., *Encyclopedia of the Dead Sea Scrolls* (2 vols.; New York: Oxford University Press, 2000) 2:710–15.

Chestnutt, Randall
"Revelatory Experiences Attributed to Biblical Women in Early Jewish Literature," in Amy Jill Levine, ed., *'Women Like This': New Perspectives on Jewish Women in the Greco-Roman World* (SBLEJL 1; Atlanta: Scholars Press, 1991) 107–25.

Childs, Brevard
The Book of Exodus: A Critical, Theological Commentary (OTL; Louisville: Westminster, 1974).

Christiansen, Ellen Juhl
The Covenant in Judaism and Paul: A Study of Ritual Boundaries as Identity Markers (AGJU 27; Leiden: Brill, 1995).

Cohen, N.
"Taryag and the Noahide Commandments," *JJS* 43 (1992) 46–57.

Cohen, Shaye J. D.
"From the Bible to the Talmud: The Prohibition of Intermarriage," *HAR* 7 (1983) 23–39.

Collins, John J., ed.
Apocalypse: The Morphology of a Genre (Semeia 14; Missoula, MT: Scholars Press, 1979).

Idem
The Apocalyptic Imagination: An Introduction to the Jewish Matrix of Christianity (New York: Crossroad, 1984).
Idem
The Apocalyptic Imagination: An Introduction to Jewish Apocalyptic Literature (2nd ed.; Biblical Resource Series; Grand Rapids: Eerdmans, 1998).
Idem
"The Genre of the Book of *Jubilees*," in Eric F. Mason, Kelley Coblentz Bautch, Angela Kim Harkins, and Daniel A. Machiela, eds., *A Teacher for All Generations: Essays in Honor of James C. VanderKam* (2 vols.; JSJSup 153/I-II; Leiden: Brill, 2012) 737–55.
Idem
"Pseudepigraphy and Group Formation in Second Temple Judaism," in Esther Chazon and Michael E. Stone, eds., *Pseudepigraphic Perspectives: The Apocrypha and Pseudepigrapha in Light of the Dead Sea Scrolls* (STDJ 31; Leiden: Brill, 1999) 43–58.
Idem
The Scepter and the Star: The Messiahs of the Dead Sea Scrolls and other Ancient Literature (ABRL; New York: Doubleday, 1995).
Idem
"The Sybilline Oracles," *OTP* 1:317–472.
Corinaldi, Michael, "The Relationship between the *Beta Israel* tradition and the *Book of Jubilees*," in Tudor Parfitt and Emanuela Trevisan Semi, eds., *Jews of Ethiopia: The Birth of an Elite* (Routledge Jewish Studies Series; London: Routledge, 2005) 193–204.
Cowley, Roger
"The Biblical Canon of the Ethiopian Orthodox Church Today," *Ostkirchlichen Studien* 23 (1974) 318–23.
Idem
Ethiopic Biblical Interpretation: A Study in Exegetical Tradition and Hermeneutics (Cambridge: Cambridge University Press, 1988).
Idem
"Old Testament Introduction in the Andemta Commentary Tradition," *Journal of Ethiopian Studies* 12 (1974) 133–75.
Crawford, Cory D.
"On the Exegetical Function of the Abraham/Ravens Tradition in Jubilees 11," *HTR* 97 (2004) 91–97.
Cresson, Bruce
"The Condemnation of Edom in Postexilic Judaism," in James M. Efird, ed., *The Use of the Old Testament in the New and Other Essays: Studies in Honor of William Franklin Stinespring* (Durham, NC: Duke University Press, 1972) 125–48.
Crislip, Andrew
"The *Book of Jubilees* in Coptic: An Early Christian *Florilegium* on the Family of Noah," *Bulletin of the American Society of Papyrologists* 40 (2003) 27–44.

Cross, Frank Moore
The Ancient Library of Qumran and Modern Biblical Studies (2nd ed.; Garden City, NY: Doubleday, 1961).
Idem
"The Development of the Jewish Scripts," in George Ernest Wright, ed., *The Bible and the Ancient Near East: Essays in Honor of William Foxwell Albright* (Garden City, NY: Doubleday, 1961) 133–202.
Idem
"The Evolution of a Theory of Local Texts," in Frank Moore Cross and Shemaryahu Talmon, eds., *Qumran and the History of the Biblical Text* (Cambridge, MA: Harvard University Press, 1975) 306–20.
Cryer, Frederick H.
"The 360-Day Calendar Year and Early Judaic Sectarianism," *SJOT* 1 (1987) 116–22.
Daly, Robert J.
"The Soteriological Significance of the Sacrifice of Isaac," *CBQ* 39 (1977) 45–75.
Davenport, Gene L.
The Eschatology of the Book of Jubilees (StPB 20; Leiden: Brill, 1971).
Davies, Philip R., and Bruce Chilton
"The Aqedah: A Revised Tradition History," *CBQ* 40 (1978) 514–46.
Day, John
"The Pharaoh of the Exodus, Josephus and Jubilees," *VT* 45 (1995) 377–78.
Dean, James Elmer
Epiphanius' Treatise on Weights and Measures: The Syriac Version (The Oriental Institute of the University of Chicago, SAOC 11; Chicago: University of Chicago Press, 1935).
Deichgräber, Reinhard
"Fragmente einer Jubiläen-Handschrift aus Höhle 3 von Qumran," *RevQ* 5/19 (1964–66) 415–22.
DeJong, David
"The Decline of Human Longevity in the Book of Jubilees," *JSP* 21 (2012) 340–65.
Idem
"The Exegetical Background to the Battle between Jacob and Esau in *Jubilees*" (Unpublished seminar paper, University of Notre Dame, 2010).
Delcor, Mathias
"Das Bundesfest in Qumran und das Pfingstfest," in idem, *Religion d'Israël et Proche Orient Ancien: Des Phéniciens aux Esséniens* (Leiden: Brill, 1976) 281–97.
Idem
"La fête des huttes dans le Rouleau du Temple et dans le livre des Jubilés," *RevQ* 15/57-58 (1991) 181–98.
Denis, Albert-Marie
Concordance latine du Liber Jubilaeorum sive Parva Genesis (Informatique et étude de textes 4; Louvain: Publications du CETEDOC, Université Catholique de Louvain, 1973).

Idem
Fragmenta pseudepigraphorum quae supersunt graeca (PVTG 3; Leiden: Brill, 1970).

Idem
Introduction aux pseudépigraphes grecs d'Ancien Testament (SVTP 1; Leiden: Brill, 1970).

Derrett, J. Duncan M.
"A Problem in the Book of Jubilees and an Indian Doctrine," *ZRGG* 14 (1962) 247-62.

Díez-Macho, Alejandro, ed.
Apocrifos del Antiguo Testamento (2 vols.; Madrid: Ediciones Christiandad, 1984).

Dillmann, August
"Beiträge aus dem Buch der Jubiläen zur Kritik des Pentateuch-Textes," *SPAW* 1 (1883) 323-40.

Idem
"Das Buch der Jubiläen oder die kleine Genesis," *JBW* 2 (1850) 230-56; 3 (1851) 1-96.

Idem
Ethiopic Grammar (2nd ed.; trans. Carl Bezold; London: Williams & Norgate, 1907).

Idem
Grammatik der äthiopischen Sprache (2nd ed.; Leipzig: Chr. Herm. Tauchnitz, 1899).

Idem
Lexicon Linguae Aethiopicae (1865; repr., New York: Frederick Ungar, 1955).

Idem
Maṣḥafa Kufālē sive Liber Jubilaeorum (Kiel: C. G. L. van Maack; London: Williams & Norgate, 1859).

Idem
Review of Bernhard Beer, *Das Buch der Jubiläen und sein Verhältniss zu den Midraschim*, *ZDMG* 11 (1857) 161-63.

Idem
"Ueber den Umfang des Bibelcanons der Abyssinischen Kirche," *JBW* 5 (1852-53) 144-51.

Dimant, Devorah
"Between Qumran Sectarian and Non-Sectarian Texts: The Case of Belial and Mastema," in Adolfo Roitman, Lawrence Schiffman, and Shani Tzoref, eds., *The Dead Sea Scrolls and Contemporary Culture: Proceedings of the International Conference Held at the Israel Museum, Jerusalem (July 6-8, 2008)* (STDJ 93; Leiden: Brill, 2011) 235-56.

Eadem
"The Biblical Basis of Non-Biblical Additions: The Binding of Isaac in Jubilees in Light of the Story of Job," in Devorah Dimant, *Connected Vessels: The Dead Sea Scrolls and the Literature of the Second Temple Period* (Asuppot 3; Jerusalem: Bialik Institute, 2010) 348-68.

Eadem
"The Biography of Enoch and the Books of Enoch," *VT* 33 (1983) 19-24.

Eadem
"The 'Fallen Angels' in the Dead Sea Scrolls and in the Apocryphal and Pseudepigraphic Books Related to Them" (PhD diss., Hebrew University of Jerusalem, 1974).

Eadem
"Judah and Tamar in Jubilees 41," in Eric F. Mason, Kelley Coblentz Bautch, Angela Kim Harkins, and Daniel A. Machiela, eds., *A Teacher for All Generations: Essays in Honor of James C. VanderKam* (JSJSup 153/I-II; Leiden: Brill, 2012) 783-97.

Eadem
"New Light from Qumran on Jewish Pseudepigrapha—4Q390," in Julio Trebolle Barrerea and Luis Vegas Montaner, eds., *The Madrid Qumran Congress: Proceedings of the International Congress on the Dead Sea Scrolls, Madrid, 18-21 March, 1991* (2 vols.; STDJ 11; Leiden: Brill, 1992) 2:405-48.

Eadem
"Noah in Early Jewish Literature," in Michael E. Stone and Theodore A. Bergren, eds., *Biblical Figures Outside the Bible* (Harrisburg, PA: Trinity Press International, 1998) 123-50.

Eadem
Qumran Cave 4:XXI: Parabiblical Texts, Part 4: Pseudo-Prophetic Texts (DJD 30; Oxford: Clarendon, 2001).

Eadem
"The Sons of Heaven—The Teaching about the Angels in the Book of Jubilees in Light of the Writings of the Qumran Community," in Moshe Idel, Devorah Dimant, and Shalom Rosenberg, eds., *A Tribute to Sarah: Studies in Jewish Philosophy and Kabbalah* (Jerusalem: Magnes Press, 1994) 97-118.

Eadem
"Two 'Scientific Fictions': The So-Called Book of Noah and the Alleged Quotation of Jubilees in CD 16:3-4," in Peter Flint, James VanderKam, and Emanuel Tov, eds., *Studies in the Hebrew Bible, Qumran, and the Septuagint Presented to Eugene Ulrich* (VTSup 101; Leiden: Brill, 2006) 230-49.

Dobos, Károly Daniel
"The Consolation of History: A Reexamination of the Chronology of the Abraham Pericope in the Book of Jubilees," *Hen* 31 (2009) 84-91.

Docherty, Susan
"Joseph the Patriarch: Representations of Joseph in Early Post-Biblical Literature," in Martin O'Kane, ed., *Borders, Boundaries and the Bible* (JSOTSup 313; Sheffield: Sheffield Academic Press, 2002) 194-216.

Doering, Lutz
"The Concept of the Sabbath in the Book of Jubilees," in Matthias Albani, Jörg Frey, and Armin Lange, eds., *Studies in the Book of Jubilees* (TSAJ 65; Tübingen: Mohr Siebeck, 1997) 179-205.

Idem
"*Jub*. 50:6-13 als Schlussabschnitt des Jubiläenbuchs: Nachtrag aus Qumran oder ursprünglicher Bestandteil des Werks," *RevQ* 20/79 (2002) 359-87.

Idem
"Jubiläen 2, 24 nach 4QJubª VII, 17 und der Aufbau von Jubiläen 2, 17-33," *BN* 84 (1996) 23-28.

Idem
Schabbat: Sabbathalacha und -praxis im antiken Judentum und Urchristentum (TSAJ 78; Tübingen: Mohr Siebeck, 1999).

Doran, Robert
"The Non-Dating of Jubilees: Jub 34–38; 23:14-32 in Narrative Context," *JSJ* 20 (1989) 1–11.

Dorman, Anke
"'Commit Injustice and Shed Innocent Blood': Motives behind the Institution of the Day of Atonement in the Book of Jubilees," in Thomas Hieke and Tobias Nicklas, eds., *The Day of Atonement: Its Interpretations in Early Jewish and Christian Traditions* (TBN 15; Leiden: Brill, 2012) 51–62.

Drawnel, Henryk
The Aramaic Astronomical Book (4Q208–4Q211) from Qumran: Text, Translation, and Commentary (Oxford: Oxford University Press, 2011).

Idem
An Aramaic Wisdom Text from Qumran: A New Interpretation of the Levi Document (JSJSup 86; Leiden: Brill, 2004).

Driver, Samuel Rolles
A Critical and Exegetical Commentary on Deuteronomy (ICC; Edinburgh: Clark, 1902).

Duncan, Julie Ann
"35. 4QDeut[h]," in Eugene Ulrich et al., eds., *Qumran Cave 4.IX: Deuteronomy, Joshua, Judges, Kings* (DJD 14; Oxford: Clarendon, 1995) 61–70.

Ego, Beate
"Abraham als Urbild der Toratreue Israels: Traditionsgeschichtliche Überlegungen zu einem Aspekt des biblischen Abrahambildes," in Friedrich Avemarie and Hermann Lichtenberger, eds., *Bund und Tora: Zur theologischen Begriffsgeschichte in alttestamentlicher, frühjüdischer und urchristlicher Tradition* (WUNT 92; Tübingen: Mohr Siebeck, 1996) 25–40.

Eadem
"Abraham's Faith in the *One* God—A Motif of the Image of Abraham in Early Jewish Literature," in Hermann Lichtenberger and Ulrike Mittmann-Richert, eds., *Biblical Figures in Deuterocanonical and Cognate Perspective* (Deuterocanonical and Cognate Literature Yearbook 2008: Berlin: de Gruyter, 2009) 337–54.

Eadem
"Heilige Zeit—heiliger Raum—heiliger Mensch: Beobachtungen zur Struktur der Gesetzesbegründung in der Schöpfungs- und Paradiesgeschichte des Jubiläenbuchs," in Matthias Albani, Jörg Frey, and Armin Lange, eds., *Studies in the Book of Jubilees* (TSAJ 65; Tübingen: Mohr Siebeck, 1997) 207–19.

Eiss, Werner
"Das Wochenfest im Jubiläenbuch und im antiken Judentum," in Matthias Albani, Jörg Frey, and Armin Lange, eds., *Studies in the Book of Jubilees* (TSAJ 65; Tübingen: Mohr Siebeck, 1997) 165–78.

Elliger, Karl, and Wilhelm Rudolph, eds.
Biblia Hebraica Stuttgartensia (Stuttgart: Deutsche Bibelstiftung, 1977).

Emerton, J. A.
"An Examination of a Recent Structuralist Interpretation of Genesis XXXVIII," *VT* 26 (1976) 79–98.

Endres, John C.
Biblical Interpretation in the Book of Jubilees (CBQMS 18; Washington, DC: Catholic Biblical Association of America, 1987).

Idem
"Prayers in Jubilees," in Lynn LiDonnici and Andrea Lieber, eds., *Heavenly Tablets: Interpretation, Identity and Tradition in Ancient Judaism* (JSJSup 119; Leiden: Brill, 2007) 31–47.

Idem
"Rebekah's Prayer (*Jubilees* 25:11-23)," in Károly D. Dobos and Miklós Kőszeghy, eds., *With Wisdom as a Robe: Qumran and Other Jewish Studies in Honour of Ida Fröhlich* (Hebrew Bible Monographs 21; Sheffield: Sheffield Phoenix, 2009) 253–62.

Idem
"Revisiting the Rebekah of the Book of *Jubilees*," in Eric F. Mason, Kelley Coblentz Bautch, Angela Kim Harkins, and Daniel A. Machiela, eds., *A Teacher for All Generations: Essays in Honor of James C. VanderKam* (2 vols.; JSJSup 153/I-II; Leiden: Brill, 2012) 765–82.

Eppel, R.
"Les tables de la loi et les tables célestes," *RHPhR* 17 (1937) 401–12.

Epstein, A.
Beiträge zur Alterthumskunde, part 1: *Abhandlungen: Midrasch Tadsche, nach Handschriften edirt* (Vienna: Ch. D. Lippe, 1887). [Its title is מקדמוניות היהודים on a page further in; apparently this is replaced by *Beiträge zur Alterthumskunde.*]

Idem
"Le Livre des Jubilés, Philon, et le Midrasch Tadsché," *REJ* 20 (1890) 80–97; 22 (1891) 1–25.

Erho, Ted
"New Ethiopic Witnesses to Some Old Testament Pseudepigrapha," *BSO(A)S* 76 (2013) 75–97.

Eshel, Esther
"Demonology in Palestine During the Second Temple Period" (Diss., Hebrew University of Jerusalem, 2000).

Eadem
"The *Imago Mundi* of the *Genesis Apocryphon*," in Lynn LiDonnici and Andrea Lieber, eds., *Heavenly Tablets: Interpretation, Identity and Tradition in Ancient Judaism* (JSJSup 119; Leiden: Brill, 2007) 111–31.

Eadem
"Isaiah 11:15: A New Interpretation Based on the Genesis Apocryphon," *DSD* 13 (2006) 38–45.

Eadem
"*Jubilees* 32 and the Bethel Cult Traditions in Second Temple Literature," in Esther Chazon, David Satran, and Ruth Clements, eds., *Things Revealed: Studies in Early Jewish and Christian Literature in Honor of Michael E. Stone* (JSJSup 89; Leiden: Brill, 2004) 21–36.

Eadem
"Mastema's Attempt on Moses' Life in the 'Pseudo-Jubilees' Text from Masada," *DSD* 10 (2003) 359–64.

Eshel, Hanan
"*Megillat Ta'anit* in Light of Holidays Found in *Jubilees* and the *Temple Scroll*," *Meghillot* 3 (2005) 253–57.

Idem
"Three New Fragments from Qumran Cave 11," *DSD* 8 (2001) 1–8 (English version of "Three New Fragments from Cave 11 at Qumran," *Tarbiz* 68 [1998] 273–78).

Ewald, Heinrich
"Ueber die Aethiopischen Handschriften zu Tübingen," *Zeitschrift für die Kunde des Morgenlandes* 5 (1844) 164–201.

Fabricius, Johann Albert
"Parva Genesis," in his *Codex Pseudepigraphus Veteris Testamenti* (Hamburg and Leipzig: Liebezeit, 1713; 2nd ed., 1722) 849–64; vol. 2, Hamburg: Felginer, 1723, 120–22.

Falk, Daniel
"Dating the Watchers: What's at Stake?" *Hen* 31 (2009) 23–29.

Idem
The Parabiblical Texts: Strategies for Extending the Scriptures among the Dead Sea Scrolls (LSTS 63; Companion to the Qumran Scrolls 8; London: T&T Clark, 2007).

Finkelstein, Louis
"The Book of Jubilees and the Rabbinic Halaka," *HTR* 16 (1923) 39–61.

Idem
The Pharisees: The Sociological Background of Their Faith (3rd ed.; 2 vols.; The Morris Loeb Series; Philadelphia: Jewish Publication Society, 1962).

Idem
"Pre-Maccabean Documents in the Passover Haggadah," *HTR* 36 (1943) 1–38 (Appendix: "The Date of the Book of Jubilees," 19–24).

Idem
Review of C. Albeck, *Das Buch der Jubiläen und die Halacha*, *MGWJ* 76 (1932) 525–34.

Idem
"Some Examples of Maccabean Halaka," *JBL* 49 (1930) 21–25.

Fitzmyer, Joseph A.
The Acts of the Apostles: A New Translation with Introduction and Commentary (AB 31; New York: Doubleday, 1998).

Idem
The Genesis Apocryphon of Qumran Cave 1 (1Q20): A Commentary (3rd rev. ed.; BibOr 18B; Rome: Pontifical Biblical Institute, 2004).

Idem
The Gospel according to Luke I–IX: A New Translation with Introduction and Commentary (AB 28; New York: Doubleday, 1981).

Idem
The Gospel according to Luke X–XXIV: A New Translation with Introduction and Commentary (AB 28A; New York: Doubleday, 1985).

Idem
"Zu Jub 13,10-16," *BO* 18 (1966) 14.

Flint, Peter W., and James C. VanderKam
The Dead Sea Scrolls after Fifty Years: A Comprehensive Assessment (2 vols.; Leiden: Brill, 1998, 1999).

Flusser, David
Judaism and the Origins of Christianity (Jerusalem: Magnes Press, 1988).

Fraade, Steven
Enosh and His Generation: Pre-Israelite Hero and History in Postbiblical Interpretation (SBLMS 30; Chico, CA: Scholars Press, 1984).

Francis, Michael
"Defining the Excluded Middle: The Case of Ishmael in *Jubilees*," *JSP* 21 (2012) 259–83.

Frankel, Zecharias
"Das Buch der Jubiläen," *MGWJ* 5 (1856) 311–16, 380–400.

Franxman, Thomas W.
Genesis and the "Jewish Antiquities" of Flavius Josephus (BibOr 35; Rome: Biblical Institute Press, 1979).

Freedman, Harry, and Maurice Simon, eds.
Midrash Rabbah (10 vols.; 3rd ed.; London/New York: Soncino, 1983).

Frevel, Christian
"Molech und Mischehen: Zu einigen Aspekten der Rezeption von Gen 34 in Jub 30," in Ulrich Dahmen and J. Schnocks, eds., *Juda und Jerusalem in der Seleukidenzeit: Herrschaft–Widerstand–Identität* (BBB 159; Göttingen: Vandenhoeck & Ruprecht, 2010) 161–87.

Idem
"'Separate Yourself from the Gentiles' (*Jubilees* 22:16): Intermarriage in the Book of *Jubilees*," in Christian Frevel, ed., *Mixed Marriages: Intermarriage and Group Identity in the Second Temple Period* (LHBOTS 547; London: T&T Clark, 2011) 220–50.

Frey, J. B.
"Apocryphes de l'Ancien Testament. 2. Le Livre des Jubilés," in Louis Pirot and André Robert, eds., *Dictionnaire de la Bible* (Paris: Letouzey et Ané, 1928) 1:371–79.

Frey, Jörg
"Zum Weltbild im Jubiläenbuch," in Matthias Albani, Jörg Frey, and Armin Lange, eds., *Studies in the Book of Jubilees* (TSAJ 65; Tübingen: Mohr Siebeck, 1997) 261–92.

Friedlander, Gerald
Pirḳê de Rabbi Eliezer (1916; repr., New York: Hermon, 1970).

Frishman, Judith, and Lucas van Rompay, eds.
The Book of Genesis in Jewish and Oriental Christian Interpretation (Traditio Exegetica Graeca 5; Louvain: Peeters, 1997).

Fuchs, G.
"Die Versuchung Abrahams im äthiopischen Jubiläenbuch (*Maṣḥafa Kufālē*)," in Stefan Beyerle, Axel Graupner, and Udo Rüterswörden, eds., *Viele Wege zu den Einen: Historische Bibelkritik–Die Vitalität der Glaubensüberlieferung in der Moderne* (Biblisch-theologische Studien 121; Neukirchen-Vluyn: Neukirchener Verlag, 2012), 193–212.

Fujita, Shozo
"The Metaphor of Plant in Jewish Literature of the Intertestamental Period," *JSJ* 7 (1976) 30–45.

Furstenberg, Yair
Purity and Community in Antiquity: Traditions of the Law from Second Temple Judaism to the Mishnah (Jerusalem: Magnes Press, 2016).

García Martínez, Florentino
"4QMess Ar and the *Book of Noah*," in idem, *Qumran and Apocalyptic: Studies on the Aramaic Texts from Qumran* (STDJ 9; Leiden: Brill, 1992) 1–44.

Idem
"The Heavenly Tablets in the Book of Jubilees," in Matthias Albani, Jörg Frey, and Armin Lange, eds., *Studies in the Book of Jubilees* (TSAJ 65; Tübingen: Mohr Siebeck, 1997) 243–60.

Idem
"Man and Woman: Halakhah Based upon Eden in the Dead Sea Scrolls," in Gerard Luttikhuizen, ed., *Paradise Interpreted: Representations of Biblical Paradise in Judaism and Christianity* (TBN 2; Leiden: Brill, 1999) 95–115.

Idem
"Las tablas celestes en el libro de los Giubileos," *Miscelanea Comillas* 41 (1983) 333–49.

García Martínez, Florentino, Eibert J. C. Tigchelaar, and Adam S. van der Woude, eds.
Qumran Cave 11.II: 11Q2–18, 11Q20–31 (DJD 23; Oxford: Clarendon, 1998).

Gaster, Moses
The Chronicles of Jerahmeel (Oriental Translation Fund; London: Royal Asiatic Society, 1899; repr., *The Chronicles of Jerahmeel: or, The Hebrew Bible Historiale* [Prolegomenon by Haim Schwarzbaum; New York: Ktav, 1971]).

Geist, Andrew, and James VanderKam
"Four Places That Belong to the Lord (*Jubilees* 4.26)," *JSP* 22 (2012) 146–62.

Gelzer, Heinrich
"Die apokryphischen Reste der Byzantiner und ihre Abstammung aus Pandorus und Africanus," in idem, *Sextus Julius Africanus und die byzantinische Chronographie*, vol. 2: *Die Nachfolger des Julius Africanus* (Leipzig: Teubner, 1885) 249–97.

Gilders, William K.
"Blood and Covenant: Interpretive Elaboration on Genesis 9.4-6 in the Book of *Jubilees*," *JSP* 15 (2006) 83–118.

Idem
Blood Ritual in the Hebrew Bible: Meaning and Power (Baltimore: Johns Hopkins University Press, 2004).

Idem
"The Concept of Covenant in Jubilees," in Gabriele Boccaccini and Giovanni Ibba, eds., *Enoch and the Mosaic Torah: The Evidence of Jubilees* (Grand Rapids: Eerdmans, 2009) 178–92.

Idem
"Where Did Noah Place the Blood? A Textual Note on *Jubilees* 7:4," *JBL* 124 (2005) 745–49.

Ginzberg, Louis
The Legends of the Jews (7 vols.; Philadelphia: Jewish Publication Society of America, 1909–38; repr., Baltimore: Johns Hopkins University Press, 1998).

Idem
"Libro dei Giubilei 16,30," *Revista Israelitica* 5 (1908) 74.

Idem
An Unknown Jewish Sect (Moreshet Series 1; New York: Jewish Theological Seminary of America, 1970 [German original, 1922]).

Glessmer, Uwe
"Calendars in the Dead Sea Scrolls," in Peter Flint and James VanderKam, eds., *The Dead Sea Scrolls after Fifty Years: A Comprehensive Assessment* (2 vols.; Leiden: Brill, 1998, 1999) 2:213–78.

Idem
"Explizite Aussagen über kalendarische Konflikte im Jubiläenbuch: Jub 6, 22-32.33-38," in Matthias Albani, Jörg Frey, and Armin Lange, eds., *Studies in the Book of Jubilees* (TSAJ 65; Tübingen: Mohr Siebeck, 1997) 127–64.

Goldingay, John
Psalms, vol. 2: *Psalms 42–89* (Baker Commentary on the Old Testament Wisdom and Psalms; Grand Rapids: Baker Academic, 2007).

Goldmann, Moshe
"The Book of Jubilees," in Avraham Kahana, ed., *The Apocryphal Books* (2 vols.; 1956; repr., Jerusalem: Maqor, 1970) 1:216–313.

Goldstein, Jonathan
"The Date of the Book of Jubilees," *PAAJR* 50 (1983) 63–86. Reprinted in Jonathan Goldstein, *Semites, Iranians, Greeks and Romans* (BJS 217; Atlanta: Scholars Press, 1990) 161–80.

Görtz-Wrisberg, I. von
"No Second Temple—No Shavuot? The Book of Jubilees as a Case Study," in Birger Olsson and Magnus Zetterholm, eds., *The Ancient Synagogue from Its Origins until 200 C.E.: Papers Presented at an International Conference at Lund University, October 14–17, 2001* (ConBNT 39; Stockholm: Almqvist & Wiksell International, 2003) 376–402.

Goudoever, J. van
Biblical Calendars (2nd ed.; Leiden: Brill, 1961).

Grabbe, Lester
Etymology in Early Jewish Interpretation: The Hebrew Names in Philo (BJS 115; Atlanta: Scholars Press, 1988).

Greenberg, Moshe
Biblical Prose Prayers as a Window to the Popular Religion of Ancient Israel (The Taubman Lectures in Jewish Studies, 6th Series; Berkeley: University of California Press, 1983).

Greenfield, Jonas, Michael Stone, and Esther Eshel
The Aramaic Levi Document: Edition, Translation, Commentary (SVTP 19; Leiden: Brill, 2004).

Gregory, Bradley
"The Death and Legacy of Leah in Jubilees," *JSP* 17 (2008) 99–120.

Grelot, Pierre
"Hénoch et ses écritures," *RB* 92 (1975) 481–500.

Idem
"Jean 8,56 et Jubilés 16,16-29," *RevQ* 13/49–52 (1988) 621–28.

Idem
"Le Livre des Jubilés et Le Testament de Levi," in Pierre Casetti, Othmar Keel, and Adrien Schenker, eds., *Mélanges Dominique Barthélemy: Études bibliques offertes à l'occasion de son 60e anniversaire* (OBO 38; Göttingen: Vandenhoeck & Ruprecht, 1981) 109–33.

Idem
"Notes sur le Testament Araméen de Lévi," *RB* 63 (1956) 391–406.

Grossfeld, Bernard
The Targum Onqelos to Exodus (ArBib 7; Wilmington, DE: Michael Glazier, 1988).

Idem
The Targum Onqelos to Genesis (ArBib 6; Wilmington, DE: Michael Glazier, 1988).

Grossman, Maxine
"Affective Masculinity: The Gender of the Patriarchs in Jubilees," *Hen* 31 (2009) 91–97.

Gunkel, Hermann
Genesis (trans. Mark E. Biddle; Mercer Library of Biblical Studies; Macon, GA: Mercer University Press, 1997; translated from the 9th German printing, 1977 = 3rd ed., 1910).

Hadas, Moses
"Jub 16:30," *AJSL* 49 (1933) 338.

Hafemann, Scott J.
"Moses in the Apocrypha and Pseudepigrapha: A Survey," *JSP* 7 (1990) 79–104.

Hagedorn, D.
"Die 'Kleine Genesis' in P.Oxy. LXIII 4365," *Zeitschrift für Papyrologie und Epigraphik* 116 (1997) 147–48.

Haile, Getatchew
"The Homily of Aṣe Zärʾa Yaʿəqob of Ethiopia in Honour of Saturday," *OLP* 13 (1982) 185–231.

Hakham, A.
The Book of Isaiah (2 vols.; Daʿat Miqraʾ; Jerusalem: Mossad Harav Kook, 1984).

Halpern-Amaru, Betsy
"Bilhah and Naphtali in Jubilees: A Note on 4QTNaphtali," *DSD* 6 (1999) 1–10.

Eadem
"Burying the Fathers: Exegetical Strategies and Source Traditions in *Jubilees* 46," in Esther Chazon, Devorah Dimant, and Ruth Clements, eds., *Reworking the Bible: Apocryphal and Related Texts at Qumran* (STDJ 58; Leiden: Brill, 2005) 135–52.

Eadem
The Empowerment of Women in the Book of Jubilees (JSJSup 60; Leiden: Brill, 1999).

Eadem
"Exile and Return in *Jubilees*," in James M. Scott, ed., *Exile: Old Testament, Jewish and Christian Conceptions* (JSJSup 56; Leiden: Brill, 1997) 127–44.

Eadem
"The Festivals of Pesaḥ and Maṣṣot in the Book of Jubilees," in Gabriele Boccaccini and Giovanni Ibba, eds., *Enoch and the Mosaic Torah: The Evidence of Jubilees* (Grand Rapids: Eerdmans, 2009) 309–22.

Eadem
"The First Woman, Wives, and Mothers in *Jubilees*," *JBL* 113 (1994) 609–26.

Eadem
"Flavius Josephus and *The Book of Jubilees*: A Question of Source," *HUCA* 72 (2001) 15–44.

Eadem
"Joy as Piety in the 'Book of Jubilees,'" *JJS* 56 (2005) 185–205.

Eadem
"The Naming of Levi in the Book of Jubilees," in Esther G. Chazon and Michael E. Stone, eds., *Pseudepigraphic Perspectives: The Apocrypha and Pseudepigrapha in Light of the Dead Sea Scrolls. Proceedings of the International Symposium of the Orion Center, 12–14 January 1997* (STDJ 31; Leiden: Brill, 1999) 59–69.

Eadem
"A Note on Isaac as First-Born in *Jubilees* and Only Son in 4Q225," *DSD* 13 (2006) 127–33.

Eadem
The Perspective from Mt. Sinai: The Book of Jubilees and the Exodus (JAJSup 21; Göttingen: Vandenhoeck & Ruprecht, 2015).

Eadem
"The Portrait of Sarah in Jubilees," in Ulf Haxen, Hanne Trautner-Kromann, and Karen Lisa Goldschmidt Salamon, eds., *Jewish Studies in a New Europe: Proceedings of the Fifth Congress of Jewish Studies in Copenhagen 1994 under the auspices of the European Association for Jewish Studies* (Copenhagen: C. A. Rietzel, 1998) 336-48.

Eadem
"Protection from Birds in the *Book of Jubilees*," in Aren Maeir, Jodi Magness, and Lawrence Schiffman, eds., *'Go Out and Study the Land' (Judges 18:2): Archaeological, Historical and Textual Studies in Honor of Hanan Eshel* (JSJSup 148; Leiden: Brill, 2012) 59-67.

Eadem
Rewriting the Bible: Land and Covenant in Post-Biblical Jewish Literature (Valley Forge, PA: Trinity Press International, 1994).

Eadem
"The Use of Bible in *Jubilees* 49: The Time and Date of the Pesaḥ Celebration," *Meghillot* 5-6 (2007) 81-100.

Hamidović, David
Les traditions du Jubilé à Qumrân (Paris: Geuthner, 2007).

Hamilton, Victor P.
The Book of Genesis: Chapters 1-17 (NICOT; Grand Rapids: Eerdmans, 1990).

Idem
The Book of Genesis: Chapters 18-50 (NICOT; Grand Rapids: Eerdmans, 1995).

Hanneken, Todd
"Angels and Demons in the Book of Jubilees and Contemporary Apocalypses," *Hen* 28 (2006) 11-25.

Idem
"Moses Has His Interpreters: Understanding the Legal Exegesis in Acts 15 from the Precedent in Jubilees," *CBQ* 77 (2015) 686-706.

Idem
"The Sin of the Gentiles: The Prohibition of Eating Blood in the Book of *Jubilees*," *JSJ* 46 (2015) 1-27.

Idem
"The Status and Interpretation of *Jubilees* in 4Q390," in Eric F. Mason, Kelley Coblentz Bautch, Angela Kim Harkins, and Daniel A. Machiela, eds., *A Teacher for All Generations: Essays in Honor of James C. VanderKam* (2 vols.; JSJSup 153/I-II; Leiden: Brill, 2012) 407-28.

Idem
The Subversion of the Apocalypses in the Book of Jubilees (SBLEJL 34; Atlanta: Society of Biblical Literature, 2012).

Idem
"The Watchers in Rewritten Scripture: The Use of the *Book of the Watchers* in *Jubilees*," in Angela Harkins, Kelley Coblentz Bautch, and John Endres, eds., *The Fallen Angels Traditions: Second Temple Developments and Reception History* (CBQMS 53; Washington, DC: Catholic Biblical Association of America, 2014) 25-68.

Hanson, Paul D.
The Dawn of Apocalyptic: The Historical and Sociological Roots of Jewish Apocalyptic Eschatology (rev. ed.; Philadelphia: Fortress Press, 1979).

Harrington, Daniel J., and Maurya P. Horgan
"Palestinian Adaptations of Biblical Narratives and Prophecies: The Bible Rewritten (Narratives)," in Robert A. Kraft and George W. E. Nickelsburg, eds., *Early Judaism and Its Modern Interpreters* (Bible and Its Modern Interpreters 2; Philadelphia: Fortress Press, 1986).

Hartom, Eliyahu S.
"The Book of Jubilees," in *The Apocryphal Literature* (7 vols.; 3rd ed.; Tel Aviv: Yavneh, 1969) 5b.7-147.

Hayes, Christine E.
Gentile Impurities and Jewish Identities: Intermarriage and Conversion from the Bible to the Talmud (New York: Oxford University Press, 2002).

Eadem
"Intermarriage and Impurity in Ancient Jewish Sources," *HTR* 92 (1999) 3-36.

Eadem
"The Midrashic Career of the Confession of Judah (Genesis xxxviii 26), Part I: The Extra-Canonical Texts, Targums and Other Versions," *VT* 45 (1995) 62-81.

Eadem
"The Midrashic Career of the Confession of Judah (Genesis xxxviii 26), Part II: The Rabbinic Midrashim," *VT* 45 (1995) 174-87.

Hayward, C. T. R.
"Genesis and Its Reception in *Jubilees*," in Craig A. Evans, Joel N. Lohr, and David L. Petersen, eds., *The Book of Genesis: Composition, Reception, and Interpretation* (VTSup 152; Leiden: Brill, 2012) 375-404.

Idem
"Jacob's Second Visit to Bethel in Targum Pseudo-Jonathan," in Philip R. Davies and Richard T. White, eds., *A Tribute to Géza Vermès: Essays on Jewish and Christian Literature and History* (JSOTSup 100; Sheffield: JSOT Press, 1990) 175-92.

Idem
Jerome's Hebrew Questions on Genesis (Oxford Early Christian Studies; Oxford: Clarendon, 1995).

Idem
"The Present State of Research into the Targumic Account of the Sacrifice of Isaac," *JJS* 32 (1981) 127-50.

Hayward, Robert
"The Sanctification of Time in Second Temple Judaism: Case Studies in the Septuagint and Jubilees," in Stephen C. Barton, ed., *Holiness: Past and Present* (London: T&T Clark, 2003) 141-67.

Heine, R. E.
Origen: Homilies on Genesis and Exodus (FC 71; Washington, DC: Catholic University of America Press, 1982).

Heinemann, Joseph
"210 Years of Egyptian Exile: A Study in Midrashic Chronology," *JJS* 22 (1971) 19-30.

Hellerman, Joseph
"Purity and Nationalism in Second Temple Literature: 1-2 Maccabees and *Jubilees*," *JETS* 46 (2003) 401-21.

Hempel, Charlotte
"The Place of the *Book of Jubilees* at Qumran and Beyond," in Timothy Lim, ed., *The Dead Sea Scrolls in Their Historical Context* (Edinburgh: T&T Clark, 2000) 187-96.

Hendel, Ronald S.
"4Q252 and the Flood Chronology of Genesis 7-8: A Text-Critical Solution," *DSD* 2 (1995) 72-79.

Idem
The Text of Genesis 1-11: Textual Studies and Critical Edition (Oxford: Oxford University Press, 1998).

Hengel, Martin
Judaism and Hellenism: Studies in Their Encounter in Palestine during the Early Hellenistic Period (2 vols.; Philadelphia: Fortress Press, 1974).

Henten, Jan W. van
"Mastemah משטמה," in *DDD*², 553-54.

Herrmann, Albert
Die Erdkarte der Urbibel mit einem Anhang über Tartessos und die Etruskerfrage (Braunschweig: Georg Westermann, 1931).

Hilgert, Earl
"The Jubilees Calendar and the Origin of Sunday Observance," *AUSS* 1 (1963) 44-51.

Hilhorst, Antonius
"Erwähnt P. Oxy. LXIII 4365 das Jubiläenbuch?" *Zeitschrift für Papyrologie und Epigraphik* 130 (2000) 192.

Hillel, Vered
"Demonstrable Instances of the Use of Sources in the Pseudepigrapha," in Charlotte Hempel, ed., *The Dead Sea Scrolls: Texts and Context* (STDJ 90; Leiden: Brill, 2010) 325-37.

Himmelfarb, Martha
"Earthly Sacrifice and Heavenly Incense: The Law of the Priesthood in *Aramaic Levi* and *Jubilees*," in Ra'anan Boustan and Annette Yoshiko Reed, eds., *Heavenly Realms and Earthly Realities in Late Antique Religions* (Cambridge: Cambridge University Press, 2004) 103-22.

Eadem
"Jubilees and Sectarianism," in *Enoch and Qumran Origins: New Light on a Forgotten Connection* (Grand Rapids: Eerdmans, 2005) 129-31.

Eadem
A Kingdom of Priests: Ancestry and Merit in Ancient Judaism (Jewish Culture and Contexts; Philadelphia: University of Pennsylvania Press, 2006).

Eadem
"Levi, Phinehas, and the Problem of Intermarriage at the Time of the Maccabean Revolt," *JSQ* 6 (1999) 1-24.

Eadem
"Sexual Relations and Purity in the Temple Scroll and the Book of Jubilees," *DSD* 6 (1999) 11-36.

Eadem
"Some Echoes of Jubilees in Medieval Hebrew Literature," in John Reeves, ed., *Tracing the Threads: Studies in the Vitality of the Jewish Pseudepigrapha* (SBLEJL 6; Atlanta: Scholars Press, 1994) 127-35.

Eadem
"Torah, Testimony, and Heavenly Tablets: The Claim to Authority in the *Book of Jubilees*," in Benjamin Wright., ed., *A Multiform Heritage: Studies on Early Judaism and Christianity in Honor of Robert A. Kraft* (Scholars Press Homage Series 24; Atlanta: Scholars Press, 1999) 19-29.

Hoenig, Sidney B.
"The Designated Number of Kinds of Labor Prohibited on the Sabbath," *JQR* 68 (1978) 193-217.

Idem
"The Jubilees Calendar and the 'Days of Assembly,'" in Abraham I. Katsh and Leon Nemoy, eds., *Essays on the Occasion of the Seventieth Anniversary of the Dropsie University* (Philadelphia: Dropsie University, 1979) 189-207.

Hoffmann, Paul
Die Toten in Christus: Eine religionsgeschichtliche und exegetische Untersuchung zur paulinischen Eschatologie (NTAbh n.F. 2; Münster: Aschendorff, 1966).

Holladay, Carl
Fragments from Hellenistic Jewish Authors (4 vols.; SBLTT 20, 30, 39-40; Atlanta: Scholars Press, 1983-96).

Holladay, William L.
Jeremiah: A Commentary on the Book of the Prophet Jeremiah (2 vols.; Hermeneia; Minneapolis: Fortress Press, 1986, 1989).

Hollander, Harm W., and Marinus de Jonge
The Testaments of the Twelve Patriarchs: A Commentary (SVTP 8; Leiden: Brill, 1985).

Hölscher, Gustav
Drei Erdkarten: Ein Beitrag zur Erdkenntnis des hebräischen Altertums (Sitzungsberichte der Heidelberger Akademie der Wissenschaften, Philosophisch-historische Klasse, 1944-48; Heidelberg: Carl Winter, Universitäts-Verlag, 1949).

Hopkins, Jamal-Dominique
"The Authoritative Status of Jubilees at Qumran," *Hen* 31 (2009) 97-104.

Idem
"Hebrew Patriarchs in the Book of *Jubilees*: A Descriptive Analysis as an Interpretative Methodology," in Károly D. Dobos and Miklós Kőszeghy, eds., *With Wisdom as a Robe: Qumran and Other Jewish Studies in Honour of Ida Fröhlich*

(Hebrew Bible Monographs 21; Sheffield: Sheffield Phoenix, 2009) 239-52.

Horgan, Maurya P.
Pesharim: Qumran Interpretations of Biblical Books (CBQMS 8; Washington, DC: Catholic Biblical Association of America, 1979).

Houtman, Cornelis
Exodus (3 vols.; Historical Commentary on the Old Testament; Kampen: Kok, 1993, 1996 [vols. 1-2]; Louvain: Peeters, 2006 [vol. 3]).

Hughes, Jeremy
Secrets of the Times: Myth and History in Biblical Chronology (JSOTSup 66; Sheffield: JSOT Press, 1990).

Huizenga, Loren A.
"The Battle for Isaac: Exploring the Composition and Function of the *Aqedah* in the Book of *Jubilees*," *JSP* 13 (2002) 33-59.

Hultgård, Anders
L'eschatologie des Testaments des Douze Patriarches, vol. 1: *Interprétation des textes* (Acta Universitatis Upsaliensis Historia Religionum 6; Uppsala: Almqvist & Wiksell, 1977).

Ibba, Giovanni
"The Evil Spirits in Jubilees and the Spirits of the Bastards in 4Q510 with Some Remarks on Other Qumran Manuscripts," *Hen* 31 (2009) 111-16.

Ilan, Tal
"Biblical Women's Names in the Apocryphal Traditions," *JSP* 11 (1993) 3-67.

Isaiah, Abraham ben, and Benjamin Scharfman
The Pentateuch and Rashi's Commentary (5 vols.; Brooklyn, NY: S. S. & R., 1949-50).

Jacob, Benno
The Second Book of the Bible: Exodus (Hoboken, NJ: Ktav, 1992).

Jacobson, Howard
A Commentary on Pseudo-Philo's Liber Antiquitatum Biblicarum *with Latin Text and English Translation* (2 vols.; AGJU 31; Leiden: Brill, 1996).

Jacobus, Helen R.
"The Curse of Cainan (Jub. 8.1-5): Genealogies in Genesis 5 and Genesis 11 and a Mathematical Pattern," *JSP* 18 (2009) 207-32.

Japhet, Sara
I & II Chronicles: A Commentary (OTL; Louisville: Westminster John Knox, 1993).

Jassen, Alex P.
Scripture and Law in the Dead Sea Scrolls (Cambridge: Cambridge University Press, 2014).

Jaubert, Annie
"Le calendrier des Jubilés et les jours liturgiques de la semaine," *VT* 7 (1957) 35-61.

Eadem
"Le calendrier des Jubilés et la secte de Qumrân: Ses origines bibliques," *VT* 3 (1953) 250-64.

Eadem
La date de la cène: Calendrier biblique et liturgie chrétienne (Paris: Librairie LeCoffre, 1957); Eng. trans., *The Date of the Last Supper: The Biblical Calendar and Christian Liturgy* (trans. I. Rafferty; New York: Society of St. Paul, 1965).

Eadem
"Jésus et le calendrier de Qumrân," *NTS* 7 (1960-61) 1-22.

Eadem
La notion d'alliance dans le Judaïsme (Patristica Sorbonensia 6; Paris: Seuil, 1963).

Jellinek, Adolph
Bet ha-Midrasch: Sammlung kleiner Midraschim und vermischter Abhandlungen aus der ältern jüdischen Literatur (2 vols., 6 parts; Leipzig: C. W. Vollrath, 1855; repr., Jerusalem: Wahrmann, 1967).

Jervell, Jacob
Imago Dei: Gen 1, 26f. im Spätjudentum, in der Gnosis und in den paulinischen Briefen (FRLANT 76; Göttingen: Vandenhoeck & Ruprecht, 1960).

Jones, F. Stanley
An Ancient Jewish Christian Source on the History of Christianity: Pseudo-Clementine Recognitions 1.27-71 (SBLTT 37, Christian Apocrypha Series 2; Atlanta: Scholars Press, 1995).

Jonge, Marinus de, and Johannes Tromp
"Jacob's Son Levi in the Old Testament Pseudepigrapha and Related Literature," in M. Stone and T. Bergren, eds., *Biblical Figures outside the Bible* (Harrisburg, PA: Trinity Press International, 1998) 203-36.

Kahana, Avraham, ed.
The Apocryphal Books (2 vols.; Jerusalem: Maqor, 1969-70).

Kawashima, Robert S.
"The Jubilee, Every 49 or 50 Years?" *VT* 53 (2003) 117-20.

Kim, Angela
"Cain and Abel in the Light of Envy: A Study in the History of the Interpretation of Envy in Genesis 4:1-16," *JSP* 12 (2001) 65-84.

Kister, Menahem
"5Q13 and the *'Avodah*: A Historical Survey and Its Significance," *DSD* 8 (2004) 136-48.

Idem
"Ancient Material in *Pirqe de-Rabbi Eli'ezer*: Basilides, Qumran, the *Book of Jubilees*," in Aren M. Maeir, Jodi Magness, and Lawrence Schiffman, eds., *'Go Out and Study the Land' (Judges 18:2): Archaeological, Historical and Textual Studies in Honor of Hanan Eshel* (JSJSup 148; Leiden: Brill, 2012) 69-93.

Idem
"Biblical Phrases and Hidden Biblical Interpretations and *Pesharim*," in Devorah Dimant and Uriel Rappaport, eds., *The Dead Sea Scrolls: Forty Years of Research* (STDJ 10; Leiden: Brill, 1992) 27-39.

Idem
"Body and Purification from Evil: Prayer Formulas and Concepts in Second Temple Literature and Their Relationship to Later Rabbinic Literature," *Meghillot* 8-9 (2010) 243-84.

Idem
"Commentary to 4Q298," *JQR* 85 (1994) 237-49.

Idem
"Newly-Identified Fragments of the Book of Jubilees: Jub. 23:21-23, 30-31," *RevQ* 12 (1987) 529-36.

Idem
"Observations on Aspects of Exegesis, Tradition, and Theology in Midrash, Pseudepigrapha, and Other Jewish Writings," in John C. Reeves, ed., *Tracing the Threads: Studies in the Vitality of Jewish Pseudepigrapha* (SBLEJL 6; Atlanta: Scholars Press, 1994) 1-34.

Idem
"On Good and Evil: The Theological Foundations of the Qumran Community," in idem, ed., *The Qumran Scrolls and Their World* (2 vols.; Between Bible and Mishnah; Jerusalem: Yitshaq ben Zvi, 2009) 2:497-528.

Idem, ed.
Qumran Scrolls and Their World (2 vols.; Between Bible and Mishnah; Jerusalem: Yitshaq Ben-Zvi, 2009).

Idem
"Some Aspects of Qumran Halakhah," in Julio Trebolle Barrera and Luis Vegas Montaner, eds., *The Madrid Qumran Congress: Proceedings of the International Congress on the Dead Sea Scrolls, Madrid, 18-21 March, 1991* (2 vols.; STDJ 11; Leiden: Brill, 1992) 2:571-88.

Idem
"Some Observations on Vocabulary and Style in the Dead Sea Scrolls," in Takamitsu Muraoka and John F. Elwolde, eds., *Diggers at the Well: Proceedings of the Third International Symposium on the Hebrew of the Dead Sea Scrolls and Ben Sira* (STDJ 36; Leiden: Brill, 2000) 137-65.

Idem
"Studies on MMT and Its World: Law, Theology, Language, and Calendar," *Tarbiz* 68 (1999) 360-63.

Idem
"Syncellus and the Sources of *Jubilees* 3: A Note on M. Segal's Article," *Meghillot* 1 (2003) 127-33.

Idem
"*Tohu wa-Bohu*, Primordial Elements and *Creatio ex Nihilo*," *JSQ* 14 (2007) 229-56.

Idem
"Towards the History of the Essene Sect: Studies in the Animal Apocalypse, the Book of Jubilees, and the Damascus Document," *Tarbiz* 56 (1986-87) 1-18.

Idem
"Two Formulae in the Book of Jubilees," *Tarbiz* 70 (2001) 289-300.

Klawans, Jonathan
Impurity and Sin in Ancient Judaism (Oxford: Oxford University Press, 2000).

Idem
"The Impurity of Immorality in Ancient Judaism," *JJS* 48 (1997) 1-16.

Klein, S.
"Palästinisches im Jubiläenbuch," *ZDPV* 57 (1934) 7-27.

Knibb, Michael
"Jubilees and the Origins of the Qumran Community," An Inaugural Lecture Delivered in the Department of Biblical Studies, King's College (London, January 17, 1989).

Idem
"A Note on 4Q372 and 4Q390," in Florentino García Martínez, A. Hilhorst, and C. J. Labuschagne, eds., *The Scriptures and the Scrolls: Studies in Honour of A. S. van der Woude on the Occasion of His 65th Birthday* (Leiden: Brill, 1992) 164-77.

Idem
"Which Parts of *1 Enoch* Were Known to *Jubilees*? A Note on the Interpretation of *Jubilees* 4.16-25," in J. Cheryl Exum and Hugh G. M. Williamson, eds., *Reading from Right to Left: Essays on the Hebrew Bible in Honour of David J. A. Clines* (JSOTSup 373; Sheffield: Sheffield Academic Press, 2003) 254-62.

Knoppers, Gary
1 Chronicles 10-29: A New Translation with Introduction and Commentary (AB 12A; New York: Doubleday, 2004).

Knowles, Michael P.
"Abram and the Birds in *Jubilees* 11: A Subtext for the Parable of the Sower," *NTS* 41 (1995) 145-51.

Koch, Klaus
"Die mysteriösen Zahlen der judäischen Könige und die apokalyptischen Jahrwochen," *VT* 28 (1978) 433-41.

Krašovec, Jože
Reward, Punishment, and Forgiveness: The Thinking and Beliefs of Ancient Israel in the Light of Greek and Modern Views (VTSup 78; Leiden: Brill, 1999).

Kraus, Hans-Joachim
Psalms 1-59: A Commentary (Minneapolis: Augsburg, 1988).

Krüger, M. J.
"Die Chronologie im Buche der Jubiläen, auf ihre biblische Grundlage zurückgeführt und berichtigt," *ZDMG* 12 (1858) 279-99.

Kugel, James L.
"4Q369 'Prayer of Enosh' and Ancient Biblical Interpretation," *DSD* 5 (1998) 119-48.

Idem
The Bible As It Was (Cambridge, MA: Belknap Press of Harvard University Press, 1997).

Idem
"Biblical Apocrypha and Pseudepigrapha and the Hebrew of the Second Temple Period," in Takamitsu Muraoka and John F. Elwolde, eds., *Diggers at the Well: Proceedings of the Third International Symposium on the Hebrew of the Dead Sea Scrolls and Ben Sira* (STDJ 36; Leiden: Brill, 2000) 166–77.

Idem
"Biblical Interpretation at Qumran," in Menahem Kister, ed., *The Qumran Scrolls and Their World* (2 vols.; Between Bible and Mishnah; Jerusalem: Yitshaq Ben-Zvi, 2009).

Idem
The Compositional History of the Book of *Jubilees*," *RevQ* 26/104 (2014) 517–37.

Idem
"Exegetical Notes on 4Q225 'Pseudo-Jubilees,'" *DSD* 13 (2006) 73–98.

Idem
"The Figure of Moses in *Jubilees*," *Hebrew Bible and Ancient Israel* 1 (2012) 77–92.

Idem
"How Old Is the *Aramaic Levi Document*?," in idem, *A Walk through* Jubilees: *Studies in the* Book of Jubilees *and the World of Its Creation* (JSJSup 156; Leiden: Brill, 2012) 343–64.

Idem
In Potiphar's House: The Interpretive Life of Biblical Texts (San Francisco: HarperSanFrancisco, 1990; 2nd ed., Cambridge, MA: Harvard University Press, 1994).

Idem
"Is the Book of Jubilees a Commentary on Genesis or an Intended Replacement?," in Christl M. Maier, ed., *Congress Volume: Munich 2013* (VTSup 163; Leiden: Brill, 2014) 67–91.

Idem
"Jubilees," in *Outside the Bible: Ancient Jewish Writings Related to Scripture*, ed. Louis H. Feldman, James L. Kugel, and Lawrence H. Schiffman (3 vols.; Philadelphia: Jewish Publication Society, 2013) 1:272–465.

Idem
"The Jubilees Apocalypse," *DSD* 1 (1994) 322–37.

Idem
"*Jubilees*, Philo, and the Problem of Genesis," in N. David, Armin Lange, Kristin De Troyer, and Shani Tzoref, eds., *The Hebrew Bible in Light of the Dead Sea Scrolls* (FRLANT 239; Göttingen: Vandenhoeck & Ruprecht, 2012) 295–311.

Idem
The Ladder of Jacob: Ancient Interpretations of the Biblical Story of Jacob and His Children (Princeton: Princeton University Press, 2006).

Idem
"Levi's Elevation to the Priesthood in Second Temple Writings," *HTR* 86 (1993) 1–64.

Idem
"A Note on Divine Names and Epithets in the Book of *Jubilees*," in Eric F. Mason, Kelley Coblentz Bautch, Angela Kim Harkins, and Daniel A. Machiela, eds., *A Teacher for All Generations: Essays in Honor of James C. VanderKam* (2 vols.; JSJSup 153/I-II; Leiden: Brill, 2012) 754–63.

Idem
"On the Interpolations in the *Book of Jubilees*," *RevQ* 94 (2009) 215–72.

Idem
"Reuben's Sin with Bilhah in the Testament of Reuben," in David Wright, David N. Freedman, and Avi Hurvitz, eds., *Pomegranates and Golden Bells: Studies in Biblical, Jewish, and Near Eastern Ritual, Law, and Literature in Honor of Jacob Milgrom* (Winona Lake, IN: Eisenbrauns, 1995) 525–54.

Idem
"The Story of Dinah in the *Testament of Levi*," *HTR* 85 (1992) 1–34.

Idem
Traditions of the Bible: A Guide to the Bible as It Was at the Start of the Common Era (Cambridge, MA: Harvard University Press, 1998).

Idem
A Walk through Jubilees: *Studies in the* Book of Jubilees *and the World of Its Creation* (JSJSup 156; Leiden: Brill, 2012).

Idem
"Which Is Older, *Jubilees* or the *Genesis Apocryphon*?," in *A Walk through* Jubilees: *Studies in the* Book of Jubilees *and the World of Its Creation* (JSJSup 156; Leiden: Brill, 2012) 305–42.

Kugel, James L., and Rowan A. Greer
Early Biblical Interpretation (Philadelphia: Westminster, 1986).

Kugler, Robert
From Patriarch to Priest: The Levi-Priestly Tradition from Aramaic Levi to Testament of Levi (SBLEJL 9; Atlanta: Scholars Press, 1996).

Kutsch, Ernst
"Der Kalender des Jubiläenbuches und das Alte und das Neue Testament," *VT* 11 (1961) 39–47.

Idem
"Die Solstitien im Kalender des Jubiläenbuches und in äth. Henoch 72," *VT* 12 (1962) 205–7.

Kvanvig, Helge
"Jubilees—Between Enoch and Moses: A Narrative Reading," *JSJ* 35 (2004) 243–61.

Idem
"Jubilees—Read as a Narrative," in Gabriele Boccaccini, ed., *Enoch and Qumran Origins: New Light on a Forgotten Connection* (Grand Rapids: Eerdmans, 2005) 75–83.

Lambdin, Thomas O.
Introduction to Classical Ethiopic (Geʻez) (HSS 24; Missoula, MT: Scholars Press, 1978).

Lambert, David
"Did Israel Believe That Redemption Awaited Its Repentance? The Case of Jubilees 1," *CBQ* 68 (2006) 631–50.

Idem
"Last Testaments in the Book of Jubilees," *DSD* 11 (2004) 82–107.

Lange, Armin
"Divinatorische Träume und Apokalyptik im Jubiläenbuch," in Matthias Albani, Jörg Frey, and Armin Lange, eds., *Studies in the Book of Jubilees* (TSAJ 65; Tübingen: Mohr Siebeck, 1997) 25–38.

Idem
"The Essene Position on Magic and Divination," in Moshe Bernstein, Florentino García Martínez, and John Kampen, eds., *Legal Texts and Legal Issues: Proceedings of the Second Meeting of the International Organization for Qumran Studies, Published in Honour of Joseph M. Baumgarten* (STDJ 23; Leiden: Brill, 1997) 377–435.

Lavee, Moshe
"The Noahide Laws: The Building Blocks of a Rabbinic Conceptual Framework in Qumran and the Book of Acts," *Meghillot* 10 (2013) 73–114.

Leach, E. R.
"A Possible Method of Intercalation for the Calendar of the Book of Jubilees," *VT* 7 (1957) 392–97.

Le Déaut, Roger
La nuit pascale (AnBib 22; Rome: Pontifical Biblical Institute, 1963).

Leslau, Wolf
Comparative Dictionary of Ge'ez (Classical Ethiopic) (Wiesbaden: Harrassowitz, 1991).

Idem
Concise Dictionary of Ge'ez (Classical Ethiopic) (Wiesbaden: Harrassowitz, 1989).

Idem
Falasha Anthology (Yale Judaica Series 6; New Haven: Yale University Press, 1951).

Levenson, Jon D.
"The Rewritten Aqedah of Jewish Tradition," in idem, *The Death and Resurrection of the Beloved Son: The Transformation of Child Sacrifice in Judaism and Christianity* (New Haven: Yale University Press, 1993) 173–99.

Idem
"Sources of Torah: Psalm 119 and the Modes of Revelation in Second Temple Judaism," in Patrick D. Miller, Paul D. Hanson, and S. Dean McBride, eds., *Ancient Israelite Religion: Essays in Honor of Frank Moore Cross* (Philadelphia: Fortress Press, 1987) 559–74.

Levine, Baruch
Numbers 1–20: A New Translation with Introduction and Commentary (AB 4A; New York: Doubleday, 1993).

Idem
Numbers 21–36: A New Translation with Introduction and Commentary (AB 4B; New Haven: Yale University Press, 2000).

Levinson, Joshua
The Twice Told Tale: A Poetics of the Exegetical Narrative in Rabbinic Midrash (Jerusalem: Magnes Press, 2005).

Levison, Jack R.
Portraits of Adam in Early Judaism: From Sirach to 2 Baruch (JSPSup 1; Sheffield: JSOT Press, 1988).

Lewis, Charlton T., and Charles Short
A Latin Dictionary (Oxford: Clarendon, 1969).

Lewis, Jack
A Study of the Interpretation of Noah and the Flood in Jewish and Christian Literature (Leiden: Brill, 1978).

Licht, Jacob S.
"The Plant Eternal and the People of Divine Deliverance," in Chaim Rabin and Yigael Yadin, eds., *Essays on the Dead Sea Scrolls in Memory of E. L. Sukenik* (Jerusalem: Heikhal ha-Sefer, 1961) 49–75.

Idem
Testing in the Hebrew Scriptures and in Judaism of the Second Temple Period (Jerusalem: Magnes Press, 1973).

Idem
The Thanksgiving Scroll: A Scroll from the Wilderness of Judaea: Text, Introduction, Commentary and Glossary (Jerusalem: Bialik, 1957).

Lichtenberger, Hermann
"Zu Vorkommen und Bedeutung von יצר im Jubiläenbuch," *JSJ* 14 (1983) 1–10.

LiDonnici, Lynn, and Andrea Lieber, eds.
Heavenly Tablets: Interpretation, Identity and Tradition in Ancient Judaism (JSJSup 119; Leiden: Brill, 2007).

Lieber, Elinor
"Asaf's 'Book of Medicines': A Hebrew Encyclopedia of Greek and Jewish Medicine, Possibly Compiled in Byzantium on an Indian Model," in *Symposium on Byzantine Medicine* (Dumbarton Oaks Papers 38; Washington, DC: Dumbarton Library and Research Collection, 1985) 233–49.

Liebreich, L. J.
"Jubilees 50:9 in a Piyyut of the Day of Atonement," *JQR* 44 (1953) 169.

Lignée, Hubert
"La place du Livre des Jubilés et du Rouleau du Temple dans l'histoire du mouvement essénien: Les deux ouvrages ont-ils été écrits par le Maître du Justice?," *RevQ* 13 (1988) 331–45.

Lincicum, David
Paul and the Early Jewish Encounter with Deuteronomy (WUNT 284; Tübingen: Mohr Siebeck, 2010).

Lipscomb, W. Lowndes
"A Tradition from the Book of Jubilees in Armenian," *JJS* 29 (1978) 149–63.

Idem
"The Wives of the Patriarchs in the Ekloge Historion," *JJS* 30 (1979) 91.

Littmann, Enno
"Das Buch der Jubiläen," in Emil Kautsch, ed., *Die Apokryphen und Pseudepigraphen des Alten Testaments*, vol. 2: *Die Pseudepigraphen des Alten Testaments* (Tübingen: Greiburg i. B. and Leipzig: J. C. B. Mohr [Paul Siebeck], 1900) 31–119.

Livneh, Atar
"'Can the Boar Change Its Skin?' Esau's Speech in *Jubilees* 37:18-23," *Hen* 34 (2012) 75–94.

Idem
"How Long Did Abraham Sojourn in Haran? Traditions on the Patriarch in Compositions from Qumran," *Meghillot* 8–9 (2010) 193–209.

Idem
"*Jubilees* 34:1-9: Joseph, the 'House of Joseph,' and the Josephites' Portion," *JSJ* 43 (2012) 22–41.

Idem
"Judgment and Revenge: The Exodus Account in *Jubilees* 48," *RevQ* 98 (2011) 161–75.

Idem
"'Love Your Fellow as Yourself': The Interpretation of Leviticus 19:17-18 in the Book of *Jubilees*," *DSD* 18 (2011) 173–99.

Idem
"Not at First Sight: Gender Love in *Jubilees*," *JSP* 23 (2013) 3–20.

Idem
"With My Sword and Bow: Jacob as Warrior in *Jubilees*," in Devorah Dimant and Reinhard Kratz, eds., *Rewriting and Interpretation: The Biblical Patriarchs in Light of the Dead Sea Scrolls* (BZAW 439; Berlin: de Gruyter, 2013) 189–213.

Loader, William R. G.
Enoch, Levi, and Jubilees on Sexuality: Attitudes towards Sexuality in the Early Enoch Literature, the Aramaic Levi Document, and the Book of Jubilees (Grand Rapids: Eerdmans, 2007).

Idem
"Jubilees and Sexual Transgression: Reflections on Enochic and Mosaic Tradition," *Hen* 31 (2009) 48–54.

Lockshin, Martin
Rashbam's Commentary on Deuteronomy: An Annotated Translation (BJS 340; Providence, RI: Brown Judaic Studies, 2004).

Machiela, Daniel A.
The Dead Sea Genesis Apocryphon: A New Text and Translation with Introduction and Special Treatment of Columns 13–17 (STDJ 79; Leiden: Brill, 2009).

Idem
"On the Importance of Being Abram: *Genesis Apocryphon* 18, *Jubilees* 10:1–13:4, and Further Thoughts on a Literary Relationship," in Eric F. Mason, Kelley Coblentz Bautch, Angela Kim Harkins, and Daniel A. Machiela, eds., *A Teacher for All Generations: Essays in Honor of James C. VanderKam* (2 vols.; JSJSup 153/I-II; Leiden: Brill, 2012) 715–36.

Maher, Michael
Targum Pseudo-Jonathan: Exodus (ArBib 2; Collegeville, MN: Liturgical Press, 1994).

Idem
Targum Pseudo-Jonathan: Genesis (ArBib 1B; Collegeville, MN: Liturgical Press, 1992).

Maier, J.
"Zu etnographisch-geographischen Überlieferungen über Japhetiten (Gen 10,2-4) im frühen Judentum," *Hen* 13 (1991) 157–94.

Maori, Yeshayahu
The Peshitta Version of the Pentateuch and Early Jewish Exegesis (Jerusalem: Magnes Press, 1995).

Marcus, Joel
The Mystery of the Kingdom of God (SBLDS 90; Atlanta: Scholars Press, 1986).

Marmorstein, A.
"Die Namen der Schwestern Kains und Abels in der midraschischen und in der apokryphen Literatur," *ZAW* 25 (1905) 141–44.

Martens, Karen
"Jubillaerbogens brug af Mastema i sin genskrivning af Exodus [The Book of Jubilees' Use of Mastema in Its Rewriting of Exodus]," *Dansk teologisk tidsskrift* 66 (2003) 161–82.

Martin, François
"Le Livre des Jubilés: But et procédés de l'auteur. Ses Doctrines," *RB* 8 (1911) 321–44, 502–33.

Mason, Eric, et al., eds.
A Teacher for All Generations: Essays in Honor of James C. VanderKam (2 vols.; JSJSup 153/I-II; Leiden: Brill, 2012).

Idem
'You Are a Priest Forever': Second Temple Jewish Messianism and the Priestly Christology of the Epistle to the Hebrews (STDJ 74; Leiden: Brill, 2008).

McNamara, Martin, and Robert Hayward
Targum Neofiti 1: Exodus (ArBib 2; Collegeville, MN: Liturgical Press, 1994).

Idem
Targum Neofiti 1: Genesis (ArBib 1; Collegeville, MN: Liturgical Press, 1992).

Meier, John P.
A Marginal Jew: Rethinking the Historical Jesus (5 vols.; ABRL; New York: Doubleday [vols. 1–3]; AYBRL; New Haven: Yale University Press [vols. 4–5], 1991–2016).

Mendels, Doron
The Land of Israel as a Political Concept in Hasmonean Literature (TSAJ 15; Tübingen: Mohr Siebeck, 1987).

Menn, Esther
Judah and Tamar (Genesis 38) in Ancient Jewish Exegesis: Studies in Literary Form and Hermeneutics (JSJSup 51; Leiden: Brill, 1997).

Mermelstein, Ari
Creation, Covenant, and the Beginnings of Judaism: Reconceiving Historical Time in the Second Temple Period (JSJSup 168; Leiden: Brill, 2014).

Meyer, R.
"Levitische Emanzipationsbestrebungen in nachexilischer Zeit," *OLZ* 41 (1938) 721–28.

Milgrom, Jacob
"The Concept of Impurity in *Jubilees* and the *Temple Scroll*," *RevQ* 16/62 (1993) 277–84.

Idem
Leviticus: A New Translation with Introduction and Commentary (3 vols.; AB 3, 3A, 3B; New York: Doubleday, 1991, 2000, 2010).

Milik, J. T.
"A propos de 11QJub," *Bib* 54 (1973) 77–78.

Idem
The Books of Enoch: Aramaic Fragments of Qumrân Cave 4 (Oxford: Clarendon, 1976).

Idem
"Fragment d'une source du Psautier (4QPs89) et fragments des Jubilés, du Document de Damas, d'un phylactère dans la grotte 4 de Qumran," *RB* 73 (1966) 94–106.

Idem
"Hénoch au pays des aromates (ch. 26 à 32): Fragments araméens de la grotte 4 de Qumran (Pl. 1)," *RB* 65 (1958) 70–77.

Idem
"Livre des Jubilés," in Dominique Barthélemy and J. T. Milik, eds., *Qumran Cave I* (DJD 1; Oxford: Clarendon, 1955) 82–84.

Idem
"Recherches sur la version grecque du Livre des Jubilés," *RB* 78 (1971) 545–57.

Idem
"Le travail d'édition des fragments manuscrits de Qumran," *RB* 63 (1956) 49–67.

Idem
"Le travail d'édition des manuscrits du désert de Juda," in *Volume du Congrès: Strasbourg 1956* (VTSup 4; Leiden: Brill, 1957) 17–26.

Idem
"Le Testament de Lévi en araméen: Fragment de la Grotte 4 de Qumrân," *RB* 62 (1955) 394–406.

Milikowsky, Chaim
Seder Olam: Critical Edition, Commentary, and Introduction (2 vols.; Jerusalem: Yishaq Ben Zvi, 2013).

Mimouni, Simon Claude,
La circoncision dans le monde judéen aux époques grecque et romaine: Histoire d'un conflit interne au judaïsme (Collection de la Revue des études juives 42; Paris-Louvain: Peeters, 2007).

Monger, Matthew Phillip
"4Q216 and the State of *Jubilees* at Qumran," *RevQ* 26/104 (2014) 595–612.

Montgomery, James A.
"An Assyrian Illustration to the Book of Jubilees," *JBL* 33 (1914) 157–58.

Moore, Carey
Tobit: A New Translation with Introduction and Commentary (AB 40A; New York: Doubleday, 1996).

Morgenstern, Julian
"The Calendar of the Book of Jubilees: Its Origin and Its Character," *VT* 5 (1955) 34–76.

Müller, Karlheinz
"Die hebräische Sprache der Halacha als Textur der Schöpfung: Beobachtungen zu Verhältnis von Tora und Halacha im Buch der Jubiläen," in Helmut Merklein, Karlheinz Müller, and Günter Stemberger, eds., *Bibel in jüdischer und christlicher Tradition* (BBB 88; Frankfurt: Anton Hain, 1993) 157–76.

Müller, Mogens
"Die Abraham-Gestalt im Jubiläenbuch: Versuch einer Interpretation," *SJOT* 10 (1996) 239–57.

Murphy, Catherine M.
Wealth in the Dead Sea Scrolls and in the Qumran Community (STDJ 40; Leiden: Brill, 2002).

Naeh, S.
"On Two Hippocratic Concepts in Rabbinic Literature," *Tarbiz* 66 (1997) 169–85.

Najman, Hindy
"Interpretation as Primordial Writing: Jubilees and Its Authority Conferring Strategies," *JSJ* 30 (1999) 379–410.

Eadem
Seconding Sinai: The Development of Mosaic Discourse in Second Temple Judaism (JSJSup 77; Leiden: Brill, 2003).

Eadem
"The Symbolic Significance of Writing in Ancient Judaism," in Hindy Najman and Judith H. Newman, eds., *The Idea of Biblical Interpretation: Essays in Honor of James L. Kugel* (JSJSup 83; Leiden: Brill, 2004) 139–73.

Eadem
"Torah of Moses: Pseudonymous Attribution in Second Temple Writings," in Craig Evans, ed., *The Interpretation of Scripture in Early Judaism and Christianity: Studies in Language and Tradition* (JSPSup 33; Studies in Scripture in Early Judaism and Christianity 7; Sheffield: Sheffield Academic Press, 2000) 202–16.

Nau, F.
"Traduction de la Chronique syriaque anonyme, éditée par Sa Béatitude Mgr. Rahmani, Patriarche des Syriens catholiques," *Revue de l'Orient Chrétien* 12 (1907) 429–40; 13 (1908) 90–99, 321–28, 436–43.

Nebe, G.-W.
"*4Q174*, 1–2, I, 6f im Lichte von *Sektenschrift* und *Jub* 2,22," *RevQ* 18/72 (1998) 581–87.

Idem
"Ergänzende Bemerkung zu 4Q176, Jubiläen 23,21," *RevQ* 14/53 (1989) 129–30.

Idem
"Qumranica V: Zu unveröffentlichen Handschriften vom Toten Meer. Die vermeintlichen Jubiläen-Texte aus Masada Mas 1276-1786 und Mas 1039-317," *ZAW* 111 (1999) 622-35.

Newsom, Carol
"379. 4QApocryphon of Joshua^b," in George J. Brooke et al., in consultation with James C. VanderKam, *Qumran Cave 4.XVII: Parabiblical Texts, Part 3* (DJD 22; Oxford: Clarendon, 1996) 263-88.

Nickelsburg, George W. E.
1 Enoch 1: A Commentary on the Book of 1 Enoch Chapters 1-36, 81-108 (Hermeneia; Minneapolis: Fortress Press, 2001).

Idem
Jewish Literature between the Bible and the Mishnah. A Historical and Literary Introduction (2nd ed.; Minneapolis: Fortress Press, 2005).

Idem
Resurrection, Immortality, and Eternal Life in Intertestamental Judaism (HTS 26; Cambridge, MA: Harvard University Press, 1972).

Nickelsburg, George W. E., and James C. VanderKam
1 Enoch 2: A Commentary on the Book of 1 Enoch Chapters 37-82 (Hermeneia; Minneapolis: Fortress Press, 2012).

Niehoff, Maren
The Figure of Joseph in Post-Biblical Jewish Literature (AGJU 16; Leiden: Brill, 1992).

Nitzan, Bilhah
"The Liturgy at Qumran: Statutory Prayers," in Menahem Kister, ed., *The Qumran Scrolls and Their World* (2 vols.; Between Bible and Mishnah; Jerusalem: Yisḥaq Ben Zvi, 2009) 1:225-60.

Eadem
"Moses' Penitential-Like Prayer in *Jubilees* 1 and Its Relation to the Penitential Tradition of Post-Exilic Judaism," *Hen* 31 (2009) 35-41.

Noack, Bent
"The Day of Pentecost in Jubilees, Qumran, and Acts," *ASTI* 1 (1962) 73-95.

Idem
"Jubilaeerbogen," in E. Hammershaimb, J. Munck, B. Noack, and P. Seidelin, eds., *De Gammeltestamentlige Pseudepigrapher* (Copenhagen: Gad, 1958) 3:175-301.

Idem
"Qumran and the Book of Jubilees," *SEÅ* 22-23 (1957-58) 191-207.

Noah, M. N.
Spr hyšr or the Book of Jasher (New York: M. M. Noah & A. S. Gould, 1840).

Nötscher, F.
"Himmlische Bücher und Schicksalsglaube in Qumran," *RevQ* 1/3 (1958-59) 405-11.

Novak, David
The Image of the Non-Jew in Judaism: An Historical and Constructive Study of the Noahide Laws (New York: Edwin Mellen, 1983).

Novick, Tzvi
"The Rabbis' Written Torah and the Heavenly Tablets," in Eric F. Mason, Kelley Coblentz Bautch, Angela Kim Harkins, and Daniel A. Machiela, eds., *A Teacher for All Generations: Essays in Honor of James C. VanderKam* (2 vols.; JSJSup 153/I-II; Leiden: Brill, 2012) 589-600.

Olyan, Saul
A Thousand Thousands Served Him: Exegesis and the Naming of Angels in Ancient Judaism (TSAJ 36; Tübingen: Mohr Siebeck, 1993).

Osswald, Eva
"Beobachtungen zur Erzählung von Abrahams Aufenthalt in Ägypten im 'Genesis Apokryphon,'" *ZAW* 72 (1960) 7-25.

Park, Sejin
Pentecost and Sinai: The Festival of Weeks as a Celebration of the Sinai Event (LHBOTS 342; New York: T&T Clark, 2008).

Parry, Donald, and Emanuel Tov, eds.
The Dead Sea Scrolls Reader (6 vols.; Leiden: Brill, 2004-5).

Paul, Shalom M.
"Heavenly Tablets and the Book of Life," *Ancient Near Eastern Society Journal* 5-6 (1973-74) 345-53.

Payne Smith, J.
A Compendious Syriac Dictionary (Oxford: Clarendon, 1903).

Paz, Yaqir
"Before the Giving of the Torah: The Fathers and the Statutes of Moses in Rabbinic Literature against the Backround of Second Temple Literature and the Fathers of the Church" (MA thesis, Hebrew University of Jerusalem, 2009).

Perrot, Charles
La lecture de la Bible dans la synagogue: Les anciennes lectures palestiniennes du Shabbat et des fêtes (Collection Massorah, Série 1: Études classiques et textes 1; Hildesheim: Gerstenberg, 1973).

Peters, Dorothy M.
Noah Traditions in the Dead Sea Scrolls: Conversations and Controversies of Antiquity (SBLEJL 26; Atlanta: Society of Biblical Literature, 2008).

Eadem
Noah Traditions in Jubilees: Evidence for the Struggle between Enochic and Mosaic Authority," *Hen* 31 (2009) 116-22.

Petersen, David L.
Zechariah 9-14 and Malachi: A Commentary (OTL; Louisville: Westminster John Knox, 1995).

Petit, Françoise
La chaîne sur la Genèse: Édition integrale I-IV (Traditio Exegetica Graeca 1-4; Louvain: Peeters, 1992-96).

Potin, Jean
La fête juive de la Pentecôte: Étude des textes liturgiques (2 vols.; LD 65; Paris: Cerf, 1971).

Poznanski, Samuel
"Zu den Namen der Frauen Kain's und Abel's," *ZAW* 25 (1905) 340-42.

Preuss, H. D.
"גלולים *gillûlîm*," *TDOT* 3:1-5.

Puech, Émile
La croyance des Esséniens en la vie future: Immortalité, resurrection, vie éternelle? Histoire d'une croyance dans le Judaïsme ancien (2 vols.; EBib 21-22; Paris: Gabalda, 1993).

Idem
"Une nouvelle copie du *Livre des Jubilés*: 4Q484 = pap4QJubilés^j," *RevQ* 19/74 (1999) 261-64.

Idem
Qumrân Grotte 4.XXII: Textes araméens première partie: 4Q529–4Q549 (DJD 31; Oxford: Clarendon, 2001).

Pummer, Reinhard
"Antisamaritanische Polemik im jüdischen Schriften aus der intertestamentarischen Zeit," *BZ* 26 (1982) 224-42.

Idem
"The *Book of Jubilees* and the Samaritans," *Eglise et théologie* 10 (1979) 147-78.

Idem
"Genesis 34 in Jewish Writings of the Hellenistic and Roman Periods," *HTR* 75 (1982) 177-88.

Qimron, Elisha
The Dead Sea Scrolls: The Hebrew Writings (2 vols.; Between Bible and Mishnah; Jerusalem: Yisḥaq Ben Zvi, 2010, 2013).

Idem
"Improving the Editions of the Dead Sea Scrolls," *Meghillot* 1 (2003) 135-45.

Qimron, Elisha, and Florentino García Martínez
The Temple Scroll: A Critical Edition with Extensive Reconstructions (Beersheba: Ben-Gurion University of the Negev Press; Jerusalem: Israel Exploration Society, 1996).

Rabin, Chaim
"Jubilees," in H. F. D. Sparks, ed., *The Apocryphal Old Testament* (Oxford: Clarendon, 1984) 1-139.

Idem
Qumran Studies (Scripta Judaica 2; Oxford: Oxford University Press, 1957).

Idem
The Zadokite Documents (2nd ed.; Oxford: Oxford University Press, 1958).

Rad, Gerhard von
Genesis: A Commentary (OTL; Philadelphia: Westminster, 1961).

Rahmani, I. E., II
Chronicon civile et ecclesiasticum anonymi auctoris (London: Charfé, 1904).

Rajak, Tessa
"The Hasmoneans and the Uses of Hellenism," in Philip R. Davies and Richard T. White, eds., *A Tribute to Géza Vermès: Essays on Jewish and Christian Literature and History* (JSOTSup 100; Sheffield: JSOT Press, 1990) 261-80.

Rapoport, S.
"Der Berg des Ostens bei den Samaritanern," *ZDMG* 11 (1857) 730-33.

Rapp, Hans
Jakob in Bet-El: Gen 35, 1-15 und die jüdische Literatur des 3. und 2. Jahrhunderts (HBS 29; Freiburg: Herder, 2001).

Rappaport, Uriel
"The Hasmonean State and Hellenism," *Tarbiz* 60 (1991) 477-503.

Ravid, Liora
"The Book of Jubilees and Its Calendar—A Reexamination," *DSD* 10 (2003) 371-94.

Eadem
"Issues in the Book of Jubilees" (PhD diss., Bar-Ilan University, 2001).

Eadem
"Purity and Impurity in the Book of *Jubilees*," *JSP* 13 (2002) 61-86.

Eadem
"The Sabbath Laws in Jubilees 50:6-13," *Tarbiz* 69 (2000) 161-66.

Eadem
"The Special Terminology of the Heavenly Tablets in the Book of Jubilees," *Tarbiz* 68 (1999) 463-71.

Reed, Annette Yoshiko
"Enochic and Mosaic Traditions in Jubilees: The Evidence of Angelology and Demonology," in Gabriele Boccaccini and Giovanni Ibba, eds., *Enoch and the Mosaic Torah: The Evidence of Jubilees* (Grand Rapids: Eerdmans, 2009) 358-63.

Eadem
"Retelling Biblical Retellings: Epiphanius, the Pseudo-Clementines, and the Reception History of *Jubilees*," in Menahem Kister, Hillel Newman, Michael Segal, and Ruth Clements, eds., *Tradition, Transmission, and Transformation from Second Temple Literature through Judaism and Christianity in Late Antiquity* (STDJ 113; Leiden: Brill, 2015) 304-21.

Reeves, John C., ed.
Tracing the Threads: Studies in the Vitality of Jewish Pseudepigrapha (SBLEJL 6; Atlanta: Scholars Press, 1994).

Idem
"What Does Noah Offer in 1QapGen X,15?" *RevQ* 12 (1986) 415-19.

Riessler, Paul
"Jubiläenbuch oder Kleine Genesis," in idem, *Altjüdisches Schrifttum ausserhalb der Bibel* (Augsburg: Filser, 1928; 2nd ed.; Darmstadt: Wissenschaftliche Buchgesellschaft, 1966) 539-666.

Ringgren, Helmer
The Faith of Qumran (trans. Emilie T. Sander; Philadelphia: Fortress Press, 1963).

Rivkin, Ellis
"The Book of Jubilees—an Anti-Pharisaic Pseudepigraph?" *Eretz-Israel* 16 (1982) 193-98.

Robinson, Ira
"*běpetaḥ ʿênayim* in Genesis 38:14," *JBL* 96 (1977) 569.

Robinson, Patricia
"To Stretch Out the Feet: A Formula for Death in the Testaments of the Twelve Patriarchs," *JBL* 97 (1978) 369-74.

Rofé, Alexander
"Fragments from an Additional Manuscript of the Book of Jubilees in Cave 3 of Qumran," *Tarbiz* 34 (1965) 333-36.

Rönsch, Hermann
Das Buch der Jubiläen oder die Kleine Genesis (Leipzig: Fue, 1874; repr., Amsterdam: Editions RODOPI, 1970).

Idem
"Die Leptogenesis und das Ambrosianische altlateinische Fragment derselben," *ZWTh* 14 (1871) 60-98.

Rook, John T.
"The Names of the Wives from Adam to Abraham in the Book of *Jubilees*," *JSP* 7 (1990) 105-17.

Idem
"A Twenty-Eight-Day Month Tradition in the Book of Jubilees," *VT* 31 (1981) 83-87.

Rothstein, David
"'And Jacob came (in)to [בוא + אל] . . .': Spousal Relationships and the Use of a Recurring Syntagm in Genesis and Jubilees," *Hen* 29 (2007) 91-103.

Idem
"Jubilees' Formulation of Gen 2:23: A Literary Motif Viewed against the Legal Matricies of the Hebrew Bible and the Ancient Near East," *Zeitschrift für Altorientalische und Biblische Rechtsgeschichte* 11 (2005) 4-11.

Idem
"Same-Day Testimony and Same-Day Punishment in the Damascus Document and Jubilees," *ZABR* 11 (2005) 12-26.

Idem
"Sexual Union and Sexual Offences in *Jubilees*," *JSJ* 35 (2004) 363-84.

Idem
"Text and Context: Domestic Harmony and the Depiction of Hagar in Jubilees," *JSP* 17 (2008) 243-64.

Idem
"Why Was Shelah Not Given to Tamar? *Jubilees* 41:20," *Hen* 27 (2005) 115-26.

Rowley, Harold Henry
"Criteria for the Dating of Jubilees," *JQR* 36 (1945-46) 183-87.

Idem
The Relevance of Apocalyptic: A Study of Jewish and Christian Apocalypses from Daniel to the Revelation (3rd ed.; New York: Association Press, 1964).

Rubenstein, Jeffrey
The History of Sukkot in the Second Temple and Rabbinic Periods (BJS 302; Atlanta: Scholars Press, 1995).

Ruiten, Jacques T. A. G. M. van
Abraham in the Book of Jubilees: The Rewriting of Genesis 11:26–25:10 in the Book of Jubilees 11:14–23:8 (JSJSup 161; Leiden: Brill, 2012).

Idem
"Abraham, Job and the Book of *Jubilees*: The Intertextual Relationship of Genesis 22:1-19, Job 1:1–2:13 and *Jubilees* 17:15–18:19," in Ed Noort and Eibert Tigchelaar, eds., *The Sacrifice of Isaac: The Aqedah (Genesis 22) and Its Interpretations* (TBN 4; Leiden: Brill, 2002) 58-85.

Idem
"Abraham's Last Day according to the Book of *Jubilees* (Jub. 22:1–23:8)," in Erkki Koskenniemi and Pekka Lindqvist, eds., *Rewritten Biblical Figures* (Studies in Rewritten Bible 3; Turku, Finland: Åbo Akademi University, 2010) 57-88.

Idem
"Abram's Prayer: The Coherence of the Pericopes in Jubilees 12:16-27," in Gabriele Boccaccini and Giovanni Ibba, eds., *Enoch and the Mosaic Torah: The Evidence of Jubilees* (Grand Rapids: Eerdmans, 2009) 211-28.

Idem
"Angels and Demons in the Book of Jubilees," in Friedrich V. Reiterer, Tobias Nicklas, and Karin Schöpflin, eds., *Angels: The Concept of Celestial Beings. Origins, Development and Reception* (Deuterocanonical and Cognate Literature Yearbook 2007; Berlin: de Gruyter, 2007) 585-609.

Idem
"Between Jacob's Death and Moses' Birth: The Intertextual Relationship between Genesis 50:15–Exodus 1:14 and Jubilees 46:1-16," in Anthony Hilhorst, Émile Puech, and Eibert Tigchelaar, eds., *Flores Florentino: Dead Sea Scrolls and Other Early Jewish Studies in Honour of Florentino García Martínez* (JSJSup 122; Leiden: Brill, 2007) 467-89.

Idem
"Biblical Interpretation in Jubilees 3:1-31," in Klaus-Dietrich Schunck and Matthias Augustin, eds., *Lasset uns Brücken bauen* (Frankfurt am Main: P. Lang, 1998) 315-19.

Idem
"The Birth of Moses in Egypt according to the Book of Jubilees (Jub 47.1-9)," in Anthony Hilhorst and Geurt H. van Kooten, eds., *The Wisdom of Egypt: Jewish, Early Christian, and Gnostic Essays in Honour of Gerard P. Luttikhuizen* (AGJU 59; Leiden: Brill, 2005) 43-65.

Idem
"The Covenant of Noah in *Jubilees* 6.1-38," in Stanley Porter and Jacqueline de Roo, eds., *The Concept of the Covenant in the Second Temple Period* (JSJSup 71; Leiden: Brill, 2003) 167-90.

Idem
"The Creation of Man and Woman in Early Jewish Literature," in Gerard Luttikhuizen, ed., *The*

Creation of Man and Woman: Interpretations of the Biblical Narratives in Jewish and Christian Traditions (TBN 3; Leiden: Brill, 2000) 34–62.

Idem
"Eden and the Temple: The Rewriting of Genesis 2:4–3:24 in the *Book of Jubilees*," in Gerard Luttikhuizen, ed., *Paradise Interpreted: Representations of Biblical Paradise in Judaism and Christianity* (TBN 2; Leiden: Brill, 1999) 63–94.

Idem
"The Garden of Eden and Jubilees 3:1-31," *Bijdr* 57 (1996) 305–17.

Idem
"Genesis herscheven en geïnterpreteert in het boek *Jubileeën* nader toelicht met een vergelijking van Genesis 17 en *Jubileeën* 15," *NTT* 64 (2010) 32–50.

Idem
"The Interpretation of Genesis 6:1-12 in Jubilees 5:1-19," in Matthias Albani, Jörg Frey, Armin Lange, eds., *Studies in the Book of Jubilees* (TSAJ 65; Tübingen: Mohr Siebeck, 1997) 57–73.

Idem
"Land and Covenant in *Jubilees* 14," in Jacques van Ruiten and J. Cornelis de Vos, eds., *The Land of Israel in Bible, History, and Theology: Studies in Honour of Ed Noort* (VTSup 124; Leiden: Brill, 2009) 259–76.

Idem
"A Literary Dependency of Jubilees on 1 Enoch?," in Gabriele Boccaccini, ed., *Enoch and Qumran Origins: New Light on a Forgotten Connection* (Grand Rapids: Eerdmans, 2005) 90–93.

Idem
"Lot versus Abraham: The Interpretation of Genesis 18:1–19:38 in Jubilees 16:1-9," in Ed Noort and Eibert Tigchelaar, eds., *Sodom's Sin: Genesis 18-19 and Its Interpretations* (Leiden: Brill, 2004) 29–46.

Idem
"Moses and His Parents: The Intertextual Relationship between Exodus 1:22–2:10 and Jubilees 47:1-9," in Antti Laato and Jacques van Ruiten, eds., *Rewritten Bible Reconsidered: Proceedings of the Conference in Karkku, Finland, August 24-26, 2006* (Studies in Rewritten Bible 1; Turku: Åbo Akademi University; Winona Lake, IN: Eisenbrauns, 2008) 43–78.

Idem
Primaeval History Interpreted: The Rewriting of Genesis 1–11 in the Book of Jubilees (JSJSup 66; Leiden: Brill, 2000).

Idem
"The Rewriting of Exodus 24:12-18 in Jubilees 1:1-4," *BN* 79 (1995) 25–29.

Idem
"Some Questions with Regard to a Supposed Interpolator in the Book of *Jubilees* Focused on the Festival of Weeks (*Jub*. 6:1-22)," *RevQ* 26/104 (2014) 539–53.

Idem
"The Use and Interpretation of the Book of *Jubilees* in the *Mäṣḥäfä Milad*," *RevQ* 26/104 (2014) 613–29.

Idem
"Van tekst tot tekst: Psalm 90 en Jubileeën 23:12-15," *NTT* 47 (1993) 177–85.

Idem
"Visions of the Temple in the *Book of Jubilees*," in Beate Ego, Armin Lange, and Peter Pilhofer, eds., *Gemeinde ohne Tempel / Community without Temple* (WUNT 118; Tübingen: Mohr Siebeck, 1999) 215–27.

Russell, David M.
The "New Heavens and New Earth": Hope for the Creation in Jewish Apocalyptic and the New Testament (Studies in Biblical Apocalyptic Literature 1; Philadelphia: Visionary Press, 1996).

Russell, David S.
The Method and Message of Jewish Apocalyptic: 200 BC–AD 100 (OTL; Philadelphia: Westminster, 1964).

Safrai, Shemuel
"Halakha in Jubilees," in idem, *The Literature of the Sages, First Part: Oral Tora, Halakha, Mishna, Tosefta, Talmud, External Tractates* (CRINT 2.3; Assen/Maastricht: van Gorcum; Philadelphia: Fortress Press, 1987) 140–43.

Safrai, Ze'ev
"The War of the Sons of Jacob in Southern Samaria," *Sinai* 100 (1987) 613–27.

Sanders, Ed P.
"The Covenant as a Soteriological Category and the Nature of Salvation in Palestinian and Hellenistic Judaism," in Robert Hamerton-Kelly and Robin Scroggs, eds., *Jews, Greeks, and Christians: Religious Cultures in Late Antiquity* (Leiden: Brill, 1976) 11–56.

Sanders, James A.
The Psalms Scroll of Qumrân Cave 11 (11QPs^a) (DJD 4; Oxford: Clarendon, 1965).

Satlow, Michael
"Jewish Constructions of Nakedness in Late Antiquity," *JBL* 116 (1997) 429–54.

Saulnier, Stéphane
Calendrical Variations in Second Temple Judaism: New Perspectives on the 'Date of the Last Supper' Debate (JSJSup 159; Leiden: Brill, 2012).

Idem
"Jub 49:14 and the [Absent] Second Passover: How [and Why] to Do Away With an Unwanted Festival," *Hen* 31 (2009) 42–47.

Schäfer, Peter
"Der Götzendienst des Enosch: Zur Bildung und Entwicklung aggadischer Traditionen im nachbiblischen Judentum," in idem, *Studien zur Geschichte und Theologie des rabbinischen Judentums* (AGJU 15; Leiden: Brill, 1978) 134–52.

Schafer, Rachel
"'One Language and One Tongue': Animal Speech in *Jubilees* 3:27-31" (Unpublished seminar paper, University of Notre Dame, 2010).

Schaller, J. B.
"Gen 1.2 im antiken Judentum: Untersuchungen über Verwendung und Deutung der Schöpfungsaussagen von Gen. 1.2 im antiken Judentum" (PhD diss., University of Göttingen, 1961).

Schechter, Solomon
Fragments of a Zadokite Work (Documents of Jewish Sectaries 1; Cambridge: University Press, 1910; repr. New York: Ktav, 1970).

Schiffman, Lawrence H.
"The Book of Jubilees and the Temple Scroll," in Gabriele Boccaccini and Giovanni Ibba, eds., *Enoch and the Mosaic Torah: The Evidence of Jubilees* (Grand Rapids: Eerdmans, 2009) 99–115.

Idem
The Courtyards of the House of the Lord: Studies on the Temple Scroll (ed. F. García Martínez; STDJ 75; Leiden: Brill, 2008).

Idem
The Halakhah at Qumran (SJLA 16; Leiden: Brill, 1975).

Idem
"The Sacrificial System of the *Temple Scroll* and the Book of Jubilees," *SBLSP* (1985) 217–33.

Schimmel, H.
Sepher Midrash Tadshe (Tel Aviv: 'Am 'Oved, 1993).

Schmid, Konrad, and Christoph Riedweg, eds.
Beyond Eden: The Biblical Story of Paradise (Genesis 2–3) and Its Reception History (FAT 2; Tübingen: Mohr Siebeck, 2008).

Schmidt, Francis
"Jewish Representations of the Inhabited Earth during the Hellenistic and Roman Periods," in Aryeh Kasher, Uriel Rappaport, and Gideon Fuks, eds., *Greece and Rome in Eretz Israel: Collected Essays* (Jerusalem: Yishaq Ben Zvi/IES, 1990) 119–34.

Idem
"Naissance d'une Géographie Juive," in Alain Desreumaux and Francis Schmidt, eds., *Moïse Géographe: Recherches sur les représentations juives et chrétiennes de l'espace* (Paris: J. Vrin, 1988) 13–30.

Schmitt, G.
Ein indirektes Zeugnis der Makkabäerkämpfe: Testament Juda 3–7 und Parallelen (Wiesbaden: Reichert, 1983).

Schodde, George H.
"The Book of Jubilees translated from the Ethiopic," *Bibliotheca Sacra* 42 (1885) 629–45; 43 (1886) 56–72, 356–71, 455–86; 44 (1887) 426–59, 602–11, 727–45.

Idem
The Book of Jubilees Translated from the Ethiopic (Oberlin, OH: E. J. Goodrich, 1888).

Schreiber, Sarah
"Is a Halakhic Redactor Necessary? A Closer Look at Jubilees 41" (Unpublished seminar paper, University of Notre Dame, 2010).

Schubert, Friedemann
"'El 'Æljôn' als Gottesname im Jubiläenbuch," *Mitteilungen und Beiträge* 8 (1994) 3–18.

Idem
Tradition und Erneuerung: Studien zum Jubiläenbuch und seinem Trägerkreis (Europäische Hochschulschriften, Reihe III: Geschichte und ihre Hilfswissenschaften 771; Frankfurt: Lang, 1998).

Schuller, Eileen
"Women of the Exodus in Biblical Retellings of the Second Temple Period," in Peggy L. Day, ed., *Gender Difference in Ancient Israel* (Minneapolis: Augsburg Fortress Press, 1989) 178–94.

Schulz, Joseph P.
"Two Views of the Patriarchs: Noahides and Pre-Sinai Israelites," in Michael A. Fishbane and Paul R. Florh, eds., *Texts and Responses: Studies Presented to Nahum N. Glatzer on the Occasion of His Seventieth Birthday by His Students* (Leiden: Brill, 1975) 43–59.

Schüpphaus, J.
"כסל *ksl*, etc.," *TDOT* 7:264–65.

Schürer, Emil
The History of the Jewish People in the Age of Jesus Christ (3 vols.; rev. and ed. Geza Vermes and Fergus Millar; trans. T. A. Burkill, Malcolm Doubles, H. Kennedy, G. Ogg, L. Olds, Max Wilcox, and Paul Winter; Edinburgh: T&T Clark, 1973–87).

Schwartz, J.
"Jubilees, Bethel and the Temple of Jacob," *HUCA* 56 (1985) 63–85.

Schwarz, Eberhard
Identität durch Abgrenzung: Abgrenzungsprozesse in Israel im 2. vorchristlichen Jahrhundert und ihre traditionsgeschichtlichen Voraussetzungen. Zugleich ein Beitrag zur Erforschung des Jubiläenbuches (Europaische Hochschulschriften 162; Frankfurt am Main: Peter Lang, 1982).

Scott, Ian W.
"Epistemology and Social Conflict in *Jubilees* and *Aristeas*," in Wayne O. McCready and Adele Reinhartz, eds., *Common Judaism: Explorations in Second-Temple Judaism* (Minneapolis: Fortress Press, 2008) 195–213.

Scott, James
"The Chronologies of the Apocalypse of Weeks and the Book of Jubilees," in Gabriele Boccaccini and Giovanni Ibba, eds., *Enoch and the Mosaic Torah: The Evidence of Jubilees* (Grand Rapids: Eerdmans, 2009) 67–81.

Idem
"The Division of the Earth in Jubilees 8:11—9:15 and Early Christian Chronography," in Matthias Albani, Jörg Frey, and Armin Lange, eds., *Studies in the Book of Jubilees* (TSAJ 65; Tübingen: Mohr Siebeck, 1997) 295–323.

Idem
"Geographic Aspects of Noachic Materials in the Scrolls at Qumran," in Stanley E. Porter and Craig A. Evans, eds., *The Scrolls and the Scriptures: Qumran Fifty Years After* (JSPSup 26; Roehampton Institute London Papers 3; Sheffield: Sheffield Academic Press, 1997) 368–81.

Idem
Geography in Early Judaism and Christianity: The Book of Jubilees (SNTSMS 113; Cambridge: Cambridge University Press, 2002).

Idem
On Earth as in Heaven: The Restoration of Sacred Time and Sacred Space in the Book of Jubilees (JSJSup 91; Leiden: Brill, 2005).

Idem
Paul and the Nations: The Old Testament and Jewish Background of Paul's Mission to the Nations with Special Reference to the Destination of Galatians (WUNT 84; Tübingen: Mohr Siebeck, 1995).

Segal, Michael
"Between Bible and Rewritten Bible," in Matthias Henze, ed., *Biblical Interpretation at Qumran* (SDSSRL; Grand Rapids: Eerdmans, 2005) 10–28.

Idem
"The Book of Jubilees: Rewritten Bible, Redaction, Ideology and Theology" (PhD diss., Hebrew University of Jerusalam, 2004).

Idem
The Book of Jubilees: Rewritten Bible, Redaction, Ideology and Theology (JSJSup 117; Leiden: Brill, 2007).

Idem
"The Dynamics of Composition and Rewriting in Jubilees and Pseudo-Jubilees," *RevQ* 16/104 (2014) 555–77.

Idem
"Law and Narrative in Jubilees: The Story of the Entrance into the Garden of Eden Revisited," *Megillot* 1 (2003) 111–25.

Idem
"The Literary Relationship between the Genesis Apocryphon and Jubilees: The Chronology of Abram and Sarai's Descent to Egypt," *Aramaic Studies* 8 (2010) 71–88.

Idem
"On the Meaning of the Expression תורה ותעודה in Jubilees," *Meghillot* 5–6 (2007) 323–45.

Idem
"Rewriting the Story of Dinah and Shechem: The Literary Development of Jubilees 30," in Nora David, Armin Lange, Kristin De Troyer, and Shani Tzoref, eds., *The Hebrew Bible in Light of the Dead Sea Scrolls* (FRLANT 239; Göttingen: Vandenhoeck & Ruprecht, 2012) 337–56.

Idem
"The Story of Shechem and Dinah in *Jubilees* 30," *Meghillot* 8 (2010) 227–41.

Segal, Moshe
The Complete Book of Ben Sira (2nd ed.; Jerusalem: Bialik, 1972).

Shemesh, Aharon
"4Q265 and the Authortiative Status of Jubilees at Qumran," in Gabriele Boccaccini and Giovanni Ibba, eds., *Enoch and the Mosaic Torah: The Evidence of Jubilees* (Grand Rapids: Eerdmans, 2009) 247–60.

Idem
"4Q265 and the Status of the Book of Jubilees in the Qumran Community," *Zion* 73 (2008) 5–20.

Idem
Halakhah in the Making: The Development of Jewish Law from Qumran to the Rabbis (The Taubman Lectures in Jewish Studies 6; Berkeley: University of California Press, 2009).

Sheridan, Mark, ed.
Genesis 12–50 (ACCS: Old Testament 2; Downers Grove, IL: InterVarsity, 2002).

Silver, Daniel J.
"'Quoth the Raven, "Nevermore"—Some Reflections on Jubilees, Chapter 11," in Herman J. Blumberg, Benjamin Braude, Bernard H. Mehlman, Jerome S. Gurland, and Leslie Y. Guttermann, eds., *"Open Thou Mine Eyes . . .": Essays on Aggadah and Judaica Presented to Rabbi William G. Braude on His Eightieth Birthday and Dedicated to His Memory* (Hoboken, NJ: Ktav, 1992) 255–72.

Singer, Wilhelm
Das Buch der Jubiläen oder die Leptogenesis (Stuhlweissenburg, Hungary: Singer, 1898).

Skehan, Patrick
"*Jubilees* and the Qumran Psalter," *CBQ* 37 (1975) 343–47.

Skinner, John
A Critical and Exegetical Commentary on Genesis (ICC; 2nd ed.; Edinburgh: T&T Clark, 1930).

Smith, Mark
"384. 4QpapApocryphon of Jeremiah B?," in M. Broshi, et al., in consultation with J. VanderKam, *Qumran Cave 4.XIV: Parabiblical Texts, Part 2* (DJD 19; Oxford: Clarendon, 1996) 137–52.

Idem
"Reading, Writing and Interpretation: Two Notes on Jubilees and Pseudo-Jubilees," in Martin F. J. Baasten and W. Th. Van Peursen, eds., *Hamlet on a Hill: Semitic and Greek Studies Presented to Professor T. Muraoka on the Occasion of his Sixty-Fifth Birthday* (Orientalia Louvaniensia Analecta 118; Leuven: Peeters, 2003) 441–47.

Sokoloff, Michael
A Dictionary of Jewish Babylonian Aramaic of the Talmudic and Geonic Periods (Ramat-Gan: Bar Ilan University Press; Baltimore: Johns Hopkins University Press, 2002).

Idem
A Dictionary of Jewish Palestinian Aramaic (2nd ed.; Ramat-Gan: Bar Ilan University Press; Baltimore: Johns Hopkins University Press, 2002).

Sollamo, Raija
"The Creation of Angels and Natural Phenomena Intertwined in the *Book of Jubilees* (4QJub^a)," in Charlotte Hempel and Judith Lieu, eds., *Biblical Traditions in Transition: Essays in Honour of Michael A. Knibb* (JSJSup 111; Leiden: Brill, 2006) 273–90.

Söllner, Peter
"Ismael und Isaak—muss der eine den anderen denn immer nur verfolgen? Zum Verhältnis der beiden Abrahamsöhne im Jubiläenbuch," in Axel von Dobbeler, Kurt Erlemann, and Roman Heiligenthal, eds., *Religionsgeschichte des Neuen Testaments: Festschrift für Klaus Berger zum 60. Geburtstag* (Tübingen: Francke, 2000) 357–78.

Steck, Odil Hannes
"Die Aufnahme von Genesis 1 in Jubiläen 2 und 4. Esra 6," *JSJ* 8 (1977) 154–82.

Idem
"Die getöteten 'Zeugen' und die verfolgten 'Tora-Sucher' in Jub 1,12: Ein Beitrag zur Zeugnis-Terminologie des Jubiläenbuches (I)," *ZAW* 107 (1995) 445–65.

Idem
"Die getöteten 'Zeugen' und die verfolgten 'Tora-Sucher' in Jub 1,12: Ein Beitrag zur Zeugnis-Terminologie des Jubiläenbuches (II)," *ZAW* 108 (1996) 70–86.

Idem
Israel und das gewaltsame Geschick der Propheten: Untersuchungen zur Überlieferung des deuteronomistischen Geschichtsbildes im Alten Testament, Spätjudentum und Urchristentum (WMANT 23; Neukirchen-Vluyn: Neukirchener Verlag, 1967).

Steindorff, George
"Der Name Josephs *Saphenat-Pa'neach* Genesis Kapitel 41, 45," *Zeitschrift für Ägyptische Sprache und Altertumskunde* 27 (1889) 41–42.

Stern, Menahem
Greek and Latin Authors on Jews and Judaism (3 vols.; Fontes ad res Judaicas spectantes; Jerusalem: Israel Academy of Sciences and Humanities, 1974–84).

Stern, Sacha
Calendar and Community: A History of the Jewish Calendar 2nd Century BCE–10th Century CE (Oxford: Oxford University Press, 2001).

Steudel, Annette
"אחרית הימים in the Texts from Qumran," *RevQ* 16/62 (1993) 225–46.

Eadem
Der Midrasch zur Eschatologie aus der Qumrangemeinde [4QMidrEschat^{a.b}] (STDJ 13; Leiden: Brill, 1994).

Stoffregen-Pedersen, Kirsten, and Tedros Abraha
"Andəmta," in Siegbert Uhlig, ed., *Encyclopaedia Aethiopica* (Wiesbaden: Harrassowitz, 2003) 1:258–59.

Stökl, Jonathan
"The Book Formerly Known as Genesis. A Study of the Use of Biblical Language in the Hebrew Fragments of the Book of Jubilees," *RevQ* 22/87 (2006) 431–49.

Idem
"A List of the Extant Hebrew Text of the Book of Jubilees, Their Relation to the Hebrew Bible and Some Preliminary Comments," *Hen* 28 (2006) 97–124.

Stökl Ben Ezra, Daniel
The Impact of Yom Kippur on Early Christianity: The Day of Atonement from Second Temple Judaism to the Fifth Century (WUNT 163; Tübingen: Mohr Siebeck, 2003).

Stone, Michael E
"Apocryphal Notes and Readings," *Israel Oriental Studies* 1 (1971) 123–31.

Idem
"The Book[s] Attributed to Noah," *DSD* 13 (2006) 4–23.

Idem
Fourth Ezra: A Commentary on the Book of Fourth Ezra (Hermeneia; Minneapolis: Fortress Press, 1990).

Stone, Michael, Aryeh Amihai, and Vered Hillel, eds.,
Noah and His Book(s) (SBLEJL 28; Atlanta: Society of Biblical Literature, 2010).

Stone, Michael E., and Jonas Greenfield
"The Fifth and Sixth Manuscripts of *Aramaic Levi Document* from Cave 4 at Qumran (4QLevi^e aram and 4QLevi^f aram)," *Le Muséon* 110 (1997) 271–92.

Strong, Justin
"Aristotle and Hippocrates in the Book of Jubilees," *JSJ* 48 (2017) 309–30.

Stuckenbruck, Loren
1 Enoch 91–108 (Commentaries on Early Jewish Literature; Berlin: de Gruyter, 2007).

Idem
"The 'Angels' and 'Giants' of Genesis 6:1-4 in Second and Third Century BCE Jewish Interpretation: Reflections on the Posture of Early Apocalyptic Traditions," *DSD* 7 (2000) 354–77.

Idem
"The Book of Jubilees and the Origin of Evil," in Gabriele Boccaccini and Giovanni Ibba, eds., *Enoch and the Mosaic Torah: The Evidence of Jubilees* (Grand Rapids: Eerdmans, 2009) 294–308.

Idem
"Pleas for Deliverance from the Demonic in Early Jewish Texts," in Robert Hayward and B. Embry, eds., *Studies in Jewish Prayer* (Oxford: Oxford University Press, 2005) 55–73.

Idem
"Prayers of Deliverance from the Demonic in the Dead Sea Scrolls and Related Early Jewish Literature," in Ian Henderson and Gerbern

Oegema, eds., *The Changing Face of Judaism, Christianity, and Other Greco-Roman Religions in Antiquity* (Studien zu den Jüdischen Schriften aus hellenistisch-römischer Zeit 2; Gütersloh: Gütersloher Verlagshaus, 2006) 146-65.

Sulzbach, Carla
"The Function of Sacred Geography in the Book of Jubilees," *Journal for Semitics* 14 (2005) 283-305.

Syrén, Roger
"Ishmael and Esau in the Book of Jubilees and Targum Pseudo-Jonathan," in Derek R. G. Beattie and Martin J. McNamara, eds., *The Aramaic Bible: Targums in Their Historical Context* (JSOTSup 166; Sheffield: JSOT Press, 1994) 310-15.

Tabory, Joseph
Jewish Festivals in the Time of the Mishnah and Talmud (3rd ed.; Jerusalem: Magnes Press, 2000).

Tafel, Gottlieb
Theodosii Meliteni qui fertur Chronographia ex codice graeco Regiae Bibliothecae monacensis (Munich: G. Franz, 1859).

Talmon, Shemaryahu
"The Beginning of the Day in the Biblical and Early Post-Biblical Periods: From Morning or From Evening?," in Sara Japhet, ed., *The Bible in the Light of Its Interpreters: Sarah Kamin Memorial Volume* (Jerusalem: Magnes Press, 1994) 73-108.

Idem
"The Calendar Reckoning of the Sect from the Judaean Desert," in Chaim Rabin and Yigael Yadin, eds., *Aspects of the Dead Sea Scrolls* (Scripta Hierosolymitana 4; Jerusalem: Magnes Press, 1958) 162-99.

Idem
"Fragments of Hebrew Writings without Identifying Sigla of Provenance from the Literary Legacy of Yigael Yadin," *DSD* 5 (1998) 149-57.

Idem
"Yom Hakkippurim in the Habakkuk Scroll," *Bib* 32 (1951) 549-63.

Ta-Shema, Y.
"On the Interpretation of a Section of the Book of Jubilees," *Bet Miqra* 11 (1966) 99-102.

Tchernowitz, Chaim
History of Hebrew Law: The Transmission and Development of the Oral Law from Its Inception to the Compilation of the Talmud, vol. 4: *From the Period of the Scribes and the Zugot to the End of the Second Commonwealth* (New York: Committee for the Publication of Rav Tzair's Collected Works, 1950) 348-88.

Teeter, D. Andrew
"On 'Exegetical Function' in Rewritten Scripture: Inner-Biblical Exegesis and the Abram/Ravens Narrative in *Jubilees*," *HTR* 106 (2013) 373-402.

Idem
"Wisdom, Torah, and Rewritten Scripture: *Jubilees* and 11QPs^a in Comparative Perspective," in Bernd U. Schipper and D. Andrew Teeter, eds., *Wisdom and Torah: The Reception of 'Torah' in the Wisdom Literature of the Second Temple Period* (JSJSup 163; Leiden: Brill, 2013) 233-72.

Tervanotko, Hanna
"'You Shall See': Rebecca's Farewell Address in 4Q364 3 ii 1-6," in Nóra Dávid, Armin Lange, Kristin De Troyer, and Shani Tzoref, eds., *The Hebrew Bible in Light of the Dead Sea Scrolls* (FRLANT 239; Göttingen: Vandenhoeck & Ruprecht, 2012) 413-26.

Testuz, Michel
Les idées religieuses du Livre des Jubilés (Geneva: E. Droz; Paris: Librairie Minard, 1960).

Thackeray, H. St. J.
Josephus, 4: Jewish Antiquities, Books I–IV (LCL 242; Cambridge, MA: Harvard University Press; London: William Heinemann, 1930).

Thiessen, Matthew
"The Text of Genesis 17:14," *JBL* 128 (2009) 625-42.

Thomas, Samuel
"Enoch, Elijah and the (Eschatological) Torah," *Hen* 31 (2009) 54-59.

Tigchelaar, Eibert J. C.
"A Cave 4 Fragment of Divre Mosheh (4QDM) and the Text of 1Q22 1:7-10 and *Jubilees* 1:9, 14," *DSD* 12 (2005) 303-12.

Idem
"Eden and Paradise: The Garden Motif in Some Early Jewish Texts (1 Enoch and Other Texts found at Qumran)," in Gerard Luttikhuizen, ed., *Paradise Interpreted: Representations of Biblical Paradise in Judaism and Christianity* (TBN 2; Leiden: Brill, 1999) 37-62.

Idem
"The Qumran *Jubilees* Manuscripts as Evidence for the Literary Growth of the Book," *RevQ* 26/104 (2014) 579-94.

Tigchelaar, Eibert, and Florentino García Martínez
"208-209. 4Q4QAstronomical Enoch^{a-b} ar," in S. J. Pfann and P. S. Alexander et al., in consultation with James VanderKam and Monica Brady, *Qumran Cave 4.XXVI: Cryptic Texts and Miscellanea, Part 1* (DJD 36; Oxford: Clarendon, 2000) 95-171 with Plates III-VII.

Tiller, Patrick
"The 'Eternal Planting' in the Dead Sea Scrolls," *DSD* 4 (1997) 312-35.

Tisserant, Eugène
"Fragments syriaques du Livre des Jubilés," *RB* 30 (1921) 55-86, 206-32.

Toorn, Karel van der, and Pieter van der Horst
"Nimrod before and after the Bible," *HTR* 83 (1990) 1-29.

Torrey, Charles Cutler
"The Aramaic of the Gospels," *JBL* 61 (1942) 71-85.

Idem
"A Hebrew Fragment of Jubilees," *JBL* 71 (1952) 39–41.
Tretti, Cristiana
"The Treasury of Heavenly Wisdom: Differing Modulations of the Concept from *1 Enoch* and *Jubilees* to Medieval Jewish Mysticism," *Hen* 31 (2009) 59–65.
Treuenfels, A.
"Die kleine Genesis בראשית זוטא," *Fürst's Literaturblatt des vorderen Orients* number 1 (1846) 7–12; number 2 (1846) 28–32; number 4 (1846) 59–64; number 5 (1846) 65–71; number 6 (1846) 81–86.
Tromp, Johannes
The Assumption of Moses: A Critical Edition with Commentary (SVTP 10; Leiden: Brill, 1993).
Trotter, Jonathan
"The Unity of *Jubilees* 5:1-18" (Unpublished paper presented at the Enoch Graduate Seminar, University of Notre Dame, 2012).
Tyloch, Witold J.
"Quelques remarques sur la provenance essénienne du Livre des Jubilés," *RevQ* 13 (1988) 347–52.
Uhden, R.
"Die Erdkreisgliederung der Hebräer nach dem Buche der Jubiläen," *Zeitschrift für Semitistik und verwandte Gebiete* 9 (1933–34) 210–33.
Ulfgard, Håkan
The Story of Sukkot: The Setting, Shaping, and Sequel of the Biblical Feast of Tabernacles (BGBE 34; Tübingen: Mohr Siebeck, 1998).
Ullendorff, Edward
Ethiopia and the Bible (Schweich Lectures, 1967; London: Oxford University Press for the British Academy, 1968).
Ulrich, Eugene
The Biblical Qumran Scrolls: Transcriptions and Textual Variants (VTSup 134; Leiden: Brill, 2010).
Urbach, Ephraim E.
The Sages: Their Concepts and Beliefs (trans. I. Abrahams; Cambridge, MA: Harvard University Press, 1987).
Vallone, G.
"Norme matrimoniali e Giubilei IV, 15-33," *Annali dell'Istituto Orientale di Napoli* 43 (1983) 201–15.
VanderKam, James C.
"2 Maccabees 6, 7a and Calendrical Change in Jerusalem," *JSJ* 12 (1981) 52–74.
Idem
"Adam's Incense Offering (Jubilees 3:27)," *Meghillot* 5–6 (2007) 141–56.
Idem
"The Angel of the Presence in the Book of Jubilees," *DSD* 7 (2000) 378–93.
Idem
"The Angel Story in the Book of Jubilees," in Esther Chazon and Michael E. Stone, eds., *Pseudepigraphic Perspectives: The Apocrypha and Pseudepigrapha in Light of the Dead Sea Scrolls: Proceedings of the International Symposium of the Orion Center, 12–14 January 1997* (STDJ 31; Leiden: Brill, 1999) 151–70.
Idem
"Another Citation of Greek *Jubilees*," in Andrés Piquer Otero and Pablo A. Torijano Morales, eds., *Textual Criticism and Dead Sea Scrolls Studies in Honour of Julio Trebolle Barrera: Florilegium Complutense* (JSJSup 157; Leiden: Brill, 2012) 377–92.
Idem
"Anthropological Gleanings from The Book of Jubilees," in Ulrike Mittmann-Richert, Friedrich Avemarie, and Gerbern S. Oegema, eds., *Der Mensch vor Gott: Forschungen zum Menschenbild in Bibel, antikem Judentum und Koran: Festschrift für Hermann Lichtenberger zum 60. Geburtstag* (Neukirchen-Vluyn: Neukirchener Verlag, 2003) 117–31.
Idem
"The *Aqedah*, *Jubilees*, and PseudoJubilees," in Craig A. Evans and Shemaryahu Talmon, eds., *The Quest for Context and Meaning: Studies in Biblical Intertextuality in Honor of James A. Sanders* (Biblical Interpretation Series; Leiden: Brill, 1997) 241–61.
Idem
"Authoritative Literature in the Dead Sea Scrolls," *DSD* 5 (1998) 382–402.
Idem
"Biblical Interpretation in 1 Enoch and Jubilees," in James H. Charlesworth and Craig A. Evans, eds., *The Pseudepigrapha and Early Biblical Interpretation* (JSPSup 14; Sheffield: JSOT Press, 1993) 96–125.
Idem
The Book of Jubilees (2 vols.; CSCO 510–11; Scriptores Aethiopici 87–88; Louvain: E. Peeters, 1989).
Idem
The Book of Jubilees (Guides to Apocrypha and Pseudepigrapha; Sheffield: Sheffield Academic Press, 2001).
Idem
"The Book of the Covenant," in Richard Bauckham, James Davila, and Alexander Panayotov, eds., *Old Testament Pseudepigrapha: More Noncanonical Scriptures* (Grand Rapids: Eerdmans, 2013) 1:28–32.
Idem
"Calendars and Calendrical Information in the Dead Sea Scrolls," *Revue Xristianskij Vostok* 7 (1999) 207–33.
Idem
Calendars in the Dead Sea Scrolls: Measuring Time (Literature of the Dead Sea Scrolls; London: Routledge, 1998).
Idem
"Das chronologische Konzept des Jubiläenbuches," *ZAW* 107 (1995) 80–100. An English version is "Studies in the Chronology of the Book of Jubilees," in VanderKam, *From Revelation to Canon: Studies in*

the Hebrew Bible and Second Temple Literature (JSJSup 62; Leiden: Brill, 2000) 522–44.

Idem
"Covenant and Biblical Interpretation in Jubilees 6," in Lawrence Schiffman, Emanuel Tov, and James C. VanderKam, eds., *The Dead Sea Scrolls Fifty Years after Their Discovery: Proceedings of the Jerusalem Congress, July 20–25, 1997* (Jerusalem: Israel Exploration Society and the Shrine of the Book, Israel Museum, 2000) 92–104.

Idem
"Covenant and Pentecost," *Calvin Theological Journal* 37 (2002) 239–54.

Idem
"The Demons in the Book of Jubilees," in Armin Lange, Hermann Lichtenberger, and K. F. Diethard Römheld, eds., *Die Dämonen: Die Dämonologie der israelitisch-jüdische und frühchristlichen Literatur im Kontext ihrer Umwelt / Demons: The Demonology of the Israelite-Jewish and Early Christian Literature in the Context of Their Environment* (Tübingen: Mohr Siebeck, 2003) 339–64.

Idem
"The End of the Matter? Jubilees 50:6-13 and the Unity of the Book," in Lynn LiDonnici and Andrea Lieber, eds., *Heavenly Tablets: Interpretation, Identity and Tradition in Ancient Judaism* (JSJSup 119; Leiden: Brill, 2007) 267–84.

Idem
Enoch: A Man for All Generations (Studies on Personalities of the Old Testament; Columbia: University of South Carolina Press, 1995).

Idem
Enoch and the Growth of an Apocalyptic Tradition (CBQMS 16; Washington: Catholic Biblical Association of America, 1984).

Idem
"Enoch Traditions in Jubilees and Other Second-Century Sources," *SBLASP* (1978) 1:229–51.

Idem
"Exegesis of Pentateuch Legislation in Jubilees and Related Texts Found at Qumran," in Gohei Hata and Akio Moriya, eds., *Pentateuch Traditions in [the] Ancient World = Kodai-sekai ni-okeru Mose-gohso no Densho* (Kyoto: Kyoto University Academic Press, 2011) 259–86 (Japanese version).

Idem
"Exegesis of Pentateuch Legislation in Jubilees and Related Texts Found at Qumran," in Akio Moriya and Gohei Hata, eds., *Pentateuch Traditions in the Late Second Temple Period: Proceedings of the International Workshop in Tokyo, August 28–31, 2007* (JSJSup 158; Leiden: Brill, 2012) 177–200.

Idem
"The Festival of Weeks and the Story of Pentecost in Acts 2," in Craig A. Evans, ed., *From Prophecy to Testament: The Function of the Old Testament in the New* (Peabody, MA: Hendrickson, 2004) 185–205.

Idem
From Revelation to Canon: Studies in the Hebrew Bible and Second Temple Literature (JSJSup 62; Leiden: Brill, 2000).

Idem
"Genesis 1 in Jubilees 2," *DSD* 1 (1994) 300–321.

Idem
"The Granddaughters and Grandsons of Noah," *RevQ* 16 (1994) 457–61.

Idem
"Greek at Qumran," in John J. Collins and Gregory E. Sterling, eds., *Hellenism in the Land of Israel* (Christianity and Judaism in Antiquity 13; Notre Dame, IN: University of Notre Dame Press, 2001) 175–81.

Idem
"Isaac's Blessing of Levi and His Descendants in Jubilees 31," in Donald W. Parry and Eugene Ulrich, eds., *The Provo International Conference on the Dead Sea Scrolls: Technological Innovations, New Texts, and Reformulated Issues* (STDJ 30; Leiden: Brill, 1999) 497–519.

Idem
"Jaubert's Solution to the Passion Chronology," *Revue Xristianskij Vostok* n.s. 4 (X) (2006) 536–50.

Idem
"*Jubilees* 46:6–47:1 and 4QVisions of Amram," *DSD* 17 (2010) 141–58.

Idem
"Jubilees and Hebrew Texts of Genesis-Exodus," *Textus* 14 (1988) 71–85.

Idem
"*Jubilees* and the Priestly Messiah of Qumran," *RevQ* 13 (1988) 353–65.

Idem
"Jubilees as Prophetic History," in Donald W. Parry, Stephen D. Ricks, and Andrew C. Skinner, eds., *The Prophetic Voice at Qumran: The Leonardo Museum Conference on the Dead Sea Scrolls, 11–12 April 2014* (STDJ 120; Leiden: Brill, 2017) 167–88.

Idem
"Jubilees as the Composition of One Author?," *RevQ* 26/104 (2014) 501–16.

Idem
"Jubilees' Exegetical Creation of Levi the Priest," *RevQ* 17/65-68 (1996) 359–73.

Idem
"The Jubilees Fragments from Qumran Cave 4," in Julio Trebolle Barrera and Luis Vegas Montaner, eds., *The Madrid Qumran Congress: Proceedings of the International Congress on the Dead Sea Scrolls, Madrid, 18–21 March, 1991* (2 vols.; STDJ 11; Leiden: Brill, 1992) 635–48.

Idem
"Made to Order: Creation in Jubilees," in Lance Jenott and Sarit Kattan Gribetz, eds., *In the Beginning: Jewish and Christian Cosmogony in Late Antiquity* (TSAJ 155; Tübingen: Mohr Siebeck, 2013) 23–38.

Idem
"The Manuscript Tradition of Jubilees," in Gabriele Boccaccini and Giovanni Ibba, eds., *Enoch and the Mosaic Torah: The Evidence of Jubilees* (Grand Rapids: Eerdmans, 2009) 3-21.

Idem
"Mastema in the Qumran Literature and the Book of Jubilees," in Joel Baden, Hindy Najman, and Eibert Tigchelaar, eds., *Sibyls, Scriptures, and Scrolls: John Collins at Seventy* (JSJSup 175; Leiden: Brill, 2017) 1346-60.

Idem
"Moses Trumping Moses: Making the Book of Jubilees," in Sarianna Metso, Hindy Najman, and Eileen Schuller, eds., *The Dead Sea Scrolls: Transmission of Tradition and Publication of Texts* (STDJ 92; Leiden: Brill, 2010) 25-44.

Idem
"The Origin, Character, and Early History of the 364-Day Calendar: A Reassessment of Jaubert's Hypotheses," *CBQ* 41 (1979) 390-11.

Idem
"The Origins and Purposes of the Book of Jubilees," in Matthias Albani, Jörg Frey, and Armin Lange, eds., *Studies in the Book of Jubilees* (TSAJ 65; Tübingen: Mohr Siebeck, 1997) 3-24.

Idem
"Psalm 90 and Isaiah 65 in Jubilees 23," in John Ashton, ed., *Revealed Wisdom: Studies in Apocalyptic in Honour of Christopher Rowland* (AJEC 88; Leiden: Brill, 2014) 73-81.

Idem
"The Putative Author of the Book of Jubilees," *JSS* 26 (1981) 209-17.

Idem
"Putting Them in Their Place: Geography as an Evaluative Tool," in John C. Reeves and John Kampen, eds., *Pursuing the Text: Studies in Honor of Ben Zion Wacholder on the Occasion of his Seventieth Birthday* (JSOTSup 184; Sheffield: Sheffield Academic Press, 1994) 47-69.

Idem
"Questions of Canon Viewed through the Dead Sea Scrolls," *Bulletin for Biblical Research* 11 (2001) 269-92.

Idem
"Questions of Canon Viewed through the Dead Sea Scrolls," in Lee M. McDonald and James A. Sanders, eds., *The Canon Debate* (Peabody, MA: Hendrickson, 2002) 91-109.

Idem
"Rebekah's Patriarchal Prayers," in Jeremy Penner, Ken M. Penner, and Cecilia Wassen, eds., *Prayer and Poetry in the Dead Sea Scrolls and Related Literature: Essays in Honor of Eileen Schuller on the Occasion of Her 65th Birthday* (STDJ 98; Leiden: Brill, 2012) 421-36.

Idem
"Recent Scholarship on the Book of Jubilees," in *CurBR* 6.3 (2008) 405-31.

Idem
"Response: Jubilees and Enoch," in Gabriele Boccaccini, ed., *Enoch and Qumran Origins: New Light on a Forgotten Connection* (Grand Rapids: Eerdmans, 2005) 162-70.

Idem
Review of James Scott, *On Earth as in Heaven: The Restoration of Sacred Time and Sacred Space, JSP* 15 (2006) 233-37.

Idem
"The Righteousness of Noah," in George W. E. Nickelsburg and John J. Collins, eds., *Ideal Figures in Ancient Judaism* (SBLSCS 12; Chico, CA: Scholars Press, 1980) 13-32.

Idem
"Sabbatical Chronologies in the Dead Sea Scrolls and Related Literature," in Timothy Lim, ed., *The Dead Sea Scrolls in Their Historical Context* (Edinburgh: Clark, 2000) 159-78.

Idem
"The Scriptural Setting of the Book of Jubilees," *DSD* 13 (2006) 61-72.

Idem
"The Scrolls, the Apocrypha, and the Pseudepigrapha," *Hebrew Studies* 34 (1993) 35-47.

Idem
"Shavu'ot," in Lawrence H. Schiffman and James C. VanderKam, eds., *Encyclopedia of the Dead Sea Scrolls* (2 vols.; New York: Oxford University Press, 2000) 2:871-72.

Idem
"Some Thoughts on the Relationship between the Book of Jubilees and the Genesis Apocryphon," in Ariel Feldman, Maria Cioată, and Charlotte Hempel, *Is There a Text in This Cave? Studies in the Textuality of the Dead Sea Scrolls in Honor of George J. Brooke* (STDJ 119; Leiden: Brill, 2017) 371-84.

Idem
"Studies on the Prologue and Jubilees 1," in Randal A. Argall, Beverly A. Bow, and Rodney A. Werline, eds., *For a Later Generation: The Transformation of Tradition in Israel, Early Judaism, and Early Christianity* (Harrisburg, PA: Trinity Press International, 2000) 266-79.

Idem
"The Temple Scroll and the Book of Jubilees," in George J. Brooke, ed., *Temple Scroll Studies* (JSPSup 7; Sheffield: JSOT Press, 1989) 211-36.

Idem
Textual and Historical Studies in the Book of Jubilees (HSM 14; Missoula, MT: Scholars Press, 1977).

Idem
"A Twenty-Eight-Day Month Tradition in the Book of Jubilees?," *VT* 32 (1982) 504-6.

Idem
"Viewed from Another Angle: Purity and Impurity in the Book of *Jubilees*," *JSP* 13 (2002) 209-15.

Idem
"The Wording of Biblical Citations in Some Rewritten Scriptural Works," in Edward D. Herbert and Emanuel Tov, eds., *The Bible as Book: The Hebrew Bible and the Judaean Desert Discoveries* (London: The British Library & Oak Knoll Press in Association with The Scriptorium: Center for Christian Antiquities, 2002) 41-56.

VanderKam, James C., and J. T. Milik
"4QJub^f (4Q**221**): A Preliminary Edition," *HAR* 14 (1994) 233-61.

Eidem
"4QJubilees^g (4Q222)," in George J. Brooke, ed., *New Qumran Texts and Studies: Proceedings of the First Meeting of the International Organization for Qumran Studies, Paris 1992* (STDJ 15; Leiden: Brill, 1994) 105-14.

Eidem
"The First *Jubilees* Manuscript from Qumran Cave 4: A Preliminary Publication," *JBL* 110 (1991) 243-70.

Eidem
"Jubilees," in H. Attridge et al., in consultation with James VanderKam, *Qumran Cave IV.VIII: Parabiblical Texts, Part 1* (DJD 13; Oxford: Clarendon, 1994) 1-185.

Eidem
"A Preliminary Publication of a Jubilees Manuscript from Qumran Cave 4: 4QJub^d (4Q219)," *Bib* 73 (1992) 62-83.

Vaux, Roland de
"La grotte des manuscrits hébreux," *RB* 56 (1949) 586-609.

Venter, Peter M.
"Intertekstuele aanduidings van de wêreld van het boek Jubileë," *Hervormde Teologiese Studies* 59 (2003) 957-89.

Vermes, Geza
"Bible and Midrash: Early Old Testament Exegesis," in idem, *Post-Biblical Jewish Studies* (SJLA 8; Leiden: Brill, 1975) 59-91.

Idem
"Genesis 1-3 in Post-Biblical Hebrew and Aramaic Literature before the Mishnah," *JJS* 43 (1992) 221-25.

Idem
"Leviticus 18:21 in Ancient Jewish Bible Exegesis," in Jacob J. Petuchowski and Ezra Fleischer, eds., *Studies in Aggadah, Targum and Jewish Liturgy in Memory of Joseph Heinemann* (Jerusalem: Magnes/Hebrew Union College Press, 1981) 108-24.

Idem
"New Light on the Sacrifice of Isaac from 4Q225," *JJS* 47 (1995) 140-46.

Idem
Scripture and Tradition in Judaism: Haggadic Studies (2nd ed.; StPB 4; Leiden: Brill, 1973).

Volz, Paul
Jüdische Eschatologie von Daniel bis Akiba (Tübingen: Mohr Siebeck, 1903).

Wacholder, Ben-Zion
"The Date of the Eschaton in the Book of Jubilees: A Commentary on Jub. 49:22–50:5, CD 1:1-10, and 16:2-3," *HUCA* 59 (1988) 87-101.

Idem
The Dawn of Qumran. The Sectarian Torah and the Teacher of Righteousness (HUCM 8; Cincinnati, OH: Hebrew Union College, 1983).

Idem
"How Long Did Abraham Stay in Egypt? A Study in Hellenistic, Qumran and Rabbinic Chronology," *HUCA* 35 (1964) 43-56.

Idem
"*Jubilees* as the Super Canon: Torah-Admonition versus Torah-Commandment," in Moshe J. Bernstein, Florentino García Martínez, and John Kampen, eds., *Legal Texts and Legal Issues: Proceedings of the Second Meeting of the International Organization for Qumran Studies, Cambridge 1995. Published in Honour of Joseph M. Baumgarten* (STDJ 23; Leiden: Brill, 1997) 195-211.

Idem
"The Relationship between 11QTorah (The Temple Scroll) and the Book of Jubilees: One Single or Two Independent Compositions," *SBLASP* 24 (1985) 205-16.

Wacholder, Ben-Zion, and S. Wacholder
"Patterns of Biblical Dates and Qumran's Calendar: The Fallacy of Jaubert's Hypothesis," *HUCA* 66 (1995) 1-40.

Wahl, Harald M.
"Die Jakoberzählungen der Genesis und der Jubiläen im Vergleich: Zur Auslegung der Genesis im 2. Jahrhundert v. Chr. und mit Anmerkungen zur Pentateuchforschung," *VT* 44 (1994) 524-46.

Wallrath, Martin, ed., with Umberto Roberto and Karl Pinggéra
Iulius Africanus Chronographiae: The Extant Fragments (trans. William Adler; GCS n.s. 15; Berlin: de Gruyter, 2007).

Weinfeld, Moshe
Deuteronomy 1-11: A New Translation with Introduction and Commentary (AB 5; New York: Doubleday, 1991).

Weitzman, Steven
"From Feasts into Mourning: The Violence of Early Jewish Festivals," *Religion* 79 (1999) 545-65.

Werman, Cana
"The Attitude towards Gentiles in The Book of Jubilees and Qumran Literature Compared with the Early Tannaic Halakha and Contemporary Pseudepigrapha" (PhD diss., Hebrew University of Jerusalem, 1995).

Eadem
The Book of Jubilees: Introduction, Translation, and Interpretation (Between Bible and Mishnah; Jerusalem: Yishaq Ben Zvi, 2015).

Eadem
"The Book of Jubilees and Its Aramaic Sources," *Meghillot* 8 (2010) 135–74.

Eadem
"The *Book of Jubilees* and the Qumran Community," *Meghillot* 2 (2004) 37–55.

Eadem
"The Book of Jubilees in Hellenistic Context," *Zion* 66 (2001) 275–96.

Eadem
"Epochs and End-Time: The 490-Year Scheme in Second Temple Literature," *DSD* 13 (2006) 229–55.

Eadem
"*Jubilees* 30: Building a Paradigm for the Ban on Intermarriage," *HTR* 90 (1997) 1–22.

Eadem
"Jubilees in the Hellenistic Context," in Lynn LiDonnici and Andrea Lieber, eds., *Heavenly Tablets: Interpretation, Identity and Tradition in Ancient Judaism* (JSJSup 119; Leiden: Brill, 2007), 133–58.

Eadem
"Levi and Levites in the Second Temple Period," *DSD* 4 (1997) 211–25.

Eadem
"Qumran and the Book of Noah," in Esther Chazon and Michael E. Stone, eds., *Pseudepigraphic Perspectives: The Apocrypha and Pseudepigrapha in Light of the Dead Sea Scrolls* (STDJ 31; Leiden: Brill, 1999) 171–81.

Eadem
"The Rules of Consuming and Covering the Blood in Priestly and Rabbinic Law," *RevQ* 16 (1995) 621–36.

Eadem
"The Shaping of the Events of the Generation of the Flood," *Tarbiz* 64 (1995) 183–202.

Eadem
"Te'udah: On the Meaning of the Term," in Gershon Brin and Bilhah Nitzan, eds., *Fifty Years of Dead Sea Scrolls Research: Studies in Memory of Jacob Licht* (Jerusalem: Yishaq Ben Zvi, 2001) 231–43.

Eadem
"Times and End-Time in Second Temple Literature," *Tarbiz* 72 (2004) 37–57.

Eadem
"The Torah and the Te'udah Written on the Tablets," *Tarbiz* 68 (1999) 473–92.

Eadem
"The תורה and the תעודה Engraved on the Tablets," *DSD* 9 (2002) 75–103.

Werman, Cana, and Aharon Shemesh
"*Halakhah* in the Dead Sea Scrolls," in Menahem Kister, ed., *The Qumran Scrolls and Their World* (2 vols.; Jerusalem: Yishaq Ben Zvi, 2009) 409–33.

Werman, Cana, and Aharon Shemesh
Revealing the Hidden: Exegesis and Halakha in the Qumran Scrolls (Jerusalem: Bialik, 2011).

Westermann, Claus
Genesis 1–11: A Commentary (Minneapolis: Augsburg, 1984).

Idem
Genesis 12–36: A Commentary (Minneapolis: Augsburg, 1985).

Idem
Genesis 37–50: A Commentary (Minneapolis: Augsburg, 1986).

Wevers, John W.
Genesis (Septuaginta: Vetus Testamentum Graecum Auctoritate Academiae Scientarum Gottingensis editum 1; Göttingen: Vandenhoeck & Ruprecht, 1974).

Wiesenberg, Ernest
"The Jubilee of Jubilees," *RevQ* 3 (1961–62) 3–40.

Wildberger, H.
Isaiah 1–12: A Commentary (CC; Minneapolis: Fortress Press, 1991).

Idem
Isaiah 13–27 (CC; Minneapolis: Fortress Press, 1997).

Williams, Frank
The Panarion *of Epiphanius of Salamis Book I [Sects 1–46]* (2nd ed.; NHMS 63; Leiden: Brill, 2009).

Idem
The Panarion *of Epiphanius of Salamis, Books II and III [Sects 47–80, De Fide]* (NHMS 36; Leiden: Brill, 1994).

Winston, David
The Wisdom of Solomon: A New Translation with Introduction and Commentary (AB 43; Garden City, NY: Doubleday, 1979).

Wintermute, O. S.
"Jubilees," in James Charlesworth, ed., *The Old Testament Pseudepigrapha* (2 vols.; Garden City, NY: Doubleday, 1983, 1985) 2:35–142.

Wise, Michael
"That Which Has Been Is That Which Shall Be: 4QFlorilegium and the מקדש אדם," in idem, *Thunder in Gemini and Other Essays on the History, Language and Literature of Second Temple Palestine* (JSPSup 15; Sheffield: Sheffield Academic Press, 1994) 152–85.

Wise, Michael O., Martin G. Abegg Jr., and Edward M. Cook
The Dead Sea Scrolls: A New Translation (rev. and updated ed.; New York: Harper, 2005).

Woude, Adam Simon van der
"Fragmente des Buches Jubiläen aus Qumran Höhle XI (11QJub)," in Gert Jeremias, Heinz-Wolfgang Kuhn, and Hartmut Stegemannn, eds., *Tradition und Glaube: Das frühe Christentum in seiner Umwelt* (Göttingen: Vandenhoeck & Ruprecht, 1971) 140–46.

Wright, Archie T.
The Origin of Evil Spirits: The Reception of Genesis 6:1-4 in Early Jewish Literature (2nd ed.; WUNT 198; Tübingen: Mohr Siebeck, 2013).

Xella, Paolo
"Resheph," *DDD²*, 700-703.

Yadin, Yigael
The Temple Scroll (3 vols.; Jerusalem: Israel Exploration Society, 1983).

Zahn, Molly
Rethinking Rewritten Scripture: Composition and Exegesis in the 4QReworked Pentateuch Manuscripts (STDJ 95; Leiden: Brill, 2011).

Idem
"Rewritten Scripture," in Timothy Lim and John Collins, eds., *The Oxford Handbook of the Dead Sea Scrolls* (Oxford: Oxford University Press, 2010) 323-36.

Zakovitch, Yair, and Avigdor Shinan
The Story of Judah and Tamar: Genesis 38 in the Bible, the Old Versions and the Ancient Jewish Literature (Research Projects of the Institute of Jewish Studies Monograph Series 15; Jerusalem: Hebrew University, 1992).

Zeitlin, Solomon
"The Book of Jubilees, Its Character and Its Significance," *JQR* 30 (1939-40) 1-31.

Idem
"The Book of 'Jubilees' and the Pentateuch," *JQR* 48 (1957) 218-35.

Idem
"Criteria for the Dating of Jubilees," *JQR* 36 (1945-46) 187-89.

Idem
"The Judaean Calendar during the Second Commonwealth and the Scrolls," *JQR* 57 (1966) 28-45.

Idem
"On the Beginning of the Day in the Calendar of Jubilees," *JBL* 78 (1959) 153-56.

Zimmerli, Walter
Ezekiel 2: A Commentary on the Book of the Prophet Ezekiel Chapters 25-48 (Hermeneia; Philadelphia: Fortress Press, 1983).

Zipor, Moshe
"The Flood Chronology: Too Many an Accident," *DSD* 4 (1997) 207-10.

Zobel, H.-J.
"עליון *'elyôn*," *TDOT* 11:121-39.

Zuurmond, Rochus
"Asshur in Jubilees 13.1?" *JSP* 4 (1989) 87-89.

Idem
"De misdaad van Ruben volgens Jubileeën 33:1-9," *Amsterdamse Cahiers* 8 (1987) 108-16.

Idem
"Oefeningen in Kufale" (PhD diss., University of Amsterdam, 1981).

Idem
"Het Oordeel over Kain in de Oud-Joodse Traditie," *Amsterdamse Cahiers* 3 (1982) 107-16.

Indexes

1. Passages

This index lists all major citations of ancient literature except those from Jubilees itself, although citations of Qumran manuscripts are included. The citation numbers are those of the standard English versions of the texts unless otherwise noted.

a / Hebrew Bible and Related Versions

Genesis

1–50	1
1–2	176, 194
1:1–2:9	174, 176
1:1–2:4	210
1:1–2:3	174, 176, 193, 200
1	17, 53, 85, 176, 178, 185, 187, 210, 224, 282
1:1-5	177–78, 184
1:1-2	177
1:1	177, 185
1:2	177–78, 182–84
1:3–2:4	446
1:3-30	174
1:3-5	177, 184
1:4	120, 184, 194
1:5	184
1:6-10	178
1:6-8	186
1:6	186, 194
1:7	186, 194
1:8	186
1:9-13	186
1:9-10	178
1:9	187, 192
1:10	187
1:11-12	41, 187, 432
1:11	210
1:12	174, 210
1:13	120
1:14-19	252
1:14-15	188
1:14	186, 189, 194, 452
1:15	186
1:16	188
1:17-18	188
1:17	186, 188
1:18	120, 189, 194
1:20-21	174
1:20	41, 182, 186, 189, 630
1:21	189, 210
1:22	1120
1:24-30	190
1:24	174, 191, 210
1:25	190, 210
1:26-27	309, 311
1:26	41, 174, 176, 189–91, 194, 210, 212, 227, 311
1:27	190, 214
1:28	6, 191, 210, 282, 309, 311, 600, 739, 1120
1:29-30	192, 282, 309
1:29	310
1:31	378
2–3	210, 216, 456
2	115, 187, 210–11, 216, 218, 1213
2:1-3	174–76, 193–94, 200, 214, 1201
2:1-2	192
2:1	165–66, 192
2:2-3	21
2:2	168, 176, 192–93
2:3	176, 194, 198, 204
2:4–3:24	210
2:4-9	174
2:4	176
2:5	221
2:7	215, 227
2:8	120, 187, 215, 374, 376
2:9	170, 174, 187
2:10-14	187, 221
2:10	374
2:11	618
2:13	373, 378
2:15	48, 210, 215–16, 221, 335
2:16-17	108, 210, 224, 265
2:16	224, 345, 354
2:17	82, 224–25, 266, 909
2:17-33	174
2:18–3:24	210
2:18-24	210
2:18-22	44
2:18-20	190
2:18	211–12, 214, 245
2:19	48, 210–11
2:20	210–11
2:21-22	212, 218
2:21	212
2:22	212–214
2:23	213, 458
2:24	83, 214, 446
2:25	210, 221–22
3	210, 225, 227, 233, 264
3:1	222, 224
3:2-3	224
3:2	224
3:3	108, 224, 266
3:4-5	225
3:5	225
3:6-7	225
3:6	224–25
3:7	62, 225, 230, 232
3:8-13	44
3:8	226
3:9-13	226
3:9	221
3:10-11	222
3:10	221
3:11	224
3:13	984
3:14-19	226
3:14-15	226
3:15	984
3:16	226
3:17-19	227, 264, 335
3:17	209–10, 224, 226–27
3:18	227

1251

Genesis (continued)		5:9	248	6:15	294
3:19	209, 226–27, 265	5:10	247, 269	6:17	292, 344, 349, 401, 689
3:20	57, 227, 233	5:12-18	247		
3:21	227, 230–32, 234	5:12	248	6:18	290
3:22	227	5:18	249	6:19-20	292, 308
3:23-24	62	5:20	411	6:19	211, 290, 349
3:23	215, 227, 232–33, 264	5:21-24	12, 249	6:22	274, 290, 292
		5:21	128, 249, 256	7–8	282
3:24	233	5:22	128, 249–50, 256–57	7:1	290
4:1-16	79, 239			7:2-3	211, 292, 308
4:1-2	239	5:23	250, 257–58, 411	7:2	80
4:1	57, 61, 210, 213, 233, 240–41	5:24	49, 100, 249–50, 259–60, 355	7:3	290
				7:4	292, 344, 507, 689
4:2-3	335	5:27	411	7:5	290, 292, 507
4:3-4	79, 309	5:28-29	264	7:6	264, 411
4:4-5	49, 241	5:29	247, 264, 336, 365	7:7-9	293
4:5	236	5:31	286	7:7	292
4:8	267	5:32	268, 338, 361, 370, 411, 448	7:8-9	211
4:9-12	265			7:8	507
4:9	241	6–8	689	7:10	292
4:10-12	242	6–7	344	7:11–8:17	293
4:10-11	267	6	275–76, 278–79, 283	7:11-16	293
4:10	242			7:11	274, 292–94
4:11	242–43, 266	6:1–9:17	274	7:12	294, 296
4:12	237, 242, 305	6:1-12	283	7:13	268, 293
4:13	240	6:1-5	274–75	7:14	211
4:14	4, 242, 460	6:1-4	24, 276, 283, 290	7:16	211, 274, 292–93
4:15	242, 267–68	6:1-2	275, 279	7:17-20	274, 293–94
4:16	376	6:3	89–90, 274, 276, 278–86, 289, 401	7:17	294
4:17-24	239			7:18	294
4:17-22	241	6:4	275–76, 279, 343, 403, 426	7:19	294
4:17	246, 267			7:20	294
4:23-25	243	6:5-12	276	7:21-23	260, 297
4:23	267	6:5	276–77, 344, 406, 454, 643, 688	7:21	292
4:24	242–43			7:22-23	689
4:25-26	239	6:6	278	7:23	292, 344
4:25	241, 244–45, 248	6:7-8	274–75	7:24	274, 293–95
4:26	246–47, 269–70	6:7	276–78, 292, 344, 689	8–9	303
5	57, 61, 239, 263–64, 266, 268, 274–75, 292–93, 410, 599			8	55, 304, 320
		6:8-9	290, 309	8:1	322, 534, 787
		6:8	278	8:2-3	296
		6:9	342, 411	8:2	293–94, 296
5:1-32	239	6:10	268	8:3-4	105, 295
5:1	309	6:11-13	344	8:4-5	274, 293
5:3	245–47	6:11	277, 344, 687	8:4	47, 304, 378
5:4-5	246	6:12	274–77, 325, 349, 688	8:5	296, 322
5:4	108, 240			8:6-12	296
5:5	265, 680	6:13	292, 344–45, 687–88	8:11	303
5:6	246–48			8:13-14	297
5:7	247	6:14-16	292	8:13	296, 322

8:14-19	297	9:14	315, 345	10:19	384
8:14	274, 293, 296–97	9:15	282, 311, 315, 787, 1182	10:21-22	334, 341
8:15	303			10:21	268, 366
8:17-19	211	9:16	301, 311, 314–15, 787	10:22	333, 341, 362, 377, 385, 420, 1047
8:18-22	303				
8:18	300	9:17	315		
8:19-20	274	9:18-19	341	10:23	385
8:19	274, 293, 303	9:18	268, 339, 341	10:24-29	385
8:20-22	303, 308, 314	9:20-27	231, 335, 357, 418	10:24-25	366
8:20	80, 300, 303–5, 307	9:20-21	334–35	10:24	362, 365, 420
		9:20	335, 354	10:25-26	385
8:21-22	277, 303, 308	9:21-27	334, 337	10:25	286, 361, 366–67, 418
8:21	282, 305, 314, 454, 688–89	9:21	332, 337		
		9:22	332, 338, 341	10:29	618
8:22	296, 308, 325	9:23	338	10:30	262, 295, 413
9-10	397	9:24	332, 338	10:32	418
9	54–55, 113–14, 282, 311–12, 315, 320, 338–39, 397, 655	9:25-27	339, 341, 385, 420, 665	11	57, 230, 361, 366, 391, 397, 411, 424, 430, 432
		9:25	338–39		
		9:26-27	339, 374	11:1-9	229, 377, 397, 411–12, 415–16
9:1-6	54	9:26	332, 339, 342, 376, 736		
9:1-7	54, 282, 303, 309, 634			11:1	115, 229, 412, 415
		9:27	117–18, 332, 339	11:2	412–13
9:1	282, 290, 309, 338, 402, 1120	9:28-29	357, 361, 397, 410	11:3	413
		9:29	410	11:4	412–13
9:2-6	303, 309	10-11	21, 361	11:5	415–16
9:2	300, 309–10	10	96, 113, 341, 361, 366–67, 369–70, 377, 384–85, 391, 415–16, 418	11:6-7	414–16
9:3-4	309			11:6	229, 396, 415
9:3	310			11:7	415
9:4-6	345, 347–48			11:8-9	416–17
9:4-5	310, 314, 349	10:1	268, 341, 370	11:8	416–17
9:4	114, 310, 313	10:2-31	370	11:9	415–18
9:5-6	309–10	10:2	334, 341, 362, 365, 378, 380, 388, 420	11:10-32	680
9:5	300, 310, 642			11:10-26	61, 365, 387, 418
9:6	53, 174–75, 191, 268, 282, 300, 310–11, 642			11:10-18	361
		10:3	380	11:10	268, 333
		10:6-12	426	11:12-15	365
9:7-20	54	10:6	338–39, 341, 378, 385	11:12-13	85, 362, 420
9:7	282, 290, 303, 309, 311, 402, 1120			11:12	198
		10:7-19	385	11:14-17	366
		10:7	385, 618	11:16-19	366
9:8-17	54, 303	10:8-12	366, 377, 426–27	11:18-21	361
9:9-17	315	10:8	426	11:18	10, 411
9:10	315	10:10-12	386	11:20-21	425
9:11-17	303, 315	10:10	377, 413, 417	11:20	425
9:11	282–83, 300, 303, 308, 311, 314–15, 688	10:11	427	11:22-25	425, 430
		10:15-19	385, 419	11:22-23	429–30
		10:15-18	392	11:24-25	430
9:12	311, 315	10:15	732	11:26-32	455
9:13	315	10:16	498	11:26-27	425, 432

Genesis (continued)		13:3	466, 474–75	14:18	485, 655, 819,
11:26	13, 433, 458, 460	13:4	469, 474, 476, 635		873, 875–76, 1046
11:27-29	433	13:5-13	477	14:19-20	655
11:27	448	13:5	474	14:19	353, 453, 875
11:28	12, 425, 427, 447–48, 451	13:6-11	477	14:20	36, 80, 481, 483, 655, 736, 772,
11:29	61, 444, 447, 590	13:9	477–78		873, 876
11:30	431, 447, 503	13:10	470, 533	14:21-24	489, 564
11:31	419, 425, 434, 444, 447–49, 459–60, 468	13:11	533	14:21	467, 482, 485, 882
		13:12-13	477	14:22-24	6, 486
		13:12	477	14:22	453, 486
11:32	13, 431, 458–61	13:13	466, 534	14:23	473
11:33	13	13:14-17	54, 470, 477–78	14:24	496, 923
12	471–72, 617, 768	13:14	478, 768	15	54, 56, 93, 435,
12:1-3	22, 54, 175, 444, 452, 455–56, 531	13:15	469, 478		437, 439, 459, 489–90, 493, 496,
12:1	49, 455, 564, 569, 1092	13:16	438, 466, 478, 598, 721, 768		498, 500, 513, 536–37, 565, 635,
12:2	195, 309, 436, 443, 456, 617, 667, 739, 850	13:17	466, 478–79, 496		1156
		13:18	80, 109, 469, 471–72, 476–77, 479,	15:1-6	489, 492–93
12:3	456, 596, 617, 740, 768, 858, 861, 1122		496, 541, 587, 654, 721, 811, 928	15:1-4	489
				15:1-2	492
		14	115, 439, 478–80, 483, 489–90, 565,	15:1	452, 455–56, 489–90, 737
12:4–14:24	467		876, 920, 923, 928	15:2-3	490–91
12:4	451–52, 458–62, 505, 705–6	14:1	479	15:2	490
12:5-6	419	14:2	479–80	15:3	491
12:5	419, 467–68, 483	14:3	479	15:4	452, 491
12:6	419, 468–69	14:5	479, 805	15:5	453, 492–93, 737
12:7	54, 80, 465, 469, 513, 541, 635, 721, 1106	14:6	618	15:6	492, 562, 565, 835, 862
		14:7	499		
		14:8-11	479	15:7-21	489, 492
12:8	465, 469–71, 541, 635, 767	14:8	479–80	15:7	425, 435, 448, 450, 488, 492, 541
		14:9	479		
12:9	471, 476	14:10	467, 479	15:8	492–93
12:10-20	62, 472, 474, 476, 713, 718	14:11	480	15:9	488, 493
		14:12	480	15:10	493, 496
12:10	564	14:13-16	920	15:11	435, 437, 497
12:11-13	472	14:13-14	480	15:12-21	497
12:11	473	14:13	457, 481, 496, 499, 587, 811, 923	15:12-16	497
12:13	23, 472			15:12	428, 497, 501
12:15	472, 564, 1027	14:14-20	467, 481	15:13	449, 459, 497–98, 537, 705, 1090
12:16	473, 475, 564, 718, 790	14:14	467, 480, 483, 491, 923, 995		
		14:15	491	15:14	498, 1153, 1157, 1163
12:17	473	14:16	482, 875–76		
12:19	23	14:17-24	479	15:15	493, 677
13	479, 768, 812, 966	14:17	485	15:16-17	499
13:1	473, 476	14:18-24	655	15:16	419, 498, 805
13:2	473	14:18-20	476, 873	15:17	493, 499, 501
				15:18-21	499, 661

15:18-19	437	17:15-22	510, 516	18:19	79, 341–42, 345, 539, 607–9, 611, 616, 626, 629, 667–68, 717, 737, 942, 958
15:18	49, 418, 437–38, 499, 501	17:15	516		
		17:16	516, 1002		
15:21	499	17:17	516–17		
16	63, 489, 502–4, 557, 560	17:19	517, 521, 532–33, 537		
				18:22-33	533–34
16:1-4	489, 502–3	17:20	517, 607, 737	18:25	419, 533
16:1-3	593	17:21	322, 508, 513, 517, 610	19:1-11	533–34
16:1-2	503			19:1	531, 533–34
16:1	503	17:22	518	19:5	534
16:2	63, 503, 785	17:23-24	564	19:8	534
16:3	474, 476–77, 489, 503–5, 510, 592	17:23	510, 518, 610, 914	19:12-23	533–34
		17:24-25	511	19:13	533
16:4-14	504, 557	17:24	518, 705	19:15	531, 534, 613
16:4-6	555	17:25-26	610–11	19:24-38	531, 533
16:6-14	23, 560	17:25	505, 518	19:24-25	533, 963
16:8-9	555	17:26-27	510, 518	19:24	533
16:10	557	17:26	518	19:26	534
16:11	504, 559–60	17:27	508, 519	19:27-28	533
16:12	504, 522	18–19	608	19:29	533–34, 787
16:13	61, 554, 560	18	121, 536, 538	19:30-38	528, 533–34
16:14	560, 713	18:1-15	531	19:37-38	534–35
16:15-16	489, 502–3	18:1-8	439	19:37	535
16:15	503, 713	18:1-2	531	19:38	535
16:16	504, 705, 713	18:1	49, 496, 530–31, 536, 561, 587, 811, 1106	20	21, 23, 62, 447, 471, 476, 536, 542, 553, 718
17	54, 56, 79, 510–12, 514, 519, 521, 526, 610, 635, 886				
		18:2-9	531	20:1	530–31, 535, 587, 719
17:1-27	510, 512	18:3	531		
17:1-8	510, 513	18:4	531	20:6	475
17:1-6	1120	18:6	744	20:7	453, 851
17:1	510, 513, 886, 1106	18:7	744	20:12	433, 447, 1139
		18:9-10	63	20:16	475, 1042
17:2	513–14, 517	18:9	531	20:18	475
17:4	513–514	18:10	518, 530–31, 533, 538	21	536–37, 553–54, 557
17:5-8	667				
17:5	514, 886	18:11	532	21:1-4	37, 530–31, 535
17:6	513–14, 517, 886	18:12-15	530–31	21:1	536, 538
17:7-8	456, 492	18:12	517, 532	21:2	536
17:7	513–14, 521, 661	18:13-15	49	21:3	537, 540
17:8	469, 478, 514	18:13-14	532	21:4	522, 536–37, 540, 610–11
17:9-14	510, 514, 526	18:14	322, 518, 532, 538		
17:9-10	610, 717	18:15	532	21:5-7	537
17:9	514	18:16—19:38	530, 533	21:5	540, 595, 705
17:10-14	515	18:16-21	533	21:8-21	537, 553
17:10	508, 514–15	18:16	533, 807	21:8-14	553, 564
17:11	509, 514–15	18:17-19	607	21:8-13	553
17:12	515	18:18-19	607	21:8	553, 562
17:13	515, 521	18:18	443, 456, 596, 617, 1122	21:9	522, 554–55, 560
17:14	515–16			21:10	64, 522, 555

1255

Genesis (continued)		22:12	44, 564, 571–73	23:19	588, 653, 811, 949, 1126
21:11	552–53, 556	22:13	567, 574	23:20-21	935
21:12	64, 530, 552, 556–57, 653	22:14	567, 569, 571, 574–75	23:20	732
21:14-21	553, 557	22:15-19	54	24	23, 449, 590–92, 763
21:14	536, 557, 569	22:15-18	195, 568, 575	24:1—25:4	586, 590
21:15	557–58	22:15	562, 575	24:2-4	734
21:16-17	559	22:16-18	575–76, 717	24:2-3	592
21:16	552, 554, 558, 560	22:16	567, 575–76, 584	24:3-4	592, 733
21:17-18	558	22:17-18	717	24:3	613, 615, 665
21:17	552, 554, 558–59	22:17	478, 576, 711, 721, 737	24:4	109, 733
21:18	557	22:18	596, 617, 1122	24:5-7	592
21:19	552, 559–60	22:19	536, 561, 568, 576, 587, 653	24:7	592, 615
21:20-21	559			24:9	592
21:20	552, 559	22:20-24	449, 460, 576, 590–91, 734, 803	24:10-33	1150
21:21	552, 559, 618, 764	22:20-23	590–91	24:10	460, 935
21:22-34	23, 553, 560, 587, 721–22, 920	22:20-21	59	24:15	109, 590–91
		22:20	591, 734	24:21	455
21:22	459	22:22	591	24:24	591
21:25	719	22:23	245, 590–91	24:27	592, 736, 862, 1107
21:30-34	719	22:24	1038		
21:30-31	536	23	499, 586–89, 613	24:28-61	803
21:31-34	536	23:1-2	587	24:29-30	591
21:31	722	23:1	561, 587, 589, 705	24:29	591, 803
21:32	722	23:2	587, 589, 653, 811	24:37-38	592, 734
21:33	459, 471, 542, 558	23:3-18	588	24:40	455, 592
21:34	561	23:3-7	732	24:42	455
22	561, 563, 569, 574–76, 579–80, 587, 635	23:3-4	588	24:47	591
		23:4	588	24:48	734
		23:5-6	588	24:53	591
22:1-19	560, 563, 568, 576	23:6	588	24:55	591
22:1-6	568	23:7-9	588	24:56	455, 592
22:1	51, 489, 553, 560–64, 566, 568	23:7	588	24:59	864
		23:8-9	588	24:62-27	593
22:2	563, 568–69 571–73, 575	23:9	588, 1126	24:62	713
		23:10-11	588	24:67	949
22:3-4	569	23:10	732	25–26	712
22:3	569	23:11	588, 1126	25	676, 964, 987
22:4	569–70	23:12-18	588	25:1-4	539, 586, 592
22:5	570–71	23:12	588, 732	25:1	592
22:6	570–71	23:13	588, 732	25:2-4	618
22:7-10	568, 570	23:14-15	588	25:2	7, 593, 929
22:7	445, 570, 574	23:15-16	588	25:3-4	593, 607
22:8	570–71, 574	23:16	588, 732, 992	25:3	385, 1153
22:9	541, 571	23:17-18	588	25:5-6	606, 618
22:10	570–71	23:17	1126	25:6	618
22:11-14	568, 571	23:18	732	25:7-11	595
22:11	49, 562, 568, 572	23:19-20	1126	25:7-8	966
				25:7	595, 607, 626–27, 680, 705, 1112

1256

25:8	626, 656, 676–77, 680, 957, 1114	26:2-4	1092	26:32	721–22
		26:2-3	716	26:33	421, 722
25:9	676, 678–79, 811, 965–66, 1126	26:2	716–17, 1093, 1106	26:34-35	665, 731–32, 734
		26:3-4	717	26:34	613, 812, 985
25:10	679	26:3	469, 598, 717, 720, 769	26:35	732, 745
25:11–26:32	712			27	598, 602, 626, 654–55, 657–58, 716, 731, 745–46, 766, 778, 850, 964, 977
25:11	712–13	26:4-5	717		
25:12-28	712–13	26:4	598, 617, 737, 959		
25:12-18	560, 713	26:5	79, 135, 607, 630, 645, 717, 909		
25:12-16	522, 560				
25:13-18	1001	26:6	712, 718	27:1-41	745
25:13-16	607	26:6-11	766	27:1-40	730–31
25:13	553, 557, 560	26:7-10	718	27:1-4	746
25:17	733	26:8	718	27:1-2	756, 762
25:18	618, 653	26:9-10	718	27:1	743, 750
25:19-28	586, 713	26:11-16	712, 718	27:2	626
25:19-27	586, 593	26:11	710, 718	27:3	746
25:19-20	591	26:12-17	718–19	27:4	743, 746–47, 896
25:19	1001	26:12-14	653	27:5-13	731
25:20	590–91, 705	26:12-13	718, 1032	27:5-10	745
25:21-22	593	26:12	710	27:5	745–47
25:21	785	26:14-16	722	27:6–28:4	760, 762
25:22-23	602, 943	26:14	710, 718, 812	27:6-9	943
25:23	593, 716, 755, 950, 987	26:15	719	27:6	747
		26:16	719, 920	27:7	747
25:24-28	596	26:17-22	712, 719	27:9	744, 747, 749, 753, 896
25:24-27	594	26:17-21	722		
25:24-26	595, 1049	26:17	719	27:10	747
25:25-26	754	26:18	719	27:11-12	748
25:25	987	26:19-25	719	27:11	594
25:26	539, 594–95, 705	26:19	710, 719	27:12	748, 762
25:27	594, 745, 765, 809, 945, 970	26:20-21	719	27:13	748–49
		26:20	710, 719–20	27:14	744, 749, 896
25:28	586, 595–97, 602, 745	26:21	710, 720	27:15	747, 749
		26:22	710–11, 719–20, 1120	27:16	749
25:29-34	712–14, 963			27:17	654, 744, 896
25:29	714	26:23-25	712, 720, 1090, 1092	27:18-19	750
25:30	709, 714–15			27:18	445
25:31	714–15	26:23	653	27:19	23, 748, 750, 753
25:32-33	715	26:24	456, 711, 716, 720–22, 769, 1106, 1122	27:20	744, 750
25:32	715			27:21-22	751
25:33	715			27:21	744, 750
25:34	714–15, 977	26:25	541, 635, 721, 959	27:22	748
26	598, 712, 719, 721–23, 725, 731, 1092	26:26-33	712, 721, 920, 959	27:23	744, 751
		26:26-31	721–22	27:24	744, 750–51
		26:26	711, 722	27:25	655, 744, 751, 862
26:1-5	712, 716	26:28	721	27:26-27	658, 751–52, 851
26:1-4	1092	26:29	722	27:26	744
26:1	712–13, 716	26:31	721	27:27-29	600, 659
26:2-6	716	26:32-33	721	27:27	744, 749

Genesis (continued)		28:5	760, 763–64, 777	29:20	761, 782
27:28-29	752, 755	28:6	665, 734	29:21-22	777
27:28	655, 744, 752, 755	28:6-9	65, 613, 665, 760, 764–65, 799, 811–12	29:21	778
27:29	598, 617, 658–59, 740, 744, 762, 858, 861, 887, 924, 937, 950			29:22	778
				29:23-24	778
		28:7	762	29:23	777–78, 783
		28:8	734	29:24	777–78
27:30	667, 753	28:9	560, 733–34, 764, 812	29:25	754, 777–79, 782
27:31	753			29:26-27	777
27:32	753	28:10-22	760, 766	29:26	777, 780
27:33	746–47, 753	28:10	767, 811	29:27-28	782
27:34	745, 754	28:11	759, 767, 769	29:27	781
27:35	754, 779	28:12-15	768	29:28-30	777
27:36-37	754	28:12	759, 768–69	29:28	781
27:36	594, 716, 754, 964	28:13-15	800, 841	29:29	782
27:37	745, 950	28:13-14	771, 865	29:30	779, 781–83, 969
27:38	755	28:13	759, 768, 1091–92, 1107	29:31–30:24	783
27:39-40	755			29:31-35	1097
27:39	655, 755	28:14	598, 617, 721, 739, 759, 768, 790, 1122	29:31-32	784
27:40–28:5	731			29:31	784, 969
27:40	745, 755, 950, 979, 986, 997			29:32-35	897
		28:15	460, 720, 768, 771, 948	29:32-34	969
27:41-45	730-31			29:32	784, 788
27:41-42	944	28:16-22	769	29:33	784
27:41	756, 760, 941, 950, 961, 976–77, 985	28:16	769–70	29:34	784, 857
		28:17	770, 887	29:35	785
		28:18-19	887	30:1-14	785
27:42–28:22	760	28:18	767, 770–71, 849, 875	30:1-8	785
27:42-46	760			30:1-2	785
27:42-45	760	28:19	767, 770, 804, 849	30:1	491, 775, 785, 787
27:42	731, 736, 747, 760	28:20-22	771, 863	30:2	785
27:44-45	761	28:20	876, 948	30:3-8	786
27:45	761–62, 864	28:21-22	846	30:3-4	783
27:46	613, 665, 730–32, 735, 762–63	28:21	771, 800, 819, 848, 850, 1107	30:3	786
				30:4-6	786
28	733, 745, 764, 849	28:22	483, 770–72, 875, 878, 885, 887	30:4	775, 783
28:1-22	760			30:7-8	786
28:1-5	730–31, 849, 862	29–30	776	30:9-13	787
28:1-4	763	29	777, 779, 788	30:9	775, 787
28:1-3	732	29:1-14	592, 1150	30:10	787
28:1-2	733, 803	29:1	764, 777, 807	30:11	787
28:1	613, 665, 731–32, 734, 762–63	29:2-14	776	30:12	775, 787
		29:4	460	30:13	775, 787
28:2-4	731	29:5	591	30:14-18	787
28:2	733–34, 807, 1097	29:12	764	30:14-16	776, 787
28:3-4	752–53, 763, 915	29:15–30:24	790	30:16	783, 820
28:3	598, 733, 752, 762, 886	29:17-20	777	30:17-21	1097
		29:17	777, 779, 969, 1008	30:17-18	787
28:4	598, 738, 752, 763–64, 868			30:17	776
		29:18	777, 779, 782	30:18	776

1258

30:19-21	787, 791	31:26-42	802	32:28	175, 808
30:21	787	31:26-27	779	32:28 (Heb. v. 29)	1089
30:22-24	787	31:29	800, 802	32:29	888
30:22	534	31:30-37	802	32:30	807
30:25-26	789	31:30-36	109	32:31	808
30:25-43	777, 788	31:30-35	803	32:32	780
30:25	789, 799	31:30	764, 789, 848	32:32 (Heb. v. 33)	81
30:27-35	789	31:32-35	848	33:1-3	969
30:27	788	31:32	801–2	33:1	808, 980, 996, 1002
30:28	776	31:36	801		
30:30	789–90	31:37	801–2	33:3	807
30:35	790	31:38	790	33:4	808
30:36	789, 799	31:41	788–90	33:5	807
30:37-43	800	31:42	800, 961	33:8	807–8
30:37-42	790	31:43	782, 803	33:9-11	808
30:37-39	789	31:44-54	802	33:10	807
30:39	789	31:44	802	33:12	808
30:42	790	31:46	755, 802–3	33:13-14	819
30:43	790	31:47	73, 803	33:13	790, 807
31-33	798	31:49	243	33:14	807, 812
31	801, 803, 841	31:50	782	33:15	807–8
31:1-2	776, 788, 790	31:51-52	803	33:16	807–9, 812
31:2	790	31:51	803	33:17	809, 879, 883
31:3	799–800	31:53	764, 800, 802–3, 961	33:18	809–10, 819
31:4-16	803			33:19-20	810
31:4-5	969	31:54	802–3	33:19	919, 992
31:4	799	31:55 (Heb. 32:1)	807	33:30	808
31:6	800	32-33	808, 841	33:32	808
31:7-9	800	32:1–33:17	23	34	23, 61, 84, 660, 810, 818-25, 830, 833-35, 838, 840-42, 919-20, 931, 1046
31:7	803	32:1-2 (Heb. vv. 2-3)	807		
31:9	790	32:1 (Heb. v. 2)	807		
31:10-13	800	32:3 (Heb. v. 4)- 33:17	799, 807		
31:10	800				
31:11	800			34:1	820, 969
31:12-13	800	32:3	812, 966	34:2	814, 820–21, 920
31:12	800	32:4	807	34:3	821–22, 903
31:13	800	32:5	807	34:4	822
31:14-16	800	32:6	980, 996, 1002	34:5	821–22, 919
31:16	800	32:7	807	34:6-10	822
31:17	800–801	32:9	764, 1107	34:7	822, 824–25, 827, 829, 919, 1045–46
31:18	764, 789–90, 801, 938	32:10	768		
		32:11	807	34:8-17	1046
31:19	109, 779, 799, 848	32:18	807	34:8-12	825
31:20	797, 801	32:20	807	34:9-10	818
31:21	801	32:22-32	808	34:9	842
31:22-55	798, 801	32:23	807–8	34:11-12	822
31:22	799	32:24	808	34:12	821–22
31:23	801	32:25	878, 948	34:13	243, 821–22
31:24	800, 802	32:26	808, 948	34:14-24	823
31:25	801	32:27-28	886	34:14-17	823

1259

Genesis (*continued*)

34:14	84, 830–31	35:16	870–71, 889, 896–97	36:20-30	1001
34:15-16	825	35:17	896	36:20	980
34:15	830	35:18-20	871, 896	36:25	980
34:16	818, 842	35:18	784, 896, 1095	36:31-39	966, 992, 1001
34:17	823, 830–31	35:19	870, 896	36:31	991, 998, 1001–2, 1111
34:18-26	818	35:20	897	36:32	992
34:20-21	934	35:21-22	901–2	36:35	1001–2
34:23	823	35:21	811, 889, 896, 902	36:37	1001
34:25-29	840	35:22-25	901, 914	36:39	1001
34:25-26	823	35:22	43, 61, 810, 835, 901, 903–6, 914, 931	36:40-43	1001
34:25	814, 823–25, 840			36:43	980
34:26-29	840	35:23-26	914	37	919, 928, 1006–7, 1062–64, 1083, 1085
34:26	820, 823–24, 840	35:23-25	914		
34:27-29	818, 823	35:23	914, 969	37:1-11	1081
34:27-28	840	35:24	914	37:1	918–19, 929, 955, 967
34:27	821, 824–25	35:25	914		
34:28	840	35:26	914–15, 969	37:1-2	929, 1006
34:29	840, 847	35:27-29	746, 764, 810–12, 849, 956, 1001	37:2-11	23, 919
34:30-31	818, 840			37:2	923, 929, 1001, 1003, 1006–7, 1030, 1097, 1122
34:30	817, 834, 837, 841	35:27	92, 889, 901–2, 914–15, 919, 957, 967, 1089		
34:31	841			37:3	930, 1084
35	846, 849, 871, 902, 906, 915, 918	35:28-29	889, 965–66	37:5-11	1062
		35:28	850, 863, 957, 965, 1112	37:10	1062
35:1-15	771–72, 810, 863			37:12-36	1006
35:1-3	847	35:29	626, 656, 957, 966, 1114	37:12-14	920
35:1	846–48, 863			37:12	919
35:2-3	847	35:35-37	918	37:13-14	918, 928–29
35:2	847	36	966, 1000– 1001, 1006	37:14	919, 1088–89
35:3	847			37:15-17	929
35:2	109	36:1-14	1002	37:15	919
35:4	109, 470, 845, 848	36:1-8	1001	37:17-18	918, 928
35:5	817, 841, 920	36:1-5	975	37:17	809, 929
35:6-7	848	36:1	1001	37:18-30	929
35:7	587, 849, 863	36:2	980	37:18-28	1081
35:8	91, 764, 767–68, 864, 871, 895	36:3	560, 996	37:18	929
		36:4-5	996	37:21-22	835
35:9-13	871, 885–86, 895	36:4	996–97	37:22	1047, 1064
35:9-12	891	36:6-9	812	37:23	1084
35:9	885, 888, 1106	36:6-8	812, 966	37:25-28	929
35:10-15	195	36:6	1000	37:25	1068–69
35:10	175, 886, 1089	36:8-9	980	37:26-27	835, 1037
35:11	886, 1002, 1120	36:9-14	1001	37:27	1037
35:12	868, 886–87	36:10	996	37:28	918, 928–29, 1007
35:13	887, 892	36:13	996	37:29-30	835
35:14-15	886–88	36:15-19	1001	37:31-35	929
35:14	770, 897	36:15	997	37:31-33	1014
35:15	849	36:19	980	37:31-32	929–30
35:16-21	810				
35:16-20	970				

37:31	918, 928, 1044	38:22	1035	40	1006, 1016, 1018
37:32-35	930	38:23	1035	40:1	1016
37:32-33	930	38:24-30	1037, 1045	40:2-3	1016
37:32	918, 928, 1047, 1084	38:24-26	1045	40:3	1016
		38:24	80, 612, 827, 906, 1035-36, 1047, 1050	40:4	1005, 1016-17
37:33-34	929			40:5-19	1017
37:33	930			40:5	1005, 1016-17
37:34	930, 932, 1077	38:25	1036, 1047, 1050	40:6-20	1016
37:35	666, 918, 928, 930-32, 1106	38:26	1036, 1040-41, 1047-49, 1051	40:6-8	1017
				40:7	1016
37:36	918, 928-29, 1003, 1007, 1014, 1016, 1030	38:27-30	1049, 1098	40:8	1017, 1022
		38:29-30	1049	40:9-19	1016
		39-40	1006	40:9-15	1017
38	61, 64, 835, 934-35, 1006-7, 1015, 1036-41, 1043, 1049, 1064, 1097	39	1007, 1015, 1030, 1037	40:12	1017
				40:14-15	1017-18
		39:1-6	1006-7	40:15	1013
		39:1	929, 1007, 1014, 1016, 1030	40:16-19	1017
38:1-5	1041, 1097			40:18	1017
38:1-2	1037	39:2	1008, 1015	40:21-22	1016
38:1	1041, 1044	39:3-6	1007-8	40:21	1005, 1017-18
38:2	59, 62, 665, 934, 1042	39:3	1008, 1015	40:22	1005, 1017-18
		39:4-5	1026	40:23	1016, 1018
38:3-5	1037	39:4	1004	41	1021-22, 1026, 1059, 1065
38:6-12	1037	39:6-20	64, 1006, 1008		
38:6-11	935	39:6-7	1038	41:1-45	1026
38:6-10	1097	39:6	1004, 1008	41:1-8	1017
38:6	1037	39:7	1009, 1122	41:1-7	1021
38:7	1039, 1097	39:8-9	1009	41:1	1016, 1021, 1123
38:8	1039	39:8	1004	41:5	1021
38:9-10	1039	39:9	687, 1008-9	41:8	1021
38:9	1034, 1038-39	39:10	1011, 1122-23	41:9-24	1021
38:10	1034, 1038, 1097	39:11-12	1012	41:9	1022
38:11	1040, 1050	39:11	1013	41:10-13	1022
38:12-26	1037, 1041	39:12	1004, 1013-14	41:14	1022
38:12-18	1037	39:13	1014	41:15-16	1022
38:12	934, 1040-41, 1097	39:14-15	1013	41:15	1022
		39:14	1013-14	41:17-24	1017, 1021-22
38:13	1034, 1045, 1050	39:15	1014	41:22	1021
38:14	1034, 1041-42, 1097	39:16-18	1013	41:24	1022
		39:17-18	1013	41:25	1020, 1022
38:15	1034, 1042, 1044	39:17	522, 1005, 1013-14	41:26	1022
38:16-19	1042			41:27	1021-22, 1099
38:16	1050	39:18	1005, 1014	41:28	1022
38:18	1034-35, 1043, 1098	39:19	1014	41:29-30	1022
		39:20	1015	41:29	1020, 1022
38:19-23	1037, 1043	39:21-23	1006, 1015-17	41:30-31	1021, 1023
38:19	1035, 1043	39:21	1005, 1015	41:30	1020
38:20-23	1044	39:22-23	1016	41:31	1020, 1023
38:20	1035	39:22	1005, 1015-16	41:32	1023
38:21	1035	39:23	1005, 1016	41:33-36	1023

Genesis (continued)

41:33	1024
41:34-36	1032
41:34	1020
41:35-36	1060
41:35	1020, 1057, 1060, 1075
41:36	1020–21, 1057
41:37-39	1023
41:37	1027
41:38	1020, 1023, 1027
41:39-40	1026
41:39	1020, 1024
41:40-41	1084
41:40	1020, 1024, 1026
41:41-44	1024
41:41	1024, 1027
41:43	1020, 1024–25, 1027, 1106
41:44	1024, 1026
41:45-46	1026
41:45	10, 62, 929, 934–35, 1007, 1027, 1029–30, 1099
41:46-53	1059
41:46	762, 1021, 1027, 1030, 1097, 1121, 1123
41:47-49	1031
41:47-48	1075
41:47	1121
41:48-49	1060
41:48	1023
41:49	1032
41:50-52	1030, 1099
41:50	10, 62, 929, 934–35, 1007, 1026, 1030
41:52	1017, 1120
41:53-54	1031
41:53	1037, 1049, 1097, 1121
41:54–44:2	1059
41:54-57	1122
41:54	1059–60, 1065
41:55-57	1060
41:55-56	1028
41:55	1060, 1065
41:56	1057, 1059–61
41:57	1027, 1057, 1060–61, 1065, 1085
42	1061, 1064, 1066
42:1-5	1061
42:1	1057, 1059, 1061
42:2	1057, 1066
42:3-5	1059, 1061
42:3	1057
42:4	1057, 1061, 1065
42:5	1057, 1061, 1068
42:6-17	1062
42:6	1062, 1069, 1078, 1085
42:7	1057, 1059, 1061–62
42:8	1059, 1061–62
42:9-20	1081
42:9	1058–59, 1061–62, 1094
42:10-11	1062
42:12	1062
42:13	1062–63
42:14-16	1062
42:14	1062
42:15-16	1071
42:16	1062
42:17	1059, 1061–62
42:18	1062, 1079
42:20	1071
42:21-22	1064, 1083
42:21	1063
42:22	835, 1063–64
42:23	1081
42:24	835, 1058, 1063, 1068, 1106
42:25	1058–59, 1061, 1063
42:26-34	1064
42:26-28	109
42:27-28	1064
42:28	1070
42:29-34	1081
42:29	1058–59, 1061
42:30-34	1064
42:30	1058–59, 1061
42:34	1058
42:35-38	1064
42:35	109, 1064, 1070
42:36-38	1064, 1066
42:36-37	1066
42:36	835, 1058–59, 1061, 1065, 1084
42:37-38	1059, 1066
42:37	835, 1064, 1066–67
42:38	1058–59, 1061, 1064–65, 1067, 1079
43	1065–66, 1068
43:1-2	1059, 1066
43:1	1058–60, 1065
43:2	1066
43:3-5	1066
43:6	1066
43:7	1066
43:8-10	835, 1066–67
43:8-9	1059, 1066–67
43:8	1059, 1066
43:10	1067, 1080
43:11-15	1067
43:11-14	1067
43:11	1059, 1066, 1068, 1089
43:15—44:2	1068
43:15-16	1068
43:15	1059, 1067–68
43:16-17	1068
43:16	1068
43:17-26	1069
43:17	1069
43:18-23	1068
43:18	1069–70
43:21	109
43:22	1058, 1063
43:23	835, 1059, 1068–69
43:24-25	1069
43:26-34	1069
43:26	1059, 1068–69, 1078
43:27	1069
43:28	1069, 1078
43:29-30	1068
43:29	1059, 1068–69
43:30	1068, 1106
43:32	1069, 1095, 1122, 1135
43:33-34	1070
43:34	1059, 1068, 1070
44–45	1070
44	1074
44:1-13	1074

44:1-2	1059, 1068–70, 1074	45:8	1025–27, 1083–84, 1106	46:11	1116
44:1	1074	45:9-11	1083	46:12	1054, 1096–98, 1101
44:2	1074	45:9	1082	46:13	1096
44:3-6	1074	45:10	1083, 1088, 1093–94, 1109	46:15	969, 1095–96, 1098
44:3	1070	45:12	1081–82	46:16-18	1095, 1098
44:4-5	1076	45:13	1082, 1084, 1106, 1122	46:16	1099
44:4	1074–75, 1078	45:14-15	851, 1082, 1106	46:18	969, 1095–96, 1098
44:5	1078	45:15	1081	46:19-22	1095, 1099
44:6	1073	45:16-20	1083	46:19	1095
44:7-9	1075	45:16	679, 1027–28	46:20	10, 929, 934–35, 1030
44:7	1076	45:18-19	1083		
44:8	1076	45:18	1083, 1094, 1109	46:22	1095–96, 1099
44:9	1076	45:19	1093	46:23	1100
44:10-13	1076	45:20	1083, 1089, 1093–94, 1109	46:23-25	1095, 1100
44:10	1076			46:25	1095–96, 1100
44:11	1077	45:21-28	1074, 1084	46:26-27	1101
44:13	1075	45:21-22	1084	46:26	934, 1093
44:14-34	835	45:21	1089	46:27	667, 1093, 1101
44:14-17	1074, 1077	45:22	1077, 1085	46:28-34	1083
44:14	1075, 1078	45:23-24	1085	46:28	1089, 1093–94
44:15	1071, 1078	45:24	1085	46:29-30	1106
44:16	1078	45:25	1085	46:29	851
44:17	1077–78	45:26-28	1085	46:30	863, 1082, 1103, 1106-7
44:18-34	1074, 1079	45:26	1027, 1073, 1084		
44:18	4, 1067, 1073, 1079	45:27	850, 1093	46:31—47:12	1108
		45:28	850, 1082, 1089, 1106-7	46:31—47:10	1108-9
44:19-29	1079			46:31-34	1095, 1108
44:20	1065, 1079	46	1089, 1091–92, 1094–95, 1097	46:32-34	1076
44:26	1066			46:32	1083, 1110
44:27-28	1065, 1079	46:1-4	1089	46:34	1095, 1108, 1122, 1135
44:27	1079	46:1	1089–90, 1094		
44:28	1079, 1084	46:2-4	1091	47:1-6	1083, 1095, 1108
44:30-33	1079	46:2	1090–91	47:1	1083, 1109–10
44:30-31	1080	46:3	456, 1088, 1093	47:5	1130
44:30	1079–80	46:4	676–77, 892, 1092, 1127	47:6	1094, 1108-9
44:31	1080			47:7-10	1108
44:32-33	1080	46:5-6	1093	47:8-9	762
44:32	1067	46:5	1088–89, 1093–94	47:8	1104
44:34	1079–80	46:6	1083, 1089, 1093–94, 1110	47:9	1108, 1112
45-47	1083			47:11-12	1108
45	1074, 1082–84	46:7	1093–94	47:11	1094, 1103, 1108-9
45:1-20	1074, 1081	46:8-27	934, 1089, 1094–96	47:12	1109
45:1	1081, 1089			47:13-26	1026–27, 1110
45:1-2	1081	46:8-15	1095-96	47:13-19	1110
45:3	1081	46:8	1093, 1095	47:13	1110
45:4	1082–83	46:9	995	47:14	1110
45:5	1082–83	46:10	59, 62, 835, 934–35, 1088, 1096	47:15-17	1110
45:6	1082, 1097, 1121				
45:7-8	1083				

Genesis (continued)		49	837, 1112–13	50:13	1088, 1114, 1126
47:15	1110	49:1-28	1112	50:14	1127
47:17-18	1110	49:1-2	1113	50:15–Exod 1:14	1119
47:18-21	1110	49:1	890, 1112–13	50:15-21	1121
47:19	1110	49:2	1113	50:15	1121
47:20-21	1110	49:3-27	1112	50:18	1082
47:21	924, 1110	49:3-4	835, 902, 909, 1112	50:19-21	1083
47:22	1111			50:19	785
47:23-25	1060, 1110	49:4	899, 902–4	50:20	1120
47:23-34	1111	49:5-7	23, 38, 834, 837, 840	50:21	799, 1120
47:23	924, 1111			50:22	1031, 1121, 1123
47:24-26	924	49:6	824, 857	50:24-26	23
47:25	1027, 1110	49:8	859	50:24-25	1123
47:26	1111	49:9	859	50:24	1123–25
47:27-31	892	49:10	859, 887	50:25	1123–24, 1126
47:27	1113, 1120–21	49:22-26	1112	50:26	1031, 1118, 1123–26, 1129
47:28–50:14	1112	49:22	1025, 1120		
47:28–48:20	851	49:24	1010, 1025		
47:28	1112	49:25-26	1120	Exodus	
47:29-31	1112, 1123	49:25	738	1–24	1
47:29-30	957	49:26	659	1:22–2:10	1138
47:29	1112	49:28	195, 1112	1:1-5	1123
47:30	410, 949, 1114	49:29-33	890, 1123	1:5	1027
48	851–52, 861, 958, 1112, 1121	49:29-32	949, 1112, 1114	1:6	1113, 1120, 1123, 1125
		49:29-31	968		
48:1-20	1112	49:29-30	957, 1126	1:7	598, 1113, 1120–21
48:1	852	49:29	957, 1114	1:8-10	1130
48:2	850	49:30	1114	1:8	1125, 1130
48:3-4	851	49:31	764, 940, 952, 957, 966, 968, 1114	1:9-13	1130
48:3	195			1:9-10	1133
48:5	852, 878	49:32	1112, 1126	1:9	1119, 1134–35
48:7	896–97	49:33–50:4	677	1:10	1119, 1133–34
48:8-20	862, 1114	49:33	677, 957, 1112, 1114	1:11	1119, 1131, 1133–34, 1157
48:8	851				
48:10	658, 851	50:1-14	1112, 1124	1:12	1119, 1133–35
48:11	861, 863	50:1-3	1124	1:13-14	1157
48:12	851, 861	50:1	678, 1093	1:13	1134–35, 1163
48:13-20	852	50:2-4	85	1:14	1176
48:14	595, 736	50:2-3	1125	1:22	1136–40, 1160
48:15-16	1112	50:3	679	2	18, 1139, 1142
48:15	1107	50:4-14	890	2:1-15	1137
48:16	850	50:4	679	2:1-9	1138
48:17	736	50:5-7	1134	2:1-2	1140
48:19-20	1120	50:5	957, 1114, 1127	2:1	1138
48:21-22	919, 1112	50:6	1129	2:2	1139–41
48:21	1126	50:7-14	1092	2:3	413, 1136, 1140–41
48:22	97, 824, 918–20, 922–24, 926, 928, 992–93, 1113, 1127	50:7-8	1129	2:4	1141
		50:7	1027	2:5-10	1144
		50:8	1127	2:5-6	1141
		50:9	1129, 1134	2:5	1136, 1141–42

2:6	1142	4:22	164, 195, 573, 601, 715	8:9	1156
2:7-9	1141–42			8:10 (Heb. v. 6)	1157, 1164
2:7	1137, 1142–43	4:24-26	51, 64, 1151–52, 1163	8:11	1156
2:8	1137, 1142, 1153			8:15 (Heb. v. 11)	1162
2:9	787, 1143, 1145	4:24	1148, 1153–54	8:16-28 Eth (Eng. v. 20-32)	
2:10	1137–38, 1143–45	4:25-26	1174		1155
2:11-15	1138, 1145	4:26	520–21, 1154	8:16	1156, 1164
2:11-12	1145	4:27	375	8:18 (Heb. v. 14)	1158
2:11	1137, 1142, 1145	4:28	1154	8:19 (Heb. v. 15)	1158, 1162
2:12	1137	4:29	1164	8:20	1156
2:13	156, 1137, 1145–46	4:30	1154	8:20 (Heb. v. 16)	1164
		4:31	1139	8:21	1156
2:14-15	1146	5:1–11:10	1150, 1153	8:22 (Heb. v. 18)	1157
2:14	1137, 1145–46	5:2	1157	8:23	569, 1154, 1190
2:15–4:31	1150	5:3	569	8:23 (Heb. v. 19)	1164
2:15-22	592, 776	5:6	1164	8:25	1164
2:15-20	1150	5:14	1164	8:27 (Heb. v. 23)	1157
2:15	1148, 1150	6	1128	8:29	1156
2:23	1150	6:2-8	54	8:29 (Heb. v. 25)	1164
2:24-25	1157	6:3	54	8:31	1156
2:24	787	6:5	1157	8:32 (Heb. v. 28)	1162
3–12	1154	6:6	1153, 1156–57	9:1	1156
3–4	536	6:9	1176	9:3	1154
3	1149, 1151, 1153	6:15	59, 62, 835, 934	9:5-6	1164
3:1	375	6:16-20	998, 1128	9:5	470
3:2	1151–52	6:16	1116	9:6	1154
3:6	143	6:20	1127, 1138	9:7	1162
3:7-12	1153	6:25	787	9:8-12	1148
3:8	378, 470	6:29	1156	9:8	1156
3:9	1139	7–12	1154	9:9	1155
3:12	216, 1151	7:3	1154, 1162	9:10	1155
3:13	1151	7:4	1153, 1156–57	9:11	1158
3:14-15	1151	7:5	1157	9:12	1162
3:15	1107, 1176	7:7	1139, 1144, 1150–51	9:13	1164
3:16-17	1153			9:14	1156–57
3:16	1107	7:8-13	1154	9:15	1154
3:17	1176	7:8-12	1157	9:16	1157
3:18	569	7:11-12	1157	9:18	1164
3:20	1154, 1176	7:13	1162	9:19	1148, 1154
3:21-22	1163	7:14	1157, 1162	9:20	1156
3:21	1163–64	7:15	1164	9:22	1156
3:22	1163	7:17	1157	9:25	1148, 1154–55
4:1-3	1154	7:19	1156	9:30	1156–57
4:17	1154	7:20	1156	9:34	1156, 1162
4:18-19	1150	7:22	1157, 1162	9:35	1162
4:19	1152	7:25	1154, 1164	10:1	1154, 1162
4:20	1150	8:4	1156	10:3	1156
4:21	1153–54, 1156, 1162	8:5	1156	10:4	1164
		8:6	1164	10:5	1155
4:22-23	578, 1157, 1171	8:7 (Heb. v. 3)	1158	10:6	1156

1265

Exodus (*continued*)		12:14-20	577	13:20-23	164
10:7	1156, 1159	12:14	577, 1150, 1157, 1169, 1177–78, 1180, 1182	13:20	1189
10:12	1155			14:2	1189
10:13	1164			14:4	1159, 1162
10:15	1155	12:15	516	14:5	1159, 1189
10:20	1162	12:18	1171, 1188	14:6-9	1189
10:21	1156	12:19	1183	14:6	1160
10:22-23	1164	12:21	1183	14:7	1149
10:27	1162	12:22	1172	14:8	1159, 1162
10:28	1159	12:23	578–79, 1172–75	14:9	1160, 1190
11–12	1172	12:24	1178, 1183	14:17-18	1159
11:1	1156, 1159, 1173	12:21-27	578	14:19-20	1160
11:2-3	1159, 1163	12:27	578, 1173	14:19	49, 164, 178, 1160
11:2	1163	12:28	1171	14:20-21	1189
11:3	1156, 1163	12:29-32	1150, 1153	14:20	1190
11:4-7	578	12:29-30	1154	14:21	1162
11:4-5	1173	12:29	1172–73	14:22	1160
11:4	1164	12:30	578, 1156, 1175–76	14:24	1162, 1189
11:5	1154, 1172–73	12:31	1161	14:26	1161
11:6	1175	12:31-32	1159	14:27-29	1190
11:7	1173	12:33-36	1150, 1157	14:27	1160, 1189
11:8	1156, 1159	12:33-34	577	15	1161
11:9-10	1154	12:33	1159, 1188	15:1	1160
11:10	1162	12:34	1162, 1188	15:4	1160
12–15	1161	12:35-36	474, 1159, 1163	15:5	1161
12–13	1170	12:35	1163	15:8	1161
12	545, 579, 1171–74, 1176, 1178–80, 1183, 1188	12:36	1163	15:11	960
		12:39	577, 1159, 1162, 1188	15:17-18	156
				15:17	155, 350
12:1-24	1180	12:40-41	449, 459, 493, 537	15:19	1160
12:1-13	580	12:40	498	15:21	1160
12:1	138	12:41	493, 537, 705	15:22-26	143
12:3	580, 1164, 1183	12:42	587, 1177–78	15:22	1189, 1193
12:5	574	12:43-50	1180–81	15:23	1193
12:6	1171, 1179–80, 1183	12:43	545	15:27	1193
		12:44	521	16	202–3, 1213–14
12:7	1172	12:46	1181, 1187	16:1-3	1194
12:8-9	1180–81	12:48	521, 545	16:1	138, 1192–94, 1214
12:8	1171, 1176, 1180, 1187	12:51	1162	16:4-21	1194
		13:2	578	16:5	202, 1194
12:9	1168, 1176, 1181, 1187	13:3-10	577, 579, 1188	16:16	1205
		13:3	1177, 1188	16:22-30	202, 1193
12:10	1168, 1180–81	13:5-7	1189	16:22-26	1194, 1204
12:12-13	578, 1173	13:5	1189	16:23	1209, 1213
12:11	1176, 1180–81	13:6-7	1188	16:24	1213
12:12	1153, 1155–57, 1171, 1173	13:6	1188	16:25	1209, 1213
		13:9-10	1182	16:28	135
12:13	578, 580, 1154, 1169, 1172–74, 1176, 1182	13:10	1177	16:29	203, 1194, 1207–8
		13:17	1189	16:30	1195, 1205
		13:19	23, 1126–27, 1130	16:31	667

16:35	1195	21:22-23	1065	27:21	204
17–18	1193	21:23-25	267, 642	28:3	658
17	439	21:24	168	28:38	150, 261, 352
17:1-7	1193	21:28-32	310	28:40	227
17:1	1193	22:18	909	28:41	658, 876
17:8-16	1193	23:8	642	28:42-43	230
17:14	725	23:10-12	1195	29:1	658
18	1193	23:10-11	1195	29:9	876
18:5	375, 1193	23:11	353	29:12	1187
18:16	135	23:16	316–17, 319, 577, 653	29:21	855
18:20	135			29:22	632
19–24	17, 54, 312	23:17	84	29:29-30	876
19	138, 1205	23:19	353	29:33	658
19:1-2	375	23:20-23	112, 179	29:34	884
19:1	132, 138, 312	23:20-22	49	29:38-46	1206
19:3-6	523	23:20	1160	29:38-42	314
19:3-4	375	23:24	615	29:38-41	631
19:3	667	23:25	617	29:38	1206
19:5-6	59, 204, 523, 539–40, 597, 659, 833, 913	23:31-33	662	29:42	314, 1206–7
		23:32	722	29:43	164
		23:33	148	29:45-46	161, 164, 375
19:5	54, 194–96, 539, 913, 1205	24	1, 76, 137–38, 493, 1195	29:45	151, 156
				29:46	151
19:6	539–40, 828, 1205	24:1-8	143	30:1-10	228, 1206
19:8	312	24:3-8	312	30:6-7	228
19:10-11	138	24:3	138, 204, 312, 501	30:7-8	261, 544, 1206
19:11	161	24:4	138, 146–47, 312, 501	30:8	228, 1206
19:14-15	1203			30:14	1169, 1183
19:15	74, 138, 214	24:6	312	30:19-21	640
19:18	161, 375, 499	24:7-8	54	30:19	640
19:20	130, 375	24:7	204, 312	30:22-38	545
19:24	375	24:8	312, 314, 318	30:22-33	545
20	74, 130, 1195	24:12-18	1, 85, 137	30:34-36	228
20:1–24:4	138	24:12	129–30, 138–39, 143	30:34-35	86, 544–45
20:4	428			30:34	228, 231, 545
20:5-6	697, 702	24:13-15	139	30:36	545
20:5	445, 615	24:13-14	137	31:12-17	86, 143, 175–77, 193–95
20:6	702, 838	24:13	139, 375		
20:8-11	194–95, 1194	24:15	137	31:13-17	194
20:8	196, 200, 1201	24:16-17	139–40	31:13	176–77, 193–96, 204, 523
20:9-10	1201	24:16	139–40, 960		
20:9	1202	24:17	130, 140, 960	31:14-16	200
20:10	200, 1193, 1201–2, 1208–9	24:18	140, 143	31:14-15	200–201, 1202
		25–40	86	31:14	201, 1202–3
20:12	941	25–31	143	31:15	201
20:21	180, 375	25	105, 909	31:16-17	312
20:22–23:33	143	25:5	637	31:16	201
20:26	230–31	25:8	151, 156	31:17	176–77, 193, 196
21:12-14	268	25:10	637	31:18	129, 139, 143
21:12	242	25:22	375	32	821

1267

Exodus (continued)		Leviticus		7	633
32:6	522, 555, 881	1–7	86	7:11-36	631, 654
32:11-14	156, 158	1	631	7:16-18	633, 881
32:15-20	139	1:3	261, 353, 1207	7:16	633
32:15-16	129	1:4	1207	7:18	633, 1182
32:15	139, 143	1:5	320, 496, 631	7:22-27	631
32:20	848	1:8-9	337	7:25-26	337
32:21	840	1:9	631	7:26-27	348, 630
32:25-29	835, 837	1:10	493	7:26	348, 630
32:25	837	1:11	496	7:36	204
32:26-29	836	1:14-17	493	7:38	1195
32:26	836	1:14	307	8:16	632
32:27	836	2	512	8:25	632
32:28	836	2:1-2	337, 631	9	631
32:29	836–37, 854	2:1	308, 337	9:12	631
32:30-31	840	2:2	1207	10:11	856
32:32-33	839	2:3	691	10:12-15	858
32:33	840	2:13	308, 635–36	11–15	834
33:1	147	2:15	308	11	662
33:3	147	3	631, 632–33, 881, 1187	11:41-45	662
33:14	178			11:44	539
33:19	616	3:1	543	12	214–18, 220–21, 233–34, 375
34	142, 147, 312	3:3-5	1187		
34:1	125, 129, 319	3:3-4	544, 631–32	12:1-2	214
34:2	130	3:3	496, 631–32	12:2-5	214
34:4	129	3:4	631–32	12:2	21, 62, 81, 86, 102, 110, 120, 215–17
34:5-7	960	3:5	633		
34:6	982	3:8	496, 1187	12:3	214, 521
34:7	312, 838	3:9-11	1187	12:4-5	21, 62, 81, 86, 102, 110, 120, 216–17
34:10-16	144	3:9-10	544		
34:12	662, 722	3:10	622	12:4	215–16
34:13	662	3:11	633	12:5	215
34:15	612, 662, 722	3:13	496	12:6-8	215
34:16	612, 826	3:14-16	1187	12:6	120
34:21	1208	3:14-15	544, 632	12:8	120
34:22	316, 319, 494, 511, 536, 653	3:15	632	15:18	213, 1203
		3:16-17	337, 544, 632	16	86, 289, 291–92, 306, 932–33
34:23	84	3:16	544, 633, 832		
34:26	353	3:17	348, 630–31	16:4	640
34:27	125, 133, 144–45, 147	3:35	622	16:6	932
		4	306, 660, 1187	16:9	306, 543, 930, 932
34:28	577	4:2	660	16:11	932
34:29	139	4:26	306, 543	16:15-16	306
35:2	200, 1202–3	4:27-31	306	16:15	930, 932
35:3	1208	4:27	660	16:16-17	932
40	784	5:1	244	16:16	833, 932
40:17	138	6:5-6 (Eng. vv. 12-13)	636	16:19	930
40:26-27	228			16:20	932
40:38	667	6:8-13	631	16:21	932–33
		6:20 (Eng. v. 27)	348, 640	16:22	932

16:23-24	640	18:30	156, 907	20:25	662
16:24	932	19	336, 342, 609	20:26	194, 539, 662, 828, 913
16:29	930, 932	19:1	913		
16:30	289, 660, 932–33	19:2	546, 828	20:27	908
16:31	82, 930	19:3	342	21:6-8	855
16:32-34	932	19:4	627, 633	21:6	857
16:34	289, 932	19:5	633	21:7	666
17-18	113	19:5-8	631, 633, 881	21:8	523, 857
17	114, 310, 348, 641	19:5	353	21:9	612, 827, 1046
17:4	348, 516, 829	19:8	516, 829	21:14	666
17:5	641	19:10	156	21:16-24	220
17:7	664	19:12	984	21:17	857
17:10-14	313, 630	19:17-18	609, 950, 958–59, 961, 1081, 1120–21	21:21	857
17:10	313–14, 348			21:22	857
17:11	301, 307, 310, 313, 320	19:17	686–87, 945, 949, 958, 984, 1121	22	880
				22:3	150
17:12	313, 348	19:18	342, 346, 608–9, 942, 945, 950, 958–60	22:4-7	214
17:13	313, 349, 641			22:18-19	880
17:14	114, 310, 313–14, 349, 641			22:21	880
		19:23-25	86, 335–36, 342, 351, 355	22:32	523
18	86, 306, 663, 685, 826, 829, 834, 907–9, 913	19:23	352	23	86, 495, 512, 1171, 1205
		19:24	352–54, 356	23:1-2	545
18:2-5	781	19:25	353	23:2-3	200
18:2-3	663	19:26	630	23:2	577, 1178
18:3	472	20	86, 662–63, 826–29, 831, 834, 907–8, 913	23:4	1177–78
18:6-21	780			23:5	1171, 1178–79
18:7-8	907, 911			23:6	577–78, 1188
18:8	43	20:1-21	662	23:8	1188
18:12	1138	20:2-5	826–27, 842	23:9-10	495
18:15	1050, 1054	20:2	815, 827–30, 908	23:9-21	316–17
18:18	80, 781	20:3	816, 828–29, 831–32	23:9-16	46, 494
18:19	685			23:10	320, 353
18:20	904	20:4-5	909	23:11	494
18:21-24	685	20:4	816, 827, 831	23:15-21	84, 316
18:21-22	685	20:5	827–29	23:15-16	316, 494
18:21	815, 820, 826–27, 841–42	20:7	828	23:16-20	319
		20:8	523, 828	23:16	318, 511, 653
18:23	643, 912	20:10-14	780	23:17-19	307, 322
18:24-30	306, 904, 907	20:10	612, 827, 1011	23:17	511, 654, 1091
18:24-27	685	20:11	43, 82, 905, 907–8, 910–11	23:18	511–12
18:24-25	685			23:19	512, 654
18:24	663, 907	20:12	912, 1050, 1052–54	23:20	511, 654
18:25	685			23:21	318
18:26-30	685	20:14	1050, 1052–53	23:23-25	323
18:27	663, 685	20:17	780	23:24	323
18:29-30	685	20:19-21	780	23:27	932
18:29	43, 827–28, 909, 911–12	20:19	1138	23:28	932
		20:23	663	23:29	930
		20:24	194, 662	23:32	930

1269

Leviticus (continued)

23:34	879, 885	26:31	832	9:8	1177
23:36	544, 893	26:33	153, 684, 689	9:10	1178, 1184
23:37	577, 1178	26:34-35	305, 1198	9:11	1179–80
23:38	1206	26:34	1195–96, 1198	9:12	1180
23:39-43	893	26:39-42	431	9:13	1168, 1178–79
23:39	546, 879, 893–94	26:40	159	9:14	1177
23:40-42	893	26:42	159	10:10	323, 1172
23:40-41	547	26:43	305, 1195–96, 1198	10:33	375
23:40	530, 540, 546, 548–50, 881	26:44	146	13–14	1197
23:41	546	26:45	156	13	473
23:42-43	542, 547	26:46	1195	13:21	469
23:42	542	27	882, 885	13:22	86, 109, 276, 465, 471, 473, 476
23:44	545, 577, 1178	27:2-8	882	13:23	470
24:5-9	1207	27:9-10	882	14:5	156
24:7	512, 1207	27:11-13	882	14:13-25	156
24:17-21	642	27:11	881	14:22	589
24:19-20	267	27:14-15	882	14:33-34	1196
24:19	267	27:16-24	882	14:41	629
24:46	143	27:28-29	882	15	660
25–26	1195	27:30-33	36, 86, 484, 882, 884	15:1-13	633
25	56, 86, 127–28, 1195, 1197, 1199	27:30-31	36	15:1-10	308, 631
25:1	1195	27:30	36, 351–53, 484–85, 882	15:3	631
25:2	1196–97, 1200	27:32	485, 876–77, 884	15:4-5	631
25:4	1195	27:34	1195	15:7	631
25:6	1195			15:10	631
25:8	127, 1195	Numbers		15:20-21	353
25:10-12	127	1:50-53	854	15:27	660
25:10	1196	1:2	1183	15:28	660
25:13	1195–96	1:3	1183	15:30	525
25:18-19	1199	2	994	15:31	629
25:19	1199	3:5-13	854	15:32-36	1203, 1208
25:39-43	1196	5:15	1182	15:39	612
25:47-55	1196	5:18	1182	16:3	1146
26	1195	6:24-26	86, 195, 460, 857	16:4	156
26:1	615, 627	6:24	459	16:8-10	854
26:4	616	6:25	616	16:10	1088
26:5	1199	6:26	154, 832	16:22	401
26:6	154	8:17	134	16:28	326
26:11-12	161	9	1178, 1184	16:30	666
26:12	156, 195	9:1-14	86, 1178	18	835, 885
26:13	1176	9:1-5	1171	18:1-7	854
26:14-15	838	9:2	1171, 1177	18:2	857, 1088
26:16	684	9:3	1171, 1177, 1179, 1181	18:6	1088
26:18	1195			18:8-32	858
26:20	688	9:5	1171	18:12	353
26:25	689	9:6-7	1184	18:19	636
26:26	135	9:6-14	1177	18:21-32	36, 484, 858
				18:21-27	86
				18:21-24	482, 484

1270

18:21	484	28:2	216	33:6	1189
18:22	644	28:3-8	314, 1206	33:7	1189
18:23	484–85	28:6	314, 631	33:8	1189
18:24	880	28:8	631	33:21-22	3, 414
18:25-32	484	28:9-10	1206	33:27	3, 432
18:25-28	882	28:10	1207	33:27-28	3
18:31	485	28:11-15	307, 323, 336	33:38-39	681
19	678	28:12	337	34:4	810
19:11-13	678	28:13	337	34:5	418
19:13	678	28:15	307, 336, 1171	34:6-7	371
19:20	909	28:16-17	578	34:8	469
20:14-16	1164	28:16	1171, 1179	35	306
20:29	679	28:17-25	577	35:16-21	267
21:13	804	28:17	1188	35:17	242
21:21-35	805, 920	28:19-24	1188	35:21	242
21:24	807	28:26-31	84, 316, 319, 500	35:23	949
21:33-35	376	28:26	318–19, 494, 511–12, 653	35:30-34	642
21:33	805			35:31-32	642
23:9	662	28:27-31	307, 322	35:31	642
24	659	28:27	512	35:33-34	306
24:9	740	28:30	512	35:33	306, 350, 642
24:14	1113	29	544		
24:17-18	659	29:1-6	323	Deuteronomy	
24:18	659	29:2	336	1:1	86, 128, 130
25	142, 875	29:3-4	337	1:3	101, 1144, 1196, 1200
25:1-15	86	29:5	307, 336		
25:1-14	836	29:7-11	307	1:4	376, 805
25:1-5	663	29:7	930, 932	1:6	101
25:2	663	29:11	307	2:5	868
25:6	836	29:12-40	544	2:11	804
25:7-8	836	29:12	879, 885, 893	2:12	980
25:9	836	29:13-34	543, 879, 893	2:19-21	804
25:12-13	78, 836	29:13	544	2:19	804
25:13	837–38	29:16	543	2:20-21	804
25:14	835	29:36-38	893–94	2:20	804
26	1054	29:36	544	2:21	805
26:2	1183	29:39	544, 880	2:23	306
26:4	1095	29:40	545	2:26–3:7	805
26:9	1146	30:2	864	3:1-14	376
26:19-22	1038, 1054	32:1	804	3:1	805
26:24	1096	32:3	805	3:8	804–5
26:26	1146	32:26	804	3:9	377
26:44	1099	32:33-42	806	3:10	805
26:45-51	1095	32:38	805	3:11	805
26:59	1138	32:29	804	3:13	805
26:64-65	1095	33	1189–90	3:25	418
27:16	401	33:3-7	1189	4:3	630
28–29	86, 307, 500, 1171	33:3	1189	4:4	160
28:1-15	631	33:4	1155, 1157	4:9	148, 912
28:1-2	545	33:5	1189	4:11	140, 180

1271

Deuteronomy (*continued*)

4:15-20	627	7:3-6	733	11:22	160, 446, 614
4:15-16	912	7:3-4	665, 820, 826	11:24	418, 886
4:19-20	539	7:3	830	11:28	611
4:19	445	7:5	662, 770, 848, 1155	12	313, 349, 641
4:20	658	7:6	172, 195–96, 198, 523, 539–40, 585, 596–97, 658–59, 733, 913	12:2-4	770
4:23-28	627			12:5	151
4:23	148, 153			12:6	880
4:25-28	153			12:11	151
4:25-26	153			12:16	310, 348–49, 641
4:26	153, 912	7:7	523	12:17	876
4:27-30	153	7:8-9	839	12:18	485, 881
4:27	153	7:9-12	147	12:21	151
4:28	153	7:9	629, 697, 817, 838	12:23-25	310, 348
4:29	627	7:13	617, 688	12:23-24	349
4:29-31	159	7:16	148, 445	12:23	641
4:29-30	154	7:19	589	12:24	641
4:31	146–48, 156	7:21	147	12:25	313
4:32	143	7:24	725	12:27	349, 496
4:39-40	147	7:25	691	12:28	616
4:40	153	7:26	149	12:29-32	149
5:8	428	8	627	13:3	602, 630
5:9-10	697, 702	8:1	148	13:5	160
5:9	445, 615	8:7-9	470	14	662
5:12	200	8:7	470	14:1	160
5:13-14	1201	8:8	470	14:2	195–96, 198, 523, 539–40, 658–59, 913
5:14	200, 1193, 1201-2	8:10	436		
5:16	941	8:11	627		
5:22-24	140	8:18	627	14:8	985
5:22	180	8:19	615, 627, 630	14:21	539, 659, 662
5:23	140	9:4-7	147	14:22-27	36, 86–87, 883
5:25	140	9:10	129, 139	14:22-26	353
5:28-29	130	9:11	139	14:22-23	82
5:30-31	137	9:16	611	14:22	883
5:31	139, 143	9:18	153, 156	14:23	151, 484, 876, 883
5:32-33	611	9:25-29	156–58	14:24	151
5:32	611, 688	9:25	156	14:26-27	881
6:1	143	9:26	156, 658	14:26	485
6:5	154, 614, 627, 959, 970	9:27	156, 158	15	1195
		9:29	658	15:1	353
6:11	436	10:6	101	15:9	353
6:13	960	10:8	837, 856, 1115	15:20	1186
6:14	630	10:16	159	16	1183
6:25	147	10:17-18	629	16:1-8	1171
7	144, 823, 839	10:17	288, 376, 948	16:1	545
7:1-6	86, 149, 661, 732	11:1	614, 645, 717	16:2	579
7:2-6	820	11:11-12	616	16:3-4	577
7:2-5	662	11:13	614	16:3	1177, 1188
7:2-4	820	11:14	616, 688	16:4	1180
7:2	662, 722	11:15	436	16:5-6	1187
		11:17	912	16:5-7	1183

16:6-7	1184	22:28-29	820–22	28:41	391, 684
16:6	1168, 1171, 1179–80	23:6	663	28:44	155, 684
		23:12-14	231	28:45	147, 684
16:7	1181, 1185	23:18	1044	28:46	391
16:8	893, 1188	23:21-23	864	28:48	684
16:9-12	316	24:1-5	780	28:49-50	692
16:9	495	24:1-4	905	28:51	688
16:10	319, 494	24:4	306, 685, 906	28:58	948
16:11	502, 654	25	1039	28:59-61	683
16:12	770	25:5-10	780, 1039	28:59	391, 682
16:13-15	893	26:2	353, 484, 629, 832	28:61	683–84
16:13	770	26:5-11	611	28:64	153
16:14-15	545	26:5	59, 1038	28:69 (Eng. 29:1)	912
16:14	502, 542, 546, 881	26:6	1176	29:2-3	589
16:15	540	26:10	353, 832	29:8 (Eng. v. 9)	912
16:16	84	26:11-12	485	29:10-15	146
16:22	770	26:12	883	29:12-15	146
17:2	153, 629	26:14	664	29:12	146
17:8-13	855, 1116	26:18	196, 539–40	29:14-15	146
17:8-11	856	26:19	539, 659	29:16	630
17:8	642	27	391	29:16 (Eng. v. 17)	149
17:9-14	717	27:7	881	29:17	149
17:11	611	27:14-25	391	29:21 (Eng. v. 22)	687
17:20	525	27:15-26	243	29:24	152
18:3-8	858	27:20	43, 82, 900, 905, 907–8, 911	29:25 (Heb. v. 24)	146, 525, 687
18:4	351, 353			29:26	539
18:5	854	27:24	82, 243–44, 367	29:28	243
18:7	854	27:26	391	30–31	74
18:18-19	130	28	617, 683–84, 693, 963	30:1-10	154, 159–60
19:21	642			30:1	133, 146–47
20:6	352, 354	28:3	616	30:6	159, 602
20:30	147	28:4	617	30:8	160, 687
21:1-9	243	28:6	944	30:10	160, 687
21:5	856	28:9	539	30:16	687
21:15-17	780	28:12	616	30:17	159
21:15	780	28:13-14	688	30:20	160, 614, 806
21:17	964	28:13	155	31–34	680
21:22-23	909	28:14	525, 611	31–32	75
22	904	28:15-67	391	31	76, 147, 328, 644
22:10	986	28:15	147, 684	31:2	1144
22:13-30	780	28:18	391	31:5	148
22:20-29	612	28:19	944	31:6	156, 668
22:20-21	1046	28:20	683, 687	31:8	156, 668
22:21	825, 900, 908	28:22	683–84	31:9	76, 142, 144–45
22:22	905	28:27	683	31:16-22	328, 347
22:23-24	904	28:29	693	31:16	146, 152, 410, 612
22:24	908	28:32	391	31:17	146–47, 152–53, 156, 683
22:25-27	904–5	28:35	683		
22:25	714	28:36	684	31:18-21	74
22:27	904	28:37	153	31:18	146, 153, 644, 687

1273

Deuteronomy (continued)		33:16	659	17:14-18	923
31:19	87, 145, 148	33:21	147	17:14	922
31:20	133, 147–48	33:28-29	737	17:15	922
31:21	76, 87, 133, 146–48, 158–59, 683, 687	34	18	17:17-18	923
		34:7	283, 681, 944, 1144, 1196	17:18	923
				18–20	368, 374
31:24-26	76, 147	34:8	679, 1200	18:1-10	368
31:24	144–45			18:1	1186
31:25-26	142	Joshua		18:12-13	767
31:26	1113	1:3	886	18:26	931
31:27-29	328, 347	1:4	371, 418, 732	19:1	370
31:27	74, 147, 158–59	1:8	455, 645, 659	19:8	472
31:29	153, 525, 611, 1113	1:15	668	19:17	370
		3:10	628	19:24	370
31:31	133	3:16	922	19:32	370
32	737	4:19	1200	19:40	370
32:1	687	5:9	605	19:50	924
32:4	147, 629, 736	5:10	1186	19:51	368
32:5-6	160	6:1	1125	20:7	587, 810
32:5	684	7:11	629	22:3	645
32:6-14	737	7:15	629	22:5	160, 614
32:6	164, 601	9–10	920	22:19	1186
32:8-9	87, 194, 523, 539–40, 948	9:1-2	921	22:29	1186
		9:10	805, 920	23:7	615
32:8	53, 160, 164, 523	9:17	931	23:8	160
32:9	164, 524, 662	10:5	498, 921	23:12	830
32:10	524	10:6	921	23:13	148
32:16-17	664	10:10	922	24	616
32:16	149	10:16-27	921	24:1	848
32:17	151, 662	10:28-43	921	24:2-3	87, 434, 455, 803
32:20	153, 643, 684	11	922, 1125	24:2	115, 430, 444, 446–47, 615–16
32:21	525, 615	11:1-15	922		
32:24	643	11:1	1132	24:14	616
32:25	684	11:3	921	24:15	498
32:39	615	11:23	126	24:18	616
32:41-42	684	12:1-6	804–5	24:20	133
32:46	145	12:1	804	24:21	616
33	737	12:2	807	24:23	848
33:2	112, 375	12:4-5	804	24:24	616
33:3	179	12:4	805	24:30	922, 924
33:6	903, 910	12:7	126, 418	24:32	23, 919, 1123, 1126–27, 1130
33:7	859	13:5	469		
33:8-11	836, 875	13:12	805		
33:8-9	836	13:17	805	Judges	
33:8	838	14:15	587	1:10	587
33:9-11	836	15:3	810	1:22-26	767
33:9	1115–16	15:24	472	1:27	809
33:10-11	1207	15:54	587	1:36	810
33:10	854, 856, 1116	16:1	767	2:2	662
33:11	836–37, 858	16:8	922	2:9	924

2:10	677	2:35	667, 944	13:13	831
2:11-22	693	4:4	375	13:15	903
2:11	153	10:2	896	13:32	751
2:17	612	12:20-21	616	15:16	905
2:20	629	12:21	445	14:7	459
3:6	826, 830	12:24	616	16:2	493
3:7	153	13:2	767	16:21-22	905
4-5	896	14:32-33	349	16:21	597
4	1125	15:7	618	15:9	459
4:2	1124, 1132	15:24	629	20:3	905-6
4:5	896	17:4	804	20:24	980
4:7	896	18:17-27	780	21:10	1141
4:13	896	20:13	459	22:11	179
4:23-24	1124	24:10	949	22:17-20	859
4:23	1132	24:21	725	22:38-43	859
4:24	1132	25:26	949	24:1	1152, 1174
5:5	375	29:7	459	24:14	149
5:21	896	31:10	809	24:16-17	1174
6	439			24:25	305, 1174
6:5	439	2 Samuel			
6:6	432	2:1-7	468	1 Kings	
6:10	498	2:7	597	2:3	645
6:11-12	439	2:9	468	2:10	410
6:15	439	2:14	522	4:12	809
6:17-21	439	3:3	1038	4:20	1122
6:25-32	439	6:2	375	4:31 (Heb. 5:11)	860
7-8	439	7	667, 860, 890, 914	5:4 (Heb. v. 18)	1122
7:11	597	7:8-11	860	5:5	1187
9:7-15	470	7:9	667	5:10	470
10:8	804	7:10-11	860	5:18 (Eng. v. 4)	675
11:14-23	805	7:10	135, 350	6:13	156
12:13-15	922	7:11	156	8:2	879, 885, 894
13:20	887	7:12	890	8:12	180
15:18	149	7:13	1187	8:19	1187
16:24	446	8:1-12	979	8:20	1187
18:6	459	8:12	979	8:22	735
18:31	1186	8:13-14	997, 1001	8:23	735
20:10	1045	10:5	980	8:28	453
21:19	922	10:6	979	8:29	668, 1187
		11:1-7	903	8:35	545
Ruth		11:1-5	87	8:43	1187
1:16	800	11:2	903	8:47-48	159
2:13	799	11:26-27	245	8:47	154
3:7-9	904	12:9	629	8:48	154, 1187
4:7	72	12:16	1051	8:52	668
4:18-22	1038, 1049	13	1038	8:53	194, 662
		13:1	903, 1038	8:57	668
1 Samuel		13:2	825	8:63-64	881
1-3	1186	13:4	903	8:65	419, 469, 885, 894
2:30	944, 1206	13:12	1045	8:66	540, 894

1275

1 Kings (continued)		21:14	153	6:20	668
9:3	1187	23:3	912	6:37-38	159
9:7	1187	23:4-20	848	6:38	154
10	860	23:13	149	6:40	668
10:1-10	860	23:21-23	1183, 1187	7:8	419, 894
10:24	860	23:22	1186	7:9	894
11:14	1001			7:10	894
11:43	410	1 Chronicles		7:15	668
12:15	751	1:9	385	7:16	151
13:1	130	1:19	286	7:19	148–49
14:13	376	1:24	362	8:13	319
14:19	376	1:29	560	10:15	751
14:23	151, 770	1:32	385	11:9	980
15:30	525	1:43	992, 1001	13:5	636
16:13	615	1:50	1001	15:10-15	654
16:24	588	2	1095	17:7-9	856, 1116
16:26	615	2:3-4	1054	19:2	1121
17–18	1060	2:3	934, 1037	19:7	288, 629
17:1	446	4–8	1095	19:8-11	855, 1116
17:21	453	4:1	1054	20:7	455, 562, 590, 838
18:4	152	4:17-18	1144	20:22-23	577
18:13	152	4:17	1142	20:25	577
19:8	375	4:18	1142	20:26	577
19:10	525	4:21	1054	20:34	73
19:14	525	5:1	902	23:6	855
21:20	333, 344	5:23	377	24:15	681
21:23	149	7:1	1096	24:18-19	151
21:26	806	16:36	391	24:18	150
		19:6	1038	24:19	152
2 Kings		21:1	1174	24:20-22	152
5:19	459, 896	21:2	1152	29:21	544
8:20-22	756	21:15-16	1174	30	577
9:20	197	21:18-27	575	30:16	1187
12:19 (Eng. v. 18)	150	21:15	580	30:21-26	1172
14:25	469	21:22	1174	30:21	1172, 1188
16:3	663	22:11	459	30:22	1172
17:7	148	22:16	459	30:23	1172, 1188
17:9-17	152	23–27	126	30:25-26	1172
17:9-10	151	23:4	855	31:2-12	484
17:10	770	23:13	856	31:4	1116
17:15	134, 148, 664	23:25	161	31:5	130, 484
17:16	148–49	24:5	855	31:6-10	884
17:18	153	24:6	1115	31:10	485, 884
17:20	153	26:29	855	33:3	151
17:23	153	27:1-15	126	33:7	151
17:35	615			33:19	151
18:6	160	2 Chronicles		34:3-4	151
19:15	375, 453	3:1	108, 575	34:13	855, 1115
19:19	453	5–7	894	34:33	1188
21:11-15	806	5:3	894	35:1-19	1187

35:1	1171	9:9	1157	2:5	573
35:3	855, 1116	9:11	1161	2:6-7	407
35:13	1181, 1184	9:13	135, 143	2:10	565
35:14	1187	9:14	143	5:7	643
35:18	1186	9:20	158	8:2	687
36:15-16	152	9:26-30	152	8:4	644
36:19	811	9:26	152	9:23	563
36:21	1195–96	9:29	152	11:5	456
36:23	445	9:30	153	15:2	785
		9:31	156	16:16	851
Ezra		9:32	948	17:13	666
1:2	445	9:34	134	22:19-20	700
2:25	931	9:35	378	22:19	697
4:9	377	10	150	33:2	456
6:2	420, 811	10:29	194	37:11	432
6:19-22	1183	10:35-39	485	38	182
6:21	194, 662	10:35-37	352, 484	38:4-7	182
9:1	194, 662, 806	10:35 (Eng. v. 34)	636	38:7	182, 185
9:2	539, 658, 733, 833	10:38	353	38:9	180
9:7	692	10:40 (Eng. v. 39)	151	38:12	184
9:9	146, 471	11:33	922	38:22	179
9:10	148–49	12:44-47	858	38:28	187
9:11	306, 663	12:44	353	38:29	179
9:12	663	13:5	203, 484	42:16	681
10:10-11	832	13:10-14	858		
10:11	627–28, 645, 662	13:11	151	Psalms	
10:16	662	13:17-18	150	2:6	375
		13:17	200	2:8	887
Nehemiah		13:19	1204	4:2	736
1:1	377	13:31	636	5:9 (Eng. v. 8)	459, 627, 646
1:4-5	445			7:2	453
1:6	668	Esther		7:12	419
5:12-13	391	1:2	377	9:5	419
7:29	931	1:5	377	9:11 (Eng. v. 10)	471
8	18	1:12	130	9:12 (Eng. v. 11)	375
8:6	390–91, 908	1:19	130	11:6	533
8:7-9	856	3:7	1011	14:5	733
8:7-8	1116			16:8	616
8:9	1116	Job		18:11 (Eng. v. 10)	179
8:13-18	893	1–2	51, 87, 406–7, 563	18:16-19	859
8:14–17	542, 547	1:1	594	18:37-42	859
8:15-16	548	1:5	569	19:10	147
8:17	540, 542	1:6-9	407	19:14 (Eng. 13)	460
8:18	893	1:8	594	19:15 (Eng. v. 14)	687
9:2	159, 194, 662	1:11	573	21:5 (Eng. v. 4)	806
9:5-6	342	1:12	407	22:1	453
9:6	453	1:21	736	22:25 (Heb. v. 24)	864
9:7-8	562	1:22	565	23:3	737
9:7	448	2:1-4	407	24:3	575
9:8	565	2:3	565, 594	25:3	616

Psalms (continued)

Reference	Page
25:5	616
25:15	616
25:21	616
27:14	616
30:13	453
31:6 (Eng. v. 7)	615
32:11	700
33:1	700
33:6	446
33:7	183
33:12	907
33:21	597
34:2	616
34:2 (Eng. v. 1)	732
34:18	148
34:20	1181
36:4 (Eng. v. 3)	687
37:10	700
37:11	154, 700
37:28	1007
39:10 (Eng. v. 9)	456
40:6	832
40:9 (Eng. v. 8)	627
41:13	907
42:3 (Eng. v. 2)	628
44:4 (Eng. v. 3)	616
47:5 (Eng. v. 4)	907
49:12 (Eng. v. 11)	267
50:6	419
50:14	864
51	87
51:4 (Eng. v. 2)	159, 660
51:5 (Eng. v. 3)	159
51:6 (Eng v. 4)	147
51:9 (Eng. v. 7)	159
51:12 (Eng. v. 10)	157, 159
51:13 (Eng. v. 11)	158
54:4 (Eng. v. 2)	687
58:3-4	984
68:4 (Eng. v. 3)	700
68:9 (Eng. v. 8)	375
68:17 (Eng. v. 16)	112, 375
69:28 (Heb. v. 29)	839
69:29 (Eng. v. 28)	962
69:31 (Eng. v. 30)	735
72:17	617
72:19	907
74:2	375
74:7	151
74:12	188
76:3 (Eng. v. 2)	375, 819
77:6	129
78:2	456
78:8	684
78:33	684
78:42-51	1155
78:48	643
78:49-51	1174
78:49	1174
78:51	1154
78:61	153
79:1-3	692
79:2-3	692
79:3	693
79:10	693
80:2	375
80:9	135, 155
80:9 (Eng. v. 8)	155
80:9 (Heb. v. 10)	598
80:13 (Heb. v. 14)	985
80:14	985
83:18	453
83:19 (Eng. v. 18)	616
84:3 (Eng. v. 2)	628
84:8 (Eng. v. 7)	163
86:10	453
86:13	401
89:9 Eth (MT 90:7)	683
89:10 LXX (MT 90:10)	682-84
89:11 Eth (MT 90:11)	682
89:13 Eth (MT 90:11)	683
89:23	859
90	87, 265, 680, 682, 694, 696, 702
90:3-4	265
90:3	266
90:4	74, 87, 266, 682, 685, 696, 732
90:5	698
90:7-9	685-86
90:7	682
90:9	685
90:10	432, 672-73, 682-86
90:13-17	686
90:14-15	698
90:15	696
90:15 (Eth 89:17)	682
90:16	696
91:15	1206
95:6	615
95:10	684
96:2	736
96:4-5	53
96:4	948
96:11	739
97:7	446
97:12	700
99:1	375
100:4	735-36
102:17 (Eng. v. 16)	163
103:1	632
103:21	178
104	342
104:3	182
104:4	178-79, 182
104:16-17	187
104:24	184
105:3	597
105:4	616
105:26-36	1155
105:33	1154
105:37	1163
105:45	135
105:27	1154
105:37-38	1159
106:13	148
106:19	428
106:23	156
106:28-31	835
106:28	663-64
106:31	835
106:34-39	664
106:35-37	53
106:36	148
106:37	151
106:41	153, 460
107:13	148
110	439, 873
110:1-4	873
112:2	733
113–118	541, 550
113	550
113:2	736
113:9	550

114	550	143:10	627–28	12:7	701
115:4	446, 615	145:1	736		
115:5	445	145:21	736	Song of Solomon (Canticles)	
115:8	446, 615	146:10	163	4:14	470
115:14	550	147:11	616	5:11	986
116:4	541	147:16-17	684		
116:6	541	148	181	Isaiah	
116:17	550	148:2	182, 185	1:13-14	150
118	550	148:4	178	1:4	629
118:1	550	148:7	183	1:12	832
118:14	541	148:8	179	2:3	856
118:15	550	148:9	187	2:8	446, 615
118:21	541			3:5	689
118:24	550	Proverbs		4:3-4	164
118:25	541, 549	3:6	459	5:24	319
118:27	550	3:16	970	6:2	182
118:28-29	550	3:17	970	6:3	179, 629
119:16	856	3:19-20	184	6:10	166
119:31-32	614	3:19	185	6:13	470, 539, 658, 733
119:31	160	7:22-23	988	8	74–78, 102, 142, 149, 152, 644
119:43	856	8	184		
119:61	148	8:22	80, 185	8:1-16	78
119:83	148	8:24	185	8:2	72
119:109	148	8:30	185	8:12-16	76
119:133	454	9:15	627	8:14-15	78, 149
119:137-38	147	10:3	432	8:14	134
119:137	736	11:5	459, 627, 646	8:15	149
119:141	148	11:16	970	8:16-20	76, 690
119:153	148	11:22	985	8:16-17	644
119:176	148	12:20	970	8:16	72, 76–77, 87, 134, 141, 253
121	642	12:22	970		
121:4	947	14:29	588	8:17	141, 153, 616
121:7	459, 642	15:1	970	8:18	161, 375
121:8	944	15:21	627	8:20	72, 76–77, 87, 141
123:2	616	16:17	644	8:23	810
127:3	490	16:33	368	9:6	154
129:4	736	22:18-19	522	9:7	860
133:1	950	22:24	663	9:11	692
134	342	23:15	597	9:17 (Eng. v. 16)	688
135:4	196, 539	23:23	970	11	986
135:6	177	26:19	944	11:1-5	860–61
135:7	446	31:23	970	11:2	860
135:16	445, 664	31:26	970	11:4	859–60
135:17	445–46, 615			11:5	860
135:18	446, 615	Ecclesiastes		11:6-7	984
136:2	376	5:4-6	864	11:6	986
136:5	188	5:4 (Heb. v. 3)	864	11:7	986
136:10	1154	7:8	588	11:8	984
139:7-12	726	10:12	687	11:14	979, 986, 1000
140:3	984	12:5	957	13:9	961

Isaiah (continued)					
13:17-18	692	41:8	455, 562, 590, 838, 857	57:1-2	699–700
14:1	523	41:10	490	57:1	681, 699
14:14	426	41:19	638	57:2	700
14:16	460	42:1	616	57:9	666
14:22	725	42:16	471, 668	57:12-13	445
14:29	725	42:17	428	57:18-19	166, 698–99
14:30	725	44:1	523	57:21	682, 700
15–16	535	44:8	615	58:8	698
19:11-13	473	44:9-20	87, 428, 445–46, 615	58:13	200–201, 204, 1203–4, 1207, 1209
19:11	476	44:9	445–46, 628, 664	59:7-8	644
19:13	476	44:10	445	60:2	180
19:25	913	44:11	446, 628	60:3	514
22:5	683, 693, 962	44:14	470	60:21	350
22:22	455	44:15	445	61:3	155, 351, 546
24:5-6	306	44:17	445	62:12	539
24:5	135, 839	44:18-19	628	63:6	981
24:17	691	44:18	664	63:9	49, 162, 178–79
24:23	163	44:19	149, 66-65	63:15	600
26:14	699	44:20	445	63:16	601
26:19	699–700, 702	44:24	183	63:17	913
27:12	393	45:1	514	63:18	539, 659
30	141, 690	45:5	615	64:8	164, 601
30:4	476	45:6	615	65–66	698
30:7	664	45:7	184	65	87, 682, 694, 697, 700
30:8-11	72, 87, 142	45:13	459	65:13-14	699
30:8-9	690	45:14	615	65:15	614
30:11	690	45:18	615	65:17-25	263
30:15	690	45:19	737	65:17-18	165
30:18-19	616	45:20	148, 664	65:18-19	698
30:19	1206	45:21-22	615	65:20	693–94, 697
30:21	690	46:7	148, 446	65:21-25	698
30:23	616	46:9	615	65:22	697
30:26	189	48:1-2	691	65:24	693
30:29	575	48:15	455, 659	65:25	698, 984, 986
30:30	961	48:22	682	66	87, 697, 700, 702
34:11	986	49:7	629	66:12	700
31:4	161	49:14-15	668, 740	66:14	698–702
35:10	739	50:5	456	66:15-16	702
37:16	453	51:3	263	66:15	700
37:19	446, 615	51:2	455, 599	66:16	390
37:20	453	51:16	599	66:22-23	165
40–45	87	52:7	163	66:22	702
40:2	799	54:1	775		
40:5	163	54:7	156	Jeremiah	
40:19	436	54:9	311	1:16	446, 615
40:28	459, 471	54:10	155	2:8	445
41:2	514	56:7	7	2:11	445
41:6	1121	57	699		
41:7	436				

2:18	374	16:19	615	33:6	154, 166, 698
2:21	350, 658	17:8	289	33:8	660
2:27	664	17:17	156	33:16	860
2:28	446, 615	17:19-27	150, 1202	33:17	859
2:31	684–85	17:21-22	1204	33:21-22	854
3:1	685	17:21	202	34:18-19	493
3:2	306	17:22	203	36:3	289
3:4	601	17:23	150	39:12	597
3:19	601	17:24-27	150	42:10	350
3:21-22	691	17:24	202	42:16-17	684
3:22	698	17:27	201–2	42:18	135, 153
4:1-2	691	18:18	856	43:12-13	1156
5:1	152	20:18	682	44:22	135, 153
6:4	1179	22:9	525	45:4	350
6:14	682	23:6	860	47:1	724
6:20	832	24:6	350	47:4	376, 724–25
6:23	692	24:7	156, 158, 195	48	535
7:6	133	25	723–24	48:47	535
7:29	684–85	25:14	514	49	535
8:2	693	25:15	724	49:2	693
8:11	682	25:16	724	49:7-22	962
8:19	525, 615	25:17-26	724	49:8	962
9:1 (Eng. v. 2)	156	25:18	723–24	49:13	962
10	628	25:20	723	49:17-18	962
10:1-10	664	25:27	724	50:9	692
10:3	446, 615	25:38	724	50:35	428
10:5	445–46	26:20-23	152	50:38	428
10:8	445, 615, 664	29:11	154	51:1	692
10:9-12	628	29:12-14	154	51:11	692
10:9	446, 615	29:14	154	51:15	446
10:12-13	184	29:18	134, 153, 614	51:16	179, 446
10:12	446	29:19	152	51:18	151, 664
10:13	446	30:5	682	51:39	677, 965
10:14	445, 615, 628, 664	30:10	666	51:57	677, 965
10:15	151, 445, 615, 664	30:17	166, 698		
10:16	445, 628	30:22	156, 195	Lamentations	
11:10	133	31:1	156	2:6-7	151
11:12	148	31:3	160	2:6	150
11:17	350	31:5	352	2:19	732
11:20	419	31:9	160, 164, 195, 601		
12:7	156	31:15	679, 896	Ezekiel	
12:12	682	31:33	156, 158	1:5-12	178
12:17	912	31:35-36	325	3:27	456
13:10	133	32:9	588	5:5	375
13:23	985	32:18	948	5:12	684
14:19	693	32:37-44	155	5:13	164
14:22	446, 615–16	32:38	156	5:15	135, 153
15:7	1125	32:39-40	159	6:10	164
16:10	687	32:39	158	7	682
16:19-20	445	32:41	135, 155, 350, 546	7:15	684

1281

Ezekiel (continued)		37:26-28	155, 161	10:13	571
7:21	153	37:27-28	161, 164	11:30	724
7:25	682	37:27	156	11:45	542
7:26	683, 856	37:28	163, 204, 523	12:1	571
14:6	149	38–39	380	12:2	699
14:11	156, 195	38:2	380	12:7	539, 659
14:14	256, 290	38:5	385		
14:20	256, 290	38:6	380	Hosea	
16:36	149	38:10	1133	2:1 (Eng. 1:10)	160, 628
16:38-40	908	38:12	375	2:4 (Eng. v. 2)	213
16:44	820	38:13	385	2:10 (Eng. v. 8)	688
16:46-52	614	38:15	380	2:13 (Eng. v. 11)	150, 326–27
17:18	629	39:1	380	2:15 (Eng. v. 13)	327
17:19	629	39:2	380	2:24 (Eng. v. 22)	689
18:12	149	40:4	145	2:25 (Eng. v. 23)	213
20	197	40:46	854	3:5	154
20:5-9	318	42	885	4:1-3	689
20:7-8	149	43:7	161, 828	4:1	643
20:12-24	150	43:9	161	4:3	689
20:12	194–95, 523	43:11	135	4:6	148, 856
20:16	149	43:24	636	4:14	1044
20:20	194	44:5	135	5:7	156
20:27	525	44:15-31	858	5:8	319
20:41	197	44:16	857–58	6:2	569
21:28	495	44:24	135, 150, 855	9:7	405
22:14	597	45:4-5	854	9:8	405
22:26	150	45:21-24	577	9:10	685
23:2-3	318	45:21	1171, 1188	11:1	160, 195, 601
23:22	692	45:23-25	543, 879	12:4	594, 888
23:46	693	45:23-24	1188	12:7 (Eng. v. 6)	616
24:7-8	641	45:25	893	13:1	644
24:13	660	46:12	622	13:2	446, 615
25:13	385	47:15-17	469	14:3	446, 615
25:14	963	47:20	469		
25:15	725	48:29	126	Joel	
25:16	376, 725	48:31-34	994	1:9	854
27:5	377			2:17	854
27:10	385	Daniel		4:2 (Eng. 3:2)	913
28:3	256	2:18	445	4:17 (Eng. 3:17)	164, 375
28:14	261	2:47	376	4:21 (Eng. 3:21)	375
28:16	261	3:52-90 LXX	181		
28:18	460	3:58	182	Amos	
30:14-19	1156	3:59 LXX	181, 185	1:8	725
33:22	456	3:64-73 LXX	181	1:11	97, 761, 981, 988, 997, 1000
34:16	744	7–12	20		
36:17	306	7:10	839	1:13-15	535
36:25	660	8:2	377	2:1-3	535
36:26-27	158	9:5	525	2:9-10	498
36:33-36	263	9:10	135	2:9	806
36:36	350	9:24-27	127, 221, 1195	2:11-12	87
				5:22	832

5:26	446	1:15	724	2:13-16	213
6:14	469	1:18	724	2:15	539
7:9	726	2	724	3:7	525
7:16	726	2:1	724	3:16	839
8:5	1204	2:5	376	3:17	196, 539
8:12	152	3:9	457–58	3:20 (Eng. 4:2)	166, 189, 698
8:14	725			4:4 (Heb. 3:22)	18
9	712, 725	Haggai			
9:1	724–26	1:5	145	Codex Basel	238–40, 248, 256,
9:2-4	81, 87, 724–26	1:7	145		268, 270, 365–66,
9:2	712	2:11	856		412, 425, 430
9:4	726	2:15	145		
9:7	376, 725	2:18	145		
9:12	1000			**b / New Testament**	
9:15	350	Zechariah			
		2:14 (Eng. v. 10)	161	Matthew	
Obadiah		2:15 (Eng. v. 11)	161	1:1-17	240
18	961	3	407	4:18	809
		3:1-10	857	5:24	809
Jonah		3:1-2	407	12:39	685
1:9	445	3:1	564	12:45	685
3:3	289	3:4	1158	13:8	1032
		8:3	161	15:29	809
Micah		8:8	661	16:4	685
1:3	161	8:9	597	17:17	685
4:2	856	8:10	944	22:32	143
4:7	163	8:13	155, 597	26:17-19	112
4:8	902	8:17	984	26:27-30	1176
4:13	860	10:7	597	26:61	156
7:20	738	14:16-19	542		
		14:17	545	Mark	
Nahum				1:16	809
1:11	1133	Malachi		4:3-8	439
3:13	1125	1:2-4	87	4:8	1032
3:7	460	1:2-3	984	4:14-20	439
		1:2	839	4:15	439
Habakkuk		1:6	601	7:31	809
1:3	682	1:7	858	8:38	685
1:6-9	693	1:10	832	9:19	685
1:7	428	1:12	858	12:26	143
1:17	693	1:13	832	12:28-34	959
2:1-2	1090	2	875	14:12-16	112
2:8	693	2:4-7	38, 87, 92, 836–37	14:23-26	1176
2:17	693	2:5	837–38	14:58	156
2:18	445, 664	2:6	837–38, 846, 856		
2:19	445, 615, 664	2:7	855–57	Luke	
3:5	643	2:8	837	1:1-4	125
		2:10	164, 601	1:55	738
Zephaniah		2:11-12	832	2:22	215
1:14	724	2:11	832	3:36	198, 362, 364
				8:8	1032

Luke (continued)			15:20	113		3:5	839
9:41	685		15:21	114		5:10	540
11:29	685		15:28-29	113		13:8	839
16:22-23	667		21:25	113		19:10	851
16:22	112					20:1-6	697
20:37	143		Romans			20:15	839
22:7-15	112		3:23	688		21:3	161
22:17	1176		4:3	492		21:12-14	994
22:20	1176		4:15	911			
23:12	809		4:19	593		**c / Apocrypha and Pseudepigrapha**	
			5:12	233			
John						Ahiqar (Syriac)	
1:29	112		1 Corinthians			2:62 (Syriac A)	986
2:19	156		2:9	398		8:7	986
4:5-6	922		15:45-46	160		8:11	986
4:5	922						
6:1	809		Galatians			Apocalypse of Moses	
8:56	541		3:19	111			398
13:1	112		3:6	492		1:1	145
13:29	112		6:15	398			
14:26	890					Aramaic Levi Document	
18:28	112		Ephesians				24, 60, 90–93, 99,
18:39	112		5:14	398			348, 637–38, 836,
19:14	112						873–74
19:36	1181		Philippians			1:3	823
			2:15	685		3	852
Acts			4:3	839		3:1-2	735
1:9-11	887					3:9	455
1:12	1207		Hebrews			3:10	854
1:21	944		2:2	112		3:16	857
2	113		11:9	595		3:17	856
2:9-11	113		11:29	1160		4	852, 872
2:40	685					4:4	872
7:4	460-61		James			4:7	91, 852, 872
7:6	497		2:23	492		4:8	91
7:15-16	1126		5:11	565		4:9	858
7:16	23					4:11	852–53, 855
7:22	1144		1 Peter			4:13	872
7:23	1145		2:9	540		5:1	91–92, 852, 875
7:25-26	1146		3:20	347		5:2-5	92
7:29	1146					5:2-3	875
7:30	1145		2 Peter			5:5-6	92
7:36	1145, 1154		2:5	347, 351		5:8–10:14	92
7:38	111-12		3:8	266		5:8	625, 852, 872
7:53	111					6–9	852
9:2	690		1 John			6–8	625
10-11	663		5:16	644		6:4	625
10:28	663					6:5	640, 857
15	113-14, 346		Revelation			7–10	625
15:5	114		1:6	540		7:1-3	640
						7:4-7	636

7:4	625, 639	48:42-43	233	10:4-6	348
7:5	637	53	144	10:4-5	278
7:7	625	59:3-12	144	10:6	155
8:1	496, 631	67:6	197	10:7	284
8:2	640–41			10:9-10	279–80
8:6	631, 639, 872	3 Baruch		10:9	96, 280, 399
9:6-9	636	3:7-8	413	10:11-15	404
10	625			10:11-13	278
10:1-2	852	1 Enoch		10:11-12	278–79, 284
10:1	639	Book of the Watchers (1–36)		10:11	259, 400
10:3	93, 625		24, 28, 34, 88, 90,	10:12	280
10:4	852		250, 257, 259, 274,	10:14	348
10:5	633		286, 290, 345, 399,	10:15	280, 399, 402
10:6-10	496		408	10:16	282, 350
10:6-8	640	1:1-3	252	10:17	697
10:6	641	1:2	179	10:19	689, 697, 1032
10:8	641	1:3-9	161	10:20-21	282
10:9-10	349	3	626, 637	10:20	400
10:9	641	5:8-9	698	12–16	259, 278
10:10-14	93	6–16	24, 89, 290, 403	12:1	259–60
10:10	92–93, 98, 408, 496, 625, 630, 634	6–11	259, 276, 278, 283–84, 290–91, 345, 363, 402	12:2	259
				12:3-4	250
10:11-14	852			12:4	249, 275
10:12-13	839	6	50	13–36	250
10:14	853	6:1–9:4	343	13:4	250
11:1	92, 98, 111, 935	6:1–7:2	276	13:6	250
11:3	1116	6:2	248–49, 259	13:8	674
11:5-7	784	6:6	248, 275, 286	14:5	278
11:5-6	1116	6:7	179–81, 270	15–16	53
11:6	91	7:1	257, 259, 400, 408	15:1	250
11:10-11	1138	7:2-5	279	15:3	249, 275
11:10	854	7:2	343	15:4	400
12:3-5	1138	7:3-6	283	15:6	278
12:6	821	7:3-5	280, 613	15:8–16:1	347, 402
13:4-6	854	7:4	343	15:8	403
13:4-5	1116	7:5	277	15:9–16:1	403
13:4	251	8	363–64	15:11	403, 613
13:6	251, 854, 1116	8:1	257	16:1	429
13:9-10	854	8:3	257, 278, 364, 408	16:3	249
13:15-16	854, 1116	9:6	257	17–36	89
13:16	91, 855	9:7	278	18:6-9	379
Greek ALD	637–38	9:8	275, 400	19:1	524, 664
11:6	91	9:9-10	280	24–25	228
		9:9	399, 613	24	98
Aristeas, Letter of		10–11	110, 282, 287	24:1-3	379
	125	10	283, 404, 697	25:3	161
151-52	663	10:1-3	98	25:6	697
		10:2-3	350	26:1-2	375
2 Baruch		10:3	546	28–32	262
29:5	1032	10:4-8	284, 404	32	228

1285

1 Enoch (*continued*)
Book of Parables/Similitudes (37–71)

37:1	599
39:2	961
45:2	682
50:4	288
54:7–55:2	98
60:7-10	98
60:8	260
60:17	180
60:24	98
63:8	682
69:13-25	960
69:14	960
69:15	960
69:16-17	960
69:20-24	960
69:25	960
70–71	260, 483

Book of the Luminaries/Astronomical Book (72–82)

	37, 45, 88–90, 105, 107, 112, 165, 250–52, 257, 277, 323–24, 494
72–76	251
72	252–53, 257, 295, 323
72:1	165, 250
72:4	188
72:13	494
72:32	45, 89, 324, 327
72:35-36	188
74	252–53
74:2	250
74:10-17	89
74:10	45, 89, 324
74:11-12	494
74:12-17	327
74:12	45, 89, 324
74:13	324
75	494
75:1-3	45, 251–52
75:1	323
75:2	45, 89, 323–24
77:1	161
78	252–53
78:10	252
78:15-16	89
79:1	252, 277
79:2	252, 277
79:4-5	89
79:5	252, 277
80:4	252
80:5	252
80:7	252
81	128, 250, 257–58
81:1-2	69
81:2	254
81:5-6	250, 257, 259
81:6	252–53
81:10	250
82:1-3	250, 252
82:2-3	251
82:1	250
82:6	250, 324
82:4-8	252
82:9-20	252
82:4-7	45, 494
82:4	252, 323
82:6	45, 89, 323–34
82:9-11	252
82:11	89, 323
82:13-14	252
82:13	323

Book of Dreams (83–90)

	34–35, 88–90, 250, 254
83–84	89
83:1-2	250
83:1	250, 252
84:6	350

Animal Apocalypse (85–90)

	20, 34–35, 89–90, 254, 343
85:1	252
85:3	90, 98, 111, 250, 256
85:4	90
85:6	244
86:4	34, 343
86:5-6	277
87:1	277
87:3-4	260–61
87:4	34, 343
88:2	34, 90, 343
89:2	294
89:3-4	294
89:6	34, 343
89:12	985
89:43	985
89:50	261
89:66	261, 985
89:73	261
89:70	839
89:76	839
90	687
90:6-7	687
90:9-18	34
90:9-16	34
90:16	34
90:17	839
90:20-27	839
90:28-37	254
90:28-29	156
90:39-42	260
90:40-42	260

Epistle of Enoch (91–107)

	88, 250–51, 253–54
91–104	253
91	253

Apocalypse of Weeks (93:1-10; 91:11-17)

	20, 69, 88, 90, 250, 252, 254
91:1-3	90, 252
91:1	250, 254
91:3	252
91:15	254
91:17	254
91:18-19	252
92:1	250–52, 254
93:1-3	252
93:1-2	250, 252
93:2	69, 90, 179, 254
93:3	254
93:10	350
94:1	252
98:6-8	244
100:5	701
101:1	252
102:4	252
102:5	403
103:1-4	252
103:2	69
103:7-8	348
103:9	682
104:12-13	250
106–107	90, 98, 260
106:2	694

106:15	297	1:13-14	231	4:9-17	31
106:19–107:2	98	1:14-15	31, 231	4:9-14	231
106:19	69	1:14	32	4:11-15	231
107:1	69	1:41	695	4:11	32
108:1	252	1:48	525	4:12	231
		1:20-28	32	6:7	547
3 Enoch		1:52	525	7:22-23	655
4:3-5	260	2	695–96	8:26	1209–10
		2:1	874	8:41	1210
Enochic Book of Giants		2:29-41	695–96, 1209	10:6	540
	90	2:29	695	11:1-12	34
		2:38	1209	12:21	806
4 Ezra		2:42-28	690	12:26	806
7:118	233	2:42	695		
14	143–44	2:46	525	**3 Maccabees**	
14:4-6	144	2:49-60	838	2:4-5	614
14:44-47	144	2:52-53	1009	4:8	547
14:45-46	144	2:52	565		
		4:26-35	34	**4 Maccabees**	
Jeremiah, Epistle of		5	30, 806, 999	14:13	739
4	446	5:1-8	999	15:23	739
8	445	5:3	999		
16	615	5:4-5	927	**Prayer of Joseph**	
19	664	5:4	806	B	889
23	615	5:5	806		
25	445, 615, 628	5:17-18	999	**Psalms of Solomon**	
26	446	5:37	924	17:22-25	859
39	446	5:43-44	806	17:24-25	887
41	446, 664	5:58-60	999	17:29-30	887
45	446, 615	5:65	999	17:30-31	860
53-55	438–39	6:55-62	690	17:34-35	887
53-54	438	7	692		
53	446	7:9	691	**Pseudo-Philo**	
		7:12-18	692	*Liber antiquitatum biblicarum*	
Joseph and Aseneth		7:17	692–93		19
4:7	1025	7:18	692	1:2-4	246
8:9	1026	7:21-25	690	4:11	425
11:7	1026	7:24	692	4:16	427
11:9	1026	7:26-50	927	6:1	427
18:1	1026	9:2	924	6:3-4	427
21:21	1026	9:50	922, 927	8:7-8	823
		9:54-57	692	8:9	1123
Judith		10:21	879	9:2	1140
5:6-9	449	10:83-85	927	9:4	1140
8:6	1209	10:83-84	927	9:5	1045
9:2	824, 835	11:8	1133	9:7-8	283
11:13	484	15:33-34	35	10:1	1155
				10:2	1162
1 Maccabees		**2 Maccabees**		10:5	1161
1:11	40, 524	1:24-25	655	10:6	1162
1:12-15	40	2:1-3	438		

Liber antiquitatum biblicarum (cont.)
11:2	74
11:15	143
13:7	545
13:8	283
32:1-2	561
32:3	557
32:4	572

Sibylline Oracles
2:154-59	694
3:97-107	417
3:100	413
3:110-20	392
3:114-19	115, 391
3:119-21	115
3:120-61	426
3:261-64	1032
11:10-13	417

Sirach
3:17	970
16:7-8	614
16:7	614
17:17	539
24	80
24:8	655
24:12	913
24:15	544
24:27	373
26:2	970
26:26	970
30:18-19	663–64
30:19	664
36:23	970
40:19	970
42:17	185
43	181
43:27-33	185
44:16	251, 260
44:17	290, 347
45:2	855
45:6	855
45:15-16	854
45:15	854
45:17	856
45:18-19	858
45:20-21	858
45:26	854
50:1-21	873
50:7	873
50:14	873
50:15-17	873
50:16	873
50:19	873
50:20	857
50:21	873
50:25-26	723

Testament of Job
1:5	565
4:5	565
26:5	565
27:4	565
27:7	565

Testament/Assumption of Moses
	14
1:2	1196
4:2	658
6:1	873

Testaments of the Twelve Patriarchs
Testament of Asher
8:1-2	1126

Testament of Benjamin
12:1-4	1126
12:3	1126
12:4	1126–27

Testament of Dan
1:1-2	1100
5:3	941
7:1	965
7:2	1126

Testament of Gad
6:1	941
6:3	941
7:7	941
8:1	941
8:2	1126
8:5	1126

Testament of Issachar
	7
7:8	1126
7:9	965

Testament of Joseph
	1006
2:2	1009
3:3	1010
3:9	1004, 1013
4:1	1004, 1013
4:4	1123
5:2	1004, 1013
7:1	1004, 1013
7:5-6	1010
8:2	1012
10:6	941
11:1	941
11:8	1123
15:1	1123
17:2-3	1121
17:2	941
18:3	1030
19:6	941
20:2	1126
20:4	965
20:5-6	1027
20:6	1122

Testament of Judah
	7, 110, 926
3–7	97, 918, 925, 927
3:1-8	925
3:1	920
3:7	860
4:1-3	925
5:1-7	925
5:1	925
6:1-2	925
6:3-5	925
6:3	925
7:1-3	925
7:1	925
7:2	920
7:4-9	925
7:7	924
7:9	924
7:10	976
7:11	860, 920
8:2	934
9	97, 975, 979–80, 982–83, 995, 998
9:1	976
9:2	976, 982
9:3-8	992

9:3	995–96	4:2	854, 872	9:3	1126
9:4-6	994	5:2	853		
9:4	991	5:4	824	Testament of Reuben	
9:7-8	998	6:3	823	1:6	907
9:7	991	6:4-5	824	1:7	910
10–12	1037	6:6	823, 841	1:9	910
10:1	1038, 1041	6:6-8	823	1:10	899, 910–11
10:2	1039	6:8-11	824	2:1	910
10:3	1039	6:8	825	3:13	902–3
10:4-5	1039	7:3	823	3:14	899, 904
10:4	1039	8	853, 872	3:15	905
10:6	934	8:2	872	4:4	910
11:3	1040	8:3	853, 867, 872	4:6-11	907
11:4-5	1040	8:10	853, 872	5:1–6:4	907
12:1-2	1042	8:11–15	855	6:9	941
12:1	1041	8:11	853, 855	7:2	1126
12:3	1042	8:16	858		
12:4	1043	8:17	855	Testament of Simeon	
12:5-7	1047	8:18	872	3:4	941
12:8	1049	9	880	4:7	941
12:10	1049	9:1-2	852, 875	8:2	1126
12:11	1049	9:1	858	8:3-4	1127
12:12	1049	9:2	853		
13:3	934	9:3-5	853	Testament of Zebulun	
15:3	1043	9:3-4	875	8:5	941
15:4	1051	9:4	868, 882	10:6-7	1126
16:4	934	9:6-14	625, 853		
17:1	934	9:6-7	625	Tobit	
17:5	858	9:7	853	1:6-7	484, 884
19:2-4	1051	9:9-14	625	1:10-11	662
19:2	1052	9:12	636	4:12	268
19:3	1052	11:1	934	5:17-18	766
19:4	1052	11:2-6	1116	5:19–6:1	766
21:2-4	858	12:5	821	5:21–6:1	766
21:5	858	13:2	1116	6:18	446
24:1	7	13:3	845	11:7-15	851
24:5	7	13:8	845	11:13	851
25:1-2	858	17–18	874	12:15	162
25:1	921	17:3	845		
26:4	1126	17:6	859	Visions of Amram	
		18:21	815		24, 95, 99, 1144
Testament of Levi		19:5	1126	1-14	1128
	60	21:6	859	3	1128
2:1–5:8	852			6	1129
2–5	852	Testament of Naphtali		8-9	1129
2:5–4:6	853	1:6-12	935	11	1138
2:10	853–54, 857	1:10-12	782		
2:12	858	3:5	343	Wisdom of Solomon	
3:5-6	853–54	8:2	860	2:7-8	547
4:2-4	853	9:1	1126	3:19	685

Wisdom of Solomon (*continued*)
4:10-14	681
8:9	593
9	184
10:17	1163
10:19	1161
11–19	1155, 1157
11:6-7	1157
13:1	628
13:10	628
13:17-18	628
14:8	628
14:9	628
14:21	664
14:27	628
14:29	628
17:15–18:16	628
18:5	1157, 1161
18:9	1176
18:10-12	1176

d / Dead Sea Scrolls

1Q17	5, 760
1	759
2	767
4	759, 767
5	759, 767
6	759
1Q18	5
1-2 1	938
1-2 2	938
1-2 3	938
3	944, 956
4	938
1Q22 (The Words of Moses [DM])	101, 103
i:1-4	101
i:1-2	101
i:3	101
i:6-8	149
i:6-7	101
i:7-10	101–2
i:7-8	147
i:7	149
i:8-10	101
i:9-10	101
i:8	153
i:10	147
i:11	101–2
iii:1-6	102
iii:7–iv:11	102
1Q23-24	90
1Q34 (1Q Liturgical Prayers[a])	
3 ii:6	317
1Q34bis	
3 ii:6	194
1QapGen (Genesis Apocryphon)	19, 93, 99, 307, 346, 367, 381, 471
i–xvii	98
ii:3	93, 111, 264
ii:8	93, 111, 264
ii:12	111, 264
v:29	634
vi:7	94, 111
vi:8-9	94
x:12	295, 304
x:13-18	303–4
x:13-17	93
x:13-14	335
x:13	300, 304–5
x:15	300, 307
x:17	307
xii	336
xii:8-9	340
xii:9-12	94, 341
xii:11	333
xii:13-17	93
xii:13	93, 295, 335–36
xii:14-16	335
xii:14	335
xii:16	337
xii:17	342
xiii–xv	94
xiv:9-14	340
xiv:15-22	93
xiv:15-17	115
xv	93
xvi–xvii	96, 361, 369, 384
xvi:8-25	370
xvi:8-12	379–80
xvi:9	371, 380
xvi:11	380
xvi:12	370
xvi:14-25	379
xvi:14	370
xvi:15	371
xvi:16-17	372
xvi:16	371–72
xvi:17	371–72
xvi:18	372–73
xvi:26	370, 373
xvi:27	378
xvii	93, 384, 387
xvii:7-15	384
xvii:7-8	376, 386
xvii:8-9	388
xvii:8	387
xvii:9-11	388
xvii:9	388
xvii:10	377
xvii:11-14	387
xvii:12	387
xvii:14	377
xvii:15	387
xvii:16-17	388
xvii:16	371, 380, 384, 388
xvii:17-18	389
xvii:17	389
xvii:18-19	389
xvii:18	389
xvii:20ff	390
xix:7-8	471
xix:7	465, 470
xix:8-10	472
xix:8-9	471
xix:8	465, 471
xix:9-10	109, 475
xix:9	476
xix:10	472
xix:13	373
xix:14-21	94
xix:14-19	472
xix:19-21	472
xix:23-24	472
xix:22	473
xix:23	475
xix:24	473
xix:25	251
xix:29	473
xx:1-9	473

xx:1	906	1QH[a]	104	ii:5-6	644
xx:11	472	v:24-25	406	ii:10	390
xx:12-30	475	vii:11	525	ii:18	390
xx:14	473	viii:16	160	ii:19-23	502
xx:15	899	ix:7-20	184	iii:1	908
xx:17-18	474–75	ix:7	184	iii:4-6	908
xx:31-32	503	ix:8-10	182	iii:10	266, 911
xx:33-34	473	ix:13-14	183	iii:18	736
xx:34	475	ix:14	184	iii:21	736
xxi:2-4	476	ix:19	184	iii:25	157
xxi:5-6	477	xii:35	525	iv:2-6	956
xxi:6	480	xiv:13	162, 178	iv:2	627, 737
xxi:7	466, 478	xiv:16	49	iv:3	588
xxi:8-9	478	xvi:10	351	iv:6-8	154
xxi:9-10	478	xvii:25	166	iv:6-7	166, 698
xxi:9	478	xvii:33	642	iv:10	588, 839
xxi:10-12	499	xviii:24	546	iv:23	736
xxi:13	478	xix:4-5	735	v:11	695
xxi:14	466, 478–79	xx:34	627	v:13-20	103, 107, 661
xxi:15-19	479	xxiii:25-26	642	v:14-15	663
xxi:15-17	499	xxvii:8	736	v:16-17	590
xxi:16	377	2 i:5-6	642	vi:12-14	231
xxi:19-20	479			viii:1	967
xxi:20	479	1QIsa[a]	162, 697	viii:4-6	155
xxi:21-22	480			viii:6	305
xxi:23-24	479	1QM		viii:9	197
xxi:24-34	479	i:1-2	723	viii:10	197, 305
xxi:32-33	479	vi:12	588	viii:15	911, 967
xxi:34–xxii:1	467	vii:6	179	viii:17	525
xxi:34	480	x:11	179	ix:4-5	197
xxii:1-2	480	xi:3	723	ix:4	305
xxii:3	480	xi:10	1149	ix:13	911
xxii:5	478	xiv:1	1156	ix:22-23	590
xxii:6-7	486			x:4	324
xxii:13	819	1QpHab		x:5	323
xxii:14-17	481	iii:12-13	961	x:7	324
xxii:15	483	vi:8-9	693		
xxii:17	483	vi:10-12	693	1QSa	
xxii:18-20	485	viii:10-13	691	i:3	305
xxii:18	467, 485	viii:12	839	i:22-24	855
xxii:19	467, 485	xii:8-10	691	i:24	855
xxii:21	486			ii:8	179
xxii:27-34	489	1QS	7, 104		
xxii:27-29	477, 489	i–ii	390	1QSb	
xxii:27	490	i:5	160	iii:4	854
xxii:30	490	i:9	266, 911	iii:6	179
xxii:31	490	i:15	525, 688	iii:25-26	857
xxii:31-32	490	i:16–iii:12	105	iv:23	857
xxii:33-34	491	i:18–ii:23	317	iv:24-26	854
xxii:34	491	i:20	390	iv:25	49, 162, 854

1QSb (continued)
iv:26   49, 162, 178
iv:27-28   855
iv:28   857
v:18   854
v:24-28   860, 887

2QJer (2Q13)
7-8 11   376

2Q19   5, 676
2   679
4   680
4   672
5   672, 680

2Q20   5
1   1120
3   1118

2Q26   90

3Q5
1   5, 676, 683
1 2   672, 682–83
2   675
3   5, 676
3 1   679
3 2   672
3 3   672
4   672

3Q7
5 3   49, 162

4Q158
6   130

4Q174 (4QFlorilegium)
                     163
1-2 i:2-3   156
1-2 i:3   156
1-2 i:6-7   197

4Q176
19-21   5
19-20   676
19 + 20 1   674
19-20 2   692
19-20 3   674–75, 692

19-20 4   675
21   675–76
21 5   676

4Q177 (4QCatena A [4QMidrEschat[b]?])
1-4   890
1-4 14   319
12-13 i:5   736

4Q185
1-2 ii:1-2   644

4Q197 (4QTob[b])
4 i:1-4   766
4 i:3   766

4QEn[a] (4Q201)   89
1 iii:7   180
1 iii:10   179–80

4Q203   90

4QEn[c] (4Q204)   89

4Q206 (4QEn[e])
2-3   90
4 i:16   294
4 i:21   343

4Q208–4Q211
(4QEnastr[a-d] ar)   45, 88, 251

4Q208–4Q209   88

4Q208   88

4Q209   88
23 3   161

4Q210–4Q211   88

4Q212 (4QEn[g] ar)
ii:22-25   251

4Q215 (4QNaph)   782, 935

4Q216 (4QJub[a])   5–6, 26, 35, 91, 181–82, 185
i–ii   137
i:3-4   125

i:3   41, 129
i:4   130
i:6   71, 132
i:7   41, 139
i:11   71, 126, 133, 141
i:13   133
i:14   133
i:15   133
i:16   133
i:17   133, 147
ii   154
ii:2   133
ii:3   148
ii:4-5   72, 148
ii:4   133
ii:5   133–34
ii:6   134
ii:7   149
ii:9   134
ii:10   134
ii:11   134
ii:12   152
ii:13   71, 134, 695
ii:14-15   692
ii:14   134
ii:15   135, 153
ii:16   135
ii:17   135
iv   137, 162
iv:3   135
iv:4   72, 126, 135
iv:5   136, 161
iv:6   136, 162
iv:7   163
iv:8   136
iv:9   136
v–vii   31, 34, 175
v   41
v:1   168
v:2   168
v:3-4   176
v:3   168
v:4   168
v:5   169, 178–79
v:6   169
v:7-8   169
v:7   169, 180
v:8   169
v:9   169, 183
v:10   169–70, 183–84
v:11   170

v:12	170	i:13	621, 626	1 7	624
v:13	170	i:14	621, 627	1 8	624
vi:3	188	i:33	622, 632	2 i	666
vi:6	170	i:35	622	2 i:1-3	652
vi:7	170, 188	i:36	622, 632	2 i:2	650
vi:8	170	i:37	622	2 i:3	650
vi:12	170	ii:7	623, 638	2 ii:1	652
vi:14	170	ii:11-12	639	3	676
vii	199	ii:11	623	3 1	672
vii:1	171	ii:17	623	3 2	672
vii:2	171, 190	ii:18	623	3 3	672
vii:3	171, 191	ii:19	623	3 5	672, 686
vii:4	171	ii:20	642	4	901
vii:5	171	ii:21	41, 623, 642	4 2-3	900
vii:6-7	171	ii:22	623, 642	4 2	390, 900
vii:6	171	ii:24	643	4 3	900
vii:7	171	ii:25	623, 644	4 4	900
vii:8	171	ii:26	623, 644	4 5	900
vii:8-9	171	ii:27	624, 644	4 6-7	900
vii:9	171	ii:28	644, 645	4 6	900
vii:10	172	ii:29	624, 645	4 7	900
vii:11	172, 195, 656	ii:30	624, 645	4 9	910
vii:12	172	ii:31	624, 646	4 10	900
vii:13	172	ii:32	624, 646	5	674, 975
vii:14	173	ii:33	624, 646	5 2	973
vii:15	173	ii:34	624	5 3	973
vii:17	71–72, 173, 193, 199, 319	ii:35-37	652	5 4	973
		ii:35	412, 648, 652, 706	5 5	973, 982
		ii:36	648	5 6	973
4Q217 (4QpapJub[b]?)	5, 102	ii:37	648, 653	5 7	973
				6	992
1	5, 136, 165	4Q220 (4QJub[e])	5, 625, 631	6 2	990
1 1-2	165	1 1	621, 630	6 3	990
2	5, 136, 165	1 2	621–22, 630	7	1006
2 1-4	126, 165	1 3	497, 622, 630–31, 635	7 1-9	1006
2 1	2, 126			7 1	1004
3	5	1 4	622, 631	7 2	1004
6	5	1 5	622	7 3	1004
7	5	1 6	622, 632	7 10	1012
		1 7	622	7 11	1004
4Q218 (4QJub[c])	5	1 8	622, 632	7b	1004, 1012
1	175	1 9	622	7b 11	1013–14
1 1-4	200	1 10	622		
1 2	200			4Q222 (4QJub[g])	5
1 3	173	4Q221(4QJub[f])	5, 625	1	731
1 4	173, 201	1 1	623	1 2	729
		1 2	623, 644	1 3-4	735
4Q219 (4QJub[d])	5, 625, 631	1 3-4	623	1 3	735
i:11	626	1 4	624, 644	1 4	735
i:12	621	1 5	644–45		

1293

4Q222 (4QJub^g) (*continued*)		iii:16	955	4Q225–227 (Pseudo-Jubilees)	
1 5	41, 736	iii:19	955		102
2	760	iv:2-15	975		
2 1	758, 762	iv:4	973, 984	4Q225 (Pseudo-Jubilees^a	
2 2	762	iv:6	974, 985	[4QpsJub^a])	102, 576
2 3	762	iv:8	974, 987	1 6-7	136
		iv:9-10	974	1 8	1153, 1158
4Q223–224 (4QpapJub^h)		iv:9	974	2 i:2	449
	5	iv:10	974	2 i:8–ii:10	102
unit 1		iv:11-12	974	2 i:8-9	563
i:1-5	871	iv:11	974, 986	2 i:9-10	564, 1161
i:1	886	iv:12	974	2 i:9	50, 429
i:2	868, 886	iv:14	975	2 i:10-12	564
i:4-5	869	iv:15-33	992	2 i:11	568
i:4	887	iv:15-17	993	2 i:12	569
unit 2		iv:16	989	2 i:13	570
i:4-5	918	iv:17	990	2 ii:1	570
i:5	917	iv:18	990	2 ii:4	571
i:45	938	iv:19	990, 993–94	2 ii:5	179
i:46	938	iv:20	990	2 ii:6-8	574
i:49	938	iv:21	990	2 ii:8-14	102
i:50	938	iv:22	990	2 ii:12	1116
i:51	938	iv:23	990	2 ii:13	50, 429, 562
i:52	939	iv:24	990	2 ii:14	50, 429
i:54	939	iv:27	980, 991		
ii:4	939	iv:29	991	4Q226	102
ii:6	939, 946	iv:31	991	1 5	102
ii:8	939	v	1006	1 6	102
ii:9-10	947	v:1-18	1006	2 3	102
ii:9	939	v:1	1004	3	102
ii:11	947	v:2	1004	7 1-7	102
ii:12-14	948	v:3	1004, 1013	7 6	179
ii:12	939	v:5	1005, 1014		
ii:13	948	v:15	1005, 1018	4Q227	102
ii:14	939	v:17	1005	1 2	102
ii:18	939	v:18-32	1021	2	102
ii:48-54	956	v:22	1020	2 1	253
ii:48	960	v:24	1020	2 2	238, 256
ii:49	961	v:25	1020	2 3-4	259
ii:51	954	v:26	1020	2 3	252
ii:52	954	v:27	1020	2 4-5	257
iii:1-19	956	v:28	1023–24		
iii:1	1037	v:29	1020	4Q228 (4QText with a	
iii:6-7	956	unit 3		Citation of Jubilees)	
iii:8	965	ii:1-3	1037		99, 107
iii:10	955, 965	frg. 9	939	1 i:2	102, 127
iii:11	955	11	939	1 i:4	100, 102
iii:12	955	12	940	1 i:7	100, 102
iii:13	955	13	940	1 i:9	102, 127
iii:15	956	41	1037		

4Q244 (4QpsDaniel[b] ar)		4Q265 (4QMiscellaneous Rules)		4Q319 (4QOtot)	100, 251, 253, 257
8	340		102, 218		
8 3	295	3	103	4Q320	
		3 3	102, 1184	4 iii–iv	105
4Q251 (4QHalakha A)		4	103	4 iii:4	1178
10 3	882	5	103	4 iii:6	323
10 4	882	6–7	103, 107	4 iv:2	323
10 5	882	6	103, 197	4 iv:9	1178
		6 4-5	203	4 v:3	1178
4Q252 (4QCommentary on Genesis A)		7	197, 214, 217–18	4 v:5	323
		7 1-6	103	4 v:12	1178
i:1–ii:5	295	7 7-10	103, 107, 197		
i:1–ii:4	105	7 9	197	4Q329	
i:1-3	286	7 11-17	102–3, 197, 217	vi:9	323
i:2	280	7 14	216, 375		
i:3-5	295	7 17	217	4Q331–333	100
i:4-5	105				
i:5-10	294	4Q266	35	4Q364 (4QRewritten Pentateuch)	
i:5-7	296	8 iii:6-9	682	3 ii:1-6	765
i:7-10	105, 295–96	11 17-18	105	3 ii:1-4	765
i:10	295			3 ii:5	765
i:11-12	322	4Q270		3 ii:7-9	765
i:20-22	322	6 ii:17	2, 99, 126	14 3-4	129
ii:2-3	105, 222, 295, 297	6 ii:18	100	14 15	143
ii:3	45, 324	6 iv:18-19	682		
ii:5	297	7 ii:11-12	105	4Q365	
ii:6-7	338			23	636
ii:8	590	4Q271			
ii:9-10	449, 459	4 ii:4-5	126	4Q369	
v:1-4	859	4 ii:5	2, 99	1 ii:6	195
v:1	859	4 ii:6	100		
		5 i:18	157	4Q372 (4QNarrative and Poetic Composition[b])	
4Q253 (4QCommentary on Genesis B)		5 i:19-21	201		
		5 i:19	150	1 29	960
1 2	305			1 30	960
1 3	305	4Q286 (4QBerakhot[a])			
2 1	305	1a ii b 8-11	126	4Q374	
2 3	305	1a ii b 11	126	2 ii:8	166
2 4	305	3 a-d 4-5	179		
				4Q379 (4QapocJosh[b])	
4Q256	103, 107			12 3-6	1200
4 ix:8	107	4Q306		12 4	1200
4 ix:8-10	662	2 3	152, 695		
4 ix:10	663			4Q384 (Apocryphon of Jeremiah B?/ 4Qpap apocrJer B?)	
		4Q317 (4QcryptA Lunisolar Calendar)			
4Q258	103, 107			9 2	103, 127
i:7	107	1 + 2a ii:11	126		
		2 30	126	4Q385a	
4Q264a (4QHalakha B)	101	4 33	126	3a-c 6	150
i:5-8	1204	9 13	126		

1295

4Q390 (4QApocryphon of Jeremiah C^e)	36–37, 97, 101, 103, 705	4Q434 (4QBarkhi Nafshi^a) 1 i:9	154	4Q512 (4QpapRitual of Purification) 29-32 vii:10	1207
1 8-10	152			29-32 vii:11	1207
1 8-9	152, 689	4Q444			
1 8	103, 148, 150, 154, 327, 704	1-4 i + 5 3	736	4Q525 (Beatitudes) 11-12 1	154
1 9-10	103, 692	4Q460		14 ii:13	154
1 9	103	9 i:12	525	15 5	643
1 11	104				
2 i:4-5	104	4Q464 (4QExposition on the Patriarchs)		4Q530–33	90
2 i:4	104, 692	1	458	4Q537 (4QTestament of Jacob)	891–92
2 i:6	689	2 2	458	1-3 1-6	890
2 i:8-9	104, 690	3 i	458	1-3 5	891
2 i:10	103	3 i:5	458		
		3 i:8-9	458	4Q542 (Testament of Qahat)	
4Q392				1 i:4-5	1116
1 3	160	4Q482–84	6	1 i:7-8	1116
				1 i:10-12	1116
4Q393		4Q482		1 ii:9-12	1116
1 ii:5-6	157	1	6		
		2	6, 956	4Q543–549 (4QVisions of Amram^{a-g})	95, 1116
4Q398					
11-13 6-8	152	4Q484	7		
11-13 7 (= C 24)	695	1	7	4Q543–547	95
		2	7		
4Q400		5	7	4Q543–544	95
1 i:6	845	7	7		
1 i:4	178	19	7	4Q543	
1 i:8	178			1 1-2	1116
		4Q502		3-4	1128
4Q409		6-10 8	546		
1 i:8	658			4Q544	
6 8	853	4Q503		1 1-8	1128
		1-6 iii:13	546	1 6	1138
4Q412		24-25 vii:3-5	195	1 8-9 [13-14]	1138
4 2	546	24-25 vii:5	195		
		24-25 vii:6	195	4Q545	
4Q418		40-41 7	179	1a-b ii:11-19	1128
70 2	179	48-50 5	546	1a i:9	1144
4Q421		4Q504–506 (Words of the Luminaries)	196	4Q546	
13 3-4	1204			2 1-4	1128
4Q422 (4QParaphrase of Genesis and Exodus)		4Q508 (4QPrFêtes^b) 2 2	289	4Q547 1-2 iii:1-8	95 1128
ii:9	305	2 3	933		
4Q427		4Q511		4Q561 (4QHoroscope ar)	98
7 ii:6	166	1 5	736		
7 ii:14	736	35 4	178		

4Q588 (DM/PAM 43.686)		4QSam[a]	751	1 9	246	
	101, 149	4QTestimonia (4Q175)		2 2	237	
30 1-4	101	1-8	130	2 3	237	
		14-20	836	3 2	237, 247	
4QDan[c]	31			7	275	
		4QXII[a]	31	7a	7, 332, 335	
4QDeut[f]				7 1	272, 275	
4-6 8	470	5Q13 (Sectarian Rule)		7 3	277	
		1 2	853	8	444	
4QDeut[h]		2 6-9	853	8 4	443	
10 1	145	2 7-13	890	9	444, 462	
11-15 3-4	836	2 7	890	9 2	443, 459	
		4 2-3	908	9 5-6	443, 460	
4QDeut[j]	53					
v:5	470	6Q8 (6QpapGiants ar)	90	11QMelchizedek (11Q13)		
xii:14	523	26 1	295		483	
4QDeut[n]		8QGen		11Q15		
i:3	470	4 2	515–16	1 6	157	
4QExod[b]		11Q5 (11QPs[a])		Temple Scroll (11Q19 [11QT[a]])		
3 i-4 8	1143	xix:15-16	407, 454		19, 105, 144, 163,	
		xix:15	454		352, 883, 904	
4QGen-Exod[a]		xxvi:9-15	104, 184	vii:8	1183	
24-25 i:1	1154	xxvi:11-12	104, 169, 184	xiv:9–xv:3	336	
		xxvi:11	183, 185	xiv:10-12	307	
4QGen[h2]		xxvi:12	169, 185	xiv:10-11	336	
Gen 2:18b	212	xxvi:13-14	184	xiv:10	336	
		xxvii:5-6	45, 324	xiv:13–xv:2	337	
4QGen[k]	187	xxviii:7-8	853	xvii:2	322	
		xxviii:7	658	xvii:4	322	
4QJer[b]	628	xxviii:8	658	xvii:7	1179, 1184	
				xvii:8-9	1169, 1184	
4QLevi[e] ar	91	11Q10 (Job Targum)		xvii:9	1184, 1187	
		xxx:5	182	xvii:10-16	1188	
4QLevi[f] ar (4Q214b)				xviii:10–xix:9	106	
	91–92, 637–38	11Q11 (11QApocryphal Psalms[a])		xviii:13	511	
			401	xviii:14	511	
4QMMT (Some of the Works				xix:2-3	512	
of the Torah)	105, 353	11Q12 (11QJubilees)		xix:6-7	511	
B 63-64	884		5, 239, 300, 332	xix:9	319, 511	
C 5-7	691	1 1	237	xix:11–xxi:10	106	
		1 2	237	xx	633	
4QpaleoJob[c]	563	1 4-6	245	xx:8	633	
		1 4	237	xx:10-13	633	
4QpHos[a] (4Q166)		1 5-6	245	xx:10	512	
ii:15-17	326	1 5	237	xxi:12–xxiii:2	106	
		1 6	237	xxiii	636	
4QpIsa[a]		1 7	245	xxiii:14-17	632	
8-10 17-21	860			xxiii:14-16	622	

Temple Scroll (continued)

xxiii:14	632
xxiii:15	632
xxv	636
xxv:3	323
xxv:9	322
xxvi:5-7	306–7
xxvi:10	289, 641
xxviii:02	544
xxviii:03–xxix:1	543
xxviii:3–xxix:1	879
xxviii:5-6	544
xxviii:10–xix:9	106
xxix:7-10	155–56, 161
xxix:8-10	136, 889
xxix:9-10	163
xxxv:8	644
xxxvii:9	885
xxxviii:14-15	885
xxxix–xli	994
xxxix:12	994
xl:9-10	885
xl:14	854
xliii:1-12	36
xliii:3-17	883
xliii:3-12	105–6
xlix:5-21	678
l:10-15	678
lii:10-12	349
liii:4-6	349
liii:5-6	641
lvii:17-18	781
lviii:9	151
lix:5-8	693
lix:7-8	153, 692
lix:8	153
lix:9-10	154
lx:3-4	353
lx:6-7	485, 885
lx:9-10	885
lx:11	856
lxiii:3	178, 856
lxvi:14-15	1138

CD	7, 36–37, 100, 107, 346
i:1-10	1198
i:9	690
ii:16–iii:16	318
ii:11	598
ii:15-16	611
ii:16–iii:7	318
iii:1-4	838
iii:11	525
iii:17	839
iii:18	289
iv:10	691
iv:12-13	691
iv:14-18	691
iv:21	781
v:7-11	447
v:9-10	1050, 1052
vi:7	695
vi:19	933
vii:9-21	36
viii:4-5	839
x:7-10	681–82
x:14–xii:6	101
x:14-17	326
x:14	1201
x:19	1203
x:20	201, 1208
x:21	1208
x:22	202
xi:1-2	202, 1204
xi:2	201, 1202
xi:3-4	681
xi:5-6	1208
xi:6	1209
xi:7-9	203, 1204
xi:17-19	1204
xi:17-18	1206
xi:18	1206
xii:1-2	1203
xii:2	157, 454
xii:4-6	201
xv:1-5	960
xv:1	311
xv:6	311
xv:8	311
xvi:1-6	518
xvi:1-4	2, 99, 107
xvi:2-4	126
xvi:2-3	68, 1198
xvi:3-4	2, 16, 35, 99–100
xvi:3	99
xvi:4-6	100
xix:5-13	36
xix:13-22	36
xix:17	839

XQ5a (XQText A) 332

Masada
Mas1j (1276–1786)

i:5	1153
i:6	1153
ii:4	1153

e / Other Jewish Texts

Artapanus

1	474
2	1028

Demetrius the Chronographer

2 9	821
2 14	1070

Ezekiel the Tragedian
Exagoge

132-51	1155
159	1174
167-71	1189

Josephus
Against Apion

1.1-4	125
1.37-38	144
1.75-90	1131
1.103-5	1131
1.227-52	1131–32
1.252-87	1132

Antiquities of the Jews

	13, 19, 107–8
1.1-4	125
1.4	229
1.15-16	144
1.20-23	144
1.26	144
1.36	213
1.39	373
1.40	108
1.41	108
1.50	229
1.52	108
1.54-57	449
1.58	243
1.69-71	108, 364
1.75	110, 281

1.92	274	2.125	1071	Philo	
1.95	295	2.161	1081	*Allegorical Interpretation*	
1.102	309–10	2.170-71	1090	1.88-89	221
1.118	417	2.178	1097	3.217-19	517
1.122	380	2.183	1099	3.218	532
1.123	380	2.191	1111	*On the Confusion of Tongues*	
1.140	337	2.192-93	1027	68	417
1.141	332, 338	2.193	1111	*On the Contemplative Life*	
1.142	339	2.194	1113	86	1160
1.144	333	2.198	1028	*On the Creation of the World*	
1.157	469	2.199	1122, 1126	29	183
1.163-65	475	2.220	1141	35	183
1.170	109, 471	2.224-25	109	*On Dreams*	
1.182	486	2.224	108, 1142	1.47-48	431
1.184	496–97	2.232	109	*On Giants*	
1.185	496	2.236	109	66	426
1.187	503	2.276	1153	*On the Life of Abraham*	
1.192	515	2.293-314	1155	68-84	449
1.196	531	2.303	1155	275-76	717
1.203	534	2.317	1188	*On the Life of Joseph*	
1.218	558	3.245	549, 893	41	1012
1.220	552, 559	3.247	893	42-44	1009
1.226	570, 575	12.1	806	52-53	1014
1.227	561	12.5.1	231	157	1027
1.234	966	12.8	806	232-35	1071
1.238	593	12.8.1	999	*On the Life of Moses*	
1.242	109	12.241	231	1.23-24	1144
1.269	749	13.301	92	1.96-139	1155
1.270-273	750	13.372	549	1.97	1155
1.274	753	16.6.2	873	2.254	1160
1.276-77	733	16.163	873	2.65	110, 281
1.301	780	19.358	547	141	1163
1.302	781	20.216-18	874	142	1163
1.304	784	*Jewish War*		*On the Migration of Abraham*	
1.310-11	109	1.1-3	125	89-93	525
1.316	109	1.70	92	176-92	449
1.322-23	109	2.129	231	*On Rewards and Punishments*	
1.339-40	823	2.147	202	31	540–41
1.340	824	2.148	231	*On the Special Laws*	
1.342	109, 848	2.169	231	1.132-36	484
1.345-46	966	2.234-35	810	1.220-22	633
1.346	965	2.568	810	*On the Virtues*	
2.39	929	2.652	810	95	484
2.41-42	1008	3.48	810	155–60	353
2.73	1018	3.49	810	*Questions and Answers on Exodus*	
2.91	1030	4.504	810	1.23	1174
2.94	1027	4.511	810	*Questions and Answers on Genesis*	
2.113	109	4.551	810	1.25	218
2.120	109	5.381	475	2.82	426
		6.426	1184		

Pseudo-Eupolemus 251

f / Rabbinic Literature and Other Later Jewish Texts

MISHNAH

m. 'Abot	565
5:3	564
m. Berakot	
1:1	1180
m. Beṣah	
5:2	1208
m. Ḥullin	
6:1	630
m. Makkot	
3:3	1184
m. Megillah	
4:9	826
4:10	826
m. Menaḥot	
8:1	1091
10:2	922
m. Mo'ed	
10	1176
m. Niddah	
3:7	218
5:6	821
5:9	821
m. Pesaḥim	
8:1	1184
9:2	1178
9:5	1171, 1182
10:9	1180
m. Qiddušin	
4:14	717
m. Roš Hašanah	
1:1	323, 452
m. Šabbat	
1:1	1205
2:1-7	1208
7:2	203, 1205, 1208–9
12:2	1208
13:5-7	1209
14:1	1209
17-18	203
19:5	515, 519
19:6	524
23:5	677
m. Sanhedrin	
7:3	267
7:4	908, 910
9:1	267
9:6	815
m. Šebu'ot	
1:6	290
m. Soṭah	
5:3	1208
m. Sukkah	
2:8	543
3:1	890
3:8	890
4:1-5	549
4:1	549
4:5	550
8	550
m. Ta'anit	
4:5	636
m. Tamid	
2:3	636, 638
m. Yoma	
3:3	640
7:4	640
8:8	289
8:9	290
m. Zebaḥim	
5:7	633
5:8	1180, 1184

TOSEFTA

t. 'Abodah Zarah	
8:4	344–45
8:6	345
t. Menaḥot	
9:14	636
t. Soṭah	
6:6	555
t. Pisḥa	
8:11-22	1182

TALMUDS

b. Baba Batra	
123a	778
147a	452
b. Berakot	
5a	643
9a	1180
18b	452
31b	1209
b. Erubin	
53a	1130
b. Ḥagigah	
12a	183
b. Ḥullin	
84a	630
92a	345
b. Keritot	
6a	544
b. Ketubbot	
3a	1203
b. Megillah	
13a	1142
13b	778
17a	733, 762
24a	815
31a	1189
b. Menaḥot	
83b	1091
b. Niddah	
30b	218
b. Nedarim	
31b-32a	1153
32b	481
38a-b	1203
61a	1201
82a	1203
b. Pesaḥim	
84b-85a	1181
93b-94b	1178
94ab	426
96a	1164, 1171
b. Qiddišin	
31b	946
72a-b	667
b. Roš Hašanah	
11b	293
18b	483, 873
b. Šabbat	
86b-87a	138
117b-118b	1209
119b	150
121b	1209
133b	524
150a	1204
151b	677
b. Sanhedrin	
38b	221

46a	1208
56a-60a	345
56a-b	345
56b	345, 1193
57a	345
58b	246, 1139
69b	268
82a	815
89b	561, 563–65
90b	699
108a	276

b. Soṭah
10a	542
12a	1140
12b	1142–43
36b	1010, 1013
58b	1139

b. Ta'anit
10b	1085

b. Tamid
29b	639

b. Yebamot
34b	1038
86a-b	874

b. Yoma
85b-86b	289

b. Zebaḥim
35a	641
113b	417

y. Beṣah
1:1, 60b	547

y. Sukkah
1:1, 51d	547

y. Yoma
4:4	544

TARGUMS

Targum to 1 Chronicles
4:23	599

Fragment Targum
Genesis
1:6	186
1:7	186
2:15	222
22:10	571
29:17	779
29:22	780
41:43	1020

Exodus
4:25	1152
4:26	1152

Targum Jonathan to the Prophets
Isaiah
61:1	851

Targum Neofiti
Genesis
1:1	185
2:15	221
2:22	575
2:25	222
3:5	225
3:16	226
4:26	247
6:3	282
9:22	338
9:26	332
9:27	339
11:1	458, 1159
11:4	413
11:9	416
11:28	448
13:16	478
15:1	490
15:2	491
15:3	491
15:6	492
15:14	1157
17:1	513
17:17	517
17:19	517
18:1-15	531
21:6	540
21:9	522, 555
22:1	561, 565
22:8	571
22:10	571
25:27	594
25:29	714
27:10	747
27:28	752
27:35	754
27:41	756
28:12	769
29:17	779
29:22	780
30:2	785

31:24	802
34:13	823
35:4	848
35:11	887
38:26	1048
39:18	1014
41:49	1031
42:9	1062
43:34	1070
44:8	1076
45:12	1081
47:6	1109
50:21	1121

Exodus
1:8	1130
1:11	1131
2:3	1141
2:9	1143
4:24	1152
4:25	1152
4:26	1152
6:20	1138
12:14	1182
12:42	579

Leviticus
20:17	246

Deuteronomy
14:23	883
14:26	883
33:16	659

Targum Onqelos
Genesis
2:22	575
3:5	225
3:16	226
4:24	243
9:22	338
9:26	332
9:27	339
13:16	478
15:1	490
15:6	492
15:9	493
17:17	517
27:35	754
29:17	779
30:2	785
34:13	823
35:8	895

Targum Onqelos					
Genesis (*continued*)		21:14-15	558	2:1-2	1140
38:26	1048	21:15	555	2:2	1139
41:45	1027	22:1	561, 565, 587	2:3	1140
42:9	1062	25:1	593	2:5	1142
45:12	1081	25:8	679	2:10	1144
Exodus		25:27	594	2:13	1145
1:8	1130	25:29	714	4:24	1152
4:24	1152	26:2	716	4:25	1152
24:7	312	26:18	719	4:26	1152
24:8	307, 312	27:5	746	8:17	1155
Numbers		27:9	749	8:20	1155
24:17	659	27:11	748	8:25	1155
Deuteronomy		27:13	749	8:27	1155
32:24	643	27:35	754	12:3	1182
		27:41	756	12:8	1180
Targum Pseudo-Jonathan		27:42	747, 760	12:11	1182
Genesis		29:12	778	12:12	1155
1:6	186	29:17	779	12:13	1173–74
1:7	186	29:22	780	12:23	1174
1:26	191	29:24	782	12:29	1172
2:15	221	29:25	778	12:40	493
4:8	267	29:29	782	12:42	579
4:24	243	30:1	785	12:46	1181
4:26	247	30:2	785	19:3	138
5:24	251	32:25	877	19:7	138
6:12	276	35:2	847	19:9	138
9:22	338	35:4	848	19:10	138
10:11-12	427	35:8	864, 895	19:14	138
11:1	415, 458, 1159	37:35	931	19:15	138
11:7	415	38:6	1046	19:16	138
11:9	416	38:14	1042	24:7	312
11:28	448	38:24	1046	24:8	312
12:6	419	38:26	1048, 1054	24:12	139
12:19	475	39:6	1008	Leviticus	
14:20-21	876	41:45	1027, 1030	2:13	636
15:2	491	41:47	1032	18:21	826
15:6	492	42:24	1063	19:18	609, 950
15:14	1157	43:34	1070	19:24	353
16:12	618	45:12	1081	20:17	246
17:1	513	45:24	1085	23:42	542, 545
17:17	517	46:3	1090	Deuteronomy	
18:1-15	531	46:4	1092	27:24	243
18:14	536	46:23	1100	29:14-15	146
18:21	827	48:22	920	32:8	523
19:5	534	49:24	1010	32:24	643
21:6	557	50:25	1124, 1127	33:16	659
21:9	522, 555	Exodus			
21:11-12	555	1:6	1125	*'Abot de Rabbi Nathan*	
21:12	556	1:8	1130	Version A ch. 16	960
		1:11	1131		

Algazi, Samuel
Toledot Adam   111

Book of Jashar   561, 918, 925, 975, 992
37-40   925

Book of Noah (Introduction to the Book of Asaph the Physician)
    4, 96–98, 110, 341, 347, 369, 398–409

Chronicles of Jerahmeel
    918, 975, 992
36   925
36:1   920
36:10   920
37   925

Echa Rabbah
1.85   667

Exodus Rabbah
1:1   555
1:7   1027
1:8   1130
1:13   1140
1:20   1140
1:25   1143
1:26   1144
1:27   1145
1:30   1145
11:3   1155
17   1173
23:9   1157
25:11   1206

Genesis Rabbah
1:3   182
1:4   80, 185
1:9   185
6:1   189
8:3-5   191
11:8   196
11:9   187
14:15   491
15:3   187
16:5   216
16:6   345
17:4   211
18:4   458
18:5   1139
18:6   221
21:9   187
22:8   267
23:1   267
23:4   43
23:6-7   247
24:5   345
25:3   264
26:3   268
26:5   534
26:7   403
28:8   276
31:5-6   345
31:5   345
32:8   293
33:7   297
34:8   345
36:6   338
36:7   338
36:8   339
37:7   268, 366
38:13   462
38:14   447
39:7   459, 461
39:15   419
39:16   471
41:1-2   475
41:2   475
41:5   419
42:7   479
42:8   457
43:5   479
44:6   490
44:9   491
44:11   452
44:12   453
44:14   493
46:4   513
50:5   534
53:11   522, 555
53:13   557
54:6   542
55:4   561
55:7   568
56:1   569–70
56:2   570
56:4   571
56:7   573
56:11   565
58:5   587
61:4   593
63:10   594
63:12   714
63:14   715
64:10   721–22
65:1   985
65:18   750
66:5   753
67:6   754
67:8   756
67:9   736, 760
67:10   761
68:5   733
68:10   767, 769
68:12   768–69
68:13   768
69:8   768
70:6   771
70:7   878
70:16   779
70:18   778
71:2   779
71:7   785
73:1   787
74:13   782, 803
79:5   819
80:1-5   820
80:10   821, 824, 920
81:1-2   847
81:5   864, 896
82:2-3   888
82:8   931
82:10   896
82:11   902
84:19   1047
84:21   931
85:9   1043–44
85:10   1046
85:12   1048
86:3   929, 1007
86:6   1008
87:7   1010
90:3   1025
90:4   1030
91:6   1063
92:5   1070
92:8   1077
93:10   1081
94:2   1085
97:6   993
98:4   903

Genesis Rabbah (continued)

98:7	859
100:3	1125
100:10	1145
100:11	1126

Leviticus Rabbah

1:3	1142, 1144

Mekilta de Rabbi Ishmael
Ba-ḥodeš

2-3	138
5	204
8.1	946

Beshallaḥ

2-3	1190
7	1161

Pisḥa

6	1180
7	1155
7.8	580
11.19	580

Shabbata

1	1202-3

Mekilta de Rabbi Shimon ben Yoḥai   196

Midrash Aggadah   110

Midrash Tadshe   4, 175, 183, 186, 188, 192, 198-99, 214, 218-19, 793

6	110
8	110
8:2-4	792
15	110

Midrash Tannaim   314

Midrash Wayyissaʿu   4, 97, 110, 918, 922, 925-26, 977, 992

unit 2

2	919-20
3-4	921
4	920
22	925
26	922
30	925
31-39	927
31	925
42	925
45	925
46-48	922
49	925
61	925
62-63	924
63-64	924
64	924
65	924

unit 3

1	1000
2-3	981
3	981, 1000
4-5	982-83
5-6	982
6	980
8-9	982
9	982
10	995
12-13	983
12	983
13	983
14-15	983
15-16	995
15	980
16-17	996
16	990
17-53	994
17-18	995
18-19	995
18	990
19-37	996
19	995
37-38	996
37	996
40-46	996
46-47	996
46	996
47-48	996
48-49	996
49	996
52-53	996
52	991
54-55	996
54	991, 996
56	991
57-58	999
58	991
74:3	976
74:4-5	976
74:7-8	976

Pesiqta Rabbati

43 §108b	667

Pirqe Rabbi Eliezer

3	183
12	221
14	244
21	267
24	413
26-31	565
30	558, 592-93
32	748-49
36	782, 791, 1030
37	854, 877, 880
38	1030
39	1090

Rashbam, Commentary on Deuteronomy   243

Seder Olam Rabbah

1	459, 474, 561, 587
1:1	265
2	733, 762, 790
4	293-94, 297
5	345, 493, 536-37, 1189, 1193
6:1	140
11	1200

Sifra
Behar

1	1195

Emor

16.11	549
17.9	543

g / Christian Literature

PATRISTIC LITERATURE

Jerome   118
Hebrew Questions on Genesis   188, 461-62, 555, 575, 593
Letter to Fabriola no. 78 [or 127]   3, 414, 431-32

Mansio 18	3, 16	2.1-3	11	Procopius of Gaza	
Mansio 24	3	2.4	11	1123	
		2.9	116		
Origen		2.11	116	Pseudo-Clement	
Hexapla (Gen 22:12)	573	3.1-3	428	*Homilies*	
Homilies on Genesis 2.1	593	3.4-5	428	8.17.4	282
		3.4	116	*Recognitions*	
OTHER CHRISTIAN LITERATURE		5.5	11	1.27-71	114–15
		6.1-5	11	1.27-35	114
Acts of Philip	404	6.1	16	1.27.8	114
		7.1-3	11	1.30.2-3	115
Catena on Genesis		7.2	11	1.30.4–1.31.1	427
(Petit, *La chaîne sur la Genèse*)		39	245–46	1.30.5	115, 458
	117, 396	39.6.1-5	116	1.31.1	115, 427
#551	12	39.6.5	246	1.31.2	115
#585	12, 239	39.7.1-2	116, 248	1.32.1-33.3	115
#590	12	66.23.1	116	1.32.4	115
#742	304	66.83-84	116	4.9	697
#805	420	66.83.3	116		
#833	12	83.1–84.5	392	Theophilus of Antioch	
#838	413	83.1	392	*Ad Autolycum*	115
#839	12, 398, 414	83.3	392		
#857	12	83.5	392	COPTIC TEXTS	
#861	12, 431	84.1	392		
#867	12, 16	*Anacephalaeosis*		P.CtYBR inv. 4995 117	
#1804b	12	I 3.1-3	427–28		
#1829	12	*On Weights and Measures*		ETHIOPIC TEXTS	
#1850	12		11, 116, 175, 181		
#2268	12, 1123	3-4	12	Andemta (Amharic) commentary	
#2270	13, 1120, 1138	21-22	12	tradition	119–20
		22	175, 198	Genesis	
Chronicle on Creation	239, 264	23-24	12	1:4	120
				1:13	120
Didymus of Alexandria	13, 16, 414	Eugippius's Anthology of Augustine,		1:18	120
Commentary on Genesis	13	*On the Trinity*	14	2:8	120
Commentary of Job	13				
		Eusebius		Emperor Zar'a Ya'qob,	
Epiphanius of Salamis		*Preparation for the Gospel*		"Homily in Honor of Saturday"	
	104, 116, 169–172,	2.2.60	365		120–21
	178–81, 183–84,				
	186, 188, 190,	Hippolytus	393	Te'zāza Sanbat (Ethiopic	
	195, 197, 199, 240,	*Chronicum*	391	Ezra Apocalypse) 118	
	393	44-239	115	14	119
Ancoratus		44-198	392	15-16	119
92	372	47-49	392	15	119
112-114	116	50	392	25	119
The Panarion (= *The Medicine Chest*)		90	392	33-34	119
	239, 420	118-30	392	38-39	119
1.2.1	304	195-97	392		
1.3	11	*Diamerismos*	369, 391		

1305

Syriac Texts

Bar Hebraeus 117

Catena of Severus
 435–37, 450–51, 462

Ephraem
Commentary on Genesis
25:2 755

Jacob of Edessa 435, 442, 448, 462

Letter to John of Litarba
 117, 436–37, 450–51

Jewish histories 117

The Names of the Wives of the Patriarchs according to the Book Called Jubilees among the Hebrews [MS BM Additional 12.154, folio 180] (Syriac list) 3, 8, 16, 111, 239–41, 248, 268, 270, 340, 362, 365, 412, 414, 425, 430–31, 433, 918, 934, 1142

Michael Syrus 117

Syriac Chronicle to the year 1234 (*Chronicum ad annum Christi 1234 pertinens*) 9, 117, 169–171, 175, 178–81, 184, 186, 188, 190–91, 198, 200, 210, 229, 237–39, 250–51, 261–62, 272, 275, 300, 303, 311, 359–61, 368, 370, 374, 378, 380, 382, 398, 418, 424–25, 433–34, 436, 442–45, 448, 453, 458–59, 462, 467–68, 480–82, 485–86, 899–900, 910, 972–75, 989–91, 1034–36, 1051

Chronographers

Annianus the Alexandrian
 13, 117, 461–62

Cedrenus, George of Byzantium
 10, 237, 250–51, 428, 430, 433, 450, 461, 531, 536, 542, 1140, 1149–50, 1161

Historiarum Compendium
 239, 361, 365, 410, 425

Julius Africanus 13, 462, 498
Chronicle 12, 14, 116–17

Logothetes 14, 117, 450, 452, 461–62

Leo Grammaticus 117

Theodosius Melitenus 117
Chronographia 398, 418

Panadorus the Alexandrian
 13, 117, 461

Syncellus, George
 13, 20, 117, 192, 197, 199, 214, 244, 248–49, 259, 263, 267, 398–402, 404–7, 409, 442, 444, 461–62, 531, 792–95

Chronography 13, 210, 256
3.8-10 188
3.4-18 186
3.14-18 198
3.16-18 186
3.16-17 16
4.20 17
4.21 17
4.29–5.2 211
5.2-24 219
5.26 17
6.25–7.23 223
7.28 239
7.29-32 223, 232
8.1-9 229
8.11-14 239
8.11 233, 240
8.12-13 240
8.15-17 240
8.16 241
8.18-19 241
8.20-22 244–45
8.20 241
8.23-24 246
9.9 246
9.10 246
9.20 245
10.3-5 247
11.1-15 266
11.1-2 246
11.4-6 266
12.10-11 343
26.32–27.5 284
27.9-11 398
27.33–28.11 398
43.18-19 415
43:26 417
46.20-22 368
46.21-22 393
46.23–47.3 372
47:10-18 393
47.20 410
88.6-7 335
90.11-12 364
111.6-7 433
111.9 549
112.4-6 458
112.7 448
112.8-9 448
120.4-5 654
120.13-15 749
120.16-17 733
122.14-15 877
123.23-25 755
124.1-3 849
124.5-7 944, 957
124.7-11 988
124.9-10 973
124.12 990
124.13 990
139.3-5 1144
207.7-10 877

h / Other Texts

Ancient Near Eastern Texts

Enuma Anu Enlil 453

Greek/Roman Texts

Aristophanes
Plutus
1054   547

Arrian
Indica
36.8   386
37.2   386
37.3   386
37.8   386
38.1   386

Geoponica   637–38
11.1   626

Herodotus
Histories
4.100   371

Hesiod
Works and Days
113-14   704
121-22   704
130-31   704
176-78   704
180-81   694
180   704
183-89   704
201   694

Hippocrates
On the Nature of the Child
    218–19

Oxyrhynchus Papyri
4365   11
4385   16

Plutarch
Moralia
Quaestiones Convivales
Question 6.2   547–48

Strabo
Geography
1.2.28   372–73
2.5.25   371
14.6.1   373
17.1.7   372–73

Tacitus
Histories
5.5.5   548

2. Names

This index lists all citations of modern authors and editors in this volume except for references to their dictionaries, lexicons, grammars, and concordances.

Aalen, Sverre
    701
Abegg, M.
    622, 642
Abraha, Tedros
    119
Adler, William
    9, 11–14, 16–17, 116–17, 188, 198, 211, 219, 223, 229, 232–33, 239–41, 245, 247, 256, 263, 266, 284, 335, 343, 364–65, 368, 372, 398, 415, 417, 433, 450, 452, 458, 461–62, 549, 654, 733, 749, 755, 793, 849, 944, 957, 973, 988, 990, 1144
Aharoni, Yohanan
    472
Albani, Matthias
    40, 45, 69, 76, 105, 130, 176, 189, 196, 262, 274, 316, 325, 327, 369, 871
Albeck, Chanoch
    83, 110, 193, 200–203, 267, 279, 289, 332, 336, 346–47, 353, 356, 484, 543, 607, 610, 612, 630, 633, 638, 826–27, 879, 881–84, 905, 910, 1046, 1176, 1180, 1183–84, 1203–10
Albright, W. F.
    30

Alehegne, Mersha
    119–20
Alexander, Loveday
    125
Alexander, Philip
    96, 368–69, 371, 373, 375–82, 386–87, 389
Alexander, Tamar
    919, 925, 996
Allegro, J. M.
    5, 674–75
Anderson, Gary A.
    41, 43, 80, 145, 211, 213–15, 265, 307, 342, 573, 906, 911, 1038, 1048, 1054
Andrei, Osvalda
    498
Argall, Randal A.
    125
Ashton, John
    682
Aune, David
    540
Avemarie, Friedrich
    53
Avigad, Nahman
    93, 377
Avi-Yonah, Michael
    472

Baden, Joel
    405
Baillet, Maurice
    5–7, 672, 675, 956
Baltzer, Klaus
    625
Barth, J.
    221
Barthélemy, Dominique
    105, 872
Basten, Martin F. J.
    189
Bauckham, Richard
    13, 414
Baumgarten, Joseph
    46, 102, 178, 215, 217–18, 223–24, 352–54, 356, 501, 518, 546, 581, 695, 808, 883, 885, 933, 1171, 1184, 1201

Bautch, Kelley Coblentz
  241, 274, 697–99, 701–2
Baynes, Leslie
  69, 118, 839, 962, 1011
Beattie, Derek R. G.
  619
Beckwith, Roger
  118, 199
Beer, Bernhard
  29, 83, 85, 97, 214, 230, 267, 429, 457, 481, 544, 547, 549, 561, 563, 565, 780, 877, 919, 1046, 1203
Begg, Christopher T.
  496, 803
Ben-Dov, Jonathan
  45, 295–96
Berger, Klaus
  33–34, 118, 134–35, 151, 161, 165, 191, 197, 203, 214, 221, 237, 242, 244, 253, 256, 266, 275, 280–81, 296, 304, 306, 318, 343–44, 347, 366–67, 390–92, 434, 438, 442, 467–68, 473, 480–81, 508, 514, 518–19, 539, 541, 546, 564, 584, 599, 609, 634, 639, 642, 652, 664, 667, 672–75, 687, 689, 693–94, 696–97, 701, 722, 724, 790, 798, 816–17, 828, 845, 855, 857, 861, 867, 870, 881, 886, 890, 894, 899–900, 910, 917, 927, 940, 943–44, 947–48, 951, 962, 968, 970, 972, 985, 987, 994, 1012, 1025, 1028–29, 1035, 1049, 1052, 1057, 1074, 1082, 1092, 1104, 1107–8, 1118, 1131, 1133, 1136, 1144, 1148–49, 1153, 1155, 1168, 1181, 1188, 1195, 1207–8, 1211
Bergren, Theodore A.
  309, 855
Bergsma, John
  89, 128, 249, 252, 276, 1195, 1200–1201
Berner, Christoph
  25–27, 141, 164, 451
Bernstein, Moshe J.
  76, 305, 327, 338, 401, 562
Bhayro, Siam
  343

Blenkinsopp, Joseph
  72–73, 141, 149, 663, 697, 699
Block, Daniel
  375
Boccaccini, Gabriele
  4, 17, 20, 54, 81, 89–90, 103, 105–7, 197, 215, 225, 241, 276, 295, 452, 1172, 1180
Bockmuehl, Markus
  114, 346
Bohn, Friedrich
  30, 33
Bokser, Baruch
  1182
Bousset, Wilhelm
  255, 921–22, 924, 926–27, 999
Boxel, Piet van
  63, 596, 600, 740, 945
Bow, Beverly A.
  125
Brady, Monica
  152
Brandt, Peter
  118
Brin, Gershon
  139, 983–86, 988
Brock, Sebastian
  434, 436–38, 442, 448–51, 461–62
Brooke, George J.
  76, 102, 105, 130, 142
Broshi, Magen
  2,
Brown, Raymond E.
  112, 1181
Brownlee, William Hugh
  104
Bruning, Brandon
  846
Büchler, Adolph
  10, 85, 183, 363, 391–92, 547–48, 869, 896, 1026, 1100
Buisch, Pauline P.
  1121
Byron, John
  241, 243, 265, 268

Calvert-Koyzis, Nancy
  625
Caquot, André
  72, 75, 178–79, 262, 281, 304, 353, 365, 390, 467, 473, 480, 482–84, 519–20, 609, 634, 639, 691, 694, 701, 769, 792–93, 812, 834, 882, 927–28, 968, 979–80, 985, 994, 998–99, 1012, 1082, 1101, 1150, 1159, 1177, 1208
Cavallin, Hans Clemens
  701–2
Ceriani, A. M.
  3, 8, 14, 674, 711, 805, 846, 917, 938, 1020, 1148, 1170
Chabot, I. B.
  9
Chazon, Esther G.
  93, 95, 98, 196, 249, 686, 784, 890, 1115
Charles, R. H.
  2–4, 8, 14, 16, 19, 30–31, 33, 35, 39–40, 46–47, 60, 66–67, 69, 80, 83–86, 88, 90, 96–98, 128–29, 133–37, 139–140, 146, 150–51, 155, 161, 163, 165, 169–70, 178–179, 183, 186, 188, 195, 197–201, 203–4, 214, 221, 229–32, 238, 240–42, 246–48, 251, 254–55, 263, 265–66, 268, 273, 277–78, 281, 288–90, 302, 304, 306, 310–11, 319–20, 324, 326, 332–33, 338, 340–41, 343–44, 347–48, 353–54, 360, 362, 364–68, 371–73, 376–77, 379, 381, 385–90, 398, 401, 404, 406–8, 412, 414, 417, 419–20, 425, 428–29, 432, 453, 458–59, 466–70, 472, 480–83, 488, 491, 498, 500, 507, 509–10, 512–14, 520–21, 523–25, 529–30, 532, 537–40, 543–45, 547, 552, 555, 558, 560–61, 563–65, 569, 571, 573, 585, 590, 594, 597, 599, 607, 609, 612, 614, 617, 621–23, 626, 628–29, 634, 636–39, 642–44, 648–50, 652–53, 655–56, 658–60, 663–64, 666, 668, 672–75, 677, 679, 681, 687, 690–91, 693–94, 696–98, 700–701, 710–12, 714, 720–21, 723–24, 733, 737–38, 744, 746, 750–51, 754–56, 762, 766, 768–70, 774–76, 781–82, 787, 792–94, 797–98, 800, 805–6, 809–10, 814–17, 819, 821, 823, 826–27,

834, 841, 845–46, 850, 856–57, 859–62, 867–70, 872–73, 877, 880–82, 886–88, 890, 895, 899–902, 910–11, 913, 917, 921–22, 924, 927, 931, 935, 937–40, 948, 954, 961, 965, 967, 973, 976, 980, 985, 987, 998–99, 1003–5, 1010, 1012, 1020, 1025, 1031, 1035, 1043, 1046, 1051–52, 1057–58, 1073–75, 1082, 1088, 1096, 1099–1101, 1103–4, 1109, 1112, 1116, 1118, 1131, 1137, 1140, 1148–51, 1167–70, 1172, 1176–77, 1180–81, 1183, 1188, 1192, 1203–4, 1208, 1210

Charlesworth, J.
518
Childs, Brevard S.
312
Chilton, B. D.
579
Christiansen, Ellen Juhl
54, 308–9, 315, 522
Clements, Ruth
95, 890, 1115
Cohen, N.
347
Cohen, Shaye J. D.
820, 827
Collins, John J.
19–20, 268, 357, 392, 417, 458, 686–87, 859
Corinaldi, Michael
118
Cowley, Roger
118, 120
Crawford, Cory D.
432, 435, 437–39
Crislip, Andrew
117–18
Cross, F. M.
4, 31

Daly, R.
579
Dan, Yosef
919, 925, 996
Davenport, Gene L.
25–27, 33, 37, 66, 134, 141, 146–47, 150, 153–56, 158, 161–64, 166, 253–55, 259–60, 263, 390–91, 666, 679–80, 687–88, 690–91, 693–701, 723–24, 727, 849, 853, 856–57, 859, 871–72, 875, 963, 1197–99, 1212
David, Nora
765, 821
Davies, Philip R.
35, 579
Davila, James
13, 414
Day, John
1142
Dean, James Elmer
12, 188
Deichgräber, Reinhard
5, 675
DeJong, David
34, 988, 1000
Delcor, Mathias
541, 543–45
Denis, A.-M.
10, 1123, 1140
Desreumaux, Alain
369
Dillmann, August
2, 4, 14, 16, 20, 29–30, 34, 39, 45–46, 85, 137, 197, 238, 253, 261, 266, 273, 302–3, 322, 366–67, 371–72, 380–81, 390, 402, 407, 418, 467, 481–82, 491, 514, 519–20, 524, 530, 552–53, 558, 560, 573, 609, 622–23, 632, 634, 637–38, 652, 673, 675, 706, 709–10, 714, 729, 769, 775, 805, 810, 834, 845, 868, 871, 881, 886, 900–901, 973, 980, 1005, 1074, 1088, 1101, 1104, 1136, 1142, 1148–49, 1153, 1188
Dimant, Devorah
2, 36, 47, 50–51, 89, 95, 98–100, 103, 126, 128, 152–53, 178–79, 249–50, 256–57, 274, 276–77, 279, 283, 309, 341, 343, 345, 363, 398–99, 402–3, 405, 562–63, 565, 569–71, 573, 635, 704, 725, 919, 1039, 1050, 1052–53, 1115
Dobbeler, Axel von
503

Dobos, Károly Daniel
63, 463, 510, 706
Docherty, Susan
919, 923, 1015, 1026, 1071, 1081
Doering, Lutz
176, 193–94, 196, 199–204, 215, 696, 1193, 1201–13
Doran, Robert
34, 928, 993, 1000–1001, 1006, 1059
Dorman, Anke
289–90, 932–33
Drawnel, Henryk
45, 91–93, 251, 348, 637–38, 735, 823, 854–55, 857, 872, 875, 935
Driver, S. R.
148, 485, 602, 685, 1171, 1181
Duke, R.
1144
Duncan, J.
145

Ego, Beate
196, 215, 263
Eiss, Werner
105, 316–17
Elwolde, John F.
77, 643
Emerton, J.
1038
Endres, John C.
54, 58, 63, 138, 274, 401, 586–87, 590, 592–95, 598, 602, 618, 629–30, 635–36, 640, 642–43, 655, 658, 665, 676–77, 679–80, 697, 701, 714, 718–19, 722–23, 730–32, 735–36, 738–40, 747–49, 753, 755, 760–61, 764, 766, 768, 770, 776–81, 783, 788–90, 799–800–803, 806, 808, 810–12, 818–19, 821, 825–26, 828, 835, 840, 848, 850, 852, 856–57, 865, 874, 888–89, 895, 905, 913, 931, 934, 940–41, 948, 951, 966–67, 969, 994, 997, 1009, 1017, 1028–29, 1038, 1049, 1071, 1081–82, 1091, 1108, 1116
Epstein, A.
25, 46, 83, 110, 166, 183, 186, 188, 199, 219, 223, 319, 793

Erho, Ted
  15
Erlemann, Kurt
  503
Eshel, Esther
  90–91, 251, 369, 372, 375, 377, 387, 400–405, 458, 637–38, 735, 823, 855, 857, 872, 875, 890–91, 1153
Eshel, Hanan
  7, 332
Evans, Craig A.
  17, 102, 113
Ewald, Heinrich
  14
Exum, J. Cheryl
  34

Fabricius, Johann Albert
  10
Falk, Daniel
  765
Finkelstein, Louis
  31–33, 83, 193, 201, 231–32, 267, 346, 520, 630, 633, 641, 821, 826, 882, 1046, 1091, 1202–6, 1208–10
Fishbane, Michael A.
  346
Fitzmyer, Joseph A.
  113, 125, 335, 388, 471, 667, 1126
Fleischer, Ezra
  826
Flint, Peter
  2, 328
Flohr, Paul R.
  346
Flusser, David
  156, 454, 959–60
Fraade, Steven D.
  247, 269
Francis, Michael
  58, 504, 522, 555, 557, 607, 612, 617, 653
Frankel, Zecharias
  10, 29, 45–46, 83, 85, 223, 363
Franklin, S.
  11

Freedman, David N.
  903
Freedman, Harry
  183, 268, 557, 750, 785
Friedlander, Gerald
  782, 880
Frevel, Christian
  612, 660, 663, 818, 820, 826, 828, 833, 840
Frey, Jörg
  40, 130, 262, 339–40, 367, 369–70, 375, 381, 385, 387–88, 391
Fuks, Gideon
  369
Furstenberg, Yair
  107

García Martínez, Florentino
  69–70, 76, 88, 98, 102, 217, 247, 341, 401, 590, 632, 689, 829, 840, 865
Gaster, Moses
  925
Geist, Andrew
  216, 261–62, 295
Gelzer, Heinrich
  13–14, 117, 248
Gilders, William
  10, 54, 56, 138, 196, 301, 305–6, 310–15, 332, 497, 522, 631
Ginzberg, Louis
  126, 202, 243, 417, 458, 518, 960, 1204, 1209
Glessmer, Uwe
  189, 327–28
Goldingay, John
  157
Goldmann, Moshe
  152, 158, 165, 197, 200, 222, 273, 281, 304, 322, 325, 344, 351, 367–68, 412, 417, 432, 452, 457, 480, 482, 520, 524, 609, 616, 634, 639, 643, 654, 663, 675, 684, 687, 695, 711, 722, 724, 738, 751, 769–770, 775–76, 816, 828, 869, 879, 886, 903, 907, 912, 917, 949, 954, 968, 973, 980, 1012, 1052, 1075, 1082, 1143, 1148–49, 1153, 1168, 1177, 1181

Goldstein, Jonathan
  32–33, 873, 927–28, 1000
Goldschmidt Salamon, Karen Lisa
  531
Goudoever, J. van
  316, 322, 578, 580–81, 801, 894, 1190
Grabbe, Lester
  417, 426, 431
Gribetz, Sarit Kattan
  41
Greenberg, Moshe
  735–36
Greenfield, Jonas
  90–91, 251, 637–38, 735, 823, 855, 857, 872, 875
Gregory, Bradley
  897, 915, 968–96, 970
Grelot, Pierre
  90, 251, 253–54, 257, 541, 855
Gressmann, Hugo
  255
Grossfeld, Bernard
  312, 314, 754
Gunkel, Hermann
  279, 294–95, 297, 305, 413, 479

Hadas, Moses
  547
Hagedorn, D.
  11
Haile, Getatchew
  121, 136
Hakham, A.
  699
Halpern-Amaru, Betsy
  54, 56–57, 61–65, 95, 108–9, 154, 158, 213, 224–27, 233, 245, 248, 264, 269–70, 305–306, 309, 340–41, 362–63, 365–66, 387, 425, 430, 433–35, 438, 447, 474–75, 503–4, 531–33, 540–42, 556–57, 559, 573, 587, 590–92, 595, 602, 617, 654, 717, 731, 736–40, 777, 780–81, 783–87, 799–800, 820, 824, 831, 848, 850, 856–57, 881, 887, 889, 897, 902–6, 915, 931, 935, 941, 947, 949, 952, 969–70, 1014–15, 1030–31, 1037, 1039, 1043, 1047–48, 1096, 1115, 1121–

22, 1124–25, 1127–29, 1133, 1138–39, 1141, 1144, 1150, 1152, 1170–72, 1177–78, 1180, 1186, 1188, 1190, 1202
Hamilton, Victor P.
211, 282, 339, 534, 557, 568–69, 589, 618, 677, 713, 716, 719, 721, 730, 752–54, 756, 769–71, 778–80, 790, 801, 807, 819, 825, 998, 1001, 1007–8, 1014–17, 1021, 1025–26, 1030, 1041–42, 1044, 1061, 1063–65, 1070, 1077–78, 1081, 1090, 1092, 1094, 1106, 1114, 1122, 1124, 1127
Hanneken, Todd
20, 33, 37, 47, 65–68, 103, 114, 152, 163, 255–56, 274, 280, 283, 286, 290–91, 349, 405, 407, 535, 600, 666, 681, 683, 686–87, 689–90, 694, 696, 698, 700, 703–4, 725, 727, 806, 963, 1017, 1022
Harkins, Angela (Kim)
242, 274
Hartom, Eliyahu S.
133, 152, 158, 200, 304, 363, 366–67, 432, 480, 609, 636, 639, 652, 654, 659, 674–75, 679, 684, 695, 711, 722, 724, 738, 744, 748, 751, 766, 770, 775–76, 783, 816, 861, 869, 900, 903, 907, 910, 912, 917, 948–49, 954, 968–69, 973, 980, 998, 1010, 1012, 1027, 1038, 1042, 1047, 1052, 1057, 1060, 1065, 1075, 1078, 1084, 1090, 1100–1102, 1107, 1114, 1139, 1142–43, 1148, 1150, 1160, 1162
Hata, Gohei
42, 79
Hayes, Christine E.
828, 833, 835, 838, 1047–48
Hayward, C. T. R.
17, 21, 47, 54, 71, 79, 84–85, 461, 555, 593
Hayward, Robert
1182
Haxen, Ulf
531
Heiligenthal, Roman
503

Heine, R. E.
593
Hellenthal, Barbara
639
Hempel, Charlotte
6, 104, 107, 181
Hendel, Ronald S.
226, 297
Henderson, Ian
401, 454
Hengel, Martin
525
Henten, J. W. van
405
Henze, Matthias
22
Herrmann, Albert
369
Hieke, Thomas
289
Hilhorst, Antonius
11, 95, 689
Himmelfarb, Martha
53, 58, 76–77, 96, 106, 110, 142, 216, 398–401, 406–8, 522, 819, 833, 836, 839, 904
Hoenig, Sidney B.
1210
Hoffmann, D.
314, 695, 698, 701
Holladay, William L.
428, 445
Hollander, H. W.
825, 858, 860, 925, 941, 976
Hölscher, Gustav
368–69, 371–73, 375–82, 386–89
Horgan, Maurya P.
327
Horst, Pieter van der
426–27
Houtman, Cornelis
139, 836, 839, 1131, 1143, 1146, 1152, 1159, 1173, 1181
Hughes, Jeremy
361
Huizenga, Loren A.
568–69, 571, 573–74, 576, 1190
Hultgård, Anders
39, 861, 873–75

Hurvitz, Avi
903

Ibba, Giovanni
4, 20, 54, 81, 89, 103, 105, 107, 197, 215, 225, 241, 276, 295, 452, 1172, 1180
Idel, Moshe
47
Isaiah, Abraham ben
1179

Jacob, Benno
545
Jacobson, Howard
74, 572
Japhet, Sara
751
Jassen, Alex P.
101
Jaubert, Annie
45, 47, 54, 112, 138, 222, 494–95, 577, 661, 1091
Jellinek, Adolph
17, 29, 39, 45, 83, 97, 219, 293, 302, 324, 398, 925–26, 996
Jenott, Lance
41
Jervell, Jacob
546
Jones, F. Stanley
114–15, 427, 458
Jonge, M. de
855, 858, 860, 925, 941, 976

Kahana, Avraham
152, 524
Kampen, John
76, 367, 401
Kasher, Aryeh
369
Kasher, Rimmon
983
Kautsch, Emil
83
Khalil, Joseph
766

Kister, Menahem
    5, 11, 32, 77-78, 81, 134, 142,
    144, 153, 183, 185, 199, 211,
    231-32, 244, 277, 297, 306, 354-
    56, 454-55, 525, 561, 607-8,
    643, 674-76, 687-89, 691-93,
    725, 881, 890, 1144, 1211-13
Klawans, Jonathan
    60, 833-34
Klein, S.
    921-22, 924, 927
Knibb, Michael
    33-34, 89-90, 101, 104-5, 107,
    251, 253-54, 257, 689
Knoppers, Gary N.
    1038
Knowles, Michael P.
    431, 438
Kort, Ann
    883
Koskenniemi, Erkki
    652
Kőszeghy, Miklós
    63
Krašovec, Jože
    159
Kraus, Hans-Joachim
    157
Kratz, Reinhard
    919
Krüger, M. J.
    29-30
Kugel, James L.
    22, 27-28, 33, 37, 40-41, 44, 49,
    55, 60, 77-78, 80-83, 90-92, 94,
    102, 128-30, 139, 141-44, 146,
    148-49, 151, 153, 161-63, 165,
    179, 181, 185, 195, 204-5, 213,
    215, 221-22, 225, 228, 232-34,
    240, 242-44, 251, 253, 262, 265-
    68, 277, 279-80, 283, 291-92,
    312, 316, 320-21, 328-29, 335,
    338-39, 345, 347-48, 353, 363,
    368, 401, 404, 407, 413, 416-17,
    427, 429, 432, 434, 446, 449,
    453, 455-58, 461, 471-72, 475-
    76, 479, 484-85, 495-96, 498-
    99, 502, 512, 517-18, 520,
    522-26, 532-35, 538, 540-42,
    544-45, 548, 550, 554-55, 557,
    560, 564-65, 569-70, 572-73,
    575, 581-82, 588, 590, 592, 594,
    596, 598, 600, 608-10, 612, 614,
    616, 627-28, 630, 639, 642-43,
    653, 664-67, 682, 686, 690, 695-
    96, 702, 715, 723-24, 726, 734,
    750-51, 755, 768-70, 779-80,
    790, 808, 811, 820-21, 823-28,
    837, 841-42, 852, 854, 859, 862-
    65, 872, 877-79, 888-89, 891-
    95, 903-4, 906-7, 910, 913, 922,
    924, 933-34, 944, 948, 950, 958,
    962, 965, 967-68, 976, 987, 997-
    98, 1000, 1008-11, 1013-15,
    1026, 1038, 1041-44, 1048-49,
    1051-53, 1065, 1070-71, 1074-
    75, 1078-79, 1084, 1090, 1101,
    1107, 1111, 1113, 1118, 1127,
    1129-30, 1133, 1139-40, 1144,
    1151, 1153, 1155, 1161, 1163-64,
    1175, 1180, 1183, 1185-86, 1189,
    1197, 1199, 1205, 1211
Kugler, Robert
    90, 835-37, 853, 855, 857, 872,
    879, 881
Kvanvig, Helge
    17-18, 81

Laato, Antti
    1138
Labuschagne, C. J.
    689
Lambert, David
    157-59, 341-42, 345, 347, 356-
    57, 607-9, 635, 941-43
Lange, Armin
    40, 52, 130, 263, 401, 408, 454,
    765, 821, 871, 1017, 1022
Lauterbach, Jacob Z.
    1161
Lavee, Moshe
    345-46
Le Déaut, Roger
    574-75, 577-80, 1190
Lehrman, S. M.
    1027
Leslau, Wolf
    118-19
Levenson, Jon D.
    574-75, 579
Levinson, Joshua
    17, 20, 22
Levine, Baruch A.
    350, 612, 805, 880, 1177, 1208
Levison, Jack R.
    190-91, 226, 231-32
Licht, Jacob
    155, 182, 546, 563-64
Lichtenberger, Hermann
    52, 158, 277, 344, 454, 944
LiDonnici, Lynn
    27, 93, 369, 401
Lieber, Andrea
    27, 93, 369, 401
Lieu, Judith
    181
Lignée, Hubert
    105
Lim, Timothy
    6, 19, 1195
Lincicum, David
    86, 159
Lindqvist, Pekka
    652
Lipscomb, W. Lowndes
    61, 111, 238, 240, 245, 340, 362,
    365-66, 412
Littmann, Enno
    83, 133, 135, 170, 186, 197, 221,
    242, 266, 273, 304, 333, 343-44,
    366-67, 390, 456, 466, 472, 480,
    520, 585, 594, 609, 621-22, 628,
    634, 637, 639, 654, 660, 673-75,
    711, 724, 744, 769, 774-76, 815-
    16, 867, 881-82, 900, 917, 931,
    940, 954, 967-68, 973, 980,
    1020, 1052, 1057, 1074, 1104,
    1148-49, 1177
Livneh, Atar
    342, 347, 449-50, 608, 919-21,
    923-26, 928, 949-50, 958-61,
    969-70, 983-87, 992-97, 1009,
    1011, 1081, 1121-22
Loader, William R. G.
    60-61, 211, 213, 218, 225, 245,
    611, 732, 734-35, 821, 828, 831,
    833, 841, 904-5, 907, 1009-10,
    1014, 1030, 1048-50, 1052
Lohr, Joel N.
    17

Luttikhuizen, Gerard P.
190, 211, 217

Machiela, Daniel A.
93–94, 96, 115, 335, 367–68, 369, 371–73, 375–81, 384, 386–89, 472

Maeir, Aren M.
244, 435, 1141, 1144

Magness, Jodi
244, 435, 1141, 1144

Maher, Michael
138, 458, 593, 749, 895, 1100, 1146

Maier, Christl M.
27

Maier, J.
369, 381, 385, 388–89

Malalas, John
364

Maori, Yeshayahu
821, 1139

Marcus, Joel
1032

Marmorstein, A.
240, 245–46

Martin, François
83, 859, 927

Mason, Eric F.
19, 37, 41, 63, 70, 94, 118, 484, 738, 1039

McNamara, Martin
458, 522, 579, 619, 754

Meier, John P.
959

Mendels, Doron
33, 35, 810, 928, 999–1000

Menn, Esther
1041, 1043–44, 1046–47, 1049–50

Merklein, Helmut
329

Mermelstein, Ari
54, 81, 315

Metso, Sarianna
72

Meyer, R.
874

Milgrom, Jacob
60, 150, 305–6, 310, 337, 351, 608, 632, 636, 640, 662, 733, 781, 827, 833, 881, 904, 930, 1011, 1195

Milik, J. T.
5, 7, 14, 31, 34, 88–90, 101–2, 104, 126, 136, 165, 169–170, 199, 251, 253–54, 257, 264, 270, 284, 294, 300, 343, 399, 624, 672, 872, 940, 948, 956, 1004, 1012, 1020, 1037, 1158

Milikowsky, Chaim
265, 294, 296, 345, 459, 474, 537, 561, 1098, 1190, 1194, 1200

Mimouni, Simon Claude
514, 523–24

Mittmann-Richert, U.
53

Moore, Carey A.
766

Monger, Matthew Phillip
6

Montgomery, James A.
436

Morales, Pablo A. Torijano Morales
13

Moriya, Akio
42, 79

Morschauer, Scott
883

Mosser, Carl
1160

Müller, Karlheinz
329, 457

Muraoka, Takamitsu
77, 643

Murphy, Catherine M.
691

Naeh, S.
219–20

Nahon, Gérard
262

Najman, Hindy
18–19, 69, 72, 80, 126, 405

Nebe, G. W.
197, 674

Neusner, Jacob
345

Newsom, Carol
1200

Nickelsburg, George W. E.
34, 69, 88, 90, 128, 250, 259, 268, 348, 364, 399, 401–3, 438, 613, 680, 697–98, 701, 927, 960

Nicklas, Tobias
47, 289

Niehoff, Maren
1011, 1015, 1026–27, 1071, 1081

Niklas, Tobias
697

Nitzan, Bilhah
139, 185, 195

Noack, Bent
321, 859

Noort, Ed
51, 563

Nötscher, F.
70

Novak, David
345–46

Novick, Tzvi
70

Oegema, Gerbern
53, 401, 454

O'Kane, Martin
919

Olyan, Saul M.
47

Osswald, Eva
471

Otero, Andrés Piquer
13

Panayotov, Alexander
13, 414

Parfitt, Tudor
118

Parry, Donald W.
93, 305

Paul, Shalom M.
69

Paz, Yaqir
41, 79–80

Penner, Jeremy
63

Penner, Ken M.
64

Peters, Dorothy M.
257, 264, 309

Petersen, David L.
    17, 838
Petit, F.
    12, 239, 304, 396, 398, 413–14,
    420, 431
Petuchowski, Jacob J.
    826
Peursen, W. Th. van
    189
Pilhofer, Peter
    263
Pinggéra, Karl
    117
Porter, Stanley
    54
Poznanski, Samuel
    240
Preuss, H. D.
    149
Puech, Émile
    7, 95, 701, 724, 891, 1128
Pummer, Reinhard
    819

Qimron, Elisha
    6, 133, 217, 1184

Rabin, Chaim
    126, 155, 354, 390, 480, 538,
    609, 634, 656, 681–82, 769, 904,
    911, 968, 980, 987, 1031, 1074,
    1101, 1208
Rad, Gerhard von
    1112
Rainey, Anson F.
    472
Rajak, Tessa
    35
Rapp, Hans
    542, 784, 847–48, 852–53, 855,
    862–63, 869, 871–72, 878–79,
    882–89, 891, 893, 895, 914
Rappaport, Uriel
    35, 153, 369, 725
Ravid, Liora
    27, 33, 46–47, 71, 140, 203, 215,
    295, 316, 328, 494–95, 678,
    1199, 1202, 1210, 1212–13
Reed, Annette Yoshiko
    11, 276

Reeves, John C.
    9, 96, 307, 367, 561
Reiterer Friedrich V.
    47, 697
Riessler, Paul
    968, 1101
Roberto, Umberto
    117
Robin, Christian
    72
Robinson, Ira
    1042
Robinson, Patricia
    677
Rofé, Alexander
    5, 675
Roitman, Adolfo
    50, 405
Römheld, K. F. Diethard
    52
Rönsch, Hermann
    3, 10, 14, 16–17, 29, 83, 114–16,
    219, 240, 261–62, 398, 404, 407,
    414, 431–32, 466, 482, 509, 530,
    536, 539, 543, 576, 589, 605, 614,
    621–22, 633, 649, 672–75, 684,
    691, 710–12, 721, 724, 733, 744,
    759, 766, 775–76, 792–94, 797–
    98, 808, 810–11, 814–17, 845–46,
    857, 867–70, 880, 895, 900, 917,
    938, 956, 967, 972, 991, 1004–5,
    1020, 1025–26, 1058, 1096, 1110,
    1140, 1148, 1167–69
Roo, Jacqueline de
    54
Rook, John T.
    46, 61, 223, 240–41, 245, 247–49,
    256, 268, 340, 362, 366, 412
Rösel, M.
    130
Rosenberg, Shalom
    47
Rothstein, David
    213, 227, 556, 559–60, 778–79,
    783, 786, 830, 899, 906, 909–10,
    1039, 1048, 1054
Rubenstein, Jeffrey
    541, 545, 548–50, 879, 884
Ruiten, Jacques T. A. G. M. van
    47, 51, 54–55, 89–90, 95, 121,
    137, 139–40, 170, 176–78, 187–
    88, 190–91, 193–97, 200–201,
    210–12, 214–16, 222, 225–27,
    229, 231–32, 239, 241–42, 244–
    46, 249, 252, 261, 263–69, 274,
    276, 278–79, 283, 286, 293, 303–
    4, 306, 308–13, 316, 334–38, 341,
    354, 356, 361, 363, 365–67, 369,
    385, 387, 410, 412–13, 415, 417,
    433–34, 436, 447, 449, 451–54,
    456–57, 468, 470, 473–74, 477,
    485, 490–91, 497, 499, 502, 504,
    512, 518–20, 523, 531–35, 537,
    550, 553–54, 563, 569, 572, 582,
    591–93, 595, 601–2, 606–9, 611–
    14, 618, 625, 629, 632–33, 636,
    640, 652, 654, 657, 661–63, 665,
    676–80, 682–83, 685, 696, 1120–
    21, 1123, 1128–30, 1133–34,
    1138–41
Russell, David M.
    165

Safrai, Ze'ev
    472
Sanders, James A.
    104, 184
Satlow, Michael
    231
Satran, David
    890
Saulnier, Stéphane
    45, 112, 1178
Schafer, A. Rahel
    229–30
Schäfer, Peter
    269–70
Scharfman, B.
    1179
Schechter, Solomon
    2, 99–100
Schiffman, Lawrence H.
    50, 54, 105, 130, 196, 202–3, 244,
    317, 336–37, 405, 435, 512, 632,
    885, 1141, 1144, 1180, 1184
Schipper, Bernd U.
    76
Schmidt, Francis
    369–70, 378–79, 381, 388
Schodde, George H.
    75, 260, 266, 609, 769, 834

Schoeps, H.
    579
Schöpflin, Karin
    47
Schreiber, Sarah
    1040, 1050, 1053
Schubert, Friedemann
    39, 615, 692, 695–96, 855, 873, 875, 1116
Schuller, Eileen
    72, 642
Schultz, Joseph P.
    346–47
Schüpphaus, J.
    632
Schwartz, D.
    518
Schwartz, J.
    885, 888–89, 891
Schwarz, Eberhard
    33, 40, 53, 57, 194–96, 198, 661–63, 665–66, 819, 907, 913
Scott, James M.
    20, 66, 68, 98, 113–15, 128, 154, 255, 257–58, 317, 369, 391–93, 499, 521, 680–81, 686, 1197–98
Segal, Michael
    22, 24–25, 28, 37, 78, 80, 142, 165, 199, 218–20, 223–24, 257, 277, 283–87, 290–91, 351, 355–57, 366, 398, 400, 403, 405, 407, 409, 412, 471, 473–76, 489, 504–5, 510–11, 516, 518–20, 522, 524, 538, 565, 573, 577–79, 581–82, 598, 706, 793–94, 815, 817, 821–22, 826, 831, 840–41, 903–4, 909–11, 913, 1040–41, 1044–46, 1049–54, 1149, 1152–53, 1155–56, 1158–59, 1162–63, 1172–75, 1186, 1211
Segal, Moshe
    185, 251
Shemesh, Aharon
    84, 103, 107, 144, 196–97, 218, 309, 322, 355, 661–63, 881–85, 893, 932–33, 1050, 1180–82, 1185, 1187, 1189
Sheridan, Mark
    593

Shinan, Avigdor
    1037–42, 1044–46, 1048, 1064, 1098
Singer, Wilhelm
    29, 459, 481, 541–42, 544, 549–50, 677, 762, 766, 826
Sippor, Moshe
    983
Skehan, Patrick W.
    104, 184
Skinner, John
    211, 221, 240, 264, 279, 282, 297, 305, 339, 373, 413, 415–16, 448, 497, 516, 557, 576, 587, 661, 680, 714, 717, 747, 752, 760, 779–80, 802, 809, 819, 864, 929, 1016, 1043, 1092, 1110, 1124
Smith, Mark
    103, 189
Sollamo, Raija
    181–82
Söllner, Peter
    503–4, 517, 554–55, 558, 560, 618, 654
Steck, Odil Hannes
    41, 75–76, 79, 142, 148, 152, 174, 176, 178, 186–87, 191–92, 695–96
Steindorff, G.
    1030
Stemberger, Günter
    329
Sterling, Gregory E.
    458
Stern, Menahem
    548
Steudel, Annette
    319, 1113
Stoffregen-Pedersen, Kirsten
    119
Stökl Ben Ezra, Daniel (Jonathan)
    5, 86, 289, 292
Stone, Michael E.
    90–91, 93, 98, 136, 143–45, 249, 251, 265, 309, 458, 635, 637–38, 686, 735, 784, 823, 855, 857, 872, 875
Strong, Justin
    985

Stuckenbruck, Loren
    225, 229, 233, 275–76, 279, 401, 408–10, 454
Syrén, Roger
    619
Tabory, Joseph
    326, 549, 893, 1171, 1179, 1184
Tafel, Gottlieb
    428, 430, 433
Talmon, Shemaryahu
    7, 102, 105, 332
Ta-Shema, Y.
    826–27, 832–33
Tchernowitz, Chaim
    83, 193, 203, 452, 485, 495, 1203–5, 1208–10
Teeter, D. Andrew
    76, 79, 143, 148, 432, 435–36, 438–39, 497
Tervanotko, Hanna
    765
Testuz, Michel
    27, 75, 177, 179, 190–91, 212, 369, 379, 381, 390, 577, 586, 596, 681, 686, 690, 694, 723, 748, 859, 888, 963, 1197–98
Thackeray, H. St. J.
    108
Thiessen, Matthew
    515–16
Tiller, Patrick A.
    155, 350
Tisserant, Eugène
    9, 180, 200, 261–62, 304, 307, 378–80, 418, 435, 482, 899, 910, 972, 980, 985
Tigchelaar, Eibert J. C.
    5–6, 51, 88, 95, 101–2, 134, 149, 153, 405, 563
Toorn, Karel van der
    426–27
Torrey, C. C.
    135
Touati, Charles
    262
Tov, Emmanuel
    2, 54
Trautner-Kromann, Hanne
    531

1315

Trebolle Barrera, Julio
    351
Treuenfels, A.
    10, 246, 414
Trevison Semi, Emanuela
    118
Tromp, Johannes
    855, 858, 873, 1196
Trotter, Jonathan
    276
Troyer, Kristin de
    765, 821
Tuffin, Paul
    16-17, 117, 188, 198, 211, 219, 223, 229, 232-33, 239-41, 245, 247, 256, 263, 266, 284, 335, 343, 364-65, 368, 372, 398, 415, 417, 433, 458, 549, 654, 733, 749, 755, 793, 849, 944, 957, 973, 988, 990, 1144
Tzoref, Shani
    50, 405, 765, 821

Uhlig, Siegbert
    118-19
Ulfgard, Håkan
    541, 548-49, 880
Ulrich, Eugene
    93, 187, 305, 516, 622
Urbach, Ephraim E.
    144, 289

VanderKam, James C.
    2, 4-5, 10, 13-16, 24-25, 27, 33-34, 38, 40-43, 45-47, 49-50, 52-55, 57, 60, 63, 68-69, 72, 79, 85-88, 90, 93-95, 102, 104-7, 112-13, 118, 121, 125, 128, 130, 133-36, 138-40, 142-43, 146, 148, 157, 162-64, 168-170, 174, 176-77, 179, 183, 186-92, 196, 198-99, 203-4, 208-9, 216, 222-23, 227-28, 231-32, 237-38, 240-43, 249-54, 256, 259-62, 266-68, 273-77, 279-80, 288, 290, 295, 300-302, 304-7, 310-12, 317-18, 320, 323-24, 326, 328, 332-33, 337-38, 341, 343-44, 353-54, 360-62, 365-69, 374, 379, 383, 385-86, 390-91, 397-98, 402, 405-7, 409, 414, 418, 420, 423, 429, 433, 435, 438, 451, 454, 456, 458, 462-63, 465-69, 478, 480-83, 488, 491, 498-99, 504, 508-9, 511-12, 514, 518-21, 523-24, 529-30, 535-37, 539-40, 543, 549, 552, 555, 558, 560-64, 567, 571, 574-75, 578, 581-82, 584-86, 589, 594-95, 597, 605, 609, 613, 621-23, 628-29, 632, 634, 637-39, 648-52, 664, 672-76, 678, 681-83, 685, 688, 692, 694, 696, 705-6, 709-13, 715, 717-23, 733, 735-37, 743-44, 748-49, 754, 758-60, 767, 770, 774-76, 786, 795, 797-98, 801, 805-6, 808-10, 814-17, 826, 828, 830, 832, 834-35, 837-38, 845-46, 850-51, 853-56, 862, 864-65, 867-71, 876, 879-81, 886-87, 899-901, 903, 910-11, 913, 917-18, 922, 924, 927, 931, 937-40, 954-57, 962, 967, 972-74, 978, 985, 990-91, 999-1000, 1003-5, 1008, 1012, 1020, 1023, 1031, 1034-36, 1052, 1057-58, 1067, 1070, 1073-75, 1082, 1088, 1090-91, 1096, 1099, 1101, 1104, 1109, 1112, 1117-20, 1123-30, 1136-38, 1142-43, 1148-49, 1153, 1158, 1160-61, 1167-69, 1177-79, 1181, 1183, 1188, 1190, 1192, 1195-98, 1201, 1204, 1211-12, 1214
Vaux, Roland de
    681
Vegas Montaner, Luis
    351
Verheyden, Jozef
    697
Vermes, Geza
    19, 574, 682, 826-27, 1152
Vervenne, Marc
    176
Volz, Paul
    255, 700-701

Wacholder, Ben Zion
    67-68, 76-78, 105, 139, 142, 163, 474, 888, 1195, 1198
Wallraff, Martin
    117
Wassen, Cecilia
    64
Weinfeld, Moshe
    611, 616, 645, 659
Werline, Rodney A.
    125
Werman, Cana
    6, 8, 31, 33, 35-37, 42, 59, 65, 70, 75, 77-78, 82, 84, 93-94, 96-98, 103, 106, 110, 134-36, 139, 141-42, 144, 146, 151-52, 154-56, 158-60, 164-65, 169-173, 177, 179-80, 188, 190-91, 193-96, 199-201, 203-4, 213, 217, 219-20, 222, 224-25, 227, 231-32, 237-38, 240, 242, 244, 247, 250-51, 254, 257, 261-62, 264, 276-77, 280-81, 284-85, 287-96, 300, 302-5, 307, 309-10, 312-14, 316-17, 322-26, 328, 337, 340, 342-44, 347, 349-50, 354-56, 365-73, 375-77, 379, 381, 383, 386-89, 391, 396, 398-99, 404, 406-8, 412-13, 416, 423, 426-27, 429-33, 445, 447, 449, 452, 454-56, 465, 467, 470, 472, 474, 480-82, 485, 488, 491, 499-500, 503-5, 508, 511, 515, 519-20, 522, 528, 530, 532, 538, 540, 542-43, 546-47, 549, 554, 557-60, 569-71, 575-76, 582, 587-88, 590, 592, 595-96, 601, 604, 610, 617-18, 621-22, 627, 629, 636-37, 639, 641, 646, 650-51, 654, 656-57, 659-60, 662-63, 665, 667-68, 672, 674-76, 678-79, 683, 685, 691-92, 694-96, 698, 700, 703-5, 713-14, 716, 720, 722, 729, 735, 737-39, 741, 744, 746, 751-52, 758-61, 764-65, 767, 769, 771, 774-75, 778-80, 785-86, 788-90, 793, 797-98, 802-5, 807, 812, 815, 817-19, 822-23, 825-26, 829-30, 831-33, 840-41, 845-46, 850, 853-54, 856-57, 868-70, 881-85, 887, 890, 893, 895, 897, 899-901, 903, 906-7, 909, 914,

917–18, 928–29, 932–35, 941, 944, 948, 956–58, 960–63, 965, 967–68, 974, 978, 980, 986, 993–96, 998, 1000, 1002, 1005, 1010–11, 1013–14, 1017, 1022–24, 1027–28, 1036, 1041, 1043–44, 1050–53, 1057–58, 1060, 1063, 1069, 1076, 1091, 1094, 1102, 1106–7, 1109, 1118, 1122, 1131–34, 1140, 1145, 1148–49, 1151, 1153–54, 1156, 1158, 1160, 1162, 1167–69, 1176, 1180–82, 1184–85, 1187, 1189, 1192–93, 1195, 1197–99, 1202, 1205

Westermann, Claus
177, 191, 211, 221, 226, 280, 282, 297, 303, 305, 310, 339, 413, 415, 431, 448, 491, 513–14, 535, 569, 576, 588–89, 594, 608, 618, 659, 677, 719, 760, 779, 788, 802, 819, 861, 864, 873, 876, 998, 1001, 1008, 1022, 1025, 1030, 1061, 1069, 1078, 1092–93, 1106, 1113–14, 1124

Wevers, John W.
303

White, Richard T.
35

Wiesenberg, Ernest
27, 57, 462–63, 706, 957, 1164–65, 1194, 1197, 1199–1200

Wildberger, H.
149, 699

Williams, Frank
11

Williamson, Hugh G. M.
34

Winston, David
1161

Wintermute, O. S.
133, 197, 242, 248, 253, 262, 266, 304, 310, 353, 373, 389–90, 407, 480, 519–20, 538, 549, 609, 611, 628, 634, 638–39, 642, 654, 725–26, 737, 769, 834, 881–82, 927, 940, 968, 980, 987, 1012, 1031, 1074, 1101, 1177, 1204

Wise, Michael
163

Woude, A. S. van der
5

Wright, Archie T.
402

Wright, Benjamin C.
77, 142

Wright, David
903

Wright, George Ernest
4

Xella, P.
643

Yadin, Yigael
93, 105–6, 144, 155–56, 307, 319, 332, 336, 349, 353, 377, 631, 633, 636, 693, 884–85, 1179, 1183–84

Yardeni, Ada
35

Zahn, Molly
19, 765

Zakovitch, Yair
1037–42, 1044–46, 1048, 1064, 1098

Zeitlin, Solomon
30, 33, 231, 316–17, 321, 495, 501

Zimmerli, W.
375

Zipor, Moshe
297

Zobel, H.-J.
875

Zuurmond, Rochus
242–43, 468, 899, 902–4, 906, 1125

Designer's Notes

In the design of the visual aspects of *Hermeneia*, consideration has been given to relating the form to the content by symbolic means.

The letters of the logotype *Hermeneia* are a fusion of forms alluding simultaneously to Hebrew (dotted vowel markings) and Greek (geometric round shapes) letter forms. In their modern treatment they remind us of the electronic age as well, the vantage point from which this investigation of the past begins. The Lion of Judah used as visual identification for the series is based on the Seal of Shema. The version for *Hermeneia* is again a fusion of Hebrew calligraphic forms, especially the legs of the lion, and Greek elements characterized by the geometric. In the sequence of arcs, which can be understood as scroll-like images, the first is the lion's mouth. It is reasserted and accelerated in the whorl and returns in the aggressively arched tail: tradition is passed from one age to the next, rediscovered and re-formed.

"Who is worthy to open the scroll and break its
seals...."
Then one of the elders said to me
"weep not; lo, the Lion of the tribe of David,
the Root of David, has conquered,
so that he can open the scroll and its seven seals."
Rev. 5:2, 5

To celebrate the signal achievement in biblical scholarship which *Hermeneia* represents, the entire series will by its color constitute a signal on the theologian's bookshelf: the Old Testament will be bound in yellow and the New Testament in red, traceable to a commonly used color coding for synagogue and church in medieval painting; in pure color terms, varying degrees of intensity of the warm segment of the color spectrum. The colors interpenetrate when the binding color for the Old Testament is used to imprint volumes from the New and vice versa.

Wherever possible, a photograph of the oldest extant manuscript, or a historically significant document pertaining to the biblical sources, will be displayed on the end papers of each volume to give a feel for the tangible reality and beauty of the source material.

The title-page motifs are expressive derivations from the *Hermeneia* logotype, repeated seven times to form a matrix and debossed on the cover of each volume. These sifted-out elements will be seen to be in their exact positions within the parent matrix.

Horizontal markings at gradated levels on the spine will assist in grouping the volumes according to these conventional categories.

The type has been set with unjustified right margins so as to preserve the internal consistency of word spacing. This is a major factor in both legibility and aesthetic quality; the resultant uneven line endings are only slight impairments to legibility by comparison. In this respect the type resembles the handwritten manuscripts where the quality of the calligraphic writing is dependent on establishing and holding to integral spacing patterns.

All of the typefaces in common use today have been designed between AD 1500 and the present. For the biblical text a face was chosen which does not arbitrarily date the text, but rather one which is uncompromisingly modern and unembellished so that its feel is of the universal. The type style is Univers 65 by Adrian Frutiger.

The expository texts and footnotes are set in Baskerville, chosen for its compatibility with the many brief Greek and Hebrew insertions. The double-column format and the shorter line length facilitate speed reading and the wide margins to the left of footnotes provide for the scholar's own notations.

Kenneth Hiebert

Category of biblical writing, key symbolic characteristic, and volumes so identified.

1
Law
(boundaries described)
  Genesis
  Exodus
  Leviticus
  Numbers
  Deuteronomy

2
History
(trek through time and space)
  Joshua
  Judges
  Ruth
  1 Samuel
  2 Samuel
  1 Kings
  2 Kings
  1 Chronicles
  2 Chronicles
  Ezra
  Nehemiah
  Esther

3
Poetry
(lyric emotional expression)
  Job
  Psalms
  Proverbs
  Ecclesiastes
  Song of Songs

4
Prophets
(inspired seers)
  Isaiah
  Jeremiah
  Lamentations
  Ezekiel
  Daniel
  Hosea
  Joel
  Amos
  Obadiah
  Jonah
  Micah
  Nahum
  Habakkuk
  Zephaniah
  Haggai
  Zechariah
  Malachi

5
New Testament Narrative
(focus on One)
  Matthew
  Mark
  Luke
  John
  Acts

6
Epistles
(directed instruction)
  Romans
  1 Corinthians
  2 Corinthians
  Galatians
  Ephesians
  Philippians
  Colossians
  1 Thessalonians
  2 Thessalonians
  1 Timothy
  2 Timothy
  Titus
  Philemon
  Hebrews
  James
  1 Peter
  2 Peter
  1 John
  2 John
  3 John
  Jude

7
Apocalypse
(vision of the future)
  Revelation

8
Extracanonical Writings
(peripheral records)

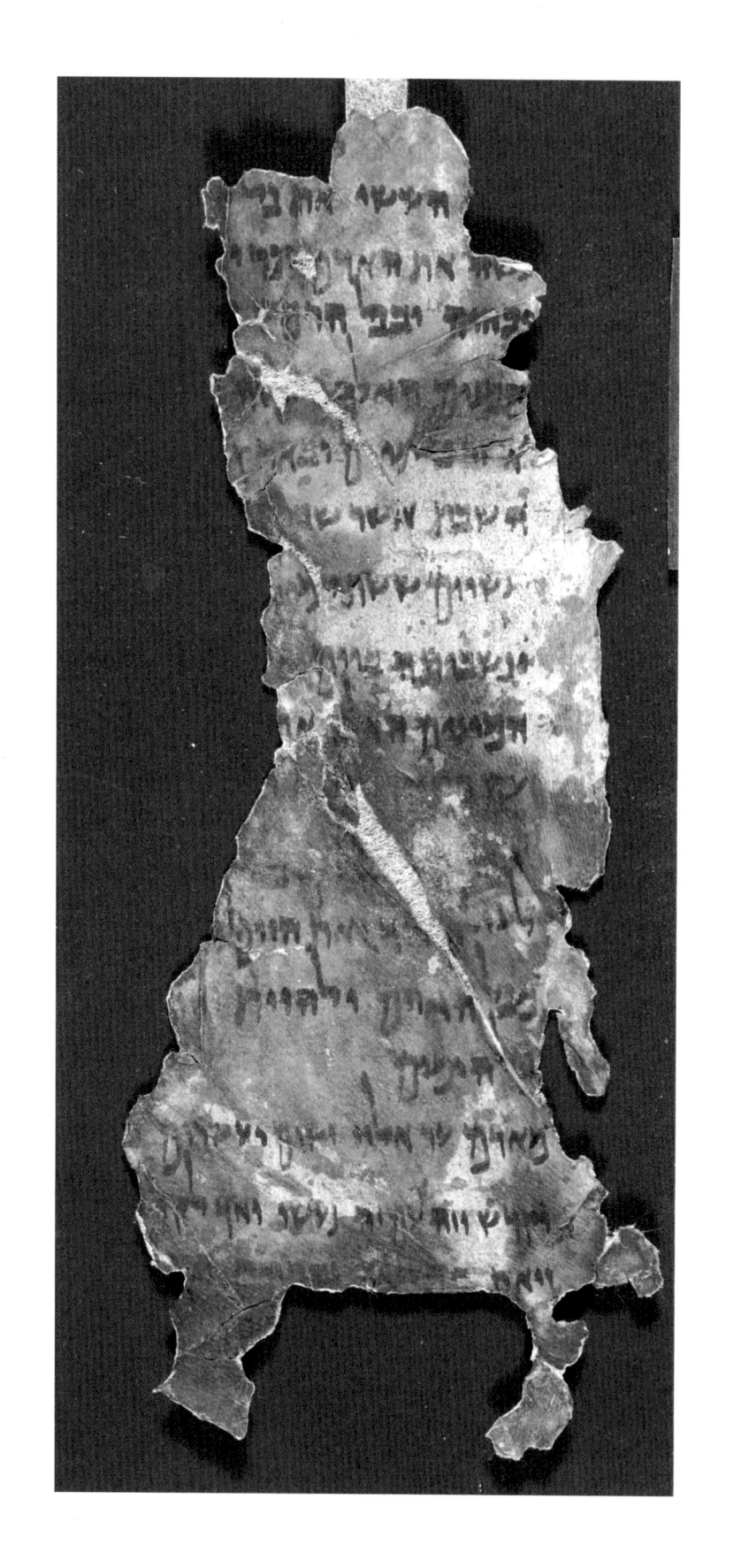

אשה את ב[
אח או אחו[
ובני אח[
יקח אשה[
אשר אמר[
ישכבנה[
אפתחו[
והמה[
יחיו ימיך[
יביאו עליך[
אשר יקים[
אל אחות אמו או א[
אשר יואיל לגלות ערו[
ויש[